1992

Sexual Harassment
in
Employment Law

Sexual Harassment
in
Employment Law

Barbara Lindemann

David D. Kadue

BNA
BOOKS

The Bureau of National Affairs, Inc., Washington, D.C.

To Nicholas H.H. Stonnington

B.T.L.

To Marjorie, Arnold, and Martha Kadue

D.D.K.

Library of Congress Cataloging-in-Publication Data

Lindemann, Barbara, 1935—
    Sexual harassment in employment law / Barbara Lindemann Schlei, David D. Kadue.
        p.   cm.
    Includes index.
    ISBN 0-87179-704-6
    1. Sexual harassment of women—Law and legislation—United States. 2. Sex discrimination in employment—Law and legislation—United States. I. Kadue, David D. II. Title.
KF3467.L56   1992
344.73'014133—dc20
[347.3041433]   91-41340
                                                                          CIP
                                                                          Rev.

Published by BNA Books, 1250 23rd St., N.W., Washington, D.C. 20037
Printed in the United States of America
International Standard Book Number: 0-87179-704-6

FOREWORD

It is a sobering revelation that every woman—*every* woman—who has spent substantial time in the work force in the last two decades can tell at least one story about being the object of sexual harassment. The phrase itself hovered at the periphery of most people's vocabulary until October 11, 1991, when Professor Anita Hill wrenched it into the vernacular during her seven hours of televised testimony before the Senate Judiciary Committee. It turns out to describe an experience that most women, but very few men, understand very well.

The stories of harassment are as varied as the women who tell them. There is the lawyer who put herself through college by waiting tables at a Hungarian restaurant, and soon discovered that the owner's son would take the opportunity to grope her as she passed through the kitchen with arms full of food. "You learned to wriggle past him without spilling the goulash," she explains. And the editor of a major newspaper who, as a junior reporter, had to repel numerous advances by one of her superiors. And the nurse who, early in her career, found herself locked in an examining room with a doctor who announced it was time for him to perform a different type of examination. And the teaching assistant who asked her psychology professor for some advice with a personal problem, only to have him turn around and demand some help with *his* personal problem. The list is endless.

The common thread to these stories, if there is one, is that they tend to involve women who are young—or at least young to their professions—and men in positions of authority who had no compunctions about using the leverage afforded them to demand or cajole sex. Sure, everyone knew or suspected that this type of thing happened occasionally, the way we know that people occasionally become the victims of crime or other misfortune. But who knew, who understood, that it was quite so pervasive? Apparently most women did, while most men did not. It was the best-kept secret of modern times.

Each woman handled these crises in her own way. Some quit. Others endured and learned to "wriggle without spilling the goulash." Some others appealed to a higher authority within the office. Still others submitted, often with a sense of violation and shame. Generally, however, the problem was viewed as a private one, to be handled by each woman alone; a personal challenge, not a matter for public policy.

The idea that harassment could be punished through the legal system is of relatively recent origin. The EEOC first issued guidelines on sexual harassment just eleven years ago, identifying it as a form of discrimination with broad societal implications, rather than just a distasteful private foible. The first Supreme Court case recognizing sexual harassment came less than six years ago. Yet, as attested by the materials in these pages, the law has progressed swiftly in a very short time. Litigation has finally come to this somewhat seamy, but highly pervasive, corner of workplace misconduct. And, for the most part, it's a good thing.

But not entirely. Lawsuits are clumsy tools for shaping human behavior: they are expensive, eat up a lot of time and usually exacerbate whatever tensions already exist; they often have unforeseen consequences; they tend to enrich the lawyers far more often than they satisfy the parties. Before our litigious society throws itself headlong into this venture, it's worth considering why a fair measure of caution and common sense is particularly advisable.

I.

There is no good side to racism; there is no redeeming value to fraud or theft. By and large the things we define as wrongs in the law cleave neatly from the things that are lawful. Sexual harassment is somewhat unusual in that offensive, prohibited conduct is often not all that dissimilar from conduct that is acceptable, even desirable, in a different context or involving different individuals. There are, to be sure, certain actions that would be unacceptable under any circumstances: "Have sex with me or you're fired" is a fine example. But much sexual harassment comes to us steeped in the ambiguities, misunderstandings, tensions and frustrations of male-female relations. No other human interaction is as shrouded in mystery, as likely to result in hurt feelings, or so deeply engages our sense of self-esteem as the human mating ritual.

Outside the work environment, these tensions and ambiguities tend to make courtship exciting and, in any event, are not matters of public concern. But when men and women are brought together in the workplace, sexual tensions and ambiguities are aggregated with the already formidable tensions and frustrations of the job. The results can be explosive.

One response might be a bright-line rule: never mix business and sexual relationships. While this rule is easy to remember, it is impossible to enforce, as men and women are drawn to each other in the workplace, as elsewhere. Even were it enforceable, do we really want to live in a society where normal flirtations, courtships and marriages are routinely banned from the office and the factory? The function of the law must be to separate the normal from the perverse, the playful from the harmful, the bumbling from the evil. No easy tasks these.

While the law and respect for decency require that we undertake the effort, it is worth considering some serious drawbacks in using litigation to resolve this conundrum. I list them, roughly, in what I see as ascending order of significance.

A. Just When You Thought it Was Safe to Go Back in the Water ...

While many frown on romance in the workplace, it is a fact of life. Indeed, I would suggest that it is an important and enduring reality and that, within bounds of propriety and good taste, romance in the workplace should be accepted rather than forbidden.

There are important personal and business reasons for this. Propinquity leads to sexual interest, which may lead to romance and marriage, or just romance and fun. Rules that prohibit or discourage interpersonal relationships can cause frustration and resentment among employees, and may cost businesses the services of one or both partners when the inevitable secret relationships develop. From the perspective of unattached employees, the work environment provides the most suitable atmosphere to find a partner of compatible interests, age, temperament and education.

The fear of a sexual harassment charge—with the humiliating personal implication and the potentially devastating professional consequences—may well discourage many employees from taking the first hesitating step toward an office romance. This may make the workplace a less collegial and inviting place, as men and women socialize less with their co-workers and turn their energies toward meeting people elsewhere.

Chilling romance in the office may be a cost we are willing to bear as a society in order to eliminate sexual harassment. But it *is* a cost, and one we ought to recognize. For young men and women, busy with their careers but also on the lookout for a lasting relationship, the burden of having to exclude their co-workers from the pool may be more than trivial.

B. She Said, He Said

Some of what is included within the concept of sexual harassment, particularly of the hostile environment type, is done openly and publicly. Consider, for example, the Washington state judge who informed a prosecutor in open court of his desire to "jump [her] bones." But charges of sexual harassment, like those of rape, child molestation and spousal abuse, can raise some of the most difficult problems of proof in the law, because some of the most egregious conduct—the nurse and doctor locked in the examining room, the professor and student in his office, the boss and his assistant traveling on business in a distant city—occurs in private, with the participants doubling as the only witnesses. Our adversarial system is at its very weakest when the evidence consists entirely of the conflicting accounts of two interested parties. While recent experience makes this point too obvious for much elaboration, the policy implications are considerable.

A charge of sexual harassment, if sustained, can have devastating consequences for the accused. There is a natural reluctance, therefore, to sustain the charges where it's one person's word against another's. Sexual harassment victims are aware of this, which makes them think twice before airing their accusations. After all, bringing an unsustained charge of harassment doesn't earn the accuser a badge of honor, and may well result in ostracizing her or impairing her advancement. And it doesn't take many cases where the accuser suffers this fate to persuade other women to remain silent.

Dealing with sexual harassment through the mechanism of the adversary process may thus have the perverse effect of suppressing the disclosure and resolution of the most egregious types of misconduct. This problem may explain why a recent Florida study found that 40 percent of female attorneys felt they had been sexually harassed at some time by a state-court judge, but only one of them had ever filed a complaint. While this problem may have no satisfactory solution, it does suggest that there are serious drawbacks in relying on litigation as the principal means of ridding the workplace of sexual harassment.

C. Congress Shall Make No Law ...

Much of what we define as sexual harassment consists of speech, and speech is normally protected against governmental interference by the First Amendment. Some speech, of course, is not protected—extortion, blackmail, obscenity—and some sexual harassment undoubtedly falls within these unprotected categories. Though there's not much law on the subject, it's safe to assume that much of quid pro quo sexual harassment—"have sex with me or you're fired"—lands on the unprotected side of the line.

But the line blurs rapidly as one moves away from the easy cases. Could Congress make a law prohibiting employees from asking each other out on dates? Could it prohibit a second or third request after a firm "no"? These are questions worth pondering, because sexual harassment law requires employers to punish employees who get too aggressive in expressing a personal interest in other employees, even when this expression is purely verbal. Title VII effectively forces the employer to become the censor for employee speech and conduct.

Things get even fuzzier when one considers some of the hostile environment cases where male employees use locker-room jargon and decorate their work spaces with pictures of scantily clad women. It is widely assumed that Congress may not outlaw such decorations unless they amount to obscenity, that it couldn't pass a law prohibiting off-color language in private discourse. Under sexual harassment law as it has developed to this point, however, an employer may be held liable for failing to curb such workplace indiscretions. The tension between the right of female employees to work in an environment free of gender-based abuse, and the right of male employees to engage in speech and conduct normally deemed constitutionally protected, has not yet attracted much judicial attention, but it soon may. At least one constitutional scholar, Professor Kingsley R. Browne of Wayne State University Law School, has suggested that much of hostile environment sexual harassment law is constitutionally suspect.

D. Whose Rights Are These, Anyway?

A complaint of sexual harassment in the work environment brings into conflict the rights and interests of two or more employees. On one side is the accuser, who is entitled to work in an environment cleansed of coercion and insults; on the other is the accused supervisor or co-worker, who has an interest in retaining his job and clearing his name. In the nature of things, it may be very difficult to reconcile these interests in a single proceeding, and the employer may be left holding the bag when one disputant or the other is dissatisfied with the outcome.

Ellison v. Brady, best known for announcing the "reasonable woman" standard for sexual harassment cases, provides a helpful illustration. Ellison worked in the San Mateo office of the Internal Revenue Service. A co-worker named Gray sent her a series of harassing letters. Ellison complained to management, which arranged for Gray to be transferred to another office. Gray brought a grievance through his union and the case was resolved by letting him return to the San Mateo office after six months. Ellison refused to work in the same office as Gray, and rejected a transfer to another office on the grounds that she, as the victim of the harassment, should not have to bear the burden. Having resolved Gray's rights in the context of *his* grievance, the employer was now stuck with a claim for damages by Ellison, who took the position that Gray had gotten off too easy, and that she was entitled not to work in close proximity to him.

As sexual harassment claims become more common, employers may frequently find themselves caught between the pit of a Title VII suit for failing to purge a hostile environment, and the pendulum of a wrongful discharge suit for disciplining an employee wrongly accused of harassment. Given the intractable problems of proof discussed earlier, how can employers protect themselves from attack by one side or the other? And even if the facts are not in dispute—let's say the accused employee admits having done or said something unacceptable—what is the proper remedy? It's a judgment call the employer must make with some regard to the entire office, not merely the parochial interests of the particular individuals involved. One concern might be to send a message to other employees that such conduct will not be tolerated. This counsels in favor of overly severe punishment, but does that then expose the employer to a claim of vindictiveness by the punished employee? Or what if the transgression is minor and the transgressor is essential to the employer's operations? Is the employer required to risk business without him or damages in a Title VII suit?

Of course, employers have always had to resolve disputes among members of the work force, but sexual harassment claims stand on somewhat different footing. First, they require the employer to police all manner of non-job-related interaction at or near the work site and, quite possibly, off the work site. A dinner date between co-workers that ends in hurt feelings or worse may well foster a sexual harassment claim. Second, sexual harassment claims are unique in that one employee can base her (or his) claim on the employer's failure to punish another employee quickly or severely enough, as happened in *Ellison.* Quite obviously, employers will have to be far more vigilant in setting and enforcing standards for employee conduct, on *and* off the job.

All of this runs against the grain of contemporary notions as to the proper relationship between employer and employees. Enlightened employers have generally shied away from the Orwellian notion of policing employee behavior outside the work environment; enlightened office policy generally grants errant employees a chance to mend their ways before they are sent packing. When it comes to accusations of sexual harassment, however, employers may deem it prudent to take the harshest measures first, lest they be accused of insensitivity to harassment in the workplace.

E. The Gilded Cage

Perhaps the most worrisome aspect of using litigation as the primary tool for eliminating sexual harassment is that it could stunt the progress of women in their long struggle to gain workplace equality. This could happen as a result of precautions—often subtle and surreptitious—that male employees might take so as to avoid spurious charges of sexual harassment. Of course, we want male employees to adjust their inappropriate behavior, and we want employers to exercise authority in purging the work environment of sexually hostile practices. But the incentives may be too great, causing male workers to run for shelter by minimizing their contact with potential female protégés. The right balance may be difficult to achieve if litigation is used as the principal lever.

The concept of workplace equality has been premised on just that—equality— whether on the basis of sex, race, or any other immutable characteristic. We all look forward to the day when employment decisions will be made only on the basis of merit, and when employees of both genders work together without regard to their biological differences. In subtle ways, sexual harassment law tends to deepen those differences, driving a wedge between the sexes in the workplace. Although anecdotal evidence is always somewhat suspect, many women have reported a distancing from male colleagues after the Thomas-Hill hearings. "My God," many male employees must have thought, "if allegations like that were raised against me, how on earth would I defend myself?" Considering the devastating consequences of a sexual harassment charge both professionally and personally, it's hard to fault men for being cautious.

"So much the better," one might say. "*Let* them be careful—it will just discourage sexual byplay and other questionable conduct that doesn't belong in the office anyway." One must keep in mind, however, that men are still in an overwhelmingly dominant position in terms of supervisory authority. This means that men tend to make a far larger share of the hiring and promotion decisions. What effect will concerns about spurious sexual harassment charges have on those decisions?

Take simple items like deciding which junior associate to take on an important business trip or which employee to keep in the office for an after-hours project. Competence may well suggest the female as the better choice; caution may lead the manager to select the male. It is impossible to tell whether and to what extent the fear of sexual harassment charges will color supervisory decisions, but as sexual harassment litigation becomes more common, male managers may end up presupposing that every time they appoint a woman to a position that brings her into close personal contact, they hand her a loaded gun with which she can blow away their careers.

To dismiss such concerns as baseless, to suggest that the failure to promote can itself be subject to a Title VII claim, is myopic. Managers have a lot of discretion in hiring, evaluating, and promoting; proving sex discrimination in such decisions is very hard and, given the choice, most managers would rather defend against a claim for discriminatory hiring than one for sexual harassment: The former is an inconvenience, the latter a sudden end to a career.

Short of adverse hiring and promotion decisions, the fear of sexual harassment suits may well isolate women in the workplace. No one wants to be accused of creating a hostile work environment or get shipped off to a branch office because another employee lodges a complaint of sexual harassment. Male employees may find it prudent to avoid lunches with colleagues of the opposite sex, and after-work socializing may well exclude female co-workers. The personal networks that are so important in building a career may exclude women, as men fear getting too chummy with female co-workers and subordinates. To the extent sexual harassment litigation raises the level of suspicion between men and women in the workplace, it may ultimately hamper efforts at gender integration.

II.

It is far easier, of course, to find fault than solutions. And litigation surely does have a place in helping rid the American workplace of the type of demeaning experiences far too many women have had to endure. I am reminded of the experience of a friend of mine who had been general counsel to a medium-sized manufacturer in the apparel business. As is prevalent in that industry, the company's field managers regularly handled the merchandise, generally as it was worn by female models; complaints came in on a fairly consistent basis. Mindful of her employer's potential liability, my friend drafted a sexual harassment policy that contained the usual advice and warnings: sexual harassment is unlawful; the company condemns it; if you feel you have been sexually harassed, you have certain remedies; and so on. The general counsel dutifully presented the policy to one of the company's top managers, who approved it for distribution. She had hundreds of copies made, which were then posted on bulletin boards and stuffed into employees' pay envelopes.

It was at that point that the company's president first became aware of the policy. He was outraged—perhaps fearful it would foment litigation—and he ordered the notices torn off bulletin boards, removed from pay envelopes and retrieved from employees who had already received them. Quite obviously, the company in question could use a swift kick in the pants by way of a sexual harassment suit; few things rivet the mind to a problem like the threat of substantial liability.

But litigation ought not be the only avenue of approach, or even the most significant one. Whatever one may think about litigation as a means of resolving other disputes, it has too many negatives as the primary means of dealing with sexual harassment. If we are to achieve a workplace free from discrimination of any kind, including sexual harassment, it must be through the moral suasion employers exercise over their employees and, indeed, employees exercise over employers. It must be made absolutely clear that there is nothing at all cool about harassing or demeaning other employees on account of their sex.

Companies must adopt stringent policies against sexual harassment. A forcefully worded policy condemning harassment, written in simple terms and aggressively backed by the company's top managers, is probably the most important ingredient in assuring a workplace where men and women can work together without discomfort or coercion. One large company managed to enhance enforcement efforts simply by rephrasing its policy in more easily understood language and putting up large posters condemning harassment.

Employee training is another obvious and essential component of a comprehensive sexual harassment policy. Men and women tend to see sexually related speech differently, which explains why much of what most women find sexually suggestive and demeaning many men consider playful and harmless. One recent study, for example, found that 67 percent of men would feel flattered if propositioned, while 63 percent of women would be offended. From their own perspective, each may feel justified, yet the result may be hurt feelings, distrust, apprehension and more hurt feelings. Many companies have been successful in using focus groups to avoid misunderstandings in the workplace, helping to educate men and women as to how they see the same events differently. Counseling, too, can be beneficial in educating men about how women perceive their actions, and vice versa.

Sexual harassment is the kind of problem supervisors hate to deal with, first because interpersonal problems are always a headache, and second because the issue is so sensitive. Training mid-level managers to deal with sexual harassment claims in a constructive, positive way is a challenge companies will have to accept if they are to avoid the quagmire of litigation. Front-line managers are in the best position to sense the atmosphere in the workplace, and to make gentle corrections before minor disagreements turn into major grievances and lawsuits. Common sense may not be enough and giving managers professional training on how to detect and deal with harassment is time and money well invested.

A fast, effective and confidential grievance procedure for dealing with harassment problems is yet another essential component of any company's office policy. One large company runs a 24-hour hotline that gives employees advice and accepts complaints (sometimes anonymously) on sexual harassment. Unions can be very helpful in this process as well, as they have traditionally helped to mediate workplace grievances through the dispute resolution mechanisms of collective bargaining agreements. Union representatives, however, are likely to need the same training in dealing with sexual harassment claims as mid-level managers, especially because they tend to be the elected representatives of male-dominated constituencies. Indeed, the overwhelming majority of union-filed grievances relating to sexual harassment have involved challenges to discipline imposed on alleged sexual harassers rather than vindication of the rights of the alleged victim. This apparent bias must be overcome if unions are to fulfill their pivotal role in resolving workplace claims of sexual harassment.

Finally, there must be a measure of restraint among employees. Men, on the one hand, must be aware of the boundaries of propriety and learn to stay well within them. Women must be vigilant of their rights, but must also have some forgiveness for human foibles: misplaced humor, misunderstanding, or just plain stupidity. Transgressions should be noted, and an apology or correction obtained. But it is important for everyone to try to mend the working relationship, not rush into a lawsuit.

Harassment tends to be less prevalent in stable workplaces where employees feel loyalty to the company and each other; only by education and awareness can the legal burden of sexual harassment law be turned into the economic benefit of developing a more productive, cohesive and comfortable workplace. The point is to learn to work together, not to turn offices into armed camps where men and women circle each other with mistrust and apprehension. This takes enlightened leadership, not crafty finagling. In other words, this is a problem far too important and delicate to be handed over to the lawyers.

HON. ALEX KOZINSKI
Judge, United States Court
of Appeals for the Ninth Circuit

FOREWORD

That this book is sorely needed should have been apparent to all from the day the authors started work on it four years ago. That it is so timely is purely fortuitous. (This introduction is being written on the evening of Clarence Thomas's confirmation as an Associate Justice of the United States Supreme Court by a 52–48 vote of the United States Senate.) The problem of sexual harassment was with us long before Anita Hill made America aware of the subject. Sexual harassment was always serious; it was always sensitive; it was always difficult; and it was always prevalent. It remains all of those things today.

But the sexual harassment issue will never again be the same in America. As the Army-McCarthy hearings changed the nation's view of red-baiting and the Watergate hearings changed our view of politics, the Judge Thomas-Professor Hill hearings transfixed America and will inevitably deeply affect our nation's views of sexual harassment, in many different ways.

The country will not soon forget the drama of Anita Hill's simple, calm, quiet and unhesitating responses to her interrogators—her unshakable reiteration of the details that seemingly shocked some of the senators so greatly. Nor will it soon forget the powerful, sweeping and angry denials of those charges by about-to-be Justice Clarence Thomas—his accusations of "high-tech lynching," his claims of racism, the oft-repeated contention that he was the victim of a conspiracy by sinister interest groups and slick liberal lawyers, and his emotional charges that the senatorial process was unfair to *him*.

Rarely, if ever, have the American people had so much difficulty in determining who was telling the truth, who was lying, what the possible motivations were, why accusations of sexual harassment are made, and how they should be resolved. Their confusion was understandable. To the untrained observer, both Professor Hill and Judge Thomas seemed like credible witnesses. And Judge Thomas's supporters deliberately played upon that confusion. They sought to create doubts by tactics fair and foul. They were relentless in their pursuit of Professor Hill, mainly when she was not present, and they quickly made it clear that the classic slash-and-burn tactics feared by all female complainants were the order of the day. Her detractors barely paid lip service to the quest for truth.

During the hearings, we heard more theories about why Anita Hill made her charges of sexual harassment than one would have thought it possible to conjure up. Among these were mental derangement, jealousy, disappointment over failure to obtain a promotion, anger that, as chairman of the EEOC,

Clarence Thomas made decisions on the basis of political expediency rather than on the merits, resentment about his employment of lighter-skinned women— and yes, always, the liberal conspiracy (even though Anita Hill was identified as a conservative Republican who had been a supporter of Robert Bork). Some of these theories were offered by senators, some by Judge Thomas's former staff, some by the nominee himself. The term "a woman scorned" became the subject of much debate and even hilarity as the chairman of the Judiciary Committee misstated the source of his misquotation. But if the theories were inconsistent, few seemed to notice—or to care. Far more time was spent complaining about extraneous matters such as leaks than on questioning Judge Thomas about the facts. The effort to focus attention on every issue but the critical one—whether the former chairman of the EEOC sexually harassed an attractive female subordinate—paid off. And Judge Thomas's own testimony reminded many of the tactics frequently used by defense counsel in criminal trials: if you don't have the facts on your side and you don't have the law on your side, pound the table and cry foul.

One senator told the American people, with a straight face, that only an insane person would talk to a female employee about sexual matters in explicit terms or encourage her to see pornographic films. He suggested that any man who behaved in the manner described by Professor Hill should be locked up in an asylum. Yet no witness was permitted to tell the senators or, more important, the American people, whether such conduct occurs in the workplace with any degree of regularity, or whether the details of Professor Hill's story are consistent with incidents of harassment experienced by other women. No expert was permitted to testify regarding how women who are the victims of sexual harassment respond, nor even whether the way the accused reacted to the charges in front of the Committee tells us something important about what really happened. Specifically, no one was permitted to testify as to whether the guilty generally respond the way Judge Thomas did or whether Judge Thomas's reactions were typical of those who are falsely charged. And, although no expert was allowed to tell us whether an individual who sexually harasses one woman is always a harasser of others, several senators eagerly offered their own assessments on the subject. (Tonight, a taxi driver, having received an instantaneous TV education from these learned gentlemen, assured me that sexual harassment never occurs on an isolated basis; there is always a pattern of conduct, he said.)

In the end, a majority of Americans were reluctant to believe that a man who had reached the pinnacle of his profession, who had overcome adversity (with a little help from affirmative action), who was trained by nuns and attended church regularly—a black Republican who wore his conservatism on his sleeve—could engage in such "bizarre" conduct. Even a majority of women could not understand how a true victim of sexual harassment could respond as Professor Hill did; they did not understand why Anita Hill didn't simply cut her ties with the man who was well on his way to becoming the most important African American in the country, the man whose favorable references would be critical to her career as long as she remained in the work force.

The large majority of the television audience was heavily influenced by the unrelenting assault on Professor Hill's character and emotional stability. Even the President of the United States joined in. He told the nation immediately after hearing Clarence Thomas's opening statement, and without waiting to hear Anita Hill's testimony, that Clarence Thomas was telling the truth. The inference was obvious. Professor Hill was publicly branded a liar even before she had a chance to tell her side of the story.

The senators who would ordinarily have defended Professor Hill were as overwhelmed by the onslaught as was the public. They appeared snake-bitten, paralyzed, powerless to respond. In the end, they simply seemed inept—unable to figure out how to deal with the problem, and particularly with the remarkable political paradox created by the opposition's cynical playing of "the race card."

It is also possible that the senators' maleness got in the way. In this respect, it is notable that almost every member of the all-male Judiciary Committee expressed his sympathy with Judge Thomas for the "ordeal he was undergoing," thereby giving the public the impression that they thought him innocent, yet almost none expressed comparable sentiments regarding the pain, anguish and humiliation Professor Hill was being forced to endure. Questions as mundane as the appropriate period for statutes of limitations were discussed at length during the Thomas-Hill hearings, while other far more fundamental concerns hung unstated over the Senate Chambers. One obvious brooding omnipresence that affected the single-gender Committee was the "there but for the grace of God go I" syndrome. In some cases, the syndrome simply reflected a concern over the possibility of false accusations. In others, more may have been involved. After all, some of what is classified as sexual harassment today was common practice less than a generation ago.

There was another problem that legitimately concerned many viewers. Sexual harassment, like date rape and child molestation, is an offense that is usually committed in private. The absence of percipient witnesses, though inherent in the nature of the offense, may make it difficult to eliminate all doubts as to what did or did not occur. Senators seeking to discredit Professor Hill artfully capitalized on this concern. With obvious glee, they forced those appearing on behalf of Anita Hill to "admit" that they had not observed the dirty deeds firsthand even though they had come to testify only that her story was not a recent fabrication, that she had told them of the harassment at the time it was occurring. As a result, critically important corroborative evidence was lost in the fog of deliberate obfuscation. Nevertheless, whether or not one believes that Professor Hill was lying or fantasizing eight to ten years before she reluctantly made her charges public, and was still lying or fantasizing at the time of the hearings, the danger of false accusations in these one-on-one sex cases is real. It is important to find ways to assure that the innocent are protected. Better methods of determining the truth must be developed. And, in cases in which the issue is solely whether a charge of sexual harassment is true (as opposed to an inquiry into whether, considering all we know about an individual, that person has demonstrated the character and qualifications necessary for confirmation to a lifetime position on the nation's highest court), the accused certainly should be given the benefit of the doubt.

There is another point the hearings illustrated. Whatever the forum, it is important that we evaluate charges of sexual harassment in the light of actual human experience rather than on the basis of unrealistic, puritanical assumptions—assumptions such as: all unmarried persons are virgins; all spouses are monogamous; no decent person ever uses profanity; and all sex acts are performed in the missionary position. People's private lives frequently involve more than appears on the surface. It is not unusual for upstanding, honorable individuals to have predilections for or to engage in occasional conduct that is not entirely consistent with all of the terms of the prevailing moral code. That is why Judge Thomas struck such a responsive chord when he told the Committee defiantly that under no circumstances would he answer questions about his private life. Although his purpose may well have been to avoid inquiries regarding his alleged interest in pornographic films, and although any such admission would have provided strong support for Anita Hill's charges that he described X-rated movies to her in the most graphic terms, the public agreed with Judge Thomas's assertion, unchallenged by any senator, that his "private" life was off limits. Most Americans, it is clear, would be extremely reluctant to undergo a public cross-examination concerning their own sexual practices and experiences.

Our public discourse regarding sexual practices often fails to match the reality of our conduct. In fact, it is not nearly as common, as several of our good senators would have us believe, for well-respected public figures to have committed at some point in their lives sexual acts that years later they themselves find wholly unacceptable. Nor is it uncommon for us to discover that well-respected priests, ministers, college presidents, and other authority figures are currently engaged in private sexual conduct that is not only illegal but appears to be wholly out of character. It happens all the time, and whenever it does, the public finds itself once again in a state of shocked disbelief.

The Thomas-Hill hearings were a mixed blessing at best. There is no doubt that the public consciousness was raised, no doubt that men will be more reluctant to take the risk of engaging in sexual harassment. On the other hand, for a while at least, women may be even less willing than before to come forward and report misconduct. Still, in the long run, Americans will undoubtedly acquire a greater understanding of what goes on in the workplace, what sexual harassment is all about, how it should be defined, who does it, how frequently it occurs, how women react, and how judgments as to what occurred can be made.

As more and more women find it necessary or choose to work for a living, the office, the factory, and other job sites are becoming the primary locations for the initiation of male-female (and even other) relationships. People who work closely together and share common interests often find that sexual attraction ensues. It is not surprising that those feelings arise even when one of the persons is a superior and the other a subordinate. What is proper workplace etiquette if the man, or the woman, decides that he or she would like to explore the possibility of a romantic relationship? When does a breach of etiquette become sexual harassment? How do men, used to being the initiating partners, know when requests for dates or even sexual advances are either inappropriate or unwanted?

Admittedly, sexual harassment is a troubling, difficult, mystifying, unexplored area. Our knowledge of how to deal with its manifold ramifications is limited. Our law on the subject is in its infancy. America has awakened to the issue, but does not know quite what to do with it. Some of the necessary next steps, however, are apparent.

1. We must try to develop a set of rules that can be easily understood and applied. This involves building a consensus as to what we can properly proscribe, what we should only discourage, and what constitutes part of normal male-female interplay. In our efforts to protect women in the workplace we should not stifle their opportunities, or those of their male co-workers, to achieve a rewarding social life as the result of contacts made at work. There can be no doubt that the rules are changing. Women are free to ask men for dates. They are no longer placed on pedestals or wrapped in cellophane. Women who work for a living cannot and should not be protected against contact with the harsh realities of the real world. Women are equals in the workplace as well as elsewhere. From now on, they must be treated with respect, but not with kid gloves. Our rules can no longer be based on the unacceptable assumption that women are more sensitive than men—whatever the truth of that assumption—or that women are in any way the weaker sex. All stereotypical notions must be dismissed before the rule-making process begins. Nevertheless, in the end, after balancing the factors, we must provide firm protection against all forms of sexual harassment.

2. We must become more open-minded and tolerant. We must try to look at the issue objectively—not as men or as women, but as human beings. True, we each bring our own perspective to the process—a perspective shaped by a variety of circumstances, including gender. But we should all want rules that are fair to *both* sexes—and, yes, to all individuals, regardless of their sexual preferences. After all, most of us are parents, or will be. We should want fairness for our daughters and for our sons alike. Unfair rules are in the end harmful to all.

3. We must proceed firmly but with caution. Our knowledge is limited. Overzealousness can only hurt the cause. As with all efforts to protect individual rights, there will be those who seek to bring the venture into disrepute. They will capitalize on any errors that are made. And a backlash can sidetrack for many years the long overdue effort to ensure fair treatment in the workplace.

4. We must be aware that whatever rules we develop will require constant reexamination, modification, and fine-tuning. The sexual, gender, and preference revolutions are not over. Society is in a constant state of evolution. In a world of mass television, fax transmittals, and supersonic flights, changes tend to occur quickly. As women begin to shatter the glass ceiling, sexual harassment by female supervisors will become a more significant part of the problem. Some differences in approach to female-conducted harassment may be necessary. Similarly, as gays and lesbians achieve equal employment opportunities, sexual harassment by persons of different sexual preferences will require our attention. Male reactions to unwanted sexual attentions from other males, even when that attention springs from a mistaken belief that an advance would be welcome, are likely to be far more vigorous and forceful than the responses we have come to expect from women. Employers will have to be trained to

handle such situations with tact and understanding, and with a full recognition of (1) the rights of all involved, (2) the need for fair and equal treatment for persons thought by some to be "different," (3) the morale problem that can arise from improper handling of explosive sexual situations, and (4) the fact that all involved have entered uncharted waters.

5. We must engage in a vigorous and intensive educational campaign. Sexual harassment must be debated and explored in the classrooms, the boardrooms, and the workplace. It must be given the serious attention the subject demands and, notwithstanding the deplorable treatment afforded Professor Hill, women must be encouraged to come forward and discuss their complaints. If they do, in many cases they may be able to resolve those grievances through frank and open discussions with supervisors previously unaware of the nature or impact of their own conduct. The educational process is key—and this book constitutes an important beginning in that effort.

Finally, three cautionary notes. First, as is the case with so many of today's issues, we must be sensitive to other, sometimes conflicting, concerns or values, not just to those directly affecting the triggering event. Specifically, we must not be so eager to eradicate what we perceive to be offensive conduct that we are willing to trample on the freedom of others. Free speech is a fragile but critical commodity. Those who would limit it are frequently persons of good will, well-motivated but zealous advocates of a worthy cause. They genuinely believe that we can bend the First Amendment where their particular cause is concerned, but stand fast with respect to all others. They are wrong. If all those who felt the way they do prevailed, there would be little left of the basic right itself. We all know that words can constitute acts. But words and pictures can also constitute legitimate expressions of views, a healthy way of asserting one's individuality, an unpleasant but protected reflection of a different philosophy, attitude, or way of life. All persons should be aware of the sensitivity of others, but the law cannot guarantee that we will not sometimes be discomforted. Not everything that is wrong can or should be made illegal. That is especially true where freedom of expression is involved.

Second, our legitimate concern over sexual harassment should not cause us to transform the male-female relationship into a hostile or adversary one. None of us should approach the workplace with a defiant attitude or a chip on our shoulder. We should not start from the premise that a person of the opposite sex with whom we work is an enemy or poses a threat to our personal or professional well-being. On the contrary, the assumption should be that he or she is someone who will be sympathetic to our problems, understanding of our needs, helpful in our efforts to succeed. That will not always be the case, of course, but it is worth a try. Men and women *should* get along well together. There is an attraction, one to the other, that transcends sexuality. In many instances, however, fear or insecurity on one side or the other will inhibit the development of the type of healthy and constructive relationship that should exist. When that occurs, it's worth the time and effort to try to overcome the barriers. Positive personal relations can make the workplace a far more pleasant place to spend one's time.

Third, we should not confuse equality and uniformity. Men are attracted to women, and women to men, because of the numerous differences that mark the sexes—not just because they are constructed differently. The two sexes complement each other in many felicitous ways. Uniformity, or even similarity, of dress, manner, attitude, or approach is not a desirable goal. Although job-related rules must not be based on stereotypes, neither fairness nor equity requires the creation of a unisex society, in the workplace or elsewhere.

The infusion of women into all aspects of the work force was largely a matter of economic necessity. Still, an important side benefit could be a significant change in the way we view members of the opposite sex. It is more important than ever that we learn to treat all individuals with respect and afford them the personal dignity they deserve. If we do, sexual harassment will largely be a thing of the past.

HON. STEPHEN REINHARDT
Judge, United States Court
of Appeals for the Ninth Circuit

PREFACE

The book Barbara Lindemann Schlei and I co-authored, *Employment Discrimination Law,* began with a telephone call in the early 1970s from then Dean of the University of Southern California Law School and now Ninth Circuit Judge Dorothy W. Nelson, inviting Barbara and me to lunch at the faculty club. As the EEOC's chief lawyer in Southern California, Barbara was an exceptionally visible and capable employment discrimination litigator on the plaintiff's side. My law firm had the southwest's largest practice representing employers.

At lunch, Vice Dean Jerry J. Wiley suggested that Professor Michael Reiss, an extraordinarily capable clinical law professor, moderate a course to be taught in a debate format by Barbara and me for practicing attorneys. I demurred because there was no book or decent materials. Barbara suggested that we put together materials. I declined, citing time pressures. Barbara, ever optimistic, said she would put together the materials if I would just "look at them." I agreed. Somehow "looking at them" turned into hundreds of hours, but we had a sixty-page single-spaced outline, with about 500 pages of edited cases behind the outline that we used to teach the course.

The course was a huge success. People heard about it around the country and wrote seeking a copy of the materials. The law was moving so fast in the area that much of what we had put together was now incomplete or out of date, and Barbara proposed that we rewrite and expand the materials. I again demurred, citing time pressures. Barbara again asked if I would "just look at them." Never one to learn from experience, I agreed. Somehow "looking at them" turned into many hundreds of hours, but we had a 125–page single-spaced outline and over a thousand pages of edited cases.

Barbara suggested that we turn the outline and edited cases into a book. I refused, citing time pressures. Barbara replied, "There'll be nothing to it. We've already done all the work. We'll just get our friends around the country to draft various chapters, starting with the outline."

"Nothing to it" turned into thousands of hours of work editing and rewriting the very excellent work done by many of our friends from around the country, and poring over galleys and page proofs. When done, we had the first edition of *Employment Discrimination Law,* followed by the 1979 supplement, and then the second edition. Happily, the American Bar Association then took over the job of supplementing; our partnership with the ABA has been very successful.

Barbara then pointed out that while *Employment Discrimination Law* had proven extremely successful, some areas it covered were either so complex or so important that they warranted a separate book. Barbara therefore conceived the idea of a series of books expanding various areas covered by *Employment Discrimination Law,* starting with sexual harassment. She again approached me, asked me to be a co-author along with her and the very capable David Kadue, with the same approach that had worked so well in the past: "Paul, there will be nothing to it. It will just be an expansion of *Employment Discrimination Law* focusing on the sexual harassment area."

I may be dense, but over the years I have learned something. I knew how much work was going to be involved. It was going to be an extraordinary amount of work. And that would be totally incompatible with being chair of the employment practice at my law firm, carrying my caseload, and trying to get ready for the third edition of *Employment Discrimination Law.* I refused, and resisted months of entreaties. Finally, I agreed to "just look at each chapter and make suggestions." I have faithfully carried out that commitment. I have been exceptionally impressed with the quality of this book, and would have expected no less from anything done by Barbara. I hope you agree with me that this book is an extremely useful expansion of the sexual harassment coverage of *Employment Discrimination Law,* and will be invaluable to both students of the law and those who must apply the law to practical and litigation situations.

PAUL GROSSMAN

Los Angeles, California
December 2, 1991

ACKNOWLEDGMENTS

This book presents the thinking of outstanding employment discrimination law specialists from all areas of the country and all aspects of the practice. The employment discrimination law practitioners who have contributed their ideas and experiences to this work include plaintiffs' attorneys, management defense attorneys, government attorneys, and law school professors.

We therefore have enormous debts to acknowledge.

The following persons drafted chapters or portions of chapters or otherwise contributed to particular chapters:

Vicki A. Abrahamson is a partner in the law firm of Vicki A. Abrahamson & Associates, Chicago, representing plaintiffs in employment litigation. She is a 1979 graduate of the University of Michigan Law School. We thank her for drafting the portion of the chapter on Asserted Defenses addressing the Federal Arbitration Act.

James N. Adler is a partner in the law firm of Irell & Manella, Los Angeles, representing management. He is a 1961 Order of the Coif graduate of the Michigan Law School, where he was Editor-in-Chief of the *Michigan Law Review.* He served as law clerk to Justice Charles E. Whittaker and to Chief Justice Earl Warren, United States Supreme Court. He drafted the chapter on Election and Exhaustion of Remedies for the first edition of *Employment Discrimination Law,* and he drafted the Equal Pay chapter for the second edition. We thank him and his associates Robert G. Barnes, Mark Daniels, David Gindler, Jeremy Gray, Jack P. Lipton, and Wendy A. Wolf for drafting the section on harassment on bases other than sex in the chapter on Forms of Harassment, and thank him and Jack P. Lipton for their contribution to the discussion of harassment based on sexual orientation or transsexualism in the chapter on Hostile Environment Harassment.

Laura Allen is a partner in the law firm of Hughes, Hubbard & Reed, New York City. A 1975 Order of the Coif graduate of Cornell Law School, she served as law clerk to Judge Inzer B. Wyatt of the United States District Court for the Southern District of New York. We thank her and Stephanie Young, an associate with Hughes, Hubbard & Reed, for substantial editing and revising of the chapters on Complainant's Litigation Strategy and Employer's Litigation Strategy.

Fred Alvarez is co-chairman of the Labor and Employment Law Group of Pillsbury, Madison & Sutro, San Francisco, representing management. He is a 1975 graduate of Stanford Law School. From 1984 to 1987 he served as a commissioner of the EEOC. From 1987 to 1989 he served as Assistant Secretary of Labor in charge of the Employment Standards Administration, which includes the Office of Federal Contract Compliance Program. We thank him and Carol L. Woodward, an associate with Pillsbury, Madison & Sutro, San Jose, for drafting the chapter on Harassment by Supervisors.

R. Lawrence Ashe, Jr., is a partner in the law firm of Paul, Hastings, Janofsky & Walker, Atlanta, representing management. He is a 1967 *cum laude* graduate of Harvard Law School. He is Management Co-Chair of the EEO Committee of the ABA's Labor and Employment Law Section. He drafted the Scored Tests chapter of both editions of *Employment Discrimination Law.* We thank him and Sarah Corley Turman, an associate with Paul, Hastings, Janofsky & Walker, for their research contribution to the section on negligence in the chapter on The Common Law.

Mark W. Atkinson is a partner in the law firm of Paul, Hastings, Janofsky & Walker, Los Angeles, representing management. He is a 1974 graduate of the University of California at Los Angeles School of Law, where he was a member of the *UCLA Law Review.* He drafted the Promotion chapter in the second edition of *Employment Discrimination Law.* We thank him for his editorial assistance with the chapters on Quid Pro Quo Harassment and Asserted Defenses.

Larry C. Backer, an associate with the law firm of Seyfarth, Shaw, Fairweather & Geraldson, Los Angeles, representing management, has now joined the faculty of the University of Tulsa College of Law, Tulsa, Oklahoma. He is a 1982 graduate of Columbia University School of Law, having received his Master of Public Policy degree in 1979 from Harvard University, and served as a law clerk to Judge L.I. Garth of the United States Court of Appeals for the Third Circuit. We thank him for drafting the chapter on Forms of Harassment.

Jeffrey C. Bannon is Regional Attorney with the Dallas office of the EEOC. He is a 1977 honor graduate of the University of Connecticut School of Law. We thank him for drafting portions of the Overview chapter and for editing and revising the chapter on The Agency Investigation.

Ralph H. Baxter, Jr., is managing partner of the law firm of Orrick, Herrington & Sutcliffe, San Francisco. He is a 1974 graduate of the University of Virginia Law School. He drafted the chapter on the National Labor Relations Act in the second edition of *Employment Discrimination Law.* We thank him and Lynne C. Hermle, an associate with Orrick, Herrington & Sutcliffe, for editorial assistance on the chapters on Harassment by Supervisors, Constructive Discharge, and Retaliation.

Renee Turkell Brook is an associate in the law firm of O'Melveny & Meyers, Los Angeles, representing management. She is a 1983 graduate of the University of California at Los Angeles School of Law. We thank her for drafting the chapter on Harassment by Co-Workers.

David W. Burcham, a partner in the law firm of Gibson, Dunn & Crutcher, Los Angeles, representing management, has now joined the faculty of the Loyola Law School, Los Angeles. A 1984 *magna cum laude* graduate of Loyola Law School, he was Chief Articles Editor of the *UCLA Law Review* and served as a law clerk for Justice Byron White of the United States Supreme

Court and for Chief Judge Ruggero Aldisert of the United States Court of Appeals for the Third Circuit. We thank him and Robin M. Bernhardt, an associate with Gibson, Dunn & Crutcher, for drafting the chapter on Fair Employment Practices Statutes.

Sarah E. Burns is Professor of Law at New York University Law School. She is a 1979 graduate of the Yale University School of Law, where she was an editor of the *Yale Law Journal*. We thank her for the substantial research and thinking that she supplied for the chapter on Hostile Environment Harassment.

David R. Cashdan is an attorney practicing in Washington, D.C., representing plaintiffs in employment litigation. He is a 1964 graduate of the University of Michigan Law School. He served from 1965 to 1970 with the General Counsel's office of the EEOC. We thank him for his ideas and research contributions to the chapter on Quid Pro Quo Harassment.

Christopher E. Cobey is a partner in the law firm of Seyfarth, Shaw, Fairweather & Geraldson, San Francisco, representing management. He is a 1974 graduate of the University of California at Davis School of Law. We thank him for his editorial assistance with the chapters on Taking Preventive Action, Responding to Internal Complaints, Complainant's Litigation Strategy, and Employer's Litigation Strategy.

Robert L. Corbin is a partner in the law firm of Corbin & Sharenow, specializing in white-collar criminal and business litigation. He is a 1972 graduate of Fordham University School of Law. We thank him for his editorial assistance with the chapter on Criminal Law.

D. Barclay Edmundson is a partner in the law firm of Munger, Tolles & Olson, Los Angeles, representing management. A 1979 Order of the Coif graduate of the University of California at Los Angeles School of Law, he served as law clerk to Judge William Matthew Byrne of the United States District Court for the Central District of California. He participated in drafting the Equal Pay chapter in the second edition of *Employment Discrimination Law*. We thank him for contributing the proof portions to the chapters on Quid Pro Quo and Hostile Environment Harassment.

Allen J. Gross heads the Labor and Employment Department of Orrick, Herrington & Sutcliffe, Los Angeles, representing management. He is a 1974 graduate of Georgetown University Law School, where he served as an executive editor of *The Tax Lawyer*. We thank him and Lori A. Bowman, an associate with Orrick, Herrington & Sutcliffe, for drafting the chapter on Attorney's Fees and Costs.

Catherine B. Hagen is a partner in the law firm of O'Melveny & Meyers, Newport Beach, California, representing management. She is a 1978 *summa cum laude* graduate of Loyola Law School and was Editor of the *Loyola of Los Angeles Law Review*. We thank her and her associates Wayne Clayton, John Manier, and Larry Walraven for drafting the chapter on Asserted Defenses.

Fay Hartog-Rapp is Of Counsel to the law firm of Seyfarth, Shaw, Fairweather & Geraldson, Chicago, representing management. She is a 1975 graduate of Loyola University of Chicago School of Law. We thank her and Lisa

A. Lopatka, an associate with Seyfarth, Shaw, Fairweather & Geraldson, for drafting the chapter on Federal Constitutional, Statutory, and Civil Rights Law.

Anne T. Harvey is a partner in the law firm of Lawless, Harvey & Horowitz, San Francisco, representing plaintiffs in employment litigation. She is a 1976 graduate of the University of California at Davis School of Law. We thank her for drafting the section on intentional infliction of emotional distress in the chapter on The Common Law.

Howard C. Hay is a partner in the law firm of Paul, Hastings, Janofsky & Walker, Costa Mesa, California, representing management. A 1969 graduate of the University of Michigan Law School, he served as law clerk to Chief Judge Frank M. Coffin of the United States Court of Appeals for the First Circuit. He drafted the chapters on Non-Scored Objective Criteria and Proof in the first edition of *Employment Discrimination Law*. We thank him and Beth J. Pearce, an associate with Paul, Hastings, Janofsky & Walker, for drafting the chapter on Taking Preventive Action.

Pamela L. Hemminger is a partner in the law firm of Gibson, Dunn & Crutcher, Los Angeles, representing management. She is a 1976 *magna cum laude* graduate of Pepperdine University School of Law, where she was an editor of the *Pepperdine Law Review*. We thank her for writing the chapter on Settlement.

James D. Henderson is Of Counsel to the law firm of Seyfarth, Shaw, Fairweather & Geraldson, Los Angeles, engaged in white-collar criminal litigation. He is a 1972 graduate of Arizona State University College of Law, where he was an editor of the *Arizona State Law Journal*. From 1972 to 1987 he served as a special attorney in the Organized Crime and Racketeering Section of the U.S. Department of Justice, and from 1978 to 1985 served as Chief of the Los Angeles Strike Force on Organized Crime. We thank him for revising and editing the chapter on Criminal Law.

Georgeanne Henshaw is a partner in the law firm of Seyfarth, Shaw, Fairweather & Geraldson, representing management. She is a 1980 *cum laude* graduate of the University of Michigan Law School. We thank her for revising and editing the chapter on Constructive Discharge.

Stuart P. Herman is a partner in the law firm of Herman and Wallach, Los Angeles, representing both plaintiffs and management. He is a 1967 graduate of the University of California Boalt Hall School of Law, and received his master's degree in Industrial Relations from the London School of Economics. He served as a senior trial attorney with the Civil Rights Division, Employment Section, Department of Justice. He drafted the chapter of Federal Employee Litigation in the first edition of *Employment Discrimination Law*, and drafted the chapter on Election and Exhaustion of Remedies in the second edition. We thank him and his associates Cheri Goldstein and Nancy Bornn for drafting the chapter on Complainant's Litigation Strategy.

Hunter R. Hughes, III, is a partner in the law firm of Roger & Hardin, Atlanta, representing management. He drafted the chapter on Election and Exhaustion of Remedies in the second edition of *Employment Discrimination Law*. We thank him and Lisa B. Golen, an associate with Rogers & Hardin, for drafting the chapter on Complainant's Litigation Strategy.

Keith A. Hunsaker, Jr., is a partner in the law firm of Seyfarth, Shaw, Fairweather & Geraldson, Los Angeles, representing management. A 1975 Order of the Coif graduate of Duke University School of Law, he was Notes & Comments Editor of the *Duke Law Journal* and served as law clerk to Judge Hanson L. Winter of the United States Court of Appeals for the Fourth Circuit. We thank him for drafting large portions of the Overview chapter and for editorial assistance with the chapter on The Alleged Harasser as Defendant.

Weyman T. Johnson, Jr., is a partner in the law firm of Paul, Hastings, Janofsky & Walker, Atlanta, representing management. He is a 1979 graduate of the University of Georgia Law School. We thank him for editing and revising the chapters on Collective Bargaining Agreements and Union Obligations, Evidence, and Discovery.

W. Carl Jordan is a partner in the law firm of Vinson & Elkins, Houston, representing management. He is a 1974 *cum laude* graduate of the Harvard Law School. We thank him and Catherine Q. Morse, an associate with Vinson & Elkins, for drafting the chapter on The Common Law.

Krista Schoenheider Kaplan is an associate with the law firm of Seyfarth, Shaw, Fairweather & Geraldson, Chicago, representing management. She is a 1987 graduate of the University of Pennsylvania School of Law, where she was Comments Editor for the *University of Pennsylvania Law Review.* We thank her for her editorial assistance with the chapter on The Common Law.

Karen Kaplowitz is a partner in the law firm of Alschuler, Grossman & Pines, representing both defendants and plaintiffs. She is a 1971 graduate of the University of Chicago Law School. She drafted the chapter on Native Americans in the second edition of *Employment Discrimination Law.* We thank her, her partner Peter Sloan, and her associate David Carman, for drafting the chapter on Federal Constitutional, Statutory, and Civil Rights Law.

Alan M. Koral is a partner in the law firm of Vedder, Price, Kaufman, Kommholz & Day, representing management. He is a 1975 graduate of the University of Chicago Law School. He drafted the Religion chapter in the second edition of *Employment Discrimination Law.* We thank him for drafting the chapter on Quid Pro Quo Harassment.

Minna J. Kotkin is a Professor of Law at Brooklyn Law School. She is a 1975 *magna cum laude* graduate of Rutgers University School of Law and was Editor-in-Chief of the *Rutgers Law Journal.* We thank her for drafting the chapter on Monetary Relief.

Michael Leech is a partner in the law firm of Hinshaw and Culbertson, representing both plaintiffs and management. He is a 1976 graduate of the University of Virginia Law School. He is co-author of Hollowing & Leech, *Employment Termination: Rights and Remedies* (BNA 1985). We thank him for drafting the sections on public policy violations, invasion of privacy, and assault and battery in the chapter on The Common Law.

Sidney F. Lewis is an associate with the law firm of Kullman, Inman, Bee, Downing & Banta, New Orleans, representing management. He is a 1985 graduate of Tulane University Law School. We thank him for drafting the chapter on Employer's Litigation Strategy.

Lloyd C. Loomis is Senior Counsel, Employee Relations, Atlantic Richfield Company, Los Angeles. He is a 1972 graduate of the University of

Missouri Law School and a contributing editor of the second edition of *Employment Discrimination Law*. We thank him for drafting the chapter on Collective Bargaining Agreements and Union Obligations.

Kathleen M. Lucas is the principal of the law offices of Kathleen M. Lucas, San Francisco, representing plaintiffs. She is a 1974 *cum laude* graduate of the George Washington University School of Law. We thank her and her associate Deborah C. England for drafting the chapter on Quid Pro Quo Harassment.

Peggy R. Mastroianni is Special Assistant to EEOC Chairman Evan J. Kemp, Jr. She is a 1974 graduate of Fordham University School of Law and received her Master of Arts in Teaching from Harvard University in 1962. We thank her for drafting the chapter on Harassment by Co-Workers.

Mary Constance T. Matthies is a principal in Matthies Law Firm, P.C., Tulsa, Oklahoma, representing management. She drafted the chapter on Title VII Coverage in the second edition of *Employment Discrimination Law*. We thank her for drafting the chapters on Evidence and Discovery.

Kathleen M. McKenna is a partner in the law firm of Proskauer, Rose, Goetz & Mendelsohn, representing management in both New York and New Jersey. She is a 1978 graduate of Boston College School of Law. We thank her for drafting the sections on timeliness and exhaustion of administrative remedies in the chapter on Asserted Defenses.

Debra A. Millenson is Senior Trial Attorney, Office of the Solicitor, U.S. Department of Labor. She was Acting Director of the Office of Systematic Programs of the EEOC, Washington, D.C. She drafted portions of the chapter on Sex in the second edition of *Employment Discrimination Law*. We thank her for drafting the section on federal executive orders in the chapter on Federal Constitutional, Statutory, and Civil Rights Law.

Joseph M. Miller is a partner in the law firm of Seyfarth, Shaw, Fairweather & Geraldson, Los Angeles, representing management in workers' compensation litigation. He is a 1965 graduate of the University of California Boalt Hall School of Law, and received his Master of Law degree in 1967 from New York University. We thank him for editorial assistance with the chapter on Workers' Compensation Statutes.

Timothy W. Millett, an associate with the law firm of Seyfarth, Shaw, Fairweather & Geraldson, Los Angeles, representing management, is now an associate with the law firm of Kindel & Anderson, Los Angeles. A 1988 graduate of Brigham Young University, J. Reuben Clark Law School, he served as a law clerk to Judge Lloyd D. George of the United States District Court for the District of Nevada. We thank him for drafting the chapter on Harassment by Nonemployees.

Paul E. Mirengoff is a partner in the law firm of Hunton & Williams, Washington, D.C., representing management. He is a 1974 graduate of Stanford University Law School, where he was an editor of the *Stanford Law Review*. He served from 1976 to 1980 with the appellate division of the Office of General Counsel of the EEOC. He drafted the chapter on Reverse Discrimination and Affirmative Action in the second edition of *Employment Discrimination Law*. We thank him for drafting the chapter on Constructive Discharge.

Richard G. Moon is a partner in the law firm of Moon, Moss & McGill, Portland, Maine, representing management. He is a 1974 graduate of the University of Michigan Law School. We thank him and Timothy J. O'Brien, an associate with Moon, Moss & McGill, for drafting the chapter on Retaliation.

Gary C. Moss is Of Counsel to the law firm of Smith & Kotchka, Las Vegas. He is a 1969 graduate of the University of Iowa Law School, where he was Notes & Comments Editor of the *Iowa Law Review.* We thank him and Charles O. Agege, an attorney practicing business and commercial litigation in Los Angeles, for drafting the chapter on Monetary Relief.

Kathleen Peratis is a partner in the New York law firm of Frank, Taback & Peratis, representing plaintiffs in employment litigation. She is a 1969 graduate of the University of Southern California Law Center. She drafted portions of the chapter on Sex in the second edition of *Employment Discrimination Law.* We thank her for drafting the chapter on Constructive Discharge.

Thomas L. Pfister is a partner in the law firm of Latham & Watkins, Los Angeles, representing management. He is a 1974 graduate of Harvard Law School. He drafted the chapter on Class Actions in the second edition of *Employment Discrimination Law.* We thank him and his associates Christopher A. Thorn and Joseph B. Farrell for drafting the chapter on Responding to Internal Complaints.

Bettina B. Plevan is a partner in the law firm of Proskauer, Rose, Goetz & Mendelsohn, New York City, representing management. She is a 1970 *magna cum laude* graduate of Boston University School of Law, where she was an editor of the *Boston University Law Review.* We thank her for drafting the chapter on Employer's Litigation Strategy.

Kaiulani Poderick contributed to this book as an associate in the law firm of Seyfarth, Shaw, Fairweather & Geraldson, Los Angeles, representing management. She is a 1982 Order of the Coif graduate of the University of Utah, where she was Managing Editor of the *University of Utah Law Review.* We thank her for writing the chapter on Unemployment Compensation Statutes.

N. Thompson Powers is a partner in Steptoe & Johnson, Washington, D.C., representing management. He was the First Executive Director of the EEOC and Editor-in-Chief of the 1987–1989 supplement to *Employment Discrimination Law.* We thank him and Monica L. Goebel, an associate with the Phoenix office of Steptoe & Johnson, for drafting the chapter on The Alleged Harasser as Plaintiff.

Susan Buckingham Reilly is Area Director of the Washington, D.C., Field Office of the EEOC. She is a 1978 graduate of the University of Virginia Law School. We thank her for drafting portions of the chapters on Evidence and Discovery.

Merrick T. Rossein is Associate Professor of Law, City University of New York Law School at Queens College. He is a 1975 graduate of Antioch School of Law. He drafted the sexual harassment section of the chapter on Sex in the second edition of *Employment Discrimination Law,* and is the author of *Employment Discrimination Law and Litigation* (Clark Boardman Co., Ltd., 1990). We thank him for drafting portions of the chapter on Harassment by Nonemployees.

Paula M. Rusak is a partner in the law firm of Matthews, Dinsdale & Clark, Toronto, Ontario, representing management. She is a 1978 graduate of McGill University School of Law. We thank her for writing a chapter on Sexual Harassment in Canada, which appears in Appendix 5.

Steven M. Schneider is a partner in the law firm of Mitchell, Silberberg & Knupp, Los Angeles, representing management. He is a 1973 graduate of the Harvard Law School. He contributed to the discussion of tolling in the first edition of *Employment Discrimination Law.* We thank him for drafting portions of the chapters on Evidence and Discovery.

Martin D. Schneiderman is a partner in the law firm of Steptoe & Johnson, Washington, D.C., representing management. He is a 1966 *magna cum laude* graduate of Columbia University School of Law. He drafted the chapter on Executive Orders in the second edition of *Employment Discrimination Law.* We thank him for his editorial review of the executive order section of the chapter on Federal Constitutional, Statutory, and Civil Rights Law.

Charles A. Shanor is a Professor of Law at Emory University and Of Counsel to the law firm of Paul, Hastings, Janofsky & Walker, Atlanta. He is a 1973 graduate of the University of Virginia School of Law, where he was an editor of the *Virginia Law Review.* He also received a law degree from Oxford University, which he attended as a Rhodes Scholar, and clerked for Judge Elbert Parr Tuttle of the United States Court of Appeals for the Fifth Circuit. From 1987 to 1990 he served as General Counsel of the EEOC. He drafted the chapter on Race and Color in the second edition of *Employment Discrimination Law.* We thank him and Kelly J. Koelker, an associate with Paul, Hastings, Janofsky & Walker and a graduate of Duke Law School who extensively assisted in this project, for drafting the chapter on Claims by Third Parties.

Gary Siniscalco heads the Labor and Employment Department of Orrick, Herrington & Sutcliffe, San Francisco, representing management. He formerly served as Regional Counsel for the San Francisco regional office of the EEOC. He is a 1968 graduate of the Georgetown University Law Center. He drafted the section on homosexuality in the chapter on Sex in the first edition of *Employment Discrimination Law.* We thank him for drafting the chapter on The Agency Investigation.

Donald R. Stacy is a partner in the law firm of Elarbee, Thompson & Trapnell. He is a 1967 graduate of the University of Mississippi Law School, and received his LL.M. in 1968 from the Yale Law School. He served as Regional Counsel, EEOC, Atlanta; Director, Cincinnati, Ohio, Legal Aid Society; and Professor of Law, Vanderbilt University Law School. He drafted the chapter on Subjective Criteria in the first and second editions of *Employment Discrimination Law.* We thank him and his associates Lisa Andrews, Douglas H. Duerr, and Sharon P. Morgan for drafting our chapter on Retaliation.

Frank H. Stewart is a partner in the law firm of Taft, Stettinius & Hollister, Cincinnati, representing management. He is a 1957 graduate of the University of Virginia Law School. He drafted the chapter on Injunctive and Affirmative Relief in the second edition of *Employment Discrimination Law.* We thank him for drafting discussions, used throughout the book, on the effect of an antiharassment policy.

Judith Vladeck is the senior partner in the law firm of Vladeck, Waldman, Elias & Engelhard, New York City, representing plaintiffs in employment litigation. She is a 1947 graduate of Columbia University Law School. We thank her for contributing to the section in the chapter on Asserted Defenses on workers' compensation preemption and for contributing to discussions in the book on failure to exhaust internal grievance procedures.

Donald R. Wager is an attorney practicing criminal law in Los Angeles. He is a 1962 graduate of Willamette University Law School. We thank him for drafting the chapter on Criminal Law.

Robert F. Walker is a partner in the law firm of Paul, Hastings, Janofsky & Walker, Santa Monica, California, representing management. He is a 1966 graduate of the Yale Law School. He drafted the chapters on Religion and Equal Pay in the first edition of *Employment Discrimination Law.* We thank him and Jon Douglas Meer, an associate with Paul, Hastings, Janofsky & Walker, for drafting the chapter on The Alleged Harasser as Defendant, and for his contribution to the chapter on Employer's Litigation Strategy.

James Weinstein is Professor of Law at the Arizona State University School of Law. He is a 1978 Order of the Coif graduate of the University of Pennsylvania Law School, where he was Research Editor of the *University of Pennsylvania Law Review.* He served as law clerk to Chief Judge James R. Browning of the United States Court of Appeals for the Ninth Circuit. We thank him for editing the constitutional sections of the chapter on Federal Constitutional, Statutory, and Civil Rights Law and for writing the section on First Amendment free speech issues in the chapter on Asserted Defenses.

Richard C. White is a partner in the law firm of O'Melveny & Meyers, Newport Beach, California, representing management. He is a 1962 graduate of Stanford University Law School. We thank him and Larry Walraven, an associate with the firm of O'Melveny & Meyers, for drafting the chapter on Workers' Compensation Statutes.

M. Kirby Wilcox heads the Labor and Employment Law Department of Morrison & Foerster, San Francisco, representing management. He received his master's degree from the London School of Economics and is a 1977 graduate of Hastings College of Law, where he was Executive Editor of the *Hastings Law Journal.* We thank him, his partner David L. Slate, and his associates Patrick J. Maher, Debra L. Perschbacher, and Anne F. Zinkin for editing the three chapters constituting the remedies section of this book, as well as drafting the chapter on Injunctive and Affirmative Relief and portions of the chapters on Monetary Relief and Attorney's Fees and Costs.

Finally, we acknowledge numerous other people who made this book possible:

We thank Marilyn Holle, an attorney with Protection and Advocacy, a nonprofit agency representing plaintiffs in disability rights litigation. She is a 1974 graduate of the University of California at Los Angeles School of Law, and served as an attorney with the Los Angeles office of the EEOC. Marilyn played an important role in both the first and second editions of *Employment Discrimination Law,* including drafting the index to the first edition. We thank her for drafting the index to this work.

We thank Thomas D. Brown, who received his Master of Journalism degree from the University of California at Los Angeles and who is a legal assistant with Seyfarth, Shaw, Fairweather & Geraldson, Los Angeles, for his important editorial assistance.

We thank the following individuals for valuable contributions to various portions of the book: Stephen M. Bernardo, Michael Dayen, Terrie L. Goldade, Roy Sommers Kaufman, and Jay K. Kupnietsky, all summer associates with Seyfarth, Shaw, Fairweather & Geraldson, Los Angeles.

We thank the following individuals for their research and editorial assistance: Lawrence P. Postol, partner in Seyfarth, Shaw, Fairweather & Geraldson, Washington, D.C., and James R. Beyer, Jean Manning, David Marshall, and Kenneth D. Sulzer, all associates with Seyfarth, Shaw, Fairweather & Geraldson.

We thank the following individuals for their research assistance: Jack Brannelly, Glenda Cameron, L. Rae Connett, William R. Gray, David L. Johnson, and Gerald Pauling, all summer associates with Seyfarth, Shaw, Fairweather & Geraldson; Roberto Dulce and Mahlon McLean, both legal assistants with Seyfarth, Shaw, Fairweather & Geraldson; Hope Jacobson and Jay D. McFadyen, both associates with Seyfarth, Shaw, Fairweather & Geraldson; and Ruben Scott, an associate with Samuelsen, Gonzalez, Valenzuala & Sorkow.

We also thank those who typed and retyped this book with extraordinary patience and kindness. They include Loretta Peller, Rosemarie Ahmed, Carolyn Hennings, Le'Kisch Laidley, NaDari Taylor, Paul Fronczek, and Jeff Holley.

Our debt to all of these individuals is immense. We wish to emphasize, however, that responsibility for the final product is ours alone. The contributions acknowledged above were all rewritten by us. We relinquished editorial control only with respect to the preface and forewords.

SUMMARY TABLE OF CONTENTS

DETAILED TABLE OF CONTENTS

PART III—OTHER SOURCES OF LEGAL PROTECTION

Part I

INTRODUCTION

CHAPTER 1

OVERVIEW

I. INTRODUCTION

For more than a quarter century, Title VII of the Civil Rights Act of 1964[1] has prohibited discrimination in employment because of an individual's sex.[2] Yet not until 1976 did a court recognize that Title VII forbids the form of sex discrimination that is now called sexual harassment,[3] and only in 1986 did the Supreme Court, in *Meritor Savings Bank v. Vinson,*[4] finally establish that Title VII prohibits harassment in employment even if the harassment does not cause a direct financial injury.

After considering the characteristics of sexual harassment,[5] this chapter describes the two basic legal theories under which sexual harassment can be analyzed as violating Title VII[6] and the legal developments leading to a recognition of these theories.[7] The chapter concludes with a brief overview of some of the legal issues arising in sexual harassment litigation that are discussed in detail throughout the remainder of this book.[8]

II. CHARACTERISTICS OF SEXUAL HARASSMENT

Narrowly and traditionally defined, sexual harassment in employment is a demand that a subordinate, usually a woman, grant sexual favors in order to

---

[1]42 U.S.C. §2000e *et seq.*

[2]Section 703(a)(1) of Title VII makes it "an unlawful employment practice for an employer ... to discriminate against any individual with respect to his compensation, terms, conditions, or privileges of employment, because of such individual's race, color, religion, sex, or national origin." 42 U.S.C. §2000e-2(a)(1). The prohibition against discrimination based on sex was added to Title VII at the last minute on the floor of the House of Representatives, *Meritor Sav. Bank v. Vinson,* 477 U.S. 57, 63, 40 FEP Cases 1822, 1825 (1986), reproduced *infra,* by opponents of the legislation in an attempt to defeat it. N. Schlei, Foreword to B.L. SCHLEI & P. GROSSMAN, EMPLOYMENT DISCRIMINATION LAW (2d ed. 1983). The attempt failed, and the bill was passed as amended. As a result, "we are left with little legislative history to guide us in interpreting the Act's prohibition against discrimination based on 'sex.' " *Meritor,* 477 U.S. at 64, 40 FEP Cases at 1826.

[3]Williams v. Saxbe, 413 F. Supp. 654, 12 FEP Cases 1093 (D.D.C. 1976), reproduced *infra.* The very term "sexual harassment" is only of recent vintage. *See* C. MACKINNON, SEXUAL HARASSMENT OF WORKING WOMEN: A CASE OF SEX DISCRIMINATION 27 & n.13 (1979)(term surfaced in 1975).

[4]*Supra* note 2.

[5]See Section II. *infra.*

[6]See Section III. *infra.*

[7]See Section IV. *infra.*

[8]See Section V. *infra.*

obtain or retain a job benefit.[9] More broadly defined, it is the imposition of any unwanted condition on any person's employment because of that person's sex.[10]

Documented accounts of sexual harassment in employment against women date back at least as far as the industrial revolution, when women began to leave the farm for the factory in significant numbers.[11] It was not until the mid-1970s, however, that sexual harassment gained prominence in the national consciousness.[12]

Studies conducted then and thereafter and congressional hearings conducted in 1979 and 1981[13] have revealed the following aspects of the problem:

(1) A majority of working women believe that they have been sexually harassed in the workplace.[14] Women's advocates have characterized harassment as the most widespread problem faced by women in the work force.[15]

---

[9]*E.g.,* C. MACKINNON, *supra* note 3, at 1 (defining sexual harassment as the "imposition of sexual requirements in the context of a relationship of unequal power").

[10]Under this broader definition, harassment in the workplace can include jokes, direct taunting, disruption of work, vandalism of property, and physical attacks. For a collection of further definitions, see Note, *The Dehumanizing Puzzle of Sexual Harassment: A Survey of the Law Concerning Harassment of Women in the Workplace,* 24 WASHBURN L.J. 574, 577–80 (1985); Vermeulen, *Employer Liability Under Title VII for Sexual Harassment by Supervisory Employees,* 10 CAP. U.L. REV. 499, 499 (1981). Harassment could also take subtle forms, such as referring to female employees as "girls."

[11]L. FARLEY, SEXUAL SHAKEDOWN: THE SEXUAL HARASSMENT OF WOMEN ON THE JOB 28–44 (1979). For an anecdotal history of sexual harassment in the late 19th and early 20th centuries, see Goodman, *Sexual Harassment: Some Observations on the Distance Travelled and the Distance Yet to Go,* 10 CAP. U.L. REV. 445, 449–52 (1981)(including story of Russian immigrant in New York's garment industry whose first phrase in English was "keep your hands off please").

[12]Following a 1975 study by the Working Women's Institute, in which 70% of respondents reported sexual harassment, *Redbook* magazine conducted a survey in 1976 in which 88% of 9,000 female respondents stated that they had experienced sexual harassment on the job. For extensive discussion of the early popular and professional literature on this subject, see Note, *supra* note 10, 24 WASHBURN L.J. at 575 n.6, 576 nn.12–13.

[13]There were 1981 hearings on Sexual Discrimination in the Workplace before the Senate Committee on Labor and Human Resources and 1979 hearings on Sexual Harassment in the Federal Government before the Subcommittee on Investigations of the House Committee on Post Office and Civil Service). Note, *supra* note 10, 24 WASHBURN L.J. at 574 n.3, 577 n.20.

[14]Although the 88% figure reported by *Redbook* in 1976 is probably overstated in that victims were more likely to respond than nonvictims, *see* C. MACKINNON, *supra* note 3, at 4, more careful studies have also reported widespread incidence of sexual harassment. Note, *supra* note 10, 24 WASHBURN L.J. at 575 (citing various studies to effect that 50% to 80% of women have experienced sexual harassment on the job); Note, *Inadequacies in Civil Rights Law: The Need for Sexual Harassment Legislation,* 48 OHIO ST. L.J. 1151, 1159 n.63 (1987)(42% to 88% of women had experienced sexual harassment). Probably the most comprehensive survey of sexual harassment was conducted by the United States Merit Systems Protection Board (MSPB). Surveying 23,000 federal employees in 1980, the MSPB found that 42% of all women reported some form of sexual harassment as defined by the surveyors. *Sexual Harassment in the Federal Workplace— Is It a Problem?* (MSPB 1981). As late as 1986, a follow-up study found no substantial change in the reported extent of sexual harassment. *Sexual Harassment in the Federal Government: An Update* 16 (MSPB 1988). For these and additional surveys, see sources collected in A. CONTE, SEXUAL HARASSMENT IN THE WORKPLACE: LAW AND PRACTICE 1–4 (1990); Pollack, *Sexual Harassment: Women's Experience vs. Legal Definitions,* 13 HARV. WOMEN'S L.J. 35, 46 n.33 (1990); Note, *Legal Remedies for Employment Related Sexual Harassment,* 64 MINN. L. REV. 151, 152 n.6 (1979).

[15]Note, *supra* note 10, 24 WASHBURN L.J. at 574 n.3 (sexual harassment cited in congressional testimony by program director of Working Women's Institute as most subtle, all-too-readily tolerated, accepted and ignored form of employer or supervisor misbehavior faced by women in work force). Sexual harassment is a continuing problem. A 1988 study by *Working Woman* magazine reported that 90% of Fortune 500 companies had received complaints from employees in one year. Los Angeles Times, Oct. 21, 1990, Part A (Sunday, Home Edition), at 1, col. 1. The National Organization for Women (NOW) has reported in a recent survey that more than 80% of women claimed to have been sexually harassed. *Id.* A recent survey for the U.S. military found that 64% of American military women who responded to the survey said they had been harassed in some manner. Reuters Library Report, Sept. 11, 1990. According to the researchers, the military study is the largest attempt ever to measure sexual harassment in the workplace. *Id.* Surveys in the private workplace have found that 30% to 40% of women complain of sexual harassment. *Id.*

(2) The incidence of sexual harassment litigation has increased dramatically during the past decade.[16]

(3) Sexual harassment occurs in a wide variety of forms, including rape, pressure for sexual favors, sexual touching, suggestive looks or gestures, sexual joking or teasing, and the display of unwanted sexual materials.[17]

(4) Sexual harassment in its severest forms (physical conduct, retaliatory discharges) tends almost exclusively to be practiced by men against women.[18]

(5) Men and women, as classes, tend to differ in assessing the acceptability of sexually related conduct, with the result that what some men consider to be normal and inoffensive conduct is highly offensive to some women.[19] Arguments for the existence of general gender-based differences in perception have persuaded several courts to endorse legal standards that direct the trier of fact to view the typical charge of sexual harassment—a man allegedly harassing a woman—from the viewpoint of the "reasonable woman."[20]

---

[16]*See, e.g.,* Note, *supra* note 14, 48 OHIO ST. L.J. at 1159–60 (prior to the 1980 Guidelines EEOC received about 1000 sexual harassment charges per year; thereafter the EEOC received 3,453 in 1981, 4,195 in 1982, 4,468 in 1983). Filing of EEOC cases decreased by about 1,500 in the period 1984–88, see Woerner & Oswald, *Sexual Harassment in the Workplace: A View Through the Eyes of the Courts,* 41 LAB. LAW. J. 786, 792 (1990). The most recent figures available from the EEOC's internal data base are that the EEOC received over 5,000 sexual harassment charges in fiscal year 1989 (of about 80,000 charges filed) and over 5,300 sexual harassment charges in fiscal year 1990 (of about 90,000 charges filed). In California, the Department of Fair Employment and Housing reports that sexual harassment complaints now make up more than 20% of their caseload, compared to only 3% one decade ago. Los Angeles Times, Oct. 21, 1990, Part A (Sunday, Home Edition), at 1, Col. 1.

[17]*See, e.g.,* Pollack, *supra* note 14, 13 HARV. WOMEN'S L.J. at 50 n.46. Of the women surveyed in studies by the MSPB in 1980 and 1987, roughly 1% reported rape or sexual assault; 10% unwanted letters, telephone calls, or sexual materials; 10% pressure for sexual favors; 20% pressure for unwanted dates; 25% deliberate touching, pinching, leaning over, or commenting; and 35% sexual remarks, teasing, jokes, or questions. See discussion at Section V. *infra.*

[18]The 1981 study by the MSPB showed that sexual harassment was perpetrated nearly three times as often by men as by women. Note, *supra* note 10, 24 WASHBURN L.J. at 575 n.4 Moreover, the litigated cases are almost exclusively by women complaining of harassment by men. *But see* Harvey v. Blake, 913 F.2d 226, 227 (5th Cir. 1990)(female-on-male harassment); Huebschen v. Wisconsin Dep't of Health & Social Servs., 716 F.2d 1167, 32 FEP Cases 1582, 1582–83 (7th Cir. 1983)(same); Johnson v. Ramsey County, 46 FEP Cases 1686, 1687 (Minn. Ct. App. 1988)(male-on-male harassment); Wright v. Methodist Youth Servs., 511 F. Supp. 307 (N.D. Ill. 1981)(same); Barlow v. Northwestern Memorial Hosp., 30 FEP Cases 223 (N.D. Ill. 1980)(female-on-female harassment); Hart v. National Mortgage & Land Co., 189 Cal. App.3d 1420, 235 Cal. Rptr. 68 (1987)(harassment of man by both man and woman).

[19]Pollack, *supra* note 14, 13 HARV. WOMEN'S L.J. at 52; Abrams, *Gender Discrimination and the Transformation of Workplace Norms,* 42 VAND. L. REV. 1183, 1203–4, 1205–6 (1989). Commentators have noted that male harassers often consider their offensive conduct to be just joking. C. MACKINNON, *supra* note 3, at 51–52; Ehrenreich, *Pluralist Myths and Powerless Men: The Ideology of Reasonableness in Sexual Harassment Law,* 99 YALE L.J. 1177, 1199 n.81, 1207 n.110 (1990); Note, *Perceptions of Harm: The Consent Defense in Sexual Harassment Cases,* 71 IOWA L. REV. 1109, 1129–30 (1986)("Men sometimes see aggressive behavior as seduction, rather than the harassment women perceive"; arguing that consent to sexual advance should not be inferred by silent acquiescence); Note, *Sexual Harassment Claims of Abusive Work Environment Under Title VII,* 97 HARV. L. REV. 1449, 1459 (1984). One study found that three times as many women as men believed that eyeing a woman up and down was a form of harassment. Collins & Blodgett, *Sexual Harassment: Some See It, Some Won't,* HARV. BUS. REV. at 92–93 (Mar./Apr. 1981). For a series of linguistic studies to the point that conversations between men and women often amount to cross-cultural communication, see D. TANNEN, YOU JUST DON'T UNDERSTAND: WOMEN AND MEN IN CONVERSATION (1990).

[20]*E.g.,* Ellison v. Brady, 924 F.2d 872, 54 FEP Cases 1346 (9th Cir. 1991) and cases cited therein (adopting "reasonable woman" rather than a "reasonable person" standard in assessing whether harassing conduct is actionable). In adopting the "reasonable woman" standard, the court in *Robinson v. Jacksonville Shipyards,* 760 F. Supp. 1486, 1505 (M.D. Fla. 1991), accepted that "Men and women respond to sex issues in the workplace to a degree that exceeds normal differences in other perceptual reactions between them," on the basis of testimony that research reveals a near flip-flop of male and female responses to sexual approaches in the workplace: "Approximately two-thirds of the men . . . would be flattered; only fifteen percent would be insulted. For the women, the proportions are reversed."

(6) Sexual harassment tends to occur most often in "gender hierarchies"[21] in which men hold power over women either as their organizational superiors[22] or because women are present in small numbers in a traditionally male job or workplace.[23] This dominance of men over women in the workplace is not likely to disappear soon. The participation of women in the labor force has risen steadily in recent years[24] because Title VII has eliminated most overt barriers to women's entry into the work force and because economic and social conditions, reflected in the increased number of households headed by women,[25] have driven many women to work out of necessity. This influx has not, however, significantly altered the distribution of managerial positions. While many women hold supervisory and managerial jobs, most continue to find themselves working under male supervisors and managers who possess power over their welfare.[26]

(7) Women who are most vulnerable economically are the most vulnerable to sexual harassment.[27]

(8) Women often remain silent when confronted with sexual harassment[28]

---

[21]The phrase is from Pollack, *supra* note 14, 13 HARV. WOMEN'S L.J. at 41 (seeing sexual harassment as "part of a larger system of oppression").

[22]C. MACKINNON, *supra* note 3, at 217–18 ("Economic power is to sexual harassment as physical force is to rape"). Professor MacKinnon defines sexual harassment as "the unwanted imposition of sexual requirements in the context of a relationship of unequal power," *id.* at 1, and argues that sexual harassment of women can occur largely because women occupy inferior job positions and job roles. She states: "American society legitimizes male sexual dominance of women and employer's control of workers . . . . [T]he structure of the work world women occupy makes them systematically vulnerable to this form of abuse." *Id.* at 1, 4. Not only do women predominantly work in jobs with relatively little power, but many of these jobs are sex-segregated and gender-defined. For example, Professor MacKinnon argues that the position of secretary is not only statistically female, but has wife-like duties that make it all the easier to see an incumbent as a sex object. *Id.* at 9–23. For a general discussion of arguments for the proposition that social and economic circumstances in the United States facilitate the subordination of women in the workplace, see B. BABCOCK, A. FREEDMAN, E. NORTON & S. ROSS, SEX DISCRIMINATION AND THE LAW: CAUSES AND REMEDIES 192–217 (1975).

[23]Goodman, *supra* note 11, 10 CAP. U.L. REV. at 454–56. The 1981 MSPB survey showed that 53% of female federal employees in nontraditional jobs reported being sexually harassed as compared to 41% in traditional jobs, and concluded that men sometimes use sexual harassment to defend their "territory" from female intruders. Note, *supra* note 14, 48 OHIO ST. L.J. at 1153 n.16. For an extensive account of the relationship between sex segregation in jobs and the efforts of males in male-dominated jobs to use sexual harassment as a means of protecting "their territory" from incursions by female workers, see Schultz, *Telling Stories About Women and Work: Judicial Interpretations of Sex Segregation in the Workplace in Title VII Cases Raising the Lack of Interest Argument,* 103 HARV. L. REV. 1749, 1832–39 (1990)(discussing "The Work Cultures of Traditionally Male Jobs").

[24]The labor force participation rate for women age 25 to 64 (noninstitutional) rose from 49% of women in 1970 to 67.1% in 1988. Bureau of the Census, U.S. Dep't of Commerce, *Statistical Abstract of the United States,* Tab. No. 627 (110th ed. 1990).

[25]Between 1970 and 1988, the number of households headed by women rose from 21.1 to 31.1%. *Id.,* Tab. No. 58.

[26]The participation rate of women in the civilian (noninstitutional) population over age 16 employed in executive, administrative, and managerial occupations is more than 39%. *Id.,* Tab. No. 389. Generally indicative of the higher status typically held by males in the workplace are the figures showing that median earnings of full-time women workers continue to be no more than two-thirds of median earnings for full-time men workers.

[27]*See* Note, *supra* note 14, 48 OHIO ST. L.J. at 1153 n.16 (arguing, on basis of 1981 MSPB survey, that "the more vulnerable a person is, the more prone she is to be harassed."). *E.g.,* Phillips v. Smalley Maintenance Servs., 711 F.2d 1524, 32 FEP Cases 975 (11th Cir. 1983)(alleged harasser knew complainant financially dependent on her job to make house payments and used this as basis to demand that she demonstrate her gratitude with sexual favors).

[28]Pollack, *supra* note 14, 13 HARV. WOMEN'S L.J. at 52 n.56 (citing study that 61% of sexual harassment victims ignored it and citing "widespread and well-founded belief that complaining will not resolve the problem and instead will cause further economic and psychological damages"). *See* Robinson v. Jacksonville Shipyards, 760 F. Supp. 1486, 1506 (M.D. Fla. 1991), reproduced in Chapter 2, Forms of Harassment:

    The coping strategy a woman selects depends on her personal style, the type of incident and her expectation that the situation is susceptible of resolution. . . . Typical coping methods include: (1)

even while suffering physically,[29] economically,[30] and pyschologically.[31] (9) Sexual harassment has significant costs for the employers of harassed employees and for the economy as a whole.[32]

III. Legal Theories of Sexual Harassment as Sex Discrimination

Sexual harassment is a violation of Title VII under either of two legal theories: "quid pro quo" and "hostile environment."

A. Quid Pro Quo Harassment

Perhaps the most vivid example of sexual harassment in employment is an unwelcome request for sexual activity: an agent of the employer—almost always, but not necessarily, a man—uses his supervisory power to induce a subordinate employee—almost always, but not necessarily, a woman—to grant sexual favors.[33] The proposed exchange of job benefits for sexual favors suggests the name "quid pro quo."[34]

---

denying the impact of the event, blocking it out; (2) avoiding the workplace or the harasser, for instance, by taking sick leave or otherwise being absent; (3) telling the harasser to stop; (4) engaging in joking or other banter in the language of the workplace in order to defuse the situation; and (5) threatening to make or actually making an informal or formal complaint.

[29]Note, *supra* note 10, 24 Washburn L.J. at 575–76 n.9 (citing studies to effect that 63% of victims of sexual harassment experience nausea, headaches, and tiredness); Goodman, *supra* note 11, 10 Cap. U.L. Rev. at 456 (common to suffer headache, backache, nausea, weight loss or gain); Rossein, *Sex Discrimination and the Sexually Charged Work Environment*, 9 N.Y.U. Rev. of L. & Soc. Change 271, 278 (1979–80). *See also* Robinson v. Jacksonville Shipyards, *supra* note 28, 760 F. Supp. at 1507 ("Physical stress also results from sexual harassment; it may manifest itself as sleeping problems, headaches, weight changes and other physical ailments.").

[30]Note, *supra* note 10, 24 Washburn L.J. at 575–76 n.9 (1985)(citing studies to effect that 66% of victims of sexual harassment have been fired or pressured into resigning); *see also* Andrews, *The Legal and Economic Implications of Sexual Harassment*, 14 N.C. Cent. L.J. 113 (1983). One oft-cited 1979 study found 25% of sexually harassed women being fired and another 40% quitting. *See* Vermeulen, *supra* note 10, 10 Cap. U.L. Rev. at 502 n.14; Note, *Employer Liability for Co-Worker Sexual Harassment Under Title VII*, 13 N.Y.U. Rev. of L. & Soc. Change 83, 84 n.6 (1985); Note, *Legal Remedies for Employment-Related Harassment*, 64 Minn. L. Rev. 151, 152 n.7 (1979); Rossein, *supra* note 29, 9 N.Y.U. Rev. of L. & Soc. Change at 277.

[31]Studies have found that 90% of sexual harassment victims experience nervousness, fear, and anger; Note, *The Dehumanizing Puzzle of Sexual Harassment: A Survey of the Law Concerning Harassment of Women in the Workplace*, 24 Washburn L.J. 574, 575–76 n.9 (1985); Note, *Relief for Hostile Work Environment Discrimination: Restoring Title VII's Remedial Powers*, 99 Yale L.J. 1611, 1615 n.31 (1990); Note, *supra* note 14, 64 Minn. L. Rev. at 152 n.8; Note, *supra* note 30, 13 N.Y.U. Rev. of L. & Soc. Change at 84–85 nn.5–6 and authorities cited therein. *See also* Robinson v. Jacksonville Shipyards, *supra* note 28, 760 F. Supp. at 1506 ("Stress as a result of sexual harassment is recognized as a specific, diagnosable problem by the American Psychiatric Association").

[32]Some studies have suggested that through lower job productivity, higher turnover, and increased absenteeism, sexual harassment costs more than $130 million annually to federal government employers alone. Pollack, *supra* note 14, 13 Harv. Women's L.J. at 51–52 n.54. A 1988 survey by *Working Woman* magazine, said to be the first "scientific sampling" of sexual harassment at major corporations, reported that 160 companies spent an average of $6.7 million per year in costs (such as absenteeism, low productivity, and employee turnover) said to be related to sexual harassment. Los Angeles Times, November 23, 1988, Part IV, at 11.

[33]We thus tend to refer to a sexual harassment complainant here as "she" and an alleged harasser as "he."

[34]"Quid pro quo" is the adjective coined by Professor Catharine MacKinnon in her ground-breaking book, Sexual Harassment of Working Women: A Case of Sex Discrimination (1979): "Women's experience of sexual harassment can be divided into two forms which merge at the edges and in the world. The first I term the *quid pro quo,* in which sexual compliance is exchanged, or proposed to be exchanged, for an employment opportunity. The second arises when sexual harassment is a persistent *condition of work.*" *Id.* at 32.

B. Hostile Environment Harassment

Under a second theory of liability, sexual harassment violates Title VII, even absent a tangible job detriment, when unwelcome conduct based on sex creates a "hostile environment."[35] In this form of harassment, an employee's co-workers, and perhaps also supervisors, engage in conduct that is unpleasant to her because of her gender. The conduct usually involves a series of incidents rather than a single episode. The conduct may consist of unwelcome sexual advances that do not necessarily evince any resentment of women in the workplace. More often, the conduct reflects hostility instead of sexuality. In many cases this conduct reflects and stems from the same kinds of prejudice and stereotyped thinking that has led to abusive conduct directed at racial and ethnic groups.[36]

A sexually hostile environment is "sexual" not because it necessarily involves or invites sexual activity, but because the offensive conduct is motivated by the victim's sex.[37] Thus, a hostile environment may or may not be expressed in sexual gestures, language, or activity.

C. Quid Pro Quo and Hostile Environment Harassment Compared

The essence of a quid pro quo claim is that an individual has been forced to choose between suffering an economic detriment and submitting to sexual demands. This "put out or get out" bargain, which makes employment benefits contingent upon sexual cooperativeness, is the kind of sexual harassment first recognized as discrimination on the basis of gender.[38]

The essence of a hostile environment claim is that an individual has been required to endure a work environment that, while not necessarily causing any direct economic harm, causes psychological or emotional harm or otherwise unreasonably interferes with the individual's job performance.

While quid pro quo and hostile environment situations thus have differing characteristics, they overlap and often converge. Victims of quid pro quo harassment often suffer a hostile environment. Indeed, the quid pro quo concept, in its widest reach, could include any situation in which individuals must accept a gender-hostile environment in order to enjoy the tangible benefits of their jobs.

Similarly, victims of hostile environments often suffer the tangible job detriments associated with quid pro quo harassment. A hostile environment

---

[35]Others have labeled this form of harassment as "abusive environment," e.g., Note, supra note 19, 97 HARV. L. REV. at 1449; Meritor Sav. Bank v. Vinson, 477 U.S. 57, 66–67, 40 FEP Cases 1822 (1986), reproduced infra (using "hostile," "abusive," and "offensive" interchangeably, or "absolute harassment"); Note, supra note 30, 13 N.Y.U. REV. OF L. & SOC. CHANGE at 85. "Hostile environment" is the most popular term, appearing to derive from the EEOC Guidelines on Discrimination Because of Sex; see text accompanying note 67 infra.

[36]For a discussion of various forms of nonsexual harassment, see Chapter 2, Forms of Harassment, Section I.

[37]A common dictionary definition of "sexual" is "of, relating to, or associated with sex or the sexes," WEBSTER'S NINTH NEW COLLEGIATE DICTIONARY 1079 (1983). The first definition of "sex" is "either of two divisions of organisms distinguished respectively as male or female." Id. at 1078. Thus, the phrase "sexual harassment," in its broadest sense, refers to harassment on the basis of manhood or womanhood, regardless of whether the harassment involves the solicitation of, or a reference to, sexual acts.

[38]See Barnes v. Costle, 561 F.2d 983, 15 FEP Cases 345 (D.C. Cir. 1977), reproduced infra.

may drive employees off the job,[39] demoralize or upset them to the extent that they are fired for absenteeism or unsatisfactory work,[40] or cause them to complain about the harassment and risk retaliatory discharge.[41]

As the overlapping natures of quid pro quo and hostile environment harassment suggest, the distinctions made between them are often "slippery,"[42] and these categories are not the only way to classify sexual harassment in employment. Another method of categorization would focus on the forms of behavior involved, classifying incidents of sexual harassment into (1) unwelcome amorous advances, (2) offensive conduct reflecting resentment of the presence of females in the workplace, and (3) ostensibly nondirected conduct that, by creating a sexually charged workplace, may have a disproportionately demeaning effect upon one sex.[43] All three forms of behavior could, singly or in combination, constitute a hostile environment; only the first would be an essential part of a claim of quid pro quo harassment.

IV. THE LEGAL RECOGNITION OF SEXUAL HARASSMENT AS SEX DISCRIMINATION

A. Sexual Harassment as Sex Discrimination

In retrospect, the great question posed by the judicial history of sexual harassment is not how it came to be regarded as a form of discrimination, but why for so long it was treated differently from other forms of discriminatory conduct. One objective of this book is to simplify the legal issues surrounding sexual harassment and show that, in most respects, it can be explained very satisfactorily using the same basic precepts that are applied in other employment discrimination cases.

Under the traditional Title VII framework, an action by a covered respondent, such as an employer, against a covered person, such as an employee, is unlawful only if the action is taken on (1) a statutory "issue" (such as a decision to hire, fire, or impose a condition of employment) (2) because of (3) a statutory "basis" (race, color, sex, religion, or national origin). Thus, Title VII forbids harassment by which one, some, or all persons of one sex suffer significantly unfavorable employment conditions as a result of acts or omissions of the employer, under circumstances that permit the conclusion that the injury would not have been sustained had the victim's sex been different.

Historically, the obstacles to recognizing sexual harassment as sex discrimination have involved both the "basis" and the "issue." Quid pro quo harassment clearly involves an issue—the deprivation of tangible job benefits—but for some time was not understood to involve a basis—sex. Courts instead

---

[39]See Chapter 9, Constructive Discharge.

[40]See Chapter 4, Hostile Environment Harassment, Section X.

[41]See Chapter 10, Retaliation.

[42]Jeppsen v. Wunnicke, 611 F. Supp. 78, 83, 37 FEP Cases 994 (D. Alaska 1985). *See also* Carrero v. New York City Hous. Auth., 890 F.2d 569, 579, 51 FEP Cases 596, 603 (2d Cir. 1989)(hostile environment and quid pro quo claims "not always clearly distinct and separate" but rather "may be complementary to each other").

[43]For a detailed discussion of these forms of sexual harassing behavior, see Chapter 2, Forms of Harassment, Section III.

thought that the basis of the adverse employment decision was a set of characteristics peculiar to the personality of the individual employee—who in the early cases was always a woman—as opposed to the characteristics of a protected group—the gender to which the employee belonged.

If the primary problem in recognizing quid pro quo harassment as sex discrimination was the basis, the primary obstacle in recognizing hostile environment harassment as sex discrimination was the issue: hostile environment harassment may not cause any tangible job detriment. A secondary obstacle involved the basis: Some courts failed (and some still fail) to see sex as the basis where the offensive conduct itself is not clearly sexual in nature. These courts have not appreciated that the sex-based nature of hostile conduct can be demonstrated by circumstantial evidence.

The history of recognizing sexual harassment as unlawful sex discrimination has therefore required a recognition that quid pro quo harassment does occur on the prohibited basis of sex, and that hostile environment harassment is sex-based conduct that can be so severe and pervasive that it affects the conditions of employment.

B. Quid Pro Quo Cases

An analogy illustrates how easily the quid pro quo case fits within traditional notions of intentional disparate treatment. Suppose that in addition to the normal duties of the job, female clerks—but not male clerks—are required to take the boss's children to school, pick up his laundry, balance his checkbook, and do his grocery shopping. There is nothing inherently improper in hiring an employee, male or female, to perform these tasks, even though they are admittedly personal in nature. When, however, they are assigned on the basis of sex, Title VII is violated. Moreover, if a woman objects to these assignments because of their discriminatory nature, any resulting reprisal would be forbidden by Title VII's antiretaliation provisions.[44]

The analysis is exactly the same where the personal tasks are sexual in nature, except that it would be superfluous to require proof that the assignment had been made on the basis of sex, because only a woman can perform sexual tasks for a heterosexual man. Harassment of men by heterosexual women stands on the same footing. So, too, does homosexual harassment. Only in the case of harassment by a bisexual supervisor is there a theoretical absence of disparate treatment.[45] Moreover, the disparate treatment is always clearly intentional. The employer is liable for this conduct to the extent that the supervisor is accomplishing discriminatory acts through use of the employer's authority to grant or deny an employment benefit.[46]

Despite the force of this reasoning, five of the first seven courts to address the issue held that the quid pro quo harassment of a female subordinate by a

---

[44]§704(a), 42 U.S.C. §2000-3(a). See Chapter 10, Retaliation, Section III.

[45]For a discussion of the bisexual supervisor, see Chapter 3, Quid Pro Quo Harassment, Section VII.A.3.

[46]For a discussion of employer liability in this respect, see Chapter 6, Harassment by Supervisors, Section II.

male superior was *not* actionable under Title VII.[47] Courts offered a series of objections to the idea that quid pro quo harassment is sex discrimination. The primary objection was that quid pro quo harassment simply reflects a conflict between personalities—a "personal proclivity, peculiarity or mannerism of the supervisor"—rather than discrimination on the basis of gender.[48] Related to this was the objection that quid pro quo harassment was based on sexual attractiveness, not gender.[49] A third objection was that the employer could not be liable for quid pro quo harassment, because an individual's sexual advances were not truly employment-related, absent an employment policy authorizing them.[50] Yet another objection was that recognizing quid pro quo harassment as employment discrimination would open the legal floodgates to a deluge of litigation presumably not intended by Congress.[51]

There are several possible historical explanations for the torpor with which courts came to conclude that quid pro quo harassment was essentially sex discrimination. One partial explanation is that there is no mention of sexual harassment in the legislative history of either Title VII or its 1972 amendments.[52]

Another explanation, partial in both senses of the word, is that the thinking of a male-dominated federal judiciary reflected "traditional forms of male socialization."[53] Under Title VII, male judges rather than juries have decided whether sexual advances by males were intimidating, hostile, or offensive and would be so to a reasonable person. That judicial task becomes even more

---

[47]Note, *Sexual Harassment and Title VII: The Foundation for the Elimination of Sexual Cooperation as an Employment Condition,* 76 MICH. L. REV. 1007, 1010–11 (1978).

[48]*E.g.,* Corne v. Bausch & Lomb, 390 F. Supp. 161, 10 FEP Cases 289, 291 (D. Ariz. 1975), *vacated on procedural grounds,* 562 F.2d 55, 15 FEP Cases 1370 (9th Cir. 1977). This idea, now rejected in Title VII jurisprudence, re-emerged in interpretations of the Constitution's equal protection clause in the context of a sexual harassment damages suit under 42 U.S.C. §1983. Huebschen v. Wisconsin Dep't of Health & Social Servs., 716 F.2d 1167, 32 FEP Cases 1582 (7th Cir. 1983)(retaliation by supervisor against subordinate for breaking off romance not gender based).

[49]*E.g.,* Barnes v. Train, 13 FEP Cases 123 (D.D.C. 1974)(supervisor solicited his subordinate because she was attractive and retaliated against her because he was rejected), *rev'd sub nom.* Barnes v. Costle, 561 F.2d 983, 3 FEP Cases 1657 (D.C. Cir. 1977), reproduced *infra; see generally* General Elec. Co. v. Gilbert, 429 U.S. 125, 12 FEP Cases 1335 (1976)(upholding exclusion of pregnancy from disability plan in that persons so disadvantaged included both men and women).

[50]*E.g.,* Miller v. Bank of Am., 418 F. Supp. 233, 13 FEP Cases 439 (N.D. Cal. 1976), *rev'd,* 600 F.2d 1211, 20 FEP Cases 462 (9th Cir. 1979)(Title VII not designed to "hold an employer liable for what is essentially the isolated and unauthorized sex misconduct of one employee to another").

[51]*Id.* at 236 (under plaintiff's theory, "flirtations of the smallest order would give rise to liability"); Corne v. Bausch & Lomb, *supra* note 48, 390 F. Supp. at 163 (fearing "a potential federal lawsuit every time any employee made amorous . . . advances toward another"); Tomkins v. Public Serv. Elec. & Gas Co., 422 F. Supp. 553, 557, 13 FEP Cases 1574 (D.N.J. 1976), *rev'd,* 568 F.2d 1044 (1977)("If the plaintiff's view were to prevail, no supervisor could, prudently, attempt to open a social dialogue with any subordinate of either sex. An invitation to dinner could become an invitation to a federal lawsuit. . . . And if an inebriated approach by a supervisor to a subordinate at the office Christmas party could form the basis of a federal lawsuit . . . if a promotion or raise is later denied to the subordinate, we would need 4,000 federal trial judges instead of 400"). For a recent effort to rehabilitate the arguments against recognizing sexual harassment as sex discrimination, see Paul, *Sexual Harassment as Sex Discrimination: A Defective Paradigm,* 8 YALE LAW & POLICY REV. 333, 345–59 (1990) (citing absence of Title VII legislative history on sexual harassment, absence of group-based animus in quid pro quo cases and some hostile environment cases, the doctrinal anomaly of the bisexual supervisor, inherently unauthorized nature of sexual harassment, and blurred line between welcome and unwelcome sexual advances).

[52]Note, *The Dehumanizing Puzzle of Sexual Harassment: A Survey of the Law Concerning Harassment of Women in the Workplace,* 24 WASHBURN L.J. 574, 581 n.44 (1985). *See also* N. Schlei, Foreword to B.L. SCHLEI & P. GROSSMAN, EMPLOYMENT DISCRIMINATION LAW (2d ed. 1983).

[53]"Because most judges are men, who have experienced the traditional forms of male socialization, their instinctive reaction is to accept the perspective of the employer." Abrams, *Gender Discrimination and the Transformation of Workplace Norms,* 42 VAND. L. REV. 1183, 1203 (1989).

difficult if, as some commentators[54] and courts[55] suggest, the conduct must be evaluated from the standpoint not of the reasonable man, but of the reasonable woman, who may see things differently.

Further, workplace relationships between men and women are often ambiguous. There is an undeniable social component of working relationships, and it is common for a successful courtship to begin at the workplace.[56] Few advocate a sterile workplace in which all flirting is proscribed. Thus, although the establishment of new norms is an important function of discrimination law, drawing the line between benign and pernicious behavior is not easily accomplished in the case of sexual behavior. By contrast, there is much less difficulty in deciding whether conduct is harassing when it is based on membership in a racial, ethnic, or religious group.[57]

An additional factor that has been suggested as inhibiting the recognition of sexual harassment as employment discrimination is the same male-harbored fear of false reporting that once led to testimonial disabilities placed on women in the prosecution of rape cases.[58] Reinforcing this fear is the fact that labeling conduct as sexual harassment often has greater personal consequences for the accused than does a finding of some other type of discrimination. Practical experience suggests that the alleged harasser is also more likely to be an individual defendant in a sexual harassment case than in other types of discrimination cases, because of advantages that a plaintiff's counsel may perceive in naming an individual defendant.[59]

Many sexual harassment cases present facts supporting traditional common-law torts such as assault, battery, false imprisonment, and intentional infliction of emotional distress,[60] as well as such crimes as solicitation of prostitution and even rape.[61] Despite the potential for greater remedies under common-law theories,[62] victims of sexual harassment have pressed their claims primarily under Title VII. The overlap of common-law torts and crimes with employment discrimination law has served as a rationalization for treating sexual harassment differently from other forms of discriminatory conduct. Some commentators

---

[54]Ehrenreich, *Pluralist Myths and Powerless Men: The Ideology of Reasonableness in Sexual Harassment Law,* 99 YALE L.J. 1177 (1990); Abrams, *supra* note 53, 42 VAND. L. REV. at 1202–6.

[55]*E.g.,* Ellison v. Brady, 924 F.2d 872, 54 FEP Cases 1346 (9th Cir. 1991) and cases cited therein.

[56]In a recent study, 75% of the respondents were either aware of or had been personally involved in an office romance. The Washington Post, Aug. 27, 1989, at H3 (citing results reported in MAINIERO, OFFICE ROMANCE: LOVE, POWER, & SEX IN THE WORKPLACE (1989)). In addition, because people are marrying later in life, they are shifting their search for spouses from the campus to the workplace. Business Wire Inc., Sept. 19, 1990 (citing The Cosmopolitan Report, a six-year study underwritten by *Cosmopolitan* magazine and the Battelle Human Affairs Research Centers). Reflecting these developments is a trend in American industry to relax anti-nepotism policies. A survey by the American Society for Personnel Management of 547 companies concluded that nearly two-thirds of the companies employing 1,000 or more relaxed nepotism policies in the 1980s. The Chicago Tribune, May 28, 1985, at 5.

[57]"We are not here concerned with racial epithets . . . which serve no one's interest, but with social patterns that to some extent are normal and expectable. It is the abuse of the practice, rather than the practice itself, that arouses alarm." Barnes v. Costle, *supra* note 38, 561 F.2d at 1001 (MacKinnon, J., concurring.)

[58]Vermeulen, *Employer Liability Under Title VII for Sexual Harassment by Supervisor Employees,* 10 CAP. U.L. REV. 499, 523–24 (1981). For a discussion of evidentiary issues in sexual harassment cases, see Chapter 25, Evidence.

[59]See Chapters 21, Complainant's Litigation Strategy, and 23, The Alleged Harasser as Defendant.

[60]See Chapter 15, The Common Law.

[61]See Chapter 16, Criminal Law.

[62]The availability of damages for nonfinancial injury under Title VII is doubtful, and punitive damages are not permitted. See Chapter 29, Monetary Relief.

can be read to suggest that sexual harassment claims might require a new legal structure.[63] This sense of novelty may have delayed the recognition that sexual harassment is a form of sex discrimination, juridically equivalent to harassment on other forbidden bases, such as race, national origin, and religion.[63a]

The 1976 decision of Judge Charles Richie in *Williams v. Saxbe* was the first to recognize sexual harassment as a form of sex discrimination.

WILLIAMS v. SAXBE

413 F. Supp. 654, 12 FEP Cases 1093
(D.D.C. 1976)

CHARLES R. RICHEY, District Judge:—Plaintiff, Diane R. Williams, brings this action to recover damages and for other relief as a result of the defendants' alleged violations of the provisions of Title VII of the Civil Rights Act of 1964, as amended by the Equal Employment Opportunity Act of 1972, 42 U.S.C. §2000e et seq., and other acts of Congress; specifically, plaintiff alleges that she has been denied equal employment opportunities in the Department of Justice because of her sex. • • •

This action is before the Court at this time for review of the administrative record. Pending before the Court are defendants' motion to dismiss, defendants' renewed motion for summary judgment, and plaintiff's motion for judgment. • • •

• • • The • • • issue is whether the retaliatory actions of a male supervisor, taken because a female employee declined his sexual advances, constitutes sex discrimination within definitional parameters of Title VII of the Civil Rights Act of 1964. • • •

• • •

I. Background

• • • During plaintiff's employment, her immediate supervisor was a Mr. Harvey Brinson. On September 11, 1972, Mr. Brinson advised the plaintiff of his intention to terminate her and, by notice dated September 21, 1972, her termination was made effective on September 22, 1972. In the interim, September 13 to be exact, plaintiff filed a formal complaint alleging sex discrimination.

Plaintiff's discrimination complaint alleged, in essence, that she had had a good working relationship with Mr. Brinson up until she refused a sexual advance made by Mr. Brinson in June. She asserted that thereafter Mr. Brinson engaged in a continuing pattern and practice of harassment and humiliation of her, including but not limited to, unwarranted reprimands, refusal to inform her of matters for the performance of her responsibilities, refusal to consider her proposals and recommendations, and refusal to recognize her as a competent professional in her field. On the other hand, the alleged basis for terminating plaintiff was her poor work performance during this same period.

• • •

---

[63]*See* C. MACKINNON, SEXUAL HARASSMENT OF WORKING WOMEN: A CASE OF SEX DISCRIMINATION 27 & n.13 (1979)(suggesting an "inequality approach" toward analysis of discrimination claims, although demonstrating that sexual harassment is sex discrimination even under traditional approaches); Note, *Inadequacies in Civil Rights Law: The Need for Sexual Harassment Legislation*, 48 OHIO ST. L.J. 1151, 1157–59 of n.54 (1987)(arguing for legislation expressly proscribing sexual harassment because the "but for" test used in *Barnes v. Costle* is unsatisfactory as a "semantic device" that "artificially combines relationship-oriented discrimination and gender-oriented discrimination under the deceptively broad title of sex discrimination").

[63a]For a discussion of harassment on bases other than sex, see Chapter 2, Forms of Harassment, Section I.

II. Retaliatory Actions of a Male Supervisor, Taken Because a Female Employee Declined his Sexual Advances, Constitutes Sex Discrimination Within the Definitional Parameters of Title VII of the Civil Rights Act of 1964.

As noted above, the motion to dismiss presents the issue of whether the retaliatory actions of a male supervisor, taken because a female employee declined his sexual advances, constitutes sex discrimination within the definitional parameters of Title VII of the Civil Rights Act of 1964, as amended. This Court finds that it does. Defendants, however, make a cogent and almost persuasive argument to the contrary.

The defendants' argument is bottomed on locating the "primary variable" in the alleged class, which must be the gender of the class member to come within the protection of Title VII of the Civil Rights Act. Defendants reason that:

"Examination of . . . cases where sex discrimination has been found reveals that the particular stereotype involved may well have caused the creation of the class. However, the impetus for creation of the class must be distinguished from the primary variable which describes the class. The impetus for creation of the class may well be a sexual stereotype, i.e. women are weak, or women are not business-minded, but the class itself cannot be described, the boundaries cannot be set in terms of stereotypes. Rather, the class is described, by a variable which distinguishes its members from people outside the class. In previous sex discrimination cases, this primary variable was gender and, therefore, the applicability of the Act was triggered. Thus, conceptually, sexual stereotypes are irrelevant to the actual determination of whether an impermissible class exists. For example, if an employer enforced a policy that only women could be "roustabouts," an impermissible classification would arise, a classification described by the primary variable, gender, and the Act would be triggered despite the absence of a sexual stereotype. Therefore, in the instant case, even assuming that a sexual stereotype was at the root of Brinson's alleged imposition of a sexual condition, such a factor is irrelevant to the description of the alleged class. Accordingly, since the primary variable in the claimed class is willingness *vel non* to furnish sexual consideration, rather than gender, the sex discrimination proscriptions of the Act are not invoked. Plaintiff was allegedly denied employment enhancement not because she was a woman, but rather because she decided not to furnish the sexual consideration claimed to have been demanded. Therefore, plaintiff is in no different class from other employees, regardless of their gender or sexual orientation, who are made subject to such carnal demands." Defendants' Brief in Support of the Motion to Dismiss, at 5-6.

While defendants' argument is appealing, it obfuscates the fact, that, taking the facts of the plaintiff's complaint as true, the conduct of the plaintiff's supervisor created an artificial barrier to employment which was placed before one gender and not the other, despite the fact that both genders were similarly situated. It is the opinion of this Court that plaintiff has therefore made out a cause of action under 42 U.S.C. §2000e-16 (a). The reason for this Court's opinion is that it rejects the defendants' narrow view of the prohibition of the statute, which is the result of what this Court perceives as an erroneous analysis of the concept of sex discrimination as found in Title VII, to which the Court now turns.

[SCOPE OF ACT]

The fact that "Congress intended to strike at the entire spectrum of disparate treatment of men and women resulting from sex stereotypes," Sprogis v. United Air Lines, Inc., 444 F.2d 1194, 1198, 3 FEP Cases 621, 623 (7th Cir. 1971),[2] does not mean that only a "sex stereotype" can give rise to sex discrimination within Title VII. The statute prohibits "*any* discrimination based on . . . sex. . . ." Subsection 717(a) of the Equal Employment Opportunity Act of 1972, 42 U.S.C. §2000e-16(a). [Emphasis added]. On its face, the statute clearly does not limit discrimination to sex stereotypes. And while there is language in the legislative

---

[1][Omitted.]
[2][Omitted.]

history of the amendment that indicates that Congress did want to eliminate impediments to employment erected by sex stereotypes, these expressions do not provide a basis for limiting the scope of the statute, particularly since there is ample evidence that Congress' intent was not to limit the scope and effect of Title VII, but rather, to have it broadly construed.[3] Furthermore, the plain meaning of the term "sex discrimination" as used in the statute encompasses discrimination between genders whether the discrimination is the result of a well-recognized sex stereotype or for any other reason. It is important in this regard to note that Title VII is applicable to men as well as to women.[4]

There therefore can be no question that the statutory prohibition of §2000e-16(a) reaches *all* discrimination affecting employment which is based on gender. While the defendants would appear to agree that it is not essential that a "sex stereotype" be the cause of the disparate treatment, it is their view that a policy or practice is not sex discrimination within the meaning of §2000e-16(a) unless the class is described by what they call the primary variable, i.e. gender. Defendants' analysis goes one step further. They contend that §2000e-16(a) sex discrimination may only be found when the policy or practice is applicable to only one of the genders because of the characteristics that are peculiar to one of the genders. When applied to this case, defendants' analysis has produced the argument that since the criteria of "willingness to furnish sexual consideration" could be applied to both men and women, then the class cannot be said to be defined *primarily* by gender and therefore there can be no §2000e-16(a) sex discrimination.

[ARGUMENT REJECTED]

Defendants' argument must be rejected because a finding of sex discrimination under §2000e-16(a) does not require that the discriminatory policy or practice depend upon a characteristic peculiar to one of the genders. That a rule, regulation, practice, or policy is applied on the basis of gender is alone sufficient for a finding of sex discrimination. Phillips v. Martin Marietta Corp., 400 U.S. 542, 3 FEP Cases 40 (1971); Sprogis v. United Air Lines, Inc., supra. In Martin Marietta, the Supreme Court, while vacating the decision of the Fifth Circuit, accepted the Fifth Circuit's finding that there was discrimination even though it was not based upon a characteristic peculiar to one gender. The Fifth Circuit had held that a policy which allowed the hiring of men who had pre-school children for certain positions, but not allowing the hiring of women with pre-school children for the same position, was sex discrimination in violation of Title VII, 411 F.2d 1, 1 FEP Cases 746, 71 LRRM 2323 (1969). The court of appeals rejected the argument that sex discrimination could only be found if the policy depended solely upon gender. Rather, the court stated:

> [2] We are of the opinion that the words of the statute are the best source from which to derive the proper construction. The statute proscribes discrimination based on an individual's race, color, religion, sex, or national origin. A per se violation of the Act can only be discrimination based solely on one of the categories i.e., in the case of sex, women vis-a-vis men. When another criterion of employment is added to one of the classifications listed in the Act, there is no longer apparent discrimination based solely on race, color, religion, sex or national origin. It becomes the function of the courts to study the conditioning of employment on one of the elements outlined in the statute coupled with the additional requirement, and to determine if any individual or group is being denied work due to his race, color, religion, sex or national origin. Id. at 3-4, 1 FEP Cases at 748.

The Supreme Court did not reject this analysis, but rather, vacated the lower court's decision because the practice could have been permissible if there was evidence to show that it was a "bona fide occupational qualification" under §703(e) of the Act. 400 U.S. at 544, 3 FEP Cases at 41.

The Sprogis case concerned a "no-marriage" rule which provided that stewardesses had to be unmarried when hired and remain unmarried under penalty of discharge. 444 F.2d at 1196, 1196 n.2, 3 FEP Cases at 622. The no-marriage rule could have been applied to

---

[3-4][Omitted.]

men as well as women, since both are capable of marriage. The criteria of marriage can also not be said to be a characteristic peculiar to one of the genders. Nevertheless, the court held that the rule resulted in sex discrimination in violation of Title VII. Id. at 1198, 3 FEP Cases at 624. The court found it sufficient that the rule was applied to women and not to men, despite the fact that they were similarly situated.[5]

The requirement of willingness to provide sexual consideration in this case is no different from the "pre-school age children" and "no-marriage" rules of Martin Marietta and Sprogis. As here, none of those rules turned upon a characteristic peculiar to one of the genders. It was and is sufficient to allege a violation of Title VII to claim that the rule creating an artificial barrier to employment has been applied to one gender and not to the other. Therefore, this Court finds that plaintiff has stated a violation of Title VII's prohibition against "any discrimination based on . . . sex. . . ."[6]

[GEDULDIG CASE]

The recent case of Geduldig v. Aiello, 417 U.S. 484, 8 FEP Cases 97 (1974) does not require that the defendant's interpretation or, rather, limitation of §2000e-16(a) sex discrimination be accepted. The Geduldig analysis has been found to be inapplicable to Title VII cases. See Lombard, *Sex: A Classification in Search of Strict Scrutiny,* 21 Wayne L. Rev. 1355, 1366, 1366 n.47-52 (1975); see also Communication Workers of America v. A.T. & T. Co., 10 FEP Cases 435, C.A. No. 461 (2d Cir. March 26, 1975). This is understandable since Geduldig concerned the question of whether the refusal to extend insurance protection to pregnancy as a covered disability under a state insurance program resulted in an individous discrimination in violation of the Constitutional standard as opposed to the statutory standard of Title VII.[7]

Nor do the so-called "hair cases" cited by the defendant, Dodge v. Giant Food, Inc., 488 F.2d 1333, 6 FEP Cases 1066 (D.C. Cir. 1973); Fagan v. National Cash Register Co., 481 F.2d 1115, 5 FEP Cases 1335 (D.C. Cir. 1973); Boyce v. Safeway Stores, Inc., 351 F.Supp. 402, 5 FEP Cases 285 (D.D.C. 1972); require that this Court adopt the analysis asserted by the defendant. In one of those cases, the regulation or policy was found applicable to both men and women, 481 F.2d at 1124 n.20, 5 FEP Cases at 1341; 351 F.Supp. at 403, 5 FEP Cases at 286. Further, the courts in all of these cases found that any disparate treatment in the regulation or policy involved was permissible under the exception found in §703(e) of the Act. E.g., 481 F.2d at 1125. But this finding should not be confused with the threshhold analysis of whether sex discrimination is extant. Disparate treatment was assumed in two of those cases. What they were then concerned with was whether the disparate treatment was permissible under the exception to the Act. See also Weeks v. Southern Bell Tel. & Tel. Co., 406 F.2d 228, 1 FEP Cases 656, 70 LRRM 2843 (5th Cir. 1969). The only case of any distinction, Dodge, refused to find sex discrimination because the Court concluded that: "Title VII never was intended to encompass sexual classifications having only an insignificant effect on employment opportunities." 488 F.2d at 1337, 6 FEP Cases at 1068.

---

[5][Omitted.]

[6]This court also rejects any argument that this cannot be sex discrimination because the application of the rule would depend upon the sexual preference of the supervisor, as opposed to some other reason. But the reason for the discrimination under Title VII is not necessary to a finding of discrimination. Cf. Griggs v. Duke Power Co., 401 U.S. 424, 432, 3 FEP Cases 175, 178 (1971) ("But Congress directed the thrust of the Act to the consequences of employment practices, not simply the motivation.") Rather, the reason for the discrimination may only be relevant in considerations of whether the policy or practice is based upon a bona fide occupational requirement. 400 U.S. at 545; 444 F.2d at 1198-1201.

It is also notable that since the statute prohibits discrimination against men as well as women, a finding of discrimination could be made where a female supervisor imposed the criteria of the instant case upon only the male employees in her office. So could a finding of discrimination be made if the supervisor were a homosexual. And, the fact that a finding of discrimination could not be made if the supervisor were a bisexual and applied this criteria to both genders should not lead to a conclusion that sex discrimination could not occur in other situations outlined above.

[7]Even restricting an examination of Geduldig to its analysis of what is sex discrimination, this Court finds Geduldig distinguishable since the Court noted that "There is no risk from which men are protected and women are not." 94 S.Ct. at 497-98 in that case.

Assuming Title VII permits a weighing of the effect of a particular policy or regulation, this Court could not find the instant policy or practice to have an insignificant effect.

Nor does this Court agree that it should adopt the agency's interpretation merely because it is entitled to be given extra consideration. Since this Court has found that the agency's interpretation does not comport with the scope and purpose of the statute, this court may reject the agency's decision. Volkswagenwerk Aktiiengesellschaft v. Federal Maritime Commission, 390 U.S. 261, 272 (1968).

[FINAL ARGUMENT]

Finally, defendants argue that plaintiff has not made out a case of sex discrimination under the Act because, the instant case was not the result of a policy or a regulation of the office, but rather, was an isolated incident which should not be the concern of the courts and was not the concern of Congress in enacting Title VII. But this argument is merely based upon defendant's view of the facts, coupled with a fear that the courts will become embroiled in sorting out the social life of the employees of the numerous federal agencies. First, whether this case presents a policy or practice of imposing a condition of sexual submission on the female employees of the CRS or whether this was a nonemployment related personal encounter requires a factual determination. It is sufficient for purposes of the motion to dismiss that the plaintiff has alleged it was the former in this case.[8] For, if this was a policy or practice of plaintiff's supervisor, then it was the agency's policy or practice, which is prohibited by Title VII. Secondly, the decision of the Court that plaintiff has stated a cause of action under Title VII will not have the feared result defendants urge. What the statute is concerned with is not interpersonal disputes between employees. Rather, the instant case reveals the statutory prohibition on the alleged discriminatory imposition of a condition of employment by the supervisor of an office of an agency.

This Court concludes that plaintiff has stated a cause of action under 42 U.S.C. §2000e-16(a). • • •

---

[8]Paragraph 21 of the Complaint alleges that the supervisor's conduct was a policy or practice imposed on the plaintiff and other women similarly situated. This is an essential allegation for presenting a cause of action. Plaintiff's theory has never been that this was merely an isolated personal incident.

Williams v. Saxbe touches on several of the issues that were to become the focus of sexual harassment litigation: whether the court should ever look at things from the alleged harasser's viewpoint, as opposed to that of the complainant; the degree of harassment that a woman must suffer before Title VII is breached; and whether the employer is responsible for the acts of a supervisor. The following year, Judge Spotswood Robinson, writing for the D.C. Circuit, confirmed that quid pro quo harassment violates Title VII, reasoning that in most cases it is simply a form of disparate treatment based on sex.

BARNES v. COSTLE

561 F.2d 983, 15 FEP Cases 345
(D.C. Cir. 1977)

ROBINSON, Circuit Judge:—This appeal launches a review of an order of the District Court awarding a summary judgment to [the employer][1] on the ground that Title VII of the Civil Rights Act of 1964[2] as amended by the Equal Employment Opportunity Act of 1972,[3] does not offer redress for appellant's complaint that her job at the Environmental Protection

---

[1-3][Omitted.]

Agency was abolished because she repulsed her male superior's sexual advances.[4] We reverse.

I

Appellant, a black woman, was hired by the director of the Agency's equal employment opportunity division, who also is black, as his administrative assistant at grade GS-5. During a pre-employment interview, she asserts, he promised a promotion to grade GS-7 within ninety days. Shortly after commencement of the employment, she claims, the director initiated a quest for sexual favors by "(a) repeatedly soliciting [her] to join him for social activities after office hours, notwithstanding [her] repeated refusal to do so; (b) by making repeated remarks to [her] which were sexual in nature; (c) by repeatedly suggesting to [her] that if she cooperated with him in a sexual affair, her employment status would be enhanced."[5] Appellant states that she "continually resisted [his] overtures ... and finally advised him that notwithstanding his stated belief that many executives 'have affairs with their personnel', she preferred that their relationship remain a strictly professional one."[6] Thereafter, she charges, the director "alone and in concert with other agents of [appellee], began a conscious campaign to belittle [her], to harrass her and to strip her of her job duties, all culminating in the decision of [appellee's] agent ... to abolish [her] job in retaliation for [her] refusal to grant him sexual favors."[7] These activities, appellant declares, "would not have occurred but for [her] sex."[8]

[COMPLAINT]

After seeking unsuccessfully an informal resolution of the matter, appellant, acting *pro se,* filed a formal complaint alleging that the director sought to remove her from his office when she "refused to have an after hour affair with" him.[9] The complaint charged discrimination based on race rather than gender,[10] a circumstance which appellant attributes to erroneous advice by agency personnel.[11] A hearing on the complaint was conducted by an appeals examiner, who excluded proffered evidence of sex discrimination and found no evidence of race discrimination.[12] In its final decision, the Agency concurred in the examiner's finding.[13]

Appellant then obtained counsel and appealed to the Civil Service Commission. There, appellant's attorney requested the Board of Appeals and Review to reopen the record to enable the presentation of sex-discrimination evidence.[14] The Board, however, affirmed the agency's negative finding on race discrimination and refused the request to reopen on the ground that appellant's allegations did not bring the case within the purview of the Commission's regulations implementing Title VII.[15]

Thereafter, appellant filed her complaint in the District Court, confining her theory, by allegations to which we have averted,[16] to sex discrimination violative of Title VII and the Fifth Amendment.[17] The court, limiting the inquiry to reexamination of the administrative record,[18] granted appellee's motion for summary judgment in the view that "the alleged discriminatory practices are not encompassed by the Act."[19] The "alleged retaliatory actions of [appellant's] supervisor taken because [appellant] refused his request for an 'after hour affair,' " the court held, "are not the type of discriminatory conduct contemplated by the 1972 Act."[20] The court reasoned:

> The substance of [appellant's] complaint is that she was discriminated against, not because she was a woman, but because she refused to engage in a sexual affair with her supervisor. This is a controversy underpinned by the subtleties of an inharmonious personal relationship. Regardless of how inexcusable the conduct of [appellant's] supervisor might have been, it does not evidence an arbitrary barrier to continued employment based on [appellant's] sex.[21]

[4–10][Omitted.]

[11]• • • The claim here is that agency personnel told appellant that the matter was solely a personnel grievance and did not amount to sex discrimination. • • •

[12–21][Omitted.]

The appeal to this court then followed.

II

• • •

[COMMITTEE REPORT]

When • • • the 1964 Act was amended by the Equal Employment Opportunity Act of 1972,[27] there was considerable discussion on the topic. Not surprisingly, it then became evident that Congress was deeply concerned about employment discrimination founded on gender, and intended to combat it as vigorously as any other type of forbidden discrimination. The report of the House Committee on Education and Labor declared in ringing tones that the statute—eight years after passage—still had much to accomplish in order to elevate the status of women in employment.[28]

> Numerous studies have shown that women are placed in the less challenging, the less responsible and the less remunerative positions on the basis of their sex alone.
>
> Such blatantly disparate treatment is particularly objectionable in view of the fact that Title VII has specifically prohibited sex discrimination since its enactment in 1964.[29]

The Committee emphasized that women's employment rights are not "judicial divertissements,"[30] and that "[d]iscrimination against women is no less serious than other forms of prohibited employment practices and is to be accorded the same degree of social concern given to any type of unlawful discrimination."[31] The report of the Senate Committee on Labor and Public Welfare reveals a similar commitment to eradication of sex discrimination:[32]

> While some have looked at the entire issue of women's rights as a frivolous divertissement, this Committee believes that discrimination against women is no less serious than other prohibited forms of discrimination, and that it is to be accorded the same degree of concern given to any type of similarly unlawful conduct. As a further point, recent studies have shown that there is a close correlation between discrimination based on sex and racial discrimination, and that both possess similar characteristics.[33]

Not unexpectedly, then, during the thirteen years since enactment of Title VII it has become firmly established that the Act invalidates all "artificial, arbitrary and unnecessary barriers to employment when the barriers operate invidiously to discriminate on the basis of . . . impermissible classification[s]."[34] Title VII has been invoked to strike down a wide variety of impediments to equal employment opportunity between the sexes, including insufficiently validated tests,[35] discriminatory seniority systems,[36] weight-lifting requirements,[37] and height and weight standards solely for those of one gender.[38] • • •

• • •

[THESIS]

We start with the statute as written and, so measured, we think the discrimination as portrayed was plainly based on appellant's gender. Her thesis, in substance, is that her supervisor retaliated by abolishing her job when she resisted his sexual advances. More particularly, she states that he repeatedly told her that indulgence in a sexual affair would enhance her employment status; that he endeavored affirmatively but futilely to consummate

---

[22-26][Omitted.]
[27-33][Omitted.]
[34]Griggs v. Duke Power Co., 401 U.S. 424, 431, 91 S.Ct. 849, 853, 28 L.Ed.2d 158, 163, 3 FEP Cases 175, 177 (1971).
[35-38][Omitted.]
[39-47][Omitted.]

his proposition; and that, upon her refusal to accede, he campaigned against her continued employment in his department and succeeded eventually in liquidating her position.[48] So it was, by her version, that retention of her job was conditioned upon submission to sexual relations—an exaction which the supervisor would not have sought from any male.[49] It is much too late in the day to contend that Title VII does not outlaw terms of employment for women which differ appreciably from those set for men,[50] and which are not genuinely and reasonably related to performance on the job.[51]

The District Court felt, however, that appellant's suit amounted to no more than a claim "that she was discriminated against, not because she was a woman, but because she refused to engage in a sexual affair with her supervisor."[52] In a similar vein, appellee has argued that "[a]ppellant was allegedly denied employment enhancement not because she was a woman, but rather because she decided not to furnish the sexual consideration claimed to have been demanded."[53] We cannot accept this analysis of the situation charged by appellant. But for her womanhood, from aught that appears, her participation in sexual activity would never have been solicited.[54] To say, then, that she was victimized in her employment simply because she declined the invitation is to ignore the asserted fact that she was invited only because she was a woman subordinate to the inviter in the hierarchy of agency personnel.[55] Put another way, she became the target of her superior's sexual desires because she was a woman, and was asked to bow to his demands as the price for holding her job. The circumstance imparting high visibility to the role of gender in the affair is that no male employee was susceptible to such an approach by appellant's supervisor.[56] Thus gender cannot be eliminated from the formulation which appellant advocates, and that formulation advances a prima facie case of sex discrimination within the purview of Title VII.

[SCOPE OF ACT]

It is clear that the statutory embargo on sex discrimination in employment is not confined to differentials founded wholly upon an employee's gender. On the contrary, it is enough that gender is a factor contributing to the discrimination in a substantial way.[57] That

---

[48][Omitted.]

[49]The vitiating sex factor thus stemmed, not from the fact that what appellant's superior demanded was sexual activity—which of itself is immaterial—but from the fact that he imposed upon her tenure in her then position a condition which ostensibly he would not have fastened upon a male employee. Appellant flatly claims that but for her gender she would not have been importuned, and nothing to the contrary has as yet appeared, and there is no suggestion that appellant's allegedly amorous supervisor is other than heterosexual. These are matters for proof at trial, and the inquiry at this stage of the litigation is solely in terms of a prima facie case of sex discrimination. In sum, the record in its current posture portrays a superior placing on a female subordinate a substantial employment condition which he would not seek to levy on a man. See note 55 infra. The situation is very different from instances of sexual affairs between an agency's employees which are not tied to employment opportunity in any way.

[50]Cf. Phillips v. Martin Marietta Corp., 400 U.S. 542, 544, 91 S.Ct. 496, 497-98, 27 L.Ed.2d 613, 615-16, 3 FEP Cases 40, 41 (1971). Title VII expressly prohibits "discriminat[ion] against any individual with respect to . . . the terms, conditions, or privileges of employment, because of such individual's . . . sex. . . ." See text supra at note 24. As we have said, the Equal Employment Opportunity Act of 1972 now confers the same protection upon federal employees. See text supra at note 43.

[51]The Act tolerates any sex-based distinction in employment which is a "bona fide occupational qualification" for the position in question. Civil Rights Act of 1964, tit. VII. §703(e), 42 U.S.C. §2000e-2(e) (1970). By appellant's assessment, her only alternatives were to submit to sexual blackmail or suffer adversity as an employee. Appellee, quite understandably, does not argue that provision of sexual services can qualify as a "bona fide occupational qualification" for women in federal employment.

[52-54][Omitted.]

[55]It is no answer to say that a similar condition could be imposed on a male subordinate by a heterosexual female superior, or upon a subordinate of either gender by a homosexual superior of the same gender. In each instance, the legal problem would be identical to that confronting us now—the exaction of a condition which, but for his or her sex, the employee would not have faced. These situations, like that at bar, are to be distinguished from a bisexual superior who conditions the employment opportunities of a subordinate of either gender upon participation in a sexual affair. In the case of the bisexual superior, the insistence upon sexual favors would not constitute gender discrimination because it would apply to male and female employees alike.

[56][Omitted.]

[57]• • • We have previously held that not every dissimilarity in employment conditions respectively set for the sexes impinges on Title VII. In Dodge v. Giant Food, Inc., 160 U.S.App.D.C. 9, 488 F.2d 1333, 6

this was the intent of Congress is readily apparent from a small but highly significant facet of the legislative history of Title VII. When the bill incorporating Title VII was under consideration in 1964, an amendment that would have expressly restricted the sex ban to discrimination based solely on gender was defeated on the floor of the house.[58] Like the Fifth Circuit, we take this as an indication of congressional awareness of the debilitating effect that such a limitation would have had on any attempt to stamp out sex-based factors irrelevant to job competence.[59]

Interpretations of the Act, both judicial and administrative, more than adequately reflect this understanding and appreciation of the legislative purpose. In Phillips v. Martin Marietta Corporation,[60] the Supreme Court held that a company's refusal of employment to mothers but not to fathers of pre-school-age children was prima facie sex discrimination within the meaning of Title VII.[61] Not all women were excluded from the employment, but only those who had pre-school-age children. Nonetheless, since gender was a criterion in the determination of employability, a prima facie violation of Title VII was shown.[62] Other courts, in analogous contexts, have similarly concluded that distinctions predicated only partly though firmly on gender are covered by Title VII's ban on sex discrimination.[63] And an administrative interpretation of the Act commanding deference[64] is the Equal Employment Opportunity Commission's pronouncement that "so long as sex is a factor in the application of" an employer's rule forbidding marriage by female employees, "such application involves discrimination based on sex."[65]

[GENDER]

In all of these situations, the objectionable employment condition embraced something more than the employee's gender, but the fact remained that gender was also involved to a significant degree. For while some but not all employees of one sex were subjected to the condition, no employee of the opposite sex was affected; and that is the picture here.[66] It does not suffice to say, as the District Court did, that appellant's position was eliminated merely because she refused to respond to her supervisor's call for sexual favors.[67] Appellant's gender, just as much as her cooperation, was an indispensible factor in the job-retention

---

FEP Cases 1066 (1973), finding that different grooming standards for men and women did not violate the statute, we observed that Title VII was not intended to encompass minor sexual classifications which "do not limit employment opportunities by making distinctions based on immutable personal characteristics, which do not represent any attempt by the employer to prevent the employment of a particular sex, and which do not pose distinct employment disadvantages for one sex." Id. at 12, 488 F.2d at 1337, 6 FEP Cases at 1068. (footnotes omitted). • • •

[58–59][Omitted.]

[60]400 U.S. at 544, 91 S.Ct. at 497-98, 27 L.Ed.2d at 615-616, 3 FEP Cases at 41.

[61–65][Omitted.]

[66]• • • An analogy is afforded by Slack v. Havens, 7 FEP Cases 885, 890 (S.D.Cal. 1973), aff'd, 522 F.2d 1091, 11 FEP Cases 57 (9th Cir. 1975), where four black women were discharged as a result of their refusal to perform heavy cleaning, assertedly not part of their duties and required of them simply because of their race. The one white woman assigned to their department, who had less seniority than three of the four, was transferred elsewhere to work for the day, id. at 887, and another black employee then on loan to another department was returned to aid in the cleaning. Id. at 889. En route to the office to collect their final pay checks, the four plaintiffs were told by their supervisor that "[c]olored folks are hired to clean because they clean better." Id. at 887. There were no allegations of racial discrimination other than with respect to this one incident. Over the employer's objection that the dispute related solely to job classification, id. at 889, the court held that the discharge was violative of Title VII because the plaintiff's supervisors

> meant to require the plaintiffs to perform the admittedly heavy and possibly dangerous work of cleaning the bonding and coating department when they would not require the same work from plaintiffs' white fellow employee. Furthermore, [they] meant to enforce the decision by firing the plaintiffs when they refused to perform that work. The consequence of the above was racial discrimination whatever the motivation of the management of defendant . . . may have been.

Id. at 890. On appeal, the Ninth Circuit affirmed the ruling on discrimination but remanded the case for recalculation of backpay. 522 F.2d at 1095, 11 FEP Cases at 30-31. Like the plaintiffs in Slack, appellant asserts that she was confronted by demands that would not have been made upon her but for her sex, and that her refusal to comply with them led to abolition of her job. That the demand here was for sexual relations is of no consequence. See note 49 supra.

[67][Omitted.]

condition of which she complains, absent a showing that the supervisor imposed a similar condition upon a male coemployee.[68]

We also note that, in disposing of this case, the District Court referred to it as "a controversy underpinned by the subtleties of an inharmonious personal relationship."[69] Were we satisfied that this characterization was but a part of the reasoning underlying the court's ruling that the discrimination was not sex-based, we would have no need to address it further.[70] The fact is, however, that we are uncertain as to the reach of the court's observation, and concerned about the implications to which it is susceptible.

[LIABILITY OF EMPLOYER]

If the court meant that the conduct attributed to appellant's supervisor fell outside Title VII because it was a personal escapade rather than an agency project, no support for a summary judgment could be derived therefrom. Generally speaking, an employer is chargeable with Title VII violations occasioned by discriminatory practices of supervisory personnel.[71] We realize that should a supervisor contravene employer policy without the employer's knowledge and the consequences are rectified when discovered, the employer may be relieved from responsibility under Title VII.[72] But, so far as we are aware, the agency involved here is not in position to claim exoneration on that theory.

If, on the other hand, the court was saying that there was no actionable discrimination because only one employee was victimized, we would strongly disagree. A sex-founded impediment to equal employment opportunity succumbs to Title VII even though less than all employees of the claimant's gender are affected.[73] The protections afforded by Title VII against sex discrimination are extended to the individual,[74] and "a single instance of discrimination may form the basis of a private suit."[75] To briefly illustrate, suits have been entertained where a woman charged that she was fired because she was pregnant and unmarried, notwithstanding the fact that no other woman was discharged for that reason,[76] and where a male nurse asserted that he was denied assignments to care for female patients, although no allegations were made with respect to the assignment of other male nurses.[77] Close analogies emerge from situations wherein a black woman was terminated ostensibly for personality conflicts but allegedly was told that she probably did not need the job anyway

---

[68]• • • On this account, we believe that General Elec. Co. v. Gilbert, supra note 64, and Geduldig v. Aiello, 417 U.S. 484, 94 S.Ct. 2485, 41 L.Ed.2d 256, 8 FEP Cases 97 (1974), are distinguishable. In General Electric, it was concluded that exclusion of benefits for pregnancy from an employer's otherwise comprehensive disability plan did not work a discrimination attributable to sex. The Court relied heavily upon its earlier holding in Geduldig that a similar state-sponsored plan did not infringe the Fourteenth Amendment. The Court reasoned that neither program foreclosed anyone from eligibility for benefits because of gender, but merely removed one risk from the coverage provided. As analyzed in each case, "[t]he program divides potential recipients into two groups—pregnant women and non-pregnant persons. While the first group is exclusively female, the second includes members of both sexes." General Elec. Co. v. Gilbert, supra note 64, 429 U.S. at 135, 97 SCt. at 407, 50 L.Ed.2d. at 353, 13 FEP Cases at 1661, quoting Geduldig v. Aiello, supra, 417 U.S. at 496-97 n.20, 94 S.Ct. at 2492 n.20, 41 L.Ed.2d at 264-265 n.20, 8 FEP Cases at 101. There was no showing that there were risks against which men were protected and women were not, or vice versa; or that the total package of benefits gave an advantage to men over women; or that the exclusion of pregnancy benefits was a subterfuge for discrimination against women.

As we read these decisions, they do not condone discrimination bottomed partly though not wholly on sex, or sex discrimination against some but not all women. By the Court's appraisal, men and women were treated equally in terms of protection conferred by the disability plans, and that led to the view that there was no discrimination at all. Moreover, the opinion in neither case suggests that the Court was retreating from its decision in Phillips v. Martin-Marietta Corp., supra note 50, which invalidated a condition barring women from employment only if they had pre-school-age children, and affected no one else at all. See text supra at notes 60-62. When, as in the case before us, a woman is subjected to an employment condition by a superior who leaves all men completely free from that condition, it cannot be said that there is parity of treatment as found in General Electric and Geduldig, or that there is not a sex-predicated discrimination as found in Phillips.

[69–71][Omitted.]

[72]See, e.g., Miller v. Bank of America, 418 F.Supp. 233, 235-236, 13 FEP Cases 439, 440 (N.D. Cal. 1976) (official policy of bank to discourage sexual conduct, and bank not advised of behavior by filing of grievance with Employer Relations Department); Howard v. National Cash Register Co., 388 F.Supp. 603, 605-606, 15 FEP Cases 341, 342-344 (S.D. Ohio 1975)(racial slurs by fellow employees always investigated and employees disciplined).

[73–77][Omitted.]

because she was married to a white male,[78] and where a white woman attributed the loss of her job to her relationship with a black man.[79] In each of these instances, a cause of action was recognized although it did not appear that any other individual of the same gender or race had been mistreated by the employer.[80]

[COVERAGE OF ACT]

At no time during our intensive study of this case have we encountered anything to support the notion that employment conditions summoning sexual relations between employees and superiors are somehow exempted from the coverage of Title VII.[81] The statute in explicit terms proscribes discrimination "because of . . . sex,"[82] with only narrowly defined exceptions completely foreign to the situation emerging here.[83] The legislative history similarly discloses a congressional purpose to outlaw any and all sex-based discrimination,[84] equally with any other form of discrimination which Title VII condemns.[85] Beyond these considerations, the courts have consistently recognized that Title VII must be construed liberally to achieve its objectives;[86] as we ourselves recently noted, it "requires an interpretation animated by the broad humanitarian and remedial purposes underlying the federal proscription of employment discrimination."[87] It would be pointless to speculate as to whether Congress envisioned the particular type of activity which the job-retention condition allegedly levied on appellant would have exacted. As Judge Goldberg of the Fifth Circuit has so well put it,

> Congress chose neither to enumerate specific discriminatory practices, nor to elucidate in extenso the parameter of such nefarious activities. Rather, it pursued the path of wisdom by being unconstrictive, knowing that constant change is the order of our day and that the seemingly unreasonable practices of the present can easily become the injustices of the morrow[88]

Against this backdrop, we cannot doubt that Title VII intercepts the discriminatory practice charged here.[89] The judgment appealed from is accordingly reversed, and the case is remanded to the District Court for further proceedings consistent with this opinion.[90]

Reversed and remanded.

[78–80][Omitted.]

[81]We are advertent to appellee's plaint that "if the claim which appellant presents were to be found to be justiciable within the framework of a Title VII action, the District Court—and, inevitably, this Court—will find itself embroiled in the resolution of controversies involving claimed denials of employment enhancement on the ground of sex discrimination when the alleged basis of the denials are personal relationships made 'inharmonious' by the influence of a wide range of sexual stereotypes upon unenlightened supervisors." Brief for Appellee at 27. This consideration is wholly beside the point in this forum. We cannot assume that Congress did not realize that any problem in this condition inheres also in claims of employment discrimination stemming from race, color, religion or national origin, and that any such difficulty is treatable by measures other than disregard of the legislative will. Cf. Miller v. Laird, 349 F.Supp. 1034, 1044 (D.D.C. 1972). In designating gender as one of the founts from which discrimination must not flow, "Congress has made the choice, and it is not for us to disturb it." Chandler v. Roudebush, supra note 18, 425 U.S. at 864, 96 S.Ct. at 1961, 48 L.Ed.2d at 433, 12 FEP Cases at 1377.

[82–90][Omitted.]

Concurring Opinion

MacKINNON, Circuit Judge, concurring:—I concur in the remand of this case, but would narrowly limit the area in which petitioner can assert her claim against the Environmental Protection Agency. In support of that position, I offer the following analysis of vicarious liability of an employer for acts of its agents.

The liability of an employer for sexual harassment imposed on an employee by a supervisor requires reference to the law of agency and tort, as well as statutory interpretation.

The starting point must be that supervisors act, generally, as agents of the employer. In certain circumstances, the relationship can be closer, so that the supervisor could be termed a servant of the employer.

An act of sexual harassment which caused the victim, because of her rejection of such advances, to be damaged in her job, would constitute a tort.• • • Where sexual favors are solicited in return for job benefits or under retaliatory threats to expose one's deficiencies on the job, the gravity of the incident might also constitute a violation of the criminal laws.[1] On the civil side, a question arises whether a principal can be held liable for the tort of the agent.

[AGENCY]

Under the general rules of agency, "A Master is not subject to liability for the torts of his servants acting outside the scope of their employment." *Restatement (Second) of Agency* § 219(2)(1958). The present case offers no suggestion that the sexual harassment was even arguably within the scope of employment and certainly it would not be so understood by any federal employee. The sexual harassment furthered no objective of the government agency, nor was it part of the supervisor's actual or ostensible authority, nor was it even within the outermost boundaries of what could be perceived to be his apparent authority.

To the general rule, however, the *Second Restatement of Agency* attaches four exceptions. The first three involve situations where culpability would naturally apply to the principal: "(a) the master intended the conduct or the consequences, or (b) the master was negligent or reckless, or (c) the conduct violated a non-delegable duty of the master . . . ." None of these are here relevant, though if the government had prior knowledge of the offending supervisor's propensity for sexual harassment of subordinate employees, liability might be based on negligence or reckless conduct. The fourth exception considers situations where "the servant purported to act or to speak on behalf of the principal and there was reliance upon apparent authority, or he was aided in accomplishing the tort by the existence of the agency relation." *Restatement (Second) of Agency,* supra.

The exception is stated in the disjunctive. The first part has no application here—it could not be reasonably believed by an employee that the supervisor's demands derived from the employer or that in complying with such demands the employee actually relied upon the authority of the employer. Concerning the second part of the exception, at first reading it seems to argue too much. In every case where vicarious liability is at issue, the agent will have been aided in some way in committing the tort by the position that he holds. In this case, the male supervisor would not have been in a position to ask petitioner for an "after-hours affair" were it not for his position as her immediate "boss."

The examples provided in the *Restatement* commentary, however, indicate that a narrower concept is involved. The tort must be one accomplished by an instrumentality, or through conduct, associated with the agency status.

> In other situations, the servant may be able to cause harm because of his position as agent, as where a telegraph operator sends false messages purporting to come from third persons. . . . Again, the manager of a store operated by him for an undisclosed principal is enabled to cheat the customers because of his position.

Restatement (Second) of Agency §219 Comment at 485. The telegraph operator commits the tort *via* a telegraph message; the store manager commits the tort through the way he charges for what he sells. If the supervisor falsified the report of the quality of the female employee's work, that might (arguably) be a tort of defamation within the stated exception; but the tort involved in the sexual advance is committed entirely outside of the employment milieu.

[SAME CONCLUSION]

Turning to the master-servant vicarious liability in tort law, the same conclusion is reached. Again, the first hurdle is to determine whether the activity is within the scope of

----

[1][Omitted.]

employment. It was not so in this case. There might still be a possibility of holding the master liable for acts outside the scope of that employment. The exception is stated with an example of another kind of tort in W.L. Prosser, *Handbook of the Law of Torts,* (4th ed. 1971) 465-66:

> The most difficult questions arise where the servant, for strictly personal reasons and not in furtherance of his employment, loses his temper and attacks the plaintiff in a quarrel which arises out of the employment . . . . Here, unless some non-delegable duty can be found, the older rule denied recovery, and this is still the holding of the majority of the decisions. There has been a tendency in the later cases, however, to allow recovery on the ground that the employment has provided a peculiar opportunity and even incentive for such loss of temper; and there have been California decisions which have found something of an analogy to the workmen's compensation acts, and have considered that the intentional misconduct arises out of and in the course of the employment.

Even if this court were to join what is admittedly a minority of jurisdictions on this point, the exception would not here apply. While the supervisor has been provided with an opportunity by the agency, it is no more than would be afforded by any employment setting, and can hardly be said to compromise an "incentive" for such tortious conduct.

There being no basis for liability by the employer in a situation like the one presented in this case, under the general law of agency and tort, there is even less basis for vicarious liability if the supervisor's action were characterized under the criminal law. See *Restatement (Second) of Agency* § 231.

Analysis of liability of an employer for violation of Title VII takes us beyond the common law of agency and tort, but rules operative in those spheres provide a necessary starting point. From this basis, we are led to the conclusion that, if liability is to be placed upon an employer, it must be because of the wording and policy of the legislation. Without the interposition of statutory law, the common law would impute no liability.

[TOMKINS CASE]

Title VII includes in its definition of employer "any agent" of one who fits the general definition. 42 U.S.C. § 2000e(b).[2] The District Court in Tomkins v. Public Service Electric & Gas Co., supra, emphasized the reference to agent in the general definition, though eventually that court found that the sexual advances involved there were outside the purview of the supervisor's authority:

> Insofar as the quoted language suggests that acts done for the private benefit of an individual supervisor cannot be imputed to the Employer for the purpose of finding a violation of Title VII, this Court respectfully disagrees. If a supervisor is acting within the purview of his authority, the doctrine of *respondeat superior* may be employed whether he is driving a company car or victimizing a female. See Title 42 United States Code, § 2000e(b) which expressly includes any agent of an employer within the meaning of "employer."

The other significant legislative scheme governing employer-employee relations, the National Labor Relations Act, defines employer in a similar way: "The term 'employer' includes any person acting as an agent of an employer, directly or indirectly." 29 U.S.C. §152(2)(1970). To the extent that the term "agency" is used, however, the usual principles of agency are invoked; and, as has been seen, those rules would deny government liability as an employer in a case such as this. The supervisor is not acting as an agent when he commits the tort complained of; hence, no unlawful employment practice has been committed by the "employer."

However, the action complained of does not terminate with the mere sexual advance. In the present case, and in others of this type, it is alleged that the employee's refusal to comply led the supervisor to take unfavorable employment-related actions against her. If

---

[2][Omitted.]   *144, 171*

those employment-related actions were unjustified, then the issue arises of holding the employer liable for those actions. Even where the tort complained of arose in the employment setting, if it was not committed within the *scope* of the supervisor's authority, the employer will not be liable.

[TAFT-HARTLEY ACT]

A different interpretation has been followed, however, where the tortious conduct is also violative of the National Labor Relations Act. While granting fullest rein to an employer's discretion to hire, promote, or fire for a "good reason, bad reason, or no reason at all," that statute, as interpreted by the courts, delineates certain impermissible reasons (such as discrimination for or against union members); and when those impermissible reasons are involved, the normal rules of vicarious liability are not applied. For example, if a supervisor singles out union members for abusive treatment, neither actual nor constructive knowledge by the personnel director is required to find a section 8(a)(3) violation. The supervisor might even be acting outside the scope of his employment and contrary to the announced policy of the employer, still, to hold that no violation occurred "would provide a simple means for evading the Act by a division of corporate functions." Allegheny Pepsi-Cola Bottling Co. v. NLRB, 312 F.2d 529, 531, 52 LRRM 2019 (3d Cir. 1962). This approach has even been extended so far as to find a violation in the combination of two acts, by two different members of management, where each was itself permissible.[3]

As it is a departure from the common law rule, the approach to liability adopted by courts applying the National Labor Relations Act must be carefully scrutinized to determine whether it should be followed in a related, but significantly distinct context.

First, whatever reliance can be drawn from the legislative history of the National Labor Relations Act, and its statement of policy to encourage collective bargaining, is inapplicable to Title VII. Combing the legislative history of the Civil Rights Act turns up no direct statement that employers are to be vicariously liable.

However, the Supreme Court has found that "The objective of Congress in the enactment of Title VII is plain from the language of the statute," Griggs v. Duke Power Co., 401 U.S. 424, 429, 3 FEP Cases 175, 177 (1971), and relying on that language alone, has developed strong rules of employer liability. See e.g., Franks v. Bowman Transportation Co., 424 U.S. 747, 12 FEP Cases 549 (1976)(retroactive seniority relief required, despite section 703(h) of Title VII); Albermarle Paper Co. v. Moody, 422 U.S. 405, 10 FEP Cases 1181 (1975) (backpay even in the absence of bad faith); McDonnell Douglas Corp v. Green, 411 U.S. 792, 5 FEP Cases 965 (1973) (prima facie case met, even in particular case, with no showing of intent to discriminate); Griggs v. Duke Power Co., 401 U.S. 424, 432, 3 FEP Cases 175, 178 (1971) ("Congress has placed on the employer the burden of showing that any given requirement must have a manifest relationship to the employment in question").

[THREE RATIONALES]

Accordingly, what legislative history cannot itself supply has been suggested by a reading of the statute's intent from its overall scheme. Common elements may be found between the liability for employer conduct under Title VII and employer liability, as traced above, under the National Labor Relations Act. Generally, liability has been premised on one of three (non-exhaustive) rationales: 1) if ambiguous conduct might be violative of the statute, the employer is in the best position to know the real cause, and to come forward with an explanation; 2) the employer, not the employee, can establish prophylactic rules which, without upsetting efficiency, could obviate the circumstances of potential discrimination; 3) the type of conduct at issue is questionable at best, and it is not undesirable to induce careful employers to err on the side of avoiding possibly violative conduct.

---

[3]In a case of selective discharge, the personnel director who orders the firing might not actually know that the employee was a union supporter, but it is sufficient if a foreman does, because his knowledge will be imputed to the employer as an entity. Texas Aluminum Co. v. NLRB, 435 F.2d 917, 919, 76 LRRM 2151 (5th Cir. 1970).

The first rationale is the premise behind many Title VII cases involving subjective decision-making. See e.g., United States v. N.L. Industries, Inc., 479 F.2d 354, 368, 5 FEP Cases 823, 834 (8th Cir. 1973); Rowe v. General Motors Corp., 457 F.2d 348, 358, 4 FEP Cases 445, 452 (5th Cir. 1972). For a fine analysis of contemporary Title VII law, see Lopatka, *A 1977 Primer on the Federal Regulation of Employment Discrimination,* 1977 U. ILL. L. FOR. 69 (1977), especially at 89 (subjective decisions). See also Stacy, *Subjective Criteria in Employment Decisions Under Title VII,* 10 GEORGIA L. REV. 732 (1976). This rationale also seems to underlie the Supreme Court's strict formulation of liability in the related field of jury discrimination: when the percentages show a large disparity, it is for the state or county to offer explanations. See, e.g., Castaneda v. Partida, 45 LW 4302 (U.S. March 23, 1977); Alexander v. Louisiana, 405 U.S. 625 (1972); Turner v. Fouche, 396 U.S. 346, 359-360 (1970).

The second rationale finds clearest expression in the Supreme Court's decisions involving employment testing. • • • Employers who use general knowledge or aptitude tests are not inherently discriminating, but such tests can be made more or less relevant and fair, and it is the employer who controls their imposition. Hence, if discrimination results, he must answer.

In labor relations law under the National Labor Relations Act, the second rationale has also been influential. Even though an employer has a statutory (and constitutional) right to address his employees on the likely effects of a union takeover, predictions about economic consequences of unionization are fraught with potential for implied or actual threat. If such threats develop, the employer is liable. This is so even if it is his supervisors who make the threats, since making predictions is inherently dangerous and the employer could have instructed his supervisors simply to avoid making predictions in talking with employees. See generally NLRB v. Gissel Packing Co., 395 U.S. 575, 618, 71 LRRM 2481 (1969).

[THIRD RATIONALE]

The National Labor Relations Act also provides several examples of the third rationale. That rationale underlies the rule adopted by the National Labor Relations Board, and sanctioned by the courts, Peerless Plywood Co., 107 NLRB 427, 33 LRRM 1151 (1953), whereby employer speeches within 24 hours before the scheduled time of an election are prohibited. Not every employer speech during that time period is coercive, but it is not a severe burden to require that employers order their campaigns without relying on that particular tactic. On the union side, the use of "dual-purpose" authorization cards provide a comparable example of an intrinsically troublesome device, and the Board, and the courts, have seen no harm in inducing an avoidance of the practice.

These general principles by no means exhaust the guiding rules of employer liability in labor relations law, but they do provide a structure useful for focusing on whether *respondeat superior* should be imposed in a particular case. Different conclusions result in varying Title VII contexts.[5] Where sexual advances are involved, it must be candidly recognized at the outset that, even when directed from a supervisor who would be difficult to refuse, the advances themselves might be welcome. It cannot be presumed as a matter of law that the employee is subjected to disfavorable treatment because of the advances. Once it is established, however, that the employee has no interest in the proposal, then the employee may suffer from the continuation of advances. And the eventual damage to her job for failing to accede, if that is a result, is undeniably harmful.

---

[4][Omitted.]

[5]At one end of the spectrum, for example, a supervisor's persistent use of racial epithets would undoubtedly lead to an employer's Title VII liability. Tracing through the three rationales: (1) If uttered often enough, the employer either actually knows of it, or should know of it. (2) A simple order announced by the employer (even before any suggestion of abuse has arisen) would obviate the problem. (3) Namecalling of any kind is close to abuse, and there is no harm from inducing its complete avoidance.

At the other end would be a foreman's unprovoked and unforeseeable attack upon the black workers on a particular job: the employer could not be expected to anticipate it; no general prophylactic rule could have been promulgated to prevent it; to order supervisors to circumvent all occasions where such incidents might arise would severely impede the efficient ordering of work.

1. *The rationale of an employer's better position to know.* Unlike the case of a standardized employment test, the employer or higher supervisor is not in the best position of anyone to know whether an employee has been unjustly damaged on her job. The sexual advance of a supervisor toward an employee is seldom a public matter; and the distinction between invited, uninvited-but-welcome, offensive-but-tolerable and flatly rejected advances ordinarily does not fall within the special ability of the employer or higher supervisor to discern.

However, once a complaint of offensive advances has been made, the employer's role becomes far more serious. One of the four district court opinions (besides the one currently before us) that have considered sexual advances, based employer liability precisely on this phase of the incident, "When a female employee registers a complaint of sexual abuse and the company chooses to fire her rather than investigate, the corporate response may constitute discrimination based on sex." Tompkins v. Public Service Electric & Gas Co., supra.

[ALLEGATIONS OF COMPLAINT]

In the present case, the complaint fairly includes allegations that the plaintiff's supervisor, whose sexual advances had been spurned, induced other agents of the Environmental Protection Agency to punish her (complaint at J.A. 29); that the Agency was guilty of wrongful action in prosecuting her complaint, informing her that she should not bring a sex but only a race discrimination claim (J.A. 30);[6] that the Civil Service Commission collaborated in frustrating her claim by refusing as a matter of law to reopen the hearings for evidence of sex discrimination (J.A. 31); that "agents and employees of the defendant" retaliated against her for having filed an EEO complaint (J.A. 37, 44—Count II of Amended Complaint); and that harassment both for refusing sexual advances and for filing the EEO complaint was not only imposed by the supervisor who had made the advances, but also by "other supervisors" within her agency. (J.A. 85).

These allegations are sufficient to raise a suspicion under the first rationale that the employer itself knew, or should have known, of the harassment, and hence the common law result of no *respondeat superior* should be considered reversed by the statute. However, under this rationale, the plaintiff still has a substantial burden to prove: as alleged, EPA officials other than Barnes' own supervisor must be shown to have incorrectly or falsely advised plaintiff in processing her complaint, and to have treated her adversely in job assignment, for the purpose of frustrating her Title VII charge and punishing her for bringing it, or with that effect. If plaintiff can prove this, she should prevail.

From a more general perspective *respondeat superior* should apply, and the common law rule should be ousted, whenever a plaintiff can show that, in addition to the particular sexual advance, and the retaliatory actions by the maker of that advance, other agents of the employer with knowledge of her charges assisted the retaliation or impeded the complaint. That type of showing suffices to shift to the defendant the burden of disproving that the agency had, at the least, a callous disregard of Title VII rights.

2. *Employer's ability to take preventive steps in advance.* An employer could promulgate a rule that no sexual advances were to be made by any supervisors to any employees. The unique problem with this kind of harassment, however, is that its potential is not confined to working hours. Even if a no-advances rule were adopted, it could only with great difficulty be made to apply to employees' own time.

Hence, there is no basis *under this rationale* to oust the common law rule against *respondeat superior* for acts outside the scope of employment. Nor do the facts of this complaint demonstrate a narrowly definable opportunity for the employer to formulate a specific preventive rule short of prohibiting all off-hours social contacts between employees and supervisors which is of course out of the question.

[PREVENTIVE MEASURES]

As the analysis under this rationale unfolds, it is apparent that an employer could somewhat insulate itself from vicarious liability by taking certain preventive measures. At

---

[6][Omitted.]

the least, an employer should be free from vicarious liability if it 1) posts the firm's (or government's) policy against sexual harassment by supervisors, and 2) provides a workable mechanism for the *prompt* reporting of sexual harassment, which mechanism 3) includes the rapid issuance of a warning to the supervisor complained of, or the mere notation of a rejected sexual advance for possible future reference in case an issue is made of voluntariness, and 4) affords the opportunity of the complainant remaining anonymous. Here, the established policy of the federal government against sex discrimination,[7] applies to the Environmental Protection Agency, and the 1972 Equal Employment Opportunity Act[8] together with Executive Order No. 11375 (1967)[9] provide a mechanism for reporting and adjusting complaints.[10] Those broad steps are important, and in the present context (where no precise preventive rule was feasible) they suffice to defeat vicarious liability. Nevertheless, detailed procedures along the lines suggested would demonstrate more sensitivity to the particular problem of sexual advances and subsequent discrimination, and, if conscientiously applied, would come close to assuring an employer of protection against vicarious liability in many cases.

3. *Inducing extra caution.* Sexual advances may not be intrinsically offensive, and no policy can be derived from the equal employment opportunity laws to discourage them. We are not here concerned with racial epithets or confusing union authorization cards, which serve no one's interest, but with social patterns that to some extent are normal and expectable. It is the abuse of the practice, rather than the practice itself, that arouses alarm.

Accordingly, there is no justification under this rationale to impose vicarious liability upon an employer.

[SUMMARY]

In summary, I concur in the remand of this case, but on a narrower ground than the majority. Barnes has brought her suit against the Environmental Protection Agency and its administrator, not against a single supervisor. Vicarious liability of an employer would not attach at common law under the facts her alleged, so the suit can be maintained only by reason of a statutory exception. Drawing from labor relations law and equal opportunity law, we can isolate three general rationales for overturning the common law and imposing • • • principal-agent liability. Only one of those provides a basis for such a ruling on these facts. That theory is brought into operation by the charge that other management personnel harassed petitioner, that they misled her in filing her complaint, that her supervisors retaliated against her for doing so and that her employer, with knowledge of the facts alleged by her, ratified the discrimination that her supervisor had improperly imposed upon her. Those allegations if true would make a case that the Environmental Protection Agency knew or should have known of the harassment involved.[11] The case should be remanded to allow petitioner a chance to prove this claim.

[7-11][Omitted.]

Barnes v. Costle thus firmly established that the sex-based assignment of duties, sexual or otherwise, violates Title VII where the employer enforces the assignment by threat of discharge or other adverse economic consequence. It left unsettled, however, whether Title VII was also violated by sex-based disparate treatment that had no economic impact.[64]

---

[64]Although discrimination having only a noneconomic effect is actionable, the remedy under Title VII is limited to declaratory and injunctive relief, see Chapter 28, and costs and attorney's fees, see Chapter 30, unless the plaintiff resigns under circumstances such that the courts will deem it to have been a constructive discharge, see Chapter 9. Companion state-law claims may be brought in these circumstances, seeking compensatory and punitive damages. See Chapter 15, The Common Law.

In 1980, the Equal Employment Opportunity Commission (EEOC) promulgated regulations, in the form of guidelines, interpreting the Title VII prohibition against discrimination on the basis of sex.[65] One subpart of the EEOC Guidelines addressed sexual harassment. In addressing quid pro quo harassment, the EEOC incorporated the holdings of such cases as *Saxbe* and *Barnes*. The EEOC Guidelines state that sexual harassment is sex discrimination in violation of Title VII, and, more specifically, that an individual's response to unwelcome conduct of a sexual nature may not lawfully be made the basis of any adverse employment decision.[66]

C. Hostile Environment Cases

While the 1980 EEOC Guidelines essentially codified judicial holdings in the area of quid pro quo harassment, they anticipated judicial developments with respect to a sexually hostile environment. In 1980, no court had yet held that a sexually hostile environment, involving no tangible job detriment, was actionable. Nonetheless, the EEOC, borrowing from analogous judicial authority in the area of race and national origin discrimination, opined that unwelcome sexual conduct violates Title VII whenever it "has the purpose or effect of unreasonably interfering with an individual's work performance or creating an intimidating, a hostile, or offensive working environment."[67]

Notwithstanding that the essence of sexual harassment is gender discrimination, the EEOC Guidelines focused on sexuality rather than gender. The EEOC defined sexual harassment as job detriments resulting from "[u]nwelcome sexual advances, requests for sexual favors, and other verbal or physical conduct of a sexual nature."[68] In so doing, the EEOC inadvertently misled some courts into supposing that sex-based harassment must necessarily involve sexual conduct.[69] Hostile environment cases are really much simpler. They present situations that, like quid pro quo cases, involve disparate treatment based on an employee's gender. In one common situation, women employees, often in occupations or workplaces traditionally dominated by men, are subjected to hazing behaviors: scorn, ridicule, and verbal abuse from males who resent their presence. The behavior consists of gestures, words, or conduct that may or may not be sexual in content. The sexual content of the conduct may suffice, but it is never necessary, to prove that the conduct is based on sex. Cases involving analogous harassment of racial and ethnic minorities are di-

---

[65]The EEOC is the federal agency charged with enforcement of Title VII. §705(a), 42 U.S.C. §2000e-4(a).

[66]29 C.F.R. §1604.11(a), EEOC Guidelines on Discrimination Because of Sex, reproduced in Appendix 1. The Guidelines on Discrimination Because of Sex appear at 29 C.F.R. §§1604.1–.11. One part, §1604.11, is on sexual harassment. The EEOC Guidelines are nonbinding but "constitute a body of experience and informed judgments to which courts and litigants may properly resort for guidance." Meritor Sav. Bank v. Vinson, 477 U.S. 57, 65, 40 FEP Cases 1822, 1826 (1986), reproduced *infra* (citation omitted).

[67]29 C.F.R. §1604.11(a), *supra* note 66.

[68]The Guidelines may have been influenced by the literature focusing on sexual harassment as the sexual exploitation of women.

[69]See Chapter 4, Hostile Environment Harassment, Section V.B. Where the abuse is not sexually oriented, the EEOC Guidelines (which speak of "sexual conduct") arguably do not apply, although the first sentence of §1604.11(a) could be read alone to bar all gender-based harassment.

rectly relevant,[70] and establish that harassment on the basis of sex, even if not sexual in content, violates Title VII.

In another common situation, a female employee is subjected to offensive sexual advances, innuendo, touching, and propositions by a male employee, who may or may not be her supervisor. The conduct, which would not necessarily be considered undesirable by all women, continues although it is unwelcome in the particular case. The woman may or may not eventually submit. She suffers emotional distress and finds it difficult to do her job. She may or may not resign.

When this conduct is not an isolated act of an individual employee, but rather is attributable to the employer, it is little different from the prototypical quid pro quo case in which an employee is fired for rebuffing the boss's advance. Unless the woman resigns, the detriment she suffers, while solely emotional and psychological, is no less real than a tangible job detriment. Her working conditions differ from those of her male colleagues, and she would not have suffered disparate treatment but for her sex. Her tolerance of an adverse condition based on her sex has been made part of the employment bargain. The fact that the offensive conduct is sexually oriented is relevant to show motivation—that she would not have been treated in the same manner had she been a man.

It was this sort of hostile environment case that confronted the Supreme Court in *Meritor Savings Bank v. Vinson.*

MERITOR SAVINGS BANK v. VINSON

477 U.S. 57, 40 FEP Cases 1822
(1986)

JUSTICE REHNQUIST delivered the opinion of the Court.

This case presents important questions concerning claims of workplace "sexual harassment" brought under Title VII of the Civil Rights Act of 1964, 78 Stat. 253, as amended, 42 U.S.C. §2000e et seq.

I

In 1974, respondent Mechelle Vinson met Sidney Taylor, a vice president of what is now petitioner Meritor Savings Bank (the bank) and manager of one of its branch offices. When respondent asked whether she might obtain employment at the bank, Taylor gave her an application, which she completed and returned the next day; later that same day Taylor called her to say that she had been hired. With Taylor as her supervisor, respondent started as a teller-trainee, and thereafter was promoted to teller, head teller, and assistant branch manager. She worked at the same branch for four years, and it is undisputed that her advancement there was based on merit alone. In September 1978, respondent notified Taylor that she was taking sick leave for an indefinite period. On November 1, 1978, the bank discharged her for excessive use of that leave.

Respondent brought this action against Taylor and the bank, claiming that during her four years at the bank she had "constantly been subjected to sexual harassment" by Taylor

---

[70]*See, e.g.,* Rogers v. EEOC, 454 F.2d 234, 4 FEP Cases 92 (5th Cir. 1971), *cert. denied,* 406 U.S. 957 (1972). For a discussion of nonsexual harassment, see Chapter 2, Forms of Harassment, Section I. The EEOC Guidelines state that the "principles involved here continue to apply to race, color, religion, or national origin." *Supra* note 66, 29 C.F.R. at §1604.11(a) n.1.

in violation of Title VII. She sought injunctive relief, compensatory and punitive damages against Taylor and the bank, and attorney's fees.

At the 11-day bench trial, the parties presented conflicting testimony about Taylor's behavior during respondent's employment. Respondent testified that during her probationary period as a teller-trainee, Taylor treated her in a fatherly way and made no sexual advances. Shortly thereafter, however, he invited her out to dinner and, during the course of the meal, suggested that they go to a motel to have sexual relations. At first she refused, but out of what she described as fear of losing her job she eventually agreed. According to respondent, Taylor thereafter made repeated demands upon her for sexual favors, usually at the branch, both during and after business hours; she estimated that over the next several years she had intercourse with him some 40 or 50 times. In addition, respondent testified that Taylor fondled her in front of other employees, followed her into the women's restroom when she went there alone, exposed himself to her, and even forcibly raped her on several occasions. These activities ceased after 1977, respondent stated, when she started going with a steady boyfriend.

Respondent also testified that Taylor touched and fondled other women employees of the bank, and she attempted to call witnesses to support this charge. But while some supporting testimony apparently was admitted without objection, the District Court did not allow her "to present wholesale evidence of a pattern and practice relating to sexual advances to other female employees in her case in chief, but advised her that she might well be able to present such evidence in rebuttal to the defendants' cases." Vinson v. Taylor, 22 EPD ¶30708, pp. 14688–14689, 23 FEP Cases 37, 38–39, n. 1 (D DC 1980). Respondent did not offer such evidence in rebuttal. Finally, respondent testified that because she was afraid of Taylor she never reported his harassment to any of his supervisors and never attempted to use the bank's complaint procedure.

Taylor denied respondent's allegations of sexual activity, testifying that he never fondled her, never made suggestive remarks to her, never engaged in sexual intercourse with her and never asked her to do so. He contended instead that respondent made her accusations in response to a business-related dispute. The bank also denied respondent's allegations and asserted that any sexual harassment by Taylor was unknown to the bank and engaged in without its consent or approval.

The District Court denied relief, but did not resolve the conflicting testimony about the existence of a sexual relationship between respondent and Taylor. It found instead that

> "If [respondent] and Taylor did engage in an intimate or sexual relationship during the time of [respondent's] employment with [the bank], that relationship was a voluntary one having nothing to do with her continued employment at [the bank] or her advancement or promotions at that institute." Id., at 42 (footnote omitted).

The court ultimately found that respondent "was not the victim of sexual harassment and was not the victim of sexual discrimination" while employed at the bank. Id., 43.

Although it concluded that respondent had not proved a violation of Title VII, the District Court nevertheless went on to address the bank's liability. After noting the bank's express policy against discrimination, and finding that neither respondent nor any other employee had ever lodged a complaint about sexual harassment by Taylor, the court ultimately concluded that "the bank was without notice and cannot be held liable for the alleged actions of Taylor." Id., at 42.

The Court of Appeals for the District of Columbia reversed. 243 U.S. App. D.C. 323, 753 F.2d 141, 36 FEP Cases 1423 (1985). Relying on its earlier holding in Bundy v. Jackson, 205 U.S. App. D.C. 444, 641 F.2d 934, 24 FEP Cases 1155 (1981), decided after the trial in this case, the court stated that a violation of Title VII may be predicated on either of two types of sexual harassment: harassment that involves the conditioning of concrete employment benefits on sexual favors, and harassment that, while not affecting economic benefits, creates a hostile or offensive working environment. The court drew additional support for this position from the Equal Employment Opportunity Commission's Guidelines on Discrimination Because of Sex, 29 CFR §1604.11(a) (1985), which set out these two types of sexual harassment claims. Believing that "Vinson's grievance was clearly of the [hostile environment] type," 243 U.S. App. D.C., at 327, 753 F.2d, at 145, 36 FEP Cases, at 1426, and that the District Court had not considered whether a violation of this type had occurred, the court concluded that a remand was necessary.

The court further concluded that the District Court's finding that any sexual relationship between respondent and Taylor "was a voluntary one" did not obviate the need for a remand. "[U]ncertain as to precisely what the [district] court meant" by this finding, the Court of Appeals held that if the evidence otherwise showed that "Taylor made Vinson's toleration of sexual harassment a condition of her employment," her voluntariness "had no materiality whatsoever." Id., at 328, 753 F.2d at 146, 36 FEP Cases, at 1427. The court then surmised that the District Court's finding of voluntariness might have been based on "the voluminous testimony regarding respondent's dress and personal fantasies," testimony that the Court of Appeals believed "had no place in this litigation." Id., at 328, n.36, 753 F.2d, at 146, n.36, 36 FEP Cases, at 1427.

As to the bank's liability, the Court of Appeals held that an employer is absolutely liable for sexual harassment practices by supervisory personnel, whether or not the employer knew or should have known about the misconduct. The court relied chiefly on Title VII's definition of "employer" to include "any agent of such a person," 42 U.S.C. §2000e(b), as well as on the EEOC guidelines. The court held that a supervisor is an "agent" of his employer for Title VII purposes, even if he lacks authority to hire, fire, or promote, since "the mere existence—or even the appearance—of a significant degree of influence in vital job decisions gives any supervisor the opportunity to impose on employees." 243 U.S. App. D.C., at 332, 753 F.2d, at 150, 36 FEP Cases, at 1430.

In accordance with the foregoing, the Court of Appeals reversed the judgment of the District Court and remanded the case for further proceedings. A subsequent suggestion for rehearing en banc was denied, with three judges dissenting. 245 U.S. App. D.C. 1330, 760 F.2d 1330, 37 FEP Cases 1266 (1985). We granted certiorari, 474 U.S. —— (1985), and now affirm for different reasons.

II

Title VII of the Civil Rights Act of 1964 makes it "an unlawful employment practice for an employer . . . to discriminate against any individual with respect to his compensation, terms, conditions, or privileges of employment, because of such individual's race, color, religion, sex, or national origin." 42 U.S.C. §2000e-2(a)(1). The prohibition against discrimination based on sex was added to Title VII at the last minute on the floor of the House of Representatives. 110 Cong. Rec. 2577-2584 (1964). The principal argument in opposition to the amendment was that "sex discrimination" was sufficiently different from other types of discrimination that it ought to receive separate legislative treatment. See id., at 2577 (Statement of Rep. Celler quoting letter from United States Department of Labor); id., at 2584 (statement of Rep. Green). This argument was defeated, the bill quickly passed as amended, and we are left with little legislative history to guide us in interpreting the Act's prohibition against discrimination based on "sex."

Respondent argues, and the Court of Appeals held, that unwelcome sexual advances that create an offensive or hostile working environment violate Title VII. Without question, when a supervisor sexually harasses a subordinate because of the subordinate's sex, that supervisor "discriminate[s]" on the basis of sex. Petitioner apparently does not challenge this proposition. It contends instead that in prohibiting discrimination with respect to "compensation, terms, conditions, or privileges" of employment, Congress was concerned with what petitioner describes as "tangible loss" of "an economic character," not "purely psychological aspects of the workplace environment." Brief for Petitioner 30-31, 34. In support of this claim petitioner observes that in both the legislative history of Title VII and this Court's Title VII decisions, the focus has been on tangible, economic barriers erected by discrimination.

We reject petitioner's view. First, the language of Title VII is not limited to "economic" or "tangible" discrimination. The phrase "terms, conditions, or privileges of employment" evinces a congressional intent " 'to strike at the entire spectrum of disparate treatment of men and women' " in employment. Los Angeles Department of Water and Power v. Manhart, 435 U.S. 702, 707, n.13, 17 FEP Cases 395, 398 (1978), quoting Sprogis

v. United Air Lines, Inc., 444 F.2d 1194, 1198, 3 FEP Cases 621, 623-624 (CA7 1971). Petitioner has pointed to nothing in the Act to suggest that Congress contemplated the limitation urged here.

Second, in 1980 the EEOC issued guidelines specifying that "sexual harassment," as there defined, is a form of sex discrimination prohibited by Title VII. As an "administrative interpretation of the Act by the enforcing agency," Griggs v. Duke Power Co., 401 U.S. 424, 433-434, 3 FEP Cases 175, 179 (1971), these guidelines, " 'while not controlling upon the courts by reason of their authority, do constitute a body of experience and informed judgment to which courts and litigants may properly resort for guidance,' " General Electric Co. v. Gilbert, 429 U.S. 125, 141-142, 13 FEP Cases 1657, 1664 (1976), quoting Skidmore v. Swift & Co., 323 U.S. 134, 140, 4 WH Cases 866 (1944). The EEOC guidelines fully support the view that harassment leading to noneconomic injury can violate Title VII.

In defining "sexual harassment," the guidelines first describe the kinds of workplace conduct that may be actionable under Title VII. These include "[u]nwelcome sexual advances, requests for sexual favors, and other verbal or physical conduct of a sexual nature." 29 CFR §1604.11(a) (1985). Relevant to the charges at issue in this case, the guidelines provide that such sexual misconduct constitutes prohibited "sexual harassment," whether or not it is directly linked to the grant or denial of an economic *quid pro quo,* where "such conduct has the purpose or effect of unreasonably interfering with an individual's work performance or offensive working environment." §1604.11(a)(3).

In concluding that so-called "hostile environment" (i.e., non *quid pro quo*) harassment violates Title VII, the EEOC drew upon a substantial body of judicial decisions and EEOC precedent holding that Title VII affords employees the right to work in an environment free from discriminatory intimidation, ridicule, and insult. See generally 45 Fed. Reg. 74676 (1980). Rogers v. EEOC, 454 F.2d 234, 4 FEP Cases 92 (CA5 1971), cert. denied, 406 U.S. 957, 4 FEP Cases 771 (1972), was apparently the first case to recognize a cause of action based upon a discriminatory work environment. In Rogers, the Court of Appeals for the Fifth Circuit held that a Hispanic complainant could establish a Title VII violation by demonstrating that her employer created an offensive work environment by giving discriminatory service to its Hispanic clientele. The court explained that an employee's protections under Title VII extend beyond the economic aspects of employment:

> "[T]he phrase 'terms, conditions or privileges of employment' in [Title VII] is an expansive concept which sweeps within its protective ambit the practice of creating a working environment heavily charged with ethnic or racial discrimination . . . . One can readily envision working environments so heavily polluted with discrimination as to destroy completely the emotional and psychological stability of minority group workers . . . ." 454 F.2d at 238, 4 FEP Cases, at 95.

Courts applied this principle to harassment based on race, e.g., Firefighters Institute for Racial Equality v. St. Louis, 549 F.2d 506, 514–15, 14 FEP Cases 1486, 1493 (CA8), cert. denied sub nom. Banta v. United States, 434 U.S. 819, 15 FEP Cases 1184 (1977); Gray v. Greyhound Lines, East, 178 U.S. App. D. C. 91, 98, 545 F.2d 169, 176, 13 FEP Cases 1401, 1406 (1976), religion, e.g., Compston v. Borden, Inc., 424 F.Supp. 157, 17 FEP Cases 310 (SD Ohio 1976), and national origin, e.g., Cariddi v. Kansas City Chiefs Football Club, 568 F.2d 87, 88, 16 FEP Cases 462, 462–463 (CA8 1977). Nothing in Title VII suggests that a hostile environment based on discriminatory *sexual* harassment should not be likewise prohibited. The guidelines thus appropriately drew from, and were fully consistent with, the existing caselaw.

Since the guidelines were issued, courts have uniformly held, and we agree, that a plaintiff may establish a violation of Title VII by proving that discrimination based on sex has created a hostile or abusive working environment. As the Court of Appeals for the Eleventh Circuit wrote in Henson v. Dundee, 682 F.2d 897, 902, 29 FEP Cases 787, 791 (1982):

> "Sexual harassment which creates a hostile or offensive environment for members of one sex is every bit the arbitrary barrier to sexual equality at the workplace that racial harassment is to racial equality. Surely, a requirement that a man or woman run

a gauntlet of sexual abuse in return for the privilege of being allowed to work and make a living can be as demeaning and disconcerting as the harshest of racial epithets."

Accord, Katz v. Dole, 709 F.2d 251, 254–255, 31 FEP Cases 1521, 1523 (CA4 1983); Bundy v. Jackson, 205 U.S. App. D. C. 444, 641 F.2d 934, 944, 24 FEP Cases 1155, 1160 (1981); Zabkowicz v. West Bend Co., 589 F.Supp. 780, 35 FEP Cases 610 (ED Wisc. 1984).

Of course, as the courts in both Rogers and Henson recognized, not all workplace conduct that may be described as "harassment" affects a "term, condition, or privilege" of employment within the meaning of Title VII. See Rogers v. EEOC, supra, at 238, 4 FEP Cases, at 95 ("mere utterance of an ethnic or racial epithet which engenders offensive feelings in an employee" would not affect the conditions of employment to sufficiently significant degree to violate Title VII); Henson, supra, at 904, 29 FEP Cases, at 793 (quoting same). For sexual harassment to be actionable, it must be sufficiently severe or pervasive "to alter the conditions of [the victim's] employment and create an abusive working environment." Ibid. Respondent's allegations in this case—which include not only pervasive harassment but also criminal conduct of the most serious nature—are plainly sufficient to state a claim for "hostile environment" sexual harassment.

The question remains, however, whether the District Court's ultimate finding that respondent "was not the victim of sexual harassment," 22 EPD ¶30708, at 14692–14693, 23 FEP Cases, at 43, effectively disposed of respondent's claim. The Court of Appeals recognized, we think correctly, that this ultimate finding was likely based on one or both of two erroneous views of the law. First, the District Court apparently believed that a claim for sexual harassment will not lie absent an *economic* effect on the complainant's employment. See ibid. ("It is without question that sexual harassment of female employees in which they are asked or required to submit to sexual demands as a *condition to obtain employment or to maintain employment or to obtain promotions* falls within protection of Title VII.") (emphasis added). Since it appears that the District Court made its findings without ever considering the "hostile environment" theory of sexual harassment, the Court of Appeals' decision to remand was correct.

Second, the District Court's conclusion that no actionable harassment occurred might have rested on its earlier "finding" that "[i]f [respondent] and Taylor did engage in an intimate or sexual relationship . . ., that relationship was a voluntary one." Id., at 14692, 23 FEP Cases, at 42. But the fact that sex-related conduct was "voluntary," in the sense that the complainant was not forced to participate against her will, is not a defense to a sexual harassment suit brought under Title VII. The gravamen of any sexual harassment claim is that the alleged sexual advances were "unwelcome." 29 CFR §1604.11(a) (1985). While the question whether particular conduct was indeed unwelcome presents difficult problems of proof and turns largely on credibility determination committed to the trier of fact, the District Court in this case erroneously focused on the "voluntariness" of respondent's participation in the claimed sexual episodes. The correct inquiry is whether respondent by her conduct indicated that the sexual advances were unwelcome, not whether her actual participation in sexual intercourse was voluntary.

Petitioner contends that even if this case must be remanded to the District Court, the Court of Appeals erred in one of the terms of its remand. Specifically, the Court of Appeals stated that testimony about respondent's "dress and personal fantasies," 243 U.S.App.D.C. at 328, n. 36, 753 F.2d, at 146, n.36, 36 FEP Cases, at 1427, which the District Court apparently admitted into evidence, "had no place in this litigation." Ibid. The apparent ground for this conclusion was that respondent's voluntariness *vel non* in submitting to Taylor's advances was immaterial to her sexual harassment claim. While "voluntariness" in the sense of consent is not a defense to such a claim, it does not follow that a complainant's sexually provocative speech or dress is irrelevant as a matter of law in determining whether he or she found particular sexual advances unwelcome. To the contrary, such evidence is obviously relevant. The EEOC guidelines emphasize that the trier of fact must determine the existence of sexual harassment in light of "the record as a whole" and "the totality of circumstances, such as the nature of the sexual advances and the context in which the alleged incidents occurred." 29 CFR §1604.11(b) (1985). Respondent's claim that any marginal relevance of the evidence in question was outweighed by the potential for unfair prejudice is the sort of argument properly addressed to the District Court. In this case the District Court concluded that the evidence should be admitted, and the Court of Appeals' contrary conclusion was based upon the erroneous, categorical view that testimony about provocative dress and publicly expressed sexual fantasies "had no place in this litigation." 243 U.S. App. D. C., at 328, n. 36, 753 F.2d, at 146, n. 36, 36 FEP Cases, at 1427. While the District Court must carefully weigh the applicable considerations in deciding whether to admit evidence of this kind, there is no *per se* rule against its admissibility.

III

Although the District Court concluded that respondent had not proved a violation of Title VII, it nevertheless went on to consider the question of the bank's liability. Finding that "the bank was without notice" of Taylor's alleged conduct, and that notice to Taylor was not the equivalent of notice to the bank, the court concluded that the bank therefore could not be held liable for Taylor's alleged action. The Court of Appeals took the opposite view, holding that an employer is strictly liable for a hostile environment created by a supervisor's sexual advances, even though the employer neither knew nor reasonably could have known of the alleged misconduct. The court held that a supervisor, whether or not he possesses the authority to hire, fire, or promote, is necessarily an "agent" of his employer for all Title VII purposes, since "even the appearance" of such authority may enable him to impose himself on his subordinates.

The parties and *amici* suggest several different standards for employer liability. Respondent, not surprisingly, defends the position of the Court of Appeals. Noting that Title VII's definition of "employer" includes any "agent" of the employer, she also argues that "so long as the circumstance is work-related, the supervisor is the employer and the employer is the supervisor." Brief for Respondent 27. Notice to Taylor that the advances were unwelcome, therefore, was notice to the bank.

Petitioner argues that respondent's failure to use its established grievance procedure, or to otherwise put it on notice of the alleged misconduct, insulates petitioner from liability for Taylor's wrongdoing. A contrary rule would be unfair, petitioner argues, since in a hostile environment harassment case the employer often will have no reason to know about, or opportunity to cure, the alleged wrongdoing.

The EEOC, in its brief as *amicus curiae,* contends that courts formulating employer liability rules should draw from traditional agency principles. Examination of those principles has led the EEOC to the view that where a supervisor exercises the authority actually delegated to him by his employer, by making or threatening to make decisions affecting the employment status of his subordinates, such actions are properly imputed to the employer whose delegation of authority empowered the supervisor to undertake them. Brief for United States and Equal Employment Opportunity Commission as *Amicus Curiae* 22. Thus, the courts have consistently held employers liable for the discriminatory discharges of employees by supervisory personnel, whether or not the employer knew, should have known, or approved of the supervisor's actions. E.g., Anderson v. Methodist Evangelical Hospital, Inc., 464 F.2d 723, 725, 4 FEP Cases 987, 988 (CA6 1972).

The EEOC suggests that when a sexual harassment claim rests exclusively on a "hostile environment" theory, however, the usual basis for a finding of agency will often disappear. In that case, the EEOC believes, agency principles lead to

> "a rule that asks whether a victim of sexual harassment had reasonably available an avenue of complaint regarding such harassment, and, if available and utilized, whether that procedure was reasonably responsive to the employee's complaint. If the employer has an expressed policy against sexual harassment and has implemented a procedure specifically designed to resolve sexual harassment claims, and if the victim does not take advantage of that procedure, the employer should be shielded from liability absent actual knowledge of the sexually hostile environment (obtained, e.g., by the filing of a charge with the EEOC or a comparable state agency). In all other cases, the employer will be liable if it has actual knowledge of the harassment or if, considering all the facts of the case, the victim in question had no reasonably available avenue for making his

or her complaint known to appropriate management officials." Brief for United States and Equal Employment Opportunity Commission as *Amici Curiae,* 26.

As respondent points out, this suggested rule is in some tension with the EEOC guidelines, which hold an employer liable for the acts of its agents without regard to notice. 29 CFR §1604.11(c) (1985). The guidelines do require, however, an "examin[ation of] the circumstances of the particular employment relationship and the job [f]unctions performed by the individual in determining whether an individual acts in either a supervisory or agency capacity." Ibid.

This debate over the appropriate standard for employer liability has a rather abstract quality about it given the state of the record in this case. We do not know at this stage whether Taylor made any sexual advances toward respondent at all, let alone whether those advances were unwelcome, whether they were sufficiently pervasive to constitute a condition of employment, or whether they were "so pervasive and so long continuing . . . that the employer must have become conscious of [them]," Taylor v. Jones, 653 F.2d 1193, 1197–1199, 28 FEP Cases 1024, 1027 (CA8 1981) (holding employer liable for racially hostile working environment based on constructive knowledge).

[7, 8] We therefore decline the parties' invitation to issue a definitive rule on employer liability, but we do agree with the EEOC that Congress wanted courts to look to agency principles for guidance in this area. While such common-law principles may not be transferable in all their particulars to Title VII, Congress' decision to define "employer" to include any "agent" of an employer, 42 U.S.C. §2000e(b), surely evinces an intent to place some limits on the acts of employees for which employers under Title VII are to be held responsible. For this reason, we hold that the Court of Appeals erred in concluding that employers are always automatically liable for sexual harassment by their supervisors. See generally Restatement (Second) of Agency §§219–237 (1958). For the same reason, absence of notice to an employer does not necessarily insulate that employer from liability. Ibid.

[9] Finally, we reject petitioner's view that the mere existence of a grievance procedure and a policy against discrimination, coupled with respondent's failure to invoke procedure, must insulate petitioner from liability. While those facts are plainly relevant, the situation before us demonstrates why they are not necessarily dispositive. Petitioner's general nondiscrimination policy did not address sexual harassment in particular, and thus did not alert employees to their employer's interest in correcting that form of discrimination. App. 25. Moreover, the bank's grievance procedure apparently required an employee to complain first to her supervisor, in this case Taylor. Since Taylor was the alleged perpetrator, it is not altogether surprising that respondent failed to invoke the procedure and report her grievance to him. Petitioner's contention that respondent's failure should insulate it from liability might be substantially stronger if its procedures were better calculated to encourage victims of harassment to come forward.

IV

In sum, we hold that a claim of "hostile environment" sex discrimination is actionable under Title VII, that the District Court's findings were insufficient to dispose of respondent's hostile environment claim, and that the District Court did not err in admitting testimony about respondent's sexually provocative speech and dress. As to employer liability, we conclude that the Court of Appeals was wrong to entirely disregard agency principles and impose absolute liability on employers for the acts of their supervisors, regardless of the circumstances of a particular case.

Accordingly, the judgment of the Court of Appeals reversing the judgment of the District Court is affirmed, and the case is remanded for further proceedings consistent with this opinion.

It is so ordered.

Concurring Opinions

JUSTICE STEVENS, concurring.

Because I do not see any inconsistency between the two opinions, and because I believe the question of statutory construction that JUSTICE MARSHALL has answered is fairly presented by the record, I join both the Court's opinion and JUSTICE MARSHALL's opinion.

JUSTICE MARSHALL, with whom JUSTICE BRENNAN, JUSTICE BLACKMUN, and JUSTICE STEVENS join, concurring in the judgment.

I fully agree with the Court's conclusion that workplace sexual harassment is illegal, and violates Title VII. Part III of the Court's opinion, however, leaves open the circumstances in which an employer is responsible under Title VII for such conduct. Because I believe that question to be properly before us, I write separately.

The issue of the Court declines to resolve is addressed in the EEOC Guidelines on Discrimination Because of Sex, which are entitled to great deference. See Griggs v. Duke Power Co., 401 U.S. 424, 433-434, 3 FEP Cases 175, 179 (1971) (EEOC Guidelines on Employment Testing Procedures of 1966); see also ante, at 6. The Guidelines explain:

> "Applying general Title VII principles, an employer . . . is responsible for its acts and those of its agents and supervisory employees with respect to sexual harassment regardless of whether the specific acts complained of were authorized or even forbidden by the employer and regardless of whether the employer knew or should have known of their occurrence. The Commission will examine the circumstances of the particular employment relationship and the job functions performed by the individual in determining whether an individual acts in either a supervisory or agency capacity.
>
> "With respect to conduct between fellow employees, an employer is responsible for acts of sexual harassment in the workplace where the employer (or its agents or supervisory employees) knows or should have known of the conduct, unless it can be shown that it took immediate and appropriate corrective action." 29 CFR §§1604.11(c), (d) (1985).

The Commission, in issuing the Guidelines, explained that its rule was "in keeping with the general standard of employer liability with respect to agents and supervisory employees. . . . [T]he Commission and the courts have held for years that an employer is liable if a supervisor or agent violates the Title VII, regardless of knowledge or any other mitigating factor." 45 Fed. Reg. 74676 (1980). I would adopt the standard set out by the Commission.

An employer can act only through individual supervisors and employees; discrimination is rarely carried out pursuant to a formal vote of a corporation's board of directors. Although an employer may sometimes adopt company-wide discriminatory policies violative of Title VII, acts that may constitute Title VII violations are generally effected through the actions of individuals, and often an individual may take such a step even in defiance of company policy. Nonetheless, Title VII remedies, such as reinstatement and backpay, generally run against the employer as an entity.[1] The question thus arises as to the circumstances under which an employer will be held liable under Title VII for the acts of its employees.

The answer supplied by general Title VII law, like that supplied by federal labor law, is that the act of a supervisory employee or agent is imputed to the employer.[2] Thus, for example, when a supervisor discriminatorily fires or refuses to promote a black employee,

---

[1]The remedial provisions of Title VII were largely modeled on those of the National Labor Relations Act (NLRA). See Albermerle Paper Co. v. Moody, 422 U.S. 405, 419, and n. 11, 10 FEP Cases 1181, 1188 (1975); see also Franks v. Bowman Transportation Co., 424 U.S. 747, 768-770, 12 FEP Cases 549, 557-558 (1976).

[2]For NLRA cases, see, e.g., Graves Trucking, Inc. v. NLRB, 692 F.2d 470, 111 LRRM 2862 (CA7 1982); NLRB v. Kaiser Agricultural Chemical, Division of Kaiser Aluminum & Chemical Corp., 473 F.2d 374, 384, 82 LRRM 2455 (CA5 1973); Amalgamated Clothing Workers of America v. NLRB, 124 U.S. App. D.C. 365, 377, 365 F.2d 898, 909, 62 LRRM 2431 (1966).

that act is, without more, considered the act of the employer. The courts do not stop to consider whether the employer otherwise had "notice" of the action, or even whether the supervisor had actual authority to act as he did. E.g., Flowers v. Crouch-Walker Corp., 552 F.2d 1277, 1282, 14 FEP Cases 1265, 1268 (CA7, 1977); Young v. Southwestern Saving and Loan Assn., 509 F.2d 140, 10 FEP Cases 522 (CA5 1975); Anderson v. Methodist Evangelical Hospital, Inc., 464 F.2d 723, 4 FEP Cases 987 (CA6 1972). Following that approach, every Court of Appeals that has considered the issue has held that sexual harassment by supervisory personnel is automatically imputed to the employer when the harassment results in tangible job detriment to the subordinate employee. See Horn v. Duke Homes, Inc., Div. of Windsor Mobile Homes, 755 F.2d 599, 604-606, 37 FEP Cases 228, 231–233 (CA7 1985); Vinson v. Taylor, 243 U.S. App. D.C. 323, 329-334, 753 F.2d 141, 147-152, 36 FEP Cases 1423, 1427–1431 (1985); Craig v. Y&Y Snacks, Inc., 721 F.2d 77, 80-81, 33 FEP Cases 187, 189–190 (CA3 1983); Katz v. Dole, 709 F.2d 251, 255, n.6, 31 FEP Cases 1521, 1524 (CA4 1983); Henson v. City of Dundee, 682 F.2d 897, 910, 29 FEP Cases 787, 798 (CA11 1982); Miller v. Bank of America, 600 F.2d 211, 213, 20 FEP Cases 462, 463–464 (CA9 1979).

The brief filed by the Solicitor General on behalf of the EEOC in this case suggests that a different rule should apply when a supervisor's harassment "merely" results in a discriminatory work environment. The Solicitor General concedes that sexual harassment that affects tangible job benefits is an exercise of authority delegated to the supervisor by the employer, and thus gives rise to employer liability. But, departing from the EEOC Guidelines, he argues that the case of a supervisor merely creating a discriminatory work environment is different because the supervisor "is not exercising, or threatening to exercise, actual or apparent authority to make personnel decisions affecting the victim." Brief for United States and EEOC as Amici Curiae 24. In the latter situation, he concludes, some further notice requirement should therefore be necessary.

The Solicitor General's position is untenable. A supervisor's responsibilities do not begin and end with the power to hire, fire, and discipline employees, or with the power to recommend such actions. Rather, a supervisor is charged with the day-to-day supervision of the work environment and with ensuring a safe, productive, workplace. There is no reason why abuse of the latter authority should have different consequences than abuse of the former. In both cases it is the authority vested in the supervisor by the employer that enables him to commit the wrong: it is precisely because the supervisor is understood to be clothed with the employer's authority that he is able to impose unwelcome-sexual conduct on subordinates. There is therefore no justification for a special rule, to be applied *only* in "hostile environment" cases, that sexual harassment does not create employer liability until the employee suffering the discrimination notifies other supervisors. No such requirement appears in the statute, and no such requirement can coherently be drawn from the law of the agency.

Agency principles and the goals of Title VII law make appropriate some limitation on the liability of employers for the acts of supervisors. Where, for example, a supervisor has no authority over an employee, because the two work in wholly different parts of the employer's business, it may be improper to find strict employer liability. See 29 CFR §1604.11(c) (1985). Those consideration, however, do not justify the creation of a special "notice" in hostile environment cases.

Further, nothing would be gained by crafting such a rule. In the "pure" hostile environment case, where an employee files an EEOC complaint alleging sexual harassment in the workplace, the employee seeks not money damages but injunctive relief. See Bundy v. Jackson, 205 U.S. App. D.C. 444, 446, 641 F.2d 934, 946, n.12, 24 FEP Cases 1155, 1162 (1981). Under Title VII, the EEOC must notify an employer of charges made against it within 10 days after receipt of the complaint. 42 U.S.C. §2000e-5(b). If the charges appear to be based on "reasonable cause," the EEOC must attempt to eliminate the offending practice through "informal methods of conference, conciliation, and persuasion." Ibid. An employer whose internal procedures assertedly would have redressed the discrimination can avoid injunctive relief by employing these procedures after receiving notice of the complaint or during the conciliation period. Cf. Brief for United States and EEOC as *Amici Curiae* 26. Where a complainant, on the other hand, seeks backpay on the theory that a hostile work environment effected a constructive termination, the existence of an internal complaint procedure may be a factor in determining not the employer's liability but the remedies available against it. Where a complainant without good reason bypassed an internal complaint procedure she knew to be effective, a court may be reluctant to find constructive termination and thus to award reinstatement or backpay.

I therefore reject the Solicitor General's position. I would apply in this case the same rules we apply in all other Title VII cases, and hold that sexual harassment by a supervisor of an employee under his supervision, leading to a discriminatory work environment, should be imputed to the employer for Title VII purposed regardless of whether the employee gave "notice" of the offense.

The *Meritor* Court recognized that a work environment that is hostile toward women may violate Title VII even apart from any question of economic disparate treatment of particular individuals.[71] *Meritor* had no occasion to address a broader question: whether Title VII prohibits sexually hostile behavior directed at no individual in particular. Where a workplace is rife with sexual insults and epithets offensive to women, but the antifemale language is simply part of the language of the shop and not directed at particular individuals, it may be difficult to argue that females are treated disparately. Yet maintaining such a workplace may nonetheless be unlawful as a practice with a significant adverse impact on members of a protected class, which is not justified by business necessity.[72] A disparate treatment approach seems satisfactory, however, for any case in which the intent of the harasser may be imputed to the employer, or where employer intent may be inferred from the fact that it tolerates sexual harassment while it polices other forms of employee misconduct.[72a]

V. ISSUES IN SEXUAL HARASSMENT CASES

The differing natures of quid pro quo and hostile environment cases require some differences in proof. In quid pro quo cases, the job detriment is tangible. Questions of proof will focus on the employer's motivation for imposing this job detriment.[73] In hostile environment cases, by contrast, the detriment is intangible; a question unique to hostile environment cases is whether this

---

[71]*Supra* note 66, 477 U.S. at 64, 40 FEP Cases at 1826–27 (Title VII not limited to economic aspects of employment; work environment can be so heavily polluted with discrimination as to alter women's conditions of employment).

[72]*See, e.g.,* Robinson v. Jacksonville Shipyards, 760 F. Supp. 1468, 1522–23 (M.D. Fla. 1991), reproduced in Chapter 2, Forms of Harassment (actionable conduct includes "behavior that is not directed at a particular individual . . . but is disproportionately more offensive or demeaning to one sex"). Courts have spent little time analyzing whether hostile environment harassment violates Title VII as a matter of disparate treatment, adverse impact, or some other theory. Some have argued for an adverse impact approach, Note, *Sexual Harassment Claims of Abusive Work Environment under Title VII,* 97 HARV. L. REV. 1449, 1456 (1984) ("abusive environment claim should be identified as a claim of either facial sex discrimination or disparate impact"); Schneider, *Sexual Harassment and Higher Education,* 65 TEX. L. REV. 525, 556 (1987), but no court seems to have found that approach necessary. *See generally* Bryan, *Sexual Harassment as Unlawful Discrimination under Title VII of the Civil Rights Act of 1964,* 14 LOY. L.A.L. REV. 25, 39 (1980)("If it is unlawful discrimination at all, sexual harassment is what has been described as 'disparate treatment' discrimination rather than 'disparate impact' discrimination").

[72a]*See, e.g.,* Hunter v. Allis-Chalmers, 797 F.2d 1417, 1423–24, 41 FEP Cases 721, 725 (7th Cir. 1986)(evidence of pervasive co-worker harassment implies employer condoned it)(Posner, J., concurring).

[73]See Chapter 3, Quid Pro Quo Harassment, Section VII.B.

detriment is sufficiently significant to warrant the application of Title VII. The significance of the detriment will depend partly on how blatant and tenacious the harassment was, and partly on how the conduct was received by the complainant—welcomed, endured, or protested. The determination sometimes will depend on whether it is made from the standpoint of the man or the woman, and whether actual subjective perceptions, or a judicially created "objective" interpretation, is used.[74]

Both quid pro quo and hostile environment cases may implicate rights of third parties—persons other than those who are the direct targets of the sexual harassment. In a quid pro quo context, when a female subordinate gains favor by submitting to the unwelcome sexual advances of her male superior, a more qualified third party, denied the job benefit in question, may have a claim under Title VII.[75] Some courts have recognized a third-party quid pro quo claim on the rationale that it is unlawful to use "sex"—in the sense of sexual activity— as a criterion. This equation of sexual activity with gender misreads "sex" for purposes of Title VII.[76] Decisions by other courts and the EEOC, by contrast, recognize the difference between sexual activity and gender, but may be some- what difficult to reconcile with the "but for" test used in *Barnes v. Costle,* in that a male who is unfairly disadvantaged because his female competitor was sexually receptive has, in a "but for" sense, lost a job opportunity because of his gender.[77]

Perhaps the most heavily litigated question in hostile environment cases is whether an employer should be held responsible for sexual harassment of which the employer was actually unaware. If the harasser is a supervisor, courts have used varying standards to determine whether the supervisor's conduct may be imputed to the employer.[78] The EEOC has equivocated on the appropri- ate standard of employer liability,[79] and the Supreme Court has said that the question must be decided in each case on the basis of agency principles.[80] If the alleged harasser is not a supervisor, courts require employer ratification, knowing acquiescence, or negligence as a condition of liability.[81]

Although Title VII has provided the occasion for most legal thinking about sexual harassment in employment, other legal sources are of equal inter- est. Canada has proscribed sexual harassment in employment in ways similar to those followed by American courts, but with a broader standard of employer

---

[74]See Chapter 4, Hostile Environment Harassment. *Compare* Rabidue v. Osceola Ref. Co., 805 F.2d 611, 42 FEP Cases 631 (6th Cir. 1986), reproduced in Chapter 2, Forms of Harassment (majority opinion reasons that offensiveness of conduct should be judged by objective, "reasonable person" standard), *cert. denied,* 481 U.S. 1041 (1987) *with* Ellison v. Brady, *supra* note 55 (reasonable woman standard).

[75]For discussion of these claims, see Chapter 5, Claims by Third Parties.

[76]Title VII bans discrimination "because of *such individual's* . . . sex." Sex in this sense is a gender, not an activity.

[77]See Chapter 5, Claims by Third Parties. Of course, were it a man who gained favor because he granted sexual favors to a homosexual male or to a heterosexual female superior, it would be disadvantaged women who might pursue a gender-based claim.

[78]See Chapter 6, Harassment by Supervisors.

[79]The EEOC, in its Guidelines, *supra* note 66, held the employer automatically responsible for all harassment by supervisors. In the *amicus curiae* brief submitted on its behalf in *Meritor Sav. Bank v. Vinson, supra* note 66, 477 U.S. at 71, the EEOC retreated from this position.

[80]*Supra* note 66, 477 U.S. at 72. The Canadian Supreme Court, interpreting an analogous statute, has taken a different point of view. For a discussion of Canadian law on sexual harassment, see Appendix 5.

[81]See Chapters 7, Harassment by Co-Workers, and 8, Harassment by Nonemployees.

liability.[82] Some government employees have been able to rely upon federal constitutional rights, such as the right to equal protection. A state or local government employee may invoke those rights under the Reconstruction Era Civil Rights Acts.[83] Complainants often may also expand upon the possibilities created by Title VII by invoking state fair employment practices (FEP) statutes, which sometimes provide greater remedies or have broader coverage.[84] Complainants may also seek less conventional remedies under state unemployment compensation[85] or workers' compensation statutes.[86] The most significant monetary remedies often will be available where the complainant can invoke a common-law theory of liability, such as intentional infliction of emotional distress.[87] Finally, while criminal law, apart from the law of rape, has added little to the development of sexual harassment law, its ramifications in any given case cannot be overlooked.[88]

Collective bargaining has provided additional sources of sexual harassment law. Unions may be liable for sexual harassment, principally under Title VII or because of a breach of the duty of fair representation.[88a] Further, collective bargaining agreements with just-cause provisions have given unions the opportunity to challenge employer discipline of employees for sexual harassment. Labor arbitrators reviewing these challenges have created an extensive set of standards concerning an employer's ability to deal with sexual harassment in the workplace, standards that have evolved further through arbitral interpretation of Title VII.[89]

The single most important source of sexual harassment law has been the EEOC. Created to enforce Title VII,[90] the EEOC has issued persuasive interpretations on the subject of sexual harassment in its official decisions,[91] in its Compliance Manual,[92] in its Policy Guidances,[93] and, most significantly, in its 1980 Guidelines on Discrimination Because of Sex.[94] Among the most important of the EEOC's contributions to the law of sexual harassment has been its interpretation that Title VII requires employers to take reasonable steps to prevent sexual harassment from occurring, steps that include creating, publishing, and enforcing internal policies against sexual harassment in employment.[95]

Employees of private employers subject to Title VII may file a charge of sexual harassment with the EEOC, which investigates to determine whether there is reasonable cause to believe that sex discrimination has occurred. The

---

[82]For a discussion of Canadian law, see Appendix 5.

[83]For a discussion of 42 U.S.C. §§1983 and 1985(3), see Chapter 11, Federal Constitutional, Statutory, and Civil Rights Law.

[84]See Chapter 12, Fair Employment Practices Statutes.

[85]See Chapter 13, Unemployment Compensation Statutes.

[86]See Chapter 14, Workers' Compensation Statutes.

[87]See Chapter 15, The Common Law.

[88]See Chapter 16, Criminal Law.

[88a]See Chapter 17, Collective Bargaining Agreements and Union Obligations.

[89]See Chapter 17, Collective Bargaining Agreements and Union Obligations.

[90]§705(a), 42 U.S.C. §2000e-4(a).

[91]*See, e.g.,* EEOC decisions cited in Chapter 8, Harassment by Nonemployees, Section II.

[92]Reproduced in part in Appendix 4 and discussed in Chapter 20, The Agency Investigation.

[93]Reproduced in Appendices 2 and 3.

[94]Reproduced in Appendix 1.

[95]See Chapters 18, Taking Preventive Action, and 19, Responding to Internal Complaints.

EEOC may resolve the dispute administratively, sue the employer itself, or simply permit the charging party to file a lawsuit.[96]

Plaintiffs and defendants in sexual harassment suits face considerations peculiar to this kind of litigation.[97] At center stage in any sexual harassment suit is the alleged harasser. The complainant may attempt to hold the alleged harasser individually liable.[98] The alleged harasser, having been subject to accusations by the complainant and possibly discipline by the employer, may decide to file his own lawsuit.[99]

Sexual harassment lawsuits by their nature tend to raise important issues of discovery[100] and evidence.[101] They also raise the same important issues regarding settlement that pertain to any employment discrimination lawsuit.[102]

Several defenses asserted in employment litigation generally, such as timeliness, workers' compensation exclusivity, and arbitral preemption, are of particular importance in sexual harassment cases.[103] Relatively novel are the First Amendment issues, which could be significant, especially in hostile environment cases involving verbal and visual messages that are not directed at individual complainants.[104]

Problems of remedy underlie much of the discussion of sexual harassment cases, which present special problems of injunctive relief,[105] monetary relief,[106] and attorney's fees and costs.[107]

Sexual harassment in the workplace has spawned a body of legal literature that is quite substantial in light of the relatively short period, since 1976, that sexual harassment complainants have had redress under Title VII.[108]

---

[96]See Chapter 20, The Agency Investigation.

[97]See Chapters 21, Complainant's Litigation Strategy, and 22, Employer's Litigation Strategy.

[98]See Chapter 23, The Alleged Harasser as Defendant.

[99]See Chapter 24, The Alleged Harasser as Plaintiff.

[100]See Chapter 26, Discovery.

[101]See Chapter 25, Evidence.

[102]See Chapter 31, Settlement.

[103]See Chapter 27, Asserted Defenses.

[104]For an extensive discussion of the neglected First Amendment issues, see Browne, *Title VII as Censorship: Hostile Environment Harassment and the First Amendment,* 52 Ohio St. L.J. 481 (1991).

[105]See Chapter 28, Injunctive and Affirmative Relief.

[106]See Chapter 29, Monetary Relief.

[107]See Chapter 30, Attorney's Fees and Costs.

[108]In addition to the literature cited in the notes above, the law of sexual harassment has received extended treatment in the following books: A. Conte, Sexual Harassment in the Workplace: Law and Practice (1990); 1 A. Larson, Employment Discrimination §§41.60–67 (1990); S. Omilian & J. Kamp, Sex-Based Employment Discrimination §§21.01–26.10 (1990); S. Omilian, Sexual Harassment in Employment (1987); M. Rossein, Employment Discrimination Law and Litigation §§6.1–6.8 (1990); C. Sullivan, M. Zimmer & R. Richards, Employment Discrimination §8.7 (1988). Even as early as 1981, one could list more than 200 articles and books on the subject of sexual harassment. Stanton, *A Sexual Harassment Bibliography,* 10 Cap. U.L. Rev. 697 (1981). *See also* Crocker, *An Annotated Bibliography on Sexual Harassment in Education,* 7 Women's Rts. L. Rep. 91 (1982). No attempt is made to provide a comprehensive bibliography here.

Chapter 2

FORMS OF HARASSMENT

I. Harassment on Bases Other Than Sex

A. Introduction

The law of sexual harassment has drawn much of its content from the law of harassment based on race, national origin, and religion.[1] This borrowing, which has been quite self-conscious,[2] has been based on the notion that each of the various forms of illegal discrimination can "poison" a working environment.[3] As Judge J. Skelly Wright explained in *Bundy v. Jackson:*[4]

> Sexual stereotyping through discriminatory dress requirements may be benign in intent, and may offend women only in a general, atmospheric manner, yet it violates Title VII. Racial slurs, though intentional and directed at individuals, may still be just verbal insults, yet they too may create Title VII liability. How then can sexual harassment, which injects the most demeaning sexual stereotypes into the general work environment and which always represents an intentional assault on an individual's innermost privacy, not be illegal?[5]

In *Meritor Savings Bank v. Vinson,* Justice William H. Rehnquist also recognized the relevance of nonsexual harassment cases, explaining that "a hostile or offensive environment for members of one sex is every bit the arbitrary barrier to sexual equality at the workplace that racial harassment is to racial equality."[6]

The EEOC has also consistently encouraged courts to borrow from the jurisprudence of nonsexual harassment.[6a] The law of nonsexual harassment

---

[1]For a discussion of the early development of the law of sexual harassment, see Chapter 1, Overview, Section III.

[2]*See, e.g.,* Henson v. City of Dundee, 682 F.2d 897, 901–5, 29 FEP Cases 787 (11th Cir. 1982), reproduced in Chapter 4, Hostile Environment Harassment; Barnes v. Costle, 561 F.2d 983, 15 FEP Cases 345 (D.C. Cir. 1977), reproduced in Chapter 1, Overview.

[3]Footnote 1 to the EEOC Guidelines on Sexual Harassment reads: "The principles involved here [in §1604.11] continue to apply to race, color, religion or national origin." 29 C.F.R. §1604.11(a) n.1, reproduced in Appendix 1. In 1980, after notice and comment, the EEOC issued its Guidelines on Discrimination Because of Sex, 29 C.F.R. §§1604.1–.11, one portion of which (§1604.11(a)–(g)) constitutes the sexual harassment guidelines. 45 Fed. Reg. 74677 (November 10, 1980). The EEOC Guidelines are nonbinding but "constitute a body of experience and informed judgments to which courts and litigants may properly resort for guidance." Meritor Sav. Bank v. Vinson, 477 U.S. 57, 65, 40 FEP Cases 1822, 1826 (1986)(citations omitted), reproduced in Chapter 1, Overview.

[4]641 F.2d 934, 24 FEP Cases 1155 (D.C. Cir. 1981)(Wright, Swygert & Robinson, JJ.).

[5]*Id.* at 945, 24 FEP Cases at 1161.

[6]*Supra* note 3, 477 U.S. at 67, 42 FEP Cases at 1827 (quoting Henson v. City of Dundee, *supra* note 2).

[6a]See note 3 *supra.* The EEOC Compliance Manual further emphasizes the conceptual interrelationship

therefore provides a useful basis for understanding sexual harassment, and is also important to study because sexual harassment sometimes occurs in combination with other types of prohibited harassment,[7] and because the facts that support a harassment claim on a basis other than sex can contribute toward a showing of the "pervasiveness" element of a hostile environment sexual harassment claim.[8]

B. Race, Color, and National Origin

In *Rogers v. EEOC,*[9] the Fifth Circuit addressed, in the context of a national origin case, an issue of first impression: whether Title VII prohibits harassment that entails no tangible job detriment. The plaintiff in *Rogers* was an optometrist's assistant who claimed that she was abused by white co-workers and that she was not allowed to attend to white optometry patients. The Fifth Circuit held that "the relationship between an employee and his working environment is of such significance as to be entitled to statutory protection."[10] In an oft-quoted passage, Judge Irving L. Goldberg explained:

> [E]mployees' psychological as well as economic fringes are statutorily entitled to protection from employer abuse .... [T]he phrase "terms, conditions, or privileges of employment" in Section 703 is an expansive concept which sweeps within its protective ambit the practice of creating a working environment heavily charged with ethnic or racial discrimination .... One can readily envision working environments so heavily polluted with discrimination to destroy completely the emotional and psychological stability of minority group workers ....[11]

Since *Rogers,* federal appellate courts, while formulating a variety of standards for evaluating hostile environment cases, have focused both upon the gravity and the frequency of the offensive conduct.[12] In *Johnson v. Bunny Bread Co.,*[13] where employees complained that their supervisors and co-workers often referred to them as "niggers," the Eighth Circuit ruled that a "steady barrage of opprobrious racial comment" was actionable under Title VII, but that Title VII does not prohibit racial comments that are merely part of casual conversation, "accidental," or sporadic.[14] In contrast, in *Davis v. Monsanto Chemical*

---

of sexual and nonsexual harassment. *E.g.,* EEOC COMPL. MAN. §615.7 (BNA) p.615:0019, reproduced in Appendix 4.

[7]Hicks v. Gates Rubber Co., 833 F.2d 1406, 45 FEP Cases 608 (10th Cir. 1987).

[8]*Id.* at 1416–17 (evidence of racial harassment considered in determining pervasiveness element of hostile environment claim). *Cf.* Wall v. AT&T Technologies, 54 FEP Cases 1540 (M.D.N.C. 1990)(allegations of separate incidents of racial and sexual harassment; evidence of racial harassment not used to support claim of sexual harassment).

[9]454 F.2d 234, 4 FEP Cases 92 (5th Cir. 1971)(Goldberg, Godbold & Roney, JJ.), *cert. denied,* 406 U.S. 957 (1972).

[10]*Id.* at 237–38, 4 FEP Cases at 94–95.

[11]*Id.*

[12]*See, e.g.,* Vance v. Southern Bell Tel. & Tel. Co., 863 F.2d 1503, 1510–11, 50 FEP Cases 742 (11th Cir. 1989).

[13]646 F.2d 1250, 1257, 25 FEP Cases 1326, 1331–32 (8th Cir. 1981).

[14]For other applications of the same general standard, see *EEOC v. Beverage Canners,* 897 F.2d 1067, 1070, 52 FEP Cases 878 (11th Cir. 1990)(racially hostile remarks "so 'commonplace, overt and denigrating' that they created an atmosphere charged with racial hostility"); Ways v. City of Lincoln, 871 F.2d 750, 49 FEP Cases 865 (8th Cir. 1989)(racially hostile work environment existed where plaintiff endured racial slurs and other offensive racially oriented incidents for six years); Hicks v. Gates Rubber Co., *supra* note 7, 833 F.2d at 1413, 45 FEP Cases at 617 (racial slurs and jokes to which plaintiff was subjected over eight-month period essentially occasional and incidental); Snell v. Suffolk County, 782 F.2d 1094, 1103, 39 FEP Cases 1590 (2d Cir. 1986)("proliferation of demeaning literature and epithets [deemed] sufficiently continuous and pervasive to establish a 'concerted pattern of harassment' in violation of Title VII").

Co.,[15] where black plaintiffs complained of racial slurs, derogatory racial graffiti on bathroom walls, restrictions on lunchroom use, and spitting on time cards, the Sixth Circuit concluded that the conduct was not sufficiently pervasive to alter the plaintiffs' conditions of employment.[16] Judge Boyce F. Martin pointed out that racial epithets were directed only once at the plaintiffs, that the company had acted quickly to correct any abusive situation reported, and that the evidence otherwise tended to contradict the assertions made by the plaintiffs.[17]

There is no bright-line standard that determines whether racially harassing conduct has become actionable. As demonstrated in *Vance v. Southern Bell Telephone & Telegraph Co.,*[18] even isolated acts, if sufficiently severe, can create a racially hostile environment. In *Vance,* a black employee twice found a noose hanging from the light fixture above her work station and found that some of her work had been sabotaged. Judge Peter T. Fay stressed that the determination of "whether a hostile environment is severe enough to adversely affect a reasonable employee" requires examination of

> not only the frequency of the incidents but the gravity of the incidents as well . . . .
> It is thus incorrect to apply mechanically an absolute numerical standard to the number of acts of harassment which must be committed by defendant before a jury may reasonably find that a hostile environment exists.[19]

Complainants who demonstrate the existence of a racially hostile environment may recover economic damages if the harassment leads to discharge. In *De Grace v. Rumsfeld,*[20] a civilian firefighter, subjected to racial harassment, feared reporting to work and was eventually discharged for excessive absenteeism.[21] The First Circuit held that the employer could not justify the discharge of an employee on the basis of absenteeism caused by racial harassment for which the employer was responsible.[22]

Racial harassment is usually evidenced by the use of racist language.[23] In *Walker v. Ford Motor Co.,*[24] the Eleventh Circuit held that racially abusive

---

[15]858 F.2d 345, 47 FEP Cases 1825 (6th Cir. 1988)(Martin, Jones & Norris, JJ.), *cert. denied,* 109 S.Ct. 3166 (1989).

[16]The *Davis* court distinguished a racial harassment case from a sexual harassment case, holding that in a case of racial harassment, the plaintiff need not prove a "pattern of harassment." The court set forth a two-part test for maintaining a racial harassment claim under Title VII: (1) whether the racial harassment created an "unreasonably abusive or offensive work-related environment or adversely affected the reasonable employee's ability to perform the tasks required by the employer"; and (2) whether management tolerated and condoned the abusive situation in that the employer knew or should have known of the alleged conduct and failed to take prompt remedial action. *Id.* at 349.

[17]*Id.* at 347, 47 FEP Cases at 1826.

[18]*Supra* note 12 (Hill, Fay, JJ., Davis, District Judge).

[19]*Id.* at 1510–11, 50 FEP Cases at 747–48. The application of this analysis in the area of sexual harassment was expressly approved in *Meritor Savings Bank v. Vinson, supra* note 3, 477 U.S. at 66–67. State courts have also adopted this approach. *See, e.g.,* Vaughn v. AG Processing, 459 N.W.2d 627, 55 EPD ¶40,555 (Iowa 1990).

[20]614 F.2d 796, 21 FEP Cases 1444 (1st Cir. 1980).

[21]*Id.* at 800–801, 21 FEP Cases at 1446–47.

[22]*Id.* at 803–4, 21 FEP Cases at 1448–50.

[23]*E.g.,* Snell v. Suffolk County, *supra* note 14 (racially hostile environment created by proliferation of demeaning literature and epithets); Erebia v. Chrysler Plastic Prods. Corp., 772 F.2d 1250, 1256, 37 FEP Cases 1820 (6th Cir. 1985)(repeated racial slurs created hostile working environment), *cert. denied,* 475 U.S. 1015 (1986); Walker v. Ford Motor Co., 684 F.2d 1355, 1359, 29 FEP Cases 1259 (11th Cir. 1982)(racially abusive language created working environment heavily charged with discrimination); Taylor v. Jones, 653 F.2d 1193, 1198–99, 28 FEP Cases 1024, 1026–30 (8th Cir. 1981)(racial slurs, epithets, and jokes characterized degrading work atmosphere).

[24]*Supra* note 23, 684 F.2d at 1358–60, 29 FEP Cases at 1261–62 (Tuttle, Kravitch & Henderson,

language over a period of a few months is sufficient to prove both the existence of a hostile environment in the workplace and that a plaintiff's termination constituted unlawful retaliation. Judge Phyllis A. Kravitch rejected the employer's argument that because racial slurs were allegedly common parlance in the relevant geographic area, they were not intended to carry racial overtones.[25]

Unlawful racial harassment may also consist of nonracial disparate treatment, such as pranks and other forms of hazing, that is shown by circumstantial evidence to be racially motivated.[26] In *Vaughn v. Pool Offshore Co.*,[27] the hazing of a black oil rig worker—by greasing his genitals, dousing him with cold water and ammonia while he was showering, and pouring hot coffee in his back pocket—were not found to amount to racial harassment, even when these "pranks" were accompanied by racially derogatory epithets. Judge Henry A. Politz emphasized that nearly all rig employees, including the white supervisor, were victims of similar pranks,[28] and reasoned that because the humiliation was dispensed on a racially equal basis, the environment was "coarse, rowdy and generally abusive, but not polluted with discrimination."[29]

Racial harassment may also be actionable under state fair employment practices (FEP) statutes,[30] the common law,[31] and 42 U.S.C. §1983.[32] Racial harassment generally is not cognizable, however, under 42 U.S.C. §1981.[33]

C. Religion

The prohibition in Title VII against religious discrimination applies to all aspects of religious observance and practice, as well as belief.[34] Thus, harassment on the basis of religion, like harassment on the basis of sex, may take the

---

JJ.)(management and employees repeatedly used offensive racial epithets toward black male trainee, "including referring to poorly repaired cars as 'nigger-rigged' and referring to the salesman with the lowest sales volume as 'the black ass' "); *see also* Erebia v. Chrysler Plastic Prods. Corp., *supra* note 23, 772 F.2d at 1251–53, 1256, 37 FEP Cases at 1821–22, 1825 (Mexican-American employee subjected to ethnic slurs for more than five years); *but see* Davis v. Monsanto Chem. Co., *supra* note 15 (racial epithets directed to complainant only once insufficient).

[25]Walker v. Ford Motor Co., *supra* note 23, 684 F.2d at 1358–59, 29 FEP Cases at 1261–62.

[26]*E.g.*, Johnson v. Lillie Rubin Affiliates, 5 FEP Cases 547 (M.D. Tenn. 1972)(referring to white employees as "Miss" or "Mrs." and black employees by first name is discriminatory).

[27]683 F.2d 922 (5th Cir. 1982).

[28]*Id.* at 925.

[29]*Id. Cf.* Barnes v. Costle, 561 F.2d 983, 990 n.55, 15 FEP Cases 345, 351 (D.C. Cir. 1977)(dictum)(no sex discrimination where bisexual supervisor insists on sexual favors from men and women alike).

[30]*E.g.*, Fisher v. Tacoma School Dist., 53 Wash. App. 591, 769 P.2d 318, 55 FEP Cases 237 (1989)(action for racial and sexual harassment brought under Washington law prohibiting discrimination in employment). For a discussion of state fair employment practices (FEP) statutes, see Chapter 12.

[31]*E.g.*, Alcorn v. Anbro Eng'g, 2 Cal.3d 493, 86 Cal. Rptr. 88 (1970)(racial epithets gave rise to cause of action for intentional infliction of emotional distress). For a detailed discussion of common-law actions for acts constituting harassment, see Chapter 15, The Common Law.

[32]*E.g.*, Day v. Wayne County Board of Auditors, 749 F.2d 1199, 1205, 36 FEP Cases 743, 747 (6th Cir. 1984)(42 U.S.C. §1983 racial discrimination case).

[33]Patterson v. McLean Credit Union, 491 U.S. 164, 49 FEP Cases 1814, 1821 (1989)(§1981 prohibits racial discrimination only in making and enforcement of private contracts).

[**Editor's Note**: The Civil Rights Act of 1991, discussed in Appendix 8, overturned *Patterson* to provide that §1981 applies to conduct that occurs during employment.]

[34]§701(j), 42 U.S.C. §2000e(j)(defining "religion" to include "all aspects of religious observance and practice, as well as belief"). *See, e.g.,* Brown Transp. Corp. v. Commonwealth of Pa., 578 A.2d 555, 133 Pa. Commw. 545 (Pa. Ct. App. 1990)(continuing practice of placing Bible verses on paycheck and religious content in company newsletter constituted religion-based harassment under Pennsylvania FEP statute against Jewish employee who had complained in vain about practice, which led him to believe company promoted Christians only).

form of quid pro quo harassment, in which a supervisor demands that an employee engage in unwelcome religious activity in order to obtain or retain a job benefit. In *Young v. Southwestern Savings & Loan Association,*[35] employees were required to attend a monthly staff meeting that began with a short religious talk and a prayer, both delivered by a Christian minister. "This theological appetizer, nondenominational though it may be, was somewhat uncongenial to plaintiff, who is an atheist."[36] Reversing the judgment of the trial court, the Fifth Circuit, again by Judge Irving L. Goldberg, held that the employer's insistence that the plaintiff attend the unwelcome religious portion of the meeting constituted a constructive discharge.[37]

Most often, religious harassment is of the hostile environment variety, taking the form of comments disparaging an employee's religious views.[38] As with other forms of unlawful harassment, complainants must show that unwelcome conduct was directed at them because of their religious practices or beliefs,[39] and that the harassment was severe or pervasive[40] and unwelcome.[41] In addition, complainants must establish that the employer had actual or constructive knowledge of the religious harassment and failed to take prompt and adequate remedial action.[42]

As in other harassment cases, in religious harassment cases the mere existence of an antiharassment policy is no defense, especially where supervisory personnel acquiesced and participated in the harassment.[43] In *Weiss v. United States,*[44] a supervisor participated in demeaning and offensive religious slurs and taunts.[45] Judge Richard L. Williams held that

> [w]hen an employer vests wide discretion over employee assignments and evaluations in the hands of a supervisor, and when the employer is put on notice that

[35]509 F.2d 140, 141–42, 10 FEP Cases 522, 522–23 (5th Cir. 1975)(Thornberry, Goldberg & Godbold, JJ.).

[36]*Id.* at 142.

[37]*Id.* at 143, 10 FEP Cases at 524–25. Constructive discharge can also be shown by evidence of retaliatory conduct after protest of discriminatory conduct, even if retaliatory actions are not based on religion. *See, e.g.,* Weiss v. United States, 595 F. Supp. 1050, 1056–57, 36 FEP Cases 1, 5–6 (E.D. Va. 1984).

[38]*E.g.,* Weiss v. United States, *supra* note 37, 595 F. Supp. at 1056 (continuous, abusive religion-based language can "pollute a healthy working environment by making an employee feel uncomfortable or unwanted . . . [and] can even severely affect the employee's emotional and psychological stability")(citing Compston v. Borden, Inc., 424 F. Supp. 157, 160–61, 17 FEP Cases 310 (S.D. Ohio 1976)(repeated demeaning and offensive religious slurs by co-worker and supervisor necessarily alter conditions of employment))(cited with approval in Meritor Sav. Bank v. Vinson, 477 U.S. 57, 66, 40 FEP Cases 1822, 1826–27 (1986), reproduced in Chapter 1, Overview); Vaughn v. AG Processing, *supra* note 19 (continuous reference to claimant as "goddamn stupid fuckin' Catholic"; "I know you're Catholic, but I haven't seen one yet that had any fuckin' brains").

[39]*Cf.* Ries v. Croft Indus., 52 FEP Cases 238 (W.D. Mo. 1989)(harassment alleged by plaintiff—that former employee flipped his hair at her in ungentlemanly-like manner and threatened her with forklift truck, and that another former employee accused plaintiff of exposing herself in Houston, Texas—does not suggest either religious focus or motivation).

[40]*Cf.* Shapiro v. Holiday Inns, No. 89 C 7458, 1990 U.S. Dist. LEXIS 3801, slip op. at 24–26 (N.D. Ill. April 5, 1990)(anti-Semitic remarks not pervasive enough to constitute actionable harassment where plaintiff could point to only a few concrete examples).

[41]*Cf. id.,* slip op. at 26 (plaintiff admitted she never complained about anti-Semitic remarks because they had no real effect on her and she thought them trivial).

[42]*See, e.g.,* Weiss v. United States, *supra* note 37, 595 F. Supp. at 1057, 36 FEP Cases at 5.

[43]Katz v. Dole, 709 F.2d 251, 31 FEP Cases 1521 (4th Cir. 1983), reproduced in Chapter 7, Harassment by Co-Workers; Weiss v. United States, *supra* note 37.

[44]*Supra* note 37.

[45]Comments included "resident Jew," "Jew faggot," "Christ killer," "nail him to the cross," and "you killed Christ, Wally, so you'll have to hang from the cross." *Supra* note 37, 595 F. Supp. at 1053, 36 FEP Cases at 2.

the supervisor has engaged in discriminatory or retaliatory actions against an employee, the employer can certainly be held liable if it relies upon that supervisor's representations to remove the employee.[46]

State FEP statutes may serve as the vehicle for religious harassment actions.[47] Successful complainants are entitled to economic damages where the harassment results in an adverse job action.[48]

D. Age

The law of sexual harassment, influenced by other developments in the law regarding other forms of harassment, has had its own influence in the developing law of age-based harassment. Claims of age-based harassment are cognizable under the Age Discrimination in Employment Act (ADEA),[49] which closely tracks the language of Title VII, and under state FEP statutes.[49a] In *Young v. Will County Department of Public Aid*,[50] the Seventh Circuit assumed that the ADEA protects older employees from a hostile work environment and adopted the analytical approach followed in sexual harassment cases.[51] Accordingly, an employee of at least 40 years of age may establish a claim under the ADEA for damages caused by a hostile work environment.[52]

While courts have not uniformly used the terms "hostile environment" or "age harassment" in analyzing an employee's allegations,[53] courts have applied the standards developed in sexual harassment cases to determine

---

[46]*Id.* at 1057–58, 36 FEP Cases at 6.

[47]*See, e.g.*, Vaughn v. AG Processing, 459 N.W.2d 627, 55 EPD ¶40,555 (Iowa 1990)(anti-Catholic harassment)(claim for religious harassment under Iowa statute must show (1) plaintiff belongs to protected class; (2) plaintiff suffered unwelcome religious harassment; (3) harassment based upon religion; (4) harassment affected term, condition, or privilege of employment; and (5) employer knew or should have known of harassment and failed to take prompt remedial action); Brown Transp. Corp. v. Commonwealth of Pa., *supra* note 34 (Pennsylvania FEP statute); Leibowitz v. Bank Leumi Trust Co., 548 N.Y.S.2d 513, 521, 31 EPD ¶33,607 (2d Dep't 1989)(wrongful discharge action for religious harassment pursuant to "Whistleblowers' Statute" (N.Y. Labor Law §740), where plaintiff frequently called "Hebe" or "kike," recharacterized as claim for wrongful discharge and dismissed on grounds New York does not recognize wrongful discharge action for sexual harassment of at-will employee); Diem v. San Francisco, 686 F. Supp. 806, 51 FEP Cases 242 (N.D. Cal. 1988)(religious harassment claims cognizable under California FEP statute and general civil rights statute giving persons right to be free from violence or threats of violence on account of religion).

[48]*E.g.*, Weiss v. United States, *supra* note 37, 595 F. Supp. at 1057, 36 FEP Cases at 5 (employer could not invoke decreased performance as legitimate basis for discharge where "diminution [was] the direct result of the employer's discriminatory behavior").

[49]29 U.S.C. §621 *et seq.* (hereinafter ADEA).

[49a]*E.g.*, Yurick v. Superior Court, 209 Cal. App.3d 1116, 257 Cal. Rptr. 665, 667, 54 FEP Cases 1196 (1989)(age harassment actionable under state FEP statute and compensatory and punitive damages available, but action dismissed for failure to exhaust administrative remedies); Stork v. International Bazaar, 54 Wash. App. 274, 774 P.2d 22, 27–29 (1989)(age harassment claim available under state FEP statute, but dismissal of action affirmed and emotional distress damages claim held to be without merit); City of Billings v. State Human Rights Comm'n, 681 P.2d 33, 34–38, 39 EPD ¶35,985 (Mont. 1984)(affirming reinstatement and back pay award to constructively discharged plaintiff taunted as "old man" and "grandpa" by fellow employees).

[50]882 F.2d 290, 50 FEP Cases 1089 (7th Cir. 1989).

[51]The court, however, affirmed summary judgment for the employer in that case because withholding of a salary increase, unfavorable work evaluations, and supervisor's referring older employees to the manual for answers do not in combination constitute actionable harassment. *Id.* at 294, 50 FEP Cases at 1093.

[52]The court in *Young* identified these elements of an ADEA claim: (1) plaintiff is a member of a protected class; (2) plaintiff was harassed because of membership in the class; and (3) the harassment affected a term, condition or privilege of employment. *Id.*

[53]*See, e.g.*, Buckley v. Hospital Corp. of Am., 758 F.2d 1525, 1530, 37 FEP Cases 1082 (11th Cir. 1985).

employer liability in ADEA cases.[54] In *Drez v. E.R. Squibb & Sons*,[55] Judge Dale E. Saffels expressly adopted the standard set forth in *Meritor*[56] to recognize a hostile environment claim under the ADEA where the plaintiff alleged that, because of his age, he was subjected to "harassment, criticism and confrontation on the job" and his personnel file included a memorandum from one of his supervisors describing him as an "absolute moron."

E. Disability

The Americans With Disabilities Act of 1990 (ADA),[57] effective July 26, 1992, prohibits employment discrimination against disabled individuals.[58] Although the ADA does not expressly prohibit disability-based harassment, the Act is modeled after §703(a) of Title VII, which has been interpreted to prohibit harassment on any basis covered by that statute.[59]

Because the ADA does not limit rights under any other federal or state law,[60] harassment on the basis of disability[61] continues to be prohibited under state FEP statutes.[62] Disability-based harassment is also actionable under statutes applicable to certain state employers[63] and federal contractors.[64]

---

[54]*E.g.*, Lewis v. Federal Prison Indus., 786 F.2d 1537, 1542–45, 40 FEP Cases 998 (11th Cir. 1986). In *Lewis*, a supervisor repeatedly encouraged the plaintiff, an elderly employee, to "go ahead and retire," and told him not to contribute to an office funeral-flowers fund because he "was not going to be around that long." The plaintiff alleged a constructive discharge because of "harassment" and age discrimination. *Id.* at 1541–42. The trial court agreed that the plaintiff had suffered age discrimination, but found the employer not liable for the behavior of its supervisory personnel. The Eleventh Circuit reversed and remanded the age harassment claim for application of the then-prevailing Title VII law on employer liability for a supervisor's sexual harassment. *Id.* at 1542–43. *Lewis* was decided before the Supreme Court considered the question of employer liability for harassment in *Meritor*.

[55]674 F. Supp. 1432, 1436, 52 FEP Cases 1661, 1664 (D. Kan. 1987)(leaving undisturbed a jury verdict of no discrimination).

[56]*Id.* at 1436–37.

[57]42 U.S.C. §§12101–12213.

[58]*Id.* at §§12111–12117.

[59]*See, e.g.*, Rogers v. EEOC, 454 F.2d 234, 238, 4 FEP Cases 92, 95 (5th Cir. 1971), *cert. denied*, 400 U.S. 957 (1972). Moreover, the ADA defines discrimination broadly to include coercing, intimidating, threatening, or interfering with any individual in the exercise or enjoyment of any right protected by the Act. This protection extends to individuals who aid or assist others in exercising or enjoying the protections of the Act. 42 U.S.C. §12203. The ADA also specifically protects individuals who "associate" with disabled persons. 42 U.S.C. §12112(b)(4). EEOC regulations interpreting the employment provisions of the ADA, 20 C.F.R. Part 1630, do not specifically address harassment on the basis of disability.

[60]42 U.S.C. §12201(a).

[61]"Disability" is now the preferred term. Many state statutes use the older term, "handicap."

[62]*E.g.*, McWilliams v. AT&T Information Sys., 728 F. Supp. 1186, 52 FEP Cases 383 (W.D. Pa. 1990)(plaintiff harassed by superiors because of record of disability—mental depression and anxiety—could invoke Pennsylvania statutory prohibition on employment discrimination against the handicapped). *Cf.* Leggett v. First Interstate Bank, 86 Or. App. 523, 739 P.2d 1083, 1087–88, 111 Lab. Cas. ¶56,040 (1987)(arachnophobic complainant, harassed by co-workers who put rubber spiders on her desk and discharged after seeking reassignment, could show handicap discrimination if she could show she "was terminated for resisting harassment relating to her spider phobia").

[63]Harassment based on disability may be actionable under 42 U.S.C. §1983. Hutchings v. Erie City & County, 516 F. Supp. 1265, 1270 (W.D. Pa. 1981). *See also* Cordero-Martinez v. Aponte Roque, 685 F. Supp. 314 (D.P.R. 1988)(Rehabilitation Act not exclusive remedy for blind applicant who alleged disability discrimination and who could maintain §1983 action without exhausting administrative remedies). *Cf.* Richardson v. City of Albuquerque, 857 F.2d 727 (10th Cir. 1988)(§1983 action by police recruit harassed for inability to see without contact lenses dismissed in that all police recruits harassed as part of intentional stress training and plaintiff not treated differently because of visual impairment).

[64]Under the Federal Rehabilitation Act (FRA) of 1973, 29 U.S.C. §701 *et seq.*, which is left undisturbed by the ADA, 42 U.S.C. §12201(a), disability harassment is actionable. *E.g.*, Graves v. Methodist Youth Servs., 624 F. Supp. 429, 39 FEP Cases 1223 (N.D. Ill. 1985)(plaintiff stated claim under Rehabilitation Act that he was "verbally harassed about . . . his mental condition by his supervisors and other employees").

II. SEXUAL HARASSMENT AS ACTIONABLE MISCONDUCT

Two characteristics of sexual harassment distinguish it from other forms of harassment. First, sexual harassment frequently consists of sexual advances, which can be and often are welcome and which have social utility, whereas typical forms of nonsexual harassment, such as racial epithets, inherently lack social value.[65]

Second, the term "sex" is ambiguous in that it describes not only a basis protected by statute, but also an activity.[66] To the extent that "sexual" harassment consists of hostile activities directed at an individual because of gender, sexual harassment analytically resembles harassment based upon any other protected basis. The resemblance is much weaker, however, when sexual harassment is of the quid pro quo variety, for then the discrimination results from an activity (rejection of sexual advances) rather than directly from a status. Although quid pro quo harassment is a relatively common form of sex discrimination, quid pro quo harassment is a rare form of discrimination on bases other than sex, occurring primarily in the context of religious harassment.[67]

The conceptual difficulties created by the dual meaning of "sex" still appear in cases involving adverse actions taken against a complainant who ends a previously consensual relationship.[68] In that situation, some federal courts have been reluctant to conclude that the adverse action was impermissibly based on gender, opining instead that any adverse action might instead be based on personal animus arising from a failed relationship.[69]

---

[65]*See* Barnes v. Costle, 561 F.2d 983, 999, 15 FEP Cases 345, 360 (D.C. Cir. 1977)(MacKinnon, J., concurring). This peculiar feature of sexual harassment accounted, in some measure, for the initial reluctance of courts to treat sexual harassment as sex discrimination. See Chapter 1, Overview, Section III.

[66]One explanation for the ambiguous use of "sexual" is that women, as a gender, are socially defined largely in sexual terms. Thus, it has been said that it is no accident that the English language uses the term "sex" to refer to both gender status and to an activity. C. MACKINNON, SEXUAL HARASSMENT OF WORKING WOMEN 182 (1979).

[67]*E.g.,* Young v. Southwestern Savings & Loan Ass'n, 509 F.2d 140, 10 FEP Cases 522 (5th Cir. 1975)(case of religious harassment involving refusal to participate in prayer meetings). The theory of quid pro quo harassment does not apply to an immutable basis such as race, but may apply to related activities such as dating persons of another race. *E.g.,* Moffett v. Gene B. Glick Co., 621 F. Supp. 244, 41 FEP Cases 671 (N.D. Ind. 1985)(white female employee subjected to unlawful racial harassment when, after she began dating black man, fellow employees used derogatory language about him in her presence and used racially oriented language).

[68]For a discussion of harassment as the form of retaliation, see Chapter 10, Retaliation, Section IV.C. See also Section III.A.2. *infra.*

[69]*E.g.,* Huebschen v. Wisconsin Dep't of Health & Social Servs., 716 F.2d 1167, 32 FEP Cases 1582 (7th Cir. 1983); Trautvetter v. Quick, 916 F.2d 1140, 54 FEP Cases 109 (7th Cir. 1990)(claim of discrimination "must show an intent to discriminate *because* of her status as a female and not because of characteristics of her gender which are personal to her . . . . If this distinction—subtle as it is—is not maintained, any consensual workplace romance involving a state supervisor and employee which soured for one reason or another could give rise to equal protection claims if the employee simply alleges that his or her supervisor's conduct during the term of the romance constituted 'sexual harassment' "); Keppler v. Hinsdale Township High School Dist., 715 F. Supp. 862, 50 FEP Cases 295 (N.D. Ill. 1989), reproduced *infra. Huebschen* and *Keppler* both involved charges that supervisors caused their former lovers to suffer tangible job detriments in retaliation for the termination of their romances. The courts distinguished between retaliation against a subordinate because of a failed romantic relationship, which in their view is not actionable, and retaliation for refusal to continue a sexual relationship, which is actionable. Huebschen v. Department of Health & Social Servs., 716 F.2d at 1172, 32 FEP Cases at 1585–86; Keppler v. Hinsdale Township High School Dist., 715 F. Supp. at 867–70, 50 FEP Cases at 299–301. Thus, actions resulting from feelings of rage, jealousy and humiliation upon termination of a relationship do not constitute sexual harassment because such actions occurred because of the rejection, not because of the victim's gender. This line of reasoning has drawn criticism for attempting to craft a distinction without a difference. *See* Babcock v. Frank, 729 F. Supp. 279, 287–88, 54 FEP Cases 1123 (S.D.N.Y. 1990), reproduced *infra* (criticizing *Huebschen* and *Keppler*).

III. FORMS OF SEXUAL HARASSMENT

Traditionally, in assessing liability for sexual harassment, courts have analyzed the conduct in terms of a quid pro quo or a hostile environment theory of discrimination.[70] However, the conduct that constitutes sexual harassment is better understood when grouped into three broad categories:[71] (A) unwelcome sexual advances,[72] (B) gender-based animosity of either a sexual or a nonsexual nature,[73] and (C) a sexually charged workplace.[74]

The conduct involved in a quid pro quo case consists of unwelcome sexual advances coupled with a tangible job detriment.[75] Evidence of gender-based animosity or of a sexually charged workplace is not necessary to establish a quid pro quo claim.[76] It might, however, evidence the sexual nature of the advances made[77] and the sex-based motivation behind the challenged job detriment.

A hostile environment case involves harassment sufficiently severe or pervasive to constitute a condition of employment. The harassment violates the prohibition against sex discrimination if the harassment results from the sex of the harassed employee—that is, the harassment would not have occurred but for the gender of the complainant.[78] A hostile environment may include some combination of unwelcome sexual advances, incidents of gender-based animosity (whether overtly sexual or not), and a sexually charged workplace.[79]

Because incidents of quid pro quo harassment involving unwelcome sexual advances can also create a hostile environment, many complainants alleging

---

[70]These basic forms of harassing behavior relate to the two standard theories of liability as follows:

Behavior	Quid Pro Quo	Hostile Environment
Sexual advances	part of case, if tied to tangible job benefit	part of case, whether made by supervisor, co-worker or nonemployee
Gender-baiting or hazing (either overtly or covertly sexual)	not part of case, but may be evidence of sex-based motive in decision making	part of case
Sexually charged workplace	not part of case, but may be evidence of motive	part of case

[71]The three forms of harassing conduct usually occur in some combination. The legal context in which these forms of harassment are analyzed are explored in Chapters 3, Quid Pro Quo Harassment, and 4, Hostile Environment Harassment. An introductory discussion to the two traditional theories of liability for harassment appears in Chapter 1, Overview.

[72]See Section III.A. *infra.*

[73]See Section III.B. *infra.*

[74]See Section III.C. *infra.*

[75]If there is no loss of a tangible job detriment, the case is usually treated as a hostile environment case with the issue being whether the unwelcome advance, together with other offensive, sex-based behavior, was so severe or pervasive as to alter the complainant's condition of employment.

[76]Of course, an "implicit quid pro quo" may exist in an atmosphere characterized by sexual favoritism. *See* Broderick v. Ruder, 685 F. Supp. 1269, 46 FEP Cases 1272 (D.D.C. 1988), reproduced *infra.*

[77]Conversely, evidence of unwelcome sexual advances, sufficient for prevailing on a quid pro quo claim, may evidence a hostile work environment. *See, e.g.,* Meritor Sav. Bank v. Vinson, 477 U.S. 57, 40 FEP Cases 1822 (1986), reproduced in Chapter 1, Overview.

[78]McKinney v. Dole, 765 F.2d 1129, 1138, 38 FEP Cases 364, 371 (quoting Bundy v. Jackson, 641 F.2d 934, 942, 24 FEP Cases 1155 (D.C. Cir. 1985)(citations omitted).

[79]In *Laughinghouse v. Risser,* 754 F. Supp. 836 (D. Kan. 1990), the complainant alleged that after her supervisor unsuccessfully propositioned her, he focused his abrasive management style on her but made no further direct sexual demands. *Id.* at 839–40. In *Babcock v. Frank, supra* note 69, 729 F. Supp. at 281–82, the complainant alleged that after she refused to resume a previously consensual relationship with her supervisor, he denied her promotions and career advancement opportunities and condoned her mistreatment by male co-workers.

quid pro quo harassment also allege hostile environment harassment,[80] and both categories of harassment can resemble retaliatory conduct forbidden by §704(a) of Title VII.[81] Consequently, more than one theory of liability might apply to the facts of a particular case.[82]

A. Unwelcome Sexual Advances

Cases involving unwelcome sexual advances can be best categorized by the nature of the response of the complainant to the sexual advance. The range of responses includes outright rejection,[83] initial rejection and later acceptance,[83a] initial acceptance followed by later rejection,[83b] ambigious conduct,[83c] coerced submission,[83d] and welcome acceptance.[84] While some of these responses are self evident, others warrant additional discussion.

1. Outright Rejection

In the typical "rejection" case, the complainant alleges that rejection of an unwelcome sexual advance motivated the employer's denial of a tangible job benefit for which the complainant was qualified. The ultimate issue in such a case—whether the employer punished the complainant for opposing the employer's sexual advances—resembles the issue present in Title VII retaliation cases.[85]

A classic rejection case, *Sparks v. Pilot Freight Carriers,* illustrates how a rejection of unwelcome sexual advances is often followed by denial of

---

[80]*See, e.g.,* Hicks v. Gates Rubber Co., 833 F.2d 1406, 45 FEP Cases 608 (10th Cir. 1987)(quid pro quo, hostile environment and racial harassment); Babcock v. Frank, *supra* note 79 (quid pro quo and hostile environment claims); Laughinghouse v. Risser, *supra* note 79 (quid pro quo and hostile environment claims).

[81]See Chapter 10, Retaliation.

[82]Thus, in *Vinson v. Taylor,* 753 F.2d 141, 36 FEP Cases 1423 (D.C. Cir. 1985), *aff'd in part and rev'd in part sub. nom. Meritor Sav. Bank v. Vinson, supra* note 77, the D.C. Circuit concluded that the plaintiff's grievance was of the hostile environment type even where the complainant, a bank employee, testified that her supervisor, Taylor, asked her to have sexual relations with him, claiming that she "owed him" because he had obtained the job for her, and where, after initially declining his invitation, she ultimately yielded, fearing that continued refusal would jeopardize her employment. She further testified that thereafter she was forced to submit to sexual advances by Taylor both during and after business hours, and that often Taylor assaulted or raped her. In addition, she alleged, Taylor caressed her on the job, followed her into the ladies' room when she was there alone, and at times exposed himself to her. The parties did not dispute that the plaintiff's advancement was based solely on merit. It is not clear why the plaintiff did not also state a claim for quid pro quo harassment, on the theory that her supervisor refrained from interfering with her merit promotions only as long as she continued to have sex with him.

[83]For a discussion of the affect of this response on proof of unwelcomeness, see Chapter 3, Quid Pro Quo Harassment, Section V.B.1.

[83a]*Id.* at Section V.B.2.

[83b]*Id.* at Section V.B.3.

[83c]*Id.* at Section V.B.4.

[83d]*Id.* at Section V.B.5.

[84]*Id.* at Section V.B.6. A threshold question, of course, is whether the advance in question was of a sexual nature. See Chapter 3, Quid Pro Quo Harassment, Section V.A.

[85]*See* Bundy v. Jackson, 641 F.2d 934, 24 FEP Cases 1155 (D.C. Cir. 1981)(referring to prima facie case of denial of promotion "in retaliation" for complainant's rejection of supervisor's sexual advances); Boyd v. James S. Hayes Living Health Care Agency, 671 F. Supp. 1155, 1167–68, 44 FEP Cases 332, 342–343 (W.D. Tenn. 1987)(analyzing termination of employee in retaliation for refusing sexual advances under §704(a)); Sowers v. Kemira, Inc., 701 F. Supp. 809, 825, 46 FEP Cases 1825, 1836–37 (S.D. Ga. 1988)(prima facie case of retaliation established because adverse employment actions occurred only days after complaints were made to harasser's supervisor about his conduct). For a discussion of retaliation in general harassment cases, see Chapter 10, Retaliation. Even if no tangible job detriment occurred, the unwelcome sexual advances may be evidence of a hostile environment.

tangible employment benefits. *Sparks* also shows how evidence of unwelcome sexual advances supports claims of sexual harassment on both quid pro quo and hostile environment grounds.[86]

SPARKS v. PILOT FREIGHT CARRIERS

830 F.2d 1554, 45 FEP Cases 160
(11th Cir. 1987)

KRAVITCH, Circuit Judge:—Barbara Sparks appeals the district court's grant of summary judgment in Sparks' sexual harassment and sex discrimination action filed against her former employer, Pilot Freight Carriers, Inc. (Pilot Freight) pursuant to Title VII, 42 U.S.C. §2000e et seq. We reverse the grant of summary judgment and remand.

I. STATEMENT OF FACTS

Appellant Sparks was employed by Pilot Freight as a billing clerk in its Duluth, Georgia trucking terminal from May 1983 until March 1984. In February 1984, Pilot Freight promoted Dennis Long, a former sales manager in the Atlanta terminal, to the position of terminal manager of the Duluth terminal. As terminal manager, Long held the highest position in the Duluth terminal and, according to Sparks, had authority to exercise virtually unfettered discretion over personnel matters, including the hiring and firing of employees. According to Sparks, the only Pilot Freight employees superior to Long were stationed in Pilot Freight's headquarters in North Carolina.

Sparks alleges that shortly after Long arrived in Duluth he began to harass her. One of the earliest instances occurred when Long called her into his office and asked her if she was married or had a boyfriend, and if she could become pregnant. Sparks claims that after she was promoted to general secretary, with Long as her boss, in March 1984, Long's unwelcomed sexual harassment of her continued. This harassment included such acts as: putting his hands on Sparks to rub her shoulders or "fool with" and smell her hair; repeatedly inquiring into Sparks' personal life; on one occasion asking her if he could come to her house with a bottle of wine, and, having been refused, calling out to her over the public address system as she was leaving the office stating that this was her "last chance;" making threatening remarks to Sparks, such as "you'd better be nice to me," "your fate is in my hands," "revenge is the name of the game;" and at least one other remark that the district court concluded was "too sexually explicit" to repeat. Sparks did not notify any of Long's superiors at Pilot Freight that he was harassing her.

In May 1984, Pilot Freight closed its Duluth terminal. Long was transferred to Atlanta where he resumed his former job as sales manager. Sparks and several other employees also were transferred to the Atlanta terminal; other Duluth employees were laid off. The terminal manager of the Atlanta terminal was Carl Connell.

Sparks was given a job as a billing clerk on the night shift where she worked for three days. On the fourth day, Thursday May 10th, Sparks allegedly called the office and asked Connell's secretary, Hilda Tatum, whether she could change her working hours. Later that day Tatum called Sparks back to tell Sparks that she could not change her hours. Sparks allegedly responded that she could not come in that night because she was sick. Curtis

---

[86]Sparks v. Pilot Freight Carriers, 830 F.2d 1554, 1557–61, 1564–65, 45 FEP Cases 160, 161–67 (11th Cir. 1987), reproduced *infra*. The plaintiff argued successfully that the quid pro quo standard for determining employer liability—that "employers are liable in such situations for the actions of their supervisors, even when such actions are unknown to them", *id.* at 1566, 45 FEP Cases at 169 (Hill, J., concurring in part and dissenting in part)—should be used to determine employer liability on the hostile environment claim, as long as the supervisor is the "agent" of the employer for Title VII purposes, including situations "where the supervisor exercises the authority actually delegated to him by his employer, by making or threatening to make decisions affecting the employment status of his subordinates." *Id.* at 1559, 45 FEP Cases at 163 (quoting Meritor Sav. Bank v. Vinson, *supra* note 77, 477 U.S. at 71, 40 FEP Cases at 1826).

Turner, a male billing clerk, also called in sick that day. The following day, Connell called Sparks at home several hours before her shift was to begin and fired her. Turner was not fired. Sparks was replaced by John Briscoe, a billing clerk who had been laid off when the Duluth terminal was closed.

Sparks filed the instant action against Pilot Freight, alleging three violations of Title VII. Her first claim is that during her tenure at the Duluth terminal she was subject to hostile working environment sexual harassment by her boss, Dennis Long. Her second two claims relate to her discharge: the first being that Connell engaged in unlawful disparate treatment because of sex when he discharged her and not Turner; the second is that her discharge resulted from *quid pro quo* sexual harassment in that Long induced Connell to fire her in retaliation for her refusal to accede to his sexual demands.

The district court granted summary judgment for Pilot Freight on all three claims. We reverse.

II. WORKING ENVIRONMENT SEXUAL HARASSMENT

• • •

A.

• • • An employee asserting a claim of hostile working environment sexual harassment by an "employer" must prove the following in order to establish a *prima facie* case: (1) that the employee belongs to a protected group, Henson, 682 F.2d at 903; (2) that the employee was subject to "unwelcome" sexual harassment, Vinson, 106 S.Ct. at 2406; Henson, 682 F.2d at 903; 29 C.F.R. §1604.11(a) (1985); (3) that the harassment complained of was based on sex, Henson, 682 F.2d at 903; and (4) that the harassment complained of affected a "term, condition, or privilege" of employment in that it was "sufficiently severe or pervasive 'to alter the conditions of [the victim's] employment and create an abusive working environment.' " Vinson, 106 S.Ct. at 2406 (brackets in original) (quoting Henson, 682 F.2d at 903).

The district court concluded that Sparks could survive summary judgment as to these four elements of her *prima facie* case. The court granted summary judgment for the defendant, however, because it concluded that Sparks failed to establish a necessary fifth element: Pilot Freight's liability for Long's actions under the theory of *respondeat superior*.

• • •

Under Title VII an "employer" is directly liable for its own sexual harassment of its employees. See 42 U.S.C. §2000e-2(a)(1), 29 C.F.R. §1604.11(c). Thus, where the harasser is plaintiff's "employer," *respondeat superior* theory does not apply and plaintiff need not establish that she gave anyone notice of the harassment.[2] Hunter v. Allis-Chalmers Corp., Engine Div., 797 F.2d 1417, 1422, 41 FEP Cases 721 (7th Cir. 1986); Horn v. Duke Homes, Div. of Windsor Mobile Homes, Inc., 755 F.2d 599, 604, 37 FEP Cases 228 (7th Cir. 1985); see Vinson, 106 S.Ct. 2408-09; Henson, 682 F.2d at 905 n.9.

The Act defines the term "employer" as a "person engaged in an industry affecting commerce ... *and any agent of such a person*."[3] 42 U.S.C. §2000e(b) (emphasis added). Therefore, if Long was acting as an "agent" of Pilot Freight when he sexually harassed Sparks, Pilot Freight is directly liable to Sparks for Long's conduct—provided Sparks can establish the four elements of her *prima facie* case outlined above. See Vinson, 106 S.Ct. at 2408; Horn, 755 F.2d at 604.

B.

Title VII does not define the term "agent." Rather, in determining whether a supervisor was acting as an "agent"·for Title VII purposes, courts must look for guidance to common

---

[1][Omitted.]
[2–3][Omitted.]

law agency principles. Vinson, 106 S.Ct. at 2408, citing, 42 U.S.C. §2000e(b) *and* Restatement (Second) of Agency §§219-237 (1958).

• • • Applying the general rule of agency that "[a] master is subject to liability for the torts of his servants committed when acting in the scope of their employment," Restatement (Second) of Agency, §219(1), the district court determined that Pilot Freight was not liable for Long's actions because Long was not acting within the scope of his employment when he harassed Sparks. The district court based this ruling on its determination that Long was not "actuated by some purpose to serve the master" when he harassed Sparks.[5] Sparks, No. C85-2941A, slip op. at 8, citing Restatement (Second) of Agency §§219(1), 228(2).

Although the district court recognized that an employer may be liable under section 291(2) of the Restatement for its servant's actions even though the servant was not acting "within the scope of his employment," the district court concluded that none of section 219 (2)'s exceptions to the general rule of Section 219(1) apply to this case. • • •

In holding that none of the enumerated exceptions to the "within the scope of employment" rule apply, the district court apparently overlooked section 219(2)(d). This section provides that a master is liable for the torts of his servants acting outside the scope of their employment where:

> (d) the servant purported to act or to speak on behalf of the principal and there was reliance upon apparent authority, or *he was aided in accomplishing the tort by the existence of the agency relationship.* (emphasis added).

Under this section, unlike under section 219(1), the master is not insulated from liability by the fact that the servant was acting entirely for his own benefit. See id. at §§219(2), 235 Comment E; see also id. at §§262, 265.

Interpreting general agency rules, and presumably relying primarily on section 219(2), the Equal Employment Opportunity Commission (EEOC) has concluded that a supervisor acts as an "agent" of the employer for Title VII purposes, thus rendering the employer directly liable for the supervisor's action, "where [the] supervisor exercises the authority actually delegated to him by his employer, by making or threatening to make decisions affecting the employment status of his subordinates." Vinson, 106 S.Ct. at 2407–08 (stating, without ruling on, the position of the EEOC in its amicus brief;)[6] • • • see §219(d)(2), Restatement (Second) of Agency; • • • This liability is direct; the employer cannot find shelter in the claim that it neither had notice of, or approved of, the unlawful conduct. Vinson, 106 S.Ct. at 2408; see Horn, 755 F.2d at 604–05; 29 C.F.R. §1604.11(c); §219(d)(2), Restatement (Second) of Agency.

Adopting this rule and applying it to the instant case,[8] we observe that it is undisputed that when Pilot Freight made Long terminal manager of the Duluth terminal it vested him with both actual and apparent authority to alter Sparks' employment status—including authority to fire her. Moreover, the evidence, considered in the light most favorable to Sparks, shows that Long used the authority delegated to him by Pilot Freight to assist him in harassing Sparks: specifically, Long repeatedly reminded Sparks that he could fire her should she fail to comply with his advances.[9] Therefore, we conclude that, when the evidence

---

[4][Omitted.]

[5]Under common law agency principles, "a master is subject to liability for the torts of his servants committed while acting in the scope of their employment." Restatement (Second) of Agency, §219(1). In order for a servant's conduct to be properly considered "within the scope of employment" it must: (1) be of the kind he is employed to perform; (2) occur substantially within the authorized time and space limits; and (3) be actuated, at least in part, by a purpose to serve the master. Id. at §228(1). Alternatively, "conduct of a servant is not within the scope of employment if it is different in kind from that authorized, far beyond the authorized time and space limits, or too little actuated by a purpose to serve the master." Id. at §228(2).

[6]See Note 9, infra.

[7][Omitted.]

[8]While we recognize that the rule of the EEOC proposed in Vinson, supra, is not an official regulation, we adopt it because we conclude that it is simply an application in the Title VII context of §219(d)(2), Restatement (Second) of Agency—the rule which, under Vinson, supra, we conclude properly governs this action. • • •

[9]The evidence before us, when considered in the light most favorable to Sparks, shows that Long did threaten to use the authority delegated to him to Sparks' detriment. Therefore, we need not address the issue raised by the EEOC, and not resolved by the Supreme Court, in Vinson: what rule should govern the

is viewed in the light most favorable to Sparks, Sparks has established a genuine issue of material fact as to whether Long was acting as Pilot Freight's agent when he engaged in the alleged sexual harassment of Sparks. She consequently has established a genuine issue of material fact as to whether Pilot Freight is directly liable to her under Title VII. See Hamilton v. Rogers, 791 F.2d 439, 442–43, 40 FEP Cases 1814 (5th Cir. 1986); Horn, 755 F.2d at 604–05. Accordingly, the district court's grant of summary judgment on Sparks' hostile working environment sexual harassment claim must be reversed. See Anderson v. Liberty Lobby, Inc., 477 U.S. 242, 106 S.Ct. 2505, 2510–11, 2513–14, 91 L.Ed. 2d 202 (1986).

C.

Pilot Freight contests this conclusion, asserting that it cannot be liable for Long's actions because Sparks did not complain to anyone at Pilot Freight about Long's conduct. Pilot Freight cannot prevail on this claim.

To the extent that Pilot Freight's claim is that an employer is not liable for sexual harassment by its supervisors absent "notice," its claim is not even colorably valid given the Supreme Court's holding in Vinson,[10] 106 S.Ct. at 2408 (employer liable for agent's acts even absent notice); accord Horn, 755 F.2d at 604; 29 C.F.R. §1604.11(c).

• • •

D.

Nor are we inclined to accept Pilot Freight's argument that, even if we reverse the district court's conclusion that Long was not acting as Pilot Freight's agent, we nevertheless should affirm the grant of summary judgment by reversing the district court's denial of summary judgment as to the first four elements of Sparks' *prima facie* case.

In particular, Pilot Freight asserts that it is entitled to summary judgment because Sparks has not established that Long's harassment was sufficiently severe to be actionable under Title VII.[11] To be actionable under Title VII, the "sexual harassment" must have affected a "term, condition, or privilege" of employment within the meaning of Title VII. See Henson, 682 F.2d at 904. The Court in Vinson interpreted this as requiring proof that the sexual harassment was "sufficiently severe or pervasive 'to alter the conditions of [the victim's] employment and create an abusive working environment.' " Vinson, 106 S.Ct. at 2406 (quoting Henson, 682 F.2d at 904). This test may be satisfied by a showing that sexual harassment was sufficiently severe or persistent "to affect seriously [the victim's] psychological well being." Henson, 682 F.2d at 904.

Applying this test, we conclude that the district court properly found that Sparks could survive a motion for summary judgment on her claim that Long's alleged conduct is actionable under Title VII as it affected a "term, condition, or privilege" of Sparks' employment. According to Sparks, Long repeatedly sexually harassed her and threatened her job—conduct which she said "frightened" and "upset" her, causing her to doubt her job security. See Sparks, No. C85-2941A, slip op. at 6. Accepting these allegations as true, we conclude that Long's sexual harassment of Sparks was sufficiently persistent and severe to satisfy the Vinson requirement that the conduct must have seriously affected the plaintiff's psychological well being.[12] Accordingly, Sparks has established a genuine issue of material

---

employer's liability for sexual harassment by its supervisors where the sexual harassment claim rests "exclusively" on a "hostile environment" theory, in that the supervisor neither explicitly nor implicitly threatened to use his authority against the victim. See Vinson, 106 S.Ct. at 2408.

[10]Pilot Freight's argument reflects a lack of understanding of the basis of its liability for Long's acts. As the Seventh Circuit recently explained in Allis-Chalmers, supra, an employer is directly liable for its supervisors' violations of Title VII because those acts are viewed as acts of the employer itself. 797 F.2d at 1422. Therefore, there is no reason to have a notice requirement because the supervisory employee is deemed to be the employer itself and thus notice to the supervisor that he is engaging in unwelcomed harassment is notice to the employer. See id.

[11][Omitted.]

[12]See 29 C.F.R. §§1604.11(a)(2) (unwelcome sexual advances constitute sexual harassment where submission to such conduct is made, explicitly or *implicitly,* a term or condition of an individual's employment) (emphasis added), 1604.11(a)(3) (unwelcome sexual advances constitutes sexual harassment where they have the purpose or effect of creating an intimidating, hostile or offensive working environment).

fact as to whether Long's conduct affected a "term, condition, or privilege" of her employ-ment; the district court therefore should have denied summary judgment for defendant on this issue.[13]

• • •

IV. QUID PRO QUO SEXUAL HARASSMENT

Sparks' third claim is one of *quid pro quo* sexual harassment. The essence of this claim is that Sparks suffered a tangible job detriment as a result of her reactions to Long's sexual harassment of her because Long, in order to get revenge, influenced Connell to fire her.

Title VII prohibits an employer from requiring sexual consideration from an employee as a *quid pro quo* for job benefits. In order to establish a *prima facie* case of *quid pro quo* sexual harassment against an employer the employee must prove: (1) that the employee belongs to a protected group, (2) that the employee was subject to unwelcome sexual harassment, (3) that the harassment complained of was based on sex, and (4) that the employee's reaction to the harassment complained of affected tangible aspects of the em-ployee's compensation or terms, conditions or privileges of employment. Henson, 682 F.2d at 909.[22]

The district court concluded that summary judgment was inappropriate as to the first three elements, but granted summary judgment based on the fourth element of Sparks' *prima facie* case. Because Sparks' *quid pro quo* sexual harassment claim is based in part on her harassment by Long, we conclude, for the reasons stated in section II of this opinion, that the district court properly found that Sparks established a genuine issue of material fact as to the first three elements of her *prima facie* case. We reverse the district court's grant of summary judgment on the fourth element.

Sparks alleges that the following evidence, drawn from the deposition testimony sub-mitted to the district court, permits the inference that Long influenced Connell to fire her as retaliation for her reaction to his sexual harassment of her: (1) Long threatened to have Sparks fired if she did not accede to his demands, (2) Long and Connell had worked together in the Atlanta terminal and apparently were friends, (3) another female employee who had refused Long's advances stated that Long had influenced Connell to reprimand her based on fictitious problems, (4) Long and Connell allegedly discussed Sparks' termination, al-though whether they discussed it prior to, or shortly after her termination is unclear, and (5) Sparks was fired for pretextual reasons after having been at the Atlanta terminal less than five days. Therefore, Sparks asserts that the grant of summary judgment was improper.

Pilot Freight retorts that Sparks' evidence is insufficient to overcome Connell's state-ments in deposition that he made the decision to fire Sparks independently of, and without consulting, Long. The district court concluded that the only deposition evidence that could possibly undermine Connell's claim that Long did not influence him was that of Pilot Freight employee Kathy Chastain, who testified that Long discussed Sparks' termination with Connell. The court found that Chastain's testimony did not refute Connell's, however, because the court construed Chastain's testimony as stating that the purported conversation

---

[13]Judge Hill's proposal that we require the factfinder to determine first whether harassing behavior was "ambiguously" or "patently" offensive before assigning liability to the employer is unnecessary. The Supreme Court has stated that "[f]or sexual harassment to be actionable, it must be sufficiently severe or pervasive 'to alter the conditions of [the victim's] employment and create an abusive working environ-ment.' " Meritor, 106 S.Ct. at 2406 (quoting Henson, 682 F.2d at 904). Not all harassment rises to a violation of Title VII. For an employer to be liable for sexual harassment, a factfinder must find that the harassment had been sufficiently offensive to be actionable.

Moreover, we question the usefulness of requiring a factfinder to distinguish between "ambiguously" and "patently" offensive actions considering that most complaints of sexual harassment are based on actions which, although they may be permissible in some settings, are inappropriate in the workplace. What can be a "compliment," as Judge Hill puts it, between two persons who have a social relationship can be abusive in the workplace—but that is, in many cases, the whole point of the sexual harassment claim. With access to all the evidence, and with the common sense to make credibility determinations, a factfinder should not find it difficult to distinguish between harassing actions that constitute a violation of Title VII and those "ambiguous" actions which simply may not "create an abusive working environment."

[14–21][Omitted.]

[22]Where the alleged harasser is the plaintiff's supervisor, the employer is directly liable; plaintiff need not prove *respondeat superior.* Henson, 682 F.2d at 909; see 42 U.S.C. §2000e(b); 29 C.F.R. §1604.11(c).

between Long and Connell occurred after Sparks was fired. Concluding that there was no evidence to refute Connell's claim, the court granted summary judgment for Pilot Freight.

The district court was incorrect both in his construction of Chastain's testimony and in his decision to grant summary judgment. As Sparks observes, Chastain did not testify to having overheard a conversation between Connell and Long, as the district court said. Rather she testified that Long recited to her, on the day Sparks was fired, a conversation between himself and Connell about Sparks. While it is clear from Chastain's deposition testimony that the conversation between Long and herself occurred after Sparks was fired, Chastain's testimony does not indicate when the conversation between Long and Connell occurred. We conclude, after reviewing the deposition testimony of Chastain, that a jury could infer, based in her testimony, that the conversation between Long and Connell occurred before Sparks was fired. Because this inference is [the] one most favorable to Sparks, the party opposing summary judgment, it is this inference that we must adopt. See Liberty Lobby, 106 S.Ct. at 2513.

Once this inference is adopted, Connell's statement that he made the decision to fire Sparks without consulting Long no longer stands unrefuted. We conclude that the testimony of Chastain, when considered in light of the rest of the evidence presented by Sparks—in particular the alleged absence of a legitimate reason for firing her and Long's purported attempts to use his relationship with Connell to retaliate against other female employees—is sufficient to establish a genuine material issue of fact as to whether Long influenced Connell to fire Sparks in retaliation for Sparks' reaction to his unwelcome advances. Given that being fired certainly is a tangible detriment, we conclude that Sparks has established a genuine issue of material fact as to the fourth and final element of her *prima facie* cases. Accordingly, we reverse the district court's grant of summary judgment of Sparks' claim of *quid pro quo* sexual harassment.

V.

In conclusion, the district court's grant of summary judgment as to each of Sparks' Title VII claims is REVERSED and the case is REMANDED for proceedings consistent with this opinion.

Concurring and Dissenting Opinion

HILL, Circuit Judge, concurring in part; and dissenting in part—While I concur in the decision to remand this case to the district court, I respectfully dissent from a portion of this opinion.

I concur with those parts of the opinion addressed to sexual discrimination which results in tangible detriment to the plaintiff. Until the Supreme Court decides otherwise I will concur with the generally accepted opinion that employers are liable in such situations for the actions for supervisors, even when such actions are unknown to them. See e.g., Henson v. City of Dundee, 682 F.2d 897, 909, 29 FEP Cases 787 (11th Cir. 1982). See also, Meritor Savings Bank, FBS v. Vinson, 477 U.S. 57, ——, 106 S.Ct. 2399, 2408, 91 L.Ed.2d 49, 40 FEP Cases 1822 (1986) (noting that the EEOC had described this trend in its brief as *amicus curiae,* but refusing to "issue a definitive rule on employer liability"). Given this standard for liability, the district court should not have granted summary judgment in those portions of the case directed to rectifying a tangible detriment to plaintiff Sparks.

At the same time, I dissent from that part of the majority opinion which deals with workplace environment discrimination. Vinson dismissed two extreme standards proposed for evaluating work environment discrimination cases: courts could neither insulate those employers who had no notice of the situation, nor hold them automatically liable. Vinson, 477 U.S. at ——, 106 S.Ct. at 2408. It is because I fear that today's decision dips into the second of the two extremes that I dissent from a part of it.[1]

---

[1] The majority opinion suggests that because plaintiff claims both work environment and quid pro quo violations of Title VII, this court need not address itself to the topic of a standard for "hostile environment"

Workplace environment discrimination deserves a special standard for two reasons. First, as the defendant in Vinson argued: "in a hostile environment case the employer often will have no reason to know about, or opportunity to cure, the alleged wrongdoing." Vinson, 477 U.S. at ——, 106 S.Ct. at 2407. By definition employers should have more reason to know of biases displayed in tangible ways than of biases woven into the environment.

Likewise, the standard the court chooses must recognize that racial and gender discrimination differ. In both instances we find patently offensive types of conduct which cannot be justified and which the law demands be rectified. And yet in cases of gender discrimination we find a second and more subtle strain of conduct which may or may not be offensive given the relationship between the parties at the given time. For example, to a given individual, the gender-based compliment may be acceptable when placed in the context of a relationship between the parties; the same statement may be offensive when that relationship does not exist or has soured. The law stands ready to protect workers against sexually harassing behavior, but it need not and ought not intervene when neither party is offended by the actions. Thus, the standard chosen by the court must be able to measure the behavior within the contours of the situation as it existed at the time of the allegedly discriminatory behavior.

I would propose the following two-step test for analyzing hostile environment situations. First, it must be determined whether or not the allegedly discriminatory behavior was ambiguously or patently offensive. Where the conduct was patently offensive and the offending individual was plaintiff's supervisor, the inquiry may end: [even] without notification of the wrong, the employer may be held liable.

However, where it is found that the supervisor's behavior was ambiguous, i.e., less than overtly offensive, a second finding must be made as to whether the plaintiff, by some objective action at the time of the allegedly offensive conduct displayed objection to the conduct of the supervisor. These expressions of dissatisfaction may not always be through formal channels of protest within the employer's structure (although such methods would be the best display of the fact that ambiguous conduct was offensive to the employee), and thus while this test will often provide notice to the employer, it will not guarantee such notice. However, the objective demonstration of displeasure will clarify and define the otherwise ambiguous actions of the supervisor, and will prevent any reinterpretation of the situation via hindsight.

I would remand the case for a trial and determinations according to the standards set forth in this concurring and dissenting opinion.

---

litigation. I disagree. Because plaintiff asserts two types of discrimination does not mean we measure both claims by the laxer standard; each claim must be examined according to the standard appropriate to that contention. Thus, I find that the majority opinion adopts, without analysis, a sweeping and controversial position on hostile environment discrimination.

---

2. Initial Acceptance Followed by Later Rejection

In a "soured romance" case, a subordinate employee terminates a consensual relationship with a superior and then suffers a tangible job detriment or a hostile environment.[87] The legal issues raised in soured romance cases resemble those raised in typical outright rejection cases—whether the adverse employ-

---

[87]Soured romances can also occur where the supervisor seeks to terminate the relationship with the subordinate. In such instances, employers fear that the subordinate may manufacture a sexual harassment claim. However, a careful reading of cases such as *Huebschen v. Department of Health & Social Servs.*, *supra* note 69, and *Trautvetter v. Quick*, *supra* note 69 (both finding against the complainant), indicates that prevailing on this basis is a formidable task for the subordinate bent on revenge against a superior.

ment action is a result of the complainant's rejection of unwelcome sexual advances. A soured romance case arguably differs from other quid pro quo cases in that the adverse job action may stem from a personal reaction to the souring of the romance rather than from the gender of the complainant.[88] This arguable difference disappears, of course, if after the romance ends the alleged harasser makes a new, unwelcome, sexual advance before taking the adverse action.[89]

In *Keppler v. Hinsdale Township High School District,* the court struggled to fashion a rule distinguishing these two types of soured romance cases.

KEPPLER V. HINSDALE TOWNSHIP HIGH SCHOOL DISTRICT

715 F. Supp. 862, 50 FEP Cases 295
(N.D. Ill. 1989)

BRIAN B. DUFF, District Judge:—Plaintiff Rose Keppler has sued Roger Miller and Hinsdale Township High School District 86 ("District 86") under Title VII of the Civil Rights Act of 1964 ("Title VII"), 42 U.S.C. §§2000e et seq., and under 42 U.S.C. §1983 ("§1983"). She alleges sexual discrimination and due process violations, but what she really wants is to make others pay for her mistakes. She will not succeed here.

FACTS

District 86 has two high schools: Hinsdale Central and Hinsdale South. The Superintendent for District 86 controls the day-to-day affairs of both schools. The Superintendent at all times relevant to this case was Dr. John Thorson. • • •
 • • •

Ms. Keppler first became employed by District 86 in 1978 as Coordinator of Education Services. Because this was an administrative position, Ms. Keppler reported directly to Superintendent Thorson. • • •

In the fall of 1982, Ms. Keppler met socially on two occasions with Dr. Miller. Dr. Miller had become employed by District 86 in 1980 as an assistant principal at Hinsdale Central. In the fall of 1982, his marriage was in trouble and he was seeking companionship and advice. Ms. Keppler provided them.

By the end of 1982, Dr. Miller's relationship with his wife was over, and he began seeing Ms. Keppler on a regular basis. They had sexual relations frequently and, when the relationship was going well, saw each other during the week as well as on weekends. In 1984, District 86 promoted Dr. Miller to principal of Hinsdale Central.

Dr. Miller and Ms. Keppler continued to see each other through the spring of 1986. Although they also saw other people, and at times contemplated terminating their relationship, they continued to have sexual intercourse on a regular basis when they were together.

By March, 1986, however, things had taken a turn for the worse. After Dr. Miller and Ms. Keppler returned from a weekend together in New Orleans in March, during which they had sexual relations, their sexual relationship was at an end.

[1] From that point on, the evidence is conflicting as to who was tired of whom, and just what transpired when the two were together. For the purposes of this summary judgment

---

[88]Huebschen v. Wisconsin Dep't of Health & Social Servs., *supra* note 69 (reversing district court judgment of violation of Title VII and equal protection clause where male employee brought suit against female supervisor after termination of employment following shortly after termination of sexual relationship). For the view that this is a distinction without a difference, see Babcock v. Frank, *supra* note 69.

[89]Keppler v. Hinsdale Township High School Dist., 715 F. Supp. 862, 50 FEP Cases 295 (N.D. Ill. 1989), reproduced *infra.*

motion, this court accepts as true all of the testimony of Ms. Keppler in her deposition and in the affidavit she provided in opposing the summary judgment motion.[1]

Ms. Keppler and Dr. Miller saw each other socially on two occasions in April, 1986. On a Sunday in mid-April, Mr. Miller invited Ms. Keppler to accompany him to his parents' home. She agreed to go. Dr. Miller drove the two of them in Ms. Keppler's car. At the end of the day, Dr. Miller drove Ms. Keppler back to his house. He asked her to come in, but she refused. He then became angry and insisted that their sexual relationship should continue. When she refused again, he threw the car keys in her lap, and went inside. Ms. Keppler went home.

Later that month, Dr. Miller asked Ms. Keppler to come to dinner with him and two other couples. Again, Ms. Keppler agreed and met Dr. Miller in the parking lot of a Marriott Hotel. After dinner, the two returned to the Marriott, and Dr. Miller requested that Ms. Keppler come to his place for sexual relations. Ms. Keppler refused, and left.

• • •

At some point in 1986, Ms. Keppler's administrative position was changed from Director of Special Services to Director of Curriculum, Instruction, Staff Development and Special Services ("Director of Curriculum"). As part of her new job, Ms. Keppler continued to have considerable responsibility for special services, but also took on additional responsibilities. She still reported directly to Superintendent Thorson.

In August 1986, Dr. Miller told Ms. Keppler that she had lost professional credibility in his eyes, and that as far as he was concerned she should leave the district. From August, 1986 through February, 1988, Dr. Miller made a number of negative comments to Superintendent Thorson about Ms. Keppler's performance as Director of Curriculum. Superintendent Thorson, noting the antagonistic relationship between Dr. Miller and Ms. Keppler, decided to transfer Ms. Keppler's office to Hinsdale South for the 1987-88 school year.

In early 1988, Superintendent Thorson met with Ms. Keppler and told her that he thought she should resign her position as Director of Curriculum. When Ms. Keppler asked why, Thorson indicated that it was because of her poor relationship with the principals of the two district high schools. The superintendent noted that she had tenure as a teacher and could therefore stay with the district in that capacity, but told her that she would have to give up her administrative role. He also indicated that he hoped she would not accept a teaching role, and would instead leave the district. Ms. Keppler told him that she would think it over.

On February 15, at a Board meeting, Superintendent Thorson recommended that the Board terminate Ms. Keppler's position as Director of Curriculum. An extensive discussion ensued, but the members agreed not to take any action until Ms. Keppler decided whether or not to resign.

On February 28, Ms. Keppler met with Dr. Richard Spiegel, president of the Board. Dr. Spiegel informed Ms. Keppler that he thought she should resign. At that point, Ms. Keppler informed Dr. Spiegel of her previous relationship with Dr. Miller, and of her belief that the principal's attitude toward her was engendered in part by the fact that she had terminated the relationship. She also stated that she would consider legal action if the Board decided to terminate her administrative position.

• • •

On April 4, 1988, the Board voted unanimously to terminate Ms. Keppler's position as Director of Curriculum, and to do away with that position, at least in the near future, for financial reasons. Ms. Keppler was then transferred to a position as special education teacher for the 1988-89 school year, and to a salary level commensurate with that position.

Ms. Keppler thereafter filed this action against Dr. Miller and District 86. Count I seeks relief under 42 U.S.C. §1983 and alleges that Dr. Miller violated her equal protection rights by discriminating against her on the basis of her sex. Count II also seeks relief under §1983, but against District 86 for violating her rights to due process by depriving her of her position as Director of Curriculum without a hearing. Count [III] arises under Title VII, and alleges that District 86, as Ms. Keppler's employer, discriminated against her on the basis of sex by relying on Dr. Miller's recommendation that her administrative position be terminated.

---

[1][Omitted.]

DISCUSSION

The Sex Discrimination Claims

Counts I and III differ in that the former seeks recovery under §1983 from Dr. Miller while the latter seeks it under Title VII from District 86. The counts are similar, however, in that both are predicated on Dr. Miller's alleged sexual harassment.[2] To prevail on either claim, Ms. Keppler must first show that Dr. Miller discriminated against her because of her sex. *See Volk* v. *Coler,* 845 F.2d 1422, 1437–38 [46 FEP Cases 1287] (7th Cir. 1988). Since Ms. Keppler cannot do so, this court need not consider whether the district could be held liable under Title VII for Dr. Miller's actions.

• • •

The complaint in this case does not specify whether it is predicated on quid pro quo sexual harassment, hostile environment sexual harassment, or both. The complaint contains allegations that, after the consensual relationship between Dr. Miller and Ms. Keppler ended, Dr. Miller subjected Ms. Keppler to "unwelcome sexual harassment, advances, and requests for sexual favors." This suggests an hostile environment claim. The complaint, however, then goes on to allege that, as a result of Ms. Keppler's refusal to comply with Dr. Miller's requests for sexual relations, Dr. Miller engaged in a campaign to have Ms. Keppler removed from her position as Director of Curriculum, a campaign that ended in success when the Board relied on his complaints about Ms. Keppler and terminated her administrative position. These allegations indicate that Ms. Keppler is seeking to recover on a quid pro quo theory.

In their motion for summary judgment, the defendants addressed the complaint as alleging both hostile environment and quid pro quo sexual harassment. They attempted to show that Dr. Miller's relationship with Ms. Keppler was primarily consensual, and that on the few occasions when Dr. Miller made unwelcome sexual advances to Ms. Keppler, his actions were neither hostile nor abusive. The defendants also sought to establish that Dr. Miller never recommended that Ms. Keppler's administrative position be terminated, and that any negative comments he did make about her played no role in the Board's ultimate decision to terminate her.

Ms. Keppler responded by introducing evidence that Dr. Miller's sexual advances had been unwelcome, and appeared at first to be setting the stage for a hostile environment claim. In the end, however, she conceded that she had not made out a case of hostile environment sexual harassment, and that the gravaman of her case was that Dr. Miller had embarked on his campaign against her in retaliation for her rejection of him—i.e., quid pro quo sexual harassment.

In support of this claim, Ms. Keppler first noted that a single incident of sexual harassment can suffice to establish a quid pro quo. She then argued that Dr. Miller's conduct following Ms. Keppler's rejection of him, and Superintendent Thorson's subsequent reliance on their failed relationship as one reason for recommending Ms. Keppler's demotion, created a jury question as to whether Ms. Keppler had suffered sex discrimination.

Ms. Keppler's quid pro quo claim, however, collides with the Seventh Circuit's ruling in *Huebschen* v. *Department of Health and Social Services,* 716 F.2d 1167 [32 FEP Cases 1582] (7th Cir. 1983). In that case, a male employee brought suit against a female supervisor under §1983 and Title VII alleging sex discrimination. The two had been involved in a consensual sexual romance, but when their relationship deteriorated, the female defendant immediately began treating her ex-lover badly, and within a week indicated that there were problems with his job. A short time later, the plaintiff was fired on the defendant's recommendation.

The Court held that, although the plaintiff had been treated unfairly, he had not established sex-based discrimination:

The proper classification, if there is one at all, was the group of persons with whom [defendant] had or sought to have an affair. It was this group, of which [plaintiff] may

---

[2][Omitted.]
[3][Omitted.]

have been the only one, that [defendant] sought to disadvantage. As unfair as [defendant's] treatment of [plaintiff] may have been, we are simply not persuaded that the Equal Protection Clause should protect such a class.

Id. at 1172.

Does *Huebschen* mean that once an employee engages in consensual sex with an employer, she forfeits any right to legal protection from that employer? Certainly not. The *Huebschen* Court specifically distinguished its case from *Woerner v. Brzeczek,* 519 F.Supp. 511 [26 FEP Cases 897] (N.D. Ill. 1981), and thereby made clear that a hostile environment claim remains available after a consensual sexual relationship comes to an end.

But what about quid pro quo claims? Here, it is more difficult to discern *Huebschen's* message. The opinion's language suggests that once a person engages in consensual sex with an employer, the employee may not thereafter complain if the employer threatens termination as a penalty for ending the relationship. But it need not be read this broadly.

To understand *Huebschen,* it is first necessary to subcategorize quid pro quo claims. The standard form of quid pro quo harassment involves express or implied demands for sexual favors in return for job benefits: "You have sex with me, and you will get a raise (or keep your job, or whatever)." A different situation arises, however, when an employer makes sexual advances to an employee, but without either expressing or implying that the employee's job will be affected by a refusal. The employee may be annoyed, or even amused, but feeling no compulsion to comply, she simply rejects the employer's efforts. The employer then fires or demotes the employee, or just makes life miserable, but without further sexual advances or innuendos. These cases are really not quid pro quo claims at all, and will be referred to here as "sexual retaliation" cases, for lack of a better term.

Courts rarely have distinguished between standard and sexual retaliation quid pro quo claims because, in the ordinary case where no prior consensual relationship has occurred, both amount to sexual discrimination. Title VII prohibits employers from using sex as a criteria for employment benefits: An employer may not penalize an employee for refusing to engage in sexual relations. Whether the refusal followed a threat of penalty does not alter the fact that the employer discriminated on the basis of sex.

Moreover, as a factual matter it is often difficult to differentiate between the two: An employee who is fired after rejecting a sexual advance may testify that she felt threatened by termination when she refused, and if her employer has penalized (or rewarded) others in the office for their response to his actions, she may indeed have faced an implied quid pro quo situation.

The distinction between standard and retaliatory quid pro quo, however, does become significant in the context of a prior consensual relationship. In such cases, the termination of the sexual relationship involves not just the cessation of copulation, but the end of a prior intimate relationship. An employer who threatens a penalty if the employee will not continue the physical relationship is using gender as a basis for job benefits. But an employer who seeks retribution because his former lover has jilted him may be reacting not to the rejection of copulation *per se,* but to the change in the status quo—that is, the termination of the intimate physical and emotional relationship.

If *Huebschen* is to be taken as anything but wrong, it must be seen as drawing a distinction between standard and retaliatory quid pro quo claims. The Court could not have meant that an employer who has engaged in consensual copulation with an employee may thereafter demand it as a condition of retaining job benefits. The Court, however, may have been saying that when an employer penalizes an employee after the termination of a consensual relationship, a presumption arises that the employer acted not on the basis of gender, but on the basis of the failed interpersonal relationship—a presumption rebuttable only if the employee can demonstrate that the employer demanded further sexual relationships before taking the action he did.

Read in this way, *Huebschen* makes a great deal of sense. Title VII prohibits discrimination in the workplace. An employee has the right to work in an atmosphere free from sexual abuse, and to obtain the privileges and benefits of her employment without having to provide sexual favors to her employer. An employee who chooses to become involved in an intimate affair with her employer, however, removes an element of her employment relationship from the workplace, and in the realm of private affairs people do have the right to react to rejection, jealousy and other emotions which Title VII says have no place in the employment setting.

Such an employee, of course, always has the right to terminate the relationship and to again sever her private life from the workplace; when she does so, she has the right, like any other worker, to be free from a sexually abusive environment, and to reject her employer's sexual advances without threat of punishment. Yet, she cannot then expect that her employer will feel the same as he did about her before and during their private relationship.[4] Feelings will be hurt, egos damages or bruised. The consequences are the result not of sexual discrimination, but of responses to an individual because of her former intimate place in her employer's life. *Compare Volk* v. *Coler,* 845 F.2d at 1433 ("Discrimination and harassment against an individual woman *because of her sex* is a violation of the equal protection clause." (emphasis added).

Ms. Keppler's case presents the latter scenario. After her relationship with Dr. Miller ended, he did not abuse her or in any way harass her at the office. Nor did he even hint that by refusing to continue their sexual relationship she was jeopardizing her job. Instead, even assuming the truth of Ms. Keppler's testimony, Dr. Miller requested on a few occasions that they resume their relationship, and became angry when she refused. Bearing a grudge, he then embarked on a campaign to denigrate her in the eyes of Superintendent Thorson, with the ultimate goal of having her removed from her administrative position.[5]

Huebschen teaches that Dr. Miller's conduct did not violate Title VII. Because the two had engaged in a prior consensual relationship, Ms. Keppler could establish sexual discrimination only by rebutting the presumption that Dr. Miller penalized her not because she was a woman, but instead because she was his former lover. To do this, she had to show (at this stage, provide evidence from which a jury could find) not merely that Dr. Miller wanted their relationship to continue, but that Dr. Miller threatened punishment if copulation or some form of erotic engagement was refused. She has not done so. Even if Dr. Miller did seek retribution against Ms. Keppler for abandoning their relationship—and it is by no means clear that he did—the most she has shown is that Dr. Miller reacted harshly to their failed relationship.[6] *Huebschen* says that this is not sexual discrimination under the anti discrimination laws.[7] Accordingly, summary judgment will be entered against Ms. Keppler on Counts I and II of her complaint.

• • •

CONCLUSION

The defendant's motion for summary judgment is granted, and judgment is entered for the defendants and against Ms. Keppler on all counts of the complaint. The defendant's motion for sanctions is denied.

---

[4]By contrast, in the ordinary case where no prior consensual relationship has occurred, an employee does have the right to expect that her employer will feel the same about her—or at least treat her the same—if she declines his sexual advances.

[5]In their reply brief, the defendants have argued that Ms. Keppler could not show a causal connection between her rejection of Dr. Miller and Dr. Miller's later negative comments about her. In support of this argument, they point to two occurrences in June, 1986, after the rejection but before the negative comments began, which suggest that Dr. Miller became annoyed with Ms. Keppler for purely professional reasons. Although this argument would have had force, this court cannot consider it. For the defendants failed to include the June events in their Rule 12(1) statement of materials facts not in dispute, and thereby deprived Ms. Keppler the opportunity to address these facts in her response to the summary judgment motion.

[6]Had Ms. Keppler presented evidence that Dr. Miller threatened her with reprisals if she declined his efforts to continue their sexual relationship, he still could have argued that it was her rejection of him, not her rejection of sex, that motivated his subsequent actions. In that case, however, it would have been for the jury to resolve the matter.

[7]Ms. Keppler attempts to distinguish *Huebschen* on the grounds that in that case there was no evidence that, after the consensual relationship ended, the defendant made further requests for sexual favors. Yet, the presence or absence of a specific request could not have served as the basis for the Seventh Circuit's ruling since, as the district court held, there was evidence supporting the jury's verdict that the plaintiff's "refusal to continue a sexual relationship motivated the decision to fire him." *Huebschen* v. *Department of Health & Social Services,* 547 F.Supp. 1168, 1176 [32 FEP Cases 1521] (N.D. Ill. 1982), *rev'd,* 716 F.2d 1167 [32 FEP Cases 1582] (7th Cir. 1983). Whether explicit or implicit, a desire to continue a prior consensual relationship is not, on its own, an impermissible basis for personnel action under Title VII.

Huebschen v. Department of Health & Social Services,[90] discussed at length and with some uneasiness in *Keppler,* is difficult to square with the majority of soured romance decisions.[91] *Babcock v. Frank* may reflect a trend to confine the *Huebschen* holding to its facts.[92]

BABCOCK v. FRANK

729 F. Supp. 279, 54 FEP Cases 1123
(S.D.N.Y. 1990)

ROBERT W. SWEET, District Judge:—Defendant Postmaster General Anthony Frank has moved pursuant to Rule 12(b)(1) and (6), Fed. R. Civ. P., for an order dismissing the Title VII action brought by plaintiff Kathryn D. Babcock ("Babcock") or, alternatively, for an order under Rule 56 granting defendant summary judgment. For the reasons set forth below, the motions for dismissal and summary judgment are denied. Defendant's request for additional relief denying Babcock's Title VII claim insofar as it seeks compensatory and punitive damages is granted.
• • •
Babcock is an employee of the United States Postal Service ("USPS"), of which Postmaster Frank is the chief officer. She was hired in January 1986 as a clerk typist and a postal operations associate. Babcock's assigned station has varied but the locale most relevant to this action is the Poughkeepsie, New York branch of the USPS.
• • •
The complaint pleads that commencing sometime in April 1988, Musso, a senior postal operations specialist who had participated in hiring Babcock and subsequently acted as her direct supervisor, made unwelcome sexual advances on Babcock (including unconsented and forcible touches, squeezes and kisses) and threatened Babcock with loss of her job if she did not submit to these sexual advances.

Although not stated in the complaint, the parties do not dispute that for a year or more prior to April 1988, Babcock and Musso had conducted a consensual physical relationship. The parties also agree that the relationship between Babcock and Musso continued in some fashion until July 4, 1988, when Babcock terminated it. She contends that prior to that time she sought to end the relationship, and apparently claims that, at least in certain instances, advances made by Musso during the period between April and July were unwelcome but that she succumbed to them, on occasion, because of Musso's threats, including job-related threats and promises.

Babcock also contends that in April she was subjected to harassment or mistreatment by other male USPS employees and that rather than attempting to discourage such conduct by taking effective disciplinary action against those employees, her supervisors discriminatorily issued her a "Letter of Warning ("LOW") in lieu of seven day suspension," asserting insubordination on her part. • • •

From July until September Babcock was posted to a separate USPS facility in Poughkeepsie and apparently had little or no contact with Musso and no trouble with other USPS employees. Upon Babcock's return in September to the unit in which she worked under

[90] 716 F.2d 1167, 32 FEP Cases 1582 (7th Cir 1983).
[91] *But see Trautvetter v. Quick,* 916 F.2d 1140, 54 FEP Cases 109 (7th Cir. 1990), the court relied on the *Huebschen* distinction to analyze the viability of the claim before it. *See also* Bohen v. City of E. Chicago, 799 F.2d 1180, 1185, 41 FEP Cases 1108 (7th Cir. 1986)(dictum)("It is a good defense if the employer can show that the harassment suffered by the plaintiff was directed at the plaintiff because of factors personal to her and not because she is a woman.")
[92] *But see Trautvetter v. Quick, supra* note 91, where the plaintiff failed to establish a quid pro quo case, in part because she was not "affirmatively or constructively discharged" and because she failed to show her supervisor's "sexual advances infringed in some manner upon her ability to obtain a promotion or other job-related benefit."

Musso's supervision, however, Musso again allegedly subjected her to harassment. According to Babcock, Musso made repeated entreaties and threats to her, at work, pressuring her to resume their relationship; Babcock rejected his advances and strove to dissuade him from continuing to inquire into her personal life; and Musso, in reaction to her resistance, threatened her that he would not take such treatment from a woman and that if she did not watch out he would destroy her career.

Musso followed up on his threat on September 19, 1988, when he issued Babcock a "Letter of Warning in lieu of a fourteen day suspension" predicated on an incident of insubordination. The LOW was issued after Musso consulted with his supervisors at the USPS facility, Peter Morrissey and Robert Corcoran, concerning what disciplinary action could appropriately be taken. Upon receiving the letter, Babcock told Musso that whatever he did to her, she would not go to bed with him and that she intended to defend herself by airing the truth. • • •

• • • Following further investigation, on October 24, 1988, Musso was given written notice of his proposed removal from the Postal Service for violation of USPS policy on sexual harassment. The notice indicated that Musso had issued a LOW against Babcock, based on an incident he had fabricated, for the purpose of harassing her in retaliation for having cut off their relationship.[3]

Prior to Musso's proposed removal, Babcock claims that she was advised by Corcoran in early October of management's decision to detail her out of her postal operations association position and into another position which she did not request and which was outside her career path. She states that Corcoran and Morrissey proposed this job assignment in reprisal for her not tolerating sexual harassment from their co-worker Musso; that Morrissey had told her that if she filed EEOC charges against Musso she would be hurting her career and would not be promoted; and that because of her complaints about Musso and others, Corcoran had unfairly concluded that she had "interrelationship problems" and should not be posted to assignments that involved working with male USPS employees.
• • •

Title VII Sexual Harassment and the Consensual Sexual Relationship

USPS contends that Babcock's claim must be dismissed because Babcock consented to Musso's advances. • • •

The parties here agree that Babcock and Musso had a consensual sexual relationship prior to April 1988 and Babcock does not assert that Musso's conduct prior to then gives rise to any Title VII violation. USPS does not attempt to negate by affidavit or otherwise Babcock's pleaded allegations that Musso at times thereafter made physical and verbal sexual advances that were unwelcome, not consented to nor condoned by Babcock nor that Musso told Babcock that he would fire her or prevent her career advancement of [at] USPS if she did not accede to his advances. These allegations, which for present purposes must be taken as true, plainly suffice to establish the element of Babcock's claim that the sexual harassment was unwelcome.

No more persuasive is USPS' contention that the complaint is subject to dismissal because it pleads harassment based not on the "sex" of the employee but rather, predicates it on a prior consensual sexual relationship between supervisor and employee. • • •
• • •

Title VII has been held to provide protection against • • • *quid pro quo* conduct and that protection ought not be withdrawn merely upon a showing that the victim of harassment had in the past entered into a consensual sexual relationship with the perpetrator. While

---

　　[1,2][Omitted.]

　　[3]The proposed removal was confirmed by letter on December 5, 1988. After appealing the decision to the Merit Systems Procedure [Protection] Board, Musso settled the appeal on June 28, 1989 by agreeing to a three grade demotion in lieu of removal and to assignment to another facility. In addition, Musso was placed on a non-pay, non-duty status during December 17, 1988 to July 3, 1989 that was deemed a period of suspension without pay.

USPS offers *Huebschen v. Dept. of Health & Human Services,* 716 F.2d 1167, 1169 1172 [32 FEP Cases 1582] (7th Cir. 1983), for this proposition, in that case plaintiff made no showing that he had been threatened by his supervisor with job-related consequences if he did not continue with or resume their relationship, as Babcock alleges here. As stated in *Keppler v. Hinsdale Township H.S. Dist. 86,* 715 F.Supp. 862, 868 [50 FEP Cases 295] (N.D. Ill. 1989), "[t]he [*Huebschen*] court could not have meant that an employer who has engaged in consensual copulation with an employee may thereafter demand it as a condition of retaining benefits." It need only be added that to the extent that such a conclusion is within the intendment of *Huebschen,* its reasoning is not binding on this court.

The Court of Appeals' decision in *Carrero v. New York City Housing Authority* confirms that an employer who exacts a penalty because of his employee's rejection of his initial sexual advances commits illegal sex-based discrimination cognizable under Title VII. *Carrero,* 890 F.2d 569, slip op. at 15, 20. To the same logical degree, "[a]n employer who threatens a penalty if the employee will not *continue* the physical relationship is using gender as the basis for job benefits," *Keppler,* 715 F.Supp. at 868 (emphasis added). To assume as a matter of law that the latter is discrimination predicated not on the basis of gender, "but on the basis of the failed interpersonal relationship," *see Keppler,* 715 F.Supp. at 869, is as flawed a proposition under Title VII as the corollary that "ordinary" sexual harassment does not violate Title VII when the employer's asserted purpose is the establishment of a "new interpersonal relationship." Under either scenario, it is the sexually coercive and unwelcome nature of the employer's behavior, directed at a member of the opposite sex, that gives rise to the violation.

The allegations that Babcock's supervisor Musso implored her to love him again and that he couldn't stand seeing her without being intimate with her, when coupled with his contemporaneous threat to destroy her career at the USPS and his subsequent issuance of a disciplinary letter against her, are more than sufficient to raise an inference in a reasonable person that Musso intended to use—and did use—his supervisorial authority to blackmail Babcock into again accepting his sexual advances. Those allegations comprise a claim of *quid pro quo* sexual harassment. Babcock, after ending her relationship with Musso, "had the right, like any other worker, to be free from a sexually abusive environment, and to reject her employer's sexual advances without threat of punishment." *Keppler,* 715 F.Supp. at 869. Nothing in *DeCintio* or *Huebschen* compels dismissal of Babcock's claims on grounds that she previously had engaged in a consensual relationship with Musso.

The final matter to be considered is USPS' suggestion that Babcock failed to state a claim of hostile environment sexual harassment, because she has not alleged offensive behavior "sufficiently severe or pervasive 'to alter the working environment.' " *Vinson,* 477 U.S. at 67 (quoting *Henson v. City of Dundee,* 682 F.2d 897, 904 [29 FEP Cases 787] (11th Cir. 1982)). • • •

• • •

Here, Babcock, in her complaint and in her affidavit, states that while she finally terminated the relationship with Musso on July 4, 1988, she felt to compelled to continue the relationship from some point in April until this time under the pressure of job-related threats by Musso. In addition, she pleads that Musso repeatedly threatened and harassed her in September when she returned to their common worksite that month. Moreover, the USPS, in the course of disciplining Musso, itself indicated in correspondence that his conduct had subjected Babcock to sexual harassment that had deleteriously impacted upon Babcock's work environment. Clearly, as pleaded, Babcock's allegations could convince a reasonable person that her working environment satisfied the requisite level of severity or pervasiveness set forth in *Vinson.*

Conclusion

For the above reasons, USPS' motion for dismissal or, in the alternative, for summary judgment must be denied. Babcock's demand for compensatory and punitive damages shall be deemed stricken from the complaint.

It is so ordered.

3. Coerced Submission Cases

In a "coerced submission" case, the complainant submits to unwelcome sexual advances because of physical, psychological or economic duress. The coerced employee might claim that economic vulnerability permitted a supervisor to prey upon her financial need to extract sexual favors.[93]

According to the EEOC, a coerced employee could prevail on a theory of quid pro quo sexual harassment, even though no job detriment has affected that employee.[94] More likely, however, the coerced employee would rely on a hostile environment harassment theory. As *Thoreson v. Penthouse International Magazine* illustrates, complainants need not necessarily rely on explicit coercion; implicit economic duress may suffice.

THORESON V. PENTHOUSE INTERNATIONAL MAGAZINE, LTD.

563 N.Y.S.2d 968, 55 EPD ¶40,457
(New York Supreme Court 1990)

WILK, J.: Plaintiff brought this action against defendants Penthouse International, Ltd. and Robert Guccione to recover damages for fraud, misrepresentation, unjust enrichment, quantum meruit, breach of contract, prima facie tort, intentional infliction of emotional harm and sexual harassment. Plaintiff also seeks an accounting.

[Background Facts]

Penthouse International, Ltd. is the publisher of Penthouse Magazine. Guccione is the founder, chairman and principal shareholder of Penthouse International, Ltd.

Plaintiff, Marjorie Thoreson, worked for Penthouse under the name Anneka diLorenzo from 1973 until 1980. She grew up in St. Paul, Minnesota. When she was twelve or thirteen, her parents were involved in a bitter divorce. When she was fifteen, plaintiff travelled to Los Angeles to seek her fortune. While in California, she had some minor brushes with the law. She found work as a cocktail waitress, a topless dancer, and a receptionist. She also studied acting and entered beauty contests. She did some work as a model and as an actress.

In 1973, she was impressed by a television interview of Guccione and sent some test photos to Penthouse. Guccione met with her in Los Angeles, after which he agreed to make her Penthouse Pet of the Month for September. Plaintiff was flown to New York and then to London, where she was photographed by Guccione. While in London, they became intimate. She was twenty years old.

---

[93]*See, e.g.,* Chamberlin v. 101 Realty, 915 F.2d 777, 54 FEP Cases 101 (1st Cir. 1990)(assessment of welcomeness issue must consider that complainant may "reasonably perceive" that protest will prompt her dismissal, especially when sexual overtures are made by owner of firm); Phillips v. Smalley Maintenance Servs., 711 F.2d 1524, 32 FEP Cases 975 (11th Cir. 1983)(proper to consider that alleged harasser knew plaintiff financially depended on job to make house payments and used this as basis to demand she demonstrate gratitude with sexual favors); Babcock v. Frank, 729 F. Supp. 279, 287–88, 54 FEP Cases 1123 (S.D.N.Y. 1990)(complainant stated claim with allegation that she was coerced by job-related threats of her supervisor into continuing sexual conduct that was no longer consensual). *Cf.* EEOC Policy Guidance on Sexual Harassment, 8 FAIR EMPL. PRAC. MAN. (BNA) 405:6685 (March 19, 1990), reproduced in Appendix 3 (victims may fear economic repercussion from complaining about the harassment).

[94]*See* EEOC Policy Guidance on Employer Liability for Sexual Favoritism, 8 FAIR EMPL. PRAC. MAN. (BNA) 405:6818 n.7 (Jan. 12, 1990), reproduced in Appendix 2. *See also* Meritor Sav. Bank v. Vinson, *supra* note 77.

Plaintiff told defendant that she aspired to a career as an actress. Defendant assured her that he would use his contacts to assist her. After about one week in London, they returned to New York. In June, 1973, plaintiff returned to Los Angeles. While in the taxi to the airport, plaintiff signed a management agreement with Penthouse.

It appears that the agreement was unique in the world of "pets." The agreement generally provided that Penthouse would guide Thoreson in her career in the entertainment field. The contract noted plaintiff's inexperience and unfamiliarity with the entertainment area and her need for "supervised guidance and specialized training to develop her talents." Penthouse agreed to act as Thoreson's personal representative, general advisor and to use its best efforts to supervise, guide and direct her career. Penthouse was to assist plaintiff in the selection of suitable roles and projects in furtherance of her career in public entertainment. In exchange, plaintiff granted defendants exclusive control over her career and exclusive rights to commissions. In addition, plaintiff executed a power of attorney to allow Penthouse to handle her finances and to receive payments on her behalf.

Plaintiff was soon contacted by defendant to appear in Viva, a magazine published by Guccione. She appeared on the cover of the December issue.

Plaintiff also accepted an opportunity to do a fall, 1973 promotion tour for Penthouse and Viva. She returned to Los Angeles after the tour.

In 1974, she took acting lessons, paid for by Penthouse, and made several promotional appearances for Penthouse. She also urged Guccione to hasten her acting career. Guccione agreed to make her Pet of the Year for 1975 and invited her to live with him in New York. In the spring of 1975, she moved into Guccione's house, where she was given a small room of her own. She did a Penthouse promotional tour after the 1975 Pet of the Year issue, which was followed by an international tour for the United States Department of Defense.

As Pet of the Year, plaintiff was to receive prizes valued at $50,000. She claims that value of what she received was considerably less than that.

[Movie Opportunity]

• • • In 1976, she began to hear about the movie Caligula, which was being produced by Penthouse. Plaintiff claims that defendant led her to believe that she might play Caligula's wife. To prepare herself to the role, at Guccione's urging, she had surgery to enlarge her breasts.

While plaintiff was recuperating from the surgery, defendant told her that Caligula's director had hired another actress to play Caligula's wife. He promised to find plaintiff another role in the film.

In the spring of 1976, plaintiff flew to Rome, where Caligula was being filmed. She made a minor appearance and returned to New York. • • •

Guccione returned to the set in January, 1977, with plaintiff and other Penthouse pets • • •. One scene graphically captured plaintiff performing oral sex on a man. The second showed plaintiff and Penthouse pet Lori Wagner having sex with each other. Plaintiff claims to have performed in the scenes reluctantly and only after having been persuaded that it would further her career.

Plaintiff returned to Rome in the spring of 1977 to do the movie Messalina, in which she had the starring role. • • •

Plaintiff returned to New York in 1978 and • • • spoke to Mr. Polenco of the William Morris Agency about working as her agent. She auditioned for the lead in Raging Bull but did not get the part. The agency never contacted her again.

[Affairs With Business Associates]

In 1978, Guccione told plaintiff that he was upset because his London based financial advisor was not spending enough time in the United States. He told plaintiff to seduce the advisor and to encourage him to move to this country. Plaintiff refused. Defendant insisted that plaintiff do so because it was important to him and to the Penthouse empire. Plaintiff capitulated. Her sexual affair with the financial advisor, carried on during his periodic trips to New York, and guided by Guccione, lasted eighteen months.

In the summer of 1980, defendant encountered difficulty in raising money to open a gambling casino in Atlantic City. Defendant asked plaintiff to sleep with a furniture manufacturer from Milan, who, defendant believed, could assist him with this venture. Plaintiff refused. Defendant told her that she had to do it because she owed him. She did.

Caligula was released in 1980. Promotions were done by plaintiff and Guccione. Defendant told plaintiff that he wanted her to promote *Caligula* in Japan. Plaintiff refused because her experience on the United States promotional tour had been humiliating. Defendant refused to discuss plaintiff's reluctance to go. Plaintiff did not go, as a consequence of which she was fired. She never did another film.

With the exception of sexual harassment, I am not persuaded that plaintiff should prevail on any of her causes of action. I believe that defendants tried to promote plaintiff's career as a performer. It is not clear that defendants beckoned plaintiff down an unwanted path or that her acting talent was intentionally subordinated to any of her other attributes. In addition, plaintiff has failed to prove that she was wrongfully denied any of the prizes to which she was entitled by virtue of her selection as Pet of the Year.

[Harrassment Claim]

I do, however, find in plaintiff's favor on her sexual harassment claim.

The New York State Human Rights Law provides that any person "aggrieved by an unlawful discriminatory practice shall have a cause of action in any court of appropriate jurisdiction for damages . . ." Exec. Law §297(9). See *Murphy v. American Home Products Corp.,* [31 EPD ¶33,607] 58 NY2d 293, 307 (1983). Actions of an employer which discriminate against an individual in the "terms, conditions, or privileges of employment" because of that person's sex are encompassed within the ambit of actionable wrongs under this section. • • • This provision, like other civil rights statutes containing similar language, has been interpreted to prohibit acts of sexual harassment in the workplace. • • • Plaintiff's cause of action based on her claim of sexual harassment is, therefore, cognizable under Executive Law §297(9).

Under the Human Rights Law ("HRL"), an employer is prohibited from exploiting a dominant position of power in the workplace by imposing sexual demands upon an employee as an implicit condition of continued employment. Any attempt by an employer to use the terms, conditions or privileges of employment to coerce an employee, targeted 'on' the basis of gender, to agree to participate in sexual activity [is] a form of sex discrimination outlawed by state law. Proof of such discriminatory conduct on the part of an employer suffices to trigger liability under the Executive Law. *See Cullen v. Nassau County Civil Service Commission* [29 EPD ¶32,792] 53 NY2d 492, 496-497 (1981). The employee need not prove that he or she resisted the abuse or refused to comply with the sexual demands, see *Meritor Savings Bank v. Vinson,* [40 EPD ¶36,159] 477 U.S. 57 (1986); *Rudow, supra,* 123 Misc. 2d at 718, quoting *Bundy v. Jackson,* [24 EPD ¶31,439] 641 F2d 934, 945 (D.C. Cir., 1981); that tangible job benefits were lost, *id.; cf. Crookston v. Brown,* 140 AD2d 868 (3rd Dept., 1988); or that the discriminatory conduct was intentional. See *Cullen, supra.* Those issues, relating to the harm suffered by the employee and the relative offensiveness of the employer's actions, are factors in determining the appropriate remedy. *Id.;* see also *Batavia Lodge v. Division of Human Rights,* 35 NY2d 143 (1974).

The credible evidence reveals that defendant Guccione utilized his employment relationship with plaintiff to coerce her to participate in sexual activity with the furniture manufacturer and with his financial advisor in order to advance his business. He compelled plaintiff to continue the relationship with his advisor, which he helped to choreograph, for a period of eighteen months.

Plaintiff's testimony concerning these matters was contraverted only by defendant Guccione's blanket denial that the events took place. I do not believe him.

[Compensatory Damages]

Because plaintiff capitulated to the demands of her employer, she was not discharged. Proof of compensatory damages was comprised of her testimony about the emotional impact of these experiences. The statute authorizes the awarding of compensatory damages for plaintiffs' subjective mental suffering, on her testimony alone. See *Cullen v. Nassau County Civil Service Commission,* 53 NY2d at 497; *Batavia Lodge v. Division of Human Rights,* 35 NY2d at 146-47. As compensatory damages, plaintiff is awarded $60,000.

[Punitive Damages]

In addition to compensatory damages, which are designed exclusively to redress actual injury, plaintiff requests punitive damages.

Although punitive damages may not be available under the HRL to a party who seeks redress before the Human Rights Division, as Justice Harold Baer observed in his well-reasoned decision in *Seitzman v. Hudson River Association,* 143 Misc.2d 1068 (Sup. Ct., N.Y. Co., 1989), they may be imposed in a judicial proceeding. • • •

An award of exemplary damages is traditionally available under the common law where "the plaintiff proves sufficiently serious misconduct on the defendant's part ..." *Smith v. Wade,* 461 US 30, 82 (1983), quoting D. Dobbs, Law of Remedies 204 (1973). • • • The function or purpose of punitive damages is to

> act as a deterrent to the offender "and to serve as a warning to others. They are intended as punishment for gross misbehavior for the good of the public and have been referred to as 'a sort of hybrid between a display of ethical indignation and the imposition of a criminal fine.' [citations omitted.] Punitive damages are allowed on the grounds of public policy.... The damages may be considered expressive of the community attitude towards one who willfully and wantonly causes hurt, or injury to another" (citations omitted). *Id.* at 203.

• • • One category of misconduct which implicates the public interest, in which punitive damages are often upheld, is "where persons in positions of power or authority wantonly misuse their authority," or betray a "relationship involving a public trust." *Id.* at 59. This is particularly true where sexual abuse is involved. Id.; see *Micari v. Mann,* 126 Misc 2d 422 (S. Ct., NY Co., 1984). Such misconduct, by its nature, "causes incalculable injury to society as well as private interests." *Laurie Marie M.,* 159 AD2d at 60.

An award of punitive damages under Exec. Law §297(9) is a particularly appropriate response to flagrant acts of discrimination. • • • An employer's prejudicial abuse of his authority to coerce sexual compliance on the part of an employee, is an egregious violation of equality principles and of a relationship in which the public has, by virtue of the HRL, demonstrated strong interest. Plaintiff's legal action, by its nature, serves the dual purpose of enabling her to vindicate her individual rights and to promote "the good of the public" by advancing society's interest in enforcing statutory proscriptions against discrimination. *Home Insurance Co.,* 75 NY2d at 203.

[Intentional Discrimination]

• • • The cold and calculating use of [Guccione's] authority as plaintiff's employer, in precisely the manner deemed by the legislature to be harmful to society, affects a public trust. Because that abuse of power within a protected relationship entailed sexual coercion, it is precisely the sort of extreme misconduct that would justify the imposition of punitive damages even under traditional common law principles.[1] *Cf.* PL §§135.60; 230.30(1).

Protection for the societal interests implicated by defendant's conduct is suggested not only by the traditional punitive damages doctrine, but by the HRL itself. The statute has

---

[1]The wrong committed by defendants in this case, statutorily defined as employment discrimination, also constitutes tortious conduct under the common-law theory of intentional infliction of emotional harm. See *Micari v. Mann, supra; Ford v. Revlon, Inc.,* 153 Ariz. 38, 734 P2d 580 (Ariz Sup. Ct., 1987). There is

long been interpreted, primarily in the context of adjudications by the State Division of Human Rights, to require consideration of these public-oriented principles in determining the appropriate remedy for acts of employment discrimination.

The HRL confers upon the State Division of Human Rights "broadly stated policy-laden discretion," in providing an appropriate remedy for acts of discrimination, in order to effectively "combat the pernicious effects of the outlawed evils." *Cullen v. Nassau County Civil Service Commission,* 53 NY2d at 496. • • •

• • •

The statutory expansion of the remedial powers usually available enables the State Division, in awarding compensatory damages, to hold an employer liable for the mental distress shown to have been suffered by the plaintiff as a result of the act of discrimination.[2] Neither actual intent to cause emotional distress, nor intent to discriminate, need be proved. The statute charges the guilty employer with the duty to foresee the mental and emotional consequences that could flow from his or her conduct.

• • •

Given the public policy aims of the HRL, which mirror the dual functions served by punitive damages—retribution and deterrence—plaintiff is entitled to punitive damages to the extent calculated to reflect the community's outrage and moral indignation, and to protect "the public good" by attempting, through deterrence, to eradicate such conduct. • • •

[Balancing of Interests]

• • •

In order to fix punitive damages, we must, in light of these principles, assess the nature of defendants' conduct, the harm caused, and the degree to which the conduct offends principles of justice. The award must be consistent with the wrong committed and the defendant's financial condition, and sufficient to punish the defendant and to act as an effective deterrent against the commission of such acts in the future. • • • Evaluation of the harm caused, and the extent to which "the wrong complained of is morally culpable," • • • is guided by the policy embodied in the prohibitions against employment discrimination generally, and sexual harassment in particular.

• • •

The coercive use of power by an employer to exact sexual compliance from an employee severely undermines the Human Rights Law guarantee of equal treatment. *Cf. Skinner v. Oklahoma,* 316 US 535 (1942); *Loving v. Virginia,* 388 US 1 (1967). Defendant's subjugation of plaintiff through the use of sexual coercion forced her to safeguard her employment by sacrificing her body. In so doing, she surrendered one of the most private and intimate aspects of her personal liberty. See *People v. Onofre,* 51 NY2d 476 (1980), cert. den., 451 US 987 (1981). Unquestionably, "[s]exual harassment in the workplace is among the most offensive, and demeaning torments an employee can undergo." • • • *cf. People v. Liberta,* 64 NY2d 152 (1984), cert. denied, 471 U.S. 1020 (1985). Unless eliminated, such conduct permits the employment structure to be permeated by attitudes and relationships which we have determined to be abhorrent. When female employees such as

---

no need, however, to address that overlapping legal claim. Under circumstances such as these, where relevant common-law tort theories are subsumed within the ban on sexual harassment, a statutorily-authorized judicial award of appropriate damages pursuant to Executive Law §297(9) will "fully redress the wrong committed." *Koerner v. State of New York,* 62 NY2d 442, 449 (1984).

[2]Under the common law, compensatory damages for mental distress are only available under certain circumstances, as in cases involving extreme misconduct. See Prosser and Keeton on Torts (5th Ed., 1984), ch. 2, §12. Under this standard, liability has often been imposed for insult and indignity inflicted by persons in positions of power or responsibility with respect to the public. *Id.* at pp. 57-59; or, "the extreme and outrageous nature of the conduct may arise not so much from what is done as from abuse by the defendant of some relation or position which gives the defendant actual or apparent power to damage the plaintiff's interests. The result is something like extortion." *Id.* at 61. The statute protects employees from acts of extortion motivated by prejudice, and the insult and indignity perpetrated by employers who discriminate. Compensatory damages are available for mental distress caused by every employment discrimination case, as long as the emotional harm is proved.

[3][Omitted.]

plaintiff are allowed to be confronted by sexual coercion on the job, women as a group are relegated to a subordinate status.

For these reasons, Guccione's request for sexual compliance, by itself, constitutes an act of sexual harassment,[4] without regard to plaintiff's response. Defendants' attempt at sexual extortion entailed precisely the type of insult and indignity that the statute is designed to eradicate. (See fn.2, *supra*). Forcing plaintiff, because she is female, to choose between her right to liberty (body and personal integrity) and property (the right to earn a living) is per se discriminatory. As employers who, abused their dominant status by forcing a female employee to choose between compromising either her job or her personal dignity, defendants are guilty of attempting to reduce plaintiff, because of her sex, into a position of servitude.

In this case, defendants' attempt at sexual extortion or coercion was successful. See also *Meritor Savings Bank v. Vinson,* 477 US 57 (1986). Defendant, by requiring plaintiff to participate, over her protestations, in sexual relationships with the salesman and the financial advisor, engaged in conduct that was reprehensible. *Cf. Micari v. Mann, supra.* It was aggravated by his insistence that plaintiff maintain one of the relationships for a year and a half, under his direct supervision. Defendant's ability to coerce plaintiff, her vulnerability to his dominating influence as her employer, and the nature of the behavior that he required, make the imposition of substantial punitive damages even more important.

[Mitigation of Damages]

The offensiveness of defendants' conduct is not mitigated by the fact that plaintiff's job as a model and actress for Penthouse involved, in part, the commercial exploitation of her physical appearance. Sexual slavery was not a part of her job description. The fact that a plaintiff accepted employment which exploited her sexuality does not constitute a waiver of her right to be free from sexual harassment in the workplace. *Cf. State Division of Human Rights v. New York State Department of Correctional Services,* [17 EPD ¶8362] 61 AD2d 25, 28-29 (4th Dept., 1978); People v. Liberta, 64 NY2d at 163-64. • • •

To ensure that the size of a damages award is reasonable as punishment and effective as a deterrent, a final inquiry must be made concerning the net worth of each defendant. See *Rupert v. Sellers,* 48 AD2d 265 (4th Dept. 1975). • • • The relative wealth of the defendants must be considered in fixing punitive damages, because

> [i]f the purpose of, punitive damages is to punish and to act as a deterrent, ... [u]nless [they] are of sufficient substance to "smart," the offender in effect purchases a right to [harm] another for a price which may have little or no effect upon him. Indeed, in such a situation a defendant, instead of being deterred from repetition of his offense, may be encouraged to renew his assault.

Reynolds v. Pegler, 123 F. Supp. 36, 41-42 (S.D.N.Y., 1954) aff'd, 223 F2d 479 (2nd Cir., 1955), cert. denied, 350 US 845 (1955). • • •

The parties have stipulated, for purposes of this action, that defendant Penthouse International possesses assets with a market value of $200 million, and that defendant Guccione's net worth is $150 million. These figures supply the subjective framework within which an appropriate award must be measured.

• • •

Accordingly, plaintiff is awarded four million ($4,000,000) dollars in punitive damages. This constitutes the decision and judgment of the court.

---

[4]The statute removes sexual advances or solicitation by an employer from the traditional rule that "there is no harm in asking." *Mitran v. Williamson,* 21 Misc 2d 106, 107 (Sup. Ct. Kings County, 1960), quoting 49 Harv. L. Rev. 1033; 1055. Between strangers, it may be true that "[m]ere words cannot amount to an assault," *Prince v. Ridge,* 32 Misc 666, 667 (Sup. Ct., Queens County, 1900), and even if they did, not all assaults give rise to damages to compensate for any "insult and indignity" and mental suffering caused. *Id.* Under the HRL, by contrast, if an employer used his or her status "to induce [an employee] to grant him the favor of sexual intercourse with her," he is guilty of sexual discrimination, and is liable for compensatory damages for the mental suffering caused. *Id.*

B. Gender-Based Animosity

Sexual harassment reflecting gender-based animosity resembles harassment based on race or national origin.[95] The hostile behavior often arises when women enter male-dominated jobs or workplaces.[96] If sufficiently severe or pervasive, gender-based animosity is actionable because it is conduct that would not occur *but for* the sex of the complainant. Behavior motivated by gender-based animosity usually takes one of two forms: (1) hostile conduct of a sexual nature (gender baiting), or (2) nonsexual hazing based on gender. The conduct complained of can be clearly sexual in nature,[97] clearly nonsexual in nature,[98] or, as is more common, both sexual and nonsexual in nature.[99] The harasser can be a supervisor, a co-worker, or both.[100]

1. Gender Baiting

Other than unwelcome sexual advances, gender baiting is the easiest form of behavior to recognize as sex-based conduct, for the behavior aims to make life unpleasant for women employees because they are women.[101] Gender baiting can take the form of speech or action.[102] Words directed specifically at women may "deriv[e] their power to wound not only from their meaning but also from 'the disgust and violence they express phonetically.' "[103] *Morris*

---

[95]*See* Section I.B. *supra.*

[96]See Chapter 7, Harassment by Co-Workers, Section I.

[97]*See, e.g.,* Morris v. American Nat'l Can Corp., 730 F. Supp. 1489, 52 FEP Cases 210 (E.D. Mo. 1989), reproduced *infra.*

[98]*See, e.g.,* McKinney v. Dole, *supra* note 78, 765 F.2d at 1139, 38 FEP Cases at 371–72 (acts of physical aggression properly considered); Laughinghouse v. Risser, *supra* note 79 (aggressive management style directed especially at complainant).

[99]*See, e.g.,* Hall v. Gus Constr. Co., 842 F.2d 1010, 46 FEP Cases 573 (8th Cir. 1988), reproduced *infra;* Robinson v. Jacksonville Shipyards, 760 F. Supp. 1486 (M.D. Fla. 1991), reproduced *infra.*

[100]An employer's liability for hostile environment harassment may depend on the status of the alleged harasser. For a complete discussion of employer liability for harassment by supervisors, see Chapter 6, Harassment by Supervisors.

[101]*See, e.g.,* Arnold v. City of Seminole, 614 F. Supp. 853, 858, 40 FEP Cases 1539, 1545 (E.D. Okla. 1985)(patrol officer sent pictures of male genitals and package of condoms; picture of nude woman displayed with complainant's name on it, with message that women do not make good cops); Brown v. City of Guthrie, 22 FEP Cases 1627, 1629 (W.D. Okla. 1980)(police dispatcher asked to compare herself with nude women displayed in photographs kept in dispatcher's desk for policemen to view in their spare time).

[102]The use of general sexual terms or expletives, such as "fuck" and "fucking," may not amount to sexual conduct. However, general use of sexual terms or expletives may serve as evidence of the pervasiveness of other, clearly harassing, conduct. See State of Illinois v. Human Rights Comm'n, 178 Ill. App.3d 1033, 128 Ill. Dec. 141, 534 N.E.2d 161 (1989). The use of gender-specific terms, however, such as "cunt," "bitch," "twat," and "raggin' it," do constitute sexual conduct. *Id.* (conduct evidenced by constant use of offensive language directed to complainant over her objection created hostile work environment). *See also* Reynolds v. Atlantic City Convention Center, 53 FEP Cases 1852, 1864–65 (D.N.J. 1990)("but for the fact that plaintiff is a woman, she would not have been called a 'cunt' or 'douche bag cunt' ").

[103]Katz v. Dole, 709 F.2d 251, 254, 31 FEP Cases 1521 (4th Cir. 1983), reproduced in Chapter 7, Harassment by Co-Workers (citing C. MILLER & K. SWIFT, WORDS AND WOMEN 109 (1977)). *See also* Zabkowicz v. West Bend Co., 589 F. Supp. 780, 784, 35 FEP Cases 610 (E.D. Wis. 1984), *aff'd in relevant part,* 789 F.2d 540, 40 FEP Cases 1171 (7th Cir. 1986)(rejecting defendants' argument that display of pornographic drawings of women and use of sexual slurs such as "slut," "bitch," and "cunt" were not sex-based conduct, in that "sexually offensive conduct and language used would have been almost irrelevant and would have failed entirely in its crude purpose had the plaintiff been a man"). *See also* Bennett v. Corroon & Black Corp., 845 F.2d 104, 106, 46 FEP Cases 1329, 1331 (5th Cir. 1988)(affirming summary judgment for employer; while posting obscene cartoons bearing plaintiff's name in public men's room was, contrary

v. American National Can Corp. offers an extreme example of sexually explicit gender baiting.

MORRIS V. AMERICAN NATIONAL CAN CORP.

730 F. Supp. 1489, 52 FEP Cases 210
(E.D. Mo. 1989)

WILLIAM L. HUNGATE, District Judge:—This matter is before the Court to determine the merits of plaintiff's claims after a five-day bench trial.

Pursuant to Title VII of the Civil Rights Act of 1964, as amended, 42 U.S.C. §2000e, et seq., plaintiff, a female employee of defendant corporation, contends that she was subjected to unlawful sexual harassment by defendant supervisors and other employees, and that her complaints of the harassment were not effectively resolved, resulting in plaintiff's constructive discharge in March 1987. • • • Defendants counter they are not liable because (a) they had no notice or knowledge of problems encountered by plaintiff until she filed an administrative charge, and (b) once they had notice or knowledge of the problem(s), they took immediate steps to ameliorate the problems. Only Counts I through III of the amended complaint are now before the Court. • • •

Findings of Fact

1. Plaintiff Jacquelyn L. Morris is a female citizen of the United States. She has been employed by defendant corporation to work at its facility in Pevely, Missouri, known as the Foster-Forbes Glass Division ("Foster-Forbes").
   • • •
3. Plaintiff has worked as a machinist (or mold-maker) in the mold department at Foster-Forbes from on or about April 13, 1981, through March 30, 1987, the effective date of her resignation. • • •
4. During the period prior to April 1986, plaintiff was one of only two females in the mold department. After April 1986, she was the only female in that department. Since 1984, the mold department has had a total of either eleven or twelve employees in it.
5. Since 1983, defendant David Scott has been the Manager of Forming Operations at Foster-Forbes. He was the immediate supervisor of defendant Glenn Besore during the relevant time period.
6. During the relevant time period, defendant Glenn Besore was the Supervisor of Mold Repair at Foster-Forbes. In this position, Mr. Besore was the immediate supervisor of plaintiff and other mold department employees. • • •
7. • • • Plaintiff timely filed this lawsuit after receiving her right-to-sue letter.
8. The credible testimony establishes that between 1984 and July 16, 1986, plaintiff was subjected to the following conduct by defendant Scott: Mr. Scott commented on more than one occasion that plaintiff "had a nice ass" and that "he'd like to have a piece of that." Additionally, Mr. Scott touched plaintiff's buttocks on occasion. While Mr. Scott denied these statements and acts, the denials are not clearly credible since other employees testified to seeing such conduct. This conduct did not continue after the filing of plaintiff's first administrative charge.
9. The credible evidence establishes that between 1984 and July 14, 1986, plaintiff was subjected to the following conduct by defendant Besore: On more than one occasion, Mr. Besore would make comments such as "did[n't] you get any last night," "do you spit or swallow," or "you have the whitest teeth I ever came across." The latter two comments

---

to trial court's finding, clearly sex-based, it was isolated incident and, therefore, not severe or pervasive enough to alter conditions of plaintiff's employment), *cert. denied,* 109 S.Ct. 1140 (1989); Walker v. Ford Motor Co., 684 F.2d 1355, 1359, 29 FEP Cases 1259, 1260–61 (11th Cir. 1982)(rejecting arguments that use of racist language common in South or in car dealerships, *i.e.,* "nigger-rigged" is not race-based).

were reported to be punch lines from dirty jokes related in the mold department. Plaintiff thought they were references to oral sex acts. Additionally, Mr. Besore would make references to plaintiff's weight, her "big butt" or her "boobs." During one staff meeting, Mr. Besore responded to plaintiff's inquiry about where she should sit by moving plaintiff's head down while saying something to the effect that she "might as well sit underneath his desk since that's where everybody says you do your best work." On one occasion when plaintiff would not leave his office while he was in a meeting with a salesperson, Mr. Besore said to her something like: "You want to go out with [the salesperson] tonight? . . . You want to show him a good time or something?" Mr. Besore explained that he was trying to embarrass her into leaving his office rather than reprimanding her in front of the salesperson. Once Mr. Besore touched plaintiff's breasts and plaintiff responded by slapping him. On several occasions, Mr. Besore would tap plaintiff's and other employees' buttocks while remarking to the employees that they should get on with or back to their work.

10. Plaintiff was embarrassed or offended by these acts and comments but did not say anything about them to Mr. Besore, to Mr. Scott or to any other managerial staff at defendant corporation.

11. Before plaintiff filed the July 16, 1986, administrative charge, plaintiff received at or near her work station:

(a) a sausage with a note "bite me baby" (found in her purse on November 4, 1985);

(b) a clay replica of a penis with steel wool testicles and semen-like substance on it (found in her workbench on April 16, 1986);

(c) a welded figure of a man with a penis (found on an unknown date);

(d) a pair of women's underwear with a sanitary napkin having a reddish substance on it and with a note attached saying something like "Jackie have you lost this" (found hanging from the light at her workbench in March or April 1986);

(e) a pile of a substance described as "semen-like" (found on her toolbox on June 23, 1986);

(f) a picture of an erect penis (found on her toolbox on July 14, 1986); and

(g) "Playboy-type" pictures (found at her workbench about once or twice a week since 1984).

12. After her first administrative charge was filed on July 16, 1986, plaintiff received the following at or near her work station:

(a) the words "bitch" or "slut" written on her desk (found July 21, 1986);

(b) a large replica of an erect penis apparently made out of a stick and hard glue, along with a note saying: "Hey Jake [sic]—Heard ya got one in your pants the same size. I never knew, think we could get together.—Your Lesbian Friend" (found on her toolbox July 23, 1986);

(c) the words "Jackie blows heads" written on a shelf sign marking where equipment called "blowheads" were kept (found at first on August 7, 1986, and remained for approximately six days);

(d) a picture of a nude woman sitting on the edge of a bathtub and touching her breasts, with a note saying something like "You should be doing this instead of a man's job;"

(e) a cartoon reading "Half ton pickup" with the word "Jackie" written across the chest of the fat woman in the cartoon (found in late August 1986, posted on a bulletin board in the mold department);

(f) a cartoon of five men with handwritten words "Jackie," "suck me asshole," and "full of shit" added to the picture (found on bulletin board near plaintiff's workbench in October 1986);

(g) the words "slut" and "whore" written on a green welding screen (first discovered in October 1986 and remained for approximately one month); and

(h) a sign reading "Jackie—Attention! Because of the outbreak of A.I.D.S. you are no longer required to kiss the boss's ass" (found in mid-October 1986 on a bulletin board in the mold department).

13. Additionally, plaintiff was subject to the following incidents:

(a) in mid-August 1986, plaintiff discovered the wires to her radio had been cut;

(b) at the end of August 1986, plaintiff discovered the fan at her work station had been damaged so that it did not function;

(c) in early September 1986, someone had put black grease in her welding helmet;

(d) in early September 1986, her roller cabinet had been "locktighted" which required the breaking and replacement of the cabinet's lock to fix it;

(e) a few days thereafter, plaintiff noticed the cabinet had been dented;

(f) in early October 1986, plaintiff discovered someone had put a substance smelling like urine in the airline she used;

(g) in October 1986, plaintiff discovered on her toolbox a substance that looked to her like phlegm;

(h) on or about November 13, 1986, plaintiff found what she considered to be a semen-like substance on the chair at her workbench;

(i) sometime during November 1986, someone stole plaintiff's tools having an approximate value of $1000 to $1200;

(j) after the tools were taken, on November 24, 1986, plaintiff found a note saying "Mold shop missing tool relief fund & tax deduction (1986 only)" at her work station with a tin can having one cent in it; and

(k) during January 1987, one of her wooden toolboxes was stolen and on one occasion she was unable to stop employees from throwing cartridges ($1\text{-}^1/_2$" rolled and glued sandpaper) at her.

14. Promptly after each incident, except upon receipt of the stick and glue replica of a penis, plaintiff reported the incident to Mr. Besore and asked that he do something to stop the incidents. While Mr. Besore characterized some of the materials received by plaintiff as "sickening," Mr. Besore did not consider any of the incidents as sexual harassment or as anything more than horseplay and pranks to which a number of mold department employees were subjected. Occasionally, during his weekly staff meetings, he would mention that horseplay would not be tolerated. Once or twice, he mentioned to defendant Scott the existence of conflict among mold department employee. On occasion, he would advise Mick Oldham, Manager of Human Relations at Foster-Forbes, of problems with pranks in the mold department. Mr. Besore does not recall specifically describing to Mr. Scott or to Mr. Oldham the precise nature of the materials received by plaintiff, although he may have done so.

Mr. Besore was not present when plaintiff received the stick and glue replica of a penis. Upon learning of that item, Mr. Besore unsuccessfully asked certain employees if anyone knew who was responsible.

15. While plaintiff reported certain incidents (such as the substance found on her toolbox or a substance in her airline) to Mr. Scott, he was not aware until after receipt of the administrative charge of the sexual nature of some of the materials received by plaintiff. From the end of July 1986 to the date of the administrative hearing in December 1986, no sexual materials received by plaintiff were brought to Mr. Scott's attention by plaintiff or others.

16. Prior to the filing of the administrative charge in July 1986, plaintiff had not notified any supervisory personnel above Mr. Scott of the materials she received.

17. Due to Mr. Besore's absence, plaintiff reported the receipt of the stick and glue replica of a penis to William Barrett, the plant manager. Mr. Barrett intimated that such incidents would stop if plaintiff stopped antagonizing the other employees.

18. Mr. Scott and Mr. Besore usually responded to plaintiff's requests that something be done about the materials by telling plaintiff to clean up the material and/or return to her work. Mr. Besore and Mr. Scott noted the conduct might stop if she didn't let it bother her so much. Additionally, plaintiff was repeatedly advised nothing could be done without knowing who was responsible.

19. No person or persons were ever identified as being responsible for the conduct toward or materials left for plaintiff.

20. Defendants indicated that plaintiff may have antagonized other employees by visiting Mr. Besore's office frequently, in particular to answer or use the telephone, or by leaving unwanted scriptures at one employee's work station. Additionally, Mr. Besore opined that plaintiff had a tendency to complain a lot. Despite this and other occasional

incidents of plaintiff's relatively inappropriate behavior,[1] no one stated that plaintiff invited, instigated, or enticed the receipt of the materials she found or the conduct toward her.

21. After receipt of plaintiff's July 16, 1986, administrative charge, (a) Mr. Oldham asked Mr. Besore and Mr. Scott twice to respond to each of plaintiff's claims; (b) Mr. Besore removed from the plant any magazines from which pictures might be taken; (c) Mr. Oldham met with mold department employees and told them the horseplay and pranks had to stop; (d) Mr. Besore reportedly distributed and posted a memorandum in response to the "AIDS" notice; [(e)] the union shop committee's aid in discovering who was responsible for the items was solicited; and [(f)] the installation of a surveillance camera was suggested and rejected.

No managerial staff spoke directly with plaintiff about the basis for the charge.

22. It was not unusual in the mold department to hear dirty jokes or vulgar language; to "goose" other employees; to "grease" employee's chairs, vices, or gloves; to throw objects; to have piles of a substance (variously referred to as "phlegm," a semen-like substance, or "waterless hand cleaner") left at a work area; or to have cartoons referencing various employees posted on the bulletin board. At weekly meetings, management discussed the need to stop this horseplay for safety reasons.

23. From October 1986 to March 1987, plaintiff saw several doctors for "nervousness," "sleeplessness," blotches or welts on her legs and back, and an occasional inability to breath or difficulty breathing. At one doctor's suggestion, she remained away from work for two weeks and her symptoms improved. Two doctors suggested she resign. The company doctor who examined plaintiff prior to her return to work in March 1988 opined that her physical problems were most likely due to "interpersonal conflicts" at the mold department.

24. Plaintiff resigned on March 24, 1987, due to her physical problems; her feeling neither she nor her tools were protected at work; and her feeling no one would do anything to help her.

25. Mr. Scott meets with his supervisors, including Mr. Besore, each morning. Additionally, Mr. Scott makes it a usual practice to tour the mold department on a regular, almost daily basis. After receipt of the July 1986 administrative charge, Mr. Scott asked each of his supervisors, including Mr. Besore, to bring anything to his attention. When he asked Mr. Besore what was going on, Mr. Besore did not mention plaintiff's receipt of sexual materials.

26. No one was aware of any formal or informal company procedure by which an employee could pursue a claim of sexual harassment by co-employees or by supervisory personnel. Defendants intimated that plaintiff was familiar with and could have pursued a union grievance.

27. In April 1986, the other female employee in the mold department quit. At first, she stated she was quitting due to a need to care for her child. The company forms she completed stated she was quitting due to harassment.

28. The week before trial of this case began, there was posted in the men's room at Foster-Forbes a cartoon of a woman lying on her back with her legs spread open. "Jackie" was written on the cartoon.

29. One female employee reported that Mr. Besore had commented "boys will be boys" in a discussion with the witness about the replicas of the penises that plaintiff had received.

30. In the months just before plaintiff's resignation, plaintiff was not at work many days due to sick leave. Plaintiff was on sick leave from approximately February 18, 1987 to the effective date of her resignation.

• • •

36. During the relevant time, the defendant corporation did not have an express policy against sexual harassment or a grievance procedure independent of the policy and procedure in the collective bargaining agreements.

---

[1]Plaintiff called Mr. Besore a "fuzzball." She stated she was referring to a "curly perm" he had. Mr. Besore didn't know whether she was referring to that or to his alleged inability to deal with other employees in a manner plaintiff reportedly deemed appropriate. Once during an argument, plaintiff referred to another male employee as "dick breath." That nickname has stuck with that employee despite his disapproval of it. On occasion, plaintiff greased other employees' equipment.

Conclusions of Law

• • •

D. • • • To prevail on a hostile environment sexual harassment claim, plaintiff must establish:

(1) [plaintiff] belongs to a protected group, (2) [plaintiff] was subject to unwelcome sexual harassment, (3) the harassment was based on sex, (4) the harassment affected a "term, condition, or privilege" of employment, and (5) the employer [knew] or should have known of the harassment in question and failed to take proper remedial action.

• • •

Here, the parties do not dispute that, as a woman, plaintiff falls within a protected group. The parties dispute each of the other required elements.

E. The Court finds plaintiff was the subject of unwelcome sexual harassment from 1984 through her resignation in March 1987. To be unwelcome, the employee must not "solicit or invite it, and the [complaining] employee [must] regard[] the conduct as undesirable or offensive." *Moylan*, 792 F.2d at 749. While the nature of the work environment might be appropriate to consider, *see Hall*, 842 F.2d at 1017-18; *Perkins*, 709 F.Supp. at 1499, a ribald work environment should not excuse nor endorse sexually harassing conduct, *Hall*, 842 F.2d at 1017-18. Indeed, evidence of conduct toward those other than plaintiff may serve to establish the hostility of the environment. *Hall*, 842 F.2d at 1015. Accordingly, the environment in and of itself does not render harassing conduct "welcome."

The plaintiff's own behavior may, however, be indicative of whether or not the challenged conduct is "unwelcome." *Vinson*, 477 U.S. at 69 ("a complainant's sexually provocative speech or dress [is relevant] in determining whether he or she found particular sexual advances unwelcome"); *Jones v. Wesco Investment, Inc.*, 846 F.2d 1154, 1155 n.4 [46 FEP Cases 1431] (8th Cir. 1988). Here, there is no contention that plaintiff's manner of dress was sexually provocative. Rather, defendants rely on plaintiff's purported use of profane language; plaintiff's frequent use of a supervisor's office; and plaintiff's distribution of religious oriented materials and statements as provoking the challenged conduct at issue here. While the court cannot condone plaintiff's conduct in the workplace, the Court does not find such conduct sufficiently provocative of the materials and comments plaintiff endured. Plaintiff's use of profane language and the greasing of other employee's equipment could be part of plaintiff's efforts to fit in to the environment at hand. Such conduct, however, does not justify the harassing conduct plaintiff then endured. Importantly, no witnesses opined there was a relationship between what plaintiff did and the materials she received.

Finally, plaintiff expressed distaste for the items and materials she received, and expressed embarrassment at the language she endured from defendant Besore.

Accordingly, the Court finds the challenged conduct toward plaintiff and the materials plaintiff received were "unwelcome."

F. This Court also determines that the harassing conduct and materials were based on sex. Defendants here point out that some of the materials received by plaintiff and some of the conduct directed toward plaintiff were not sexual in nature. This, however, does not make the conduct irrelevant to the inquiry. So long as the Court finds "the incidents of harassment and unequal treatment . . . would not have occurred but for the fact" plaintiff was a woman, the Court may properly consider them in its analysis. *Hall*, 842 F.2d at 1014.

Here, the most offending conduct is clearly sexual in nature. The welded man with an erect penis, the hand-made models of penises, and the magazine pictures of a nude woman and of a penis, among other things, clearly have sexual overtones. The "slut," "did you get any last night," and "Jackie blows heads" references are clearly sexual in nature. The broken fans, radios, stolen tools, vandalized toolboxes, and the like, more likely than not were generated by the same animus that generated the note, "This is what you should be doing instead of a man's job." Defendants have not suggested that any male employee was subjected to a campaign of harassment comparable to that of plaintiff. The totality of the circumstances in the workplace, the pattern of harassment to which plaintiff was subjected, and its relatedness to the overtly sexual conduct, all indicate that the so-called non-sexual harassment more likely than not was due to plaintiff's sex. Thus, plaintiff has met the third element of the inquiry.

G. Furthermore, the harassment affected "a term, condition or privilege" of employment. In his report, the doctor selected by defendant corporation opined that plaintiff's allergic reactions, reactions acquired from 1985 and later years, were more probably due to interpersonal relationships at work than a reaction to a physical exposure to chemicals and other substances at the workplace. She became so ill that she ultimately left her employment. Thus, the conduct by Besore and others was consistent enough and pervasive enough to alter the conditions of plaintiff's employment.

The Court does not find, however, that defendant Scott's challenged conduct was sufficiently pervasive or severe to constitute actionable conduct.

H. Plaintiff has provided credible evidence of a sexually hostile environment by co-workers and defendant Besore at Foster-Forbes, Pevely, Missouri, between 1984 and March 1987. Plaintiff has established that she consistently advised her supervisor, Glenn Besore, about many individual incidents. While defendants urge plaintiff should have done more, it is not clear there was more she should do. The only grievance procedure available to her was in the relevant collective bargaining agreements, and that procedure does not clearly allow an individual employee to go beyond the first step without support of the local union shop committee. Moreover, neither the policy statement in the relevant collective bargaining agreements nor any other policy statement of defendant corporation expressly prohibited sexual harassment. The fact that Mr. Besore was incapable of communicating or unable to communicate to other supervisory personnel the actual nature of the materials and incidents should not excuse the employer's inattention to such materials and incidents.

I. Neither defendant corporation nor defendant Besore took remedial actions which were reasonably calculated to be effective in ending the harassment. *See Ways v. City of Lincoln,* 871 F.2d 750, 755 [49 FEP Cases 865] (8th Cir. 1989) (district court finding that employer's efforts were "not impressively effective" in ridding workplace of racially hostile language and incidents was not clearly erroneous). Those defendants unreasonably relied on plaintiff's co-workers to police themselves, although some among them were most likely culprits. Those defendants failed to interview plaintiff about the harassment. Those defendants apparently expected that occasional, mild rebukes of employees about "horseplay" and "pranks" would put a stop to what, in fact and law, was serious sexual harassment. It was particularly unreasonable for defendant corporation to leave Mr. Besore in a supervisory position over the mold department when he himself had engaged in sexually harassing conduct, and his efforts to stop the harassment of plaintiff were not effective over the course of two and one-half years. Most significantly, defendants' efforts were never completely effective in putting an end to the harassment of plaintiff.

J. The corporate defendant and defendant Besore are liable to plaintiff for both the conditions plaintiff experienced at work and for constructive discharge. Plaintiff has shown that the harassment directed at her continued up to within a few weeks of the date she went on sick leave. The conclusions of corporate defendant's doctor support plaintiff's contention that the stress and tension she experienced at work because of the harassment and the threat of harassment were the source of her health problems. Although the harassment plaintiff experienced in the weeks just prior to her sick leave may not have been overtly sexual, it was part of a continuing campaign of clearly sexual harassment which dated back at least two and one-half years, and which was directed at her because she is a female. Plaintiff has proven that she was subjected to unlawful sexual harassment which defendants' ineffectual measures failed to curtail. Under these circumstances, the Court is left with the impression that defendant corporation and defendant Besore were at best indifferent to plaintiff's situation, and at worst intended to let it run its course with the foreseeable possibility that plaintiff would eventually resign. A reasonable person would have found the conditions intolerable, particularly when they did not abate within a reasonable time after the defendant corporation received the administrative charge. Thus, the Court finds defendant corporation's and defendant Besore's conduct was deliberate, *see Taylor v. Jones,* 653 F.2d 1193, 1199 [28 FEP Cases 1024] (8th Cir. 1981) (on constructive discharge claim, employer liable for black employee's resignation due to racial atmosphere resulting from employer's deliberate acts), or "intentional," *see Craft v. Metro-Media, Inc.,* 766 F.2d 1205, 1217 [38 FEP Cases

404] (8th Cir. 1985) (on constructive discharge claim, employer must be found to have taken actions with intent to force employee to quit), *cert. denied,* 475 U.S. 1058 [40 FEP Cases 272] (1986), for purposes of plaintiff's constructive discharge claim.

• • •

—————————

2. *Nonsexual Hazing Based on Sex*

Hazing consists of offensive conduct, usually not overtly sexual in nature, that is visited upon a complainant because of gender. Acts of physical aggression,[104] threats of physical violence,[105] and arguably ambiguous conduct, such as urinating in a female co-worker's gas tank,[106] though not inherently sexual in nature, can nonetheless constitute harassment on the basis of sex. The purpose of this behavior, as in explicit gender-baiting cases, is to harass, intimidate, and make life unpleasant for the complainant.[107] Thus, the complainants in *Hall v. Gus Construction Co.* were permitted to introduce evidence of acts and speech not obviously based on the complainants' sex (such as failing to fix a complainant's truck) in addition to evidence of conduct clearly sexual in nature (such as solicitations to engage in sexual intercourse).

HALL V. GUS CONSTRUCTION CO.

842 F.2d 1010, 46 FEP Cases 573
(8th Cir. 1988)

ROGER L. WOLLMAN, Circuit Judge:—Gus Construction Co., Inc., and one of its foremen, John Mundorf, appeal from a judgment[1] imposing liability under Title VII of the Civil Rights Act of 1964, 42 U.S.C. §2000e *et seq.* (1982), and the Iowa Civil Rights Act, Iowa Code Chapter 601A (1985), for their having failed to protect Darla Hall, Patty Baxter, and Jeannette Ticknor from sexual harassment by their coworkers. The hostile and abusive working environment resulted in the women's constructive discharge. • • •

Mundorf hired Ms. Hall, Ms. Baxter and Ms. Ticknor in April 1984 to work for Gus Construction Co. as "flag persons" or traffic controllers at road construction sites in various Iowa counties. All of the women were in their thirties. Ms. Baxter and Ms. Hall were single mothers who sought employment so as to be better able to support young children. No other women worked on the crew. One flag person stood at one end of the section of the road under construction, another at the other end, and the third drove a pilot truck leading the motor vehicle traffic through the construction area.

Immediately after the women started work, male members of the construction crew began to inflict verbal sexual abuse on the women. The men incessantly referred to the women as "fucking flag girls." The men nicknamed Ms. Ticknor "Herpes" after she developed a skin reaction due to a sun allergy. On one occasion, Ms. Baxter returned to her car and found the name "Cavern Cunt" written in the dust on the driver's side, and "Blond

—————————

[1][Omitted.]

—————————

[104]McKinney v. Dole, 765 F.2d 1129, 1139, 38 FEP Cases 364 (D.C. Cir. 1985).
[105]Hicks v. Gates Rubber Co., 883 F.2d 1406, 1415, 45 FEP Cases 608 (10th Cir. 1987).
[106]Hall v. Gus Constr. Co., *supra* note 99, 942 F.2d at 1013–14, 46 FEP Cases at 574.
[107]*See generally* discussion in Chapter 4, Hostile Environment Harassment, for legal issues respecting this kind of claim.

Bitch" written on the passenger side where Ms. Hall sat. Male crew members repeatedly asked Ms. Hall if she "wanted to fuck" and requested that Ms. Hall and Ms. Baxter engage in oral sex with them. Mundorf was present during some of these incidents, and on one occasion used the term "fucking flag girls." Each of the women told Mundorf that the verbal abuse offended and upset her. Mundorf talked to the crew members about their conduct, but the verbal abuse soon resumed and continued up to the time the women quit their jobs.

In addition to the verbal abuse, male coworkers subjected Ms. Hall and Ms. Baxter to offensive and unwelcomed physical touching. Male crew members would corner the women between two trucks, reach out of the windows and rub their hands down the women's thighs. They grabbed Ms. Hall's breasts. One crew member picked up Ms. Hall and held her up to the cab window so other men could touch her. Mundorf observed this incident but did nothing.

All three women also experienced other types of abuse at work. Male crew members frequently pulled down their pants and "mooned" the women while they were working. One crew member exposed himself to Ms. Hall. Male crew members flashed obscene pictures of naked couples engaged in oral intercourse at the women. A male crew member urinated in Ms. Hall's water bottle. Several men urinated in the gas tank of Ms. Ticknor's car, causing it to malfunction. When carbon monoxide fumes leaked from the pilot truck causing the driver to become drowsy, the mechanic ignored the women's complaints. The women were forced to rotate their positions so that no one was in the truck for more than a short period of time. Later, a male crew member used the truck, and it was immediately repaired. Male crew members would refuse to give the women a truck to take to town for bathroom breaks. When the women would relieve themselves in the ditch, male crew members observed them through surveying equipment. Mundorf knew about this practice, but he disciplined no one.

The women quit their jobs with Gus Construction Co. in August 1984. After complying with the procedural prerequisites regarding right-to-sue notices from the Equal Employment Opportunity Commission (EEOC) and the Iowa Civil Rights Commission, the women commenced this action, claiming that they were constructively discharged from their employment as a result of the opprobrious conduct of their male coworkers and foreman Mundorf. The court awarded the women back pay, damages for emotional distress and attorney's fees.

I.

Sexual discrimination that creates a hostile or abusive work environment is a violation of Title VII of the Civil Rights Act of 1964.[2] *Meritor Sav. Bank, FSB v. Vinson,* 477 U.S. 57, 106 S.Ct. 2399, 2405–06, 40 FEP Cases 1822 (1986). Unlike *quid pro quo* sexual harassment, which "occurs when submission to sexual conduct is made a condition of concrete employment benefits," *Hicks v. Gates Rubber Co.,* 833 F.2d 1406, 1413 (10th Cir. 1987), hostile work environment harassment arises when sexual conduct " 'has the purpose or effect of unreasonably interfering with an individual's work performance or creating an intimidating, hostile, or offensive working environment.' " *Meritor Sav. Bank, FSB v. Vinson,* 106 S.Ct. at 2405 (quoting 29 C.F.R. §1604.11(a)(3) (1985)). To prevail on a sexual harassment claim, a plaintiff must show that "(1) she belongs to a protected group, (2) she was subject to unwelcome sexual harassment, (3) the harassment was based on sex, (4) the harassment affected a 'term, condition, or privilege' of employment, and (5) the employer knew or should have known of the harassment in question and failed to take proper remedial action." • • •

Appellants argue that each of the women failed to prove all of the elements necessary to establish her sexual harassment claim.[3] Appellants concede that the women belong to a protected group. They contend, however, that in finding that the women were subject to

---

[2][Omitted.]

[3]Appellants assume that the elements of a sexual harassment claim under the Iowa Civil Rights Act are the same as under Title VII. Brief of Appellant at 9.

unwelcome sexual harassment the district court erred in not distinguishing between conduct of a sexual nature and other forms of harassment. Appellants also contend that the harassment against individual women was not sufficiently severe or pervasive to affect a condition of employment. They argue that the court erred by considering all three of the women's claims as a unit rather than individually. Finally, appellants contend that the offending crew members were not agents of Gus Construction Co.

• • •

In arguing that only conduct of a sexual nature should be considered in a sexual harassment claim, appellants rely on the language of 29 C.F.R. §1604.11(a) (1986), which defines sexual harassment as "[u]nwelcome sexual advances, requests for sexual favors, and other verbal or physical conduct of a sexual nature." *Id.* Appellants point to various incidents that they contend were not sexual and should not have been considered. For example, they argue that calling Ms. Ticknor "Herpes" might have been cruel, but that it was not conduct of a sexual nature.[4] The incident in which the male crew members urinated in Ms. Ticknor's gas tank was a practical joke, they argue, not conduct of a sexual nature. Likewise, not fixing the pilot truck that gave off fumes was not conduct of a sexual nature and should not have been considered.

Although we have not previously considered this issue, other courts of appeals have held that the predicate acts underlying a sexual harassment claim need not be clearly sexual in nature. *See Hicks v. Gates Rubber Co.,* 833 F.2d at 1415 (evidence of threats of physical violence and incidents of verbal abuse—calling plaintiff "Buffalo Butt"—properly considered); *McKinney v. Dole,* 765 F.2d 1129, 1139, 38 FEP Cases 364 (D.C. Cir. 1985) (acts of physical aggression properly considered). In *McKinney,* the court stated:

> We have never held that sexual harassment or other unequal treatment of an employee or group of employees that occurs because of the sex of an employee must, to be illegal under Title VII, take the form of sexual advances or of other incidents with clearly sexual overtones. And we decline to do so now. Rather, we hold that any harassment or other unequal treatment of an employee or group of employees that would not occur but for the sex of the employee or employees may, if sufficiently patterned or pervasive, comprise an illegal condition of employment under Title VII.

Id. at 1138 (footnote omitted).

We agree with the rationale expressed in *McKinney,* and we hold that the district court correctly considered incidents of harassment and unequal treatment that would not have occurred but for the fact that Ms. Hall, Ms. Ticknor and Ms. Baxter were women. Intimidation and hostility toward women because they are women can obviously result from conduct other than explicit sexual advances. • • • Although appellants correctly note that the definition of sexual harassment in the EEOC regulation emphasizes explicitly sexual behavior, the regulations do not state that other types of harassment should not be considered. Furthermore, an enforcing agency's guidelines are not controlling upon the courts. *Meritor Sav. Bank, FSB v. Vinson,* 106 S.Ct. at 2405.

Appellants also argue that requiring a plaintiff to prove both "unwelcome sexual harassment" and that "the harassment was based on sex" implies that the harassment must be sexual in nature. We discussed the element of unwelcome sexual harassment in *Moylan v. Maries County,* 792 F.2d at 749, focusing on the word "unwelcome." "In order to constitute harassment, the conduct must be 'unwelcome' in the sense that the employee did not solicit or invite it, and the employee regarded the conduct as undesirable or offensive." *Id.* at 749. Thus, none of our previous cases hold that the offensive conduct must have explicit sexual overtones.

We also reject appellants' contention that the district court erroneously considered all of the women's claims together in determining that the harassment was sufficiently pervasive and severe to constitute a violation of Title VII. We are convinced that the harassment directed toward each woman was sufficiently severe or pervasive to alter the conditions of her employment and create an abusive working environment. *See Meritor Sav. Bank, FSB*

---

[4]Appellants argue that the nickname "Herpes" is analogous to the appellation "Scarface," which Al Capone wore proudly but which might bother a more sensitive person. Brief of Appellant at 16.

v. Vinson, 106 S.Ct. at 2406. Each of the women was subjected to a plethora of offensive incidents. The circumstances presented here are no less compelling than in other cases finding a hostile and abusive environment. • • • All of the women were subjected to sexual insults that were systematically directed to them throughout their employment with Gus Construction Co. Although Ms. Ticknor was not subject to sexual propositions and offensive touching, evidence of sexual harassment directed at employees other than the plaintiff is relevant to show a hostile work environment. *Hicks v. Gates Rubber Co.,* 833 F.2d at 1415–16; *see also Jones v. Flagship Int'l,* 793 F.2d 714, 721 n.71, 41 FEP Cases 358 (5th Cir. 1986) (incidents of sexual harassment reported by other females bear on plaintiff's claim only if there is evidence that incidents affected plaintiff's psychological well-being), *cert. denied,* 107 S.Ct. 952, 43 FEP Cases 80 (1987).

Appellants' final challenge to the district court's finding of sexual harassment is that the trial court erred in imposing employer and supervisory liability. Appellants argue that the offending employees were not agents of Mundorf or Gus Construction Co. and that the employees acted outside the scope of their employment. • • •

In *Meritor,* the Supreme Court declined to announce a definitive rule on employer liability under Title VII, but determined that "Congress wanted courts to look to agency principles for guidance in this area." 106 S.Ct. at 2408. The Court reasoned that Congress' decision to define "employer" as an "agent" of an employer, 42 U.S.C. §2000e(b), suggests that Congress did not intend to hold employers strictly liable for the acts of their supervisors. *Id. But cf.* 29 C.F.R. §1604.11(c) (1986) (holding an employer liable for the acts of its agents without regard to notice). Nevertheless, "absence of notice to an employer does not necessarily insulate that employer from liability." 106 S.Ct. at 2408.

Meritor involved harassment by a supervisor. This case involves harassment mainly by coworkers. In *Hunter v. Allis-Chalmers Corp., Engine Div.,* 797 F.2d 1417, 1421, 41 FEP Cases 721 (7th Cir. 1986), a race discrimination case, the court considered whether a corporation could be held liable for employment discrimination when the perpetrators of the harassment were the plaintiff's fellow workers. The court reasoned that a company cannot be held liable for an isolated racial slur. But a company will be liable if management-level employees knew, or in the exercise of reasonable care should have known, about a barrage of offensive conduct.

• • •

In this case, Mundorf, as the agent of Gus Construction Co., had both actual and constructive notice of the campaign of harassment against the three women. Each of the women met with Mundorf individually to complain of the treatment they were receiving from their coworkers. The women also met with Mundorf as a group to discuss the hostile work environment. Furthermore, Mundorf observed many of the incidents. He knew that the men bombarded the women with sexual insults and abusive treatment. Even if Mundorf did not know everything that went on, the incidents of harassment here, as in *Hunter,* were so numerous that Mundorf and Gus Construction Co. are liable for failing to discover what was going on and to take remedial steps to put an end to it.

II.

Appellants next contend that the district court erred in awarding damages for emotional distress under the Iowa Civil Rights Act, Iowa Code Chapter 601A. • • •

• • •

• • • We therefore uphold the award of damages for emotional distress under the Iowa Civil Rights Act.

III.

Appellants' final assessment of error is that the damage awards for emotional distress were excessive. • • •

We conclude that awards of $15,000 and $20,000 do not constitute a shocking result. Similar amounts have been awarded in prior cases. *See, e.g., Hunter v. Allis-Chalmers Corp., Engine Div.,* 797 F.2d at 1425 (upholding an award of $25,000 for the humiliation and distress of being harassed and then fired on racial grounds); *Block v. R.H. Macy & Co.,* 712 F.2d 1241, 1245, 32 FEP Cases 609 (8th Cir. 1983) (upholding $12,402 award for mental anguish, humiliation, embarrassment and stress). The district court found that the women "suffered considerable emotional distress, including embarrassment, humiliation, personal degradation and loss of self-esteem." Mem. op. and order at 16. We will not second-guess the trial judge's assessment of intangible harms.

IV.

In affirming the district court's finding of liability and determination of damages, we note that the conduct and language complained of went far beyond that which even the most sensitive of persons is expected to tolerate in this era of gradually impoverished discourse. In this day when certain so-called comedians command millions for spewing forth on film language of the drill field, perhaps each of us, consciously or not, has become inured to that which even two short decades ago might have been considered beyond the pale of colloquial speech. Title VII does not mandate an employment environment worthy of a Victorian salon. Nor do we expect that our holding today will displace all ribaldry on the roadway. One may well expect that in the heat and dust of the construction site language of the barracks will always predominate over that of the ballroom. What occurred in this case, however, went well beyond the bounds of what any person should have to tolerate. These women acknowledged that they had anticipated hearing a good deal of profanity when they accepted their jobs as flag persons. Indeed, Ms. Baxter acknowledged that she, Ms. Hall, and Ms. Ticknor had probably uttered profanity themselves out on the job site. They did not expect, however, the unrelenting pattern of verbal, physical, and psychic abuse to which they were ultimately subjected. They gave fair notice of the intolerable conditions under which they were being forced to work and from which they were entitled to protection under Title VII. Having prevailed in the trial court on their claim of sexual harassment, they should not now be denied that which is their legal due.

The judgment is affirmed.

C. Sexually Charged Workplace

A hostile environment might exist where the cultural norms of the workplace are sexually charged. A sexually charged workplace exists where (1) promotions and other job benefits are based on sexual favoritism,[108] or (2) management condones sexually offensive language or visual displays.[109] These cases do not necessarily reflect any conduct inspired by or directed at a complainant. Indeed, the sexually charged workplace may have existed for years prior to the complainant's arrival and might well have been considered inoffensive in a work environment in which women had no place.[110]

1. Sexual Favoritism Cases

In the typical sexual favoritism case, a supervisor favors subordinates who satisfy the sexual demands of supervisors, thereby creating an implicit

---

[108]See Section III.C.1. *infra.*

[109]See Section III.C.2. *infra.*

[110]*E.g.,* Robinson v. Jacksonville Shipyards, *supra* note 99 (sexually suggestive calendars of women prominently displayed for years). Cases involving verbal or visual conduct, especially when it is not directed at the complainant, raise First Amendment issues not yet fully addressed by the courts. See Chapter 27, Asserted Defenses.

quid pro quo. In this situation, even though sexual activity may not be directly required of the complainant, the complainant is nonetheless disadvantaged.[111]

BRODERICK V. RUDER

685 F. Supp. 1269, 46 FEP Cases 1272
(D.D.C. 1988)

JOHN H. PRATT, District Judge:—Trial of the above-captioned matter took place from June 22, 1987 through July 1, 1987. In addition to the oral testimony of some twenty-five (25) witnesses, there has been extensive discovery on both sides in the form of depositions and documents. The matter has been fully briefed. On the basis of the foregoing submissions, the Court enters the following Findings of Fact and Conclusions of Law.

Findings of Fact

The Parties

1. Plaintiff, a 35 year-old white female, is currently employed as a staff attorney in the Division of Corporation Finance of the Securities and Exchange Commission ("Commission" or "SEC"). She has been continuously employed as a staff attorney since August 12, 1979, a period of more than eight years. She filed this action on June 30, 1984, pursuant to Title VII of the Civil Rights Act of 1964 ("Title VII"), 42 U.S.C. §2000e-16 *et seq*, asserting two causes of action. These are, 1) that defendant is responsible for creating and refusing to remedy a sexually hostile work environment at the Washington Regional Field Office ("WRO") of the SEC, and 2) that plaintiff's supervisors at the WRO retaliated against her for opposing actions of the WRO's management that she considered to be illegal under Title VII.

• • •

Plaintiff's Reasons For Her Inability to Interact With Her Supervisors

14. Covering the entire period of her employment with the Enforcement Division, 1979 to 1984, plaintiff testified at length concerning her perception that an atmosphere of sexual harassment by persons in positions of management pervaded the WRO. Her testimony was corroborated by other witnesses. Except for her initial encounter with John Hunter, when during her first week on the job, he repeatedly importuned her to accept his offer for a ride home, and her being kissed by Leonard at a farewell part for Jack Kiefner at Brooks' house in the spring of 1982, none of the incidents complained of by plaintiff were directed at plaintiff personally, nor did they involve the conditioning of employment benefits in return for sexual favors by plaintiff. Rather, it was the occurrence of numerous other incidents[2] of which plaintiff early on became aware which, for her, created a sexually hostile or offensive working environment. This in turn poisoned any possibility of plaintiff's having the proper professional respect for her superiors and, without any question, affected her motivation and her performance of her job responsibilities.

15. Both plaintiff and defendant presented expert testimony concerning the mental condition of plaintiff. These experts examined the plaintiff at some length and their conclusions are in sharp conflict. Dr. James Titchener, M.D., a psychiatrist, testifying for the plaintiff, diagnosed plaintiff's condition as a dysthymic disorder, a "new term for depressive reaction." In plaintiff's case, he stated "it is a classic sadness, feeling of melancholy, hopelessness . . . the discouragement, the demoralization of the office atmosphere in which

---

[1][Omitted.]
[2]Some of these incidents are related in Finding of Fact 17.

---

[111]This kind of case may result in both a quid pro quo and a hostile environment claim.

she had to work." He allied this condition to a "post-traumatic stress disorder" arising from her working conditions,[3] but denied that plaintiff suffered from a paranoid personality disorder. He admitted that plaintiff had developmental and relationship problems prior to coming to the SEC, but stated that these had not reached the level of a clinical diagnosis. Ms. Karen Wagner, a social worker with broad experience, was the plaintiff's other expert. She testified generally on the stress effects of sexual harassment on women in plaintiff's position, with particular reference to the plaintiff's hostile working environment and its effect on the plaintiff and her associates in having to work in such an environment. On the other hand, Dr. Martin Stein, M.D., also a psychiatrist, diagnosed plaintiff as suffering from a paranoid personality disorder, which he defined as a "selective way that people fall into to deal with stress, insecurity, discomfort within themselves." He stated that plaintiff exhibited the characteristics of a paranoid personality disorder, *i.e.,* a pervasive mistrust and suspicion of all supervisors, refusal to accept responsibility, questioning of loyalty and, *inter alia,* the excessive use of the terms "they" and "team player". Each of these psychiatric experts was highly qualified and had long experience in psychiatric diagnosis.

16. Despite defendant's evidence to the contrary, we decline to make a judgment as to whether plaintiff suffered from a paranoid personality disorder or some lesser mental disorder, except to find that plaintiff was a sensitive person who had adjustment problems before she came to the SEC, that the environment in which she worked exacerbated these problems and that the environment affected her motivation and consequently her work performance. As discussed in Finding of Fact 13, her performance evaluations for 1982, 1983 and 1984 reflect a gradually declining overall rating (from "Superior" to "Unacceptable"), as well as a declining rating in the category of "Interaction with Supervisors" (from "Minimally Acceptable" to "Unacceptable").

17. Plaintiff and others testified at length concerning specific conduct by those in supervisory positions, which in their judgment constituted a sexually hostile work environment. These instances include, but are not limited to the following:

a. *Leonard,* the Regional Administrator, at an office party, became drunk, and, among other matters, untied plaintiff's sweater and kissed her. He also kissed one other female employee. On another occasion, at an office retreat in Lancaster, Pennsylvania in September 1983, Kennedy approached Patty Toftoy, his administrative assistant, put his hands on her hips, remarking that she had "sexy, wide hips." These facts are not disputed. Plaintiff also testified that Leonard and Regional Trial Counsel Jack Kiefner made sexually suggestive remarks about plaintiff's dress and figure. Leonard, as Regional Administrator, was head of the WRO.

b. *Hunter* admittedly came to plaintiff's apartment during plaintiff's first week with the SEC. Plaintiff testified that he had repeatedly offered her a ride home, and when she finally acceded, he barged into her apartment, and toured the premises, including her bedroom. Hunter testified that he was with his wife, and that the purpose of the visit was to obtain packing boxes. We credit plaintiff's testimony. Nelson testified that Hunter was foul-mouthed and has a penchant for crude and dirty jokes. White corroborated Nelson's testimony. More importantly, Hunter admitted that he had on ongoing sexual relationship with Mary Bour, a secretary, from December 1981 to June 1984. In August or September 1983, Hunter was called into Leonard's office and was asked whether he knew that "people in the office were talking about his [i.e., Hunter's] personal life." In fact, according to defendant's witness, Stanley Hecht, Hunter's liaison with Mary Bour "became a matter of common knowledge." This subject again came up at a meeting with Leonard and others in October 1983. During the period from January 1980 to her resignation in November 1984, Mary Bour received three promotions, a commendation and two cash awards.[4] Though Mary Bour was not under

---

[3]We decline to accept Dr. Titchener's diagnosis that plaintiff suffered "post-traumatic stress disorder." His analogy relating the Buffalo Creek, West Virginia, flood and the Beverly Hills nightclub fire to plaintiff's reaction to a sexually hostile work environment is not convincing.

[4]At the same time, Cheryl White was deprived of her paralegal responsibilities which Hunter, on at least one occasion, assigned to Mary Bour, who was a secretary. As a consequence, White asked Kennedy to be assigned to a new supervisor.

Hunter's direct supervision, Hunter admitted he had had a direct input into Mary Bour's performance evaluations. Hunter was never disciplined for this conduct, but instead received ten salary increases between October 1983 and January 1987.

c. *Kennedy*—There is no direct evidence that Kennedy, an ARA, had a sexual relationship with Joan Sarles. There is, however, extensive testimony that Kennedy was noticeably attracted to Sarles and that there was extensive socializing between them during business hours, both within and outside the office, and that their relationship was the subject of a discussion in Kennedy's office in October 1983, a meeting at which Hunter was also present. It is also undisputed that Kennedy promoted her career from the time she joined WRO as a grade 11 employee in March 1982. In three months, she was appointed to a grade 12 attorney position, and approximately one year thereafter, shortly upon becoming eligible, was promoted to grade 13. Six months later, in December 1983, she applied for and received a promotion to Branch Chief,[5] and six months thereafter to grade 14. In summary, Sarles advanced from a grade 11 to grade 14 in slightly over two years.

d. *Brooks*—There is compelling evidence that Brooks had a sexual relationship with Alice McDonald beginning in early 1983. A number of undisputed incidents confirm the fact that they frequently had long lunches together, occasionally dined and drank together, and jogged together. On one occasion during a luncheon for National Secretaries Week, Alice McDonald, who was in Brooks' company, got drunk and had to be taken home later in the afternoon by Brooks. On another occasion, McDonald accompanied Brooks on a trip to Ocean City, where they spent the night in the same hotel room. Brooks denied having sexual relations with McDonald on this occasion, but said they spent the night discussing her theological problems. As Brooks put it, "she had some difficulty with the things she had done in the past and her feelings about God and the Catholic Church." McDonald, who joined the Commission in September 1982 as a clerk typist at grade 3 and departed in November 1984, also made rapid progress with the assistance of Brooks, her supervisor. During a single twelve-month period, she received two grade promotions, a $300 cash award and a perfect score in each element of her performance appraisal in 1984.

18. We find that the conduct of Leonard, Hunter, Kennedy and Brooks was a matter of common knowledge throughout the WRO and created an atmosphere of hostile work environment offensive to plaintiff, Cheryl White, Karen Nelson and several other witnesses for plaintiff whose testimony we deem not necessary to recite in detail.[6]

19. Leonard (by deposition), Hunter, Kennedy and Brooks appeared and testified at trial. With due consideration for the compromising position in which they found themselves, we find that the testimony of Hunter and Kennedy was less than forthright and that Brooks' testimony was in material respects false and incredible. In the face of countervailing evidence, we regard the testimony of all these witnesses as deserving of little credence.

Subsequent Administrative Proceedings

• • •

22. The final EEO report, a copy of which the Commission sent to plaintiff, concluded, *inter alia,* as follows:

> Romantic involvements between supervisors and those working for them have occurred at the WRO, and some of the liaisons were common knowledge to the employees. There were frequent parties, afternoon long lunch "hours", and certain WRO employees went drinking together during the work day. All in all, an atmosphere

---

[5]When this position was opened in December 1983, there were four applicants: Joan Sarles, Ronald Crawford, Aldie Lapins and plaintiff. The selection panel consisted of Kennedy, Hunter and Thomas Monahan, the ARA for enforcement for the Philadelphia Branch Office. The panel also met with Stan Hecht. Sarles was selected as the best qualified. We are satisfied that this selection was based on merit and that plaintiff's claim of retaliation as it relates to this non-selection lacks evidentiary support.

[6][Omitted.]

existed at the WRO where drinking and sexual involvements among staff were not unusual, and where most of it was engaged in by members of upper management.

Specifically, there were relationships going on between John Hunter and his secretary, Mary Bour, and Herbert Brooks, Jr., and his secretary, Alice McDonald, of which most WRO employees were well aware. Impartial witnesses also stated that Mr. Leonard had been romantically involved with Linda Cole, an attorney no longer at the SEC, and that Mr. Kiefner had had liaisons with Debbie Forbes and Helena Wertlieb.

This conclusion submitted by the EEO office fully corroborates the basic gravamen and thrust of the evidence presented by plaintiff at trial.

• • •

The Commission's Knowledge of WRO's Hostile Work Environment

24. The Commission's Office of Personnel was aware in 1983 of the conditions at the WRO. In September 1983, plaintiff brought these matters to the attention of the Personnel Office when she protested her 1983 performance appraisal. She was advised by James L. Foster, Director of the Commission's Office of Personnel, that "if you feel that you have been unlawfully discriminated against, you should confer with the Commission's EEO office."

25. On February 16, 1984, plaintiff complained to her supervisor, Hilton Foster, in response to the latter's February 10, 1984 letter, stating that "I believe it to be another example of your harassment and discrimination against me because of my sex and because I have brought to your attention instances of sexual discrimination and sexual harassment adversely affecting my and others' work performance in this office."

26. The then-Chairman of the Commission, John S.R. Shad, and Executive Director Kundahl were sent copies of plaintiff's February 16, 1984 memorandum and thus became aware at that time, if not before, of plaintiff's allegations of sexual discrimination and harassment. This was done at the suggestion of Phillip H. Savage, the EEO Office Director at that time, because of the "nature and seriousness of the allegations." He also advised plaintiff to file a formal EEO complaint. The investigation of the complaint was assigned to Jeffrey Puretz, a staff attorney with the Investment Management Division of the Commission. Plaintiff's EEO complaint, filed February 16, 1984, was amended at least once to encompass events occurring thereafter, including the claim of retaliation stemming from her 1984 performance evaluation.

• • •

Conclusions of Law

• • •

Plaintiff's Sexual Harassment Claim

2. The parties stipulated that the definition of sexual harassment contained in the Equal Employment Opportunity Commission's Guidelines on Discrimination Because of Sex, 29 C.F.R. §1604.11 (1986), is the definition that should be applied in this case. Section 1604.11(a) defines sexual harassment as follows: "Unwelcome sexual advances, requests for sexual favors, and other verbal or physical conduct of a sexual nature constitute sexual harassment when (1) submission to such conduct is made either explicitly or implicitly a term or condition of an individual's employment, (2) submission to or rejection of such conduct by an individual is used as the basis for employment decisions affecting such individual, or (3) *such conduct has the purpose or the effect of unreasonably interfering with an individual's work performance or creating an intimidating, hostile or offensive working environment."* (emphasis supplied.) Additionally, section 1604.11(g) provides that "[w]here employment opportunities or benefits are granted because of an individual's submission to the employer's sexual advances or requests for sexual favors, the employer may be held liable for unlawful sex discrimination against other persons who were qualified for but denied that employment opportunity or benefit."

3. The United States Supreme Court recently held that a violation of Title VII may be predicated on either of two types of sexual harassment: (a) harassment that involves the conditioning of concrete employment benefits in return for sexual favors,[8] and (b) harassment that, while not directly affecting economic benefits, creates a hostile or offensive working environment. *Meritor Savings Bank, F.S.B. v. Vinson,* 477 U.S. 57, 62-67, 40 FEP Cases 1822 (1986); *see also Yates v. AVCO Corp.,* 819 F.2d 630, 634, 43 FEP Cases 1595 (6th Cir. 1987); *Hicks v. Gates Rubber Co.,* 833 F.2d 1406, 1413, 45 FEP Cases 608 (10th Cir. 1987); *Bundy v. Jackson,* 641 F.2d 934, 943-46, 24 FEP Cases 1155 (D.C. Cir. 1981); *Henson v. City of Dundee,* 682 F.2d 897, 901-02, 29 FEP Cases 787 (11th Cir. 1982); *Jones v. Lyng,* 669 F.Supp. 1108, 1121, 42 FEP Cases 587 (D.D.C. 1986).

4. A "hostile work environment" claim is actionable under Title VII if unwelcome sexual advances, requests for sexual favors, and other verbal or physical conduct of a sexual nature are so pervasive that it can reasonably be said that they create a hostile or offensive work environment. *Meritor,* 477 U.S. at 65-67. Whether the sexual conduct is sufficiently pervasive to amount to harassment and create a hostile or offensive work environment must be determined from the totality of the circumstances. *Id.* at 69; *Hicks,* 833 F.2d at 415-16. Additionally, Title VII is also violated when an employer affords preferential treatment to female employees who submit to sexual advances or other conduct of a sexual nature and such conduct is a matter of common knowledge. *King v. Palmer,* 778 F.2d 878, 880, 39 FEP Cases 877 (D.C. Cir. 1985); *Priest v. Rotary,* 634 F.Supp. 571, 581, 40 FEP Cases 208 (N.D. Cal. 1986); *Toscano v. Nimmo,* 570 F.Supp. 1197, 1199, 32 FEP Cases 1401 (D. Del. 1983); *see also* 29 C.F.R. §1604.11(g).

5. Evidence of the general work atmosphere, involving employees other than the plaintiff, is relevant to the issue of whether there existed an atmosphere of hostile work environment which violated Title VII. • • • This is so because "[e]ven a woman who was never herself the object of harassment might have a Title VII claim if she were forced to work in an atmosphere in which such harassment was pervasive." *Vinson v. Taylor,* 753 F.2d at 146.

6. Ms. Broderick established a prima facie case of sexual harassment because of having to work in a hostile work environment. The evidence at trial established that such conduct of a sexual nature was so pervasive at the WRO that it can reasonably be said that such conduct created a hostile or offensive work environment which affected the motivation and work performance of those who found such conduct repugnant and offensive. Ms. Broderick was herself sexually harassed by Leonard, Hunter, Kennedy and possibly others. But we need not emphasize these isolated incidents. More importantly, plaintiff, without any doubt, was forced to work in an environment in which the WRO managers by their conduct harassed her and other WRO female employees, by bestowing preferential treatment upon those who submitted to their sexual advances. Further, this preferential treatment undermined plaintiff's motivation and work performance and deprived plaintiff, and other WRO female employees, of promotions and job opportunities. The record is clear that plaintiff and other women working at the WRO found the sexual conduct and its accompanying manifestations which WRO managers engaged in over a protracted period of time to be offensive. The record also establishes that plaintiff and other women were for obvious reasons reluctant to voice their displeasure and, when they did, they were treated with a hostile response by WRO's management team.

• • •

The Defendant's Failure to Rebut the Prima Facie Case

12. In the ordinary gender bias case, once the plaintiff has established a *prima facie* case of discrimination or retaliation, the burden shifts to the defendant "to articulate some

---

[7][Omitted.]

[8]This is colloquially known as "*quid pro quo*" sexual harassment. Since there is no credible evidence that plaintiff herself was offered economic benefits in return for sexual favors, this type of conduct is not the subject of plaintiff's basic complaint in the instant case, except to the extent that it created and contributed to a pervasive atmosphere of sexual hostility in the work environment.

legitimate non-discriminatory reason" for the actions taken. *Texas Dept. of Community Affairs v. Burdine,* 450 U.S. 248, 252, 25 FEP Cases 113 (1981); *McDonnell Douglas Corp. v. Green,* 411 U.S. 797, 802-05, 5 FEP Cases 965 (1973); *Williams v. Boorstin,* 663 F.2d 109, 23 FEP Cases 1669 (D.C. Cir. 1980), *cert. denied,* 451 U.S. 985, 25 FEP Cases 1192 (1981). In a sexual harassment case involving the claim of hostile work environment, the burden on the defendant employer is markedly heavier. Once a plaintiff has established a *prima facie* case of sexual harassment or retaliation for opposing sexual harassment, the burden shifts to the employer to rebut the plaintiff's harassment claims and to show *by clear and convincing evidence* that the plaintiff would not have been treated differently if she had not opposed the harassment. *Bundy,* 641 F.2d at 952-53; *Day v. Mathews,* 530 F.2d 1083, 1085, 12 FEP Cases 1131 (D.C. Cir. 1976); *Baxter v. Savannah Sugar Refining Corp.,* 495 F.2d 437, 444-45, 8 FEP Cases 84 (5th Cir.), *cert. denied,* 419 U.S. 1033, 8 FEP Cases 1142 (1974). This is a higher standard than that required of an employer in a simple gender discrimination case. *Bundy,* 641 F.2d at 953. The reason for this different rule in sexual harassment cases is that "once a plaintiff establishes that she was harassed . . . it is hard to see how an employer can justify [the] harassment." *Moffett v. Gene B. Glick Co., Inc.,* 621 F.Supp. 244, 266, 41 FEP Cases 671 (N.D. Ind. 1985).

13. In this case, the Commission failed to rebut Ms. Broderick's hostile atmosphere, sexual harassment and retaliation claims by clear and convincing evidence, or even by a preponderance of the evidence. The Commission attempted to meet Ms. Broderick's harassment claims by arguing that Ms. Broderick "was paranoid." Admittedly, plaintiff had problems of personal adjustment before being employed by the Commission in 1979. Whether diagnosed either as "paranoia" or as a "post traumatic stress disorder", we are satisfied that plaintiff's mental condition was caused and exacerbated by the hostile atmosphere in which she worked. Even assuming that the assertion that plaintiff was a paranoid personality has support in Dr. Stein's testimony, it does not rebut similar testimony from other witnesses presented by the plaintiff as to the conditions of sexual harassment and retaliation at the WRO.

14. With respect to plaintiff's opposition and retaliation claims, the Commission's argument that Ms. Broderick's tardiness and her diminished work performance accounted for her performance evaluations and were legitimate reasons for reprimands and threats to terminate her are not persuasive in the overall context of this case. The Commission's allegations of excessive tardiness when tardiness by others was overlooked is sheer "make weight" and pretext. Ms. Broderick amply demonstrated, through both lay and expert witnesses, that any alleged deficiencies in her work performance, which rested largely on her failure to interact with her supervisors, were directly attributable to the atmosphere in which she worked.[10]

15. Defendant in effect argues that this is a *"quid pro quo"* sex harassment case and, except for isolated instances, plaintiff was not sexually harassed. This contention is in error, and misses the mark. The Commission's attempt to justify the sexual misconduct on the part of supervisory personnel as "social/sexual interaction between and among employees" which Title VII never intended to regulate is unacceptable on the facts of this case. However relaxed one's views of sexual morality may be in a different context, such views do not cover the pattern of conduct disclosed by the record in this case. We hold, and plaintiff has proved, that consensual sexual relations, in exchange for tangible employment benefits, while possibly not creating a cause of action for the recipient of such sexual advances who does not find them unwelcome, do, and in this case did, create and contribute to a sexually hostile working environment.

16. The SEC was the employer of, and had authority over, the personnel who persisted in this activity of which it had actual, as well as constructive, knowledge. It took

---

[9][Omitted.]

[10]Plaintiff's diminished performance cannot be asserted as a legitimate basis for her removal when that diminution is the direct result of the employer's discriminatory behavior. *Delgado v. Lehman,* 665 F.Supp. at 467; *Moffett,* 621 F.Supp. at 281; *Weiss v. United States,* 595 F.Supp. 1050, 1057, 36 FEP Cases 1 (E.D. Va. 1984); *Lamb v. Drilco Div. v. Smith Int'l.,* 32 Fair Empl. Prac. Cas. (BNA) 105, 107 (S.D. Tex. 1983). *See also Henson v. City of Dundee,* 682 F.2d 897, 910, 29 FEP Cases 787 (11th Cir. 1982).

no action. It is therefore liable under agency principles for the acts of these high-ranking subordinates.

The Court's Order

Based upon the entire record in this case, and the Findings of Fact and Conclusions of Law set forth above, it is by the court this 13th day of May, 1988,

ORDERED that judgment be and the same hereby is entered in favor of plaintiff for defendant's violation of Title VII of the Civil Rights Act of 1964, and it is

ORDERED that the parties appear for a hearing on the 26th day of May, 1988, at 1:30 p.m. to consider the appropriate relief to be granted plaintiff.

Broderick stands for the proposition that the complainant need not be the direct victim of the harassing conduct in a sexually charged workplace to maintain an action under Title VII. The *Broderick* claimant suffered harassment because she was denied opportunities available to those who participated in the sexual politics of the office and because the atmosphere of sexual politics based on explicit sexual favoritism created a hostile, offensive, and intimidating environment.[112]

2. Sexually Charged Workplace Cultures

A workplace replete with sexually explicit posters and reading material (*e.g.,* magazines depicting partially clad or nude women in sexually suggestive poses) may create a hostile environment for women. Although the displays may not be directed at any particular woman, a woman may nevertheless feel demeaned by such materials to the point that her employment is affected.

In virtually all cases, visual displays of graffiti or pornography have constituted only one part of a pattern of offensive activities.[113] Examples of such visual displays include failing to remove obscene cartoons about women in a men's bathroom,[114] showing a pornographic movie and distributing pornographic magazines,[115] showing a videotape of rabbits mating at a business meeting where the complainant was the only female present,[116] wearing a T-shirt stating, "I gagged Linda Lovelace,"[117] displaying sexually oriented

---

[112]*But see* DeCintio v. Westchester County Medical Center, 807 F.2d 304, 42 FEP Cases 921 (2d Cir. 1986), reproduced in Chapter 5, Claims by Third Parties (Title VII provided no relief where a male supervisor favored his female paramour over six male applicants in promotion decision, because the men could not complain they were denied job benefits because they refused sexual favors), *cert. denied,* 484 U.S. 825 (1987).

[113]*See, e.g.,* Brooms v. Regal Tube Co., 881 F.2d 412, 50 FEP Cases 1499 (7th Cir. 1989)(white supervisor showed black subordinate depiction of black woman engaging in interracial sodomy and told her that she had been hired for purpose shown in photograph, and later showed her racist picture featuring bestiality while saying that that was how she "was going to end up"; when complainant tried to grab one of the pornographic pictures, supervisor grabbed her arm and told her he would kill her if she moved; she broke free, ran away, and fell down a flight of stairs, never returning to work).

[114]Bennett v. Corroon & Black Corp., *supra* note 103.

[115]Boyd v. James S. Hayes Living Health Care Agency, 671 F. Supp. 1155, 44 FEP Cases 332, 335 (W.D. Tenn. 1987).

[116]Kinnally v. Bell of Pa., 748 F. Supp. 1136, 1138, 54 FEP Cases 329, 330 (E.D. Pa. 1990).

[117]Priest v. Rotary, 634 F. Supp. 571, 575, 40 FEP Cases 208, 210 (N.D. Cal. 1986). Linda Lovelace was the protagonist in the X-rated film *Deep Throat,* in which she "finds sexual ecstasy in fellatio because her clitoris is in her throat." C. MACKINNON, FEMINISM UNMODIFIED: DISCOURSES ON LIFE AND LAW 10 (1987). For a discussion of *Deep Throat* and the legal controversies concerning it, see *id.* at 10–11, 13, 128–29, 180–81. *Deep Throat* has been discussed in more than a dozen judicial decisions focusing on whether it is

pictures and cartoons in the workplace,[118] and placing sexually oriented draw-ings or graffiti on pillars and other conspicuous places in the workplace.[119]

Perhaps the one case that has come closest to holding that visual displays alone can create a hostile environment is *Robinson v. Jacksonville Shipyards,* excerpted below.[120] Although *Jacksonville Shipyards* involved more than suffi-cient conduct directed specifically at the complainant, the court's language suggests that sexually suggestive visual displays can be inherently discrimina-tory.

The decision in *Jacksonville Shipyards* addresses many important issues, often in more detail than most of the decisions that have been published to date.[121] Among these issues are: (1) the degree to which offensive visual displays directed at no particular individual may constitute part of a sexually hostile environment;[122] (2) the admissibility of a plaintiff's second-hand knowl-edge of harassment against her co-workers;[123] (3) the circumstances under which an individual defendant may be liable for sexual harassment as a Title VII "employer";[124] (4) the theory, based on expert testimony, that sexually oriented displays are discriminatory by contributing to sexual stereotyping;[125] (5) the use of expert testimony to evaluate the adequacy of sexual harassment policies;[126] (6) the appropriateness of a "reasonable woman" standard;[127] (7) the significance of a "social context" in which sexually explicit depictions or behavior are generally tolerated;[128] (8) the degree of corporate knowledge necessary to establish employer liability;[129] (9) the degree to which the First Amendment protects sexually offensive speech in the workplace;[130] and (10) the applicability of the Federal Executive Order.[131]

---

obscene for purposes of removing it from the constitutional protection of freedom of speech. See *id.* at 234 n.30.

[118]Shrout v. Black Clawson Co., 689 F. Supp. 774, 779–80, 46 FEP Cases 1339, 1343 (S.D. Ohio 1988)(leaving copy of the magazine *Sex Over Forty* on complainant's desk); Barbetta v. Chemlawn Servs. Corp., 669 F. Supp. 569, 573, 44 FEP Cases 1563, 1565–66 (W.D.N.Y. 1987)(denying motion for summary judgment, given presence of pornographic magazines in workplace, vulgar employee comments concerning them, sexually oriented pictures in company-sponsored slide presentation, and sexually oriented pictures and calendars; proliferation of pornography and demeaning comments "may be found to create an atmosphere in which women are viewed as men's sexual playthings rather than as their equal co-workers"). *See generally* Ehrenreich, *Pluralist Myths and Powerless Men: The Ideology of Reasonableness in Sexual Harassment Law,* 99 YALE L.J. 1176, 1197 n.75 (1990)(characterizing pornography as example of mechanism by which women are "sexualized").

[119]Zabkowicz v. West Bend Co., *supra* note 103, 589 F. Supp. at 782–83, 35 FEP Cases at 613; Robinson v. Jacksonville Shipyards, *supra* note 99, 760 F. Supp. at 1494–99. *See generally* Waltman v. International Paper Co., 875 F.2d 468, 50 FEP Cases 179 (5th Cir. 1989)(evidence of ongoing sexual graffiti in the workplace, not all of which was directed at plaintiff, relevant to claim of harassment); *but see* Waltman v. International Paper Co., 875 F.2d at 782 (Jones, J. dissenting).

[120]Robinson v. Jacksonville Shipyards, *supra* note 99.

[121]Indicated in the footnotes below is whether the discussion is excerpted in this chapter or elsewhere in the book and in what chapters of the book further discussion of the issue appears.

[122]See pp. 111–14 *infra.*

[123]See p. 100 *infra* and Chapter 25, Evidence, Section VI.D.

[124]See excerpts of *Robinson v. Jacksonville Shipyards* in Chapter 23, The Alleged Harasser as Defendant, Section II.B.4.

[125]See pp. 101–4 *infra.*

[126]See pp. 104–5 *infra* and Chapter 25, Evidence, Section VIII.D.

[127]See pp. 112–14 *infra* and Chapter 4, Hostile Environment Harassment, Section VI.C.3.a.

[128]See pp. 112–13 *infra* and Chapter 4, Hostile Environment Harassment, Section VI.C.3.b.

[129]See Chapters 4, Hostile Environment Harassment; 6, Harassment by Supervisors; and 7, Harassment by Co-Workers.

[130]See Chapter 27, Asserted Defenses, Section VII.

[131]See p. 116 *infra* and Chapter 11, Federal Constitutional, Statutory, and Civil Rights Law, Section IX.

ROBINSON V. JACKSONVILLE SHIPYARDS

760 F. Supp. 1486
(M.D. Fla. 1991)

MELTON, District Judge.

This action was commenced by plaintiff Lois Robinson pursuant to Title VII of the Civil Rights Act of 1964, as amended, 42 U.S.C. § 2000e, et seq., and Executive Order No. 11246, as amended. Plaintiff asserts defendants created and encouraged a sexually hostile, intimidating work environment. Her claim centers around the presence in the workplace of pictures of women in various stages of undress and in sexually suggestive or submissive poses, as well as remarks by male employees and supervisors which demean women. • • •

This non-jury action was tried by the Court over the course of eight days in January and February 1989, • • •. Each side presented two expert witnesses. • • • [T]he Court finds that certain of the defendants violated Title VII through the maintenance of a sexually hostile work environment and thereby discriminated against plaintiff because of her sex. • • •

FINDINGS OF FACT
Parties

1. Plaintiff Lois Robinson ("Robinson") is a female employee of Jacksonville Shipyards, Inc., ("JSI"). She has been a welder since September 1977. Robinson is one of a very small number of female skilled craftworkers employed by JSI. • • •

2. JSI is a Florida corporation that runs several shipyards engaged in the business of ship repair, including the Commercial Yard and the Mayport Yard. • • • As a federal contractor, JSI has affirmative action and non-discrimination obligations. • • •

• • •

10. • • • Robinson's job assignments at JSI have required her to work at both the Commercial Yard and the Mayport Yard.

• • •

13. Robinson's job assignments at the Mayport Yard have included "combination jobs," in which she sometimes works as a welder in combination with shipfitters. At times, Robinson has been directed by her supervisors to stand in front of the shipfitters' trailer to get her assignment from the shipfitters' leaderman. When welders work with shipfitters at the Mayport Yard, it is not unusual for them to go into the shipfitters' trailer. Robinson has, for example, gone into the shipfitters' trailer to check on paperwork or her assignment.

• • •

The JSI Working Environment

16. JSI is, in the words of its employees, "a boys club," • • • and "more or less a man's world," • • •. Women craftworkers are an extreme rarity. The company's EEO-1 reports from 1980 to 1987 typically show that women form less than 5 percent of the skilled crafts. • • • Leslie Albert, Lawanna Gail Banks, and Robinson each testified that she was the only woman in a crowd of men on occasions when each was sexually harassed at JSI. • • • JSI has never employed a woman as a leaderman, quarterman, assistant foreman, foreman, superintendent, or coordinator. Nor has any woman ever held a position of Vice-President or President of JSI.

17. Pictures of nude and partially nude women appear throughout the JSI workplace in the form of magazines, plaques on the wall, photographs torn from magazines and affixed to the wall or attached to calendars supplied by advertising tool supply companies ("vendors' advertising calendars"). Two plaques consisting of pictures of naked women, affixed to wood and varnished, were introduced into evidence, • • • and identified by several witnesses as having been on display for years at JSI in the fab shop area under the supervision of defendant Lovett • • •.

18. Advertising calendars, such as Joint Exhibits Nos. 1–5, have been delivered for years to JSI by vendors with whom it does business. JSI officials then distribute the advertising calendars among JSI employees with the full knowledge and approval of JSI management. JSI employees are free to post these advertising calendars in the workplace. (It is not a condition of JSI's contracts with the vendors that the advertising calendars be

posted.) • • • Generally speaking, these calendars feature women in various stages of undress and in sexually suggestive or submissive poses. • • •

19. JSI has never distributed nor tolerated the distribution of a calendar or calendars with pictures of nude or partially nude men. • • •

20. JSI employees are encouraged to request permission to post most kinds of materials; however, prior approval by the company is not required for the posting of advertising calendars with pictures of nude or partially nude women. JSI management has denied employees' requests to post political materials, advertisements and commercial materials.

21. Bringing magazines and newspapers on the job is prohibited, • • • but male JSI employees read pornographic magazines in the workplace without apparent sanctions • • •. Although JSI employees are discouraged by management from reading on the job, they are not prohibited from tearing sexually suggestive or explicit pictures of women out of such magazines and displaying them on the workplace walls at JSI. • • • Leach Depo. at 19–21, 26 (*Playboy* and *Penthouse* magazines in desk drawers in shipfitting shop and trailer office; Leach showed them to other men in the fab shop); McMillan Depo. at 46–47 (magazines showing nude women kept in storeroom and transportation department for JSI male employees to read).

22. Management employees from the very top down condoned these displays; often they had their own pictures. McIlwain, for example, has been aware for years of *Playboy*- and *Penthouse*-style pictures showing nude women posted in the workplace; he refused to issue a policy prohibiting the display of such pictures. • • • Both Brown and Stewart have encountered pictures of nude or partially nude women in the work environment at JSI. Nevertheless, both men have concluded, and agreed with each other, that there is nothing wrong with pictures of naked or partially naked women being posted in the JSI workplace. Ahlwardt kept a "pin-up" himself • • •; Lovett, like some other foremen, had vendors' advertising calendars in his office. • • • Coordinators, who are members of management, • • • and who are responsible for ensuring that government contracts are performed to the satisfaction of the federal government, have had pornographic magazines in the desks of their trailers • • •.

Sexual Harassment of Plaintiff

23. Robinson credibly testified to the extensive, pervasive posting of pictures depicting nude women, partially nude women, or sexual conduct and to the occurrence of other forms of harassing behavior perpetrated by her male coworkers and supervisors. Her testimony covered the full term of her employment, from 1977 to 1988. The Court considered those incidents that fall outside the time frame of a Title VII complaint for the purpose of determining the context of the incidents which are actionable (i.e., whether the more recent conduct may be dismissed as an aberration or must be considered to be a part of the work environment) and for the purpose of assessing the reasonableness of the response by defendants to the complaints that Robinson made during the Title VII time frame. • • •

24. Robinson's testimony provides a vivid description of a visual assault on the sensibilities of female workers at JSI that did not relent during working hours. She credibly testified that the pervasiveness of the pictures left her unable to recount every example, but those pictures which she did describe illustrate the extent of this aspect of the work environment at JSI. She testified to seeing in the period prior to April 4, 1984, the three hundredth day prior to the filing of her EEOC charge:

   (a) a picture of a woman, breasts and pubic area exposed, inside a drydock area in 1977 or 1978. • • •
   (b) a picture of a nude Black woman, pubic area exposed to reveal her labia, seen in the public locker room. • • •
   (c) drawings and graffiti on the walls, including a drawing depicting a frontal view of a nude female torso with the words "USDA Choice" written on it, at the Commercial Yard in the late 1970's or early 1980's, in an area where Robinson was assigned to work. • • •
   (d) a picture of a woman's pubic area with a meat spatula pressed on it, observed on a wall next to the sheetmetal shop at Mayport in the late 1970's. • • •

(e) centerfold-style pictures in the Mayport Yard toolroom trailer, which Robinson saw daily in the necessary course of her work for over one month in the late 1970s. • • • Neal McCormick, a toolroom worker from 1975 to 1980, verified that the toolroom personnel had indeed displayed pictures of nude women "of the Playboy centerfold variety" during the time he worked there. • • •

(f) pictures of nude or partially nude women in the fab shop lockers at the Commercial Yard through 1980. • • •

(g) a pornographic magazine handed to Robinson by a male coworker in front of other coworkers in the early 1980s. • • •

(h) a magazine containing pictures of nude and partially nude women in the possession of a pipefitter, in 1980, who was reading it in the engine room of a ship. • • •

(i) pictures in the shipfitters' shop at the Commercial Yard, in 1983, observed by Robinson while she was walking to the welding shop, including a frontal nude with a shaved pubic area and corseted nude with her breasts and buttocks area exposed. • • • Robinson complained to John Robinson, the quarterman on the third shift in the shipfitting department, about the second picture; he took it down that night and she never saw the picture again. • • •

(j) a picture of a woman with her breasts exposed, on the outside of a shack on a ship in the Commercial Yard. • • • Robinson enlisted the assistance of union vice-president Leroy Yeomans to have the picture removed. • • • It was removed within a day or two.

25. Robinson's testimony concerning visual harassment in the period commencing April 4, 1984, includes:

(a) a picture of a nude woman with long blonde hair wearing high heels and holding a whip, waved around by a coworker, Freddie Dixon, in 1984, in an enclosed area where Robinson and approximately six men were working. • • • Robinson testified she felt particularly targeted by this action because she has long blonde hair and works with a welding tool known as a whip. • • • Dixon admitted that he had indeed waved the picture around for other male employees to see, but denied that he intended to target or offend Robinson. • • • In fact, Dixon claimed that he was unaware that Robinson was in the area and that he was unaware that Robinson was a blonde. • • • The Court does not find his denials credible; the evidence more readily supports the conclusion that Dixon intended to offend Robinson, or acted with such disregard for her that the harassment could be equated with intent.

(b) calendars posted in the pipe shop in the Commercial Yard, in 1983 or 1984, including a picture in which a nude woman was bending over with her buttocks and genitals exposed to view. • • • (Joint Exh. No. 1 was admitted as illustrative of this type of calendar. It is a Whilden Valve and Gauge calendar for 1984. The naked breasts or buttocks of each model are exposed in every month; the pubic areas are also visible on the models featured in April and September. Several of the pictures are suggestive of sexually submissive behavior.) Robinson testified that she observed at least three pictures posted in the pipe shop. *Id.* Although this was not Robinson's work area, she was in that shop with a leaderman to find the pipe shop leaderman to clarify a work matter. *Id.* at 122.

(c) a picture of a nude woman with long blond hair sitting in front of a mirror brushing her hair, in a storage area on a ship. • • • Robinson mentioned to either a leaderman or the assistant foreman that she considered it a "very dirty ship," and she was subsequently reassigned to a different location. • • •

(d) Joint Exh. No. 3, a Whilden Valve & Gauge calendar for 1985, which features *Playboy* playmate of the month pictures on each page. • • • The female models in this calendar are fully or partially nude. In every month except February, April, and November, the model's breasts are fully exposed. The pubic areas are exposed on the women featured in August and December. Several of the pictures are suggestive of sexually submissive behavior.

(e) several pictures of nude or partially nude women posted in the fab shop area in the backyard of the Mayport Yard, in January 1985, visible to her from her path to and from the time clock building. • • •

(f) pictures in the shipfitters' trailer on board the *U.S.S. Saratoga,* in January 1985, including one picture of two nude women apparently engaged in lesbian sex. • • • Robinson later observed a calendar • • • in this office. • • • This calendar, distributed by Whilden Valve and Gauge, features pictures of nude and partially nude women each month. The breasts of each model are exposed; the pubic areas of the models also are exposed for May, October and December. Several of the pictures are suggestive of sexually submissive behavior.

(g) pictures in the toolroom trailer aboard the *U.S.S. Saratoga,* in January 1985, including one of a nude woman with long blond hair lying down propped up on her elbow and a smaller black and white photograph of a female nude. • • • These pictures formed a part of Robinson's complaint that forms the foundation of this lawsuit. • • •

(h) pictures in the fab shop area, in January 1985, including one of a woman wearing black tights, the top pulled down to expose her breasts to view, and one of a nude woman in an outdoor setting apparently playing with a piece of cloth between her legs. • • •

(i) Joint Exh. No. 4, a Whilden Valve & Gauge calendar for 1986, which features *Playboy* playmate of the month pictures on each page. 1 T.T. at 103–04. The female models in this calendar are fully or partially nude. In every month except April, the model's breasts are fully exposed. The pubic areas are exposed on the women featured in May, June and December. Several of the pictures are suggestive of sexually submissive behavior.

(j) a picture of a nude woman left on the tool box where Robinson returned her tools, in the summer of 1986. • • • The photograph depicted the woman's legs spread apart, knees bent up toward her chest, exposing her breasts and genitals. • • • Several men were present and laughed at Robinson when she appeared upset by the picture. • • •

(k) pictures seen in the shipfitters' trailer, in 1986, including one of a woman with short blond hair, wearing a dark vest pulled back to expose her breasts. • • • Robinson complained to shipfitter leaderman Danny Miracle about the photograph of the blond woman. Miracle removed the photograph, with some reluctance, but it was posted again shortly thereafter. • • • It was not visible from outside the trailer when it was posted the second time. • • •

(l) a sexually-oriented cartoon, • • •, posted in the safety office, in 1986, at the Mayport Yard. • • •

(m) pictures observed in the fab shop area office, in 1986, including • • • a picture of a topless brown haired woman. • • • Joint Exh. No. 6 is a wooden plaque consisting of a picture of a very young-looking woman with one breast fully exposed and the other breast partially exposed. Robinson also remarked that another plaque was present in that shop, without further identifying it. Other testimony indicated that Jt.Exh. No. 7 hung in the fab shop at the time. Jt.Exh. No. 7 shows a nude woman straddling a hammock with her head tossed back and her back arched. Her exposed breasts are fully visible as is some pubic hair.

(n) a life-size drawing of a nude woman on a divider in the sheetmetal shop, in April 1987, which remained on the wall for several weeks. • • •

(o) a drawing on a heater control box, approximately one foot square, of a nude woman with fluid coming from her genital area, in 1987, at the Commercial Yard. • • •

(p) Joint Exh. No. 5, a Valve Repair, Inc. calendar for 1987, which features *Playboy* playmate of the month pictures on each page. • • • (Defendants have admitted that this calendar was displayed during 1987 in the foreman's and leaderman's offices of the pipe shop at the Commercial Yard.) The female models in this calendar are fully or partially nude. In every month the model's breasts are fully exposed. The pubic areas are exposed on the women featured in March and September. Several of the pictures are suggestive of sexually submissive behavior.

(q) a dart board with a drawing of a woman's breast with her nipple as the bull's eye, in 1987 or 1988, at the Commercial Yard. • • •

(r) pornographic magazines, including *Players,* on a table by the gangway of a ship, in 1987 or 1988, where JSI machinists were looking through them and commenting on the pictures, • • • a *Club* magazine, held out by coworker Thomas Adams in the bow of a ship, • • • several magazines being read by pipefitters, in 1986, aboard a ship at the Mayport Yard, • • • and various other instances of welders with magazines throughout the 1980's • • •.

(s) pictures of nude and partially nude women posted in the engine room of the *M/V Splay,* in 1988, at the Commercial Yard, including a picture of a nude woman in a kneeling position and a calendar featuring photographs of nude women. • • • Robinson complained to her leaderman, who in turn found a person associated with the ship to remove and cover the pictures. • • • Later, however, the pictures were again posted and uncovered. • • •

(t) a shirt worn by the shop steward, in December 1988, with a drawing of bare female breasts and the words "DALLAS WHOREHOUSE" written on it.

26. In January 1985, following a complaint by Robinson concerning a calendar in the shipfitters' trailer, the words "Men Only" were painted on the door to that trailer. • • •

27. Robinson also testified about comments of a sexual nature she recalled hearing at JSI from coworkers. In some instances these comments were made while she was also in the presence of the pictures of nude or partially nude women. Among the remarks Robinson recalled are: "Hey pussycat, come here and give me a whiff," • • •; "The more you lick it, the harder it gets," • • •; "I'd like to get into bed with that," • • •; "I'd like to have some of that," • • •; "Black women taste like sardines," • • •; "It doesn't hurt women to have sex right after childbirth," • • •; "That one there is mine" (referring to a picture in a magazine) • • •; "Watch out for Chet. He's Chester the Molester" (referring to a cartoon character in a pornographic magazine who molests little girls) • • •; "You rate about an 8 or a 9 on a scale of 10," • • •. She recalled one occasion on which a welder told her he wished her shirt would blow over her head so he could look, • • • another occasion on which a fitter told her he wished her shirt was tighter (because he thought it would be sexier), • • • an occasion on which a foreman candidate asked her to "come sit" on his lap, *id.* at 130, and innumerable occasions on which a coworker or supervisor called her "honey," "dear," "baby," "sugar," "sugar-booger," and "momma" instead of calling her by her name, • • •. Robinson additionally related her exposure to joking comments by male coworkers about a woman pipefitter whose initials are "V.D." • • •.

28. Robinson encountered particularly severe verbal harassment from a shipfitter, George Nelson ("Nelson"), while assigned to work with him on a number of different nights in 1986 at the Mayport Yard. Nelson regularly expressed his displeasure at working with Robinson, making such remarks as "women are only fit company for something that howls," and "there's nothing worse that having to work around women." • • • When Robinson confronted Nelson over her perception of his behavior as sexual harassment, Nelson denied he was engaging in harassment because he had not propositioned her for sexual favors. • • • Nelson subsequently made Robinson's perception of "harassment" a new subject of ridicule and accused her of "crusading on a rabbit." • • •

29. On one occasion, George Leach told an offensive joke in Robinson's presence, the subject matter of which concerned "boola-boola," a reference to sodomous rape. • • • He admitted telling the joke but maintained that he told it quietly and Robinson had taken steps to avoid hearing the joke. The Court credits Robinson's testimony and further observes that the work environment is not rendered less hostile by a male coworker's demand of a female worker that she "take cover" so that the men can exchange dirty jokes. Leach later teased Robinson in a threatening fashion by yelling "boola-boola" at her in the parking lot at JSI. Robinson subsequently learned that some shipfitters had dubbed her "boola-boola" as a nickname arising out of these events. • • •

30. Robinson testified concerning the presence of abusive language written on the walls in her working area in 1987 and 1988. Among this graffiti were the phrases "lick me you whore dog bitch," "eat me," and "pussy." This first phrase appeared on the wall over a spot where Robinson had left her jacket. • • • The second phrase was freshly painted in Robinson's work area when she observed it. • • • The third phrase appeared during a break after she left her work area to get a drink of water. • • •

31. Donald Furr, Robinson's leaderman, attested to further evidence of the frequency with which this abusive graffiti occurred. He stated that he had seen words like "pussy" and "cunt" written on the walls in the JSI workplace. • • • He added that at one point "it was getting to be an almost every night occasion [Robinson] wanted something scribbled out or a picture tooken [sic] down. . . ." • • •

Sexual Harassment of Other Female Craftworkers

32. The Court heard testimony from two of Robinson's female coworkers, Lawanna Gail Banks ("Banks") and Leslie Albert ("Albert"), concerning incidents of sexual harassment to which they were subjected, including incidents that did not occur in Robinson's presence. The Court heard this evidence for several reasons. First, as with the incidents outside the time frame of a Title VII complaint involving Robinson, incidents involving other female employees place the conduct at issue in context. The pervasiveness of conduct constituting sexual harassment outside Robinson's presence works to rebut the assertion that the conduct of which Robinson complains is isolated or rare. Second, the issue in this case is the nature of the work environment. This environment is shaped by more than the face-to-face encounters between Robinson and male coworkers and supervisors. The perception that the work environment is hostile can be influenced by the treatment of other persons of a plaintiff's protected class, even if that treatment is learned second-hand. Last, other incidents of sexual harassment are directly relevant to an employer's liability for the acts of employees and to the issue of an appropriate remedy for the sexual harassment perpetrated against Robinson.

33. Banks and Albert both confirmed the description of the work environment related by Robinson. Each of these other women endured many incidents of sexually harassing behavior. • • •

34. • • • Among the incidents to which [Banks] credibly testified:

(a) being pinched on the breasts by a foreman, • • •.
(b) having her ankles grabbed by a male coworker who pulled her legs apart and stood between them, • • •.
(c) hearing such comments as "it's a cunt hair off," • • •, "are you on the rag," • • • and "what do you sleep in?" • • •.
(d) receiving verbal abuse from a rigger named Hawkins. • • • Hawkins humiliated Banks by stating, in front of a large group of male coworkers, "if you fell into a barrel of dicks, you'd come up sucking your thumb." • • •
(e) receiving a variety of harassment from a rigger named John Fraser. Fraser sniffed at Banks' behind while she was walking up a gangway, producing laughter from the group of men observing the incident. • • • Fraser also placed a large flashlight in his pants in Banks' presence to create the illusion of a large penis. • • •
(f) suffering the embarrassment of having a shipfitter leaderman, Ernie Edenfield ("Edenfield"), hold a chipping hammer handle, which was whittled to resemble a penis, near her face while he told her to open her mouth. • • •
(g) enduring the unwelcome advances of a coworker, a pipefitter named Romeo Bascuguin, who pursued her for dates and talked explicitly about his reputed sexual prowess. • • • Banks also testified to two other incidents involving calls to her home by JSI employees, including a supervisor, who expressed sexual interest in her. • • •[3]

35. Banks observed pictures of nude and partially nude women throughout the workplace at JSI. • • • She did not take as great offense at the pictures as Robinson did, but Banks stated that she steered clear of men who worked where such pictures were displayed because she came to expect more harassment from those men. • • •

[1, 2][Omitted.]

[3]While incidents outside the workplace do not provide a basis for concluding that the workplace is sexually hostile, the circumstances of these two incidents make them worthy of this brief notation in order to develop fully the record respecting the degree to which the work environment shaped attitudes that transcended the confines of the shipyards.

36. • • • On two occasions when Banks was the only woman on the company bus, male coworkers displayed or read from pornographic magazines. • • • Banks also testified concerning two occasions in which male coworkers posted pictures with an apparent animus toward Robinson. A coworker, Chris Lay, showed a number of men, and Banks, a picture of a nude woman with a welding shield. He remarked, "Lois would really like this," and placed it on the wall in the welding trailer aboard the *U.S.S. Saratoga*. • • • Banks removed the picture when the men had left. • • • Approximately the same time, some male pipefitters placed a picture of a nude woman on Robinson's toolbox. Banks removed it, but another picture was placed there and subsequently discovered by Robinson. • • •

37. Albert, a machinist at JSI from 1976 to 1986, testified to a description of the work environment consistent with that described by Robinson and Banks. She related sexual comments identical to or similar to those heard by Robinson and Banks, • • •, and noted that the recollection of specific events was hampered by the commonplace, daily nature of the comments • • •. In one noteworthy incident, a male coworker persistently propositioned Albert, prompting her to complain to her leaderman and assistant foreman. The propositions continued after those individuals spoke to the coworker. When he finally put his hands on Albert, she responded both verbally and physically. Thereafter the coworker was fired, although the circumstances in the record of his discharge do not indicate whether the discharge was for the sexually harassing behavior or for drunkenness and sleeping on the job. • • •

38. Albert also testified to the pervasive presence of pictures of nude and partially nude women throughout the shipyards, and the increase of male employee attention to such pictures following Robinson's complaints over the presence of the pictures. • • •

41. Based on the foregoing, the Court finds that sexually harassing behavior occurred throughout the JSI working environment with both frequency and intensity over the relevant time period. Robinson did not welcome such behavior.

Effect of JSI Work Environment on Women

42. The foregoing evidence was supplemented with the testimony of various experts. Plaintiff called experts in the fields of sexual stereotyping and sexual harassment; defendants presented expert testimony on the relative offensiveness of pornographic materials to men and women.

Plaintiff's Expert Witness Testimony

43. Dr. Susan Fiske appeared as an expert witness on plaintiff's behalf to testify on the subject of sexual stereotyping. • • •

44. The study of stereotyping is the study of category-based responses in the human thought and perceptual processes. Stereotyping, prejudice, and discrimination are the three basic kinds of category-based responses. Stereotyping exists primarily as a thought process, prejudice develops as an emotional or an evaluative process, primarily negative in nature, while discrimination manifests itself as a behavioral response. • • • Discrimination in this context is defined by the treatment of a person differently and less favorably because of the category to which that person belongs. • • • Either stereotyping or prejudice may form the basis for discrimination.

45. To categorize people along certain lines means their suitability will be evaluated in these terms as well. In the process of perceiving people as divided into groups, a person tends to maximize the differences among groups, exaggerating those differences, and mini-mize the differences within groups. • • • In practice, this translates into a perception that women are more similar to other women and more different from men (and vice versa) than they actually may be. • • • This perceptual process produces the in-group/out-group phe-nomenon: members of the other group or groups are viewed less favorably. • • • This categorizing process can produce discriminatory results in employment settings if it leads a person in that job setting to judge another person based on some quality unrelated to job performance into which the other person falls.

46. For example, when a superior categorizes a female employee based on her sex, that superior evaluates her in terms of characteristics that comport with stereotypes assigned to women rather than in terms of her job skills and performance. • • • Thus, to categorize a female employee along the lines of sex produces an evaluation of her suitability as a "woman" who might be expected to be sexy, affectionate and attractive; this female employee would be evaluated less favorably if she is seen as not conforming to that model without regard for her job performance. • • • Interestingly, this example is borne out in testimony by several witnesses called by defendants, who expressed disapproval of Robinson's demeanor because she did not meet the expectation of "affectionate" female behavior, • • • or who expressed disapproval of Banks' use of "crude" language as inappropriate behavior for a "lady," • • •.

47. Dr. Fiske • • • concluded, "the conditions exist for sex stereotyping at Jacksonville Shipyards and . . . many of the effects of sex stereotyping exist. . . ." • • • Dr. Fiske described the sex stereotyping at JSI as a situation of "sex role spillover," where the evaluation of women employees by their coworkers and supervisors takes place in terms of the sexuality of the women and their worth as sex objects rather than their merit as craft workers. • • •

48. Dr. Fiske identified several preconditions that enhance the presence of stereotyping in a workplace. The four categories of preconditions are: (1) rarity; (2) priming (or category accessibility); (3) work environment structure; and (4) ambience of the work environment. Stereotyping may occur in the absence of these conditions; studies have demonstrated, however, a statistically significant correlation between these preconditions and the prevalence of stereotyping. • • • All of the preconditions are present in the work environment at JSI.

49. "Rarity" exists when an individual's group is small in number in relation to its contrasting group, so that each individual member is seen as one of a kind—a solo or near solo. Rarity or "solo" status exists when an individual's group comprises fifteen to twenty percent or less of the work force in the relevant work environment. • • • Women at JSI in general occupy solo status and rarity is extreme for women in the skilled crafts. • • •

50. Solos capture the attention of the members of the majority group, providing fodder for their rumors and constantly receiving their scrutiny. • • • The solo is far more likely to become the victim of stereotyping than a member of the majority group, and the stereotype develops along the dimension that makes the solos rare. • • • Solos typically elicit extreme responses from members of the majority group. Thus, mildly substandard work performance or workplace behavior is perceived as much worse when a solo is the worker than when a member of the majority group is responsible. • • • According to Dr. Fiske, the studies concerning the perception of solo work performance and behavior demonstrate that the solo status *per se,* not the behavior, produces the extreme reaction from other people. • • •

51. The second precondition for stereotyping, "priming" or "category accessibility", is a process in which specific stimuli in the work environment prime certain categories for the application of stereotypical thinking. • • • The priming impact created by the availability of photographs of nude and partially nude women, sexual joking, and sexual slurs hold particular application in the JSI workplace. • • •

52. Dr. Fiske testified these stimuli may encourage a significant proportion of the male population in the workforce to view and interact with women coworkers as if those women are sex objects. • • •

53. The testimony of witnesses confirms a correlation between the presence of pictures and sexual comments and the level of sexual preoccupation of some of the male workers whose conduct had sexual overtones observable by female workers.

54. The third precondition for an increased frequency of stereotyping is the nature of the power structure or hierarchy in the work environment. This factor examines the group affiliation of the persons in the positions of power and the degree to which particular groups are given a sense of belonging. At JSI, this precondition arises because the people affected by the sexualized working conditions are women and the people deciding what to do about it are men. The in-group/out-group effect diminishes the impact of the women's concerns. The men who receive the complaints perceive those complaints less favorably and take them less seriously because they come from women. • • • Specific instances of handling of

complaints of sexual harassment, developed *infra,* demonstrate the phenomenon of male supervisors trivializing the valid complaints of Robinson and other female workers.

55. Dr. Fiske addressed a hypothetical concerning the effect of a sexualized workplace on a complaint lodged by a female employee. • • • This hypothetical involved a work environment where women are solos and men control the power structure. A woman complains about a man who exposed himself to her. Dr. Fiske predicted that, where sexualization of the workplace has occurred, the woman lodging the complaint would be the focus of attention, rather than the misconduct of which she complains. The woman would be perceived as the problem; she might be subject to ridicule and become the subject of rumors. The man likely would not be disciplined commensurate with the misconduct. Dr. Fiske's prediction is borne out in part by Albert's testimony concerning two male coworkers' discussion of an incident at JSI in which a male employee had exposed himself to a female employee. • • •

56. In a like manner, Dr. Fiske predicted that a female employee who complained about sexual pictures of women would, in the hypothetical environment, find that she is perceived as the problem and dismissed as a complainer. • • • The content of the speculations and reactions to the complainer, in a sexualized work environment, would focus on her sexuality. Aspersions may be cast on the sexuality of the complaining employee regarding, for example, her sexual preference, background, experiences or traumas. Dr. Fiske found it unsurprising that male employees at JSI entertained such derogatory rumors concerning Robinson. • • •

57. The fourth precondition is the ambience of the work environment. According to Dr. Fiske, studies show that the tolerance of nonprofessional conduct promotes the stereotyping of women in terms of their sex object status. For instance, when profanity is evident, women are three times more likely to be treated as sex objects than in a workplace where profanity is not tolerated. • • • When sexual joking is common in work environment, stereotyping of women in terms of their sex object status is three to seven times more likely to occur. • • •

58. Nonprofessional ambience imposes much harsher effects on women than on men. The general principle, as stated by Dr. Fiske, is "when sex comes into the workplace, women are profoundly affected . . . in their performance and in their ability to do their jobs without being bothered by it." • • • The effects encompass emotional upset, • • • reduced job satisfaction, • • •, the deterrence of women from seeking jobs or promotions, • • • and an increase of women quitting jobs, getting transferred, or being fired because of the sexualization of the workplace • • •. By contrast, the effect of the sexualization of the workplace is "vanishingly small" for men. • • •

59. Men and women respond to sex issues in the workplace to a degree that exceeds normal differences in other perceptual reactions between them. • • • For example, research reveals a near flip-flop of attitudes when both men and women were asked what their response would be to being sexually approached in the workplace. Approximately two-thirds of the men responded that they would be flattered; only fifteen percent would feel insulted. For the women the proportions are reversed. • • •

60. The sexualization of the workplace imposed burdens on women that are not borne by men. • • • Women must constantly monitor their behavior to determine whether they are eliciting sexual attention. They must conform their behavior to the existence of the sexual stereotyping either by becoming sexy and responsive to the men who flirt with them or by becoming rigid, standoffish, and distant so as to make it clear that they are not interested in the status of sex object. • • •

61. Two major effects of stereotyping were described by Dr. Fiske. One effect is selective interpretation. The individual who engages in stereotyping of another person because of that person's membership in a minority group selectively interprets behavior of the other person along the lines of the stereotypes applied to the group. • • • Thus, an employer may respond to a complaint by a female employee by stereotyping her as "an overly emotional woman," and thereafter ignore her complaints as exaggerated or insignificant. • • • (Behavior of this sort is apparent in JSI's responses to female complaints concerning sexual harassment described *infra*.). A second effect of stereotyping is denigration of

the individual merit of the person who is stereotyped. *Id.* The presence of stereotyping in the workplace affects the job turnover and job satisfaction of the members of the group subjected to stereotyping. • • •

62. Dr. Fiske's testimony provided a sound, credible theoretical framework from which to conclude that the presence of pictures of nude and partially nude women, sexual comments, sexual joking, and other behaviors previously described creates and contributes to a sexually hostile work environment. Moreover, this framework produces an evidentiary basis for concluding that a sexualized working environment is abusive to a woman because of her sex. Defendants did not provide any basis to question the theory of stereotyping and its relationship to the work environment. • • •

63. Ms. K.C. Wagner appeared as an expert witness on plaintiff's behalf to testify on common patterns and responses to sexual harassment and remedial steps. • • • The Court accepted Ms. Wagner, over the objection of defendants, as an expert on common patterns and responses to sexual harassment and accepted her, without objection, as an expert in education and training relative to sexual harassment.

64. According to Ms. Wagner, women in nontraditional employment who form a small minority of the workforce are at particular risk of suffering male worker behaviors such as sexual teasing, sexual joking, and the display of materials of a sexual nature. • • •

65. Ms. Wagner expressed her expert opinion that sexually harassing conditions for female employees exist at JSI. Her conclusion rests on the presence of indicators of sexually harassing behaviors and of a sexually hostile work environment, including evidence of a range of behaviors and conditions that are considered sexually harassing, evidence of common coping patterns by individual victims of sexual harassment, evidence of stress effects suffered by those women, evidence of male worker behavior and attitudes, and evidence of confused management response to complaints of sexual harassment. • • •

66. According to Ms. Wagner, women respond to sexually harassing behavior in a variety of reasonable ways. The coping strategy a woman selects depends on her personal style, the type of incident, and her expectation that the situation is susceptible to resolution. • • • Typical coping methods include: (1) denying the impact of the event, blocking it out; (2) avoiding the workplace or the harasser, for instance, by taking sick leave or otherwise being absent; (3) telling the harasser to stop; (4) engaging in joking or other banter in the language of the workplace in order to defuse the situation; and (5) threatening to make or actually making an informal or formal complaint. • • •

67. Of these five categories, formal complaint is the most rare because the victim of harassment fears an escalation of the problem, retaliation from the harasser, and embarrassment in the process of reporting. • • • Victims also often fear that nothing will be done and they will be blamed for the incident. • • • Thus, the absence of reporting of sexual harassment incidents cannot be viewed as an absence of such incidents from the workplace. • • • An effective policy for controlling sexual harassment cannot rely on ad hoc incident-by-incident reporting and investigation. • • •

68. Victims of sexual harassment suffer stress effects from the harassment. Stress as a result of sexual harassment is recognized as a specific, diagnosable problem by the American Psychiatric Association. • • • Among the stress effects suffered is "work performance stress," which includes distraction from tasks, dread of work, and an inability to work. • • • Another form is "emotional stress," which covers a range of responses, including anger, fear of physical safety, anxiety, depression, guilt, humiliation, and embarrassment. • • • Physical stress also results from sexual harassment; it may manifest itself as sleeping problems, headaches, weight changes, and other physical ailments. • • • A study by the Working Women's Institute found that ninety-six percent of sexual harassment victims experienced emotional distress, forty-five percent suffered work performance distress, and thirty-five percent were inflicted with physical stress problems. • • •

69. Sexual harassment has a cumulative, eroding effect on the victim's well-being. • • • When women feel a need to maintain vigilance against the next incident of harassment, the stress is increased tremendously. • • • When women feel that their individual complaints will not change the work environment materially, the ensuing sense of despair further compounds the stress. • • •

70. Management's perception concerning the scope and range of sexual harassment provides an important indicator of the hostility of the work environment. • • • The more subtle forms of sexual harassment, such as sexual comments, sexual teasing, and leering, often fall outside management's perception. • • • As a general proposition, the higher an individual is on the management ladder, the more likely he is to regard sexual harassment as an exaggerated problem and the more likely he is to minimize complaints from women concerning what they perceive to be harassing behavior. • • •

71. Men and women perceive the existence of sexual harassment differently. • • • Ms. Wagner testified that the differential perception of sexual harassment is borne out by her own experiences and by survey research. A study of federal employees by the Merit Systems Protection Board found that 11 to 12 percent more women than men characterized sexual remarks or materials of a sexual nature in the workplace as sexual harassment. • • • Regarding the second of these categories, which consisted of letters, calls and materials of a sexual nature, including materials depicting sexually provocative poses, nude, and partially nude pictures, 87 percent of the women considered this behavior to constitute sexual harassment, in contrast to 76 percent of the men. • • •

72. Male coworkers often fail to see any potential for harassment in their behavior because they believe that only the behavior of supervisors can contribute to a sexually hostile work environment. • • •

73. Ms. Wagner's testimony provided a credible, sound explanation for the variety of responses to harassing behavior at JSI to which other witnesses testified.[4] Moreover, her framework explains why some women may not feel offended by some behaviors in the workplace that offend other women • • • (testimony of Donna Martin that she was not offended by sexual joking in workplace), and yet the work environment remains hostile to most women.

Defendants' Expert Witness Testimony

74. Dr. Donald Mosher appeared as an expert witness on defendants' behalf to testify in the area of the psychological effects of sexual materials. • • •

75. Dr. Mosher prepared for his testimony by reviewing Robinson's deposition and all of the visual materials contained in Joint Exh. Nos. 1 through 7. • • • He expressed his expert opinion that those pictures do not create a serious or probable harm to the average woman. • • •

• • •

78. The Court does not accept Dr. Mosher's ultimate conclusions concerning the impact of sexual materials as pertinent to deciding issues in this case. Dr. Mosher's study and the studies upon which he relies do not address the matter of workplace exposure to sexual materials under conditions comparable to those existing at JSI. • • • Dr. Mosher conceded that the element of control is a factor in a woman's reaction to sexual materials. • • • The more specific studies and observations undertaken by plaintiff's experts deserve greater weight. • • •

79. Dr. Joseph Scott appeared as an expert witness on defendants' behalf to testify in the area of the effects of sexual materials on behavior and generally on men and women. • • •

---

[4]In *Lipsett v. University of Puerto Rico,* 740 F.Supp. 921 (D.P.R.1990), *on remand from* 864 F.2d 881 (1st Cir.1988) (*rev'g* 669 F.Supp. 1188 (D.P.R.1987)), Judge Pieras denied a motion to qualify Ms. Wagner as an expert witness in a hostile work environment sex discrimination suit. The *Lipsett* case, however, is a jury action and may be distinguished for this reason. For instance, Ms. Wagner's testimony on common patterns and responses to sexual harassment directly informs the inquiry into the effect of the conditions at JSI on the psychological well-being of the hypothetical reasonable woman. Whatever merit lies in the argument that jurors may draw on their common experiences to assess the issue, the Court risks injustice if it attempts to fashion a reasonable woman's reaction out of whole cloth. The general rule applied, particularly in nonjury cases, is that "the decision by a trial court on the competency of, and what weight should be give to the testimony of, an expert is a highly discretionary one." *IMPACT v. Firestone,* 893 F.2d 1189, 1195 (11th Cir.), *cert. denied,* — U.S. —, 111 S.Ct. 133, 112 L.Ed.2d 100 (1990). This Court is satisfied that the potential sources of bias, strengths, and weaknesses in Ms. Wagner's qualifications and testimony have been considered fully.

80. Dr. Scott prepared for his testimony by reviewing Robinson's deposition and the visual materials contained in Joint Exh. Nos. 1 through 7. • • • He expressed his expert opinion that "the average female would not be substantially effective [sic] in a negative manner" by the materials, that is, she would not take offense at them. • • • He further stated that women in the workforce would be slightly more offended by such materials than men. • • • He based his opinion on surveys which he conducted himself and surveys conducted by other people on the effects of sexual materials. • • • One of the studies upon which he relied is a study of the offensiveness to the raters of the contents of *Hustler* magazine. • • •

81. • • • In this study the females rated the cartoons and the pictorials to be less offensive than the males did, • • • although the level of offensiveness was low for both groups • • •. The methodology of the study, however, diminishes its application to the workplace. The subjects were twelve college student volunteers, six men and six women. • • • They viewed the materials at their own leisure, alone or at their own table in a room with three tables. • • •

• • •

83. The Court does not accept Dr. Scott's expert testimony as useful to the determination of the issues in this case. His opinions provide a basis for evaluating the offensiveness of sexual materials in the abstract only. The important element of context is missing; the sexually harassing impact of the materials must be measured in the circumstances of the JSI work environment. Dr. Scott's testimony does not assist in this effort.

Defendants' Social Context Evidence

84. Defendants introduced into evidence several examples of magazines often purchased by women in which complete or partial nudity, sexual cartoons, and sexually frank articles appear. *See* D.Exh. Nos. 13 (*Cosmopolitan,* Sept. 1987), 14 (*Glamour,* Sept. 1987), 15 (*Ms.,* Sept. 1987), 16 (*Vanity Fair,* Oct.1987). Dr. Scott testified that the sexual explicitness of these magazines reflects a recent trend for "women's magazines." • • • In addition, a picture of a statue in the Duval County Courthouse, in which a female figure's breasts are exposed, was introduced into evidence. • • •

85. Defendants also solicited evidence about the conditions at two other shipyards, Norfolk Shipbuilding and Drydock Corp. (NORSHIPCO) and Colona Shipyard. Harvey Williams worked in employee relations positions at both facilities • • •. • • • Both have workforces in which approximately 10 to 15 percent of the employees are female. Pictures of nude and partially nude women are posted in the shops and locker rooms, but no complaints about the pictures were filed at either site during Williams' tenure. • • •

86. For the reasons stated in Conclusions of Law ("COL") ¶15, the Court finds that this "social context" evidence has little to no value in determining the issues of this case. If this type of evidence were material, the Court finds considerable weakness in defendants' presentation. The magazines introduced into evidence do not form a basis to suggest the extent to which sexually frank or sexually explicit materials are accepted by women; no circulation figures were introduced and no evidence suggests the acceptance of the sexually frank material by female subscribers or readers. The absence of formal complaints at NORSHIPCO and Colona does not tell whether their work environments are hostile; plaintiff's expert witnesses testified that a lack of complaints does not indicate the level of hostility. Moreover, the professional relations between men and women may be otherwise so favorable that the presence of sexually-oriented pictures does not threaten the relationship; the percentage of women in the workforces at both shipyards is much higher than at JSI. Because of these weaknesses, the Court finds the social context evidence inadequate to draw reliable conclusions concerning the reaction of women to sexually-oriented pictures in the workplace.

• • •

Sexually-Oriented Pictures

94. Complaints about the pictures of nude and partially nude women yielded little success. On some occasions pictures were removed but subsequently were posted again or

like pictures were posted in their place. • • • In one instance, a calendar about which Robinson complained was merely removed from one wall to another on the assumption that the lower visibility of the objectionable pictures would adequately address the complaint of sexual harassment. • • •

95. The display of pictures of, and calendars featuring pictures of, nude and partially nude women was left to the discretion of the foremen of the respective shops. • • • The evidence shows only one foreman, Ben West of the outside machine shop at the Mayport Yard, ordered the pictures of nude and partially nude women, whether pinups or calendars, off his shop's walls. This bold action, however, was attenuated by the replacement of the calendars bearing nudes with calendars showing women in provocative swimwear. • • •

Robinson's January 1985 Complaints (Events Precipitating Lawsuit)

96. The present lawsuit stems from Robinson's complaints in January 1985 that pictures of nude and partially nude women were posted in the toolroom trailer and in the shipfitters' trailer aboard the *U.S.S. Saratoga* at the Mayport Yard. • • • Robinson initially complained to Kiedrowski, her leaderman and the most senior person in the welding department aboard ship, • • •, and later to Fred Turner ("Turner"), the welding department foreman.

97. Kiedrowski's reaction to Robinson's complaint to him left her feeling embarrassed. • • • Robinson observed that one of the pictures in the toolroom about which she complained, a color photograph of a nude blond woman, was removed shortly after her complaint to Kiedrowski; another picture in the toolroom trailer, a black and white photograph, remained posted for several more days. • • • Kiedrowski disclaimed any ability to assist Robinson in securing removal of the calendar in the shipfitters' trailer. • • • Kiedrowski also told Robinson that she had no business in the shipfitters' office. • • • The basis for his scolding her on this point is unclear; Kiedrowski had previously assigned Robinson to work with the shipfitters on occasion, • • • and, when he worked as a welder, he had occasion to enter the shipfitters' office himself • • •.

98. In the case of Turner, Robinson approached him and expressed her complaint over the "pornography" she had seen. Turner responded, "the what?"; Robinson repeated the term "pornography" three times before Turner acknowledged that he understood that she was referring to the pinup and calendar pictures in the shipyards. • • • While Turner received a report from his group that the offending pictures had been removed, deposition and trial testimony by Owens indicate that either some pictures were missed or new pictures were posted after Turner's order. • • •

• • •

100. Robinson then telephoned Lovett, the shipfitting foreman, to complain. Lovett advised Robinson he would "look into it," but he did not subsequently speak to her about it again. • • • Robinson had requested that the calendar be removed, but Lovett did not grant this request. Lovett testified that he instructed Cooney to move the calendar about which Robinson complained so that the calendar was no longer visible from outside the trailer. • • • Cooney relayed this instruction to Leach, who carried it out. • • • Lovett stopped by the trailer the next day to confirm that his instruction had been followed.

101. Robinson's complaints became common knowledge around the shipyards and the catalyst for a new wave of harassing behavior directed against her and other women. • • • Many specific incidents of sexual harassing behavior arising at this time are set forth *supra* in these findings.

102. A "Men Only" sign appeared on the door to the shipfitters' trailer after the calendar was removed. • • •

103. Robinson decided to make a formal complaint about the discriminatory sign and the continuing presence of the pictures of nude and partially nude women. On January 23, 1985, Robinson met with Owens, Turner and Chief Shop Steward Quentin McMillan ("McMillan") to complain about the pictures. In route to Owens' office for the meeting, Robinson observed several pictures on the wall and a lewd comment was directed at the woman escorting Robinson to the office. Robinson told the men at this meeting that she felt the pictures were degrading and humiliating to her, that they nauseated her, and that she wanted them removed. She complained about the "Men Only" sign and told the men that

the sign and pornography constituted discrimination, promoted harassment, and were harassment.

104. Owens told Robinson that the company had no policy against the pictures, which had been posted throughout the shipyards for at least nineteen years. • • • Owens asserted that the nudity on television was as bad as the pictures at JSI, and she should look the other way just as she would turn off the television if she were offended. • • • He told her that she chose the JSI work environment and that the men had "constitutional rights" to post the pictures. • • • He would not order the removal of the pictures. He told Robinson she had no business going into the shipfitters' trailer, but he would have the sign removed because JSI had "lady shipfitters." • • • Owens made it clear to Robinson that the shipyards were a man's world and that the rules against vulgar and abusive language did not apply to the "cussing" commonly heard there. • • • She asserted, in response to a question, that she [had] been verbally harassed more often than she could count, • • • but his definition of sexual harassment did not admit her complaint into its scope • • •.

105. Owens did not investigate the details of Robinson's complaints. He directed that the "Men Only" sign be painted over, but he did not initiate any investigation to determine who perpetrated the deed. • • • He did not take any opportunity to view the calendar about which Robinson complained. • • • He told the Mayport Yard foremen at a meeting shortly thereafter that pictures showing sexual intercourse should be removed, but pictures of nude or partially nude women could remain. • • • He specifically directed the foremen to leave up vendors' advertising calendars • • •.

106. Robinson next took her complaint to Ahlwardt, Owens' superior at the Mayport Yard. On January 23, 1985, Robinson called Ahlwardt and told him of her complaints to Owens regarding the pictures and the "Men Only" sign. Robinson testified that after she explained the course of events involving her complaint to Owens and her desire to have the pictures removed, Ahlwardt stated that he would not order the pictures removed. • • •
• • •

108. Ahlwardt also spoke to two persons in policymaking positions. He called Stewart to discuss whether JSI had a policy forbidding the posting of pictures such as those about which Robinson had complained. He told Stewart that a "breast shot" was at issue. Stewart told Ahlwardt that no policy prohibited such pictures, that Robinson's complaint was baseless, and that the calendars and pictures should be left alone. • • • Thereafter Ahlwardt spoke to Brown. Brown likewise expressed his opinion that the materials should not be removed and that Robinson's complaint lacked merit. Brown specifically instructed Ahlwardt that an order prohibiting the display of pictures of nude and partially nude women should not be issued. • • • Neither Stewart nor Brown conducted any investigation of Robinson's complaint prior to rendering advice to Ahlwardt.

109. Following these phone calls, Ahlwardt met with Robinson. • • • Robinson initiated the conversation by requesting the removal of the offending pictures and calendars. She explained her position, including her representation that other women at JSI took offense at the presence of the pictures. Ahlwardt replied that he did not know of any "pornographic" pictures in any offices or shops at the Mayport Yard; his definition of pornography is limited to pictures depicting intercourse, masturbation, or other sexual activity. • • • Robinson pressed her point by referring to the company rule against obscenity; Ahlwardt belittled her concern by looking up the term in a dictionary and dismissing it as vague. • • • Ahlwardt further told Robinson that nautical people always had displayed pinups and other images of nude or partially nude women, like figureheads on boats, and that the posting of such pictures was a "natural thing" in a nautical workplace. Ahlwardt opined that there was nothing wrong with pinups in the shipyards, that he himself previously had posted such pictures, • • • and that they certainly were not intended to intimidate, embarrass or cause concern for anyone • • •. Robinson attempted to raise a comparison between the effect of pornography on women and the effect of Ku Klux Klan propaganda on black people, • • • but Ahlwardt dismissed this comparison with the retort that there were Klan members working in the shipyards • • •. The focus of the meeting then shifted to an inquiry whether Robinson had been physically assaulted or sexually propositioned in the course of her work. • • • Robinson stated that she had not been harassed in those manners, but she considered the pictures to be harassment and to promote harassment. • • •

• • •

111. Turner was first to leave the meeting. He stated the problem was taken care of because he was transferring Robinson to the Commercial Yard. • • • Robinson left thereafter, visibly upset from the encounter. • • • Robinson received the transfer downtown.

112. Following the meeting with Robinson, Ahlwardt instructed Owens not to issue any prohibition of pictures of nude and partially nude women in the workplace. Ahlwardt took no action of his own to remove any pictures, although he visited the shipfitters' trailer the next day, when he was scheduled to be aboard the *U.S.S. Saratoga,* to observe the Whilden Valve calendar. • • •

113. Robinson testified that she filed a union grievance about the pictures and the "Men Only" sign. • • • She further testified that the third-shift shop steward told her that the grievance was pulled—withdrawn by the union leadership. • • •

114. The Court further finds that use of the grievance procedure would have been futile for Robinson. The chief steward at the Mayport Yard, McMillan, considered the pictures to be acceptable; indeed, he recounted his statement to Owens that he would grieve any rule banning the pictures as an infringement on the freedom of expression of shipyard workers. • • • Further, since the offensive pictures originated in the conduct of the majority of the bargaining unit members, it is unrealistic to expect the union to press for sanctions. Moreover, the supervisory personnel who would rule on the various steps of the grievance, Lovett, Owens, and Stewart, clearly expressed their unwillingness to take action against the posting of sexually-oriented pictures in the shipyards.

115. Robinson filed her complaint with the Jacksonville Equal Opportunity Commission ("JEOC"), an authorized state referral agency. • • • Robinson subsequently received a right to sue letter from the Equal Employment Opportunity Commission, together with a determination that no reasonable cause existed to believe that "she was discriminated against . . . by being subjected to sexually explicit pornography and harassment because of her sex, female." • • • The Court places little weight on this "no cause" determination because the investigation apparently was cursory and the only decided case relevant to this issue at that time, *Rabidue v. Osceola Refining Corp.,* 805 F.2d 611 (6th Cir.1986), *cert. denied,* 481 U.S. 1041, 107 S.Ct. 1983, 95 L.Ed.2d 823 (1987), may have provided the misleading impression that Robinson had not raised an actionable claim.

• • •

1987 Sexual Harassment Policy

117. In April 1987, during the pendency of this lawsuit, JSI adopted a new sexual harassment policy. • • • This policy is virtually verbatim a model policy distributed by JSI's parent corporation. • • • JSI's policy did not include any alternate person to receive complaints. • • •

118. The new policy was distributed solely through posting on the bulletin boards in the shops and the general bulletin boards. • • • It was not incorporated into the General Safety Instruction and Company Rule Book, the contract book, the affirmative action plan, or on the EEO posters. • • •

119. The 1987 policy had little or no impact on the sexually hostile work environment at JSI. Employees and supervisors lacked knowledge and training in the scope of those acts that might constitute sexual harassment. • • • The pictures of nude and partially nude women remained posted throughout the workplace. In fact, in January 1988, after the issuance of the new policy, Stewart objected strongly when O.C. McBride, a superintendent at the Mayport Yard, removed three *Playboy-* and *Penthouse-*style calendar pictures from the shipfitters' shop and the electrical shop in anticipation of a tour of the shipyards conducted by Stewart. • • • The naming of only one company representative, Stewart, to hear sexual harassment complaints diminished the policy's value to an employee, such as Robinson, whose prior experiences with Stewart left her without confidence in his willingness to handle such complaints. • • •

120. The Court finds that the policies and procedures at JSI for responding to complaints of sexual harassment are inadequate. The company has done an inadequate job of communicating with employees and supervisors regarding the nature and scope of sexually harassing

behavior. This failure is compounded by a pattern of unsympathetic response to complaints by employees who perceive that they are victims of harassment. This pattern includes an unwillingness to believe the accusations, an unwillingness to take prompt and stern remedial action against admitted harassers, and an express condonation of behavior that is and encourages sexually harassing conduct (such as the posting of pictures of nude and partially nude women). In some instances, the process of registering a complaint about sexual harassment became a second episode of harassment.

Remedial Aspects

121. Plaintiff seeks injunctive relief to force JSI to implement a comprehensive, effective and enforced sexual harassment policy. She also seeks make-whole relief for financial loss she alleges she suffered due to the harassing work environment. The components of this loss include days of absenteeism taken to recover from or to avoid the work environment, foregone opportunities for overtime and holiday pay, and passed opportunities for advancement through certain welding certification tests. She additionally seeks expungement of warnings she has received for excessive absenteeism.

122. Ms. Wagner, plaintiff's expert whose expertise on education and training to combat sexual harassment was accepted without objection, testified regarding the elements of a comprehensive, effective sexual harassment policy. • • • In her experience and according to the research conducted in this field, sexual harassment can be eliminated through a program that trains key supervisors how to investigate sexual harassment complaints, that teaches male and female employees what conduct is prohibited, and that includes a strong policy statement signed by a top-ranking company executive. The training of key supervisors in investigatory techniques encourages active monitoring of the environment and relieves some barriers to reporting of sexual harassment by placing the burden on management. The policy statement should: (1) describe with specificity the behaviors that constitute sexual harassment; (2) advise employees that sexual harassment may result from the behavior of coworkers as well as the behavior of supervisors; (3) promise and provide confidentiality and protection from retaliation for complainants and witnesses; and (4) provide a number of avenues through which a complaint may be initiated. The policy statement must receive wide, effective distribution.

• • •

125. Regarding lost days of work, Robinson testified that she missed several days each year because she could not face entering the hostile work environment. • • • She did not identify this as the reason for her absenteeism when providing her reason to her employer because it did not fit into the acceptable categories for absence. • • •

126. Robinson estimated her total lost time attributable to her inability to cope with the hostile work environment. • • •

127. Robinson's estimate of days missed are an admitted approximation. • • • Robinson made and kept notes of various events throughout the course of her struggle to get JSI to recognize the sexually harassing nature of the pictures of nude and partially nude women. Her asserted inability to identify more precisely the dates at issue lacks credibility in this light. If her estimate of the number of days is based on something more than a guess, then she should be able to identify the dates with a greater degree of specificity. • • • Moreover, the standard for evaluating her claim for compensation for lost time requires that she show that conditions rose to or existed at a level equivalent to an intermittent constructive discharge. See 118 F.R.D. at 531. Defendants require a list of the specific dates on which plaintiff was absent in order to determine if the degree of harassment in the workplace on those dates rises to the level of this higher standard; plaintiff's failure to provide specific dates unfairly deprives defendants of the opportunity to argue that the work environment may be sufficiently hostile to create liability under Title VII without being sufficiently hostile to warrant plaintiff's absence from the job. • • •

128. The Court finds that Robinson's testimony on the financial loss alleged to flow from her missed opportunities and days off is insufficient to form a basis to calculate an entitlement to make-whole monetary relief. Likewise, the vagueness of the testimony relating to absences is an insufficient basis upon which to expunge warnings concerning absenteeism.

CONCLUSIONS OF LAW

Title VII

[The court's discussion of the "employer" status and liability of individual defendants is excerpted in Chapter 23, The Alleged Harasser as Defendant.]

• • •

4. Five elements comprise a claim of sexual discrimination based on the existence of a hostile work environment: (1) plaintiff belongs to a protected category; (2) plaintiff was subjected to unwelcome sexual harassment; (3) the harassment complained of was based upon sex; (4) the harassment complained of affected a term, condition or privilege of employment; and (5) *respondeat superior,* that is, defendants knew or should have known of the harassment and failed to take prompt, effective remedial action.[7] • • •

5. Robinson indisputably belongs to a protected category.

6. The threshold for determining that sexually harassing conduct is unwelcome is "that the employee did not solicit it or incite it, and . . . that the employee regarded the conduct as undesirable or offensive." *Henson,* 682 F.2d at 903 (citations omitted).

7. The relevant conduct in this case is the posting of pictures of nude and partially nude women in the workplace, the sexually demeaning remarks and jokes made by male workers, and harassment lacking a sexually explicit content such as the "Men Only" sign. The credible testimony of Robinson, corroborated by the observations of her supervisors and coworkers, attests to the offense she took at this behavior. *Cf. Vinson,* 477 U.S. at 68, 106 S.Ct. at 2406 ("the question whether particular conduct was indeed unwelcome presents difficult credibility determinations committed to the trier of fact"). Moreover, not a scintilla of evidence suggests that she solicited or incited the conduct. Robinson did not welcome the conduct of which she complains.

8. The third element imposes a requirement that Robinson "must show that but for the fact of her sex, she would not have been the object of harassment." *Henson,* 682 F.2d at 904. This causation requirement encompasses several claims. For example, harassing behavior lacking a sexually explicit content but directed at women and motivated by animus against women satisfies this requirement. • • • Second, sexual behavior directed at women will raise the inference that the harassment is based on their sex. • • • A third category of actionable conduct is behavior that is not directed at a particular individual or group of individuals, but is disproportionately more offensive or demeaning to one sex. • • • This third category describes behavior that creates a barrier to the progress of women in the workplace because it conveys the message that they do not belong, that they are welcome in the workplace only if they will subvert their identities to the sexual stereotypes prevalent in that environment. That Title VII outlaws such conduct is beyond peradventure. *Cf. Price Waterhouse v. Hopkins,* 490 U.S. 228, 249–51, 109 S.Ct. 1775, 1790–91, 104 L.Ed.2d 268 (1989) (plurality opinion); *id.* at 262–67, 109 S.Ct. at 1797–99, 104 L.Ed.2d 557 (O'Connor, J., concurring in judgment) (use of gender stereotypes to evaluate female employees violates Title VII); *Griggs v. Duke Power Co.,* 401 U.S. 424, 431, 91 S.Ct. 849, 853, 28 L.Ed.2d 158 (1971) (Title VII was passed to remove "artificial, arbitrary, and unnecessary barriers to employment when the barriers operate invidiously to discriminate on the basis of . . . [an] impermissible classification").

9. The harassment of which Robinson complains was based upon her sex. The Findings of Fact reflect examples of the three aforementioned types of behavior. She suffered non-sexual harassing behavior from coworkers such as George Leach, who verbally abused or shunned her because she is a female. The "Men Only" sign also illustrates this type of harassment. She suffered incidents of directed sexual behavior both before and after she

---

[5, 6][Omitted.]

[7]Although this fifth element bears the label "respondeat superior," it actually embraces a negligence standard for employer liability that essentially restates the "fellow servant" rule. *See, e.g., Hirschfield v. New Mexico Corrections Dep't,* 916 F.2d 572, 577 n.5 (10th Cir.1990); *Guess v. Bethlehem Steel Corp.,* 913 F.2d 463, 465 (7th Cir.1990); *Hall v. Gus Constr. Co.,* 842 F.2d 1010, 1015 (8th Cir.1988).

lodged her complaints about the pictures of the nude and partially nude women. The pictures themselves fall into the third category, behavior that did not originate with the intent of offending women in the workplace (because no women worked in the jobs when the behavior began) but clearly has a disproportionately demeaning impact on the women now working at JSI. The expert testimony of Dr. Fiske provides solid evidence that the presence of the pictures, even if not directed at offending a particular female employee, sexualizes the work environment to the detriment of all female employees.

10. The fourth element tests the impact of the harassing behavior on the employee and the work environment, • • •.

11. Element four must be tested both subjectively and objectively. Regarding the former, the question is whether Robinson has shown she is an "affected individual," that is, she is at least as affected as the reasonable person under like circumstances. *See Robinson,* 118 F.R.D. at 530. The evidence reflects the great upset that Robinson felt when confronted with individual episodes of harassment and the workplace as a whole. Further, the impact on her work performance is plain. For essentially the same reasons that she successfully proved her case on the second element of this cause of action, Robinson likewise carriers her burden as to the subjective part of the fourth element. (Defendants, having urged throughout these proceedings that Robinson is hypersensitive, appear to concede the point.) The contested issue in this case is the objective evaluation of the work environment at JSI.

12. The objective standard asks whether a reasonable person of Robinson's sex, that is, a reasonable woman, would perceive that an abusive working environment has been created. • • • [T]he contours of what comprises "severe" and "pervasive" are not defined with precision. An interaction between the two is plain; greater severity in the impact of harassing behavior requires a lesser degree of pervasiveness in order to reach a level at which Title VII liability attaches. • • • Moreover, the analysis cannot carve the work environment into a series of discrete incidents and measure the harm adhering in each episode. Rather, a holistic perspective is necessary, keeping in mind that each successive episode has its predecessors, that the impact of the separate incidents may accumulate, and that the work environment created thereby may exceed the sum of the individual episodes. • • • It follows naturally from this proposition that the environment viewed as a whole may satisfy the legal definition of an abusive working environment although no single episode crosses the Title VII threshold.

13. The objective evaluation must account for the salient conditions of the work environment, such as the rarity of women in the relevant work areas. This important qualification explains why the Court places little value on the expert testimony of Drs. Mosher and Scott regarding the level of offensiveness to women of pornographic materials as measured in the abstract. Correspondingly, the need to identify the context in which harassing conduct arises weights heavily in the Court's acceptance of the expert opinions of Dr. Fiske and Ms. Wagner.

14. A reasonable woman would find that the working environment at JSI was abusive. This conclusion reaches the totality of the circumstances, including the sexual remarks, the sexual jokes, the sexually-oriented pictures of women, and the nonsexual rejection of women by coworkers. The testimony by Dr. Fiske and Ms. Wagner provides a reliable basis upon which to conclude that the cumulative, corrosive effect of this work environment over time affects the psychological well-being of a reasonable woman placed in these conditions. This corollary conclusion holds true whether the concept of psychological well-being is measured by the impact of the work environment on a reasonable woman's work performance or more broadly by the impact of the stress inflicted on her by the continuing presence of the harassing behavior. The fact that some female employees did not complain of the work environment or find some behaviors objectionable does not affect this conclusion concerning the objective offensiveness of the work environment as a whole. • • •

15. The Court recognizes the existence of authority supporting defendants' contention that sexually-oriented pictures and sexual remarks standing alone cannot form the basis for Title VII liability. The Court concludes that the reasoning of these cases is not consistent with Eleventh Circuit precedent and is otherwise unsound.

(a) Defendants' authority, which hails from other jurisdictions, proceeds from premises that are inconsistent with authority that is binding on this Court. For example, the Sixth

Circuit in *Rabidue* quoted with approval the conclusion of the district court that

> it cannot seriously be disputed that in some work environments, humor and language are rough hewn and vulgar. Sexual jokes, sexual conversations and girlie magazines may abound. Title VII was not meant—or can—change this. It must never be forgotten that Title VII is the federal court mainstay in the struggle for equal employment opportunity for the female workers of America. But it is quite different to claim that Title VII was designed to bring about a magical transformation in the social mores of American workers.

805 F.2d at 620–21 (quoting in full 584 F.Supp. 419, 430).[8] • • • The *Rabidue* court further expounded on the social context argument:

> The sexually oriented poster displays had a de minimis effect on the plaintiff's work environment when considered in the context of a society that condones and publicly features and commercially exploits open displays of written and pictorial erotica at the newsstands, on prime-time television, at the cinema, and in other public places.

Id. at 622. These propositions, however, cannot be squared with the Eleventh Circuit's holding in *Walker v. Ford Motor Co.,* 684 F.2d 1355, 1359 & n. 2 (11th Cir.1982), that the social milieu of the area and the workplace does not diminish the harassing impact of racial slurs. (As previously noted, the analysis is not different for racial and sexual harassment claims.) The point is made more directly for sexual harassment claims in *Sparks,* wherein the appellate court explained that often "the whole point of the sexual harassment claim" is that behavior that "may be permissible in some settings ... can be abusive in the workplace...." 830 F.2d at 1561 n. 13; *see also Wyerick v. Bayou Steel Corp.,* 887 F.2d 1271, 1275 n. 11 (5th Cir.1989) ("heavy pollution defense" inconsistent with *Vinson* and *Henson*). • • •

    (b) the "social context" argument also lacks a sound analytical basis. Professor Kathryn Abrams has written an insightful critique of this argument:

> The *Rabidue* court's proposed standard is wholly inappropriate for several reasons. • • • Pornography in the workplace may be far more threatening to women workers than it is to the world at large. Outside the workplace, pornography can be protested or substantially avoided—options that may not be available to women disinclined to challenge their employers or obliged to enter certain offices. Moreover, while publicly disseminated pornography may influence all viewers, it remains the expression of the editors of *Penthouse* or *Hustler* or the directors of *Deep Throat.* On the wall of an office, it becomes the expression of a coworker or supervisor as well.
>   In this context the effect of pornography on workplace equality is obvious. • • • Depending upon the material in question, it may communicate that women should be the objects of sexual aggression, that they are submissive slaves to male desires, or that their most salient and desirable attributes are sexual. • • •

Abrams, *Gender Discrimination and the Transformation of Workplace Norms,* 42 Van.L.Rev. 1183, 1212 n. 118 (1989) (citation omitted); • • •. Professor Catherine MacKinnon makes the point in a pithy statement: "If the pervasiveness of an abuse makes it nonactionable, no inequality sufficiently institutionalized to merit a law against it would be actionable." C. MacKinnon, Feminism Unmodified 115 (1987).

    (c) The "social context" argument cannot be squared with Title VII's promise to open the workplace to women. • • • A pre-existing atmosphere that deters women from entering or continuing in a profession or job is no less destructive to and offensive to workplace equality than a sign declaring "Men Only." • • •

    (d) The *Rabidue* analysis violates the most basic tenet of the hostile work environment cause of action, the necessity of examining the totality of the circumstances. • • • The Court cannot ignore the expert testimony, or the Court's own perception of the work environment evaluated as a whole; it would have to do so in order to adopt the *Rabidue* conclusion that

---

[8][Omitted.]

a sexually charged environment has only a "de minimis" effect on the psychological well-being of a reasonable woman who works in the skilled crafts at JSI.

16. Having determined that the first four elements of a sexual harassment claim have been satisfied, the Court faces the task of assessing the liability of the employers in this case. The corporate employer, JSI, is subject only to vicarious liability, an issue more fully developed *infra*. The individual employers, however, pose a distinct liability issue.

[For excerpts, see Chapter 23, The Alleged Harasser as Defendant.]

• • •

JSI is liable for the hostile work environment to which Robinson was subjected. Corporate defendant liability may be proved under either of two theories. Direct liability is incurred when an agent of the corporate employer is responsible for the behavior that comprises the hostile work environment and the agent's actions were taken within the scope of the agency. *See Steele v. Offshore Shipbuilding, Inc.,* 867 F.2d 1311, 1316 n. 1 (11th Cir.1989); *Vance,* 863 F.2d at 1512. Indirect liability attaches where the hostile environment is created by one who is not the plaintiff's employer, such as a coworker, or by an agent of the employer who is acting outside the scope of the agency, and the plaintiff can establish that the employer knew or should have known of the harassment and failed to take prompt, effective remedial action. *See Steele,* 867 F.2d at 1316; *Vance,* 863 F.2d at 1512; *Henson,* 682 F.2d at 910. The Court concludes that Robinson has demonstrated JSI's liability under both theories.

26. • • •

(a) The policymaking agents of the corporate defendant condoned the distribution of the vendors' advertising calendars that formed part of the basis for Robinson's 1985 complaint. The work rules at JSI did not permit the posting of many kinds of materials, required permission for the posting of other kinds of materials, but did not restrict the posting of pictures of nude or partially nude women. Direct liability is apparent when an employer's policy subjects female employees to sexual harassment on the job. *See Priest,* 634 F.Supp. at 581; *EEOC v. Sage Realty Corp.,* 507 F.Supp. 599, 608–10 (S.D.N.Y.1981); *Marentette v. Michigan Host, Inc.,* 506 F.Supp. 909, 911 (E.D.Mich.1980).

(b) Brown and Stewart occupied the key positions at JSI for controlling the quality of the work environment. When faced with Robinson's complaint over sexually-oriented pictures, they did not merely fail to act to remedy the hostile environment, they affirmatively endorsed and ratified a portion of it. • • •

(c) The aforementioned actions came within the scope of the agency relationship between JSI and its supervisors who acted as policymaking agents. *Cf. Sparks,* 830 F.2d at 1558–59 & n. 5 (setting forth relevant common law agency principles). The supervisors acted as the company. *See Hunter v. Allis-Chalmers Corp.,* 797 F.2d 1417, 1422 (7th Cir.1986) ("to say that the 'corporation' has committed some wrong ... simply means that someone at the decision-making level in the corporate hierarchy has committed the wrong"). Liability therefore flows directly to the corporate employer, JSI. *See* RESTATMENT (SECOND) OF AGENCY § 218 (common law agency principles of ratification; *see also Rosenthal & Co. v. Commodity Futures Trading Comm'n,* 802 F.2d 963, 966 (7th Cir.1986) ("Principals are strictly liable for their agents' acts ... if the principals authorize or ratify the acts or even just create an appearance that the acts are authorized.").

27. Liability also flows to JSI indirectly. JSI may be charged with actual or constructive knowledge of the harassing conduct. • • • Both types of knowledge exist in this case.

28. Actual complaints of sexual harassment are documented for several instances. In this regard, two points merit discussion.

(a) One, JSI must assume knowledge for complaints to quartermen and leadermen. As noted *supra,* quartermen and leadermen are not agents of JSI to the extent that they may be held as employers under Title VII. The facts show, however, that JSI relied upon these quasi-supervisory bargaining unit employees to monitor work performance, particularly on remote job sites within the compounds. Employees perceived that quartermen and leadermen were appropriate persons to whom to complain about work conditions. • • • Accordingly, the company must accept responsibility for the reporting of sexual harassment complaints to the individuals occupying the positions of quartermen and leadermen. Moreover, JSI must bear the responsibility of deterred reports of sexual harassment caused by the treatment of female employees by the quartermen and leadermen.

(b) Two, JSI cannot stand on an "ostrich defense" that it lacked knowledge of many of the complaints, because its handling of sexual harassment complaints deterred reporting and it did not conduct adequate investigation of the complaints it did receive. JSI received reports at the supervisory level and at the line level (quartermen and leadermen) concerning incidents of sexual harassment. Additionally, many supervisory personnel admitted that they knew of the sexually-oriented pictures throughout the workplace. • • • The evidence reveals a supervisory attitude that sexual harassment is an incident-by-incident matter; records were not maintained that would have permitted an analysis of sexual harassment complaints to determine the level of sexual hostility in the workplace. Under these circumstances, the Court concludes that JSI received adequate actual knowledge of the state of the work environment but, like an ostrich, the company elected to bury its head in the sand rather than learn more about the conditions to which female employees, Robinson in particular, were subjected.[10]

29. The Court additionally imposes constructive knowledge on JSI for the sexually hostile state of its work environment. Constructive knowledge is measured by a practical threshold. • • • The sexually harassing behaviors described in the Findings of Fact are too pervasive to have escaped the notice of a reasonably alert management. • • •

30. Given that JSI should have responded and did respond to some aspects of the sexually hostile work environment, the effectiveness of its response must be evaluated. Two methods of measuring effectiveness have received endorsement. One, the employer's total response is evaluated on the basis of the circumstances as then existed. *See, e.g,. Brooms,* 881 F.2d at 421. The employer's response is ineffective if "it delay[ed] unduly ... [and] the action it [did] take, however promptly, [was] not reasonably likely to prevent the misconduct from recurring." *Guess v. Bethlehem Steel Corp.,* 913 F.2d 463, 465 (7th Cir. 1990). Two, an employer can defend successfully by showing that the conduct brought to the company's attention was not repeated after the employer took action. *See, e.g., Steele,* 867 F.2d at 1316 (special importance attached to the fact that harassment ended after employer took remedial steps). In this regard, the employer must show the effectiveness of the actions, not merely that actions were taken. *See, e.g., Sanchez,* 720 F.Supp. at 981–82 (remedial action of new sexual harassment policy and procedures constituted change in form, not in substance).

31. JSI did not respond to complaints of sexual harassment with prompt, effective remedial measures. In some instances in which a complaint was made, offending graffiti and pictures were removed promptly; in many other instances, no action was taken or the action was taken after considerable delay. It is noteworthy that the company did not either seek to identify the perpetrators of most harassing incidents (such as the "Men Only" sign and the pictures and graffiti that were removed), • • • or take steps to communicate with other male employees concerning the nature of the offending behavior and the need to show respect to female employees • • •.

32. Not only were the behaviors repeated throughout the workplace and over time, but examples show that the same individuals would repeat sexually harassing misconduct following intervention from management. Moreover, JSI cannot escape the burden of responsibility for many unreported instances of sexual harassment. Although JSI did not receive the opportunity to respond to these instances due to the lack of a formal complaint, the fact that a complaint was not made resulted from the failure to maintain an effective sexual harassment complaint procedure and other circumstances in the work environment that deterred the reporting of episodes of sexual harassment.

---

[9][Omitted.]

[10]The phrase used here is intended to call attention to the analogy between these circumstances and the concept of deliberate ignorance, covered by the so-called ostrich instruction, in the criminal law. • • •

[11][Omitted.]

33. The response to Robinson's complaint demonstrated a lack of appreciation for the gravity of the conduct of which she complained. In doing so, management condoned and encouraged further harassment. The small steps taken in response, such as the moving of an offensive calendar and the removal of some pictures, are outweighed by the continuing abuse that went unremedied.

Executive Order No. 11246

34. Plaintiff asserts that liability may be imposed for violation of the anti-discrimination provisions of Executive Order No. 11246 as a breach of contract enforced by plaintiff as a third-party beneficiary to the United States Navy contracts entered into by JSI. The Court rejects these theories of liability. • • • In *Farkas v. Texas Instruments, Inc.,* 375 F.2d 629, 633 (5th Cir.), *cert. denied,* 389 U.S. 977, 88 S.Ct. 480, 19 L.Ed.2d 471 (1967), the appellate court found no private cause of action under the predecessor order to Executive Order No. 11246. *Farkas* is binding precedent, and its continuing validity received a boost from dictum in *Eatmon v. Bristol Steel & Iron Works, Inc.,* 769 F.2d 1503, 1515 (11th Cir.1985), that states that no private cause of action is available under Executive Order No. 11246. These cases seem to settle the issue, but if this precedent is not in fact dispositive, the Court adopts the analysis finding no private cause of action which appears in *Utley v. Varian Assocs.,* 811 F.2d 1279, 1284–86 (9th Cir.), *cert. denied,* 484 U.S. 824, 108 S.Ct. 89, 98 L.Ed.2d 50 (1987). *Accord Women's Equity Action League v. Cavazos,* 906 F.2d 742, 750 (D.C.Cir.1990). The third-party beneficiary theory is merely derivative of the private cause of action theory and the former cannot be entertained given the disposition of the latter.

Remedy

[The court's discussion of First Amendment issues is excerpted in Chapter 27, Asserted Defenses.]

• • •

41. The National Labor Relations Act does not impede the grant of injunctive relief to require a policy and procedures to handle sexual harassment complaints. The Court does not perceive that the obligations imposed by the policy and procedures are inconsistent with the collective bargaining agreement between JSI and Local 805 of the International Brotherhood of Boilermakers. • • • The unilateral institution of sexual harassment policies by JSI in 1980 and 1987 suggests that the company does not view this area as one subject to bargaining. Defendants' argument regarding the failure to join the union as a party is not well-taken. Joinder of the union in a discrimination suit is not necessary where the relief does not compel revision of the collective bargaining agreement, but only affects the application of its neutral terms to individuals. • • • Plaintiff alleged no wrongdoing by the union and she seeks, at most, only to clarify the application of the nondiscrimination and just cause clauses within the collective bargaining agreement. Under these circumstances, JSI's apparent concern about conflicting obligations placed the onus on it to join the union as a party. An employer may be required to grant relief to victims of discrimination that conflicts with expectations otherwise created by a collective bargaining agreement. • • • To the extent that the employer incurs conflicting obligations due to its compliance with a decree to remedy past discrimination, the burden of reconciling the conflict falls on the employer, not the victims of discrimination. • • •

42. The right of unionized employees to representation during some investigatory interviews, based in § 7 of the NLRA, *see NLRB v. J. Weingarten, Inc.,* 420 U.S. 251, 256–64, 95 S.Ct. 959, 963–67, 43 L.Ed.2d 171 (1975), does limit the procedures that the Court may order. The proposal submitted by plaintiff and adopted by the Court, however, does not impose any restriction on the right to representation during investigations. The requirement of confidentiality where possible does not exclude the lawful role of the union in representation of its members. The policy and procedures should be implemented in a fashion that does not abridge *Weingarten* rights.

43. Based on the foregoing, the Court will affirmatively enjoin defendant JSI to adopt, implement, and enforce a policy and procedures for the prevention and control of sexual harassment . . . .

––––––––––

In sharp contrast to *Robinson* is *Rabidue v. Osceola Refining Co.*[132] In *Rabidue,* the court emphasized that much of the sexual conduct complained of was not directed at the complainant and that the "lexicon of obscenity" complained of would have persisted regardless of the complainant's presence.

RABIDUE V. OSCEOLA REFINING COMPANY

805 F.2d 611, 42 FEP Cases 631
(6th Cir. 1986)

KRUPANSKY, Circuit Judge:—The plaintiff Vivienne Rabidue (plaintiff or Rabidue) timely appealed the district court's judgment in favor of defendant Osceola Refining Co. (Osceola), a division of Texas-American Petrochemicals, Inc. (defendant or Texas-American), after a bench trial on plaintiff's charges of sex discrimination and sexual harassment. In her complaint, the plaintiff asserted charges of sex discrimination and sexual harassment in violation of Title VII of the Civil Rights Act of 1964, 42 U.S.C. §2000e et seq., Michigan's Elliott Larsen Act, Mich. Comp. Laws Ann. §37.2101 et seq., and the Equal Pay Act, 29 U.S.C. §206(d). A memorandum opinion and judgment of the district court concluded that: (1) the defendant Texas-American, a successor corporation, was not liable for any preacquisition sex discrimination; (2) evidence of the plaintiff's hostile personality, willful rudeness, and disregard for company policies satisfied the burden of proof placed upon the defendant to articulate nondiscriminatory reasons in support of her discharge; (3) the plaintiff failed to produce evidence in support of her charge that the defendants articulated nondiscriminatory reasons for discharge were pretextual; (4) a male employee's language and sexual poster displays constituted "verbal conduct of a sexual nature" within the meaning of the sexual harassment guidelines promulgated by the Equal Employment Opportunity Commission (EEOC); (5) the language and posters did not create an environment of harassment necessary to support a charge of sexual harassment; (6) the plaintiff failed to establish sexual harassment under Michigan's Elliott Larsen Act; and (7) the plaintiff failed to establish Equal Pay Act violations. Rabidue v. Osceola Refining Co., 584 F.Supp. 419, 36 FEP Cases 183 (E.D.Mich. 1984).

A review of the record disclosed that the plaintiff entered the employ of Osceola during December of 1970, at which time Osceola was an independently owned company. In 1974, United Refineries of Warren, Ohio, acquired Osceola and operated it as a separate division. On September 1, 1976, Osceola was acquired by Texas-American, which corporation is the defendant in this lawsuit.

The plaintiff initially occupied the job classification of executive secretary. In that position, she performed a variety of duties, which included attending the telephone, typing, and a limited amount of bookkeeping. In 1973, the plaintiff was promoted to the position of administrative assistant and became a salaried rather than hourly employee. • • •

The plaintiff was a capable, independent, ambitious, aggressive, intractable, and opinionated individual. The plaintiff's supervisors and co-employees with whom plaintiff interacted almost uniformly found her to be an abrasive, rude, antagonistic, extremely willful, uncooperative, and irascible personality. She consistently argued with co-workers and company customers in defiance of supervisor direction and jeopardized Osceola's business relationships with major oil companies. She disregarded supervisory instruction and company policy whenever such direction conflicted with her personal reasoning and conclusions. In sum, the plaintiff was a troublesome employee.

––––––––––

[132]805 F.2d 611, 42 FEP Cases 631 (6th Cir. 1986).

The plaintiff's charged sexual harassment arose primarily as a result of her unfortunate acrimonious working relationship with Douglas Henry (Henry). Henry was a supervisor of the company's key punch and computer section. Occasionally, the plaintiff's duties required coordination with Henry's department and personnel, although Henry exercised no supervisory authority over the plaintiff nor the plaintiff over him. Henry was an extremely vulgar and crude individual who customarily made obscene comments about women generally, and, on occasion, directed such obscenities to the plaintiff. Management was aware of Henry's vulgarity, but had been unsuccessful in curbing his offensive personality traits during the time encompassed by this controversy. The plaintiff and Henry, on the occasions when their duties exposed them to each other, were constantly in a confrontation posture. The plaintiff, as well as other female employees, were annoyed by Henry's vulgarity. In addition to Henry's obscenities, other male employees from time to time displayed pictures of nude or scantily clad women in their offices and/or work areas, to which the plaintiff and other women employees were exposed.

The plaintiff was formally discharged from her employment at the company on January 14, 1977 as a result of her many job-related problems, including her irascible and opinionated personality and her inability to work harmoniously with co-workers and customers. • • • • • •

The plaintiff anchored her charges of sex discrimination and sexual harassment in Title VII of the Civil Rights Act of 1964, 42 U.S.C. §2000e et seq., and the Michigan Elliott Larsen Act, Mich. Comp. Laws Ann. §37.2101 et seq. A comparative analysis of the foregoing legislation disclosed that the language of the Elliott Larsen Act disparate treatment statutory provision, enacted some ten years subsequent to the effective date of Title VII, essentially tracked the disparate treatment language of Title VII. It is apparent that the similarity was intentional. Moreover, as the district court indicated in its opinion:

> [T]he Michigan Civil Rights Commission has issued interpretive regulations indicating that Title VII should be used as a guide in the interpretation of the Elliott Larsen Act. Because the Civil Rights Commission is the state's chief civil rights administrative agency, the Commission's guidelines are a fairly strong argument cutting in favor of applying the Title VII disparate treatment model to plaintiff's Elliott Larsen disparate treatment claim.
>
>   Finally, and most importantly, the Michigan judiciary seems inclined toward this interpretation of the Elliott Larsen Act. While Michigan Courts have not adopted wholesale the federal employment discrimination standards, . . . it remains that a good number of Michigan decisions resolve Elliott Larsen issues by reference to the legal standards codified in Title VII and the federal Age Discrimination Act.

Rabidue, 584 F.Supp. at 426 (footnotes omitted) (citing, *inter alia,* Adama v. Doehler-Jarvis, 115 Mich. App. 82, 320 N.W.2d 298, 33 FEP Cases 503 (1982), rev'd on other grounds, 419 Mich. 905, 353 N.W.2d 438, 42 FEP Cases 683 (1984); Gallaway v. Chrysler Corp., 105 Mich. App. 1, 306 N.W.2d 368, 33 FEP Cases 500 (1981); Michigan Department of Civil Rights v. Taylor School District, 96 Mich. App. 43, 292 N.W.2d 161, 36 FEP Cases 233 (1980); Michigan Department of Civil Rights v. General Motors Corp., 93 Mich. App. 366, 287 N.W.2d 240, 26 FEP Cases 326 (1979), affd, 412 Mich. 610, 317 N.W.2d 16, 35 FEP Cases 957 (1982)). In light of the foregoing, the district court's conclusion that the Elliott Larsen Act disparate treatment provisions, Mich. Comp. Laws Ann. §37.2202(1)(a) & (c), should be construed in the same manner as §703(a)(1) of Title VII, 42 U.S.C. §2000e-(2)(a)(1), is AFFIRMED.[2]

This court has examined the trial court's disposition of the plaintiff's Title VII and Elliott Larsen Act sex discrimination claims and the error assigned thereto. In arriving at its decision, the district court viewed the plaintiff's disparate treatment sex discrimination

---

[1][Omitted.]
[2][Omitted.]

charge as alleging continuing sex-based discriminatory conduct on the part of the defendant culminating in the plaintiff's discharge. Rabidue, 584 F.Supp. at 424. A review of the record disclosed that the trial court's findings, namely that the company's predischarge actions toward the plaintiff did not evince an anti-female animus, were not clearly erroneous. Consequently, the trial court's conclusion that the plaintiff failed to establish violations of Title VII or the Elliott Larsen Act in this regard is AFFIRMED.

In addressing the plaintiff's discriminatory discharge claim, the trial court noted that the plaintiff's allegations paralleled classic disparate treatment charges addressed by § 703(a)(1) of Title VII and articulated the classic assertions that she was discharged because she was a female. • • • [T]he trial court concluded that the plaintiff had failed to satisfy her burden of proof to support her contention that the defendant's advanced legitimate, nondiscriminatory reasons for her termination were pretextual and consequently had failed to sustain a disparate treatment claim that resulted from her discharge under either Title VII or the Elliott Larsen Act. Rabidue, 584 F.Supp. at 426–27. The lower court's determination that the plaintiff's discharge was not the result of gender-based discrimination was a factual finding subject to the clearly erroneous standard of review. • • • This court, having scrutinized the record, is of the opinion that the findings of fact and conclusions of law articulated in the trial court's cogent reasoning are not clearly erroneous and are accordingly AFFIRMED.[3]

The plaintiff's claim of sexual harassment derives from Title VII's proscription that "[i]t shall be an unlawful employment practice for an employer . . . to discriminate against any individual with respect to his . . . terms, conditions, or privileges of employment, because of such individual's . . . sex . . . . " 42 U.S.C. §2000e-2(a)(1)(§703(a)(1) of Title VII). The case law in this area has recognized two basic variants of sexual harassment: "harassment that creates an offensive environment ('condition of work') and harassment in which a supervisor demands sexual consideration in exchange for job benefits (*'quid pro quo'*)." • • •

This circuit has entertained cases involving a spectrum of sexual harassment issues; however, it has not directly addressed a claim asserting a violation of Title VII based upon an alleged sexually discriminatory work environment which had not resulted in a tangible job detriment as joined by the issues of the plaintiff's charges herein. • • •

In addressing the issues presented by such a sexual harassment charge, this court's attention is initially directed to the guidelines issued by the Equal Employment Opportunity Commission (EEOC) as an informed source of instruction to assist its efforts to probe the parameters of Title VII sexual harassment.[4] Those guidelines define sexual harassment in the following terms:

> (a) Harassment on the basis of sex is a violation of Sec. 703 of Title VII. Unwelcome sexual advances, requests for sexual favors, and other verbal or physical conduct of a sexual nature constitute sexual harassment when (1) submission to such conduct

---

[3]The dissent has cited evidence developed exclusively by the plaintiff without noting the wide disparity between the plaintiff's evidence when compared to the totality of the record as it bears upon her charges of disparate treatment, sexually hostile work environment, and discriminatory discharge. With particularity, the dissent has alluded to Henry's vulgarity and obscene characterizations as well as purported acts of disparate treatment and gender-based discrimination which, the trial record affirmatively disclosed, occurred while Osceola operated as an independent company or during its ownership by United Refineries—all before the Texas-American acquisition. Apart from the foregoing transcript disclosures, the plaintiff's probative evidence, at best, was vague and obscure in failing to reflect a continuation of those actions after the Texas-American acquisition or the extent and circumstances of that alleged discriminatory conduct and sexual harassment, if it did in fact persist, that purportedly implicated Texas-American. Moreover, where, as here, the evidence was in conflict, credibility issues come within the discretion of the district court for resolution. In the instant case, the district court clearly assigned greater credibility and weight to the defendant's witnesses and its testimony than to the plaintiff and her witnesses as is evidence by its opinion. This court, having reviewed the district court's interpretation of the evidence and its assignments of credibility pursuant to the clearly erroneous standard, cannot conclude that the trial court's interpretation of the evidence was clearly erroneous.

[4][Omitted.]

is made either explicitly or implicitly a term or condition of an individual's employment, (2) submission to or rejection of such conduct by an individual is used as the
basis for employment decisions affecting such individual, or (3) such conduct has the
purpose or effect of unreasonably interfering with an individual's work performance
or creating an intimidating, hostile, or offensive working environment.

29 C.F.R. §1604.11(a) (footnote omitted).

After having considered the EEOC guidelines and after having canvassed existing legal
precedent that has discussed the issue, this court concludes that a plaintiff, to prevail in a
Title VII offensive work environment sexual harassment action, must assert and prove that:
(1) the employee was a member of a protected class; (2) the employee was subjected to
unwelcomed sexual harassment in the form of sexual advances, requests for sexual favors,
or other verbal or physical conduct of a sexual nature; (3) the harassment complained of
was based upon sex; (4) the charged sexual harassment had the effect of unreasonably
interfering with the plaintiff's work performance and creating an intimidating, hostile, or
offensive working environment that affected seriously the psychological well-being of the
plaintiff; and (5) the existence of respondeat superior liability. • • •

Thus, to prove a claim of abusive work environment premised upon sexual harassment,
a plaintiff must demonstrate that she would not have been the object of harassment but for
her sex. Henson, 682 F.2d at 904 (citations omitted). It is of significance to note that instances
of complained of sexual conduct that prove equally offensive to male and female workers
would not support a Title VII sexual harassment charge because both men and women were
accorded like treatment. • • •

• • • To accord appropriate protection to both plaintiffs and defendants in a hostile
and/or abusive work environment sexual harassment case, the trier of fact, when judging the
totality of the circumstances impacting upon the asserted abusive and hostile environment
placed in issue by the plaintiff's charges, must adopt the perspective of a reasonable person's
reaction to a similar environment under essentially like or similar circumstances. Thus, in
the absence of conduct which would interfere with that hypothetical reasonable individual's
work performance and affect seriously the psychological well-being of that reasonable
person under like circumstances, a plaintiff may not prevail on asserted charges of sexual
harassment anchored in an alleged hostile and/or abusive work environment regardless of
whether the plaintiff was actually offended by the defendant's conduct. Assuming that the
plaintiff has successfully satisfied the burden of proving that the defendant's conduct would
have interfered with a reasonable individual's work performance and would have affected
seriously the psychological well-being of a reasonable employee, the particular plaintiff
would nevertheless also be required to demonstrate that she was actually offended by the
defendant's conduct and that she suffered some degree of injury as a result of the abusive
and hostile work environment.

Accordingly, a proper assessment or evaluation of an employment environment that
gives rise to a sexual harassment claim would invite consideration of such objective and
subjective factors as the nature of the alleged harassment, the background and experience
of the plaintiff, her co-workers, and supervisors, the totality of the physical environment of
the plaintiff's work area, the lexicon of obscenity that pervaded the environment of the
workplace both before and after the plaintiff's introduction into its environs, coupled with
the reasonable expectation of the plaintiff upon voluntarily entering that environment. Thus
the presence of actionable sexual harassment would be different depending upon the personality of the plaintiff and the prevailing work environment and must be considered and
evaluated upon an ad hoc basis. As Judge Newblatt aptly stated in his opinion in the district
court:

Indeed, it cannot seriously be disputed that in some work environments, humor and
language are rough hewn and vulgar. Sexual jokes, sexual conversations and girlie
magazines may abound. Title VII was not meant to—or can—change this. It must
never be forgotten that Title VII is the federal court mainstay in the struggle for equal
employment opportunity for the female workers of America. But it is quite different
to claim that Title VII was designed to bring about a magical transformation in the

social mores of American workers. Clearly, the Court's qualification is necessary to enable 29 C.F.R. §1604.11(a)(3) to function as a workable judicial standard.

Rabidue, 584 F.Supp. at 430.[5]

To prevail in an action that asserts a charge of offensive work environment sexual harassment, the ultimate burden of proof is upon the plaintiff to additionally demonstrate respondeat superior liability by proving that the employer, through its agents or supervisory personnel, knew or should have known of the charged sexual harassment and failed to implement prompt and appropriate corrective action.• • • The promptness and adequacy of the employer's response to correct instances of alleged sexual harassment is of significance in assessing a sexually hostile environment claim and the employer's reactions must be evaluated upon a case by case basis. • • •[6]

In considering an order of proof to implement the resolution of Title VII sexually hostile working environment controversies, this court has reviewed the procedure enunciated in McDonnell Douglas Corp. v. Green, • • •, and has concluded that the order of proof and procedures enunciated therein are not readily adaptable to developing the proofs and defenses in this type of Title VII action. It would appear that the most effective and efficient procedural format would implement the traditional practice of placing the ultimate burden of proof by a preponderance of the evidence upon the claimant followed by a proffer of defense and an opportunity for a plaintiff's rebuttal.

A review of the Title VII sexual harassment issue in the matter *sub judice* prompts this court to conclude that the plaintiff neither asserted nor proved a claim of "sexual advances," "sexual favors," or "physical conduct," or sexual harassment implicating subparts (a)(1) or (a)(2) of the EEOC definition, more specifically, those elements typically at issue in a case of *quid pro quo* sexual harassment. Thus, the plaintiff to have prevailed in her cause of action against the defendant on this record must have proved that she had been subjected to unwelcomed verbal conduct and poster displays of a sexual nature which had unreasonably interfered with her work performance and created an intimidating, hostile, or offensive working environment that affected seriously her psychological well-being.

In the case at bar, the record effectively disclosed that Henry's obscenities, although annoying, were not so startling as to have affected seriously the psyches of the plaintiff or other female employees. The evidence did not demonstrate that this single employee's vulgarity substantially affected the totality of the workplace. The sexually oriented poster displays had a de minimis effect on the plaintiff's work environment when considered in the context of a society that condones and publicly features and commercially exploits open displays of written and pictorial erotica at the newsstands, on prime-time television, at the cinema, and in other public places. In sum, Henry's vulgar language, coupled with the sexually oriented posters, did not result in a working environment that could be considered

---

[5]Such an approach is not inconsistent with the EEOC guidelines, which emphasize the individualized nature of a probative inquiry:

> (b) In determining whether alleged conduct constitutes sexual harassment, the Commission will look at the record as a whole and at the totality of the circumstances, such as the nature of the sexual advances and the context in which the alleged incidents occurred. The determination of the legality of a particular action will be made from the facts, on a case by case basis.

29 C.F.R. §1604.11(b).

The dissent's focus on certain of the above factors in isolation is misplaced. The district court possesses broad discretion as to the evidence to be considered in evaluating the totality of the circumstances and the context of the alleged incidents. This court has merely attempted to identify in general terms some criteria that may potentially enter into a case-by-case examination of the totality of the evidence in such a case, without inferring the weight to be accorded in the first instance by district court to any particular factor.

[6]Although the Supreme Court in Vinson declined to issue a definitive rule on employer liability arising from the acts of supervisory personnel in sexually hostile environment cases, it stated that Congress intended the courts to look to common law principles of agency for guidance in this area. 106 S.Ct. at 2408.

The court emphasizes that the instant case does not involve alleged acts of sexual harassment by a supervisor. Henry exercised no supervisory authority over the plaintiff nor the plaintiff over him, but rather the two parties were peers at Osceola and at all times pertinent hereto. Accordingly, the majority opinion, like the Vinson Court, expresses no view as to the scope of respondeat superior liability in the context of a charge of a sexually hostile working environment where alleged acts of harassment by a plaintiff's supervisor are at issue and not, as here, the alleged acts of a peer in the workplace.

intimidating, hostile, or offensive under 29 C.F.R. §1604.11(a)(3) as elaborated upon by this court.[7] The district court's factual findings supporting its conclusion to this effect were not clearly erroneous. It necessarily follows that the plaintiff failed to sustain her burden of proof that she was the victim of a Title VII sexual harassment violation.[8] Accordingly, the trial court's disposition of this issue if AFFIRMED.

• • •

For the reasons stated herein, the plaintiff having failed to sustain any of the claims which she has asserted, the judgment of the district court in favor of defendant is hereby AFFIRMED.

---

[7]The precedential cases addressing a sexually hostile and abusive environment within the context of Title VII of the Civil Rights Act of 1964, 42 U.S.C. §2000e et seq., and 29 C.F.R. §1604.11(a)(3) have all developed more compelling circumstances than are presented herein. In Bundy, both the plaintiff's co-employees and supervisors harassed her with conduct that included continual personal and telephonic sexual propositions both at work and at her home and the plaintiff's complaints inspired her supervisor to also proposition her. 641 F.2d at 939–40. In Henson, the plaintiff was subjected to numerous harangues and demeaning inquiries into her sexual proclivities, vulgarities, and repeated requests for sexual relations from her supervisor, the police chief. 682 F.2d at 899–901. In Katz, several supervisory personnel and co-workers bombarded the plaintiff with sexual slurs, insults, innuendo, and propositions, the plaintiff's complaints to her supervisor generated further harassment from him, and the plaintiff's supervisors admitted having heard co-workers direct obscenities to the plaintiff. 709 F.2d at 253–54. In the case at bar, the charges of sexually hostile and abusive environment were limited to pictorial calendar type office wall displays of semi-nude and nude females and Henry's off-color language. Unlike the facts of Bundy, Henson, and Katz, this case involved no sexual propositions, offensive touchings, or sexual conduct of a similar nature that was systematically directed to the plaintiff over a protracted period of time.

[8]As noted in the trial court's opinion, the successorship defense would have precluded preacquisition liability even if the sexual harassment ruling had not been in favor of the defendant. Rabidue, 584 F.Supp. at 433. However, this court's disposition of the sexual harassment charges renders the successorship argument a redundant defense.

[9, 10][Omitted.]

Concurring and Dissenting Opinions

KEITH, Circuit Judge, concurring in part, dissenting in part:—I concur in the portion of the majority opinion which finds no successor liability. However, as I believe the majority erroneously resolves plaintiff's substantive claims, I dissent.

I dissent for several reasons. First, after review of the entire record I am firmly convinced, that although supporting evidence exists, the court is mistaken in affirming the findings that defendant's treatment of plaintiff evinced no anti-female animus and that gender-based discrimination played no role in her discharge. The overall circumstances of plaintiff's workplace evince an anti-female environment. For seven years plaintiff worked at Osceola as the sole woman in a salaried management position. In common work areas plaintiff and other female employees were exposed daily to displays of nude or partially clad women belonging to a number of male employees at Osceola. One poster, which remained on the wall for eight years, showed a prone woman who had a golf ball on her breasts with a man standing over her, golf club in hand, yelling "Fore." And one desk plaque declared "Even male chauvanist pigs need love." Plaintiff testified the posters offended her and her female coworkers.

In addition, Computer Division Supervisor Doug Henry regularly spewed anti-female obscenity. Henry routinely referred to women as "whores," "cunt", "pussy" and "tits." See Rabidue v. Osceola, 5584 F.Supp 419, 423, 36 FEP Cases 183 (E.D. Mich. 1984). Of plaintiff, Henry specifically remarked "All that bitch needs is a good lay" and called her "fat ass." Plaintiff arranged at least one meeting of female employees to discuss Henry and repeatedly filed written complaints on behalf of herself and other female employees who feared losing their jobs if they complained directly. Osceola Vice President Charles Muetzel stated he knew that employees were "greatly disturbed" by Henry's language. However, because Osceola needed Henry's computer expertise, Muetzel did not reprimand or fire Henry. In response to subsequent complaints about Henry, a later supervisor, Charles Shoemaker, testified that he gave Henry "a little fatherly advice" about Henry's prospects if he learned to become "an executive type person."

In addition to tolerating this anti-female behavior, defendant excluded plaintiff, the sole female in management, from activities she needed to perform her duties and progress in her career. Plaintiff testified that unlike male salaried employees, she did not receive free lunches, free gasoline, a telephone credit card or entertainment privileges. Nor was she invited to the weekly golf matches. Without addressing defendant's disparate treatment of plaintiff, the district court dismissed these perks and business activities as fringe benefits. After plaintiff became credit manager defendant prevented plaintiff from visiting or taking customers to lunch as all previous male credit managers had done. Plaintiff testified that upon requesting such privileges, her supervisor, Mr. Muetzel, replied that it would be improper for a woman to take male customers to lunch and that she "might have car trouble on the road." Plaintiff reported that on another occasion, Muetzel asked her "how would it look for me, a married man, to take you, a divorced woman, to the West Branch Country Club in such a small town?" However, defendant apparently saw no problem in male managers entertaining female clients regardless of marital status. Plaintiff's subsequent supervisor, Charles Shoemaker, stated to another female worker, Joyce Solo, that "Vivienne (plaintiff) is doing a good job as credit manager, but we really need a man on that job," adding "She can't take customers out to lunch." Aside from this Catch-22, Mr. Shoemaker also remarked plaintiff was not forceful enough to collect slow-paying jobs. How plaintiff can be so abrasive and aggressive as to require firing but too timid to collect delinquent accounts is, in my view, an enigma.

My review of the record also shows plaintiff was consistently accorded secondary status. Plaintiff recounted that at a meeting convened to instruct clerical employees on their duties after the United States Refineries takeover, plaintiff was seated with female hourly employees. The male salaried employees, apparently pre-informed of the post-takeover procedures, stood at the front of the room. Plaintiff confronted Muetzel to express surprise at being addressed as a clerical employee and to ask what her post-takeover role would entail. Muetzel responded plaintiff would have whatever role was handed to her. At the suggestion of her former boss, Mr. Hansen, plaintiff wrote a memo summarizing her qualifications and pleading for non-sex based consideration for post-takeover positions. She received no response to this memo.

In contrast to the supervisors' reluctance to address Henry's outrageous behavior, plaintiff was frequently told to tone down and discouraged from executing procedures she felt were needed to correct waste and improve efficiency as her job required. Not only did plaintiff receive minimal support, but she was repeatedly undermined. For example, supervisor Doug Henry once directed his employees to ignore plaintiff's procedure for logging time and invoices, a particularly damaging directive given plaintiff's responsibility of coordinating the work of Henry's computer staff. In another example, plaintiff returned from her vacation to find that none of the check depositing procedures agreed upon had been implemented and that some of her duties had been permanently transferred to the male who filled in during her vacation. In contrast to the fatherly advice and the praise for potential which Henry received, plaintiff was informed that she had set her goals too high. After dismissal, but prior to final notice, plaintiff received instructions not to return to the refinery. In contrast, male employees were allowed to return to clean out their desks. Upon dismissal, plaintiff reported that Shoemaker advised her to get a secretarial job.

The record establishes plaintiff possessed negative personal traits. These traits did not, however, justify the sex-based disparate treatment recounted above. Whatever undesirable behavior plaintiff exhibited, it was clearly no worse than Henry's. I conclude the misogynous language and decorative displays tolerated at the refinery (which even the district court found constituted a "fairly significant" part of the job environment), the primitive views of working women expressed by Osceola supervisors and defendant's treatment of plaintiff as the only female salaried employee clearly evince anti-female animus.

Second, I dissent because I am unable to accept key elements of the standard for sexual harassment set forth in the majority opinion. Specifically, I would not impose on the plaintiff alleging hostile environment harassment an additional burden of proving respondeat superior liability where a supervisor is responsible for the harm. In Meritor Savings Bank v. Vinson,

54 LW 4703, 40 FEP Cases 1822 (June 19, 1986), the Supreme Court instructed courts to determine employer liability according to agency principles. Id. at 4707. Agency principles establish that an employer is normally liable for the acts of its supervisors and agents. Id. Because a supervisor is "clothed with the employer's authority" and is responsible for the "day-to-day supervision of the work environment and with ensuring a safe, productive workplace," his abusive behavior in violation of that duty should be imputed to the employer just as with any other supervisory action which violates Title VII. Id. at 4709 (J. Marshall concurring, joined by JJ. Brennan, Blackmun and Stevens). The creation of a discriminatory work environment by a supervisor can only be achieved through the power accorded him by the employer. I see insufficient reason to add an element of proof not imposed on any other discrimination victim, particularly where agency principles and the "goals of Title VII law" preclude the imposition of automatic liability in all circumstances. Id. As Justice Marshall concludes:

> There is therefore no justification for a special rule, to be applied only in "hostile environment" cases, that sexual harassment does not create employer liability until the employee suffering the discrimination notifies other supervisors. No such requirement appears in the statute, and no such requirement can coherently be drawn from the law of agency. . . .
>
> I would apply in this case the same rules we apply in all other Title VII cases, and hold that sexual harassment by a supervisor of an employee under his supervision, leading to a discriminatory work environment, should be imputed to the employer for Title VII purposes regardless of whether the employee gave "notice" of the offense.

Id.

In cases of hostile work environment harassment by coworkers, I would follow guidelines set forth by the Equal Employment Opportunity Commission:

> With respect to conduct between fellow employees, an employer is responsible for acts of sexual harassment in the workplace where the employer (or its agents or supervisory employees) knows or should have known of the conduct, unless it can show that it took immediate and appropriate corrective action.

29 C.F.R. §§1604.11(d) (1985).

Nor do I agree with the majority holding that a court considering hostile environment claims should adopt the perspective of the reasonable person's reaction to a similar environment. Slip op. at 12. In my view, the reasonable person perspective fails to account for the wide divergence between most women's views of appropriate sexual conduct and those of men. See Comment, *Sexual Harassment Claims of Abusive Work Environment Under Title VII*, 97 Harv.L.Rev. 1449, 1451 (1984). As suggested by the Comment, I would have courts adopt the perspective of the reasonable victim which simultaneously allows courts to consider salient sociological differences as well as shield employers from the neurotic complainant. Id. at 1459. Moreover, unless the outlook of the reasonable woman is adopted, the defendants as well as the courts are permitted to sustain ingrained notions of reasonable behavior fashioned by the offenders, in this case, men. Id.

Which brings me to the majority's mandate to consider the "prevailing work environment," "the lexicon of obscenity that pervaded the environment both before and after plaintiff's introduction into its environs," and plaintiff's reasonable expectations upon "voluntarily" entering that environment. Slip op. at 14. The majority suggests through these factors that a woman assumes the risk of working in an abusive, anti-female environment. Moreover, the majority contends that such work environments somehow have an innate right to perpetuation and are not to be addressed under Title VII:

> Indeed, it cannot seriously be disputed that in some work environments, humor and language are rough hewn and vulgar. Sexual jokes, sexual conversations and girlie magazines may abound. Title VII was not meant to—or can—change this. It must never be forgotten that Title VII is the federal court mainstay in the struggle for equal employment opportunity for the female workers in America. But [it] is quite different to claim that Title VII was designed to bring about a magical transformation in the

social mores of American workers. Clearly, the Court's qualification is necessary to enable 29 C.F.R. §1604.11(a)(3) to function as a workable judicial standard.

Slip op. at 15 (quoting the direct court opinion, Osceola v. Rabidue, 584 F.Supp. at 430.)

In my view, Title VII's precise purpose is to prevent such behavior and attitudes from poisoning the work environment of classes protected under the Act. To condone the majority's notion of the "prevailing workplace" I would also have to agree that if an employer maintains an anti-semitic workforce and tolerates a workplace in which "kike" jokes, displays of nazi literature and anti-Jewish conversation "may abound," a Jewish employee assumes the risk of working there, and a court must consider such a work environment as "prevailing." I cannot. As I see it, job relatedness is the only additional factor which legitimately bears on the inquiry of plaintiff's reasonableness in finding her work environment offensive. In other words, the only additional question I would find relevant is whether the behavior complained of is required to perform the work. For example, depending on their job descriptions, employees of soft pornography publishers or other sex-related industries should reasonably expect exposure to nudity, sexually explicit language or even simulated sex as inherent aspects of working in that field. However, when that exposure goes beyond what is required professionally, even sex industry employees are protected under the Act from non-job related sexual demands, language or other offensive behavior by supervisors or co-workers. As I believe no woman should be subjected to an environment where her sexual dignity and reasonable sensibilities are visually, verbally or physically assaulted as a matter of prevailing male prerogative, I dissent.

The majority would also have courts consider the background of plaintiff's co-workers and supervisors in assessing the presence of actionable work environment sex harassment. The only reason to inquire into the backgrounds of the defendants or other co-workers is to determine if the behavior tolerated toward female employees is reasonable in light of those background. As I see it, these subjective factors create an unworkable standard by requiring the courts to balance a morass of perspectives. But more importantly, the background of the defendants or other workers is irrelevant. No court analyzes the background and experience of a supervisor who refuses to promote black employees before finding actionable race discrimination under Title VII. An equally disturbing implication of considering defendants' backgrounds is the notion that workplaces with the least sophisticated employees are the most prone to anti-female environments. Assuming *arguendo** this notion is true, by applying the prevailing workplace factor, this court locks the vast majority of working women into workplaces which tolerate anti-female behavior. I conclude that for actionable offensive environment claims, the relevant inquiry is whether the conduct complained of is offensive to the reasonable woman. Either the environment affects her ability to perform or it does not. The backgrounds and experience of the defendant's supervisors and employees is irrelevant.

Nor can I agree with the majority's notion that the effect of pin-up posters and misogynous language in the workplace can have only a minimal effect on female employees and should not be deemed hostile or offensive "when considered in the context of a society that condones and publicly features and commercially exploits open displays of written and pictorial erotica at newsstands, on prime-time television, at the cinema and in other public places." Slip op. at 17. "Society" in this scenario must primarily refer to the unenlightened; I hardly believe reasonable women condone the pervasive degradation and exploitation of female sexuality perpetuated in American culture. In fact, pervasive societal approval thereof and of other stereotypes stifles female potential and instill the debased sense of self worth which accompanies stigmatization. The presence of pin-ups and misogynous language in the workplace can only evoke and confirm the debilitating norms by which women are primarily and contemptuously valued as objects of male sexual fantasy. That some men would condone and wish to perpetuate such behavior is not surprising. However, the relevant inquiry at hand is what the reasonable woman would find offensive, not society, which at one point also condoned slavery. I conclude that sexual posters and anti-female language

---

*I do not assert any correlation exists between the level of social sophistication present in a work environment and anti-female behavior.

can seriously affect the psychological well being of the reasonable woman and interfere with her ability to perform her job.

• • •

In conclusion, I dissent because the record shows that defendant's treatment of plaintiff evinces anti-female animus and that plaintiff's gender played a role in her dismissal. I also believe the hostile environment standard set forth in the majority opinion shields and condones behavior Title VII would have the courts redress. Finally, in my view, the standard fails to encourage employers to set up internal complaint procedures or otherwise seriously address the problem of sexual harassment in the workplace.

Interestingly, the dissent of Judge Keith in *Rabidue* has drawn more support than has the majority opinion.[133]

---

[133]For other criticisms of the *Rabidue* decision, see Chapter 4, Hostile Environment Harassment, Section VI. *See also* Robinson v. Jacksonville Shipyards, 760 F. Supp. 1486 (M.D. Fla. 1991). At least one panel of the Sixth Circuit itself has distanced itself from *Rabidue*. Davis v. Montsanto Chem. Co., 858 F.2d 345, 351, 47 FEP Cases 1825, 1829–30 (6th Cir. 1988)(Norris, J., concurring and dissenting).

Part II

THEORIES OF LIABILITY UNDER TITLE VII

Chapter 3

QUID PRO QUO HARASSMENT

I. Overview

The essence of the quid pro quo theory of sexual harassment as a violation of Title VII is that someone "relies upon his apparent or actual authority to extort sexual consideration from an employee."[1] Quid pro quo harassment occurs whenever "a supervisor conditions the granting of an economic or other job benefit upon the receipt of sexual favors from a subordinate, or punishes that subordinate for refusing to comply."[2]

The EEOC Guidelines identify two basic varieties of quid pro quo harassment:

> Unwelcome sexual advances, requests for sexual favors, and other verbal or physical conduct of a sexual nature constitute sexual harassment when (1) submission to such conduct is made either explicitly or implicitly a term or condition of an individual's employment, [or] (2) submission to or rejection of such conduct by an individual is used as the basis for employment decisions affecting such individual . . . .[3]

In a quid pro quo case, the link between the sexual favors and the job detriment may be either explicit or implicit.[4] Further, the nexus may appear at the time of the sexual advance, or only later, in connection with an adverse job

---

[1]Henson v. City of Dundee, 682 F.2d 897, 910, 29 FEP Cases 787, 799 (11th Cir. 1982), reproduced in Chapter 4, Hostile Environment Harassment. For a discussion of whether the alleged harasser possessed the authority to effect a tangible job detriment, see Section VII.B.3. *infra.*

[2]Lipsett v. University of P.R., 864 F.2d 881, 897, 54 FEP Cases 230, 242–43 (1st Cir. 1988)(Title IX and §1983 case); *see also* Spencer v. General Elec. Co., 894 F.2d 651, 658, 51 FEP Cases 1725, 1730 (4th Cir. 1990)(quid pro quo harassment occurs when "sexual consideration is demanded in exchange for job benefits"); Highlander v. KFC Nat'l Mgmt. Co., 805 F.2d 644, 648, 42 FEP Cases 654, 657 (6th Cir. 1986)(quid pro quo harassment "is anchored in an employer's sexually discriminatory behavior which compels an employee to elect between acceding to sexual demands and forfeiting job benefits, continued employment or promotion, or otherwise suffering tangible job detriments").

[3]29 C.F.R. §1604.11(a), reproduced in Appendix 1. In 1980, after notice and comment, the EEOC issued its Guidelines on Discrimination Because of Sex, 29 C.F.R. §§1604.1–.11, one part of which (§1604.11) is on sexual harassment. The EEOC Guidelines are nonbinding but "constitute a body of experience and informed judgments to which courts and litigants may properly resort for guidance." Meritor Sav. Bank v. Vinson, 477 U.S. 57, 65, 40 FEP Cases 1822, 1826 (1986), reproduced in Chapter 1, Overview (citations omitted). Subsections 1604.11(a)(1) and (2) describe quid pro quo harassment, while subsection 1604.11(a)(3) describes hostile environment harassment.

[4]See *supra* note 3, 29 C.F.R. §1604.11(a)(1).

action.[5] The sexual advances may be unwelcome at the outset, or may later become unwelcome, as in the case of a soured romance.

The typical quid pro quo case, in which a job detriment follows a sexual advance, fits easily within the conceptual framework of disparate treatment analysis.[6] The question is whether the job detriment was motivated by a nondiscriminatory reason, such as the complainant's relative qualifications, or by a forbidden reason, such as the complainant's rejection of sexual advances.[7]

II. THE FRAMEWORK FOR ANALYZING QUID PRO QUO CLAIMS

The order and allocation of proof in a quid pro quo case follows that of any employment discrimination case alleging disparate treatment:

(1) The complainant must produce evidence giving rise to an inference of unlawful discrimination. This evidence involves proof that an employment benefit had been conditioned—expressly or implicitly—on acquiecence in sexual activity.

(2) The defendant then may produce evidence that no unwelcome sexual advance occurred, or that any adverse employment decision was motivated by a nondiscriminatory reason rather than by the complainant's reaction to such an advance.

(3) The complainant, retaining the burden of persuasion, must ultimately show that the reason proffered by the defendant is pretextual, in that "but for" her reaction to an unwelcome sexual advance she would not have been so treated.[8]

The prima facie case does not explicitly address the element of discriminatory intent, which is subsumed in the element of causal connection. Thus, although "discriminatory motive is critical," it may sometimes "be inferred

---

[5]See *supra* note 3, 29 C.F.R. §1604.11(a)(2). For a discussion of the distinction between a contemporaneously apparent nexus and a nexus that appears only later, see *Keppler v. Hinsdale Township High School Dist.,* 715 F. Supp. 862, 50 FEP Cases 295 (N.D. Ill. 1989), reproduced in Chapter 2, Forms of Harassment, and discussed in Section VII.B. *infra.*

[6]Christoforou v. Ryder Truck Rental, 668 F. Supp. 294, 302, 51 FEP Cases 98, 104 (S.D.N.Y. 1987)("well known formula for proving a Title VII case of illegal discrimination in hiring, promotion and employment generally . . . is equally applicable in the somewhat specialized situation of a lawsuit alleging sexual harassment").

[7]*See, e.g.,* Henson v. City of Dundee, *supra* note 1, 682 F.2d at 911–12, 29 FEP Cases at 800 (female police dispatcher alleged quid pro quo claim by alleging she was denied opportunity to attend police academy because she rejected her supervisor's request for sexual favors); *cf.* Hicks v. Gates Rubber Co., 833 F.2d 1406, 1413–14, 45 FEP Cases 608, 613–14 (10th Cir. 1987)(female employee not subjected to sexual quid pro quo where record disclosed no suggestion her employment was conditioned on granting sexual favors to supervisors, and where job consequences arose solely from inadequate performance, not rejection of sexual advances).

[8]For cases developing this analytical framework in Title VII cases generally, see *McDonnell Douglas Corp. v. Green,* 411 U.S. 792, 804–5, 5 FEP Cases 965, 970 (1973); *Texas Dep't of Community Affairs v. Burdine,* 450 U.S. 248, 253–54, 25 FEP Cases 113, 115 (1981); B.L. SCHLEI & P. GROSSMAN, EMPLOYMENT DISCRIMINATION LAW 1286–1324 (2d ed. 1983). While virtually all decisions take this approach in quid pro quo cases, the D.C. Circuit has opined that the employer must show that the reasons for its job action were nondiscriminatory by "clear and convincing evidence." Bundy v. Jackson, 641 F.2d 934, 953, 24 FEP Cases 1155, 1166–68 (D.C. Cir. 1981). The Eleventh Circuit, in rejecting this approach, noted that *Bundy* was decided before the Supreme Court's decision in *Burdine,* which clarified the allocation of proof in disparate treatment cases. Henson v. City of Dundee, *supra* note 1, 682 F.2d at 907, 29 FEP Cases at 796. The Supreme Court in *Meritor* cited both *Bundy* and *Henson,* but did not find it necessary to resolve this issue. For a discussion of the complainant's proof of pretext, see Section X. *infra.*

from the mere fact of differences in treatment."[9] This analytical framework permits the complainant to raise the inference of quid pro quo harassment with relatively slight circumstantial evidence;[10] proof of a single incident of quid pro quo harassment may suffice to establish a prima facie case.[11]

While circumstantial evidence alone may suffice to prove intentional discrimination under the foregoing framework,[12] the complainant can obviate that framework with direct evidence of discriminatory intent. In that event the defendant may avoid liability only by proving by a preponderance of the evidence that "the same decision would have been reached even absent the presence of discrimination."[13]

III. THE PRIMA FACIE CASE

Justice Lewis F. Powell, Jr., in *McDonnell Douglas Corp. v. Green,* stated the elements of a prima facie case of discriminatory denial of employment,[14] recognizing that the elements would have to be adapted to fit the circumstances of other Title VII cases.[15] In the traditional disparate treatment claim of sex discrimination under Title VII, the complainant makes out a prima facie case by proving the basis (gender), the issue (a tangible job detriment), and the causal connection between the basis and the issue (but for the complainant's gender the complainant would not have suffered the job detriment).

In *Henson v. City of Dundee,* Judge Robert Vance for the Eleventh Circuit drew upon *McDonnell Douglas* to suggest the elements of a prima facie case

---

[9]Teamsters v. United States, 431 U.S. 324, 335 n.15, 14 FEP Cases 1514, 1519 (1977).

[10]"The burden of establishing a prima facie case of disparate treatment is not onerous." Texas Department of Community Affairs v. Burdine, *supra* note 8, 450 U.S. at 253, 25 FEP Cases at 115; Christoforou v. Ryder Truck Rental, *supra* note 6.

[11]*See, e.g.,* Shrout v. Black Clawson Co., 689 F. Supp. 774, 780 n.5, 46 FEP Cases 1339, 1344 (S.D. Ohio 1988)(where employer withheld pay increase following complainant's employment anniversary, quid pro quo claim may be predicated upon single incident); Barnes v. Costle, 561 F.2d 983, 15 FEP Cases 345 (D.C. Cir. 1977), reproduced in Chapter 1, Overview (where complainant's job abolished after she repulsed superior's sexual advances, single instance of discrimination was sufficient to support suit); Keppler v. Hinsdale Township High School Dist., *supra* note 5, 715 F. Supp. at 866, 50 FEP Cases at 298 (single incident of sexual harassment can give rise to quid pro quo claim); Neville v. Taft Broadcasting Co., 42 FEP Cases 1314 (W.D.N.Y. 1987)(discharged employee made prima facie, quid pro quo showing by proving supervisor grabbed her, forcibly kissed her, and told her if she did everything right she would go a long way), *aff'd mem.,* 857 F.2d 1461, 51 FEP Cases 1832 (2d Cir. 1987); Boyd v. James S. Hayes Living Health Care Agency, 671 F. Supp. 1155, 44 FEP Cases 332 (W.D. Tenn. 1987) (supervisor's conduct during single business trip sufficient to support quid pro quo harassment claim); *contra* Morley v. New England Tel. Co., 47 FEP Cases 917, 924 (D. Mass. 1987)(employee who had personality conflict with supervisor and demonstrated discriminatory denial of promotion not sexually harassed when only two statements made by supervisor could be considered to have sexual overtones).

[12]Texas Dep't of Community Affairs v. Burdine, *supra* note 8, 450 U.S. at 252–56, 25 FEP Cases at 115–16; Delgado v. Lehman, 665 F. Supp. 460, 466, 43 FEP Cases 593, 597–98 (E.D. Va. 1987).

[13]Sowers v. Kemira, Inc., 701 F. Supp. 809, 823, 46 FEP Cases 1825, 1835 (S.D. Ga. 1988). *See also* Price Waterhouse v. Hopkins, 490 U.S. 228, 252, 49 FEP Cases 954, 964 (1989)(direct evidence in "mixed-motive" case triggers stricter burden of proof on rebuttal); Chamberlin v. 101 Realty, 915 F.2d 777, 782 n.7, 54 FEP Cases 101, 105 (1st Cir. 1990)(where complainant presented prima facie case, burden of persuasion and burden of production passes to defense to show that same decision would have been made absent discrimination).

[14]*Supra* note 8, 411 U.S. at 802 n.13, 5 FEP Cases at 969 (elements stated were (1) belonging to a racial minority; (2) had applied and was qualified for job for which employer was seeking applicants; (3) despite qualifications was rejected; and (4) after rejection, position remained open and employer continued to seek applicants from persons of complainant's qualifications).

[15]*Id.* at 802.

of quid pro quo harassment.[16] As the *Henson* court suggested, in quid pro quo cases the causal connection is two-pronged: the tangible job detriment would not have occurred "but for" (1) the complainant's reaction to the supervisor's request for sexual favors, which request would not have occurred "but for" (2) the complainant's gender. *Henson* thus connected the employment detriment with the complainant's sex by reasoning that if the sexual request was on the basis of the complainant's sex, and if her discharge was on the basis of her response to the sexual request, then her discharge was ultimately on the basis of her sex.[17]

This basic formulation of the prima facie quid pro quo case, with some variation, has been widely followed,[18] although some courts have collapsed the redundant elements of the *Henson* standard into a simpler formulation.[19]

The elements of the prima facie case identified in *Henson* can be reformulated as follows. The complainant must show:

(1) the basis: membership in a protected group;

(2) the activity: unwelcome sexual advances;

(3) the issue: an adverse employment action;

(4) the causal connection: (a) that the sexual advance was because of the complainant's sex, and (b) that the complainant's reaction to the sexual advance affected a tangible aspect of the complainant's term, condition, or privilege of employment; and

(5) employer responsibility.[20]

This reformulation of the *Henson* prima facie case emphasizes the features peculiar to a sexual harassment case—the employer is motivated by an activity

---

[16]The *Henson* court identified the elements as: (1) the employee belongs to a protected group; (2) the employee was subject to unwelcome sexual conduct; (3) the conduct was based upon sex; (4) the employee's reaction to the harassment affected a "term, condition, or privilege" of employment; and (5) *respondeat superior.* Henson v. City of Dundee, *supra* note 1, 682 F.2d at 903–4, 29 FEP Cases at 792–94.

[17]*Id.* at 904, 29 FEP Cases at 793–94 (citing Bundy v. Jackson, 641 F.2d 934, 953, 24 FEP Cases 1155, 1166–68 (D.C. Cir. 1981)).

[18]*Second Circuit:* Koster v. Chase Manhattan Bank, 687 F. Supp. 848, 861, 46 FEP Cases 1436, 1447 (S.D.N.Y. 1988);

Fourth Circuit: Walker v. Sullair Corp., 736 F. Supp. 94, 99, 52 FEP Cases 1313, 1316–17 (W.D.N.C. 1990);

Fifth Circuit: Jones v. Flagship Int'l, 793 F.2d 714, 728, 41 FEP Cases 358, 369 (5th Cir. 1986), *cert. denied,* 479 U.S. 1065 (1987);

Sixth Circuit: Highlander v. KFC Nat'l Mgmt. Co., *supra* note 2, 805 F.2d at 648, 42 FEP Cases at 657; Boyd v. James S. Hayes Living Health Care Agency, *supra* note 11, 671 F. Supp. at 1164, 44 FEP Cases at 340;

Eighth Circuit: Moylan v. Maries County, 792 F.2d 746, 749, 40 FEP Cases 1788, 1790 (8th Cir. 1986); *Eleventh Circuit:* Sparks v. Pilot Freight Carriers, 830 F.2d 1554, 1564, 45 FEP Cases 160, 167 (11th Cir. 1987), reproduced in Chapter 2, Forms of Harassment.

[19]*See, e.g.,* Lipsett v. University of P.R., *supra* note 2, 864 F.2d at 898, 54 FEP Cases at 243 (§1983 and Title IX)("plaintiff must show that (1) he or she was subject to unwelcome sexual advances by a supervisor ... and (2) that his or her reaction to these advances affected tangible aspects of his or her compensation, terms, conditions, or privileges of employment").

[20]We use "employer responsibility" in place of the *"respondeat superior"* label used by the court in *Henson v. City of Dundee, supra* note 1, 682 F.2d at 909, 29 FEP Cases at 798, and by several other courts, *e.g., Chamberlin v. 101 Realty, supra* note 13, 915 F.2d at 785, 54 FEP Cases at 107–8; *Jones v. Flagship Int'l, supra* note 18, 793 F.2d at 721–22, 41 FEP Cases at 364. The employer liability standard actually used by the courts embraces not only principles of *respondeat superior* but also much broader principles, such as employer negligence. *See, e.g.,* Hirschfeld v. New Mexico Corrections Dep't, 916 F.2d 572, 577 n.5, 54 FEP Cases 268, 272 (10th Cir. 1990)(addressing three theories of liability); Guess v. Bethlehem Steel Corp., 913 F.2d 463, 465, 53 FEP Cases 1547, 1549 (7th Cir. 1990); Hall v. Gus Constr. Co., 842 F.2d 1010, 1015, 46 FEP Cases 573, 576–77 (8th Cir. 1988), reproduced in Chapter 2, Forms of Harassment. *See generally* Chapter 6, Harassment by Supervisors, Section II.

rather than by merely a protected status, and the causal connection has two prongs.

IV. THE BASIS: MEMBERSHIP IN A PROTECTED CLASS

The first "element"—membership in a protected class—requires only a simple stipulation of gender.[21] This element will be present in every sexual harassment case. In analyzing sexual harassment cases courts appear to have adopted the "membership" element from standard formulations of the prima facie case[22] without considering that the "because of sex" element in a sexual harassment case necessarily takes the complainant's gender into account.[23]

V. THE ACTIVITY: UNWELCOME SEXUAL ADVANCES

This element of the prima facie case is twofold: (A) a sexual advance that (B) was "unwelcome" to the complainant.

A. The Advance Must Be "Sexual"

The EEOC Guidelines describe sexual harassment as involving "unwelcome sexual advances, requests for sexual favors, and other verbal or physical conduct of a sexual nature."[24] In the typical quid pro quo case, the sexual nature of the request is plain: a supervisor demands that a subordinate employee provide sexual favors to obtain or retain a tangible job benefit. In this kind of case the complainant usually testifies to a direct sexual proposition.[25]

---

[21]Chamberlin v. 101 Realty, *supra* note 13, 915 F.2d at 784, 54 FEP Cases at 106 ("simple gender stipulation met the first test"); Boyd v. James S. Hayes Living Health Care Agency, *supra* note 11, 671 F. Supp. at 1165, 44 FEP Cases at 340 ("Plaintiff [a woman] is obviously a member of the protected group"). *Cf.* Williams v. Saxbe, 413 F. Supp. 654, 658 n.6, 12 FEP Cases 1093, 1098 (D.D.C. 1976), reproduced in Chapter 1, Overview (rejecting defendant's contention that because willingness to furnish sexual consideration can be applied to both men and women, class of discriminatees cannot be defined primarily by gender).

[22]Traditional analysis of an employment discrimination case begins by identifying the protected class to which the individual belongs. The function of this exercise is to identify what the complainant must causally connect to the alleged job detriment. Courts have continued that tradition in sexual harassment cases, even though the fact that just about everyone is either male or female tends to make the element of membership in a protected class always available and logically unnecessary to address separately from other elements.

[23]*Cf.* Sowers v. Kemira, Inc., *supra* note 13, 701 F. Supp. at 823, 46 FEP Cases at 1835 (it is "redundant" to require that harassment was "based on sex" after already requiring that there be "sexual harassment").

[24]29 C.F.R. §1604.11(a), reproduced in Appendix 1. This description fits quid pro quo cases. But note that a hostile environment claim may be maintained even where the offensive conduct is of a nonsexual nature, so long as it was because of the complainant's gender. See Chapter 4, Hostile Environment Harassment, Section III.B.2.

[25]*E.g.,* Spencer v. General Elec. Co., 894 F.2d 651, 659, 51 FEP Cases 1725, 1731 (4th Cir. 1990)(plaintiff satisfied prima facie case by showing she "suffered sexual harassment at the hands of her immediate supervisor . . . in the form of unwanted sexual solicitations and sexual horseplay"); Barnes v. Costle, *supra* note 11, 561 F.2d at 985, 15 FEP Cases at 346 (refusal to grant sexual favors to supervisor was condition for enhancement of employment status, and refusal to grant favors resulted in elimination of job); Tomkins v. Public Serv. Elec. & Gas Co., 568 F.2d 1044, 1047, 16 FEP Cases 22, 24 (3d Cir. 1977)(supervisor told plaintiff "that her continued success and advancement . . . were dependent upon her agreeing to his sexual demands"); Sowers v. Kemira, Inc., *supra* note 13, 701 F. Supp. at 823, 46 FEP Cases at 1835 (complainant's rejection of sexual advances by supervisor led him to delay her promotion and salary increase); Neville v. Taft Broadcasting Co., *supra* note 11 (one sexual advance, rebuffed by plaintiff, may establish prima facie case of "quid pro quo" harassment even if not severe enough to create a hostile environment); Heelan v.

The complainant need not prove that the demand included sexual intercourse, or that it was sexually explicit.[26] In *Boyd v. James S. Hayes Living Health Care Agency,*[27] a supervisor's conduct during an out-of-town business trip was found to constitute quid pro quo harassment when he invited the complainant to his hotel room, gave her wine, turned on a pornographic movie, put his hand on her shoulder, and offered her sexually explicit magazines.[28]

Whether conduct is sexual in nature is judged by an objective standard. Behavior interpreted by the complainant as sexual may not result in a finding of sexual harassment if another motive is established.[29] In *Chamberlin v. 101 Realty,*[30] where the boss on various occasions invited the complainant to meet customers of the firm at his house and to have lunch at the beach, the court rejected the complainant's characterizations of these events as sexual advances, reasoning that "social invitations extended to an employee by a supervisor cannot alone be considered conduct of a sexual nature."[31] Similarly, the EEOC has stated that it "is not conduct of a sexual nature" for a male superior to invite a female subordinate to dine together for "business or social purposes."[32] The EEOC has disavowed any intention of "regulating commonly accepted business practices which are purely social in nature."[33]

Johns-Manville Corp., 451 F. Supp. 1382, 1387–88, 20 FEP Cases 251, 253–54 (D. Colo. 1978)(rejection of explicit sexual invitations from supervisor resulted in dismissal).

[26]In *Pease v. Alford Photo Indus.,* 667 F. Supp. 1188, 49 FEP Cases 497 (W.D. Tenn. 1987), the plaintiff established a quid pro quo as well as a hostile environment case where she was constructively discharged after complaining about a manager who had a practice of sexually fondling his female employees and who fondled the complainant's breast. "Quid pro quo" harassment was found even though he never expressly propositioned the victims. The case could also have proceeded as an "opposition clause" retaliation case. See Chapter 10, Retaliation, Section II. *But see* Morley v. New England Tel. Co., *supra* note 11 (employee who had personality conflict with supervisor and demonstrated that she was discriminatorily denied promotion was not victim of quid pro quo sexual harassment when only two statements by supervisor could be considered to have sexual overtones: "I don't want a reluctant bride" and "you couldn't look good if you tried"); Lipsett v. Rive-Mora, 669 F. Supp. 1188, 1200 (D.P.R. 1987)("Plaintiff never established that [the defendant] demanded, explicitly or implicitly, that she submit to sexual acts"), *rev'd on other grounds,* 864 F.2d 881, 54 FEP Cases 230 (1st Cir. 1988).

[27]*Supra* note 11.

[28]*Id.* at 1165, 44 FEP Cases at 340. *See also* Neville v. Taft Broadcasting Co., *supra* note 11 (supervisor engaged in quid pro quo sexual harassment when he grabbed employee, forcibly kissed her, and told her if she did everything right she would go a long way).

[29]Jackson-Colley v. Army Corps of Eng'rs, 655 F. Supp. 122, 43 FEP Cases 617 (E.D. Mich. 1987)(defendant's gawking was actually eye problem, groin-scratching stemmed from medical condition, gifts and encouragement did not imply request for sexual favors and excessive use of vulgar language aimed at all employees).

[30]*Supra* note 13.

[31]*Id.* at 779 n.2, 54 FEP Cases at 103. Other conduct in the *Chamberlin* case, however, did constitute sexual advances, notwithstanding the absence of an explicit proposition. The conduct included telling the complainant that she had a good body, telling her that she looked good in tight jeans, and taking her hand and saying "My women are special. I like to put them on a pedestal." *Id.* at 780, 54 FEP Cases at 103. Judge Cyr concluded: "Whether or not each or any sexual overture was sufficiently crude or heavy-handed to exclude absolutely all ambiguity as to its intendment, there can be no significant question that their common aim was sexual in nature." *Id.* at 785, 54 FEP Cases at 107.

[32]EEOC Dec. 82-2, 28 FEP Cases 1843, 1844 (1982). *See also* Hanson v. American Express, 53 FEP Cases 1193, 1195 (D. Utah 1986)(citing EEOC Decision 82-2, 28 FEP Cases 1843, 1844 (1982)), *aff'd mem.,* 53 FEP Cases 1624 (10th Cir. 1988).

[33]EEOC Dec. 82-2, *supra* note 32. *Cf.* EEOC Dec. 81-18, 27 FEP Cases 1793 (1981)(constant unwelcome luncheon invitations constituted sexual harassment when viewed together with express sexual intentions and other verbal and sexual conduct).

B. The Advance Must Be "Unwelcome"

The Supreme Court in *Meritor Savings Bank v. Vinson* stated that the "gravamen of any sexual harassment claim is that the alleged sexual advances were 'unwelcome.' "[34] The court in *Henson v. City of Dundee* defined unwelcome conduct as conduct that "the employee did not solicit or incite ... and ... that the employee regarded ... as undesirable or offensive."[35]

The "unwelcome" requirement is peculiar to sexual harassment. Harassment as a general matter is considered to be inherently unwelcome.[36] Thus, potentially offensive conduct based on race or national origin is presumably offensive and unwelcome to whomever it is directed. Sexual advances are different, in that sexual advances, while potentially offensive, may reflect a friendly, romantic interest in the recipient and often are welcome, or at least not offensive.

Because sexual advances often have social utility and often are not inherently offensive,[37] "the distinction between invited, uninvited-but-welcome, offensive-but-tolerated, and flatly rejected" sexual advances may be difficult to discern.[38] Yet it is essential to distinguish welcome from unwelcome conduct, because consensual sexual relationships do not violate Title VII.[39] The focus of inquiry, therefore, is often on the complainant's response rather than on the advance itself. The complainant's possible responses include (1) outright rejection, (2) initial rejection and later acceptance, (3) initial acceptance followed by later rejection, (4) ambiguous conduct, (5) coerced submission, and (6) welcome acceptance.

1. Outright Rejection

Express contemporaneous rejection will strongly support the conclusion that a sexual advance was unwelcome.[40] The complainant need not, however,

---

[34]477 U.S. 57, 68, 40 FEP Cases 1822, 1829 (1986), reproduced in Chapter 1, Overview (citing 29 C.F.R. §1604.11(a)); *see generally* EEOC Policy Guidance on Sexual Harassment, 8 FAIR EMPL. PRAC. MAN. (BNA) 405:6684–87 (March 19, 1990), reproduced in Appendix 3. Some commentators urge that the "welcomeness" of the sexual advance is really in the nature of a defense and therefore should be part of the defendant's case. *E.g.*, Comment, *The Harms of Asking: Towards a Comprehensive Treatment of Sexual Harassment,* 55 U. CHI. L. REV. 328, 344–47 (1988).

[35]682 F.2d 897, 903, 29 FEP Cases 787 (11th Cir. 1982), reproduced in Chapter 4, Hostile Environment Harassment. *Accord* Moylan v. Maries County, *supra* note 18.

[36]See Chapter 2, Forms of Harassment, Section II.

[37]Some commentators question whether any social utility could outweigh the disadvantages to women. They emphasize that work is critical to survival and independence and that sexual advances can degrade a woman and undercut her potential. By this view, sexual advances, while having societal benefits at a social event, do not belong in the workplace. *E.g.*, C. MACKINNON, SEXUAL HARASSMENT OF WORKING WOMEN 7 (1979).

[38]Barnes v. Costle, 561 F.2d 983, 999, 15 FEP Cases 345, 358 (D.C. Cir. 1977), reproduced in Chapter 1, Overview (MacKinnon, J., concurring).

[39]*See, e.g.*, Walker v. Sullair Corp., 736 F. Supp. 94, 52 FEP Cases 1313 (W.D.N.C. 1990)(consensual sexual relationship will not give rise to sex discrimination claim).

[40]*E.g.*, Jones v. Wesco Investments, 846 F.2d 1154, 46 FEP Cases 1431 (8th Cir. 1988)(plaintiff pushed her supervisor away, informed him she was interested only in business relationship, and left room). *See generally* EEOC Policy Guidance on Sexual Harassment, 8 FAIR EMPL. PRAC. MAN. (BNA) 405:6685 n.7

directly confront the harasser to show that his conduct was unwelcome.[41] Even where the complainant has never told the alleged harasser explicitly that his sexual advances were unwelcome, "evidence that the employee consistently demonstrated her unalterable resistance to all sexual advances is enough to establish their unwelcomeness."[42] In *Lipsett v. University of Puerto Rico*,[43] Judge Hugh Bownes, writing for the First Circuit, addressed the difficult situation where the alleged harasser is making what he believes to be "innocent or invited overtures":

> The man must be sensitive to signals from the woman that his comments are unwelcome, and the woman, conversely, must take responsibility for making those signals clear. In some instances, a woman may have the responsibility for telling the man directly that his comments or conduct is unwelcome. In other instances, however, a woman's consistent failure to respond to suggestive comments or gestures may be sufficient to communicate that the man's conduct is unwelcome.

2. Initial Rejection and Later Acceptance

An initial rejection implies but does not necessarily establish that later sexual advances were unwelcome. In *Trautvetter v. Quick*,[44] the Seventh Circuit affirmed a summary judgment for the employer, in which the trial court had concluded that the plaintiff had failed to create a genuine issue as to whether the employer's sexual advances were unwelcome. The complainant, a second-grade school teacher, had rejected several sexual and social invitations from the school principal over a period of weeks, but had never told him that his conduct was inappropriate. The trial court concluded that the complainant eventually accepted and even invited the principal's sexual advances, which led to sexual intercourse, although she did so with the secret feeling that she was pressured to comply. The Seventh Circuit affirmed the summary judgment on other grounds, but observed that the record "appears to substantiate the district court's findings that Ms. Trautvetter grew to 'welcome' [the] advances and even participated in an active way as to encourage them."[45]

3. Initial Acceptance Followed by Later Rejection

Special problems of proof arise when a consensual relationship has come to an end. Although the complainant's prior consent is not a defense to a claim

---

(March 19, 1990), reproduced in Appendix 3 ("For a complaint to be 'contemporaneous,' it should be made while the harassment is ongoing or shortly after it has ceased.").

[41]Zowayyed v. Lowen Co., 735 F. Supp. 1497, 52 FEP Cases 1350 (D. Kan. 1990)(employer's motion for summary judgment denied based on plaintiff's declaration testimony that sexual advances she laughed about at time were actually unwelcome to her); EEOC Dec. 84-1, 33 FEP Cases 1887, 1888, 1890 (1984)(two of three charging parties, although not directly confronting harassment for fear of losing their jobs, showed that supervisor's sexual remarks and gestures were unwelcome by making diverting comments and sarcastic remarks).

[42]Chamberlin v. 101 Realty, 915 F.2d 777, 784, 54 FEP Cases 101, 106 (1st Cir. 1990)(citing Lipsett v. University of P.R., 864 F.2d 881, 898, 54 FEP Cases 230, 243 (1st Cir. 1988)).

[43]864 F.2d 881, 898, 54 FEP Cases 230, 243 (1st Cir. 1988)(Campbell, C.J., Bownes & Breyer, JJ.).

[44]916 F.2d 1140, 1149, 54 FEP Cases 109, 116 (7th Cir. 1990).

[45]*Id.* at 1149, 54 FEP Cases at 116.

of later harassment,[46] the prior consent, at a minimum, complicates the complainant's proof.[47]

The EEOC has stated that where the complainant has previously consented to the relationship, she "must clearly notify the harasser that his conduct is no longer welcome."[48] Her failure to complain of conduct that once was (but no longer is) welcome would indicate that the "continued conduct is, in fact, welcome."[49] The EEOC has stated that "Particularly when the alleged harasser may have some reason . . . to believe that the advances will be welcomed, it is important for the victim to communicate that the conduct is unwelcome."[50]

Judge Charles Richey, by contrast, has suggested that the supervisor has a duty to report to upper management the termination of a previously consensual sexual relationship with his subordinate, to ensure that work-related factors alone are considered in decisions affecting the subordinate's job.[51]

4. Ambiguous Response

The complainant, because of politeness, indecision or fear, may not express an outright rejection. In *Kouri v. Liberian Services,*[52] the court rejected a sexual harassment claim on the ground that the complainant had failed to show that her supervisor's attentions were unwelcome to her. Although she was bothered by his frequent friendly notes, his practice of escorting her to the

---

[46]*See, e.g.,* Boddy v. Dean, 821 F.2d 346, 45 FEP Cases 586 (6th Cir. 1987)(complainant could establish sexual discrimination by showing she was not selected for promotional position because of negative input by supervisor she had formerly dated); Prichard v. Ledford, 55 FEP Cases 755, 757 (E.D. Tenn. 1990)(earlier voluntary sexual activity not defense to sexual harassment claim); Babcock v. Frank, 729 F. Supp. 279, 287, 54 FEP Cases 1123, 1129–30 (S.D.N.Y. 1990), reproduced in Chapter 2, Forms of Harassment (protection of Title VII not withdrawn "merely upon a showing that the victim of harassment had in the past entered into a consensual sexual relationship with the perpetrator"); Shrout v. Black Clawson Co., 689 F. Supp. 774, 779, 46 FEP Cases 1339, 1343 (S.D. Ohio 1988)(employee who terminated relationship with supervisor brought successful harassment claim when supervisor attempted to force complainant to submit to sexual advances by withholding performance evaluations and salary reviews); Williams v. Civiletti, 487 F. Supp. 1387, 22 FEP Cases 1311 (D.D.C. 1980)(complainant fired for denying sexual favors to supervisor with whom she had once had affair). *Cf.* Huebschen v. Wisconsin Dep't of Health & Soc. Serv., 716 F.2d 1167, 32 FEP Cases 1582 (7th Cir. 1983)(male subordinate who jilted female supervisor has §1983 claim on basis that she retaliated against him by ending his probationary promotion).

[47]*See, e.g.,* Koster v. Chase Manhattan Bank, 687 F. Supp. 848, 861, 46 FEP Cases 1436, 1447 (S.D.N.Y. 1988)("not a scintilla of evidence was proffered that even hinted that the affair . . . was unwelcome" and "plaintiff's own witnesses support the conclusion plaintiff welcomed the relationship with defendant"); Walker v. Sullair Corp., *supra* note 39, 736 F. Supp. at 99, 52 FEP Cases at 1317 (evidence does not show "*unwelcome* sexual conduct," where "relationship began as consenting adults getting together" and there was no evidence that complainant "resisted any . . . sexual overtures"); Evans v. Mail Handlers, 32 FEP Cases 634, 637 (D.D.C. 1983)(unwelcomeness claim denied where complainant secretary and male boss had intermittent sexual relations over three-year period and where complainant did not consider conduct of boss "offensive or intimidating until the relationship began to deteriorate").

[48]EEOC Policy Guidance on Sexual Harassment, *supra* note 40, at 405:6687.

[49]*Id.*

[50]*Id.* at 405:6685.

[51]Williams v. Civiletti, *supra* note 46, 487 F. Supp. at 1389, 22 FEP Cases at 1312–13:

If a supervisor chooses to accept the sexual favors offered by a subordinate employee and such a relationship sours and as a result the working relationship deteriorates, no sanctions against the employee can be taken without a candid disclosure of the nature of the problem to the actual authority making the decision. Otherwise, the opportunity for abuse is excessive: the supervisor is able to take advantage of his position and remove his former lovers on the ground that a personality conflict has developed. It is hoped that accurate disclosure to the proper authorities will chill the willingness of supervisors to engage in such activity. Perhaps with disclosure, the people in authority will be willing to remove the supervisor who has taken advantage of his position of power. The detrimental effects of such working-place relationships are obvious.

[52]55 FEP Cases 124 (E.D. Va. 1991).

bathroom and to her car, and his visits to her at home and in the hospital, she "never made any realistic effort to cut it off."[53] Although she concocted elaborate schemes to let the supervisor know in a subtle way that she was happily married, each scheme "was a hopelessly indirect action that delivered an attenuated message."[54]

5. Coerced Submission

In a coercion case, the complainant submits to unwelcome sexual advances. The duress resulting in the submission to unwelcome sexual conduct may be physical,[55] economic,[56] or psychological.[57]

a. Voluntary submission not welcomeness. Voluntary submission to sexual conduct does not necessarily mean that the conduct was welcome. As Justice William H. Rehnquist made clear in *Meritor,* the correct inquiry "is whether [the complainant] by her conduct indicated that the alleged sexual advances were unwelcome, not whether her actual participation in sexual intercourse was voluntary."[58] The *Meritor* Court thus refused to reject out of hand the sexual harassment claim of a woman who had had sexual intercourse forty to fifty times with her alleged harasser. In rejecting the trial court's "voluntariness" finding as legally irrelevant, the Supreme Court clarified that sexual participation alone does not defeat a claim of sexual harassment.

Courts both before and after *Meritor* have recognized that a claim for sexual harassment may be viable notwithstanding conduct by the complainant

---

[53]*Id.* at 129.

[54]*Id. See also* Trautvetter v. Quick, *supra* note 44, 916 F.2d at 1149, 54 FEP Cases at 116 (suggesting that school teacher who initially rejected series of sexual propositions by principal before finally having sexual intercourse with him in motel could not show "unwelcome" requirement and suggesting that test is extent to which plaintiff "made it known that the sexual advances were 'unwelcome' ").

[55]*See, e.g.,* Gilardi v. Schroeder, 672 F. Supp. 1043, 45 FEP Cases 283 (N.D. Ill. 1986)(complainant drugged and then raped), *aff'd,* 833 F.2d 1226, 45 FEP Cases 346 (7th Cir. 1987); Moylan v. Maries County, 792 F.2d 746, 747–48, 40 FEP Cases 1788, 1789 (8th Cir. 1986)(remanding for trial of hostile environment case in which sheriff allegedly raped dispatcher, who did not scream or physically resist and who reported incident to police three months later).

[56]*See, e.g.,* Chamberlin v. 101 Realty, 915 F.2d 777, 54 FEP Cases 101 (1st Cir. 1990)(assessment of welcomeness issue must consider what complainant may "reasonably perceive" that protest will prompt dismissal, especially when sexual overtures made by owner of firm); Phillips v. Smalley Maintenance Servs., 711 F.2d 1524, 32 FEP Cases 975 (11th Cir. 1983)(proper to consider that alleged harasser knew complainant needed job to make house payments and exploited her financial need to demand sexual favors); Showalter v. Allison Reed Group, 56 FEP Cases 989, 994 (D.R.I. 1991)(two male workers succumbed to general manager's demand to have sex with his secretary because they feared for their jobs); Babcock v. Frank, *supra* note 46, 729 F. Supp. at 287–88, 54 FEP Cases at 1129–30 (complainant stated claim with allegation that she was coerced by job-related threats by supervisor into continuing sexual conduct that was no longer consensual). *See also* EEOC Policy Guidance on Sexual Harassment, *supra* note 40, at 405:6685–86 (fear of losing job can explain delay in complainant's report of sexual harassment).

[57]*Cf.* EEOC Policy Guidance on Sexual Harassment, *supra* note 40, at 405:6685 ("victims may fear repercussion from complaining about the harassment and . . . such fear may explain a delay in opposing the conduct. If the victim failed to complain or delayed in complaining, the investigation must ascertain why. The relevance of whether the victim has complained varies depending upon 'the nature of the sexual advances and the context in which the alleged incidents occurred.' 29 C.F.R. §1604.11(b)").

[58]477 U.S. 57, 68, 40 FEP Cases 1822, 1826–27 (1986), reproduced in Chapter 1, Overview. *See also* Cummings v. Walsh Constr. Co., 561 F. Supp. 872, 31 FEP Cases 930 (S.D. Ga. 1983)(motion for summary judgment denied even though complainant acquiesced to initial sexual advances by supervisor, where complainant asserts acquiescence was due to intimidation); EEOC Dec. 84-1, 33 FEP Cases 1887 (1984)("acquiescence in sexual conduct at the workplace may not mean that the conduct is welcome to the individual").

that could be construed as "acquiescence" or "participation."[59] Acquiescence without fear of any adverse consequences, however, obviously would undermine a claim of unwelcomeness.[60]

b. Failure to protest not welcomeness. Often a complainant who submits to sexual advances because of coercion will not have protested the sexual advances.[61] One commentator has argued against requiring proof of protest:

> The failure to complain, a form of silence, ... serves as evidence ... that the harassment is welcome. But ... the failure to complain ... does not necessarily mean that a victim welcomed the harasser's conduct. The failure to complain may actually be an emblem of the power of the harassment. At the very least, silence in the face of harassment requires a court to examine why the victim did not complain before concluding that the harasser's conduct was welcome.[62]

---

[59]*See generally* EEOC Policy Guidance on Sexual Harassment, *supra* note 40, at 405:6686.

    See, e.g., D.C. Circuit: Vinson v. Taylor, 753 F.2d 141, 146, 36 FEP Cases 1423, 1427 (D.C. Cir. 1985)(in response to harassing conduct, choice of any option—acquiescence, opposition, or resignation— equal in eyes of law), *aff'd sub nom.* Meritor Sav. Bank v. Vinson, *supra* note 58;

    Second Circuit: Babcock v. Frank, *supra* note 46, 729 F. Supp. at 287–88, 54 FEP Cases at 1129–30 (complainant stated claim with allegation she was coerced by job-related threats of supervisor into continuing sexual conduct that was no longer consensual);

    Fourth Circuit: Swentek v. USAir, 830 F.2d 552, 557, 44 FEP Cases 1808, 1812 (4th Cir. 1987)(trial court erred when it used Swentek's own past conduct and foul language to conclude that sexually harassing comments were "welcome" to her; "use of foul language or sexual innuendo in a consensual setting does not waive" legal protections); Katz v. Dole, 709 F.2d 251, 254 n.3, 31 FEP Cases, 1521, 1523 (4th Cir. 1983), reproduced in Chapter 7, Harassment by Co-Workers (private and consensual sexual conduct does not constitute waiver); Llewellyn v. Celanese Corp., 693 F. Supp. 369, 372, 47 FEP Cases 993, 995 (W.D.N.C. 1988)(complainant succeeded on sexual harassment claim notwithstanding her public comment that a male co-worker "has a cute ass," where she did not want co-workers to see her true feelings of embarrassment, anger, and humiliation); Spencer v. General Elec. Co., 697 F. Supp. 204, 215 n.13, 51 FEP Cases 1696, 1705 (E.D. Va. 1988)(even if complainant had engaged in "horseplay," legal protections would not be waived), *aff'd,* 894 F.2d 651, 51 FEP Cases 1725 (4th Cir. 1990);

    Fifth Circuit: Cummings v. Walsh Constr. Co., *supra* note 58 (complainant proved sexual harassment consisting of foremen's repeated requests for sexual favors, although complainant twice engaged in sexual relations with one foreman);

    Sixth Circuit: Boyd v. James S. Hayes Living Health Care Agency, 671 F. Supp. 1155, 1165, 44 FEP Cases 332, 340 (W.D. Tenn. 1987)(complainant's voluntary actions, such as going to supervisor's hotel room or accepting ride in his car, did not prevent finding that she was offended by his touching and his sexually explicit movie and magazines);

    Seventh Circuit: Moffett v. Gene B. Glick Co., 621 F. Supp. 244, 268 (N.D. Ind. 1985)(complainant's use of vulgar language not dispositive, for she need not be a "saint in a den of sinners");

    Eighth Circuit: Barrett v. Omaha Nat'l Bank, 584 F. Supp. 22, 29, 35 FEP Cases 585, 591 (D. Neb. 1983)(sexual harassment found even though complainant "was not, in every instance, a mere bystander when it came to talk of sexual activity"), *aff'd,* 726 F.2d 424, 35 FEP Cases 593 (8th Cir. 1984);

    West Virginia: Westmoreland Coal Co. v. West Virginia Human Rights Comm'n, 382 S.E.2d 562, 565 n.2, 54 EPD ¶40,101 (W. Va. 1989)(lower court erred in rejecting quid pro quo claim of coal company employee that she had finally relented to supervisor's multiple demands for sex because she "felt pushed" and thought "this will get him off my back").

[60]EEOC Dec. 82-2, 28 FEP Cases 1843, 1844 (1982)(where complainant accepted supervisor's invitation to have drinks with him and did not fear adverse action if she had declined, she failed to show that conduct was unwelcome).

[61]*See, e.g.,* Bohen v. City of E. Chicago, 622 F. Supp. 1234, 1240, 39 FEP Cases 917, 920 (N.D. Ind. 1985)(expert testimony that reticence about complaining and diminished sense of self-worth are common in cases of sexual harassment), *rev'd on other grounds,* 799 F.2d 1180, 41 FEP Cases 1108 (7th Cir. 1986).

[62]Note, *Perceptions of Harm: The Consent Defense in Sexual Harassment Cases,* 71 IOWA L. REV. 1109, 1120 (1986). *See also* C. MACKINNON, SEXUAL HARASSMENT OF WORKING WOMEN 46 (1979)("[I]t would be paradoxical if, so long as a superior has the power to force sexual attentions by adopting forms of sexual expression that do not require compliance—for example, sitting naked in his office in her presence while giving dictation—a woman would be precluded from legal action or other complaint because she had not properly refused").

In *Bundy v. Jackson*,[63] the D.C. Circuit ruled that complainants need not prove that they resisted the alleged harassment:

> It may even be pointless to require the employee to prove that she "resisted" the harassment at all. So long as the employer never literally forces sexual relations on the employee, "resistance" may be a meaningless alternative for her. If the employer demands no response to his verbal or physical gestures other than good-natured tolerance, the woman has no means of communicating her rejection. She neither accepts nor rejects the advances; she simply endures them. She might be able to contrive proof of rejection by objecting to the employer's advances in some very visible and dramatic way, but she would only do so at the risk of making her life on the job even more miserable. It hardly helps that the remote prospect of legal relief under [a quid pro quo theory] remains available if she objects so powerfully that she provokes the employer into firing her.[64]

6. Advances Found Welcome

Although the complainant must prove that a sexual advance was unwelcome, as a practical matter the employer may need to produce evidence that the advances were in fact welcome. Typically this proof takes the form of evidence that the complainant invited the advances. In *Highlander v. KFC National Management Co.*,[65] Judge Robert B. Krupansky, in upholding a finding that complainant's conduct had "induced" the advances in question, noted that the complainant had invited her supervisor to discuss opportunities for promotion during a meeting she had proposed in a bar. It was there that he had placed his arm around her and stated that, if she was really interested in becoming a co-manager, "there was a motel across the street."[66]

Similarly, in *Reichman v. Bureau of Affirmative Action*,[67] the court relied upon plaintiff Reichman's initiation of the sexual conduct in deciding that she had failed to prove that defendant Harley's attempted kiss was unwelcome to her:

> Reichman behaved in a very flirtatious and provocative manner around Harley. Despite his repeated refusals, Reichman asked Harley to have dinner at her house on several occasions. . . . In addition, Reichman continued to conduct herself in a similar manner after the kissing incident. The court is thus persuaded that no unwelcome sexual advances were made by Defendant Harley.[68]

---

[63]641 F.2d 934, 24 FEP Cases 1155 (D.C. Cir. 1981).

[64]*Id.* at 946, 24 FEP Cases at 1161–62 (citations omitted). *See also* Moylan v. Maries County, *supra* note 55.

[65]805 F.2d 644, 649, 42 FEP Cases 654, 657 (6th Cir. 1986)(Krupansky, Wellford & Peck, JJ.).

[66]*Id.* at 646, 42 FEP Cases at 655. *See also* Lipsett v. Rive-Mora, 669 F. Supp. 1188, 1200 (D.P.R. 1987)(plaintiff who "smiled back" at defendant's "flirtations" did not demonstrate that comments were unwelcome); Jensen v. Kellings Fine Foods, 51 FEP Cases 1752 (D. Kan. 1987)(rejecting sexual harassment claim of complainant who admittedly had voluntary sexual intercourse with her boss on 100 occasions over three years, until she was fired after she and boss were discovered together by his wife; court cited complainant's failure to complain to anyone during this period and her gift of pen-and-pencil set to boss just days before surprise visit by the wife); Reichman v. Bureau of Affirmative Action, 536 F. Supp. 1149, 30 FEP Cases 1644 (M.D. Pa. 1982)(discussed in text at notes 67–68 *infra*); Gan v. Kepro Circuit Sys., 28 FEP Cases 639 (E.D. Mo. 1982)(complainant initiated sexually suggestive physical conduct and had sexually explicit conversations with other employees).

[67]536 F. Supp. 1149, 30 FEP Cases 1644 (M.D. Pa. 1982).

[68]*Id.* at 1177, 30 FEP Cases at 1665–66.

7. Objective Versus Subjective Standard

The Supreme Court in *Meritor* suggested that deciding whether sexual advances were unwelcome requires use of an objective standard rather than consideration of the complainant's subjective secret feelings.[69] The EEOC has similarly stated that an objective rather than a subjective standard should be used in determining welcomeness.[70]

In *Sardigal v. St. Louis National Stockyards Co.,*[71] the complainant's allegation of unwelcomeness was rejected because, after the alleged harassment occurred, she visited her alleged harasser at the hospital, visited him at his brother's home, and allowed him to enter her house alone at night. Similarly, in *Christoforou v. Ryder Truck Rental,*[72] where the complainant continued to accept rides from the alleged harasser, even after an alleged sexual assault, the court refused to find that the conduct was unwelcome. Again, in *Reichman v. Bureau of Affirmative Action,*[73] advances were held not to be unwelcome where the complainant continued to invite her supervisor to dinner and flirted with him after the complained-of incident, which involved a kiss and a proposition.[74]

An objective standard may differ depending on whether it adopts a "male" or "female" perspective. The First Circuit in *Lipsett* noted that an issue of proof not settled by *Meritor* is "the question of whose perspective—that of the harasser or that of the victim—should be used in assessing 'unwelcomeness.' "[75] Judge Bownes observed:

> [O]ften a determination of sexual harassment turns on whether it is found that the plaintiff misconstrued or over-reacted to what the defendant claims were innocent or invited overtures. A male supervisor might believe, for example, that it is legitimate for him to tell a female subordinate that she has a "great figure" or "nice legs." The female subordinate, however, may find such comments offensive.[76]

The standard used by *Henson*—that the complainant regard the conduct as undesirable or offensive[77]—appears to be subjective. If the court uses a subjective standard, summary judgment on the unwelcomeness element will be rare. In *Zowayyed v. Lowen Co.,*[78] the company president allegedly made sexually suggestive comments to the complainant and repeatedly tried to brush up against her. The complainant told others that she found the incidents to be

---

[69]477 U.S. 57, 58, 40 FEP Cases 1822, 1826 (1986), reproduced in Chapter 1, Overview (welcomeness ascertained by determining if complainant, by her conduct, indicated advances were unwelcome).

[70]"Investigators and triers of fact rely on objective evidence, rather than subjective, uncommunicated feelings." EEOC Policy Guidance on Sexual Harassment, 8 FAIR EMPL. PRAC. MAN. (BNA) 405:6686 n.10 (March 19, 1990), reproduced in Appendix 3.

[71]42 FEP Cases 497 (S.D. Ill. 1986).

[72]668 F. Supp. 294, 51 FEP Cases 98 (S.D.N.Y. 1987).

[73]536 F. Supp. 1149, 30 FEP Cases 1644 (M.D. Pa. 1982).

[74]*See also* cases cited in note 66 *supra.*

[75]864 F.2d 881, 898, 54 FEP Cases 230, 243 (1st Cir. 1988)(Campbell, C.J., Bownes & Breyer, J.J.).

[76]*Id.* at 898, 54 FEP Cases at 243. Some commentators have suggested that courts typically use the male perspective. Note, *Perceptions of Harm: The Consent Defense in Sexual Harassment Cases,* 71 IOWA L. REV. 1109, 1130 (1986)(men sometimes see aggressive behavior as seduction rather than the harassment women perceive, thus a man's failure to ensure consent may be normal and reasonable by male standards).

[77]682 F.2d 897, 903, 29 FEP Cases 787, 792 (11th Cir. 1982), reproduced in Chapter 4, Hostile Environment Harassment.

[78]735 F. Supp. 1497, 1504–5, 52 FEP Cases 1350, 1356 (D. Kan. 1990).

humorous and that she had the president wrapped around her finger. Despite this evidence, the court held that it could not find that the sexual advances were welcome as a matter of law, because, in opposition to the employer's summary judgment motion, the complainant declared that she found the advances "to be a source of significant mental pain and anguish," which she made light of only to relieve the tension they created. Thus, the court found a factual dispute as to whether the conduct was welcome.

C. Proof of Unwelcome Sexual Advance

In many cases there will be no direct evidence, other than the complainant's testimony, that the supervisor made any advance.[79] The complainant's testimony alone can suffice to avoid a summary judgment for the employer on this element,[80] but at trial the complainant's testimony must be examined in light of the direct and circumstantial evidence that tends to corroborate or refute her testimony.[81] As the Supreme Court noted in *Meritor,* "the question whether particular conduct was indeed unwelcome presents difficult problems of proof and turns largely on credibility determinations committed to the trier of fact."[82] Thus, "in a case of alleged sexual harassment which involves close questions of credibility and subjective interpretation, the existence of corroborative evidence or the lack thereof is likely to be crucial."[83] Some courts have admitted corroborating evidence in the form of testimony that an alleged harasser used his supervisory power to sexually exploit other female subordinates.[84]

When confronted with conflicting evidence as to welcomeness, the trier of fact looks "at the record as a whole and at the totality of circumstances,"

---

[79]For an exception to the rule, see *Sparks v. Pilot Freight Carriers,* 830 F.2d 1554, 1556, 45 FEP Cases 160, 161 (11th Cir. 1987), reproduced in Chapter 2, Forms of Harassment, in which the supervisor, after the plaintiff rebuffed his advance, apparently told her over the plant's public address system that "you'd better be nice to me," "your fate is in my hands," "revenge is the name of the game," and at least one other remark that the district court found "too sexually explicit" to repeat.

[80]A defendant's motion for summary judgment on the issue of whether sexual advances were welcome would rarely be granted because the plaintiff's affidavit would almost always raise a question of fact. *See, e.g.,* Zowayyed v. Lowen Co., *supra* note 78 (triable issue whether sexual advances laughed off at time were actually offensive). *Cf.* Godfrey v. Defense Mapping Agency, 54 FEP Cases 770, 771 (W.D. Mo. 1988)(where complainant produces no admissible evidence of sexual overture in response to defense motion for summary judgment, motion will be granted).

[81]*See, e.g.,* Jackson-Colley v. Army Corps of Engineers, 655 F. Supp. 122, 127, 43 FEP Cases 617, 621 (E.D. Mich. 1987)(plaintiff's allegations of sexual propositions, vulgar gestures and language "grossly aggrandized, contrived and otherwise entirely without merit").

[82]*Supra* note 69, 477 U.S. at 68, 40 FEP Cases at 1827. *See, e.g.,* Horn v. Duke Homes, 755 F.2d 599, 602, 37 FEP Cases 228, 230 (7th Cir. 1985)("district judge reasoned that the case hinged on a simple credibility determination and concluded that [alleged harasser's] testimony was not credible").

[83]Henson v. City of Dundee, 682 F.2d 897, 913 n.25, 29 FEP Cases 787, 800 (11th Cir. 1982), reproduced in Chapter 4, Hostile Environment Harassment; *see also* Hall v. F.O. Thacker Co., 24 FEP Cases 1499, 1503 (N.D. Ga. 1980)(declining to find the plaintiff's testimony of a sexual advance credible because it was "virtually uncorroborated").

[84]*See, e.g.,* Horn v. Duke Homes, *supra* note 82, 755 F.2d at 602, 37 FEP Cases at 230 (other women vulnerable because of marital or financial problems); Toscano v. Nimmo, 570 F. Supp. 1197, 1200, 32 FEP Cases 1401, 1403–4 (D. Del. 1983)(alleged harasser a self-described womanizer). See also Chapter 25, Evidence, Section VI.

evaluating each situation on a case-by-case basis.[85] An inquiry into "welcomeness" may properly consider the complainant's contemporaneous clothing, conduct, and speech.[86] The inquiry does not extend, however, to the entirety of the complainant's sexual history. The general rule is that "evidence concerning a [complainant's] general character and past behavior toward others has limited, if any, probative value and does not substitute for a careful examination of her behavior toward the alleged harasser."[87]

The most probative conduct offered to show "welcomeness" is the complainant's conduct toward the alleged harasser. Evidence of whether specific conduct was "unwelcome" will consist in large part of how the complainant reacted to the initial sexual advance. The complainant's contemporaneous report of harassment to the employer, while not required in a quid pro quo case, strongly evidences unwelcomeness.[88]

The reported cases in which the complainant's "unwelcomeness" showing ultimately failed are usually cases in which the complainant's conduct was deemed to have invited or encouraged the advances.[89] Not all forms of friendly conduct will support a finding of welcomeness. In *Wangler v. Hawaiian Electric Co.*,[90] Judge David A. Ezra held that the complainant's conduct did not establish welcomeness for summary judgment purposes even though the complainant had baked birthday cakes for her supervisor, had sent him cards signed "Love, Andrea," and had given him a picture of herself in a belly-dancing costume. The complainant undermined the summary judgment motion by submitting a letter in which her supervisor had told her: "[O]ur relationship was never mutual. You looked to me for paternal love, whereas I desperately wanted you for my Lolita."[91]

---

[85]29 C.F.R. §1604.11(b), reproduced in Appendix 1.

[86]Meritor Sav. Bank v. Vinson, *supra* note 69, 477 U.S. at 69, 40 FEP Cases at 1828. Although the *Meritor* Court did not require consideration of the plaintiff's dress and conduct, other courts have done so: Jones v. Wesco Investments, 846 F.2d 1154, 1155 n.4, 46 FEP Cases 1431, 1432 (8th Cir. 1988)(court *must* consider "any provocative speech or dress of the plaintiff in a sexual harassment case") and cases cited in Chapter 25, Evidence, Section III.

[87]EEOC Policy Guidance on Sexual Harassment, *supra* note 70, at 405:6687. See Swentek v. USAir, 830 F.2d 552, 44 FEP Cases 1808 (4th Cir. 1987)(complainant's conduct and use of foul language did not show she welcomed sexual behavior by alleged harasser when she told him to leave her alone); Mitchell v. Hutchings, 116 F.R.D. 481, 44 FEP Cases 615 (D. Utah 1987)(evidence of sexual history in workplace discoverable, but evidence of sexual proclivities and past sexual conduct barred); Jennings v. DHL Airlines, 101 F.R.D. 549, 34 FEP Cases 1423 (N.D. Ill. 1984)(psychiatric records not discoverable); Priest v. Rotary, 98 F.R.D. 755, 32 FEP Cases 1064 (N.D. Cal. 1983)(same); Katz v. Dole, 709 F.2d 251, 254 n.3, 31 FEP Cases 1521, 1523 (4th Cir. 1983), reproduced in Chapter 7, Harassment by Co-Workers (improper for trial judge to suggest plaintiff's past conduct meant she welcomed harasser's behavior). For a discussion of the defendant's limited ability to inquire into the complainant's sexual history, see Chapters 25, Evidence, and 26, Discovery.

[88]EEOC Policy Guidance on Sexual Harassment, *supra* note 70, at 405:6685.

[89]*See, e.g.,* Trautvetter v. Quick, 916 F.2d 1140, 1149, 54 FEP Cases 109, 116 (7th Cir. 1990)(suggesting that school teacher who initially rejected series of sexual propositions by principal before finally having sexual intercourse with him in motel could not show "unwelcome" requirement and suggesting that test is extent to which plaintiff "made it known that the sexual advances were 'unwelcome' "). See also cases cited in note 66 *supra.*

[90]742 F. Supp. 1458, 53 FEP Cases 943 (D. Haw. 1990).

[91]*Id.* at 1463, 53 FEP Cases at 947. *Lolita* is the title of a 1955 novel by Vladimir Nabokov focusing on a middle-aged man's sexual fascination with a prepubescent girl. The novel begins: "LOLITA, light of my life, fire of my loins. My sin, my soul." V. NABOKOV, LOLITA 11 (1955)(Perigee paperback ed. 1980).

VI. The Issue: The Adverse Employment Action

A quid pro quo case ordinarily requires proof of economic harm. In the classic rejection case, the complainant must prove that following her rejection of sexual advances she suffered a detriment to some tangible aspect of her terms, conditions, or privileges of employment. The tangible detriment may be termination of employment,[92] denial of a promotion or pay increase,[93] denial of training,[94] or failure to rehire the complainant after a layoff.[95]

Courts have rejected quid pro quo claims in the absence of a clear economic loss.[96] In *Jones v. Flagship International*,[97] the court upheld a finding of no quid pro quo harassment where the record failed to establish that the purported sexual harassment affected the complainant's promotion or responsibilities.[98] In *Walker v. Sullair Corp.*,[99] the alleged harasser failed to promote the complainant, allegedly because she rebuffed his sexual advances. The employer, however, eventually granted the promotion and gave the complainant a retroactive pay increase to the date that the raise was first sought. The court rejected the quid pro claim because, in part, "the plaintiff has not demonstrated a tangible loss which can be attributed to the *defendant*."[100]

The EEOC would treat a coercion case as an actionable quid pro quo case on the theory that a violation occurred in the imposition of the employer's sexual bargain, even though the coerced employee has suffered no tangible job detriment but rather has received the job benefit or avoided the job detriment that was involved in the illicit sexual bargain.[101] In that event, although no economic harm resulted, a complainant presumably could sue for injunctive relief under Title VII, and for compensatory and punitive damages under broader theories of recovery.

---

[92]*See* Sparks v. Pilot Freight Carriers, *supra* note 79, 830 F.2d at 1565, 45 FEP Cases at 168 ("[b]eing fired certainly is a tangible detriment").

[93]Sowers v. Kemira, Inc., 701 F. Supp. 809, 823, 46 FEP Cases 1825, 1835 (S.D. Ga. 1988).

[94]Carrero v. New York City Hous. Auth., 890 F.2d 569, 579, 51 FEP Cases 596, 603 (2d Cir. 1989)(complainant prevailed on allegation that job detriment was denial of training and subsequent demotion despite defendant's argument that mere failure to train was not denial of tangible job benefit).

[95]Joyner v. AAA Cooper Transp., 597 F. Supp. 537, 540–42, 36 FEP Cases 1644, 1647–49 (M.D. Ala. 1983), *aff'd*, 749 F.2d 732, 41 FEP Cases 496 (11th Cir. 1984).

[96]*E.g.*, Trautvetter v. Quick, *supra* note 89, 916 F.2d at 1148, 54 FEP Cases at 115 (finding no quid pro quo case where complainant not "affirmatively or constructively discharged" and where she failed to show supervisor's "sexual advances infringed in some manner upon her ability to obtain a promotion or other job-related benefit"). *But see* Highlander v. KFC Nat'l Mgmt. Co., 805 F.2d 644, 648, 42 FEP Cases 654, 657 (6th Cir. 1986)(implying that quid pro quo case would be established even absent job detriment, if submission to unwelcome advances made an express or implied condition of employment).

[97]793 F.2d 714, 41 FEP Cases 358 (5th Cir. 1986), *cert. denied*, 479 U.S. 1065 (1987).

[98]*Id.* at 723–24, 41 FEP Cases at 365–66.

[99]736 F. Supp. 94, 99–100, 52 FEP Cases 1313, 1316–17 (W.D.N.C. 1990).

[100]*Id.* at 99, 52 FEP Cases at 1317.

[101]EEOC Policy Guidance on Employer Liability for Sexual Favoritism, 8 Fair Empl. Prac. Man. (BNA) 405:6818 n.6 (January 12, 1990), reproduced in Appendix 2. *See, e.g.*, Thoreson v. Penthouse Int'l, 563 N.Y.S.2d 968, 55 EPD ¶40,457 (N.Y. Sup. Ct. 1990), reproduced in Chapter 2, Forms of Harassment. *But see* Trautvetter v. Quick, *supra* note 89 (dismissing Title VII case where allegedly coerced affair resulted in no tangible job detriment).

VII. THE CAUSAL CONNECTION

In a quid pro quo case, unlike a typical disparate treatment case, the job detriment does not occur directly because of the complainant's gender, but because of her reaction to a sexual advance that itself was based on her gender. The causual connection thus has two prongs: (1) that because of the complainant's sex she was subjected to a sexual advance, and (2) that because of her reaction to the sexual advance she was subjected to (or avoided) a tangible job detriment. The analytic difficulty once experienced in quid pro quo cases seems to have stemmed largely from this double nexus, where the activity is because of sex and the tangible employment detriment is because of the activity.

A. On the Basis of Sex

1. Early Decisions

Courts initially were reluctant to find that adverse action taken against the complainant for rejecting sexual advances was based on gender rather than her personal characteristics.[102] Even when submission to sexual demands was clearly a condition of employment, most courts initially concluded that unwelcome sexual advances were not discrimination "based on sex."[103]

One reason that courts were slow to find quid pro quo harassment unlawful was that the proximate cause of the adverse employment action was the female complainant's *activity* (her rejection of sexual advances) rather than her *gender*. Yet protection of an activity (the refusal to grant sexual favors), as opposed to a *status* (the individual's membership in a protected group), has precedents throughout discrimination law. Analogies to this form of discrimination appear in cases forbidding discrimination on the basis of religion—a complainant who suffers loss of employment opportunities by refusing to submit to an employer's religious practices has been discriminated against on the basis of religion, regardless of the complainant's religious beliefs.[104]

Further analogies appear in authorities forbidding discrimination on the basis of retaliation for an activity that is in opposition to unlawful employment

---

[102]*See, e.g.,* Barnes v. Train, 13 FEP Cases 123, 124 (D.D.C. 1974), *rev'd sub nom.* Barnes v. Costle, 561 F.2d 983, 15 FEP Cases 345 (D.C. Cir. 1977), reproduced in Chapter 1, Overview. One history of this issue appears in Comment, *The Harms of Asking: Towards a Comprehensive Treatment of Sexual Harassment,* 55 U. CHI. L. REV. 328, 331–33 (1988).

[103]*E.g.,* Corne v. Bausch & Lomb, 390 F. Supp. 161, 163, 10 FEP Cases 289, 290–91 (D. Ariz. 1975), *vacated,* 562 F.2d 55, 15 FEP Cases 1370 (9th Cir. 1977); Barnes v. Train, *supra* note 102 (discrimination not because plaintiff was a woman but because she rejected "sexual affair with her supervisor" and thus had "inharmonious personal relationship with him"); Miller v. Bank of Am., 418 F. Supp. 233, 236, 13 FEP Cases 439, 440–41 (N.D. Cal. 1976), *rev'd on other grounds,* 600 F.2d 211, 20 FEP Cases 462 (9th Cir. 1979). In *Miller,* the court found that sexual demands could not have been contemplated as falling within the prohibitions of Title VII, because "the attraction of males to females and females to males is a natural sex phenomenon and it is probable that this attraction plays at least a subtle part in most personnel decisions." For a discussion of other grounds once used for excluding sexual harassment from Title VII coverage, see Chapter 1, Overview, Section IV.

[104]For a discussion of the interrelationship of sexual and other forms of harassment, see Chapter 2, Forms of Harassment, Section I.

practices.[105] A retaliation case often may be co-extensive with a classic quid pro quo case, where the employer has expressly conditioned a job benefit on the employee's provision of sexual favors. The employee who opposes this condition is opposing a violation of §703—the discriminatory practice of sexual harassment. If the harasser then withholds a job benefit, his action is arguably a violation of §703 or §704(a), or both.[106]

Courts now uniformly find quid pro quo harassment unlawful, without any need for these analogies, simply by reasoning that when an employer conditions an individual's employment opportunities upon services as a sexual partner, it is discriminating on the basis of gender.[107]

2. The "But For" Test

In *Barnes v. Costle,*[108] the D.C. Circuit ruled that quid pro quo harassment is on the basis of the complainant's gender:

> But for her womanhood ... [the complainant's] participation in sexual activity would never have been solicited. To say, then, that she was victimized in her employment simply because she declined the invitation is to ignore the asserted fact that she was invited only because she was a woman subordinate to the inviter. ... Put another way, she became the target of her superior's sexual desires because she was a woman and was asked to bow to his demands as the price of holding her job.[109]

In *Henson v. City of Dundee,*[110] the Eleventh Circuit incorporated the "but for" test used in *Barnes,* thus allowing the complainant to prove that the harassment occurred on the basis of sex simply by showing that, but for her sex, the harassment would not have occurred. Judge Vance noted that, ordinarily, this element is easily established:

> In the typical case in which a male supervisor makes sexual overtures to a female worker, it is obvious that the supervisor did not treat male employees in the same fashion. It will therefore be a simple matter for the plaintiff to prove that, but for her sex, she would not have been subjected to sexual harassment.[111]

Following *Barnes* and *Henson,* courts have had no difficulty in finding this element of the prima facie case in all but the most unusual harassment cases, even where the supervisor selects the complainant because of her per-

---

[105]For a discussion of retaliation, see Chapter 10. *See also* Moffett v. Gene B. Glick Co., 621 F. Supp. 244 (N.D. Ind. 1985)(white employee harassed for dating black man).

[106]*See generally* Dockter v. Rudolf Wolff Futures, 913 F.2d 456, 461–62, 53 FEP Cases 1642, 1646–47 (7th Cir. 1990)(analyzing quid pro quo claim of administrative assistant fired after rejecting unwelcome advance that was never source of complaint to management; court put question as whether dismissal was "retaliatory under Title VII"); Holland v. Jefferson Nat'l Life Ins. Co., 883 F.2d 1307, 1316, 50 FEP Cases 1215, 1222 (7th Cir. 1989)(female employee established prima facie case of retaliation by evidence that her supervisor, who had promised to hold her job open during maternity leave, refused to do so after she complained to him of harassment by another manager).

[107]See Section VII.A.2. *infra.*

[108]561 F.2d 983, 15 FEP Cases 345 (D.C. Cir. 1977), reproduced in Chapter 1, Overview (reversing *Barnes v. Train*).

[109]*Id.* at 990, 15 FEP Cases at 350–51.

[110]682 F.2d 897, 29 FEP Cases 787 (11th Cir. 1982), reproduced in Chapter 4, Hostile Environment Harassment.

[111]*Id.* at 904, 29 FEP Cases at 793.

sonal characteristics and even where not all female employees are subject to sexual advances.[112]

Quid pro quo harassment on the basis of sex is not limited to heterosexual advances by male superiors toward female subordinates. Although the vast majority of quid pro quo cases involve the harassment of women by men, female supervisors who attempt to exact sexual favors from male subordinates through the threat of adverse employment action are similarly harassing their subordinates on the basis of sex.[113]

Homosexual quid pro quo harassment is similarly a violation of Title VII, for it, too, is based on gender.[114] Liability thus can exist where women have been sexually harassed by women,[115] and where men have been sexually harassed by men.[116] As noted by one commentator:

> In practice, the courts have reduced the necessary showing to a simple inquiry into sexual orientation. Thus, I need only state that heterosexual B would not have harassed A had A not been a member of the opposite sex, or that homosexual B would not have harassed A had A not been of B's gender.[117]

3. The "Bisexual Defense"

An issue raised by courts in *dicta* is the possibility of a "bisexual defense": an employer theoretically could defeat the "because of sex" element

---

[112]*See, e.g.,* Chamberlin v. 101 Realty, 915 F.2d 777, 784, 54 FEP Cases 101, 107 (1st Cir. 1990)(because supervisor did not make sexual advances to male employees, "there can be no question that, but for the fact that Chamberlin is female, she would not have been subjected to sexual harassment"). In the context of 42 U.S.C. §1983, some courts continue to distinguish between advances because of gender and advances because of personal characteristics. *E.g.,* Trautvetter v. Quick, 916 F.2d 1140, 1151, 54 FEP Cases 109, 117–18 (7th Cir. 1990).

[113]*See, e.g.,* Huebschen v. Wisconsin Dep't of Health & Soc. Serv., 716 F.2d 1167, 32 FEP Cases 1582 (7th Cir. 1983)(male alleged he was demoted for ending sexual relationship with female supervisor); Barnes v. Costle, *supra* note 108, 561 F.2d at 990 n.55, 15 FEP Cases at 351 (*dictum*)(male can establish prima facie case of quid pro quo harassment by showing that harassing conduct based on gender); Bundy v. Jackson, 641 F.2d 934, 942 n.7, 24 FEP Cases 1155 (D.C. Cir. 1981)(*dictum*)(sexual harassment no less "because of sex" when it is female harassing subordinate male or superior of either sex harassing subordinate of the same sex); *cf.* Ross v. Comsat, 34 FEP Cases 260, 265 (D. Md. 1984)(summary judgment against male employee's sexual harassment claim based on sexual propositions from female co-worker, given absence of evidence that plaintiff had to "acquiesce to sexual advances as condition of his employment"), *rev'd on other grounds,* 759 F.2d 355, 37 FEP Cases 797 (4th Cir. 1985).

[114]"A woman who is fired for refusal to submit to a lesbian supervisor is just as fired—and her firing is just as related to gender—as if the perpetrator were a man." C. MACKINNON, SEXUAL HARASSMENT OF WORKING WOMEN 206 (1979). Courts are unanimous in recognizing that homosexual harassment is unlawful as a form of discrimination "because of sex." Bundy v. Jackson, *supra* note 113, 641 F.2d at 942 n.7, 24 FEP Cases at 1159 (*dictum*); Barnes v. Costle, *supra* note 108, 561 F.2d at 990 n.55, 15 FEP Cases at 351; Wright v. Methodist Youth Servs., 511 F. Supp. 307, 25 FEP Cases 563 (N.D. Ill. 1981)(alleged discharge for rejecting supervisor's homosexual advances states claim under Title VII); Barlow v. Northwestern Memorial Hosp., 30 FEP Cases 223, 224 (N.D. Ill. 1980)(complainant, a female secretary, stated Title VII claim in alleging her female supervisor demoted her because complainant refused to accede to supervisor's sexual advances); Joyner v. AAA Cooper Transp., *supra* note 95, 597 F. Supp. at 542, 36 FEP Cases at 1648 (plaintiff subject to sexual advances on basis of sex where he was male and his male supervisor had "homosexual proclivities"); Johnson v. Ramsey County, 424 N.W.2d 800, 46 FEP Cases 1686 (Minn. Ct. App. 1988)(male state judge made unwelcome sexual advances to male court reporter on his staff; conduct actionable under Minnesota FEP statute).

[115]Polk v. Yellow Freight Sys., 801 F.2d 190, 196, 41 FEP Cases 1279, 1283 (6th Cir. 1986)(female office manager accused of unwanted touching, sexual suggestions, and homosexual advances to office staff, creating intimidating and hostile environment); *see also* cases cited in note 114 *supra*.

[116]*See* Joyner v. AAA Cooper Transp., 597 F. Supp. 537, 542, 36 FEP Cases 1644, 1648 (M.D. Ala. 1983)(male plaintiff who alleged he was discriminated against after declining supervisor's homosexual advances "is a member of the protected class (males)"); Bundy v. Jackson, *supra* note 113.

[117]Comment, *supra* note 102, 55 U. CHI. L. REV. at 348.

in a quid pro quo case by showing that the harasser treated members of both genders equally as his sexual prey.[118] The sexual overtures of this bisexual supervisor would not be actionable under Title VII because they would not reflect differential treatment of either sex.[119] As Professor Catharine A. Mac-Kinnon has stated, "a sexual condition [placed on an employment opportunity] that disadvantages both sexes ... is probably not sex discrimination—it is merely exploitative, oppressive and an abuse of power."[120]

Although a methodically bisexual harasser thus would not discriminate against a victim on the basis of gender, a fact-finder in any given case could infer that gender motivated that particular encounter. A bisexual individual may select which employee to solicit for any particular liaison with that employee's sex as the motivating factor, thus satisfying the "but for sex" leg of the prima facie case. Moreover, the mere fact that the supervisor is bisexual, or has had bisexual relationships, would in no event be sufficient to defend a harassment action absent some showing that the supervisor actually made similar, or even equal, demands upon employees of both sexes.[121]

B. "Affecting": The Link Between Harassment and the Adverse Employment Action

The complainant must show a causal connection between an unwelcome sexual advance and an adverse employment action by showing that such an

---

[118]Henson v. City of Dundee, *supra* note 110, 682 F.2d at 905 n.11, 29 FEP Cases at 794 (court states that it should be clear that sexual harassment is discrimination based upon sex except in the "exceedingly atypical case of a bisexual supervisor"); Vinson v. Taylor, 760 F.2d 1330, 1333 n.7, 37 FEP Cases 1266, 1269 (D.C. Cir. 1985)(Bork, J., dissenting from denial of rehearing *en banc*); Bundy v. Jackson, *supra* note 113, 641 F.2d at 942 n.7, 24 FEP Cases at 1159 (court rejects argument that sexual harassment could not be gender discrimination because any homosexual supervisor could harass an employee of the same gender: "[o]nly by a reductio ad absurdum could we imagine a case of harassment that is not sex discrimination where a bisexual supervisor harasses men and women alike"); Barnes v. Costle, *supra* note 108, 561 F.2d at 990 n.55, 15 FEP Cases at 351 (under "because of sex" analysis, gender discrimination not applicable to conduct by bisexual supervisor).

[119]No reported case appears to have decided this "bisexual harasser" issue. The obvious practical difficulties an employer might create for itself in making this showing have led Professor MacKinnon to term this the "kamikaze defense," C. MacKinnon, FEMINISM UNMODIFIED (1987), although it has demonstrated utility in hostile environment cases. *E.g.*, Sheehan v. Purolator, Inc., 839 F.2d 99, 105, 49 FEP Cases 1000, 1006 (2d Cir. 1988)(supervisor whose temper was manifested indiscriminately toward all employees did not commit sexual harassment), *cert. denied*, 488 U.S. 891 (1988); Walker v. Sullair Corp, *supra* note 100, 736 F. Supp. at 99, 52 FEP Cases at 1317 (third element of a quid pro quo harassment case not satisfied because several witnesses said supervisor "treat[ed] both male and female employees with contempt"); Halpert v. Wertheim & Co., 27 FEP Cases 21 (S.D.N.Y. 1980)(same).

[120]C. MacKinnon, *supra* note 114, at 203. Prior to *Barnes v. Costle, supra* note 108, 561 F.2d at 990 n.55, 15 FEP Cases at 351, some courts used the possibility of a bisexual defense as a basis for excluding sexual harassment from Title VII's protections altogether. *See, e.g.*, Corne v. Bausch & Lomb, *supra* note 103, 390 F. Supp. at 163, 10 FEP Cases at 291 ("it would be ludicrous to hold that [harassment of female employees] was contemplated by the Act because to do so would mean that if the conduct complained of was directed equally to males, there would be no basis for suit").

[121]One commentator has suggested that the possibility of a bisexual loophole exposes a deeper need to reformulate the "but for sex" requirement to ensure that any loss of an employment benefit based upon refusal of a sexual overture is actionable. This result could be accomplished simply by reading the phrase "on the basis of sex" as including not only actions based on gender, but also all actions based on sexuality. In doing so, the focus of the inquiry in all sexual harassment cases would remain on the nature of the unwelcome advance and the adverse employment action rather than on the sexual orientation of the supervisor. Comment, *supra* note 102, 55 U. CHI. L. REV. at 348 nn.85–86 (liability for bisexual supervisor not inconceivable).

action resulted from the refusal to accede to a supervisor's sexual advances,[122] or was avoided only by a coerced submission. The existence of this causal connection is a question of fact, decided on the basis of direct or circumstantial evidence.[123]

In *Keppler v. Hinsdale Township High School District*,[124] the court suggested that the causal connection might be more difficult for the complainant to establish in a soured romance case than it is in a rejection case. Judge Brian Barnett Duff first identified "the standard form" of quid pro quo harassment— "express or implied demands for sexual favors in return for job benefits: 'You have sex with me and you will get a raise (or keep your job, or whatever).' "[125] In this standard case, the court would presume that a subsequent adverse employment action resulted from sex discrimination.

Judge Duff then distinguished the standard harassment case from a soured romance case, where initial acceptance is followed by rejection, which is followed by an adverse job action. Judge Duff would presume that the action, if retaliatory at all, stemmed from "the termination of the intimate physical and emotional relationship," not from "the rejection of copulation *per se*."[126] This presumption reflects the view that while an "employer who threatens a penalty if the employee will not continue the physical relationship is using gender as a basis for job benefits," the employer who simply retaliates for the termination of the relationship is not.[127] As the court acknowledges, this distinction will often be difficult to maintain in practice.[128]

1. Lapse of Time

A significant factor in proving the causal connection is the time period between the sexual conduct and the adverse employment action. In the classic quid pro quo case, rejection of a sexual advance promptly leads to economic retaliation. In *Horn v. Duke Homes*,[129] the complainant's supervisor commented on the complainant's "sexual needs now that her husband had left her" and told her that he would make it easy on her if she would go out with him. After the complainant's final rejection of these advances, she was reprimanded for

---

[122]*See, e.g.,* Highlander v. KFC Nat'l Mgmt. Co., 805 F.2d 644, 649, 42 FEP Cases 654, 657 (6th Cir. 1986)(record "totally devoid of any evidence tending to demonstrate that plaintiff was denied a job benefit or suffered a job detriment as a result of her failure to engage in the activity suggested by [her supervisor]"); Walker v. Sullair Corp., 736 F. Supp. 94, 100, 52 FEP Cases 1313, 1317 (W.D.N.C. 1990)("Without some connection between the sexual conduct and some economic benefit or detriment, there is no case of quid pro quo sexual harassment").

[123]*See, e.g.,* Boyd v. James S. Hayes Living Health Care Agency, 671 F. Supp. 1155, 1166, 44 FEP Cases 332, 341 (W.D. Tenn. 1987)(plaintiff proved that supervisor's increased criticism of her work following her rebuffing his advances was result of supervisor's deliberate attempt "to create a situation in which plaintiff could not succeed"). For a discussion of the allocation of proof in a quid pro quo case, see Section II. *supra.*

[124]715 F. Supp. 862, 50 FEP Cases 295 (N.D. Ill. 1989), reproduced in Chapter 2, Forms of Harassment.

[125]*Id.* at 868, 50 FEP Cases at 299–300.

[126]*Id.*

[127]*Id.*

[128]*Id.* (court noted that an employee fired after rejecting sexual advance may testify that she felt threatened by termination when she refused, and if employer has penalized (or rewarded) others in office for their response to his actions, she may indeed have faced implied quid pro quo situation).

[129]755 F.2d 599, 601, 37 FEP Cases 228, 229 (7th Cir. 1985).

substandard work and transferred to a different position. One week later, she was fired. The close proximity in time between the complainant's rejections and the adverse employment action helped convince the Seventh Circuit to affirm the finding of a quid pro quo violation.[130]

While delays of several months are not necessarily fatal to a quid pro quo claim,[131] the closer the two events are in time, the more likely it is that a trier of fact will find a causal connection.[132] Where there is a significant gap in time between the sexual advance and the adverse employment decision, courts have been reluctant to find that the adverse employment decision was in retaliation for the employee's rejection of the sexual advances.[133]

The amount of time that must elapse before the connection will be considered too tenuous is determined in light of the facts of each case. In *Chamberlin v. 101 Realty*,[134] the First Circuit found that an interval of ten weeks between the last sexual advance and the discharge "does not preclude a finding that the discharge was a consequence of [the plaintiff's] rejection of [her supervisor's] sexual advances," especially considering that the supervisor was on vacation for a month during that period of time.[135] In *Tomkins v. Public Service Electric & Gas Co.*,[136] a gap of one year between the sexual advance and the firing did not bar the Third Circuit from affirming a finding of causal connection.

2. Comparative Evidence

The complainant who has rejected a sexual advance may establish a causal connection by showing that while suffering no direct adverse job detriment, the complainant failed to obtain an employment benefit granted to another employee who submitted to the alleged harasser's advances.[137] It may also be

---

[130]*Id.* at 603, 37 FEP Cases at 230–31. *See also* Sparks v. Pilot Freight Carriers, 830 F.2d 1554, 1556–57, 45 FEP Cases 160, 161–62 (11th Cir. 1987), reproduced in Chapter 2, Forms of Harassment (quid pro quo case established where supervisor, after rejection of his sexual advances, began harassing plaintiff, including use of company loudspeaker to warn her that "revenge is the name of the game," and supervisor enlisted help of other management personnel to fire plaintiff when she called in sick two weeks after her last rejection of a sexual advance).

[131]*See, e.g.,* Bertoncini v. Schrimpf, 712 F. Supp. 1336, 1337 (N.D. Ill. 1989)(15 months between sexual advance and employer's alleged efforts to embarrass, discredit and punish her for sexual rejection of employer). *See generally* Note, *The Aftermath of Meritor: A Search for Standards in the Law of Sexual Harassment*, 98 YALE L.J. 1717 (1989).

[132]*See, e.g.,* Sparks v. Pilot Freight Carriers, *supra* note 130, 830 F.2d at 1565, 45 FEP Cases at 168 (plaintiff raised sufficient factual question to preclude summary judgment for employer by evidence that alleged harasser influenced plaintiff's supervisor to fire her for pretextual reasons following her refusal to meet alleged harasser's sexual demands); Boyd v. James S. Hayes Living Health Care Agency, *supra* note 123, 671 F. Supp at 1165–66, 44 FEP Cases at 340–41 (causal connection found between supervisor's sexual advances and his increasingly harsh treatment of plaintiff, in part because his attitude toward her became markedly more negative immediately after she rebuffed his sexual overtures during seminar trip).

[133]*See generally* Note, *supra* note 131, 98 YALE L.J. at 1728 (some courts tend to analyze cases involving elements of quid pro quo sexual harassment under environmental sexual harassment standard where there has been a "protracted period between the advances and adverse employment decisions").

[134]915 F.2d 777, 54 FEP Cases 101 (1st Cir. 1990).

[135]*Id.* at 785 n.10, 54 FEP Cases at 107.

[136]568 F.2d 1044, 16 FEP Cases 22 (3d Cir. 1977).

[137]*See* Spencer v. General Elec. Co., 894 F.2d 651, 659, 51 FEP Cases 1725, 1731 (4th Cir. 1990)(this element of the prima facie case satisfied by "evidence that another female employee . . . who succumbed to [her supervisor's] sexual desires received larger pay increases than she received" and by evidence that plaintiff was denied promotion for which she was qualified after rebuffing supervisor's advances); King v. Palmer, 778 F.2d 878, 880, 39 FEP Cases 877, 879 (D.C. Cir. 1985)(promotion of complainant's fellow employee who was having sexual relations with employer found to be "clearly pretextual"); Broderick v.

relevant if employees of the opposite gender were afforded opportunities that the complainant was denied.[138]

3. The Alleged Harasser's Involvement in the Adverse Employment Decision

To establish a causal link between the employment detriment and the harassment, the complainant must show that the alleged harasser made, or substantially affected, the decision that caused the job detriment. In *Sparks v. Pilot Freight Carriers*,[139] the complainant alleged that she was sexually harassed and threatened by her manager, Long. However, the decision to fire her was made by Long's superior, Connell. The district court had granted summary judgment against the quid pro quo claim for want of a causal connection. The Eleventh Circuit reversed, holding that the complainant had submitted sufficient evidence to support the inference that Long had influenced Connell into firing the complainant in retaliation for her reaction to Long's sexual advances:

> (1) Long threatened to have Sparks fired if she did not accede to his demands, (2) Long and Connell had worked together in the Atlanta terminal and apparently were friends, (3) another female employee who had refused Long's advances stated that Long had influenced Connell to reprimand her based on fictitious problems, (4) Long and Connell allegedly discussed Sparks' termination . . . and (5) Sparks was fired for pretextual reasons after having been at the Atlanta terminal for less than five days.[140]

Judge Phyllis A. Kravitch concluded that this evidence was sufficient "to overcome Connell's statements in deposition that he made the decision to fire Sparks independently of, and without consulting, Long."[141]

Ruder, 685 F. Supp. 1269, 1278, 46 FEP Cases 1272, 1281 (D.D.C. 1988), reproduced in Chapter 2, Forms of Harassment (evidence of other employee behavior found relevant in hostile work environment action); Priest v. Rotary, 634 F. Supp. 571, 581, 40 FEP Cases 208, 215 (N.D. Cal. 1986)(complainant waitress assigned to less-profitable coffee shop rather than lounge or dining room and eventually discharged because of negative reaction to defendant's requests for sexual favors); Toscano v. Nimmo, 570 F. Supp. 1197, 1199, 32 FEP Cases 1401, 1403 (D. Del. 1983)(granting sexual favors was condition for receiving position in Veteran's Administration hospital that female plaintiff sought and constituted employment practice that discriminated against plaintiff upon basis of sex).

[138]*See* Henson v. City of Dundee, 682 F.2d 897, 911–12, 29 FEP Cases 787, 800 (11th Cir. 1982) reproduced in Chapter 4, Hostile Environment Harassment (giving male employees opportunity to attend police academy may be relevant to plaintiff's claim that she was denied similar opportunity because she rejected supervisor's sexual advances).

[139]*Supra* note 130 (Hill, Kravitch & Tuttle, JJ.).

[140]*Id.* at 1565, 45 FEP Cases at 168. *See also* Sowers v. Kemira, Inc., 701 F. Supp. 809, 823, 46 FEP Cases 1825, 1835 (S.D. Ga. 1988)(sufficient causal link between harassment and plaintiff's failure to receive promotion where harasser, although not "ultimate decision maker," had "great amount of influence" over decision). *Cf.* Highlander v. KFC Nat'l Mgmt. Co., *supra* note 122, 805 F.2d at 649, 42 FEP Cases at 657 ("evidence adduced at trial also disclosed that [the harassing supervisor] did not participate in the decision to terminate plaintiff's employment"); Dockter v. Rudolf Wolff Futures, 913 F.2d 456, 461–62, 53 FEP Cases 1642, 1646–47 (7th Cir. 1990)(trial court's determination that termination of plaintiff did not result from rejection of her supervisor's advances was buttressed by fact that managers other than harassing supervisor suggested her termination, over initial objections of harassing supervisor); Koster v. Chase Manhattan Bank, 687 F. Supp. 848, 46 FEP Cases 1436 (S.D.N.Y. 1988)(former bank vice president failed to establish that salary decisions were likely due to discriminatory animus; vice president had received three-level promotion and another salary increase six months after promotion; she merely showed that all except three male employees at her level or below received higher salaries); Sheekey v. Nelson, 40 FEP Cases 1216 (D.N.J. 1986)(manager who allegedly harassed plaintiff did not terminate her and had, on one occasion, saved her job).

[141]*Supra* note 130, 830 F.2d at 1565, 45 FEP Cases at 168.

Where the district court has found a causal link between the sexual over-ture and the adverse employment decision, the appellate court will overturn the finding only if it is clearly erroneous.[142]

VIII. EMPLOYER RESPONSIBILITY

Courts have found employers automatically liable for the actions of their supervisory personnel in quid pro quo cases both before[143] and after[144] the Supreme Court's decision in *Meritor*.[145] The discriminatory act is imputed to the employer without regard to whether it knew or should have known of the discrimination or granted the actual authority to discriminate.[146] The EEOC similarly takes the position that "[a]n employer will always be held responsible for acts of quid pro quo harassment."[147]

Quid pro quo harassment may be perpetrated only by the employer through someone who has the power to grant or deny the job benefit in question. If the alleged harasser lacks authority to make or influence employment decisions, no quid pro quo case ordinarily is possible.[148] A harasser's conduct may form the basis of liability under Title VII, however, if he subsequently acquires and

---

[142]*See, e.g.,* Hicks v. Gates Rubber Co., 833 F.2d 1406, 1414, 45 FEP Cases 608, 614 (10th Cir. 1987)("We cannot say that the trial court's finding of no quid pro quo sexual harassment was clearly erroneous . . . . The record fails to disclose any suggestion to [the plaintiff]—either explicitly or implicitly—that her employment was conditioned on granting sexual favors [to her supervisors]. Similarly, the trial court found that the adverse job consequences [the plaintiff] suffered did not arise from her refusal to acquiesce in her supervisors' sexual conduct, but rather, were due solely to her inadequate job performance").

[143]*E.g.,* Highlander v. KFC Nat'l Mgmt. Co., 805 F.2d 644, 648, 42 FEP Cases 654, 657 (6th Cir. 1986); Horn v. Duke Motor Homes, *supra* note 129, 755 F.2d at 605, 37 FEP Cases at 232; Crimm v. Missouri Pacific R.R., 750 F.2d 703, 710, 36 FEP Cases 883, 888 (8th Cir. 1984); Katz v. Dole, 709 F.2d 251, 255 n.6, 31 FEP Cases 1521, 1524 (4th Cir. 1983), reproduced in Chapter 7, Harassment by Co-Workers; Bundy v. Jackson, 641 F.2d 934, 947, 24 FEP Cases 1155, 1159, 1162–63 (D.C. Cir. 1981); Henson v. City of Dundee, *supra* note 138, 682 F.2d at 909–10, 29 FEP Cases at 798–99; Miller v. Bank of Am., 600 F.2d 211, 213, 20 FEP Cases 462, 463–64 (9th Cir. 1979); Barnes v. Costle, 561 F.2d 983, 993, 15 FEP Cases 345, 352–53 (D.C. Cir. 1977), reproduced in Chapter 1, Overview; Toscano v. Nimmo, *supra* note 137, 570 F. Supp at 1203–4, 32 FEP Cases at 1407.

[144]*E.g.,* Spencer v. General Elec. Co., *supra* note 137, 894 F.2d at 658 n.10, 51 FEP Cases at 1730 ("Of course, in a case such as this where the sexual harassment is being committed by one of the employer's supervisors, this element [employer liability] is automatically met because under 42 U.S.C. §2000e(b) knowledge of the harassment is imputed to the employer through its agent-supervisor"); Carrero v. New York City Hous. Auth., 890 F.2d 569, 579, 51 FEP Cases 596, 603 (2d Cir. 1989); Lipsett v. University of P.R., 864 F.2d 881, 901, 54 FEP Cases 230, 246 (1st Cir. 1988)(Title IX case).

[145]For a discussion of employer liability in quid pro quo cases, see Chapter 6, Harassment by Supervisors, Section II.

[146]*See, e.g.,* Schroeder v. Schock, 42 FEP Cases 1112 (D. Kan. 1986)(employer liable for "quid pro quo" harassment by supervisor who had authority to recommend plaintiff's discharge even if supervisor's acts—sexual advances at a restaurant after work hours—are beyond scope of his employment, in that supervisor was within the scope of authority when making or recommending employment decisions that affected plaintiff).

[147]EEOC Policy Guidance on Sexual Harassment, 8 FAIR EMP. PRAC. MAN. (BNA) 405:6694 (March 19, 1990), reproduced in Appendix 3.

[148]Morgan v. Massachusetts Gen. Hosp., 901 F.2d 186, 192, 53 FEP Cases 1780, 1785 (1st Cir. 1990)(quid pro quo case failed for lack of proof "perpetrator of the alleged harassment [had] supervisory authority over the plaintiff"); Koster v. Chase Manhattan Bank, *supra* note 140 (allegation that complainant's former lover impeded her transfer to another position without merit because he did not participate in decision and exercised only limited authority to make recommendations).

exercises the authority to make an adverse employment decision.[149] Similarly, a supervisor who harasses the subordinate of another supervisor may still possess the authority to control the terms, conditions, or privileges of the complainant's employment through his relationship with the other supervisor.[150]

Courts have rebuffed employers' attempts to avoid liability for the actions of their supervisors on the theory that the supervisor, in harassing an employee, was acting contrary to the explicit policies of the employer. As Judge Luther M. Swygert explained in *Horn v. Duke Homes*,[151] the fact that the agent may have "acted outside the scope of his employment" will not insulate the employer from liability:

> It could be argued that because [the supervisor] was not authorized to discriminate on the basis of sex and because his sexual proclivities were wholly unconnected to the well-being of the employer, he was acting outside the scope of his employment. On the other hand, by delegating power to [the supervisor] the "employer" and [the supervisor] essentially merged; as long as the tort complained of was caused by the exercise of this supervisory power, [the supervisor] should be deemed as acting within the scope of his employment and the employer should be held liable for the tort.[152]

IX. EMPLOYER REBUTTAL

A. Disputing Elements of the Prima Facie Case

The first line of defense for an employer is to rebut elements of the prima facie case. The employer may bar the complainant's recovery by showing, for example, that no sexual advances occurred, that if they occurred they were welcomed, or that no job detriment resulted. This aspect of the employer's defense most frequently tends to attack the unwelcome element.

B. Articulating a Legitimate Nondiscriminatory Reason

In response to the prima facie case, the employer may "articulate some legitimate, nondiscriminatory reason" for the adverse employment decision.[153] The employer will attempt to prove that the adverse employment action was based on legitimate factors and not on the complainant's reaction to any sexual advance. Thus, the employer may introduce evidence of poor work perform-

---

[149]Simmons v. Lyons, 746 F.2d 265, 36 FEP Cases 410 (5th Cir. 1984)(plaintiffs alleged that sheriff-elect conditioned their reappointment on submission to his sexual advances and thereafter failed to hire them).

[150]Sparks v. Pilot Freight Carriers, *supra* note 130.

[151]755 F.2d 599, 37 FEP Cases 228 (7th Cir. 1985)(Swygert, Coffey & Eschback, JJ.).

[152]*Id.* at 605, 37 FEP Cases at 232–33. The Seventh Circuit went on to hold that "whatever the result under the common law of agency, Title VII demands that employers be held strictly liable for the discriminatory employment decisions of their supervisory personnel who are delegated the power to make such employment decisions." *Id.*

[153]Texas Dep't of Community Affairs v. Burdine, 450 U.S. 248, 254, 25 FEP Cases 113, 116 (1981); Bundy v. Jackson, *supra* note 143, 641 F.2d at 950–52, 24 FEP Cases at 1165–67.

ance,[154] excessive tardiness or absenteeism,[155] insubordination,[156] a violation of company policy,[157] or a lack of work.[158]

Where the complainant has produced direct evidence in a "mixed-motive" case, the employer may still avoid liability by proving that it would have made the same decision absent consideration of the discriminatory factor.[159]

X. THE COMPLAINANT'S PROOF OF PRETEXT

The complainant has the opportunity to prove that the reason the employer has articulated for its job decision is actually a pretext for sex discrimination.[160] The complainant's proof of pretext tends to reiterate facts indicating a causal link between the harassment and the adverse job action. Thus, in evaluating the complainant's proof of pretext, courts consider whether the employer's reason for its adverse employment decision was actually motivated by the complainant's rejection of sexual advances.[161]

---

[154]Dockter v. Rudolf Wolff Futures, *supra* note 140 (discharge not result of sex discrimination, but rather of inability to do job); Hicks v. Gates Rubber Co., *supra* note 142 (complainant not subjected to quid pro quo harassment where employment not conditioned on granting sexual favors to supervisors; rather, job consequences arose solely from inadequate performance); Tunis v. Corning Glass Works, 698 F. Supp. 452 (S.D.N.Y. 1988); Koster v. Chase Manhattan Bank, *supra* note 140 (former bank employee failed to establish she was qualified for certain position and transfer and thus discriminatorily denied position); Neville v. Taft Broadcasting Co., 42 FEP Cases 1314 (W.D.N.Y.)(complainant's job performance, which had been satisfactory and then deteriorated, offered as evidence against quid pro quo sexual harassment), *aff'd,* 857 F.2d 1461, 51 FEP Cases 1832 (2d Cir. 1987).

[155]*Cf.* Ambrose v. United States Steel Corp., 39 FEP Cases 30 (N.D. Cal. 1985)(documented absences held to be pretextual defense because complainant had been absent far fewer times than she had during previous appraisal year when her attendance had been rated satisfactory).

[156]Christoforou v. Ryder Truck Rental, 668 F. Supp. 294, 302–3, 51 FEP Cases 98, 105 (S.D.N.Y. 1987)(despite evidence of plaintiff's resistance to sexual advances by supervisor and sexual "tension" and "hostility" toward plaintiff, her discharge did not occur because of sex, but because of plaintiff's insubordination and other work-related shortcomings); Bohen v. City of E. Chicago, 622 F. Supp. 1234, 1237, 39 FEP Cases 917, 923–24 (N.D. Ind. 1985)(plaintiff sexually harassed but fired because of insubordination and obstinate behavior), *rev'd on other grounds,* 799 F.2d 1180, 41 FEP Cases 1108 (7th Cir. 1986).

[157]*Cf.* Sparks v. Pilot Freight Carriers, 830 F.2d 1554, 45 FEP Cases 160 (11th Cir. 1987), reproduced in Chapter 2, Forms of Harassment (employer applied disparate standards to work rule requiring same-day notification for sick days); Priest v. Rotary, 634 F. Supp. 571, 40 FEP Cases 208 (N.D. Cal. 1986)(employer's defenses that waitress violated policy of socializing in lounge as well as failure to perform other duties found clearly pretextual).

[158]*Cf.* Hallquist v. Max Fish Plumbing & Heating Co., 46 FEP Cases 1855 (D. Mass. 1987)(female plumber's discharge for lack of work held pretextual where two male colleuages kept on and supervisor had recently received complaint from client for sending female plumber), *aff'd,* 843 F.2d 18, 47 FEP Cases 323 (1st Cir. 1988).

[159]Price Waterhouse v. Hopkins, 490 U.S. 228, 49 FEP Cases 954 (1989); Sowers v. Kemira, Inc., 701 F. Supp. 809, 824, 46 FEP Cases 1825, 1835 (S.D. Ga. 1988)("defendant has failed to establish that plaintiff's promotion would have been delayed even absent discrimination"); Bohen v. City of E. Chicago, 799 F.2d 1180, 39 FEP Cases 917 (7th Cir. 1986)(complainant, even though sexually harassed, was lawfully discharged). *But see* Moylan v. Maries County, 792 F.2d 746, 40 FEP Cases 1788 (8th Cir. 1986)(pervasive and repeated sexual harassment, including alleged rape, cannot be defended on grounds that plaintiff was properly discharged); Bundy v. Jackson, *supra* note 143 (burden shifts to defendant to disprove that sex played part in decisions where there was pervasive sexual harassment).

[160]McDonnell Douglas v. Green, 411 U.S. 792, 5 FEP Cases 965 (1973); Texas Dep't of Community Affairs v. Burdine, *supra* note 153, 450 U.S. at 253–54, 25 FEP Cases at 115. *See, e.g.,* Spencer v. General Elec. Co., 894 F.2d 651, 659, 51 FEP Cases 1725, 1730–31 (4th Cir. 1990)(citations omitted); King v. Palmer, 778 F.2d 878, 881, 39 FEP Cases 877, 880 (D.C. Cir. 1985); Joyner v. AAA Cooper Transp., 597 F. Supp. 537, 541, 36 FEP Cases 1644, 1647–48 (M.D. Ala. 1983), *aff'd,* 749 F.2d 732, 41 FEP Cases 496 (11th Cir. 1984).

[161]*See, e.g.,* EEOC v. FLC & Brothers Rebel, 663 F. Supp. 864, 44 FEP Cases 362 (W.D. Va. 1987), *aff'd mem.,* 846 F.2d 70 (4th Cir. 1988)(sexually harassed female employee victim of sex discrimination

If the employer has alleged that a complainant's dismissal was due to lack of work, the complainant may attempt to prove pretext by showing that the employer added employees to the work force after the complainant's termination.[162] The complainant may also show that the employer failed to follow company procedures in taking the adverse employment action at issue.[163]

If the employer has cited the complainant's excessive absenteeism as a reason for its employment decision, then the complainant may attempt to prove (1) that the facts recited by the employer are not true,[164] (2) that her attendance at the time of her discharge was no worse than it had previously been, when no adverse job action had been taken,[165] or (3) that similarly absent employees who did not reject sexual advances were not fired.[166] A fourth item of proof, but one that does not necessarily impugn the employer's motivation would be that the complainant's absenteeism resulted from the harassment.[167]

Whether the stated reason for the adverse employment action was a pretext for sex discrimination is a factual question, based largely on the trier of fact's credibility findings. Courts make that factual determination by reviewing such evidence as the relative qualifications of employees vying for a particular promotion[168] and whether the complainant's job performance was sufficiently poor to merit discharge in the absence of a discriminatory intent.[169] A trial

---

where employer's defense was she was terminated for using "unlady-like language"); Boyd v. James S. Hayes Living Health Care Agency, 671 F. Supp. 1155, 1165–67, 44 FEP Cases 332, 340–41 (W.D. Tenn. 1987)(plaintiff's performance of job duties did not deteriorate after she rebuffed supervisor's sexual advances and he gave her additional responsibilities in order to have basis for criticizing her work because she had rejected him); Joyner v. AAA Cooper Transp., *supra* note 160, 597 F. Supp. at 544, 36 FEP Cases at 1650 ("plaintiff's bid to return to work would not have been rejected *but for* plaintiff's refusal to cooperate with the terminal manager's homosexual demands and [plaintiff's] action of reporting the incident").

[162]Hallquist v. Max Fish Plumbing & Heating Co., *supra* note 158, 46 FEP Cases at 1859 ("lay off" as explanation for plaintiff's dismissal not persuasive explanation, given gender-baiting and fact that man "laid off" at same time actually had job protected); Joyner v. AAA Cooper Transp., *supra* note 160, 597 F. Supp. at 544, 36 FEP Cases at 1650 (failure to recall experienced employee whose work had always been satisfactory was pretextual).

[163]Craig v. Y & Y Snacks, 721 F.2d 77, 79, 33 FEP Cases 187, 188 (3d Cir. 1983)(employer failed to give complainant mandatory three-day suspension before discharge, making discharge "which might otherwise have been legitimately supportable . . . pretextual and in violation of Title VII"). *Id.* at 80, 33 FEP Cases at 189.

[164]*See, e.g.,* Boyd v. James S. Hayes Living Health Care Agency, *supra* note 161, 671 F. Supp. at 1166, 44 FEP Cases at 341 ("plaintiff and her witnesses were much more credible than the defendants' proof" on issue of whether supervisor's increased criticism of plaintiff's work following her rebuffing his advances was result of supervisor's deliberate attempt "to create a situation in which plaintiff could not succeed").

[165]Ambrose v. United States Steel Corp., *supra* note 155. *See also* Mays v. Williamson & Sons Janitorial Servs., 775 F.2d 258, 259, 39 FEP Cases 106, 107 (8th Cir. 1985)(complainant placed under surveillance in attempt to document excuse to discharge her after she reported sexual harassment).

[166]*See generally* B.L. SCHLEI & P. GROSSMAN, EMPLOYMENT DISCRIMINATION LAW 1291–92 (2d ed. 1983).

[167]See text accompanying note 171 *infra.*

[168]*See, e.g.,* King v. Palmer, *supra* note 160, 778 F.2d at 880, 39 FEP Cases at 879 (rejecting as "clearly pretextual" testimony of doctors responsible for promoting Ms. Grant [an employee other than the plaintiff] that they promoted Grant because of her superior qualifications); Toscano v. Nimmo, 570 F. Supp. 1197, 1202–3, 32 FEP Cases 1401, 1405–7 (D. Del. 1983)(granting sexual favors as condition for position sought by female at hospital constituted employment practice discriminative on basis of sex).

[169]*See* Chamberlin v. 101 Realty, 915 F.2d 777, 785, 54 FEP Cases 101, 107 (1st Cir. 1990)(agreeing with district court "that Chamberlin's firing was not precipitated by Chamberlin's work performance or by any shortcomings in her employment skills or aptitude, but by her unwavering determination to resist [her supervisor's] sexual advances"); Boyd v. James S. Hayes Living Health Care Agency, *supra* note 161, 671 F. Supp. at 1165, 44 FEP Cases at 340–41 (rejecting defendant's argument that "plaintiff performed her job poorly," and finding that "plaintiff's overall performance continued to be satisfactory"); Horn v. Duke Motor Homes, *supra* note 151, 755 F.2d at 603 n.1, 37 FEP Cases at 230–31 (plaintiff "succeeded in proving that [the employer's] legitimate reasons for discharging her were pretextual, and that she had in fact been terminated because she refused his sexual advances"). *But see* Dockter v. Rudolf Wolff Futures, 913 F.2d 456, 461, 53 FEP Cases 1642, 1646 (7th Cir. 1990)("Consistent with the overwhelming nature of the

court's factual finding will not be overturned unless the appellate court concludes that it is clearly erroneous.[170]

A complainant might also assert that the diminished work performance cited by the employer was the result of sexual harassment. This kind of case is probably best analyzed as a hostile environment rather than a quid pro quo case, for if the reasons asserted by the employer are factually true and represent the employer's motivation for the employment action, then the employer's reasons are not pretextual and the employer's action is unlawful only if it was ultimately caused by a hostile work environment.[171]

---

evidence presented at trial, the district court held that Ms. Dockter's termination was the result of her inability to become proficient as an operator of the IBM personal computer").

[170]Dockter v. Rudolf Wolff Futures, *supra* note 169 (determining intent under Title VII is "factual determination subject to a clearly erroneous standard of review"); Hicks v. Gates Rubber Co., 833 F.2d 1406, 45 FEP Cases 608 (10th Cir. 1987)(affirming finding, under "clearly erroneous" standard, that "adverse job consequences Hicks suffered did not arise from her refusal to acquiesce in her supervisors' sexual conduct, but rather, were due solely to her inadequate job performance"); Horn v. Duke Homes, 755 F.2d 599, 603 n.1, 37 FEP Cases 228, 230–31 (7th Cir. 1985)(fact that district court's findings, that plaintiff had successfully proven that defendant's legitimate reasons for discharging her were pretextual, were implicitly rather than explicitly stated in the opinion did not support reversal under the "clearly erroneous" standard).

[171]For a further discussion, see Chapter 4, Hostile Environment Harassment, Section XI.

HOSTILE ENVIRONMENT HARASSMENT

I. OVERVIEW

The 1980 EEOC Guidelines interpret Title VII to prohibit "[u]nwelcome sexual advances, requests for sexual favors, and other verbal or physical conduct of a sexual nature" that "has the purpose or effect of unreasonably interfering with an individual's work performance or creating an intimidating, hostile, or offensive working environment."[1] In 1986, the Supreme Court in *Meritor Savings Bank v. Vinson*[2] unanimously endorsed the EEOC's concept that sexually harassing conduct can be so severe or pervasive that it alters an employee's working conditions and thus violates Title VII even when no tangible job detriment has occurred.[3]

The facts that support a hostile environment theory of liability will often appear in quid pro quo cases.[4] Courts have considered all incidents of harassment, whether quid pro quo or hostile environment, as each case is decided by looking "at the totality of the circumstances."[5] The line between the two theories of harassment blurs to the extent that a hostile environment involves

---

[1] 29 C.F.R. §1604.11(a)(3), reproduced in Appendix 1. In 1980, after notice and comment, the EEOC issued its Guidelines on Discrimination Because of Sex, 29 C.F.R. §§1604.1–.11, one portion of which (§1604.11(a)(g)) constitutes the sexual harassment guidelines. 45 FED. REG. 74677 (November 10, 1980). The EEOC Guidelines are nonbinding but "constitute a body of experience and informed judgments to which courts and litigants may properly resort for guidance." Meritor Sav. Bank v. Vinson, 477 U.S. 57, 65, 40 FEP Cases 1822, 1826 (1986), reproduced in Chapter 1, Overview (citations omitted). Subsection 1604.11(a)(3) describes hostile environment harassment, while subsections 1604.11(a)(1) and (2) describe quid pro quo harassment.

[2] *Supra* note 1, 477 U.S. at 67–68, 40 FEP Cases at 1826–27 (citing Rogers v. EEOC, 454 F.2d 234, 238, 4 FEP Cases 92 (5th Cir. 1972), *cert. denied*, 406 U.S. 957 (1972)); Bundy v. Jackson, 641 F.2d 934, 944, 24 FEP Cases 1155 (D.C. Cir. 1981); Katz v. Dole, 709 F.2d 251, 254–55, 31 FEP Cases 1521 (4th Cir. 1983), reproduced in Chapter 7, Harassment by Co-Workers; and Henson v. City of Dundee, 682 F.2d 897, 902, 29 FEP Cases 787 (11th Cir. 1982), reproduced *infra*.

[3] *See generally* Ellison v. Brady, 924 F.2d 872, 54 FEP Cases 1346, 1351 (9th Cir. 1991)(although EEOC Guidelines speak of intimidating, hostile, or offensive environment *or* unreasonable interference with work, whereas *Meritor* spoke of altering conditions of employment *and* creating an abusive environment, EEOC and Supreme Court standards are "not . . . inconsistent"). *But see* Pollack, *Sexual Harassment: Women's Experience vs. Legal Definitions,* 13 HARV. WOMEN'S L.J. 35, 60 (1990)(criticizing *Meritor* as adopting narrow standard of liability implied by *Rogers* court instead of broader standard of liability expressed in EEOC Guidelines).

[4] *E.g.,* Henson v. City of Dundee, 682 F.2d 897, 29 FEP Cases 787 (11th Cir. 1982), reproduced *infra;* Bundy v. Jackson, 641 F.2d 934, 24 FEP Cases 1155 (D.C. Cir. 1981).

[5] Meritor Sav. Bank v. Vinson, *supra* note 1, 477 U.S. at 69, 40 FEP Cases at 1828 (citing with approval 29 C.F.R. §1604.11(b))("trier of fact must determine the existence of sexual harassment in light of 'the record as a whole' and 'the totality of circumstances such as the nature of the sexual advances and the context in which the alleged incidents occurred' "); *see also* Hicks v. Gates Rubber Co., 833 F.2d 1406, 1415, 45 FEP Cases 608, 613 (10th Cir. 1987); Henson v. City of Dundee, *supra* note 4, 682 F.2d at 904.

sexual advances and results in a constructive or retaliatory discharge, or so interferes with work performance that it ultimately leads to a complainant's discharge for absenteeism or poor performance.[6] The EEOC Policy Guidance on Sexual Harassment recognizes the potentially overlapping nature of quid pro quo harassment and hostile environment harassment:

> hostile environment harassment may acquire characteristics of quid pro quo harassment if the offending supervisor abuses his authority over employment decisions to force the victim to endure or participate in the sexual conduct. Sexual harassment may culminate in a retaliatory discharge if a victim tells the harasser or her employer she will no longer submit to the harassment, and is then fired in retaliation for this protest.[7]

Nonetheless, a sexually hostile environment typically differs from a quid pro quo case in several important respects. First, whereas quid pro quo harassment requires action by a supervisor, a hostile environment may result entirely from the actions of co-workers or even nonemployees. Second, a hostile environment is not limited to sexual advances, or even to targeted sexual behavior; it also may involve nonsexual behavior directed at the complainant because of gender, and sexual activity that is not directed at the complainant at all but that nonetheless affects the complainant's working conditions. Third, hostile environment harassment, unlike quid pro quo harassment, does not require any proof of economic injury. It is sufficient to prove that the harassing actions were so severe or pervasive that they effectively changed the complainant's working conditions. Fourth, while the employer's liability is generally considered to be automatic in a quid pro quo case under Title VII, in a hostile environment case employer liability is determined on a case-by-case basis, through use of traditional agency principles.[8]

As a result of these differences, hostile environment claims emphasize different issues than do quid pro quo claims. Indeed, the two issues most frequently litigated in hostile environment cases—the level of harassment an employee is not expected to endure in the workplace and the employer's accountability for its employees' harassing actions—are seldom significant in quid pro quo cases.

The overlapping nature of the two basic theories of liability, and their relationship to retaliatory conduct forbidden by §704(a) of Title VII,[9] is reflected in the leading case of *Henson v. City of Dundee,* which examined all three theories of liability.

---

[6]Note, *The Aftermath of Meritor: A Search for Standards in the Law of Sexual Harassment,* 98 YALE L.J. 1717 (1989)(arguing that subtle quid pro quo case lurks beneath many hostile environment claims and that courts should look for connections between environmental violation and adverse decisions, examining claim as a quid pro quo claim, with hostile environment seen as unwelcome sexual behavior). For a discussion of constructive discharge, see Chapter 9. For a discussion of Retaliation, see Chapter 10. For a discussion of discharges based on work performance or absenteeism or disability that itself resulted from sexual harassment, see Sections VI.E. and X.B. *infra.*

[7]EEOC Policy Guidance on Sexual Harassment, 8 FAIR EMPL. PRAC. MAN. (BNA) 405:6682 (March 19, 1990), reproduced in Appendix 3. *See generally* Carrero v. New York City Hous. Auth., 890 F.2d 569, 579, 51 FEP Cases 596, 603 (2d Cir. 1989)(hostile environment and quid pro quo claims "not always clearly distinct and separate" but rather "may be complementary to one another").

[8]For a discussion of employer liability, see Section VIII. *infra;* Chapters 6, Harassment by Supervisors; 7, Harassment by Co-Workers; and 8, Harassment by Nonemployees.

[9]42 U.S.C. §2000e-3(a). For a discussion of §704 claims by sexual harassment complainants, see Chapter 10, Retaliation.

HENSON V. CITY OF DUNDEE

682 F.2d 897, 29 FEP Cases 787 (11th Cir. 1982)

VANCE, Circuit Judge:— • • •[W]e must determine the proper application of Title VII principles to claims of sexual harassment at the workplace. Appellant, Barbara Henson, filed a Title VII action against the City of Dundee, Florida alleging sexual harassment on her job with the police department. At the close of appellant's case, the district court entered judgment for the City of Dundee and this appeal followed.

Henson was hired as a dispatcher in the five-officer Dundee police department on January 14, 1975. • • •

Henson claims that during the two years she worked for the Dundee police department, she and her female coworkers were subjected to sexual harassment by the chief of the Dundee police department, John Sellgren. She alleges that this harassment led her to resign under duress • • •

At trial, Henson attempted to prove three types of sexual harassment. First, she claimed that Sellgren created a hostile and offensive working environment for women in the police station. She • • • testified that Sellgren subjected them to numerous harangues of demeaning sexual inquiries and vulgarities throughout the course of the two years during which Henson worked for the police department. Henson stated that in addition to these periodic harangues, Sellgren repeatedly requested that she have sexual relations with him. • • • Henson testified further that she complained of Sellgren's conduct in 1976 to the city manager, Jane Eden, but that Eden took no action to restrain Sellgren.

Henson also claimed that her resignation on January 28, 1977 was tantamount to a constructive discharge based upon sex in violation of Title VII. Specifically, she testified that on January 18, 1977 Sellgren suspended her for two days on the pretext that she had violated an office policy by bringing food into the dispatch room. According to Henson, this policy had not been previously enforced, and she regarded the suspension as a warning by Sellgren that she would be fired if she did not accede to his sexual requests. She therefore claimed that her resignation was involuntary.

Finally, Henson claimed that Sellgren prevented her from attending the local police academy because she refused to have sexual relations with him. She testified that Sellgren made it clear to her that if she agreed to have a relationship with him, he would help her gain the approval of the city manager to attend the academy. • • • [D]uring this period two of the male CETA dispatchers were sent to the police academy. • • • Henson was qualified to attend the police academy and • • • [Eden] would have permitted Henson to attend if Sellgren had informed her of Henson's interest in the academy.

• • • At the close of Henson's case, the district court granted the city's motion to dismiss the action pursuant to rule 41(b) of the Federal Rules of Civic Procedure.[3] • • • [W]e discern the following bases for dismissal:

(1) Henson's claim that she suffered under a hostile and demeaning work environment standing alone did not state a cognizable claim under Title VII. Although Henson's superior, Sellgren, subjected her and her female coworker to "crude and vulgar language, almost daily inquiring of these two women employees as to their sexual habits and proclivities," the trial judge concluded that there was no violation of Title VII unless Sellgren's conduct inflicted upon Henson some tangible job detriment.

(2) Henson's claim that she was compelled to resign because of an intolerable, sexually demeaning work environment stated a claim upon which relief could be granted for constructive discharge under Title VII. However, the district court did not credit Henson's testimony that she resigned from the Dundee police force because of an intolerable work environment. Specifically, the court found that Henson resigned because a Dundee police officer with whom she was having an affair, Robert Owens, had been forced to resign in January 1978.

(3) Henson's claim that she was prevented from attending the police academy because of her refusal to have sexual relations with Sellgren stated a claim under Title VII. At the

---

[1, 2][Omitted.]
[3][Omitted.]

same time, her testimony regarding Sellgren's demands for sex as a condition to attendance at the academy was "not believed by me, as the Trial Judge." The court specifically found, however, that none of the male CETA dispatchers had been sent to the academy. The court also found that Sellgren had never made any sexual advances to Henson's coworker, Carolyn Dicks.

On appeal, Henson argues that her work environment allegations stated a claim under Title VII for sexual harassment. She also argues that the district court erred in its holdings on her constructive discharge and police academy claims.

I.

Sexual harassment and work environment

Henson contends that a plaintiff states a claim under Title VII by alleging that sexual harassment perpetrated or condoned by an employer has created a hostile or offensive work environment. She argues that the trial court erred by holding that a Title VII plaintiff must allege in addition that she suffered some tangible job detriment as a result of working in such an environment. We agree that under certain circumstances the creation of an offensive or hostile work environment due to sexual harassment can violate Title VII irrespective of whether the complainant suffers tangible job detriment. We therefore reverse the district court's order as to this claim and remand a new trial on Henson's work environment claim.

Title VII prohibits employment discrimination on the basis of gender, and seeks to remove arbitrary barriers to sexual equality at the workplace with respect to "compensation, terms, conditions, or privileges of employment." 42 U.S.C. §2000e-2(a)1; Griggs v. Duke Power Co., 401 U.S. 424, 431, 91 S.Ct. 849, 853, 28 L.Ed.2d 158, 3 FEP Cases 175 (1971). The former fifth circuit has held that "terms, conditions, or privileges of employment" include the state of psychological well being at the workplace. In the area of race discrimination, Judge Goldberg stated:

> the phrase "terms, conditions, or privileges of employment" in [Title VII] is an expansive concept which sweeps within its protective ambit the practice of creating a working environment heavily charged with ethnic or racial discrimination.

Rogers v. EEOC, 454 F.2d 234, 238, 4 FEP Cases 92 (5th Cir. 1971), cert. denied, 406 U.S. 957, 92 S.Ct. 2058, 32 L.Ed.2d 343, 4 FEP Cases 771 (1972). Therefore, courts have held that an employer violates Title VII simply by creating or condoning an environment at the workplace which significantly and adversely affects an employee because of his race or ethnicity, regardless of any other tangible job detriment to the protected employee. See, e.g., Calcote v. Texas Educational Foundation, Inc., 458 F.Supp. 231, 237, 20 FEP Cases 1680 (W.D.Tex.1976) (racial harassment of white employee created discriminatory working conditions), aff'd, 578 F.2d 95, 20 FEP Cases 1685 (5th Cir. 1978).[4]

Sexual harassment which creates a hostile or offensive environment for members of one sex is every bit the arbitrary barrier to sexual equality at the workplace that racial harassment is to racial equality. Surely, a requirement that a man or woman run a gauntlet of sexual abuse in return for the privilege of being allowed to work and make a living can be as demeaning and disconcerting as the harshest of racial epithets.[5] A pattern of sexual

---

[4]Accord, Friend v. Leidinger, 588 F.2d 61, 68-69, 18 FEP Cases 1052 (4th Cir. 1978) (Butzner, J., concurring in part and dissenting in part) (numerous derogatory references to blacks by supervisors and coworkers created discriminatory working conditions); Firefighters Inst. for Racial Equality v. City of St. Louis, 549 F.2d 506, 514-15, 14 FEP Cases 1486 (8th Cir.), cert. denied, 434 U.S. 819, 98 S.Ct. 60, 54 L.Ed.2d 76, 15 FEP Cases 1184 (1977) (employee eating clubs segregated by race created discriminatory work environment for black employees); Lucero v. Beth Israel Hosp. & Geriatric Center, 479 F.Supp. 452, 454, 21 FEP Cases 266 (D.Colo.1979) (pattern of racial slurs created discriminatory working environment for black employees); United States v. City of Buffalo, 457 F.Supp. 612, 631-35, 19 FEP Cases 776 (W.D. N.Y.1978) (same conclusion), modified in part, 633 F.2d 643, 24 FEP Cases 313 (2d Cir. 1980). Cf. Gray v. Greyhound Lines, East, 545 F.2d 169, 176, 13 FEP Cases 1401 (D.C.Cir. 1976) (employee has standing to challenge employer's hiring practices that create a discriminatory work environment).

[5]The problem of sexual harassment in the workplace apparently is widespread. It was recently the focus of hearings before the Senate Committee on Labor and Human Resources. At those hearings, the acting

harassment inflicted upon an employee because of her sex is a pattern of behavior that inflicts disparate treatment upon a member of one sex with respect to terms, conditions, or privileges of employment. There is no requirement that an employee subjected to such disparate treatment prove in addition that she has suffered tangible job detriment.

We are bolstered in our conclusion that a hostile or offensive atmosphere created by sexual harassment can, standing alone, constitute a violation of Title VII by a recent decision of the United States Court of Appeals for the District of Columbia circuit. In Bundy v. Jackson, 641 F.2d 934, 943-46, 24 FEP Cases 1155 (D.C.Cir.1981), the court found that the principle of law equating illegal sex discrimination with a hostile work environment caused by sexual harassment "follows ineluctably from numerous cases finding Title VII violations where an employer created or condoned a substantially [racially] discriminatory work environment, regardless of whether the complaining employees lost any tangible job benefits." Id. at 943-44 (citing Rogers v. EEOC, 454 F.2d at 238) (emphasis omitted). See also Walter v. KFGO Radio, 518 F.Supp. 1309, 1315-16, 26 FEP Cases 982 (D.N.D.1981); Morgan v. Hertz Corp., — F.Supp. —, 27 Fair Empl.Prac.Cas. (BNA) 990, 994 (W.D.Tenn.1981); Brown v. City of Guthrie, 22 Fair Empl.Prac.Cas. (BNA) 1627, 1631-33 (W.D.Okla.1980).[6]

Additionally, the E.E.O.C. has recently issued regulations that provide a useful and informative set of guidelines on sexual harassment.[7] In pertinent part the guidelines provide

---

chairman of the Equal Employment Opportunity Commission cited the rising number of charges filed with the agency that complained of sexual harassment. See Sex Discrimination in the Workplace, 1981: Hearings before the Senate Comm. on Labor and Human Resources, 97th Cong., 1st Sess. 336, 342 (1981)(statement of J. Clay Smith, Jr., acting chairman of E.E.O.C.); 106 L.R.R. News & Background Inf. 333-35 (April 27, 1981). See also U.S. Merit Systems Protection Board, Sexual Harassment in the Federal Workplace: Is it a Problem? (1981); 45 Fed. Reg. 25,024 (April 11, 1980)(commentary accompanying E.E.O.C. interim guidelines on sexual harassment).

[6]Cf. Rogers v. Loews L'Enfant Plaza Hotel, 526 F.Supp. 523, 28 Empl.Prac.Dec. (CCH) ¶32,553 at 24,470-73, 29 FEP Cases 828 (D.D.C.1982) (sexual harassment gives rise to common law tort claims for invasion of right to privacy assault and battery, and intentional infliction of emotional distress); Woerner v. Brzeczek, 519 F.Supp. 517, 519, 26 FEP Cases 897 (N.D.Ill.1981)(cause of action for offensive work environment caused by sexual harassment can be stated under 42 U.S.C. §1983); Guyette v. Stauffer Chem. Co., 518 F.Supp. 521, 525-26, 26 FEP Cases 634 (D.N.J. 1981) (non-supervisory employee could not be held individually liable for sexual harassment under Title VII); Kyriazi v. Western Elec. Co., 461 F.Supp. 894, 950, 18 FEP Cases 924 (D.N.J. 1978) (plaintiff prevailed on pendent New Jersey state claim of tortious interference with contract due to sexual harassment causing hostile work environment); Smith v. Rust Eng'g Co., 18 Empl.Prac. Dec. (CCH) ¶8698, at 4784, 20 FEP Cases 1172 (N.D.Ala.1978) (no cause of action for hostile work environment caused by sexual harassment committed by co-worker where there was no allegation that management knew of the harassment); Caldwell v. Hodgeman 25 Fair Empl.Prac.Cas. (BNA) 1647, 1649-50 (Mass.D.Ct.1981) (offensive environment caused by sexual harassment resulted in constructive discharge entitling employee to unemployment benefits); Continental Can Co. v. State, 297 N.W.2d 241, 248-49, 22 FEP Cases 1808 (Minn.1980) (cause of action for hostile work environment due to sexual harassment under Minn.Stat. 363.03(I)(2)(c) (1978)). But see Hill v. BASF Wyandotte Corp., 27 Fair Empl.Prac. Cas. (BNA) 66, 71-72 (E.D.Mich.1981); Neeley v. American Fidelity Assurance Co., 17 Empl. Prac.Dec. (CCH) ¶8395, at 6009, 17 FEP Cases 482 (W.D.Okla.1978).

[7]In General Elec. Co. v. Gilbert, 429 U.S. 125, 97 S.Ct. 401, 50 L.Ed.2d 343, 13 FEP Cases 1657 (1976), the Supreme Court suggested the degree to which courts should defer to the E.E.O.C.'s interpretation of Title VII:

"We consider that the rulings, interpretations and opinions of the Administrator under this Act, while not controlling upon the courts by reason of their authority, do constitute a body of experience and informed judgment to which courts and litigants may properly resort for guidance. The weight of such a judgment in a particular case will depend upon the thoroughness evident in its consideration, the validity of its reasoning, its consistency with earlier and later pronouncements, and all those factors which give it power to persuade, if lacking power to control."

Id. at 141-42, 97 S.Ct. at 410-11 (quoting Skidmore v. Swift & Co., 323 U.S. 134, 140, 65 S.Ct. 161, 164, 89 L.Ed. 124, 4 WH Cases 866 (1944)). The E.E.O.C. guidelines on sexual harassment are well founded in Title VII principles previously enunciated by the courts, see Rogers v. EEOC, 454 F.2d 234, 238, 4 FEP Cases 92 (5th Cir. 1971), cert. denied, 406 U.S. 957, 92 S.Ct. 2058, 32 L.Ed.2d 343, 4 FEP Cases 771 (1972), and of the agency itself. A number of other courts have found the guidelines to be valuable. See, e.g., Bundy v. Jackson, 641 F.2d 934, 947, 24 FEP Cases 1155 (D.C.Cir.1981); Walter v. KFGO Radio, 518 F.Supp. 1309, 1315, 26 FEP Cases 982 (D.N.D.1981); Caldwell v. Hodgeman, 25 Fair Empl.Prac.Cas. (BNA) 1647, 1649 (Mass.D.Ct.1981); Continental Can Co. v. State, 297 N.W.2d 242, 248, 22 FEP Cases 1808 (Minn.1980); see also Note, Sexual Harassment and Title VII, 76 U.Mich.L.Rev. 1007, 1019 n.91 (1978). See generally Development, New EEOC Guidelines on Discrimination Because of Sex: Employer Liability for Sexual Harassment Under Title VII, 61 B.U.L.Rev. 535 (1981) (discussing development of guidelines in light of Title VII principles).

that "[u]nwelcome sexual advances, requests for sexual favors, and other verbal or physical conduct of a sexual nature constitute sexual harassment when ... such conduct has the purpose or effect of unreasonably interfering with an individual's work performance or creating an intimidating, hostile, or offensive working environment." 29 C.F.R. §1604.11(a) (1981).

Of course, neither the courts nor the E.E.O.C. have suggested that every instance of sexual harassment gives rise to a Title VII claim against an employer for a hostile work environment. Rather, the plaintiff must allege and prove a number of elements in order to establish her claim. These elements include the following:

(1) *The employee belongs to a protected group.* As in other cases of sexual discrimination, this requires a simple stipulation that the employee is a man or a woman.

(2) *The employee was subject to unwelcome sexual harassment.* The E.E.O.C. regulations helpfully define the type of conduct that may constitute sexual harassment: "sexual advances, requests for sexual favors, and other verbal or physical conduct of a sexual nature . . . ." 29 C.F.R. §1604.11(a) (1981). See also E.E.O.C. Dec. No. 81-18, 27 Fair Empl.Prac.Cas. (BNA) 1793, 1802-05 (April 3, 1981). In order to constitute harassment, this conduct must be unwelcome in the sense that the employee did not solicit or incite it, and in the sense that the employee regarded the conduct as undesirable or offensive. Gan v. Kepro Circuit Systems, Inc., 27 Empl.Prac.Dec. (CCH) ¶32,379, at 23,648, 28 FEP Cases 639 (E.D.Mo.1982); Vinson v. Taylor, 23 Fair Empl.Prac.Cas. (BNA) 37, 42 (D.D.C.1980); 29 C.F.R. § 1604.11(a) (1981) (only unwelcome sexual advances generate Title VII liability); Development, *New EEOC Guidelines on Discrimination Because of Sex: Employer Liability for Sexual Harassment Under Title VII,* 61 B.U.L.Rev. 535, 561 (1981) ("[w]hether the advances are unwelcome ... becomes an evidentiary question well within the court's ability to resolve").

(3) *The harassment complained of was based upon sex.* The essence of a disparate treatment claim under Title VII is that an employee or applicant is intentionally singled out for adverse treatment on the basis of a prohibited criterion. • • • In proving a claim for a hostile work environment due to sexual harassment, therefore, the plaintiff must show that but for the fact of her sex, she would not have been the object of harassment. See Bundy v. Jackson, 641 F.2d at 942-43 • • •

In the typical case in which a male supervisor makes sexual overtures to a female worker, it is obvious that the supervisor did not treat male employees in a similar fashion. It will therefore be a simple matter for the plaintiff to prove that but for her sex, she would not have been subjected to sexual harassment. See Bundy v. Jackson, 641 F.2d at 942 n.7. However, there may be cases in which a supervisor makes sexual overtures to workers of both sexes or where the conduct complained of is equally offensive to male and female workers. See Barnes v. Costle, 561 F.2d 983, 990 n.55, 15 FEP Cases 345 (D.C.Cir.1977); Bradford v. Sloan Paper Co., 383 F.Supp. 1157, 1161, 8 FEP Cases 634 (N.D.Ala.1974); Note, *Sexual Harassment and Title VII,* supra, at 1020-21 & n.99, 1033 & n.178; Comment, *Sexual Harassment and Title VII,* 51 N.Y.U.L.Rev. 148, 151-52 (1976). In such cases, the sexual harassment would not be based upon sex because men and women are accorded like treatment. Although the plaintiff might have a remedy under state law in such a situation, the plaintiff would have no remedy under Title VII. • • •

(4) *The harassment complained of affected a "term, condition, or privilege" of employment.* The former fifth circuit has held that the state of psychological well being is a term, condition, or privilege of employment within the meaning of Title VII. Rogers v. EEOC, 454 F.2d at 238. The court in Rogers made it clear, however, that the "mere utterance of an ethnic or racial epithet which engenders offensive feelings in an employee" does not affect the terms, conditions, or privileges of employment to a sufficiently significant degree to violate Title VII. Id.[8] For sexual harassment to state a claim under Title VII, it must be sufficiently pervasive so as to alter the conditions of employment and create an abusive working environment. Whether sexual harassment at the workplace is sufficiently severe and persistent to affect seriously the psychological well being of employees is a question

---

[8][Omitted.]

to be determined with regard to the totality of the circumstances. 29 C.F.R. §1604.11(b) (1981); • • •

(5) *Respondeat superior.* Where, as here, the plaintiff seeks to hold the employer responsible for the hostile environment created by the plaintiff's supervisor[9] or co-worker, she must show that the employer knew or should have known of the harassment in question and failed to take prompt remedial action. See Bundy v. Jackson, 641 F.2d at 943 & n.8; Vinson v. Taylor, 23 Fair Empl.Prac.Cas. (BNA) at 41-42. The employee can demonstrate that the employer knew of the harassment by showing that she complained to higher management of the harassment, Bundy v. Jackson, 641 F.2d at 943; Brown v. City of Guthrie, 22 Fair Empl.Prac.Cas. (BNA) at 1633, or by showing the pervasiveness of the harassment, which gives rise to the inference of knowledge or constructive knowledge, Taylor v. Jones, 653 F.2d 1193, 1199, 28 FEP Cases 1024 (8th Cir. 1981).[10]

In this case, Henson has made a prima facie showing of all elements necessary to establish a violation of Title VII. Dismissal of her claim was therefore erroneous. She is entitled to prove her claim on remand to the district court for a new trial.[11]

• • •

II.

Henson asserts two other claims of sexual harassment, that she was constructively discharged from employment because of her sex and that she was denied the opportunity to attend the police academy because she refused Sellgren's sexual importunities. The district court dismissed each claim, largely because it disbelieved crucial portions of Henson's testimony regarding historical facts in the case. • • •

A. *Standard of Review.*

• • •

Henson urges that normal deference to the district court's findings is not warranted in this case because the district judge operated under an erroneous conception of the law regarding sexual harassment and work environment. • • • We disagree. • • •

---

[9]We assume for purposes of this discussion that Sellgren was Henson's supervisor rather than her employer. If Sellgren was her employer, then the City of Dundee would be liable for his actions without the operation of respondeat superior. See Heelan v. Johns-Manville Corp., 451 F.Supp. 1382, 1390, 20 FEP Cases 251 (D.Colo.1978). On remand, the parties should offer evidence on this point. See generally Ginsburg & Kroeski, *Sexual Advances by an Employee's Supervisor: A Sex Discrimination Violation of Title VII?*, 3 Employee Rel.L.J. 83, 92 (1977).

[10]We note that Henson testified at trial that she complained of Sellgren's alleged harassment to the town manager of the City of Dundee. According to Henson's testimony, the manager not only failed to restrain Sellgren, but actually suggested that a sexual liaison between Henson and Sellgren would be mutually beneficial.

Our treatment of the respondeat superior issue in the case of sexual harassment that creates an offensive work environment differs from our treatment of the issue when sexual harassment results in tangible job detriment. • • •

[11]Generally in cases of disparate treatment the employee may establish a prima facie case by means of a lesser evidentiary showing than that which would be necessary to prevail on the merits. See McDonnell Douglas Corp. v. Green, 411 U.S. 792, 802-04, 93 S.Ct. 1817, 1824-25, 36 L.Ed.2d 668, 5 FEP Cases 965 (1973). The role of the prima facie case in disparate treatment litigation is to shift the burden of production to the employer after the employee has eliminated the most common nondiscriminatory reasons for the adverse treatment to which the employee has been subjected. Texas Dep't of Community Affairs v. Burdine, 450 U.S. 248, 253-54, 101 S.Ct. 1089, 1094-95, 67 L.Ed.2d 207, 25 FEP Cases 113 (1981). This procedure serves to "progressively sharpen the inquiry into the elusive factual question of intentional discrimination," id. at n.8, in a case where prohibited criteria and legitimate job related criteria often blend in the employment decision.

In contrast, the case of sexual harassment that creates an offensive environment does not present a factual question of intentional discrimination which is at all elusive. Except in the exceedingly atypical case of a bisexual supervisor, it should be clear that sexual harassment is discrimination based upon sex. We therefore see no reason to suggest a specific prima facie case for the hostile environment claim. In trying these cases, the district courts should employ normal principles of pleading and proof allocation. These principles may, in some cases, dictate that the allocation scheme vary in the individual case because of superior knowledge on the part of one party or other similar factors.

In this case, • • • the district court's legal error did not involve a principle of law that was controlling with respect to either the constructive discharge or the police academy claims. The district court erred only in its legal theory that sexual harassment must be coupled with tangible job detriment in order to give rise to Title VII liability. This error warrants reversal on Henson's first claim for a hostile work environment as a matter of law. However, the error did not affect the district court's treatment of the remaining claims which specifically complain of sexual harassment coupled with tangible job detriment. Indeed, the district court applied the correct legal principles in passing upon Henson's remaining claims.[14] • • •

We proceed to determine whether the district court committed clear error in making findings of historical fact that warranted the dismissal of either remaining claim of sexual harassment coupled with tangible job detriment.

B. *Constructive Discharge*

• • • In this case, the judge disbelieved Henson's testimony that she resigned from the Dundee Police Department because of sexual harassment, finding instead that she resigned because the man with whom she had been having an affair was forced to resign from the department. Cf. Privette v. Union Carbide Corp., 395 F.Supp. 372, 375, 13 FEP Cases 349 (W.D.N.C.1975) (court finds that the cause of plaintiff's resignation was unrelated to alleged harassment). Although the evidence on this point presents close questions of credibility and conflicting inferences, we cannot say that the finding of the district judge was clearly erroneous.

• • •

C. *Permission to attend the police academy*

An employer may not require sexual consideration from an employee as a *quid pro quo* for job benefits.[18] See, e.g., Miller v. Bank of America, 600 F.2d 211, 20 FEP Cases 462 (9th Cir. 1979); Tomkins v. Public Service Electric & Gas Co., 568 F.2d at 1044; Barnes v. Costle, 561 F.2d at 983; Garber v. Saxon Business Products, Inc., 552 F.2d 1032, 15 FEP Cases 344 (4th Cir. 1977) (per curiam); 29 C.F.R. §1604.11(a) (1981). In order to establish a violation of Title VII on grounds of sexual harassment of this kind, an employee must prove a number of elements, many of which are similar to the proof required to establish the existence of a hostile or offensive work environment:

(1) *The employee belongs to a protected group.*
(2) *The employee was subject to unwelcome sexual harassment.*

[12, 13][Omitted.]

[14]In concluding that the trial court used the correct standard in evaluating Henson's claims of *quid pro quo* sexual harassment, we implicitly reject a suggestion by the District of Columbia circuit that would alter the allocation of the burden of proof in cases such as this one. In Bundy v. Jackson, 641 F.2d 934, 952, 24 FEP Cases 1155 (D.C.Cir. 1981), the court held that a defendant who had created an offensive work environment through sexual harassment must bear an onerous burden of persuasion to rebut the prima facie case of the employee who claims in addition that she was deprived of tangible job benefits due to sexual harassment. • • •

• • •

We think that this burden shifting procedure is peculiarly suited to the remedy phase of a Title VII action • • • We would not apply the procedure • • • to the first phase of a disparate treatment case as Bundy suggests. Indeed, such an application may run afoul of the decision in the Supreme Court in Texas Dep't of Community Affairs v. Burdine, 450 U.S. 248, 101 S.Ct. 1089, 67 L.Ed.2d 207, 25 FEP Cases 113 (1981), which was handed down shortly after the decision of the District of Columbia circuit in Bundy. • • •

[15-17][Omitted.]

[18]In her book on sexual harassment, Professor MacKinnon makes a useful distinction between harassment that creates an offensive environment ("condition of work") and harassment in which a supervisor demands sexual consideration in exchange for job benefits ("*quid pro quo*"). C. MacKinnon, Sexual Harassment of Working Women, 32-47 (1979); see Kay & Brodsky, Book Review, 58 Texas L.Rev. 671, 679 (1980).

On a practical level, of course, there are many cases that could be characterized interchangeably as condition of work or *quid pro quo*. See, e.g., Tomkins v. Public Serv. Elec. & Gas Co., 568 F.2d 1044, 1046 & n.1, 16 FEP Cases 22 (3d Cir. 1977).

(3) *The harassment complained of was based upon sex.*

(4) *The employee's reaction to harassment complained of affected tangible aspects of the employee's compensation, terms, conditions, or privileges of employment.* The acceptance or rejection of the harassment by an employee must be an express or implied condition to the receipt of a job benefit or the cause of a tangible job detriment in order to create liability under this theory of sexual harassment. 29 C.F.R. §1604.11(a)(1) & (2) (1981). As in the typical disparate treatment case, the employee must prove that she was deprived of a job benefit which she was otherwise qualified to receive because of the employer's use of a prohibited criterion in making the employment decision. See Bundy v. Jackson, 641 F.2d at 953; • • •

(5) *Respondeat superior.* In a typical Title VII case, an employer is held liable for the discriminatory actions of its supervisors which affect the tangible job benefits of an employee on the basis of race, religion, or national origin. • • • The reason for this stern rule is readily apparent:

> When [the employer gave] its [supervisory personnel] authority to fire employees, it also accepted responsibility to remedy any harm caused by [the supervisors'] unlawful exercise of that authority. The modern corporate entity consists of the individuals who manage it, and little, if any, progress in eradicating discrimination in employment will be made if the corporate employer is able to hide behind the shield of individual employee action.

Tidewell v. American Oil Co., 332 F.Supp. at 436 (citation omitted).

• • • Sexual harassment resulting in tangible job detriment is a form of sex discrimination every bit as deleterious to the remedial purposes of Title VII as other unlawful employment practices. We hold that an employer is strictly liable for the actions of its supervisors that amount to sexual discrimination or sexual harassment resulting in tangible job detriment to the subordinate employee. See Miller v. Bank of America, 600 F.2d at 213; 29 C.F.R. §1604.11(c) (1981); 45 Fed.Reg. 74,676-77 (Nov. 10, 1980) (commentary issued in conjunction with proposed E.E.O.C. guidelines on sexual harassment). But see Tomkins v. Public Service Electric & Gas Co., 568 F.2d at 1048-49 (requiring actual or constructive knowledge of supervisor's conduct and failure to take remedial action before holding employer liable for sexual harassment involving tangible job detriment.[19]

We recognize that this holding requires differing treatment of respondeat superior claims in the two types of sexual harassment cases. In the classic *quid pro quo* case an employer is strictly liable for the conduct of its supervisors, while in the work environment case the plaintiff must prove that higher management knew or should have known of the sexual harassment before the employer may be held liable. The rationale underlying this difference in the treatment of the two cases is easily stated. • • • The capacity of any person to create a hostile or offensive environment is not necessarily enhanced or diminished by any degree of authority which the employer confers upon that individual. When a supervisor gratuitously insults an employee, he generally does so for his reasons and by his own means. He thus acts outside the actual or apparent scope of the authority he possesses as a supervisor. His conduct cannot automatically be imputed to the employer any more so than can the conduct of an ordinary employee.[20]

The typical case of *quid pro quo* harassment is fundamentally different. In such a case, the supervisor relies upon his apparent or actual authority to extort sexual consideration from an employee. Therein lies the *quid pro quo.* In that case the supervisor uses the means furnished to him by the employer to accomplish the prohibited purpose. He acts within the scope of his actual or apparent authority to "hire, fire, discipline or promote." • • • Because

---

[19]We reject the argument in Tomkins that an employer may escape "responsibility" for sexual harassment of this type merely by taking subsequent remedial action. Such action by the employer may, of course, mitigate damages, but it in no way affects an employer's liability.

[20]• • •
Under the rule in this case, employer responsibility for the acts of a supervisor in creating an offensive environment is coextensive with its liability for the acts of an employee. Under the E.E.O.C. regulations, an employer is responsible for the acts of its employees if the employer "knows or should have known of the conduct [and does not take] immediate and appropriate corrective action." 29 C.F.R. §1604.11(d) (1981).

the supervisor is acting within at least the apparent scope of the authority entrusted to him by the employer when he makes employment decisions, his conduct can fairly be imputed to the source of his authority.[21]

In this case, Henson has alleged all of the elements of a *quid pro quo* sexual harassment claim.[22] The district judge, however, • • • found that two circumstances which would have corroborated Henson's story did not exist. Specifically, he found that Sellgren had never propositioned Henson's female coworker, Dicks, and that no male dispatcher had ever attended the police academy.

Both of these specific factual findings are clearly erroneous. • • •

• • • In this case, • • • there is a substantial risk that the district judge based his evaluation of Henson's credibility upon a clearly erroneous view of the availability of corroborating evidence.[25] When the finder of the fact proceeds upon a faulty theory to assess credibility, its finding based solely upon that assessment cannot stand.[26] • • • Here, the district judge's thorough misapprehension of the factual situation surrounding Henson's testimony on the issue of the police academy assignment prevents us from deferring to his credibility finding. We conclude that Henson is entitled to a new trial on her claim for sexual harassment which allegedly prevented her from attending the police academy.

---

[21]The common law rules of respondeat superior will not always be appropriate to suit the broad remedial purposes of Title VII. See Note, supra note 7, at 1026-29. In this case, however, the imposition of liability upon an employer for *quid pro quo* sexual harassment committed by supervisors appears to be in general agreement with common law principles. See Restatement (Second) of Agency §219(2)(d) (master is liable for tort of his servant if the servant "was aided in accomplishing the tort by the existence of the agency relation"). *But cf.* Barnes v. Costle, 561 F.2d 983, 995, 15 FEP Cases 345 (D.C.Cir. 1976) (McKinnon, J., concurring) (supervisor not acting within apparent scope of employment when he extorts sexual consideration from subordinate in exchange for favorable job action).

[22]For the benefit of the district court on remand, we will discuss the elements of a prima facie case for *quid pro quo* sexual harassment. The prima facie case is, of course, a variation upon the pattern established in McDonnell Douglas Corp. v. Green, 411 U.S. 792, 802-04 & n.13, 93 S.Ct. 1817, 1824-25 & n.13, 36 L.Ed.2d 668, 5 FEP Cases 965 (1973). • • •

We would phrase the prima facie case in terms that • • • closely track McDonnell Douglas, although our version is not substantially different from those of the other two courts:

(1) The employee is a member of the protected class;

(2) She was subjected to unwelcome sexual harassment to which members of the opposite sex had not been subjected;

(3) She applied and was qualified for a position for which the employer was accepting applications;

(4) That despite her qualifications she was rejected;

(5) That after her rejection, the position remained open and the employer continued to accept applicants who possessed complainant's qualifications.

While the above prima facie case is applicable to Henson's claim on remand, the prima facie case may vary depending upon the specific facts. McDonnell Douglas v. Green, 411 U.S. at 802 n.13, 93 S.Ct. at 1824 n.13. Specifically, there will be cases in which submission to unwelcome sexual advances is an express or implied condition to the receipt of a job benefit. 29 C.F.R. §1604.11(a)(1). In such cases, an employee need not prove as part of the prima facie case that she actually applied for a given position since such an application would have been futile. Cf. International Bhd. of Teamsters v. United States, 431 U.S. 324, 367, 97 S.Ct. 1843, 1870, 52 L.Ed.2d 396, 14 FEP Cases 1514 (1977)(plaintiff who was deterred from applying for position because of employer's known discrimination policies is not barred from relief).

[23, 24][Omitted.]

[25]We note that in a case of alleged sexual harassment which involves close questions of credibility and subjective interpretation, the existence of corroborative evidence or the lack thereof is likely to be crucial. In this case, for all we know, the judge based his credibility finding wholly upon his erroneous perception of the lack of corroborating evidence. Cf. Hall v. F. O. Thacker Co., 24 Fair Empl.Prac.Cas. (BNA) 1499, 1503 (N.D.Ga.1980) (district judge did not credit plaintiff's testimony on sexual advances because it was "virtually uncorroborated"); Neidhardt v. D. H. Holmes Co., 21 Fair Empl.Prac.Cas. (BNA) 452, 457 (E.D.La.1979), aff'd mem., 624 F.2d 1097, 24 FEP Cases 746 (5th Cir. 1980) (the district judge did not believe plaintiff's account of sexual harassment because "there is not a scintilla of credible evidence to corroborate [plaintiff's] version"); E.E.O.C. Dec. No. 81-23, 27 Fair Empl.Prac.Cas. (BNA) 1816, 1819 (June 3, 1981) (no reasonable cause to support claim of sexual harassment because there was "absolutely no evidence that her supervisor had ever subjected any other employees to sexual advances . . . [and because] no other corroborative evidence exist[ed] to substantiate the Charging Party's claim that her supervisor made sexual advances toward her").

[26][Omitted.]

[27][Omitted.]

AFFIRMED IN PART, REVERSED IN PART, AND REMANDED WITH IN-STRUCTIONS.

Concurring and Dissenting Opinion
[Omitted.]

II. THE FRAMEWORK FOR ANALYZING ENVIRONMENTAL HARASSMENT CLAIMS

The *McDonnell Douglas/Burdine* shifting-burden-of-proof approach, applied in quid pro quo cases,[10] often is not appropriate in a hostile environment case.[11] Most often, the harassment consists of either unwelcome sexual advances based on the gender of the complainant or commentary that demeans the complainant's gender. In these cases, most courts would hold that the conduct itself is obviously on the basis of sex and satisfies any need to show discrimination because of sex.[12] The Fourth Circuit in *Katz v. Dole*[13] thus compressed the three-part *McDonnell Douglas/Burdine* approach into two steps for purposes of the typical hostile environment claim:

> First, the plaintiff must make a *prima facie* showing that sexually harassing actions took place, and if this is done, the employer may rebut the showing either directly, by proving that the events did not take place, or indirectly, by showing that they were isolated or genuinely trivial. Second, the plaintiff must show that the employer knew or should have known of the harassment, and took no effectual action to correct the situation. This showing can also be rebutted by the employer directly, or by pointing to remedial action reasonably calculated to end the harassment.[14]

Judge Sam J. Ervin, III, justified this modification by noting that while the employer's motive is the fundamental issue in a classic disparate treatment

---

[10]For a discussion of the *McDonnell Douglas/Burdine* framework, see Chapter 3, Quid Pro Quo Harassment, Section II.

[11]*E.g.,* Rabidue v. Osceola Ref. Co., 805 F.2d 611, 621, 42 FEP Cases 631 (6th Cir. 1986), reproduced in Chapter 2, Forms of Harassment (*McDonnell Douglas/Burdine* "not readily adaptable" to hostile environment claim), *cert. denied,* 481 U.S. 1041 (1987); Henson v. City of Dundee, *supra* note 4, 682 F.2d at 905 n.11 (unlike quid pro quo case, hostile environment "does not present a factual question of intentional discrimination which is at all elusive" and does not require "specific prima facie case" as opposed to "normal principles of pleading and proof allocation"); Note, *Sexual Harassment Claims of Abusive Work Environment Under Title VII,* 97 HARV. L. REV. 1149, 1156 (1984)(environmental harassment claim "difficult to square with the *McDonnell Douglas* model of Title VII disparate treatment analysis, which is designed primarily to assess the relationship between a demonstrable injury and a specific employment decision and to determine the motive behind the employer's decision").

[12]*E.g.,* Cline v. G.E. Credit Auto Lease, 748 F. Supp. 650, 54 FEP Cases 419, 423 (N.D. Ill. 1990)(*McDonnell Douglas* does not apply to harassment cases based on sexual activity in that "the discriminatory nature of the charged conduct speaks for itself"). See Section VII.A.1. *infra. But see* note 49 and Section VII.A.3. *infra.*

[13]709 F.2d 251, 31 FEP Cases 1521 (4th Cir. 1983), reproduced in Chapter 7, Harassment by Co-Workers (Phillips, Ervin & Chapman, JJ.).

[14]*Id.* at 256, 31 FEP Cases at 1524.

case, in an environmental case involving sexually explicit conduct the proof of the sexual harassment itself provides proof of the motive.[15]

The *McDonnell Douglas/Burdine* analysis remains useful, however, in hostile environment claims based on nonsexual hazing. In those cases, because the harassment is not overtly sexual, an issue may arise as to whether the hostile conduct is because of the complainant's sex, as opposed to the harasser's dislike of the complainant as an individual or the harasser's generally misanthropic personality.[16]

The *McDonnell Douglas/Burdine* analysis has little to offer in the case of a sexually charged workplace featuring widespread sexual favoritism, sexually suggestive posters, sexually oriented graffiti, sexual language, or pornography, none of which may be directed specifically toward the complainant and all of which may even have existed in the workplace prior to the complainant's arrival. In order to prove that the harassment was because of sex, the complainant may need to rely upon a disparate treatment theory showing intent by evidence that the employer systematically refused to correct conduct offensive to one sex and thereby discriminated against that sex,[17] or an adverse impact theory that the employer's tolerance of gender-demeaning conduct had a foreseeably adverse impact on members of that gender without any justifying business necessity.[18]

III. THE PRIMA FACIE CASE

In the widely followed Eleventh Circuit decision in *Henson v. City of Dundee*,[19] Judge Robert Vance identified the elements of a prima facie case of hostile environment harassment, which can be stated as:

(1) the basis: membership in a protected group;
(2) the activity: unwelcome conduct of a sexual [sex-based] nature;
(3) the issue: affecting a term and condition of employment;

---

[15]*Id.* ("once the plaintiff in such a case proves that harassment took place, the most difficult legal question typically will concern the responsibility of the employer for that harassment"). *See also* Broderick v. Ruder, 685 F. Supp. 1269, 46 FEP Cases 1272 (D.D.C. 1988), reproduced in Chapter 2, Forms of Harassment (in hostile environment cases, defendant must show by clear and convincing evidence that no harassment existed, as opposed to articulating legitimate, nondiscriminatory reason); Moffett v. Gene B. Glick Co., 621 F. Supp. 244, 266, 41 FEP Cases 671, 685 (N.D. Ind. 1985)(racial harassment)("once a plaintiff establishes that she was harassed and that the employer was involved . . . , it is hard to see how an employer can justify harassment").

[16]*See* Cline v. GE Credit Auto Lease, *supra* note 12, 54 FEP Cases at 423 (where "harassment is unrelated to sexual activity, the question of discriminatory intent reappears—and with it, the need for either direct proof of discrimination or an inference of discrimination resulting from the *McDonnell Douglas* analysis"). For citations to further cases, see Section VII.A.2. *infra.*

[17]*See generally* Bohen v. City of E. Chicago, 799 F.2d 1180, 41 FEP Cases 1108, 1115–17 (7th Cir. 1986)(Posner, J., concurring)(§1983 case).

[18]*See* Robinson v. Jacksonville Shipyards, 760 F. Supp. 1486, 1522–23 (M.D. Fla. 1991), reproduced in Chapter 2, Forms of Harassment (nondirected conduct disproportionately offensive to one sex may create unlawful barrier to employment). *See generally* Lynch v. Freeman, 817 F.2d 380, 387–89 (6th Cir. 1987)(rule barring access to inside sanitary bathroom facilities and penalizing construction workers for failure to use unsanitary portable toilets had disparate impact upon female construction workers, who were more physically prone than males to cystitis and other diseases due to unsanitary conditions). For a further discussion, see Section VII.A.3 *infra.*

[19]*Supra* note 4.

(4) the causal connection: on the basis of sex; and

(5) employer responsibility.[20]

Although some courts have reformulated these elements,[21] the *Henson* formulation is still commonly followed and guides the discussion here.

IV. THE BASIS: MEMBERSHIP IN A PROTECTED GROUP

Both men and women can bring actions for a hostile environment under Title VII.[22] Men bring few environmental harassment cases, a fact thought to be related to the different positions of men and women in society.[23] Nonetheless, any hostile environment action predicated on the maleness or the femaleness of the complainant will satisfy the first element of a sexual harassment claim.[24]

---

[20]The *Henson* court identified the elements as (1) the employee belongs to a protected group; (2) the employee was subject to unwelcome sexual conduct; (3) the conduct was based upon sex; (4) the employee's reaction to the harassment affected a "term, condition, or privilege" of employment; and (5) *respondeat superior. Id.* at 903–4, 29 FEP Cases at 792–94. We use the term "employer responsibility" in place of "*respondeat superior*" because the standard that courts actually apply incorporates negligence concepts far broader than the traditional standard of *respondeat superior. E.g.,* Hirschfeld v. New Mexico Corrections Dep't, 916 F.2d 572, 577 n.5, 54 FEP Cases 268, 272 (10th Cir. 1990); Guess v. Bethlehem Steel Corp., 913 F.2d 463, 465, 53 FEP Cases 1547, 1549 (7th Cir. 1990)("standard has been mislabeled. It is not respondeat superior"). *See generally* EEOC v. Hacienda Hotel, 881 F.2d 1504, 1515–16, 50 FEP Cases 877 (9th Cir. 1989)(recognizing judicial difficulty in "developing a standard to govern the liability of an employer for sexual harassment perpetrated by its supervisory personnel or by co-workers of the Title VII claimant," and questioning whether *respondeat superior* test is operative after *Meritor*). For further discussion of employer responsibility, see Section VIII. *infra.*

[21]*E.g., Second Circuit*: Carrero v. New York Housing Auth., 890 F.2d 569, 578, 51 FEP Cases 596, 602–3 (2d Cir. 1989)((1) unwelcome conduct (2) prompted by gender and (3) sufficiently pervasive to create an "offensive environment antithetical" to "priority of merit"; but more must be shown to establish employer liability for the hostile environment);

　　Third Circuit: Andrews v. City of Philadelphia, 895 F.2d 1469, 1482, 54 FEP Cases 184, 195 (3d Cir. 1990)((1) intentional discrimination because of sex; (2) discrimination "pervasive and regular"; (3) detrimental effect on plaintiff; (4) discrimination would "detrimentally affect a reasonable person of the same sex in that position"; and (5) "existence of respondeat superior liability");

　　Fourth Circuit: Paroline v. Unisys Corp., 879 F.2d 100, 105, 50 FEP Cases 306, 310 (4th Cir. 1989)((1) conduct in question was unwelcome, (2) harassment was based on sex, (3) harassment was sufficiently pervasive or severe to create an abusive working environment, and (4) some basis exists for imputing liability to the employer), *vacated in part on other grounds,* 900 F.2d 27, 52 FEP Cases 845 (4th Cir. 1990); Swentek v. USAir, 830 F.2d 552, 557, 44 FEP Cases 1808, 1812 (4th Cir. 1987)(same); Katz v. Dole, *supra* note 13 (discussed in text accompanying notes 13–14 *supra*);

　　Ninth Circuit: EEOC v. Hacienda Hotel, *supra* note 20 ((1) subjected to sexual advances, requests for sexual favors, or other verbal or physical conduct of a sexual nature; (2) conduct was unwelcome; (3) conduct was sufficiently severe or pervasive to alter conditions of employment and create abusive working environment; and (4) employer failed to remedy or prevent hostile environment "of which management level employees knew, or in the exercise of reasonable care should have known");

　　Federal Circuit: Downes v. FAA, 775 F.2d 288, 292, 39 FEP Cases 70, 74 (Fed. Cir. 1985)((1) offensive conduct must be sufficiently pervasive so as to alter conditions of employment, and (2) be sufficiently severe and persistent to affect seriously psychological well-being of employee).

[22]Moylan v. Maries County, 792 F.2d 746, 749, 40 FEP Cases 1788, 1790 (8th Cir. 1986)(that plaintiff belongs to protected class is "not usually disputed").

[23]*See* Drinkwater v. Union Carbide Corp., 904 F.2d 853, 861 n.15, 56 FEP Cases 483 (3d Cir. 1990)(because hostile environment theory "posits . . . sexual power assymetry between men and women" and "because men's sexuality does not define men as men in this society, a man's hostile environment claim, although theoretically possible, will be much harder to plead and prove"); Goluszek v. Smith, 697 F. Supp. 1452, 48 FEP Cases 317 (N.D. Ill. 1988)(discussed in text at notes 135–38 *infra*)(rejecting hostile environment claim by man because harassment in question did not stem from sexual "imbalance of power"). *Cf.* Morgan v. Massachusetts Gen. Hosp., 901 F.2d 186, 53 FEP Cases 1780, 1785 (1st Cir. 1990)(affirming summary judgment against hostile environment claim by male claiming homosexual harassment but relying on ground that harassment not severe or pervasive).

[24]*See, e.g.,* Moylan v. Maries County, *supra* note 22.

V. THE ACTIVITY: UNWELCOME CONDUCT OF A SEX-BASED NATURE

A. Unwelcome Conduct

1. Sexual Advances

Hostile environments can be created by sexual advances, if the advances are unwelcome. Thus, the words of the Supreme Court in *Meritor* can apply as much in a hostile environment case as in a quid pro quo case: "the gravamen of any sexual harassment claim is that the alleged sexual advances were 'unwelcome.' "[25]

2. Gender-Based Animosity

Women who encounter gender-baiting, teasing, hazing, and sabotage of their work performance ordinarily need no further proof of unwelcomeness. The conduct by its nature is unwelcome,[26] even though a complainant may choose to endure it to retain her job.

3. Sexually Charged Workplace

In a sexually charged workplace it may be difficult to distinguish welcomeness of the conduct from the complainant's effort to adjust to the prevailing workplace culture. In *Ukarish v. Magnesium Elektron,*[27] a hostile environment claim failed for lack of unwelcomeness where the complainant, although subjectively disliking the vulgar language of her male co-workers, appeared to accept it "and joined in it as one of the boys."[28]

Similarly, in *Gan v. Kepro Circuit Systems,*[29] a hostile environment claim failed where the complainant herself regularly used "crude and vulgar language," initiated sexually oriented conversations with male and female co-workers, "frequently asked male employees about their marital sex lives and whether they engaged in extra-marital sexual relationships," and made her own marital sexual relationships "a regular topic of office conversation." The court decided that the complainant "was not subjected to unprovoked propositions and sexually suggestive remarks, as she alleges. Any such propositions that did occur were prompted by her own sexual aggressiveness and her sexually explicit conversations."[30]

---

[25]477 U.S. 57, 68, 40 FEP Cases 1822, 1829 (1986)(citing 29 C.F.R. §1604.11(a)). For a discussion of welcomeness of sexual advances, see Chapter 3, Quid Pro Quo Harassment, Section V. When a supervisor conditions tangible job benefits upon a subordinate's response to such an advance, the case is a quid pro quo case.

[26]*See, e.g.,* Kotcher v. Rosa & Sullivan Appliance, 53 FEP Cases 1148, 1150 (N.D.N.Y. 1990)(where supervisor pretended to masturbate and ejaculate behind complainant's back, actions were of "such a degrading nature that no ordinary person would welcome them").

[27]31 FEP Cases 1315 (D.N.J. 1983).

[28]*Id.* at 1319.

[29]28 FEP Cases 639 (E.D. Mo. 1982)

[30]*Id.* at 640. *See also* Tindall v. Housing Auth., 55 FEP Cases 22, 26 (W.D. Ark. 1991)(plaintiff not truly offended where she "acted like 'one of the boys' and freely joined in sexual jokes with the men");

General participation in sexual conduct notwithstanding, a complainant can establish proof of unwelcomeness with respect to particular conduct by expressing opposition to it. In *Swentek v. USAir*,[31] the Fourth Circuit criticized a district court for relying upon the complainant's general conduct and use of foul language to find that "she was the kind of person who could not be offended by such comments and therefore welcomed them generally."[32] What the trial court must do instead, Judge James Harvie Wilkinson, III, emphasized, is to determine whether the complainant welcomed the particular conduct in question from the alleged harasser.[33] Thus, the complainant's "use of foul language or sexual innuendo in a consensual setting does not waive 'her legal protections against unwelcome harassment.' "[34]

4. Proof of Unwelcomeness

a. General approach. Whether unwelcome conduct has occurred is an issue of fact. A trial court's findings on such an issue will not be disturbed unless clearly erroneous.[35] A court may consider all of the circumstances surrounding the conduct to determine whether it was welcome, including the complainant's "sexually provocative speech or dress,"[36] participation in sexual horseplay and use of foul language at work,[37] friendly association with the

---

Weinsheimer v. Rockwell Int'l Corp., 754 F. Supp. 1559, 54 FEP Cases 828, 831–32 (M.D. Fla. 1990)(claim denied where sexual banter and vulgarity abounded and complainant "among the most prevalent and graphic participants"); Perkins v. General Motors Corp., 709 F. Supp. 1487, 1498, 51 FEP Cases 1684, 1693 (W.D. Mo. 1989)(rejecting unwelcomeness claim where complainant engaged in sexually explicit talk and aggressively touched men), *aff'd in part and rev'd in part on other grounds sub nom.* Perkins v. Spivey, 911 F.2d 22, 53 FEP Cases 973 (8th Cir. 1990), *cert. denied,* 55 FEP Cases 352 (1991); cases cited in notes 36–38 *infra.*

[31]*Supra* note 21 (Phillips, Ervin & Willeinson, JJ.).

[32]*Id.* at 557, 44 FEP Cases at 1812.

[33]*Id.*

[34]*Id.* (quoting Katz v. Dole, 709 F.2d 251, 254 n.3, 31 FEP Cases 1521, 1523 (4th Cir. 1983), reproduced in Chapter 7, Harassment by Co-Workers). *See also* Danna v. New York Tel. Co., 54 FEP Cases 1638, 1652 (S.D.N.Y. 1990)(co-workers' graffiti and comments associating complainant with fellatio and anal intercourse unwelcome notwithstanding her own resort to graffiti and verbal profanity, where her graffiti was defensive and not profane, where she had ceased her own foul language to supervisors after warning, and where she complained to supervisors about graffiti); Department of Fair Empl. & Hous. v. Livermore Joe's, Inc., Cal. FEHC Dec. 90–07 at 14 (1990)(rejecting "assumption that one can infer automatically from a woman's voluntary sexual conduct with some persons her similar response to sexual conduct to which she is involuntarily subjected by others, especially where consensual conduct was "a joke with the girls").

[35]*E.g.,* Anderson v. City of Bessemer City, 470 U.S. 564, 37 FEP Cases 396 (1985)(trial court's factual determination may be overturned only where appellate court is " 'left with the definite and firm conviction that a mistake has been committed' "); *see also* Jordan v. Clark, 847 F.2d 1368, 1375, 46 FEP Cases 1558, 1563 (9th Cir. 1988)(affirming finding that alleged harasser had not made harassing calls to plaintiff at home or touched her or told her she would have to sleep with him two or three times a week to keep job and get promotion), *cert. denied,* 109 S.Ct. 786 (1989).

[36]Meritor Sav. Bank v. Vinson, *supra* note 25, 477 U.S. at 69, 40 FEP Cases at 1828; Jones v. Wesco Investments, 846 F.2d 1154, 1155 n.4, 46 FEP Cases 1431, 1432 (8th Cir. 1988)("court must consider any provocative speech or dress of the plaintiff in a sexual harassment case").

[37]*E.g.,* cases cited in notes 27–30 *supra. See also* Smith v. Acme Spinning Co., 40 FEP Cases 1104, 1105 (W.D.N.C. 1986)(rejecting unwelcomeness claim as to two "rubbing" incidents where complainant "frequently participated in on-the-job horseplay that included a good deal of rubbing and touching of male employees"). *But see* Wyerick v. Bayou Steel Corp., 887 F.2d 1271, 1275, 51 FEP Cases 491 (5th Cir. 1989)(overturning summary judgment for employer granted, in part, on ground that complainant's sexual comments at work proved that sexual comments of co-workers were not unwelcome to her); Swentek v. USAir, *supra* note 21 (error for trial court to have held complainant's "own past conduct and use of foul language meant that [the purported harasser's] comments were 'not unwelcome' even though she told [him] to leave her alone").

alleged harasser,[38] and failure to report alleged incidents of harassment to superiors.[39]

Courts generally have not permitted defendants to explore a complainant's sexual history with persons other than the alleged harasser to prove that the sexual conduct was actually welcomed.[40]

     b. After welcome participation. Conduct that is initially welcome may become unwelcome. A complainant in that situation has waived no rights by initially accepting the behavior, but has complicated any attempt to prove unwelcomeness. Thus, the EEOC has found that no harassment occurred where a complainant had joined others in using dirty remarks and telling dirty jokes during her first two months on the job, and then failed to give notice that the conduct was no longer welcome. Simply ceasing to participate in the conduct was insufficient to show that the continuing activity was not welcome.[41] This situation is analogous, of course, to a quid pro quo case in which a romance has gone sour.[42]

B. "Sexual Nature" of Unwelcome Conduct

     The EEOC Guidelines are potentially misleading as to whether the unwelcome conduct must be of a "sexual nature" to be actionable. After stating correctly the general proposition that "[h]arassment on the basis of sex is a violation of Sec. 703 of Title VII," the Guidelines state that sexual harassment consists of unwelcome "sexual advances ... and other verbal or physical conduct of a sexual nature."[43] Read in isolation, this more specific description

---

[38]Staton v. Maries County, 868 F.2d 996, 49 FEP Cases 309, 310 (8th Cir. 1989)(affirming finding that harassment may have been invited in that complainant and alleged harasser were "close and confided in one another"); Evans v. Mail Handlers, 32 FEP Cases 634, 635, 637 (D.D.C. 1983)(plaintiff told defendants intimate details of her sexual activity and did not consider sexual conduct of supervisor "to be offensive or intimidating" until after their voluntary sexual relationship began to deteriorate); Reichman v. Bureau of Affirmative Action, 536 F. Supp. 1149, 1177, 30 FEP Cases 1644, 1665–66 (M.D. Pa. 1982)(rejecting unwelcomeness claim regarding supervisor's sexual advances and attempt to kiss complainant where complainant "behaved in a very flirtatious and provocative manner" around alleged harasser and where her behavior did not change after incident).

[39]Dockter v. Rudolf Wolff Futures, 913 F.2d 456, 53 FEP Cases 1642, 1645 (7th Cir. 1990)(affirming finding of no liability where administrative assistant did not complain to management during two weeks she was subject to unwelcome advances by supervisor, including fondling her breast and attempted kiss, which she immediately rebuffed; even if environment was hostile, plaintiff suffered no damages cognizable by Title VII); Tindall v. Housing Auth., *supra* note 30, 55 FEP Cases at 25 (relying on undisputed fact that complainant never reported alleged harassment to manager who had "open door" policy); Loftin-Boggs v. City of Meridian, 633 F. Supp. 1323, 1326–27, 41 FEP Cases 532, 535 (S.D. Miss. 1986)(complainant who herself participated in crude language and storytelling cannot prove conduct unwelcome where she failed to report conduct had become unwelcome), *aff'd*, 824 F.2d 971, 51 FEP Cases 1832 (5th Cir. 1987), *cert. denied*, 484 U.S. 1063 (1988).

[40]See Chapter 25, Evidence, Section VI.

[41]EEOC Dec. 84-1, 33 FEP Cases 1887, 1890 (1983) (because complainant had participated in sexual conduct for first two months on job in order to "fit in," she had "affirmative duty" to notify alleged harasser that conduct no longer welcome), discussed in EEOC Policy Guidance on Sexual Harassment, 8 FAIR EMPL. PRAC. MAN. (BNA) 405:6687 n.12 (March 19, 1990), reproduced in Appendix 3. *See also* Weinsheimer v. Rockwell Int'l Corp., *supra* note 30, 754 F. Supp. at 1564 n.12, 54 FEP Cases at 832 (complainant's frequent, willing involvement in sexual innuendo prevalent in workplace does not "completely bar" claim of sexual harassment, but does require proof "that at some point she clearly made her co-workers and superiors aware that in the future such conduct would be considered 'unwelcome' "); Loftin-Boggs v. City of Meridian, *supra* note 39 (same).

[42]For a discussion of problems of proof attending a sexual harassment case involving a soured romance, see Chapter 2, Forms of Harassment, Section III.A.2.

[43]29 C.F.R. §1604.11(a), reproduced in Appendix 1.

in the Guidelines implies that the predicate acts underlying a sexual harassment claim must be sexual in nature,[44] an implication that has misled some courts.[45]

The sexual nature of conduct is always relevant, of course, to whether the conduct was because of a complainant's gender. Courts have erred, however, in requiring proof that the offensive conduct be sexual in nature.[46] Any such requirement would make coverage of Title VII under-inclusive, for Title VII would then not bar claims of sex-based harassment consisting of nonsexual acts.[47] Any such requirement could also make Title VII over-inclusive, for Title VII would then cover all offensive sexual conduct, even where the conduct is directed without regard to gender.[48] Focusing on whether conduct was of a sexual nature thus may obscure the need, present in every claim of sex-based harassment, to show that the conduct was because of the complainant's gender.[49]

The EEOC, recognizing that its Guidelines are potentially misleading, has made clear that proof of sexual activity is not necessary for proof of unlawful harassment:

> Although the Guidelines specifically address conduct that is sexual in nature, the Commission notes that sex-based harassment—that is, harassment not involving sexual activity or language—may also give rise to Title VII liability (just as in the case of harassment based on race, national origin or religion) if it is

---

[44]A similar focus on sexuality rather than gender led the EEOC to decide that it was not discriminatory for a retail store to require female managers and sales clerks selling female sportswear to wear revealing swimwear, as a sales promotion tactic, even though the women found the requirement so offensive they refused to wear the swimwear and were discharged. Focusing narrowly on whether the conduct was "of a sexual nature," the EEOC reasoned that the swimwear requirement would violate Title VII only if it was both sexually revealing and likely to elicit unwelcome sexual conduct. While the outfits were revealing, the EEOC concluded that they likely would attract only stares and compliments rather than explicitly sexual comments or gestures. EEOC Dec. 85-9, 37 FEP Cases 1893, 1895–96 (1985).

[45]*E.g.,* Reynolds v. Atlantic City Convention Center, 53 FEP Cases 1852, 1867–68 (D.N.J. 1990)(refusal of complainant's male co-workers to work with her because she was a woman would not be "within the regulation's proscription of 'other verbal or physical conduct of a sexual nature,' " "and so does not figure into the calculus of a sexually offensive working environment"), *aff'd mem.,* 925 F.2d 419, 54 FEP Cases 1560 (3d Cir. 1991); Walker v. Sullair Corp., 736 F. Supp. 94, 52 FEP Cases 1313 (W.D.N.C. 1990)(rejecting hostile environment claim because conduct complained of—reprimands and close monitoring—not sexual in nature).

[46]*See, e.g.,* Andrews v. City of Philadelphia, 895 F.2d 1469, 1485 n.6, 54 FEP Cases 184, 197 (3d Cir. 1990)(district court may have been misled by language of EEOC Guidelines into believing that "only explicit sexual harassment would be actionable," a reading that "does not appear to be consistent with either the wording of the EEOC Guidelines or the prevailing case law").

[47]Such a requirement would be analogous to requiring that racial harassment be of a racial nature, whereas the actual requirement is simply that the harassment be because of race. See Chapter 2, Forms of Harassment, Section I.B.

[48]This point prompted a criticism of the EEOC Guidelines when they were first proposed:
The guideline's definition of sexual harassment as "[u]nwelcome sexual advances, requests for sexual favors, and other verbal or physical conduct of a sexual nature" reflects a position that such conduct is *per se* gender-based. The types of conduct which the guideline describes as sexual harassment, however, need not be directed toward an employee because of his or her sex. For example, verbal conduct of a sexual nature, if directed at and affecting both male and female employees, would appear to be actionable under the guideline, although it would not be discriminatory under Title VII.
McLain, *The EEOC Sexual Harassment Guidelines: Welcome Advances Under Title VII?,* 10 U. BALT. L. REV. 275, 292 (1981).

[49]Conduct of a sexual nature is not always "because of sex." Weinsheimer v. Rockwell Int'l Corp., *supra* note 30, 754 F. Supp. at 1565, 54 FEP Cases at 832–33 (sexual comments were "gender-neutral, participated in by men and women alike"). *Cf.* Wyerick v. Bayou Steel Corp., *supra* note 37, 887 F.2d at 1274–75, 51 FEP Cases at 493–94 (co-workers' offensive sexual commentary actionable as based on gender as it consisted of "highly personalized lewd statements and gestures" rather than "general banter around the workplace that often took a sexual tone"). For additional authorities, see Section VII.A.3. *infra.*

"sufficiently patterned or pervasive" and directed at employees because of their sex.[50]

Courts now generally recognize that offensive gender-based conduct need not be sexual in nature to be actionable as sex discrimination forbidden by Title VII.[51]

The leading case on this point is *McKinney v. Dole*,[52] in which Judge J. Skelly Wright held that nonsexual physical aggression by a male supervisor against a female employee because of her sex could constitute part of a sexually hostile environment in violation of Title VII:

> We have never held that sexual harassment or other unequal treatment of an employee or group of employees that occurs because of the sex of the employee must, to be illegal under Title VII, take the form of sexual advances or of other incidents with clearly sexual overtones.... Rather, we hold that any harassment or other unequal treatment of an employee or group of employees that would not occur but for the sex of the employee or employees may, if sufficiently patterned or pervasive, comprise an illegal condition of employment under Title VII.[53]

VI. THE ISSUE: AFFECTING A TERM OR CONDITION OF EMPLOYMENT

A. The Effect on Conditions of Employment Must Be "Severe or Pervasive"

Not every instance of disparate treatment in working conditions on the basis of sex rises to the level of a violation of Title VII. For example, certain

---

[50]EEOC Policy Guidance on Sexual Harassment, *supra* note 41, at 405:6692. The EEOC nonetheless persists in defining sex-based harassment that does not involve sexual conduct as something other than "sexual harassment." EEOC COMPL. MAN. (BNA) §615.6, p. 615:0017–18, reproduced in Appendix 4. This definition is misleading and conflicts with the EEOC sexual harassment guidelines themselves, which begin with the sentence, "Harassment on the basis of sex is a violation of . . . Title VII." 29 C.F.R. §1604.11(a), *supra* note 43.

[51]*D.C. Circuit:* McKinney v. Dole, 765 F.2d 1129, 38 FEP Cases 364 (D.C. Cir. 1985)(discussed in text at notes 52–53 *infra*);

First Circuit: Lipsett v. University of P.R., 864 F.2d 881, 905, 54 FEP Cases 230, 249 (1st Cir. 1988)(male co-workers' "constant verbal attack," "although not explicitly *sexual*, was nonetheless charged with antifemale animus, and therefore could be found to have contributed significantly to the hostile environment");

Third Circuit: Andrews v. City of Philadelphia, *supra* note 46, 895 F.2d at 1485, 54 FEP Cases at 197 (rejecting narrow interpretation of EEOC Guidelines and holding "pervasive use of derogatory and insulting terms relating to women generally and addressed to female employees personally" may evidence sexually hostile environment);

Fourth Circuit: Delgado v. Lehman, 665 F. Supp. 460, 43 FEP Cases 593 (E.D. Va. 1987)(sexual harassment may consist of verbal abuse of women if it is sufficiently patterned and caused by sex of harassed employee);

Eighth Circuit: Hall v. Gus Constr. Co., 842 F.2d 1010, 46 FEP Cases 573 (8th Cir. 1988), reproduced in Chapter 2, Forms of Harassment (trial court must consider hostile nonsexual conduct of complainant's male co-workers, such as co-workers' urination into complainants' water bottle and gas tank);

Tenth Circuit: Hicks v. Gates Rubber Co., 833 F.2d 1406, 1414–15, 45 FEP Cases 608, 614–15 (10th Cir. 1987)(threats of physical violence and incidents of physical abuse should be considered in sexual harassment claim); *but see id.* at 1419–20, 45 FEP Cases at 618–19 (Seth, J., dissenting);

Eleventh Circuit: Bell v. Crackin Good Bakers, 777 F.2d 1497, 1503, 39 FEP Cases 948, 952–53 (11th Cir. 1985)(reversing summary judgment granted because of complainant's failure to prove sexual conduct; it would suffice to prove "threatening, bellicose, demeaning, hostile, offensive conduct . . . because of the sex of the victim");

But see Ninth Circuit: Ellison v. Brady, 924 F.2d 872, 875 n.5, 54 FEP Cases 1346, 1350 (9th Cir. 1991)(reserving question whether conduct must be sexual to create "sexually discriminatory working environment").

[52]*Supra* note 51 (Wright, Mikra & Starr, JJ.).

[53]*Id.* at 1138, 38 FEP Cases at 371.

appearance standards for male and female employees, such as those involving hair length for men, do not rise to the level of sex discrimination cognizable under Title VII.[54]

The Supreme Court in *Meritor* stated that sexual harassment, to be actionable under Title VII, "must be sufficiently severe or pervasive to alter the conditions of the victim's employment and create an abusive working environment."[55] By this standard, actionable harassment must be pervasive enough to be distinguishable from the ordinary tribulations of the workplace, such as the sporadic use of abusive language,[56] gender-related jokes, and occasional teasing.[57]

Most cases suggest that determining whether conduct has created an "intimidating, hostile or offensive working environment" will depend on whether the conduct was (1) severe enough to alter the recipient's workplace experience even though the conduct occurred but once or but rarely,[58] or (2) pervasive enough so as to be more than merely an accidental or isolated event and thus to become a defining condition of the workplace, even if no act in itself was actionable.[59] Severity and pervasiveness are interrelated, in that "the required showing of severity or seriousness varies inversely with the pervasiveness or frequency of the conduct."[60]

The foregoing is not the only formulation of the test. Judge Robert Krupansky, writing for the majority of the Sixth Circuit panel in *Rabidue v. Osceola Refining Co.*,[61] stated that to be actionable, sexual harassment must "unreasonably interfer[e] with the plaintiff's work performance *and* creat[e] an intimidating, hostile, or offensive working environment that affect[s] seriously the psychological well-being of the plaintiff."[62] This language would qualify hostile environment claims in that (1) the language makes conjunctive rather than disjunctive the factors of "interference with job performance" and "creating a ... hostile working environment," and (2) the phrase "affected seriously" describes the effect on the complainant in retrospective terms, raising the issue of whether the harassment must actually affect the complainant's psychological

---

[54]B.L. Schlei & P. Grossman, Employment Discrimination Law 410–17 (2d ed. 1983), Five-Year Supp. at 144.

[55]477 U.S. 57, 67, 40 FEP Cases 1822 (1986)(citing with approval *Rogers* and *Henson* on this interpretation of "hostile or abusive work environment").

[56]*Id.* at 67, 40 FEP Cases at 1827 ("mere utterance of an ethnic or racial epithet which engenders offensive feelings in an employee" not itself actionable). In *Meritor,* the Supreme Court expressly treated cases involving racial and sexual harassment as equivalent.

[57]Hallquist v. Max Fish Plumbing & Heating Co., 46 FEP Cases 1855, 1860 (D. Mass. 1987)("gender-related jokes and occasional teasing" relevant to motive for complainant's discharge but insufficient without more to establish claim for hostile environment), *aff'd,* 843 F.2d 18, 47 FEP Cases 323 (1st Cir. 1988). For a larger sample of conduct considered too trivial or isolated to be actionable, see cases cited in note 70 *infra.*

[58]*See generally* EEOC Policy Guidance on Sexual Harassment, *supra* note 41, at 405:6689.

[59]*See generally id.* at 405:6690–91.

[60]Ellison v. Brady, *supra* note 51, 924 F.2d at 878 n.8, 54 FEP Cases at 1352.

[61]805 F.2d 611, 42 FEP Cases 631 (6th Cir. 1986), reproduced in Chapter 2, Forms of Harassment (Krupansky & Milburn, JJ., with Keith, J., dissenting).

[62]*Id.* at 619, 42 FEP Cases at 637 (emphasis added). *See also* Brooms v. Regal Tube Co., 881 F.2d 412, 419, 50 FEP Cases 1499 (7th Cir. 1989); Highlander v. KFC Nat'l Mgmt. Co., 805 F.2d 644, 42 FEP Cases 654, 658 (6th Cir. 1986); Shrout v. Black Clawson Co., 689 F. Supp. 774, 46 FEP Cases 1339, 1344 (S.D. Ohio 1988); Jackson-Colley v. Army Corp of Engineers, 655 F. Supp. 122, 43 FEP Cases 617, 621 (E.D. Mich. 1987); Bennett v. New York City Dep't of Corrections, 705 F. Supp. 979, 49 FEP Cases 134, 140 (S.D.N.Y. 1989).

well-being or whether it is sufficient that the harassment reasonably could be expected to have that effect.[63]

B. Factors Determining Whether the Harassment Is Severe or Pervasive

Whether harassment is "severe or pervasive" is determined by "the totality of the circumstances."[64] The EEOC Guidelines point to such considerations as "the nature of the sexual advances and the context in which the alleged incidents occurred."[65]

The EEOC has identified several factors that affect whether a hostile environment exists: (1) whether the conduct was verbal or physical, or both; (2) how frequently it was repeated; (3) whether the conduct was hostile and patently offensive; (4) whether the alleged harasser was a co-worker or a supervisor; (5) whether others joined in perpetrating the harassment; and (6) whether the harassment was directed at more than one individual.[66]

1. Physical Conduct

Physical incidents may constitute actionable harassment even if they occur but once. In *Barrett v. Omaha National Bank,*[67] one incident was sufficient to constitute actionable harassment where the harasser talked to the complainant about sexual activities and touched her in an offensive manner while they were inside a vehicle from which she could not escape.[68]

---

[63]*Cf.* Henson v. City of Dundee, 682 F.2d 897, 29 FEP Cases 787, 794 (11th Cir. 1982), reproduced *supra* ("sufficiently severe and persistent to affect seriously the psychological well-being," which suggests complainant need not wait for harm). For a discussion of the split in authority regarding whether actual psychological harm must be proved, see Section VI.C.2. *infra.*

[64]29 C.F.R. §1604.11(b), quoted in note 5 *supra.*

[65]*Id.* The Eleventh Circuit addressed the importance of context in a case of racial harassment:

[A] hostile environment case is likely to consist of evidence of many or a very few acts or statements by the defendant which, taken together, constitute harassment. . . .

We stress also that the determination of whether the defendant's conduct is sufficiently "severe and pervasive" to constitute racial harassment does not turn solely on the number of incidents alleged by the plaintiff. . . . Thus, in order to determine whether a hostile environment is severe enough to adversely affect a reasonable employee, the law requires that the finder of fact examine not only the frequency of the incidents, but the gravity of the incidents as well.

Vance v. Southern Bell Tel. & Tel. Co., 863 F.2d 1503, 1510–11, 50 FEP Cases 742, 747 (11th Cir. 1989). For purposes of analysis, the Eleventh Circuit treated case analyses pertaining to racial and sexual harassment as the same, *id.* at 1510–15, 50 FEP Cases at 747–50.

[66]EEOC Policy Guidance on Sexual Harassment, 8 FAIR EMP. PRAC. MAN. (BNA) 405:6689 (March 19, 1990), reproduced in Appendix 3. The district court in *Ross v. Double Diamond,* 672 F. Supp. 261, 270–71, 45 FEP Cases 313, 320 (N.D. Tex. 1987)(citations omitted), identified a similar list of factors:

First, a court should consider the nature of the unwelcome sexual acts or words. Generally, unwelcome touching is more offensive than unwelcome verbal abuse. However, this is only a generalization and in specific situations the type language used may be more offensive than a type of physical touching. Second, a court should consider the frequency of the offensive encounters. It is less likely that a hostile work environment exists when, for instance, the offensive encounters occur once every year than if the encounters occur once every week. Third, the Court should consider the total number of days over which all of the offensive meetings occur. Lastly, the Court should consider the context in which the sexually harassing conduct occurred. The Court emphasizes that none of these factors should be given more weight than the others. In addition, the nonexistence of one of these factors does not, in and of itself, prevent a Title VII claim as the trier of fact must consider the "totality of the circumstances."

[67]584 F. Supp. 22, 35 FEP Cases 585 (D. Neb. 1983), *aff'd,* 726 F.2d 424, 35 FEP Cases 593 (8th Cir. 1984).

[68]*Id.* at 30, 35 FEP Cases at 591. *See also* Jones v. Wesco Investments, 846 F.2d 1154, 46 FEP Cases 1431 (8th Cir. 1988)(kissing, touching, pinching, patting, putting hand under dress); Watts v. New York City Police Dep't, 54 FEP Cases 1131, 1136 (S.D.N.Y. 1989)(two sexual assaults enough: "Physical assaults of a sexual nature obviously constitute incidents that tend to satisfy this criterion of severity"); EEOC Dec.

The EEOC presumes that the unwelcome, intentional touching of "intimate body areas" is sufficiently offensive to alter the conditions of a working environment in violation of Title VII:

> More so than in the case of verbal advances or remarks, a single unwelcome physical advance can seriously poison the victim's working environment. If an employee's supervisor sexually touches that employee, the [EEOC] normally would find a violation. In such situations, it is the employer's burden to demonstrate that the unwelcome conduct was not sufficiently severe to create a hostile work environment.[69]

2. Frequency of Conduct

Unless the conduct is quite severe, a single incident or isolated incidents of offensive sexual conduct will not create an abusive environment. Thus, a hostile environment claim that does not involve "severe" conduct will require a showing of multiple instances of offensive conduct.[70]

83-1, 31 FEP Cases 1852, 1854–55 (1982)(violation found where harasser forcibly grabbed and kissed charging party while they were alone in store room); EEOC Dec. 84-3, 34 FEP Cases 1887, 1888, 1890 (1984)(violation found where harasser slid hand under complainant's skirt and squeezed her buttocks).

[69]EEOC Policy Guidance on Sexual Harassment, *supra* note 66, at 405:6691. *Cf.* Graham v. American Airlines, 53 FEP Cases 1390, 1396 (N.D. Okla. 1989)(certain instances of touching by *co-workers* not sufficiently severe or persistent to affect seriously complainant's psychological well-being).

[70]*E.g., D.C. Circuit:* Robinson v. Thornburgh, 54 FEP Cases 324, 326 (D.D.C. 1990)(no sexual harassment where deputy U.S. marshal asked out on dates by two co-workers, where she declined invitations and did not feel job would be threatened by declining them);

First Circuit: Chamberlin v. 101 Realty, 915 F.2d 777, 54 FEP Cases 101, 106 (1st Cir. 1990)(five mild "sexual advances" by supervisor, without more, insufficient); Morgan v. Massachusetts Gen. Hosp., 901 F.2d 186, 192–93, 53 FEP Cases 1780, 1785–86 (1st Cir. 1990)(conduct not severe or pervasive where homosexual co-worker engaged in bumping incident, "peeped" at complainant's "privates" in men's restroom, "hung around him a lot," and asked him to dance at Christmas party);

Second Circuit: Christoforou v. Ryder Truck Rental, 668 F. Supp. 294, 301, 51 FEP Cases 98, 104 (S.D.N.Y. 1987)(although level of behavior needed to create hostile environment "cannot be precisely defined," it is "clearly more abusive, pervasive and persistent" than three specific incidents of sexual harassment over a year-and-a-half period); Neville v. Taft Broadcasting Co., 42 FEP Cases 1314, 1317 (W.D.N.Y 1987)(one sexual advance, rebuffed by plaintiff, may establish prima facie case of "quid pro quo" harassment but is not severe enough to create hostile environment), *aff'd,* 857 F.2d 1461, 51 FEP Cases 1832 (2d Cir. 1987);

Third Circuit: Drinkwater v. Union Carbide Corp., 904 F.2d 853, 863, 56 FEP Cases 483 (3d Cir. 1990)(New Jersey FEP statute)(hostile environment claim must demonstrate "continuous period of harassment, and two comments do not create an atmosphere"); Reynolds v. Atlantic City Convention Center, 53 FEP Cases 1852, 1866 (D.N.J. 1990)(awarding summary judgment against hostile environment claim where evidence showed that, over two-year period, one male co-worker once shook his crotch at plaintiff and occasionally gave her "the finger," second co-worker once called her a "cunt," and third co-worker once called her a "douche bag cunt"), *aff'd mem.,* 925 F.2d 419, 54 FEP Cases 1560 (3d Cir. 1991); Freedman v. American Standard, 41 FEP Cases 471, 476 (D.N.J. 1986)(no hostile environment created by obscene message from co-workers and sexual solicitation by one co-worker);

Fourth Circuit: cf. Katz v. Dole, 709 F.2d 251, 256, 31 FEP Cases 1521 (4th Cir. 1983), reproduced in Chapter 7, Harassment by Co-Workers (plaintiff's claims "nontrivial");

Fifth Circuit: Sapp v. City of Warner Robins, 655 F. Supp. 1043, 1049, 43 FEP Cases 486 (M.D. Ga. 1987)(co-worker's single blatantly unwelcome sexual invitation that plaintiff travel out of state with him did not create abusive working environment);

Sixth Circuit: Highlander v. KFC Nat'l Mgmt. Co., *supra* note 62, 42 FEP Cases at 658 (while quid pro quo case may rest on single incident, "hostile environment claims are characterized by varied combinations and frequencies of hostile sexual exposures"); Hollis v. Fleetguard, Inc., 668 F. Supp. 631, 44 FEP Cases 1527, 1532–33 (M.D. Tenn. 1987)(co-worker's four requests, over four-month period, that complainant have sexual affair with him, followed by his avoidance of her, did not constitute hostile environment where he did not coerce, pressure, or abuse plaintiff after she rejected his advances); Vermett v. Hough, 627 F. Supp. 587, 606, 42 FEP Cases 1432 (W.D. Mich. 1986)("[a]busive environments consist of multiple, even though perhaps individually nonactionable, incidents of unwelcome sexual harassment");

Seventh Circuit: Scott v. Sears, Roebuck & Co., 798 F.2d 210, 214, 41 FEP Cases 805, 808 (7th Cir. 1986)(offensive comments and conduct of co-workers "too isolated and lacking the repetitive and debilitating

3. Hostility of Conduct

The inherent nature of the conduct is an obvious factor in gauging whether it was severe or pervasive enough to alter the conditions of employment. Unwelcome sexual conduct can range from well-intended romantic overtures to misogynist epithets or a physical assault. Some forms of unwelcome sexual conduct are so trivial that they are not actionable.[71] Obviously, the more hostile the activity is, the less pervasive it need be to be actionable.[72]

4. Whether the Harasser Is a Supervisor

The supervisory status of one who engages in unwelcome conduct bears on the effect that the behavior will have on the complainant. A supervisor's capacity to create a hostile environment for a subordinate is enhanced by the degree of authority conferred on the supervisor by the employer. Further, a supervisor may rely upon apparent authority to force a subordinate to endure a harassing environment for fear of retaliation.[73]

5. Whether Others Engaged in Harassment

A complainant's feeling of powerlessness is compounded if the complainant and other employees are subjected to harassment by more than one co-worker or supervisor.[74] An over-the-road truck driver proved a hostile environment by persuading the court that her "innermost privacy was intentionally assaulted" by the seemingly coordinated conduct of her co-workers.[75] The

---

effect necessary to maintain a hostile environment claim"); Sardigal v. St. Louis Nat'l Stockyards Co., 42 FEP Cases 497, 500 (S.D. Ill. 1986)(alleged incident in which plaintiff told by supervisor to remove her skirt and stand in leotards and hose "was a single event which by all evidence did not reoccur and did not constitute sexual harassment in violation of Title VII");

    Eighth Circuit: Moylan v. Maries County, 792 F.2d 746, 750, 40 FEP Cases 1788, 1790 (8th Cir. 1986)(single or isolated incidents of harassment not sufficient to establish violation; harassment must be "sustained and nontrivial"); Johnson v. Bunny Bread Co., 646 F.2d 1250, 1257, 25 FEP Cases 1326, 1332 (8th Cir. 1981)(merely casual, accidental, or sporadic offensive comments cannot sustain racial harassment claim); Cariddi v. Kansas City Chiefs Football Club, 568 F.2d 87, 88, 16 FEP Cases 462 (8th Cir. 1977)(same);

    Tenth Circuit: Wolf v. Burum, 1990 U.S. Dist. LEXIS 6700 (D. Kan. 1990)(manager's suggestion that complainant sit on his face was "opprobrious and vulgar" but "not an incident which pervades and poisons the work atmosphere");

    Federal Circuit: Downes v. FAA, 775 F.2d 288, 293, 39 FEP Cases 70, 74 (Fed. Cir. 1985)(no claim of sexual harassment for "each and every crude joke or sexually explicit remark on the job by employees, even supervisors"; pattern of offensive conduct must be proved).

    Iowa: Lynch v. City of Des Moines, 454 N.W.2d 827, 54 EPD ¶40,097 (Iowa 1990)(doubting that sexually hostile environment could be shown with "only one incident of sexual harassment").

    [71]Ferguson v. E.I. du Pont de Nemours & Co., 560 F. Supp. 1172, 1197–98, 31 FEP Cases 795, 813 (D. Del. 1983)("not every sexual innuendo or flirtation gives rise to an actionable wrong") and cases cited therein; see also cases cited in note 70 *supra.*

    [72]*See* Ellison v. Brady, 924 F.2d 872, 54 FEP Cases 1346 (9th Cir. 1991).

    [73]*See* Meritor Sav. Bank v. Vinson, *supra* note 55, 40 FEP Cases at 1831 (Marshall, J., dissenting)(in both quid pro quo and hostile environment cases "it is the authority vested in the supervisor by the employer that enables him to commit the wrong"); Rabidue v. Osceola Ref. Co., 805 F.2d 611, 42 FEP Cases 631, 642 (6th Cir. 1986), reproduced in Chapter 2, Forms of Harassment (Keith, J., dissenting)(same), *cert. denied,* 481 U.S. 1041 (1987).

    [74]*E.g.,* Waltman v. International Paper Co., 875 F.2d 468, 50 FEP Cases 179, 186–87 (5th Cir. 1989)(complainant raised issue of hostile environment with evidence that several different employees touched her in sexual manner and directed sexual comments toward her); Hunter v. Allis-Chalmers Corp., 797 F.2d 1417, 41 FEP Cases 721, 722 (7th Cir. 1986)(racial harassment complainant faced with graffiti, destruction of property, and derogatory notes by co-workers).

    [75]Llewellyn v. Celanese Corp., 693 F. Supp. 369, 380, 47 FEP Cases 993, 1001 (W.D.N.C. 1988).

conduct included exposing the complainant to nude male co-workers, threats of violence, removing the pin that connected her trailer to her tractor, verbal sexual advances and threats of harm if she reported them, grabbing her around the chest from behind, attempting to drag her into the sleeper compartment of a truck cab, placing a live snake on the floor of her cab, and forming the "37 Club," a group of 37 male drivers who bet on which man would be first to have sexual intercourse with the complainant.[76]

6. Harassment Directed at Others

Hostile conduct directed toward other members of the complainant's protected group (*e.g.,* women) may help determine the existence of a hostile environment.[77]

C. Standard for Determining Severe or Pervasive Conduct

The severity or pervasiveness of particular offensive conduct is a matter of perspective. Therefore, a threshold concern is the point of view one should adopt in evaluating the evidence.

1. Objective Standard

Courts and the EEOC agree that in determining whether harassment is sufficiently severe or pervasive to create a hostile environment, the harasser's

---

[76]*Id.* at 371–74, 47 FEP Cases at 994–97.

[77]*E.g., D.C. Circuit:* Vinson v. Taylor, 753 F.2d 141, 146, 36 FEP Cases 1423, 1427 (D.C. Cir.)(trial court erred in excluding testimony of other female employees: "Even a woman who was never herself the object of harassment might have a Title VII claim if she was forced to work in an atmosphere in which such harassment was pervasive"), *aff'd in part and rev'd in part sub nom.* Meritor Sav. Bank v. Vinson, 477 U.S. 57, 40 FEP Cases 1822 (1986), reproduced in Chapter 1, Overview; Broderick v. Ruder, 685 F. Supp. 1269, 1277, 46 FEP Cases 1272, 1280–81 (D.D.C. 1988), reproduced in Chapter 2, Forms of Harassment (general evidence of atmosphere and attitudes toward other women relevant);

Fourth Circuit: Delgado v. Lehman, 665 F. Supp. 460, 468, 43 FEP Cases 593, 599 (E.D. Va. 1987)(citing alleged harasser's treatment of other women in workplace); *but see* Ross v. Double Diamond, *supra* note 67, 45 FEP Cases at 322 (finding no hostile environment as to complainant Stoudenmire without expressly considering fact that Stoudenmire was personally aware of hostile environment that did exist as to her sister and co-worker, complainant Ross);

Fifth Circuit: Waltman v. International Paper Co., *supra* note 74, 875 F.2d at 477, 50 FEP Cases at 187 (trial court must consider sexual graffiti even if not directed at complainant); *contra id.* at 484, 50 FEP Cases at 192 (Jones, J., dissenting)(criticizing "gratuitous extension of an actionable claim to encompass harassment of which plaintiff was not even a target"); *cf.* Jones v. Flagship Int'l, 793 F.2d 714, 721 n.7, 41 FEP Cases 358, 363 (5th Cir. 1986)(incidents of sexual harassment reported by other females bear on plaintiff's claim only if incidents affected plaintiff's psychological well-being), *cert. denied,* 479 U.S. 1065 (1987);

Sixth Circuit: Shrout v. Black Clawson Co., *supra* note 62, 689 F. Supp. at 776, 46 FEP Cases at 1341 (citing incidents not involving complainant for conclusion that workplace atmosphere was "pervasively sexual"); Pease v. Alford Photo Indus., 667 F. Supp. 1188, 49 FEP Cases 497 (W.D. Tenn. 1987)(hostile environment created by owner's touching, rubbing, and fondling bodies of several women employees in workplace);

Seventh Circuit: EEOC v. Gurnee Inn Corp., 48 FEP Cases 871, 879 (N.D. Ill. 1988)(hostile environment created where complainant forced to observe sexual conduct in workplace and where she was unsuccessful in efforts to help employees under her avoid unwelcome sexual advances);

Eighth Circuit: Hall v. Gus Constr. Co., 842 F.2d 1010, 1015, 46 FEP Cases 573, 576 (8th Cir. 1988), reproduced in Chapter 2, Forms of Harassment (sexual harassment directed at employees other than plaintiff relevant to question of severity or pervasiveness);

Tenth Circuit: Hicks v. Gates Rubber Co., 833 F.2d 1406, 45 FEP Cases 608, 615 (10th Cir. 1987)(evidence of general atmosphere and treatment of other employees relevant to whether there was hostile environment). For a discussion of the admissibility of harassment directed at others, see Chapter 25, Evidence, Section VI. For a discussion of a claim based solely upon sexual messages and conduct directed at others, see Chapter 5, Claims by Third Parties, Sections IV. and V.

conduct should be evaluated from the objective standpoint of a "reasonable person." Courts have rejected a subjective standard by which a trier of fact would rely solely on whether a complainant genuinely found the level of harassment so severe or pervasive that she believed her work environment was altered. A wholly subjective standard would make the complainant the arbiter of acceptable workplace conduct. It would make employers guess at what conduct is acceptable and could yield inequitable results by making Title VII serve "as a vehicle for vindicating the petty slights suffered by the hypersensitive."[78] Thus, if the challenged conduct would not substantially affect the work environment of a reasonable person, no actionable sexual harassment has occurred. Under this standard, the trier of fact must "adopt the perspective of a reasonable person's reaction to a similar environment under similar or like circumstances."[79]

2. Dual Objective-Subjective Standard

Several courts, following the Sixth Circuit in *Rabidue,* have adopted a dual standard by which the fact-finder considers, in objective terms, the likely effect of the offensive conduct upon a reasonable person's ability to perform work and upon that person's well-being, and also considers, in subjective terms, the actual effect upon the particular complainant. The complainant by this standard must show not only that the work environment of a reasonable person in the same position would have been substantially affected, but that the complainant in fact suffered psychological injury.[80]

---

[78]Zabkowicz v. West Bend Co., 589 F. Supp. 780, 784, 35 FEP Cases 610, 613 (E.D. Wis. 1984), *aff'd in relevant part,* 789 F.2d 540, 40 FEP Cases 1171 (7th Cir. 1986). Some individual employees are far more sensitive to offensive comments and actions than others. *See, e.g.,* Ellison v. Brady, *supra* note 72, 54 FEP Cases at 1353 (referring to "idiosyncratic concerns of the rare hyper-sensitive employee"); Andrews v. City of Philadelphia, 895 F.2d 1469, 1483, 54 FEP Cases 184, 195 (3d Cir. 1990)(objective standard of severe or pervasive needed to protect employer from "hypersensitive" employee while removing discrimination that deprives women of "self-respecting employment").

[79]Highlander v. KFC Nat'l Mgmt. Co., *supra* note 62, 805 F.2d at 650, 42 FEP Cases at 658. *See, e.g.,* Graham v. American Airlines, 53 FEP Cases 1390, 1396 (N.D. Okla. 1989)(certain instances of touching by co-workers not sufficiently severe or persistent to affect seriously complainant's psychological well-being).

[80]*E.g., Second Circuit:* Koster v. Chase Manhattan Bank, 687 F. Supp. 848, 862, 46 FEP Cases 1436, 1448 (S.D.N.Y. 1988)(complainant must show actual offense and injury); *cf.* Christoforou v. Ryder Truck Rental, *supra* note 70 (plaintiff admitted that alleged harassment did not interfere with work);
Third Circuit: Andrews v. City of Philadelphia, *supra* note 78, 895 F.2d at 1482, 54 FEP Cases at 195 (plaintiff must show discrimination "injured this particular plaintiff" and would detrimentally affect reasonable person of same sex in that position);
Fourth Circuit: Paroline v. Unisys Corp., 879 F.2d 100, 105, 50 FEP Cases 306, 311 (4th Cir. 1989)(plaintiff must demonstrate "harassment interfered with her ability to perform her work or significantly affected her psychological well-being"), *vacated in part on other grounds,* 900 F.2d 27, 52 FEP Cases 845 (4th Cir. 1990); Smith v. Acme Spinning Co., 40 FEP Cases 1104, 1108 (W.D.N.C. 1986)(finding from plaintiff's own testimony that "even if the incident occurred, she neither regarded it as serious nor did it influence her decision to leave her job");
Sixth Circuit: Yates v. Avco Corp., 819 F.2d 630, 633, 43 FEP Cases 1595 (6th Cir. 1987)(plaintiff must show psychological injury); Rabidue v. Osceola Ref. Co., 805 F.2d 611, 620, 42 FEP Cases 631, 638 (6th Cir. 1986), reproduced in Chapter 2, Forms of Harassment (harassment must have seriously affected psychological well-being), *cert. denied,* 481 U.S. 1041 (1987);
Seventh Circuit: Dockter v. Rudolf Wolff Futures, 913 F.2d 456, 53 FEP Cases 1642, 1644 (7th Cir. 1990)(court should consider "likely effect of a defendant's conduct upon a reasonable person's ability to perform his or her work and upon his or her well-being, as well as the actual effect upon the particular plaintiff bringing the claim")(quoting Brooms v. Regal Tube Co., 881 F.2d 412, 419, 50 FEP Cases 1499, 1503 (7th Cir. 1989)); Scott v. Sears, Roebuck & Co., *supra* note 70 (demeaning conduct and sexual

The EEOC takes the position that no such additional showing of actual psychological harm is required,[81] a position that is consistent with, if not necessarily echoed by, the statements of several courts.[82]

3. The "Reasonable Woman" Standard

a. Relevance of gender-based differences in perception. There is some dispute concerning whether the reasonable person standard should consider what some presume to be gender-based differences in perception. In *Rabidue v. Osceola Refining Co.,*[83] a divided Sixth Circuit panel upheld a finding that no hostile environment had occurred in a workplace where a male supervisor called women "whores," "cunt," "pussy," and "tits," called plaintiff a "fat ass," and said of her that "all that bitch needs is a good lay."[84] The panel majority held that these remarks and the concurrent display in the workplace of pictures of nude or semi-nude women had only a "de minimis effect on the plaintiff's work environment when considered in the context of a society that condones and publicly features and commercially exploits open displays of written and pictorial erotica at the newsstands, on prime-time television, at the cinema, and in other public places."[85]

Critics of *Rabidue* accuse it of adopting the perspective of a "reasonable male" rather than that of a "reasonable victim":

> The traditional perspective [of the "reasonable person"] abounds with myths based on male perceptions that it is harmless kidding around, that women really welcome the sexual overtures, that "no" is really a coy way of saying "yes," and that women who complain, far from being reasonable, are overly sensitive or prudish or are too assertive and unable to get along with people. When courts allow these male myths to infect their measurement of a reasonable person, they bias the formulation of the standard itself and trivialize sexual harassment by assuming that the complained-of conduct is not really serious or harmful.
>
> This is precisely what happened in *Rabidue....*
>
> The district court and the majority of the court of appeals held that a reasonable person could not find this work environment offensive, because obscenities are merely annoying, and the posters could not have such impact on a person in a society where pornography is widely consumed, and displayed and condoned. Consumed, displayed, and condoned by whom, one must ask? It is painfully obvious that the court's assessment is based on a very male view of the world. It

---

stereotyping not sufficiently pervasive or psychologically debilitating that they affected complainant's ability to perform job).

[81]EEOC Policy Guidance on Sexual Harassment, *supra* note 66, at 405:6690 n.20.

[82]*See, e.g., Second Circuit:* Blesedell v. Mobil Oil Co., 708 F. Supp. 1408, 1418–19, 53 FEP Cases 391, 398 (S.D.N.Y. 1989)(whether hostile environment existed is based on reasonableness standard); Bennett v. New York City Dep't of Corrections, 705 F. Supp. 979, 987, 49 FEP Cases 134, 140 (S.D.N.Y. 1989)(lack of effect on job performance may affect avenues of compensation but does not bar claim where complainant has shown discriminatory hostility sufficiently pervasive to change work atmosphere);

Fifth Circuit: Bennett v. Corroon & Black Corp., 845 F.2d 104, 106, 46 FEP Cases 1329 (5th Cir. 1988)(cartoons of complainant in men's restroom rose to level of "pervasive severity" because "highly offensive"), *cert. denied,* 489 U.S. 1020 (1989).

[83]805 F.2d 611, 42 FEP Cases 631 (6th Cir. 1986), reproduced in Chapter 2, Forms of Harassment (Krupansky & Milburn, JJ., with Keith, J., dissenting).

[84]*Id.* at 624, 42 FEP Cases at 641 (Keith, J., dissenting).

[85]*Id.* at 622, 42 FEP Cases at 639. *Cf.* Walker v. Ford Motor Co., 684 F.2d 1355, 1359, 29 FEP Cases 1259 (11th Cir. 1982)(persistent use of terms such as "nigger-rigged," "dumb nigger," "black ass" sufficiently pervasive to create racially hostile environment, notwithstanding defendant's claim that terms were common usage in the South or not directed at plaintiff).

is largely men who make, purvey and condone misogynistic pornography. It is only by completely leaving women out of the reasonable person standard that a court could use this standard to hold that a work environment, repeatedly complained of by women workers as being harmful, degrading, disruptive of their ability to work and the source of extreme physical stress, was acceptable to the reasonable person . . . .[86]

Several courts, including another panel of the Sixth Circuit,[87] have held, in accord with the EEOC,[88] that the objective standard in a case of antifemale harassment ought to be based on the viewpoint of the reasonable woman.[89] In *Ellison v. Brady*,[90] the Ninth Circuit panel majority decided to "adopt the perspective of a reasonable woman primarily because . . . a sex-blind reasonable person standard tends to be male-biased and tends to systematically ignore the experiences of women."[91] The court explained:

> We realize that there is a broad range of viewpoints among women as a group, but we believe that many women share common concerns which men do not necessarily share. For example, because women are disproportionately victims of rape and sexual assault, women have a stronger incentive to be concerned with sexual behavior. Women who are victims of mild forms of sexual harassment may understandably worry whether a harasser's conduct is merely a prelude to violent sexual assault. Men, who are rarely victims of sexual assault, may view sexual conduct in a vacuum without a full appreciation of the social setting or the underlying threat of violence that a woman may perceive.[92]

Judge Albert Stephens argued in dissent:

> It is clear that the authors of the opinion intend a different result between the "reasonable woman" and the "reasonable man" in Title VII cases on the assumption that men do not have the same sensibilities as women. This is not necessarily true. A man's response to circumstances faced by women and their effect upon

---

[86]Finley, *A Break in the Silence: Including Women's Issues in a Torts Course,* 1 YALE J.L. & FEMINISM 41, 60–62 (1989). *See also* Note, *Perceptions of Harm: The Consent Defense in Sexual Harassment Cases,* 71 IOWA L. REV. 1109, 1123, 1130 n.139 (1986)("[*Rabidue*] court recognized that the environment was vulgar, and yet the court said the environment was not abusive enough to affect the female psyche. Perhaps what the court meant was that the average female should not be offended by hearing 'tits,' 'cunts,' or 'pussy.' Or perhaps, after all, what the court really meant was that the female psyche should be more like the male psyche").

[87]Yates v. Avco Corp., *supra* note 80, 819 F.2d at 637 n.2, 43 FEP Cases at 1600 (Martin, Wellford & Nelson, JJ.)("men and women are vulnerable in different ways and offended by different behavior").

[88]EEOC Policy Guidance on Sexual Harassment, 8 FAIR EMP. PRAC. MAN. (BNA) 405:6690 (March 19, 1990), reproduced in Appendix 3 ("consider the victim's perspective and not stereotyped notions of acceptable behavior").

[89]*E.g., Third Circuit:* Andrews v. City of Philadelphia, *supra* note 78, 54 FEP Cases at 197 (obscene language and pornography could be highly offensive to woman as creating professional barrier of sexual differentiation and abuse, although men may find actions "harmless and innocent");
    See also Fisher v. San Pedro Peninsula Hosp., 262 Cal. Rptr. 842, 852 n.7, 54 FEP Cases 584, 591 (Cal. Ct. App. 1989)(California FEP statute)(in hostile environment case reasonable employee is one of same sex as complainant); Department of Fair Empl. & Hous. v. Rosenberg, Cal. FEHC Dec. 90-09 (1990)(car saleswoman subjected to harassment by male car dealer who was "just joking" when he told complainant she would have to sleep with him, told complainant she should try to sell more cars by bending over to pick up pennies so men could look up her dress and "check out" her butt, told others that complainant was a "coke whore" who would "spread her legs" for cocaine, told customers in her presence that she was "trashy," and threw tennis balls into complainant's office when he did not "like" her); Department of Fair Empl. & Hous. v. Livermore Joe's, Inc., Cal. FEHC Dec. 90-07 (1990)(male restaurant management harassed female subordinate with such horseplay as slapping her buttocks, lifting her skirt with kitchen tongs, sticking loaf of French bread between her legs, inquiring whether complainant did it "dog style," and occasionally shaping hamburger meat in form of a penis and asking complainant, "Is this big enough?").

[90]*Supra* note 72.

[91]924 F.2d at 879, 54 FEP Cases at 1353.

[92]*Id.,* 54 FEP Cases at 1352–53 (citations omitted).

women can be and in given circumstances may be expected to be understood by men.[93]

b. Relevance of workplace cultural norms. Courts assessing harassment claims have differed on whether Title VII forbids only harassment that exceeds the bounds of current social acceptability, or forbids all harassment in the workplace, even if most people historically have tolerated it. Some courts hold that in determining whether an environment is hostile to a complainant, the court must consider prevailing workplace norms.[94] Other courts take a contrary view, giving no weight to current workplace practices.[95] Thus, where sexually crude language, pornography, and graffiti have been accepted in the workplace prior to the complainant's employment, courts are divided over whether the offensiveness of the conduct should be discounted on the basis that it reflects the traditional workplace "culture"—a group norm that, however, unpleasant, is not illegal.[96]

The *Rabidue* court evaluated the offensiveness of conduct on the basis of "the lexicon of obscenity that pervaded the environment of the workplace both before and after the plaintiff's introduction into its environs, coupled with the reasonable expectations of the plaintiff upon voluntarily entering that environment."[97] The court observed that in some work environments, " 'humor and language are rough hewn and vulgar. Sexual jokes, sexual conversations, and girlie magazines may abound. Title VII was not meant to—or can—change this.' "[98]

Similarly, in her dissent in *Waltman v. International Paper Co.,* Judge Edith Jones observed: "We have so little social consensus in sexual mores nowadays that, short of incidents involving unwanted physical contact, it is impossible generally to categorize unacceptable sexual etiquette. It is likewise impossible to eradicate sexual conduct from the workplace—without unthinkable intrusiveness."[99]

---

[93]*Id.* at 884, 54 FEP Cases at 1357. For a further criticism of the reasonable woman standard, particularly insofar as it might justify government-imposed prohibitions that would discourage the use of constitutionally protected speech, see Browne, *Title VII as Censorship: Hostile-Environment Harassment and the First Amendment,* 52 OHIO ST. L.J. 481 (1991).

[94]See cases cited in notes 96, 100–105 *infra.*

[95]*See, e.g.,* Ellison v. Brady, 924 F.2d 872, 54 FEP Cases 1346, 1352 (9th Cir. 1991)(declining to examine harassment from perspective of "reasonable person" engaging in allegedly harassing conduct because that perspective "would run the risk of reinforcing the prevailing level of discrimination"); Wyerick v. Bayou Steel Corp., 887 F.2d 1271, 1275, 51 FEP Cases 491, 494 (5th Cir. 1989) (overturning summary judgment for defendant to extent trial court held plaintiff "was barred as a matter of law from maintaining a claim for hostile environment because her work atmosphere, as a whole, was heavily charged with sexual comments and gestures"); Arnold v. City of Seminole, 614 F. Supp. 853, 870, 40 FEP Cases 1539 (E.D. Okla. 1985)(Title VII requires employer to institute "educational efforts" to eliminate pervasive harassment). *See also* cases cited in note 108 *infra.*

[96]*Compare* Robinson v. Jacksonville Shipyards, 760 F. Supp. 1486, 1525–27 (M.D. Fla. 1991), reproduced in Chapter 2, Forms of Harassment ("social context" argument inconsistent with Title VII promise to open workplace to women) *and* Sparks v. Pilot Freight Carriers, 830 F.2d 1554, 1561 n.13, 45 FEP Cases 160, 165 (11th Cir. 1987), reproduced in Chapter 2, Forms of Harassment (whole point of sexual harassment claim is abusiveness in workplace of behavior arguably acceptable elsewhere) *with* Rabidue v. Osceola Ref. Co., 805 F.2d 611, 42 FEP Cases 631 (6th Cir. 1986), reproduced in Chapter 2, Forms of Harassment (use by co-worker of extremely vulgar language, which included referring to women as "cunts" and "pussies," held permissible given generally crude behavior of men at worksite), *cert. denied,* 481 U.S. 1041 (1987).

[97]*Supra* note 96, 805 F.2d at 620, 42 FEP Cases at 638.

[98]*Id.* at 620–21, 42 FEP Cases at 638 (quoting district court opinion of Judge Newblatt).

[99]875 F.2d 468, 484, 50 FEP Cases 179, 192 (5th Cir. 1989)(footnote omitted).

Courts have found no hostile environment at a chemical plant where sexually oriented dialogue was "customary plant language" and "no better or no worse than it had been before [the complainant] arrived,"[100] at a security trading house where coarse references to male and female genitalia and to sexual activity were "the language of this marketplace,"[101] at a patrol station where nearly everyone used profanity,[102] in a "back shop" environment "replete with sexual innuendo, joke telling and general vulgarity,"[103] and in a convention center work environment "permeated by profanity."[104] Similarly, where the complainant alleged several touching incidents by, and between, her male fellow janitors, the court dismissed the hostile environment claim with the observation that "the most we have is conduct not accepted in polite society."[105]

A critic of judicial reliance on historical workplace norms calls it a theory of "what is good for the gander is good for the goose."[106] Similarly critical is the EEOC, which contends that workplace culture only "rarely will be relevant."[107] By the EEOC's view, "In general, a woman does not forfeit her right to be free from sexual harassment by choosing to work in an atmosphere that has traditionally included vulgar, antifemale language."[108]

---

[100]Ukarish v. Magnesium Elektron, 31 FEP Cases 1315, 1321–22 (D.N.J. 1983)(female factory worker who continually engaged in sexual banter with male employees throughout workday, exchanging sexually oriented language and candid discussions of sexual exploits, failed to establish impact on condition of employment).

[101]Halpert v. Wertheim & Co., 27 FEP Cases 21, 23–24 (S.D.N.Y. 1980)(female securities trader failed to establish that she was subjected to harassment where evidence established that traders, including complainant, used coarse sexual language throughout trading day).

[102]Klink v. Ramsey County, 397 N.W.2d 894, 43 FEP Cases 1476, 1482 (Minn. Ct. App. 1986)(applying Title VII law in suit alleging violation of Minnesota FEP statute).

[103]Weinsheimer v. Rockwell Int'l Corp., 754 F. Supp. 1559, 54 FEP Cases 828, 829, 833 (M.D. Fla. 1990)(alleged requests by male co-worker that complainant "suck him" and "give him head" were "consistent with the general environment in the back shop" and not "sufficiently severe" to violate Title VII).

[104]Reynolds v. Atlantic City Convention Ctr., 53 FEP Cases 1852, 1866 (D.N.J. 1990)("we must discount the impact of these obscenities in an atmosphere otherwise pervaded by obscenity"; "gestures and remarks [in question] were not made in church").

[105]Collins v. Pfizer, Inc., 39 FEP Cases 1316, 1330 (D. Conn. 1985)(female porter assigned to clean restrooms, claiming co-workers "slapped her on the rear end" and encouraged her to "gra[b] the testicles of a supervisor," failed to establish hostile environment).

[106]Pollack, *Sexual Harassment: Women's Experience vs. Legal Definitions,* 13 HARV. WOMEN'S L.J. 35, 65 (1990)(characterizing majority's approach in *Rabidue v. Osceola Refining Co., supra* note 96). *See also* Abrams, *Gender Discrimination and the Transformation of Workplace Norms,* 42 VAND. L. REV. 1183, 1212 (1989); Ehrenreich, *Pluralist Myths and Powerless Men: The Ideology of Reasonableness in Sexual Harassment Law,* 99 YALE L.J. 1177, 1201–10 (1990); Strauss, *Sexist Speech in the Workplace,* 25 HARV. C.R.-C.L. L. REV. 1, 11–16 (1990); Note, *The Aftermath of Meritor: A Search for Standards in the Law of Sexual Harassment,* 98 YALE L.J. 1717, 1737–38 (1989)(standards must reflect "women's sensitivity").

[107]EEOC Policy Guidance on Sexual Harassment, *supra* note 88, at 405:6691.

[108]*Id.* at 405:6692.

See also Second Circuit: Bennett v. New York City Dep't of Corrections, 705 F. Supp. 979, 986, 49 FEP Cases 134, 139 (S.D.N.Y. 1989)(corrections officer raised factual issue of hostile environment by alleging coarse humor, obscene graffiti, sexual advances, and unwanted touching by co-workers; fact that prisons are coarse and rowdy "does not mean that anything goes"); Barbetta v. Chemlawn Servs. Corp., 669 F. Supp. 569, 573 & n.2, 44 FEP Cases 1563, 1566 (W.D.N.Y. 1987)(disagreeing with *Rabidue* in holding that pornography in workplace can help create hostile environment);

Fifth Circuit: Bennett v. Corroon & Black Corp., 845 F.2d 104, 106, 46 FEP Cases 1329 (5th Cir. 1988), *cert. denied,* 489 U.S. 1020 (1989);

Eleventh Circuit: Robinson v. Jacksonville Shipyards, 760 F. Supp. 1486, 1525–27 (M.D. Fla. 1991), reproduced in Chapter 2, Forms of Harassment (rejecting defendants' "social context" defense on basis that behavior "permissible in some settings . . . can be abusive in the workplace" (citing Sparks v. Pilot Freight Carriers, *supra* note 96)).

D. Proof of Severe or Pervasive Harassment

The heart of the hostile environment claim is proof that the incidents of harassment were "sufficiently severe or pervasive 'to alter the conditions of [the victim's] employment and create an abusive work environment.' "[109] This necessarily fact-intensive inquiry requires a balance between the complainant's right to be free from sexual offense and the fact that the law does not address every discomfort and trivial offense.[110] Findings concerning whether incidents of harassment occurred are reviewed only for clear error,[111] but a trial court's ultimate finding as to the existence of a hostile work environment is reviewed *de novo*.[112] Some courts have indicated that whether a hostile environment has existed in a given case will rarely be resolved by summary judgment.[113]

Courts have admitted evidence of other forms of discrimination, such as racial discrimination, in determining whether workplace incidents have been sufficiently severe or pervasive to create a hostile environment. In *Hicks v. Gates Rubber Co.,*[114] where a black woman alleged race and sex discrimination, the Tenth Circuit affirmed findings of no quid pro quo sexual harassment and no *racially* hostile environment, but remanded for the trial court to determine whether there was a *sexually* hostile working environment. The trial court was to consider not only the overtly sexual conduct directed at the complainant, but also (1) sexual conduct directed at other female employees;[115] (2) acts that were not overtly sexual but that represented sex-based disparate treatment harassment; and (3) incidents of *racial* harassment that may, combined with the sexually harassing conduct, have contributed to pervasive harassment.[116]

E. Unreasonable Interference With Work

In some cases a hostile environment may affect more than merely the psychological conditions of work. The EEOC Guidelines expressly endorse the theory that sexual harassment is actionable whenever it unreasonably interferes

---

[109]Meritor Sav. Bank v. Vinson, 477 U.S. 57, 67, 40 FEP Cases 1822, 1827 (1986), reproduced in Chapter 1, Overview (quoting from Henson v. City of Dundee, 682 F.2d 897, 904, 29 FEP Cases 787 (11th Cir. 1982)).

[110]*See, e.g.,* Bundy v. Jackson, 641 F.2d 934, 943 n.9, 24 FEP Cases 1155, 1160 (D.C. Cir. 1981).

[111]EEOC v. Hacienda Hotel, 881 F.2d 1504, 1515, 50 FEP Cases 877, 885 (9th Cir. 1989); Brooms v. Regal Tube Co., 881 F.2d 412, 420, 50 FEP Cases 1499, 1503 (7th Cir. 1989); Swentek v. USAir, 830 F.2d 552, 556, 44 FEP Cases 1808 (4th Cir. 1987).

[112]Brooms v. Regal Tube Co., *supra* note 111; *accord* EEOC v. Hacienda Hotel, *supra* note 111; Jordan v. Clark, 847 F.2d 1368, 1375 n.7, 46 FEP Cases 1558, 1563 (9th Cir. 1988), *cert. denied,* 109 S.Ct. 786 (1989).

[113]*Compare* Blesedell v. Mobil Oil Co., 708 F. Supp. 1408, 1418–19, 53 FEP Cases 391 (S.D.N.Y. 1989)(question whether reasonable person's work performance or psychological well-being would have been adversely affected "must be answered on a full record and upon evaluation of live testimony") *with* Reynolds v. Atlantic City Convention Center, 53 FEP Cases 1852, 1865–66 (D.N.J. 1990)(consideration of effect on "reasonable person" is threshold matter susceptible to summary judgment) *and* Bennett v. New York City Dep't of Corrections, *supra* note 108 (denying defendant's summary judgment motion despite incidents of "little probative value," because finder of fact drawing all reasonable inferences in complainant's favor could find "a pattern of something beyond the occasional crude joke, trivial remark, or accidental slip of the tongue").

[114]833 F.2d 1406, 45 FEP Cases 608 (10th Cir. 1987).

[115]For cases citing harassment directed at persons other than the complainant, see Section VI.C.6. *supra.*

[116]*Supra* note 114, 833 F.2d at 1414, 45 FEP Cases at 615–16. On remand, the district court, affirmed by the Tenth Circuit on appeal, found that there were only "a few isolated incidents of racial enmity" and found that evidence of racial and sexual harassment, even though aggregated, did not create a hostile work environment." See 928 F.2d 966, 972–73 (10th Cir. 1991).

with "work performance."[117] Under this theory, the employer who is responsible for that unreasonable interference with work is also responsible for the direct consequences of the interference when these consequences take the form of an adverse employment decision that is based on the complainant's absenteeism or other work-performance problems that the complainant can trace to a sexually hostile environment.[118]

VII. THE CAUSAL CONNECTION: ON THE BASIS OF SEX

A. Harassment Based on Sex

To establish a hostile environment claim, the complainant must show that "but for the fact of her sex, she would not have been the object of harassment."[119] Whether unwelcome conduct is obviously because of the complainant's sex will depend upon whether the situation involves (1) sexual advances, (2) gender-based animosity, or (3) a sexually charged workplace.

1. Sexual Advances

Judge Robert Vance, in *Henson v. City of Dundee,* observed that a hostile environment consisting of unwelcome sexual advances "does not present a factual question of intentional discrimination which is at all elusive. Except in the exceedingly atypical case of a bisexual supervisor, it should be clear that sexual harassment is discrimination based upon sex."[120] The *Henson* court thus observed that proof of unwelcome sexual advances goes well beyond the ordinary "disparate treatment" evidence, such as evidence that the employer treats some people less favorably than similarly situated people of the opposite sex;[121] proof of this sexual conduct generally is enough to show the complainant's proof of intent to discriminate on the basis of sex.[122]

2. Gender-Based Animosity

Many varieties of sex-based hostile conduct are, like sexual advances and gender baiting, obviously on the basis of sex.[123] Misogynist epithets are an example. In *Reynolds v. Atlantic City Convention Center,* "but for the fact

---

[117]29 C.F.R. §1604.11(a)(3), quoted in text accompanying note 1 *supra.*

[118]See Section X.B. *infra.*

[119]Henson v. City of Dundee, 682 F.2d 897, 904, 29 FEP Cases 787 (11th Cir. 1982), reproduced *supra.*

[120]*Id.* at 905 n.11, 29 FEP Cases at 794. For a discussion of the "bisexual harasser defense," see Chapter 3, Quid Pro Quo Harassment, Section VII.A.3.

[121]International Bhd. of Teamsters v. United States, 431 U.S. 324, 335 n.15, 14 FEP Cases 1514 (1977).

[122]*See* Walker v. Ford Motor Co., 684 F.2d 1355, 1358–59, 29 FEP Cases 1259, 1261–62 (11th Cir. 1982)(affirming trial court's rejection of argument that racial comments such as "black ass" and "nigger-rigged" were not intended to carry racial overtones). *See also* Zabkowicz v. West Bend Co., 589 F. Supp. 780, 784, 35 FEP Cases 610, 613 (E.D. Wis. 1984)(rejecting defense that harassing conduct was not on basis of sex where sexually offensive conduct "would have failed entirely in its crude purpose had the plaintiff been a man"), *aff'd in relevant part,* 789 F.2d 540, 40 FEP Cases 1171 (7th Cir. 1986). The sexuality of conduct, however, does not always mean that the conduct is based on gender. See cases cited in notes 128–29 *infra.*

[123]*See, e.g.,* Hall v. Gus Constr. Co., 842 F.2d 1010, 46 FEP Cases 573 (8th Cir. 1988), reproduced in Chapter 2, Forms of Harassment ("Cavern Cunt," "Blonde Bitch"); Rabidue v. Osceola Ref. Co., 805 F.2d 611, 42 FEP Cases 631 (6th Cir. 1986), reproduced in Chapter 2, Forms of Harassment ("bitch," "whores," "cunt," "pussy," "tits"); Zabkowicz v. West Bend Co., *supra* note 122 ("slut," "bitch," "fucking cunt").

that plaintiff is a woman she would not have been called 'cunt' or 'douche bag cunt.' "[124]

In cases of nonsexual hazing based on sex, the hostile treatment is not explicitly sexual in nature, and the employer may contend that the hostility is explained by the complainant's own personality,[125] or that women and men alike received the same hostile treatment.[126] It is in these hazing cases that the question of intentional discrimination becomes elusive and that circumstantial evidence therefore becomes necessary. In these cases, courts may use a burden-shifting framework featuring a prima facie case, employer rebuttal, and the plaintiff's proof of pretext, as they do in traditional disparate treatment cases, to determine if the harassment is because of the complainant's gender. In *Cline v. General Electric Capital Auto Lease*,[127] the alleged harasser was generally abusive to subordinates of both sexes and of various racial and ethnic backgrounds. The employer argued that this rough treatment simply reflected the harasser's "mother hen" personality and was for the good of his department, but Judge Brian B. Duff found that explanation insufficient because the harassment of women, which included yelling and pinching, was disproportionate, both quantitatively and qualitatively. Judge Duff thus concluded that the harassment of the complainant was because of her gender.[128]

3. Sexually Charged Workplace

In a sexually charged workplace, if the conduct is directed at the complainant or at other women in the workplace, the complainant ordinarily can show without great difficulty that the conduct was on the basis of sex. A special problem arises where sexually explicit material, such as pornographic pictures or graffiti, is directed at no individual in particular, and was an accepted part of the workplace prior to the complainant's arrival. The complainant may then attempt to establish the "because of sex" element by showing that the activity

---

[124]*Supra* note 104, 53 FEP Cases at 1864–65. *See also* Danna v. New York Telephone Co., 54 FEP Cases 1638, 1651 (S.D.N.Y. 1990)(complainant's workplace poisoned because of her sex where she was daily forced to confront pictures such as those depicting her as engaged in oral and anal sex).

[125]*See, e.g.,* Fekete v. United States Steel Corp., 353 F. Supp. 1177, 1186 (W.D. Pa. 1973)(no Title VII violation where "individual is harassed occasionally because he is unconventional and unduly sensitive or a hypochondriac, or because he does not have a sense of humor." *See also* Goluszek v. Smith, 697 F. Supp. 1452, 48 FEP Cases 317 (N.D. Ill. 1988)(antifemale sexual banter not actionable in claim by male plaintiff).

[126]*See, e.g., Second Circuit:* Sheehan v. Purolator, Inc., 839 F.2d 99, 105, 49 FEP Cases 1000, 1006 (2d Cir.)(affirming judgment against hostile environment claim where supervisor's "temper was manifested indiscriminately toward men and women, even his superiors"), *cert. denied,* 488 U.S. 891 (1988);

Fourth Circuit: Walker v. Sullair Corp., 736 F. Supp. 94, 99, 52 FEP Cases 1313, 1317 (W.D.N.C. 1990)(where alleged harasser "treat[ed] both male and female employees with contempt," "harassment was not of sexual origin");

Fifth Circuit: Jackson-Colley v. Army Corps of Engineers, 655 F. Supp. 122, 127, 43 FEP Cases 617, 621–22 (E.D. Mich. 1987)(supervisor "swore and cursed in front of all employees, male and female");

Seventh Circuit: Cline v. G.E. Credit Auto Lease, 54 FEP Cases 419, 424 (N.D. Ill. 1990)(prima facie case made out because complainant showed "harsh treatment she received was qualitatively different from the treatment received by men in her department");

Tenth Circuit: Hicks v. Gates Rubber Co., 928 F.2d 966 (10th Cir. 1991)(affirming finding that no harassment based on sex was shown where supervisor patted bottoms of both male and female security guards).

[127]55 FEP Cases 498 (N.D. Ill. 1991).

[128]*Id.* at 505–16. The abusive behavior included calling the complainant, Phyllis Cline, "Filly," and then, when she complained about that nickname, telling the staff to call her "Syphilis, the gift that keeps on giving." *Id.* at 500. *See generally* Hall v. Gus Constr. Co., 842 F.2d 1010, 46 FEP Cases 573 (8th Cir. 1988)(rejecting employer's argument that nicknaming a female co-worker "Herpes" was not harassment based on her gender).

by its nature is demeaning to members of one sex and is permitted to continue despite their protests. This evidence implies an intent to discriminate on the basis of sex. Alternatively, the evidence may be analyzed as reflecting an employer policy or custom that has an adverse impact on one sex not justified by any business necessity.[129]

Where men and women alike have engaged in vulgar sexual comments and activities,[130] or where the conduct complained of is equally offensive to men and women,[131] the evidence may not support a finding of sex-based conduct. In *Weinsheimer v. Rockwell International*,[132] the complainant testified that a male co-worker would ask her to "suck him" or "give him head," point to her crotch and say "give me some of that stuff," request an "ice-cube job," and grab at her crotch and breast.[133] The court found that the complainant failed to show that the conduct complained of was based on sex, as opposed to "contentiousness and vulgarity" that was gender neutral: "In sum, the witnesses ... attributed the bulk of the back shop's problems, and [complainant's] in particular, to general causes that were not sexually motivated."[134]

4. Hostile Environment Claims by Men

In *Goluszek v. Smith*,[135] the court held that sexually oriented harassment of a male by other males in a male-dominated environment was not because of sex, because the harassment did not "treat[] males as inferior." The plaintiff was a sexually inexperienced male who "blushes easily" and who had never lived anywhere but in his mother's home. His work as a maintenance mechanic brought him into contact with machine operators who belonged to the Teamsters union. Although, or perhaps because, the plaintiff was "abnormally sensitive" to sexual comments, his male co-workers repeatedly questioned his manhood—offering to get him "fucked," asking if he had gotten any oral sex or "pussy," and suggesting that he "get some of that soft pink smelly stuff that's between the legs of women." The shop routine also featured poking the plaintiff in the buttocks with a stick and discussions about "butt fucking in the ass."[136] The plaintiff's employer scoffed at or ignored his complaints about this offensive conduct. Judge Ann Williams found that a woman in the plain-

---

[129]Robinson v. Jacksonville Shipyards, 760 F. Supp. 1486, 1522–23 (M.D. Fla. 1991), reproduced in Chapter 2, Forms of Harassment (suggesting "because of sex" element might be shown by adverse impact analysis in that demeaning pin-ups may constitute barrier of women's entry into workplace).

[130]*E.g.*, Halpert v. Wertheim & Co., 27 FEP Cases 21, 23–24 (S.D.N.Y. 1980)(female securities trader failed to establish she was subjected to harassment where traders, including complainant, used coarse sexual language throughout trading day).

[131]*E.g.*, Fair v. Guiding Eyes for the Blind, 742 F. Supp. 151 (S.D.N.Y. 1990)(rejecting hostile environment claim based on homosexual discussion by male supervisor that would be equally offensive to both sexes). *See also* Vaughn v. Pool Offshore Co., 683 F.2d 922, 925 (5th Cir. 1982)(black employee subjected to rude pranks not singled out because of race, because "obnoxious treatment" was shared with other employees); Bradford v. Sloan Paper Co., 383 F. Supp. 1157 (N.D. Ala. 1974)(both white and black employees felt they were overworked and harassed).

[132]754 F. Supp. 1559, 54 FEP Cases 828, 832 (M.D. Fla. 1990).

[133]*Id.* at 1561 & n.4, 54 FEP Cases at 829.

[134]*Id.* at 1565, 54 FEP Cases at 833.

[135]*Supra* note 125.

[136]*Id.* at 1544, 48 FEP Cases at 318.

tiff's situation would have been subjected to pervasive harassment.[137] Nonetheless, the plaintiff, as a male, had no claim because

> the defendant's conduct was not the type of conduct Congress intended to sanction when it enacted Title VII. . . . The discrimination Congress was concerned about when it enacted Title VII is one stemming from an imbalance of power and an abuse of that imbalance by the powerful which results in discrimination against a discrete and vulnerable group. . . . The "sexual harassment" that is actionable under Title VII "is the exploitation of a powerful position to impose sexual demands or pressures on an unwilling but less powerful person." . . . In effect, the offender is saying by words or actions that the victim is inferior because of the victim's sex. . . .
>
> . . . [Plaintiff] was a male in a male-dominated environment. . . . The argument that [plaintiff] worked in an environment that treated males as inferior consequently is not supported by the record. In fact, [plaintiff] may have been harassed "because" he is a male, but that harassment was not of a kind which created an antimale environment in the workplace. . . . A wooden application of the verbal formulations created by the courts would salvage [plaintiff's] sexual-harassment claim. The court, however, chooses instead to adopt a reading of Title VII consistent with the underlying concerns of Congress . . . .[138]

B. Harassment Based on Sexual Orientation or Transsexualism

1. Sexual Orientation

Employment discrimination against homosexuals is a widespread phenomenon[139] that may conceptually resemble discrimination on the basis of gender.[140] Nonetheless, both the EEOC[141] and courts have uniformly held that Title VII's ban on sex discrimination does not prohibit employment discrimination because of an individual's sexual orientation.[142] Nor does Title VII protect "effeminate" males.[143]

---

[137]*Id.*

[138]*Id.* at 1544, 48 FEP Cases at 320 (citations omitted). *See also* Drinkwater v. Union Carbide Corp., 904 F.2d 853, 861 n.15, 56 FEP Cases 483 (3d Cir. 1990), quoted in note 23 *supra.* The *Goluszek* court did not address the possibility that the plaintiff had standing to assert a claim on the basis that he, although male, could proceed on a theory that he was injured by an antifemale work environment. For a discussion of a complainant's reliance on conduct offensive to others, see Chapter 5, Claims by Third Parties, Sections II.A. and IV. *See generally* Torrey, *Indirect Discrimination under Title VII: Expanding Male Standing to Sue for Injuries Received as a Result of Employment Discrimination Against Females,* 64 WASH. L. REV. 365 (1989).

[139]*See* M. SAGHIR & E. ROBINS, MALE AND FEMALE HOMOSEXUALITY: A COMPREHENSIVE INVESTIGATION 173, 311 (1973)(16% of gay men and 12% of lesbians in survey reported they were fired, asked to resign, or threatened with job loss because of their homosexuality); Levine, *Employment Discrimination Against Gay Men,* in HOMOSEXUALITY: AN INTERNATIONAL PERSPECTIVE 27 (J. Harry & M. Das eds. 1980)(nearly one-third of gay men in survey reported job discrimination); Levine & Leonard, *Discrimination Against Lesbians in the Workforce,* 9 SIGNS 700, 706 (1984)(approximately 25% of lesbians reported job discrimination); *see generally* Comment, *Challenging Sexual Preference Discrimination in Private Employment,* 41 OHIO ST. L.J. 501 (1982). It has been argued that "[h]omosexuals in our society have suffered from the extreme hatred and fear of the heterosexual majority. They have at various times been viewed as psychotic, immoral, and generally repulsive." Note, *Sexual Orientation Discrimination in the Wake of Bowers v. Hardwick,* 22 GA. L. REV. 773, 773–74 (1988)(footnotes omitted). For extensive citations to literature on discrimination on the basis of sexual orientation, see *Jantz v. Muci,* 759 F. Supp. 1543 (D. Kan. 1991).

[140]For a reference to a rejected argument in this respect, see text accompanying notes 144–45 *infra.*

[141]EEOC Dec. 76-75, 19 FEP Cases 1823 (1976)(charging party denied employment because he was admitted homosexual).

[142]B.L. SCHLEI & P. GROSSMAN, EMPLOYMENT DISCRIMINATION LAW 430 (2d ed. 1983), Five-Year Supp. at 157. *See also* Williamson v. A.G. Edwards & Sons, 876 F.2d 69, 70, 50 FEP Cases 95, 96 (8th Cir. 1989)(Title VII does not prohibit discrimination against homosexuals), *cert. denied,* 110 S.Ct. 1158 (1990).

[143]SCHLEI & GROSSMAN, *supra* note 142, at 430. *See also* Goluszek v. Smith, *supra* note 125, 697 F. Supp. at 1453, discussed in Section IV.A.3. *supra.*

Accordingly, if an employer harasses a homosexual employee solely because of the employee's sexual orientation, the employer does not thereby violate Title VII, for the harassment is not considered to be "because of sex." In *DeSantis v. Pacific Telephone & Telegraph Co.,*[144] the Ninth Circuit rejected the argument that discrimination against homosexuals was based on gender, in that males who chose male partners were adversely treated, whereas females who chose male partners were not. The court also rejected the argument that homosexual discrimination was unlawful because it had a disproportionate impact against men.[145]

Homosexual complainants are thus limited to whatever remedies they may have under federal and state constitutions,[146] the common law,[147] state statutes,[148] local ordinances,[149] and executive orders.[150]

On the other hand, if the harassment of an employee consists of homosexual advances, Title VII forbids the harassment without regard to the sexual orientation of the harassed employee. What is important for purposes of Title VII is that the homosexual harasser, because of sexual orientation, made the advances on the basis of the complainant's gender.[151]

---

[144]608 F.2d 327, 19 FEP Cases 1493 (9th Cir. 1979). *See also* Carreno v. Electrical Workers (IBEW) Local 226, 54 FEP Cases 81, 82–83 (D. Kan. 1990)(granting summary judgment against hostile environment claim because harassment not based on employee's sex: "undisputed facts indicate that the plaintiff was not harassed because he is a male, but rather because he is a homosexual male"). In *Carreno,* male electricians evinced their disapproval of their co-worker's homosexual lifestyle with physical assaults and terms such as "Mary" and "faggot." In rejecting the complainant's hostile environment claim, the court distinguished those cases that have found liability on the basis of homosexual harassment by noting that those cases were quid pro quo cases. A more fundamental distinction is that in the quid pro quo cases the homosexual harasser picks his victim because of the victim's sex, not the victim's sexual orientation.

[145]*Supra* note 144, 608 F.2d at 330–31. It has been estimated that homosexuals make up 4% to 5% of the adult male population. The percentage of female homosexuals is approximately half that of males. See W. POMER, HOMOSEXUALITY, THE SAME SEX: AN APPRAISAL OF HOMOSEXUALITY (1968).

[146]*See generally* Law, *Homosexuality and the Social Meaning of Gender,* 1988 WIS. L. REV. 187, 188 (1988); Gay Law Students Ass'n v. Pacific Tel. & Tel. Co., 24 Cal.3d 458, 474, 595 P.2d 592, 156 Cal. Rptr. 14, 24, 19 FEP Cases 1419, 1426 (1979)(privately owned public utility forbidden by state constitution from excluding class of homosexuals from employment opportunities); Jantz v. Muci, 759 F. Supp. 1543 (D. Kan. 1991)(equal protection claim by man who alleged he was denied job as high school athletics coach because principal believed he had homosexual orientation cognizable under 42 U.S.C. §1983). *Cf.* Padula v. Webster, 822 F.2d 97, 104, 44 FEP Cases 174, 179 (D.C. Cir. 1987)(FBI may discriminate based on homosexual conduct, if not on basis of homosexual status, in that this conduct is criminalized in roughly one-half of the states).

[147]Zaks v. American Broadcasting Co., 626 F. Supp. 695, 697, 121 LRRM 2624 (C.D. Cal. 1985)(assault and battery claim by complainant stabbed in back and arm and stuffed unconscious into closet by fellow workers because of his homosexuality).

[148]The District of Columbia and a few states, such as Hawaii, Massachusetts, and Wisconsin, prohibit employment discrimination on the basis of sexual orientation. See DAILY LAB. REP. (BNA) No. 72, A-17 (April 15, 1991). California has a statute, Labor Code §1102, which prohibits discrimination on the basis of political affiliation; it has been interpreted to protect homosexual status.

[149]*See, e.g.,* Rudow v. New York City Comm'n on Human Rights, 474 N.Y.S.2d 1005, 1014 n.11, 41 FEP Cases 1402, 1411 (1984), *aff'd,* 109 A.D.2d 1111, 487 N.Y.S.2d 453 (1st Dep't 1985)(executive order prohibits discrimination by any city agency on account of "sexual orientation or affectional preference in any matter of hiring or employment"); *see also* SANTA MONICA (Cal.) MUN. CODE §§4940(d)(1988)("compelling interest in eradicating discrimination based on . . . sexual orientation [or] (AIDS)").

[150]*See, e.g.,* Under 21 v. City of N.Y., 108 A.D.2d 250, 488 N.Y.S.2d 669, 671 (1985)(upholding executive order forbidding discrimination based on "sexual orientation or affectional preference"); Robinson v. Shapp, 23 Pa. Commw. 153, 350 A.2d 464 (1976), *aff'd,* 473 Pa. 315, 374 A.2d 533 (1977)(court refused to enjoin enforcement of similar executive order).

[151]See Chapter 3, Quid Pro Quo Harassment, Section VII.A.

2. Transsexualism

Courts uniformly have held that the prohibition against sex discrimination in Title VII does not protect individuals who undergo sex-change surgery or announce an intention to undergo sex-change surgery.[152]

Courts interpreting state discrimination statutes have reached the same result. The Iowa Supreme Court, concluding that discrimination against transsexuals is not sex discrimination, ruled against a transsexual who alleged that her employer excluded her from company restrooms and fired her because of her transsexualism.[153]

VIII. EMPLOYER RESPONSIBILITY

The Supreme Court in *Meritor* addressed the issue of employer liability in hostile environment cases but "declin[ed] the parties' invitation to issue a definitive rule."[154] The Court did resolve that employers are *not* automatically liable in hostile environment cases,[155] and that the liability of the employer should be determined based on agency principles.[156]

Lower courts have since confirmed that the employer may be liable for a hostile environment either indirectly under an agency theory or directly because of the employer's negligence in supervising the workplace. Whether the hostile environment is created by supervisors, co-workers, or nonemployees, the same general principles of employer liability will apply:[157] the employer will be liable for a sexually hostile environment if the employer (1) knew[158] or should

---

[152]SCHLEI & GROSSMAN, *supra* note 142, at 430, Five-Year Supp. at 157. Nor is transsexualism protected as a disability. Blackwell v. United States Dep't of Treasury, 830 F.2d 1183, 1183–84, 44 FEP Cases 1856, 1857 (D.C. Cir. 1987)(failure to hire transvestite not actionable under Rehabilitation Act even though transvestites may experience rejection in workplace as result of mental ailment made apparent by cross-dressing life-style); Sommers v. Iowa Civil Rights Comm'n, 337 N.W.2d 470, 47 FEP Cases 1217 (Iowa 1983)(Iowa FEP statute)(same). The Americans With Disabilities Act of 1990 specifically excludes transsexuals from its definition of disability. 42 U.S.C. §12211. Also expressly excluded as disabilities are homosexuality, bisexuality, transvestism, sexual behavior disorders, and "gender identity disorders not resulting from physical impairments." *Id.*

[153]Sommers v. Iowa Civil Rights Comm'n, *supra* note 152, 337 N.W.2d at 471, 474, 47 FEP Cases at 1218, 1220. Nor was the plaintiff's transsexualism considered a disability. *Id.* at 473, 47 FEP Cases at 1219. *But see* Richards v. United States Tennis Ass'n, 400 N.Y.S.2d 267, 272 (Sup. Ct. 1977)(requirement that transsexual tennis player submit to a sex-chromatin test to participate in tournament violated New York Human Rights Law).

[154]477 U.S. 57, 72, 40 FEP Cases 1822, 1829 (1986), reproduced in Chapter 1, Overview.

[155]*Id.*

[156]*Id.*

[157]For a discussion of employer liability for hostile environment harassment by supervisors, see Chapter 6; for a discussion of employer liability for co-worker harassment, see Chapter 7; for a discussion of employer liability for harassment by nonemployees, see Chapter 8.

[158]Actual knowledge is proved by evidence of firsthand observation, the victim's internal complaint to supervisors or managers, or a charge of discrimination. If the hostile environment was perpetuated or known to a supervisor, the supervisor's knowledge is imputed to the employer if the supervisor was an "agent" of the employer for that purpose, as defined by common law. EEOC Policy Guidance on Sexual Harassment, 8 FAIR EMP. PRAC. MAN. (BNA) 405:6696–97 (March 19, 1990), reproduced in Appendix 3.

have known of the alleged sexual harassment[159] and (2) failed to prevent the harassment[160] or take prompt and appropriate corrective action.[161]

An employer with notice of a hostile environment must promptly conduct a thorough investigation. A failure to investigate properly, or a failure to take appropriate corrective action at the conclusion of an investigation, can lead to liability.[162]

IX. EMPLOYER'S REBUTTAL

A. Disputing Elements of the Prima Facie Case

The employer may defend a hostile environment charge by disputing one of the elements of the prima facie case: that there were sex-based incidents, that the incidents were unwelcome, or that the incidents were sufficiently severe or pervasive to alter the conditions of the complainant's employment.

B. Articulating a Nondiscriminatory Reason

If the situation involves sexual advances, overt gender-baiting, or a sexually charged workplace, then the harassment is facially sex-based discrimination,[163] and no nondiscriminatory reason is likely to exist for the defendant's actions.

If the complained-of conduct is unrelated to any sexual activity, such as in a case of nonsexual hazing, then the employer may argue that the conduct was based on factors other than sex.[164] The employer may attempt to show, for example, that the conduct complained of was motivated by the complainant's

---

[159]Knowledge of sexual harassment may be imputed to the employer as a matter of law if it is openly practiced in the workplace or well-known among employees. *E.g.,* Lipsett v. University of P.R., 864 F.2d 881, 54 FEP Cases 230 (1st Cir. 1988)(employer liable where it should have known of concerted harassment of plaintiff and other female medical residents by more senior male residents); Hall v. Gus Constr. Co., 842 F.2d 1010, 46 FEP Cases 573 (8th Cir. 1988), reproduced in Chapter 2, Forms of Harassment (knowledge imputed to supervisor). The EEOC reasons that an employer should be presumed to know of sexual harassment if it has failed to establish a "reasonably available avenue by which victims of sexual harassment can make their complaints known to appropriate officials who are in a position to do something about these complaints." EEOC Policy Guidance on Sexual Harassment, *supra* note 158, at 405:6695.

[160]Employer liability is usually a matter of failing to correct harassment. In some cases, employer liability has been litigated on the basis that the employer should have foreseen sexual harassment and failed to take reasonable steps to prevent it. Paroline v. Unisys Corp., 879 F.2d 100, 50 FEP Cases 306, 312 (4th Cir. 1989), reproduced in Chapter 9, Constructive Discharge (court may impute liability, in certain circumstances, to employer who failed to take steps to *prevent* sexual harassment), *aff'd in part and vacated in part,* 900 F.2d 27, 52 FEP Cases 845 (4th Cir. 1980). *See also* CAL. GOVT. CODE §12940(h)(employer must "take all reasonable steps to prevent harassment from occurring"). For a discussion of this and other respects in which it is critical for an employer to have a written antiharassment policy, see Chapter 18, Taking Preventive Action.

[161]For an extended discussion of employer liability, see Chapters 6, Harassment by Supervisors, Section IV.; 7, Harassment by Co-Workers; and 8, Harassment by Nonemployees.

[162]For a further discussion of investigation and follow-up activities, see Chapter 19, Responding to Internal Complaints.

[163]*But see* Waltman v. International Paper Co., 875 F.2d 468, 50 FEP Cases 179, 194 (5th Cir. 1989)(Jones, J, dissenting)(questioning whether graffiti that "included male and female references" was discriminatory); Fair v. Guiding Eyes for the Blind, 742 F. Supp. 151 (S.D.N.Y. 1990)(homosexual discussion equally offensive to both sexes).

[164]See text accompanying note 16 *supra.*

personality,[164a] was directed indiscriminately against men and women,[165] or that men as well as women were offended by certain abusive conduct.[166]

C. Rebutting Employer Responsibility

The employer may also argue that it cannot be held legally responsible for the harassment because it neither knew nor should have known of the alleged misconduct or because upon learning of the misconduct the employer took prompt and effective remedial action.[167]

1. The Plaintiff's Failure to Use Effective Internal Grievance Procedures

a. Adequacy of policy. In *Meritor,* where the complainant had failed to report the alleged harassment through the internal grievance procedures, the Supreme Court "reject[ed] [the employer's] view that the mere existence of a grievance procedure and a policy against discrimination, coupled with [the complainant's] failure to invoke that procedure, must insulate [the employer] from liability."[168]

The mere existence or issuance of some policy does not show effective action.[169] In *Yates v. Avco Corp.,*[170] a company policy provided no defense: "Though the intent of this policy was commendable, the facts of the case demonstrate that not only was it vague on paper, it was vague and ad hoc in its implementation and did not function effectively to eliminate harassment in the Avco Nashville plants."[171] In *Robinson v. Jacksonville Shipyards,*[172] the employer's "model policy" was found insufficient because, among other things, it specified only one person to receive sexual harassment complaints, a person in whom the complainant reasonably lacked confidence, and the policy failed to identify any alternative avenue for complainants.[173]

b. Effect of adequate policy. The Supreme Court in *Meritor* stressed that such facts as an adequate policy against discrimination and a related grievance

---

[164a]*See* cases cited in note 193 *infra.*

[165]See cases cited in note 126 *supra.*

[166]*See* cases cited in note 163 *supra. But see* Wyerick v. Bayou Steel Corp., 887 F.2d 1271, 1274–75, 51 FEP Cases 491 (5th Cir. 1989)(rejecting argument that proof of hostile environment requires that sexual conduct was not equally offensive to men and women alike)(citing Bennett v. Corroon & Black Corp., 845 F.2d 104, 46 FEP Cases 1329 (5th Cir. 1988), *cert. denied,* 109 S.Ct. 1140 (1989)); Spencer v. General Elec. Co., 697 F. Supp. 204, 218 n.15, 51 FEP Cases 1696, 1707 (E.D. Va. 1988)(mere fact that male also offended by sexual harassment of females does not mean harassment not based on sex), *aff'd,* 894 F.2d 651, 51 FEP Cases 1725 (4th Cir. 1990).

[167]Guess v. Bethlehem Steel Corp., 913 F.2d 463, 53 FEP Cases 1547 (7th Cir. 1990)(standard is negligence, not *respondeat superior*); Swentek v. USAir, 830 F.2d 552, 44 FEP Cases 1808 (4th Cir. 1987)(test is whether employer had knowledge and took corrective action); Hall v. Gus Constr. Co., *supra* note 159 (co-worker harassment at construction site; foreman informed of and witnessed harassment and did not correct it).

[168]*Supra* note 154.

[169]For a discussion of what constitutes an adequate sexual harassment policy, see Chapter 18, Taking Preventive Action, Section II.

[170]819 F.2d 630, 43 FEP Cases 1595 (6th Cir. 1987).

[171]*Id.* at 635, 43 FEP Cases at 1599.

[172]760 F. Supp. 1486 (M.D. Fla. 1991), reproduced in Chapter 2, Forms of Harassment.

[173]*Id.* at 1510. *See also* EEOC v. Hacienda Hotel, 881 F.2d 1504, 50 FEP Cases 877, 886 (9th Cir. 1989)(unreasonable to require use of policy that did not specifically proscribe sexual harassment and whose internal procedures required initial resort to supervisor who engaged in or condoned harassment). The policy in *Meritor* itself had similar faults.

procedure "are plainly relevant" to employer liability in hostile environment cases, particularly where the procedures are well calculated "to encourage victims of harassment to come forward."[174]

Thus, although a complainant has no statutory obligation to use the employer's grievance system to report sexual harassment, the existence of an adequate internal grievance procedure can be decisive where a complainant has failed to invoke it. In that event, courts have found that the employer lacked notice of the sexual harassment, and therefore had no opportunity to take prompt corrective action.[175] A policy identifying persons to whom to report harassment will undermine a complainant's claim that complaints to co-workers were sufficient to impute knowledge to the employer.[176] An employer might also challenge the complainant's credibility on the basis of a failure to make any timely complaint about the alleged sexual harassment.[177]

2. The Employer's Prompt Corrective Action

a. Promptness of the employer's action. The EEOC Guidelines suggest that an employer with knowledge of sexual harassment must "immediate[ly]" take remedial measures.[178] In *Baker v. Weyerhaeuser Co.,*[179] the employer waited six months to discharge a known sexual harasser after the complainant's first reports of sexual harassment. The court held that the employer had failed to promptly remedy the hostile environment, and was thus liable.[180] In *Bennett v. Corroon & Black Corp.,*[181] the employer failed to act with sufficient promptness by waiting one day before removing "obscene" cartoons, depicting the complainant, from the men's restroom. The court concluded that the cartoons were so obviously offensive that the employer should have acted immediately rather than waiting for the complainant's reaction.[182]

---

[174]477 U.S. 57, 72–73, 40 FEP Cases 1822, 1829 (1986).

[175]*See, e.g.,* Kotcher v. Rosa & Sullivan Appliance Center, 53 FEP Cases 1148 (N.D.N.Y. 1990)(claim dismissed where employees knew of employer's grievance procedure but chose not to use it; once complaints made, employer took immediate action); Valdez v. Church's Fried Chicken, 683 F. Supp. 596, 47 FEP Cases 1155, 1169–70 (W.D. Tex. 1988)(existence of policy itself no defense, but Title VII claim against employer nonetheless dismissed because complainant failed to notify employer of harassment); Slate v. Kingsdown, Inc., 46 FEP Cases 1495, 1497 (M.D.N.C. 1987)(no employer liability where complainant never reported to management two assaults by her supervisor); Silverstein v. MetroPlex Communications, 678 F. Supp. 863, 46 FEP Cases 67 (S.D. Fla. 1988)(plaintiff failed to complain to anyone even though she had opportunity to do so, and harassment not so pervasive as to put employer on constructive notice); Collins v. Pfizer, Inc., 39 FEP Cases 1316, 1330 (D. Conn. 1985)(plaintiff never complained of alleged hostile environment). *See also* Waltman v. International Paper Co., *supra* note 163, 875 F.2d at 485–86, 50 FEP Cases at 194 (Jones, J., dissenting)(plaintiff's failure to employ grievance procedure should adversely affect her claim).

[176]Juarez v. Ameritech Mobile Communications, 53 FEP Cases 1722, 1726 (N.D. Ill. 1990)(because employer policy specified where employees were to file sexual harassment complaints, knowledge of accounts payable supervisor who had no apparent connection to human resources department did not constitute notice to employer itself).

[177]Monroe-Lord v. Hytche, 668 F. Supp. 979, 983–84 (D. Md. 1987)(plaintiff's testimony unworthy of credence because during seven years of employment she never filed grievance), *aff'd,* 854 F.2d 1317 (4th Cir. 1988).

[178]29 C.F.R. §1604.11(d)(cited in Lipsett v. University of P.R., 864 F.2d 881, 901 n.22, 54 FEP Cases 230 (1st Cir. 1988)).

[179]903 F.2d 1342, 52 FEP Cases 1872 (10th Cir. 1990).

[180]*Id.* at 1345, 52 FEP Cases at 1874–75. Indeed, the *Baker* court concluded that the employer "*did not* take corrective measures." *Id.* at 1346, 52 FEP Cases at 1875 (emphasis added). Presumably, the employer waited so long that its action was no longer "corrective."

[181]845 F.2d 104, 46 FEP Cases 1329 (5th Cir. 1988), *cert. denied,* 109 S.Ct. 1140 (1989).

[182]*Id.* at 106 (trial court's finding that employer took prompt corrective action clearly erroneous).

Conversely, in *Barrett v. Omaha National Bank,*[183] the employer avoided liability where it immediately investigated claims and, within four days of the report of improper harassment, reprimanded the alleged harassers, informed them that their conduct would not be tolerated, and told one of them that he would be fired for any further misconduct. Similarly, Judge Edith Jones, writing for the Fifth Circuit in *Dornhecker v. Malibu Grand Prix Corp.,* determined that "prompt" remedial action need not necessarily be "immediate."[184] In a case "[w]here the offending conduct spanned only two days to begin with," and where the employer told the complainant that the sexual harasser "would only work with her one-and-a-half more days," the Fifth Circuit found the employer's action to be prompt and reversed the district court's contrary finding under the "clearly erroneous" standard.[185] Judge Jones held that "prompt" is relative, depending on the severity and pervasiveness of the specific facts; the employer's promptness "may be assessed proportionately to the seriousness of the offense."[186]

b. Sufficiency of the employer's action. The employer's remedial action must be "appropriate" and " 'reasonably calculated' to end the harassment."[187] The appropriateness of the employer's action "will necessarily depend on the particular facts of the case—the severity and persistence of the harassment, and the effectiveness of any initial remedial steps."[188] Particularly important in assessing the sufficiency of the remedial action is whether the sexual harassment in fact ended without undue cost to the complainant.[189]

---

[183]726 F.2d 424, 35 FEP Cases 593 (8th Cir. 1984).

[184]828 F.2d 307, 309, 44 FEP Cases 1604, 1605 (5th Cir. 1987)("Since the demise of the institution of dueling, society has seldom provided instantaneous redress for dishonorable conduct").

[185]*Id.*

[186]*Id.* ("clownish and boorish" behavior over two days that did not include threats or proposition not sufficiently serious to require quicker response). *See also* Tunis v. Corning Glass Works, 54 EPD ¶40,170 (S.D.N.Y. 1990)(rejecting hostile environment claim of female process engineer based on posting pictures of nude women in sexually provocative poses, whistling and catcalls by co-workers, and prevalent use of gender-based language, *e.g.,* "tank man" instead of "tank person," where every complaint by complainant prompted swift remedial action).

[187]Waltman v. International Paper Co., 875 F.2d 468, 479, 50 FEP Cases 179, 188 (5th Cir. 1989)(quoting Jones v. Flagship Int'l, 793 F.2d 714, 719–20, 41 FEP Cases 358, 362–63 (5th Cir. 1986), *cert. denied,* 479 U.S. 1065 (1987)). *See also* Sanchez v. City of Miami Beach, 720 F. Supp. 974, 981, 55 FEP Cases 439 (S.D. Fla. 1989)(employer must do more than indicate existence of official policy against sexual harassment).

[188]Waltman v. International Paper Co., *supra* note 187. *E.g.,* Huddleston v. Roger Dean Chevrolet, 845 F.2d 900, 46 FEP Cases 1361 (11th Cir. 1988)(employer admonished alleged sexual harasser and threatened to fire him if incident was repeated; full investigation undertaken); Barrett v. Omaha Nat'l Bank, *supra* note 183 (employer undertook full investigation of alleged sexual harassment); Hunter v. Countryside Ass'n for the Handicapped, 723 F. Supp. 1277, 51 FEP Cases 344 (N.D. Ill. 1989)(employer placed alleged sexual harasser on unpaid leave while he stood trial on rape charges and persuaded him not to return to work after he was acquitted); Taylor v. Faculty-Student Ass'n, 40 FEP Cases 1292, 1294–95 (W.D.N.Y. 1986)(employer conducted "formal investigation with the assistance of legal counsel," arranged to transfer plaintiff to different department with same pay, and arranged for employee discussion and instruction on sexual harassment policy); *cf.* Hollis v. Fleetguard, Inc., 668 F. Supp. 631, 44 FEP Cases 1527 (M.D. Tenn. 1987)(employer's action, "albeit meager, was 'reasonably responsive to the employee's complaint,' " particularly where plaintiff declined to initiate investigation).

[189]Steele v. Offshore Shipbldg., 867 F.2d 1311, 1316, 49 FEP Cases 522, 526 (11th Cir. 1989)(employer not liable after it promptly issued reprimand and harassment stopped); Swentek v. USAir, 830 F.2d 552, 558, 44 FEP Cases 1808, 1813 (4th Cir. 1987)(after employer issued written warning, no more complaints received; warning was adequate remedial action); Brooms v. Regal Tube Co., 881 F.2d 412, 421, 50 FEP Cases 1499, 1505 (7th Cir. 1989)(employer held liable even though it made supervisor apologize to victim, postponed merit salary increase, and threatened supervisor with termination, because a few weeks after these actions harassment began anew).

Accordingly, the sufficiency of the employer's actions is a question of fact. In *Waltman v. International Paper Co.,*[190] where a co-worker made sexual comments regarding the complainant over the public address system, the employer told him to stop but did not reprimand him or record the incident in his personnel file. The employer reacted to the complainant's report of harassment first by transferring her to another shift, and then by having supervisors read the company policy against sexual harassment to the employees. Moreover, although the complainant allegedly did not seek an investigation of the purported harassment, the employer allegedly attempted to dissuade her from seeking an investigation. These allegations foreclosed a partial summary judgment for the employer on the issue of prompt remedial action.[191]

X. THE PLAINTIFF'S ULTIMATE PROOF OF CAUSATION

A. Proof of Pretext

The ultimate task of a complainant is to prove that harassment, attributable to an employer, was because of sex and adversely affected her employment. How a complainant approaches that task will depend on the evidence and on the employer's defense.

In cases of sexual advances, a complainant will have no need to present proof of pretext with respect to the creation of the hostile environment, because, absent a bisexual harasser, the issue of a sex-based motive will not be in controversy.[192]

A traditional pretext analysis may apply in a hazing case where the employer disputes that harassment occurred because of the complainant's sex. In cases involving friction between the complainant and other employees, for example, the employer may argue that the complainant's personality, rather than gender, caused the friction,[193] or that the harassment in question affected

---

[190]*Supra* note 187.

[191]*Id.* at 479–81, 50 FEP Cases at 188–89; *see also* Harrison v. Reed Rubber Co., 603 F. Supp. 1457, 1461, 37 FEP Cases 1545, 1548 (E.D. Mo. 1985)(remedial action insufficient where employer's instructions that alleged harasser stay away from plaintiff "were apparently based on productivity considerations and did not include directives to cease all sexual harassment," employer failed to monitor "whether all harassment ceased," and "harassment never finally ceased," forcing plaintiff to switch departments); Paroline v. Unisys Corp., 879 F.2d 100, 107, 50 FEP Cases 306, 312 (4th Cir. 1989), reproduced in Chapter 9, Constructive Discharge (reasonable fact-finder could infer from manager openly joking about sexual harassment complaints after ostensibly warning male employees not to engage in sexual harassment that employer did not really intend to take serious corrective action), *aff'd in part and rev'd in part,* 900 F.2d 27, 52 FEP Cases 845 (4th Cir. 1990).

[192]See Sections II. and VII.A.1. *supra.* Of course, if the complainant alleges that a job detriment has resulted directly from her reaction to sexual harassment, the complainant is making a quid pro quo or retaliation claim rather than a hostile environment claim. If the allegation is that a job detriment has resulted indirectly from a hostile environment, in that the hostile environment has interfered with work performance that in turn resulted in a job detriment, then the case may proceed as a hostile environment claim, as to which any proof of unlawful motive regarding the ultimate job decision would be unnecessary. See Section X.B. *infra.*

[193]*See* Huddleston v. Roger Dean Chevrolet, *supra* note 188, 845 F.2d at 902–3, 46 FEP Cases at 1362 (plaintiff told by general manager of car dealership that both she and chief sexual harasser would be fired if problems continued); Snell v. Suffolk County, 782 F.2d 1094, 1098, 39 FEP Cases 1590, 1592 (2d Cir. 1986)(corrections officer complaining of national origin harassment accused of trying to "make waves"); Bohen v. City of E. Chicago, 622 F. Supp. 1234, 1243, 39 FEP Cases 917, 923 (N.D. Ind. 1985)(victim of sexual harassment fired for being obstinate), *rev'd on other grounds,* 799 F.2d 1180, 41 FEP Cases 1108 (7th Cir. 1986). *See also* cases cited in note 125 *supra.*

men and women alike.[194] Here, because the employer disputes the gender-related basis of the conduct, proof of pretext is appropriate to show that the conduct was in fact on the basis of sex. In this kind of hostile environment case a burden-shifting analysis would apply just as it would in any case in which the sexual basis of the adverse treatment was disputed.[195]

Most cases, however, often contain too much sex-specific conduct to make the "personality clash" defense possible to sustain. In *Zabkowicz v. West Bend Co.,*[196] where the complainant's co-workers were exposing themselves, verbally abusing her, and making obscene gestures, a federal district court found that the harassing conduct was on the basis of sex notwithstanding the defense that this behavior merely reflected a "personality clash." Similarly, in *Morris v. American National Can Corp.,*[197] an employer was unsuccessful in arguing that the complainant had "antagonized" the co-workers who threw objects at her, sabotaged her work, made her the target of openly displayed sexual graffiti, and adorned her work station with replicas and pictures of penises, and obscene pictures and notes. In *Kyriazi v. Western Electric Co.,*[198] where the complainant alleged that sexual remarks, lewd gestures, and an obscene cartoon were directed at her—and the employer responded by challenging her ability to "get along" with others—a court concluded that she was simply a "strong-willed" woman who "refused to supinely accede to the male-female stereotyping which confronted her at [work]."[199]

B. Proof of Unreasonable Interference With Work

Even where the employer can prove that the immediate cause of an adverse employment decision was a nondiscriminatory business reason, such as poor work performance or excessive absenteeism, complainants have prevailed by adducing proof that the performance or attendance problems were themselves the result of a hostile environment.[200]

1. Interference With Job Performance

In *Weiss v. United States,*[201] where a Jewish plaintiff was debilitated by repeated slurs such as "Jew faggot" and "Christ-killer," the employer could not rely on the plaintiff's decreased performance as a basis for discharge because the decreased performance was itself the result of the employer's

---

[194]See cases cited in note 126 *supra.*

[195]See Sections II. and VII.A.2. *supra.*

[196]589 F. Supp. 780, 784, 35 FEP Cases 610, 613 (E.D. Wis. 1984), *aff'd in relevant part,* 789 F.2d 540, 40 FEP Cases 1171 (7th Cir. 1986).

[197]730 F. Supp. 1489, 1492–93, 52 FEP Cases 210, 213–14 (E.D. Mo. 1989).

[198]461 F. Supp. 894, 18 FEP Cases 924 (D.N.J. 1978), *vacated in part on other grounds,* 473 F. Supp. 786, 25 FEP Cases 86 (D.N.J. 1979), *aff'd,* 647 F.2d 388 (3d Cir. 1981).

[199]*Id.* at 925, 934, 18 FEP Cases at 947, 953. *But see* Weinsheimer v. Rockwell Int'l Corp., 754 F. Supp. 1559, 54 FEP Cases 828, 832–33 (M.D. Fla. 1990)(sexual comments were "gender-neutral, participated in by men and women alike").

[200]*See* 29 C.F.R. §1604.11(a)(3), reproduced in Appendix 1, discussed in Section VI.E. *supra.*

[201]595 F. Supp. 1050, 36 FEP Cases 1 (E.D. Va. 1984).

discriminatory behavior.[202] Several courts have reached analogous results in sexual harassment cases.[203]

Proof that the harassment actually caused the poor work performance will often be difficult because of the speculative nature of the proof. In *Bohen v. City of East Chicago*,[204] Judge Frank H. Easterbrook found that the complainant, although proving sexual harassment and disparate treatment, did not prove unlawful discrimination with regard to the reasons for her discharge:

> Now it might be that the department could not have fired Bohen for obstinate conduct if the sexual harassment were the cause of her attitude. I conclude, however, that it was not.... Bohen was in trouble in February 1980, only two months into her employment; ours is not the case of a mild-mannered person slowly driven mad by unwanted sexual attention. A conclusion that the sexual harassment caused the attitudes that led to Bohen's discharge would be pure speculation.[205]

2. Interference With Attendance

In *DeGrace v. Rumsfeld*,[206] a civilian firefighter received three threatening notes and found some of his equipment damaged after complaining to his supervisor of derogatory racial slurs by his co-workers. The plaintiff, who alleged that the threats caused him to fear reporting to work, was eventually discharged for excessive absenteeism. The First Circuit concluded that because the absenteeism resulted from racial harassment, it could not be said that the discharge was free of racial discrimination even if the ultimate decision-maker acted on legitimate reasons.

In an analogous sexual harassment case, the complainant may attempt to

---

[202]*Id.* at 1055, 36 FEP Cases at 4.

[203]Note, *The Aftermath of Meritor: A Search for Standards in the Law of Sexual Harassment,* 98 YALE L.J. 1717 (1989).

E.g., D.C. Circuit: Broderick v. Ruder, 685 F. Supp. 1269, 1280 n.10, 46 FEP Cases 1272, 1283 (D.D.C. 1988), reproduced in Chapter 2, Forms of Harassment, and cases cited therein (employer could not rely on tardiness and diminished work performance "directly attributable" to hostile environment);

Second Circuit: Carrero v. New York City Hous. Auth., 668 F. Supp. 196, 203 (S.D.N.Y. 1987)(sexual harassment of assistant building superintendent prevented her from receiving appropriate training and fair evaluation of her performance), *aff'd in part, rev'd in part, and remanded,* 890 F.2d 569, 51 FEP Cases 596 (2d Cir. 1989);

Fourth Circuit: Delgado v. Lehman, 665 F. Supp. 460, 467, 43 FEP Cases 593, 600 (E.D. Va. 1987)(employer, having created hostile environment, "cannot complain about plaintiff's diminished job performance");

Seventh Circuit: Bohen v. City of E. Chicago, *supra* note 193, 39 FEP Cases at 923 ("it might be that [employer] could not have fired [complainant] for obstinate conduct if the sexual harassment were the cause of her attitude"), *rev'd on other grounds,* 799 F.2d 1180, 41 FEP Cases 1108 (7th Cir. 1986);

See also EEOC v. Gurnee Inn Corp., 48 FEP Cases 871, 879–80 (N.D. Ill. 1988)(complainant fired for absenteeism really was constructively discharged because a sexually hostile environment caused stress that induced her to avoid work).

[204]*Supra* note 193.

[205]*Supra* note 193, 39 FEP Cases at 923 (N.D. Ind. 1985).

[206]614 F.2d 796, 804, 21 FEP Cases 1444, 1449 (1st Cir. 1980).

prove that the excessive absenteeism cited by the employer as the basis for its action was itself the result of sexual harassment,[207] or that the sexual harassment otherwise prevented the complainant from working.[208]

---

[207]A review of circuit court sexual harassment cases suggests that about a fourth of them have involved increased absenteeism after incidents of harassment.

E.g., First Circuit: Lipsett v. University of P.R., 864 F.2d 881, 890, 54 FEP Cases 230 (1st Cir. 1988)(complainant put on probation by defendant employer for leaving workplace without authorization after incident of harassment);

Third Circuit: Andrews v. City of Philadelphia, 895 F.2d 1469, 1474–75, 54 FEP Cases 184 (3d Cir. 1990)(complainant used up sick leave and vacation time after incident of harassment; plaintiff penalized for absenteeism in violation of mediation agreement); Craig v. Y&Y Snacks, 721 F.2d 77, 79, 33 FEP Cases 187 (3d Cir. 1983)(complainant terminated for failure to report to work for seeking medical care, although she returned the next day with doctor's note);

Fifth Circuit: Waltman v. International Paper Co., *supra* note 187, 875 F.2d at 472, 50 FEP Cases at 182 (complainant took two months of sick leave for recovery from severe debilitating depression caused by incidents of harassment); Jones v. Flagship Int'l, 793 F.2d 714, 716, 41 FEP Cases 358 (5th Cir. 1986)(complainant so distressed by harassment that she left job for two weeks, only agreeing to return on supervisor's promise harassment would not recur), *cert. denied,* 479 U.S. 1065 (1987);

Sixth Circuit: Wheeler v. Southland Corp., 875 F.2d 1246, 1248, 50 FEP Cases 86, 88 (6th Cir. 1989)(complainant used all sick leave and vacation time and did not return to work after incident of harassment); Highlander v. KFC Nat'l Mgmt. Co., 805 F.2d 644, 646, 42 FEP Cases 654, 656 (6th Cir. 1986)(complainant discharged for absenteeism);

Seventh Circuit: Swanson v. Elmhurst Chrysler-Plymouth, 882 F.2d 1235, 1237, 50 FEP Cases 1082, 1083 (7th Cir. 1989)(complainant discharged for absenteeism; court found that reason given for discharge was probably pretext);

Eighth Circuit: Barrett v. Omaha Nat'l Bank, 726 F.2d 424, 426–27, 35 FEP Cases 593 (8th Cir. 1984)(plaintiff took extended sick leave after receiving negative performance evaluation in retaliation for rebuffing sexual harassment);

Tenth Circuit: Hicks v. Gates Rubber Co., 833 F.2d 1406, 1410, 45 FEP Cases 608 (10th Cir. 1987)(plaintiff missed six days of work due to injury she alleged was caused by supervisor in retaliation for her complaints of sexual harassment).

[208]*See, e.g.,* Cline v. General Elec. Capital Auto Lease, 55 FEP Cases 498, 506 (N.D. Ill. 1991)(complainant medically disabled by harassment-induced stress was constructively discharged and entitled to back pay for period of her disability). *Cf.* Robinson v. Jacksonville Shipyards, 760 F. Supp. 1486 (M.D. Fla. 1991), reproduced in Chapter 2, Forms of Harassment (denying for failure of proof plaintiff's claim for sick leave because of absences caused by hostile environment).

CHAPTER 5

CLAIMS BY THIRD PARTIES

I. INTRODUCTION

While Title VII obviously protects persons who are the targets of quid pro quo or hostile environment harassment in employment, it is less clear whether Title VII also protects a person who is injured by sex-based conduct in the workplace that is directed at someone else or that is directed at no one in particular.[1] This difficult issue arises in two basic situations.

In the first situation, a heterosexual male employer hires, promotes, or otherwise favors his female lover, L, while passing over two better-qualified candidates—female X and male Y. Does either X or Y have a viable sex discrimination claim? Does it matter whether the employer's sexual advances to L were unwelcome[2] or welcome?[3]

In the second situation, female X or male Y objects to the employer's tolerance of a workplace that condones sexual advances, verbal sexual references, and the public display of pornographic pictures and graffiti, none of which is specifically directed at X or Y. Does either X or Y have a viable hostile environment claim? Does it matter whether others in the workplace find the conduct unwelcome[4] or welcome?[5]

The 1980 EEOC Guidelines endorsed third-party claims in general terms: "Where employment opportunities or benefits are granted because of an individual's submission to the employer's sexual advances or requests for sexual favors, the employer may be liable for unlawful sex discrimination against other persons who were qualified for but denied that employment opportunity or benefit."[6] The Guidelines do not consider the significance of (1) whether

---

[1]For secondary literature on this subject, see Shearer, *Paramour Claims Under Title VII*, 15 EMPL. REL. L.J. 57 (1989); Machlowitz & Machlowitz, *Preventing Sexual Harassment*, 73 A.B.A. J. 78 (Oct. 1987); Waks & Starr, *Sexual Harassment in the Workplace: The Scope of Employer Liability*, 7 EMPL. REL. L.J. 369, 382 (1981–82); Comment, *The Meaning of "Sex" in Title VII: Is Favoring an Employee Lover a Violation of the Act?*, 83 NW. U.L. REV. 612 (1989); Annot., *Nature and Burden of Proof in Title VII Action Alleging Favoritism in Promotion or Job Assignment Due to Sexual or Romantic Relationship Between Supervisor or Another*, 86 A.L.R. FED. 230 (1988).

[2]For a discussion of claims by X or Y relating to unwelcome advances to L, see Section II. *infra.*

[3]For a discussion of claims by X or Y relating to welcome sexual advances to L, see Section III. *infra.*

[4]For a discussion of claims by X or Y in the context of sexual harassment of their colleagues, see Section IV. *infra.*

[5]For a discussion of claims by X or Y in the context of widely accepted sexual conduct that X or Y finds offensive to observe, see Section V. *infra.*

[6]29 C.F.R. §1604.11(g), reproduced in Appendix 1. The EEOC's Guidelines are interpretive regulations that do not have the force of law but are entitled to appropriate deference. *See* City of Los Angeles Dep't

the favored employee's relationship with the supervisor was consensual or (2) the sexual orientation of the harasser and the sex of the complainants.

In January 1990 the EEOC issued a Policy Guidance on Employer Liability for Sexual Favoritism Under Title VII,[7] which elaborates upon the EEOC's view as to whether Title VII is violated under the circumstances described in the Guidelines. The Policy Guidance groups workplace sexual favoritism into three categories: (1) favoritism based upon coerced sexual conduct (quid pro quo harassment),[8] (2) isolated instances of favoritism toward a lover,[9] and (3) widespread favoritism (environmental harassment).[10]

This chapter addresses third-party claims in these three situations and also in a fourth situation: a sexually hostile environment not involving sexual favoritism.[11] The chapter is organized as follows:

	Effect on Complainant	
	Tangible Job Detriment	**Hostile Environment**
Unwelcome Conduct	Section II	Section IV
Consensual Conduct	Section III	Section V

II. THIRD-PARTY CLAIMS BASED ON UNDERLYING QUID PRO QUO HARASSMENT

A. Theories of the Third-Party Claim

The typical claim of quid pro quo sexual harassment is by a female who shows that she has been subjected to an adverse job action that would not have occurred "but for" her gender.[12] For example, a woman who is passed over for a promotion because she rebuffed her supervisor's sexual advances can characterize her claim as discrimination "because of . . . sex" under Title VII.[13]

The issue presented here arises where a woman is coerced into accepting her supervisor's unwelcome sexual advances and as a result secures some job benefit that is denied to some other employee. Under these circumstances, do disappointed competitors of the woman have a viable sex discrimination claim?

---

of Water & Power v. Manhart, 435 U.S. 702, 714 n.26, 17 FEP Cases 395, 401 (1978); General Elec. Co. v. Gilbert, 429 U.S. 125, 141, 13 FEP Cases 1657, 1664 (1976).

[7]Policy Guidance on Sexual Favoritism, 8 FAIR EMPL. PRAC. MAN. (BNA), 405:6817–21 (Jan. 12, 1990), reproduced in Appendix 2. Unlike the EEOC Guidelines, the Policy Guidance on Sexual Favoritism is an interpretive memorandum that was not issued pursuant to the notice and comment rulemaking provisions of the Administrative Procedure Act, 5 U.S.C. §553.

[8]Discussed in Section II. *infra.*

[9]Discussed in Section III. *infra.*

[10]Discussed in Section IV. *infra.*

[11]Discussed in Section V. *infra.*

[12]The elements of a prima facie case of quid pro quo sexual harassment are (1) the basis: membership in a protected group; (2) the activity: unwelcome conduct of a sexual nature; (3) the issue: tangible effects on a term, condition, or privilege of employment; (4) the causal connection: the activity was because of the basis, and the complainant's reaction to the activity affected a tangible aspect of term, condition, or privilege of employment; and (5) employer responsibility. *See* Henson v. City of Dundee, 682 F.2d 897, 904–5, 29 FEP Cases 787, 792–94 (11th Cir. 1982).

[13]For a detailed discussion of quid pro quo claims, see Chapter 3, Quid Pro Quo Harassment.

This claim, which the EEOC Guidelines endorse,[14] is the subject of extended discussion in the EEOC Policy Guide on Sexual Favoritism.[15] The EEOC describes two alternative theories in support of such a claim: (1) a disappointed female could claim that she was denied job benefits as an "implicit quid pro quo" that had become a general condition of employment, and (2) a disappointed female *or* male could advance a derivative claim on the basis of the unlawful sex-based coercion of the favored employee.

1. Submission as a General Condition of Employment

If an employee obtains a job benefit as a result of submitting to unwelcome sexual advances, other employees of the same sex who were qualified for but denied that benefit may be able to establish that exchanging sexual favors for job conditions was an implicit quid pro quo, a general condition of employment.

This theory of recovery is available only to members of the same sex as the favored employee. It applies when submission to sexual advances is an implicit condition of employment, a condition that, assuming the presence of heterosexual male decision-makers, disadvantages only women.[16] In support of this theory, the EEOC cites *Toscano v. Nimmo,*[17] in which Judge Walter K. Stapleton awarded judgment to a woman who was denied a promotion that was awarded to a female competitor. The court found that granting sexual favors to the male decision-maker, a self-described "life-long 'womanizer' " who had propositioned many female workers, was a condition for receiving the employment position in question. The favored employee's sexual encounter with the male decision-maker shortly before her promotion was evidence of this condition.[18]

The EEOC's *Toscano*-based theory is consistent with the view that Title VII forbids discrimination that is based on gender, not discrimination that is based solely on sexual cooperativeness. This EEOC theory provides that an employer does discriminate on the basis of gender when it implicitly requires that females, and only females, submit to sexual advances to receive job benefits. Thus understood, the *Toscano*-based theory is of limited practical utility. Proof of a general requirement of sexual submission is relatively rare.[19]

---

[14]See text accompanying note 6 *supra.*

[15]Policy Guidance on Sexual Favoritism, *supra* note 7, part B at 405:6818–19.

[16]*See generally* Barnes v. Costle, 561 F.2d 983, 989 n.49, 15 FEP Cases 345, 350 (D.C. Cir. 1977), reproduced in Chapter 1, Overview (female plaintiff must prove supervisor was heterosexual to prevail on claim that submission to sexual relations with supervisor was condition of employment that would not have been imposed on a male).

[17]570 F. Supp. 1197, 32 FEP Cases 1401 (D. Del. 1983).

[18]*Id.* at 1200–1202, 32 FEP Cases at 1404–5. The EEOC states that *Priest v. Rotary,* 634 F. Supp. 571, 40 FEP Cases 208 (N.D. Cal. 1986), and *Broderick v. Ruder,* 685 F. Supp. 1269, 46 FEP Cases 1272 (D.D.C. 1988), reproduced in Chapter 2, Forms of Harassment, are also "implicit quid pro quo" cases. Both cases involved allegations or evidence that females were advantaged or disadvantaged depending upon their reaction to sexual advances by a supervisor. The EEOC implies that *Spencer v. General Elec. Co.,* 697 F. Supp. 204, 51 FEP Cases 1696 (E.D. Va. 1988), *aff'd,* 894 F.2d 651, 51 FEP Cases 1725 (4th Cir. 1990), also supports a theory of "implicit quid pro quo" harassment. EEOC Policy Guidance on Sexual Favoritism, *supra* note 7, part C at 605:6821 n.14. *See also* EEOC v. Gurnee Inn Corp., 48 FEP Cases 871, 879 (N.D. Ill. 1988)(complainant Carolyn Brucci prevailed on hostile environment and constructive discharge claims with evidence that female employees who tolerated sexual advances complainant rebuffed were treated better than she).

[19]Policy Guidance on Sexual Favoritism, *supra* note 7, part B at 405:6818–19 ("Many times, a third party female will not be able to establish that sex was generally made a condition for the benefit in question").

2. Derivative Claim

In many quid pro quo cases, a supervisor limits unwelcome sexual advances to one woman in whom he is interested. Where he has extracted favors and conferred rewards as part of a sexual quid pro quo, the EEOC considers that both female and male co-workers who are better qualified for the benefit in question have "standing to challenge the favoritism on the basis that [each was] injured as a result of the discrimination leveled against the woman who was coerced."[20] This "derivative" theory of recovery is consistent with the EEOC's historical view of standing under Title VII,[21] and is supported by cases holding that any person injured by an unlawful employment practice, regardless of whether that person was the target of the practice, has standing to sue under Title VII.[22]

The EEOC's derivative standing theory has not been fully tested in the courts. The third-party standing cases cited in the Policy Guidance on Sexual Favoritism involve nonminority workers' assertions of *their own right* to be free from workplace discrimination.[23] None of the plaintiffs' claims in those cases was antithetical to the claims of the minority worker subject to the discrimination. In contrast, an employee who has gained favor by submitting to sexual advances would not seek to undo the job benefit received and might actually oppose the third party's lawsuit because of embarassment or because of concerns about the appropriate remedy.[24]

In further support of the EEOC's theory, however, is the argument that third-party standing might be particularly compelling in a case of sexual harassment and favoritism for the very reason that the direct victim of the sexual harassment, the favored employee, is not likely to be an effective plaintiff to redress the unlawful discrimination that has occurred.

---

[20]*Id.* at 405:6819 (footnotes omitted).

[21]"The EEOC interprets Title VII to afford standing to anyone protesting any form of alleged employer discrimination, on the theory that all employees have a right to work in an atmosphere free from unlawful employment practices." Allen v. American Home Foods, 644 F. Supp. 1553, 1557, 42 FEP Cases 407, 409 (N.D. Ind. 1986)(citing cases and EEOC decisions).

[22]The Policy Guidance on Sexual Favoritism, *supra* note 7, part B at 405:6819, cites examples of third-party standing cases: Clayton v. White Hall School Dist., 875 F.2d 676, 679–80, 49 FEP Cases 1618, 1621 (8th Cir. 1989)(white employee who lost employment benefit discriminatorily denied to black employees had standing to sue for hostile working environment because her "interest in a work environment free of racial discrimination is clearly within the zone of interest protected by Title VII"); EEOC v. T.I.M.E.-D.C. Freight, 659 F.2d 690, 692 n.2, 27 FEP Cases 10, 11 (5th Cir. 1981)(white bus drivers personally injured by a "no-transfer" policy allegedly designed to exclude blacks have Title VII standing); Allen v. American Home Foods, *supra* note 21, 644 F. Supp. at 1556–57, 42 FEP Cases at 408–10 (males who lost jobs when plant closed because of sex of female co-workers could sue under Title VII). *See also* EEOC Dec. 71-909, 3 FEP Cases 269 (1970)(maintenance of working environment in which racial insults against blacks are habitual also violates white employees' statutory rights). *See generally* Torrey, *Indirect Discrimination under Title VII: Expanding Male Standing to Sue for Injuries Received as a Result of Employment Discrimination Against Females,* 64 WASH. L. REV. 365 (1989).

[23]In one of the cases cited by the EEOC, *Clayton v. White Hall School Dist., supra* note 22, Judge Theodore McMillian held that a white plaintiff had standing to challenge antiblack discrimination only for purposes of asserting a hostile environment claim. The same court, in an earlier decision in the same case, had held that "loss of an economic benefit was not within the zone of interests protected by the civil rights laws." 875 F.2d at 679, 49 FEP Cases at 1620 (characterizing the court's earlier decision in *Clayton v. White Hall School Dist.,* 778 F.2d 457, 460, 39 FEP Cases 945, 946 (8th Cir. 1985)).

[24]Remedial problems exist when there are antithetical claimants. For instance, the disadvantaged competitor might seek as a remedy to "bump" the favored employee from his or her position. *See, e.g.,* Lander v. Lujan, 888 F.2d 153, 51 FEP Cases 157 (D.C. Cir. 1989)(no abuse of discretion in ordering innocent incumbent "bumped" to remedy past discrimination); Walters v. City of Atlanta, 803 F.2d 1135, 1148–50, 42 FEP Cases 387, 397–98 (11th Cir. 1986)(affirming bumping of innocent incumbent to remedy earlier discrimination).

B. Sex of the Third-Party Complainant

Under the EEOC's theory of submission to sexual favors as a general condition of employment, only a disadvantaged female competitor could claim that women, but not men, are generally required to submit to the sexual advances of a heterosexual male supervisor in order to enjoy the job benefit in question.

Under the EEOC's theory of derivative liability, however, a discrimination action is available to the better-qualified competitor, male or female. In derivative cases, the "basis of sex" element of the claim is satisfied by the underlying discriminatory relationship, making the sex of the third party irrelevant.[25]

III. THIRD-PARTY CLAIMS BASED ON UNDERLYING CONSENSUAL SEXUAL FAVORITISM

A. Theory of the Third-Party Claim

When a disadvantaged competitor challenges a decision based on a *consensual* sexual relationship, the EEOC[26] and most courts[27] have rejected claims of sex discrimination under Title VII. Nonetheless, a decision by a panel of the D.C. Circuit, in *King v. Palmer*,[28] assumed that the disappointed competitor would have a Title VII claim under those circumstances. District Court Judge Gerhard Gesell had ruled that a female nurse could state a claim that she was unlawfully denied a promotion where her supervisor had awarded the promotion to another female nurse on the basis of his intimate relationship with her.[29] Judge Gesell articulated the elements of the plaintiff's prima facie case as (1) membership in a protected class, (2) application and qualifications for a job for which the employer was seeking applicants, (3) rejection for the position in favor of another applicant, and (4) a sexual relationship between the employer and the accepted applicant, which was a "substantial factor" in the accepted applicant's promotion.[30] Impliedly, Judge Gesell assumed that dis-

---

[25]It is the sexual harassment of the favored employee, not the sex of the disadvantaged competitor, that establishes the requisite causal connection between the basis (sex) and the issue (the job benefit). See note 12 *supra*.

[26]Policy Guidance on Sexual Favoritism, *supra* note 7, part A at 405:6817–18.

[27]*E.g.*, DeCintio v. Westchester County Medical Center, 807 F.2d 304, 42 FEP Cases 921 (2d Cir. 1986), reproduced *infra, cert. denied*, 484 U.S. 825 (1987); cases cited in note 35 *infra*.

[28]598 F. Supp. 65, 35 FEP Cases 1302 (D.D.C. 1984), *aff'd in part and rev'd in part*, 778 F.2d 878, 39 FEP Cases 877 (D.C. Cir. 1985), *rehearing en banc denied*, 778 F.2d 883, 40 FEP Cases 190 (D.C. Cir. 1986).

[29]As discussed more fully in Section II.A.1. *supra*, several cases are consistent with *King* to the extent they hold that widespread sexual favoritism amounting to an "implicit quid pro quo" harassment is actionable under Title VII. *E.g.*, Broderick v. Ruder, 685 F. Supp. 1269, 1277, 46 FEP Cases 1272, 1280 (D.D.C. 1988), reproduced in Chapter 2, Forms of Harassment (citing *King* in concluding that Title VII violated "when an employer affords preferential treatment to female employees who submit to sexual advances or other conduct of a sexual nature and such conduct is a matter of common knowledge"); Priest v. Rotary, *supra* note 18 (violation of Title VII where supervisor's consensual sexual partner and other females who tolerated supervisor's sexual conduct given job assignment preference); Toscano v. Nimmo, *supra* note 17 (Title VII violated when female promoted on basis of sexual relationship with supervisor where condition imposed on female applicants that would not be imposed on males). *But see* Malarkey v. Texaco, 559 F. Supp. 117, 122, 34 FEP Cases 1818, 1821–22 (S.D.N.Y. 1982)(female plaintiff passed over in favor of more "physically attractive" females has no Title VII claim; because "only women were promoted to the positions in question, the ultimate choice of which women to hire could not have been based on discrimination between men and women"), *aff'd*, 704 F.2d 674 (2d Cir. 1983).

[30]*Supra* note 28, 598 F. Supp. at 67, 35 FEP Cases at 1303.

crimination "because of ... sex" would include discrimination because of *sexual conduct* or a *sexual relationship*. He ultimately found against the plaintiff, however, for failing to provide direct evidence of "an explicit sexual relationship" between the favored employee and the supervisor.[31]

On appeal, the D.C. Circuit assumed without analysis that alleging sexual favoritism "presents a cognizable cause of action under statutes prohibiting sex discrimination in employment."[32] Although this question was not squarely presented on appeal,[33] both the district court and circuit court decisions in *King* assumed that Title VII's prohibition against sex discrimination is violated whenever sex is " 'for no legitimate reason a substantial factor in the discrimination.' "[34] The *King* court did not focus on the sex of the individual asserting the Title VII claim.

In the leading judicial decision rejecting *King*, the Second Circuit held that Title VII does not forbid isolated cases of consensual sexual favoritism.

DeCINTIO v. WESTCHESTER COUNTY MEDICAL CENTER

807 F.2d 304, 42 FEP Cases 921 (2d Cir. 1986),
cert. denied, 484 U.S. 825 (1987)

MINER, Circuit Judge: • • • seven male respiratory therapists employed by appellant Westchester County Medical Center ("WCMC"), brought suit in the United States District

---

[31]*Id.* at 69, 35 FEP Cases at 1304; *see also* Kersul v. Skulls Angels, 130 Misc.2d 345, 495 N.Y.S.2d 886, 42 FEP Cases 987 (N.Y. Sup. Ct. 1985)(refusing to dismiss claims under state discrimination law where plaintiff claimed there was "close personal relationship" between employer and another female employee resulting in favorable treatment of that employee despite unsatisfactory performance; court directed plaintiff to amend pleadings to specify, "without euphemisms," that employer and favored employee were having sexual relationship); *cf.* Anderson v. University Health Center, 623 F. Supp. 795, 798, 41 FEP Cases 1197, 1199 (W.D. Pa. 1985)(allegations of sexual relationship between plaintiff's supervisor and plaintiff's co-worker irrelevant to discharged plaintiff's sex discrimination claims where not shown that co-worker was favored, promoted, or replaced plaintiff).

[32]*Supra* note 28, 778 F.2d at 880, 39 FEP Cases at 879 (Wright, McGowan & Edwards, JJ.).

Some linguistic support for this view can be found in the cases. *See, e.g.,* Barnes v. Costle, *supra* note 16, 561 F.2d at 990, 15 FEP Cases at 351 ("[T]he statutory embargo on sex discrimination in employment is not confined to differentials founded wholly upon an employee's gender. ... [I]t is enough that gender is a factor contributing to the discrimination in a substantial way"); Meritor Sav. Bank v. Vinson, 477 U.S. 57, 64, 40 FEP Cases 1822, 1826 (1986), reproduced in Chapter 1, Overview ("The phrase 'terms, conditions, or privileges of employment' evinces a congressional intent ' "to strike at the entire spectrum of disparate treatment of men and women." ' ")(quoting Los Angeles Dep't of Water & Power v. Manhart, 435 U.S. 702, 707 n.13, 17 FEP Cases 395, 398 (1978)(quoting Sprogis v. United Air Lines, 444 F.2d 1194, 1198, 3 FEP Cases 621, 623–24 (7th Cir.), *cert. denied,* 404 U.S. 991 (1971))). *See generally* Comment, *The Meaning of "Sex" in Title VII: Is Favoring an Employee Lover a Violation of the Act?,* 83 Nw. U.L. Rev. 612, 615 (1989)(arguing that hiring or promoting one's lover to detriment of more-qualified candidate violates Title VII).

[33]The parties had agreed that there was a claim cognizable under Title VII, thereby not raising the issue of whether Title VII bars claims based on consensual sexual favoritism. Dissenting from the denial of the employer's petition for rehearing *en banc,* Judge Robert H. Bork voiced a concern that the panel's decision " 'may represent a significant expansion of Title VII coverage.' " King v. Palmer, *supra* note 28, 778 F.2d at 883, 40 FEP Cases at 191 (Bork, J., joined by Ruth Bader Ginsburg, Scalia, Starr, Silberman & Buckley, JJ.)(quoting motion of the United States for an extension of time to file *amicus curiae* brief). The majority of the D.C. Circuit decided that rehearing the Title VII coverage issue was inappropriate because the issue was not raised on appeal. *See* Comment, *supra* note 32, 83 Nw. U.L. Rev. at 630 n.123.

[34]*Supra* note 28, 778 F.2d at 880, 39 FEP Cases at 879 (quoting Judge Gesell, 798 F. Supp. at 66–67, 35 FEP Cases at 1302 (quoting Bundy v. Jackson, 641 F.2d 934, 942, 24 FEP Cases 1155, 1159 (D.C. Cir. 1981))). Rather than address the theoretical viability of the plaintiff's claim under Title VII, the D.C. Circuit in *King* focused on whether the plaintiff could recover even without proving an "explicit sexual relationship" between the favored employee and the supervisor. Rejecting the district court's contrary holding, the circuit court ruled that "direct evidence of a sexual relationship, *i.e.,* kisses, embraces and other amorous behavior, which concededly played a substantial role in [the favored employee's] selection for promotion ... was more than enough to satisfy plaintiff's burden of proof on the point." *Id.* at 882, 39 FEP Cases at 881.

Court for the Southern District of New York (Brieant, J.), alleging that WCMC and appellant Westchester County had discriminated against them on the basis of sex in violation of Title VII • • •. The gravamen of their complaint was that they had been unfairly disqualified from promotion to the position of Assistant Chief Respiratory Therapist. They alleged that when the Program Administrator of the Respiratory Therapy Department, James Ryan, initiated the suggestion that registration by the National Board of Respiratory Therapists ("NBRT") be required of all applicants for the Assistant Chief position, he did so in order to disqualify them and to enable him to hire Jean Guagenti, a woman with whom he was engaged in a romantic relationship. The district court held that • • • Title VII • • • [was] violated • • •.

• • •

II. DISCUSSION

The dispositive issue in this action is whether, under Title VII • • •, the phrase "discrimination on the basis of sex" encompasses disparate treatment premised not on one's gender, but rather on a romantic relationship between an employer and a person preferentially hired. The meaning of "sex," for Title VII purposes, thereby would be expanded to include "sexual liaisons" and "sexual attractions." Such an overbroad definition is wholly unwarranted.

Title VII • • • prohibits discrimination in employment "against any individual with respect to his compensation, terms, conditions, or privileges of employment, because of such individual's race, color, religion, sex, or national origin." 42 U.S.C. §2000e-2(a)(1). • • • "Sex," when read in this context, logically could only refer to membership in a class delineated by gender, rather than sexual activity regardless of gender. As the Supreme Court noted in Trans World Airways v. Hardison, 432 U.S. 63, 14 FEP Cases 1697 (1977), "[t]he emphasis of both the language and the legislative history of [Title VII] is on eliminating discrimination in employment; similarly situated employees are not to be treated differently *solely because they differ* with respect to race, color, religion, sex, or national origin." Id. at 71 (emphasis added). The proscribed differentiation under Title VII, therefore, must be a distinction based on a person's sex, not on his or her sexual affiliations. • • •

In King v. Palmer, 778 F.2d 878, 39 FEP Cases 877 (D.C. Cir. 1985), the D.C. Circuit implicitly recognized a Title VII action alleging discrimination premised on a voluntary sexual relationship. The court noted, however, that the question whether a consensual sexual relationship can form the basis of a Title VII claim had not been presented on appeal. Id. at 880. Additionally, six judges of that court, in denying a suggestion for rehearing *en banc* and a motion by the government regarding the filing of an *amicus* brief, emphasized that the applicability of Title VII to the facts before them was not raised on appeal, and thus was not the proper subject of a rehearing *en banc.* Id. at 883, 40 FEP Cases 190. To the extent that King and cases following King, e.g., Kersul v. Skulls Angels Inc., 130 Misc. 2d 345, 495 N.Y.S.2d 886, 42 FEP Cases 987 (Sup. Ct. 1985), can be interpreted as recognizing Title VII claims for non-gender based sex discrimination, we decline to adopt such a broad extension of Title VII protection.

Title VII claims have been employed successfully to combat instances of sex discrimination with respect to terms and conditions of employment, e.g., Mills v. Ford Motor Co., 800 F.2d 635, 41 FEP Cases 1397 (6th Cir. 1986), as well as sexual harassment in the workplace, e.g., Meritor, 106 S.Ct. 2399, 40 FEP Cases 1822 (1986) ("hostile environment" sexual harassment); see generally Annot., 78 A.L.R. Fed. 252 (1986). In all of these cases, however, there existed a causal connection between the gender of the individual or class and the resultant preference or disparity. Many courts have limited the word "sex" to its "traditional definition." Sommers v. Budget Marketing, Inc., 667 F.2d 748, 750, 27 FEP Cases 1217 (8th Cir. 1982), and refused to extend Title VII proscriptions beyond gender-based discrimination. See, e.g., Ulane v. Eastern Airlines, 742 F.2d 1081, 35 FEP Cases 1348 (7th Cir. 1984)(transsexuality), cert. denied, 471 U.S. 1017, 37 FEP Cases 784 (1985); Sommers v. Budget Marketing, Inc., 667 F.2d 748, 27 FEP Cases 1217 (8th Cir. 1982) (same); DeSantis v. Pacific Telephone & Telegraph Co., 608 F.2d 327, 19 FEP Cases 1493 (9th Cir. 1979) (homosexuality); Smith v. Liberty Mutual Insurance Co., 569 F.2d 325, 17 FEP Cases 28 (5th Cir. 1978) (effeminacy). We can adduce no justification for defining "sex," for Title VII purposes, so broadly as to include an ongoing, voluntary, romantic engagement.

Toscano v. Nimmo, 570 F.Supp. 1197, 32 FEP Cases 1401 (D. Del 1983), relied on by appellees, does not mandate a contrary result. In Toscano, a female employee alleged, and the district court found, that the granting of sexual favors was a condition to receiving promotion, in violation of Title VII. Although the district court permitted the female employee to prove her claim with circumstantial evidence of the sexual relationship between the employer and the successful applicant, the claim itself was premised on the coercive nature of the employer's acts, rather than the fact of the relationship itself. The Title VII action at issue in Toscano, therefore, was the substantial equivalent of a "sexual harassment" suit. The decision in Toscano lends no support to the contention that a voluntary amorous involvement may form the basis of a Title VII claim.

The EEOC's guidelines fail to buttress appellees' contentions. The guidelines provide that "[w]here employment opportunities or benefits are granted because of an individual's *submission* to the employer's sexual advances or requests for sexual favors, the employer may be held liable for unlawful sex discrimination against other persons who were qualified for but denied that employment opportunity or benefit." 29 C.F.R. §1604.11(g) (1986) (emphasis added). The word "submission," in this context, clearly involves a lack of consent and implies a necessary element of coercion or harassment. In addition, the EEOC has indicated that sexual relationships between co-workers not be subject to Title VII scrutiny, so long as they are personal, social relationships. See *Preamble to Interim Guidelines on Sex Discrimination,* 45 Fed. Reg. 25024 (1980). While appellees do claim that the liaison between Ryan and Guagenti became more than a private affair when it affected their professional lives, appellees do not claim that they or any other staff members, including Guagenti, were forced to submit to Ryan's sexual advances in order to win promotion.

Even assuming that appellees' allegations are true and that the district court's findings are correct, appellees have not set forth a cognizable Title VII claim for sex discrimination. Appellees allege, and the district court found, that Ryan and Guagenti were engaged in a romantic partnership; that Ryan established a special requirement for the Assistant Chief position solely as a pretext to enable him to cause Guagenti to be hired; that appellees were precluded from applying for the position due to the special requirement; and that Guagenti was hired on the recommendation of Ryan. Ryan's conduct, although unfair, simply does not violate Title VII. Appellees were not prejudiced because of their status as males; rather, they were discriminated against because Ryan preferred his paramour. Appellees faced exactly the same predicament as that faced by any woman applicant for the promotion: No one but Guagenti could be considered for the appointment because of Guagenti's special relationship to Ryan. That relationship forms the basis of appellees' sex discrimination claims. Appellees' proffered interpretation of Title VII prohibitions against sex discrimination would involve the EEOC and federal courts in the policing of intimate relationships. Such a course, founded on a distortion of the meaning of the word "sex" in the context of Title VII, is both impracticable and unwarranted.

The *DeCintio* decision is frequently cited for the proposition that the sex discrimination forbidden by Title VII is discrimination based on gender, not discrimination based on a sexual or other personal relationship.[35]

---

[35]*E.g., Federal Circuit Courts:* Platner v. Cahs & Thomas Contractors, 908 F.2d 902, 905, 53 FEP Cases 940, 942–43 (11th Cir. 1990)(where boss fired female employee whom boss's daughter-in-law suspected was having an affair with boss's son, employment decision may have been "unseemly and regrettable" nepotism but not sex discrimination under Title VII); Drinkwater v. Union Carbide Corp., 904 F.2d 853 (3d Cir. 1990)(discussed at text accompanying notes 71–73 *infra*); Autry v. North Carolina Dep't of Human Resources, 820 F.2d 1384, 1386, 44 FEP Cases 169, 171 (4th Cir. 1987)(no Title VII violation where black plaintiff alleged successful white promotion candidate was friend of person who conducted interview and

The EEOC Policy Guidance on Sexual Favoritism follows *DeCintio* rather than *King:*

> Not all types of sexual favoritism violate Title VII. It is the Commission's position that Title VII does not prohibit isolated instances of preferential treatment based upon consensual romantic relationships. An isolated instance of favoritism toward a "paramour" (or a spouse, or a friend) may be unfair, but it does not discriminate against women or men in violation of Title VII, since both are disadvantaged for reasons other than their genders. A female charging party who is denied an employment benefit because of such sexual favoritism would not have been treated more favorably had she been a man nor, conversely, was she treated less favorably because she was a woman.[36]

---

made promotion decision; "voluntary ongoing friendship would be an inappropriate basis for a Title VII suit");

    Federal District Courts: Candelore v. Clark County Sanitation Dist., 54 FEP Cases 1312 (D.C. Nev. 1990)(granting summary judgment against older female employee who claimed younger female employee got better treatment because of sexual relationship with supervisors, where there was no evidence of any unwelcome sexual advances by supervisors; preferential treatment of paramour not discrimination on basis of sex); Handley v. Phillips, 715 F. Supp. 657, 675, 52 FEP Cases 195, 208 (M.D. Pa. 1989)("specific allegation as to dissimilar treatment resulting from [supervisor's] alleged desire to promote another female is not the basis for a Title VII claim"); Cairo v. OH Material Corp., 710 F. Supp. 1069, 1071–72, 50 FEP Cases 372, 374 (M.D. La. 1989)(no sex discrimination or sexual harassment where male employee claimed he was discharged for refusing to allow supervisor to date his wife; claimed reason for discharge was not employee's gender and discharge was therefore not "because of . . . sex" within the meaning of Title VII); Freeman v. Continental Technical Servs., 710 F. Supp. 328, 330–31, 48 FEP Cases 1398, 1399 (N.D. Ga. 1988)(rejecting female employee's claim that Title VII was violated when she was discharged after becoming pregnant as result of consensual affair with employer's president; "plaintiff was not terminated because she was a woman, but because of her sexual relationship with [the president] and the consequences thereof"); Miller v. Aluminum Co. of Am., 679 F. Supp. 495, 501, 45 FEP Cases 1775, 1779 (W.D. Pa.)("preferential treatment on the basis of a consensual romantic relationship between a supervisor and an employee is not gender-based discrimination"), *aff'd without opinion,* 856 F.2d 184, 52 FEP Cases 1472 (3d Cir. 1988); Yatvin v. Madison Metro. School Dist., 653 F. Supp. 945, 951, 45 FEP Cases 1852, 1857 (W.D. Wis. 1987)(female plaintiff's claim that members of promotion selection committee chosen on basis of predisposition in favor of male candidates viable only if she could show predisposition "was based on considerations of gender rather than personal bias in favor of a particular male or against plaintiff"), *aff'd,* 840 F.2d 412, 45 FEP Cases 1862 (7th Cir. 1988);

    State Courts: Erickson v. Marsh & McLennan Co., 117 N.J. 539, 558, 569 A.2d 793, 802, 55 FEP Cases 1179 (1990)(where male complainant alleged he was fired so that supervisor's paramour could be promoted, New Jersey Supreme Court held complainant could not state claim for sex discrimination because discharge could not have been "because of sex"); Nicolo v. Citibank N.Y. State, 147 Misc.2d 111, 554 N.Y.S.2d 795, 798, 56 FEP Cases 563 (N.Y. Sup. Ct. 1990)(discussed at text accompanying notes 37–41 *infra*); Polk v. Pollard, 539 So.2d 675, 677, 52 FEP Cases 538, 539 (La. Ct. App. 1989)(consistent with FEP statute to fire plaintiff at request of boss's girlfriend, where complainant not pressured for sexual favors or subject to verbal or physical harassment and where "employee of the male gender could have been discharged in the same situation"). *See also* Hickman v. W-S Equip. Co., 176 Mich. App. 17, 438 N.W.2d 872, 51 FEP Cases 247, 248 (1989)(not citing *DeCintio* but dismissing action where claim was that boss fired complainant to give job to his girlfriend; "discharge would likely have occurred regardless of plaintiff's sex").

    But see Gilardi v. Schroeder, 833 F.2d 1226, 1233, 45 FEP Cases 346 (7th Cir. 1987)(Title VII violated where male supervisor who raped female subordinate later fired her at his wife's insistence; "it is obvious that the discharged employee was discriminated against 'because of such individual's . . . sex' ")(quoting 42 U.S.C. §2000e-2(a)(1)).

    Cf. Babcock v. Frank, 729 F. Supp. 279, 287, 54 FEP Cases 1123, 1130 (S.D.N.Y. 1990), reproduced in Chapter 2, Forms of Harassment (distinguishing *DeCintio* where plaintiff, who admitted having earlier consensual sexual relationship with supervisor, claimed that supervisor thereafter made unwelcome sexual advances and told plaintiff she would not advance if she did not accede).

    [36]Policy Guidance on Sexual Favoritism, 8 FAIR EMP. PRAC. MAN. (BNA), part A at 405:6817 (Jan. 12, 1990), reproduced in Appendix 2 (footnotes omitted). The Policy Guidance cites *Benzies v. Illinois Dep't of Mental Health,* 810 F.2d 146, 148, 42 FEP Cases 1537, 1538 (7th Cir.)(denial of promotion to woman is not violation if motivated by personal or political favoritism or grudge), *cert. denied,* 483 U.S. 1006 (1987) and *Bellissimo v. Westinghouse Elec. Corp.,* 764 F.2d 175, 180, 37 FEP Cases 1862 (3d Cir. 1985)(discharge of female employee violates Title VII only if on basis that would not result in discharge of male employee), *cert. denied,* 475 U.S. 1035 (1986). The Policy Guidance does not cite *Phillips v. Martin Marietta Corp.,* 400 U.S. 542, 3 FEP Cases 40 (1971), in which the Court found that discrimination on a "sex plus" basis (female plus having preschool children) is unlawful. One difference is that *some* women, but *no* men, were injured in *Phillips;* in the voluntary lover cases, *all* men *and* all women, other than the lover, are disadvantaged.

In *Nicolo v. Citibank New York State*,[37] the court relied on *DeCintio* and the EEOC Policy Guidance on Sexual Favoritism to abandon *Kersul v. Skulls Angels*,[38] an earlier New York decision that endorsed a claim based on favoritism toward a consensual sexual partner. In *Nicolo,* the court stated that the complainant must allege that the intimate relationship between a supervisor and another employee "must somehow have resulted in discrimination not only against the individual complainant, but other employees of the same gender."[39] The court concluded that although one isolated act of sexual favoritism did not state a claim, allegations of sexual favoritism could give rise to a sexual harassment claim in the following circumstances:

> [I]n a situation where a policy has evolved, or it is generally understood, that the sexual favors by members of one gender will be the quid pro quo for promotions, or other benefits, this Court would certainly recognize a cause of action in the favor of employees of the opposite gender, as well as employees of the same gender, who did not wish to submit to such conditions.... Likewise, sexual favoritism, which became pervasive to the extent of creating a hostile work environment, would also be actionable.[40]

The *Nicolo* court thus rejected the disadvantaged male employee's claim, noting that "Title VII does not prohibit isolated incidents of preferential treatment based upon consensual romantic relationships and, although unfair, does not constitute discrimination against other female or male employees."[41]

B. Sex of the Third-Party Complainant

1. Male Complainant

The position of the EEOC, consistent with the reasoning of the *Nicolo* court, is that an "isolated instance of favoritism toward a [female] 'paramour' ... may be unfair, but it does not discriminate against women *or* men in violation of Title VII, since both are disadvantaged for reasons other than their genders."[42]

The EEOC thus would reject an argument by a male complainant that he suffered sex discrimination by a heterosexual male's sexual favoritism toward the complainant's female competitor. The male complainant would argue that he was discriminated against on the basis of his sex in that his gender was a "but for" cause of his job detriment, in much the same way as the gender of the female plaintiff in *Barnes v. Costle* was a "but for" cause of her job detriment. This argument would apply regardless of whether the underlying sexual activity was consensual.

DeCintio and the EEOC Policy Guidance on Sexual Favoritism do not fully explain why they reject this argument. The *DeCintio* court relied on the

---

[37]*Supra* note 35.

[38]130 Misc.2d 345, 495 N.Y.S.2d 886, 42 FEP Cases 987 (N.Y. Sup. Ct. 1985)(female employee replaced by another female employee who was having consensual sexual relationship with supervisor has sex discrimination claim).

[39]*Supra* note 35, 554 N.Y.S.2d at 798, 56 FEP Cases at 565.

[40]*Id.* at 799 (citations omitted), 56 FEP Cases at 566.

[41]*Id.* at 798, 56 FEP Cases at 565.

[42]Policy Guidance on Sexual Favoritism, *supra* note 36, part A at 405:6817.

term "submission" in §1604.11(g) of the EEOC Guidelines[43] to conclude that favoritism based upon a *consensual* relationship is not forbidden under the Guidelines. That reading of the Guidelines is probably correct, but does not recognize that the EEOC's sexual harassment guidelines address only one form of sex discrimination. Thus, while the term "submission" in §1604.11(g) impliedly excludes consensual sexual relations from the scope of a third-party *sexual harassment* claim, nothing in the EEOC Guidelines necessarily excludes the consideration of sexual relations as part of a third-party *sex discrimination* claim.

A second rationale of the *DeCintio* court—that women as well as men are passed over when a male supervisor favors his female lover—is similarly inconclusive.[44] Given that the promoting official in *DeCintio* was presumably a heterosexual male, the male plaintiffs, because of their gender, could not have occupied the favored position of the female promotee, who allegedly got the job in question because of the selecting official's sexual interest in her.[45]

Whatever may be the logical appeal of the male complainant's argument, it would require scrutiny into consensual personal relationships and it is hard to reconcile with the widespread recognition that nepotism does not constitute sex discrimination, even when the reason for the nepotism may be sexual in part, as in the case of marriage.[45a] Accordingly, there is little support for the theory that a supervisor's sex-related favoritism toward a particular member of the opposite gender is in itself actionable by a disadvantaged member of the supervisor's own gender.[45b]

Other appellate decisions follow *DeCintio* in holding that consensual sexual favoritism provides no basis for a sex discrimination claim even when the favored employee and the disadvantaged competitor are of different sexes. In *Erickson v. Marsh & McLennan Co.,*[46] the New Jersey Supreme Court concluded that a male who claimed that he was fired to make room for his supervisor's girlfriend had not stated a prima facie case of sex discrimination. Citing the word "submission" in the EEOC Guidelines, the court noted: "The adverse employment action allegedly resulted from a consensual, non-coercive

---

[43]Reprinted at text accompanying note 6 *supra.*

[44]*Compare* General Elec. Co. v. Gilbert, 429 U.S. 125, 13 FEP Cases 1657 (1976)(pregnancy exclusion from insurance coverage not sex discrimination because some women as well as all men fully covered)(overruled by Pregnancy Discrimination Act, codified at 42 U.S.C. §2000e(k)) *with* Phillips v. Martin Marietta Corp., *supra* note 36 (rule disadvantaging women with preschool children is sex discrimination even though it does not disadvantage all women) *and* Newport News Shipbldg. & Dry Dock v. EEOC, 462 U.S. 669, 32 FEP Cases 1 (1983)(health plan excluding pregnancy benefits of employees' spouses discriminated against male employees under Pregnancy Discrimination Act amendment to Title VII).

[45]Possibly reinforcing the *DeCintio* court's rejection of the male plaintiffs' discrimination claim is the belief that male claimants must show that their employer is "the unusual employer who discriminates against the majority." Erickson v. Marsh & McLennan Co., *supra* note 35. *But see* Drinkwater v. Union Carbide Corp., *supra* note 35 ("In quid pro quo cases, sexual harassment claims are equally available to men and women . . . .").

[45a]See generally cases cited in note 35 *supra.*

[45b]*Compare* Davis v. Connecticut Gen'l Life Ins. Co., 53 FEP Cases 1172, 1174 (M.D. Tenn. 1990)(male complainant had triable sex discrimination claim that female was chosen over him because she had romantic relationship with supervisor) *with* Miller v. Aluminum Co. of Am., *supra,* note 35 (preferential treatment on basis of consensual romance between supervisor and employee is not gender-based discrimination) *and* Polk v. Pollard, *supra* note 35, 52 FEP Cases at 539 (not discriminatory for male boss to fire female complainant at request of boss's female lover: "employee of the male gender could have been discharged in the same situation").

[46]*Supra* note 35, 569 A.2d 793, 55 FEP Cases 1179.

relationship between [the complainant's supervisor] and [his girlfriend]. As such, it is insufficient to establish a claim of sexual harassment."[47] The court further concluded: "More importantly, we find no reason to extend the protection of [the New Jersey fair employment practices statute] to sex-discrimination claims based on voluntary personal relations in the work place."[48] In reaching this conclusion, the court did not formulate the issue in terms of whether the male plaintiff was disadvantaged vis-à-vis his supervisor's girlfriend because of his sex.

2. Female Complainant

In *Miller v. Aluminum Co. of America,*[49] a female employee claimed that a female co-worker received preferential treatment, including retaining her job during a reduction in force, because of her consensual romantic relationship with the plant manager. Citing *DeCintio,* Judge Gustavo Diamond dismissed this claim:

> Male employees in [plaintiff's] workplace shared with her the same disadvantage relative to Ms. Hollihan: none could claim the special place in [the plant manager's] heart that Ms. Hollihan occupied. Favoritism and unfair treatment, unless based on a prohibited classification, do not violate Title VII. . . . Because they underestimate the essential element of disparate treatment based on gender, we reject those cases cited by [plaintiff] which permit "paramour" claims.[50]

IV. THIRD-PARTY HOSTILE ENVIRONMENT CLAIMS BASED ON UNDERLYING SEXUAL HARASSMENT

A. Theory of the Third-Party Claim

The typical hostile environment claim is by a female who has been the target of sexual harassment that was sufficiently severe or pervasive to affect the conditions of her employment.[51] The issue raised here is whether a hostile environment claim can be maintained by someone in the workplace who was not the target of the harassment.[52]

In the context of widespread sexual favoritism, the EEOC supports a hostile environment claim by employees who were not themselves specific targets of the harassment. According to the EEOC, both men and women who

---

[47]*Id.,* 55 FEP Cases at 1185.

[48]*Id.*

[49]*Supra* note 35.

[50]*Id.* at 501, 45 FEP Cases at 1779 (citations omitted)(expressly rejecting King v. Palmer, 598 F. Supp. 65, 35 FEP Cases 1302 (D.D.C. 1984) *and* Kersul v. Skulls Angels, *supra* note 31). *See also* Malarkey v. Texaco, 559 F. Supp. 117, 122, 34 FEP Cases 1818, 1821–22 (S.D.N.Y. 1982)(favoring more attractive over less attractive women is not gender discrimination), *aff'd,* 704 F.2d 676 (2d Cir. 1983).

[51]The elements of a prima facie case of hostile environment include: (1) unwelcome conduct (2) on the basis of sex (3) that is so severe or pervasive as to create an intimidating, hostile, or offensive work environment, thus affecting a term or condition of employment; and (4) the defendant knew or should have known and failed to take prompt remedial action. Meritor Sav. Bank v. Vinson 477 U.S. 57, 40 FEP Cases 1822 (1986), reproduced in Chapter 1, Overview.

[52]This chapter does not address the case in which a complainant who is the target of harassment uses evidence of harassment against others in the workplace to bolster her own claim as a target. For a discussion of cases addressing admissibility of this evidence, see Chapter 25, Evidence, Section VI.

object to an "atmosphere demeaning to women" can establish a violation if the conduct is sufficiently severe or pervasive to alter the conditions of their employment and create a hostile working environment.[53] Under this theory, liability exists "regardless of whether those who were granted favorable treatment willingly bestowed the sexual favors."[54] The EEOC, in the hostile environment context, thus does not distinguish between third-party claims where the targets of the objectionable conduct submitted to it and third-party claims where the targets did not submit:

> If favoritism based upon the granting of sexual favors is widespread in a workplace, both male and female colleagues who do not welcome this conduct can establish a hostile work environment in violation of Title VII regardless of whether any objectionable conduct is directed at them and regardless of whether those who were granted favorable treatment willingly bestowed the sexual favors. In these circumstances, a message is implicitly conveyed that the managers view women as "sexual playthings," thereby creating an atmosphere that is demeaning to women. . . .
>
> Managers who engage in widespread sexual favoritism may also communicate a message that the way for a woman to get ahead in the workplace is by engaging in sexual conduct or that sexual solicitations are a prerequisite to their fair treatment. This can form the basis of an implicit "quid pro quo" harassment claim for female employees, as well as a hostile environment claim for both women and men who find this offensive.[55]

Relatively few authorities squarely support the EEOC's theory of a third-party claim of sexual harassment based upon environmental harassment directed at employees other than the complainant.[56] Title VII standing cases would apply here, as in the quid pro quo context.[57] In *Fisher v. San Pedro Peninsula Hospital*,[58] the court recognized a nurse's sexual harassment claim against a doctor whose offensive remarks and touchings were directed at other nurses, but in the plaintiff's presence. Thus, even if the plaintiff were not the intended object of sexual harassment, she could state a claim as a result of witnessing the doctor's hugging and kissing of other nurses, grabbing their breasts, making offensive sexual statements, and making lewd comments concerning the breasts of anesthetized female patients.[59]

---

[53]Policy Guidance on Sexual Favoritism, *supra* note 36, part C at 405:6819–21.

[54]*Id.*

[55]Policy Guidance on Sexual Favoritism, *supra* note 36, part C at 405:6819–20 (footnotes omitted).

[56]Cases do support the EEOC theory in *dictum* or by citing the complainant's knowledge of sexual harassment directed at others as additional evidence to support the complainant's claim of a hostile environment. *See, e.g.,* Vinson v. Taylor, 753 F.2d 141, 146, 36 FEP Cases 1423, 1427 (D.C. Cir. 1985) (*dictum*)("Even a woman who was never herself the object of harassment might have a Title VII claim if she were forced to work in an atmosphere in which such harassment was pervasive"), *aff'd sub nom.* Meritor Sav. Bank v. Vinson, 477 U.S. 57, 40 FEP Cases 1822 (1986), reproduced in Chapter 1, Overview; EEOC v. Gurnee Inn Corp., 48 FEP Cases 871, 879 (N.D. Ill. 1988)("[o]bservance of sexual harassment of others can, and in this case . . . did, create a 'hostile working environment' "). For additional authorities on the use of harassment against others to support the complainant's own claim, see Chapter 25, Evidence, Section VI.

[57]See notes 20–23 *supra.* In *Clayton v. White Hall School Dist.,* 875 F.2d 676, 49 FEP Cases 1618 (8th Cir. 1989), Clayton, a white school employee who lost her right to have her child attend the school where she worked as a result of a school policy change allegedly aimed at the predominantly black work force to which Clayton belonged, had standing, the EEOC argued, to challenge the new policy, although she herself was not the direct target of racial discrimination, because she was injured as a result of it. The court ruled that the plaintiff had standing to maintain that this job action created a hostile work environment. *Id.* at 679, 49 FEP Cases at 1820.

[58]214 Cal. App.3d 590, 262 Cal. Rptr. 842, 54 FEP Cases 584 (1989).

[59]*Id.,* 262 Cal. Rptr. at 854.

In contrast, in *Ross v. Double Diamond,*[60] even though the plaintiff was allegedly the target of some environmental harassment, Judge Eldon Mahon declined to consider harassment against others in the workplace in deciding her hostile environment claim.[61] After finding that another plaintiff, Ross, had presented enough evidence to support her claim of a hostile work environment,[62] the court refused to consider this evidence in hearing the claim of Ross's co-worker, Stoudenmire. Even though Stoudenmire knew about Ross's mistreatment and actively helped Ross address it, the court apparently concluded that the sexual harassment of others was not relevant to Stoudenmire's claim of a hostile work environment.[63]

B. Sex of the Complainant

Courts and commentators have concluded that a sexually hostile environment in the form of widespread sexual favoritism, or in the form of widespread verbal and visual abuse, tends inevitably to demean the status of women.[64] Women therefore have the clearest claim as third-party complainants in hostile environment cases.[65]

The EEOC position is that when sexually offensive conduct occurs, "co-workers of any . . . sex can claim that this conduct, which communicates a bias against protected class members, creates a hostile environment for them," even if the actual targets of the conduct themselves do not object.[66]

V. Third-Party Hostile Environment Claims Based on Underlying Consensual Conduct

A. Theory of the Third-Party Claim

Third-party hostile environment claims may also challenge an atmosphere that *other* employees accept, and perhaps even enjoy, as a part of the culture of the workplace. These claims might arise with respect to any one or more of

---

[60]672 F. Supp. 261, 45 FEP Cases 313 (N.D. Tex. 1987).

[61]The *Ross* court relied on *Rabidue v. Osceola Ref. Co.,* 805 F.2d 611, 42 FEP Cases 631 (6th Cir. 1986), *cert. denied,* 481 U.S. 1041 (1987), reproduced in Chapter 2, Forms of Harassment.

[62]Ross was asked if she "fooled around," was asked to pull her dress above her knees for a photograph, was asked by a manager to "pant heavily" on the phone, was subjected to the taking of a picture under her dress, was pulled onto her manager's lap, and was trapped in his office where he asked her to bend over and clean mustard off the wall.

[63]Stoudenmire failed to establish a hostile environment claim with evidence that she was segregated from male employees for three days while in training, was denied the right to take her books home, and was subjected to her manager's speculation that she liked to wear black boots and carry a whip in the bedroom.

[64]*See, e.g.,* Drinkwater v. Union Carbide Corp., 904 F.2d 853, 861 n.15, 56 FEP Cases 483 (3d Cir. 1990)("[N]on-quid pro quo hostile environment cases depend on the underlying theory that '[w]omen's sexuality largely defines women as women in this society, so violations of it are abuses of women as women.' 'The relationship of sexuality to gender is the critical link in the argument that sexual harassment is sex discrimination.' C. MacKinnon, Sexual Harassment of Working Women 174, 151 (1979). This theory posits that there is a sexual power asymmetry between men and women and that, because men's sexuality does not define men as men in this society, a man's hostile environment claim, although theoretically possible, will be much harder to plead and prove").

[65]Some courts have concluded that a "reasonable woman" may find offensive behavior that a "reasonable person" might not. Ellison v. Brady, 924 F.2d 872, 54 FEP Cases 1346 (9th Cir. 1991) and cases cited therein.

[66]Policy Guidance on Sexual Favoritism, 8 Fair Emp. Prac. Man. (BNA), 405:6820 (Jan. 12, 1990), reproduced in Appendix 2. *But see* Goluszek v. Smith, 697 F. Supp. 1452, 48 FEP Cases 317 (N.D. Ill.

three categories of sexual activity in the workplace: (1) consensual sexual relationships between supervisors and employees, (2) sexual "horseplay" among male and female employees, and (3) displays of sexual graffiti or pornography.

The consensual nature of the conduct is not a defense. As the EEOC has stated in the context of sexual favoritism, "the fact that it was exclusively voluntary and consensual would not have defeated a claim that it created a hostile work environment for other people in the workplace."[67] The consensual nature of the conduct does mean that the complainant may not proceed on a derivative theory. Instead, the complainant must resort to a theory of adverse impact[68] or contend that the employer intended to discriminate against her because of sex in that the employer knew that the complainant found the work environment harassing and yet failed to correct it.[69]

1. Consensual Sexual Relationships

In *Drinkwater v. Union Carbide Corp.*,[70] a Third-Circuit diversity case applying New Jersey law, a female employee claimed that an affair between her male supervisor and the plaintiff's subordinate made the working environment sexually hostile. Judge Edward Becker discussed whether a consensual romantic relationship can give rise to a claim of hostile environment:

> The *DeCintio* decision was recently endorsed by the New Jersey Supreme Court in *Erickson v. Marsh & McLennan Co., Inc.*, 117 N.J. 539, 569 A.2d 793 [55 FEP Cases 1179] (1990). *Erickson,* is, of course, binding on this court sitting in diversity. In *Erickson,* a male plaintiff claimed that he had been wrongfully discharged and discriminated against on the basis of sex when his superior fired him in order to promote a woman with whom the superior had allegedly been romantically involved.
>
> • • •
>
> Defendants' counsel have urged that *Erickson* controls this case and effectively eviscerates any colorable claim that plaintiff may have had. We disagree. . . . *Erickson* held that a consensual relationship cannot form the basis of a sex discrimination claim not founded on sexual harassment, and that a consensual relationship cannot, by itself, without additional evidence of sexual hostility, give rise to a hostile environment sexual harassment claim. . . .
>
> This case is distinguishable. Plaintiff has alleged a sexual harassment claim, not just a sex discrimination claim. To the extent that plaintiff argues that the Kahwaty/ Schembri relationship gives her a cause of action for nonharassment sex discrimination, or that it, by itself, gives her a cause of action for sexual harassment,

---

1988)(male plaintiff, even though himself the object of harassment, had no hostile environment claim based upon sexually charged workplace consisting of conduct that would be demeaning to women; court thought that no claim exists unless offender says by words or actions that "victim is inferior because of the victim's sex").

[67]*Id.* at 405:6820 n.13 (emphasis added)(rejecting statement in *Miller v. Aluminum Co. of Am.,* 679 F. Supp. 495, 501–2, 45 FEP Cases 1775, 1780 (W.D. Pa. 1988) that sexual favoritism based on consensual relationship cannot create hostile environment for others in workplace); *cf.* Parrish v. English Am. Tailoring Co., 1988 U.S. Dist. LEXIS 14240 (D. Md. 1988)(dismissing allegations of sexual relationship between supervisor and another female employee, because "Title VII does not prohibit discrimination based upon sexual affiliations").

[68]*See, e.g.,* Robinson v. Jacksonville Shipyards, 760 F. Supp. 1486, 1522–23 (M.D. Fla. 1991), reproduced in Chapter 2, Forms of Harassment (behavior not directed at particular individual but disproportionately more demeaning to one sex may create barrier to progress in workplace).

[69]*See, e.g.,* Hunter v. Allis-Chalmers, 797 F.2d 1417, 1423–24, 41 FEP Cases 721, 725 (7th Cir. 1986)(evidence of pervasive co-worker harassment implies employer condoned it)(Posner, J., concurring).

[70]904 F.2d 853 (3d Cir. 1990).

Erickson clearly defeats her argument. Plaintiff has attempted to allege more, however. Unlike Erickson, she alleged an "oppressive and intolerable environment," which, she argues, was created by the Kahwaty/Schembri affair. And there are at least hints in this record that the environment was so charged with sexual innuendo as to create an atmosphere that discriminated against her as a woman. We believe that there is a critical difference between this kind of hostile environment claim and the harassment claims pled in cases like *Erickson: in hostile environment cases, it is the environment, not the relationship, that is actionable. The relationship may contribute to the environment, but it is the workplace atmosphere that is critical.* Thus, we predict that the Supreme Court of New Jersey would distinguish *Erickson* and recognize hostile environment claims.

In fact, however, this plaintiff's sexual harassment claim cannot survive. Although she makes remote references to the effect that the Kahwaty/Schembri affair had on the environment at [the workplace], there is insufficient evidence in the record for plaintiff to survive summary judgment on that count. . . .

Such an atmosphere might have discriminated against plaintiff if sexual discourse displaced standard business procedure in a way that prevented plaintiff from working in an environment in which she could be evaluated on grounds other than her sexuality. Thus, we believe that evidence of a sufficiently oppressive environment could, in theory, give courts enough evidence to infer . . . intentional discrimination . . . even absent evidence of the harasser's subjective intent to discriminate. However, there is no evidence that Kahwaty and Schembri flaunted the romantic nature of their relationship, nor is there evidence that these kinds of relationships were prevalent at [the workplace]. *Cf. Broderick v. Ruder, supra.*[16]

Plaintiff apparently wants us to assume that the atmosphere was sexually charged or that Kahwaty was making implicit sexual demands on her. We decline to make such assumptions. A sexual relationship between a supervisor and a co-employee could adversely affect the workplace without creating a hostile sexual environment. A supervisor could show favoritism that, although unfair and unprofessional, would not necessarily instill the workplace with oppressive sexual accentuation. The boss could treat everyone but his or her paramour badly and all of the subordinates, save the paramour, might be affected in the same way. *Erickson* clearly states that this kind of situation does not create a claim for sexual harassment.[71]

---

[16]In *Broderick* the court found that a *prima facie* sexual harassment claim had been made out with plaintiff's evidence of pervasive sexual conduct in the office. This conduct included managers who continually referred to female employees' sexuality and bestowed preferential treatment upon those who submitted, apparently consensually, to sexual advances. There was also evidence that this atmosphere undermined plaintiff's motivation and affected job opportunities.

The dictum in *Drinkwater,* that a consensual sexual relationship may contribute to a hostile environment, is consistent with the EEOC's position regarding widespread favoritism.[72]

Similarly, in *Priest v. Rotary,*[73] the court found that a restaurant owner had created a sexually hostile working environment where his "consensual

---

[71]*Id.* at 860–62 (emphasis added, footnotes 15 and 17 omitted).
[72]*See* text accompanying note 55 *supra.*
[73]634 F. Supp. 571, 40 FEP Cases 208 (N.D. Cal. 1986).

sexual partner" received preferential job assignments and where other female employees also received preferential assignments for tolerating his conduct.[74]

2. Sexual "Horseplay"

In a leading "horseplay" case, *Broderick v. Ruder*,[75] the complainant alleged that male managers and co-workers on several occasions touched or made sexual comments to female employees, used vulgar language, and told dirty jokes. The complainant further alleged that two managers had sexual relationships with female staff members who received promotions, a commendation, and two cash awards, and that another manager was "noticeably attached" to a female subordinate whose career he promoted. Judge John Pratt described the law as follows:

> Evidence of the general work atmosphere, involving employees other than the plaintiff, is relevant to the issue of whether there existed an atmosphere of hostile work environment which violated Title VII. *Vinson v. Taylor*, 753 F.2d 141, 146, 36 FEP Cases 1423 (D.C. Cir. 1985), *aff'd in relevant part and rev'd in part*, 477 U.S. 57, 106 S. Ct. 2399, 91 L. Ed. 2d 49, 40 FEP Cases 1822 (1986); *Delgado v. Lehman*, 665 F. Supp. 460, 43 FEP Cases 593 (E.D. Va. 1987). *See also Rogers v. EEOC*, 454 F.2d 234, 4 FEP Cases 92 (5th Cir. 1971), *cert. denied*, 406 U.S. 957, 92 S. Ct. 2058, 32 L. Ed. 2d 343 (1972). This is so because "[e]ven a woman who was never herself the object of harassment might have a Title VII claim if she were forced to work in an atmosphere in which such harassment was pervasive." *Vinson v. Taylor*, 753 F.2d at 146.

Judge Pratt found that the plaintiff had established a prima facie case of hostile environment sexual harassment, even though much of it involved conduct not directed toward her:

> [P]laintiff, without any doubt, was forced to work in an environment in which the WRO [Washington Regional Field Office] managers by their conduct harassed her and other WRO female employees, by bestowing preferential treatment upon those who submitted to their sexual advances. Further, this preferential treatment undermined plaintiff's motivation and work performance and deprived plaintiff, and other WRO female employees, of promotions and job opportunities. The record is clear that plaintiff and other women working at the WRO found the sexual conduct and its accompanying manifestations which WRO managers engaged in over a protracted period of time to be offensive. The record also establishes that plaintiff and other women were for obvious reasons reluctant to voice their displeasure and, when they did, they were treated with a hostile response by WRO's management team.[76]

---

[74]*Id.* at 581–82, 40 FEP Cases at 219.

[75]685 F. Supp. 1269, 1277–78, 46 FEP Cases 1272, 1280–81 (D.D.C. 1988), reproduced in Chapter 2, Forms of Harassment; *see also* Spencer v. General Elec. Co., 697 F. Supp. 204, 51 FEP Cases 1696 (E.D. Pa. 1988)(where supervisor engaged in daily horseplay with female subordinates who joined in and generally found horseplay inoffensive and funny, and even though virtually none of horseplay was directed at plaintiff, Title VII was violated because supervisor's conduct would have interfered with work performance and have seriously affected psychological well-being of reasonable employee), *aff'd*, 894 F.2d 651, 51 FEP Cases 1725 (4th Cir. 1990). The EEOC cites *Spencer* for "the proposition that pervasive sexual conduct can create a hostile work environment for those who find it offensive even if the targets of the conduct welcome it and even if no sexual conduct is directed at the persons bringing the claim." Policy Guidance on Sexual Favoritism, *supra* note 66, part C at 405:6821 n.14.

[76]*Supra* note 75, 685 F. Supp. at 1278, 46 FEP Cases at 1281.

3. Displays of Sexual Material

Sexual material may appear in the public areas of a workplace in the form of graffiti, cartoons, and sexually suggestive posters or pin-ups. To the extent that this material remains on display, and thus is tolerated, the display may be characterized as consensual conduct. While no court yet has ruled that the display of pornography or sexual graffiti can itself constitute a hostile environment, courts have cited these displays as evidence in support of a hostile environment claim.[77]

In *Waltman v. International Paper Co.*,[78] the Fifth Circuit reversed a summary judgment for the employer, holding that the court below should consider not only harassment directed at the plaintiff, but visual forms of harassment not specifically directed at her, such as graffiti on walls, in restrooms, in the elevator, "sexually explicit calendars" on walls and in lockers, and "used tampons" hanging from lockers.[79] Similarly, in *Robinson v. Jacksonville Shipyards*,[80] the court found for the plaintiff on a hostile environment claim based on evidence that largely consisted of the public display in the workplace of male-oriented pornographic or quasi-pornographic material.

The *Waltman* court's decision to consider graffiti not directed at the plaintiff herself prompted a dissent from Circuit Judge Edith Jones.[81] Noting that the Supreme Court in *Meritor* had required plaintiffs to show that sexual harassment was so "severe or pervasive" as to "create an abusive environment," Judge Jones observed:

> Such language does not . . . suggest that whenever a victim *feels* abused, she has a cause of action under Title VII. . . .
>
> This case . . . [should] not raise any question whether a woman who was *not* the target of unwanted physical contact or obscene remarks or graffiti might assert a Title VII claim. To render such a claim actionable, as the majority does, not only contravenes *Meritor* but also creates the unpalatable possibility that a woman might sue her employer for consensual conduct that others undertook among themselves. Surely, such invasions of privacy cannot have been the object of banning sexual harassment in the workplace.
>
> • • •
>
> From [plaintiff's] testimony, it appears that most of the graffiti had nothing to do with her personally.[12] The graffiti was arguably nondiscriminatory because it included male and female references. Using evidence of generalized sexual graffiti to bolster an otherwise nonactionable complaint against an employer highlights the subjectivity of the majority's holding. . . . [S]exual mores in our society are in rapid flux. Depictions that were only recently regarded as taboo in movies and television are now *de rigueur* for programs that even children will

---

[12]With the exception of a phrase scratched in paint on one wall, [plaintiff] simply wiped away graffiti she found offensive. She had no idea who wrote the graffiti. The plant employed over 350 people.

---

[77]*See* Robinson v. Jacksonville Shipyards, *supra* note 68, 760 F. Supp. at 1522–23 and cases cited therein.

[78]875 F.2d 468, 50 FEP Cases 179 (5th Cir. 1989).

[79]*Id.* at 471, 50 FEP Cases at 181–82. *Accord* Robinson v. Jacksonville Shipyards, *supra* note 68, 760 F. Supp. at 1522–26. *See also* cases cited in note 52 *supra*.

[80]*Supra* note 68, 760 F. Supp. at 1494–99.

[81]Judge Jones's dissent also discussed whether the evidence of harassment directed at plaintiff herself was "sufficiently pervasive" to meet the *Meritor* standards, whether the employer had notice of the harassment, and whether the employer took adequate steps to control sexually oriented behavior of employees. *Supra* note 78, 875 F.2d at 482, 50 FEP Cases at 191.

watch. The public use of lewd and suggestive language is as commonplace on the playground as in the workplace. Against such trends, it is quaint but also naive to rule that employers are legally required to eradicate all sexual graffiti from their establishments. The EEOC guidelines and policy statement never go so far. This case, moreover, is distinguishable from *Bennett v. Corroon & Black Corp.*, 845 F.2d 104, 46 FEP Cases 1329 (5th Cir. 1988), in which the employee was viciously satirized and suffered emotional injury solely because of the graffiti about her.[82]

B. Sex of the Complainant

Male or female employees could challenge a hostile sexual environment not directed at them personally.[83] Some offensive workplace conduct arguably is equally offensive to both sexes,[84] while other conduct may affect one sex disproportionately.[85]

---

[82]*Supra* note 78, 875 F.2d at 484–86, 50 FEP Cases at 192–94 (footnote 13 omitted).

[83]See cases discussed in Section IV.C. *supra. But see* Goluszek v. Smith, 697 F. Supp. 1452, 48 FEP Cases 317 (N.D. Ill. 1988)(male could not complain of hostile environment that would be offensive to women even though he himself was object of harassment).

[84]Fair v. Guiding Eyes for the Blind, 742 F. Supp. 151 (S.D.N.Y. 1990)(rejecting female employee's claim that supervisor's open discussion of his homosexuality constituted sexual harassment; "If the acts complained of would be equally offensive to both sexes, then the subject of the harassment cannot claim to have been singled out because of her sex"); Bennett v. Corroon & Black Corp., 517 So.2d 1245, 48 FEP Cases 675, 677 (La. Ct. App. 1987)(cartoons in men's restroom depicting crude sexual deviant behavior not actionable; cartoons were labeled with names of both male and female employees and "sexual conduct that would prove equally offensive to male and female workers would not support a Title VII sexual harassment claim"), *cert. denied,* 520 So.2d 425 (1988). For citation to the differing ruling on the same facts by the Fifth Circuit on the plaintiff's Title VII claim, see text accompanying note 82 *supra.*

[85]Robinson v. Jacksonville Shipyards, *supra* note 68, 760 F. Supp. at 1522–23 (behavior may be actionable if "disproportionately more offensive or demeaning to one sex").

CHAPTER 6

HARASSMENT BY SUPERVISORS

I. OVERVIEW

An important issue in virtually every sexual harassment case is whether an individual harasser's conduct may be imputed to the employer. Whether an employer is liable for harassment by one of its employees is of great significance not only to the employer but to the complainant, who, absent employer liability, has potential remedies only against the alleged harasser. If the harassment is engaged in by a rank-and-file employee, no employer liability will exist absent proof that the employer knew or should have known of the conduct and failed to take appropriate action. If the harassment is by a supervisor, however, the employer may be held liable for the harassment even though the employer knew nothing about it, and even though the employer had expressly forbidden any harassment.

Read literally, the EEOC Guidelines favor liability for the employer in all cases of harassment by a supervisor.[1] The Guidelines state that an employer is liable for harassment by its supervisors and agents "regardless of whether the specific acts complained of were authorized or even forbidden by the employer and regardless of whether the employer knew or should have known of their occurrence."[2] Notwithstanding that general proposition, courts, and

---

[1] 29 C.F.R. §1604.11(c). In 1980, the EEOC issued its Guidelines on Discrimination Because of Sex, 29 C.F.R. §§1604.1–.11, one part of which (§1604.11) is on sexual harassment. The EEOC Guidelines are nonbinding but "constitute a body of experience and informed judgments to which courts and litigants may properly resort for guidance." Meritor Sav. Bank v. Vinson, 477 U.S. 57, 65, 40 FEP Cases 1822, 1826 (1986), reproduced in Chapter 1, Overview (citations omitted). The sexual harassment guidelines in §1604.11 are reproduced in Appendix 1.

[2] 29 C.F.R. §1604.11(c), *supra* note 1. Imposing automatic liability for harassment by a supervisor contrasts with the EEOC's treatment of employer liability where sexual harassment is committed by co-workers or by nonemployees. In the latter situations, the Guidelines would hold the employer liable only where it "knows or should have known of the conduct, unless it can show that it took immediate and appropriate corrective action." *Id.* at §1604.11(d), (e); see Chapters 7, Harassment by Co-Workers, and 8, Harassment by Nonemployees.

Supervisors generally are defined as employees who have the employer's power to do such things as hire, fire, direct or discipline other employees, or the power effectively to recommend those kinds of decisions. *See* National Labor Relations Act §2(11), 29 U.S.C. §152(11). Whether the harasser will be considered a supervisor or merely a co-worker depends on "the circumstances of the particular employment relationship and the job functions performed by the individual." 29 C.F.R. *§1604.11(c). *See, e.g.,* Scott v. Sears, Roebuck & Co., 605 F. Supp. 1047, 37 FEP Cases 878, 884 (N.D. Ill. 1985), *aff'd*, 798 F.2d 210, 41 FEP Cases 805 (7th Cir. 1986)(co-worker who trained plaintiff and occasionally gave evaluation of plaintiff's performance to management was not considered supervisor and therefore his knowledge of his own harassment of complainant was not imputed to employer).

the EEOC itself, have used two separate analyses, one for quid pro quo harassment and the other for hostile environment harassment.

In *Meritor Savings Bank v. Vinson*,[3] the Supreme Court expressly declined to issue a definitive rule on an employer's liability for harassment by a supervisor. Rather, the Court generally endorsed the use of agency principles in determining employer liability, with the proviso that "such common-law principles may not be transferable in all their particulars to Title VII."[4] Application of those agency principles has led courts to impose automatic employer liability in cases of quid pro quo sexual harassment involving a tangible job detriment.[4a] In cases of hostile environment harassment, however, the application of agency principles has depended upon various factors, such as the means by which the harassment was effected, whether the employer had notice of the harassment, what opportunity the complainant had to report the harassment, and the employer's response to its knowledge of the harassment.

II. EMPLOYER LIABILITY FOR QUID PRO QUO HARASSMENT BY SUPERVISORS

The EEOC has consistently stated—in its Guidelines,[5] in the brief submitted on its behalf to the Court in *Meritor*,[6] and in its post-*Meritor* policy statements[7]—that the employer is automatically liable for supervisory misconduct in quid pro quo cases involving tangible job detriments.[8] By this view,

---

[3]*Supra* note 1.

[4]*Supra* note 1, 477 U.S at 72, 40 FEP Cases at 1829 (court stated record on appeal not adequate to decide the employer liability issue directly). For a sample of the secondary literature on this issue, see Sykes, *The Boundaries of Vicarious Liability: An Economic Analysis of the Scope of Employment Rule and Related Legal Doctrines*, 101 HARV. L. REV. 563, 606–8 (1988); Note, *Sexual Harassment in the Workplace: Employer Liability for a Sexually Hostile Environment*, 66 WASH. U.L.Q. 91 (1988); Holtzman & Trelz, *Recent Developments in the Law of Sexual Harassment: Abusive Environment Claims After Meritor Savings Bank v. Vinson*, 31 ST. LOUIS U.L.J. 239 (1987); Comment, *An Employer's Guide to Understanding Liability for Sexual Harassment Under Title VII: Meritor Savings Bank v. Vinson*, 55 U. CIN. L. REV. 1181 (1987); Comment, *When Should an Employer Be Liable for the Sexual Harassment by a Supervisor Who Creates a Hostile Work Environment? A Proposed Theory Of Liability*, 19 ARIZ. ST. L.J. 285 (1987).

[4a]We refer to employer liability as "automatic" because alternative terms such as "strict liability" and "vicarious liability" do not seem entirely appropriate. Strict liability implies liability without fault, Note, *Perceptions of Harm: The Consent Defense in Sexual Harassment Cases*, 71 IOWA L. REV. 1109, 1117–18 n.57 (1986), whereas proof of fault by at least one individual is required in a case of sexual harassment. *See generally* Chapter 23, The Alleged Harasser as Defendant. Vicarious liability is generally a function of the doctrine of *respondeat superior*, a doctrine that does not adequately describe an employer's liability for sexual harassment by its employees. See note 47 *infra*. An employer may be held automatically liable for sexual harassment by a supervisor in circumstances in which it would not be vicariously liable in tort under the doctrine of *respondeat superior*. See Section IV. *infra*. The Supreme Court in *Meritor* used the terms "automatic" and "vicarious" interchangeably.

[5]29 C.F.R. §1604.11(c), *supra* note 1.

[6]Brief for the United States and the EEOC as *Amici Curiae,* Meritor Sav. Bank v. Vinson, *reprinted in* 241 DAILY LAB. REP. E-1 (BNA Dec. 16, 1985).

[7]*See* EEOC Policy Guidance on Current Issues of Sexual Harassment (March 19, 1990), §D1 and cases cited therein, 8 FAIR EMPL. PRAC. MAN. (BNA) 405: 6681–6701, reproduced in Appendix 3.

[8]The EEOC's argument in favor of this rule is that when an employer empowers an individual to fire employees, it also accept[s] responsibility to remedy any harm caused by his unlawful exercise of that authority. The modern corporate entity consists of the individuals who manage it, and little, if any, progress in eradicating discrimination in employment will be made if the corporate employer is able to hide behind the shield of individual employee action. EEOC Post-Trial Memorandum of Law (cited in Tidwell v. American Oil Co., 332 F. Supp. 424, 436, 3 FEP Cases 1007, 1016 (D. Utah 1971)). In *Tidwell,* the court held the employer liable because a middle-level

where a supervisor exercises authority delegated by the employer to make employment decisions, the supervisor's actions are properly imputed to the employer, without regard to whether the employer knew of the supervisor's discriminatory intent or whether the supervisor had actual authority to discriminate on that basis. Courts generally endorse this view.[9]

To establish the requisite degree of supervisory authority, the complainant must show that the alleged harasser possessed the apparent or actual authority

---

manager discharged a supervisor who refused to disqualify minority applicants for entry-level positions. *See also* Flowers v. Crouch-Walker Corp., 552 F.2d 1277, 1282, 14 FEP Cases 1265, 1268 (7th Cir. 1977)(employer liable as principal where employee, in authorized capacity as supervisor, discriminated on basis of race); Anderson v. Methodist Evangelical Hosp., 464 F.2d 723, 725, 4 FEP Cases 987, 988 (6th Cir. 1972)(employer liable for racially motivated discharge by supervisor even where upper management has "exemplary" record on race relations).

[9]*D.C. Circuit:* Bundy v. Jackson, 641 F.2d 934, 947, 24 FEP Cases 1155, 1159 (D.C. Cir. 1981).

First Circuit: Lipsett v. University of P.R., 864 F.2d 881, 901, 54 FEP Cases 230 (1st Cir. 1988).

Second Circuit: Carrero v. New York City Hous. Auth., 890 F.2d 569, 579, 51 FEP Cases 596, 603 (2d Cir. 1989)(employer automatically liable for supervisor's unlawful acts in quid pro quo case).

Third Circuit: Compare Tomkins v. Public Serv. Elec. & Gas Co., 568 F.2d 1044, 1048–49, 16 FEP Cases 22, 25 (3d Cir. 1977)(actual or constructive knowledge by employer required in quid pro quo case) *with* Craig v. Y&Y Snacks, 721 F.2d 77, 80, 33 FEP Cases 187 (3d Cir. 1983)(when supervisor has plenary authority over dismissal, his employment decision may be imputed to employer) *and* Toscano v. Nimmo, 570 F. Supp. 1197, 32 FEP Cases 1401, 1407 (D. Del. 1983)(finding that employer knew or should have known of supervisor's actions not required in quid pro quo case).

Fourth Circuit: Katz v. Dole, 709 F.2d 251, 255 n.6, 31 FEP Cases 1521, 1524 (4th Cir. 1983), reproduced in Chapter 7, Harassment by Co-Workers (employer automatically liable for quid pro quo harassment by supervisory personnel).

Fifth Circuit: Cummings v. Walsh Constr. Co., 561 F. Supp. 872, 878, 31 FEP Cases 930 (S.D. Ga. 1983)(employer bound by acts of official with power to hire and fire).

Sixth Circuit: Highlander v. K.F.C. Nat'l Mgmt. Co., 805 F.2d 644, 649, 42 FEP Cases 654, 657 (6th Cir. 1986)("knowledge of an employment decision based on impermissible sexual factors is imputed to the employer"); Shrout v. Black Clawson Co., 689 F. Supp. 774, 780, 46 FEP Cases 1339, 1344 (S.D. Ohio 1988)(employer "strictly liable for the conduct of supervisory employees having plenary authority over hiring, advancement, dismissal and discipline")(quoting *Highlander*); Boyd v. James S. Hayes Living Health Care Agency, 671 F. Supp. 1155, 1167, 44 FEP Cases 332, 342 (W.D. Tenn. 1987)(harassing supervisor had "authority to make employment decisions about discipline and termination, and therefore his employer is liable for his conduct").

Seventh Circuit: Horn v. Duke Homes, 755 F.2d 599, 605, 37 FEP Cases 228, 232 (7th Cir. 1985)(employer automatically liable for discrimination by supervisor who had "absolute" authority to hire and fire and used that authority to "extort" sexual favors; in that situation, "supervisor *is*, for all intents and purposes, the company"); Horbaczewsky v. Spider Staging Sales Co., 621 F. Supp. 749, 750, 41 FEP Cases 1008 (N.D. Ill. 1985).

Eighth Circuit: Crimm v. Missouri Pac. R.R., 750 F.2d 703, 36 FEP Cases 883, 888 (8th Cir. 1984)(in quid pro quo case, automatic liability applies).

Ninth Circuit: Miller v. Bank of Am., 600 F.2d 211, 213, 20 FEP Cases 211 (9th Cir. 1979)(employer liable for acts of supervisor who had authority to "hire, fire, discipline or promote, or at least to participate or recommend such actions," even if supervisor's actions violated employer's policy); Ambrose v. United States Steel Corp., 39 FEP Cases 30, 35 (N.D. Cal. 1985)(employer automatically liable for conduct of its supervisors in quid pro quo cases); EEOC v. Judson Steel Co., 33 FEP Cases 1286, 1295 (N.D. Cal. 1982)(employer liable for supervisor's discriminatory conduct where supervisor had authority to make employment decisions).

Tenth Circuit: Schroeder v. Schock, 42 FEP Cases 1112, 1114 (D. Kan. 1986)(employer liable for acts of supervisor who had authority to recommend plaintiff's discharge, where supervisor used authority to extort sexual consideration from employee, even where extortion took place away from work after work hours).

Eleventh Circuit: Henson v. City of Dundee, 682 F.2d 897, 909–10, 29 FEP Cases 787, 798 (11th Cir. 1982), reproduced in Chapter 4, Hostile Environment Harassment ("employer is strictly liable for sexual discrimination by supervisors that causes tangible job detriment"); Steele v. Offshore Shipbldg., 867 F.2d 1311, 1316, 49 FEP Cases 522 (11th Cir. 1989)(employer automatically liable for supervisor's quid pro quo harassment; "[w]hen a supervisor requires sexual favors as quid pro quo for job benefits, the supervisor, by definition, acts as the company"); Huddleston v. Roger Dean Chevrolet, 845 F.2d 900, 904, 46 FEP Cases 1361 (11th Cir. 1988)(same); Sparks v. Pilot Freight Carriers, 830 F.2d 1554, 1560, 45 FEP Cases 160, 164 (11th Cir. 1987), reproduced in Chapter 2, Forms of Harassment (employer liable for harassment by supervisor where employer vested supervisor with authority to fire subordinates and supervisor used this authority to sexually harass plaintiff).

to execute the relevant employment decision.[10] The capacity to recommend or otherwise influence employment decisions may be sufficient.[11]

Moreover, a harasser who lacks authority to make employment decisions but who subsequently attains that authority may be considered to have supervisorial authority, which may form the basis of liability under Title VII.[12] A harasser who has lost direct supervisory control over a subordinate because the subordinate has a new supervisor may still possess the authority to influence the terms, conditions, or privileges of employment through a relationship with the new supervisor.[13] Additionally, the harasser may be individually liable as an agent of the employer.[14]

Despite the consensus of the EEOC and lower courts on automatic employer liability for quid pro quo harassment, it is worth noting that the Court in *Meritor* did not squarely address the issue. The court did refer approvingly to arguments in the EEOC *amicus curiae* brief that, when a supervisor exercises authority delegated by the employer "by making or threatening to make decisions affecting the employment status of his subordinates, such actions are properly imputed to the employer whose delegation of authority empowered the supervisor to undertake them."[15]

Nonetheless, it is conceivable that an employer could argue that a clearly articulated and publicized policy prohibiting sexual harassment, and providing for retaliation-free reporting to an individual with authority to remedy the problem, deprives a supervisor not only of actual but also of apparent authority to use personnel decisions to coerce subordinates into cooperation with sexual demands.[16]

III. Employer Liability for Environmental Harassment by Supervisors—The Decision in *Meritor*

A. The Supreme Court's General Endorsement of Agency Principles

In the developments leading up to *Meritor,* the principal issue dividing courts was whether an employer was automatically liable for environmental

---

[10]Henson v. City of Dundee, *supra* note 9, 682 F.2d at 910; Flowers v. Crouch-Walker Corp., 552 F.2d 1277, 1282, 14 FEP Cases 1265, 1268 (7th Cir. 1977); *cf.* Koster v. Chase Manhattan Bank, 687 F. Supp. 848, 861–62 (S.D.N.Y. 1988)(plaintiff did not show that defendant participated in decision not to allow her to interview for desired position, or that he had authority to prevent her transfer or terminate her).

[11]Miller v. Bank of Am., *supra* note 9, 600 F.2d at 213; Sowers v. Kemira, Inc., 701 F. Supp. 809, 46 FEP Cases 1825 (S.D. Ga. 1988); *cf.* Koster v. Chase Manhattan Bank, *supra* note 10, 687 F. Supp. at 862 (*dictum*) (no liability where alleged harasser only had power to recommend adverse decision).

[12]Simmons v. Lyons, 746 F.2d 265, 270, 36 FEP Cases 410, 414 (5th Cir. 1984)(sheriff-elect allegedly conditioned complainant's reappointment on submission to his sexual advances).

[13]Sparks v. Pilot Freight Carriers, *supra* note 9, 830 F.2d at 1565, 45 FEP Cases at 168.

[14]Title VII, §701(b), 42 U.S.C. §2000e(b). *See* Hunter v. Allis-Chalmers Eng'g Div. Corp., 797 F.2d 1417, 1419–20 (7th Cir. 1986). For a discussion of individual liability, see Chapter 23, The Alleged Harasser as Defendant.

[15]*Supra* note 1, 477 U.S. at 70, 40 FEP Cases at 1828. The brief is cited in note 6 *supra. See also* Lipsett v. University of P.R., *supra* note 9 (Title IX case)(*Meritor* implicitly left intact the standard developed in lower courts of automatic liability in cases of quid pro quo sexual harassment).

[16]One early decision stated that if the harassing supervisor's conduct contravenes the employer's policy without the employer's knowledge, and the employer rectifies the situation upon discovery of it, the employer will be relieved of liability for the harassment. Barnes v. Costle, 561 F.2d 983, 993, 15 FEP Cases 345, 353 (D.C. Cir. 1977), reproduced in Chapter 1, Overview; *see also* Tomkins v. Public Serv. Elec. & Gas Co., *supra* note 9; *but see* Miller v. Bank of Am., *supra* note 9 (vicarious liability imposed upon employer without regard to employer's knowledge and even though supervisor's acts violated company policy).

harassment perpetrated by a supervisor without the knowledge of the employer's upper management. While courts had uniformly imputed liability to the employer in quid pro quo cases involving a tangible job detriment,[17] they had split on what facts establish employer liability where harassment by a supervisor did not entail a tangible job detriment. Some courts had denied relief absent proof that management (other than the harassing supervisor) knew or should have known of the harassment.[18] Other courts, following a literal interpretation of the EEOC Guidelines,[19] had held the employer automatically liable for harassment by a supervisor, regardless of what the employer had authorized, known, or should have known regarding the harassment.[20]

In *Meritor,* the Solicitor General, on behalf of the United States and the EEOC, submitted an *amicus curiae* brief that developed an intermediate approach. The Solicitor General's brief argued that when the harassing supervisor is not exercising authority to make personnel decisions, the employer should not be liable if it had an effective policy against sexual harassment that the victim had failed to invoke.[21] The Solicitor General contended that the EEOC Guidelines, read as a whole, effectively distinguish between quid pro quo and hostile environment situations by directing that the "circumstances of the particular employment relationship" be examined.[22] The brief argued that an employer should not be held liable for a hostile environment created by a supervisor unless the employer knew or had reason to know of the sexually offensive atmosphere. The Solicitor General argued further that an employer

---

[17]*See, e.g.,* cases cited in notes 9–10 *supra* and in EEOC Policy Guidance on Current Issues, *supra* note 7.

[18]*E.g.,* Henson v. City of Dundee, *supra* note 9, 682 F.2d at 905, 29 FEP Cases at 794 (complainant who seeks to hold employer responsible for hostile environment created by supervisor *must* show that employer knew or should have known of harassment and failed to take action). *See also* Katz v. Dole, *supra* note 9, 709 F.2d at 255, 31 FEP Cases at 1523–24 (in "condition of work" case, where workplace "pervaded with sexual slur, insult, and innuendo," complainant must demonstrate employer had actual or constructive knowledge of harassment and took no prompt and adequate remedial action); Bundy v. Jackson, *supra* note 9, 641 F.2d at 943, 24 FEP Cases at 1159 (employer liable where higher officials had full notice of harassment by supervisors and did nothing to stop practice); Barnes v. Costle, *supra* note 16, 15 FEP Cases at 353 (employer may be relieved from liability under Title VII where supervisor contravened employer's policy without employer's knowledge and consequences were rectified upon discovery); Spoon v. American Agriculturalist, 120 A.D.2d 857, 858, 502 N.Y.S.2d 296, 298 (N.Y. App. Div. 1986)(summary judgment precluded where issue existed as to whether employer was aware of supervisor's harassment); Kersul v. Skulls Angels, 130 Misc.2d 345, 349, 495 N.Y.S.2d 886, 889, 42 FEP Cases 987, 989 (N.Y. Sup. Ct. 1985)(knowledge imputed to company where harasser was president of company).

But note that the *Henson* court assumed for purposes of the decision that the harasser "was [complainant's] supervisor *rather than her employer,*" 682 F.2d at 905, 29 FEP Cases at 794 n.9 (emphasis added). The court explained that if the harasser were her employer, then defendant would be automatically liable. *Id.* *See also* Salvatore v. N.Y. State Div. of Human Rights, 118 A.D.2d 715, 716, 500 N.Y.S.2d 47, 48–49 (N.Y. App. Div. 1986)(requirement of employer knowledge satisfied where employer and harasser are same).

[19]29 C.F.R. §1604.11(c), *supra* note 1.

[20]*E.g.,* Vinson v. Taylor, 753 F.2d 141, 151, 36 FEP Cases 1423, 1431 (D.C. Cir. 1985), *aff'd on other grounds sub nom.* Meritor Sav. Bank v. Vinson, 477 U.S. 57, 40 FEP Cases 1822 (1986), reproduced in Chapter 1, Overview ("To hold that an employer cannot be reached for Title VII violations unknown to him is . . . to open the door to circumvention of Title VII by the simple expedient of looking the other way"); Miller v. Bank of Am., *supra* note 9, 600 F.2d at 213, 20 FEP Cases at 463 (not holding employer liable would "create an enormous loophole in the statutes"); Mitchell v. OsAir, 629 F. Supp. 636, 642–43, 45 FEP Cases 580, 584 (N.D. Ohio 1986)(applying strict liability while noting that "[h]ostile environment is merely one position on the continuum of sexual harassment, and the threat of job detriment is no less real for being implied rather than explicit"), *appeal dismissed,* 816 F.2d 681 (6th Cir. 1987); Jeppsen v. Wunnicke, 611 F. Supp. 78, 83, 37 FEP Cases 994, 997 (D. Alaska 1985)(expressly rejecting *Henson, supra* note 9, and adopting appellate court decision in *Meritor,* noting that distinction between quid pro quo cases and hostile environment cases is "extremely slippery"); Ambrose v. United States Steel Corp., *supra* note 9, 39 FEP Cases at 35 (position as supervisor gave power to harass; therefore, employer must answer for supervisor's conduct).

[21]*Supra* note 6, 241 DAILY LAB. REP. at E-9.

[22]29 C.F.R. §1604.11(c), *supra* note 1.

who lacks actual knowledge of sexual harassment generally has no reason to know of such harassment if it has created a "reasonable avenue" by which a victim might complain to company officials in a position to rectify the problem.[23]

The Solicitor General found support for this view in common-law principles of agency law. He reasoned that while an employer is automatically liable for quid pro quo harassment because the supervisor is wielding authority delegated by the employer, a supervisor who creates a hostile environment without the use of such authority is not acting as the employer's agent.[24]

In addition to the positions advanced by the Solicitor General, the Supreme Court faced the employer's and complainant's diametrically opposed views on the issue of employer liability. The employer argued that its ignorance of any sexual harassment by its branch manager was an absolute defense, especially since the employer had an antiharassment policy that the complainant had failed to use.[25] The complainant, arguing for affirmance of the ruling of the D.C. Circuit, maintained that the employer was automatically liable for each act of sexual harassment that its supervisor had committed, regardless of whether the employer knew or should have known about it. She reasoned that because Title VII defines "employer" to include an "agent" of the employer, knowledge of the supervisor amounts to notice to the employer.[26]

The lead opinion of the Court, representing the view of five justices, expressly rejected both of these positions.[27] Yet, because unresolved questions as to whether sexual harassment had actually occurred lent an "abstract quality" to the debate over the appropriate standard for employer liability, the Court declined to issue any definitive rule.[28] The lead opinion in *Meritor* did agree with the EEOC that "Congress wanted the courts to look to agency principles for guidance in this area."[29] The Court cited with approval the Restatement (Second) of Agency §§219–237 (1958).[30] The Restatement provides that employers are liable for wrongful acts committed by employees "in the scope of their employment,"[31] and also for acts outside the scope of employment if circumstances show that it would be fair and reasonable to impose such liability.[32]

---

[23]*Supra* note 6.

[24]*Id.*

[25]Meritor Sav. Bank v. Vinson, 477 U.S. 57, 70, 40 FEP Cases 1822, 1828 (1986).

[26]*Id.* For the same view of the D.C. Circuit, see note 20 *supra*.

[27]The lead opinion by Justice Rehnquist was signed by Chief Justice Burger and Justices White, Powell, and O'Connor. Justice Stevens joined both the lead opinion and the concurring opinion by way of a one-sentence separate opinion in which he stated that he found no inconsistency between the lead opinion and the concurring opinion of Justices Marshall, Brennan, and Blackmun, which advocated automatic employer liability.

[28]*Supra* note 25, 477 U.S. at 72, 40 FEP Cases at 1829.

[29]*Id.*

[30]*Id.*

[31]Restatement (Second) of Agency §219(1)(1958). Conduct is within the scope of employment if "actuated, at least in part, by a purpose to serve the [employer]," *id.* at §228, and may be within the scope of employment even if the employer specifically forbids it, lest the employer escape liability merely by disavowing wrongful conduct. *Id.* at §230. Conduct not authorized by the employer may still be within the scope of employment if it is sufficiently similar or incidental to authorized acts, bearing in mind such factors as (1) whether the conduct is common among employees; (2) the time, place, and purpose of the act; (3) whether the employer has "reason to expect" the act will be done; and (4) whether "the instrumentality by which the harm is done has been furnished by the [employer]." *Id.* at §229.

[32]An employer is liable for acts of an employee acting outside the scope of employment if the employer "intended the conduct or consequences," Restatement (Second) of Agency §219(2)(a)(1958), the employer

The *Meritor* Court gave no special guidance as to how these agency principles should apply, noting that these "common-law principles may not be transferable in all their particulars to Title VII."[33] The Court did state that employer liability is not automatic in a hostile environment case, and that the employer's knowledge of harassment and the adequacy of its sexual harassment grievance procedure are "plainly relevant" to, though "not necessarily dispositive" of, the issue of employer liability.[34]

B. The Concurring Opinion's Advocacy of Strict Liability

While the *Meritor* majority thought that employer liability was not squarely before the Court, Justice Thurgood Marshall disagreed. His concurring opinion, discussing the issue in detail, advocated automatic liability, even for hostile environment cases.[35] He chided the Solicitor General for "departing from the EEOC Guidelines," which, read literally, would impose automatic employer liability for harassment by supervisors regardless of whether the context is quid pro quo or hostile environment.[36] Justice Marshall reasoned that a supervisor's abuse of authority over the day-to-day work environment, just as the abuse of his authority to hire, fire, and discipline, should automatically lead to liability for the employer: "It is precisely because the supervisor is understood to be clothed with the employer's authority that he is able to impose unwelcome sexual conduct on subordinates."[37]

Thus, the concurring opinion would impose automatic liability on the employer whenever an employee is sexually harassed by a direct supervisor. The opinion acknowledged that automatic liability might not be appropriate where the harassing supervisor lacks authority over the employee, such as where the two persons work in different departments.[38]

IV. EMPLOYER LIABILITY FOR HOSTILE ENVIRONMENT HARASSMENT BY SUPERVISORS—THE POST-*MERITOR* LAW

Under the law as articulated in *Meritor,* an employer's liability for environmental harassment under Title VII is not automatic.[39] In *Meritor,* the Supreme

---

was negligent, *id.* at §219(2)(b), "the conduct violated a nondelegable duty" of the employer, *id.* at §219(2)(c), the employee "purported to act or to speak on behalf of the [employer] and there was reliance upon apparent authority, or the employee was aided in accomplishing the tort by the existence of the agency relation," *id.* at §219(2)(d).

[33]*Supra* note 25, 477 U.S. at 72, 40 FEP Cases at 1829.

[34]*Id.* The Court further stated that "the mere existence of a grievance procedure and a policy against discrimination, coupled with [the victim's] failure to invoke that procedure" do not necessarily insulate the employer from liability. *Id.* at 72, 40 FEP Cases at 1829. See Section IV.D. *infra.*

[35]*Id.* at 74–78, 40 FEP Cases at 1830–31.

[36]*Id.* at 76–77, 40 FEP Cases at 1831.

[37]*Id.*

[38]*Id.* at 77, 40 FEP Cases at 1831. The concurring opinion would appear to restrict questions concerning employer liability for supervisory harassment to whether the supervisor had actual or apparent authority over the victimized employee. The fact that Justice Stevens joined both the lead and the concurring opinions might perhaps be explained by the fact that the supervisor in *Meritor* clearly had the requisite authority. For a more recent exposition of the argument for automatic employer liability, see Note, *Hostile Environment Sexual Harassment and the Imposition of Liability Without Notice: A Progressive Approach to Traditional Gender Roles and Power Based Relationships,* 24 NEW ENGLAND L. REV. 917 (1990) (advocating as the Note's title might suggest, automatic employer liability for sexual harassment by supervisors).

[39]*Supra* note 25, 477 U.S. at 72, 40 FEP Cases at 1829. Note, however, that under some state fair employment practices acts, the statutory language appears to make the employer automatically liable for

Court declined to specify the circumstances under which employer liability attaches, instead instructing lower courts to "look to agency principles for guidance in this area."[40] Accordingly, analysis of employer liability for environmental harassment has focused on three potential bases for employer liability: (A) harassment within the harasser's scope of employment, (B) harassment within the harasser's apparent authority, and (C) employer negligence in failing to prevent or remedy the harassment.[41]

In any given case a court might consider any of these three theories as a basis for employer liability.[42] The scope-of-employment and apparent-authority theories are likely to apply, if at all, only in the context of harassment by supervisors, for only supervisors, by definition, will be able to exercise the employer's power to affect conditions of the complainant's employment. The negligence theory, by contrast, depends upon the employer's failure to control the workplace, and is equally applicable to cases of harassment by co-workers, although the employer's duty to prevent and remedy harassment may often be greater where the harasser is a supervisor.

A. Scope of Employment

Under agency principles, liability is imputed to the employer for the torts of its employees committed while acting in the scope of their employment.[43] This doctrine, sometimes referred to as *respondeat superior,* is almost never suitable in a sexual harassment case.[44] Nonetheless, *"respondeat superior"* is the term courts routinely use to refer to the employer's liability for sexual harassment.[45]

---

harassment by a supervisor. *E.g.,* CAL. GOV'T CODE §12940(h). For a discussion of the scope of employer liability under state fair employment practices statutes, see Chapter 12, Fair Employment Practices Statutes, Section IV. For a discussion of employer liability under 42 U.S.C. §1983, see Chapter 11, Federal Constitutional, Statutory, and Civil Rights Law, Section III.E.

[40]*Id.* The court cited generally to Restatement (Second) of Agency §§219–237 (1958).

[41]*See* Restatement (Second) of Agency §219 (1958).

[42]*See, e.g.,* Hirschfeld v. New Mexico Corrections Dep't, 916 F.2d 572, 54 FEP Cases 268, 271 (10th Cir. 1990)(employer not liable for hugging and kissing of prison typist by a correctional officer because (A) sexual harassment not within officer's scope of authority, (B) officer's hugging and kissing not aided by status as employer's agent other than that he would not have been there but for his job, and (C) employer's prompt investigation and demotion of officer following complaint showed employer not negligent or reckless).

One commentator has argued with force that regardless of the standard used, the *de facto* rule is automatic liability for hostile environment harassment by supervisors, in that whenever harassment is severe and pervasive enough to be otherwise actionable, it triggers employer liability under such principles as apparent agency and constructive employer knowledge. Note, *The Aftermath of Meritor: A Search for Standards in the Law of Sexual Harassment,* 98 YALE L.J. 1717, 1730–31 (1989).

[43]Section 228(1) of the Restatement provides:

Conduct of a servant is within the scope of employment if, but only if:

   (a) it is of the kind he is employed to perform; (b) it occurs substantially within the authorized space and time limits; (c) it is actuated, at least in part, by a purpose to serve the master, and (d) if force is intentionally used by the servant against another, the use of force is not unexpectable by the master.

[44]See notes 47–51 *infra* and accompanying text.

[45]Courts have found *respondeat superior* liability on the basis that the employer knew or should have known of the harassment and failed to take prompt and adequate remedial action, without considering whether the supervisor's actions were done in furtherance of the employer's business. *E.g.,* Henson v. City of Dundee, 682 F.2d 897, 905, 29 FEP Cases 787, 794 (11th Cir. 1982), reproduced in Chapter 4, Hostile Environment Harassment (under heading of *respondeat superior,* court considered whether the employer knew or should have known of the harassment and failed to take remedial action); Rabidue v. Osceola Ref. Co., 805 F.2d 611, 621, 42 FEP Cases 631, 638 (6th Cir. 1986), *cert. denied,* 481 U.S. 1041 (1987)(same), reproduced in

More accurate labels for the source of employer liability for sexual harassment would be "negligence," "direct liability," or "agency by estoppel."[46] In *Hunter v. Allis-Chalmers Corp.,* Judge Richard Posner observed, in a racial harassment setting, that *respondeat superior* applies only to intentional wrongs that the agent believes he is committing to further his employer's business: "[i]t would be the rare case where ... harassment against a co-worker could be thought by the author of the harassment to help the employer's business."[47]

Nonetheless, some decisions have in fact based employer liability on the doctrine of *respondeat superior,* in the scope-of-employment sense, even when the court could have relied on the sounder ground of direct employer liability for negligence.[48]

The case of *Davis v. United States Steel Corp.*[49] illustrates the distinctions among various standards of employer liability. In *Davis,* the three-judge panel split on which common-law standard should govern employer liability for hostile environment harassment by a supervisor. The complainant alleged fifteen months of sexual harassment by her supervisor, which continued even after his manager witnessed incidents of verbal sexual advances and physical touching; the manager took no action because he thought the conduct was innocent and friendly. The lower court granted summary judgment for the employer on the common-law claims that were based on these acts of sexual harassment. The Fourth Circuit reversed because the employer could be held directly liable for its own inaction after its manager had witnessed the sexual advances.

Chapter 2, Forms of Harassment; Jones v. Flagship Int'l, 793 F.2d 714, 720, 41 FEP Cases 358, 362 (5th Cir. 1986)(same); Katz v. Dole, 709 F.2d 251, 255, 31 FEP Cases 1521, 1523–24 (4th Cir. 1983)(same).

[46]*See* EEOC Policy Guidance on Current Issues, *supra* note 7, §D2(b). For a discussion of direct employer liability, see Section IV.C. *infra.* For a traditional definition of *respondeat superior,* see BLACK'S LAW DICTIONARY 1311–12 (West 1990)(employer liable for injury to others from acts of employee "done within scope of employment in the employer's service"; "doctrine is inapplicable where injury occurs while employee is acting outside legitimate scope of authority").

[47]797 F.2d 1417, 1422, 41 FEP Cases 721, 724 (7th Cir. 1986). For a further discussion of the mistaken use of the term *respondeat superior,* see Chapter 4, Hostile Environment Harassment, note 20.

The traditional limits of *respondeat superior* have led some to argue that the doctrine be expanded, perhaps as a matter of federal common law, to address the problem of sexual harassment. *See, e.g.,* Note, *Legal Remedies for Employment-Related Harassment,* 64 MINN. L. REV. 151, 174–75 (1979).

[48]*See, e.g.,* Yates v. Avco Corp., 819 F.2d 630, 43 FEP Cases 1595 (6th Cir. 1987). In *Yates,* the court could have upheld employer liability for a supervisor's hostile environment harassment simply on the basis that the employer knew or should have known of the harassment and failed to deal with it effectively. *Id.* at 636, 43 FEP Cases at 1599. The court went on, however, to reason that, "even under traditional agency principles, [the] employer should be liable." The court set out three factors for determining whether an employee acts within the scope of employment: "*when* the act took place, *where* it took place, and whether it was *foreseeable.*" *Id.,* 43 FEP Cases at 1600. The court thought that the harassment was within the scope of employment because it (1) occurred during working hours; (2) occurred in the office; (3) was carried out by someone with the authority to hire, fire, promote, and discipline employees; and (4) was foreseen by the company's sexual harassment policy. *Id.,* 43 FEP Cases at 1600. *See also* Shrout v. Black Clawson Co., 689 F. Supp. 774, 781, 46 FEP Cases 1339, 1345 (S.D. Ohio 1988)(following *Yates* scope-of-authority test to find employer liability for hostile environment harassment by supervisor, even though court could have relied solely on finding that employer knew or reasonably should have known of the harassment and failed to remedy the problem). The *Yates* court's application of this test is questionable under the Restatement (Second) of Agency. In finding that the supervisor's conduct was within the scope of his employment, the court ignored whether the conduct was of the kind for which the supervisor was employed, §228(1)(a), and whether the supervisor acted to serve the employer, §228(1)(c). Furthermore, foreseeability should be a factor in determining scope of employment only where the servant intentionally uses force, §228(1)(d). Finally, it is ironic to use the employer's sexual harassment policy, which courts and the EEOC urge employers to implement, to make the employer liable for sexual harassment.

[49]779 F.2d 209, 39 FEP Cases 955 (4th Cir. 1985).

The three-judge panel in *Davis* could not agree, however, on whether liability should be imputed to the employer for the sexual harassment that had preceded the notice to the manager. The majority held that imputed liability was inappropriate because the supervisor's sexual advances effected his own independent purpose, not his employer's.[50] The majority reasoned that imputed liability could not rest solely on the fact that the advances were made possible, or even more easily accomplished, by virtue of the employment setting and relationship.[51]

Dissenting, Judge John Butzner, Jr., saw a triable issue of vicarious liability on the theory that the sexual harassment was committed within the scope of employment. He emphasized that by the facts alleged the employer had delegated supervisory authority to a person who committed acts of harassment "interwoven" with the performance of supervisory duties.[52] Judge Butzner noted that sexual harassment at the workplace is foreseeable, and reasoned that a jury could find that the supervisor's sexual harassment was "part and parcel of his supervision" of the plaintiff.[53]

B. Apparent Authority

Principles of apparent authority[54] might appear to render an employer liable whenever its supervisor explicitly or implicitly uses the delegated authority to hire, fire, direct, and evaluate employees so as to create a hostile environment.[55] Under traditional agency principles, however, apparent authority exists only if it flows from the act of the supervisor's principal, not simply from the subjective personal beliefs of the harassed employee.[56]

Obviously, an employer is not likely to communicate that supervisors have any authority to commit sexual harassment. Indeed, the employer is likely to have published policies that expressly forbid sexual harassment, thereby disavowing any apparent authority that may be observed.[57] In that setting, absent some evidence that the employer tolerates deviations from these poli-

---

[50]*Id.* at 211–12, 39 FEP Cases at 956–57. *See also* Barnes v. Costle, 561 F.2d 983, 995–96, 15 FEP Cases 345, 355 (D.C. Cir. 1977), reproduced in Chapter 1, Overview (MacKinnon, J., concurring)(common law would not impose employer liability for harassment by supervisor because no employee could understand that sexual harassment furthered an objective of employer, or that harassment fell within supervisor's actual or apparent authority).

[51]Davis v. United States Steel Corp., *supra* note 49, 779 F.2d at 214, 39 FEP Cases at 958 (Phillips, J., concurring). *But see* Restatement (Second) of Agency §219(d)(1958)("A master is not subject to liability for the torts of his servants acting outside the scope of their employment, unless . . . [the servant] was aided in accomplishing the tort by existence of the agency relation"); EEOC Policy Guidance on Current Issues, *supra* note 7, §D2(c)2 ("A supervisor's capacity to create a hostile environment is enhanced by the degree of authority conferred on him by the employer").

[52]*Supra* note 49, 779 F.2d at 213, 39 FEP Cases at 954 (Butzner, J., dissenting).

[53]*Id.* at 213, 39 FEP Cases at 957–58. The concurring opinion responded that the dissent's analysis would make the scope-of-employment test no more than an "on-the-job" test. *Id.* at 214, 39 FEP Cases at 958 (Phillips, J., concurring). *See also* note 48 *supra.*

[54]"Apparent authority is the power to affect the legal relations of another person by transactions with third persons, professedly as agent for the other, arising from and in accordance with the other's manifestations to such third persons." Restatement (Second) of Agency §8 (1958).

[55]*See generally* Comment, *An Employer's Guide to Understanding Liability for Sexual Harassment Under Title VII: Meritor Savings Bank v. Vinson,* 55 U. CIN. L. REV. 1181 (1987).

[56]*Id.*

[57]Liability on an apparent agency will be routine, however, wherever the harasser himself is the employer. *See, e.g.,* Ross v. Twenty-Four Collection, 681 F. Supp. 1547, 1552, 48 FEP Cases 1590 (S.D. Fla. 1988)(harasser was president, director, and majority shareholder; no doubt that his knowledge of his own harassment could be imputed to corporation), *aff'd,* 875 F.2d 873, 50 FEP Cases 600 (11th Cir. 1989).

cies, an employee will not have any reasonable belief that a harasser is acting within the scope of a supervisor's authority.[58] As the Eleventh Circuit noted in *Henson v. City of Dundee:*

> The environment in which an employee works can be rendered offensive in an equal degree by the act of supervisors, . . . co-workers, . . . or even strangers to the workplace . . . . *The capacity of any person to create a hostile or offensive environment is not necessarily enhanced or diminished by any degree of authority which the employer confers upon that individual.* When a supervisor gratuitously insults an employee, he generally does so for his reasons and by his own means. He thus acts outside the actual or apparent scope of the authority he possesses as a supervisor. His conduct cannot automatically be imputed to the employer any more so than can the conduct of an ordinary employee.[59]

The EEOC has approached the issue of apparent authority from the point of view of the employee's access to mechanisms that can correct improper supervisory conduct. Its position is that employer inattention to those mechanisms may create the basis for liability under a theory of apparent authority:

> The Commission believes that in the absence of a strong, widely disseminated, and consistently enforced employer policy against sexual harassment, and an effective complaint procedure, employees could reasonably believe that a harassing supervisor's actions will be ignored, tolerated, or even condoned by upper management . . . . If the employer has not provided an effective avenue to complain, then the supervisor has unchecked, final control over the victim and it is reasonable to impute his abuse of this power to the employer.[60]

Notwithstanding the traditional limits to theories of liability based on apparent authority, some courts have held that automatic employer liability is appropriate in hostile environment cases because of the supervisor's apparent authority to control the work environment. Thus, the supervisor may use or threaten to use that authority to help create a hostile environment and make the victim reluctant to report it to higher management.[61] Some judges would therefore impute liability for supervisory harassment to the employer, even absent

---

[58]Fields v. Horizon House, 1987 U.S. Dist. LEXIS 11315 (E.D. Pa. 1987).

[59]682 F.2d 897, 910, 29 FEP Cases 787, 799 (11th Cir. 1982), reproduced in Chapter 4, Hostile Environment Harassment (emphasis added). The opinion in *Henson* distinguished the foregoing discussion of a supervisor's activity in an abusive environment case from a supervisor's activity in a quid pro quo case:

> The typical case of quid pro quo sexual harassment is fundamentally different. In such a case, the supervisor relies upon his apparent or actual authority to extort sexual consideration from an employee. Therein lies the quid pro quo. In that case the supervisor uses the means furnished to him by the employer to accomplish the prohibited purpose. He acts within the scope of his actual or apparent authority to "hire, fire, discipline or promote." . . . Because the supervisor is acting within at least the apparent scope of the authority entrusted to him by the employer when he makes employment decisions, his conduct can fairly be imputed to the source of his authority.

Id., 29 FEP Cases at 799. *See also* Katz v. Dole, 709 F.2d 251, 255, 31 FEP Cases 1521, 1523–24 (4th Cir. 1983), reproduced in Chapter 7, Harassment by Co-Workers.

[60]EEOC Policy Guidance on Current Issues, *supra* note 7, §D2(c)2 ("A supervisor's capacity to create a hostile environment is enhanced by the degree of authority conferred on him by the employer"); *see also* Section IV.C. *infra* (employer's duty to prevent and remedy harassment).

[61]*See, e.g.,* Mitchell v. OsAir, 629 F. Supp. 636, 643, 45 FEP Cases 580, 585 (N.D. Ohio 1986)(decided before *Meritor*):

> [A] supervisor confronted by a woman subordinate who refuses to tolerate a hostile environment can alter working conditions in subtle ways which would probably not be recognized by a *quid pro quo* claim . . . . [The] contention that hostile environment claims against supervisors involve conduct that does not threaten a noncompliant employee with job losses cannot be accepted.

Similarly, in *Jeppsen v. Wunnicke,* 611 F. Supp. 78, 82, 37 FEP Cases 994, 997 (D. Alaska 1985)(another pre-*Meritor* case), the court noted:

> The practical problem is that the employee who stays on the job the longest and puts up with the most

any tangible job detriment, if the supervisor is clothed with the employer's authority to supervise the day-to-day working environment.[62]

The Eleventh Circuit opinion in *Sparks v. Pilot Freight Carriers*[63] illustrates how a supervisor's ability to effectuate quid pro quo harassment can supply apparent authority to sustain employer liability for hostile environment harassment. In *Sparks,* a trucking company terminal manager had wide discretion over all personnel matters in the terminal. He paid special attention to his new billing clerk. Calling her into his office, he asked her if she was married, if she had a boyfriend, and if she could become pregnant. As weeks went by, he would rub her shoulders, play with her hair, and ask her if he could visit her at home with a bottle of wine. He coupled his advances with comments such as "you'd better be nice to me" and "your fate is in my hands."[64] The company's upper management, located in another state, did not know of this conduct until the complainant filed suit. The district court granted summary judgment for the employer on the environmental harassment claim because the supervisor was not acting within the scope of his employment when he harassed the plaintiff, and thus the employer could not be held liable for his acts.[65]

The Eleventh Circuit reversed, holding that the employer could be liable for the harassment even though it was beyond the scope of employment. The court concluded that the supervisor "was aided in accomplishing the tort by the existence of the agency relationship" within the meaning of §219(2)(d) of the Restatement (Second) of Agency.[66]

Application of the *Sparks* apparent agency theory would be doubtful in the absence of explicit threats to misuse supervisorial authority, or in cases where the supervisor lacked power to affect the complainant's tangible job benefits.[67]

---

offensive sexual harassment is more likely than not going to be the employee who is the most dependent on retaining the job . . . [and] likely to be the most reticent to complain.

[62]*E.g.,* Rabidue v. Osceola Ref. Co., *supra* note 45, 805 F.2d at 625, 42 FEP Cases at 642 (Keith, J., dissenting) ("The creation of a discriminatory work environment by a supervisor can only be achieved through the power accorded him by the employer"). *See also* Ross v. Double Diamond, 672 F. Supp. 261, 274, 45 FEP Cases 313, 323 (N.D. Tex. 1987)(harassment by manager of facility who had power to hire and fire imputed to employer under EEOC Guidelines and Justice Marshall's concurring opinion in *Meritor*); Huddleston v. Roger Dean Chevrolet, 845 F.2d 900, 904–5, 46 FEP Cases 1361, 1363 (11th Cir. 1988)(court found "direct" liability under agency principles; when harasser acts as agent of employer, then harasser is employer for purposes of Title VII; plaintiff's harasser was her supervisor who had actual and apparent authority to alter plaintiff's employment status); *see also* cases cited in notes 11–12 *supra. See generally* Sykes, *The Boundaries of Vicarious Liability: An Economic Analysis of the Scope of Employment Rule and Related Legal Doctrines,* 101 HARV. L. REV. 563, 606–8 (1988)(arguing on grounds of economic analysis that employers should be strictly liable for supervisory harassment whether it be quid pro quo or hostile environment).

[63]830 F.2d 1554, 45 FEP Cases 160 (11th Cir. 1987), reproduced in Chapter 2, Forms of Harassment.

[64]*Id.* at 1556, 45 FEP Cases at 161.

[65]*Id.* at 1558–59, 45 FEP Cases at 162–63 (supervisor not "actuated by some purpose to serve the master").

[66]*Id.* at 1559, 45 FEP Cases at 163. The court reasoned that it was unnecessary for the complainant to give notice to the employer because the supervisor was the employer's agent under the circumstances and because Title VII defines "employer" to include any "agent" of an employer. *See also* Levendos v. Stern Entertainment, 909 F.2d 747, 751–53, 53 FEP Cases 779, 783–84 (3d Cir. 1990)(actions of and notice to harassing supervisors were enough to constitute notice to employer, because supervisors threatened complainant with loss of job and had decision-making authority to make their threats good); Rauh v. Coyne, 744 F. Supp. 1186, 1190 (D.D.C. 1990)(employer could be liable for supervisor's harassment under §219(2)(d) of Restatement (Second) of Agency where supervisor was able to harass complainant only because he, as supervisor, had key to enter locked room where complainant worked).

[67]*See* Steele v. Offshore Shipbldg., 867 F.2d 1311, 1316–17, 49 FEP Cases 522 (11th Cir. 1989)(limiting *Sparks* to situations involving quid pro quo as well as hostile environment harassment). *But see* M. ROSSEIN,

C. Direct Liability—Breach of Duty to Prevent and Remedy Harassment

Employer liability for a hostile environment most often stems from a negligent failure to prevent or remedy sexual harassment. This basis for liability is not unique to harassment by supervisors and may also apply in cases of harassment by co-workers and even by a nonemployee.[67a] Courts and the EEOC agree that employers have an affirmative duty under Title VII to institute, communicate, and administer an effective program to prevent sexual harassment.[68] If the employer fails to prevent harassment, then it has a further duty to "investigate ... and deal appropriately with the offending personnel."[69] Conversely, if the employer satisfies its duty to prevent and remedy harassment, it effectively avoids liability.[70]

Courts and the EEOC have attached various labels to this theory of employer liability, including negligence,[71] agency by estoppel,[72] and direct liability.[73] Other courts, using no label, have simply required some level of employer knowledge and failure to prevent or remedy known harassment before imposing liability for environmental harassment by a supervisor.[74] Finally,

---

EMPLOYMENT DISCRIMINATION LAW AND LITIGATION, §6.7(1), at 6-25 n.78 (1990)(arguing for general application of the *Sparks* rationale even absent explicit threats of firing).

[67a]See Chapters 7, Harassment by Co-Workers, Sections IV. and V., and 8, Harassment by Nonemployees. See also Chapters 4, Hostile Environment Harassment, Sections VIII. and IX.C., and 19, Responding to Internal Complaints.

[68]*E.g.*, 29 C.F.R. §1604.11(f), *supra* note 1; Policy Guidance on Current Issues, *supra* note 7, §D2(c)2, and cases cited therein; *see also* Yates v. Avco Corp., 819 F.2d 630, 635–36, 43 FEP Cases 1595, 1599 (6th Cir. 1987)(duty to act upon harassment problem arose earlier when complaints by other female employees were reported); Ross v. Double Diamond, *supra* note 62, 672 F. Supp. at 273, 45 FEP Cases at 322 (knowledge of earlier harassment of a female worker weighed heavily in decision to hold employer liable for same employee's later harassment of other women). For a detailed discussion of the employer's duty to promulgate an effective sexual harassment policy, see Chapter 18, Taking Preventive Action.

[69]Mumford v. James T. Barnes & Co., 441 F. Supp. 459, 466, 17 FEP Cases 107, 112 (E.D. Mich. 1977). For a detailed discussion of the employer's duty to investigate, see Chapter 19, Responding to Internal Complaints.

[70]*E.g.*, Steele v. Offshore Shipbldg., 867 F.2d 1311, 1316, 49 FEP Cases 522, 525 (11th Cir. 1989)(employer escaped liability because it took "prompt remedial action" of sending EEO manager from New York headquarters to Florida to interview employees and bringing harasser home from Saudi Arabia to be reprimanded). See Chapter 27, Asserted Defenses, Section V.

[71]*E.g.*, Policy Guidance on Current Issues, *supra* note 7, §D2(c)3; Restatement (Second) Agency §219(2)(b); Fields v. Horizon House, *supra* note 58 (analyzing employer liability under various theories including negligence and estoppel, court found no liability because of employer's prompt remedial action).

[72]Policy Guidance on Current Issues, *supra* note 7, §D2(c)3, Restatement (Second) Agency §8B; Fields v. Horizon House, *supra* note 58.

[73]Policy Guidance on Current Issues, *supra* note 7, §D2(b). For a collection of pre-*Meritor* decisions adopting these approaches, see *Davis v. Western-Southern Life Ins. Co.,* 34 FEP Cases 97, 101 (N.D. Ohio 1984)(plaintiff must show that employer knew or should have known of supervisor creating abusive environment and failed to take prompt remedial action). For a collection of post-*Meritor* decisions uniformly applying a negligence-like standard, see *Hirschfeld v. New Mexico Corrections Dep't,* 916 F.2d 572, 54 FEP Cases 268, 272 (10th Cir. 1990).

[74]*E.g.*, EEOC v. Hacienda Hotel, 881 F.2d 1504, 1515–16, 50 FEP Cases 877, 886 (9th Cir. 1989)("employers are liable for failing to remedy or prevent a hostile or offensive work environment of which management-level employees knew, or in the exercise of reasonable care, should have known")(citing Hall v. Gus Constr. Co., 842 F.2d 1010, 1015, 46 FEP Cases 573 (8th Cir. 1988), reproduced in Chapter 2, Forms of Harassment, and Hunter v. Allis-Chalmers Corp., 797 F.2d 1417, 1421–22, 41 FEP Cases 721 (7th Cir. 1986)); *see also* Sanchez v. City of Miami Beach, 720 F. Supp. 974, 980 (S.D. Fla. 1989)(proof that employer knew or should have known of harassment required to make out prima facie case of sexual harassment); Baker v. Weyerhaeuser Co., 903 F.2d 1342, 1345, 52 FEP Cases 1872, 1874–75 (10th Cir. 1990)(liability founded not on occasional supervisory role of harasser but on fact that management knew of harassment and did not act to stop it). *But cf.* Waltman v. International Paper Co., 875 F.2d 468, 478, 50 FEP Cases 179, 187 (5th Cir. 1989)("There is some uncertainty in the law concerning the type and extent of notice to the employer necessary to sustain a sexual harassment claim under Title VII"; avoids resolution by finding both actual and constructive notice).

many courts have applied the same standard, but with the misleading label of *respondeat superior*.[75]

D. The Role of the Employer's Grievance Procedure as a Defense

If the employer has in place a preventive procedure "calculated to encourage victims of harassment to come forward,"[76] and a hostile environment complainant fails to report the sexual harassment to upper management, then that failure may be a defense for the employer.[77] The grievance procedure in *Meritor* was deemed inadequate because it required the harassed employee to complain first to her supervisor, who in that case was the harasser.[78] To be effective as a defense to liability, an employer's sexual harassment policy should be easily accessible, well-publicized within the workplace, and provide for prompt, adequate remedial action.[79]

Once an employer is notified that sexual harassment has occurred, the employer may escape liability by taking remedial action, but only if that action is "reasonably calculated to end the harassment."[80] The promptness and adequacy of the employer's response must be evaluated on a case-by-case basis.[81] Whether the sexual harassment ended after the remedial actions were taken is of particular importance.[82]

---

[75]See Section IV.A. *supra*.

[76]Meritor Sav. Bank v. Vinson, 477 U.S. 57, 73, 40 FEP Cases 1822, 1829 (1986), reproduced in Chapter 1, Overview.

[77]The necessary implication of this rationale is that the knowledge of the harasser who has created an abusive environment is not automatically imputed to the employer even though the harasser is a supervisor. *See, e.g.,* Kotcher v. Rosa & Sullivan Appliance Center, 54 EPD ¶40,304 (N.D.N.Y. 1990)(abusive supervisor conduct, including references to plaintiff's breasts and "bodily equipment" and gestures simulating masturbation and ejaculation, not imputed to employer where plaintiffs knew of employer's procedure for reporting sexual harassment, and where immediate action occurred once report was finally made); Davis v. Western-Southern Life Ins. Co., 34 FEP Cases 97, 102 (N.D. Ohio 1984)(no employer liability for harassment by supervisor because plaintiff never reported it to the "appropriate supervisors"). *But see* Hopkins v. Shoe Show of Va., 678 F. Supp. 1241, 1245 (S.D.W. Va. 1988)(denying defendant's motion for summary judgment, given question of material fact as to whether plaintiff had a "reasonably available avenue of complaint"); Salazar v. Church's Fried Chicken, 44 FEP Cases 473 (S.D. Tex. 1987)(court excused employee from giving notice because manager, to whom employee was to complain, was roommate of harasser).

[78]Meritor Sav. Bank v. Vinson, *supra* note 76.

[79]Policy Guidance on Current Issues, *supra* note 7, §E; Meritor Sav. Bank v. Vinson, *supra* note 76. *See also* Yates v. Avco Corp., 819 F.2d 630, 635, 43 FEP Cases 1595, 1599 (6th Cir. 1987)(policy was inadequate because it assumed that supervisor was not harasser and gave supervisor responsibility for both reporting and correcting the harassment; the court noted that policy was "vague on paper, [and] vague and ad hoc in its implementation and did not function effectively to eliminate harassment").

[80]*See, e.g.,* Sanchez v. City of Miami Beach, 720 F. Supp. 974, 981 (S.D. Fla. 1989)(employer must do more than indicate the existence of an official policy against sexual harassment)(quoting Katz v. Dole, 709 F.2d 251, 256, 31 FEP Cases 1521, 1524 (4th Cir. 1983), reproduced in Chapter 7, Harassment by Co-Workers. For a more detailed discussion of remedial action, see Chapter 19, Responding to Internal Complaints.

[81]Dornhecker v. Malibu Grand Prix, 828 F.2d 307, 309–10, 44 FEP Cases 1604, 1605 (5th Cir. 1987)(employer's remedial action taken within 12 hours of incident decided case for employer); Rabidue v. Osceola Ref. Co., 805 F.2d 611, 621, 42 FEP Cases 631, 638–39 (6th Cir. 1986), reproduced in Chapter 2, Forms of Harassment, *cert. denied*, 481 U.S. 1041 (1987); Bennett v. New York City Dep't of Corrections, 705 F. Supp. 979, 987–88, 49 FEP Cases 134, 141 (S.D.N.Y. 1989)(employee's claim survived summary judgment in part because employer took four weeks to respond to incident).

[82]Brooms v. Regal Tube Co., 881 F.2d 412, 421, 50 FEP Cases 1499, 1505 (7th Cir. 1989)(employer held liable even though it made supervisor apologize to victim, postponed merit salary increase, and threatened supervisor with termination, because a few weeks following these actions, harassment began anew); Steele v. Offshore Shipbldg., 867 F.2d 1311, 1316, 49 FEP Cases 522, 525 (11th Cir. 1989)(employer not liable after it promptly issued a reprimand and harassment stopped); Swentek v. USAir, 830 F.2d 552, 558, 44 FEP Cases 1808, 1813 (4th Cir. 1987)(after employer issued written warning, no more complaints were received; warning was an adequate remedial action).

CHAPTER 7

HARASSMENT BY CO-WORKERS

I. THE NATURE OF CO-WORKER HARASSMENT

Sexual harassment in the workplace is perpetrated not only by supervisors, but also by co-workers. Indeed, harassment by co-workers may well be the most prevalent form of sexual harassment.[1] Co-worker harassment is hostile environment harassment.[2] Quid pro quo analysis does not apply because co-worker harassment, by definition, does not involve the abuse of power delegated by the employer.[3]

The lack of formal authority does not mean that the co-worker lacks the power to harm the victim.[4] As one commentator has observed:

> Women in many nontraditional blue collar occupations are not only dependent upon ... co-workers for their training and job assignments, but also for their physical safety. The ability to "get along" takes on a whole new meaning when you are working in a 40-story elevator shaft, handling "hot" wires, or walking a 12-inch beam over a busy expressway with a load of two-by-fours or steel rods.[5]

The power of peers to inject fear and anxiety into the workplace is evident in many co-worker harassment cases. One sexual harassment complainant asserted that a co-worker pulled a ladder out from under her and shoved a steel pipe into her ribs while they were both on a plumbing job.[6] Another sexual harassment complainant alleged that a co-worker stuck his tongue in her ear while she was carrying a vial of hot liquid through the powerhouse of a paper mill.[7] In racial harassment cases, courts have emphasized a black firefighter's concern that his co-workers might not work as a team with him in a firefighting

---

[1]Note, *Employer Liability for Co-Worker Sexual Harassment Under Title VII*, 13 N.Y.U. REV. L. & SOC. CHANGE 83, 86 (1985)(citing statistics that hostile environment harassment is perpetrated by co-workers more often than supervisors, and "is at least as prevalent" as quid pro quo harassment, although it may not trigger as much litigation in that it does not necessarily cause direct economic harm). *See also* Pollack, *Sexual Harassment: Women's Experience vs. Legal Definitions*, 13 HARV. WOMEN'S L.J. 35, 51 n.52 (1990)(same, citing additional sources); Allegretti, *Sexual Harassment of Female Employees by Nonsupervisory Co-Workers: A Theory of Liability*, 15 CREIGHTON L. REV. 437, 438 n.7 (1982) (same).

[2]See Chapter 4, Hostile Environment Harassment.

[3]See Chapters 3, Quid Pro Quo Harassment, and 6, Harassment by Supervisors.

[4]Pollack, *supra* note 1, 13 HARV. WOMEN'S L.J. at 50–51 (arguing male co-workers have power to harm by virtue of the "existing gender hierarchy").

[5]*Id.* at 73 n.151.

[6]Egger v. Plumbers Local 276, 644 F. Supp. 795, 797, 41 FEP Cases 1465, 1467 (D. Mass. 1986).

[7]Waltman v. International Paper Co., 875 F.2d 468, 471, 50 FEP Cases 179, 181–82 (5th Cir. 1989).

situation,[8] and a black corrections officer's fears that white officers might not respond to his calls for assistance.[9]

Personal fear of co-workers is not confined to blue collar settings. In *Lipsett v. University of Puerto Rico,*[10] a female resident in a general surgery training program was warned by the chief resident of a "reign of terror" against women, and was advised that, as a low-level female resident, she should "keep a relationship" with a senior male resident.

The co-workers themselves generally are not individually liable under Title VII.[11] Their liability would fall under common-law theories,[12] state discrimination statutes,[13] or, possibly, criminal statutes.[14]

The employer is not necessarily liable for co-worker harassment. Rather, the inquiry as to employer liability focuses on whether the employer had actual or constructive notice of the harassment and, if so, whether the employer acted appropriately to control the harassment.[15] Because co-worker harassment involves no abuse of the employer's authority, the employer's liability for co-worker harassment is a matter of its failure to exercise control over the workplace. Supervisor acquiescence in co-worker harassment may rise to the level of ratification, making co-worker harassment tantamount to supervisor harassment.[16]

Co-worker harassment tends to occur most often in situations where women have entered jobs or workplaces traditionally occupied by male incumbents.[17] Thus, plaintiffs in many co-worker harassment cases are women who have entered traditionally "male" jobs such as police officer,[18] firefighter,[19] plumber,[20] electrician,[21] truck driver,[22] engineer,[23] car salesperson,[24] pilot,[25] air traffic

---

[8]DeGrace v. Rumsfeld, 614 F.2d 796, 801, 21 FEP Cases 1444, 1446 (1st Cir. 1980).

[9]Snell v. Suffolk County, 782 F.2d 1094, 1098, 39 FEP Cases 1590, 1593 (2d Cir. 1986).

[10]864 F.2d 881, 887, 888, 54 FEP Cases 230 (1st Cir. 1988)(harassment suit brought under Title IX and §1983).

[11]Zabkowicz v. West Bend Co., 589 F. Supp. 780, 35 FEP Cases 610 (E.D. Wis. 1984)(complainant cannot sue nonsupervisory co-workers for sexual harassment under Title VII), *aff'd in relevant part,* 789 F.2d 540, 546, 40 FEP Cases 1171, 1176 (7th Cir. 1986). For a discussion of potential Title VII liability for individual harassers, see Chapter 23, The Alleged Harasser as Defendant.

[12]See Chapter 15, The Common Law.

[13]See Chapter 12, Fair Employment Practices Statutes.

[14]See Chapter 16, Criminal Law.

[15]See Sections IV. and V. *infra.*

[16]*See* Katz v. Dole, 709 F.2d 251, 255 n.6, 31 FEP Cases 1521, 1524 (4th Cir. 1983), reproduced *infra.* See Chapter 6, Harassment by Supervisors.

[17]Pollack, *supra* note 1, 13 HARV. WOMEN'S L.J. at 66 n.122 (harassment most prevalent with women in jobs where they comprise 15% or less of work force).

[18]Andrews v. City of Philadelphia, 895 F.2d 1469, 54 FEP Cases 184 (3d Cir. 1990); Arnold v. City of Seminole, 614 F. Supp. 853, 40 FEP Cases 1539 (E.D. Okla. 1985); Sapp v. City of Warner Robins, 655 F. Supp. 1043, 43 FEP Cases 486 (M.D. Ga. 1987); Vermett v. Hough, 627 F. Supp. 587, 42 FEP Cases 1432 (W.D. Mich. 1986).

[19]Downum v. City of Wichita, 675 F. Supp. 1566, 49 FEP Cases 162 (D. Kan. 1986).

[20]Egger v. Plumbers Local 276, *supra* note 6, 644 F. Supp. at 798, 41 FEP Cases at 1467 (plaintiff told to "psychologically become a man").

[21]Reynolds v. Atlantic City Convention Ctr., 53 FEP Cases 1852 (D.N.J. 1990)(journeyman electrician called "douche bag cunt" by co-workers).

[22]Llewellyn v. Celanese Corp., 693 F. Supp. 369, 47 FEP Cases 993 (W.D.N.C. 1988); Martin v. Norbar, Inc., 537 F. Supp. 1260, 30 FEP Cases 103 (S.D. Ohio 1982).

[23]Kyriazi v. Western Elec. Co., 461 F. Supp. 894, 18 FEP Cases 924 (D.N.J. 1978), *vacated in part,* 473 F. Supp. 786, 25 FEP Cases 86 (D.N.J. 1979), *aff'd,* 647 F.2d 388 (3d Cir. 1981).

[24]Huddleston v. Roger Dean Chevrolet, 845 F.2d 900, 46 FEP Cases 1361 (11th Cir. 1988).

[25]Freedman v. American Standard, 41 FEP Cases 471 (D.N.J. 1986).

controller,[26] securities trader,[27] surgeon,[28] miner,[29] automobile mechanic,[30] airline mechanic,[31] and railroad engineer.[32] Other plaintiffs are women who work in traditionally "male" work environments such as fire stations,[33] warehouses,[34] assembly line manufacturing operations,[35] prisons,[36] oil refining companies,[37] paper mills,[38] construction sites,[39] steel plants,[40] and the military.[41]

Explanations for co-worker harassment of members of a female minority are varied. Some theorize that the harassment stems from the male workers' own "sense of disempowerment";[42] men may perceive female newcomers as economically or psychologically threatening and want to keep a woman "in her place."[43] One commentator has explained co-worker harassment as an attempt to resurrect the barriers that excluded women from the workplace prior to the enactment of Title VII:

---

[26]Katz v. Dole, *supra* note 16.

[27]Halpert v. Wertheim & Co., 27 FEP Cases 21 (S.D.N.Y. 1980).

[28]Lipsett v. University of P.R., 864 F.2d 881, 906–7, 54 FEP Cases 230 (1st Cir. 1988).

[29]*See* Goodman, *Sexual Harassment: Some Observations on the Distance Travelled and the Distance Yet to Go,* 10 Cap. U.L. Rev. 445, 454–55 (1981)(citing newspaper accounts of female miners being stripped, greased, tied, blindfolded, and hung from coal-loading silo).

[30]Scott v. Sears, Roebuck & Co., 798 F.2d 210, 41 FEP Cases 805 (7th Cir. 1986).

[31]Graham v. American Airlines, 53 FEP Cases 1390 (N.D. Okla. 1989)(airline mechanic touched by co-workers).

[32]Masiello v. Metro-North Commuter R.R., 54 FEP Cases 172 (S.D.N.Y. 1990)(engineer forcibly hugged, kissed, and grabbed by co-workers).

[33]Bohen v. City of E. Chicago, 622 F. Supp. 1234, 39 FEP Cases 917 (N.D. Ind. 1985)(dispatcher in fire station), *aff'd in part and rev'd in part,* 799 F.2d 1180, 41 FEP Cases 1108 (7th Cir. 1986).

[34]Zabkowicz v. West Bend Co., 589 F. Supp. 780, 35 FEP Cases 610 (E.D. Wis. 1984)(general warehouse worker), *aff'd in relevant part,* 789 F.2d 540, 546, 40 FEP Cases 1171, 1176 (7th Cir. 1986).

[35]Perkins v. General Motors Corp., 709 F. Supp. 1487, 51 FEP Cases 1684 (W.D. Mo. 1988)(supervisor at automobile manufacturing plant); Goodman, *supra* note 21, 10 Cap. U.L. Rev. at 455–56.

[36]Minteer v. Auger, 844 F.2d 569, 46 FEP Cases 1173 (8th Cir. 1988)(correctional officer); Bennett v. New York City Dep't of Corrections, 705 F. Supp. 979, 49 FEP Cases 134 (S.D.N.Y. 1989)(same).

[37]Rabidue v. Osceola Ref. Co., 805 F.2d 611, 42 FEP Cases 631 (6th Cir. 1986), reproduced in Chapter 2, Forms of Harassment (sole woman in salaried management position), *cert. denied,* 481 U.S. 1041 (1987).

[38]Waltman v. International Paper Co., 875 F.2d 468, 50 FEP Cases 179 (5th Cir. 1989), reproduced in Chapter 2, Forms of Harassment (worker in powerhouse); Baker v. Weyerhaeuser Co., 903 F.2d 1342, 52 FEP Cases 1872 (10th Cir. 1990)(clean-up worker).

[39]Hall v. Gus Constr. Co., 842 F.2d 1010, 46 FEP Cases 573 (8th Cir. 1988)(flag person); *see also* Goodman, *supra* note 29, 10 Cap. U.L. Rev. at 455 & n.66.

[40]Bradford v. Guardsmark, Inc., 53 FEP Cases 1732 (N.D. Ind. 1990)(only female emergency technician at steel plant).

[41]Goodman, *supra* note 29, 10 Cap. U.L. Rev. at 455 & n.67 (describing studies on harassment in the armed forces). *See generally* Pollack, *Sexual Harassment: Women's Experience vs. Legal Definitions,* 13 Harv. Women's L.J. 35, 66–67 n.122 (1990)(citing studies to effect that women suffer most harassment when holding nontraditional jobs and when working in predominantly male work groups); Lab. Law. Reports (CCH)(Nov. 19, 1990)(22% of active duty military personnel experienced sexual harassment in 1989, with women four times as likely as men to experience sexual harassment).

[42]Some commentators go so far as to suppose that employers have granted male workers the freedom to harass their female co-workers as some kind of no-cost status benefit. *E.g.,* Ehrenreich, *Pluralist Myths and Powerless Men: The Ideology of Reasonableness in Sexual Harassment Law,* 99 Yale L.J. 1176, 1228–29 (1990)("male worker's acquiescence in the hierarchical and regimented structuring of the capitalist workplace is 'bought' by allowing him to retain some sense of power through subordinating women"); Note, *Employer Liability for Co-Worker Sexual Harassment Under Title VII,* 13 N.Y.U. Rev. L. & Soc. Change 83, 102 n.121 (1985)(co-worker harassment as status benefit conferred by male supervisors upon male subordinates).

[43]L. Farley, Sexual Shakedown (1978); Comment, *The Harms of Asking: Towards a Comprehensive Treatment of Sexual Harassment,* 55 U. Chi. L. Rev. 328, 341 (1988)(men uncomfortable with women in a work role); Note, *supra* note 42, 13 N.Y.U. Rev. L. & Soc. Change at 102 n.121 (characterizing co-worker harassment as "competition-reducing device . . . [to] protect [male] salaries, positions, and egos by limiting the number of females in the workplace"). For an extensive account of the relationship between sex segregation in jobs and the efforts of males in male-dominated jobs to use sexual harassment as a means of protecting "their territory" from incursions by female workers, see Schultz, *Telling Stories About Women and Work: Judicial Interpretations of Sex Segregation in the Workplace in Title VII Cases Raising the Lack of Interest Argument,* 103 Harv. L. Rev. 1749, 1832–39 (1990)(discussion under the heading of "The Work Cultures of Traditionally Male Jobs").

Sexist speech, like rape, is not only—and perhaps not at all—about sex. It is about power. It is the way that some men respond to the threat posed by the reality of women in the workplace, especially when women enter a field traditionally dominated by men. In essence, sexist speech reinstitutionalizes barriers in the workplace based on gender. When women subjected to sexist speech leave the job, or persist but with decreased productivity, it serves to perpetuate male dominance in the workplace.[43a]

Others have suggested that what a new female worker perceives as sexually harassing is simply the preexisting condition of the environment.[44]

II. Judicial Recognition of Co-Worker Harassment as Actionable

Some early decisions, comparing the co-worker's authority to the employer's authority, rejected claims of co-worker harassment on the ground that co-workers lack the power to affect the complainant's terms and conditions of employment.[45] Courts now recognize that the formal authority of the harasser does not control whether the harassment had made the complainant's environment so hostile, offensive, or intimidating as to alter the terms and conditions of work.[46] As the Eleventh Circuit stated in *Henson v. City of Dundee*, "[t]he capacity of any person to create a hostile or offensive work environment is not necessarily enhanced or diminished by any degree of authority which the employer confers on that individual."[47]

The analysis of employer liability for co-worker sexual harassment evolved largely from cases involving racial harassment.[48] In the ground-breaking case of *Rogers v. EEOC*,[49] the Fifth Circuit in 1971 held that Title VII, in forbidding discrimination as to "terms, conditions, and privileges of employment," forbids "working environments so heavily polluted with discrimination as to destroy completely the emotional and psychological stability of minority group workers."[50] Employer liability for unchecked racial harassment by co-workers was well-established by 1980, when the First Circuit decided *DeGrace v.*

[43a]Strauss, *Sexist Speech in the Workplace,* 25 HARV. CIV. C.R.-C.L. L. REV. 1, 13–14 (1990)(citations omitted).

[44]See cases cited in Chapter 4, Hostile Environment Harassment, Section VI.C.3.b. (opinions emphasizing relevance of workplace cultural norms).

[45]*E.g.,* Smith v. Rust Eng'g Co., 20 FEP Cases 1172 (N.D. Ala. 1978)(no Title VII violation where harassing co-worker "did not promise [plaintiff] anything with respect to her employment and the plaintiff does not claim that acquiescence in the sexual advances . . . was impliedly or expressly required as a condition of employment").

[46]The formal authority of the harasser may be relevant to the issue of the employer's automatic liability for quid pro quo harassment, but even a subordinate can perpetrate co-worker hostile environment harassment. Moffett v. Gene B. Glick Co., 621 F. Supp. 244, 272, 41 FEP Cases 671, 689–90 (N.D. Ind. 1985)(factual dispute whether harassers were plaintiff's subordinates immaterial to question whether plaintiff could be racially harassed in violation of Title VII).

[47]682 F.2d 897, 910, 29 FEP Cases 787, 799 (11th Cir. 1982), reproduced in Chapter 4, Hostile Environment Harassment.

[48]The EEOC's 1980 Guidelines, while codifying judicial decisions on quid pro quo harassment, were proposing new law with respect to employer liability for hostile environment harassment. Comment, *supra* note 43, 55 U. CHI. L. REV. at 335–36 (EEOC wanted to align sexual harassment with racial, religious, national origin harassment). For a detailed discussion of how the law of harassment on other bases has served as a background for the development of sexual harassment law, see Chapter 2, Forms of Harassment.

[49]454 F.2d 234, 4 FEP Cases 92 (5th Cir. 1971).

[50]*Id.,* 4 FEP Cases at 95.

Rumsfeld.[51] The plaintiff in *DeGrace* was the only black civilian firefighter at a naval air station, where his co-workers referred to him in derogatory racial terms, damaged his equipment, subjected him to the "silent treatment," and put threatening notes in his locker.[52] The First Circuit held that an employer "may not stand by and allow an employee to be subjected to a course of racial harassment by co-workers."[53] While an employer "cannot change the personal beliefs of his employees he can let it be known ... that racial harassment will not be tolerated, and he can take all reasonable measures to enforce this policy."[54] "[M]ore than mere verbal chastisements of those employees who used racial epithets was needed in order ... forcefully to convey the message that racism would not be tolerated."[55]

In promulgating its guidelines on sexual harassment, the EEOC acknowledged its debt to the holdings of such cases as *Rogers* and *DeGrace.*[56] The EEOC Guidelines address employer liability for co-worker harassment as follows: "With respect to conduct between fellow employees, an employer is responsible for acts of sexual harassment in the workplace where the employer (or its agents or supervisory employees) knows or should have known of the conduct, unless it can show that it took immediate and appropriate corrective action."[57]

The first court to adopt the EEOC's view of employer liability for co-worker sexual harassment was the Minnesota Supreme Court in *Continental Can Co. v. Minnesota.*[58] Courts have consistently followed this view.[59]

---

[51]614 F.2d 796, 21 FEP Cases 1444 (1st Cir. 1980).

[52]*Id.* at 799–800, 21 FEP Cases at 1445–46 (One note read: "If we end up having a fire, you'll be staying in it and getting a lot blacker.").

[53]*Id.* at 803, 21 FEP Cases at 1448.

[54]*Id.* at 805, 21 FEP Cases at 1449.

[55]*Id.* at 805 & n.5, 21 FEP Cases at 1450.

[56]In ruling that harassment on the basis of sex violates Title VII, the EEOC stated in a footnote that "the principles involved here continue to apply to race, color, religion or national origin." 29 C.F.R. §1604.11(a)(1990), reproduced in Appendix 1.

[57]29 C.F.R. §1604.11(d), reproduced in Appendix 1. In 1980, after notice and comment, the EEOC issued its Guidelines on Discrimination Because of Sex, 29 C.F.R. §§1604.1–.11, one part of which (§1604.11) was on sexual harassment. The EEOC Guidelines are nonbinding but "constitute a body of experience and informed judgments to which courts and litigants may properly resort for guidance." Meritor Sav. Bank v. Vinson, 477 U.S. 57, 65, 40 FEP Cases 1822, 1826 (1986), reproduced in Chapter 1, Overview (citation omitted). *See also* Henson v. City of Dundee, 682 F.2d 897, 903 n.7, 29 FEP Cases 787, 792 (11th Cir. 1982), reproduced in Chapter 4, Hostile Environment Harassment.

[58]297 N.W.2d 241, 249, 22 FEP Cases 1808, 1813 (Minn. 1980). The plaintiff alleged that co-workers engaged in verbal advances, sexually motivated touching, and sexually derogatory comments, such as one pining for a return to slavery days so that the complainant could be trained as her co-worker's sexual servant. The case was one of first impression under the Minnesota Human Rights Act. Reversing the lower court judgment for the defendant, the court followed applicable Title VII authority, including the then-interim EEOC Guidelines on co-worker harassment. *Id.* at 248, 22 FEP Cases at 1812–13. The court held that the Minnesota statute "imposes a duty on the employer to take prompt and appropriate action when it knows or should have known of co-employees' conduct in the workplace amounting to sexual harassment." *Id.* at 249, 22 FEP Cases at 1814.

[59]*E.g., Fourth Circuit:* Katz v. Dole, 709 F.2d 251, 256, 31 FEP Cases 1521, 1524 (4th Cir. 1983), reproduced *infra;*

Fifth Circuit: Waltman v. International Paper Co., 875 F.2d 468, 477, 50 FEP Cases 179, 186–87 (5th Cir. 1989);

Sixth Circuit: Rabidue v. Osceola Ref. Co., 805 F.2d 611, 621, 42 FEP Cases 631, 638 (6th Cir. 1986), reproduced in Chapter 2, Forms of Harassment, *cert. denied,* 481 U.S. 1041 (1987);

Eighth Circuit: Barrett v. Omaha Nat'l Bank, 726 F.2d 424, 427, 35 FEP Cases 593, 594 (8th Cir. 1984);

Tenth Circuit: Baker v. Weyerhaeuser Co., 903 F.2d 1342, 1345, 52 FEP Cases 1872, 1875 (10th Cir. 1990);

Eleventh Circuit: Huddleston v. Roger Dean Chevrolet, 845 F.2d 900, 904, 46 FEP Cases 1361, 1363 (11th Cir. 1988).

Hostile environment harassment by co-workers can occur even where the harassers are subordinates of the complainant.[60] However, one court has held that where the complainant is capable of stopping the unwelcome conduct by means of supervisory power, a hostile environment claim will fail.[61]

III. Elements of Employer Liability for Co-Worker Harassment

Employer liability for co-worker harassment depends upon a showing that the complainant, because of gender and with the actual or constructive knowledge of the employer, was subjected to harassment so severe or pervasive as to affect the terms and conditions of employment and that the employer failed to take prompt corrective action.[62]

In *Katz v. Dole,* the Fourth Circuit proposed the following elements and order of proof. First, the plaintiff must produce evidence that sexually harassing actions occurred, evidence that the employer may rebut by showing that the events did not occur or that they were "isolated or genuinely trivial." Second, the plaintiff must produce evidence that the employer knew or should have known of the harassment and took no prompt remedial action. This evidence, too, is subject to employer rebuttal.

KATZ v. DOLE

709 F.2d 251, 31 FEP Cases 1521 (4th Cir. 1983)

ERVIN, Circuit Judge:—

Deborah Ann Katz is a former federal air traffic controller whose employment was terminated by the Federal Aviation Administration (FAA) in September, 1981, for alleged participation in an illegal strike against the FAA. • • • Katz' complaint claimed that she had been subjected to sexual harassment and to disparate and adverse personnel actions amounting to gender discrimination in violation of Title VII • • • At the close of the trial, that court found Katz had not been the object of intentional discrimination on the basis of her sex and • • • granted Katz limited relief on her prayer for a correction of her government employment files. Katz appeals. We conclude that Katz did make out a case of sexual harassment

---

[60]*E.g.,* Erebia v. Chrysler Plastic Prods. Corp., 772 F.2d 1250, 37 FEP Cases 1820 (6th Cir. 1985)(affirming liability verdict in favor of Mexican-American supervisor harassed by subordinates; issue of plaintiff's supervisory status not raised), *cert. denied,* 475 U.S. 1015 (1986). *See* Moffett v. Gene B. Glick Co., *supra* note 46 (degree of harasser's authority not dispositive as to existence of hostile environment). For a skeptical view of alleged harassment by co-workers, see *Waltman v. International Paper Co.,* 875 F.2d 468, 50 FEP Cases 179 (5th Cir. 1989)(Jones, J., dissenting). Noting that " '[h]arassment' and 'power' are active nouns that embody an exercise of will," Judge Jones takes a limited view of the circumstances in which the acts of co-workers "can render the employer liable for . . . the noxious exercise of power that Title VII forbids." *Id.* at 482, 50 FEP Cases at 191.

[61]Perkins v. General Motors Corp., 709 F. Supp. 1487, 1500–1501, 51 FEP Cases 1684, 1695 (W.D. Mo. 1988)(female supervisory employee authorized to discipline subordinates failed to establish sexually hostile work environment when she declined to formally punish subordinate who touched her breast).

[62]*See* Note, *Employer Liability for Co-Worker Sexual Harassment Under Title VII,* 13 N.Y.U. Rev. L. & Soc. Change 83, 90 (1985):

In a co-worker sexual harassment case, a plaintiff must plead and prove six elements: (1) that she belongs to a protected class; (2) that she was subjected to unwelcome sexual harassment; (3) that the sexual harassment was based upon her sex; (4) that the sexual harassment was intentional; (5) that it adversely affected her compensation, terms, conditions, or privileges of employment . . .; and (6) that the employer is responsible for the sexual harassment.

See Chapter 4, Hostile Environment Harassment.

actionable under Title VII but find no error in the district court's handling of Katz' disparate treatment claim. We therefore affirm in part and reverse in part.[1]

I.

Katz entered the federal air traffic controller training program in 1974. In 1977, she was assigned to the Washington Air Traffic Control Center, and in August, 1980, she was certified as a fully trained controller. At the Washington Center, Katz was assigned to controller crew 1F, supervised by John J. Sullivan. She was the only woman on the crew. She was transferred to another crew in May, 1982, at her own request. While working on crew 1F and under Sullivan's supervision, Katz alleges she was subjected to substantial sexual harassment by FAA employees, including Sullivan and other supervisory personnel. She also asserts that she brought this harassment to the attention of Sullivan, who responded with further sexual harassment, and of Sullivan's superior, who reacted with indifference.

The record[2] confirms Katz' allegations. The FAA workplace was pervaded with sexual slur, insult and innuendo, and Katz was personally the object of verbal sexual harassment by her fellow controllers. This harassment took the form of extremely vulgar and offensive sexually related epithets addressed to and employed about Katz by supervisory personnel as well as by other controllers. The words used were ones widely recognized not only as improper but as intensely degrading, deriving their power to wound not only from their meaning but also from "the disgust and violence they express phonetically." C. Miller & K. Swift, *Words and Women* 109 (1977).

FAA supervisory personnel had been alerted to the problem. One of the Secretary's witnesses, the manager of the controller training program, testified that he was aware from female workers' complaints that sexual intimidation was a "common" experience at the agency. Sullivan testified that he had heard controllers referring to Katz by obscenities. Sullivan himself admitted that he had suggested to Katz that her problems with another controller, about whose sexual advances Katz was complaining, might be solved if Katz submitted to him. Uncontradicted testimony by Katz indicated that the supervisor of crew 2F once stated in her presence that he would consider accepting her transfer to his crew because of her sexual abilities. Katz' witnesses corroborated Katz' testimony that Sullivan and other crew members frequently referred to Katz by obscene words.[3]

The record is devoid of significant evidence to contradict Katz' claims that her employment by the FAA was conditioned by a pattern of personally directed sexual insult and innuendo. Furthermore, despite their knowledge of this harassment, her employer's supervisory personnel did nothing effectual to stop it, and indeed, in Sullivan's case, took part in it.

In Garber v. Saxon Business Products, Inc., 552 F.2d 1032, 15 FEP Cases 344 (4th Cir. 1977), we recognized that "an employer policy or acquiescence in a practice" of sexual harassment can constitute a violation of Title VII. When such harassment pervades the workplace, or is condoned or carried out by supervisory personnel, it becomes an illegal and discriminatory condition of employment that poisons the work environment. See 42 U.S.C. §2000e-2(a)(1). Sexual harassment erects barriers to participation in the work force of the sort Congress intended to sweep away by the enactment of Title VII. See Bundy v. Jackson, 641 F.2d 934, 944, 24 FEP Cases 1155 (D.C. Cir. 1981). See generally Los Angeles Dept. of Water & Power v. Manhart, 435 U.S. 702, 707 n.13, 17 FEP Cases 395 (1978) (in

---

[1]This case is not moot. Katz is appealing her termination through administrative proceedings which are still ongoing. In the event Katz prevails on this appeal, and subsequently is reinstated by the FAA, the award of injunctive or declaratory relief could be appropriate. In addition, even if she does not regain her job, Katz might be entitled to nominal damages and attorneys fees. See Joshi v. Florida State University, 646 F.2d 981, 991 n.33, 26 FEP Cases 300 (5th Cir. 1981), cert. denied, 456 U.S. ___, 72 L.Ed. 2d 845, 28 FEP Cases 1391 (1982).

[2][Omitted.]

[3]One of Katz' witnesses, a male controller in another crew, and a friend of Katz, testified that he and Katz used nicknames for one another with possible sexual connotations. There is no evidence, however, that this linguistic intimacy was known to other, unfriendly and harassing FAA employees. A person's private and consensual sexual activities do not constitute a waiver of his or her legal protections against unwelcome and unsolicited sexual harassment.

forbidding gender discrimination Congress intended to prohibit the "entire spectrum" of disparate treatment on the basis of sex).

Sexual harassment, like other forms of gender discrimination, can take many forms, but the Eleventh Circuit has identified two basic varieties: "harassment that creates an offensive environment ('condition of work') and harassment in which a supervisor demands sexual consideration in exchange for job benefits *('quid pro quo')."* Henson v. City of Dundee, 682 F.2d 897, 908 n.18, 29 FEP Cases 787 (11th Cir. 1982), citing C. MacKinnon, *Sexual Harassment of Working Women* 32-47 (1979). See 29 C.F.R. §1604.11(a) (similar analysis in EEOC guidelines on sexual harassment). Katz' primary claim falls within the "condition of work" category: she alleged in her complaint and proved at trial that her fellow employees' unwelcome and demeaning sexually related behavior toward her created "an intimidating, hostile [and] offensive working environment." 29 C.F.R. §1604.11(a)(3). The evidence also indicates that Katz was made *quid pro quo* propositions at times.

Although such a claim of sexual harassment might be analyzed under the familiar Title VII disparate treatment formula,[4] we think that a somewhat different order of proof is appropriate. See McDonnell Douglas Corp. v. Green, 411 U.S. 792, 802 n.13, 5 FEP Cases 965 (1973) (disparate treatment analysis not necessarily applicable in every aspect to all factual situations). In the usual case involving allegations of disparate treatment, once the plaintiff establishes that he or she was disadvantaged in fact by some employment decision or practice, the crux of the matter is the question of motive: was there an intent to discriminate along legally impermissible lines such as race or gender?[5] In cases involving claims of sexual harassment, on the other hand, the sexual advance or insult almost always will represent "an intentional assault on an individual's innermost privacy." Bundy, 641 F.2d at 945. Therefore, once the plaintiff in such a case proves that harassment took place, the most difficult legal question typically will concern the responsibility of the employer for that harassment. Except in situations where a proprietor, partner or corporate officer participates personally in the harassing behavior, the plaintiff will have the additional responsibility of demonstrating the propriety of holding the employer liable under some theory of *respondeat superior.* We believe that in a "condition of work" case the plaintiff must demonstrate that the employer had actual or constructive knowledge of the existence of a sexually hostile working environment and took no prompt and adequate remedial action. Henson, 682 F.2d at 905; Bundy, 641 F.2d at 943; 29 C.F.R. §1604.11(d). The plaintiff may do this by proving that complaints about the harassment were lodged with the employer or that the harassment was so pervasive that employer awareness may be inferred.[6] Thus, we posit a two step analysis. First, the plaintiff must make a *prima facie* showing that sexually harassing actions took place, and if this is done, the employer may rebut the showing either directly, by proving that the events did not take place, or indirectly, by showing that they were isolated or

---

[4]First, the plaintiff has the burden of proving by the preponderance of the evidence a prima facie case of discrimination. Second, if the plaintiff succeeds in proving the prima facie case, the burden shifts to the defendant "to articulate some legitimate, nondiscriminatory reason for the [employment decision.]" Third, should the defendant carry this burden, the plaintiff must then have an opportunity to prove by a preponderance of the evidence that the legitimate reasons offered by the defendant were not its true reasons, but were a pretext for discrimination.
Texas Dept. of Community Affairs v. Burdine, 450 U.S. 248, 252-53, 25 FEP Cases 113 (1981) (citations omitted).

[5]The McDonnell Douglas scheme is intended "to bring the litigants and the court expeditiously and fairly to [the] ultimate question" of whether "the defendant intentionally discriminated against the plaintiff." Burdine, 450 U.S. at 253.

[6]Where the plaintiff's complaint is of *quid pro quo* harassment by supervisory personnel, the employer is strictly liable. Henson, 682 F.2d at 910; 29 C.F.R. §1604.11(c). It is arguable that Katz meets this less stringent standard for imposing liability. The district court specifically found that Katz' supervisor responded to Katz' complaint about sexual harassment by a co-worker, whom the supervisor had designated to oversee part of Katz' on-the-job training, with the suggestion that the problem might be solved by acquiescing in the co-worker's propositions. (We note that the identical result occurred when the plaintiff in Henson attempted to complain about a co-worker's advances. 682 F.2d at 905 n.10. Sexually abusive supervisors are, it appears, short on originality as well as rectitude.) In addition, Katz testified, and her testimony was unrebutted, that during a discussion with another crew's supervisor on the possibility of transferring to his crew, the supervisor suggested that the transfer could be arranged in consideration of Katz' sexual favors. These facts probably make out a *quid pro quo* case. We need not resolve this question, however, since Katz' complaint was framed in condition of work terms, and we conclude that she meets the requirements to prevail on those terms.

genuinely trivial. Second, the plaintiff must show that the employer knew or should have known of the harassment, and took no effectual action to correct the situation. This showing can also be rebutted by the employer directly, or by pointing to prompt remedial action reasonably calculated to end the harassment. Title VII is not a clean language act, and it does not require employers to extirpate all signs of centuries-old prejudices. But to avoid liability under Title VII, an employer on notice of sexual harassment must do more than indicate the existence of an official policy against such harassment. Where, as here, the employer's supervisory personnel manifested unmistakable acquiescence in or approval of the harassment, the burden on the employer seeking to avoid liability is especially heavy.[7]

Katz satisfied the requirements for proving sexual harassment actionable under Title VII. Her testimony and that of her witnesses that she was the object of sustained and non-trivial harassment was corroborated by the Secretary's own witnesses. Furthermore, the record shows that the FAA was or should have been aware of the problem both because of its pervasive character and because of Katz' specific complaints directed to her superiors. No significant effort was made to end the harassment. While the agency did have an articulated policy against sexual harassment which involved seminars on the issue for its supervisors, this policy was not effective, and was known not to be effective by FAA supervisory personnel. On the basis of the undisputed facts in the record, we hold that Katz was entitled to prevail on her claim of sexual harassment.

II.

• • •

Katz argues that because the district court incorrectly found that she was not the victim of sexual harassment, its findings on her other claims of gender discrimination must also be set aside. We disagree. Katz' sexual harassment claim required the district court to apply Title VII in an area almost totally unexplored by our previous decisions. In contrast, her disparate treatment claims presented no novel legal questions. Since the record supports the district court's factual findings on those claims, we must uphold its conclusions.

III.

The district court's judgment for the Secretary on Katz' disparate treatment claims is affirmed. The judgment against Katz on the issue of sexual harassment is reversed, and the case remanded for a consideration of remedies.

AFFIRMED IN PART; REVERSED IN PART; AND REMANDED.

---

[7]Under this order of proof, the ultimate burden remains throughout on the plaintiff to prove the existence and the intentional nature of the harassment. This burden was satisfied in this case by the showing that Katz was subjected to sustained verbal sexual abuse.

IV. NOTICE TO THE EMPLOYER

A. Actual Notice

Unless the employer has actual or constructive knowledge of co-worker harassment, it has no Title VII liability.[63] Courts will find actual knowledge on the part of the employer where complaints of co-worker harassment have

---

[63]*E.g.,* Collins v. Pfizer, Inc., 39 FEP Cases 1316, 1331 (D. Conn. 1985)(no liability where isolated incidents not reported); Faris v. Henry Vogt Mach. Co., 813 F.2d 786, 787 (6th Cir. 1987)(no liability where no evidence company knew or should have known of alleged harassment).

been lodged with any representative of the employer who holds a position sufficiently high within the organization to make notice to that person notice to the employer.[64] These positions have included police chief,[65] sales manager,[66] department chief,[67] and medical school program director.[68] A complaint to a first-line supervisor has been characterized as a complaint to "higher management."[69]

Some courts have found that the employer had actual knowledge of co-worker harassment even where a complaint was made to such lower-level supervisors as a foreman[70] and a dispatcher.[71] Actual knowledge has been found even where the lower-level supervisor failed to report the complaint "upstairs."[72] However, other courts have held that the employer had no liability where the complainant did not notify management above the first-line supervisor.[73]

Where supervisors have witnessed co-worker harassment firsthand, courts have held that the employer had actual knowledge. Thus, actual employer knowledge of co-worker harassment has been found where a police chief saw obscene pictures and photos on the walls of the police department,[74] where a CEO saw obscene cartoons in the men's room,[75] and where a foreman was present when a crew member picked up the plaintiff and held her so that other co-workers could touch her.[76]

B. Constructive Notice

Constructive knowledge may exist where the "harassment was so pervasive that employer awareness may be inferred."[77] If the harassment takes a

---

[64]Katz v. Dole, 709 F.2d 251, 255, 31 FEP Cases 1521, 1524 (4th Cir. 1983), reproduced *supra*. For a discussion of which employees may be employer representatives for this purpose, see *Robinson v. Jacksonville Shipyards,* 760 F. Supp. 1486, 1529–30 (M.D. Fla. 1991)(employer's quartermen and leadmen considered responsible enough so that complaints to them amounted to complaints to employer).

[65]Arnold v. City of Seminole, 614 F. Supp. 853, 870, 40 FEP Cases 1539, 1551 (N.D. Okla. 1985).

[66]Huddleston v. Roger Dean Chevrolet, 845 F.2d 900, 904, 46 FEP Cases 1361, 1363 (11th Cir. 1988).

[67]Kyriazi v. Western Elec. Co., 461 F. Supp. 894, 935, 18 FEP Cases 924, 953 (D.N.J. 1978), *vacated in part on other grounds,* 473 F. Supp. 786, 25 FEP Cases 86 (D.N.J. 1979), *aff'd,* 647 F.2d 388 (3d Cir. 1981).

[68]Lipsett v. University of P.R., 864 F.2d 881, 906–7, 54 FEP Cases 230 (1st Cir. 1988)(suit brought under Title IX and §1983). *See also* Robinson v. Jacksonville Shipyards, *supra* note 64 (quarterman and leadman).

[69]Waltman v. International Paper Co., 875 F.2d 468, 478, 50 FEP Cases 179, 187 (5th Cir. 1989).

[70]Hall v. Gus Constr. Co., 842 F.2d 1010, 1016, 46 FEP Cases 573, 577 (8th Cir. 1988), reproduced in Chapter 2, Forms of Harassment (foreman of construction crew was agent of employer).

[71]Llewellyn v. Celanese Corp., 693 F. Supp. 369, 380, 47 FEP Cases 993, 1001 (W.D.N.C. 1988)(actual knowledge where dispatcher responsible for passing complaint up hierarchy).

[72]Morris v. American Nat'l Can Corp., 730 F. Supp. 1489, 1496, 52 FEP Cases 210, 216 (E.D. Mo. 1989), reproduced in Chapter 2, Forms of Harassment (fact that first-line supervisor did not report "upstairs" does not excuse employer); *see also* Baker v. Weyerhaeuser Co., 903 F.2d 1342, 1345, 1348, 52 FEP Cases 1872, 1874, 1877 (10th Cir. 1990)(defendant "permitted a known sex maniac to run amok in the workplace").

[73]Ukarish v. Magnesium Elektron, 31 FEP Cases 1315, 1322 (D.N.J. 1983)(complaint to foreman); Wimberly v. Shoney's, Inc., 39 FEP Cases 444, 453 (S.D. Ga. 1985)(complaint to area manager and area training supervisor).

[74]Arnold v. City of Seminole, 614 F. Supp. 853, 870, 40 FEP Cases 1539, 1551 (N.D. Okla. 1985).

[75]Bennett v. Corroon & Black Corp., 845 F.2d 104, 106, 46 FEP Cases 1329, 1331 (5th Cir. 1988), *cert. denied,* 109 S.Ct. 1140 (1989).

[76]Hall v. Gus Constr. Co., *supra* note 70, 842 F.2d at 1012, 46 FEP Cases at 574 (alternative holding of constructive notice). *See also* EEOC v. Murphy Motor Freight Lines, 488 F. Supp. 381, 385–86, 22 FEP Cases 892, 896 (D. Minn. 1980)(company had actual knowledge of race harassment where supervisory personnel saw derogatory notice placed on bulletin board and racial slurs placed on equipment).

[77]Katz v. Dole, *supra* note 64, 709 F.2d at 255, 31 FEP Cases at 1524.

variety of forms and occurs with the acquiescence of supervisory personnel, then the employer's constructive notice seems clear. In *Hall v. Gus Construction Co.*,[78] the Eighth Circuit held that the employer had constructive notice of co-worker harassment where male construction crew members verbally abused female traffic controllers. The crew members called the traffic controllers "fucking flag girls," "Herpes," "Cavern Cunt," and "blonde bitch"; repeatedly asked one plaintiff if she "wanted to fuck," requested oral sex, touched the plaintiffs' thighs and grabbed one plaintiff's breasts; exposed themselves to plaintiffs; denied plaintiffs access to restroom facilities and then used surveying equipment to watch them urinate in the ditch; and posted obscene drawings and pictures. The court concluded that this "unrelenting pattern of verbal, physical, and psychic abuse" involved incidents "so numerous" that the employer would have had to know of them.[79]

In *Lipsett v. University of Puerto Rico*,[80] the First Circuit found sufficient evidence of constructive notice in the literature displayed in a rest facility where all members of a medical residency program got their meals, had meetings, and checked the bulletin board.[81] In that facility the complainant's male co-workers posted a list of obscene sexual nicknames for all female residents on the bulletin board[82] and posted a sexually explicit drawing of the plaintiff's body on the wall. The men also "plastered the walls of their rest facility with Playboy centerfolds."[83] The First Circuit ruled that the employer had constructive notice of a hostile environment in that the surgery training program director would have entered the rest facility where these materials were prominently displayed.[84]

Pervasive graffiti and pornography can give rise to an inference of knowledge on the part of the employer. In *Waltman v. International Paper Co.*,[85] where the plaintiff demonstrated that there was graffiti on the walls of the powerhouse, the restroom, and the elevator, the Fifth Circuit held that she had created a factual issue regarding the employer's constructive knowledge of co-worker harassment.[86]

When courts rule that the employer has no constructive knowledge, it is usually because the co-worker harassment is isolated, rather than pervasive.[87]

---

[78]842 F.2d 1010, 1012, 1016, 46 FEP Cases 573, 574, 577 (8th Cir. 1988), reproduced in Chapter 2, Forms of Harassment.

[79]*Id.* at 1016, 1018, 46 FEP Cases at 577, 579. The Eighth Circuit found constructive notice on similarly egregious facts in the earlier race harassment case of *Taylor v. Jones*, 653 F.2d 1193, 1199, 28 FEP Cases 1024, 1027 (8th Cir. 1981)(employer must have become conscious of harassment consisting of continuing slurs, epithets, jokes, threats, and fights, and hanging of noose in workplace).

[80]864 F.2d 881, 54 FEP Cases 230 (1st Cir. 1988)(applying Title VII law in harassment suit brought under Title IX and §1983).

[81]*Id.* at 888.

[82]Complainant's was "Selastraga," translated to mean "she swallows them." *Id.* at 888.

[83]*Id.*

[84]*Id.* at 906 n.25. *See also* Andrews v. City of Philadelphia, 895 F.2d 1469, 54 FEP Cases 184 (3d Cir. 1990)(constructive knowledge existed where employee experienced sexual comments by co-workers and found pornographic materials in her desk and posted on walls).

[85]875 F.2d 468, 478, 50 FEP Cases 179, 187 (5th Cir. 1989).

[86]*See also* Barbetta v. Chemlawn Servs. Corp., 669 F. Supp. 569, 573, 44 FEP Cases 1563, 1566 (W.D.N.Y. 1987)(plaintiff defeated employer's summary judgment motion with evidence of pornographic magazines, pictures, and calendars in workplace, and use of sexual pictures in company-sponsored film presentation).

[87]*E.g.*, Hunter v. Allis-Chalmers Corp. 797 F.2d 1417, 1422, 41 FEP Cases 721, 724 (7th Cir. 1986)(race harassment); Wimberly v. Shoney's, Inc., 39 FEP Cases 444, 453 (S.D. Ga. 1985)(touching, indecent

However, in *Ukarish v. Magnesium Elektron*,[88] the court held that the employer had no constructive knowledge because the plant atmosphere, albeit "distasteful," was simply a "fact of life." The reasoning in *Ukarish* seems to be that, because the prevailing environment in the plant had always been coarse,[89] and because the plaintiff, "as far as anyone working with her could tell, appeared to accept [the coarse atmosphere] and joined in it as one of the boys,"[90] there was nothing to put the employer on notice that there was anything unwelcome about that atmosphere. Similarly, the dissent of Judge Edith Jones in *Waltman v. International Paper Co.* argues that the existence of sexual graffiti throughout the workplace is too "ordinary" to put the employer on constructive notice that the sexually charged environment was unwelcome.[91] Thus, while evidence of the culture of the workplace may be part of an employer's effort to rebut the complainant's prima facie case of hostile environment,[92] it arguably may also evidence that the employer lacked constructive notice of a hostile environment.

V. THE EMPLOYER'S REMEDIAL RESPONSE

Once notified of harassment, the employer must take prompt remedial action "reasonably calculated to end the harassment."[93] In *Waltman v. International Paper Co.*, the Fifth Circuit summarized this obligation:

> What is appropriate remedial action will necessarily depend on the particular facts of the case—the severity and persistence of the harassment, and the effectiveness of any initial remedial steps. ... [N]ot every response by an employer will be sufficient to discharge its legal duty. Rather, the employer may be liable despite having taken remedial steps if the plaintiff can establish that the employer's response was not "reasonably calculated" to halt the harassment.[94]

---

propositions, lewd comments, profanity, and obscene pranks not so pervasive to impute constructive knowledge to employer); Silverstein v. Metroplex Communications, 678 F. Supp. 863, 870, 46 FEP Cases 67, 73 (S.D. Fla. 1988)(no constructive knowledge found despite allegations that co-worker asked complainant about marital status, that another told complainant he had sexual dream about her, that still another telephoned complainant at home to ask that she spend night with him); Freedman v. American Standard, 41 FEP Cases 471, 476 (D.N.J. 1986)(no constructive knowledge found where female pilot received obscene message from co-worker on one occasion, was treated rudely by co-workers on two occasions, and was "treated coolly" by one co-worker after rejecting his sexual solicitation).

[88]31 FEP Cases 1315, 1319, 1322 (D.N.J. 1983).

[89]*Id.* at 1319 (sexually oriented dialogue between workers was "customary plant language").

[90]*Id.*

[91]*Supra* note 85, 875 F.2d at 486, 50 FEP Cases at 194 (Jones, J., dissenting)("Depictions that were only recently regarded as taboo in movies and television are now *de rigueur* for programs that even children will watch"). *See also* Valdez v. Church's Fried Chicken, 683 F. Supp. 596, 620, 47 FEP Cases 1155, 1170 (W.D. Tex. 1988)(no constructive knowledge where assistant manager saw co-worker flirting with and touching female employees, because "[f]lirting, some casual touching, and sexual innuendos or jokes do not by themselves constitute actionable sexual harassment").

[92]See Chapter 4, Hostile Environment Harassment, Section VI.C.3.b. For a more detailed discussion of possible employer remedial actions, see Chapter 19, Responding to Internal Complaints.

[93]Katz v. Dole, 709 F.2d 251, 256, 31 FEP Cases 1521, 1524 (4th Cir. 1983), reproduced *supra. See, e.g.,* Waltman v. International Paper Co., *supra* note 85; Swentek v. USAir, 830 F.2d 552, 558, 44 FEP Cases 1808, 1813 (4th Cir. 1987); Barrett v. Omaha Nat'l Bank, 726 F.2d 424, 427, 35 FEP Cases 593, 595 (8th Cir. 1984).

[94]*Supra* note 85, 875 F.2d at 479, 50 FEP Cases at 188 (citations omitted). *See also* Dornhecker v. Malibu Grand Prix Corp., 828 F.2d 307, 309, 44 FEP Cases 1604, 1605 (5th Cir. 1987)(adequacy of remedial action may be assessed proportionately to seriousness of offense); Swentek v. USAir, *supra* note 93, 830 F.2d at 558, 44 FEP Cases at 1813 (employer obligated to investigate allegations and present reasonable basis for its subsequent actions).

Obviously, the employer risks liability where it takes no action at all in response to known incidents of sexual harassment. In *Katz v. Dole*,[95] the court held the employer liable for co-worker sexual advances and sexually related epithets directed to a female air traffic controller, where it did nothing to stop the harassment.[96] The employer's remedial obligation does not, however, require it to ensure a work environment completely free of harassment.[97]

The degree of remedial action that courts require of employers in a case of co-worker harassment depends upon various factors, including: the severity of the harassment,[98] the degree of acquiescence in the harassment by supervisors,[99] the promptness of the employer's responsive action,[100] the credibility of the complainant's accusations,[101] and the apparent sincerity of the employer's efforts to eradicate the harassment.[102] Depending on which of the above factors are present, the same court may reach different conclusions as to whether an employer's response is adequate.

---

[95]*Supra* note 93.

[96]*See also* Lipsett v. University of P.R., 864 F.2d 881, 907, 54 FEP Cases 230 (1st Cir. 1988)(employer liable where it took no action against alleged harassers); Hall v. Gus Constr. Co., 842 F.2d 1010, 1016, 46 FEP Cases 573, 577 (8th Cir. 1988)(employer liable where it knew of harassment but failed to investigate or take remedial action); Waltman v. International Paper Co., *supra* note 85, 875 F.2d at 478, 50 FEP Cases at 187 (failure to investigate or reprimand co-workers who made sexually suggestive comments to plaintiff, sent her pornographic notes, and propositioned her, and failure to remove and prohibit sexual graffiti raised issue regarding adequacy of remedial measures and precluded summary judgment for employer).

[97]Katz v. Dole, *supra* note 93, 709 F.2d at 256, 31 FEP Cases at 1524 ("Title VII is not a clean language act, and it does not require employers to extirpate all signs of centuries-old prejudices"); *see also* Barrett v. Omaha Nat'l Bank, 726 F.2d at 427, 35 FEP Cases at 595 (same); Moffett v. Gene B. Glick Co., 621 F. Supp. 244, 270–71, 41 FEP Cases 671, 688 (N.D. Ind. 1985)("employers cannot be responsible for every offensive remark made at the workplace precisely because an employer cannot change the personal beliefs of its employees").

[98]*See* Minteer v. Auger, 844 F.2d 569, 46 FEP Cases 1173 (8th Cir. 1988)(reprimand of co-workers who made unwelcome sexual remarks sufficient for employer to avoid liability); Vermett v. Hough, 627 F. Supp. 587, 607, 42 FEP Cases 1432, 1448 (W.D. Mich. 1986)(employer not liable for sexual harassment where, in response to single corroborated incident in which co-worker raised a flashlight between employee's legs at knee level while she was standing with another co-worker, employer counseled, reprimanded, and gave damaging performance evaluation to offending employee); Ross v. Comsat, 34 FEP Cases 260, 265 (D. Md. 1984)(employer not liable for harassment where male employee alleged that female co-worker made "verbal passes" unaccompanied by physical acts and employer attempted to insulate the victim from further advances), *rev'd on other grounds,* 759 F.2d 355, 37 FEP Cases 797 (4th Cir. 1985); Durant v. Owens-Ill. Glass Co., 517 F. Supp. 710, 725, 31 FEP Cases 215, 227 (E.D. La. 1980)(employer that promptly reprimanded co-worker for verbally harassing another employee on two occasions not liable for sexual harassment).

[99]Katz v. Dole, *supra* note 93, 709 F.2d at 256, 31 FEP Cases at 1524 ("Where, as here, the employer's supervisory personnel manifested unmistakable acquiescence in or approval of the harassment, the burden on the employer seeking to avoid liability is especially heavy"); Andrews v. City of Philadelphia, 895 F.2d 1469, 54 FEP Cases 184 (3d Cir. 1990)(same); Snell v. Suffolk County, 782 F.2d 1094, 1105, 39 FEP Cases 1590, 1598 (2d Cir. 1986)(many employees complained of racial harassment, but only three complaints investigated).

[100]*Compare* Baker v. Weyerhaeuser Co., 903 F.2d 1342, 1345, 52 FEP Cases 1872, 1874–75 (10th Cir. 1990)(employer held liable for harassment even though offending employee ultimately discharged, where no action was taken against offending employee until several months after plaintiff's complaint) *with* Dornhecker v. Malibu Grand Prix Corp., *supra* note 94 (no liability where employer acted within 12 hours of complaint and assured plaintiff she would not have to work with harassing employee after completion of current project in day and a half).

[101]Swentek v. USAir, *supra* note 93, 830 F.2d at 558, 44 FEP Cases at 1813 (employer need not credit all complainant accusations to escape liability); Vermett v. Hough, *supra* note 98, 627 F. Supp. at 598, 42 FEP Cases at 1441 (court did not credit plaintiff's accusations where she offered no corroborating testimony).

[102]Paroline v. Unisys Corp., 879 F.2d 100, 108, 50 FEP Cases 306, 313 (4th Cir. 1989), reproduced in Chapter 9, Constructive Discharge (warning alleged harasser that he would be fired if harassment recurred and delaying his planned promotion and salary increase held insufficient to support summary judgment where head of office joked about complainant's report of sexual harassment after giving warning and where alleged harasser had earlier been warned to cease harassing co-workers), *rev'd in relevant part,* 900 F.2d 27, 52 FEP Cases 845 (1990)(*en banc*).

The Fifth Circuit, observing that "society has seldom provided instantaneous redress for dishonorable conduct," has held that an employer avoided liability with a promise to the complainant that she would not have to work with the harasser after their current business trip, which had a day and one-half remaining.[103] The same circuit has upheld liability where a manager permitted obscene cartoons labeled with the complainant's name to remain on the wall of the men's room for one day after he first saw them.[104]

Courts have approved remedial action where a co-worker was reprimanded with the threat of suspension,[105] a co-worker received a suspension without pay that led him to resign,[106] and a threat to fire the complainant's chief harasser was followed by his termination for other reasons.[107]

An appropriate remedial response may include a transfer of the complainant or the harassing co-worker to a different work area or shift.[108] Transfer of the complainant may sometimes be an adequate response,[109] but a failure to even consider a transfer of the harassing co-worker may trigger liability,[110] and a transfer that leaves the complainant worse off in terms of employment opportunities may be an inadequate response per se, at least where there has actually been a finding (as opposed to a mere allegation) of sexual harassment.[111]

Initial steps, sufficient in themselves, may not suffice where harassment

---

[103]Dornhecker v. Malibu Grand Prix Corp., 828 F.2d 307, 309–10, 44 FEP Cases 1604, 1605 (5th Cir. 1987).

[104]Bennett v. Corroon & Black Corp., 845 F.2d 104, 106, 46 FEP Cases 1329, 1331 (5th Cir. 1988)(emphasizing that complainant's male co-workers were seeing cartoons, which showed complainant "engaged in crude and deviant sexual activities," and that employer's chief executive officer allowed cartoons to remain in place), cert. denied, 109 S.Ct. 1140 (1989). The court held that although the employer was liable because of its failure to act promptly, its later remedial actions were sufficiently thorough to preclude any relief. The subsequent remedial efforts included removing the CEO who had left the cartoons in place, asking the plaintiff to return to work, paying the plaintiff's salary until she got a new job, and paying the full cost of psychiatric counseling. Id. at 106, 46 FEP Cases at 1330–31.

[105]Swentek v. USAir, supra note 93, 830 F.2d at 558, 44 FEP Cases at 1813. See also Vermett v. Hough, supra note 98, 627 F. Supp. at 607, 42 FEP Cases at 1448 (appropriate remedial action where co-worker counseled and disciplined); Friend v. Leidinger, 446 F. Supp. 361, 18 FEP Cases 1030, 1043 (E.D. Va. 1977)(no employer acquiescence where fire chief disciplined white co-workers who engaged in racial harassment), aff'd, 588 F.2d 61, 18 FEP Cases 1052 (4th Cir. 1978).

[106]Schirmer v. Eastman Kodak Co., 49 FEP Cases 1585, 1587 (E.D. Pa. 1988), aff'd, 869 F.2d 591, 49 FEP Cases 1640 (3d Cir. 1989).

[107]Huddleston v. Roger Dean Chevrolet, 845 F.2d 900, 902–4, 46 FEP Cases 1361, 1362–63 (11th Cir. 1988)(supervisor, in response to complaints of harassment from co-workers, threatened to fire co-workers if complaints continued).

[108]See, e.g., Watts v. New York City Police Dep't, 724 F. Supp. 99, 107 (S.D.N.Y. 1989)(issue of inadequate remedial action raised where employer refused to allow police academy trainee to transfer to another class to avoid co-worker who was harassing her and failed to investigate allegations of harassment until after victim resigned, even though employer docked offending co-worker's pay and advised him to stay away from her); Martin v. Norbar, Inc., 537 F. Supp. 1260, 30 FEP Cases 103 (S.D. Ohio 1982)(adequacy of employer response at issue where employer rejected complainant's request that she be transferred to avoid further harassment by co-worker). For a more detailed discussion of transfer as an appropriate remedial action, see Chapter 19, Responding to Internal Complaints, Section IV.C.2.c.

[109]See Howard v. National Cash Register, 388 F. Supp. 603, 605–6 (S.D. Ohio 1975)(racial harassment); Bell v. St. Regis Paper Co., 425 F. Supp. 1126, 1129–30, 1137–38 (N.D. Ohio 1976)(harassment based on plaintiff's interracial marriage).

[110]See, e.g., College-Town v. Massachusetts Comm'n Against Discrimination, 400 Mass. 156, 508 N.E.2d 587, 46 FEP Cases 1406, 1412 (1987).

[111]Guess v. Bethlehem Steel Corp., 913 F.2d 463, 53 FEP Cases 1547 (7th Cir. 1990)(dictum)(where foreman picked up complainant and pressed her face against his crotch in front of onlooking co-workers, transfer that left complainant worse off could not satisfy employer's duty to take remedial action).

continues unabated. In those circumstances, it is not enough to simply remind employees of antiharassment rules[112] and hold "sporadic pep talks."[113]

The employer cannot excuse its failure to act solely on the ground that it does not know which co-workers are responsible for known acts of harassment.[114] Courts have held that where harassment takes the form of graffiti throughout the workplace, the employer has an affirmative duty to address the problem even if the authorship is unknown.[115]

---

[112]Zabkowicz v. West Bend Co., 589 F. Supp. 780, 785, 35 FEP Cases 610, 613, *aff'd in relevant part,* 789 F.2d 540, 40 FEP Cases 1171 (7th Cir. 1986); Arnold v. City of Seminole, 614 F. Supp. 853, 40 FEP Cases 1539 (E.D. Okla. 1985)(memorandum directing police officers not to direct immoral language or objects insufficient where plaintiff continued to be subject to harassment in the form of pornographic pictures posted in workplace with her name on them, a picture showing a man having sex with a goat with plaintiff's name written on it, displays of female genitalia with plaintiff's name written over them, and delivery to plaintiff's workplace mailbox of envelope containing photographs of male sex organs and a package of condoms).

[113]DeGrace v. Rumsfeld, 614 F.2d 796, 805, 21 FEP Cases 1444, 1450 (1st Cir. 1980)(employer tolerated racially hostile climate).

[114]Morris v. American Nat'l Can Corp., 730 F. Supp. 1489, 1492, 52 FEP Cases 210, 213 (E.D. Mo. 1989)(no adequate remedial action where plaintiff was told employer could do nothing unless it knew which co-workers left obscene artifacts at her work station).

[115]Waltman v. International Paper Co., 875 F.2d 468, 480, 50 FEP Cases 179, 189 (5th Cir. 1989)(where employer failed to remove and prohibit graffiti, plaintiff raised factual issue regarding adequacy of remedial response). *See also* Arnold v. City of Seminole, *supra* note 112.

Chapter 8

HARASSMENT BY NONEMPLOYEES

I. Overview

Sexual harassment in employment does not occur only among employees of a common employer. Employees are also harassed by vendors, independent contractors, and customers. This chapter focuses on the circumstances under which the employer of a complainant may be held liable for sexual harassment by persons who are not employees of the employer. This chapter also reviews the manner in which nonemployees may themselves be liable to the complainant under common-law theories, civil statute, or criminal law.[1]

The EEOC Guidelines provide that employers are liable for sexual harassment perpetrated by nonemployees "in the workplace, where the employer (or its agents or supervisory employees) knows or should have known of the conduct, and fails to take immediate and appropriate corrective action."[2] The Guidelines further provide that "[i]n reviewing these cases the Commission will consider the extent of the employer's control and any other legal responsibility which the employer may have with respect to the conduct of such nonemployees."[3]

The relatively few reported decisions on sexual harassment by nonemployees have endorsed the EEOC Guidelines.[4] These decisions indicate that employers will be held liable for harassment by nonemployees when: (1) the employer imposes a job requirement, such as a dress code, that is not necessary for the performance of an employee's duties and that subjects the employee to sexual harassment, or (2) the employer knows or should have known of sexual harassment by nonemployees and fails to take prompt corrective action within its control.

---

[1]See Section IV. *infra*.

[2]29 C.F.R. §1604.11(e), reproduced in Appendix 1. In 1980, after notice and comment, the EEOC issued its Guidelines on Discrimination Because of Sex, 29 C.F.R. §§1604.1–.11, one part of which (§1604.11) concerns sexual harassment. The EEOC Guidelines are nonbinding but "constitute a body of experience and informed judgment to which courts and litigants may properly resort for guidance." Meritor Sav. Bank v. Vinson, 477 U.S. 57, 65, 40 FEP Cases 1822, 1826 (1986), reproduced in Chapter 1, Overview.

[3]*Id.*

[4]*See* B.L. Schlei & P. Grossman, Employment Discrimination Law 425 (2d ed. 1983), Five-Year Supplement 150 (1989).

II. JOB REQUIREMENTS FORESEEABLY SUBJECTING EMPLOYEES TO SEXUAL HARASSMENT

Most decisions that have addressed allegations of harassment by nonemployees have involved employer dress codes. Generally, dress codes that impose different standards for the sexes (*e.g.,* dresses for women, business suits for men) are not violative of Title VII.[5] However, a dress code is unlawful if it reflects demeaning sexual stereotypes, regardless of whether the required attire encourages sexual advances.[6] Thus, a requirement that women wear provocative attire in an effort to portray them as sexual playthings would in itself violate Title VII.[7]

A dress code for women may also violate Title VII when the employer fails to modify it after learning that it encourages sexual advances. In the leading case of *EEOC v. Sage Realty Corp.,*[8] a female lobby attendant in a large Manhattan office building was required to wear a special red, white, and blue uniform to commemorate the 1976 Bicentennial. The employer ordered Bicentennial uniforms in one standard size for all of its female lobby attendants. The complainant, the tallest attendant, found that the uniform, with slits down the front and up the sides, exposed portions of her thighs, midriff, and buttocks as she made the motions required by her job. The uniform prompted various nonemployees to whistle "Yankee Doodle" and "The Stars and Stripes Forever," and one to offer to "run it up the flagpole anytime you want to." The complainant was discharged because she then refused to wear the uniform. The court found the employer liable under Title VII, reasoning that its requirement that the complainant wear the Bicentennial uniform, knowing that it would subject her to sexual harassment, constituted sex discrimination.[9]

Similarly, in *Marentette v. Michigan Host,* Judge Julian Abele Cook, Jr., opined that a "dress code ... which subjects [employees] to sexual harassment" could violate Title VII.[10] The employer's dress code required cocktail waitresses to wear sexually provocative uniforms. The waitresses alleged that wearing the uniforms subjected them to sexual harassment from customers and that the employer was aware of the harassment and failed to take any corrective action.[11]

---

[5]*Id.* at 410–17, Five-Year Supplement at 144.

[6]Carroll v. Talman Fed. Sav. & Loan Ass'n, 604 F.2d 1028, 20 FEP Cases 764 (7th Cir. 1979)(requirement that women but not men wear uniforms is sex discrimination), *cert. denied,* 445 U.S. 929 (1980); Tamimi v. Howard Johnson Co., 807 F.2d 1550, 42 FEP Cases 1289 (11th Cir. 1987)(Title VII violated by requiring pregnant woman to wear makeup).

[7]The EEOC Compliance Manual provides that "in some cases the mere requirement that females wear sexually provocative uniforms may itself be evidence of sexual harassment." EEOC COMPL. MAN. (BNA) §619.4, Grooming Standards, p. 619:0008–10, reproduced in Appendix 4. *See also* Barbetta v. Chemlawn Servs. Corp., 669 F. Supp. 569, 44 FEP Cases 1563 (W.D.N.Y. 1987)(requirement that female employees wear skirts or dresses because visiting supervisor liked to look at legs was evidence of hostile working environment); Priest v. Rotary, 634 F. Supp. 571, 40 FEP Cases 208 (N.D. Cal. 1986)(Title VII violated where restaurant employer required cocktail waitresses to wear sexually suggestive attire as condition of employment).

[8]507 F. Supp. 599, 24 FEP Cases 1521 (S.D.N.Y. 1981).

[9]*Id.* at 609, 24 FEP Cases at 1524.

[10]506 F. Supp. 909, 912, 24 FEP Cases 1665, 1666 (E.D. Mich. 1980)(*dictum*).

[11]*Id.* at 910, 24 FEP Cases at 1665.

In *EEOC v. Newtown Inn Associates,* hotel cocktail waitresses complained of retaliation for protesting a marketing scheme that required them "to project an air of sexual availability to customers through the use of provocative outfits" and that had elicited unwelcome sexual advances from customers.[12] The suit alleged that waitresses were told to flirt with customers, to dance with customers in "a sexually provocative and degrading fashion," and to dress in revealing, thematic attire for events such as "Bikini Night," "P.J. Night," and "Whips and Chains Night."[13]

EEOC decisions on nonemployee harassment have also involved dress codes. In one case, the EEOC found that the employer had constructively discharged its receptionist by requiring her to wear a sexually revealing costume that elicited verbal abuse from male visitors.[14] She had been told to dress as an "Indian maiden" while performing duties as a hostess for visiting VIPs. Her costume consisted of a halter-bra top and a midi-skirt with a slit in front that ran up her thighs. The EEOC determined that the costume requirement had the purpose and effect of unreasonably interfering with her work and that it created a hostile, intimidating, and offensive working environment.

The Commission reached a contrary decision regarding a retail women's clothing store that required salespersons to wear swim attire as part of a swimwear promotion.[15] Female co-managers objected to the requirement on their own behalf and on behalf of their sales clerks. The women who refused to wear the swimsuits were discharged. The EEOC found no cause to believe that discrimination had occurred, reasoning that the swimwear requirement was not sexual in nature. The EEOC stated that a costume requirement is unlawful only if (1) the outfit required to be worn was sexually provocative or revealing and (2) wearing the outfit would likely have resulted in the wearer's being subjected to unwelcome verbal or physical sexual activity.[16] Citing *EEOC v. Sage Realty,* the EEOC held that the employer was not liable because, although the swimwear caused some disturbances, the reaction by customers and others to the costume was not vulgar and did not subject the employees to explicit sexual remarks, references, or gestures. In reaching its decision the EEOC considered the nature of the job in relation to the swimwear requirement and found that the outfit was reasonably related to the sales job that the female employees were hired to perform.

III. FAILURE TO TAKE PROMPT CORRECTIVE ACTION

Even absent a dress code policy, employer liability for harassment by nonemployees may arise if the employer fails to exercise reasonable control to prevent it. Where employers can control the conduct of nonemployees, the

---

[12]647 F. Supp. 957, 958, 42 FEP Cases 480 (E.D. Va. 1986).
[13]*Id.*
[14]EEOC Dec. 81-17, 27 FEP Cases 1791 (1981). This and other EEOC decisions are precedential decisions concerning whether there exists reasonable cause to believe that discrimination had occurred.
[15]EEOC Dec. 85-9, 37 FEP Cases 1893 (1985).
[16]*Id.* at 1895.

analysis strongly resembles that used in determining employer liability for co-worker harassment.[16a]

A. Independent Contractors

In a case brought under the New York State Human Rights Law, an employer had retained a polygraph examiner to administer pre-employment lie detector tests.[17] While administering the tests, the examiner allegedly touched the breasts of female applicants and asked them non-job-related questions of a sexual nature. The employer incurred liability for this conduct by continuing to use the polygraph examiner after it had notice of his improper conduct.[18]

B. Customers

The EEOC determined that a restaurant employer violated Title VII where its waitress was subject to unwelcome sexual conduct by a male customer and where the employer, although knowing of the harassment, took no corrective action.[19] Two factors that bore significantly on the employer's ability to take corrective action were that the harasser was a frequent customer and that he had a friendly relationship with the employer. The employer therefore was in an advantageous position to take corrective action.[20]

C. Consultants

In *Dornhecker v. Malibu Grand Prix Corp.,*[21] the complainant was "playfully" choked at a business convention by the employer's consultant after she complained to co-workers that he had dropped his pants in public, grabbed her hips, and touched her breasts. The Fifth Circuit upheld the employer's defense, and though assuming that the employer had a duty to prevent harassment by a nonemployee, the court believed that the employer's handling of the problem was prompt and decisive.[22]

D. Vendors

Although there appear to be no reported decisions on the subject, sexual harassment by vendors of the complainant's employer is a problem that has

---

[16a]See Chapter 7, Harassment by Co-Workers. *See generally* Danna v. New York Tel. Co., 54 FEP Cases 1638, 1652 (S.D.N.Y. 1990)(employer responsible for failing to remove graffiti from airport terminal even though employer did not own or exclusively control terminal, where employer failed to exercise control it did have and failed to contact terminal management to see what could be done to remove graffiti.).

[17]People v. Hamilton, 42 FEP Cases 1069 (N.Y. Sup. Ct. 1986). Tests of this sort are no longer permissible, by virtue of the 1988 Employee Polygraph Protection Act, 29 U.S.C. §§2001–2009.

[18]*See also* Waltman v. International Paper Co., 875 F.2d 468 (5th Cir. 1989)(triable issue whether employer had failed to take prompt remedial action in response to complaints of sexual harassment, one of which involved employee of independent contractor at paper mill sticking his tongue in complainant's ear).

[19]EEOC Dec. 84-3, 34 FEP Cases 1887 (1984).

[20]*See also* Churchman v. Pinkerton's, Inc., 756 F. Supp. 515, 55 FEP Cases 81 (D. Kan. 1991)(female security officer alleged sexual harassment by employee of security company's client); Llewellyn v. Celanese Corp., 693 F. Supp. 369, 371–72, 47 FEP Cases 993, 994 (W.D.N.C. 1988)(employer liable where complainant's breast touched by customer and where her report to employer led to reminder that "the customer is always right").

[21]828 F.2d 307, 44 FEP Cases 1604 (5th Cir. 1987).

[22]*Id.* at 309, 44 FEP Cases at 1605.

drawn sustained attention. One state fair employment practices agency has issued an internal memorandum detailing sample complaints by which an employee sexually harassed by a visiting salesperson may proceed against the employer for failing to prevent or correct the harassment.[23]

IV. DIRECT LIABILITY OF THE NONEMPLOYEE HARASSER

Although a sexual harassment claim directly against a nonemployee is very rare, several theories of liability would support such a claim: (1) common-law claims,[24] (2) state fair employment statutes,[25] (3) state civil rights statutes,[26] (4) federal employment or civil rights law,[27] and (5) criminal law.[28]

In *Seritis v. Hotel & Restaurant Employees*,[29] two teenage waitresses secured a judgment of $200,000 against a union and its chief executive for intentional infliction of emotional distress and breach of the duty of fair representation.[30] The union controlled the hiring of waitresses through its collective bargaining agreements with restaurants and also could influence firing decisions. One of the plaintiffs was fired through union influence after she rejected certain job opportunities the union made available to her, such as a monthly salary for being a "live-in sexual playmate" for two men, providing sexual services at parties, and having sex with a dog in a stage show in Nevada.[31] The union denied the other plaintiff access to waitress jobs after she, too, declined union-offered job opportunities, such as working as a topless waitress on a bus, working as a prostitute at a convention, living with a lesbian, and having sex with a dog on a stage in Las Vegas.[32]

---

[23]Internal Memorandum of the California Department of Fair Employment and Housing Commission, Enforcement Division (Aug. 13, 1990).

[24]For a discussion of common-law theories of liability, see Chapter 15, The Common Law.

[25]*See, e.g.,* CAL. GOV'T CODE §12940(h)(forbidding harassment by any "employer . . . or any other person"); Department of Fair Employment & Hous. v. Madera County, Cal. FEHC Dec. 90-03 at 28 (1990)(interpreting §12940(h) to impose liability on individual who was not employer); Internal Memorandum, *supra* note 23 (detailing sample administrative complaints under California discrimination statute that would impose liability on both salesman and his employer for harassment of customer's employee). For a discussion of state employment discrimination statutes, see Chapter 12, Fair Employment Practices Statutes.

[26]*See, e.g.,* People v. Hamilton, 42 FEP Cases 1069 (N.Y. Sup. Ct. 1986)(polygraph examiner could be directly liable under law forbidding discrimination in public accommodations); CAL. CIV. CODE §51.5 (forbidding sex discrimination by any business establishment); CAL. CIV. CODE §51.7 (establishing general right to freedom from violence or intimidation by threat of violence on basis of sex).

[27]For a discussion of possible individual liability under 42 U.S.C. §1985(3), see Chapter 11, Federal Constitutional, Statutory, and Civil Rights Law. For a discussion of how an individual may be directly liable under Title VII as an agent of the employer, see Chapter 23, The Alleged Harasser as Defendant. For a discussion of possible liability under the National Labor Relations Act, see text accompanying notes 29–32 *infra.* Yet another way in which a nonemployee harasser may be held to account would be disciplinary action by the harasser's employer, which has an obvious interest in controlling misconduct in its work force directed against its customers, clients, and other nonemployees. *See, e.g.,* Dow Chem. Co., 90-2 ARB ¶8602 (1990)(Sartain, Arb.)(male employee challenging discipline for sexual harassment of female outside contractors). For a discussion of a unionized employer's discipline of employees for harassment of persons outside the work force, see Chapter 17, Collective Bargaining Agreements and Union Obligations, Section IV.

[28]For a discussion of criminal law theories associated with sexual harassment, see Chapter 16, Criminal Law.

[29]167 Cal. App.3d 78, 213 Cal. Rptr. 588, 37 FEP Cases 1501 (1985).

[30]The duty of fair representation is imposed upon unions by the National Labor Relations Act. Ford Motor Co. v. Huffman, 345 U.S. 330, 31 LRRM 2548 (1953).

[31]*Supra* note 29, 213 Cal. Rptr. at 591, 37 FEP Cases at 1503.

[32]*Id.* For further discussion of union obligations to avoid or prevent sexual harassment, see Chapter 17, Collective Bargaining Agreements and Union Obligations, Section IX.

CHAPTER 9

CONSTRUCTIVE DISCHARGE

I. OVERVIEW

An employee who is discharged as a result of sexual harassment is entitled to relief under Title VII.[1] The same result will occur even absent a formal discharge, if the employee reasonably has quit to avoid sexual harassment that can no longer be endured. In that event the employee has been "contructively" discharged and is entitled to the same remedies as if there had been a formal discharge.[2]

II. THE PRIMA FACIE CASE

To establish a prima facie case of a constructive discharge in violation of Title VII, a sexual harassment complainant must prove:

(1) The issue: that the complainant resigned[3] or otherwise experienced some job detriment;[4]

---

[1]Remedies would include back pay and reinstatement, or front pay in lieu of reinstatement. Economic relief under Title VII is available whenever the plaintiff loses salary or benefits as a result of an unlawful employment decision. B.L. SCHLEI & P. GROSSMAN, EMPLOYMENT DISCRIMINATION LAW, Chapter 38 (2d ed. 1983).

[2]If an employee is not discharged formally or constructively but quits voluntarily, the employee is not entitled to back pay even though subjected to a sexually hostile environment. Brooms v. Regal Tube Co., 881 F.2d 412, 423, 50 FEP Cases 1499 (7th Cir. 1989)("district court may award back pay . . . only . . . if a plaintiff can demonstrate that the defendant discharged him or her, either actually or constructively"). *But see* Huddleston v. Roger Dean Chevrolet, 845 F.2d 900, 905, 46 FEP Cases 1361, 1364 (11th Cir. 1988)(finding of sexual harassment, even without finding of constructive discharge, could entitle plaintiff to nominal damages and thus eligibility for attorney's fees).

[3]Courts have rejected constructive discharge claims by plaintiffs who were formally fired. Lynch v. Freeman, 817 F.2d 380, 385, 43 FEP Cases 1120, 1125 (6th Cir. 1987)(employee who is actually discharged has no basis for asserting claim of constructive discharge); Ross v. Double Diamond, 672 F. Supp. 261, 278, 45 FEP Cases 313, 326 (N.D. Tex. 1987)(essential element of constructive discharge claim is resignation, which cannot be shown if plaintiff was fired). *But see* EEOC v. Gurnee Inn Corp., 48 FEP Cases 871, 880 (N.D. Ill. 1988)(employee fired when she did not show up for work was constructively discharged because failure to report to work resulted, at least in part, from stress caused by sexual harassment).

[4]Although by definition a constructive "discharge" involves termination of employment, the analysis has been applied to other losses of employment opportunities. *E.g.,* Llewellyn v. Celanese Corp., 693 F. Supp. 369, 381, 47 FEP Cases 993, 1002 (W.D.N.C. 1988)("Even though [plaintiff] did not quit, her medical leave without pay was caused by her intolerable work situation. As such, it was a constructive discharge for purposes of back pay liability"); Sowers v. Kemira, Inc., 46 FEP Cases 1825, 1838 n.1 (S.D. Ga. 1988)(disability caused by sexual harassment constitutes constructive discharge); Robinson v. Jacksonville Shipyards, 118 F.R.D. 525, 54 FEP Cases 83, 88 (M.D. Fla. 1988)(plaintiff may obtain back pay for harassment-induced sick leave by proving "functional equivalent of an intermittent constructive discharge, that is . . . that working

(2) The basis: that the complainant is a member of a protected group, male or female;

(3) The causal connection: that because of the complainant's gender the complainant was harassed,[5] and that the harassment caused the complainant to resign;[6]

(4) Objectively intolerable work conditions: that the sexual harassment created working conditions so aggravated that a reasonable person in the same position would have felt compelled to resign;[7] and

(5) Employer responsibility: that the employer is responsible for the employee's action because, depending upon which of two standards applies, (a) the employer intended to force the complainant's resignation, or (b) the employer or its agent was aware of the harassment and failed to take corrective action before the complainant reasonably resigned.[8]

Application of the constructive discharge analysis is a "heavily fact-driven determination."[9] Some courts have indicated that a trial court's finding of the issue of constructive discharge is rarely subject to reversal even if the appellate court would have drawn a different conclusion on the same facts.[10]

---

conditions were so difficult and unpleasant that a reasonable person in her shoes would have felt compelled to resign, or to take time off, in order to cope with the working conditions").

"Constructive demotion" may also be actionable. In one case, a plaintiff claimed that she took a demotion to escape intolerable conditions. The court recognized her claim:

> Although the suggested extension of this theory to cover a demotion is apparently novel, it is a logical one. I see no reason to distinguish the situation where an employer makes conditions so intolerable that the employee, in response, reasonably decides to take a demotion from one where the employee resigns. To reject such a constructive demotion theory would, in effect, penalize an employee for conduct amounting to a mitigation of damages.

Toscano v. Nimmo, 570 F. Supp. 1197, 32 FEP Cases 1401, 1409 (D. Del. 1983)(finding no constructive demotion on facts presented).

[5]Absent proof of underlying sexual harassment, there can be no constructive discharge predicated on the harassing conduct. Barrett v. Omaha Nat'l Bank, 726 F.2d 424, 428, 35 FEP Cases 593, 595 (8th Cir. 1984)("[h]aving failed to prove her claim of sexual harassment . . . Barrett has not established the underlying illegality necessary to support a constructive discharge claim"); Vermett v. Hough, 627 F. Supp. 587, 607–8, 42 FEP Cases 1432, 1448 (W.D. Mich. 1986)(claim of constructive discharge "must of necessity fail" if there is no finding of sexual harassment); Wimberly v. Shoney's, 39 FEP Cases 444, 453 (S.D. Ga. 1985)(no constructive discharge where plaintiff failed to prove existence of sexual harassment); Brandon v. Cook Paint & Varnish Co., 562 F. Supp. 1244, 31 FEP Cases 1598 (W.D. Mo. 1983)(no constructive discharge where evidence did not support claims of quid pro quo sexual harassment or environment hostile to women).

[6]See Section III. *infra.*

[7]See Section IV. *infra.* For a comparison of the standard of "aggravated" with the standard of "severe and pervasive," see Section IV.B. *infra.*

[8]See Section V. *infra. See also* Note, *Choosing a Standard for Constructive Discharge in Title VII Litigation,* 71 CORNELL L. REV. 587 (1986)(discussing application of various standards of liability).

[9]Levendos v. Stern Entertainment, 860 F.2d 1227, 1230, 48 FEP Cases 443 (3d Cir. 1988)(material issues of fact preclude summary judgment as to whether female constructively discharged).

[10]Although some courts have held that a finding of constructive discharge is, "at least partially, a question of law and must therefore be reviewed . . . *de novo,*" Yates v. Avco Corp., 819 F.2d 630, 636, 43 FEP Cases 1595 (6th Cir. 1987), *see also* Wheeler v. Southland Corp., 875 F.2d 1246, 1249, 50 FEP Cases 86, 88–89 (6th Cir. 1989), most courts apply a "clearly erroneous" standard. *See, e.g.,* Huddleston v. Roger Dean Chevrolet, *supra* note 2 (constructive discharge question of fact reviewed under clearly erroneous standard; lower court determination that plaintiff's resignation not result of constructive discharge affirmed); Hirschfeld v. New Mexico Corrections Dep't, 916 F.2d 572, 54 FEP Cases 268, 274–75 (10th Cir. 1990)(lower court's determination that plaintiff's evidence, although uncontroverted, was not credible not clearly erroneous and thus affirmed).

III. THE CAUSAL CONNECTION

The complainant must prove that the termination of employment resulted because of gender. The first prong in the proof of this causal connection is that the complainant was sexually harassed because of gender. This proof is identical to the complainant's proof of the underlying sexual harassment case.[11]

The second prong of the causal connection requires proof that it was sexual harassment that caused the complainant's resignation. Under liberal rules of pleading, an allegation that the complainant was "unable to continue her employment . . . because of acts committed against her" is sufficient to state a constructive discharge claim.[12] Often, the allegation of causal connection is proven simply with testimony from the complainant; expert testimony may also be very useful in this regard.[13]

The timing of the complainant's resignation will often be important evidence, just as the timing of a job detriment will be significant in a quid pro quo case.[14] A close proximity in time between the sexual harassment and the resignation will strongly support the claim of a causal connection. Conversely, long delays will tend to undermine the claim. Although constructive discharge may be found even where the resignation did not closely follow the last act of harassment,[15] delays of one month and four months between the last instance of harassment and the resignation have been found to be too long to support a constructive discharge claim.[16] Even a delay of eleven days between the employer's corrective action and the resignation has been found to be too lengthy to justify a finding of causal connection.[17]

---

[11]Proof that the sexual harassment was on the basis of sex is discussed in Chapter 3, Quid Pro Quo Harassment, Section II.D.1., and Chapter 4, Hostile Environment Harassment, Section III.C. If the plaintiff fails to prove the underlying sexual harassment, there can be no claim of constructive discharge predicated on the harassing conduct. See cases cited in note 5 *supra.*

[12]Hunter v. Countryside Ass'n for the Handicapped, 710 F. Supp. 233, 238, 49 FEP Cases 790, 793 (N.D. Ill. 1989). *See generally* Blesedell v. Mobil Oil Co., 708 F. Supp. 1408, 1420, 53 FEP Cases 391 (S.D.N.Y. 1989)(amended complaint's claim of constructive discharge deemed reasonably related to original complaint of sexual harassment).

[13]*See* Ross v. Twenty-Four Collection, 681 F. Supp. 1547, 1551–52, 48 FEP Cases 1590 (S.D. Fla.)(expert testimony regarding exacerbation of plaintiff's disease because of sexual harassment established that harassment affected plaintiff's psychological well-being, forcing her to resign), *aff'd mem.,* 875 F.2d 873, 50 FEP Cases 600 (11th Cir. 1989). The employer may rebut a plaintiff's proof with evidence of other reasons for resignation. See Section VI.B. *infra.*

[14]See Chapter 3, Quid Pro Quo Harassment.

[15]*E.g.,* Barbetta v. Chemlawn Servs. Corp., 669 F. Supp. 569, 572, 44 FEP Cases 1563, 1565 (W.D.N.Y. 1987)(delay of four months between last incident of harassment and plaintiff's resignation not dispositive in disproving a causal connection, because act of harassment need not be straw that broke camel's back).

[16]*E.g.,* Benton v. Kroger Co., 640 F. Supp. 1317, 46 FEP Cases 1356 (S.D. Tex. 1986)(rejecting plaintiff's allegations because "the last incident of alleged sexual harassment took place a month before plaintiff's termination of employment" and "an outspoken employee whose rights had been violated would not have remained silent for that period"); Hirschfeld v. New Mexico Corrections Dep't, *supra* note 10 (affirming, under "clearly erroneous" standard, finding of no constructive discharge where plaintiff did not resign until four months after last act of harassment). *But see* Barbetta v. Chemlawn Servs. Corp., *supra* note 15 (delay of four months not dispositive).

[17]Steele v. Offshore Shipbldg., 867 F.2d 1311, 1317–18, 49 FEP Cases 522 (11th Cir. 1989)(plaintiff quit 11 days after employer took effective action to stop harassment; district court's finding of no constructive discharge affirmed).

IV. ESTABLISHING OBJECTIVELY INTOLERABLE WORK CONDITIONS

A. Objective Versus Subjective Standard

To establish constructive discharge, complainants must prove not only that they felt compelled to resign but that the sexual harassment experienced was such that a reasonable person in the same position would have resigned. The test is thus objective in part and subjective in part: the harassment must not only have actually caused the resignation but must have been of such a nature that it could have caused a reasonable person to resign.[18] The Fourth Circuit has held that the intolerability of the complainant's working conditions must be "assessed by the objective standard of whether a 'reasonable person' in complainant's position would have felt compelled to resign."[19]

The Sixth Circuit has stated that the "reasonable person" hypothesized in this test is someone of the same sex as the complainant: "We acknowledge that men and women are vulnerable in different ways and offended by different behavior."[20]

B. Aggravating Factors

Courts generally hold that in order to establish constructive discharge, a complainant must establish more than a resignation causally connected to illegal discrimination. Usually there must be proof of "other aggravating factors" beyond the evidence required to establish a mere violation of Title VII.[21] Thus, in order to prove that a resignation amounted to a discharge, complainants

---

[18]Downey v. Isaac, 622 F. Supp. 1125, 1132, 38 FEP Cases 52, 58 (D.D.C. 1985)("A claim of constructive discharge must be supported by more than an employee's subjective opinion that her position has become so intolerable and difficult that she must resign.").

[19]Bristow v. Daily Press, 770 F.2d 1251, 1255, 38 FEP Cases 1145, 1147 (4th Cir. 1985), *cert. denied*, 475 U.S. 1082 (1986). *See also* Jordan v. Clark, 847 F.2d 1368, 1377 n.10, 46 FEP Cases 1558, 1564 (9th Cir. 1988)(constructive discharge occurs when looking at totality of circumstances reasonable person would have felt forced to quit due to intolerable and discriminatory working conditions).

[20]Yates v. Avco Corp., 819 F.2d 630, 637, 43 FEP Cases 1595, 1600 (6th Cir. 1987). *See generally* Ellison v. Brady, 924 F.2d 872, 54 FEP Cases 1346, *republished as amended*, 55 FEP Cases 111 (9th Cir. 1991) and cases cited therein (adopting "reasonable woman" standard in determining whether environment is sufficiently severe or pervasive to be actionable under hostile environment theory of sexual harassment).

[21]*See, e.g., D.C. Circuit:* Hopkins v. Price Waterhouse, 825 F.2d 458, 473, 44 FEP Cases 825 (D.C. Cir. 1987)("mere fact of discrimination, without more, is insufficient to make out a claim of constructive discharge"), *rev'd on other grounds,* 490 U.S. 228, 49 FEP Cases 954 (1989).

First Circuit: Contardo v. Merrill Lynch, 54 FEP Cases 1269, 1273 (D. Mass. 1990)(no constructive discharge found because sex discrimination, including sexual harassment, was "relatively covert, and habitual, even mindless, rather than pre-meditated," and because the discrimination was not "career-ending").

Fifth Circuit: Bourque v. Powell Elec. Mfg. Co., 617 F.2d 61, 65–66, 22 FEP Cases 1191, 1194 (5th Cir. 1980)(employer's failure to provide equal pay for equal work violated Title VII but was in itself insufficient predicate for finding constructive discharge, especially given societal goal of having discrimination attacked, where possible, within context of existing employment relationships).

Sixth Circuit: Geisler v. Folsom, 735 F.2d 991, 996, 34 FEP Cases 1581, 1585 (6th Cir. 1984)(no constructive discharge even though plaintiff's supervisor had "deplorable attitude" toward women); Pease v. Alford Photo Indus., 667 F. Supp. 1188, 1202–3, 49 FEP Cases 497, 508 (W.D. Tenn. 1987)("Proof of discrimination alone is not a sufficient predicate for a finding of constructive discharge. There must be other aggravating factors").

Ninth Circuit: Sanchez v. City of Santa Ana, 915 F.2d 424, 431 (9th Cir. 1990)(generally isolated incident is insufficient as matter of law to support finding of constructive discharge, which instead requires "aggravating factors" such as "a continuous pattern" of discriminatory treatment).

may be required to prove that they were subjected to a continuous course of sexual harassment, as opposed to isolated incidents.[22] Unless complainants can prove a series of sexually harassing incidents by supervisors or co-workers, such as unwanted touchings,[23] repeated propositions,[24] and other vulgar conduct,[25] they generally will be unable to support a claim of constructive discharge.[26] Although a single incident of sexual harassment could be egregious enough to justify a resignation,[27] generally the "aggravating circumstances" that would support a claim of constructive discharge consist of a pattern of discriminatory behavior.[28]

Where the employer's corrective action is mild in comparison to the severity of the harassment, or where remedial action is promised but not

---

[22]*E.g., Fifth Circuit:* Pittman v. Hattiesburg Municipal Separate School Dist., 644 F.2d 1071, 1077, 25 FEP Cases 1349 (5th Cir. 1981)(unequal pay, absent other aggravating factors, insufficient support for constructive discharge claim); Wimberly v. Shoney's, *supra* note 5, 39 FEP Cases at 453 (random, sometimes meaningless encounters between female employees and male supervisor and co-workers did not create sexually hostile work environment justifying resignation, there being no evidence of continuous, sustained, or pervasive sexually oriented misconduct).

Sixth Circuit: Wheeler v. Southland Corp., *supra* note 10 (constructive discharge in sexual harassment context not established simply by proof of discrimination; there must be other aggravating factors); Yates v. Avco Corp., *supra* note 10, 819 F.2d at 637, 43 FEP Cases at 1600 (no constructive discharge, which requires aggravating factors, particularly where employee's resignation not reasonable under circumstances); Held v. Gulf Oil Co., 684 F.2d 427, 432, 29 FEP Cases 837, 841 (6th Cir. 1982)("continuous course of discriminatory conduct" causing constructive discharge included "sex-based opprobrium" such as implying that sexual charms would improve plaintiff's sales, lecturing plaintiff about her sex life, using plaintiff as an "errand girl" and requiring her to unstop toilets).

Ninth Circuit: Watson v. Nationwide Ins. Co., 823 F.2d 360, 361, 46 FEP Cases 1606, 1607 (9th Cir. 1987)(plaintiff alleging constructive discharge must show some "aggravating factors" such as continuous pattern of discriminatory treatment, because Title VII best served when parties attack discrimination within context of existing relationships); Nolan v. Cleland, 686 F.2d 806, 813, 29 FEP Cases 1732 (9th Cir. 1982)(continuous pattern of discrimination treatment in assignments and evaluations for two years constitutes sufficient aggravated situation to support constructive discharge finding).

See also cases cited in note 21 *supra.*

[23]Paroline v. Unisys Corp., 879 F.2d 100, 50 FEP Cases 306 (4th Cir. 1989), reproduced in Section IV. *infra* (sexually suggestive remarks, repeated forced kisses, and back rubbing), *aff'd in part and rev'd in part,* 900 F.2d 27, 52 FEP Cases 845 (4th Cir. 1990)(*en banc*); Llewellyn v. Celanese Corp., *supra* note 4, 693 F. Supp. at 380, 47 FEP Cases at 1001 (repeated advances and sexual touching of plaintiff's body including her breast, and male employee exposing genitals); Wheeler v. Southland Corp., *supra* note 10, 875 F.2d at 1247, 50 FEP Cases at 87 (supervisor repeatedly called plaintiff "honey" and "baby" while leaning against her and touching her hips).

[24]Llewellyn v. Celanese Corp., *supra* note 4, 693 F. Supp. at 380, 47 FEP Cases at 1001 (sexual advances); Brooms v. Regal Tube Co., 881 F.2d 412, 50 FEP Cases 1499 (7th Cir. 1989)(sexual advances)(Cummings, Flaum & Kanne, JJ.); Sowers v. Kemira, Inc., *supra* note 4 (repeated requests to date, go "skinny-dipping," "make out," have sex, and repeated implied promises of job benefits and threats of detrimental job action).

[25]Huddleston v. Roger Dean Chevrolet, 845 F.2d 900, 46 FEP Cases 1361 (11th Cir. 1988)(expelling gas, ridiculing plaintiff's appearance, and calling plaintiff a bitch and a whore in front of customers); Llewellyn v. Celanese Corp., 693 F. Supp. 369, 47 FEP Cases 993 (W.D.N.C. 1988)(nude male employee exposing genitals to plaintiff).

[26]*Cf.* Benton v. Kroger Co., *supra* note 16 (plaintiff's allegations of "sexual gestures" were uncorroborated and not believed by court); Wimberly v. Shoney's, 39 FEP Cases 444 (S.D. Ga. 1985)(court either disbelieved testimony of four plaintiffs to myriad incidents or deemed them trivial); Kramer-Navarro v. Bolger, 586 F. Supp. 677, 683, 38 FEP Cases 450, 455 (S.D.N.Y. 1984)(plaintiff's claim that she feared coming to work was "belied by her failure to identify . . . the basis for her fears").

[27]See cases cited in note 35 *infra.*

[28]*E.g.,* Clark v. Marsh, 665 F.2d 1168, 1173–74, 26 FEP Cases 1156, 1160 (D.C. Cir. 1981)(continuous pattern of deprivation of promotional, transfer, and educational opportunities provided aggravating factor needed to sustain constructive discharge claim); Pease v. Alford Photo Indus., *supra* note 21 (aggravating factors present where sexual harassment was "an everyday fact" at defendant's workplace); *see also* cases cited in notes 22–25 *supra.*

delivered, courts are likely to sustain a claim of constructive discharge.[29] The Seventh Circuit upheld a finding that the complainant's resignation was reasonable even though the employer had hired an attorney to investigate her complaint, had caused the harasser to apologize, had withheld the harasser's scheduled salary increase, and had threatened him with dismissal.[30] Judge Michael S. Kanne compared the employer's response with the nature of the alleged incidents of harassment and declined to overrule the district court's conclusion that a reasonable employer facing a similar situation would have acted differently. Specifically, the employer's admonitions to the alleged harasser were found to be unsuccessful in preventing further abuse, which included racial slurs with sexual innuendoes, propositioning the complainant with a photograph depicting interracial acts of sodomy, telling her that a racist pornographic picture involving bestiality showed how she was going to end up, and then grabbing her arm and threatening to kill her when she tried to run away.[31]

C. Proof of Sexual Harassment as Proof of Constructive Discharge

A plaintiff who proves a sexually hostile environment often has gone a long way toward showing the existence of aggravating factors, because by definition a hostile sexual environment involves harassment sufficiently severe and pervasive to affect the psychological well-being of the complainant, thereby affecting a term, condition, or privilege of employment.[32] Thus, the same evidence that is adduced to show a hostile environment will generally be offered as proof of the circumstances compelling the complainant's resignation from employment. A Fourth Circuit panel found that a reasonable person could resign from a work environment in which a supervisor made sexually offensive remarks to her, rubbed his hands on her back, and grabbed and kissed her against her will.[33] Similarly, a court found that a reasonable woman in the

---

[29]Fawcett v. IDS Fin. Servs., 41 FEP Cases 589, 593 (W.D. Pa. 1986). The employer may also be liable for misrepresentation where it fails to make good on a promise to a complainant to fire the alleged harasser or to transfer the plaintiff to a job free of the alleged harasser's presence. For a discussion of common-law claims by a constructively discharged employee, see Chapter 15, The Common Law.

[30]Brooms v. Regal Tube Co., *supra* note 24.

[31]*Id.* at 423, 50 FEP Cases at 1506. *See also* Maturo v. National Graphics, 722 F. Supp. 916 (D. Conn. 1989)(offer of reinstatement, made after commencement of lawsuit while harasser still employed and without serious pledge that plaintiff would not be subjected to further sexual harassment, was empty gesture that plaintiff reasonably rejected); Coley v. Consolidated Rail Corp., 561 F. Supp. 645, 651, 34 FEP Cases 129, 134 (E.D. Mich. 1982)(failure to take prompt remedial action caused resignation and thus employer constructively discharged plaintiff); Morris v. American Nat'l Can Corp., 730 F. Supp. 1489, 1496–97, 52 FEP Cases 210, 216–17 (E.D. Mo. 1989)(company's lack of prompt remedial action at best showed indifference to plaintiff's predicament and thus justified finding of constructive discharge); Llewellyn v. Celanese Corp., *supra* note 25, 693 F. Supp. at 380, 47 FEP Cases at 1001–2 (failure to take prompt remedial action led to finding of constructive discharge where placing warning notice in harasser's file was inadequate response to plaintiff's complaints of being threatened with physical violence and having offender intentionally expose himself to her).

[32]*E.g.,* Henson v. City of Dundee, 682 F.2d 897, 904, 29 FEP Cases 787, 793–94 (11th Cir. 1982), reproduced in Chapter 4, Hostile Environment Harassment (psychological well-being of victim must be affected to constitute actionable hostile environment harassment); Barbetta v. Chemlawn Servs. Corp., *supra* note 15 (complainant attempting to establish hostile atmosphere must prove more than isolated incidents of sexual harassment and must prove more than casual comments or accidental or sporadic offensive conversation).

[33]Paroline v. Unisys Corp., *supra* note 23.

complainant's position might have found intolerable a work environment featuring pornographic magazines, offensive sexual comments, and offensive touching by a male employee.[34]

Theoretically, a single instance of quid pro quo harassment might constitute a constructive discharge.[35] Ordinarily, however, conduct that itself is not sufficient to cause a constructive discharge is coupled with additional aggravating circumstances to create a constructive discharge, such as where a promotion is lost to another employee who has submitted to sexual advances that the complainant had rejected.[36]

V. EMPLOYER RESPONSIBILITY

All courts agree that an employee is discharged constructively where the employer informally shares its intent to discharge and the employee then quits before the employer's intent is ever formally expressed. All courts further agree that this intent may be inferred when an employer deliberately makes the working conditions intolerable, by sexual harassment or otherwise.

Courts differ, however, as to whether a constructive discharge may occur even when the employer does not actually intend to force the complainant's resignation. The controversy is thus whether an employer is responsible for a constructive discharge only when the employer specifically intends to oust the complainant, or whenever the employer is responsible for the offensive conduct that causes the complainant to resign.[37] Most courts take the latter position, holding that, regardless of the employer's specific intent to retain the complainant in its employ, the complainant is constructively discharged if the work environment is so intolerable that a reasonable employee would have felt forced to resign, and the complainant in fact did feel forced to resign.[38]

Under either theory, the degree of sexual harassment must have rendered the working conditions objectively intolerable.[39]

---

[34]Barbetta v. Chemlawn Servs. Corp., *supra* note 15, 669 F. Supp. at 572–73, 44 FEP Cases at 1565–66. *See also* Maturo v. National Graphics, *supra* note 31, 722 F. Supp. at 924 ("deliberate inaction of supervisors in face of two years of oral harassment and two physical attacks justified resignation"); Coley v. Consolidated Rail Corp., *supra* note 31 (pattern of sexually explicit and demeaning remarks by supervisor, coupled with defendant's failure to take prompt remedial action, would have caused reasonable person to feel compelled to resign).

[35]Sowers v. Kemira, Inc., 46 FEP Cases 1825, 1838 n.1 (S.D. Ga. 1988)("It could be argued that every instance of *quid pro quo* sexual harassment per se constitutes a constructive discharge"). See also Levendos v. Stern Entertainment, 860 F.2d 1227, 1232, 48 FEP Cases 443, 447 (3d Cir. 1988)(rejecting proposition that single nontrivial incident of discrimination can never be egregious enough to compel reasonable person to resign). *But see generally* Wardwell v. Palm Beach County, 786 F.2d 1554, 1557, 40 FEP Cases 1006, 1009 (11th Cir. 1986)(discriminatory denial of promotion does not itself provide sufficient evidence to prove a constructive discharge); *see also* cases cited in note 21 *supra*.

[36]*See generally* EEOC v. Gurnee Inn Corp., 48 FEP Cases 871, 879 (N.D. Ill. 1988)(finding constructive discharge where woman who had rebuffed supervisor's advances observed that other employees who tolerated them were better treated). *Cf.* Hicks v. Gates Rubber Co., 833 F.2d 1406, 1415–16, 45 FEP Cases 608, 615 (10th Cir. 1987)(woman may buttress her Title VII claim with evidence of treatment of others).

[37]See Section V.B. *infra. See generally* Note, *Choosing a Standard for Constructive Discharge in Title VII Litigation,* 71 CORNELL L. REV. 587 (1986).

[38]See Section V.A. *infra.* An employer's liability for sexual harassment is discussed in Chapters 6, Harassment by Supervisors; 7, Harassment by Co-Workers; and 8, Harassment by Nonemployees.

[39]See Section IV.A. *supra.*

A. Objectively Intolerable Work Environment; Intent to Force the Resignation Not Required

Courts in the First,[40] Third,[41] Fifth,[42] Seventh,[43] Ninth,[44] Tenth,[45] and Eleventh[46] Circuits hold, in agreement with the EEOC,[47] that a constructive discharge occurs whenever the complainant's resignation results from intolerable working conditions, for which the employer is responsible, that would have caused a reasonable person in the plaintiff's position to resign.

---

[40]Calhoun v. Acme Cleveland Corp., 798 F.2d 559, 41 FEP Cases 1121 (1st Cir. 1986)(applying "objective standard" whether reasonable person in employee's shoes would have felt compelled to resign; pattern of actions—demotion for refusal to retire, improper reprimand, exclusion from training, threatened increase in work hours—sufficed to warrant submitting constructive discharge issue to jury).

[41]Goss v. Exxon Office Sys., 747 F.2d 885, 36 FEP Cases 344 (3d Cir. 1984)("no finding of specific intent to bring about discharge is required for application of the constructive discharge doctrine"; test is whether "employer knowingly permitted conditions of discrimination in employment so intolerable that a reasonable person subjected to them would resign"; test satisfied where series of events shattered plaintiff's confidence in her ability to sell).

[42]Dornhecker v. Malibu Grand Prix Corp., 828 F.2d 307, 310, 44 FEP Cases 1604, 1606 (5th Cir. 1987)(constructive discharge occurs only when employer deliberately makes employee's working conditions so intolerable that employee is forced into involuntary resignation; issue is whether reasonable person in employee's position would have felt compelled to resign); Bourque v. Powell Elec. Mfg. Co., 617 F.2d 61, 65–66, 22 FEP Cases 1191, 1193–94 (5th Cir. 1980)(constructive discharge does not require employer intent to rid itself of employee; rather, issue turns on analysis of conditions imposed; requirement of working for unequal pay does not constitute condition of employment so intolerable as to force reasonable person to resign); Wimberly v. Shoney's, *supra* note 26, 39 FEP Cases at 453 (even though incidents of touching and crude language made plaintiff "uncomfortable," and, "in an ideal world, a woman should not have to encounter such antics," no constructive discharge shown in that conditions were not "intolerable"); Benton v. Kroger Co., 640 F. Supp. 1317, 1322, 46 FEP Cases 1356, 1360 (S.D. Tex. 1986)(constructive discharge results only when job conditions so unpleasant that reasonable person in employee's shoes would have felt compelled to resign).

[43]Brooms v. Regal Tube Co., *supra* note 24, 881 F.2d at 423, 50 FEP Cases at 1506 (test focuses upon "the impact of [the employer's] action on a reasonable person"); Hunter v. Countryside Ass'n for Handicapped, 710 F. Supp. 233, 238 n.6, 49 FEP Cases 790, 793 (N.D. Ill. 1989)(although Seventh Circuit has not decided issue, majority of district courts in Seventh Circuit and majority of other circuit courts hold that employer need not have intended to force plaintiff's resignation).

[44]Watson v. Nationwide Ins. Co., 823 F.2d 360, 361, 46 FEP Cases 1606, 1606–07 (9th Cir. 1987)(objective standard: looking at totality of circumstances, would reasonable person have felt forced to quit because of intolerable and discriminatory working conditions; plaintiff need not show employer subjectively intended to force resignation).

[45]Derr v. Gulf Oil Corp., 796 F.2d 340, 344, 41 FEP Cases 166, 169 (10th Cir. 1986)(court clarifies prior ambiguity in Tenth Circuit law by "unqualified adoption" of objective standard; case remanded for determination of constructive discharge issue under that standard).

[46]Garner v. Wal-Mart Stores, 807 F.2d 1536, 42 FEP Cases 1141 (11th Cir. 1987)(for constructive discharge, working conditions must have been so difficult that reasonable person in plaintiff's position would have felt compelled to resign; test not satisfied where plaintiff resigned after one day's disappointment with her assignment to "floater" position); Steele v. Offshore Shipbldg., 867 F.2d 1311, 1317, 49 FEP Cases 522 (11th Cir. 1989)(plaintiff must show working conditions so intolerable that reasonable person would feel compelled to resign); Ross v. Twenty-Four Collection, 681 F. Supp. 1547, 48 FEP Cases 1590 (S.D. Fla. 1988)(court is to apply objective standard), *aff'd mem.*, 875 F.2d 873, 50 FEP Cases 600 (11th Cir. 1989).

[47]The EEOC maintains:

[A]n employer is liable for constructive discharge when it imposes intolerable working conditions in violation of Title VII when those conditions foreseeably would compel a reasonable employee to quit, whether or not the employer specifically intended to force the victim's resignation. *See Derr v. Gulf Oil Corp.*, 796 F.2d 340, 343–44, 41 EPD ¶36,468 [41 FEP Cases 166] (10th Cir. 1986); *Goss v. Exxon Office Systems Co.*, 747 F.2d 885, 888, 35 EPD ¶34,768 [36 FEP Cases 344] (3d Cir. 1984); *Nolan v. Cleland*, 686 F.2d 806, 812–15, 30 EPD ¶33,029 [29 FEP Cases 1732] (9th Cir. 1982); *Held v. Gulf Oil Co.*, 684 F.2d 427, 432, 29 EPD ¶32,968 [29 FEP Cases 837] (6th Cir. 1982); *Clark v. Marsh*, 665 F.2d 1168, 1175 n.8, 26 EPD ¶32,082 [26 FEP Cases 1156] (D.C. Cir. 1981); *Bourque v. Powell Electrical Manufacturing Co.*, 617 F.2d 61, 65, 23 EPD ¶30,891 [22 FEP Cases 1191] (5th Cir. 1980); Commission Decision 84-1, CCH EOC Decision ¶6839 [33 FEP Cases 1887 (1983)]. However, the Fourth Circuit requires proof that the employer imposed the intolerable conditions with the intent of forcing the victim to leave. *See EEOC v. Federal Reserve Bank of Richmond*, 698 F.2d 633, 672, 30 EPD ¶33,269 [30 FEP Cases 1137] (4th Cir. 1983). But [*Federal Reserve Bank*] is not a sexual harassment case and the Commission believes it is distinguishable because specific intent is not as likely to be present in "hostile environment" cases.

EEOC Policy Guidance on Sexual Harassment, 8 FAIR EMPL. PRAC. MAN. (BNA), Part C.5 at 405:6693 (March 19, 1990), reproduced in Appendix 3.

B. Intent to Force the Complainant's Resignation Required

Courts in the D.C.,[48] Second,[49] Fourth,[50] Sixth,[51] and Eighth[52] Circuits have required an additional element. They have held that no constructive discharge occurs unless the employer intended to force the employee to resign, or at least has deliberately created the intolerable working conditions.

C. Comparison of the Standards

The distinction between the two standards may be more theoretical than practical, for most of the cases that articulate the requirement that the employer intended to force a resignation do not turn on whether the employer intent existed, but rather on whether the complainant was treated sufficiently poorly.[53] As Judge J. Harvie Wilkinson pointed out in his dissent in *Paroline v. Unisys Corp.,* it may be irrelevant whether the plaintiff is required to prove an improper intent, for intent can be inferred from the circumstances.[54]

The Sixth Circuit, while requiring "an inquiry into both the objective feelings of an employee, and the intent of the employer,"[55] permits a complainant to prove employer intent by proving that a reasonable employer would

---

[48]Bishopp v. District of Columbia, 788 F.2d 781, 789–90, 40 FEP Cases 903, 911 (D.C. Cir. 1986)("a finding of constructive discharge depends on whether the employer deliberately made working conditions intolerable and drove the employee to an 'involuntary quit' ").

[49]Martin v. Citibank, 762 F.2d 212, 221, 37 FEP Cases 1580, 1587 (2d Cir. 1985)(no constructive discharge unless employer deliberately made employee's working conditions so intolerable as to force resignation); Watts v. New York City Police Dep't, 724 F. Supp. 99, 108–9, 54 FEP Cases 1131, 1136 (S.D.N.Y. 1989)(although complainant suffered two sexual assaults within three days and subsequently was ostracized for complaining, court found that even if facts established working conditions so difficult a reasonable person would have felt compelled to resign, no constructive discharge because allegations fail to establish that employer intended to make her work environment intolerable or that employer sought to force her to resign).

[50]Bristow v. Daily Press, 770 F.2d 1251, 1255, 38 FEP Cases 1145, 1147 (4th Cir. 1985)(constructive discharge occurs only if actions complained of were intended by employer as effort to force plaintiff to quit, but intent can be inferred from employer's failure to act in face of known intolerable conditions), *cert. denied,* 475 U.S. 1082 (1986); cf. Llewellyn v. Celanese Corp., 693 F. Supp. 369, 381, 47 FEP Cases 993, 1002 (W.D.N.C. 1988)(intent of supervisors to force plaintiff to resign can be inferred from lack of prompt remedial action in response to reports of harassment).

[51]*Compare* Easter v. Jeep Corp., 750 F.2d 520, 522, 42 FEP Cases 666, 668 (6th Cir. 1984)(constructive discharge claim "requires an inquiry into the intent of the employer") *with* Coley v. Consolidated Rail Corp., *supra* note 31 ("[T]o establish constructive discharge in the Sixth Circuit the intent of the employer need not be to induce the employee to resign but only that the working conditions imposed [are] such that a reasonable person would terminate his employment"). *See also* Held v. Gulf Oil Co., 684 F.2d 427, 432, 29 FEP Cases 837, 840–41 (6th Cir. 1982)(requiring inquiry into intent of employer and "reasonably forseeable impact" of employer's conduct on employee). For other Sixth Circuit cases, see note 55 *infra.*

[52]Johnson v. Bunny Bread Co., 646 F.2d 1250, 1256, 25 FEP Cases 1326, 1331 (8th Cir. 1981)("to constitute a constructive discharge, the employer's actions must have been taken with the intention of forcing the employee to quit").

[53]*See, e.g.,* Bristow v. Daily Press, supra note 50 (no constructive discharge because circumstances not intolerable and resignation resulted from financial dispute); Martin v. Citibank, *supra* note 49 (no constructive discharge because reasonable person would not have felt compelled to resign by employer's conduct); Johnson v. Bunny Bread Co., *supra* note 52 (no constructive discharge because employer treated all employees similarly and conditions not intolerable).

[54]Paroline v. Unisys Corp., 879 F.2d 100, 114 n.2, 50 FEP Cases 306, 318 (4th Cir. 1989) reproduced *infra* (Wilkinson, J. dissenting)("While other courts have adopted an objective test, dependent upon the reasonableness of the employer's action and the reasonableness of the employee's perception of the intolerable conditions, the result under either standard is the same"), *aff'd in part and rev'd in part,* 900 F.2d 27, 52 FEP Cases 845 (4th Cir. 1990)(*en banc*). *See also* Bristow v. Daily Press, *supra* note 50, 770 F.2d at 1255, 38 FEP Cases at 1147 (employer's specific intent to force plaintiff to leave can be inferred through circumstantial evidence such as failing to act in the face of known intolerable conditions).

[55]Yates v. Avco Corp., 819 F.2d 630, 636, 43 FEP Cases 1595, 1600 (6th Cir. 1987). *See also* Wheeler v. Southland Corp., 875 F.2d 1246, 1249, 50 FEP Cases 86, 88 (6th Cir. 1989)(employer deemed to intend

have foreseen that the complainant would resign under the circumstances.[56] This proof might consist of little more than proof that a reasonable person in the complainant's position would have resigned under the circumstances, for it is likely that a reasonable employer, assuming some notice of these circumstances, would foresee that the complainant would resign. Thus, once an employee's resignation as a result of sexual harassment becomes reasonable, it generally, if not invariably, becomes foreseeable to the employer.[57]

Nonetheless, a finding of intent need not follow automatically from a finding that the employer failed to take fully effective remedial action. The employer can argue that its failure to act resulted from miscalculation or poor judgment rather than a specific intent to cause the resignation or to make the complainant's life unpleasant.[58] The court may also give weight to requests by the employer that the complainant not resign.[59] Thus, mere conclusory allegations that the employer's agent acted deliberately to force the complainant to quit will not withstand an employer's motion for summary judgment.[60]

The majority and dissenting opinions in *Paroline v. Unisys Corp.* demonstrate contrasting applications of the Fourth Circuit's requirement of proof of specific intent by the employer to force the complainant to resign. The opinion also illuminates the competing policy considerations that are present in constructive discharge cases involving sexual harassment, regardless of which

---

forseeable consequences of its conduct; employee constructively discharged where employer should have foreseen employee would resign when employer did not tell her it would replace offending supervisor, but merely told her to "hang in there"); Lynch v. Freeman, 817 F.2d 380, 43 FEP Cases 1120 (6th Cir. 1987)(finding of intent required but can be met when employer engages in conduct that has reasonably forseeable effect of causing employee to feel compelled to quit); Easter v. Jeep Corp., *supra* note 51, 750 F.2d at 522–23 (constructive discharge occurred where plaintiff told by employees under her supervision that they would not submit to her authority, that women had no business telling men what to do, that women were useful only as sex objects, and that she should be humble, and where management in face of plaintiff's complaints took no action to correct or discourage this behavior).

[56]Wheeler v. Southland Corp., *supra* note 55; Yates v. Avco Corp., *supra* note 55.

[57]See Paroline v. Unisys Corp., *supra* note 54. Both the panel majority and the dissent agreed that intent to force a resignation could be inferred from a failure to act in the face of known intolerable conditions. *Id.,* 50 FEP Cases at 314, 318. *See also* Llewellyn v. Celanese Corp., *supra* note 50 (failure of defendant's supervisory personnel to take adequate remedial action "evinces an intent to force [plaintiff] to quit"); Bristow v. Daily Press, *supra* note 50 (intent can be inferred from failure to remedy known intolerable conditions).

[58]E.g., Paroline v. Unisys Corp., *supra* note 54. Judge Wilkinson, whose dissent was adopted by the Fourth Circuit *en banc,* noted that although the defendant's remedial action of withdrawing the harasser's access to a certain facility actually increased his level of contact with the complainant, that action did not imply an intent to force the plaintiff to quit where the plaintiff had requested that the defendant take that particular remedial action.

[59]See Watts v. New York City Police Dep't, *supra* note 49 (summary judgment granted to defendant as to constructive discharge claim even though plaintiff's allegations could allow fact-finder to conclude that resignation was reasonable, because those allegations did not raise inference that defendant deliberately made working conditions intolerable; when plaintiff first notified defendant she was resigning it persuaded her to file complaint instead and when, after additional harassment, she again stated intention to resign, defendant sought to prevent resignation by acceding to plaintiff's prior request for change in schedule). *Compare* Paroline v. Unisys Corp., *supra* note 54 (although employer's request that complainant not quit "may provide a powerful defense . . . at trial . . . it does not compel or justify summary judgment"; "We refuse to adopt a rule that would allow clever or sophisticated employers automatically to avoid Title VII liability merely by asking harassment victims not to resign") *with id.* (dissent of Judge Wilkinson, in opinion adopted by the Fourth Circuit *en banc,* giving weight to defendant's request that plaintiff not resign). *See also* Wheeler v. Southland Corp., *supra* note 55, 875 F.2d at 1249, 50 FEP Cases at 89 (finding that employer could not avoid liability simply by telling complainant to "hang in there" in the face of discrimination).

[60]Hopkins v. Shoe Show, 678 F. Supp. 1241, 1245 (S.D.W.Va. 1988)(summary judgment denied as to claim of hostile environment but granted as to constructive discharge claim because of lack of specific facts showing intent to force resignation).

standard a court applies. Judge Wilkinson's dissent was adopted by the Fourth Circuit when it decided the case *en banc*.[61]

PAROLINE v. UNISYS CORP.

879 F.2d 100, 50 FEP Cases 306 (4th Cir. 1989),
aff'd in part and rev'd in part,
900 F.2d 27, 52 FEP Cases 845 (4th Cir. 1990)(en banc)

FRANCIS D. MURNAGHAN, Jr., Circuit Judge:—We must decide whether the district court erred in granting summary judgment in favor of the Unisys Corporation and Edgar L. Moore on various federal and state law claims arising out of the alleged sexual harassment of Elizabeth M. Paroline, the appellant. Paroline asserted claims of sexual harassment and constructive discharge against Unisys and Moore under Title VII of the Civil Rights Act of 1964, 42 U.S.C. §2000e *et seq*. She claims that Moore, a Unisys employee, made improper sexual advances toward her both on and off the job. Paroline also brought pendent state law claims against both defendants for intentional infliction of emotional distress, a claim against Moore for assault and battery, and a claim against Unisys for negligent failure to warn and reckless endangerment.

• • • As for the Title VII claims, the district court ruled that Unisys and Moore could not be held liable for sexual harassment or constructive discharge because Unisys took prompt remedial action after Paroline's complaint, and because Paroline quit before giving Unisys' remedy a chance to work. On the two remaining state law claims, the court first ruled that the exclusive remedies of the Virginia Workers' Compensation Act barred Paroline's action for negligent failure to warn and reckless endangerment. The court also held that Paroline could not proceed on her intentional infliction of emotional distress action because she could pursue a full remedy for her injury through her assault and battery claim against Moore. Paroline appealed.

We conclude that the district court erred in granting summary judgment against Paroline on the sexual harassment and constructive discharge claims under Title VII and on the Virginia state law claim for negligent failure to warn and reckless endangerment. However, we affirm the grant of summary judgment on the claims for intentional infliction of emotional distress, but for reasons different than those expressed by the district court.

I.

BACKGROUND

Not surprisingly, the parties present different versions of the events that prompted Paroline's lawsuit. However, because this is an appeal from a grant of summary judgment, we will present Paroline's version of the facts wherever the parties' evidence conflicts, at least to the degree that her allegations have support in affidavits, depositions or other documentary evidence. • • • •

Management at Unisys had received complaints well before Paroline started work there that Moore had made sexually suggestive remarks to and had engaged in unwelcome touching of female clerical workers. Such complaints were brought to the attention of Jo Anne Scott, who supervised the clerical and word processing staff, and of Charles Peterson, who had overall responsibility for the Unisys office in Rosslyn, Virginia, where Paroline worked. Other men in the office also allegedly engaged in improper sexual comments and touching of female employees.

Peterson convened a staff meeting to warn the men not to engage in conduct that could be construed as sexual harassment. He also met privately with Moore to caution him against sexual harassment of female employees.

---

[61]900 F.2d 27, 52 FEP Cases 845 (4th Cir. 1990)

However, Paroline's evidence casts doubts on the effectiveness and sincerity of the warnings. Other former female employees contend that Moore continued his sexual innuendo and improper touching of women workers (other than Paroline) after the warning from Peterson. Furthermore, there was evidence that after Peterson's warning, a number of men, including Peterson himself, began joking about the women's complaints of sexual harassment.

Paroline entered the scene in the fall of 1986, when she applied for a job as a word processor at Unisys. Moore participated in her job interview. During the interview, Moore asked Paroline what she would do if subjected to sexual harassment in the workplace. Although Peterson, who also interviewed Paroline, found the question inappropriate, he never criticized or reprimanded Moore for asking it. Moore recommended Paroline for the job, and Unisys hired her.

Shortly after Paroline started work in November 1986, Moore directed his attention toward her. He made sexually suggestive remarks to Paroline that she considered offensive. Sometime in December of 1986, Moore approached Paroline as she was working and started rubbing his hands on her back, and continued even though she indicated that he should stop.

The event that sparked the lawsuit, however, did not occur until January 22, 1987, when a severe snowstorm hit Northern Virginia. The Unisys office closed early because of the bad weather, and Paroline had no way home. She accepted a ride with Moore. During the trip, he made remarks which she interpreted as sexually suggestive. He also kissed her and repeatedly tried to hold her hand during the ride. When they reached Paroline's apartment, Moore insisted on coming in despite her objections. After several minutes in the apartment, Moore grabbed Paroline and began kissing her and rubbing his hand up and down her back, despite her demands that he stop. At first, he refused to remove his hands from her body. She eventually persuaded him to leave.

The next day, Paroline informed Peterson of the incident. According to Paroline's deposition testimony, Peterson indicated his awareness of previous complaints of sexual harassment in the office, and promised that it would not happen again.

Unisys launched a formal investigation of Moore's conduct. Afterwards, the company disciplined Moore. Unisys management warned him in writing that "[i]f there are any recurrences or if any form of retaliation occurs ... such will be grounds for immediate termination of your employment with Unisys." Furthermore, Unisys officials instructed Moore to seek counseling and to limit contact with female employees to official company business. Unisys also terminated his access to the company's Sensitive Compartmented Intelligence Facility ("SCIF").

Unisys notified Paroline on January 29, 1987 about the actions taken against Moore. She considered them inadequate. Paroline had since learned of Moore's alleged sexual harassment of other female workers at Unisys and the failure of the company's previous warnings to deter Moore from striking again. Paroline also feared that banning Moore from the SCIF area would actually increase her contact with him because she had not yet obtained a security clearance to enter the SCIF, and thus would be forced to remain in the same part of the office where Moore would be working. There is no evidence that Moore made any inappropriate remarks or sexual overtures toward Paroline after she complained to Peterson.

Knowing she was upset, company officials offered Paroline two weeks off. Although Unisys officials asked her not to quit, she submitted her resignation on February 15, 1987. Paroline later filed suit against Moore and Unisys.

• • •

III.

SEXUAL HARASSMENT

Paroline claims that Moore engaged in sexual harassment that created a hostile work environment in violation of Title VII. The Supreme Court has recognized that sexual harassment that creates a hostile atmosphere in the workplace may give rise to a claim of sex discrimination under Title VII. *See Meritor Savings Bank v. Vinson,* 477 U.S. 57, 66 [40

FEP Cases 1822] (1986). To prove a hostile work environment claim under Title VII, the plaintiff must show (1) that the conduct in question was unwelcome, (2) that the harassment was based on sex, (3) that the harassment was sufficiently pervasive or severe to create an abusive working environment, and (4) that some basis exists for imputing liability to the employer. *Swentek v. USAIR, Inc.,* 830 F.2d 552, 557 [44 FEP Cases 1808] (4th Cir. 1987). Unisys argues that Paroline has failed to produce evidence that the harassment was sufficiently severe or pervasive. Unisys also argues that no basis exists for holding the company liable for Moore's conduct. We disagree with both arguments.

A. *Severity or Pervasiveness of Harassment*

Whether Moore's harassment was sufficiently severe or pervasive is quintessentially a question of fact. Summary judgment was inappropriate unless, accepting Paroline's evidence as true and drawing all justifiable inferences in her favor, a fact finder could not reasonably conclude that Moore's conduct was so severe or pervasive as to create an abusive work environment. *See Anderson,* 477 U.S. at 250-52, 255 (standard for summary judgment). We conclude that summary judgment was inappropriate here because "reasonable minds could differ" as to whether Moore's behavior created a hostile atmosphere. *See id.* at 250.

To determine whether the harassment was sufficiently severe or pervasive, the fact finder must examine the evidence both from an objective perspective and from the point of view of the victim. *See Rabidue v. Osceola Refining Co.,* 805 F.2d 611, 620 [42 FEP Cases 631] (6th Cir. 1986), *cert. denied,* 481 U.S. 1041 [43 FEP Cases 631] (1987). We decline to focus solely on the plaintiff's subjective reaction, because "[a]n employee may not be unreasonably sensitive to his [or her] working environment." *Bristow v. Daily Press. Inc.,* 770 F.2d 1251, 1255 [38 FEP Cases 1145] (4th Cir. 1985), *cert. denied,* 475 U.S. 1082 [40 FEP Cases 608] (1986), *quoting Johnson v. Bunny Bread Co.,* 646 F.2d 1250, 1256 [25 FEP Cases 1326] (8th Cir. 1981). To succeed on a hostile environment claim, the plaintiff must first demonstrate that the harassment interfered with her ability to perform her work or significantly affected her psychological well-being. *See Rabidue,* 805 F.2d at 620. If the plaintiff satisfies that burden, the fact finder must then decide whether the harassment would interfere with the work performance or significantly affect the psychological well-being of a reasonable person in the plaintiff's position.

With those standards in mind, we examine the evidence to determine whether Paroline's claim should survive summary judgment. Paroline has raised a genuine issue as to whether Moore's conduct interfered with her work performance or significantly affecter her psychological well-being. Paroline testified in a deposition that she feared coming to work because of Moore's behavior. She also testified that Moore's conduct had adversely affected her ability to concentrate on her work. Others testified in deposition that Paroline appeared upset, even visibly shaken, by Moore's conduct. Furthermore, Paroline asserted in answers to interrogatories that her psychologist was prepared to testify at trial that she had suffered "depressive neurosis" as a result of Moore's actions. Accepting such evidence as true and drawing all justifiable inferences in Paroline's favor, a fact finder could reasonably conclude that Moore's behavior significantly affected Paroline's psychological well-being and adversely affected her work performance.

Paroline has also raised a genuine issue as to whether Moore's unwelcome touching and sexual innuendo would significantly affect the psychological well-being or the job performance of a reasonable person in like circumstances. Moore's alleged transgressions were far from trivial. Paroline alleged that Moore's unwanted sexual touchings and innuendo escalated into an assault and battery the day of the snowstorm. A reasonable person could find such behavior not merely offensive, but traumatic as well. Furthermore, a reasonable person could especially fear Moore upon discovering, as Paroline did, that Moore allegedly had pursued a campaign of harassment against other women in the office and had failed to heed warnings from Unisys management to cease such behavior. A person in Paroline's position could reasonably fear that Moore's behavior during the snowstorm, in the face of Unisys' orders that he desist, represented yet another stage in an ever-intensifying ordeal of sexual harassment. Moore's sexual overtones might reasonably produce strong reactions of fear and intimidation because Moore held a superior position to Paroline's in the company and perhaps even exercised supervisory authority over her. • • • Certainly, a victim of harassment might experience less stress and fear if the sexual advances had come from a person who held an equal or lower rank in the company.

A fact finder could reasonably conclude that Moore's behavior created a hostile and abusive working environment from the perspectives of both the reasonable person and Paroline herself. We, therefore, cannot say as a matter of law that the alleged harassment was insufficiently severe or pervasive to support a sex discrimination claim under Title VII.

B. *Imputing Liability to Moore and Unisys*

If the fact finder concludes that Moore exercised sufficient supervisory authority over Paroline to qualify as an "employer" under Title VII, • • •, Moore may be held liable for any actionable sexual harassment in which he personally participated. *See Sparks v. Pilot Freight Carriers, Inc.,* 830 F.2d 1554, 1557-58 [45 FEP Cases 160] (11th Cir. 1987) (employer directly liable for its own sexual harassment of employees). However, whether to impute liability to Unisys is a more complicated matter. In a hostile environment claim such as we have here, an employer is liable for one employee's sexual harassment of another worker if the employer had "actual or constructive knowledge of the existence of a sexually hostile working environment and took no prompt *and adequate* remedial action." *Swentek,* 830 F.2d at 558, *quoting Katz v. Dole,* 709 F.2d 251, 255 [31 FEP Cases 1521] (4th Cir. 1983) (emphasis added).

Paroline advances two theories by which to impute liability to Unisys for Moore's conduct. First, she contends that Unisys failed to take adequate remedial action after she complained about Moore. Furthermore, she argues that Moore's prior conduct toward other female employees should have alerted Unisys to the likelihood that he would, despite warnings, also try to harass Paroline. Such notice, Paroline argues, imposed a duty on Unisys to take adequate steps to try to prevent her harassment, not merely to act after the event. Both theories represent valid means of imputing Title VII liability to an employer in sexual harassment cases involving a hostile work environment. Paroline has produced evidence sufficient to survive summary judgment under either theory of imputed liability.

Neither party disputes that Paroline's complaint to Unisys officials about Moore's behavior represented sufficient notice to the company. However, Unisys argues that it cannot be held liable for Moore's actions because the company took prompt and adequate remedial steps once Paroline complained and after the deed was done to try to deter Moore from further harassment.

The adequacy of Unisys' remedy is a question of fact which a court may not dispose of at the summary judgment stage if reasonable minds could differ as to whether the remedial action was "reasonably calculated to end the harassment." *Katz,* 709 F.2d at 256. Although Unisys warned Moore that a recurrence of the harassment would result in his firing and took punitive measures such as delaying his planned promotion and salary increase, Paroline's evidence, if true, would cast doubt on the adequacy of those remedies. Paroline's work arrangement still exposed her to contact with Moore. Although the company ostensibly revoked Moore's SCIF access as punishment for his actions, Paroline produced evidence that the clearance revocation actually increased her chance of encountering Moore in the office. Furthermore, Paroline produced evidence that previous reprimands of Moore for alleged sexual harassment of other female employees had failed to deter him from striking again.

Indeed, a reasonable finder of fact could infer that Unisys intended Moore's earlier reprimand as nothing more than a slap on the wrist or perhaps even an outright sham. Paroline produced evidence that Peterson, the head of Unisys' Rosslyn office, openly joked about female workers' sexual harassment complaints after ostensibly warning Moore and other male employees not to engage in harassment of women. The fact finder could reasonably infer that Peterson's joking sent a message to Moore and other male employees that Unisys did not intend to take serious action to stop sexual harassment. In that light, a fact finder might also justifiably conclude that Unisys' reprimand of Moore following Paroline's complaint would have had no greater deterrent effect than the company's earlier warnings to him about sexual harassment.

We, of course, express no views on the merits. The fact finder might choose not to believe Paroline's evidence or might refuse to draw the inferences she advocates. We conclude only that summary judgment was inappropriate because a fact finder could reasonably conclude that Unisys' remedy was inadequate under the circumstances.

Paroline also argues that Unisys not only had a duty to remedy the sexual harassment after it occurred, but also had an obligation to try to prevent her harassment from occurring in the first place. Prevention is generally more efficacious than cure. In previous sexual harassment cases involving hostile workplace environments, we have focused on the adequacy of an employer's remedies *after* the harassment had occurred. See Swentek, 830 F.2d at 558; Katz, 709 F.2d at 254, 256. However, the logic of Swentek and Katz also allows us to impute liability, under certain circumstances, to an employer who failed to take steps to try to *prevent* sexual harassment of the plaintiff.

In a hostile environment case under Title VII, we will impute liability to an employer who anticipated or reasonably should have anticipated that the plaintiff would become a victim of sexual harassment in the workplace and yet failed to take action reasonably calculated to *prevent* such harassment. An employer's knowledge that a male worker has previously harassed female employees other than the plaintiff will often prove highly relevant in deciding whether the employer should have anticipated that the plaintiff too would become a victim of the male employee's harassing conduct. See Yates v. Avco, 819 F.2d 630, 636 [43 FEP Cases 1595] (6th Cir. 1987) ("[A]lthough Avco took remedial action once the plaintiffs registered complaints, its duty to remedy the problem, or at a minimum, inquire, was created earlier when the initial allegations of harassment [against other female employees] were reported."); Id. at 639 (Nelson, J., concurring); Ross v. Double Diamond, Inc., 672 F.Supp. 261, 273 [45 FEP Cases 313] (N.D. Tex. 1987) (company's knowledge of male employee's earlier harassment of a female worker weighed heavily in decision to hold employer liable for same employee's later harassment of other women). Of course an employer's knowledge of previous incidents of sexual harassment of other female workers will not necessarily indicate that an employer should have anticipated the plaintiff's harassment as well. But that is generally an issue for the fact finder, not one for disposal on summary judgment, for example, if it were clear that the male employee had previously targeted only women under a certain age or in a certain job classification, it might be unreasonable to expect an employer to anticipate the harassment of a plaintiff who falls outside those categories.

Paroline has raised a genuine issue as to whether Unisys should have anticipated her harassment by Moore. Unisys had received complaints that Moore had made improper sexual overtures toward female workers, and according to Paroline's evidence, the complaints of sexual harassment continue even after Unisys has warned Moore and other male employees to refrain from such behavior. Moreover, at least one Unisys official knew that Moore had asked Paroline in her job interview how she would respond if subjected to sexual harassment at work. One could interpret that question as an effort to gauge Paroline's willingness to tolerate sexual harassment. After the interview, Moore recommended that Unisys hire Paroline. The fact finder could reasonably infer from the evidence that Unisys should have recognized Moore's question as a warning signal that he planned to target Paroline for sexual harassment.

Assuming that Unisys should have anticipated the harassment of Paroline, we must next decide whether Paroline has raised a genuine issue as to whether the company took action reasonably calculated to prevent that harassment. As we have noted, Paroline's evidence could support an inference that Unisys' prior warning to Moore and other male employees about sexual harassment was nothing but a sham. Furthermore, Peterson never criticized or reprimanded Moore for asking Paroline in her job interview how she would respond to sexual harassment, even though he realized the question was inappropriate. Viewing the evidence most favorably to Paroline, the fact finder could reasonably conclude that Unisys should have anticipated Paroline's harassment, but took inadequate steps to try to prevent it. Therefore, the district court erred in granting summary judgment on Paroline's sexual harassment claims against Moore and Unisys.

IV.

CONSTRUCTIVE DISCHARGE

Paroline also asserts claims for constructive discharge under Title VII. Constructive discharge occurs only when an employer deliberately makes the work conditions intolerable in an effort to induce the employee to quit. *Bristow*, 770 F.2d at 1255.

Intolerability of the plaintiff's working conditions must be "assessed by the objective standard of whether a 'reasonable person' in the employee's position would have felt compelled to resign." *Bristow*, 770 F.2d at 1255. If Paroline's evidence is true, a reasonable person could have found the Unisys work environment intolerable. The sexual overtures and the attack to which Paroline was allegedly subjected could traumatize a reasonable person in Paroline's position. A reasonable person might especially fear Moore if she knew, as Paroline's evidence suggests, that Moore had a history of sexual harassment of women and had persisted in such behavior despite warnings and reprimands from his superiors. Paroline has produced evidence that Unisys management was well aware of the persisting problem created by Moore. Specifically, she claims, and Unisys has not denied, that upon hearing of Moore's alleged harassment of Paroline, Peterson responded, "Oh no, not again." Moore's superior position in the company in comparison with Paroline could increase the reasonable person's sense of vulnerability. Paroline's increased risk of encountering Moore in the office, which resulted from Unisys' revocation of his SCIF clearance, could intensify the stress and distraction of the work environment. The fact finder who believed Paroline's evidence and drew all justifiable inferences in her favor could plausibly conclude that a reasonable person would have found the work environment so intolerable that he or she would have felt compelled to resign. Summary judgment, therefore, was inappropriate, though again we emphasize that we have, and intend to express, no opinion on the merits.

We also believe a reasonable fact finder could conclude that Unisys and Moore intended to force Paroline to quit. Although the plaintiff must prove that her employer had specific intent to force her to quit, such "[i]ntent may be inferred through circumstantial evidence, including a failure to act in the face of known intolerable conditions." *Id, Accord, Holsey v. Armour & Co.*, 743 F.2d 199, 209 [35 FEP Cases 1064] (4th Cir. 1984), *cert. denied*, 470 U.S. 1028 [37 FEP Cases 192] (1985). There is evidence that Unisys management officials, as well as Moore, knew that Paroline was highly upset at the prospect of encountering Moore at the office. The evidence also showed that Unisys' remedial action increased the risk of contact between Moore and Paroline, precisely at a time when Paroline wanted to avoid Moore altogether. Our dissenting brother unsuccessfully attempts to minimize the import of such evidence by noting that Paroline herself recommended that Moore lose his security clearance. Paroline did not, however, request that Unisys accomplish revocation of Moore's SCIF clearance in such a way as to increase her day-to-day contact with her alleged harasser. Paroline lacked a SCIF clearance at the time Unisys revoked Moore's and did not know how long she might wait before obtaining one. Her increased daily contact with Moore thus would have continued indefinitely.[1] The evidence suggests that Unisys could have delayed revoking Moore's clearance until after Paroline received permission to

---

[1]Our dissenting colleague implies that Unisys would have solved the problem with the security clearances during the two-week leave it granted to Paroline following her alleged harassment. That assumption simply has no support in the evidence. The deposition testimony of Charles Peterson, Unisys' own witness, demonstrates that Unisys never anticipated that Paroline would gain immediate access to SCIF upon her return to work after the leave. In fact, the company could not predict when she would receive the clearance, as evidenced by the following deposition testimony from Peterson:

Q Well, until her clearances came through were you planning to keep her on an emergency leave status so that she wouldn't be in the office?

A [Peterson]: I had—it was my hope that that amount of time would not be required. *No, that was not my intention* . . . .

Q You had no control, I assume, over when her clearances would come through?

A No, unfortunately.

Q It's not done by [Unisys]?

A No, it's done by the government Defense Investigative Service.

Q So you're at their mercy basically?

A Oh, boy are we.

(Emphasis added).

enter the SCIF. By such delay Unisys could have punished Moore as Paroline suggested, therefore, ironically ameliorating the punishment, without increasing the risk of encounters between the two in the office. Unisys' choice of a different option at least allows inference that the company intended to increase Paroline's contact with Moore and thus exacerbate her fear and sense of vulnerability in the workplace.

We do not deny that a fact finder might reasonably conclude, as does Judge Wilkinson, that Unisys acted with noble intentions in response to Paroline's complaints of harassment. We are not triers of fact, however, and do not have the authority to usurp the fact finder's function of deciding which of two permissible inferences about Unisys' intent to draw from the evidence. To allow summary judgment at this point would make a mockery of the Supreme Court's admonition that "[c]redibility determinations, the weighing of the evidence and the drawing of legitimate inferences from the facts" are functions exclusively for the trier of fact. *Anderson,* 477 U.S. at 255.

Questions of intent are quintessentially ones for the fact finder under most circumstances, and we see no reason to depart from that principle here. The evidence, if believed by the fact finder, could support an inference that Unisys not merely "fail[ed] to act in face of known intolerable conditions," *Bristow,* 770 F.2d at 1255, but specifically tried to make life at the office less pleasant for Paroline. If, in fact Unisys' "remedy" was merely a ploy to force Paroline to quit, the fact finder could also reasonably infer that Moore, by acquiescing in Unisys' action, also intended to provoke Paroline's resignation.

Unisys argues that Paroline has failed to show, as a matter of law, that the company intended to cause her resignation. Unisys emphasizes that it asked Paroline not to quit. Although such evidence may provide a powerful defense for Unisys at trial on the constructive discharge claim, it does not compel or justify summary judgment in Unisys' favor. Even if Unisys officials did ask Paroline not to resign, a reasonable fact finder could conclude, based on Paroline's evidence, that the company was not sincere and actually wanted her to quit. We refuse to adopt a rule that would allow clever or sophisticated employers automatically to avoid Title VII liability merely by asking harassment victims not to resign. It is conceivable that some employers, in an effort to insulate themselves from liability, might ask discrimination victims not to quit and yet simultaneously strive to make those employees' workplace environment intolerable. We refuse to adopt a legal rule that encourages such duplicity. The issue of Unisys' intent is a factual, not legal, question on the record here.

With due respect to Judge Wilkinson, we believe he mischaracterizes the implications of our opinion for employers' proper handling of sexual harassment complaints. He claims that employers who receive complaints of harassment will henceforth feel compelled to fire the accused first and ask questions later. Our opinion neither requires nor condones such a cavalier disregard for the rights of accused employees in sexual harassment cases. Nothing in our opinion suggests that an employer may avoid liability only by firing the accused harasser. Nor do we mean to suggest that a constructive discharge claim will automatically survive summary judgment unless the employer has terminated the alleged harasser. The plaintiff must produce some evidence that the employer intended to force her to quit. Mere failure to fire the accused does not necessarily constitute the evidence of intent required to avoid summary judgment. But where, as here, the employer not merely declines to fire the accused but also unnecessarily takes action (by eliminating Moore's SCIF clearance before one has been secured for Paroline) which forces the plaintiff to increase contact with her alleged attacker, whose anticipated presence causes dread and fear, a fact finder could reasonably infer intent to provoke the plaintiff's resignation.

In sum, Paroline has raised genuine issues of material fact crucial to resolution of her constructive discharge claims. We reverse the grant of summary judgment because a reasonable fact finder could resolve the disputed factual issues in Paroline's favor.[2]

---

[2]Paroline raises two additional arguments that are either meritless or premature. First, she argues that the district court premised its decision on an erroneous belief that a plaintiff may recover under Title VII only if she demonstrates tangible or economic injury. We see nothing in the record to suggest that the district court operated under that assumption. Second, Paroline argues that Unisys' alleged failure to pay her for two weeks of administrative leave represents an economic injury for which she can recover under Title VII. We need not reach that issue. That argument is properly addressed to the district court if Paroline succeeds in proving a Title VII violation at trial.

· · ·

VII.

CONCLUSION

We uphold the district court's grant of summary judgment in favor of Unisys on Paroline's claims for intentional infliction of emotional distress. However, we reverse the grant of summary judgment on Paroline's Title VII claims against Moore and Unisys for sexual harassment and constructive discharge and her state law claim against Unisys for negligent failure to warn and reckless endangerment. We remand those claims to the district court for further proceedings consistent with this opinion.

We once again emphasize that our partial reversal of the district court judgment should in no way be construed as an indication of how the fact finder should ultimately decide the merits of Paroline's surviving claims.

AFFIRMED IN PART, REVERSED IN PART, AND REMANDED.

Concurring and Dissenting Opinion

J. HARVIE WILKINSON, Circuit Judge, concurring in part and dissenting in part:—I agree with the majority that Paroline has raised a triable issue of a hostile sexual environment at the company which made working conditions for her a source of considerable apprehension. I thus concur in part III of the majority opinion. I do not think, however, that there is any attempt to discharge Paroline, "constructively" or otherwise. I thus dissent from part IV. The issue is of more than theoretical import; a finding of constructive discharge carries an award of back pay.[1]

A constructive discharge is not an actual discharge; like a claim of "constructive notice" or "constructive possession" it will always have its fictional elements. In this, as in other claims of construction discharge, no one was actually terminated; instead the employee quit. Because the claim of constructive discharge is so open to abuse by those who leave employment of their own accord, this circuit has insisted that it be carefully cabined.

A plaintiff alleging constructive discharge must thus prove two elements: "deliberateness of the employer's action, and intolerability of the working conditions . . . . Deliberateness exists only if the actions complained of 'were intended by the employer as an effort to force the employee to quit.' " *Bristol v. Daily Press, Inc.,* 770 F.2d 1251, 1255 [38 FEP Cases 1145] (4th Cir. 1985), *quoting EEOC v. Federal Reserve Bank of Richmond,* 698 F.2d 633, 672 [30 FEP Cases 1137] (4th Cir. 1983), *rev'd on other grounds,* 467 U.S. 867, 104 S.Ct. 2794 [35 FEP Cases 13] (1984).[2] Although a failure to act in the face of known intolerable conditions may create an inference that the employer was attempting to force the plaintiff to resign, *Holsey v. Armour & Co.,* 743 F.2d 199, 209 [35 FEP Cases 1064] (4th Cir. 1984), such an inference depends upon some evidence that the inaction of the employer was directed *at the plaintiff.* The fact that all employees were treated identically rebuts any

---

[1] I would also hold that upon remand, Paroline's claim against Unisys for negligent failure to warn and reckless endangerment must be considered in light of the Virginia Supreme Court's failure to recognize a tort of negligent supervision of employees in *Chesapeake & Potomac Telephone Co. v. Dowdy,* 365 S.E.2d 751 [3 IER Cases 19] (Va. 1988). I do not understand the majority's discussion of *J. v. Victory Tabernacle Baptist Church,* 372 S.E.2d 391 [4 IER Cases 576] (Va. 1988), to foreclose the district court's consideration of the applicability of the *Dowdy* decision as well. With that understanding, I concur in all of the majority opinion with the exception of part IV.

[2] While other courts have adopted an objective test, dependent upon the reasonableness of the employer's action and the reasonableness of the employee's perception of the intolerable conditions, the result under either standard is the same. *Levendos v. Stern Entertainment,* 860 F.2d 1227 [48 FEP Cases 443] (3d Cir. 1988); *Calhoun v. Acme Cleveland Corporation,* 798 F.2d 559 [41 FEP Cases 1121] (1st Cir. 1986); *Derr v. Gulf Oil Corporation,* 796 F.2d 340 [41 FEP Cases 166] (10th Cir. 1986); *Lojek v. Thomas,* 716 F.2d 675 (9th Cir. 1983).

inference that the treatment of the plaintiff was done "with the intention of forcing him to resign. Certainly ... [the employer] did not wish to force all of its employees to resign." *Johnson v. Bunny Bread Co.,* 646 F.2d 1250, 1256 [25 FEP Cases 1326§ (8th Cir. 1981).

In this case, there is no evidence that Unisys engaged in any adverse action or inaction directed at the plaintiff Paroline. To the contrary, Unisys took remedial action when presented with Paroline's complaint. The company told Moore that if there were any more such incidents he would be fired. There were, in fact, no more such incidents. A written memorandum, setting forth the conditions of his continued employment, was placed in Moore's personnel file. Moore was required to seek counseling; his planned promotion and salary increase were delayed; and his contact with female employees was limited to official company business. Moreover, Unisys asked Paroline not to quit. The company also gave Paroline two weeks off in which to recuperate. Finally, Unisys offered to pay for counseling for Paroline. How this course of conduct amounts to a constructive discharge of Paroline on the part of Unisys is beyond me. Paroline did not, however, give these remedies the opportunity to work. *See Garner v. Wal-Mart Stores,* 807 F.2d 1536, 1539 [42 FEP Cases 1141] (11th Cir. 1987).

The majority bases its argument that there was a genuine issue as to Unisys' intent upon one fact: that Unisys' remedial action of withdrawing Moore's access to its Sensitive Compartmented Intelligence Facility actually "increased the risk of contact between Moore and Paroline, precisely at a time when Paroline wanted to avoid Moore altogether." The majority speculates this might conceivably be evidence of a ploy by a "clever or sophisticated" employer from which a factfinder could reasonably infer that Unisys intended to provoke Paroline to resign. The majority, however, overlooks the fact that Paroline herself, in an interview during Unisys' investigation of her complaint, requested that Unisys withdraw Moore's SCIF access. Unisys was in the process of getting Paroline a transfer so that she would be able to work in the section of the building that Moore could not enter. The fact that issuance of a SCIF clearance for Paroline rests with the Department of Defense does nothing to meet the point that Unisys was acting in accordance with Paroline's wishes in the matter.

The majority contends that, while the response of Unisys to Paroline's complaint may well have been satisfactory, the claim of constructive discharge in this case must nonetheless be submitted to the fact-finder. If, however, a claim this thin is one for the trier of fact, it is hard to imagine any claim of constructive discharge on which summary judgment would be appropriate. The implications of the majority's holding are most troubling. To protect itself as a matter of law against a claim of constructive discharge an employer may now be prompted to immediately dismiss any employee against whom a complaint of harassment is lodged. Whether this rule comports with any basic sense of moral fairness or due process, the majority neglects to ask. The workplace is to become the world of the accuser, where the slightest hesitancy in discharging the target of an accusation may lead the accuser to quit and later hold the company liable for constructive discharge.

One may take quite seriously the problems of sexual harassment in the workplace without subscribing to part IV of the majority opinion. Title VII suits for sexual harassment implicate several interests. The victim has an interest in not having to run a daily gauntlet of unwelcome pressures and advances at work. The accused also has an interest, however, in not losing a job or reputation on the basis of an accusation which turns out to be mistaken or downright false. The rule of law must reflect some equation of interests in a controversy. With all respect for the majority, it has left companies little incentive to inquire. Under the majority's view, the safe legal course is to act upon accusation, and not risk a claim of constructive discharge by waiting for the facts.

Instead of indicating an intent to force Paroline to leave, the company's actions here reflect the opposite; Unisys actively took action to improve Paroline's conditions of employment. Because there was no evidence presented of any intent to force Paroline to leave, and in fact substantial evidence of an intent to persuade her to stay, I would affirm the district court's grant of summary judgment for Unisys on the claim of constructive discharge.

VI. EMPLOYER REBUTTAL

A. Defeating the Underlying Case of Sexual Harassment

1. Lack of Harassing Conduct

An effective defense to the underlying claim of sexual harassment will also defeat a claim of constructive discharge based on the same conduct.[62] In *Gan v. Kepro Circuit Systems*,[63] the complainant resigned from her job when a supervisor disclosed to other employees that she was having her menstrual period—although she had just announced this fact to her co-workers. The court refused to consider the complainant's resignation a "constructive discharge," because it believed that she had contributed heavily to the sexually laden environment from which she supposedly sought escape. The court found that "[d]uring the course of her employment at defendant, plaintiff regularly used crude and vulgar language and initiated sexually oriented conversations with her male and female co-workers. She frequently asked male employees about their marital sex lives and whether they engaged in extra-marital sexual relationships. Plaintiff also made her own marital sexual relationships a regular topic of office conversation."[64] The evidence also showed that although a male co-worker had grabbed the complainant by her breasts, he had done so only in retaliation for her calling him a "nigger" and pinching his buttocks. The court decided that "[p]laintiff was not subjected to unprovoked propositions and sexually suggestive remarks, as she alleges. Any such propositions that did occur were prompted by her own sexual aggressiveness and her own sexually explicit conversations."[65]

2. Lack of Employer Responsibility

The success of a defense to constructive discharge based upon a claim that the employer lacked knowledge of the harassment will depend upon whether the employer "should have known" of the harassment.[66] Where the harasser is a supervisor, employer knowledge is more likely to be found, but constructive discharge has been found even where the harasser was a subordinate of the complainant.[67]

If the employer has a policy offering appropriate methods to correct sexual harassment, constructive discharge generally will not be found where the com-

---

[62]See note 5 *supra*.

[63]28 FEP Cases 639 (E.D. Mo. 1982)

[64]*Id.* at 640.

[65]*Id.*

[66]Levendos v. Stern Entertainment, 909 F.2d 747, 753–54, 53 FEP Cases 779, 784 (3d Cir. 1990)(notice to executive management of unwelcome sexual conduct is factor but not crucial in determining whether a constructive discharge has occurred; evidence in present case compels finding of "imputed notice" even though no formal complaint was made).

[67]Easter v. Jeep Corp., *supra* note 51, 750 F.2d at 523, 42 FEP Cases at 668 (constructive discharge found where *subordinate* employees sexually harassed female supervisor and employer took no remedial steps).

plainant quit before giving the employer a fair opportunity to correct the harassing behavior.[68] The Sixth Circuit found it unreasonable for a complainant to have resigned when, following her complaint to management, the harasser told her that he had been assigned to a desk adjacent to hers. In fact, the harasser had been demoted and moved to a different work area. The complainant's resignation was found unreasonable because she failed to seek official confirmation of the harasser's claim before resigning and she declined to return to work even after a manager explained the situation and asked her to return.[69] Similarly, in *Dornhecker v. Malibu Grand Prix Corp.,*[70] the Fifth Circuit found it unreasonable for the complainant to have resigned where, the day after she first complained about the conduct of a consultant, the company president told her that she would not have to work with the offender after the end of the current business trip.[71] Similarly, no constructive discharge was established where the complainant could have easily escaped the supervision of the alleged harasser by working on another shift or at another mill near her home and yet chose not to do so.[72]

B. Showing Other Reasons for the Employee's Action

In some cases the employer has shown that factors other than sexual harassment motivated the complainant's resignation. In *Henson v. City of Dundee,*[73] the district court concluded that no constructive discharge had occurred because the complainant, although sexually harassed, had resigned because the police officer with whom she was romantically involved had been forced to resign from the police force on which they both worked. The Eleventh Circuit affirmed, holding that the lower court was not clearly erroneous in finding that the complainant's resignation resulted from reasons other than sexual harassment.[74] Similarly, in *Huddleston v. Roger Dean Chevrolet,*[75] the Eleventh Circuit upheld a finding that the complainant's resignation resulted primarily from a private dispute unrelated to the sexual harassment where, in her resignation letter, the complainant had stated that she was resigning because

---

[68]*See generally* Section IV. *supra. See, e.g.,* Barrett v. Omaha Nat'l Bank, 726 F.2d 424, 427, 35 FEP Cases 593, 595 (8th Cir. 1984)(threat to fire alleged harasser for further misconduct constituted prompt remedial action such that claim against employer fails).

[69]Yates v. Avco Corp., *supra* note 55 (reversing finding of constructive discharge). *See also* Kramer-Navarro v. Bolger, 586 F. Supp. 677, 684, 38 FEP Cases 450, 455 (S.D.N.Y. 1984)(plaintiff told supervisor to "go to hell" without giving him chance to speak his piece).

[70]828 F.2d 307, 44 FEP Cases 1604 (5th Cir. 1987)(reversing finding of constructive discharge).

[71]Id. at 309–10, 44 FEP Cases at 1605–6. *See also* Steele v. Offshore Shipbldg., 867 F.2d 1311, 1316–17, 49 FEP Cases 522, 525 (11th Cir. 1989)(affirming finding of no constructive discharge where resignation occurred after corporate officials verbally reprimanded harasser and assured complainants that offensive conduct would stop and for remaining 12 days of complainants' employment no additional harassment occurred).

[72]Smith v. Acme Spinning Co., 40 FEP Cases 1104, 1109 (W.D.N.C. 1986).

[73]682 F.2d 897, 29 FEP Cases 787 (11th Cir. 1982), reproduced in Chapter 4, Hostile Environment Harassment.

[74]*Id.* at 908. *See also* Bristow v. Daily Press, 770 F.2d 1251, 1256, 38 FEP Cases 1145, 1148 (4th Cir. 1985)(judgment for age discrimination plaintiff reversed; no constructive discharge because it was obvious that plaintiff's resignation arose from financial dispute with supervisors rather than from any intolerable working conditions), *cert. denied,* 475 U.S. 1082 (1986).

[75]845 F.2d 900, 906, 46 FEP Cases 1361 (11th Cir. 1988).

of fear for her safety and the safety of her daughter.[76] The district court found that those fears stemmed from threats relating to an off-duty dispute that was not connected to any sexual harassment at the workplace. Even though the individual who allegedly had made the threats had also participated in the alleged sexual harassment, the lower court's finding that the resignation was due primarily to the nonwork-related incident was upheld as not clearly erroneous.[77]

---

[76]The complainant's failure to identify sexual harassment as a grievance in a resignation letter is probative but not dispositive of whether the resignation resulted from harassment. *See, e.g.,* Hunter v. Countryside Ass'n for the Handicapped, 710 F. Supp. 233, 238, 49 FEP Cases 790, 793 (N.D. Ill. 1989)(plaintiff may have omitted reference to alleged rape for variety of reasons); Henson v. City of Dundee, *supra* note 73, 682 F.2d at 908, 29 FEP Cases at 797 (written resignation that did not specify sexual harassment, though it did cite "work conditions", suggested voluntary resignation); Huddleston v. Roger Dean Chevrolet, 845 F.2d 900, 906, 46 FEP Cases 1361, 1364 (11th Cir. 1988)(letter of resignation citing other causes for resignation supported conclusion that other causes predominated); Kirkland v. Brinias, 741 F. Supp. 692 (E.D. Tenn. 1990)(although sexual harassment of waitresses occurred, waitresses quit because of unjust treatment cited in resignation letter, not because of "any overtly sexual conduct"). *See also* Barbetta v. Chemlawn Servs. Corp., 669 F. Supp. 569, 571–72, 44 FEP Cases 1563, 1564 (W.D.N.Y. 1987)(court noted, but did not rely upon, fact that plaintiff's letter of resignation cited "personal reasons" but found that substantial questions of fact precluded entry of summary judgment in defendant's favor on constructive discharge claim).

[77]*Supra* note 75, 845 F.2d at 905, 46 FEP Cases at 1364. *See also* Steele v. Offshore Shipbldg., *supra* note 71, 867 F.2d at 1317–18, 49 FEP Cases at 526–27 (although sexual harassment had occurred, it had stopped prior to plaintiff's resignation and did not motivate resignation); Smith v. Acme Spinning Co., *supra* note 72 (no constructive discharge despite finding of sexual harassment where plaintiff had resigned in anger after another employee received desirable assignment).

CHAPTER 10

RETALIATION

I. OVERVIEW

Section 704(a) of Title VII prohibits retaliation against those who participate in Title VII processes or oppose discriminatory employment practices.[1] Section 704(a) thus prohibits discrimination on the basis of participation or opposition, just as §703 prohibits discrimination on the basis of a protected group status.

The two bases protected by §704(a) are set forth in two separate clauses: the participation clause, which forbids discrimination "because [an individual] has made a charge, testified, assisted, or participated in any manner in an investigation, proceeding, or hearing under [Title VII]," and the opposition clause, which forbids discrimination "because [an individual] has opposed any practice made an unlawful employment practice by [Title VII]."

A claim under either the participation clause or the opposition clause requires proof:

(1) of the basis—that the complainant engaged in statutorily protected participation[2] or opposition;[3]

(2) of the issue—an adverse employment action, such as a discharge;[4]

(3) of a causal connection between the protected activity (participation or opposition) and the adverse employment action;[5] and

(4) that the adverse action was taken against a covered person[6] by a covered respondent.[7]

---

[1]42 U.S.C. §2000e-3(a) provides:

   It shall be an unlawful employment practice for an employer to discriminate against any of his employees or applicants for employment, for an employment agency, or joint labor-management committee controlling apprenticeship or other training or retraining . . . to discriminate against any individual, or for a labor organization to discriminate against any member thereof or applicant for membership, because he has opposed any practice made an unlawful employment practice by this [title], or because he has made a charge, testified, assisted, or participated in any manner in an investigation, proceeding, or hearing under this [title].

For references to alternative sources of relief, see Section VIII. *infra.*

[2]See Section II. *infra.*

[3]See Section III. *infra.*

[4]See Section IV. *infra.*

[5]See Section V. *infra.*

[6]See Section VI.A. *infra.*

[7]See Section VI.B. *infra.*

The defenses commonly raised to such a claim are that the form of the complainant's protest was too extreme, that the employment practice challenged could not reasonably have been believed to be unlawful under Title VII, that the respondent was not aware of the protest, and that the discipline of the complainant was for legitimate business reasons rather than in retaliation for opposition or participation.[8]

This chapter discusses what constitutes participation or opposition by a sexual harassment complainant, what constitutes an adverse employment action in the retaliation context, and what problems exist in establishing and rebutting the causal connection between (1) the participation or opposition and (2) the adverse employment action.

II. THE PARTICIPATION CLAUSE

A. Activities Protected as Participation

The participation clause affords absolute protection for nearly any activity related to communicating, or refusing to communicate, information to a civil rights enforcement agency.[9]

1. Filing EEOC Charges

The participation clause prohibits retaliation against a complainant for filing an administrative charge of employment discrimination with the EEOC. If the employer does retaliate, the complainant may file a second charge, for the retaliation, or the EEOC may simply exercise jurisdiction to investigate and decide the retaliation issue in the context of the original charge.[10] Similarly, some courts have permitted a complainant to include a retaliation claim in a lawsuit without filing a separate administrative charge to satisfy the requirement that the complainant first exhaust administrative remedies.[11]

2. Other Forms of Participation

The participation clause also protects those who have taken steps short of actually filing an EEOC charge. The participation clause has been held to

---

[8]See Section VII. *infra.*

[9]For a more thorough discussion of the participation clause, see B.L. SCHLEI & P. GROSSMAN, EMPLOYMENT DISCRIMINATION LAW 535–42 (2d ed. 1983), Five-Year Supplement 222 (1989).

[10]*See* EEOC COMPL. MAN. (BNA), §614.2, at 614:0007.

[11]*E.g.,* Howze v. Jones & Laughlin Steel Corp., 750 F.2d 1208, 1212, 36 FEP Cases 1026, 1029 (3d Cir. 1984)(mere adding of claim of retaliation to amended complaint is insufficient reason to deny motion to amend where employer did not argue it would be prejudiced); Thompson v. Machinists, 33 FEP Cases 641, 642–43 (D.D.C. 1983)(plaintiff allowed to amend complaint by adding claim of retaliatory discharge although only race and sex discrimination were alleged in EEOC charge, because facts presented to EEOC were same facts on which retaliation claim was based); Lazic v. University of Pa., 513 F. Supp. 761, 767–68, 29 FEP Cases 1652, 1656–57 (E.D. Pa. 1981)(failure of former university faculty member to raise retaliation claim before EEOC did not preclude her from litigating that issue in Title VII action where claim was related to original charge and reasonably might be expected to grow out of investigation of that charge). *But see* Steffen v. Meridian Life Ins. Co., 859 F.2d 534, 544–46, 48 FEP Cases 173, 182 (7th Cir. 1988)(dischargee who consulted attorney and did not allege retaliation in complaining of discharge cannot raise new theory of liability at trial), *cert. denied,* 109 S.Ct. 3191 (1989); Espinoza v. Fry's Food Stores, 55 EPD ¶40,387 (D. Ariz. 1990)(retaliation claim not maintainable in court where no retaliation charge filed with administrative agency and retaliation claim not sufficiently related to underlying claim of discrimination).

protect an employee who has merely communicated an intent to file a charge,[12] who has testified on behalf of a co-worker who has filed a sexual harassment charge,[13] who has refused to testify on behalf of the employer,[14] or who has filed charges against other employers.[15]

3. Internal Complaints

In *Vasconcelos v. Meese,*[16] the complainant sued her former employer for retaliation because the employer fired her for lying during an internal investigation of her complaint of sexual harassment. The complainant and another employee had drinks together in a bar and then engaged in kissing and petting in a nearby parking lot. The federal district court found that the complainant had invited the sexual advances. The fact that she had lied during the internal investigation emerged during the subsequent investigation of her EEOC charge based on the same allegations. On appeal, the Ninth Circuit affirmed a judgment for the defendants. Judge David Thompson rejected the complainant's argument that §704(a) protects all statements, even lies, made in internal investigations: "[a]ccusations made in the context of charges before the Commission are protected by statute; charges made outside of that context are made at the accusers' peril."[17]

4. State-Agency Complaints

The participation clause expressly protects participation in proceedings under Title VII. Its language does not address state-agency proceedings. A federal district court addressed the application of §704(a) to such a proceeding in *Proulx v. CitiBank,*[18] which involved a warehouseman fired for filing a false and malicious sexual harassment complaint with a state fair employment practices agency. Treating the issue as one of first impression, Judge Charles Haight, Jr., held that the warehouseman could state a claim for unlawful retaliation: "where an employee files with an appropriate agency a Title VII

---

[12]EEOC COMPL. MAN. (BNA), §614.5(a), at 614:0018–19, citing Gifford v. Atchison, Topeka & Santa Fe Ry. Co., 685 F.2d 1149, 1156 n.3, 34 FEP Cases 240, 245 (9th Cir. 1982)(no legal distinction between filing charge and threatening to file charge); Morley v. New England Tel. Co., 47 FEP Cases 917, 924 (D. Mass 1987)(§704 protects employee who communicated to management intent to file charge); Croushorn v. Board of Trustees, 518 F. Supp. 9, 20, 30 FEP Cases 168, 176–77 (M.D. Tenn. 1980)(same).

[13]Ramos v. Roche Prods., 694 F. Supp. 1018, 1024, 50 FEP Cases 815, 818–19 (D.P.R. 1988)(executing affidavit on behalf of co-worker in EEOC proceedings protected under participation clause), *remanded,* 880 F.2d 621, 50 FEP Cases 822 (1st Cir. 1989); Aquino v. Sommer Maid Creamery, 657 F. Supp. 208, 210, 45 FEP Cases 796, 797 (E.D. Pa. 1987)(employee's participation in state FEP proceedings on behalf of his wife, who was also employee, protected under participation clause). *Cf.* Richards v. ATE Mgmt. & Serv. Co., 54 FEP Cases 401 (N.D. Ala. 1990)(Hancock, J.)(granting summary judgment against plaintiff allegedly fired for testifying adversely to employer in non-Title VII race discrimination case and for interacting with black politicians to secure government contract for minority contractors).

[14]Smith v. Columbus Metro. Housing Auth., 443 F. Supp. 61, 64–65, 17 FEP Cases 315, 317–18 (S.D. Ohio 1977)(employee's decision not to assist employer in Title VII investigation constitutes "participation" under §704(a)); EEOC Dec. 71-2312, 3 FEP Cases 1246, 1247 (1971)(retaliation for refusal to participate in Title VII proceeding on behalf of employer is violation of §704(a)).

[15]Barela v. United Nuclear Corp., 462 F.2d 149, 152, 4 FEP Cases 831, 833 (10th Cir. 1972)(unlawful to deny employment to applicant for filing EEOC charge against prior employer).

[16]907 F.2d 111, 53 FEP Cases 616 (9th Cir. 1990).

[17]*Id.* at 113, 53 FEP Cases at 618. The court did not expressly consider the application of the opposition clause, presumably because the opposition clause, unlike the participation clause, does not protect groundless complaints.

[18]659 F. Supp. 972, 44 FEP Cases 371 (S.D.N.Y. 1987).

discrimination claim which, albeit false and malicious, facially falls within the statute, the employer is forbidden by Section 704(a) from unilaterally discharging the employee because of the filing or prosecution of the claim."[19]

B. Challenged Employment Practice Need Not Be Illegal

A plaintiff may establish a violation of the participation clause without proving that the underlying claim of discrimination is valid.[20] Courts have not imposed any requirement that a plaintiff even had a good-faith belief in the illegality of the challenged practice.[21] Accordingly, protection under the participation clause is not lost if the charges are false, malicious, or defamatory.[22]

III. THE OPPOSITION CLAUSE

A. Form and Subject of Opposition

The first issue that arises under the opposition clause is what forms of activity constitute "opposition." The opposition clause, by definition, applies in the absence of a formal charge of discrimination. It protects a variety of precharge and noncharge conduct, ranging from the informal voicing of complaints to supervisors[23] to the formal invocation of an employer's internal grievance procedures.[24]

The opposition must be to conduct that allegedly violates Title VII. Other forms of opposition, such as union activities, are protected only by the National Labor Relations Act,[24a] not §704(a).[24b]

Courts have construed the opposition clause as protecting a communication between a waitress and an attorney about sexual harassment from custom-

---

[19]*Id.* at 979, 44 FEP Cases at 376. For further discussion of this issue, see SCHLEI & GROSSMAN, *supra* note 9, at 540–42, Five-Year Supp. at 222.

[20]Drinkwater v. Union Carbide Corp., 904 F.2d 853, 866 (3d Cir. 1990)(plaintiff protected by opposition clause when she protested sexual favoritism because she had plausible legal basis at time, even though later legal developments undermined claim); Womack v. Munson, 619 F.2d 1292, 1298, 22 FEP Cases 1079, 1083 (8th Cir. 1980)(allegation that employer required black deputies to beat black prisoners protected even if allegation unwarranted), *cert. denied,* 450 U.S. 979 (1981); Abramson v. University of Haw., 594 F.2d 202, 211, 19 FEP Cases 439, 446 (9th Cir. 1979)(charge filed before employer covered by Title VII; retaliation occurred after employer was covered); Sutton v. National Distillers Prods., 445 F. Supp. 1319, 1327, 16 FEP Cases 1031, 1038 (S.D. Ohio 1978)(female guard's challenge to policy of restricting body searches to employees of same sex protected, although policy itself was business necessity), *aff'd,* 628 F.2d 936, 27 FEP Cases 323 (6th Cir. 1980). For citation to additional authorities, and for a discussion of parallel doctrine in the context of First Amendment cases, see SCHLEI & GROSSMAN, *supra* note 9, at 541.

[21]The protection of the opposition clause is more limited in this respect. See Section III. *infra.* The EEOC would require a good-faith belief in the underlying charge even in a participation clause case. Absent good faith, the EEOC would seek only injunctive relief and not individual relief on behalf of the charging party. EEOC COMPL. MAN. (BNA), §614.5(c), at 614:0019.

[22]Pettway v. American Cast Iron Pipe Co., 411 F.2d 998, 1007, 1 FEP Cases 752, 758 (5th Cir. 1969)(employer liable for unlawful retaliation when complainant discharged for malicious material contained in letter to EEOC); Booker v. Brown & Williamson Tobacco Co., 879 F.2d 1304, 1312, 50 FEP Cases 365, 370 (6th Cir. 1989)(protection not lost if charge is malicious and defamatory).

[23]Rollins v. Florida Dep't of Law Enforcement, 868 F.2d 397, 400, 49 FEP Cases 763, 765 (11th Cir. 1989)(protection under §704(a) not limited to filed formal complaints but extends to those who informally complain to supervisors); Armstrong v. Index Journal Co., 647 F.2d 441, 448, 25 FEP Cases 1081, 1086 (4th Cir. 1981)(opposition clause encompasses voicing complaints to employers).

[24]Ferguson v. E.I. du Pont de Nemours & Co., 560 F. Supp. 1172, 1200, 31 FEP Cases 795, 815 (D. Del. 1983) (precharge complaint to management protected).

[24a]See note 80 *infra* and accompanying text.

[24b]Morgan v. Massachusetts Gen'l Hosp., 901 F.2d 186, 193 (1st Cir. 1990)(union activities not basis for §704 violation).

ers[25] and a complaint by a loan officer to a bank vice president that she was sexually harassed by a co-worker.[26] The opposition clause also protects an employee who, although not a direct victim of any discriminatory practice, opposes discrimination against other employees, such as a male employee who reports that his supervisor sexually harasses female employees.[27]

B. Activities So Disruptive as to Exceed Protection

The second issue that arises under the opposition clause is when the form of an employee's opposition is so excessive as to lose the protection of the opposition clause.[28] The question of the form of the protest typically arises only under the opposition clause; under the participation clause the use of Title VII procedures is itself the form of the protest.

In determining whether the form of the opposition was excessive, courts balance the individual's right to oppose discrimination against the employer's right to operate its business.[29] Section 704(a) does not protect conduct that disrupts the workplace[30] or that so interferes with the opposer's job performance that the opposer is rendered ineffective.[31]

---

[25]EEOC Dec. 84-3, 34 FEP Cases 1887 (1984).

[26]Barrett v. Omaha Nat'l Bank, 584 F. Supp. 22, 35 FEP Cases 585 (D. Neb. 1983)(female employee sexually harassed by male co-employee, but employer not liable under Title VII because it investigated misconduct and disciplined co-employee within four days of learning of misconduct), aff'd, 726 F.2d 424, 35 FEP Cases 593 (8th Cir. 1984).

[27]Fielder v. Southco, 699 F. Supp. 577, 578, 48 FEP Cases 1895, 1896 (W.D. Va. 1988)(§704(a) protects male employee who reported that supervisor was sexually harassing females); Jones v. Lyng, 669 F. Supp. 1108, 1121, 42 FEP Cases 587, 598 (D.D.C. 1986)(§704(a) protects male employee who protested sexual harassment of female employees); Jenkins v. Orkin Exterminating Co., 646 F. Supp. 1274, 1278, 42 FEP Cases 152, 154 (E.D. Tex. 1986)(§704(a) protects male employee who informed district manager that branch manager was sexually harassing female employee). Cf. Prichard v. Ledford, 55 FEP Cases 755, 758 (E.D. Tenn. 1990)(brother of sexual harassment complainant did not engage in protected activity when he led her "astray" by taking her to nightspot with another man at a time when alleged harasser wanted her to continue romantic relationship exclusively with him; brother's activities not motivated by opposition to sexual harassment of his sister).

[28]For an extensive discussion of this issue, see SCHLEI & GROSSMAN, supra note 9, at 549–52, Five-Year Supp. at 225–26. E.g., Rosser v. Laborers Int'l Union of N. Am., 616 F.2d 221, 225, 22 FEP Cases 1274, 1276 (5th Cir.)(employee's conduct in protesting unlawful employment practice not protected by §704(a) if it so interferes with job performance that it renders him ineffective), cert. denied, 449 U.S. 886 (1980).

[29]Booker v. Brown & Williamson Tobacco Co., supra note 22, 879 F.2d at 1312, 50 FEP Cases at 370–71 (courts required to balance protection afforded by §704(a) to persons who oppose discriminatory practices with employer's right to select and control its personnel); Jones v. Flagship Int'l, 793 F.2d 714, 728, 41 FEP Cases 358, 369 (5th Cir. 1986)(employee's conduct must be "reasonable in light of the circumstances" and employer's right to run its business must be balanced against rights of employee to "express his grievances and promote his own welfare"), cert. denied, 479 U.S. 1065 (1987); Payne v. McLemore's Wholesale & Retail Stores, 654 F.2d 1130, 1144, 26 FEP Cases 1500, 1508 (5th Cir. 1981)(ex-employee not rehired after picketing to protest employer's employment practices has §704(a) claim where employer failed to show how ex-employee's activity was hostile or detrimental); Ross v. Double Diamond, 672 F. Supp 261, 265, 45 FEP Cases 313, 323–24 (N.D. Tex. 1987)(decision of sexual harassment complainant to contact local sheriff was reasonable where alleged harasser was top management representative at facility and action did not significantly interfere with employer's ability to operate its business); EEOC v. Kallir, Philips, Ross, Inc., 401 F. Supp. 66, 74, 11 FEP Cases 241, 245 (S.D.N.Y. 1975)(not excessive or disruptive to obtain information from employer's client to provide to agency investigating charge where no adverse effect on employer's relationship with client), aff'd, 559 F.2d 1203, 15 FEP Cases 1369 (2d Cir.), cert. denied, 434 U.S. 920 (1977).

[30]Hochstadt v. Worcester Found. for Experimental Biology, 545 F.2d 222, 233, 13 FEP Cases 804, 812 (1st Cir. 1976)(political activist for women's liberation forfeited §704(a) protection because she (1) constantly complained about alleged sex discrimination to colleagues, thereby damaging relationships among members of group; (2) circulated rumors that employer might lose its grant and disclosed confidential files undermining employer's fundraising; and (3) tried to get assistant director to side with her in ongoing dispute with director).

[31]Jones v. Flagship Int'l, supra note 29 (manager of EEOC programs who filed discrimination suit against employer and solicited others to join suit rendered herself ineffective in her job).

C. Need to Analyze Legality of the Challenged Employment Practice

The third issue that arises under the opposition clause is whether the practice opposed as an "unlawful employment practice" must actually be illegal under Title VII.

Although opposing a practice that actually violates Title VII generally is protected, more difficult questions arise if the practice opposed does not violate Title VII. The EEOC and most courts have stated that §704(a) protects opposition so long as the employee has a reasonable and good-faith belief that the practice opposed constituted a violation of Title VII; the employee need not show that the practice actually violated the Act.[32] The minority view is that for the opposition clause to apply the practice opposed must actually have violated Title VII.[33]

The rationale for the broader scope of protection afforded by the majority view is that although the opposition clause linguistically could be limited to cases of actual Title VII violations, following that "narrow interpretation" would have two effects contrary to the policy of Title VII: It would chill the legitimate assertion of employee rights and it would encourage employees to file formal charges rather than seek the informal adjustment of grievances.[34]

The opposition clause does not, however, protect complaints that have absolutely no basis. An employer may impose discipline, consistent with the opposition clause, on a complainant who is acting unreasonably or in bad faith in opposing conduct alleged to be sexual harassment.[35]

---

[32]*See, e.g.,* Drinkwater v. Union Carbide Corp., *supra* note 20 (reversing summary judgment against plaintiff's retaliation claim where plaintiff allegedly fired for protesting sexual favoritism of plaintiff's female subordinate by plaintiff's male superior; plaintiff reasonably believed she had sex discrimination claim as law then stood); Holland v. Jefferson Nat'l Life Ins. Co., 883 F.2d 1307, 1314, 50 FEP Cases 1215, 1221 (7th Cir. 1989)(employee who has good-faith belief that challenged practice violates Title VII protected under §704(a) even if challenged practice turns out to be lawful); Ross v. Double Diamond, *supra* note 29, 45 FEP Cases at 322–24 (despite absence of hostile environment, complainant prevailed on retaliation claim based on protest of alleged hostile environment).

[33]*See, e.g.,* Jordan v. Clark, 847 F.2d 1368, 1376, 46 FEP Cases 1558, 1564 (9th Cir. 1988)(practice opposed must be in fact unlawful under Title VII), *cert. denied,* 488 U.S. 1006 (1989). Some courts have indicated that the plaintiff must demonstrate a subjective "good-faith" or "honestly held" belief in addition to or instead of the more objective reasonableness standard. Monteiro v. Poole Silver Co., 615 F.2d 4, 8, 22 FEP Cases 90, 92 (1st Cir. 1980)("plaintiff must show that opposition was in response to some honestly held, if mistaken, feeling that discrimination practices existed"); EEOC COMPL. MAN. (BNA), §614.4(a) at 614:0010. For a more detailed discussion of the majority and minority views on this issue, see B.L. SCHLEI & P. GROSSMAN, EMPLOYMENT DISCRIMINATION LAW 543–48 (2d ed. 1983), Five-Year Supp. 223–24 (1989)(overwhelming majority view is that employee need only believe, in good faith, that opposed practice violates Title VII).

[34]Sias v. City Demonstration Agency, 588 F.2d 692, 695, 18 FEP Cases 981, 982–83 (9th Cir. 1978)(violation of Title VII to fire employee for writing letter alleging discriminatory practices; employee's action protected because based on reasonable though erroneous belief that practices violated Title VII).

[35]For cases in which a claim of sexual harassment was rejected as being based on the complainant's idiosyncratic reaction, see Sand v. Johnson Co., 33 FEP Cases 716, 720 (E.D. Mich. 1982)(standard is that of reasonable rather than hypersensitive person; mere flirtation and compliments on appearance do not support sexual harassment claim); EEOC Dec. 82-2, 28 FEP Cases 1843, 1844–45 (1983)(supervisor's invitation for drinks or dinner alone does not support inference of sexual harassment). Nonetheless, even a frivolous complaint, made pursuant to an employer's sexual harassment policy, may be protected as a matter of contract, if not by Title VII, see Chapters 15, The Common Law, Section IX.A., and should be taken seriously. See Chapter 19, Responding to Internal Complaints.

IV. ISSUE: THE ADVERSE EMPLOYMENT ACTION

A. Scope of Cognizable Employment Actions

After proving statutorily protected participation or opposition, complainants must prove that they have suffered an adverse employment action.

Types of job detriments found to be sufficient to meet this requirement are myriad,[36] including the failure to hire,[37] failure to promote,[38] withholding pay increases,[39] poor performance reviews,[40] assignment of more onerous work,[41] withdrawing "friendly courtesies,"[42] spreading rumors of an affair between the complainant and the alleged harasser,[43] abolishment of a position,[44] demotion,[45] and discharge.[46]

---

[36]For a comprehensive sample of employment actions cognizable under §704(a), see SCHLEI & GROSSMAN, *supra* note 33, at 554–57, Five-Year Supp. at 227–29.

[37]Simmons v. Lyons, 746 F.2d 265, 270, 36 FEP Cases 410, 414 (5th Cir. 1984)(alleged submission to sexual advances condition of reemployment with new sheriff); Rinkel v. Associated Pipeline Contractors, 17 FEP Cases 224, 225 (D. Alaska 1978)(alleged employer refused to hire female because she would not acquiesce to sexual advances of senior management official).

[38]Broderick v. Ruder, 685 F. Supp. 1269, 1278, 46 FEP Cases 1272, 1282 (D.D.C. 1988), reproduced in Chapter 2, Forms of Harassment (unlawful to delay promotion because complainant opposed managers' sexual conduct); Morley v. New England Tel. Co., 47 FEP Cases 917, 924 (D. Mass. 1987)(notwithstanding employee's failure to prove sexual harassment by supervisor, unlawful to deny promotion).

[39]Sowers v. Kemira, Inc., 701 F. Supp. 809, 824–25, 46 FEP Cases 1825, 1836 (S.D. Ga. 1988)(female employee proved both sexual harassment and retaliation by showing that manager made unwelcome sexual advances and that rejection and complaints to management led him to impede promotion and salary increase); Shrout v. Black Clawson Co., 689 F. Supp. 774, 780, 46 FEP Cases 1339, 1344 (S.D. Ohio 1988)(after female terminated voluntary consensual sexual relationship with supervisor, she was subjected to his unwelcome and degrading sexual conduct and was refused annual performance appraisals and salary reviews).

[40]Holland v. Jefferson Nat'l Life Ins. Co., *supra* note 32, 883 F.2d at 1314–15, 50 FEP Cases at 1220–21; Broderick v. Ruder, *supra* note 38, 685 F. Supp. at 1279, 46 FEP Cases at 1282 (plaintiff demonstrated she was subjected to adverse employment action by denial of promotion and bad performance review after she complained about manager's sexual harassment); Morley v. New England Tel. Co., *supra* note 38, 47 FEP Cases at 924 (prima facie case of retaliation stated where defendants gave plaintiff "not promote" rating after she communicated intent to file discrimination claim; plaintiff failed to prove she was subjected to sexual harassment); EEOC Dec. 81-18, 27 FEP Cases 1793, 1805-16 (1981)(employer violated Title VII when it required four female employees to permit two male supervisors to engage in unwanted verbal and physical sexual conduct).

[41]EEOC Dec. 81-18, 27 FEP Cases 1793, 1805 (1981)(reassignment of complainant's typist). *See also* Robson v. Eva's Supermarket, 538 F. Supp. 857, 861, 30 FEP Cases 1212, 1215 (N.D. Ohio 1982)(alleging complainant got more onerous work after she rejected sexual advances).

[42]Sims v. Madame Paulette Dry Cleaners, 580 F. Supp. 593, 596, 34 FEP Cases 305, 308 (S.D.N.Y. 1984)(after EEOC sex discrimination charge, employer required complainant to arrive exactly on time for work whereas previously she was permitted to arrive late).

[43]Toscano v. Nimmo, 570 F. Supp. 1197, 1204–6, 32 FEP Cases 1401, 1405 (D. Del. 1983)(after employee complained that supervisor gave promotion to another woman who gave him sexual favors, supervisor and his wife participated in conduct intended to create false impression among employee's co-workers that she had engaged in affair with him).

[44]Barnes v. Costle, 561 F.2d 983, 990, 15 FEP Cases 345, 350 (D.C. Cir. 1977), reproduced in Chapter 1, Overview (female employee asserted that job was abolished because of resistance to supervisor's sexual advances).

[45]Harrison v. Reed Rubber Co., 603 F. Supp. 1457, 1461–62, 37 FEP Cases 1545, 1549 (E.D. Mo. 1985)(female employee demoted after she complained about superintendent's sexual harassment).

[46]Horn v. Duke Homes, 755 F.2d 599, 37 FEP Cases 228 (7th Cir. 1985)(female employee discharged by plant superintendent because she refused to respond to sexual advances); Garber v. Saxon Business Prods., 552 F.2d 1032, 15 FEP Cases 344 (4th Cir. 1977)(female employee discharged for rebuffing sexual advances of male supervisor); Boyd v. James S. Hayes Living Health Care Agency, 671 F. Supp. 1155, 1167, 44 FEP Cases 332, 342 (W.D. Tenn. 1987)(plaintiff terminated because she rejected and complained about advances of employer's administrator); Crockwell v. Blackmon-Mooring Steamatic, 627 F. Supp. 800, 807, 43 FEP Cases 1451, 1456 (W.D. Tenn. 1985)(employee fired after expressing opposition to suggestive remarks made by employer's customer); Heelan v. Johns-Manville Corp., 451 F. Supp. 1382, 1390, 20 FEP Cases

Not every job change made in reaction to a complaint of sexual harassment would necessarily be an adverse employment action.[47] In *Yates v. Avco Corp.*,[48] the Sixth Circuit reversed a finding of retaliation where an employee complaining of sexual harassment was transferred to a lower-grade secretarial position and was requested to acknowledge in writing that the transfer was at her request. Judge Boyce Martin, Jr., reasoned that the request itself was not an adverse employment action and that no adverse employment action had otherwise occurred, in that the complainant received the same salary and benefits as before and was assured that she would receive the next available position at her former grade.[49]

B. Harassment as the Adverse Employment Action

Further harassment of an employee who has reported harassment can itself be retaliatory discrimination in violation of §704(a), if the harassment is motivated by the report and if, like actionable sexual harassment, it is "sufficiently severe so as to alter the conditions of employment."[50] Retaliation has also been found where the employer caused fellow employees to harass the complainant.[51] In *Toscano v. Nimmo*,[52] retaliation was found where a supervisor made harassing telephone calls to the employee at home, failed to provide her with information needed for her job, and attempted to create a false impression among co-workers that he had engaged in an affair with her.

251, 256 (D. Colo. 1978)(female employee alleged she was discharged for rejecting sexual advances of male supervisor); Williams v. Saxbe, 413 F. Supp. 654, 12 FEP Cases 1093, 1096 (D.D.C. 1976), reproduced in Chapter 1, Overview (female employee alleged she was fired for rejecting sexual advances of supervisor), *rev'd on other grounds,* Williams v. Bell, 587 F.2d 1240, 17 FEP Cases 1662 (D.C. Cir. 1978), *on remand,* Williams v. Civiletti, 487 F. Supp. 1387, 22 FEP Cases 1311 (D.D.C. 1980).

[47]Miller v. Aluminum Co. of Am., 679 F. Supp. 495, 504–5, 45 FEP Cases 1775, 1782 (W.D. Pa.)("snubbing" of sexual harassment complainant by supervisor and co-workers not actionable; court cannot compel supervisors "to act cordially toward one who had sued them"), *aff'd,* 856 F.2d 184, 52 FEP Cases 1472 (3d Cir. 1988); Petrosky v. Washington-Green County Branch, 663 F. Supp. 821, 825, 45 FEP Cases 673, 676 (W.D. Penn. 1987)(female executive director placed on probation after complaint of sexual harassment suffered no damages thereby), *aff'd,* 845 F.2d 1014, 47 FEP Cases 2 (3d Cir. 1988); Ferguson v. E.I. du Pont de Nemours & Co., 560 F. Supp. 1172, 1201, 31 FEP Cases 795, 815 (D. Del. 1983)(temporary transfer to secretarial pool not "adverse employment action" where complainant retains same pay and benefits).

[48]819 F.2d 630, 43 FEP Cases 1595 (6th Cir. 1987).

[49]*Id.* at 1601.

[50]Cobb v. Anheuser-Busch, 54 FEP Cases 451, 479 (E.D. Mo. 1990)(citing *Meritor*); Calcote v. Texas Educ. Found., 578 F.2d 95, 97, 20 FEP Cases 1685, 1687 (5th Cir. 1978)(white employee harassed by black supervisor); Hyland v. Kenner Prods. Co., 13 FEP Cases 1309, 1315 (S.D. Ohio 1976)(removal of duties and responsibilities, barring attendance at meetings, restricting communication to written form constitute actionable retaliation).

[51]Tanner v. California Physicians' Serv., 27 FEP Cases 593 (N.D. Cal. 1978)(employer created atmosphere of hostility among co-workers that made normal performance of duties by employee impossible); EEOC v. Bank of Ariz., 12 FEP Cases 527 (D. Ariz. 1976)(employer incitement of co-worker hostility in retaliation for filing EEOC sex discrimination charge).

[52]*Supra* note 43, 32 FEP Cases at 1408.

C. The Investigation as the Retaliatory Action

Nothing in §704(a) prevents an employer from conducting an otherwise lawful investigation.[53] Nonetheless, certain investigations may be unacceptable under Title VII because they intimidate witnesses.[54]

D. Defamation Actions as the Retaliatory Action

The accusations made by a sexual harassment complainant in an EEOC proceeding often will be defamatory in nature and may lead to a libel or slander suit by the employer or the alleged harasser.[55] Some courts would hold such a suit to be violative of §704(a), reasoning that §704(a) made the complainant's statements to the EEOC absolutely privileged.[56] Other courts have suggested that an employer is entitled to vindicate its reputation by filing a defamation suit on the basis of a malicious EEOC charge.[57]

The federal district court, in *EEOC v. Levi Strauss & Co.*,[58] took a middle-ground approach, holding that §704(a) bars some but not all defamation suits based upon a complainant's allegations of employment discrimination. When the complainant in *Levi Strauss* filed an EEOC charge accusing her supervisor of making sexual advances, he sued her in state court for defamation. The EEOC then asked a federal court to enjoin both the supervisor and his employer from pursuing the defamation action. The EEOC alleged that the supervisor had the implicit approval of the employer to file the state-court defamation action, and that consequently the defamation action violated the employer's

---

[53]*See* Whitaker v. Carney, 778 F.2d 216, 220–21, 39 FEP Cases 987, 990 (5th Cir. 1985)(Title VII does not require employer to withhold complainant's identity from alleged harasser), *cert. denied,* 479 U.S. 813 (1986); Burrows v. Chemed Corp., 567 F. Supp. 978, 986–87, 32 FEP Cases 851, 857 (E.D. Mo. 1983)(supervisory questioning of charging party not adverse employment action), *aff'd,* 743 F.2d 612, 35 FEP Cases 1410 (8th Cir. 1984); Wintz v. Port Auth. of N.Y. & N.J., 551 F. Supp. 1323, 32 FEP Cases 1621 (S.D.N.Y. 1982)(personnel director did not retaliate by asking employee who had filed EEOC charge to come to his office to help him investigate charge). *See also* EEOC Dec. 86-6, 40 FEP Cases 1890, 1892 (1986)(questioning sexual harassment complainant and co-workers to determine whether employer needed to take remedial action not unlawful retaliation). For a discussion of investigating incidents of sexual harassment, see Chapter 19, Responding to Internal Complaints.

[54]*See, e.g.,* EEOC v. Plumbers Local 189, 311 F. Supp. 464, 2 FEP Cases 807, 810–11 (S.D. Ohio 1970)(forbidding respondent to use statements taken from black plumbers who had been approached individually by foreman on the job and taken to company-owned trailer where respondent's attorney asked them questions to be answered under oath before shorthand reporter concerning charges of race discrimination against respondent).

[55]For a discussion of the defamation problems faced by a complainant and an employer in investigating a complainant's report of harassment, see Chapter 19, Responding to Internal Complaints. For a discussion of the alleged harasser's defamation action against the complainant or the employer, see Chapter 24, The Alleged Harasser as Plaintiff. For a discussion of the complainant's defamation action against the alleged harasser or the employer, see Chapter 15, The Common Law, Section VI.

[56]*E.g.,* EEOC v. Virginia Caroline Veneer Corp., 495 F. Supp. 775, 777–78, 27 FEP Cases 340, 343 (W.D. Va. 1980)(violative of §704(a) for employer to file defamation action against employee solely on basis of sex discrimination charge filed with EEOC).

[57]*E.g.,* Pettway v. American Cast Iron Pipe Co., 411 F.2d 998, 1007 n.22, 1 FEP Cases 752, 758 (5th Cir. 1969)(Title VII does not forbid defamation actions against complainant who defames employer's reputation); Proulx v. CitiBank, 659 F. Supp. 972, 978 n.12, 44 FEP Cases 371, 376 (S.D.N.Y. 1987)(suggesting, with *Pettway,* that employer could sue malicious complainant for defamation); Bartulica v. Paculdo, 411 F. Supp. 392, 397, 21 FEP Cases 497, 500 (W.D. Mo. 1976)(rejecting complainant's contention that §704(a) immunizes her from defamation action).

[58]515 F. Supp. 640, 641, 27 FEP Cases 346, 347 (N.D. Ill. 1981).

Title VII duty not to retaliate. When the supervisor and his employer moved to dismiss the EEOC suit, Judge James Moran granted the employer's motion on the procedural ground that it was not a necessary party, in that only the alleged harasser was a party to the state-court action.[59]

With respect to the alleged harasser's motion to dismiss, the district court ruled that §704(a), read literally, "obviously bars all retaliatory acts including lawsuits filed in state tribunals."[60] At the same time, Judge Moran noted that the defamation suit alleged that slanderous statements regarding the complainant were made to her co-workers. He reasoned:

> it cannot be concluded that all defamation actions in the wake of sexual harassment charges filed before the Commission are violations of Title VII. Rather, those suits initiated in state court in good faith and as an attempt to rehabilitate the employer's reputations [sic] which may have been tarnished by the charges are not necessarily violations of the Act.[61]

At a minimum, the *Levi Strauss* decision suggests that it is not necessarily retaliatory to sue a complainant for defamatory remarks made outside a pending EEOC proceeding. The decision is more ambiguous concerning whether it is retaliatory to sue a complainant solely on the basis of an EEOC charge if the employer believes in good faith that the EEOC charge was false and malicious.

V. CAUSAL CONNECTION

The final element of the prima facie case is proof of a causal connection between the opposition or participation and the subsequent employment detriment. A causal connection must be sufficient to show that a retaliatory motive played a part in the adverse treatment. Proving such a motive will require a showing that the employer had actual or imputed knowledge of the opposition or participation.[62]

Several common types of circumstantial evidence can imply that the adverse treatment of the employee was retaliatory. The evidence might be that, after learning of the protected activity, the employer treated the employee differently from similarly situated nonprotesting employees,[63] deviated from

---

[59]*Id.* at 642, 27 FEP Cases at 347.

[60]*Id.* at 643, 27 FEP Cases at 349.

[61]*Id.* at 644, 27 FEP Cases at 350.

[62]*E.g.,* Mandia v. Arco Chem. Co., 618 F. Supp. 1248, 1253, 39 FEP Cases 793, 794–95 (W.D. Pa. 1985)(employee claiming he was dismissed because he participated in his wife's EEOC charge of sexual harassment failed to prove causal connection where plaintiff failed to prove that company official knew of wife's charge at relevant time).

The retaliatory-intent requirement may render an employer's liability insurance coverage inapplicable. Three courts have held that sexual harassment and retaliation are intentional acts falling within the exclusionary clauses of the employer's comprehensive insurance policy. American Guar. & Liab. Ins. Co. v. Vista Medical Supply, 699 F. Supp. 787 (N.D. Cal. 1988)(summary judgment decision holding that acts of sexual harassment were intentional acts not covered by insurance policy); Continental Ins. Co. v. McDaniel, 772 P.2d 6, 48 FEP Cases 522 (Ariz. App. 1988)(sexual harassment constitutes intentional act not covered by insurance policy); Seminole Point Hosp. Corp. v. Aetna Casualty & Sur. Co., 675 F. Supp. 44 (D.N.H. 1987)(actions of sexual harassment fall within exclusion for discriminatory and intentional acts).

[63]*See, e.g.,* Mosely v. General Motors Corp., 497 F. Supp. 583, 591, 23 FEP Cases 1637, 1643 (E.D. Mo. 1980)(§704(a) violation where harsher penalty imposed for work stoppage protesting alleged racial discrimination than for work stoppages for other reasons); Francis v. American Tel. Co., 55 F.R.D. 202, 4 FEP Cases 777 (D.D.C. 1972)(surveillance limitations imposed on plaintiff not imposed on persons who had not filed charges).

its own written procedures to carry out the adverse action against the protesting employee,[64] or began surveillance of the protesting employee.[65] Additional circumstantial evidence of retaliation would include the closeness in time between the employer's knowledge of the protected activity and the adverse action,[66] and employer attempts to conceal that the person who decided on the adverse action knew at that time that the employee had engaged in protected participation or opposition.[67]

VI. THE PARTIES

A. Person Retaliated Against

Persons protected by §704(a) include an employee, an applicant,[68] and a former employee.[69]

An employer also may be liable for actions it takes against an employee's relative,[70] employees who are merely potential witnesses,[71] and persons who have opposed discrimination by other employers.[72] However, an employer

---

[64]*See, e.g.,* EEOC v. Operating Eng'rs Locals 14 & 15, 438 F. Supp. 876, 883–84, 16 FEP Cases 325, 330 (S.D.N.Y. 1977)(union's variation from written procedures for relief from dues obligations and suspensions).

[65]Surveillance often is important not simply as proof of adverse treatment, but because it suggests a search for a pretextual basis for discipline, which in turn suggests that subsequent discipline was for purposes of retaliation. *See, e.g.,* Mead v. United States Fidelity & Guar. Co., 442 F. Supp. 114, 18 FEP Cases 140 (D. Minn. 1977)(surveillance and drop in evaluations following protected activity).

[66]*See, e.g.,* Minor v. Califano, 452 F. Supp. 36, 17 FEP Cases 756 (D.D.C. 1978)(retaliation implied by immediate supervisor's withdrawal of complainant's assignments one day after complainant interviewed regarding EEO complaint); Hochstadt v. Worcester Found. for Experimental Biology, 425 F. Supp. 318, 324, 11 FEP Cases 1426, 1431 (D. Mass)(prima facie case of retaliation requires proof that adverse action followed protected activity "within such period of time that the court can infer retaliatory motivation"; discharge six months after settlement of civil action and one month after complaint of discrimination meets this standard), *aff'd*, 545 F.2d 222, 13 FEP Cases 804 (1st Cir. 1976). *Cf.* Juarez v. Ameritech Mobile Communications, 53 FEP Cases 1722 (N.D. Ill. 1990)(summary judgment granted against retaliation claim where six months elapsed between sexual harassment complaint and dismissal for poor performance).

[67]Macey v. World Airways, 14 FEP Cases 1426, 1429–30 (N.D. Cal. 1977)(although employer denied knowledge of state FEP charge before discharge, contrary conclusion reached from fact that other employees not discharged for absences).

[68]42 U.S.C. §2000e-3(a). Thus, an employer would be liable under §704(a) if it refused to hire an individual because of involvement in protected activity during previous employment. Barela v. United Nuclear Corp., 462 F.2d 149, 155 n.3, 4 FEP Cases 831, 833 (10th Cir. 1972).

[69]Although §704(a) mentions only "employees or applicants for employment," courts have extended protection to ex-employees. *See, e.g.,* Bailey v. USX Corp., 850 F.2d 1506, 1509, 47 FEP Cases 729, 731 (11th Cir. 1988)(former employees can sue for retaliation); Shehadeh v. Chesapeake & Potomac Tel. Co., 595 F.2d 711, 722, 18 FEP Cases 614, 621 (D.C. Cir. 1978)(derogatory references constitute actionable retaliation against ex-employee who filed EEOC charge); Pantchenko v. C.B. Dolge Co., 581 F.2d 1052, 1054–55, 18 FEP Cases 691, 692 (2d Cir. 1978)(retaliatory refusal to provide former employee with letter of recommendation); Rutherford v. American Bank of Commerce, 565 F.2d 1162, 1166, 16 FEP Cases 26, 27–28 (10th Cir. 1977)(former employer notified potential employer of EEOC charge).

[70]Wu v. Thomas, 863 F.2d 1543, 1544, 52 FEP Cases 3, 6 (11th Cir. 1989)(chairman of department removed from position and invited to seek employment elsewhere in reprisal for his wife's filing of EEOC charges); Aquino v. Sommer Maid Creamery, 657 F. Supp. 208, 210, 45 FEP Cases 796, 797 (E.D. Pa. 1987)(man who testified on behalf of his wife in state FEP proceedings fired); De Medina v. Reinhardt, 444 F. Supp. 573, 580, 20 FEP Cases 280 (D.D.C. 1978)(applicant cannot be denied employment because of spouse's antidiscrimination activities on behalf of employer's employees); EEOC Dec. 77-34, 21 FEP Cases 1803 (1977)(discrimination against employee because of familial relationship with person who has filed charge of discrimination violates §704(a)).

[71]EEOC v. Plumbers Local 189, *supra* note 54, 2 FEP Cases at 807 (black union members who were potential witnesses interviewed by respondent in coercive manner; since manner of interviews violated §704(a), evidence would be suppressed).

[72]Barela v. United Nuclear Corp., *supra* note 68 (respondent refused to hire applicant who had filed EEOC charge against prior employer). *See also* EEOC COMPL. MAN. (BNA), §614.4(b)(5), at 614:0013 (plaintiff need not be employee of employer whose discriminatory practices are being opposed).

would not be liable for retaliation when one of its own employees has suffered retaliation at the hands of another employer.[73]

B. Respondents

Employers, employment agencies, joint apprenticeship councils, and unions can be held liable for unlawful retaliation under §704(a).[74] To establish respondent liability, the complainant generally will prove that an agent of the respondent, with authority to affect the complainant's conditions of employment, has exercised that authority.[75]

VII. THE EMPLOYER'S REBUTTAL

Discharges have been held not to be retaliatory where the evidence showed that they were based solely upon such business reasons as excessive absenteeism, the physical limitations of the complainant, and changing workloads at the employer's plant.[76] The employer's proof that similarly situated nonprotesters were disciplined just as harshly for the same infraction suggests nonretaliation.[77] In *Barrett v. Omaha National Bank*,[78] the complainant, a personal banker, failed to show that her employer began to review her loans as a result of her complaints of sexual harassment. The bank showed that loan reviews were not unusual and that the complainant had been selected for review before her reports of harassment.

---

[73]*E.g.,* Hale v. Marsh, 808 F.2d 616, 619, 42 FEP Cases 944, 945 (7th Cir. 1986)(Title VII protects only employee's protests against practices of employee's own employer).

[74]Section 701(b), (c), (d), and (e), 42 U.S.C. §2000e-(b), (c), (d) and (e).

[75]Just as an employer may be liable under §703 for sexual harassment by co-workers, *e.g.,* Robson v. Eva's Super Market, 538 F. Supp. 857, 861, 30 FEP Cases 1212, 1215 (N.D. Ohio 1982), or customers, *e.g.,* EEOC v. Sage Realty Corp., 507 F. Supp. 599, 608-9, 24 FEP Cases 1521, 1530 (S.D.N.Y. 1981), employer liability may exist when a supervisor acquiesces in or adopts the retaliatory harassment of co-workers. *Cf.* Barrett v. Florida Power & Light Co., 42 FEP Cases 1816, 1817 (S.D. Fla. 1987)(no evidence current supervisor who denied pay increase was influenced by former supervisor who allegedly made sexual advances that plaintiff rejected).

The retaliation clause does not require the employer to prevent nonworkplace retaliation by nonemployees. The Fifth Circuit, in *Whitaker v. Carney,* 778 F.2d 216, 39 FEP Cases 987, 990 (5th Cir. 1985), *cert. denied,* 479 U.S. 813 (1986), thus held that an employer was compelled to disclose to an alleged sexual harasser who had since resigned the names of those employees who had complained about him. Title VII did not require the employer to keep the sexual harassment complainants confidential.

[76]*See, e.g.,* Tunis v. Corning Glass Works, 54 EPD ¶40,170 (S.D.N.Y. 1990)(complainant fired for failing to perform assignments and for inability to get along with colleagues, not for complaining about co-worker harassment); Mitchell v. Safeway Stores, 624 F. Supp. 932, 39 FEP Cases 1213 (D. Kan. 1985)(black employees alleged that they were physically unable, due to work-related injuries, to remain on job without absenteeism because of increased workload). *See generally* Zowayyed v. Lowen Co., 52 FEP Cases 1350, 1356–57 (D. Kan. 1990)(triable issue existed as to whether discharge of plaintiff resulted from complaints of unwelcome sexual advances or from her flirtatious behavior and braggadocio).

[77]*See, e.g.,* Kellin v. ACF Indus., 460 F. Supp. 952, 25 FEP Cases 1306 (E.D. Mo. 1978)(other employees discharged for comparable and lesser infractions), *aff'd in part, rev'd, and remanded in part,* 629 F.2d 532, 25 FEP Cases 1309 (8th Cir. 1980); Watford v. Birmingham Stove & Range Co., 14 FEP Cases 626, 631 (N.D. Ala. 1976)(charging party and others missing work received similar discipline).

[78]726 F.2d 424, 428, 35 FEP Cases 593, 595 (8th Cir. 1984).

VIII. ALTERNATIVE SOURCES OF PROTECTION AGAINST RETALIATION

Section 704(a) is not always an adequate source of protection for a number of reasons: the employer might not be subject to Title VII; the Title VII filing period might have elapsed; an alternative forum might be more accessible or promising; or the monetary relief sought might be damages not fully recoverable under Title VII.

Possible alternative sources of protection include the Reconstruction Era Civil Rights Acts,[79] §7 of the National Labor Relations Act,[80] state whistleblower statutes,[81] and various common-law theories.[82]

---

[79]See B.L. SCHLEI & P. GROSSMAN, EMPLOYMENT DISCRIMINATION LAW 564–65 (2d ed. 1983), Five-Year Supp. 236 (1989). See also Chapter 11, Federal Constitutional, Statutory, and Civil Rights Law.

[80]See SCHLEI & GROSSMAN, *supra* note 79, at 565–66, Five-Year Supp. at 236–37. *E.g.,* NLRB v. Yellow Freight Sys., 930 F.2d 316 (3d Cir. 1991)(upholding NLRB determination that dock worker must be reinstated because he supported a co-worker's complaint of sexual harassment against two managers).

[81]Sandom v. Travelers Mortgage Servs., 752 F. Supp. 1240, 54 FEP Cases 1259 (D.N.J. 1990)(plaintiff may sue under New Jersey Conscientious Employee Protection Act for retaliation based on filing EEOC charge); CAL. LAB. CODE §1102.5(b)(prohibiting retaliation against employee "for disclosing information to government or law enforcement agency, where the employee has reasonable cause to believe that the information discloses a violation of state or federal statute").

[82]See SCHLEI & GROSSMAN, *supra* note 79, at 567, Five-Year Supp. at 237–38. See also Chapter 15, The Common Law.

Part III

OTHER SOURCES OF LEGAL PROTECTION

CHAPTER 11

FEDERAL CONSTITUTIONAL, STATUTORY, AND CIVIL RIGHTS LAW

I. OVERVIEW

Sources of federal law available to redress sexual harassment, other than Title VII, may be more advantageous to a complainant insofar as they provide for a jury trial, compensatory damages, or a direct avenue to court without the need to exhaust administrative remedies.

Government employees may maintain that sexual harassment committed or condoned by governmental superiors has deprived them of the constitutional right to equal protection.[1] The most common vehicle for this claim is the Civil Rights Act of 1871, 42 U.S.C. §1983, which generally authorizes lawsuits by state and local government employees against their governmental superiors for violations of federal constitutional and statutory law.[2]

Other sources of federal law potentially available to sexual harassment complainants include the Civil Rights Act of 1871, 42 U.S.C. §1985(3)(covering conspiracies to deprive persons of federal rights),[3] Title IX of the Education Amendments (applying to federally funded educational institutions),[4] the Federal Employers' Liability Act (protecting railroad workers),[5] the Racketeer Influenced and Corrupt Organizations Act,[6] and Federal Executive Order 11246 (covering federal government contractors).[7]

II. CLAIMS DIRECTLY UNDER THE UNITED STATES CONSTITUTION

Sexual harassment, when perpetrated by a government official, may amount to a violation of the Constitution, particularly the constitutional guarantee of

---

[1]This alternative generally is not available to private employees because private employees generally are not subject to constitutional restraints. See Section II. *infra.*

[2]See Section III. *infra.*

[3]See Section IV. *infra.*

[4]See Section V. *infra.*

[5]See Section VI. *infra.*

[6]See Section VII. *infra.*

[7]See Section IX. *infra.*

equal protection. In *Davis v. Passman,*[8] Justice William Brennan, Jr., held that it was violative of the equal protection component of the Fifth Amendment for a United States congressman to replace a female deputy administrative assistant because he had decided that her position should be held by a man, and that she could sue her employer for damages directly under the Constitution.

Only a very narrow class of individuals appears eligible to bring this kind of a direct constitutional claim in a case of sexual harassment. First, only a government employee will generally be in a position to argue that sexual harassment by an employer has involved the governmental action necessary to create a constitutional violation. Second, courts recognize a direct constitutional claim only where there appears to be no alternative means of relief.[9]

An alternate means of relief is nearly always available, for in the vast majority of circumstances Congress has authorized redress for state and local employees under §1983,[10] and both state and federal governmental employees often have remedies available under Title VII,[11] which generally covers public as well as private-sector employees.[12] Indeed, Title VII has been held to provide the exclusive remedies for claims of employment discrimination by federal employees subject to its protection.[13]

Thus, although federal employees theoretically could assert equal protection claims against their governmental superiors directly under the Constitution, that option is available only to federal employees who are not protected by Title VII. The plaintiff in *Davis* could maintain a claim directly under the Constitution only because, as a congressional employee who was not in the competitive service, she had no protection under Title VII.[14]

---

[8]442 U.S. 228, 248–49, 19 FEP Cases 1390, 1398 (1979)(allowing claim by female congressional employee not protected by Title VII against United States congressman for alleged sex discrimination under equal protection component of due process clause of Fifth Amendment, following *Bivens* rationale).

[9]*See, e.g.,* Bivens v. Six Unknown Agents, 403 U.S. 388 (1971)(creating direct cause of action against federal agents for violation of plaintiff's Fourth Amendment rights because §1983 does not address constitutional violations committed by federal officers acting under federal laws); Carlson v. Green, 446 U.S. 14 (1980)(federal prison officials could be liable for damages under Eighth Amendment for failure to provide prisoner with proper medical attention).

[10]*E.g.,* Thomas v. Shipka, 818 F.2d 496 (6th Cir.)(disallowing claims directly under First and Fourteenth Amendments where plaintiff already had §1983 claim based on First and Fourteenth Amendment violations), *reh'g in part on other grounds,* 829 F.2d 570 (6th Cir. 1987), *vacated on other grounds,* 109 S.Ct. 859 (1989); Ward v. Caulk, 650 F.2d 1144, 1148, 26 FEP Cases 536, 538 (9th Cir. 1981)(county employee who alleged discriminatory failure to promote precluded from First, Fifth, and Fourteenth Amendment claims because of theoretical availability of §1983 claim, although this claim was time-barred); Turpin v. Mailet, 591 F.2d 426 (2d Cir. 1979)(*en banc*)(reversing prior decision and disallowing direct claim against municipality under Fourteenth Amendment in light of Supreme Court decision in *Monell v. Department of Social Servs.,* which had allowed local governments to be sued under §1983). Section 1983, being limited to deprivations by persons acting under color of state law, does not authorize lawsuits against the federal government.

[11]*E.g.,* Otto v. Heckler, 781 F.2d 754, 757, 39 FEP Cases 1754, 1756 (9th Cir.)(federal employee's constitutional claim for sexual harassment barred as identical to claim under Title VII), *modified on other grounds,* 802 F.2d 337, 42 FEP Cases 64 (9th Cir. 1986).

[12]§701(f), 42 U.S.C. §2000e(f)(excepting elected or appointed public officials and staff not subject to civil service laws).

[13]Brown v. Government Servs. Admin., 425 U.S. 820, 833–35, 12 FEP Cases 1361, 1366 (1976)(black federal employee could not bring claim under 42 U.S.C. §1981; limited to Title VII); Owens v. United States, 822 F.2d 408, 410, 44 FEP Cases 247, 248 (3d Cir. 1987)(Title VII provides exclusive claim for federal relief for federal employee complaining of sexual harassment in employment; constitutional claims thus barred); Kizas v. Webster, 707 F.2d 524, 542, 31 FEP Cases 905, 915 (D.C. Cir. 1983)(Title VII precludes Fifth Amendment claim by federal employees complaining of employment discrimination).

[14]*Supra* note 8, 442 U.S. at 247, 19 FEP Cases at 1397–98. Nor could she sue under §1983. *Id.* at 238 n.16, 19 FEP Cases at 1394.

III. Section 1983

A. Introduction

Section 1983 authorizes lawsuits to rectify the deprivation of federal constitutional or statutory rights by persons who were acting under color of state law:

> Every person who, under color of any statute, ordinance, regulation, custom, or usage, of any State or Territory or the District of Columbia subjects, or causes to be subjected, any person within the jurisdiction thereof to the deprivation of any rights, privileges, or immunities secured by the Constitution and laws, shall be liable to the party injured in an action at law, suit in equity, or other proper proceeding for redress.[15]

Sexual harassment by a state governmental official may violate both Title VII and the equal protection clause of the Fourteenth Amendment, and thus may be actionable under both Title VII and §1983. The existence of a remedy under Title VII does not preempt a §1983 claim; courts routinely permit Title VII and §1983 actions to proceed concurrently.[16]

When compared to a Title VII claim, a §1983 claim has significant advantages for a sexual harassment complainant: it provides for a jury trial, does not require exhaustion of administrative remedies, and provides for compensatory damages.[17] However, a §1983 claim requires a showing of "color of state law"[18] and, in the equal protection context, possibly presents a more difficult intent standard for complainants to meet.[19]

While virtually all courts have ruled that a jury trial is not available under Title VII,[20] a §1983 plaintiff typically is entitled to a jury trial.[21]

---

[15]42 U.S.C. §1983. For a general discussion of §1983 in the employment context, see B.L. Schlei & P. Grossman, Employment Discrimination Law (2d ed. 1983), Chapter 21, Section II.B.

[16]E.g., Starrett v. Wadley, 876 F.2d 808, 814, 51 FEP Cases 608, 611 (10th Cir. 1989)(§1983 claim for sexual harassment not preempted by parallel Title VII claim); Dwyer v. Smith, 867 F.2d 184, 192, 48 FEP Cases 1886, 1891 (4th Cir. 1989)(same); Berl v. County of Westchester, 849 F.2d 712, 716, 46 FEP Cases 1740, 1742 (2d Cir. 1988)(allowing concurrent §1983 and Title VII claims in sex discrimination case); Huebschen v. Wisconsin Dep't of Health & Social Serv., 716 F.2d 1167, 32 FEP Cases 1582 (7th Cir. 1983)(allowing parallel Title VII and §1983 actions in sexual harassment case); Rivera v. Wichita Falls, 665 F.2d 531, 27 FEP Cases 1352 (5th Cir. 1982)(judgment on both Title VII claims and §1983 claims based on the same grounds); Formica v. Galantino, 1989 U.S. Dist. LEXIS 10256 (E.D. Pa. Aug. 29, 1989)(concluding, after extensive analysis of legislative history of Title VII, that Congress did not intend to preempt §1983 actions of state and local government employees); Russell v. Moore, 714 F. Supp. 883, 886, 50 FEP Cases 409, 411 (M.D. Tenn. 1989)(sexual harassment). But see Carrero v. New York City Hous. Auth., 890 F.2d 569, 575, 51 FEP Cases 596, 600 (2d Cir. 1989)(noting lack of Supreme Court decision on point and considering it "unsettled" whether Title VII is exclusive remedy of state and local government employees for employment discrimination).

[17]See generally Note, The Emerging Law of Sexual Harassment: Relief Available to the Public Employee, 62 Notre Dame L. Rev. 677, 687 (1987)(§1983 provides "the favorable recovery for the public employee in a sexual harassment case").

[18]See Section III.C. infra.

[19]See Section III.D.1.b. infra.

[20]Compare Zowayyed v. Lowen Co., 52 FEP Cases 1350, 1354 (D. Kan. 1990)(jury trial denied under Title VII by "near unanimous weight of authority") with Walker v. Anderson Electrical Connectors, 736 F. Supp. 253 (N.D. Ala. 1990)(one of a series of spirited decisions by Judge William M. Acker, Jr., holding that Title VII does permit jury trial). For further discussion of the Title VII jury trial issue, see Chapter 21, Complainant's Litigation Strategy, Section III.A.2.

[21]A §1983 action usually involves rights and remedies of the sort typically enforced in an action at law, thus entitling the plaintiff to a jury trial upon demand. E.g., Whiting v. Jackson State Univ., 616 F.2d 116, 122 & n.4 (5th Cir. 1980); Hildebrand v. Board of Trustees, 607 F.2d 705, 707–9 (6th Cir. 1979); Burt v. Abel, 585 F.2d 613, 616 n.7 (4th Cir. 1974)(per curiam).

A §1983 plaintiff need not exhaust state administrative remedies before bringing a judicial action.[22] Before commencing a Title VII claim, by contrast, a plaintiff must "unsuccessfully pursue certain avenues of potential administrative relief."[23]

Compensatory damages are available under §1983,[24] but are not available under Title VII.[25]

Section 1983 creates no substantive rights, but provides redress for the deprivation, under color of state law, of any rights already secured by the federal Constitution and federal statutes. To prevail on a §1983 claim for sexual harassment, the complainant must prove (1) that the deprivation was by a "person" subject to §1983, (2) that the person was acting under color of state law, and (3) that the harassment deprived the complainant of rights under the United States Constitution or a federal statute.[26]

B. "Person" Liable Under §1983

Liability under §1983 is limited to entities that qualify as a "person" under §1983. The term "person" includes private parties, municipalities, counties, other political subdivisions of a state, and state officials who are sued in their individual capacities.[27] However, the term "person" does not include a state or a state official sued in an official capacity.[28]

C. Action Under Color of State Law

Liability under §1983 can exist only if the conduct in question was "under color of [a] statute, ordinance, custom, or usage of [a] State or Territory or the District of Columbia."[29] This "color of state law" requirement is met when the defendant's conduct constitutes "[m]isuse of power, possessed by virtue of state law and made possible only because the wrongdoer is clothed with the authority of state law . . . ."[30]

Generally, one acts under color of state law while "acting in his official capacity or while exercising his responsibilities pursuant to state law."[31] Ac-

---

[22]Patsy v. Board of Regents, 457 U.S. 496, 29 FEP Cases 12 (1982)(plaintiff not required to exhaust state administrative remedies before bringing §1983 action for race and sex discrimination).

[23]Love v. Pullman Co., 404 U.S. 522, 523, 4 FEP Cases 150, 150 (1972).

[24]Carey v. Piphus, 435 U.S. 247, 255 (1978)(damages available under §1983 for compensable injuries).

[25]*E.g.,* King v. Board of Regents, 898 F.2d 533, 537, 52 FEP Cases 809, 813 (7th Cir. 1990)(compensatory, punitive, and nominal damages not available under Title VII); Carrero v. New York City Hous. Auth., *supra* note 16, 890 F.2d at 581, 51 FEP Cases at 605 (*dictum*)(neither compensatory nor punitive damages available under Title VII); Bennett v. Corroon & Black Corp., 845 F.2d 104, 106, 46 FEP Cases 1329, 1331 (5th Cir. 1988)(only equitable relief available under Title VII; damages for mental anguish unobtainable), *cert. denied,* 109 U.S. 1140 (1989). For further discussion, see Chapter 29, Monetary Relief.

[26]In the Fifth Circuit it appears that a plaintiff must also prove that the sexual harassment constituted an abuse of government power. Collins v. City of Harver Heights, 916 F.2d 284, 288–91 (5th Cir. 1990)(affirming dismissal of §1983 action brought by wife of asphyxiated city worker who allegedly died because of city policy of failing to train and equip its workers; case was properly dismissed because husband's association with city was no less voluntary than relationship with private employer would have been).

[27]Hafer v. Melo, 112 S.Ct. 358 (1991)(state official can be personally liable for §1983 damages for actions taken in official capacity); Monell v. Department of Social Servs., 436 U.S. 685, 691, 17 FEP Cases 873, 884 (1978).

[28]Will v. Michigan Dep't of State Police, 109 S.Ct. 2304 (1989).

[29]42 U.S.C. §1983, reproduced in text accompanying note 15 *supra.*

[30]National Collegiate Athletic Ass'n v. Tarkanian, 109 S.Ct. 454, 461 (1988)(quoting United States v. Classic, 313 U.S. 299, 326 (1941)).

[31]West v. Atkins, 487 U.S. 42, 50 (1988).

cordingly, although supervisors who perpetrate or condone sexual harassment often are acting under color of state law, co-workers in that situation typically would not be acting under color of state law, for they would not be exercising state-granted responsibilities.[32]

Because of the "color of state law" requirement, §1983 claims for sexual harassment in employment generally are limited to employees of state or local governments. A §1983 action will not be an option for employees of private employers or the federal government, except in those rare instances in which a nonstate employer "is a willful participant in joint action with the State or its agents."[33] The mere fact of "state licensing" does not place an employer's conduct under color of state law.[34]

D. Deprivation of Federal Constitutional or Statutory Rights

Sexual harassment complainants have invoked §1983 to enforce federal rights secured by the Constitution or by federal statute. The sources of federal law most frequently invoked are the equal protection clause of the Fourteenth Amendment,[35] the due process clause of the Fourteenth Amendment,[36] the First Amendment,[37] and federal statutes.[38]

1. The Equal Protection Clause

Numerous decisions have held that sexual harassment by a state or municipal employer can violate the equal protection clause of the Fourteenth Amendment.[39] Although the Supreme Court has not yet specifically held that sexual

---

[32]Murphy v. Chicago Transit Auth., 638 F. Supp. 464, 467–68, 49 FEP Cases 1514, 1516 (N.D. Ill. 1986)(sexual harassment by co-worker staff attorneys not under color of state law since harassment had nothing to do with, and bore no similarity to, nature of staff attorney job).

[33]Dennis v. Sparks, 449 U.S. 24, 27–28 (1980)(private persons could be sued under §1983 on theory that they conspired with state judge to invade constitutional rights).

[34]Kerans v. Porter Paint Co., 656 F. Supp. 267 (S.D. Ohio 1987)(dismissing §1983 sexual harassment claim against employer and its manager for lack of "color of state law"; licensure and engaging in business in state insufficient for this purpose).

[35]See Section III.D.1. *infra.*

[36]See Section III.D.2. *infra.*

[37]See Section III.D.3. *infra.*

[38]See Section III.D.4. *infra.*

[39]*E.g., Third Circuit:* Andrews v. City of Philadelphia, 895 F.2d 1469, 1479–80, 54 FEP Cases 184, 191–92 (3d Cir. 1990)(government supervisor liable for denial of equal protection under §1983 for participating in and condoning sexual harassment of municipal employee); Skadegaard v. Farrell, 578 F. Supp. 1209, 1216, 33 FEP Cases 1528, 1533–34 (D.N.J. 1984)(sexual harassment by government supervisor would violate equal protection);

Sixth Circuit: Poe v. Haydon, 853 F.2d 418, 430, 52 FEP Cases 80, 88 (6th Cir. 1988)(case law as early as 1981 established that sexual harassment by government employers violates equal protection clause), *cert. denied,* 488 U.S. 1007 (1989); Estate of Scott v. deLeon, 603 F. Supp. 1328, 1332, 37 FEP Cases 563, 566 (E.D. Mich. 1985)(sexual harassment violates equal protection);

Seventh Circuit: Bohen v. City of E. Chicago, 799 F.2d 1180, 1185, 41 FEP Cases 1108, 1112 (7th Cir. 1986)("Sexual harassment of female employees by a state employer constitutes sex discrimination for purposes of the equal protection clause of the fourteenth amendment. Creating abusive conditions for female employees and not for male employees is discrimination."); Woerner v. Breczek, 519 F. Supp. 517, 519, 26 FEP Cases 897, 898 (N.D. Ill. 1981)(sexual harassment violates equal protection);

Tenth Circuit: Starrett v. Wadley, 876 F.2d 808, 814, 51 FEP Cases 608, 611 (10th Cir. 1989)("sexual harassment of the sort alleged by plaintiff can violate the Fourteenth Amendment right to equal protection of the laws").

But see Formica v. Galantino, 1989 U.S. Dist. LEXIS 10256 (E.D. Pa. Aug. 29, 1989)("Sexual harassment at the place of employment does not . . . amount to a constitutional violation")(citing, inappositely, Patterson v. McLean Credit Union, 484 U.S. 814, 49 FEP Cases 1814 (1989)(racial harassment on

harassment can violate the equal protection clause,[40] that holding would follow from Supreme Court equal protection doctrine pertaining to gender discrimination: Purposeful gender discrimination that is not justified by an important governmental interest violates the equal protection clause.[41] Because no defendant has yet demonstrated any legitimate state interest in sexual harassment, the only real equal protection question is whether sexual harassment constitutes *purposeful* discrimination *on the basis of gender.*[42]

a. Discrimination on the basis of gender. Where the sexual harassment consists of anti-female hazing or a sexually charged workplace,[43] the conduct is indistinguishable from any other form of purposeful gender-based discrimination and thus violates the equal protection clause so long as it is state action and is sufficiently severe or pervasive.[44] Where, however, the offensive conduct consists of friendly amorous advances, a more difficult conceptual problem arises. Unlike hostile conduct motivated by a desire to drive women from the workplace, a supervisor's unwelcome amorous advances are not so clearly purposeful discrimination on the basis of gender.

In *King v. Board of Regents*,[45] a divided panel of the Seventh Circuit upheld a jury verdict that a university dean, Steven Sonstein, was liable under §1983 in violation of the equal protection clause for creating a hostile environment with unwelcome sexual advances. The object of his attentions was a female professor, Katherine King. Judge Daniel Manion dissented:

> It does not appear that Sonstein harassed King because ... he did not like having women in the department. Rather, he harassed King ... because she was, in his mind, an attractive woman. ... Sonstein put King in a class by herself as his romantic target.
>
> • • •
>
> Sonstein's boorish advances were confined to King on account of his attraction to her personal qualities. Sonstein harassed King because she was Katherine King, not because she was female.[46]

This distinction between a lawful personal sexual attraction and unlawful discrimination on the basis of sex clearly would be untenable in a Title VII case.[47] The D.C. Circuit, in *Barnes v. Costle*,[48] held that a woman employee who lost a promotion because she rejected the sexual advances of her male supervisor was the victim of gender discrimination because, "[b]ut for her

---

job does not violate 42 U.S.C. §1981, which prohibits infringing black person's right to make and enforce contracts)).

[40]*Cf.* Meritor Sav. Bank v. Vinson, 477 U.S. 57, 40 FEP Cases 1822 (1986), reproduced in Chapter 1, Overview (sexual harassment can violate Title VII).

[41]*E.g.*, Mississippi Univ. for Women v. Hogan, 458 U.S. 718, 724 (1982)(government classification by gender requires "exceedingly persuasive classification"); Davis v. Passman, 442 U.S. 228, 234–35, 19 FEP Cases 1390, 1392–93 (1979)(equal protection principle of due process clause of Fifth Amendment prohibits gender discrimination by federal employer).

[42]Because analyses of what is "purposeful" and what is "on the basis of gender" inevitably overlap, the organization of the discussion of these points into the two subsections below is to some extent arbitrary.

[43]For a description of these forms of harassment, see Chapter 2, Forms of Harassment.

[44]*See, e.g.,* Lipsett v. University of P.R., 864 F.2d 881, 54 FEP Cases 230 (1st Cir. 1988)(harassment of female resident in male-dominated medical residency program); Bohen v. City of E. Chicago, *supra* note 39 (harassment of female dispatcher in male-dominated city fire department).

[45]*Supra* note 25.

[46]*Supra* note 25, 898 F.2d at 542, 52 FEP Cases at 817.

[47]See Chapter 3, Quid Pro Quo Harassment, Section II.C.

[48]561 F.2d 983, 15 FEP Cases 345 (D.C. Cir. 1977), reproduced in Chapter 1, Overview.

womanhood, ... participation in sexual activity would never have been solicited."[49] Similarly, the allegations of hostile environment harassment that the Supreme Court in *Meritor* held to be actionable under Title VII involved sexual advances by a supervisor allegedly motivated by sexual desire for a particular individual rather than hostility toward women in the workplace.[50]

As a theoretical matter, it is conceivable that conduct "on the basis of gender" for purposes of Title VII might not be considered to be "on the basis of gender" for equal protection purposes.[51] But there are no differences between Title VII law and equal protection doctrine that would suggest a reason for differentiating between them as far as the definition of the basis of the discrimination is concerned.[52] It would thus seem irrelevant that a state actor is not discriminating against all persons of a given gender but only a subset of that class, *i.e.,* those persons "with whom [the actor] had or sought to have an affair."[53] Discrimination against a subset of a protected class is discrimination on a protected basis.[54]

Nonetheless, for equal protection purposes, the Seventh Circuit has maintained a distinction in sexual advance cases between (1) lawful discrimination on the basis of the complainant's personality and (2) unlawful discrimination based on gender.[55] In *Trautvetter v. Quick,* a Seventh Circuit panel including Judge Manion considered a case in which an elementary school teacher brought a §1983 equal protection claim on the basis of a series of sexual advances by her school principal.[56] Affirming a summary judgment against the complainant, the court held that the unwelcome sexual advances were made on the basis of the complainant's personal characteristics, not her gender:

> [A] sexual discrimination claim under the fourteenth amendment based solely upon acts of discrimination directed towards [an individual] ... must show an intent to discriminate *because of* her status as a female and not because of characteristics of her gender which are personal to her. ... If this distinction—subtle as it is—is not maintained, any consensual workplace romance involving a state supervisor and employee which soured for one reason or another could give rise to equal protection claim if the employee simply alleges that his or her supervisor's conduct during the term of the romance constituted "sexual harassment." Such a scenario constitutes precisely the type of claim which the equal protection clause's "intent to discriminate" requirement was meant to discourage.[57]

---

[49]*Id.* at 990, 15 FEP Cases at 350.

[50]*Supra* note 40, 477 U.S. at 60, 40 FEP Cases at 1824. See Chapter 4, Hostile Environment Harassment, Section III.C.

[51]*Compare* Griggs v. Duke Power Co., 401 U.S. 424, 3 FEP Cases 175 (1971)(no proof of intent to discriminate required for violation of Title VII) *with* Washington v. Davis, 426 U.S. 229, 12 FEP Cases 1415 (1976)(proof of intent to discriminate required for violation of equal protection clause).

[52]*Compare* Gilbert v. General Elec. Co., 429 U.S. 125, 13 FEP Cases 1657 (1976) *with* Geduldig v. Aiello, 417 U.S. 484, 8 FEP Cases 97 (1974).

[53]Huebschen v. Wisconsin Dep't of Health & Social Servs., 716 F.2d 1167, 1172, 32 FEP Cases 1582, 1585 (7th Cir. 1983).

[54]*See generally* B.L. SCHLEI & P. GROSSMAN, EMPLOYMENT DISCRIMINATION LAW, 403–17 (2d ed. 1983)("sex plus" discrimination—discrimination against defined subset of protected class—generally unlawful).

[55]*Compare* Volk v. Coler, 845 F.2d 1422, 1433, 46 FEP Cases 1287, 1295 (7th Cir. 1988)("harassment against an individual woman *because of her sex* is a violation of the equal protection clause" (emphasis added)) *with* Huebschen v. Wisconsin Dep't of Health & Social Servs., *supra* note 53 (no constitutional violation where female supervisor retaliated against male subordinate for ending consensual romance in that reason she retaliated was that he had jilted her, not that he was male; his gender was "merely coincidental" to supervisor's reaction).

[56]916 F.2d 1140, 1149, 54 FEP Cases 109, 116 (7th Cir. 1990).

[57]*Id.* at 1151, 54 FEP Cases at 117–18.

The *Quick* decision and the Manion dissent in *King* both rely on an earlier Seventh Circuit decision, *Huebschen v. Department of Health and Social Services*.[58] In that case, a female supervisor in a state agency had a consensual relationship with Huebschen, a male subordinate. When Huebschen ended the relationship, the supervisor retaliated by demoting him.[59] The court held that the retaliation did not violate the equal protection clause, because the supervisor's "motivation in [demoting Huebschen] was not that Huebschen was male, but that he was a former lover who had jilted her."[60] The court concluded that "Huebschen's gender was merely coincidental" to his supervisor's action.[61]

Beyond the Seventh Circuit,[62] courts that have considered the issue have held that under the equal protection clause, as under Title VII, unwelcome sexual advances constitute discrimination "on the basis of sex."[63]

b. Purposeful discrimination. The allegation of a denial of equal protection on the basis of gender requires proof that "the sexual harassment constitutes intentional discrimination."[64] The equal protection clause, unlike Title VII, prohibits only intentional discrimination; the clause does not prohibit facially neutral conduct that has an adverse impact on a protected group.[65] To violate the equal protection clause, the discrimination must be purposeful or *de jure,* not accidental or *de facto.*[66]

This distinction between the equal protection clause and Title VII is rarely significant in that virtually every sexual harassment case is brought under a disparate treatment theory.[67] Intent is not particularly difficult to prove. When a supervisor makes unwelcome sexual advances toward an employee, or acts vindictively toward an employee who rejects those advances, the supervisor is acting intentionally. Thus, if the unwanted attentions are by their very nature

---

[58]*Supra* note 53.

[59]*Id.* at 1169, 32 FEP Cases at 1583.

[60]*Id.* at 1172, 32 FEP Cases at 1585. The court noted the absence of any evidence that the female supervisor "had discriminated against other men in the office or that she attempted to have romances with other men in the office."

[61]*Id.*

[62]Although the Seventh Circuit has never overruled *Huebschen,* cases following *Huebschen* have distinguished it in other decisions in which the court found sexual advances violative of equal protection despite arguments that the advances were made on the basis of personality rather than gender. *E.g., King v. Board of Regents,* 898 F.2d 533, 539, 52 FEP Cases 809, 814 (7th Cir. 1990)(rejecting defendant's argument that harassment based on sexual desire not based on gender); *Keppler v. Hinsdale Township High School Dist. 86,* 715 F. Supp. 862, 867–70, 50 FEP Cases 295, 298–301 (N.D. Ill. 1989), reproduced in Chapter 2, Forms of Harassment (*Huebschen* does not apply to hostile environment claims and to cases where there is retaliation for rejecting sexual advances, as opposed to cases where there is retaliation for ending relationship). In *Trautvetter v. Quick, supra* note 56, however, the Seventh Circuit reaffirmed *Huebschen.*

[63]*See, e.g.,* Starrett v. Wadley, 876 F.2d 808, 814, 51 FEP Cases 608, 611 (10th Cir. 1989) and cases cited therein. *See also* cases cited in note 39 *supra.*

[64]Bohen v. City of E. Chicago, 799 F.2d 1180, 1187, 41 FEP Cases 1108, 1113 (7th Cir. 1986); Trautvetter v. Quick, *supra* note 56 (although both Title VII and §1983 require showing of sexual harassment, "intent to discriminate must be shown under equal protection while Title VII requires no such showing").

[65]Washington v. Davis, *supra* note 51, 426 U.S. at 238–39, 12 FEP Cases at 1418–19 (official act is not violative of equal protection solely on basis of racially discriminatory impact).

[66]Batson v. Kentucky, 476 U.S. 79, 93 (1986) (disproportionate impact evidences invidious intent but does not necessarily prove it in preemptory exclusions of black jurors in case convicting black man of crime); Personnel Adm'r v. Feeney, 442 U.S. 256, 274, 19 FEP Cases 1377, 1385 (1979)(veterans' preference not sexually discriminatory even though it favors men disproportionately); Washington v. Davis, *supra* note 51, 426 U.S. at 238–39, 12 FEP Cases at 1418–19; Bohen v. City of E. Chicago, *supra* note 63 ("ultimate inquiry" under equal protection clause is whether sexual harassment constitutes intentional discrimination whereas inquiry under Title VII is whether harassment altered conditions of plaintiffs' employment).

[67]*But see* Robinson v. Jacksonville Shipyards, 760 F. Supp. 1486, 1522–23 (M.D. Fla. 1991), reproduced in Chapter 2, Forms of Harassment (suggesting that display of sexually suggestive pictures of women in workplace may be matter of adverse impact).

limited to one gender, the supervisor is intentionally treating an employee adversely on the basis of gender.[68]

Some judges, however, would rely upon the purposeful discrimination required by the equal protection clause to reject a §1983 claim based on amorous advances directed toward a particular individual.[69] In *King v. Board of Regents*,[70] the dissenting opinion of Judge Manion emphasized that the alleged harasser, a university dean, did not harass the complainant, an assistant professor, because he disliked "having women in the department," but because he was personally attracted to her.[71]

The majority opinion in *King* suggested that the Manion dissent confused *intent*, which is required for an equal protection claim, with *bad animus* toward a group, which is not required:

> While violation of the equal protection clause requires discriminatory intent, we can find no hatred requirement in either the fourteenth amendment itself or the case law. In fact, the opposite may very well be true: a desire to protect women because of paternalism and admiration may be the cause of discriminatory action. For example, state protective laws have been invalidated on Title VII grounds, as have laws that require women to take maternity leave. Similarly, pension systems that presumably benefit women have been invalidated. None of these discriminatory actions evidence a hatred or even a dislike of women. All that is required is that the action be motivated by the gender of the plaintiff. No hatred, no animus, and no dislike is required.[72]

Nonetheless, it will always be easier for a court to find the requisite intent under the equal protection clause where the conduct can be characterized as demeaning or where the conduct was addressed to more than one woman.[73]

c. Scope of the equal protection clause. The scope of protection afforded by the equal protection clause, in a sexual harassment case, should ordinarily be the same as in a Title VII case, except for the "color of state law" requirement.[74] Assuming a state actor, sexually harassing conduct that would violate Title VII should also violate the equal protection clause, and conduct too tame to violate the statute would not breach the Constitution. However, the different sources of the restriction (contrast the detail of the EEOC Guidelines and their call for prevention of harassment[75] with the text of the equal protection clause

---

[68]Only if the supervisor is bisexual and visits unwanted sexual attentions without regard to gender is purposeful discrimination absent. See generally Chapter 3, Quid Pro Quo Harassment, Section II.D.1.c.

[69]*See, e.g.*, Trautvetter v. Quick, *supra* note 56, 916 F.2d at 1149–52, 54 FEP Cases at 116–19 (*dictum*)("intent to discriminate" requirement of equal protection clause defeats case of plaintiff singled out for sexual advance because of characteristics of gender personal to her).

[70]*Supra* note 62.

[71]*Id.* at 542, 52 FEP Cases at 817.

[72]*Id.* at 538–39, 52 FEP Cases at 814.

[73]*See, e.g.*, Trautvetter v. Quick, *supra* note 56, 916 F.2d at 1152, 54 FEP Cases at 118–19 (distinguishing case of amorous advances from cases involving "demeaning and cruel sexual abuse" or pattern of unwelcome sexual advances).

[74]*Id.* at 1149–52, 54 FEP Cases at 116–19 ("parameters of a cause of action alleging sexual harassment as a violation of the equal protection clause have not been precisely defined" but "such a claim generally follows the contours of a Title VII allegation of sexual harassment"); Reynolds v. Atlantic City Convention Center, 53 FEP Cases 1852 (D.N.J. 1990)(both §1983 and Title VII "apply the same standards for determining the merit of plaintiff's claims" for discriminatory discharge).

[75]29 C.F.R. §1604.11(a). In 1980, the EEOC issued its Guidelines on Discrimination Because of Sex, 29 C.F.R. §§1604.1–.11, one part of which, §1604.11, is on sexual harassment. The EEOC Guidelines are

and its requirement of "intent") arguably call for different measures of what is actionable harassment.

Cases in which the respective scopes of Title VII and the equal protection clause could differ might include those where an employer negligently failed to investigate harassment in the workplace.[76] That conduct may not be intentional or conscious enough to constitute intentional discrimination for purposes of the equal protection clause, but could violate Title VII.[77] Nonetheless, it would be a rare case in which a court would use the intent requirement to deny §1983 liability where Title VII liability would exist.[78]

2. The Due Process Clause

A sexual harassment complainant may assert a §1983 claim on the basis of the Fourteenth Amendment right not to be deprived of property or liberty without due process of law. This right ordinarily would entail a hearing to test the validity of the reasons for the complainant's discharge from employment. Sexual harassment cases have proceeded on both property and liberty theories.

a. Property interest. Under certain circumstances a dismissal in retaliation for opposing sexual harassment may deprive a public employee of a property interest without due process of law.[79] To make this claim, the complainant must prove a property right in continued employment.[80] Property interests "are created and their dimensions are defined by existing rules or understandings that stem from an independent source such as state law."[81] To create a property interest, those rules or understandings must create more than "an abstract need or desire" for, or a "unilateral expectation" of, continued employment.[82] They must create "a legitimate claim of entitlement" to continued employment absent cause for dismissal.[83]

b. Liberty interests. Sexual harassment may be the basis for a §1983 claim that a public employee was deprived of a liberty interest without due process

---

nonbinding but "constitute a body of experience and informed judgments to which courts and litigants may properly resort for guidance." Meritor Sav. Bank v. Vinson, 477 U.S. 57, 65, 40 FEP Cases 1822, 1826 (1986), reproduced in Chapter 1, Overview (citations omitted). The sexual harassment guidelines in §1604.11 are reproduced in Appendix 1.

[76]See *id.* at §1604.11(f)("employer should take all steps necessary to prevent sexual harassment from occurring").

[77]*See, e.g.,* Bohen v. City of E. Chicago, *supra* note 64 ("ultimate inquiry" under equal protection analysis is "intentional discrimination" whereas under Title VII it is whether sexual harassment altered conditions of employment).

[78]See *id.* at 1189–92, 41 FEP Cases at 1115–17, where Judge Richard Posner, in his concurring opinion, reasoned that an employer's inattention to problems of sexual harassment in the workplace could evidence the intent requisite in an equal protection case.

[79]*See* McGraw v. City of Huntington Beach, 882 F.2d 384 (9th Cir. 1989)(city employee who had passed probationary period had legitimate expectation of continued employment and could therefore assert property interest in employment allegedly affected by continuous sexual harassment); Keppler v. Hinsdale Township High School Dist. 86, *supra* note 62, 715 F. Supp. at 870, 50 FEP Cases at 301–2 (high-school administrator alleging her position was eliminated in sexual retaliation by principal had property interest in a school district job but not in the particular position she held and thus could not challenge transfer under due-process clause).

[80]McGraw v. City of Huntington Beach, *supra* note 79, 882 F.2d at 388; Keppler v. Hinsdale Township High School Dist. 86, *supra* note 62, 715 F. Supp. at 870, 50 FEP Cases at 302.

[81]Board of Regents v. Roth, 408 U.S. 564, 577 (1972).

[82]*Id.*

[83]*Id.* An obvious example of a legitimate claim of entitlement to continued employment would be a contract of employment for a term of years.

of law. The liberty interest may involve reputation, physical freedom, or privacy.

i. Reputational interest. In instances where the firing of a public employee in retaliation for opposing sexual harassment jeopardizes the employee's good name, reputation, honor, integrity, or freedom to follow other employment opportunities, a liberty interest is implicated.[84] A liberty interest on this basis does not exist, however, unless "the employer creates and disseminates a false and defamatory impression about the employee in connection with [the] termination."[85]

ii. Interest in freedom from physical restraint. Sexual harassment may implicate the liberty interest in being free of physical restraint. In *Stoneking v. Bradford Area School District*,[86] the plaintiff alleged that while she had been a public school student she had been sexually abused by the high-school band leader. Her §1983 action against the school district and three of its employees claimed that they had established a custom, policy, or practice of deliberate indifference to misconduct by teachers, which had resulted in the alleged abuse and harassment.[87] Judge Dolores Sloviter held that the plaintiff had alleged a deprivation of her liberty interest in being free "from invasion of her personal security through sexual abuse," without due process of law.[88] Thus, if sexual harassment has involved physical restraint by a government official, that activity itself may be actionable under §1983.

iii. Interest in privacy. Another liberty interest is in privacy, which entails interests "in avoiding disclosure of personal matters, and . . . in independence in making certain kinds of important decisions."[89] In *Eastwood v. Department of Corrections*,[90] the complainant stated a §1983 claim for deprivation of her constitutional right to privacy by alleging that, after reporting co-worker sexual harassment, she was forced by her employer's investigator to reveal facts about her sexual history.

3. The First Amendment

Retaliation against a public employee who has complained of sexual harassment can be the basis of a §1983 action for deprivation of rights secured by the First Amendment, as incorporated into the Fourteenth Amendment. A First Amendment retaliation suit by a public employee generally is available whenever the employee's speech is on a matter of "public concern" and the employee's interests as a citizen outweigh the efficiency interests of the public

---

[84]*Cf.* Downum v. City of Wichita, 675 F. Supp. 1566, 1572, 49 FEP Cases 162, 167 (D. Kan. 1986)(transfer of probationary female firefighter did not implicate liberty interest because reason for transfer—curvature of spine—was not made public by defendant and was not sufficiently stigmatizing).

[85]Codd v. Velger, 429 U.S. 624, 628 (1977)(no hearing required where fired police officer did not challenge substantial truth of material in question).

[86]882 F.2d 720 (3d Cir. 1989), *cert. denied,* 110 S.Ct. 840 (1990).

[87]The chief basis of liability asserted in *Stoneking* was a practice, custom, or policy of reckless indifference to known or suspected sexual abuse of students by teachers. *Id.* at 724–25.

[88]*Id.* at 726–27.

[89]Whalen v. Roe, 429 U.S. 589, 599–600 (1977).

[90]846 F.2d 627, 630–31, 46 FEP Cases 1869, 1871 (10th Cir. 1988).

employer.[91] Several sexual harassment retaliation claims have been maintained under §1983 and the First Amendment. In *Fuchilla v. Prockop*,[92] the complainant stated a §1983 claim by alleging that a state university had discharged her in retaliation for filing a state-court sexual harassment action against her employer and her supervisor. Judge Harold Ackerman held that the complainant had alleged a deprivation of "her right to access to the courts," which is "protected under the first amendment."[93] Similarly, in *Woerner v. Breczek*,[94] two female police officers stated a constitutional violation actionable under §1983 by alleging that their supervisors had retaliated against them for complaining that one of the two officers had been sexually harassed by a police supervisor. In addition, the Tenth Circuit has upheld a jury verdict against an employer and supervisor on the basis that the complainant's dismissal had resulted from her allegations of sexual harassment, thus depriving her of freedom of expression secured by the First Amendment.[95]

4. Asserted Statutory Bases

Plaintiffs may bring §1983 claims on the basis of a federal statute as well as the Constitution. Not every federal statute, however, is necessarily enforceable under §1983.[96] The principal example of a federal discrimination statute enforceable under §1983 is Title IX of the Education Amendments of 1972, which prohibits sex discrimination in educational programs or activities that receive federal funding.[97] Because Title IX has no express damages remedy,[98] a plaintiff might decide to invoke Title IX in a §1983 claim against a state school. A §1983 damages action against a state school, however, has been held to be barred by the Eleventh Amendment.[99]

Another potential statutory basis for a §1983 suit would be Title VII, but courts have concluded that Title VII, with its detailed set of remedies, was intended to provide the exclusive remedy for any violation of its provisions.[100]

---

[91]*See, e.g.*, Starrett v. Wadley, 876 F.2d 808, 815, 51 FEP Cases 608, 612 (10th Cir. 1989).

[92]682 F. Supp. 247, 52 FEP Cases 259 (D.N.J. 1987).

[93]*Id.* at 262, 52 FEP Cases at 269.

[94]519 F. Supp. 517, 521–22, 26 FEP Cases 897, 900 (N.D. Ill. 1981)(denying employer's motion to dismiss).

[95]Starrett v. Wadley, *supra* note 91, 876 F.2d at 815–16, 51 FEP Cases at 612–13. The court did hint, however, that the defendants might have prevailed had they challenged the plaintiff's theory that her complaints were truly matters of public concern. *Id.* at 816 & n.10, 51 FEP Cases at 613. *See also* Dwyer v. Smith, 867 F.2d 184, 193, 48 FEP Cases 1886 (4th Cir. 1989)(sexual harassment complainant had no First Amendment claim on allegation that she was fired for complaining about lack of safety equipment and the like in that these complaints were not matters of public concern).

[96]Alexander v. Polk, 750 F.2d 250 (3d Cir. 1984)(violation of federal statute under color of state law actionable under §1983 unless Congress foreclosed enforcement of statute under §1983 or statute does not create enforceable rights).

[97]20 U.S.C. §1681(a). Title IX is discussed more fully in Section V. *infra.*

[98]Lieberman v. University of Chicago, 660 F.2d 1185, 1188 (7th Cir. 1981).

[99]*E.g.,* Lipsett v. University of P.R., 745 F. Supp. 793, 795–96 (D.P.R. 1990)(defendant university protected from Title IX damages suit by Eleventh Amendment; Title IX does not abrogate Eleventh Amendment); *see also* cases cited in Lipsett v. University of P.R., 864 F.2d 881, 885 n.6, 54 FEP Cases 230, 232–33 (1st Cir. 1988).

[100]Starrett v. Wadley, *supra* note 91, 876 F.2d at 813, 51 FEP Cases at 610 ("right created solely under Title VII cannot serve as the basis for an independent remedy under Section 1983, lest Congress' prescribed remedies under Title VII be undermined"). *See also* Day v. Wayne County Bd. of Auditors, 749 F.2d 1199, 1204, 36 FEP Cases 743, 746 (6th Cir. 1984)(claimant who suffered retaliation in violation of Title VII does not have §1983 claim: "Title VII provides the exclusive remedy where the §1983 claim is based solely on Title VII"); Lipsett v. Rive-Mora, 669 F. Supp. 1188, 1195 (D.P.R. 1987)(§1983 cannot be used to sustain action for violation of Title VII only), *rev'd sub nom. on other grounds,* Lipsett v. University of P.R., 864

Further, Title VII cannot be the basis of a §1983 claim against a person, such as a harassing supervisor who is not a Title VII "employer," when that person could not be liable under Title VII itself.[101]

E. Standards for Municipal and Individual Liability

1. Municipal Liability

Section 1983 liability for a municipality attaches only when an injury is inflicted by a municipal official through the "execution of a government's policy or custom."[102] Liability of a municipality cannot be predicated on a *respondeat superior* theory.[103] Thus, a municipality cannot be held liable merely because it employs a wrongdoer.

A single act may be sufficient to establish municipal liability if the act is by a municipal employee who qualifies as a "policymaker."[104] The municipality is liable for actions by nonpolicymakers only if their harassment or failure to prevent harassment constitutes a well-settled practice; thus, isolated misconduct or abuses of discretion by individuals who lack authority will not establish municipal liability.[105]

F.2d 881, 54 FEP Cases 230 (1st Cir. 1988); Talley v. De Soto, 37 FEP Cases 375 (N.D. Tex 1985)(if defendant not amenable to suit under Title VII, suit under §1983 cannot be maintained); Torres v. Wisconsin Dep't of Health & Social Servs., 592 F. Supp. 922, 35 FEP Cases 1041 (E.D. Wis. 1984)(same).

[101]Huebschen v. Wisconsin Dep't of Health & Social Servs., 716 F.2d 1167, 1171, 32 FEP Cases 1582, 1584 (7th Cir. 1983)(defendant who is not "employer" under Title VII not amenable to suit under §1983 claim based on Title VII).

[102]Monell v. Department of Social Servs., 436 U.S. 658, 694, 17 FEP Cases 873, 886 (1978). *See generally* Comment, *Employer Liability and Sexual Harassment under Section 1983: A Comment on Starrett v. Wadley,* 4 DENVER UNIV. L. REV. 571 (1990)(analyzing "policy or custom" rule). *See also* Pembaur v. City of Cincinnati, 475 U.S. 469, 481 (1986)(actions pursuant to instructions of county official with authority to establish county policy could subject county to liability under §1983); Andrews v. City of Philadelphia, 895 F.2d 1469, 1480–81, 54 FEP Cases 184, 193 (3d Cir. 1990)(city did not "support" sexual harassment because official policymaker neither authorized nor acquiesced in alleged sexual harassment; "even in 'custom' type cases, it is impossible for the delivery of a kick to inculpate the head and find no fault with the kick"); Gray v. County of Dane, 854 F.2d 179, 47 FEP Cases 886 (7th Cir. 1988)(alleged sexual harassment by some county officials did not constitute "custom" or "policy" when county made significant efforts to address plaintiff's harassment complaints); Garza v. City of Omaha, 814 F.2d 553, 43 FEP Cases 572 (8th Cir. 1987)(discrimination instigated and ratified by city employees at management and supervisory levels constituted a "custom"); Bohen v. City of E. Chicago, 799 F.2d 1180, 1189, 41 FEP Cases 1108, 1114 (7th Cir. 1986)(general and ongoing practice of sexual harassment within city fire department was "custom" or "policy" because it was known, tolerated, and participated in by officials responsible for working conditions).

[103]Monell v. Department of Social Servs., *supra* note 102, 436 U.S. at 691, 17 FEP Cases at 885.

[104]Spell v. McDaniel, 824 F.2d 1380, 1389–90 (4th Cir. 1987)(municipal establishment of deficient training program for police officers constituted "policy"), *cert. denied,* 484 U.S. 1027 (1988). *Cf.* Collins v. City of San Diego, 841 F.2d 337, 341, 46 FEP Cases 562, 565 (9th Cir. 1988)(no municipal liability for police sergeant's sexual harassment of police officer where state law established that chief of police, rather than sergeant, was in charge of city's police department).

The identification of policymakers is a function for the court; the existence of an official policy or custom is a jury question. Jett v. Dallas Indep. School Dist., 109 S.Ct. 2702, 2723, 50 FEP Cases 27, 40 (1989). Whether a person is a "policymaker" is a question of state law. City of St. Louis v. Praprotnik, 485 U.S. 112, 124 (1988)(state law determines identification of policymaking officials).

[105]*E.g.,* Kelsey-Andrews v. City of Philadelphia, 713 F. Supp. 760, 765–66, 52 FEP Cases 300, 303 (E.D. Pa 1989)(police sergeant's failure to investigate alleged sexual harassment not actionable; only police commissioner was policymaker), *aff'd in part and vacated in part,* 895 F.2d 1469, 54 FEP Cases 184 (3d Cir. 1990); Carrero v. New York City Hous. Auth., 890 F.2d 569, 577, 51 FEP Cases 596, 601 (2d Cir. 1989)(city not liable under §1983 for sexual harassment by plaintiff's supervisor even though supervisor had discretion regarding plaintiff's training and evaluation, where supervisor acted contrary to municipal policies against sexual harassment); Gray v. County of Dane, *supra* note 102, 859 F.2d at 183, 47 FEP Cases at 889 (alleged sexual harassment by some county officials not "custom" or "policy" where county made significant efforts to address plaintiff's complaints).

An informal course or pattern of sexual harassment, however, may rise to the level of an unofficial policy or custom.[106] In *Bohen v. City of East Chicago*,[107] the Seventh Circuit found the defendant municipality liable for tacitly approving the sexual harassment of an employee by supervisory and other personnel. Judge William Bauer found that "sexual harassment was the general, on-going, and accepted practice ... and high-ranking, supervisory, and management officials responsible for working conditions ... knew of, tolerated, and participated in the harassment."[108]

2. Individual Liability

Individuals acting under color of state law may be sued in their individual as well as official capacities.[109] Individual officials obviously may be liable for their own harassing conduct. More difficult is the question of when individuals are liable under §1983 for harassment by their subordinates. Individual officials are not liable for harassment by others, absent some affirmative link to the sexual harassment.[110] Individual officials can, however, be liable for any action or inaction on their part that constitutes encouragement, condonation, acquiescence, or gross negligence amounting to deliberate indifference.[111]

In *Lipsett v. University of Puerto Rico*,[112] the supervisor's personal failure to investigate and stop the sexual harassment directed at the complainant was found to constitute negligence amounting to indifference, condonation, and acquiesence in the violation of the complainant's rights. Judge Hugh Bownes emphasized the importance of notice in determining an official's liability:

> An important factor in making the determination of liability is whether the official was put on some kind of notice of the alleged violations, for one cannot make a "deliberate" or "conscious" choice to act or not to act unless confronted with a

---

[106]Monell v. Department of Social Serv., *supra* note 102, 436 U.S. at 690, 17 FEP Cases at 884.

[107]*Supra* note 102.

[108]*Id.* at 1189, 41 FEP Cases at 1114–15. *Cf.* Andrews v. City of Philadelphia, 895 F.2d 1469, 1481–82, 54 FEP Cases 184, 193–94 (3d Cir. 1990)(no municipal liability where official policymaker neither authorized nor acquiesced in sexual harassment of plaintiff, but rather took prompt action in response to complaints).

[109]Hafer v. Melo, 112 S.Ct. 358 (1991)(state official can be personally liable for damages). Official-capacity suits generally represent only another way of suing the entity of which an officer is an agent. Monell v. Department of Social Servs., *supra* note 102, 436 U.S. at 690 n.55. If the individual is sued in an official capacity, a judgment against the official may result in liability against the governmental entity. Brander v. Holt, 469 U.S. 464, 471–72 (1985)(judgment against city's director of police imposed liability on city).

[110]*See, e.g.,* Poe v. Haydon, 853 F.2d 418, 52 FEP Cases 80 (6th Cir. 1988)(no supervisory liability where supervisor alleged only to be "aware" of sexual harassment), *cert. denied,* 488 U.S. 1007 (1989); Volk v. Coler, 845 F.2d 1422, 1431–32, 46 FEP Cases 1287, 1294 (7th Cir. 1988)(supervisory officials not liable where they did not personally participate in sexual harassment); Scott v. City of Overland Park, 595 F. Supp. 520, 524, 41 FEP Cases 1211, 1213 (D. Kan. 1984)(city manager entitled to summary judgment on plaintiff's claim of sexual harassment under §1983 because he did not personally participate in or know of any harassment).

[111]*See, e.g.,* Bohen v. City of E. Chicago, *supra* note 102 (supervisors liable for failure to address plaintiff's complaints of sexual harassment); Williams v. Smith, 781 F.2d 319, 323–24 (2d Cir. 1986)(supervisor directly responsible for conducting hearing at which plaintiff's rights were violated could be liable under §1983); McClelland v. Facteau, 610 F.2d 693, 697 (10th Cir. 1979)(supervisors could be liable under §1983 if they knew of misconduct by subordinates but failed to correct it). *Cf.* Haynesworth v. Miller, 820 F.2d 1245, 1262 (D.C. Cir. 1987)(supervisor not liable for conduct of subordinate absent duty to instruct subordinate to refrain from conduct); Hays v. Jefferson County, 668 F.2d 869, 874 (6th Cir.)(supervisory personnel not liable for misconduct of subordinates unless training of subordinates so grossly negligent that misconduct substantially certain to occur), *cert. denied,* 459 U.S. 833 (1982).

[112]*Supra* note 99 (court reversed summary judgment in favor of defendants on basis that plaintiff established triable issue as to officials' acquiescence in discriminatory behavior of plaintiff's fellow residents in surgical residency program).

problem that requires the taking of affirmative steps. Once an official is so notified, either actually or constructively, it is reasonable to infer that the *failure* to take such steps, as well as the actual *taking* of them constitutes a choice "from among various alternatives." One obvious "alternative" is to do something to make the violations stop.[113]

F. Defenses to §1983 Claims

1. Official Immunity

Government officials who are sued in their individual capacity are entitled to qualified immunity from civil liability if their conduct does not violate "clearly established statutory or constitutional rights of which a reasonable person would have known."[114] Reasonableness is measured by an objective standard; an official's subjective belief that a matter was handled properly is irrelevant.[115] Defendants bear the burden of showing that they are entitled to qualified immunity.[116]

The purpose of qualified immunity is to protect public officials from liability when they neither knew nor objectively should have known of the appropriate legal standard.[117] Accordingly, officials who objectively should have known of the applicable legal standards are not protected by qualified immunity in treating, or allowing their subordinates to treat, employees differently on the basis of gender.[118] Because the general right to be free of sexual harassment is well-grounded and widely known to the public, in most cases it will be difficult to invoke official immunity against charges of participating in harassment or allowing it to continue.[119]

2. Sovereign Immunity

States generally have absolute immunity from §1983 liability by virtue of the Eleventh Amendment, although they may be sued for injunctive relief, including reinstatement of employment.[119a] Absent a waiver of sovereign immunity, the Eleventh Amendment bars damages suits in federal court against a state and—what amounts to the same thing—damages suits against the state's

---

[113]*Supra* note 99, 864 F.2d at 902, 54 FEP Cases at 246.

[114]*E.g.,* Eastwood v. Department of Corrections, 846 F.2d 627, 630–31, 46 FEP Cases 1867, 1870–71 (10th Cir. 1988)(immunity denied because plaintiff clearly established right to be free from disclosing information regarding personal sexual matters). *Cf.* Poe v. Haydon, *supra* note 110, 853 F.2d at 422, 52 FEP Cases at 83 (immunity granted because plaintiff did not have clearly established right to specific outcome following investigation of sexual harassment complaint), *cert. denied,* 488 U.S. 1007 (1989).

A court's denial of a claim of qualified immunity, although interlocutory in nature, is immediately appealable. Mitchell v. Forsyth, 472 U.S. 511, 528 (1985).

[115]Anderson v. Creighton, 483 U.S. 635, 641 (1987).

[116]Poe v. Haydon, *supra* note 110, 853 F.2d at 424, 52 FEP Cases at 84 (sexual harassment); Fuchilla v. Prockop, 682 F. Supp. 247, 254, 52 FEP Cases 259, 263 (D.N.J. 1987)(same).

[117]Harlow v. Fitzgerald, 457 U.S. 800 (1982)(case remanded for determination of whether defendants knew or should have known actions they were alleged to have taken violated certain civil service regulations).

[118]Andrews v. City of Philadelphia, 895 F.2d 1469, 1479–80, 54 FEP Cases 184, 192–93 (3d Cir. 1990)(no qualified immunity available in that police sergeant and captain should have known it was illegal to discriminate against female employees).

[119]*See id.* at 1480; Eastwood v. Department of Corrections, *supra* note 114.

[119a]Melo v. Hafer, 912 F.2d 628, 635–36 (3d Cir. 1990)(permitting §1983 suit for reinstatement), *aff'd on other grounds,* 112 S.Ct. 358 (1991).

officials in their official capacities.[120] A damages suit has been allowed to proceed, however, against a state official sued in her personal capacity for allegedly misusing her power to fire state employees.[121]

The Eleventh Amendment does not bar suits against a state's political subdivisions, such as municipalities.[122]

3. Statute of Limitations

Section 1983 itself has no statute of limitations. The proper statute of limitations to apply in a §1983 action is the relevant state's statute of limitations for personal injury actions.[123]

G. Remedies in §1983 Cases

Relief available for a §1983 violation includes injunctive relief, tort remedies, and attorney's fees.[124]

IV. Section 1985(3)

Section 1985(3), which codifies part of the Civil Rights Act of 1871,[125] authorizes damages suits by those who have suffered injury from a conspiracy to deprive them of equal protection of rights under the Constitution or federal law.[126] Like §1983, §1985 does not create substantive rights but provides redress for violation of a federal right established elsewhere. Section 1985 cannot be used to address violations of Title VII,[127] but may be used to assert federal rights that have a source independent of Title VII.[128]

Section 1985 covers conspiracies to discriminate against those who have opposed sexual harassment.[129] A §1985 claim requires proof of (1) a conspiracy, (2) a purpose of depriving one of equal protection or privileges under the law, (3) an act in furtherance of the conspiracy, and (4) resulting injury.[130]

---

[120]Will v. Michigan Dep't of State Police, 485 U.S. 1005, 49 FEP Cases 1664, 1667 (1989). *See* Eastwood v. Department of Corrections, *supra* note 114, 846 F.2d at 628, 46 FEP Cases at 1869 (Eleventh Amendment bars §1983 suit for sexual harassment against Oklahoma Department of Corrections and its officials in official capacities).

[121]Melo v. Hafer, *supra* note 119a, 912 F.2d at 636–37.

[122]Monell v. Department of Social Servs., *supra* note 103, 436 U.S. at 690, 17 FEP Cases at 884.

[123]Wilson v. Garcia, 471 U.S. 261, 280 (1985).

[124]For a discussion of §1983 monetary remedies, see Chapter 29, Monetary Relief. For a discussion of attorney's fees, see Chapter 30, Attorney's Fees and Costs.

[125]42 U.S.C. §1985(3). For a general discussion of §1985(3) in the context of employment discrimination, see B.L. Schlei & P. Grossman, Employment Discrimination Law (2d ed. 1983), Chapter 21, Section IV.

[126]Griffin v. Breckenridge, 403 U.S. 88, 102–3, 9 FEP Cases 1196, 1201 (1971)(plaintiffs alleged, *inter alia,* that defendants conspired to deprive them of rights of free speech, assembly, association, and movement); Bougher v. University of Pittsburgh, 882 F.2d 74, 79 (3d Cir. 1989)(plaintiff alleged that defendants conspired to deprive her of due-process rights).

[127]Great Am. Fed. Sav. & Loan Ass'n v. Novotny, 442 U.S. 366, 19 FEP Cases 1482 (1979)(complainant cannot use §1985(3) to assert rights created solely by Title VII).

[128]*See, e.g.,* Scott v. City of Overland Park, *supra* note 110, 595 F. Supp. at 527, 41 FEP Cases at 1216 (§1985 may be used to assert rights of city employees under Fourteenth Amendment).

[129]*See* Volk v. Coler, *supra* note 110, 845 F.2d at 1434, 46 FEP Cases at 1296–97 (complaints of sexual harassment and conspiracy to retaliate for same in violation of First Amendment); Scott v. City of Overland Park, *supra* note 110, 595 F. Supp. at 529, 41 FEP Cases at 1216 (alleging sexual harassment and discriminatory conspiracy in violation of equal protection).

[130]Trautvetter v. Quick, 916 F.2d 1140, 1153, 54 FEP Cases 109, 119 (7th Cir. 1990). In this case, the §1985 claim failed on summary judgment because, *inter alia,* the plaintiff could not prove an alleged

Plaintiffs must show that a conspiracy existed to deprive them of the right to equal treatment with members of the opposite sex.[131] At least one court has held that a §1985 plaintiff need not prove class-based animus.[132]

Courts differ as to whether agents of a single legal entity may "conspire" for purposes of §1985(3).[133]

V. TITLE IX OF THE EDUCATION AMENDMENTS OF 1972

Title IX prohibits sex discrimination, and thus sexual harassment, in any educational program or activity receiving federal funds.[134] In *Lipsett v. University of Puerto Rico,*[135] a female member of a hospital's surgical residency program was subjected to hostile environment harassment by fellow residents and was subjected to quid pro quo sexual harassment by her supervisor. The First Circuit allowed a claim against the university under Title IX,[136] reasoning that a student or employee may sue an educational institution for sexual harassment under Title IX *"if* an official representing the institution knew, or in the exercise of reasonable care, should have known, of the harassment's occurrence, *unless* that official can show that he or she took appropriate steps to halt it."[137] Judge Hugh Bownes further confirmed that Title VII standards for proving discriminatory treatment apply to claims under Title IX.[138]

Remedies available for Title IX violations include recovery of attorney's fees,[139] injunctive relief,[140] and federal administrative action.[141] An educational institution is subject to the loss of federal funding for violations of Title IX.[142]

---

conspirator's failure to prevent sexual harassment was an act in furtherance of a conspiracy; she could not prove that he was aware of the unwelcome sexual advances alleged by the plaintiff. *Id.*

[131]Volk v. Coler, 845 F.2d 1422, 1434, 46 FEP Cases 1287, 1296–97 (7th Cir. 1988).

[132]*Id. Cf.* Griffin v. Breckenridge, *supra* note 126, 403 U.S. at 102, 9 FEP Cases at 1201 ("there must be some racial or perhaps otherwise class-based invidiously discriminatory animus behind the conspirators' action").

[133]*Compare* Volk v. Coler, *supra* note 131, 845 F.2d at 1434–35, 46 FEP Cases at 1296 (intra-entity conspiracies are possible) *with* Scott v. City of Overland Park, 595 F. Supp. 520, 41 FEP Cases 1211 (D. Kan. 1984)(action allowed against defendants in individual capacities but dismissed against same defendants in official capacities).

[134]"No person in the United States shall, on the basis of sex, be excluded from participation in, be denied the benefits of, or be subjected to discrimination under any education program or activity receiving Federal financial assistance . . . ." 20 U.S.C. §1681(a). *See generally* Ingulli, *Sexual Harassment in Education.* 18 RUTGERS L.J. 281 (1987); Schneider, *Sexual Harassment and Higher Education,* 65 TEX. L. REV. 525 (1987).

[135]864 F.2d 881, 54 FEP Cases 230 (1st Cir. 1988).

[136]*Id.* at 884–85. The court did not express any opinion on the availability of sovereign immunity or whether the university "received federal funding."

[137]*Id.* at 901, 54 FEP Cases at 245 (emphasis in original)(citing Meritor Sav. Bank v. Vinson, 477 U.S. 57, 40 FEP Cases 1822 (1986)); *but see* Bougher v. University of Pittsburgh, *supra* note 126, 882 F.2d at 77 (declining to decide whether evidence of hostile environment sufficient to sustain claim of sexual discrimination under Title IX).

[138]*Id.* at 896–97, 54 FEP Cases 230, 241–42 (1st Cir. 1988)(legislative history confirms Title VII standards to apply under Title IX). *See also* Moire v. Temple Univ. School of Medicine, 613 F. Supp. 1360, 1366–69 (E.D. Pa. 1985)(entertaining Title IX claim based on alleged sexual harassment of medical student tolerated by medical school and suggesting that standards of EEOC Guidelines should apply, but rejecting claim on facts), *aff'd,* 800 F.2d 1136 (3d Cir. 1986).

[139]42 U.S.C. §1988.

[140]Lipsett v. University of P.R., *supra* note 135, 864 F.2d at 884 n.3, 54 FEP Cases at 232 (implied right of action clearly extends to claims for injunctive and declaratory relief).

[141]20 U.S.C. §1682.

[142]For citations to this and other elements of relief, see Schneider, *supra* note 134, 65 TEX. L. REV. at 572–74.

Courts have differed on whether private plaintiffs are entitled to monetary relief for Title IX violations.[143]

Title IX contains no statute of limitations. The appropriate statute of limitations to apply in Title IX Cases, as with §1983, is the relevant state statute of limitations for personal injury actions.[144]

VI. FEDERAL EMPLOYERS' LIABILITY ACT

In *Masiello v. Metro-North Commuter Railroad*,[145] a federal district court held that a female railroad engineer who alleged that she had been forcibly kissed, hugged, and grabbed by co-workers stated a claim against the railroad employer under the Federal Employers' Liability Act (FELA),[146] on a theory of the employer's negligent failure to prevent harm. Judge Charles Tenney held that the FELA claim was not preempted by Title VII: "merely because a plaintiff can bring a Title VII action should not bar her from bringing an action under the FELA."[147]

The Sixth Circuit, however, has upheld a summary judgment dismissing a FELA sexual harassment claim. Judge R. Allen Edgar noted that there was "no legislative history supporting the proposition that Congress in enacting the FELA [in 1908] had any thought of providing a remedy for racial or sexual harassment."[148]

VII. RACKETEER INFLUENCED AND CORRUPT ORGANIZATIONS ACT

The Racketeer Influenced and Corrupt Organizations Act (RICO)[149] can, under certain limited circumstances, be the basis of a civil action to redress sexual harassment.[150] The RICO statute prohibits one from operating an "enterprise" through a "pattern of racketeering activity."[151] "Racketeering activity"

---

[143]*Compare* Franklin v. Gwinnett County Public Schools, 911 F.2d 617, 619–22 (11th Cir. 1990)(private right of action under Title IX may exist, but does not include right to compensatory damages), *cert. granted,* 59 U.S.L.W. 3823 (June 10, 1991) *and* Lieberman v. University of Chicago, 660 F.2d 1185 (7th Cir. 1981)(damages not consistent with legislative purpose of Title IX) *and* Storey v. Board of Regents, 604 F. Supp. 1200 (D. Wis. 1985)(no implicit monetary or injunctive relief in employment-related discrimination under Title IX) *with* Beehler v. Jeffes, 664 F. Supp. 931, 939–40 (M.D. Pa. 1986)(money damages available under Title IX).

[144]Bougher v. University of Pittsburgh, *supra* note 126, 882 F.2d at 78.

[145]54 FEP Cases 172 (S.D.N.Y. 1990).

[146]45 U.S.C. §51 *et seq.*

[147]Supra note 145, 54 FEP Cases at 175.

[148]Griggs v. National R.R. Passenger Corp., 900 F.2d 74, 77, 52 FEP Cases 916, 917 (6th Cir. 1990)(FELA suit precluded by Title VII). In this case, the court reasoned that FELA protects railroad workers only from common-law torts and that permitting a FELA action for negligent failure to prevent sexual harassment would circumvent the administrative processes of Title VII. The *Masiello* court found this analysis in *Griggs* to be "unpersuasive." *Supra* note 145, 54 FEP Cases at 175.

[149]18 U.S.C. §§1961–1968 (1988).

[150]For a discussion of RICO as a theory of recovery for sexual harassment, see Dworkin, Ginger & Mallor, *Theories of Recovery for Sexual Harassment: Going Beyond Title VII,* 25 SAN DIEGO L. REV. 125, 158 (1988). A successful civil claim would provide for the recovery of treble damages, costs of suit, and reasonable attorney's fees.

[151]An "enterprise" would include a partnership or corporation or any group of individuals associated in fact. 18 U.S.C. §1961(4).

is not defined to include sexual activity of the sort involved in sexual harass-ment.[152] Nonetheless, in *Hunt v. Weatherbee*,[153] a female carpenter was able to maintain a civil RICO action against her union by alleging that union officials used a practice of sexual harassment to force the complainant and other female union members to support the union's political fund. The com-plainant alleged that union officers had committed the racketeering activities of extortion and obstruction of justice to force her to withdraw a state court sexual harassment complaint against a co-worker.

A sexual harassment claim of retaliatory discharge is not likely to be maintainable under RICO, even apart from any difficulty in meeting its techni-cal pleading requirements. Courts generally have held that employees lack standing under RICO to challenge the termination of their employment.[154]

VIII. FEDERAL TORT CLAIMS ACT

The Federal Tort Claims Act (FTCA)[154a] permits suits against the federal government for certain common-law torts that are committed by federal em-ployees acting within the scope of their employment, while shielding the employees themselves from personal liability for those torts.[154b] Whether the acts of the federal employee are within the scope of employment is determined by the law of *respondeat superior* of the state in which the wrongful conduct occurred.[154c] In *Wood v. United States*,[154d] a military secretary sued her boss, an Army major, for sexual harassment that allegedly included caresses in his office and an invitation to a hotel. Applying the local law of *respondeat superior,* the federal district court determined that the alleged acts were beyond the scope of employment, meaning that the United States was not liable under the FTCA, and that the Army major could be sued personally in tort and under a state fair employment practices statute.[154e]

---

[152]18 U.S.C. §1961(1). *See also* Puckett v. Tennessee Eastman Co., 889 F.2d 1481, 1489–90 (6th Cir. 1989)(affirming dismissal of civil RICO claim based on sexual harassment and employer's alleged cover-up; alleged interference with state fair employment practices agency investigating claims of sexual harassment did not qualify as "racketeering activity"); Fowler v. Burns Int'l Security Servs., 763 F. Supp. 862, 56 FEP Cases 38 (N.D. Miss. 1991)(reported in 112 DAILY LAB. REP. A-2 (June 11, 1991)(granting summary judgment against RICO claim of complainant alleging coerced sexual relations over nine-month period with supervisor in that activity did not qualify as predicate act of the crime of extortion).

[153]626 F. Supp. 1097, 39 FEP Cases 1469 (D. Mass. 1986).

[154]*E.g.,* Hecht v. Commerce Clearing House, 713 F. Supp. 72, 74–76 (S.D.N.Y. 1989)(employee allegedly fired for either protesting or refusing to participate in employer's fraudulent billing practices lacks RICO standing under either theory; discharge of employee who is not target of RICO violation lacks standing under RICO).

[154a]28 U.S.C. §2671 *et seq.*

[154b]Nasuti v. Scannell, 906 F.2d 802, 804 (1st Cir. 1990).

[154c]*Id.* at 805 n.3.

[154d]55 FEP Cases 1220 (D. Mass. 1991).

[154e]*Id.* at 1221–22. *Compare* Doe v. United States, 618 F. Supp. 503, 505 (D.S.C. 1984)(Air Force major's exposing himself and suggesting sexual acts while counseling complainant "far beyond the scope of his employment"), *aff'd,* 769 F.2d 174 (4th Cir. 1985) *and* Turner v. United States, 595 F. Supp. 708 (W.D. La. 1984)(Army employee acted beyond scope of employment in deceiving women joining Louisiana National Guard that they had to submit to complete physical examinations by him) *with* Simmons v. United States, 805 F.2d 1363 (9th Cir. 1986)(Indian Health Service counsel wrongfully entering into sexual relation-ship with complainant was acting within scope of employment).

IX. EXECUTIVE ORDER 11246

Executive Order 11246[155] prohibits discrimination in employment by certain federal contractors.[156] The Secretary of Labor has delegated enforcement of the order to the Office of Federal Contract Compliance Programs (OFCCP).[157]

A. Nondiscrimination and Affirmative Action Obligations

If a federal contractor or subcontractor is covered by the order, then it has a twofold obligation: (1) nondiscrimination in employment and (2) affirmative action to utilize women and minorities in the contractor's work force.[158] The nondiscrimination component resembles Title VII,[159] and it is OFCCP policy to apply Title VII principles in enforcing this aspect of the order.[160]

Neither the order nor its implementing regulations specifically discusses sexual harassment.[161] The OFCCP policy, however, is that the order imposes upon contractors an obligation to maintain a workplace free of unwelcome sexual conduct.[162]

Covered contractors and subcontractors must formulate and annually update a written affirmative action program,[163] which will include assurances that supervisory personnel will prevent harassment of employees "placed through affirmative action efforts."[164]

B. Enforcement of the Executive Order

Executive Order 11246 provides the Department of Labor with broad enforcement authority, which it exercises through administrative proceedings[165] that can result in a final agency order subject to judicial review under the

---

[155]3 C.F.R. §339 (1964–65 Compilation), reprinted as appendix to 42 U.S.C. §2000e, issued Sept. 24, 1965, as amended by Executive Order 11375, 32 FED. REG. 14303 (Oct. 13, 1967), and Executive Order 12086, 43 FED. REG. 46501 (Oct. 5, 1978). For a general discussion of the executive order, see B.L. SCHLEI & P. GROSSMAN, EMPLOYMENT DISCRIMINATION LAW (2d ed. 1983), Chapter 25.

[156]Federal executive orders relating to discrimination in employment date back 50 years. For a history, see *Contractors Ass'n v. Shultz,* 442 F.2d 159, 168–71 (3d Cir.), *cert. denied,* 404 U.S. 854 (1971). Executive Order 11246 as first issued did not prohibit sex discrimination, but was amended to include that issue in 1968. Executive Order 11375, *supra* note 155.

[157]41 C.F.R. §60-1.2.

[158]Both the order's nondiscrimination and affirmative action provisions apply to contractors, regardless of size, which have contracts of at least $10,000. 41 C.F.R. §60-1.5(a). In general, every facility of a covered contractor or subcontractor must follow the executive order even where that facility itself performs no work on the contract that gives rise to jurisdiction under the order. Executive Order 11246, §204, 41 C.F.R. §60-1.5.

[159]Indeed, pursuant to a Memorandum of Understanding between the two enforcement agencies, individual complaints of discrimination filed with the OFCCP under the executive order are referred to the EEOC for investigation and are treated as though they had been filed under Title VII. *See* 41 C.F.R. §60-1.24(a).

[160]OFCCP's policy statements appear in the Federal Contract Compliance Manual (FCCM), which was revised and reissued beginning in 1988. It provides that the OFCCP will look to Title VII "principles" in enforcing the order. FCCM 7-3.

[161]*See* OFCCP Sex Discrimination Guidelines, 41 C.F.R. Part 60-20.

[162]*E.g.,* OFCCP v. Florida Nat'l Bank, 85-OFC-6 (July 29, 1987). While not identifying sexual harassment as a separate violation, the FCCM discusses harassment as an example of the type of violation that OFCCP might confront during a compliance review or the complaint investigation. *See, e.g.,* FCCM 7-7.

[163]Contractors with 50 or more employees and a contract or subcontract of at least $50,000 must develop their plans within 120 days of the commencement of the contract. 41 C.F.R. §60-1.40(a) and (b).

[164]*See* 41 C.F.R. §60-2.22(a) and (b)(9). Similar language is contained in the regulations setting forth the obligations of construction contractors. 41 C.F.R. §60-4.3.

[165]41 C.F.R. §60-1.26.

Administrative Procedure Act.[166] Sanctions for violating the order include debarment from contract eligibility, termination or cancellation of existing contracts, and withholding of progress payments.[167]

Courts have held that aggrieved individuals have no private right of action either directly under the order or as a third-party beneficiary of the order.[168]

---

[166]5 U.S.C. §701 *et seq.*

[167]Executive Order 11246, *supra* note 154, §209(a); 41 C.F.R. §§60-1.27, 1.30, and 1.31.

[168]*E.g.,* Utley v. Varian Assocs., 811 F.2d 1279, 1284–86 (9th Cir. 1987)(no private judicial remedy to redress violation of executive order); Robinson v. Jacksonville Shipyards, 760 F. Supp. 1486, 1532 (M.D. Fla. 1991), reproduced in Chapter 2, Forms of Harassment (federal contractor not liable for sexual harassment under executive order or theory that complainant was third-party beneficiary of federal contract).

CHAPTER 12

FAIR EMPLOYMENT PRACTICES STATUTES

I. Overview

Fair employment practices (FEP) statutes exist in virtually every state. FEP statutes resemble Title VII in the scope of their prohibition of discrimination in employment, and in their creation of administrative agencies to enforce their statutory provisions.[1] Certain features of the FEP statutes, however, differ significantly from Title VII or otherwise merit special mention.

First, many state FEP agencies have the power to adjudicate employment discrimination claims.[2] Thus, an employer accused of violating an FEP statute may be required to submit to an administrative hearing, which can result in a judicially enforceable order of liability and award of damages.[3] The EEOC, by contrast, has limited power. It may seek to address violations of Title VII

---

[1]This chapter is not a comprehensive state-by-state survey of sexual harassment law; the approach here is thematic, with emphasis on common issues that arise from state statutory and regulatory schemes. For a state-by-state survey of sexual harassment law, see A. Conte, Sexual Harassment in the Workplace: Law and Practice, 281–409 (1990). For the language of state FEP statutes and regulations, see 8A, 8B Fair Empl. Prac. Man. (BNA), tab 53.

[2]*E.g., Cal.:* State Personnel Bd. v. FEHC, 39 Cal.3d 422, 428, 217 Cal. Rptr. 16, 19, 703 P.2d 354, 44 FEP Cases 1050 (1985)(commission "performs adjudicatory and rule-making functions");
Fla.: Florida Comm'n on Human Relations v. Human Dev. Center, 413 So.2d 1251, 1252 (Fla. Ct. App. 1982)(commission has "responsibility of investigating and adjudicating claims of employment discrimination");
Ill.: Jabbari v. Illinois Human Rights Comm'n, 173 Ill. App.3d 227, 123 Ill. Dec. 17, 527 N.E.2d 480, 483 (1988)(commission is adjudicatory agency); Lewis v. Collinsville, 158 Ill. App.3d 411, 110 Ill. Dec. 722, 511 N.E.2d 899, 900 (1987)(discrimination statute provides for investigation and adjudication of alleged human rights violations by state FEP agency);
Kan.: Bush v. City of Wichita, 223 Kan. 651, 576 P.2d 1071, 1076, 17 FEP Cases 720 (1978)("determination of probable cause is an investigatory function which must be satisfied before the commission may begin adjudicatory functions");
Md.: Soley v. State of Md. Comm'n on Human Relations, 277 Md. 521, 356 A.2d 254, 257 (1976)(word "proceedings" encompasses "both the investigative and adjudicative functions of an administrative agency"); Banach v. State of Md. Comm'n on Human Relations, 277 Md. 502, 356 A.2d 242, 30 FEP Cases 1829 (Md. 1976)(implicit in holding same);
Minn.: Travelers Indem. Co. v. Hayes Contractors, 389 N.W.2d 257 (Minn. Ct. App. 1986)(agency conducts hearing and, if finding discrimination, issues written findings, conclusions and an order, subject to judicial review);
Pa.: Pennsylvania Human Relations Comm'n v. Freeport Area School Dist., 359 A.2d 724, 727 (Pa. 1976)(implicit in holding that nothing in statute limits commission's power to investigate, conciliate, or adjudicate, depending upon source of complaint);
W. Va.: Allen v. Human Rights Comm'n, 324 S.E.2d 99, 120, 54 FEP Cases 2 (W. Va. 1984)(commission has mandatory duty to hold adjudicatory hearings within 180 days from date of filing of complaint).

[3]For a further discussion of state administrative proceedings, see Section V.A. *infra.*

by means of informal conciliation, and may itself sue in court to enforce a claimant's rights, but it has no adjudicative powers of its own.[4]

Second, many FEP statutes provide for compensatory and punitive damages in agency proceedings, in judicial actions, or in both, in addition to the limited equitable relief that is available in an action under Title VII.[5]

Third, many FEP statutes, unlike Title VII, cover some or all employers with fewer than fifteen employees.[6]

Fourth, the statutory language of many FEP statutes, unlike Title VII, specifically addresses sexual harassment.[7] The language of the 1980 EEOC Guidelines[8] has served as a model for numerous state statutes[9] as well as administrative regulations.[10] Even without that specific language, however, courts applying the sex discrimination provisions of FEP statutes have relied heavily on judicial interpretations of Title VII and the EEOC Guidelines,[11] so that virtually any FEP statute could be interpreted to encompass both the quid pro quo and the hostile environment theories of sexual harassment.[12]

---

[4]§706, 42 U.S.C. §2000e-5.

[5]See Section V.B. *infra.*

[6]For a collection of current state FEP statutes, see 8A FAIR EMPL. PRAC. MAN., *supra* note 1. *See also* statutes cited in note 75 *infra.*

[7]For citations to states whose rules, regulations, and executive orders specifically prohibit sexual harassment, see Note, *Inadequacies in Civil Rights Law: The Need for Sexual Harassment Legislation,* 48 OHIO ST. L.J. 1131, 1164 n.108 (1987). Maine has enacted a statute, effective June 21, 1991, that requires employee education and training programs to ensure a workplace free of sexual harassment. 1991 ME. LAWS ch. 474, to be codified at ME. REV. STAT. ANN. tit. 26, §806 (1991).

[8]29 C.F.R. §1604.11(a), reproduced in Appendix 1.

[9]*E.g.,* ILL. REV. STAT. 1987, ch. 68, ¶2-101(E)(1989); MASS. GEN. L. ch. 151B, §25(e)(1989); MICH. COMP. LAWS ANN. §37.2103(h)(West 1985); MINN. STAT. §363.01(10a)(1966 and Supp. 1990); N.D. CENT. CODE §14-02.4-02(3)(a)(Supp. 1987).

[10]For a comprehensive summary of statutes and regulations, see A. CONTE, *supra* note 1, and FAIR EMPL. PRAC. MAN., *supra* note 1.

[11]*E.g., Cal.:* Fisher v. San Pedro Peninsula Hosp., 214 Cal. App.3d 590, 262 Cal. Rptr. 842, 54 FEP Cases 584 (1989)(adopting elements of prima facie case of environmental sexual harassment from Title VII law);

Mich.: Rabidue v. Osceola Ref. Co., 805 F.2d 611, 42 FEP Cases 631 (6th Cir. 1986), reproduced in Chapter 2, Forms of Harassment (no violation of Michigan's FEP statute, modeled closely after Title VII, because no violation of Title VII), *cert. denied,* 481 U.S. 1041 (1987); Coley v. Consolidated Rail Corp., 561 F. Supp. 645, 34 FEP Cases 129 (E.D. Mich. 1982)(in finding violation of state FEP statute, court applied Title VII law); Langlois v. McDonald's Restaurants of Mich., 149 Mich. App. 309, 385 N.W.2d 778, 45 FEP Cases 134 (1986)(applied elements of Title VII prima facie case to state FEP claim);

Minn.: Continental Can Co. v. State of Minn., 297 N.W.2d 241, 22 FEP Cases 1808 (Minn. 1980)(court turned to federal law for guidance in deciding claim under Minnesota Human Rights Act); Klink v. Ramsey County, 397 N.W.2d 894, 43 FEP Cases 1476 (Minn. Ct. App. 1986)(adopting requirements of prima facie case of sexual harassment from Title VII law); Johnson v. Ramsey County, 424 N.W.2d 800, 46 FEP Cases 1686 (Minn. Ct. App. 1988)(applying Title VII test adopted in *Klink*);

N.J.: Drinkwater v. Union Carbide Corp., 904 F.2d 853 (3d Cir. 1990)(recognizing that New Jersey Supreme Court has not decided issue, court applied federal law to sexual harassment claim under New Jersey FEP statute); Porta v. Rollins Envtl. Servs., 654 F. Supp. 1275 (D.N.J. 1987)(applying federal law to state FEP claim);

N.Y.: Kersul v. Skulls Angels, 130 Misc.2d 345, 495 N.Y.S.2d 886, 42 FEP Cases 987 (N.Y. Sup. Ct. 1985)(sustaining sexual harassment claim based on EEOC Guidelines); Rudow v. New York City Comm'n on Human Rights, 123 Misc.2d 709, 474 N.Y.S.2d 1005, 41 FEP Cases 1402 (N.Y. Sup. Ct. 1984)(adopting federal law as applicable to state sexual harassment claims), *aff'd,* 487 N.Y.S.2d 453 (1985);

Wash.: Glasgow v. Georgia-Pacific Corp., 103 Wash.2d 401, 693 P.2d 708, 51 FEP Cases 880 (Wash. 1985)(adopting requirements of prima facie case from federal law); Fisher v. Tacoma School Dist., 53 Wash. App. 591, 769 P.2d 318 (Wash. Ct. App.)(applying Title VII test adopted in *Glasgow*), *review denied,* 112 Wash.2d 1027 (1989).

[12]*E.g., Cal.:* Fisher v. San Pedro Peninsula Hosp., *supra* note 11, 214 Cal. App.3d at 607, 262 Cal. Rptr. at 850 ("two distinct categories of sexual harassment claims: quid pro quo and hostile work environment");

Ill.: Board of Directors, Green Hills Country Club v. Illinois Human Rights Comm'n, 162 Ill. App.3d 216, 220, 113 Ill. Dec. 216, 514 N.E.2d 1227, 1230 (1987)(Illinois statute indicates employers liable for

Fifth, some FEP statutes broaden the scope of liability available under Title VII by subjecting persons to liability,[12a] by relaxing the plaintiff's burden of proof,[12b] and by making employers automatically liable for sexual harassment by supervisors, even in hostile environment situations.[13]

Sixth, FEP statutes sometimes preempt other state-law claims for employment discrimination, while Title VII expressly does not affect any state-law remedy.[14]

II. EXHAUSTION OF ADMINISTRATIVE REMEDIES

Courts vary with respect to whether aggrieved parties must exhaust their state FEP administrative remedies before commencing a judicial action for relief under the FEP statute. In California,[15] Illinois,[16] Kansas,[17] Maryland,[18] Massachusetts,[19] Montana,[20] and Pennsylvania,[21] exhaustion of administrative remedies is a prerequisite to an action under the FEP statute. In Michigan,

---

sexual harassment by supervisory personnel regardless of whether quid pro quo or hostile environment claim);
  Mich.: Langlois v. McDonald's Restaurants of Mich., *supra* note 11 (recognizing both theories);
  Wash.: Glasgow v. Georgia-Pacific Corp., *supra* note 11 (recognizing both theories).
  [12a]See note 80 *infra* and accompanying text.
  [12b]*See, e.g.,* Woods v. Graphic Communications, 925 F.2d 1195, 55 FEP Cases 242, 247 (9th Cir. 1991)(under Washington FEP statute, hostile environment need only be offensive to employee in question, not necessarily to reasonable person in employee's position).
  [13]See Section IV.B. *infra.* For a discussion of the standards used under Title VII, see Chapter 6, Harassment by Supervisors.
  [14]See Section III. *infra.*
  [15]*E.g.,* Peralta Community College Dist. v. FEHC, 52 Cal.3d. 40, 276 Cal. Rptr 114, 54 FEP Cases 1239 (1990)(exhaustion required for statutory FEP claim).
  [16]*E.g.,* Mein v. Masonite Corp., 124 Ill. App. 617, 619, 80 Ill. Dec. 154, 156, 464 N.E.2d 1137, 1139, 44 FEP Cases 188 (comprehensive remedies and administrative procedures indicate legislative intent that statute is exclusive source of redress for civil rights violations), *aff'd,* 109 Ill.2d 1, 92 Ill. Dec. 501, 44 FEP Cases 189, 191 (1985); Armstrong v. Freeman United Coal Mining Co., 112 Ill. App.3d 1020, 68 Ill. Dec. 1020, 446 N.E.2d 296, 37 FEP Cases 939 (1983)(claim under FEP statute dismissed for failure to exhaust administrative remedies). *Cf.* Williams v. Naylor, 147 Ill. App.3d 258, 100 Ill. Dec. 912, 497 N.E.2d 1274 (1986)(FEP statute bars direct action in court for discrimination in housing because of sex or marital status); Briggs v. Lawrenceville Indus., 136 Ill. App.3d 1073, 91 Ill. Dec. 788, 484 N.E.2d 347 (1985)(plaintiff must exhaust administrative remedies before bringing constitutional claim for sex discrimination in state court); Dilley v. Americana Healthcare Corp., 129 Ill. App.3d 537, 84 Ill. Dec. 636, 472 N.E.2d 596, 53 FEP Cases 1536 (1984)(plaintiff may not sue directly under constitution for discrimination without first exhausting administrative remedies set forth in FEP statute).
  [17]Van Scoyk v. St. Mary's Assumption Parochial School, 224 Kan. 304, 580 P.2d 1315 (1978)(in religious discrimination case, administrative remedies with commission must first be exhausted).
  [18]Maryland Comm'n on Human Relations v. Baltimore Gas & Elec. Co., 296 Md. 46, 459 A.2d 205 (Md. 1983)(unlawful employment practices case dismissed where action of administrative agency not final; administrative remedies must be exhausted); Maryland Comm'n on Human Relations v. Mass Transit Admin., 449 A.2d 385, 38 FEP Cases 1505 (Md. 1982)(handicap discrimination suit dismissed where administrative remedies not exhausted).
  [19]*Compare* Melley v. Gillette Corp., 19 Mass. App. 511, 475 N.E.2d 1227, 1228 (statute's "clear suggestion that a litigant is first to follow the administrative route accords with the usual requirement that administrative remedies are to be exhausted before resort is had to the courts"), *aff'd,* 491 N.E.2d 252 (1985) *and* Sereni v. Star Sportswear Mfg. Corp., 24 Mass. Ct. App. 428, 509 N.E.2d 1203, 53 FEP Cases 739 (1987)(no resort to courts permitted for age discrimination claim absent timely complaint to commission) *with* Christo v. Edward G. Boyle Ins. Agency, 402 Mass. 815, 525 N.E.2d 643 (1988)(although statutory scheme rejects principles of exhaustion of remedies, aggrieved party may maintain civil action only if timely complaint with commission previously filed, and either 90 days have passed or commissioner has assented to earlier filing).
  [20]Harrison v. Chance, 797 P.2d 200 (Mont. 1990)(statutory procedures to redress sexual harassment in workplace exclusive and cannot be bypassed); Romero v. J & J Tire, 777 P.2d 292, 50 FEP Cases 620 (Mont. 1989)(FEP statute requires complaint first with commission, which has 12 months to issue "right-to-sue" letter before aggrieved party may bring civil action).
  [21]Clay v. Advanced Computer Applications, 522 Pa. 86, 559 A.2d 917, 51 FEP Cases 346 (1989)(to assert civil action cognizable under FEP statute, aggrieved party must first utilize administrative remedies).

complainants have been able to use the administrative machinery and the court system simultaneously.[22] In Minnesota,[23] New Jersey,[24] New York,[25] and Oregon,[26] a complainant may elect between administrative and judicial remedies under the relevant FEP statute.

III. EXCLUSIVITY OF FEP STATUTES

A. FEP Preemption

Acts of sexual harassment may form the basis of several common-law causes of action available under state law. These claims include not only traditional torts such as battery and intentional infliction of emotional distress, but also the modern tort of discharge in breach of public policy. A sexual harassment complainant may invoke this public-policy tort in various situations: (1) the complainant is discharged for resisting sexual advances; (2) the complainant is discharged in retaliation for protesting sexual harassment; (3) the complainant is constructively discharged by sexual harassment that makes the work environment intolerable.[27]

Courts have grappled with the question of whether FEP statutes provide the exclusive state-law remedies for claims based upon acts constituting discrimination in employment. Employers typically argue that the FEP statute is intended to provide the exclusive remedy, and thus displaces any common-law tort action based on acts alleged to constitute employment discrimination. Complainants generally argue that FEP statutes have no effect on their common-law claims and simply provide a cumulative remedy.

---

[22]Walters v. Department of Treasury, 148 Mich. App. 809, 385 N.W.2d 695 (1986)(plaintiff may simultaneously pursue FEP sex discrimination claim in court and civil rights department); Hillman v. Consumers Power Co., 90 Mich. App. 627, 282 N.W.2d 422, 33 FEP Cases 498 (1979)(race or age discrimination plaintiff need not exhaust state administrative remedies before pursuing cumulative judicial remedy).

[23]Sigurdson v. Isanti County, 363 N.W.2d 476 (aggrieved individuals may redress alleged sex discrimination in judicial proceedings even though no charges filed with commission), *modified,* 386 N.W.2d 715 (Minn. Ct. App. 1985).

[24]Gray v. Serruto Builders, 110 N.J. Super. 297, 265 A.2d 404 (N.J. Sup. Ct. Ch. Div. 1970)(civil suit for racial discrimination in housing permitted under FEP statute even though proceeding with commission not instituted; jurisdiction with commission exclusive only when proceeding pending before it).

[25]Meschino v. IT&T Corp., 563 F. Supp. 1066, 34 FEP Cases 1634 (S.D.N.Y. 1983)(persons seeking redress of discrimination in employment may file judicial claim or administrative complaint, but not both); West v. Technical Aid Corp., 111 Misc.2d 23, 443 N.Y.S.2d 318, 34 FEP Cases 1668 (N.Y. App. Term. 1981)(person claiming to be aggrieved because of wrongful discharge for refusal to accede to sexual advances may elect between administrative and judicial remedies).

In New York, election of the administrative remedy is binding unless the complaint is dismissed on the ground of administrative convenience. Long v. AT&T Information Sys., 733 F. Supp. 188, 197 (S.D.N.Y. 1990)("direct filing of a complaint with the state division by the aggrieved party constitutes an election of remedies and results in the loss of the right to sue in state court"); Koster v. Chase Manhattan Bank, 609 F. Supp. 1191, 1196 (S.D.N.Y. 1985)(aggrieved individual has choice of judicial or administrative remedies but "may not, however, resort to both forums; having invoked one procedure, he has elected his remedies"); Goosley v. Binghamton City School Dist. Bd. of Educ., 101 A.D.2d 942, 475 N.Y.S.2d 924 (1984)(filing administrative complaint constitutes binding election of remedies, and civil suit permitted only when complaint dismissed upon ground of administrative convenience).

[26]Holien v. Sears, Roebuck & Co., 298 Or. 76, 689 P.2d 1292, 36 FEP Cases 137 (1984)(FEP statute does not require filing of administrative complaint as condition precedent to civil suit under the statute).

[27]For a discussion of common-law actions potentially available to a sexual harassment complainant, see Chapter 15, The Common Law.

B. Impact of Exclusivity

Where the FEP statute provides the exclusive remedy for an adverse employment action, the exclusivity of the FEP statutory remedy will have three potential consequences: (1) precluding *any* state-law claim, if the complainant has failed to perfect the FEP statutory claim; (2) confining the complainant to the sometimes limited remedies of the FEP statute; and (3) imposing on the complainant a different and possibly more difficult burden of proof.

1. Complete Preclusion

The potential impact of FEP exclusivity is greatest where the FEP statute makes the timely exhaustion of administrative remedies a prerequisite to a civil suit. A complainant who has forfeited an FEP statutory remedy (*e.g.*, by failing to make a timely claim or by failing to meet exhaustion requirements) would thereby be left without any state-law remedy.

2. Different Remedies

In states where the FEP statute, like Title VII, provides for only equitable relief, FEP exclusivity could deprive a sexual harassment complainant of the ability to seek the compensatory and punitive damages that would be available in a common-law tort action.[28]

By the same token, in states where an FEP claim would entitle a complainant to full, tort-like relief, the impact of the exclusivity doctrine is considerably diminished. For example, in Illinois, the FEP statute provides the exclusive remedies for employment discrimination, but those remedies include the compensatory damages that would be available in a tort action.[29] Similarly, although the Massachusetts FEP remedy is exclusive,[30] the FEP agency may award compensatory damages.[31]

3. Different Burden of Proof

FEP exclusivity may also be significant because of the burden of proof. A claim under the FEP statute may be more difficult to prove than a common-law claim based on the same conduct.[32]

C. Standards Used to Determine Exclusivity

In determining whether an FEP statute provides the exclusive state-law remedies for employment discrimination, courts have considered whether the

---

[28]*See, e.g.,* Agnello v. Adolph Coors Co., 695 P.2d 311 (Colo. Ct. App. 1984)(FEP remedies limited to equitable relief); Midland Heights Homes v. Pennsylvania Human Relations Comm'n, 387 A.2d 664 (Pa. 1978)(FEP agency lacks authority to award compensatory damages to persons injured by unlawful employment discrimination); Hannah v. Philadelphia Coca-Cola Bottling Co., 53 FEP Cases 9 (E.D. Pa. 1989)(claim for punitive damages may not be brought directly under Pennsylvania FEP statute).

[29]See text accompanying notes 57 and 104 *infra*.

[30]See text accompanying notes 61–62 *infra*.

[31]See text accompanying note 101 *infra*.

[32]"[T]he burden of proof for discrimination under the [FEP] statute is quite different from any existing common-law tort and has its own elements and presumptions." Helmick v. Cincinnati Word Processing, 45 Ohio St.3d 131, 543 N.E.2d 1212, 50 FEP Cases 1554, 1556 (Ohio 1989). For a discussion on proving common-law claims, see Chapter 15, The Common Law.

language and structure of the FEP statute is such that the legislature must have intended to occupy the field of regulation.[33] Courts are more likely to find FEP exclusivity for a sexual harassment claim where comprehensive remedies are available to a complainant under the FEP statute,[34] and less likely to find exclusivity where common-law remedies for sex discrimination predated the enactment of the FEP statute.[35]

D. Impact of Exclusivity on Traditional Common-Law Torts

Courts in many states have held that FEP statutes do not displace traditional common-law claims, such as claims for intentional and negligent infliction of emotional distress, assault, battery, negligence, intentional misrepresentation, invasion of privacy, and defamation, even in those states in which the FEP statute would displace a claim for discharge in violation of the public policy against employment discrimination.[36]

---

[33]*Cal.:* Ficalora v. Lockheed Corp., 193 Cal. App.3d 489, 238 Cal. Rptr. 360, 48 FEP Cases 817 (1987)(language of California FEP statute demonstrated legislature's intent to occupy entire field of employment discrimination); Robinson v. Hewlett-Packard Corp., 183 Cal. App.3d 1108, 228 Cal. Rptr. 591, 40 FEP Cases 819 (1986)(legislature expressly declared intent to occupy field of race discrimination law); Cook v. Lindsay Olive Growers, 911 F.2d 233 (9th Cir. 1990)(claim for wrongful discharge based on religion preempted in that legislature intended statute to provide exclusive remedy); *cf.* Rojo v. Kliger, 52 Cal.3d 65, 276 Cal. Rptr. 130, 54 FEP Cases 1146 (1990)(superseding analysis of above cases by reading statutory language differently);
Mont.: Harrison v. Chance, *supra* note 20, 797 P.2d at 203 (language of FEP statute establishes statute as exclusive remedy for acts constituting alleged violation of statute);
Pa.: Clay v. Advanced Computer Applications, *supra* note 21 (legislature intended statute to provide exclusive remedy).
[34]*Compare* Strauss v. A.L. Randall, 144 Cal. App.3d 514, 194 Cal. Rptr. 520, 37 FEP Cases 1531 (1983)(California FEP statute provides comprehensive remedy to redress age discrimination) *and* Ficalora v. Lockheed Corp., *supra* note 33 (California's FEP statute must be exclusive in that statute provides comprehensive remedy) *and* Mouradian v. General Elec. Co., 23 Mass. App. Ct. 538, 503 N.E.2d 1318 (1987)(no common-law action for wrongful discharge because of age in that FEP statute provides comprehensive remedial scheme) *and* Melley v. Gillette Corp., 19 Mass. App. 511, 475 N.E.2d 1227 (1985)(employee could not bring action against employer for wrongful termination on basis of age in that creation of common-law claim would interfere with comprehensive remedial scheme) *with* Holien v. Sears, Roebuck & Co., *supra* note 26 (by providing only equitable relief, statute fails to make plaintiff whole). The California cases are persuasive only for the general approach they follow, for the California Supreme Court in *Rojo v. Kliger, supra* note 33, has superseded their analyses by holding that the California FEP statute by its very terms was intended only to provide a cumulative remedy.
[35]Strauss v. A.L. Randall, *supra* note 34 (no common-law claim for wrongful discharge based on age in that California's FEP statute was sole source of public policy against age discrimination; FEP statute and public policy against age discrimination coeval). *Cf.* Merrell v. All Seasons Resorts, 720 F. Supp. 815, 52 FEP Cases 1412 (C.D. Cal. 1989)(California's FEP statute does not preempt claim for wrongful discharge based on pregnancy because private right to redress sex discrimination predated that statute); Froyd v. Cook, 681 F. Supp. 669, 48 FEP Cases 808 (E.D. Cal. 1988)(plaintiff could bring claim for wrongful discharge based on sexual harassment in that source of public policy against sex discrimination predated California's FEP statute). The California Supreme Court in *Rojo v. Kliger, supra* note 33, superseded this analysis for purposes of the California FEP statute by ruling that the express terms of that statute disclaim any intent that the FEP remedies be exclusive.
[36]*E.g., Ill.:* Ritzheimer v. Insurance Counselors, 173 Ill. App.3d 953, 123 Ill. Dec. 506, 527 N.E.2d 1281 (1988)(FEP statute does not preclude claim for intentional infliction of emotional distress); Bailey v. Unocal Corp., 700 F. Supp. 396 (N.D. Ill. 1988)(same); Clay v. Quartet Mfg. Co., 644 F. Supp. 56, 45 FEP Cases 51 (N.D. Ill. 1986)(claims for intentional infliction of emotional distress and battery rooted in allegations of sexual harassment not preempted);
Ind.: Fields v. Cummins Emp. Fed. Credit Union, 540 N.E.2d 631, 53 FEP Cases 1613 (Ind. Ct. App. 1989)(claims for assault, battery, infliction of emotional distress, and interference with advantageous business relationship not preempted by FEP statute);
Mich.: Melsha v. Wickes Cos., 459 N.W.2d 707 (Mich. Ct. App. 1990)(negligent infliction of emotional distress claim based on same facts as sexual harassment claim improper);
Minn.: Wirig v. Kinney Shoe Corp., 461 N.W.2d 374, 54 FEP Cases 352, 355 (Minn. 1990)(battery claim not preempted by FEP statutory sexual harassment action, although double recovery not permitted);
Ohio: Helmick v. Cincinnati Word Processing, *supra* note 32 (tort claims for intentional and negligent

E. Impact of Exclusivity on Wrongful Discharge in Breach of Public Policy Against Sexual Harassment

Cases specifically deciding whether FEP remedies supplant a public-policy claim of sexual harassment are rare.[37] Guidance nonetheless exists in state court opinions that address the exclusivity of FEP remedies in related contexts, such as claims of employment discrimination on the basis of pregnancy, race, or religion. No basis exists to distinguish these claims from sexual harassment claims if the court holds broadly that the legislature intended, or did not intend, the FEP statute to provide the exclusive remedies for discrimination in employment. The same is true if a court's decision turns on whether the FEP remedies are deemed to be inadequate. Analysis of a sexual harassment claim may merit special treatment, however, if the determination of exclusivity hinges on whether the public policy relied upon predated the enactment of the FEP statute and created a private right of action for sexual harassment.[38]

Courts in various states have split on whether an FEP statute preempts a complainant's allegations that a discriminatory discharge was in violation of state public policy. Below is a summary of developments that have occurred in a few representative states.

1. Arizona

The Arizona FEP statute does not foreclose a common-law claim for wrongful discharge in violation of the public policy against sexual harassment. In *Broomfield v. Lundell*,[39] the court permitted a claim for tortious wrongful discharge because of pregnancy, on the basis that pregnancy discrimination violates public policy as established by the Arizona FEP statute.[40] The *Broomfield* court noted that the FEP statute had no express language indicating that the statutory remedy was exclusive.[41]

---

infliction of emotional distress, assault and battery, invasion of privacy, and defamation not preempted);

Or.: Kofoid v. Woodard Hotels, 78 Or. App. 283, 716 P.2d 771, 775 (1986)(claim for intentional infliction of emotional distress resulting from wrongful discharge not precluded simply because defendant's conduct also may have violated state FEP statute);

Pa.: Fawcett v. IDS Fin. Servs., 41 FEP Cases 589 (W.D. Pa. 1986)(where former employee claimed that supervisor made physical advances and conditioned employment on submission to sexual relations with him, claims for assault, battery, negligence, and intentional misrepresentation not foreclosed by state FEP statute); Schaffer v. National Can Corp., 35 FEP Cases 840 (E.D. Pa. 1984)(FEP statute did not foreclose claim for intentional infliction of emotional distress by employee who resigned to avoid supervisor's sexual harassment);

Wis.: Beck v. Automatic Garage Door Co., 156 Wis.2d 409, 456 N.W.2d 888, 890 (Wis. Ct. App. 1990)(battery claim not preempted by FEP statute; "irrelevant" that complainant could have also pursued a statutory claim).

But see Mont.: Harrison v. Chance, *supra* note 20, 797 P.2d at 205 (because gravamen of tort claims for battery, intentional infliction of emotional distress, wrongful discharge, and implied covenant of good faith and fair dealing was sexual harassment, FEP statute provides exclusive remedy).

[37]For a case deciding not to decide, see *Erickson v. Marsh & McLennan Co.,* 117 N.J. 539, 569 A.2d 793, 55 FEP Cases 1179 (1990), where the New Jersey Supreme Court reserved the issue of whether the New Jersey FEP statute provides the exclusive remedy for wrongful discharge based on sexual harassment, noting that it might be unnecessary to create a common-law wrongful discharge action.

[38]*See* cases cited in note 35 *supra.*

[39]159 Ariz. 349, 767 P.2d 697 (1988)(common-law tort action for wrongful discharge of scrub nurse allegedly discharged because of pregnancy not preempted by Arizona FEP statute).

[40]ARIZ. REV. STAT. ANN. §41-1401 *et seq.*

[41]*Supra* note 39, 159 Ariz. at 356, 767 P.2d at 704.

2. California

In *Rojo v. Kliger*,[42] the California Supreme Court superseded several lower-court and federal court decisions on FEP preemption. These decisions generally had held that the California FEP statute preempted various common-law claims. The *Rojo* court, interpreting the language of the FEP statute,[43] held that it expressly disclaims any intention to preempt state-law claims for sexual harassment.

Prior interpretations of California law are of interest for their reasoning that the same FEP statute provided the exclusive state-law remedies for employment discrimination. In *Strauss v. A.L. Randall*,[44] a California appellate court had held that a plaintiff suing for age discrimination does not have a common-law claim for tortious wrongful discharge in breach of public policy.[45] The court reasoned that the FEP statute was the sole source of any public policy against age discrimination; prior to the FEP statute California had no public policy against discrimination on the basis of age. The court noted also that the FEP statute provides comprehensive remedies for age discrimination. The factor of comprehensive remedies was particularly important in *Ficalora v. Lockheed Corp.*,[46] in which another appellate court had held that the FEP statute displaced a common-law tort claim for retaliation, even if a public policy predating the FEP statute had already prohibited retaliation.[47] The court read the FEP statute to demonstrate the legislature's intent to occupy the entire field of employment discrimination.[48] The court concluded that the statutory remedy must be exclusive because the statute not only expressed the public policy but supplied a remedy to redress discrimination.[49]

The reasoning of *Ficalora* was rejected by a federal district court in *Froyd v. Cook*,[50] where a police dispatcher claimed that she was fired for rejecting the sexual advances of a police sergeant. The court applied the same "cumulative remedy doctrine" applied in *Strauss* but reached a different result in the context of sexual harassment. The court observed that long before the California FEP statute, California's constitution forbade employment discrimination on the basis of sex.[51] Thus, because the cumulative remedy doctrine provides that a statutory remedy is merely cumulative for a right established before the statutory remedy existed,[52] enactment of the FEP statute "provided a

---

[42]*Supra* note 33.

[43]CAL. GOV'T CODE §12900 *et seq.*

[44]*Supra* note 34.

[45]Discharges in breach of public policy generally are actionable in California. Tameny v. Atlantic Richfield Co., 27 Cal.3d 167, 164 Cal. Rptr. 839, 610 P.2d 1330 (1980)(plaintiff allegedly fired for refusing to participate in illegal price-fixing may sue employer in tort).

[46]*Supra* note 33.

[47]*Id.* at 492, 238 Cal. Rptr. at 362, 48 FEP Cases at 818–19. *Cf.* Carmichael v. Alfano Temporary Personnel, 223 Cal. App.3d 363, 272 Cal. Rptr. 737 (1990)("retaliation claims did not exist at common-law and hence are governed exclusively by the FEHA").

[48]*Id.,* 193 Cal. App.3d at 492, 238 Cal. Rptr. at 361, 48 FEP Cases at 818 (construing CAL. GOV'T CODE §12993(c)). *See also* cases cited in note 34 *supra.*

[49]*Id.* at 493, 238 Cal. Rptr. at 361, 48 FEP Cases at 819.

[50]*Supra* note 35.

[51]*Id.* at 673, 48 FEP Cases at 811.

[52]*Id.* at 674, 48 FEP Cases at 812.

cumulative remedy and did not displace a plaintiff's right to sue under California's doctrine of wrongful discharge."[53]

3. Hawaii

A discharge because of sexual harassment does not appear to be actionable as a tort in Hawaii. Several federal judges, interpreting Hawaii law, have held that the tort of discharge in breach of public policy, which Hawaii recognizes as a general matter, does not apply in an employment discrimination case. Thus, in *Lapinad v. Pacific Oldsmobile-GMC*,[54] Judge Alan Kay dismissed the wrongful-discharge claim of a management trainee who alleged that she had been fired for reporting that a manager had grabbed her breast and buttock. Judge Kay reasoned that the "public policy" exception to the employment-at-will doctrine does not apply where "the statutory or regulatory provisions which evidence the public policy themselves provide a remedy for the wrongful discharge."[55] Thus, the plaintiff could not rely on the antiharassment policies of either Title VII or the Hawaii FEP statute for a common-law tort claim because these statutes already provided a remedy for breaches of those policies.[56]

4. Illinois

Complainants in Illinois presumably are barred from suing in tort for wrongful discharge based on sexual harassment. In *Mein v. Masonite Corp.*,[57] the plaintiff sued for wrongful discharge in violation of the state's public policy against age discrimination. The Illinois Supreme Court, reasoning that the legislature intended the FEP statute, with its comprehensive scheme of administrative procedures and remedies, to be the exclusive source of redress for human rights violations, concluded that the plaintiff could not state a common-law claim for wrongful discharge.

5. Maryland

A common-law claim for wrongful discharge based on sexual harassment is probably foreclosed by Maryland law. A Maryland appellate court held in *Makovi v. Sherwin-Williams*[58] that the tort of abusive discharge based on pregnancy is foreclosed because the public policy sought to be vindicated is expressed in the Maryland FEP statute, which provides a remedy for sex

---

[53]*Id.* at 677, 48 FEP Cases at 814. *See also* Merrell v. All Seasons Resorts, *supra* note 35 (FEP statute does not preempt claim for wrongful discharge on basis of pregnancy; private rights to redress sex discrimination predated statute, pregnancy discrimination is form of sex discrimination, and language of statute does not "preempt" common-law claims).

[54]679 F. Supp. 991, 50 FEP Cases 752 (D. Haw. 1988).

[55]*Id.* at 993.

[56]*See also* Hew-Len v. F.W. Woolworth, 737 F. Supp. 1104, 1106–8 (D. Haw. 1990)(claim of discharge because of sexual harassment not actionable as "public policy" tort in that employment discrimination statute is sufficient in itself); Lui v. Intercontinental Hotels Corp., 634 F. Supp. 684, 688, 47 FEP Cases 99, 102 (D. Haw. 1986)(claim for constructive discharge based on sexual harassment barred for failure to file action under FEP statute).

[57]109 Ill.2d 1, 92 Ill. Dec. 501, 485 N.E.2d 312, 44 FEP Cases 189 (1985).

[58]316 Md. 603, 561 A.2d 179 (1989).

discrimination. Maryland appellate courts have twice addressed exclusivity in the context of sexual harassment. The plaintiff in *Chappell v. Southern Maryland Hospital*[59] claimed that he was wrongfully discharged because he insisted that the hospital take steps to stop sexual harassment. The court denied his claim, reasoning that the tort remedy of wrongful discharge was not available where statutory remedies already existed under state and federal law. In *Peoples Security Life Insurance Co. v. Watson*,[60] the plaintiff allegedly was fired in retaliation for her sexual harassment suit. The court held that the plaintiff failed to cite any clear mandate of public policy that prohibited the private employer from discharging the plaintiff. Thus, the court held that "the necessary predicate" to a claim of wrongful discharge was lacking.

6. Massachusetts

The reasoning of the court in *Melley v. Gillette Corp.*[61] forecloses a tort claim for wrongful discharge in violation of the public policy against sexual harassment. In refusing to permit a common-law age discrimination claim, the *Melley* court stated that the justification for recognizing a common-law action is that no other remedy exists to vindicate the public policy. Because Massachusetts has a comprehensive FEP statute against employment discrimination, the court decided that recognizing an additional common-law remedy was unnecessary and would only interfere with the remedial scheme.[62]

7. Montana

The Supreme Court of Montana held in *Harrison v. Chance*[63] that the state FEP statute provides the exclusive remedy for sexual harassment, reasoning that the timing of the passage of the exclusive remedy provision, as well as the plain language of the statute, indicates that the legislature intended the FEP statute to provide an exclusive remedy for discrimination in employment.

8. Ohio

Although the issue has not been decided directly, a common-law claim for wrongful discharge based on sexual harassment could be barred by Ohio law as a "pure employment discrimination claim." In *Helmick v. Cincinnati Word Processing*,[64] the Supreme Court of Ohio considered whether the Ohio FEP statute barred common-law remedies for sexual misconduct in the workplace. The complainants, who were not discharged, alleged claims for tortious interference with contract, intentional infliction of emotional distress, assault and battery, invasion of privacy, and defamation. Concluding that the statute provided a cumulative, not exclusive, remedy for these claims, the court reasoned

---

[59]320 Md. 483, 578 A.2d 766, 55 EPD ¶40,502 (1990).

[60]81 Md. App. 420, 568 A.2d 835 (1990).

[61]19 Mass. App. 511, 475 N.E.2d 1227, *aff'd*, 491 N.E.2d 252 (1985).

[62]*See also* Mouradian v. General Elec. Co., 23 Mass. App. Ct. 538, 503 N.E.2d 1318 (claim for wrongful discharge based on age foreclosed by *Melley*), *review denied*, 399 Mass. 1105, 507 N.E.2d 1056 (1987).

[63]797 P.2d 200, 203 (Mont. 1990)(statute stated that it provides "exclusive remedy for acts constituting an alleged violation" and that no other claim "based upon such acts may be entertained by a district court").

[64]45 Ohio St.3d 131, 543 N.E.2d 1212, 50 FEP Cases 1554 (1989).

that nothing in the statutory language or legislative history barred these common-law remedies, that the burden of proof under the FEP statute would be different, and that the FEP statute provided only for equitable relief at the time that the action was commenced. However, the court stated that the statute should provide the exclusive remedy for "pure" employment discrimination claims.[65]

9. Oregon

A complainant in Oregon who has been discharged for resisting a supervisor's sexual advances may bypass the FEP statute and proceed under the common-law tort of wrongful discharge, where the tort is based on a public policy against retaliatory discharge and possibly also where it is based on a public policy against sexual harassment. In *Holien v. Sears, Roebuck & Co.*,[66] the plaintiff alleged that her rejection of her supervisor's sexual advances ultimately resulted in her discharge. Holding that the plaintiff could maintain a common-law action for wrongful discharge, the Oregon Supreme Court reasoned that "an employee has a legal right which is of important public interest not to be discharged for resisting sexual harassment on the job."[67] The court added, however, that "it is not the supervisor's demand, or discriminatory sexual harassment, for which plaintiff seeks common-law tort damages; it is for a tortious discharge following her rightful resistance to those demands or harassment."[68]

In holding further that the common-law wrongful discharge claim was not displaced by the FEP statute, the *Holien* court saw no basis "to conclude that the legislature either was aware of a common-law remedy or intended to eliminate it and substitute a statutory suit for equitable relief."[69] The court also noted that the FEP statute, by providing only equitable relief, fails to make the plaintiff whole.[70]

Lower courts have limited the holding of *Holien* to retaliation claims. In *Kofoid v. Woodard Hotels*,[71] a waitress alleging discriminatory discharge because of her sex could not maintain a tort action on that basis. Conceding that *Holien* permits a "tort action for wrongful discharge,"[72] the Oregon appellate court in *Kofoid* noted that *Holien* did not recognize a common-law action when the only claimed basis for the discharge was the sex of the plaintiff.[73]

---

[65]*Id.*, 50 FEP Cases at 1556.

[66]298 Or. 76, 689 P.2d 1292, 36 FEP Cases 137 (1984).

[67]*Id.* at 90, 689 P.2d at 1300, 36 FEP Cases at 143. *See also* Dias v. Sky Chefs, 919 F.2d 1370, 54 FEP Cases 852, 854 (9th Cir. 1990)(affirming $625,000 jury verdict under Oregon law for plaintiff wrongfully discharged after resisting sexual harassment), *vacated on other grounds*, 111 S.Ct. 2791 (1991); Carlson v. Crater Lake Lumber Co., 103 Or. App. 190, 796 P.2d 1216 (1990)(court erred in granting summary judgment against employee's claim for wrongful discharge for resistance to sexual harassment).

[68]Holien v. Sears, Roebuck & Co., *supra* note 66.

[69]*Id.*, 298 Or. at 96, 689 P.2d at 1303, 36 FEP Cases at 145. The court first purported to determine whether the legislature intended to abrogate a common-law remedy for retaliatory discharge, but later shifted the focus of its analysis and found that the statute provides an additional remedy for wrongful sex discrimination.

[70]*Id.* at 97, 689 P.2d at 1303–4, 36 FEP Cases at 146.

[71]78 Or. App. 283, 716 P.2d 771 (1986).

[72]*Id.* at 286, 716 P.2d at 774.

[73]*Id. See also* Cross v. Eastlund, 103 Or. App. 138, 796 P.2d 1214 (1990)(although noting that the *Kofoid* court's distinction of *Holien* "appears thin," court held plaintiff had no common-law claim for wrongful discharge based on pregnancy). Under the distinction, a complainant in Oregon would have no

The *Kofoid* court thus distinguished *Holien* on the basis that the claim of the plaintiff in *Kofoid* was that she was fired not "for pursuing a private right, but because she is a female."[74]

10. Pennsylvania

In *Clay v. Advanced Computer Applications*,[75] where the plaintiff allegedly was fired for rebuffing a manager's sexual advances, the Pennsylvania Supreme Court held that the FEP statute "provides a statutory remedy that precludes assertion of a common-law tort action for wrongful discharge based upon discrimination."[76]

IV. SCOPE OF EMPLOYER LIABILITY

A. Who Can Be Sued as a Defendant

Most FEP statutes generally apply to public and private employers, employment agencies, and labor organizations.[77] Certain small employers, religious organizations, domestic employers, and family employers may be excluded from coverage by the statute,[78] but many FEP statutes, unlike Title VII,

---

public-policy claim for a sexually hostile environment but would have such a claim if fired for resisting that environment.

[74]*Supra* note 71, 78 Or. App. at 287, 716 P.2d at 774.

[75]522 Pa. 86, 559 A.2d 917, 918, 51 FEP Cases 346, 347 (Pa. 1989).

[76]*See also* Wolk v. Saks Fifth Avenue, 728 F.2d 221, 34 FEP Cases 193 (3d Cir. 1984)(under Pennsylvania law, no common-law tort cause of action to redress retaliation for refusal to submit to sexual advances); Aquino v. Sommer Maid Creamery, 657 F. Supp. 208, 45 FEP Cases 796 (E.D. Pa. 1987)(FEP statute provides exclusive state remedy for wrongful discharge based on sex discrimination); Hooten v. Pennsylvania College of Optometry, 601 F. Supp. 1151, 36 FEP Cases 1826 (E.D. Pa. 1984)(FEP statute is exclusive remedy for sexual harassment discrimination and that remedy forfeited by filing civil action); Shaffer v. National Can Corp., 565 F. Supp. 909, 913, 34 FEP Cases 172, 176 (E.D. Pa. 1983)(FEP statute supplants claim for wrongful discharge based on sexual harassment).

[77]*See* ALASKA STAT. §18.80.220 (1986 & Supp. 1988)(also including communications media); ARIZ. REV. STAT. ANN. §41-1463 (1985 & Supp. 1988); CAL. GOV'T CODE §12940 (West 1987 & Supp. 1990); COLO. REV. STAT. §24-34-402 (1988); CONN. GEN. STAT. ANN. §46a-60 (West Supp. 1986 & 1989); DEL. CODE ANN. tit. 19, §711 (1985 & Supp. 1988); D.C. CODE ANN. §1-2512 (1987 & Supp. 1988); FLA. STAT. ANN. §760.10 (West 1986 & Supp. 1989); HAW. REV. STAT. §378-2 (1985 & Supp. 1988); IDAHO CODE ANN. §67-5909 (1980 & Supp. 1988); ILL. ANN. STAT. ch. 68, §2-102 (Smith-Hurd 1989); IND. CODE ANN. §22-9-1-3 (Burns 1986 & Supp. 1988); IOWA CODE §§601A.2, 601A.6 (West 1988 & Supp. 1989); KAN. STAT. ANN. §44-1002(b)(1986 & Supp. 1988)(also including organizations engaged in social work); KY. REV. STAT. §344.040–.060. (Michie/Bobbs Merrill 1983 & Supp. 1988); LA. REV. STAT. ANN. §23-1006 (1985 & Supp. 1989); ME. REV. STAT. ANN. tit. V, §§4553, 4572 (1979 & Supp. 1988); MD. ANN. CODE art. 49B, §§15, 16 (1986 & Supp. 1988); MASS. GEN. L. ch. 151B, §4 (Mass./Law. Co-op. 1976 & Supp. 1989); MICH. COMP. LAWS §§37.2202–.2204 (1985); MINN. STAT. §§363.01, 363.03 (West 1966 & Supp. 1989); MO. ANN. STAT. §213.055 (Vernon 1983 & Supp. 1989); MONT. CODE ANN. §§49-2-303, 49-2-308 (1987); NEB. REV. STAT. §§48-1102,A 48-1104, 48-1106 (1988); NEV. REV. STAT. §613-330 (1987); N.H. REV. STAT. §354-A:8 (1984 & Supp. 1988); N.J. REV. STAT. §§10:5-5, 10:5-12 (1976 & Supp. 1988); N.M. STAT. ANN. §§28-1-2, 28-1-7 (1987 & Supp. 1988); N.Y. EXEC. LAW §296 (McKinney 1982 & Supp. 1989); N.D. CENT. CODE §§14-02.403–.405, (Supp. 1987); OHIO REV. CODE ANN. §§4112.01(2), 4112.02 (1980 & Supp. 1988); OKLA. STAT. ANN. tit. 25, §§1301(1), 1302–6 (West 1987 & Supp. 1989); OR. REV. STAT. §§659.010(6), 659.030 (1989); 43 PA. CONS. STAT. ANN. §§954(b), 955 (Purdon 1964 & Supp. 1988); R.I. GEN. LAWS §§28-5-6(B) to -7 (1986 & Cum. Supp. 1989); S.C. CODE ANN. §1-13-80 (1986); S.D. CODIFIED LAWS ANN. §§20-13-10 to -12 (1987 & Supp. 1988); TENN. CODE ANN. §§4-21-102(4), 4-21-401 to -404 (1985 & Supp. 1988); TEX. REV. CIV. STAT. ANN. art. 5221K, §§2.01(5), 5.01–.05 (Vernon 1987); UTAH CODE ANN. §§34-35-2, 34-35-6 (1988 & Supp. 1989); VT. STAT. ANN. tit. 21, §§495, 495d (1987 & Supp. 1988); WASH. REV. CODE ANN. §§49.60.040, 49.60.180–.200 (1962 & Supp. 1988–89); W. VA. CODE §§5-11-3(d), 5-11-9 (1987 & Supp. 1988); WIS. STAT. ANN. §§111.32(6)(a), 111.322, 111.325 (1988); WYO. STAT. §§27-9-102(2), 105 (1987).

[78]*E.g.,* ALASKA STAT. §§18.80.300(2)–(3)(1986 & Supp. 1988)(excluding social clubs, nonprofit religious, fraternal, charitable, or educational organizations, and domestic employment); ARIZ. REV. STAT. ANN. §§41-1461(1)–(2)(1985 & Supp. 1988)(excluding employers with fewer than 15 employees, noncivil-service

cover at least some employers with fewer than fifteen employees.[79] California's FEP statute covers not only the traditional respondents but any "person" (including a vendor or a customer) who engages in sexual harassment of an employee or applicant.[80]

B. Employer Liability for Supervisor Harassment

States differ on whether an employer is liable for sexual harassment by a supervisor when upper management neither knew nor should have known of the harassing activities. Several state courts have held that an employer is automatically liable for supervisory harassment regardless of whether it is the quid pro quo or hostile environment variety. Under the Illinois FEP statute, which forbids "any employer, employee, agent of any employer, employment agency or labor organization to engage in sexual harassment,"[81] an employer was held automatically liable because its club manager used lewd and derogatory language and made unwelcome sexual propositions to a waitress.[82] The court interpreted the Illinois statute to make employers automatically liable for sexual harassment of employees by supervisory personnel.[83] Similarly, under interpretations of the FEP statutes of California[84] and Massachusetts,[85] an

---

staff of elected public officials, the United States, Native American tribes, and private membership clubs); CAL. GOV'T CODE §12940(h)(West 1987 & Supp. 1990)(covering all employers in cases of sexual harassment, regardless of size, and excluding nonprofit religious organizations only); COLO. REV. STAT. §§24-34-401(2)–(3) (1988)(excluding certain religious organizations and domestic service); CONN. GEN. STAT. ANN. §§46a-51(9), (10)(West Supp. 1986 & 1989)(excluding employers of fewer than three persons, employment by parent, spouse, or child, and domestic employment); FLA. STAT. ANN. §760.02(6)(West 1986 & Supp. 1989)(excluding employers with fewer than 15 employees); HAW. REV. STAT. §378-1 (1985 & Supp. 1988)(excluding domestic employment and the United States); ILL. ANN. STAT. ch. 68, §§2-101(A)–(B)(Smith-Hurd 1989)(excluding employers with fewer than 15 employees, elected public officials, principal administrative officers of governmental bodies, domestic service, nonprofit religious organizations and persons in certain rehabilitation programs); LA. REV. STAT. ANN. §23-1006 (1985 & Supp. 1989)(excluding employers of fewer than 15 employees, private educational or religious institutions or nonprofit corporations and certain religion-affiliated organizations); MD. ANN. CODE. art. 49B, §15 (1986 & Supp. 1988)(excluding employers of fewer than 15 employees, bona fide membership clubs and certain noncivil-service employees); MASS. GEN. L. ch. 151B, §1.5 (Mass./Law. Co-op. 1976 & Supp. 1989)(excluding employers of fewer than six employees and nonprofit clubs and fraternal organizations); MICH. COMP. LAWS §37.2202(3)(1985)(excluding family members); MINN. STAT. §363.02(1)(West 1966 & Supp. 1989)(excluding employment by certain family members and domestic employment); MONT. CODE ANN. §49-2-101(8)(1987)(excluding certain nonprofit fraternal, charitable, and religious organizations); N.J. REV. STAT. §10:5-5(f)(1976 & Supp. 1988)(excluding domestic employment and employment by parent, spouse, or child); N.Y. EXEC. LAW §292(5) (McKinney 1982 & Supp. 1989)(excluding employers of fewer than four employees and domestic employment); OHIO REV. CODE ANN. §§4112.01(2), (3)(1980 & Supp. 1988)(excluding employers of fewer than four employees and domestic service); OR. REV. STAT. §659.010(5)(1989)(excluding domestic service and close family members); 43 PA. CONS. STAT. ANN. §954 (Purdon 1964 & Supp. 1988)(excluding employers of fewer than four employees, employment by certain family members, religious organizations, agricultural work, domestic employment, and persons residing in employer's residence as part of employment); TEX. REV. CIV. STAT. ANN. art. 5221K, §§2.01, 5.06 (Vernon 1987)(excluding employers with fewer than 15 employees, certain public officials and appointees, employment by parent, spouse, or child); WASH. REV. CODE ANN. §49.60.040 (1962 & Supp. 1988–89)(excluding employers of fewer than eight persons, nonprofit religious organizations, employment by parent, spouse, or child, and domestic employment).

[79]See note 78 *supra*.
[80]CAL. GOV'T CODE §12940(h).
[81]ILL. REV. STAT. ch. 68, ¶2-102(D)(1989).
[82]Board of Directors, Green Hills Country Club v. Illinois Human Rights Comm'n, 162 Ill. App.3d 216, 113 Ill. Dec. 216, 514 N.E.2d 1227 (1987).
[83]*Id.* at 220, 514 N.E.2d at 1230.
[84]Fisher v. San Pedro Peninsula Hosp., 214 Cal. App.3d 590, 608 n.6, 262 Cal. Rptr. 842, 851, 54 FEP Cases 584 (1989)(employer strictly liable for harassing conduct of agents and supervisor).
[85]College-Town v. Massachusetts Comm'n Against Discrimination, 400 Mass. 156, 508 N.E.2d 587,

employer is automatically liable for the harassing conduct of its agents and supervisors.

Other state courts have rejected automatic employer liability in hostile environment cases. Employer liability under the Michigan FEP statute follows the Title VII model. In *Coley v. Consolidated Rail Corp.*,[86] the court held that although an employer is automatically liable for the actions of its supervisors in a quid pro quo case, the employer must have actual or constructive knowledge to be liable in a hostile environment case.[87] The Supreme Court of Washington similarly held in *Glasgow v. Georgia-Pacific Corp.*[88] that in order to find an employer liable for a hostile environment created by a supervisor, the complainant must show that the employer authorized, knew, or should have known of the harassment and that the employer failed to take reasonably prompt and adequate corrective action.[89]

C. Employer Liability for Co-Worker Harassment

Courts applying FEP statutes generally have held, consistent with interpretations of Title VII, that an employer is liable for sexual harassment by a nonmanagerial co-worker only when the employer either authorized the harassment or knew or should have known of the harassment and then failed to take prompt corrective action.[90] New York's standard requires proof of acquiescence instead of simply a lack of corrective action, although acquiescence is generally shown by an absence of corrective action.[91] The knowledge of an employer's agents or supervisors may be imputed to the employer.[92]

V. FEP STATUTORY REMEDIES

A. FEP Agency Proceedings

Many state FEP agencies, unlike the EEOC, have power to adjudicate employment discrimination claims.[93] Matters decided in a state adjudicative

---

46 FEP Cases 1406, 1410–11 (1987)(legislature intended FEP statute to impose vicarious liability on employer for hostile environment created by its supervisor).

[86]561 F. Supp. 645, 34 FEP Cases 129 (E.D. Mich. 1982).

[87]*Id.* at 650, 34 FEP Cases at 133.

[88]103 Wash.2d 401, 693 P.2d 708, 51 FEP Cases 880 (1985).

[89]*Id.* at 407, 693 P.2d at 712, 51 FEP Cases at 882. *See also* Fisher v. Tacoma School Dist., 53 Wash. App. 591, 596, 769 P.2d 318, 320 ("court in *Glasgow* rejected the strict liability standard for holding employers liable in work environment cases"), *review denied,* 112 Wash.2d 1027 (1989). *Accord* Bersie v. Zycad Corp., 417 N.W.2d 288, 291 (Minn. Ct. App. 1987)(employer must know or should have known of harassment and failed to take timely and appropriate action).

[90]*E.g.,* Glasgow v. Georgia-Pacific Corp., *supra* note 88; Continental Can Co. v. State, 297 N.W.2d 241, 249, 22 FEP Cases 1808, 1814 (Minn. 1980)(statute prohibits co-worker harassment when employer knew or should have known of employee's conduct and failed to take timely and appropriate action).

[91]*E.g.,* Berlin v. Fort Howard Paper Co., 83 A.D.2d 505, 441 N.Y.S.2d 87 (1981)(employee could not maintain sexual harassment claim based on conduct by fellow employee absent evidence that employer condoned acts).

[92]*E.g.,* Fisher v. San Pedro Peninsula Hosp., *supra* note 84, 214 Cal. App.3d at 608 n.6, 262 Cal. Rptr. at 851, 54 FEP Cases at 591 (employer liable for co-worker harassment if employer or employer's agents or supervisors knew or should have know of harassment and failed to take immediate and appropriate corrective action).

[93]See cases cited in note 2 *supra* and accompanying text.

proceeding can have preclusive effect in subsequent judicial proceedings.[94]

Courts have reached varied conclusions with respect to whether state administrative agencies are empowered by FEP statutes to award compensatory and punitive damages to victims of employment discrimination. In Alaska,[95] California,[96] Maryland,[97] Ohio,[98] Pennsylvania,[99] and Washington,[100] FEP statutes do not authorize state agencies to award either compensatory or punitive relief. By contrast, in Massachusetts,[101] Minnesota,[102] New Jersey,[103] Illinois,[104] Iowa,[105] and Oregon,[106] courts have held that FEP agencies may award compensatory damages or both compensatory and punitive damages.

B. Judicial Actions Under FEP Statutes

FEP statutes, unlike Title VII, generally permit a litigant to seek all forms of relief typically granted to tort plaintiffs, such as compensatory and punitive damages.[107]

---

[94]*Compare* Kremer v. Chemical Constr. Corp., 456 U.S. 461, 28 FEP Cases 1412 (1982)(federal court in Title VII case must give *res judicata* effect to state court decision upholding FEP agency's rejection of discrimination claim where state court decision would be *res judicata* in state courts) *with* University of Tenn. v. Elliott, 478 U.S. 788, 41 FEP Cases 177, 179 (1986)(no preclusive effect in Title VII case to be given to state agency findings that were not judicially reviewed).

[95]McDaniel v. Cory, 631 P.2d 82 (Alaska 1981)(FEP agency has only remedial power and lacks authority to award compensatory and punitive damages).

[96]Dyna-Med v. FEHC, 43 Cal.3d 67, 241 Cal. Rptr. 67, 743 P.2d 1323, 46 FEP Cases 1143 (1987)(FEP agency lacks power to award punitive damages); Peralta Community College Dist. v. FEHC, 52 Cal.3d. 40, 276 Cal. Rptr. 114, 54 FEP Cases 1239 (1990)(FEP agency also lacks power to award compensatory damages).

[97]Makovi v. Sherwin-Williams Co., 316 Md. 603, 561 A.2d 179 (1989)(remedy under state FEP statute limited to equitable relief including back pay).

[98]Ohio Civil Rights Comm'n v. Lysy, 38 Ohio St.2d 217, 313 N.E.2d 3 (1974)(no authority to grant compensatory or punitive damages), *cert. denied*, 419 U.S. 1108 (1975).

[99]Midland Heights Homes v. Pennsylvania Human Relations Comm'n, 387 A.2d 664 (Pa. 1978)(FEP agency lacks statutory authority to award compensatory damages to persons injured by unlawful employment discrimination). *See also* Hannah v. Philadelphia Coca-Cola Bottling Co., 53 FEP Cases 9 (E.D. Pa. 1989)(claim for punitive damages may not be brought directly under Pennsylvania FEP statute).

[100]Washington State Human Rights Comm'n v. Cheney School Dist., 97 Wash.2d 118, 641 P.2d 163, 51 FEP Cases 928 (1982)(FEP agency lacks authority to award compensatory damages to victims of unlawful age discrimination).

[101]Franklin Publishing Co. v. Massachusetts Comm'n Against Discrimination, 25 Mass. App. Ct. 974, 519 N.E.2d 798 (1988)(mental distress compensable in commission proceedings); College-Town v. Massachusetts Comm'n Against Discrimination, *supra* note 85 (FEP agency warranted in awarding damages for emotional distress in sexual harassment case).

[102]Continental Can Co. v. State of Minn., 297 N.W.2d 241, 22 FEP Cases 1808 (Minn. 1980)(upon finding unfair discriminatory employment practice, hearing examiner may award compensatory and punitive damages).

[103]Zaherian v. Russell Fitt Real Estate Agency, 62 N.J. 399, 301 A.2d 754 (N.J. 1973)(complainant awarded incidental compensatory damages for pain and suffering).

[104]Village of Bellwood Fire & Police Comm'rs v. Human Rights Comm'n, 184 Ill. App.3d 339, 133 Ill. Dec. 810, 541 N.E.2d 1248 (1989)(FEP statute, which provides for agency award of "actual damages," contemplates compensation for emotional harm and mental suffering).

[105]Teamsters Local 238 v. Iowa Civil Rights Comm'n, 394 N.W.2d 375 (Iowa 1986)(FEP agency may award compensatory damages for emotional distress, but not punitive damages).

[106]Williams v. Joyce, 479 P.2d 513 (Or. Ct. App. 1971)(award of damages to compensate for victim's humiliation reasonably calculated to eliminate effects of discrimination).

[107]*See, e.g., Cal.:* Commodore Home Sys. v. Superior Court of San Bernardino County, 32 Cal.3d 211, 185 Cal. Rptr. 270, 649 P.2d 912, 31 FEP Cases 1058 (1982)(all relief generally available in noncontractual actions, including punitive damages, may be obtained in civil action under California FEP statute); Monge v. Superior Court, 176 Cal. App.3d 503, 222 Cal. Rptr. 64 (1986)(sexual harassment claimant may seek punitive damages);

Iowa: Ridenour v. Montgomery Ward & Co., 786 F.2d 867, 869, 40 FEP Cases 764 (8th Cir. 1986)(FEP statute authorizes recovery of compensatory damages);

Mass.: Contardo v. Merrill Lynch, 54 FEP Cases 1269 (D. Mass. 1990)(stockbroker subjected to pattern of sexual harassment that included placing pornographic pictures in her desk, sexual innuendoes and improper

VI. SPECIAL OBLIGATIONS OF STATE CONTRACTORS

Nearly half of the states and the District of Columbia require certain state contractors to refrain from discrimination as a condition of their government contract. These legal obligations are in addition to those imposed by state FEP statutes, Title VII, and the federal executive orders.[108] These state contractual provisions do not appear to have been implemented to any great extent. One explanation for the limited resort to sanctions against state contractors as a means of prohibiting employment discrimination is that few state provisions are self-enforcing, *i.e.,* few states investigate compliance independent of other proceedings.[109] Generally, sanctions are imposed only where there has been a finding of a violation under a state FEP statute.[110]

---

touchings at office gatherings, and male "locker room" atmosphere featuring lewd jokes and phallus shaped birthday cake and exotic female dancers did not prove economic or emotional distress damages, but awarded $1.00 in nominal damages plus attorney's fees plus $250,000 in punitive damages);

Minn.: Melsha v. Wickes Cos., 459 N.W.2d 707, 53 EPD ¶39,815 (Minn. Ct. App. 1990)(treble damages available in addition to punitives); Tretter v. Liquipak Int'l, 356 N.W.2d 713, 43 FEP Cases 1522 (Minn. Ct. App. 1984)(trial court did not err in awarding punitive damages to employee who prevailed on sexual harassment claim);

N.Y.: Thoreson v. Penthouse, 55 EPD ¶40,457 (N.Y. Sup. Ct. 1990), reproduced in Chapter 2, Forms of Harassment ("sexual slavery" case involving no tangible job loss but award of $4.06 million in punitive and emotional distress damages);

N.J.: Levinson v. Prentice-Hall, 868 F.2d 558 (3d Cir. 1989)(punitive damages permitted under New Jersey FEP statute); McMillan v. Lincoln Fed. Sav. & Loan Ass'n, 678 F. Supp. 89 (D.N.J. 1988)(traditional forms of relief, including compensatory and punitive damages, available in civil suit under FEP statute); Jackson v. Consolidated Rail Corp., 223 N.J. Super. 467, 538 A.2d 1310, 51 FEP Cases 712 (1988)(punitive damages may be awarded in civil action under New Jersey FEP statute);

Tenn.: Cripps v. United Biscuit, 53 FEP Cases 519, 521–22 (E.D. Tenn. 1989)(statutory entitlement to "actual damages" includes compensatory damages);

Wash.: Glasgow v. Georgia-Pacific Corp., *supra* note 88 (civil litigants' recovery of damages for mental and emotional suffering in sexual harassment suit appropriate); Ellingson v. Spokane Mortgage Co., 19 Wash. App. 48, 573 P.2d 389, 25 FEP Cases 90 (1978)(in sex discrimination suit, trial court erred in not awarding damages for mental anguish and emotional distress).

But see Colo: Agnello v. Adolph Coors Co., 695 P.2d 311 (Colo. Ct. App. 1984)(remedies in civil employment discrimination suit limited to reinstatement with back pay);

Or.: Holien v. Sears, Roebuck & Co., 298 Or. 76, 689 P.2d 1292, 36 FEP Cases 137 (1984)(general and punitive damages properly stricken from statutory employment discrimination claim for retaliatory discharge after resisting sexual advances).

[108]For a discussion of Federal Executive Order 11246, see Chapter 11, Federal Constitutional, Statutory, and Civil Rights Law.

[109]*But see* Rules of Ohio Bureau of Equal Employment Opportunity for Construction, §123:2-5.01, *et seq., reprinted in* 8B FAIR EMPL. PRAC. MAN. (BNA) 457:286 (providing mechanism for compliance reviews of construction contractors); CAL. ADMIN. CODE tit. 2, §8101 (establishing Office of Compliance Programs with authority to investigate complaints of noncompliance with state's affirmative action requirements or of discrimination by state contractors); WIS. STAT. §16.765 (requiring individual contracting departments to implement programs to assure compliance with nondiscrimination and affirmative action provisions of that section).

[110]*See, e.g.,* OKLA. STAT. ANN. tit. 25, §1505(d)(order of FEP agency finding violation by state contractor shall be certified to contracting agency).

CHAPTER 13

UNEMPLOYMENT COMPENSATION STATUTES

Sexual harassment often results in the severance of the employment relationship (whether it be of the complainant or of the alleged harasser) and therefore may become an issue in connection with claims for benefits under state unemployment compensation laws. In this context, the most frequently recurring legal issues are (I) whether a claimant who has "voluntarily" resigned employment because of sexual harassment is eligible to receive unemployment compensation benefits,[1] (II) whether a claimant who has been discharged for engaging in sexual harassment may collect benefits,[2] and (III) whether an unemployment compensation decision on a sexual harassment issue precludes relitigation of the same issue in separate litigation.[3]

This chapter discusses each of these issues and then provides some practical suggestions for employers and claimants in dealing with the impact of sexual harassment in the unemployment compensation setting.[4]

I. BENEFIT CLAIMS BY CLAIMANTS WHO VOLUNTARILY TERMINATE THEIR EMPLOYMENT BECAUSE OF SEXUAL HARASSMENT

A. Sexual Harassment as Good Cause for Voluntary Termination

State unemployment compensation statutes generally provide that employees who voluntarily terminate their employment are disqualified from receiving benefits, either completely or for a designated period of time, unless the termination is for good cause.[5] The statutes of several states expressly provide that the good cause requirement is satisfied where a voluntary termina-

---

[1]See Section I. *infra.* For a discussion of forced resignations outside the unemployment compensation context, see Chapter 9, Constructive Discharge.

[2]See Section II. *infra. See generally* Chapter 24, The Alleged Harasser as Plaintiff.

[3]See Section III. *infra. See generally* Chapter 22, Employer's Litigation Strategy.

[4]See Section IV. *infra.*

[5]ALA. CODE §25-4-78(2); ALASKA STAT. §23.20.379(a)(1); ARIZ. REV. STAT. ANN. §23-775(1); ARK. STAT. ANN. §11-10-513; CAL. UNEMP. INS. CODE §1256; COLO. REV. STAT. §8-73-108(4)(o); CONN. GEN. STAT. §31-236(a)(2)(A); DEL. CODE ANN. tit. 19, §3315(1); D.C. CODE ANN. §46-111(a); FLA. STAT. §443.101(1); GA. CODE ANN. §34-8-158(1); HAW. REV. STAT. §383-30(1); IDAHO CODE §72-1366(e); ILL. REV. STAT. ch. 48, ¶431, §601; IND. CODE §22-4-15-1(a); IOWA CODE §96.5(1); KAN. STAT. ANN. §44-706(a); KY. REV. STAT. ANN. §341.370(c); LA. REV. STAT. ANN. §23:1601(1); ME. REV. STAT. ANN. tit. 26, §1193(1); MD. ANN. CODE art. 95A, §6(a); MASS. ANN. LAWS ch. 151A, §25(e); MICH. COMP. LAWS §421.29(1)(a); MINN. STAT. §268.09(1)(a); MISS. CODE ANN. §71-5-513(A)(1)(a); MO. REV. STAT. §288.050(1)(1); MONT. CODE ANN. §39-51-2302; NEB. REV. STAT. §48.628(a)(1); NEV. REV. STAT. §612.380(1)(a); N.H. REV. STAT. ANN. §282-A:32(I)(a); N.J. REV. STAT. §43:21-5(a); N.M. STAT. ANN. §51-1-7(A); N.Y. LAB. LAW art. 18, §593(1)(a);

tion results from sexual harassment.[6] In a number of other states, good cause has been interpreted by the courts to include sexual harassment.[7]

1. Nature of the Harassment

In states where sexual harassment is designated by statute as good cause for quitting, the term typically is defined to encompass the same types of conduct proscribed under Title VII, including both quid pro quo harassment and hostile environment harassment.[8] In states where sexual harassment is not expressly designated as good cause under the unemployment compensation statutes, courts generally evaluate the harassing conduct to determine whether it would compel a reasonably prudent person under similar circumstances to resign.[9]

N.C. GEN. STAT. §96-14(1); N.D. CENT. CODE §52-06-02(1); OHIO REV. CODE ANN. §4141.29(D)(2)(a); OKLA. STAT. tit. 40, §2-404; OR. REV. STAT. §657.176(2)(c); PA. STAT. ANN. tit. 43, §802(b)(1); R.I. GEN. LAWS §28-44-17; S.C. CODE ANN. §41-35-120(1); S.D. CODIFIED LAWS ANN. §61-6-13; TENN. CODE ANN. §50-7-303(1); TEX. REV. CIV. STAT. ANN. art. 5221b-3(a); UTAH CODE ANN. §35-4-5(a); VT. STAT. ANN. tit. 21, §1344(a)(2); VA. CODE ANN. §60.2-618(1); WASH. REV. CODE ANN. §50.20.050(1); W. VA. CODE §21A-6-3(1); WIS. STAT. §108.04(7); WYO. STAT. §27-3-311(a).

[6]CAL. UNEMP. INS. CODE §1256.7; ILL. REV. STAT. ch. 48, ¶431, §601(B)(4); MASS. ANN. LAWS ch. 151A, §25(e); MINN. STAT. §268.09(1)(a); R.I. GEN. LAWS §28-44-17; WIS. STAT. §108.04(7)(i). *See also* COLO. REV. STAT. §8-73-108(4)(o)(employee entitled to unemployment benefits where employee quits "because of personal harassment by the employer not related to the performance of the job"); KAN. STAT. ANN. §44-706(a)(7)(employee not disqualified from receiving unemployment benefits if employee "left work because of unwelcome harassment . . . by the employer or another employee of which the employing unit had knowledge"); OKLA. STAT. tit. 40, §2-404 (good cause includes "unfair treatment of the employee or the creating of unusually difficult working conditions by the employer"); D.C. MUN. REGS. tit. 7, §311.7 (good cause for voluntarily leaving employment includes "sexual discrimination or harassment").

[7]*See, e.g.,* Clay v. Everett, 4 Ark. App. 122, 628 S.W.2d 339 (1982); Colorado Div. of Employment & Training v. Hewlett, 777 P.2d 704 (Colo. 1989); Grubb v. Standard Chlorine, No. 85A-FE-7 (Del. Super. Ct. 1986)(LEXIS, States Library); Small v. Jacklin Seed Co., 109 Idaho 341, 709 P.2d 114 (1985); McClodden v. Gerace, 522 So.2d 1379 (La. Ct. App. 1988); Wyandot Mental Health Ctr. v. Kansas Employment Sec. Bd. of Review, 763 P.2d 16 (Kan. 1988)(unpublished decision)(LEXIS, States Library); Doering v. Board of Review, 203 N.J. Super. 241, 496 A.2d 720 (1985); Krawczyszyn v. Ohio Bureau of Employment Serv., 54 Ohio App.3d 35 (1988); McCain v. Employment Div., 17 Ore. App. 442, 522 P.2d 1208 (1974); Homan v. Commonwealth, 107 Pa. Commw. 172, 527 A.2d 1109 (1987); Sweitzer v. State, 43 Wash. App. 511, 718 P.2d 3 (1986).

[8]*See generally* Arnett-Kremian, *Unemployment Compensation Benefits: Part of a Balanced Package of Relief for Sexual Harassment Victims,* 18 UNIV. RICHMOND L. REV. 1 (1983); Note, *Unemployment Compensation Benefits for the Victim of Work-Related Sexual Harassment,* 3 HARV. WOMEN'S L.J. 173 (1980). *Compare* CAL. UNEMP. INS. CODE §1256.7 *and* ILL. REV. STAT. ch. 48, ¶431, §601(B)(4) *and* MASS. ANN. LAWS ch. 151A, §25(e) *and* MINN. STAT. §268.09(1)(a) *with* EEOC Guidelines on Sexual Harassment, 29 C.F.R. §1604.11(a). *Cf.* WIS. STAT. §108.04(7)(i)(no disqualification from receiving benefits if "employee terminated his or her work because the employer made work, compensation or job assignments contingent upon the employee's consent to sexual contact or sexual intercourse"). *But cf.* Jensen v. Siemsen, 794 P.2d 271, 274–75 (Idaho 1990)(declining to apply EEOC sexual harassment guidelines in determining good cause under Idaho unemployment compensation statute).

[9]*See, e.g.,* McEwen v. Everett, 6 Ark. App. 32, 34–35, 637 S.W.2d 617, 619 (1982)(sexual harassment constitutes good cause to quit if it "would reasonably impel the average able-bodied, qualified worker to give up his or her employment"); McClodden v. Gerace, 522 So.2d 1379, 1381 (La. Ct. App. 1988)(claimant must show that harassment would "reasonably motivate, in a similar situation, the average able-bodied and qualified worker to give up his or her employment"); Doering v. Board of Review, 203 N.J. Super. 241, 245–46, 496 A.2d 720, 723 (1985)(harassment must be "sufficient to justify an employee's voluntarily leaving ranks of employed and joining ranks of unemployed"); Harmony v. Ohio Bureau of Employment Serv., 1990 Ohio App. LEXIS 1432 (1990)(harassment sufficient to constitute just cause for quitting is "that which, to an ordinarily intelligent person, is a justifiable reason for doing or not doing a particular act"); McCain v. Employment Div., 17 Ore. App. 442, 445, 522 P.2d 1208, 1209 (1974)(claimant must establish that sexual harassment was "sufficiently grievous to compel a reasonably prudent person to quit under similar circumstances"); St. Barnabas, Inc. v. Commonwealth, 106 Pa. Commw. 191, 194, 525 A.2d 885, 887 (1987)(claimant must show that decision to resign was "consistent with ordinary common sense and prudence and that the circumstances which prompted the severance of the employment relationship were real, not imaginary, substantial, not trifling, and reasonable, not whimsical"); Curry v. Gatson, 376 S.E.2d 166, 168 (W. Va. 1988)(employee not disqualified from receiving unemployment benefits if harassment would cause "a reasonably prudent person to resign").

One indicator of whether a sexual harassment complainant has good cause for quitting is the severity of the harassing conduct. In an Arkansas case, the court held that a claimant was justified in terminating her employment based on evidence that her employer had kissed her, grabbed her breasts, and patted her on the back and face.[10] The court rejected the administrative agency's conclusion that the harassment had to be "unbearable" before it could constitute good cause.

Similarly, a Pennsylvania court held that sexually offensive remarks made by one of the claimant's co-workers were sufficiently severe to constitute good cause for terminating employment.[11] The co-worker had told the claimant that "he would stick it in and do it easy," and that he wanted to have the claimant "in the back of his car and have an affair with [her]." In addition, on the claimant's last day of employment, the same co-worker had told the claimant that he was "going to get [her] and have charge of [her]."[12]

By contrast, in *McCain v. Employment Division*,[13] an Oregon court held that a claimant had not shown good cause for quitting based on certain evidence of the employer's sexual attitude: the plant manager displayed a postcard on his desk showing a woman with bare breasts; a poster hung on the office wall showed a bikini-clad woman whom male employees described as having "gorgeous tits"; and a cartoon on the lunchroom wall, entitled "The Perfect Woman," showed a woman's naked legs, hips, buttocks, breasts, and pubic area, with no arms, head, or upper torso. According to the court, these displays may have been vulgar and offensive, but did not constitute good cause because they did not result in any "actual discrimination, undue harassment, or other grievous cause."[14]

2. Claimant's Duty to Notify the Employer

A good cause determination may also require a showing that the claimant made a reasonable effort to notify the employer of the harassing conduct and to have the problem corrected before resigning.[15] In a Pennsylvania case, the

---

[10]McEwen v. Everett, 6 Ark. App. 32, 637 S.W.2d 617 (1982).

[11]United States Banknote Co. v. Unemployment Compensation Bd., 575 A.2d 673 (Pa. Commw. Ct. 1990).

[12]*Id.* at 674–75. *See also* Doering v. Board of Review, 203 N.J. Super. 241, 496 A.2d 720 (1985)(claimant was subjected to sexual harassment and had good cause for resigning where evidence showed that supervisor had asked claimant about having sexual relationship with him, made sexual advance toward her, called her at home, asked her to cook breakfast for him, threatened her with physical harm, and made racial comment about claimant in presence of co-worker); Weissman v. Commonwealth, 94 Pa. Commw. 67, 502 A.2d 782 (1986)(record supported administrative finding of good cause based on evidence that employer had made several sexually oriented and embarrassing remarks to and about claimant in front of co-workers and customers over five-year period, including an incident in which employer kissed claimant's hand and arm and said, "I want your body," and that employer's wife had falsely accused claimant of being rude to a customer).

[13]17 Ore. App. 442, 522 P.2d 1208 (1974).

[14]*Id.* at 445, 522 P.2d at 1210. *See also* Jensen v. Siemsen, 794 P.2d 271, 276 (Idaho 1990)(substantial evidence supported administrative decision that employer's practice of unzipping his pants and tucking in his shirt and directing sexual innuendos to claimant did not rise to level of sexual harassment).

[15]*See, e.g.,* Grubb v. Standard Chlorine, No. 85-A-FE-7 (Del. Super. Ct. 1986)(LEXIS, States Library)(claimant cannot establish good cause without attempt to have situation corrected by proper notice to employer followed by reasonable opportunity to correct); Jensen v. Siemsen, 794 P.2d 271, 274 (Idaho 1990)(claimant must prove that all reasonable alternatives were pursued prior to terminating employment); Doering v. Board of Review, 203 N.J. Super. 241, 248, 496 A.2d 720, 724 (1985)(claimant must do what is necessary and reasonable to remain employed); Harmony v. Ohio Bureau of Employment Serv., *supra* note 9 (claimant must make reasonable effort to deal with problem before leaving employment); Tedesco v.

evidence demonstrated that the claimant's termination was prompted by repeated sexual remarks and physical contacts by the employer's office manager over a three-year period, but the claimant failed to report the situation to her employer.[16] The court concluded that by not giving the employer an opportunity to correct the problem before resigning, the claimant had failed to "take the required common sense action to obviate the problem so that she would not have to leave."[17]

Courts have expressed differing views about the specific actions required of a claimant who is being subjected to sexual harassment. In some cases courts have held that claimants must report incidents of sexual harassment through grievance or claim procedures established for that purpose.[18] Other courts have held that a claimant need not register a formal complaint, but simply must make a reasonable effort to make the employer aware of the problem before voluntarily terminating employment.[19] Where the alleged harasser is the claimant's supervisor, some courts have held that the claimant has a duty to report the matter to upper management,[20] while other courts have held that the claimant has good cause for resigning if the harassing supervisor is aware of the complaints and fails to take corrective action.[21]

Commonwealth, 122 Pa. Commw. 549, 553, 552 A.2d 754, 756 (1989)(claimant who voluntarily terminates employment because of sexual harassment must show that employer was made aware of problem); CAL. UNEMP. INS. CODE §1256.7 (sexual harassment constitutes good cause to leave employment "provided the individual has taken reasonable steps to preserve the working relationship"); MINN. STAT. §268.09(a)(sexual harassment constitutes good cause for leaving employment where "employer knows or should know of the existence of the harassment and fails to take timely and appropriate action"); WASH. ADMIN. CODE §192-16-009(1)(good cause for leaving work voluntarily requires proof that claimant exhausted all reasonable alternatives prior to termination).

[16]Colduvell v. Commonwealth, 48 Pa. Commw. 185, 408 A.2d 1207 (1979).

[17]Id. at 187, 408 A.2d at 1208.

[18]See, e.g., Grubb v. Standard Chlorine, No. 85A-FE-7 (Del. Super. Ct. 1986)(LEXIS, States Library)(affirming decision to deny unemployment compensation based on evidence that claimant was aware of employer's sexual harassment claims procedure, but failed to raise matter of harassment during meeting with plant manager); Krawczyszyn v. Ohio Bureau of Employment Serv., 54 Ohio App.3d 35 (1988)("where an employer provides its employees with a mechanism to air their grievances concerning such misconduct in the workplace, a victim of sexual harassment must make a good-faith effort to employ that mechanism so that the employer is made aware of the problem and is afforded an opportunity to correct the problem"); St. Barnabas, Inc. v. Commonwealth, 106 Pa. Commw. 191, 196, 525 A.2d 885, 888 (1987)(holding that claimant had not made sufficient effort to remain on the job where she notified company personnel director of sexual harassment, but did not utilize employer's grievance procedure or report problem to company president).

[19]See, e.g., McNabb v. Cub Foods, 352 N.W.2d 378 (Minn. 1984)(holding that employer had sufficient notice of alleged sexual harassment where evidence showed that immediate supervisor had actual knowledge of harassment, claimant advised first-line supervisor that co-worker was touching and harassing her and claimant had never received copy of employer's sexual harassment policy); Homan v. Commonwealth, 107 Pa. Commw. 172, 177, 527 A.2d 1109, 1111 (1987)(holding that claimant acted reasonably by reporting incidents of harassment to supervisors; "[t]he law does not require a claimant to complain of each and every incident of sexual harassment nor does it require a formal complaint to be filed").

[20]See, e.g., West v. Commonwealth, 53 Pa. Commw. 431, 417 A.2d 872 (1980)(holding that claimant who alleged sexual harassment by supervisor had not allowed employer adequate opportunity to correct problem where claimant had not discussed sexual harassment with owner and, after her resignation, had ignored phone calls and letters from owner asking for explanation of termination).

[21]See, e.g., Caldwell v. Hodgeman, 25 FEP Cases 1647 (Mass. Dist. Ct. 1981)(rejecting administrative decision that claimant failed to take appropriate steps to resolve sexual harassment claims where employer was the harasser); Clark v. K-Mart Store, 372 N.W.2d 847 (Minn. Ct. App. 1985)(holding that claimant had given employer sufficient notice of sexual harassment where she informed employer of existence of harassment in three-week written notice of resignation, and where alleged harasser was claimant's supervisor whose knowledge could be imputed to employer); Doering v. Board of Review, 203 N.J. Super. 241, 496 A.2d 720 (1985)(holding that claimant who resigned because of sexual harassment by supervisor was not disqualified from receiving unemployment compensation by failure to file formal grievance or report incidents to supervisor's supervisor); Harmony v. Ohio Bureau of Employment Serv., supra note 9 (holding that claimant had done all that was reasonably necessary by complaining to manager about his sexually offensive remarks).

A claimant's obligation to exhaust alternative remedies before resigning may be excused where there is reason to believe that any effort to exhaust would have been futile. In *Hussa v. Employment Security Department,*[22] a Washington court upheld an administrative decision to award unemployment compensation even though the claimant concededly failed to await the outcome of the employer's investigation into her claim of sexual harassment by co-workers. Evidence introduced at the administrative hearing showed that male workers employed in a mill referred to the three female millworkers as "slut," "bitch," and "cunt," frequently patted their buttocks and, on two separate occasions, exposed themselves to the women. One of the men who had exposed himself warned the claimant not to report these incidents. When the claimant's supervisor learned of the incidents and questioned the claimant, she reported that she had been offended by abusive language in the mill, but declined to provide details or names of the offenders. The supervisor's inquiry led to the suspension of two men pending further investigation, one of whom then told the claimant that he was going to "get [her] one way or another."[23]

In determining whether the claimant had an obligation to await the outcome of this investigation before she quit, the *Hussa* court noted testimony that the atmosphere at the mill was "pro-male," that the claimant's supervisor had told her and her female co-workers that they "had more or less brought it on [themselves]," and that the claimant believed that management was "more on the man's side than on the woman's side," so that reporting the incidents of sexual harassment would be futile. The court held that under these circumstances, "a genuine apprehension and fear would have been created in the mind of an ordinarily prudent woman," so as to excuse the claimant's failure to await the employer's attempt to remedy the situation.[24]

B. The Issue of Causation

In voluntary termination cases, the employer may argue that even if the sexual harassment occurred, it was not the "real" reason for the claimant's decision to resign. In these instances, agencies and courts must address the issue of causation.

In some cases, claimants have been denied unemployment compensation based on a finding that the alleged harassment was not a factor in the decision

[22]34 Wash. App. 857, 664 P.2d 1286 (1983).
[23]*Id.* at 858–59, 664 P.2d at 1287.
[24]*Id.* at 864, 664 P.2d at 1290. *See also* McEwen v. Everett, 6 Ark. App. 32, 637 S.W.2d 617 (1982)(claimant had no obligation to resolve complaints with alleged harasser who was company president, and because there was no other supervisor or official to whom she could turn, claimant was justified in resigning); Krawczyszyn v. Ohio Bureau of Employment Serv., 54 Ohio App.3d 35 (1988)(while employee ordinarily is required to utilize internal grievance mechanism, "there may exist circumstances that would excuse the employee from pursuing the employer's internal grievance procedure, such as where the procedure would be futile . . . or where the employee's previous complaints produced no change in behavior"); Sweitzer v. State, 43 Wash. App. 511, 718 P.2d 3 (1986)(holding that claimant excused from submitting sexual harassment claims to employer's grievance committee where harassment continued after claimant registered complaint with her supervisor, grievance committee member told claimant not to submit grievance and member of employer's board of directors told claimant it would be useless to go to grievance committee and called her a whore); CAL. UNEMP. INS. CODE §1256.7 (employee who voluntarily terminates employment because of sexual harassment need not take steps to preserve working relationship if such steps "would have been futile").

to terminate employment. In *Zirelli v. Division of Employment Security*,[25] a Massachusetts court affirmed a decision to deny unemployment compensation to a claimant who resigned her job as a housekeeper after claiming that a co-worker had altered her time sheet. Although the claimant had told her supervisor that the alteration had been made by a co-worker who had been sexually harassing her for a year before, she specifically requested that no action be taken against the co-worker. Based on the claimant's initial explanation for quitting, her failure to complain about the alleged harassment, and her lack of desire to pursue the harassment claim, the court held that there was substantial evidence to support the administrative hearing examiner's conclusion that sexual harassment was not the cause of the claimant's decision to resign.[26]

Evidence that sexual harassment was a factor in the claimant's decision to resign, but not the only factor, presents a more difficult issue. Some reported decisions have held that the claimant is entitled to compensation so long as the harassment is a contributing factor in the decision. In a Minnesota case, the court upheld an award of unemployment benefits to a claimant who resigned after being sexually harassed, even though the employer claimed that her termination was caused by her dissatisfaction with the postponement of the Christmas party and the lack of cost-of-living increases.[27] According to the court: " 'The law does not require that cause attributable to the employer be the sole reason for the termination' ... 'The disqualification statute does not require that all causal factors in a termination flow from the employer, but that termination be wholly without good cause attributable to the employer.' "[28]

---

[25]394 Mass. 229, 475 N.E.2d 375 (1985).

[26]*See also* Biegner v. Bloomington Chrysler/Plymouth, 426 N.W.2d 483 (Minn. Ct. App. 1988)(record supported administrative decision that claimant's resignation was not result of sexual harassment based on evidence that employer had taken appropriate and timely action in response to claimant's complaints about co-workers' remarks concerning his sex life, that remarks had ended approximately three months before claimant's resignation, and that claimant had resigned shortly after he received written warning concerning his performance); Kampa v. Normandale Tennis Club, 393 N.W.2d 195 (Minn. Ct. App. 1986)(record supported administrative decision that claimant resigned due to scheduling problems and not because of sexual harassment, based on evidence that claimant had been reprimanded for failing to report as scheduled and resigned immediately after she was informed that scheduling difficulties could not continue); Gantenbein-Field v. Labor & Indus. Review Comm'n, 128 Wis.2d 556, 381 N.W.2d 621 (Ct. App. 1985)(limited precedent decision)(substantial evidence supported administrative decision that work scheduling problems rather than sexual harassment caused claimant's resignation; while claimant testified that supervisor touched her throughout her employment, her written resignation notice did not mention sexual harassment, she had numerous conflicts with supervisor over scheduling issues, and resigned approximately one week after being notified of scheduling change).

[27]Dura Supreme v. Kienholz, 381 N.W.2d 92 (Minn. Ct. App. 1986).

[28]*Id.* at 96 (quoting Burtman v. Dealers Discount Supply, 347 N.W.2d 292, 294 (Minn. Ct. App. 1985); Hanson v. IDS Properties Mgmt. Co., 308 Minn. 422, 424, 242 N.W.2d 833, 835 (1976)). In *Colorado Div. of Employment & Training v. Hewlett*, 777 P.2d 704 (Colo. 1989), the Colorado Supreme Court similarly held that an employee was not disqualified from receiving unemployment benefits if the employee quit because of sexual harassment even if the harassment was not the sole factor in the decision to quit. In reaching this conclusion, the court rejected a decision by the court of appeals to apply the burden-shifting approach of *Mt. Healthy City School Dist. Bd. of Educ. v. Doyle*, 429 U.S. 274 (1977), which was developed to analyze "mixed-motive" cases involving adverse employment actions based on both permissible factors and constitutionally protected rights, and which would have required the employee to show that sexual harassment played a substantial part in the decision to resign, after which the burden would shift to the employer to prove that the employee would have resigned even in the absence of sexual harassment. According to the *Hewlett* court, this test was inappropriate in the unemployment compensation setting, where employees were entitled to receive benefits, as a matter of statute, so long as sexual harassment was a reason for termination.

C. Procedural Issues

1. Burden of Proof

In most jurisdictions, claimants who voluntarily terminate their employment have the burden of establishing the existence of good cause.[29] The notable exception is California, where courts have held that the unemployment compensation statute creates a presumption that employees who have voluntarily terminated employment have done so for reasons that allow them to receive benefits. To overcome this presumption, the burden is on the employer to prove by a preponderance of the evidence that the claimant quit the employment without good cause.[30]

2. Judicial Review

While specific procedures vary from one jurisdiction to another, in all states the functions of determining and reviewing unemployment compensation claims are delegated to administrative agencies.[31] Judicial review of administrative decisions is generally limited to issues of whether the agency has committed legal error, and whether the agency's factual findings are supported by substantial evidence.[32] Thus, if an issue of good cause involves a factual dispute—for example, whether a claimant was subjected to sexual harassment or reported the harassment to her employer—the administrative agency's findings will not be overturned by a court as long as they have a substantial basis in the record.[33]

Where the facts are not in dispute, the issue of good cause generally is treated as a question of law.[34] Most courts have held that they are entitled to review the evidence *de novo,* independent of the administrative agency's deci-

---

[29]*See, e.g.,* Colorado Div. of Employment & Training v. Hewlett, 777 P.2d 704, 707 (Colo. 1989); Gunty v. Department of Employment Serv., 524 A.2d 1192, 1195 n.1 (D.C. Ct. App. 1987); Uniweld Prod. v. Industrial Relations Comm'n, 277 So.2d 827, 829 (Fla. Dist. Ct. App. 1973); Jensen v. Siemson, 794 P.2d 271, 274 (Idaho 1990); McClodden v. Gerace, 522 So.2d 1379, 1381 (La. Ct. App. 1988); Biegner v. Bloomington Chrysler/Plymouth, 426 N.W.2d 483, 485 (Minn. Ct. App. 1988); Krawczyszyn v. Ohio Bureau of Employment Serv., 54 Ohio App.3d 35 (1988); McCain v. Employment Div., 17 Ore. App. 442, 445, 522 P.2d 1208, 1210 (1974); Colduvell v. Commonwealth, 48 Pa. Commw. 185, 186, 408 A.2d 1207, 1208 (1979); Murphy v. Employment Sec. Dep't, 47 Wash. App. 252, 256, 734 P.2d 924, 926 (1987).

[30]Prescod v. Unemployment Ins. Appeals Bd., 57 Cal. App.3d 29, 37–38, 127 Cal. Rptr. 540, 545–46 (1976).

[31]For a general discussion of the procedures relating to the adjudication and appeal of unemployment compensation claims, see S.D. SHAWE & W.J. ROSENTHAL, EMPLOYMENT LAW DESKBOOK §12.03 (1990); UNEMPL. INS. REP. (CCH) ¶2020.

[32]*See, e.g.,* Sanchez v. Unemployment Ins. Appeals Bd., 36 Cal.3d 575, 585, 685 P.2d 61, 68, 205 Cal. Rptr. 501, 508 (1984); Grubb v. Standard Chlorine, No. 85A-FE-7 (Del. Super. Ct. 1986)(LEXIS, States Library); Jensen v. Siemsen, 794 P.2d 271, 273 (Idaho 1990); Biegner v. Bloomington Chrysler/Plymouth, 426 N.W.2d 483, 485 (Minn. Ct. App. 1988); Palumbo v. Board of Review, 1988 Ohio App. LEXIS 3069 (1988); St. Barnabas, Inc. v. Commonwealth, 106 Pa. Commw. 191, 194, 525 A.2d 885, 887 (1987).

[33]*See, e.g.,* Grubb v. Standard Chlorine, No. 85A-FE-7 (Del. Super. Ct. 1986)(LEXIS, States Library); Jensen v. Siemsen, 794 P.2d 271, 273 (Idaho 1990); Zirelli v. Division of Employment Sec., 394 Mass. 229, 231, 475 N.E.2d 375, 376 (1985); Kampa v. Normandale Tennis Club, 393 N.W.2d 195, 197 (Minn. Ct. App. 1986); Palumbo v. Board of Review, *supra* note 32.

[34]*See, e.g.,* Prescod v. Unemployment Ins. Appeals Bd., 57 Cal. App.3d 29, 38, 127 Cal. Rptr. 540, 546 (1976); Biegner v. Bloomington Chrysler/Plymouth, 426 N.W.2d 483, 485 (Minn. Ct. App. 1988); McPherson v. Employment Div., 285 Ore. 541, 548, 591 P.2d 1381, 1385 (1979); Homan v. Commonwealth, 107 Pa. Commw. 172, 176, 527 A.2d 1109, 1110 (1987) *Cf.* Sweitzer v. State, 43 Wash. App. 511, 515, 718 P.2d 3, 5–6 (1986)(whether claimant leaves employment for good cause is mixed question of law and fact).

sion.[35] In some cases, however, courts have held that the question of what constitutes good cause must be left to the agency's discretion, with the court's role limited to determining whether the agency's assessment is reasonably defensible.[36]

II. BENEFIT CLAIMS BY ALLEGED HARASSERS WHO ARE DISCHARGED FOR SEXUAL HARASSMENT

Unemployment benefits may also be sought by claimants who have been discharged for alleged sexual harassment of their subordinates or co-workers. In these cases, a benefit entitlement issue arises because state unemployment compensation statutes disqualify claimants who have engaged in conduct rising to a specified level of fault. The specific standard for disqualification varies from state to state, ranging from "just cause"[37] to "misconduct."[38] Under any of these standards, however, claimants who are discharged for sexual harassment will often face a denial of unemployment benefits.[39]

Where the employer challenges a claimant's right to receive unemployment benefits on the ground that the discharge was for sexual harassment, the

---

[35]*See, e.g.,* Biegner v. Bloomington Chrysler/Plymouth, 426 N.W.2d 483, 485 (Minn. Ct. App. 1988); Sweitzer v. State, 43 Wash. App. 511, 515, 718 P.2d 3, 5–6 (1986).

[36]*See, e.g.,* Lyons v. District of Columbia Dep't of Employment Serv., 551 A.2d 1345, 1346 (D.C. Ct. App. 1988)(in determining whether claimant's reason for leaving employment constitutes good cause, court must defer to agency's interpretation and application of regulations it administers); McPherson v. Employment Div., 285 Ore. 541, 557, 591 P.2d 1381, 1388–90 (1979)(agency's role is to determine the kind of reasons that constitute good cause to leave employment, with judicial review limited to determining whether agency's assessment is "unlawful in substance").

[37]DEL. CODE ANN. tit. 19, §3315(2); IND. CODE §22-4-15-1(a); OHIO REV. CODE ANN. §4141.29(d)(2)(a); S.C. CODE ANN. §41-35-120(2); UTAH CODE ANN. §35-5-5(b).

[38]ALASKA STAT. §23.20.379(a)(2); ARK. STAT. ANN. §11-10-514; CAL. UNEMP. INS. CODE §1256; D.C. CODE ANN. §46-111(b); FLA. STAT. §443.101(1); HAW. REV. STAT. §383-30(2); IDAHO CODE §72-1366(e); ILL. REV. STAT. ch. 48, ¶432, §602; IOWA CODE §96.5(2); KAN. STAT. ANN. §44-706(b); KY. REV. STAT. ANN. §341.370(b); LA. REV. STAT. ANN. §1601(2); ME. REV. STAT. ANN. tit. 26, §1193(2); MICH. COMP. LAWS §421.29(1)(b); MINN. STAT. §268.09(1)(b); MISS. CODE ANN. §71-5-513(A)(1)(b); MO. REV. STAT. §288.050(2); MONT. CODE ANN. §39-51-2303; NEB. REV. STAT. §48-628(b); NEV. REV. STAT. §512.385; N.H. REV. STAT. ANN. §282-A:32(I)(b); N.J. REV. STAT. §43:21-5(b); N.M. STAT. ANN. §51-1-7(B); N.Y. LAB. LAW art. 18, §593(3); N.C. GEN. STAT. §96-14(2); N.D. CENT. CODE §52-06-02(2); OKLA. STAT. tit. 40, §2-406; OR. REV. STAT. §657.176(2)(a); R.I. GEN. LAWS §28.44-18; S.D. CODIFIED LAWS ANN. §61-6-14; TEX. REV. CIV. STAT. ANN. art. 5221b-3(b); VA. CODE ANN. §60.2-618(2); WASH. REV. CODE ANN. §50.20.060(1); W. VA. CODE §21A-6-3(2); WIS. STAT. §108.04(5); WYO. STAT. §27-3-311(c). *Cf.* ALA. CODE §25-4-78(3)(actual or threatened misconduct repeated after previous warning); ARIZ. REV. STAT. ANN. §23-775(2)(willful or negligent misconduct); COLO. REV. STAT. §8-73-108(3)(c), (e), (g)(disqualified for 26 weeks if discharged for gross misconduct or for 10 weeks if discharged for insubordination, violation of statute or company rule, willful neglect or damage to employer's interests or rudeness, insolence or offensive behavior); CONN. GEN. STAT. §31-236(a)(2)(B)(repeated willful misconduct or just cause); GA. CODE ANN. §34-8-158(2)(failure to obey orders, rules or instructions or failure to discharge duties); MD. ANN. CODE art. 95A §6(b), (c)(disqualified until earnings from reemployment exceed 10 times weekly benefit if discharged for gross misconduct, or for 4–9 weeks if discharged for misconduct); MASS. ANN. LAWS ch. 151A, §25e (deliberate misconduct or willful disregard of employer's interest); PA. STAT. ANN. tit. 43, §802(e)(willful misconduct); TENN. CODE ANN. §50-7-303(2)(A), (B)(disqualified completely if discharged for gross misconduct or until earnings from reemployment exceed 10 times weekly benefit if discharged for misconduct); VT. STAT. ANN. tit. 21, §1344(a)(1), (2)(B)(disqualified for 6–12 weeks if discharged for misconduct or until earnings from reemployment exceed six times weekly benefit amount if discharged for gross misconduct).

[39]*See, e.g.,* Sears, Roebuck & Co. v. Florida Unemp. Appeals Comm'n, 463 So.2d 465 (Fla. Dist. Ct. App. 1985)(upholding administrative decision that claimant who made advances to female co-workers had been discharged for misconduct); Ervin v. Review Bd., 173 Ind. App. 592, 364 N.E.2d 1189 (1977)(evidence supported decision that claimant who grabbed female co-worker's buttocks and tried to kiss her had been discharged for just cause); Crane v. Iowa Dep't of Job Serv., 412 N.W.2d 194 (Iowa Ct. App. 1987)(affirming administrative decision that claimant who partially exposed his buttocks in presence of female co-workers had been discharged for misconduct); Reed v. Minnesota Dep't of Transp., 422 N.W.2d 537 (Minn. Ct. App. 1988)(holding that actions of claimant who had been discharged for off-duty harassment constituted

threshold issue is whether the harassing conduct actually occurred. Courts generally have placed this burden of proof on the employer.[40]

A second issue is whether the harassing conduct, if proved by the employer, justifies a denial of unemployment compensation.[41] In states that require proof of "misconduct" to disqualify a claimant from receiving unemployment compensation, evidence that the employer had cause for the termination will not necessarily support a denial of unemployment benefits.[42] Courts in these jurisdictions have emphasized that the disqualification issue differs from the issue of whether the employer had a legal or contractual right to discharge the employee.[43]

In some cases, courts have analyzed the disqualification issue by measuring the alleged harasser's conduct against statutory definitions of sexual harassment. In a Minnesota case, the court looked to definitions of sexual harassment in the state's fair employment practices statute, and the voluntary termination provisions of the unemployment compensation statute, to uphold an administrative decision that an alleged harasser was not disqualified from receiving unemployment benefits.[44] The claimant in that case was a college employee

---

misconduct and disqualified him from receiving unemployment benefits); Schienda v. Transportation Research Ctr., 17 Ohio App.3d 119, 477 N.E.2d 675 (1984)(upholding administrative decision that claimant who patted female employee on buttocks had been discharged for just cause); Zuraw v. Commonwealth, 61 Pa. Commw. 548, 434 A.2d 1312 (1981)(affirming administrative decision of willful misconduct where claimant hugged and touched female co-workers, continued his contacts after told by employer to stop, and removed his pants while alone with female co-worker); Kohler v. Labor & Indus. Review Comm'n, 47 FEP Cases 424 (Wis. Cir. Ct. 1988)(holding that claimant who had subjected two female co-workers to sexual innuendos had been discharged for misconduct).

[40]See, e.g., Sears, Roebuck & Co. v. Florida Unemp. Appeals Comm'n, 463 So.2d 465, 466 (Fla. Dist. Ct. App. 1985); Reed v. Minnesota Dep't of Transp., 422 N.W.2d 537, 539 (Minn. Ct. App. 1988); Katsur & Assoc. v. Commonwealth, 97 Pa. Commw. 332, 334, 509 A.2d 926, 927 (1986). A recurring issue in misconduct cases is whether a denial of unemployment benefits may be based on hearsay evidence. Hearsay evidence generally is admissible in unemployment compensation proceedings. See Annot., *Hearsay Evidence in Proceedings Before State Administrative Agencies,* 36 A.L.R.3d 12 (1989). However, the weight accorded such evidence upon judicial review differs from one jurisdiction to another. In some states, hearsay will support a finding of fact involving misconduct so long as the evidence is received without objection. See, e.g., Edwards v. Stiles, 23 Ark. App. 96, 100, 743 S.W.2d 12, 14–15 (1988); Jackson v. Department of Labor, 168 Ill. App.3d 494, 500, 523 N.E.2d 5, 9–10 (1988); Mark Twain Homes, Inc. v. Labor & Indus. Relations Comm'n, 616 S.W.2d 145, 147 (Mo. Ct. App. 1981). In other states, a finding and decision of misconduct may be based on uncorroborated hearsay unless it is contradicted by other credible evidence. See, e.g., Seeman v. Little Crow Trucking, 412 N.W.2d 422, 426 (Minn. Ct. App. 1987); Galloway v. Unemployment Compensation Bd., 1990 Ohio App. LEXIS 2818 (1990). In a number of other states, however, hearsay must be corroborated by other competent evidence. See, e.g., Florida Mining & Materials Corp. v. Florida Unemp. Appeals Comm'n, 530 So.2d 426, 427 (Fla. Ct. App. 1988); Cornell v. Review Bd., 179 Ind. App. 17, 22–23, 383 N.E.2d 1102, 1106 (1979); McConnell v. Iowa Dep't of Job Serv., 327 N.W.2d 234, 237 (Iowa 1982); Ray v. Whitfield, 521 So.2d 726, 728–29 (La. Ct. App. 1988); Ford v. Commonwealth, 91 Pa. Commw. 502, 506, 498 A.2d 449, 451 (1985); Johnson v. Neel, No. 86-150-II (Tenn. Ct. App. 1986)(LEXIS, States Library).

[41]The issue of what conduct constitutes "just cause" or "misconduct" sufficient to disqualify a claimant from receiving unemployment compensation is treated by some courts as a question of fact, see, e.g., Western-Southern Life Ins. Co. v. Fridley, 1990 Ohio App. LEXIS 3576 (1990), and by others as a question of law, see, e.g., Gradine v. College of St. Scholastica, 426 N.W.2d 459, 463 (Minn. Ct. App. 1988); Zuraw v. Commonwealth, 61 Pa. Commw. 548, 551, 434 A.2d 1312, 1314 (1981).

[42]See, e.g., Commonwealth (Pa. State Police) v. Commonwealth, 578 A.2d 1360 (Pa. Commw. Ct. 1990)(upholding administrative decision that transcript of court-martial hearing in which claimant was found guilty of unbecoming conduct, discrimination and harassment was not relevant or competent evidence to support decision of willful misconduct for unemployment compensation purposes).

[43]See, e.g., Gradine v. College of St. Scholastica, 426 N.W.2d 459, 464 (Minn. Ct. App. 1988); Commonwealth (Pa. State Police) v. Commonwealth, 578 A.2d 1360, 1361 (Pa. Commw. Ct. 1990). Cf. City of Colorado Springs v. Industrial Comm'n, 749 P.2d 412, 414 (Colo. 1988)(nonsexual harassment case holding that question of whether claimant had been properly discharged was distinct from whether he should be disqualified from receiving unemployment benefits).

[44]Gradine v. College of St. Scholastica, 426 N.W.2d 459 (Minn. Ct. App. 1988). In *Reed v. Minnesota Dep't of Transp.,* 422 N.W.2d 537, 540–41 (Minn. Ct. App. 1988), the court emphasized that a decision to

who was discharged after a student/employee complained that he had written letters to her, telephoned her and massaged her neck and shoulders. Emphasizing that sexual harassment required "unwelcome" advances, the court cited evidence that the claimant simply had expressed his affection for a particular woman who did not inform him that his letters and telephone calls were unwelcome, and that he had touched the woman only once and had stopped when asked to do so. Under these circumstances, the court concluded that the claimant's actions did not amount to sexual harassment.

Another factor considered by courts is whether the alleged harasser's actions violated an employer rule or policy concerning sexual conduct. In a Florida case,[45] the claimant, who had been discharged for making advances to two female co-workers, maintained that his actions, including kissing one of the workers on the cheek, were innocuous. Reversing an administrative award of unemployment benefits, the court rejected the claimant's characterization of his conduct: "The point is that the act constituted a clear violation of an express policy of his employer which was adopted in order to prevent, to the extent possible, actions against the employer based on sexual harassment."[46]

Finally, in a number of cases, courts have reviewed issues of disqualification based on general standards of expected workplace behavior, holding generally that sexual advances, displays, or remarks directed toward employees of the opposite sex violate these standards.[47]

III. THE EFFECT OF UNEMPLOYMENT DECISIONS ON SEPARATE LITIGATION

A unemployment compensation claim involves a specialized administrative proceeding, seeking a particular form of benefits. A sexual harassment complainant may also bring a wide range of other claims, seeking other forms of compensation, in the form of a lawsuit, an administrative complaint, or a grievance against her employer.[48] One question raised by this multiplicity of

---

deny unemployment benefits based on sexual harassment did not require a finding that the claimant's actions would give rise to a cause of action against the employer under federal or state civil rights statutes; rather, it was sufficient if the discharge was based on the employer's reasonable belief that such litigation was possible.

[45]Sears, Roebuck & Co. v. Florida Unemp. Appeals Comm'n, 463 So.2d 465 (Fla. Dist. Ct. App. 1985).

[46]*Id.* at 466. *See also* Western-Southern Life Ins. Co. v. Fridley, *supra* note 41 (supervisor discharged for carrying on extramarital sexual affair with subordinate was disqualified from receiving unemployment benefits based on provision in employment contract and employer policy manual prohibiting immoral conduct or harassment); Schienda v. Transportation Research Ctr., 17 Ohio App.3d 119, 477 N.E.2d 675 (1984)(claimant discharged for patting female employee on her buttocks properly denied unemployment benefits based on employer policy prohibiting any nonconsensual sexual contact).

[47]*See, e.g.,* Ervin v. Review Bd., 173 Ind. App. 592, 596–97, 364 N.E.2d 1189, 1192 (Ind. Ct. App. 1977)(unemployment review board could properly conclude that employee owes his employer duty to refrain from making improper sexual advances toward other employees); Crane v. Iowa Dep't of Job Serv., 412 N.W.2d 194, 196–97 (Iowa Ct. App. 1987)(claimant's deliberate action in exposing his buttocks was in "violation or disregard of standards of behavior which [employer] had the right to expect of employees"); Strickhouser v. Commonwealth, 80 Pa. Commw. 587, 588–89, 471 A.2d 1338, 1339 (1984)(claimant's conduct in dropping his pants in front of two female co-workers was "in disregard of the standard of behavior which the employer has the right to expect of an employee"); Kohler Co. v. Labor & Indus. Review Comm'n, 47 FEP Cases 424, 424 (Wis. Cir. Ct. 1988)("In this day and age the court is satisfied that young women in their employment do not have to be subjected to subtleties and innuendos of a sexual nature").

[48]See Chapters 3, Quid Pro Quo Harassment; 4, Hostile Environment Harassment; 5, Claims by Third Parties; 9, Constructive Discharge; 10, Retaliation; 11, Federal Constitutional, Statutory, and Civil Rights

forms is whether a decision in the unemployment compensation proceeding on an issue of sexual harassment will preclude the parties from relitigating the same issue in the separate action.

The preclusive effect of unemployment compensation decisions generally is governed by common-law principles of *"res judicata"* or "collateral estoppel."[49] Under these doctrines, decisions of administrative agencies can have a binding effect in subsequent proceedings so long as the agency is acting in a judicial capacity and affords the parties a full and fair opportunity to be heard.[50]

Several states have, by statute, reversed the common-law rule so that decisions made in unemployment compensation proceedings cannot be used in separate actions.[51] In many jurisdictions, however, the preclusive effect of unemployment compensation decisions depends on the particular circumstances.[52]

In determining the preclusive effect of an unemployment compensation decision, the primary consideration is whether the issues decided in the unemployment proceeding are the same as those to be decided in the separate action. In some cases courts have found a sufficient similarity of issues to preclude relitigation.[53]

Law; 12, Fair Employment Practices Statutes; 14, Workers' Compensation Statutes; 15, The Common Law; 16, Criminal Law; and 17, Collective Bargaining Agreements and Union Obligations.

[49]In general, *res judicata,* or claim preclusion, prevents the parties from relitigating issues that were or could have been raised in connection with a prior judgment on the *same cause of action.* Collateral estoppel, or issue preclusion, precludes relitigation of issues on a different cause of action if the issues were actually adjudicated and necessary to the prior judgment. *See* Kremer v. Chemical Constr. Corp., 456 U.S. 461, 467 n.6 (1982); 18 C. WRIGHT, A. MILLER & E. COOPER, FEDERAL PRACTICE AND PROCEDURE §4402 (1981).

[50]See United States v. Utah Constr. & Mining Co., 384 U.S. 394, 422 (1966); Restatement (Second) of Judgments §83 (1980).

[51]*See* ARK. STAT. ANN. §11-10-314(a)(2); CAL. UNEMP. INS. CODE §1960; COLO. REV. STAT. §8-74-108; CONN. GEN. STAT. §31-249g(b); IDAHO CODE §72-1368(k)(2); ILL. REV. STAT. ch. 48, ¶640, §1900; LA. REV. STAT. ANN. §23:1636; MICH. COMP. LAWS §421.11(b)(1); MO. REV. STAT. §288.215; N.H. REV. STAT. ANN. §282-A:180; N.Y. LAB. LAW art. 18, §623(2); S.D. CODIFIED LAWS ANN. §61-7-24; UTAH CODE ANN. §35-4-10(f)(2); WASH. REV. CODE §50.32.097; WYO. STAT. §27-3-406(c).

[52]*See generally* Committee on Benefits to Unemployed Persons, *The Preclusive Effect of Unemployment Decisions in Subsequent Litigation,* 4 LAB. L.J. 69 (1988). The preclusive effect of unemployment compensation decisions may be decided by federal as well as state courts, depending on the forum of the separate action. In diversity actions, a federal court must decide such issues by applying the law of the case where it sits. *See* Erie R.R. Co. v. Tompkins, 304 U.S. 64 (1938); Spearman v. Delco Remy Div., 717 F. Supp. 1351, 1357 n.4 (S.D. Ind. 1989)(federal court sitting in diversity must apply state law to determine collateral estoppel effect of state unemployment compensation decision). Where suit is brought on a substantive federal right, *e.g.,* under Title VII, a state administrative agency decision that has been reviewed by a state court must be given the same preclusive effect that it would be given by the courts of the particular state. Kremer v. Chemical Constr. Corp., 456 U.S. 461 (1982). Where an administrative agency decision has not been reviewed, the preclusive effect depends on the type of action. The Supreme Court has held that, based on congressional intent, unreviewed state administrative decisions may not be given preclusive effect in Title VII actions. University of Tenn. v. Elliott, 478 U.S. 788, 796 (1986). In other types of cases, federal courts generally apply federal common-law principles of *res judicata* and collateral estoppel. *Id.* at 799; Mack v. South Bay Beer Distrib., 798 F.2d 1279, 1283 (9th Cir. 1986).

[53]*See, e.g.,* Mitchell v. Humana Hosp., 54 FEP Cases 416 (N.D. Ala. 1990)(claimant who lost unemployment compensation claim in a *de novo* trial before a state court judge on issue of whether she had voluntarily resigned was issue-precluded in her Title VII constructive discharge claim); Despain v. Emery Worldwide, 1990 U.S. Dist. LEXIS 1296 (S.D. Ohio 1990)(applying Ohio law to hold that unemployment compensation determination that claimant was terminated for falsifying records precluded him from litigating just-cause issue in breach of contract action); Leong v. Hilton Hotels Corp., 698 F. Supp. 1496 (D. Haw. 1988)(decision made in unemployment compensation proceeding, and affirmed by state court, that claimant had resigned employment for personal reasons precluded her from relitigating issues of constructive discharge in action brought under Title VII and pendent state-law theories); Mays v. Envelope House, 1987 U.S. Dist. LEXIS 11043 (E.D. Ky. 1987)(unemployment compensation decision that claimant had resigned because of dissatisfaction with pay estopped her from relitigating reason for termination in subsequent action brought under Title VII and 42 U.S.C. §1981; Gear v. City of Des Moines, 514 F. Supp. 1218 (S.D. Iowa 1981)(under Iowa law, employee was precluded from relitigating, in suit brought under 42 U.S.C. §§1981 and 1983, factual issues relating to her termination and allegations of sexual harassment that previously had been decided against her in unemployment compensation proceeding); Pullar v. Upjohn Health Care Serv., 21

In the majority of cases, however, courts have declined to give preclusive effect to unemployment compensation decisions, reasoning that the issues determined in the unemployment proceeding were not identical to those raised in the separate proceeding.[54] In *Cooper v. City of North Olmstead*,[55] an employee filed suit against her former employer under Title VII and §1981, alleging that she had been discharged because of race and sex. Earlier, a state administrative agency, in a decision affirmed by a state court, had denied the plaintiff's claim for unemployment benefits, finding that the claimant had been discharged for just cause. Although the employer argued that this decision should bar the plaintiff's discrimination claims, the *Cooper* court held that the question of whether the plaintiff was discharged because of race or sex was not at issue in the unemployment compensation proceeding, which had addressed only whether she was at fault in causing her termination.

The preclusive effect of an unemployment compensation decision also depends on whether the parties had a full and fair opportunity to litigate. While unemployment compensation proceedings are generally less formal than civil actions and do not afford full discovery or the right to a jury trial, these differences may not be sufficient to avoid the application of collateral estoppel.[56] However, courts have declined to afford preclusive effect to unemployment compensation decisions where the losing party was not represented,

---

Ohio App.3d 288, 488 N.E.2d 486 (1984)(unemployment compensation decision that claimant had been discharged for insubordination barred subsequent claim for age discrimination under state fair employment practices statute); Frederick v. American Hardware Supply Co., 384 Pa. Super. 72, 557 A.2d 779, *appeal denied*, 523 Pa. 636, 565 A.2d 445 (1989) (unemployment compensation decision that claimants had been discharged for violating employer's rules and procedures operated as collateral estoppel in subsequent suit for breach of implied employment contract).

[54] *See, e.g.,* Kelley v. TYK Refractories Co., 860 F.2d 1188 (3d Cir. 1988)(under Pennsylvania law, unemployment compensation decision that claimant voluntarily terminated employment without good cause did not preclude litigation of claim for race discrimination, because administrative agency made no findings concerning presence or absence of discrimination); Comeaux v. Uniroyal Chem. Corp., 849 F.2d 191 (5th Cir. 1988)(determination made in unemployment compensation proceeding that claimant had not violated employer's safety rule and was eligible for benefits did not have preclusive effect on question whether employee's termination was racially motivated); Teamsters Local Union No. 273 v. Grandstaff, 687 F. Supp. 985 (W.D. Pa. 1988)(unemployment compensation decision awarding benefits to claimant did not estop employer from defending claim for breach of collective bargaining agreement, because issue of willful misconduct differed from issue of just cause); Mays v. Envelope House, *supra* note 53 (in action for race discrimination and harassment under Title VII and 42 U.S.C. §1981, employee estopped from relitigating reason for resigning, which had been decided in unemployment compensation proceeding, but was not precluded from litigating remaining issues); Sewall v. Taylor, 672 F. Supp. 542 (D. Me. 1987)(under Maine law, unemployment compensation decision that claimant was dismissed for misconduct did not estop employer from defending claim that employee had been discharged for exercising First Amendment rights); Niles v. Weissman & Sons, 786 P.2d 662 (Mont. 1990)(unemployment compensation decision that claimant left employment voluntarily did not preclude claim in separate action for wrongful discharge and breach of covenant of good faith, because question of employer's good faith could not have been considered in unemployment proceeding); Adams v. Harding Mach. Co., 56 Ohio App.3d 150, 565 N.E.2d 858 (1989)(unemployment compensation decision that claimant was discharged without just cause was not entitled to preclusive effect in subsequent wrongful discharge suit, because issue of just cause for purposes of benefit eligibility was not the same as just cause for discharge under employer's handbook); Santilli v. Strouss Dep't Store, No. 84 C.A. 164 (Ohio Ct. App. 1985)(LEXIS, States Library)(decision in unemployment compensation proceeding that claimant had been discharged for theft did not estop her claims for false imprisonment, defamation, and intentional and negligent infliction of emotional distress; her lawsuit did not challenge reason for discharge, but only reasonableness and legality of means used in carrying it out); Griffith v. Hodes, 96 Ore. App. 387, 772 P.2d 1370 (unemployment compensation decision that claimant was discharged for refusing to perform assigned work did not preclude claim that discharge was because of physical handicap, complaints about unsafe working conditions, and was in violation of employer's personnel manual), *review denied*, 308 Or. 197, 777 P.2d 410 (1989).

[55] 795 F.2d 1265 (6th Cir. 1986).

[56] *See, e.g.,* Gear v. City of Des Moines, 514 F. Supp. 1218, 1221–23 (S.D. Iowa 1981)(unemployment compensation decision properly could be given collateral estoppel effect where parties had right to present

where the losing party was denied an opportunity to present evidence, or where the amount in controversy in the separate action was significantly larger than the size of the claim for unemployment benefits.[57]

Another determining factor is the nature of the separate action. Courts have shown particular reluctance to give preclusive effect to unemployment compensation decisions in the context of separate administrative proceedings. In an Arizona case,[58] the court held that a judgment entered in an unemployment compensation proceeding could not be given *res judicata* or collateral estoppel effect in an employment termination case decided by the state personnel board. To do so, said the court, would nullify the function of the board to hear and review personnel matters arising out of state employment.[59]

Courts are least likely to give preclusive effect to unemployment compensation decisions where an employee attempts to use such a decision offensively, as a means of barring an employer's defense in a separate action.[60] Courts

---

evidence, to cross-examine opposing witnesses, and claimant had right to be represented by counsel); Pullar v. Upjohn Health Care Serv., 21 Ohio App.3d 288, 293–94, 488 N.E.2d 486, 492 (1984)(rejecting plaintiff's argument that unemployment compensation proceeding should not be given *res judicata* effect where she was represented by counsel, had full opportunity to produce evidence, give testimony and cross-examine witnesses, and then failed to pursue her right to appeal). *But see* Mack v. South Bay Beer Distrib., 798 F.2d 1279 (9th Cir. 1986)(as matter of federal common law, unreviewed decision by unemployment compensation board did not operate as collateral estoppel in subsequent age discrimination suit; nature of unemployment compensation proceedings, including relatively small amount in controversy, remedial purpose of benefit program, absence of legal counsel and informal procedures did not allow parties adequate opportunity to litigate employment discrimination issues).

[57]*See, e.g.,* Fox v. Devereaux Found., 1990 U.S. Dist. LEXIS 8525 (E.D. Pa. 1990)(under Pennsylvania law, unemployment compensation decision that claimant was terminated for willful misconduct did not bar his suit for sex discrimination, breach of contract, and defamation where claimant was not represented by counsel in administrative proceeding); Rucker v. State, 156 Wis.2d 824, 458 N.W.2d 390 (Wis. Ct. App. 1990)(decision in unemployment compensation proceeding that claimant was discharged for misconduct did not preclude claim under state fair employment statute that he was discharged in retaliation for opposing race and sex discrimination, because claimant was denied opportunity to present evidence of discrimination in unemployment compensation hearing).

[58]Ferris v. Hawkins, 135 Ariz. 329, 660 P.2d 1256. (Ct. App. 1983).

[59]*Id.* at 333, 660 P.2d at 1260. The Iowa Supreme Court reached a similar conclusion in *Kjos v. City of Sioux City,* 346 N.W.2d 25, 29 (Iowa 1984), where it held that an adjudication of misconduct by the state unemployment appeal board did not preclude an employee from challenging his discharge before the civil service commission: "[B]y establishing one administrative remedy for challenging the discharge and a separate remedy for seeking unemployment compensation the legislature has provided a scheme of remedies in which an adjudication of one claim will not bar the other."

[60]*See, e.g.,* Comeaux v. Uniroyal Chem. Corp., 849 F.2d 191 (5th Cir. 1988)(unemployment compensation decision that claimant was not discharged for misconduct did not preclude employer from defending claim that claimant had been discharged based on his race); Sewall v. Taylor, 672 F. Supp. 542 (D. Me. 1987)(applying Maine law to hold that unemployment compensation decision that claimant had not been terminated for misconduct did not collaterally estop employer from litigating claim that employee had been discharged for exercising his First Amendment rights); Neidhart v. Pioneer Fed. Sav. & Loan Ass'n, 498 So.2d 594 (Fla. Ct. App. 1986)(unemployment compensation decision that claimant was not discharged for misconduct did not operate as *res judicata* in subsequent civil action by claimant on theory that he had been wrongfully discharged for responding to jury summons); Luft v. Sears, Roebuck & Co., 117 LRRM 2704 (Iowa Dist. Ct. 1984)(unemployment compensation decision that claimant had not been terminated for willful misconduct did not preclude employer from defending issue of just cause termination under collective bargaining agreement); Roberts v. Wake Forest Univ., 55 N.C. App. 430, 286 S.E.2d 120 (1982)(decision in unemployment compensation proceeding that claimant was entitled to benefits did not have *res judicata* effect in subsequent breach of contract action because issues in separate proceeding were not the same); Adams v. Harding Mach. Co., *supra* note 54 (unemployment compensation decision that claimant was discharged without just cause was not entitled to preclusive effect in subsequent wrongful discharge suit because issue of just cause for purposes of eligibility for unemployment benefits differed from issue of discharge for cause under employee handbook); Tedesco v. Glenbeigh Hosp., No. 54899 (Ohio Ct. App. 1989)(finding in unemployment compensation proceeding that employer breached provision of employee handbook did not collaterally estop employer from relitigating issue in wrongful termination suit; issue regarding existence of employment contract was not relevant to determination of eligibility for unemployment benefits). *But see* Spearman v. Delco Remy Div., 717 F. Supp. 1351 (S.D. Ind. 1989)(applying Indiana law to hold that unemployment compensation decision that employee was not discharged for cause barred employer from relitigating issue in wrongful discharge case).

rarely have addressed whether a finding of sexual harassment in an unemployment compensation proceeding can be accorded collateral estoppel effect against an employer in a subsequent administrative proceeding or civil action. In *Valerio v. Dahlberg*,[61] a claimant was awarded unemployment compensation benefits based on an administrative decision that she had been discharged without just cause, and then brought a federal court action against her employer, alleging that she had been terminated in retaliation for her complaints of sexual harassment and because of her refusal to tolerate harassment by her supervisor. The court held that the unemployment compensation decision did not preclude the employer from relitigating the issue of discharge. The court emphasized that the employer's motivation, which was critical to the employee's legal claims, had not been litigated in the administrative proceeding.[62]

IV. Practical Considerations in Dealing With Unemployment Compensation Claims

At the pre-claim stage, the practical considerations of establishing or avoiding liability for unemployment compensation in sexual harassment cases do not differ greatly from those involved in civil actions. From the employer's perspective, establishing and publishing an appropriate sexual harassment policy, providing a meaningful reporting mechanism, and vigorously following up on employee complaints will help to avoid or minimize liability no matter what the forum. Similarly, from the employee's perspective, reporting allegations of harassment through established procedures and allowing the employer an opportunity to correct any problems will assist in establishing liability.[63]

Of far more practical importance is how the parties deal with unemployment compensation cases involving allegations of sexual harassment *after* an unemployment compensation claim has been filed. In some states, findings made in an unemployment compensation proceeding may have a preclusive effect in a separate action. Even where they do not, the unemployment compensation decision may dissuade or encourage the settlement of related civil claims. Furthermore, evidence given and findings made in the unemployment compensation proceeding may be admissible and thus bolster or undercut claims in a subsequent civil action.[63a]

In states that permit unemployment compensation decisions to have preclusive effect, the parties should consider a number of factors in litigating—or deciding not to litigate—such claims. First, in some states, the administrative agency responsible for unemployment compensation claims may be seen as more "pro-employee" than the state's court system, with the result that litigating unemployment compensation claims in that forum is less desirable for

---

[61]716 F. Supp. 1031 (S.D. Ohio 1988).

[62]*Id.* at 1038. In *Moody v. Westin Renaissance Co.,* 162 Mich. App. 743, 413 N.W.2d 96 (1987), the employer argued that it was not bound by an unemployment compensation decision that the claimant had left her employment because of sexual harassment. The court did not reach the question, holding that Michigan statute precluded the use of unemployment compensation decisions in subsequent civil actions.

[63]*See* Chapters 18, Taking Preventive Action, and 19, Responding to Internal Complaints.

[63a]Barfield v. Orange County, 911 F.2d 644 (11th Cir. 1990)(trial court within its discretion, in Title VII case, in admitting findings and conclusions of unemployment compensation commission that plaintiff had been discharged for misconduct).

employers and more desirable for employees. Where the unemployment compensation agency tends to favor employees, the employer may decide not to challenge an employee's claim at all, on the theory that the risk of preclusion is significantly less where the issues have not been litigated than if the agency renders an adverse decision on the merits. Based on similar considerations, an employee might decide to forgo the unemployment compensation forum, although, for many employees, financial considerations may preclude this option.

Procedural considerations should also inform a party's decision as to whether and how to litigate an unemployment compensation claim. In the unemployment compensation setting, little if any discovery is available, and the parties are much less likely to be represented by counsel than in a civil action. In such cases, the parties may be less likely to prosecute their respective cases vigorously, and may make damaging admissions that could be used in a subsequent civil action.[64] In addition, unemployment compensation cases are usually tried fairly soon after the employee's termination, when the recollections of both the employee and the employer's witnesses are fresh. While this does not necessarily benefit one party over the other, it is a factor that should be considered.

If the unemployment decision can be given preclusive effect, parties that decide to litigate the claim must present the best possible case in the administrative forum. This may mean that the party's witnesses will be tied to their testimony early on in the litigation process without the benefit of discovery or advice of counsel. In addition, the employer should consider that if it loses in the unemployment compensation proceeding, it may have established liability in a civil claim that otherwise might not have been pursued. Indeed, in some situations, the employer's decision to oppose a claim for unemployment compensation, even if successful, may prompt an administrative complaint or a lawsuit that otherwise would not have been filed—either by forcing the employee to obtain an attorney in connection with the unemployment compensation claim, or by making the employee feel compelled to seek vindication in a legal proceeding.

In states where unemployment compensation decisions cannot be given preclusive effect, the proceeding may still be used as a discovery tool for potential civil litigation. For employers this can be particularly advantageous, because they can obtain information from the claimant without necessarily subjecting their own witnesses to the same process. If the employer believes that the risk of a civil suit outweighs the cost of an unemployment compensation award, it can choose not to present witnesses and proceed only through cross-examination of the claimant. While this strategy is more likely to produce an adverse decision in the unemployment compensation proceeding, it can be a useful technique where civil litigation is pending or expected.

---

[64]If a party intends to elicit testimony for potential use in a later proceeding, it is critical to have some method for preserving the record of the unemployment compensation hearing. A court reporter's transcript of the proceeding is preferable, but a tape recording may be adequate in some cases. *See, e.g.,* Rauh v. Coyne, 744 F. Supp. 1181 (D.D.C. 1990)(admitting defendant's statement, tape-recorded in unemployment compensation hearing, that plaintiff had not been discharged for misconduct). It is important to check in advance on local practice. Agencies in some jurisdictions routinely record unemployment compensation hearings; in other jurisdictions it may be necessary to request in advance that a recording or transcription be made. Depending on local practice, it also may be possible for a party to provide its own court reporter if the agency does not provide one.

CHAPTER 14

WORKERS' COMPENSATION STATUTES

I. OVERVIEW

Employees who are sexually harassed in the workplace may have a remedy under a state workers' compensation statute.[1] In many states this remedy may bar any common-law action for the same injury.[2] Federal civilian employees who are sexually harassed may be entitled to compensation under the Federal Employees' Compensation Act.[3]

All states have enacted some type of workers' compensation system designed to compensate employees for workplace injuries.[4] Typically, workers' compensation statutes have emerged as legislative compromises between the interests of employees and those of employers. The statutes are intended to give employees an efficient and effective remedy for workplace injuries without regard to fault. Thus, injured employees avoid the traditional pitfalls of personal

---

[1]In addition, in most states an employee who has filed or made known the intent to file a workers' compensation claim has statutory protection against employer retaliation on that account. *See generally* 4 A. LARSON, WORKMEN'S COMPENSATION LAW, app. A-7A-1 to 16 (1990). *See, e.g.,* ALA. CODE §25-5-11.1 (1986); ARK. CODE ANN. §11-9-107 (1987); CAL. LAB. CODE §132a (West 1989); CONN. GEN. STAT. ANN. §31-290a (1987); HAW. REV. STAT. §378-32(2)(1988); KY. REV. STAT. ANN. §348.197 (Michie/Bobbs-Merrill 1988); LA. REV. STAT. ANN. §23:1361 (West 1985); ME. REV. STAT. ANN. tit. 39, §111 (1989); MD. CODE ANN. §101-39A (1985); MICH. STAT. ANN. §17.237 (301)(Callaghan 1988); MO. ANN. STAT. §287.780 (1990 Supp.); MONT. CODE ANN. §39-71-317 (1989); N.J. STAT. ANN. §34.15-39.1 (1988); N.Y. WORK. COMP. LAW §120 (McKinney Supp. 1990); N.C. GEN. STAT. §97-6.1 (1985); OHIO REV. CODE ANN. §4123.90 (Baldwin 1989 Supp.); OKLA. STAT. ANN. tit. 85, §5 (1990 Supp.); OR. REV. STAT. §659.410 (1989); S.C. CODE ANN. §41-1-80 (Law. Co-op. Supp. 1989); TEX. REV. CIV. STAT. ANN. art. 8307c (Vernon Supp. 1990); VT. STAT. ANN. tit. 21, §720 (1987); VA. CODE ANN. §65.1-40.1 (1987); WIS. STAT. ANN. §102.35 (1988).

[2]For a discussion of workers' compensation exclusivity as an employer defense, see Section II. *infra* and Chapter 27, Asserted Defenses, Section IV. Cases that address workers' compensation exclusivity are discussed in this chapter because these cases, in deciding the issue of exclusivity, logically must also address the scope of workers' compensation coverage, which is the subject of this chapter.

[3]5 U.S.C. §8101 *et seq. E.g.,* Nichols v. Frank, 732 F. Supp. 1085, 1087, 52 FEP Cases 951, 954 (D. Or. 1990)(postal employee received benefits equal to 75% of her wages as disability compensation for injuries caused by sexual harassment). Other specialized workers' compensation statutes are the Longshoremen's and Harbor Workers' Compensation Act, 33 U.S.C. §§901–950 (covering non-seamen workers on navigable waters and adjoining facilities such as shipbuilding facilities) and the Defense Base Act, 42 U.S.C. §§1651–1654, 1701–1717.

[4]*See* 1 A. LARSON, WORKERS' COMPENSATION LAW, §5.30 (1990). For a comprehensive listing of workers' compensation statutes, see 4 A. LARSON, *supra* note 1, at 511–23.

injury litigation, such as contributory negligence, assumption of the risk, and the fellow-servant doctrine.[5]

The corresponding benefit to the employer provided by the legislative compromise is that many previously available tort remedies are precluded and replaced with administrative remedies that are far more limited than traditional tort remedies.[6]

The object of state workers' compensation benefits is to compensate injured employees for the economic consequences of work-related injuries. Workers' compensation benefits usually consist of three components: (1) medical expenses connected to the injury, (2) periodic payments based on lost earnings during the healing period following the injury, and (3) compensation based on lost earning capacity.[7]

The principal issues raised by a claim for workers' compensation benefits are whether the employee suffered an injury as defined by the particular state statute;[8] whether the injury arose out of and occurred in the course of the employment;[9] whether workers' compensation is the exclusive remedy for covered injuries, thus precluding certain common-law claims;[10] and whether the employee has satisfied the requisite notice requirements.

Because victims of sexual harassment have historically been reluctant to complain about it contemporaneously, the time limits provided in each state workers' compensation statute for notifying the employer of an injury could become particularly important. Employees injured by sexual harassment who fail to notify the employer of the injury or to make a claim within the time specified by the statute could jeopardize their chances for a workers' compensation recovery.[11]

Incidents of sexual harassment raising workers' compensation issues include a supervisor or co-worker requesting sexual favors of an employee,[12] commenting on the employee's sexual anatomy,[13] making lewd comments to

---

[5]For a discussion of the origins of the American workers' compensation system, see 1 A. LARSON, *supra* note 4, §§4.00–5.00, at 23–40.

[6]*Id.* §2.40, at 10 ("[i]n compensation, unlike tort, the only injuries compensated for are those which produce disability and thereby presumably affect earning power").

[7]For a discussion of workers' compensation remedies, see Section IV. *infra*.

[8]See Section III.A. *infra*.

[9]See Section III.B. *infra*.

[10]See note 2 *supra*.

[11]*E.g.,* Murdock v. Michigan Health Maintenance Org., 391 N.W.2d 757, 759 (Mich. Ct. App. 1986)(remanding to determine whether employer had notice of plaintiff's injuries from sexual harassment). *See generally* Tropser v. Town of Oneida, 776 S.W.2d 72 (Tenn. 1989)(plaintiff not allowed to recover workers' compensation benefits for back injury because she did not notify employer within 30 days of injury).

[12]*E.g.,* Fields v. Cummins Employees Fed. Credit Union, 540 N.E.2d 631, 633 (Ind. Ct. App. 1989)(supervisor repeatedly promised to promote employee "if she would sleep with him"); Cummings v. Walsh Constr. Co., 561 F. Supp. 872, 876, 31 FEP Cases 930, 931 (S.D. Ga. 1983)(employee alleged that her supervisors approached her several times for sexual favors and solicited her for oral sex on at least one occasion).

[13]*E.g.,* Busby v. Truswal Sys. Corp., 551 So.2d 322, 324 (Ala. 1989)(employees complained of supervisor's stare and his comment that one employee's nipples were as large as another employee's entire breasts).

the employee,[14] threatening the employee,[15] touching and grabbing the employee,[16] and raping the employee.[17]

II. WORKERS' COMPENSATION EXCLUSIVITY

While workers' compensation statutes provide a no-fault system of compensation to employees, they also shield employers from tort liability arising from work-related injuries to their employees by providing that the workers' compensation remedy is exclusive. Thus, if an injury is compensable under workers' compensation, the benefits recovered may be the exclusive state-law remedy for that injury.

When acts of sexual harassment in employment have provided a complainant with a basis for a common-law claim,[18] the defendant will often argue that the applicable state workers' compensation statute bars the claim on the ground that workers' compensation provides the exclusive remedy.[18a] Accordingly, many cases addressing workers' compensation coverage for sexual harassment injuries arise in the context of the employer attempting to invoke, and the employee attempting to avoid, the exclusivity provision of a workers' compensation statute. In these cases, the employer is in the ironic position of arguing that it was liable to the employee under the workers' compensation statute, and the employee is in the ironic position of arguing that the employer had no liability so far as the workers' compensation statute was concerned.

III. INJURIES COGNIZABLE UNDER WORKERS' COMPENSATION

A threshold issue in any question of workers' compensation coverage is whether the employee has suffered an "injury" as that term is defined by the particular state statute.

---

[14]*E.g.*, Brooms v. Regal Tube Co., 881 F.2d 412, 417, 50 FEP Cases 1499, 1501 (7th Cir. 1989)(supervisor showed employee pornographic photograph depicting act of sodomy while commenting that employee was hired for purpose indicated in photograph); Brown v. Alos Micrographics Corp., 540 N.Y.S.2d 911, 912 (N.Y. App. Div. 1989)(employee's supervisor continually told her about the "very nice" dreams he had about her).

[15]*E.g.*, Cremen v. Harrah's Marina Hotel Casino, 680 F. Supp. 150, 152 (D.N.J. 1988)(after locking employee in his office, supervisor told her that if she "wanted the job, to prove it"); Pikop v. Burlington N. Ry. Co., 390 N.W.2d 743, 745, 42 FEP Cases 1822, 1823 (Minn. 1986)(employee alleged that her supervisor coerced her, through threats and promises relating to her employment, to perform sexual acts against her will); Cox v. Brazo, 303 S.E.2d 71, 71–73 (Ga. Ct. App. 1983)(supervisor threatened to fire employee and give her extra duties because she rejected his sexual advances).

[16]*E.g.*, O'Connell v. Chasdi, 511 N.E.2d 349, 350, 50 FEP Cases 574, 575 (Mass. 1987)(during business trip, employee's supervisor repeatedly made physical advances toward her by placing his hand on her knee, hugging her, stroking her hair and face, and attempting to hold her hand); Hollrah v. Freidrich, 634 S.W.2d 221, 222 (Mo. Ct. App. 1982)(supervisor allegedly grabbed hold of and touched private parts of employee's body); Schwartz v. Zippy Mart, 470 So.2d 720, 721, 50 FEP Cases 464, 465 (Fla. Dist. Ct. App. 1985)(employee alleged her supervisor pinched, grabbed and patted her shoulders, buttocks, and other parts of her body against her will).

[17]*E.g.*, Carr v. USW Direct Co., 98 Or. App. 30, 32, 779 P.2d 154 (Or. Ct. App. 1989)(while accompanying her supervisor on several business calls, employee harassed, assaulted, and raped by him).

[18]See Chapter 15, The Common Law.

[18a]For detailed discussion of this defense, see Chapter 27, Asserted Defenses, Section IV.

A. Nature of the Injury

1. Disabling or Requiring Medical Treatment

Workers' compensation statutes generally provide that an injury is not compensable unless it causes a disability or the need for medical attention.[19] This requirement will preclude a claim for workers' compensation benefits where sexual harassment has neither disabled the employee nor required medical care.[20] Thus, while an employee may have suffered some emotional distress as a result of sexual harassment, the employee may not be entitled to workers' compensation if the injury is not disabling.[21]

2. Physical Versus Mental or Psychological Injury

The most common injury suffered by sexual harassment complainants is mental and emotional stress,[22] which may have physical manifestations.[23] Some states limit workers' compensation to "physical" injuries and thus deny benefits to employees who, although suffering emotional stress, have not been physically injured by the sexual harassment.[24] Nonetheless, in many states an employee who has suffered emotional stress that has caused a physical injury may be able to recover benefits.[25]

Some states, however, seem to observe no distinction between physical and nonphysical injuries and provide workers' compensation benefits for purely mental or psychological injuries as well as physical injuries.[26] States that allow

---

[19] 1 A. LARSON, WORKERS' COMPENSATION LAW §2.40 (1990).

[20] Generally, "disability" in the workers' compensation context means an impairment or incapacity, temporary or permanent, caused by an injury, that renders an employee unable to earn the wages that the employee was receiving at the time of the injury in the same or other employment. *See generally* 2 A. LARSON, WORKERS' COMPENSATION LAW §57 (1990). *See, e.g.,* ALASKA STAT. §23.30.265(10)(1989); ARK. STAT. ANN. 81-1302(e)(Supp. 1983); FLA. STAT. ANN. §440.02(9)(1981); ILL. ANN. STAT. ch. 48, ¶172.36(e)(Smith-Hurd 1986); IND. CODE ANN. §22-3-7-9 (Burns 1986); KY. REV. STAT. ANN. §342.620(12)(1987); MD. ANN. CODE §101-67 (1985); MINN. STAT. ANN. §176.131(8)(West 1966); MISS. CODE ANN. §71-3-3(i)(1989); NEV. REV. STAT. §616.117 (1986); N.C. GEN. STAT. §97-2(9)(1986); R.I. GEN. LAWS §23-34-1(a)(1986); S.C. CODE ANN. §42-1-120 (1985); UTAH CODE ANN. §35-2-12(a)(1988).

[21] *E.g.,* Murdock v. Michigan Health Maintenance Org., 391 N.W.2d 757, 759 (Mich. Ct. App. 1986)("disability" means inability to perform or obtain work in employee's general field or capacity, not just inability to work for harassing employer).

[22] *E.g.,* Byrd v. Richardson-Greenshields Sec., 552 So.2d 1099, 1100, 51 EPD ¶39,446 (Fla. 1989)(employee claimed that repeated touching and verbal sexual advances by male employees resulted in emotional anguish and stress); Ramada Inn Surfside v. Swanson, 560 So.2d 300, 302 (Fla. Dist. Ct. App. 1990)(employee diagnosed as suffering from severe major depressive disorder and adjustment disorder as result of sexual harassment and assault by supervisor); Palmer v. Bi-Mart Co., 92 Or. App. 470, 472, 758 P.2d 888, 890 (1988)(employee claimed to have suffered stress syndrome due to harassment by supervisor).

[23] *E.g.,* Brooms v. Regal Tube Co., 881 F.2d 412, 416–17, 50 FEP Cases 1499, 1501 (7th Cir. 1989)(employee suffered severe debilitating depression and physical illness caused by her supervisor's repeated abuse); Ford v. Revlon, Inc., 734 P.2d 580, 583, 43 FEP Cases 213, 215 (Ariz. 1987)(during harassment, employee developed high blood pressure, a nervous tic in her left eye, chest pains, rapid breathing, and other symptoms of emotional distress).

[24] *E.g.,* Busby v. Truswal Sys. Corp., 551 So.2d 322, 325 (Ala. 1989)("Act provides compensation only for physical injuries to the body and does not provide recovery for purely psychological injuries"); Cummings v. Walsh Constr. Co., 561 F. Supp. 872, 880, 31 FEP Cases 930, 935 (S.D. Ga. 1983)("it is well settled in Georgia that mental trauma alone brought about by psychic stimulus is not compensable as an injury").

[25] 1B A. LARSON, WORKMEN'S COMPENSATION LAW §42.21(a)(1990)(nearly all decisions find compensability where mental impact or stimulus results in distinct physical injury). *Cf.* Cummings v. Walsh Constr. Co., *supra* note 24 (no compensable injury occurred absent evidence of any physical injury precipitating mental distress or any physical disability arising from the distress).

[26] *E.g.,* CAL. LAB. CODE §3208.3 (West Supp. 1990)(providing that psychiatric injuries are "compensa-

recovery for purely psychological injuries, however, still require that the injury be disabling or require medical treatment.[27]

B. Nexus With Employment

Any injury must be sufficiently connected to work in order to be compensable. The typical statutory formula is that the employee's injury must "arise out" of employment and "occur in the course" of employment. Whether sexual harassment injuries meet these criteria may depend on which of the different tests a particular state follows in resolving this question.[28]

1. Injuries Arising Out of Employment

The requirement that the injury arise out of the employment addresses the causal connection between the injury and the employee's work. States follow differing tests for resolving whether the requisite causal connection exists.

a. The "but for" standard. Some courts have taken a very expansive view of this requirement, holding that for an injury to arise out of employment there need be only some connection to the employee's job.[29] This type of analysis has been described as "positional risk" or "but for" analysis, because the injury is viewed as arising out of employment if the employment put the employee in the position to be injured.[30] Thus, assaults by co-workers have

---

ble"); WIS. STAT. ANN. §102.01(2)(c)(West Supp. 1985)(covered injury includes "mental or physical harm to an employee").

[27]*E.g.,* CAL. LAB. CODE §3208.3 (West Supp. 1990)("psychiatric injury shall be compensable if it is a mental disorder which causes disability or need for medical treatment").

[28]*Compare* Bennett v. Furr's Cafeterias, 549 F. Supp. 887, 30 FEP Cases 93 (D. Colo. 1982)(substantial questions exist as to whether employee's alleged injuries resulting from alleged sexual harassment are job-related) *with* Johnson v. International Minerals & Chem. Corp., 40 FEP Cases 1651 (D.S.D. 1986)(common-law battery claim not barred by workers' compensation, despite fact that nonconsensual kiss constituting battery occurred at work, for kiss had no association with job itself).

[29]*E.g.,* Cremen v. Harrah's Marina Hotel Casino, 680 F. Supp. 150, 153 (D.N.J. 1988)(applying positional risk analysis, which requires only that employment in some manner physically facilitated occurrence of incident); Lui v. Intercontinental Hotels Corp., 634 F. Supp. 684, 688, 47 FEP Cases 99, 101 (D. Haw. 1986)(requiring only tenuous connection to work); Baker v. Wendy's of Mont., 687 P.2d 885, 892 (Wyo. 1984)(injuries caused by supervisor's harassment arose out of employment because sufficient causal connection exists if there is nexus between injury and some condition, activity, environment, or requirement of employment); Ramada Inn Surfside v. Swanson, 560 So.2d 300, 303 (Fla. Dist. Ct. App. 1990)(employee's injury arose out of and in the course of employment when her supervisor sexually assaulted her while they were inspecting potential investment property).

[30]Professor Larson advocates the positional risk analysis. He separates the risks of injury into three categories: (1) work-related, (2) neutral, and (3) personal. At one extreme are work-related risks—all the things that go wrong in modern employment, such as machinery breaking, objects falling, and fingers getting caught in gears. Personal risks, at the other extreme, are risks clearly personal to the employee, such as the risk of being found at work and assaulted by a mortal enemy. Neutral risks are neither distinctly personal nor distinctly employment-related. Injuries due to work-related risks are generally compensable; injuries due to personal risks are generally not. As to injuries due to neutral risks, Larson's positional risk analysis would determine if the conditions of employment put the employee in a position to be injured. 1 A. LARSON, WORKERS' COMPENSATION LAW §§7.00–7.30 (1990). Several courts have used this categorical examination to determine whether an employee assaulted at work was covered by workers' compensation. Stamper v. Hiteshew, 54 FEP Cases 209 (Col. Ct. App. 1990)(plaintiff's injuries were not compensable—and thus workers' compensation exclusivity did not apply—where employer touched employee's buttocks and rubbed his body against her body; employer's conduct did not arise out of employment; conduct did not fall within Larson's category of "neutral" acts because it was "specifically targeted" at the employee); Parker v. Tharp, 409 N.W.2d 915, 917 (Minn. Ct. App. 1987)(applying the three-group method of analysis to find injury compensable because assault would not have occurred if the employees did not work together); Hollrah v. Freidrich, 634 S.W.2d 221, 223 (Mo. Ct. App. 1982)(court could not say with certainty into which category sexual assault by a fellow employee fell, therefore premature to grant summary judgment that workers' compensation was exclusive remedy).

been compensable, even if the subject of the dispute was unrelated to work, so long as the work of the participants brought them together and created the conditions for the clash. In *Cremen v. Harrah's Marina Hotel Casino*,[31] a casino cocktail server was asked to report to her supervisor's office at the end of the day. When she did so, the supervisor locked the office door and sexually assaulted her. Employing the "positional risk" analysis used by New Jersey courts, the *Cremen* court observed that because the workplace brought the employee and her supervisor together, the employment in some manner physically facilitated the occurrence. Thus, the sexual assault arose out of her employment, rendering the injuries compensable under the New Jersey workers' compensation statute.[32] The *Cremen* court noted that this broad construction of the workers' compensation statute furthers the policy of extending the "salutary aspects of workers' compensation . . . to the broadest possible spectrum of work situations."[33]

b. The "normally expected risk" standard. Some courts have held that an injury arises out of employment only if the injury is the result of a risk that one would normally expect in the workplace.[34] Courts that frame the issue in this manner generally are reluctant to find that the risk of sexual harassment is one that an employee should expect when entering the workplace.[35] Thus, these courts tend to hold that sexual harassment injuries do not arise out of the employment. These cases arise largely in the context of whether the employee's common-law claim is barred by the exclusivity provisions of the workers' compensation statute. Taking a narrow view of the "arising out of employment" requirement therefore permits a plaintiff to pursue civil remedies, but is not logically consistent with the philosophy of extending workers' compensation coverage to all work-related injuries.[36]

---

[31]680 F. Supp. 150 (D.N.J. 1988).

[32]*Id.* at 153.

[33]*Id.* at 154.

[34]*E.g.,* Bennett v. Furr's Cafeterias, 549 F. Supp. 887, 890, 30 FEP Cases 93, 95 (D. Colo. 1982)("[a]n injury 'arises out of the employment where it has been caused by employment related risks"; "it would appear to lie outside the bounds of reason" that the sort of sexual assault and harassment that employee suffered was caused by risk inherent in position of manager trainee); Carr v. USW Direct Co., 98 Or. App. 30, 35, 779 P.2d 154, 156–57 (1989)("[t]here must be some causal link between the occurrence of injury and a risk connected with the employment"); City of Richmond v. Braxton, 230 Va. 161, 335 S.E.2d 259, 289 (1985)(employee's injuries caused by her supervisor's harassment not compensable because injuries could not be traced to employment as a contributing cause and came from a hazard to which employee would have been equally exposed apart from employment); Harrison v. Edison Bros. Apparel Stores, 724 F. Supp. 1185, 1191 (M.D.N.C. 1989)(injuries from sexual harassment not natural and probable consequence or incident of employment or one of its risks); Pryor v. United States Gypsum Co., 585 F. Supp. 311, 316, 470 FEP Cases 159, 163 (W.D. Mo. 1984)(employee's injuries from sexual harassment did not arise out of employment because court "not prepared to say that a female who goes to work . . . in a predominately male workplace should reasonably expect sexual harassment as part of her job"); Johnson v. Ramsey County, 424 N.W.2d 800, 805, 46 FEP Cases 1686, 1690 (Minn. Ct. App. 1988)(court clerk kissed at work by judge for whom he worked not covered by workers' compensation because "kiss had no association with the job itself").

[35]*E.g.,* Hart v. National Mortgage & Land Co., 189 Cal. App.3d 1420, 1431, 235 Cal. Rptr. 68, 74 (1987)(workplace behavior of employee's supervisor, which included grabbing employee's testicles, pinching his buttocks, mounting him, and showing him a dildo, was not subject to workers' compensation because it was not a risk, incident, or normal part of employment relationship); Doney v. Tambouratgis, 42 Cal. Comp. Cas. 882, 884 (Cal. Ct. App. 1977)(denying workers' compensation benefits to employee assaulted by her supervisor when he had ordered her to his office after work); *see also* cases cited in note 34 *supra.*

[36]*See* 1 A. LARSON, *supra* note 30, at §2.40.

2. Injuries Occurring in the Course of Employment

The additional requirement that an injury occur in the course of employment refers to the time and place of the incident causing the injury.[37] To satisfy this requirement, the incident causing the injury must occur while the employee is at the workplace, or a place where the employee is reasonably expected to be, and performing services for the employer.[38] This requirement should present no problem to an employee who is sexually harassed at work. However, if the employee is harassed by a supervisor or co-worker outside of the workplace, in a social setting, the injury may not have occurred "in the course of" the victim's employment.[39]

C. Requirement That the Injury Be Accidental

Some states limit workers' compensation coverage to injuries that are "accidental."[40] Courts have taken varying views of what is considered to be "accidental."

1. Employee's Perspective

One test is whether the injury was accidental from the perspective of the injured employee. Under this test, injuries from sexual harassment in employment would be covered by workers' compensation on the basis that they are not normally expected or foreseen, i.e., the injured person did not foresee or expect the injury.[41]

---

[37]E.g., Cremen v. Harrah's Marina Hotel Casino, 680 F. Supp. 150, 153 (D.N.J. 1988)(in the course of employment "means that it must have happened within the period of employment, at a place where the worker might reasonably be, and while she was performing her duties of employment or doing something incidental to it").

[38]E.g., Ramada Inn Surfside v. Swanson, 560 So.2d 300, 303 (Fla. Ct. App. 1990)(employee sexually harassed and assaulted by supervisor while employee and supervisor were inspecting potential investment property was injured in the course of employment because assault occurred at location where employee had been directed to go).

[39]E.g., Paroline v. Unisys Corp., 879 F.2d 100, 111, 50 FEP Cases 306, 309 (4th Cir. 1989), reproduced in Chapter 9, Constructive Discharge (because supervisor's assault on employee in her apartment, after giving her a ride home from work, did not occur in course of employment, workers' compensation act not exclusive remedy and did not bar common-law claims, *vacated in part on other grounds,* 900 F.2d 27, 52 FEP Cases 845 (4th Cir. 1990)(*en banc*).

[40]For statutes that limit workers' compensation coverage to those injuries that are "accidental" or occur by "accident," see ALASKA STAT. §23.30.265(17)(1989); COLO. REV. STAT. §8-41-108(2)(1986); CONN. GEN. STAT. ANN. §31-275(8)(1987); DEL. CODE ANN. tit. 19, §2301(15)(1985); FLA. STAT. §440.02(16)(1990); HAW. REV. STAT. §386.3 (1988); IDAHO CODE §72-102(15)(1989); IND. CODE ANN. §22-3-6-1(e)(1986); KAN. STAT. ANN. §44-508(d)(1986); MISS. CODE ANN. §71-3-3(b)(1989); MO. REV. STAT. §287.020(2)(1990 Supp.); NEB. REV. STAT. §48-151(2)(1988); NEV. REV. STAT. §616.020 (1986); N.H. REV. STAT. ANN. §281:2.V (1987); N.J. REV. STAT. ANN. §34:15-7 (1988); N.C. GEN. STAT. §97-2(6)(1985); OHIO REV. CODE ANN. §4123.01(c)(1989 Supp.); OKLA. STAT. tit. 85, §3(7)(West Supp. 1990); OR. REV. STAT. §656.005(7) (1989 Supp.); UTAH CODE ANN. §35-1-44(5)(1989 Supp.); VA. CODE ANN. §65.1-7 (1987); WIS. STAT. §102.01(2)(c)(1988).

[41]E.g., Haddon v. Metropolitan Life Ins. Co., 389 S.E.2d 712, 713–14, 52 FEP Cases 478, 479 (Va. 1990)(injury caused by intentional act of another could be accidental because, in Virginia, an accident is an event not expected by person to whom it happens); Fields v. Cummins Employees Fed. Credit Union, 540 N.E.2d 631, 634 (Ind. Ct. App. 1989)(sexual harassment by supervisor was accident because injury is by accident "where the sufferer did not intend or expect that injury would on that particular occasion result from what he was doing"); Zabkowicz v. West Bend Co., 789 F.2d 540, 545, 40 FEP Cases 1171, 1175 (7th Cir. 1986)(injuries from sexual harassment could be accidental because "it is sufficient if the injury itself is unexpected"); Miller v. Lindenwood Female College, 616 F. Supp. 860, 861, 40 FEP Cases 510, 511 (E.D. Mo. 1985)("intentional acts of fellow employees causing emotional distress to a complainant fall within the statutory definition of 'accident' ").

2. Harasser's Perspective

The alternative test is whether the injury was accidental from the harasser's perspective. Under this test, injuries from sexual harassment, which is inherently intentional, would not be considered accidental, and thus workers' compensation would not be applicable.[42] In *Ford v. Revlon, Inc.*,[43] the employer argued that workers' compensation was the plaintiff's exclusive remedy for the injuries caused by sexual harassment. The workers' compensation statute limited its exclusivity provisions to employees injured by "accident."[44] Analyzing this term from the harasser's perspective, the court held that the acts of the supervisor and employer were not accidents but intentional acts.[45]

IV. REMEDIES

A workers' compensation claimant who suffers a disabling injury due to sexual harassment may be entitled to an award of past and future medical care, a percentage of lost salary during the healing period, and compensation for the permanent residuals of the injury.[46]

In some states, workers' compensation statutes provide added benefits or additional remedies for employees injured by an employer's willful conduct.[47] However, workers' compensation statutes provide compensation only for medical expenses and disability; pain and suffering are not separate compensable items even in states that allow recovery for psychological injuries.[48]

---

[42]*See, e.g.,* Ford v. Revlon, Inc., 734 P.2d 580, 586, 43 FEP Cases 213, 218 (Ariz. 1987)(employee's injury not compensable because defendants' acts were intentional, not accidental); Pursell v. Pizza Inn, 786 P.2d 716, 717 (Okla. Ct. App. 1990)(supervisors' intentional or willful conduct took employee's claims outside exclusive remedy provision because employee's injuries were not an accident).

[43]*Supra* note 42.

[44]For a discussion of the intentional tort exception to the exclusivity provisions of workers' compensation statutes, see Chapter 27, Asserted Defenses, Section C.

[45]*Id.* at 583, 43 FEP Cases at 218.

[46]*E.g.,* Ramada Inn Surfside v. Swanson, *supra* note 38 (affirming administrative award of temporary total disability benefits and medical expenses for psychiatric condition caused by sexual harassment); CAL. LAB. CODE §4600 (employer shall provide medical treatment "reasonably required to cure or relieve from the effects of the injury"). *See also* City of La Habra v. Workers' Comp. Appeals Bd., 48 Cal. Comp. Cas. 21, 23 (Cal. Ct. App. 1983)(leaving undisturbed administrative award of workers' compensation benefits for permanent partial disability of fire dispatcher sexually harassed by battalion chief).

[47]*See generally* 4 A. LARSON, WORKMEN'S COMPENSATION LAW, app. A-7B-1 to 5 (1990). *E.g.,* ALA. CODE §25-5-11 (1986); ARIZ. REV. STAT. ANN. §23-1022 (1983); CAL. LAB. CODE §4553 (West 1989); MD. CODE ANN. §101-44 (1985); MASS. GEN. LAWS ANN. Ch. 152, §28 (West 1988); MONT. CODE ANN. §39-71-413 (1989); NEB. REV. STAT. §48-111 (1988); OR. REV. STAT. §656.156(2)(1989); WASH. REV. CODE §51.24.020 (1990); W. VA. CODE §23-4-2 (1985).

[48]Renteria v. Orange County, 82 Cal. App.3d 833, 835, 21 FEP Cases 179, 181 (Ct. App. 1978)("[w]e are aware of no decisional or statutory authority for the proposition that mental suffering, *as such,* is a compensable injury"). *Cf.* Horn v. Bradco. Int'l, 232 Cal. App.3d 653, 283 Cal. Rptr. 721 (1991)(contrary to application of *Renteria,* workers' compensation does address disabling effects of emotional distress).

CHAPTER 15

THE COMMON LAW

I. OVERVIEW

Many forms of sexual harassment in the workplace are actionable under a variety of theories grounded in the common law.[1] Tort actions give complainants access to jury trials[2] and the opportunity to recover compensatory and punitive damages—benefits not fully available under Title VII.[3] As a result, common-law claims, which may be brought concurrently with Title VII claims,[4] often may be more important for purposes of obtaining relief.[5]

Where factual circumstances warrant, a complainant may assert any number of common-law claims, either alone or in conjunction with a Title VII action.[6] This chapter discusses the following common-law theories of recovery available to victims of sexual harassment in the workplace: infliction of

---

[1]Guyette v. Stauffer Chem. Co., 518 F. Supp. 521, 524–25, 26 FEP Cases 634, 636 (D.N.J. 1981)(sexual harassment as theory of liability "bears direct similarities to" and "arises out of" several common-law torts). *See generally* Montgomery, *Sexual Harassment in the Workplace: A Practitioner's Guide to Tort Actions,* 10 GOLDEN GATE U.L. REV. 879 (1980).

This chapter is limited to the common law. For a discussion of remedies available under state employment statutes, see Chapters 12, Fair Employment Practices Statutes; 13, Unemployment Compensation Statutes; and 14, Workers' Compensation Statutes. For a discussion of federal remedies, see Chapter 11, Federal Constitutional, Statutory, and Civil Rights Law.

[2]For a discussion of controversies over Title VII jury trials, see Chapter 21, Complainant's Litigation Strategy, Section III.

[3]For a discussion of Title VII remedies, see Chapter 29, Monetary Relief, Section II., and the Civil Rights Act of 1991, discussed in Appendix 8.

[4]Stewart v. Thomas, 538 F. Supp. 891, 894–97, 30 FEP Cases 1609 (D.D.C. 1982).

[5]*See* Paul, *Sexual Harassment as Sex Discrimination: A Defective Paradigm,* 8 YALE L. & POLICY REV. 333, 359–63 (1990)(sexual harassment is really an invasion of individual rights rather than example of group-based discrimination and would be better addressed as independent tort rather than as sex discrimination); Schoenheider, *A Theory of Tort Liability for Sexual Harassment in the Workplace,* 134 U. PA. L. REV. 1461, 1475 (1986)(tort law provides more relief than Title VII where sexual harassment complainant suffers physical, psychological, or dignitary harm); Wald, *Alternatives to Title VII: State Statutory and Common-Law Remedies for Employment Discrimination,* 5 HARV. WOMEN'S L.J. 35, 38–40, 44–46 (1982)(administrative delays and narrow statutory relief in Title VII cases render common-law claims more appealing); Note, *The Emerging Law of Sexual Harassment: Relief Available to the Public Employee,* 62 NOTRE DAME L. REV. 677 (1987)(comparing elements of various tort theories available to address sexual harassment).

Title VII has its own advantages, of course, such as the availability of attorney's fees. *See* B.L. SCHLEI & P. GROSSMAN, EMPLOYMENT DISCRIMINATION LAW 739–40 (2d ed. 1983); *see also* Note, *The Dehumanizing Puzzle of Sexual Harassment: A Survey of the Law Concerning Harassment of Women in the Workplace,* 24 WASHBURN L.J. 574, 596 (1985)(state-law claims create disadvantages of possible retaliation from employer and longer delays in state court).

[6]*See* Phillips v. Smalley Maintenance Serv., 711 F.2d 1524, 1532, 32 FEP Cases 975 (11th Cir. 1983)(upholding federal jurisdiction over state-law claims pendent to plaintiff's Title VII claim). For a discussion of pendent (or supplemental) jurisdiction, see Chapter 22, Employer's Litigation Strategy, Section III.

emotional distress,[7] assault and battery,[8] false imprisonment,[9] invasion of privacy,[10] defamation,[11] misrepresentation,[12] breach of public policy,[13] implied contract and covenant of good faith and fair dealing,[14] tortious interference with contractual relations,[15] loss of consortium,[16] and negligent hiring or retention.[17] No court appears to have recognized a common-law claim for sexual harassment as such.[18]

This chapter also discusses *respondeat superior,* the common-law doctrine by which courts impute liability to an employer for acts of sexual harassment committed by its employees.[19]

Two frequently asserted defenses to common-law claims, mentioned briefly here and discussed in more detail in other chapters, are workers' compensation preemption[20] and preemption by state fair employment practices statutes.[21]

II. INFLICTION OF EMOTIONAL DISTRESS

A. Intentional Infliction of Emotional Distress

In sexual harassment actions, intentional infliction of emotional distress is the most litigated common-law theory of recovery. As one court has observed, "[t]he evidence necessary to prove sexual harassment overlaps to a significant extent with that necessary to prove intentional infliction of emotional distress."[22]

The tort has four elements: (1) extreme and outrageous conduct; (2) an intent to cause, or reckless disregard of the probability of causing, emotional distress; (3) severe emotional distress suffered by the complainant; and (4) that the conduct complained of caused the complainant's severe emotional distress.[23]

---

[7]See Section II. *infra.*
[8]See Section III. *infra.*
[9]See Section IV. *infra*
[10]See Section V. *infra.*
[11]See Section VI. *infra.*
[12]See Section VII. *infra.*
[13]See Section VIII. *infra.*
[14]See Section IX. *infra.*
[15]See Section X. *infra.*
[16]See Section XI. *infra.*
[17]See Section XII. *infra.*
[18]*See generally* Schoenheider, *supra* note 5, 134 U. PA. L. REV. at 1485–94 (proposing new tort of sexual harassment in workplace). *See, e.g.,* Smith v. Prudential Fin. Servs., 739 F. Supp. 1042, 1044 (D.S.C. 1990)(no common-law cause of action for sexual harassment recognized).
[19]See Section XIII. *infra.*
[20]For discussion of workers' compensation preemption of sexual harassment claims, see Section XII. *infra* and Chapter 27, Asserted Defenses, Section IV.
[21]For discussion of state FEP statutory preemption, see Section VIII.B. *infra* and Chapter 12, Fair Employment Practices Statutes, Section III.
[22]Glezos v. Amalfi Ristorante Italiano, 651 F. Supp. 1271, 1277, 45 FEP Cases 1092 (D. Md. 1987); *see also* Schoenheider, *supra* note 5, 134 U. PA. L. REV. at 1481 (theory provides strong basis for recovery of money damages to remedy harassment).
[23]3 DEVITT, BLACKMAR & WOLFF, FEDERAL JURY PRACTICE AND INSTRUCTIONS, §81.05 (4th ed. 1987); W. PROSSER & P. KEETON, HANDBOOK ON THE LAW OF TORTS, §12 at 60 (5th ed. 1984)("liability for conduct exceeding all bounds usually tolerated by decent society, of a nature which is especially calculated to cause, and does cause, mental distress of a very serious kind").

1. Outrageous Conduct

The element on which liability in sexual harassment cases almost always hinges is whether the conduct was sufficiently outrageous.[24] Findings of outrageous conduct typically have occurred where the harasser has engaged in violent conduct,[25] sexual exposure,[26] or offensive touching of intimate areas of the complainant's body.[27]

Several complainants have lost emotional distress claims that were based solely on verbal harassment or unwanted touching of a nonvulgar nature.[28] In *Class v. New Jersey Life Insurance Co.,*[29] Judge George W. Lindberg found that the conduct of the male supervisor with respect to the female complainant would not have been sufficiently outrageous had it remained purely verbal, even though his comments to her over an eight-week period consisted of telling daily sex-related jokes, recounting personal episodes of group sex, inviting the

---

[24]The Restatement (Second) of Torts (1977) defines outrageous conduct as follows:
Liability has been found only where the conduct has been so outrageous in character, and so extreme in degree, as to go beyond all possible bounds of decency, and to be regarded as atrocious, and utterly intolerable in a civilized community. Generally, the case is one in which the recitation of the facts to an average member of the community would arouse his resentment against the actor, and lead him to exclaim, "Outrageous!"
Id. at §46, comment d. An emotional distress claim failed for lack of "actionable outrageous behavior" in *Miller v. Aluminum Co. of America,* 679 F. Supp. 495, 45 FEP Cases 1775 (W.D. Pa. 1988), *aff'd,* 856 F.2d 184, 52 FEP Cases 1472 (3d Cir. 1988), where the complainant alleged that she was assigned to menial routine work, disadvantaged by sexual favoritism, and subjected to a male plant manager's commentary on her breasts. *Id.* at 1779, 1784.

[25]*E.g.,* Arnold v. City of Seminole, 614 F. Supp. 853, 857, 861, 40 FEP Cases 1539, 1541, 1544 (E.D. Okla. 1985)($150,000 compensatory damage award for intentional infliction of emotional distress; complainant pushed across room and into file cabinet).

[26]*E.g.,* Priest v. Rotary, 634 F. Supp. 571, 575, 40 FEP Cases 208, 209 (N.D. Cal. 1986)(defendant exposed himself to plaintiff as she had coffee at end of shift).

[27]*E.g.,* Shrout v. Black Clawson Co., 689 F. Supp. 774, 779–82, 46 FEP Cases 1339, 1343–46 (S.D. Ohio 1988)($75,000 in compensatory damages awarded where defendant touched the complainant intimately); Gilardi v. Schroeder, 672 F. Supp. 1043, 1047, 45 FEP Cases 283 (N.D. Ill. 1986)(court awarded $100,000 to complainant who was drugged, sexually assaulted while unconscious, and then put in bed with assailant's wife), *aff'd,* 833 F.2d 1226, 45 FEP Cases 346 (7th Cir. 1987); Pease v. Alford Photo Indus., 667 F. Supp. 1188, 1190, 1203, 49 FEP Cases 497, 498, 507–9 (W.D. Tenn. 1987)(complainant awarded $2,500 compensatory damages for "serious mental injury" caused by conduct including "sexually harassing and humiliating touching" that "culminated in . . . fondling her breast while she was at work"); Priest v. Rotary, *supra* note 26, 634 F. Supp. at 584, 40 FEP Cases at 217 (awarding $95,000 compensatory damages for conduct including touching complainant's breasts and unzipping front of her uniform, which caused "highly unpleasant mental reactions, including fright, humiliation, shock, surprise, sickness, nervousness, apprehension, disgust, emotional pain, intimidation, embarrassment, anger, sleeplessness, nausea, and anxiety"); Bushell v. Dean, 781 S.W.2d 652, 52 FEP Cases 746 (Tex. Ct. App. 1989)(affirming jury finding that it was "outrageous" for supervisor to comment on complainant's body, touch her, tell her he wanted sex with her, and then—after she spurned his advances—treating her more formally and assigning new duties to her, including some of his own).

[28]*E.g.,* Paroline v. Unisys Corp., 879 F.2d 100, 112–13, 50 FEP Cases 306 (4th Cir. 1989), reproduced in Chapter 9, Constructive Discharge (alleged harassment, including suggestive remarks, rubbing plaintiff's back, and kissing plaintiff, insufficient under Virginia law), *vacated in part on other grounds,* 900 F.2d 27, 52 FEP Cases 845 (4th Cir. 1990); Studstill v. Borg-Warner Leasing, 806 F.2d 1005, 1007–8, 50 FEP Cases 427 (11th Cir. 1986)(dirty jokes, off-color comments, and profane suggestions insufficient); Kinnally v. Bell of Pa., 748 F. Supp. 1136, 1138, 1144–45, 54 FEP Cases 329 (E.D. Pa. 1990)(misogynist comments and "regime of derision and intimidation, including showing of film of copulating rabbits at business meeting where complainant was only female present" not sufficiently outrageous under Pennsylvania law); Hooten v. Pennsylvania College of Optometry, 601 F. Supp. 1151, 1155 (E.D. Pa. 1984)(harassment by co-workers, while "likely to cause distress," is "not the type of action to arouse resentment, by the average member of the community, against the actor"); Forde v. Royals, Inc., 537 F. Supp. 1173, 31 FEP Cases 213 (S.D. Fla. 1982)(unwelcome verbal sexual advances and breach of employment contract insufficient absent physical injury). *But see* Valdez v. Church's Fried Chicken, 683 F. Supp. 596, 612, 47 FEP Cases 1155, 1164 (W.D. Tex. 1988)(Texas law recognizes cause of action for mental anguish from sexual assault even in absence of physical contact).

[29]53 FEP Cases 1583 (N.D. Ill. 1990).

complainant to visit his home over the weekend, asking her if she swallowed during oral sex, disclosing that he enjoyed anal sex with women, and describing the size of his sexual organ.[30] Like the *Class* court, other courts have sustained claims only where the harasser has engaged in both sexual harassment and some kind of retaliatory job-threatening conduct.[31]

Some courts have held that allegations of sexual advances, verbal abuse, and sexual solicitations are themselves sufficient to state a claim of outrageous conduct.[32]

The workplace context of sexual harassment makes the outrageous element easier to prove than in some other claims for emotional distress, because a complainant can emphasize that the nature of the employment relationship gave the harasser extraordinary power to damage the complainant's interests.[33] As one court has observed: "The standards for intent and for socially tolerable conduct depend on the type of relationship which exists between plaintiff and defendant. An employer-employee relationship . . . imposes a greater obligation to refrain from inflicting mental distress than the obligation which exists between strangers."[34]

The standard for determining whether the conduct is "outrageous" for tort purposes and the standard for determining whether conduct is "severe" or "pervasive" for Title VII purposes are similar, if not practically equivalent. In *Fisher v. San Pedro Peninsula Hospital*,[35] the California Court of Appeal held that "[g]iven an employee's fundamental, civil right to a discrimination

---

[30]*Id.* at 1585–86. The conduct in *Class* was outrageous because the harasser engaged in pattern of harassment in retaliation for the complainant's complaints.

[31]*See, e.g.,* Andrews v. City of Philadelphia, 895 F.2d 1469, 1487, 54 FEP Cases 184, 198 (3d Cir. 1990)(employer must have retaliated against complainant for turning down his propositions; "sexual harassment alone" generally not sufficiently outrageous); Beeman v. Safeway Stores, 724 F. Supp. 674, 680–81, 51 FEP Cases 482, 484–85 (W.D. Mo. 1989)(allegations of sexual advances, verbal comments, *and* threats of discharge stated claim). *See also* Rogers v. Loews L'Enfant Plaza Hotel, 526 F. Supp. 523, 531, 29 FEP Cases 828, 833 (D.D.C. 1981)(implying that supervisor's series of sexual invitations and "leering" sexual comments by themselves not sufficiently outrageous, while holding that abusive language and other conduct after plaintiff's rejections of sexual advances could be construed as outrageous).

[32]Bailey v. Unocal Corp., 700 F. Supp. 396, 53 FEP Cases 1529 (N.D. Ill. 1988)(supervisor's alleged conduct, ranging from sexual innuendo to indecent exposure, stated claim); Coleman v. American Broadcasting Cos., 38 FEP Cases 65, 71 (D.D.C. 1985)(sexual advances, verbal comments, and sexual solicitations); Young v. Stensrude, 664 S.W.2d 263, 265 (Mo. Ct. App. 1984)(allegation that male director of medical center showed complainant pornographic film in place of instructional film during which he uttered sexual obscenities), *appeal after remand,* 773 S.W.2d 143 (Mo. Ct. App. 1989), *cert. denied,* 110 S.Ct. 738 (1990).

[33]*See generally* W. PROSSER & P. KEETON, *supra* note 23, 1988 Supp. at 18 (sexual harassment on job "undoubtedly an intentional infliction of emotional distress"). *E.g.,* Dias v. Sky Chefs, 919 F.2d 1370, 54 FEP Cases 852 (9th Cir. 1990)(affirming jury verdict of liability where manager created hostile work environment and recommended discharge of plaintiff in retaliation for complaints; duty under Oregon law to refrain from abusive employment behavior closer to that of physician toward patient than that of police officer toward citizen not in custody), *vacated on other grounds,* 111 S.Ct. 2791 (1991); Lucas v. Brown & Root, Inc., 736 F.2d 1202, 1206, 35 FEP Cases 1855 (8th Cir. 1984)(alleged sexual advances that threatened plaintiff's job security, coupled with misrepresentations respecting plaintiff's unemployment compensation, stated claim); Stewart v. Thomas, 538 F. Supp. 891, 894, 30 FEP Cases 1609 (D.D.C. 1982)(supervisor made advances, used abusive language, engaged in offensive touching, and threatened complainant with adverse job consequences if she rejected advances); Rice v. United Ins. Co., 465 So.2d 1100, 36 FEP Cases 1641 (Ala. 1984)(sustaining claim that supervisor tried to force complainant to take disability leave following pregnancy and misrepresented vital business information); Howard Univ. v. Best, 484 A.2d 958, 36 FEP Cases 482 (D.C. App. 1984)(sustaining claim brought by discharged employee stressing history of female subordination in workplace). *See also* Dworkin, Ginger & Mallor, *Theories of Recovery for Sexual Harassment: Going Beyond Title VII,* 25 SAN DIEGO L. REV. 125, 140 (1988)(predicting success of theory, because "society . . . increasingly abhors the abuse of power and expresses that abhorrence through a variety of legal principles aimed at curbing such abuses").

[34]Dias v. Sky Chefs, *supra* note 33, 54 FEP Cases at 854 (quotation omitted).

[35]214 Cal. App.3d 590, 262 Cal. Rptr. 842, 54 FEP Cases 584 (1989).

free work environment" under the California Fair Employment and Housing Act, sexual harassment in the workplace is inherently outrageous "as it exceeds all bounds of decency usually tolerated by a decent society."[36] Conversely, as held by a court applying Virginia law, conduct that is not egregious enough to create a hostile environment under Title VII will not be "outrageous" for purposes of tort law.[36a]

2. Direct Employer or Union Liability

Employers or unions may be directly liable for outrageous conduct for failing to respond appropriately to complaints of sexual harassment.[37] In *Ford v. Revlon, Inc.*,[38] the Supreme Court of Arizona held that the employer acted outrageously when it made no timely response to a female employee's numerous complaints of sexual harassment. The court noted that even if the employer had not intended to cause the complainant emotional distress, its conduct demonstrated a reckless disregard for her welfare. The employer's failure to comply with its own policy and guidelines for handling sexual harassment claims contributed to the outrageousness of its inaction. In *Woods v. Graphic Communications*,[38a] a union was liable for the tort of outrage when it intentionally failed to take actions to combat racial harassment in the workplace.

B. Negligent Infliction of Emotional Distress

Although emotional distress can also result from negligent conduct, a sexual harassment complainant generally cannot recover for negligent infliction of emotional distress unless a physical injury was also suffered.[39] In *Olson v. Connerly*,[40] a case involving sexual harassment outside the employment context, the plaintiff's "panic attacks" resulting from sexual harassment by her former physician were held to be a sufficient physical manifestation to allow recovery for mental distress arising from the physician's negligent conduct. Other explanations for why this theory of liability is invoked so rarely are that sexual harassment is virtually always intentional as to the individual perpetrator and that the employer's negligence in preventing sexual harassment more traditionally is analyzed as a matter of statutory discrimination law or as the separate tort of negligent retention or supervision.[40a]

---

[36]*Id.*, 54 FEP Cases at 596.

[36a]Dwyer v. Smith, 867 F.2d 184, 194–95, 48 FEP Cases 1886 (4th Cir. 1989)(would "defy reason" to permit claim for intentional infliction of emotional distress to proceed when court already has determined that no hostile environment existed).

[37]*E.g.*, Baker v. Weyerhaeuser Co., 903 F.2d 1342, 52 FEP Cases 1872 (10th Cir. 1990)(employer failed to respond to plaintiff's complaints of known harasser); Lapinad v. Pacific Oldsmobile-GMC, 679 F. Supp. 991, 50 FEP Cases 752 (D. Haw. 1988)(jury question whether employer's failure to address complaints of sexual harassment constituted extreme and outrageous conduct); Ford v. Revlon, Inc., 734 P.2d 580, 43 FEP Cases 213 (Ariz. 1987)(employer liable based on its reckless disregard for plaintiff's welfare). *Cf.* Juarez v. Ameritech Mobile Communications, 53 FEP Cases 1722 (N.D. Ill. 1990)(employer could not be directly liable because it did not direct, encourage, or commit extreme and outrageous conduct). Of course, an employer may be indirectly, or vicariously, liable. See Section XIII. *infra (respondeat superior)*.

[38]*Supra* note 37.

[38a]925 F.2d 1195, 55 FEP Cases 542 (9th Cir. 1991)(Washington law).

[39]*See, e.g.*, Rogers v. Loew's L'Enfant Plaza Hotel, *supra* note 31, 526 F. Supp. at 529–30 (citing rule); Miller v. Aluminium Co. of Am., *supra* note 24, 45 FEP Cases at 1784 (negligent infliction actionable only with physical impact or threat thereof or contemporary observance of injury by family member).

[40]445 N.W.2d 706, 151 Wis.2d 663 (1988), *aff'd*, 156 Wis.2d 488, 457 N.W.2d 479 (1990).

[40a]See Section XII. *infra*.

III. ASSAULT AND BATTERY

The traditional torts of assault and battery provide a common-law remedy for workers threatened with and subjected to offensive physical contact in the workplace. Although assault and battery constitute separate torts, usually they are asserted as companion causes of action in sexual harassment cases.[41]

Liability for assault requires a showing that (1) the actor intended to cause harmful or offensive physical contact, and (2) the victim was put in apprehension of such conduct.[42] Verbal harassment alone does not constitute an assault unless the circumstances somehow warrant an expectation of imminent physical contact.[43] Consequently, an employee who is the target only of sexual insults and innuendo must pursue an alternative theory of relief.[44]

Liability for battery requires a harmful or offensive contact with a person resulting from an act intended to cause the complainant or a third person to suffer the contact.[45] A battery results whenever the offensive contact extends to any part of the complainant's body or to practically anything attached to it,[46] although there may be no mental or physical harm to justify any award of damages.[47]

To satisfy the element of offensive touching, the plaintiff need not allege any sexual touching; a claim of offensive or harmful touching, regardless of its nature, is sufficient.[48] In the context of sexual harassment, however, assault and battery claims usually do allege offensive physical contact of a sexual nature.[49] Civil assault and battery actions are particularly appropriate to include among the torts pleaded in a complaint whenever an employee has been sexually assaulted by an employer or co-workers.[50] Although the individual harasser

---

[41]*E.g.,* Fields v. Cummins Employees Fed. Credit Union, 540 N.E.2d 631, 53 FEP Cases 1613, 1618 (Ind. Ct. App. 1990)(claims for assault and battery stated on basis of unwelcome touching of face, shoulders and buttocks and attempted kiss); Garcia v. Williams, 704 F. Supp. 984, 1000, 51 FEP Cases 255 (N.D. Cal. 1988)(allegations of touching complainant's private parts); Waltman v. International Paper Co., 47 FEP Cases 671 (W.D. La. 1988)(allegations of unwelcome touching and pinching of complainant's breasts and thighs and placing of air hose between her legs by male co-workers supported claims for assault and battery), *rev'd on other grounds,* 875 F.2d 468, 50 FEP Cases 179 (5th Cir. 1989); Dockter v. Rudolf Wolff Futures, 684 F. Supp. 532, 46 FEP Cases 1129 (N.D. Ill. 1988)(unwelcome petting and breast fondling by supervisory employee constituted assault and battery under Illinois law), *aff'd,* 913 F.2d 456, 53 FEP Cases 1642 (7th Cir. 1990); Valdez v. Church's Fried Chicken, *supra* note 28 (awarding $46,525 for sexual assault by male co-worker); Pease v. Alford Photo Indus., *supra* note 27 (compensatory and punitive damages for assault and battery resulting from employer's physical sexual harassment); Priest v. Rotary, *supra* note 26, 634 F. Supp. at 584 (battery consisted of repeated offensive touchings not made in self-defense); O'Reilly v. Executone of Albany, 121 A.D.2d 772, 503 N.Y.S.2d 185 (App. Div. 1986)(assault-and-battery claims arising from allegations of intentional, repeated, and malicious sexual touching by male co-workers); Skousen v. Nidy, 90 Ariz. 215, 367 P.2d 248, 250 (1961)(employer liable for assault and battery for touching private parts of 65-year-old female employee as he tried to seduce her).

[42]Restatement (Second) of Torts §21 (1965).

[43]*Id.* at §31.

[44]Schoenheider, *A Theory of Tort Liability for Sexual Harassment in the Workplace,* 134 U. PA. L. REV. 1461, 1477–78 (1986)(discussing limitations of theory).

[45]Restatement (Second) of Torts §§13, 18.

[46]*Id.*

[47]Boyd v. James S. Hayes Living Health Care Agency, 671 F. Supp. 1155, 44 FEP Cases 332 (W.D. Tenn. 1987)(where plaintiff sustained no compensable damage from offensive touching, judgment entered for defendant on battery claim).

[48]*See* Newsome v. Cooper-Wiss, Inc., 179 Ga. App. 670, 347 S.E.2d 619, 621–22 (1986)(plaintiff stated claim for assault and battery even though defendant never touched private areas of her body).

[49]*See* Waltman v. International Paper Co., *supra* note 41.

[50]*See, e.g.,* Valdez v. Church's Fried Chicken, 683 F. Supp. 596, 47 FEP Cases 1155 (W.D. Tex. 1988)(plaintiff awarded damages against co-worker in assault-and-battery action arising from sexual assault

is the obvious defendant, the employer may also be sued under a theory of negligence or *respondeat superior*.[51]

IV. FALSE IMPRISONMENT

The tort of false imprisonment involves an act intended to confine another person, "within boundaries fixed by the actor," which results in such a confinement of which the other person is conscious.[52] The sexual advances alleged in sexual harassment cases sometimes involve aggressive physical conduct that can constitute false imprisonment. In *Priest v. Rotary*,[53] false imprisonment was proven with respect to two separate incidents: the restaurant owner picked up a cocktail waitress and carried her across the room, then later physically trapped her while he fondled her body.[54]

V. INVASION OF PRIVACY

Several different torts fall under the general heading of invasion of privacy. The privacy claims commonly asserted in the context of sexual harassment actions are (A) intrusion upon seclusion, (B) false-light publicity, and (C) public disclosure of private facts. As with assault and battery, the individual perpetrator is the most common defendant, although the employer could also be sued under theories of negligence or *respondeat superior*.[55]

A. Intrusion Upon Seclusion

The tort of intrusion involves an intentional interference with the solitude or seclusion of one's person or private affairs and concerns.[56] The intrusion must be offensive or objectionable to a reasonable person, and it must encompass a truly private matter.[57] If interpreted broadly, the intrusion theory could become a dominant tort claim for redressing sexual harassment.[58]

Sexual harassment sometimes involves persistent unwelcome intrusions into the complainant's home, by telephone calls or otherwise, and on that basis has been held to give rise to a cause of action for invasion of privacy.[59] In a potentially far-reaching decision, the Alabama Supreme Court has held that

---

in workplace); Gilardi v. Schroeder, 672 F. Supp. 1043, 1047, 45 FEP Cases 283 (N.D. Ill. 1986)(female employee entitled to punitive damages for civil battery after employer drugged her and engaged in sexual intercourse with her while she was unconscious), *aff'd*, 883 F.2d 1226, 45 FEP Cases 346 (7th Cir. 1987).

[51]See Sections XII. and XIII. *infra*.

[52]Restatement (Second) of Torts §35.

[53]634 F. Supp. 571, 40 FEP Cases 208 (N.D. Cal. 1986).

[54]*Id.* at 583–84, 40 FEP Cases at 216–17.

[55]See Sections XII. and XIII. *infra*.

[56]W. PROSSER & P. KEETON, HANDBOOK ON THE LAW OF TORTS, §117 at 854 (5th ed. 1984).

[57]*Id.* at 855; Restatement (Second) of Torts §652B.

[58]See Dworkin, Ginger & Mallor, *Theories of Recovery for Sexual Harassment: Going Beyond Title VII*, 25 SAN DIEGO L. REV. 125, 141–43 (1988).

[59]Rogers v. Loew's L'Enfant Plaza Hotel, 526 F. Supp. 523, 29 FEP Cases 828 (D.D.C. 1981)(sustaining intrusion claim based on plaintiff's allegations that immediate supervisor repeatedly called her at home and at work when he was off duty and made "leering comments" to her about her personal and sexual life despite her requests that he stop).

invasion of privacy may lie with respect to a series of intrusive sexual inquiries made by a supervisor in the workplace even absent an intrusion into the complainant's home.[60]

Sexual touching and vulgar sexual propositions may also support a claim for intrusion.[61] In *Waltman v. International Paper Co.*,[62] the complainant supported a claim for invasion of privacy with allegations that a co-worker placed a high-pressure air hose between her legs.

The right to privacy may be waived. In *Cummings v. Walsh Construction Co.*,[63] the court dismissed an intrusion claim where the complainant, intimidated, yielded to her foreman's sexual advances. The court held that by failing to reject the foreman's advances, the complainant "waived whatever right to privacy she had as to her personal seclusion or solitude."[64] Employees may also waive their right to privacy as to any private matter that they openly discuss in a work environment.[65]

B. False-Light Publicity

A second form of invasion of privacy consists of publicity that places the complainant in a false light before the public.[66] The false light need not be defamatory, but must be objectionable to a reasonable person under the circumstances.[67]

In *Tomson v. Stephan*,[68] the court held that a sexual harassment complainant stated a false-light publicity action on the basis of statements that the defendant made at a news conference, in violation of the confidentiality provi-

---

[60]Phillips v. Smalley Maintenance Servs., 435 So.2d 705 (Ala. 1983), *reprinted in relevant part at* 711 F.2d 1533–37, 32 FEP Cases 982–86 (plaintiff's employer subjected her to intrusive demands and threats, including inquiry into sexual relationship with her husband; on one occasion, he slapped her buttocks; on another, he covered his office window with paper, thereby obscuring the view of others, after telling her that sexual services were part of her job). *See also* Priest v. Rotary, *supra* note 53, 634 F. Supp. at 582, 40 FEP Cases at 215 ("sexually suggestive comments to and about [complainant] in the presence of others" violated her right to privacy).

[61]*See* Pease v. Alford Photo Indus., 667 F. Supp. 1188, 1191, 1203, 49 FEP Cases 497 (W.D. Tenn. 1987)(touching thighs, breasts, and buttocks of female employees in workplace "obviously" invasion of privacy); Rogers v. Loew's L'Enfant Plaza Hotel, *supra* note 59, 526 F. Supp. at 528 (employer's repeated telephone calls to complainant coupled with "leering" comments regarding her sexual life supported claim for intrusion); Busby v. Truswal Sys. Corp., 551 So.2d 322, 328 (Ala. 1989)(employer allegedly stared at complainant's sexual anatomy, invited her for a nude swim in his pool, and suggested she come braless to work); *see generally* Bundy v. Jackson, 641 F.2d 934, 945, 24 FEP Cases 1155 (D.C. Cir. 1981)(sexual harassment is "an intentional assault on an individual's innermost privacy").

[62]47 FEP Cases 671 (W.D. La. 1988), *rev'd on other grounds,* 875 F.2d 468, 50 FEP Cases 179 (5th Cir 1989).

[63]561 F. Supp. 872, 31 FEP Cases 930 (S.D. Ga. 1983).

[64]*Id.* at 884. The court viewed the tort of intrusion as "directed to protecting the integrity and sanctity of *physical* areas a person would naturally consider private and off limits to uninvited, unwelcomed prying persons." *Id.* (emphasis added). *See also* Steele v. Offshore Shipbldg., 867 F.2d 1311, 49 FEP Cases 522 (11th Cir. 1989)(absent physical intrusion, complainant's invasion of privacy claim not actionable unless it also alleges publication).

[65]Moffett v. Gene B. Glick Co., 621 F. Supp. 244, 41 FEP Cases 671 (N.D. Ind. 1985)(complainant's open discussions about her interracial relationship waived privacy claim arising from racial comments and threats by supervisory personnel), *overruled on other grounds,* 644 F. Supp. 983 (N.D. Ind. 1986); Cummings v. Walsh Constr. Co., *supra* note 63, 561 F. Supp. at 884–85 (where plaintiff tells third party of sexual encounter with foreman, she waives right to complain of foreman's disclosure of same).

[66]W. PROSSER & P. KEETON, *supra* note 56, §117 at 863.

[67]*Id.* at 864; Restatement (Second) of Torts §652E.

[68]696 F. Supp. 1407, 1410, 48 FEP Cases 42 (D. Kan. 1988).

sions of the parties' settlement agreement, that described the complainant's lawsuit as "without merit" and "totally unfounded."[69]

C. Public Disclosure of Private Facts

Public disclosure of private facts is a third tort falling under invasion of privacy. The elements of this tort are (1) the public disclosure of a private fact, (2) publicity that would be highly offensive and objectionable to a person of ordinary sensibilities, (3) no legitimate public interest in having the information made available, and (4) injury to the complainant as a result of the publicity.[70]

In *Cummings v. Walsh Construction Co.*,[71] an employee alleged that her supervisor's public disclosure of their sexual relationship amounted to an actionable invasion of privacy. The court dismissed her claim, holding that her discussion of the relationship with third persons effectively stripped her of the "veil of privacy."[72]

VI. DEFAMATION

Sexual harassment itself sometimes consists of defamatory statements,[72a] and in any event has a way of generating defamatory statements. Consequently, defamation claims occasionally appear in connection with claims of sexual harassment.[73] In response to such accusations, alleged harassers frequently

---

[69]*Id.* at 1412. The court stressed that the defendant's unprefaced, unqualified statements could only be interpreted as assertions of fact rather than expressions of opinion. However, in *Coleman v. American Broadcasting Cos.*, 38 FEP Cases 65 (D.D.C. 1985), the court dismissed a defamation claim based on a similar statement released by the defendant to the press shortly after the plaintiff had filed a sexual harassment claim against the defendant. The court concluded that the statement was a standard response by a defendant in active litigation and, as such, should be interpreted only as an expression of opinion.

[70]Restatement (Second) of Torts §652D (1977); W. PROSSER & P. KEETON, *supra* note 56, §117 at 856–57. Under Florida law, the publication must be to the public in general or to a large number of persons. *See* Steele v. Offshore Shipbldg., *supra* note 64, 867 F.2d at 1315.

[71]*Supra* note 63, 561 F. Supp. at 884.

[72]*Id.* at 885.

[72a]One such case is *Carpenter v. County of Chenango*, 135 A.D.2d 936, 522 N.Y.S.2d 339 (N.Y. Sup. Ct. 1987), where a male police officer allegedly was responsible for posting in the workplace photographs of a nude, life-size inflatable doll posed in lewd positions and posting a teletype stating that the subject of the photographs was wanted for impersonating the complainant. The court ruled that the complainant had a triable case of defamation.

[73]*E.g.*, Dwyer v. Smith, 867 F.2d 184, 195, 48 FEP Cases 1886 (4th Cir. 1989)(police officer alleging sexual harassment claimed she was falsely accused of lying to investigating officer); Handley v. Phillips, 715 F. Supp. 657, 52 FEP Cases 195 (M.D. Pa. 1989)(plaintiff claimed employer slandered her by alleging she was drug user); Locklear v. Dubliner, Inc., 721 F. Supp. 1342, 1343, 50 FEP Cases 1386 (D.D.C. 1989)(defamation action brought by female employee arising from alleged sexual harassment and retaliation); Garcia v. Williams, 704 F. Supp. 984, 1000, 51 FEP Cases 255 (N.D. Cal. 1988)(plaintiff stated defamation claim against former boss, a district judge, based on allegation that he falsely told others that plaintiff was romantically interested in him); Chamberlin v. 101 Realty, 626 F. Supp. 865, 871 (D.N.H. 1985)(employer's statement that former employee unlawfully retained property could support defamation action), *aff'd on other grounds*, 915 F.2d 777, 54 FEP Cases 101 (1st Cir. 1990); Schomer v. Smidt, 113 Cal. App.3d 828, 833–35, 170 Cal. Rptr. 662, 664–66 (1980)(affirming jury verdict against airline captain for slandering airline flight attendant when, after she rebuffed his sexual advances, captain told other co-workers that he had seen plaintiff engaged in lesbian activity with another flight attendant). *See generally* CAL. CIV. CODE §46 (slander is false and unprivileged communication, orally uttered, which imputes impotence or want of chastity); Kersul v. Skulls Angels, 130 Misc.2d 345, 495 N.Y.S.2d 886, 890, 42 FEP Cases 987 (Sup. Ct. 1985)(female employee brought defamation action after her employer broadcasted to other employees that plaintiff was crazy); Howard Univ. v. Best, 484 A.2d 958, 988, 36 FEP Cases 482 (D.C. App. 1984)(plaintiff alleged outside consultant's report, describing plaintiff as actively opposed to present school administration, was defamatory and related to alleged instances of sexual harassment).

have brought defamation actions against both complainants[74] and employers.[75]

A defamation action requires proof that (1) the defendant made a false or defamatory statement; (2) the statement constituted an unprivileged communication to a third party; (3) the defendant was at least negligent in communicating the statement; and (4) the communication was the proximate cause of harm to the plaintiff, or the communication was actionable regardless of special harm.[76] Defamatory matter in written form has historically been regarded as libel, while orally communicated defamation constitutes slander.[77] Libel is actionable without any proof of special harm.[78] Slander, by contrast, is generally not actionable unless actual damage is proved.[79] However, proof of damage is not required where the slander involves the plaintiff's business, trade, or profession; the commission of a crime by the plaintiff; the unchasteness of a female plaintiff; or the contraction of a loathsome disease.[80]

In *Garcia v. Williams*,[81] the court sustained a slander claim brought by a federal judge's former secretary, where she alleged that the judge had told others that she was romantically interested in him. In *Chamberlin v. 101 Realty*,[82] the court held that a female employee who was dismissed for allegedly rebuffing her employer's improper sexual advances stated a claim for defamation arising from statements by the employer that implicated her in unlawful activity.[83] By contrast, an employer's publicized statement that an employee's sexual harassment claims were meritless was held to be an opinion protected by the First Amendment.[84]

VII. MISREPRESENTATION AND PROMISSORY ESTOPPEL

The torts of fraudulent and negligent misrepresentation can occur when one misrepresents facts or intentions for the purpose of inducing another to act or to refrain from acting, when justifiable reliance on the misrepresentation causes pecuniary loss.[85] One or both of these torts could potentially be maintained where a sexual harassment complainant has been persuaded to remain

---

[74]*E.g.,* Lawson v. Boeing Co., 58 Wash. App. 261, 792 P.2d 545, 549 (1990)(alleged harasser claimed he was defamed by employees accusing him of sexual harassment).

[75]*E.g.,* Feldleit v. Long Island R.R., 723 F. Supp. 892 (E.D.N.Y. 1989)(male employee brought defamation action against employer following employee's termination for sexual harassment); Stockley v. AT&T Information Sys., 687 F. Supp 764, 769, 47 FEP Cases 28 (E.D.N.Y. 1988)(employee brought defamation action against employer arising from statements concerning plaintiff during sexual harassment investigation). For a more thorough discussion, see Chapter 24, The Alleged Harasser as Plaintiff.

[76]Restatement (Second) of Torts §558 (1977); W. PROSSER & P. KEETON, *supra* note 56, §111 at 774.

[77]W. PROSSER & P. KEETON, HANDBOOK ON THE LAW OF TORTS, §112 at 786–87 (5th ed. 1984)(libel includes pictures, signs, statues and motion pictures, though debate continues regarding the characterization of radio and television broadcasts).

[78]*Id.*

[79]*Id.* at 788; Kersul v. Skulls Angels, *supra* note 73 (action for slander, which arose from employer's broadcast to others that plaintiff was crazy, deficient for failure to plead special damages).

[80]W. PROSSER & P. KEETON, *supra* note 77, §112 at 788–93.

[81]*Supra* note 73, 704 F. Supp. at 1001, 51 FEP Cases at 268.

[82]*Supra* note 73, 626 F. Supp. at 865.

[83]*Id.* at 872 (fact issue existed as to whether employer's allegations that plaintiff improperly removed property from employer's office were defamatory).

[84]*See* Coleman v. American Broadcasting Cos., *supra* note 69, 38 FEP Cases at 72 (expressed opinions protected by First Amendment and therefore not actionable).

[85]*See, e.g.,* Restatement (Second) of Torts §525 (1977)(fraudulent misrepresentation); W. PROSSER & P. KEETON, *supra* note 77, §105 at 728 (same).

on the job by the employer's false assurances that the harassment will not recur.[86]

The same facts could also support a contractual claim for promissory estoppel.[87] In *Kinnally v. Bell of Pennsylvania*,[88] the court recognized that an employer's assurances of remedial action to address sexual harassment might form part of a promissory estoppel claim, but held on the facts that the employer's letter promising an investigation did not induce the complainant to undertake reasonable substantial action or forbearance.[89]

VIII. BREACH OF PUBLIC POLICY

A. Basis of Cause of Action

Courts in most states recognize that "public policy" may limit an employer's right to discharge even an at-will employee.[90] Courts typically have recognized a "public policy" cause of action where an employee has been discharged for refusing to commit an unlawful act.[91] The New Hampshire Supreme Court, in *Monge v. Beebe Rubber Co.*,[92] applied this exception to a sexual harassment case. Although analyzing the problem as a matter of contract law, the court held that dismissing a female employee for refusing to submit to her employer's sexual advances would be actionable as a breach of public policy.[93] Since *Monge*, many sexual harassment complainants have successfully asserted wrongful discharge claims as tortious breaches of public policy. Bases cited for the public-policy claim have included the state's FEP statute,[94]

---

[86]*E.g.*, Fawcett v. IDS Fin. Serv., 41 FEP Cases 589, 594 (W.D. Pa. 1986)(plaintiff stated claim for intentional and negligent misrepresentation with allegations that employer promised to take remedial action against harassment but failed to do so, resulting in plaintiff's constructive discharge).

[87]Restatement (Second) of Contracts §90.

[88]748 F. Supp. 1136, 54 FEP Cases 329 (E.D. Pa. 1990)

[89]*Id.* at 1145.

[90]*E.g.*, Petermann v. Teamsters Local 396, 174 Cal. App.2d 184, 344 P.2d 25 (1959)(termination of employee for refusing to participate violated public policy of state as reflected in penal code). For a chart of the 39 states that recognize the tort of wrongful discharge in violation of public policy, see IND. EMPL. RIGHTS MAN. (BNA), 505:51–52.

[91]*E.g.*, Tameny v. Atlantic Richfield Co., 27 Cal.3d 167, 610 P.2d 1330, 164 Cal. Rptr. 839 (1980)(unlawful to discharge employee who refused to participate in illegal price fixing); Sabine Pilot Serv. v. Hauck, 687 S.W.2d 733, 735, 119 LRRM 2187 (Tex. 1985)(unlawful to fire employee for refusing to illegally dump bilge into bay waters); Trombetta v. Detroit, Toledo & Ironton R.R., 81 Mich. App. 489, 265 N.W.2d 385 (1978)(unlawful to discharge employee who refused to falsify pollution records).

[92]114 N.H. 130, 316 A.2d 549, 115 LRRM 4755 (1973).

[93]The court reasoned:

In all employment contracts, whether at-will or for a definite term, the employer's interest in running his business as he sees fit must be balanced against the interest of the employee in maintaining his employment and the public's interest in maintaining a proper balance between the two. We hold that a termination by the employer of a contract of employment at-will which is motivated by bad faith or malice or based on retaliation is not in the best interest of the economic system or the public good and constitutes a breach of the employment contract.

Id., 316 A.2d at 551.

[94]*E.g.*, Dias v. Sky Chefs, 919 F.2d 1370, 1374, 54 FEP Cases 852 (9th Cir. 1990)(under Oregon law, unlawful to discharge employee for complaining about sexual harassment on the job, given that sexual harassment is prohibited under state and federal law), *vacated on other grounds*, 111 S.Ct. 2791 (1991); Chamberlin v. 101 Realty, 915 F.2d 777, 54 FEP Cases 101 (1st Cir. 1990)(female employee discharged for rebuffing employer's sexual advances had claim under New Hampshire law for wrongful termination based on public policy); Holien v. Sears, Roebuck & Co., 298 Or. 76, 689 P.2d 1292, 36 FEP Cases 137 (1984)(sexual harassment supports wrongful discharge claim based on public policy under both state and federal law prohibiting harassment).

the state's constitution,[95] statutory prohibitions of prostitution[95a] and indecent exposure,[95b] and general policies against retaliation for performing an act that the public would encourage or for refusing to do an act that the public would condemn.[96]

B. Effect of Employment Discrimination Statutes

When an employee brings a public-policy claim alleging discharge in violation of the public policy against sexual harassment (as articulated in Title VII, a state FEP statute, or elsewhere), courts have raised two basic questions as to whether such a claim will be recognized. First, some courts have questioned the need to recognize a "public policy" tort action for sexual harassment, as a common-law action should be available only where there would otherwise be no remedy. Under this doctrine, existing remedies under Title VII and any state FEP statute undermine the justification for judicial recognition of a "public policy" tort.[97] Second, although Title VII by its terms does not preempt any state-law action, courts in several states have held that the state FEP statute was intended to provide the exclusive state-law remedy for acts of employment discrimination.[98] Other courts have permitted complainants to pursue public-policy claims, notwithstanding any existing statutory remedies.[99]

---

[95]Drinkwalter v. Shipton Supply Co., 225 Mont. 380, 732 P.2d 1335, 1336, 50 FEP Cases 616, 617 (1987)(sexual harassment violates public policy embodied in Montana Constitution); Rojo v. Kliger, 52 Cal.3d 65, 276 Cal. Rptr. 130, 54 FEP Cases 1146 (1990)(citing California Constitution in deciding that plaintiff may pursue public-policy claim without regard to state statutory remedies).

[95a]Harrison v. Edison Bros. Apparel Stores, 924 F.2d 530 (4th Cir. 1991)(rejecting manager's sexual overtures amounted to refusal to engage in prostitution under North Carolina law and related retaliatory discharge would fall within public policy exception to rule of employment at will); Lucas v. Brown & Root, Inc., 736 F.2d 1202, 1205, 35 FEP Cases 1855 (8th Cir. 1984)(discharge of female employee for denying sex to boss breached Arkansas public policy against prostitution).

[95b]Wagenseller v. Scottsdale Mem. Hosp., 147 Ariz. 370, 710 P.2d 1025, 1035 & n.5 (Ariz. 1985)(employee allegedly fired for refusing to "moon" her co-workers could invoke public-policy exception; being fired for refusing to bare one's buttocks implicates public policy embodied in criminal statute forbidding exposure of anus or genitalia, even though court, ignorant of the techniques involved, cannot say as matter of law that mooning would necessarily violate the statute).

[96]Handley v. Phillips, 715 F. Supp. 657, 676, 52 FEP Cases 195 (M.D. Pa. 1989)(allegations that dismissal for rejecting defendant's sexual advances constituted breach of public policy under Pennsylvania law); Clemens v. Gerber Scientific, 1989 U.S. Dist. LEXIS 376 (E.D. Pa. 1989)(public-policy claim stated under Pennsylvania law for retaliation against female for resisting sexual advances, with specific intent to harm her).

[97]E.g., Hew-Len v. F.W. Woolworth Co., 737 F. Supp. 1104, 1106–8 (D. Haw. 1990)(where plaintiff sues for breach of public policy that inheres in employment discrimination statute, statutory remedy is exclusive); Harrison v. Edison Bros. Apparel Stores, 724 F. Supp. 1185, 1191–93 (M.D.N.C. 1989)(no "public policy" exception to employment-at-will where statutory remedy exists).

[98]E.g., Wolk v. Saks Fifth Avenue, 728 F.2d 221, 34 FEP Cases 193 (3d Cir. 1984). For a more thorough discussion of this preemption issue, see Chapters 12, Fair Employment Practices Statutes, and 27, Asserted Defenses.

[99]Hallquist v. Max Fish Plumbing & Heating Co., 46 FEP Cases 1855, 1860 (D. Mass. 1987), aff'd, 843 F.2d 18, 47 FEP Cases 323 (1st Cir. 1988)(laid-off sexual harassment complainant entitled to both back pay under Title VII and compensatory damages for termination in violation of public policy under Massachusetts law); Rojo v. Kliger, supra note 95 (California FEP statute does not bar "public policy" claim; sexual harassment victims may pursue administrative or common-law remedies, or both).

IX. BREACH OF IMPLIED CONTRACT OR COVENANT

A. Breach of Implied Contract

Under the general common-law rule, employment contracts for an indefinite term are terminable at the will of either the employee or the employer.[100] A plaintiff may rebut the presumption that employment is at will by proving that the parties expressly or impliedly agreed to specific terms regarding the employment relationship.[101] The proof may include employment manuals, private agreements, or announced personnel policies.[102]

In *Wolk v. Saks Fifth Avenue*,[103] the Third Circuit dismissed a female employee's claim under Pennsylvania law that her discharge, which allegedly stemmed from her refusal to submit to her employer's sexual advances, constituted a breach of contractual guarantees in the employer's personnel manual. The court expressed a willingness to recognize an enforceable implied contract arising from a personnel manual, but affirmed the district court's finding that the complainant had presented no evidence that her employer violated any contractual provisions in its own personnel manual when it terminated her.

Where an employer has published detailed policies and guidelines specifically addressing sexual harassment and has not contractually reserved its right to terminate employment at will, a complainant has a particularly strong argument that sexual harassment and any consequential retaliation is a breach of an implied employment contract.[104]

B. Breach of Covenant of Good Faith and Fair Dealing

The covenant of good faith and fair dealing, which arises as a matter of law, requires the employer to refrain from intentionally injuring an employee's

---

[100]Vegelahn v. Gunter, 167 Mass. 92, 44 N.E. 1077 (1896)(absent contract for specific duration, employment contract terminable at will of either party).

[101]*See, e.g.,* Pugh v. See's Candies, 116 Cal. App.3d 311, 171 Cal. Rptr. 917, 115 LRRM 4002 (1981)(factors such as personnel policies, longevity of service, and verbal assurances may establish an implied-in-fact contract); Berube v. Fashion Centre, Ltd., 771 P.2d 1033 (Utah 1989)(at-will presumption is rebuttable by policy manuals and personnel policies). For a chart listing the states in which an employee may allege an implied contract of continuing employment, see IND. EMPL. RIGHTS MAN. (BNA), 505:51–52.

[102]*See* Tuttle v. ANR Freight Sys., 5 IER Cases 1103 (Col. Ct. App. 1990)(employment handbook, which stated employer would not discriminate based on sex and which was highlighted as integral part of employment relationship, gave female employee enforceable contract rights). *See generally* Foley v. Interactive Data Corp., 47 Cal.3d 654, 254 Cal. Rptr. 211 (1989)(implied employment contract restricting employer's right to terminate at will may be inferred from various factors including personnel practices, employee longevity, and practices of industry); Woolley v. Hoffman-LaRoche, Inc., 99 N.J. 284, 491 A.2d 1257, *modified,* 101 N.J. 10, 499 A.2d 515 (1985)(job security provisions in personnel policy manual supported by consideration and constituted binding commitment of employer); Toussaint v. Blue Cross & Blue Shield, 408 Mich. 579, 292 N.W.2d 880, 155 LRRM 4708 (1980)(employer's written statements in manual of personnel policies raised issue of whether employment was terminable only for cause).

[103]*Supra* note 98 (sole restriction on employee termination in employer's manual was requirement of warning and personal discussion before discharge).

[104]*See, e.g.,* Hew-Len v. F.W. Woolworth Co., *supra* note 97, 737 F. Supp. at 1107–8 (where employer had employee handbook containing policies and guidelines with respect to sexual harassment and "other issues," plaintiff arguably had breach-of-contract claim); Noye v. Hoffman-LaRoche Inc., 238 N.J. Super. 430, 570 A.2d 12 (1990) (employer may breach contract by failing to follow company procedures on sexual harassment). *Cf.* Martin v. Baer, 928 F.2d 1067 (11th Cir. 1991)(assuming arguendo that sexual harassment policy implied a contractual duty to investigate, plaintiff could not invoke a duty because he made no formal complaint of sexual harassment).

right to receive the contractual benefits of the employment relationship.[105] Courts in most states have not recognized the implied covenant of good faith and fair dealing in the employment context.[106] In states where the theory has been applied, an employer may be held to have violated the covenant.[107]

In *Drinkwalter v. Shipton Supply Co.*,[108] the Montana Supreme Court concluded that sexual harassment can constitute a breach of the implied covenant of good faith and fair dealing in an employment relationship. Similarly, in *Lucas v. Brown & Root, Inc.*,[109] the Eighth Circuit sustained the complainant's claim of a breach of covenant of good faith and fair dealing under Arkansas law, based on her allegation that she was fired because she refused to sleep with her foreman.[110]

X. CONTRACTUAL INTERFERENCE

Employees sexually harassed by co-workers have sued on a contractual interference theory.[111] To prevail under this theory, the complainant must show that the harasser intentionally and improperly interfered with the complainant's performance of the employment contract, either by inducing the employer to discharge the complainant or in some other way.[112] Proof of an unlawful motive is necessary. In *Fisher v. San Pedro Peninsula Hospital*,[113] the court rejected a nurse's claim that a doctor's sexual harassment of other nurses created a

---

[105]*See* Foley v. Interactive Data Corp., *supra* note 102, 254 Cal. Rptr. at 232 (covenant read into contracts to protect express promises of contract, not to advance general public policy interests); Fortune v. National Cash Register Co., 373 Mass. 96, 364 N.E.2d 1251, 115 LRRM 4658 (1977)(termination of employment-at-will contract motivated by bad faith constitutes breach of employment contract); Wallis v. Superior Court, 160 Cal. App.3d 1109, 207 Cal. Rptr. 123 (1984)(as party in stronger position, employer had "duty not to act unreasonably in breaching the [employment] contract," precise scope of duty depending on parties' legitimate expectations).

[106]*See, e.g.,* Noye v. Hoffman-LaRoche Inc., *supra* note 104 (refusing to recognize claim of breach of implied covenant of good faith and fair dealing in employment relationship); *see also* Dworkin, Ginger & Mallor, *Theories of Recovery for Sexual Harassment: Going Beyond Title VII,* 25 SAN DIEGO L. REV. 125, 146 (1988)(theory is rarely recognized).

[107]*See, e.g.,* Foley v. Interactive Data Corp., *supra* note 102 (employer procedures for addressing employee disputes, coupled with longevity of employee's service, obligated employer to treat employee with good faith and fair dealing).

[108]*Supra* note 95 (employee who resigned in response to sexual comments and actions by supervisor may bring action for breach of implied covenant, because "[g]ood faith and fair dealing preclude sexual harassment").

[109]*Supra* note 96.

[110]*Id.* The court analogized the plaintiff's refusal to submit to her foreman's demands to a refusal to engage in the crime of prostitution. *Id.* at 1205. Reasoning that "it is an implied term of every contract of employment that neither party be required to do what the law forbids," *id.*, the court concluded that the plaintiff could seek damages for breach of contract. Thus, the court couched the covenant of good faith and fair dealing in terms of public policy. See Section VIII. *supra.*

[111]*See* Romero v. Mason & Hanger-Silas Mason Co., 739 F. Supp. 1472 (D.N.M. 1990)(harasser allegedly induced employer into terminating employment of union-represented security inspector, who relied on state-created rights independent of collective bargaining agreement); Fisher v. San Pedro Peninsula Hosp., 214 Cal. App.3d 590, 262 Cal. Rptr. 842, 54 FEP Cases 584 (1989)(allegations that sexual harasser created hostile environment that disrupted complainant's relationship with employer); Fields v. Cummins Employees Fed. Credit Union, 540 N.E.2d 631, 53 FEP Cases 1613, 1620 (Ind. Ct. App. 1990)(contractual interference claim stated against co-workers whose harassment allegedly contributed to complainant's decision to accept demotion); Favors v. Alco Mfg. Co., 186 Ga. App. 480, 367 S.E.2d 328 (1988)(question of fact whether alleged sexual harasser interfered with complainant's contractual relationship); Lewis v. Oregon Beauty Supply Co., 302 Or. 616, 733 P.2d 430 (1987)(evidence supported plaintiff's claim that defendant's sexual harassment interfered with business relationship).

[112]Romero v. Mason & Hanger-Silas Mason Co., *supra* note 111, 739 F. Supp. at 1477 (citing Restatement (Second) of Torts §766 (1977)).

[113]*Supra* note 111.

hostile work environment that disrupted her employment relationship with the hospital. Significantly, the court found no evidence that the doctor intended to disrupt the individual plaintiff's employment relationship through his harassment of other nurses.

Contractual interference requires the existence of an enforceable employment contract,[114] although at least one jurisdiction has recognized that an at-will employee may claim tortious interference with a business relationship.[115] Because liability is founded only upon the acts of an interfering third party,[116] co-workers or supervisors cannot be liable for contractual interference unless they are shown to have acted outside their scope of authority.[117] The tort is designed to compensate only for economic harm resulting from the interference.[118] Normally the claim of contractual interference is asserted against the individual alleged to have perpetrated the harassment rather than the employer with whom the contract existed.

Sexual harassment victims have stated claims of contractual interference under a variety of factual allegations. In *Favors v. Alco Mfg. Co.*,[119] the complainant alleged that her supervisor tortiously interfered with her employment contract when he facilitated her discharge after she rejected his advances. In *Lewis v. Oregon Beauty Supply Co.*,[120] the court awarded punitive damages for contractual interference where a male co-worker's threats, insults, and intimidation forced the complainant to abandon her job.[121]

XI. LOSS OF CONSORTIUM BY THE COMPLAINANT'S SPOUSE

A claim for loss of consortium is a derivative action for the loss of sexual attentions, society, and affection resulting from an injury to one's marital partner.[122] In the context of sexual harassment, loss of consortium claims have been asserted by men whose wives have suffered physical and emotional injuries arising from sexual harassment in the workplace.[123]

---

[114]*See* Cummings v. Walsh Constr. Co., 561 F. Supp. 872, 883 (S.D. Ga. 1983)(no interference claim viable if plaintiff an at-will employee).

[115]Fields v. Cummins Employees Fed. Credit Union, *supra* note 111, 53 FEP Cases at 1620 (sustaining allegation that harassment by co-worker forced plaintiff to accept demotion). The elements of a claim of tortious interference with a business relationship are the same as those for a claim of contractual interference, except that a valid contract is not required. *Id.*

[116]Restatement (Second) of Torts §766 (1977).

[117]Favors v. Alco Mfg. Co., *supra* note 111 (supervisory employee liable only when acting outside scope and course of employment).

[118]See Schoenheider, *A Theory of Tort Liability for Sexual Harassment in the Workplace,* 134 U. PA. L. REV. 1480 (1986)(arguing that contractual interference theory has limited value to sexual harassment plaintiffs).

[119]*Supra* note 111; Newsome v. Cooper-Wiss, Inc., 179 Ga. App. 670, 347 S.E.2d 619, 622 (1986)(allegations that former supervisor encouraged complainant's dismissal supported action for tortious interference).

[120]*Supra* note 111.

[121]*Id.* at 433. *See also* Kyriazi v. Western Elec. Co., 461 F. Supp. 894, 950, 18 FEP Cases 924 (D.N.J. 1978)(male co-workers and supervisor liable for pattern of sexual harassment that interfered with complainant's employment contract). In a later proceeding, the court held the individual defendants liable for punitive damages. Kyriazi v. Western Elec. Co., 476 F. Supp. 335, 336, 26 FEP Cases 413, 417 (D.N.J. 1979).

[122]W. PROSSER & P. KEETON, HANDBOOK ON THE LAW OF TORTS, §125 at 931–32 (5th ed. 1984).

[123]*E.g.,* Handley v. Phillips, 715 F. Supp. 657, 662, 52 FEP Cases 195 (M.D. Pa. 1989)(granting summary judgment on husband's consortium claim); Bowersox v. P.H. Glatfelter Co., 677 F. Supp. 307, 312, 45 FEP Cases 1443 (M.D. Pa. 1988)(husband stated claim against wife's former supervisor for loss of consortium); Eide v. Kelsey-Hayes Co., 427 N.W.2d 488, 489, 47 FEP Cases 1050 (Mich. 1988)(sexual

Claims brought by the complainant's spouse may accompany the complainant's own actions for assault and battery, intentional infliction of emotional distress, etc.[124] In *Eide v. Kelsey-Hayes Co.*,[125] the court concluded that a derivative claim for loss of consortium was cognizable under Michigan's FEP statute.

A loss-of-consortium claim does not require that the harassed spouse suffer a physically disabling injury. In *Bowersox v. P.H. Glatfelter Co.*,[126] Judge Sylvia H. Rambo held that manifestations of sexual harassment such as depression, headaches, nausea, and severe emotional distress can easily result in the deprivation of society and companionship, thereby warranting a remedy for loss of consortium.

XII. NEGLIGENT RETENTION OR SUPERVISION

Negligent retention or supervision claims are sometimes asserted against employers in an attempt to hold them liable for the sexually harassing acts of their employees.[127] Liability for negligent retention is predicated on an employer's knowledge of an employee's propensity to engage in sexual harassment, and the subsequent failure to address this inappropriate conduct.[128] An employer charged with negligent retention may not assert an assumption of risk defense against the complainant.[129]

An employer may be found liable for negligent retention or supervision only if, in the exercise of ordinary care, the employer should have known of,

---

harassment victim's husband awarded $28,000 in damages for loss of consortium); Spoon v. American Agriculturalist, 120 A.D.2d 857, 502 N.Y.S.2d 296 (1986)(husband of complainant stated derivative claim for loss of consortium arising from employer's alleged intentional torts against wife).

[124]*See supra* note 123 and cases cited therein.

[125]*Supra* note 123, 427 N.W.2d at 489, 47 FEP Cases at 1051 (husband stated viable derivative claim for loss of consortium where wife stated sexual harassment claim under Michigan's statute). In contrast, a loss of consortium claim cannot be sustained to the extent it is predicated on a Title VII sexual harassment claim, because Title VII provides only equitable relief. Pryor v. United States Gypsum Co., 585 F. Supp. 311, 317, 47 FEP Cases 159 (W.D. Mo. 1984).

[126]*Supra* note 123.

[127]Paroline v. Unisys Corp., 879 F.2d 100, 50 FEP Cases 306, 315–16 (4th Cir. 1989)(remanding for determination whether complaint has cause of action under Virginia law), reproduced in Chapter 9, Constructive Discharge, *vacated on other grounds,* 900 F.2d 27, 52 FEP Cases 845 (4th Cir. 1990)(*en banc*); Harrison v. Edison Bros. Apparel Stores, 724 F. Supp. 1185, 1190 (M.D.N.C. 1989)(negligent retention claim asserted against employer arising from tortious acts of co-worker); Byrd v. Richardson-Greenshields Sec., 552 So.2d 1099, 51 EPD ¶39,446 (Fla. 1989)(negligent hiring and retention action brought by female plaintiff who alleged repeated touching and verbal sexual advances by supervisor); Carr v. U.S. West Direct Co., 98 Or. App. 30, 779 P.2d 154 (1989)(negligent supervision claim against employer arising from supervisor's sexual harassment and rape of female sales representative); Kresko v. Rulli, 432 N.W.2d 764, 769 (Minn. Ct. App. 1988)(negligent retention claim against employer for alleged sexual harassment by supervisor); Hart v. National Mortgage & Land Co., 189 Cal. App.3d 1420, 235 Cal. Rptr. 68 (1987)(male plaintiff asserted negligent retention claim against employer based on sexual harassment by male supervisor); Drinkwalter v. Shipton Supply Co., 225 Mont. 380, 732 P.2d 1335, 50 FEP Cases 616 (1987)(claim stated for negligent supervision as result of alleged tortious conduct by supervisor).

[128]*E.g.,* Kresko v. Rulli, *supra* note 127 ("to find negligent retention, the court must find that the employer knew or should have known of the employee's negative activities"); Perkins v. Spivey, 911 F.2d 22, 53 FEP Cases 973 (8th Cir. 1990)(although employer has no duty under Kansas common law to maintain workplace free from psychological harm of sexual harassment, it does have duty not to retain employee it knows or should know is emotionally harming co-workers to the extent they suffer physical injuries); Cox v. Brazo, 303 S.E.2d 71, 73 (Ga. Ct. App. 1983)(action stated if employer should have known of employee's reputation for sexual harassment and sexual harassment of fellow employee was foreseeable).

[129]Perkins v. Spivey, *supra* note 128, 53 FEP Cases at 978–79 (rejecting defense as inconsistent with modern views toward women and abuse).

and responded to, an employee's sexual harassment of other workers.[130] In *Carr v. U.S. West Direct Co.*,[131] the employer was held not to be liable for the negligent supervision of a supervisor accused of raping a female sales representative, even though the company had previously placed that supervisor on probation for sexual harassment, because the evidence showed that the employer had no reason to believe the supervisor was dangerous at the time of the rape. A manager's failure to follow company procedures when reporting and investigating sexual harassment charges against an alleged harasser has been held to constitute only a breach of contract, not an independent tort based on negligence.[132]

Claims for negligent retention or supervision usually accompany claims against the individual alleged harasser.[133] In *Harrison v. Edison Bros. Apparel Stores*,[134] however, the court held that the voluntary dismissal of the complainant's underlying tort claims against the alleged sexual harasser did not prevent her from pursuing a negligent retention claim against her employer, because the voluntary dismissal did not constitute a final judgment for purposes of collateral estoppel.

The common-law duty to maintain a safe workplace concerns only physical injuries,[134a] and some jurisdictions still do not recognize the tort of negligent supervision or retention absent some bodily injury.[135]

A negligent supervision or retention claim may be barred by the exclusivity provisions of state workers' compensation statutes.[136] However, in *Byrd v. Richardson-Greenshields Securities*,[137] the Florida Supreme Court declined to apply an exclusivity provision to negligent hiring and retention claims based on sexual harassment in the workplace. The court reasoned that workers' compensation laws were never intended to encompass acts of sexual harassment, particularly because state and federal policies are strongly committed to outlawing and eliminating sexual discrimination in the workplace.[138]

---

[130]Coleman v. Housing Auth., 191 Ga. App. 166, 381 S.E.2d 303, 307 (1989)(employer may be liable for negligent retention if ordinarily careful employer acting upon present knowledge could have reasonably discovered one of its employees was engaging in sexual harassment).

[131]*Supra* note 127.

[132]Noye v. Hoffman-LaRoche, Inc., 238 N.J. Super. 430, 570 A.2d 12 (1990).

[133]*See* Coleman v. Housing Auth., *supra* note 130, 381 S.E.2d at 304 (failure to state underlying action for intentional infliction of emotional distress would result in dismissal of negligent hiring and retention claims); Hogan v. Forsyth Country Club Co., 79 N.C. App. 483, 340 S.E.2d 116 (1986)(because plaintiff failed to support action for intentional infliction of emotional distress, no tort upon which to base employer's liability for negligent retention).

[134]*Supra* note 127, 724 F. Supp. at 1190–91.

[134a]EEOC v. General Motors Corp., 53 FEP Cases 994, 995 (D. Kan. 1989).

[135]*E.g.,* Spencer v. General Elec. Co., 894 F.2d 651, 656, 51 FEP Cases 1725, 1729 (4th Cir. 1990)(no common-law duty under Virginia law to protect employees from harassment). *See also* Perkins v. Spivey, *supra* note 128 (Kansas law).

[136]*E.g.,* Fields v. Cummins Employees Fed. Credit Union, 540 N.E.2d 631, 53 FEP Cases 1613 (Ind. Ct. App. 1989)(negligent retention claims barred by exclusivity of Indiana's workers' compensation act); Brooms v. Regal Tube Co., 881 F.2d 412, 421, 50 FEP Cases 1499, 1509 (7th Cir. 1989)(Illinois workers' compensation act precluded plaintiff's negligence action against employer arising from sexual harassment in workplace). For a discussion of workers' compensation exclusivity, see Chapters 14, Workers' Compensation Statutes, Section II., and 27, Asserted Defenses, Section IV.

[137]*Supra* note 127.

[138]*Id.* at 1103–4; *see also* Hogan v. Forsyth Country Club Co., *supra* note 133, 340 S.E.2d at 124 (plaintiff's negligent retention claim not barred by workers' compensation statute).

XIII. RESPONDEAT SUPERIOR

Under each of the common-law torts discussed in this chapter (except the tort of contractual interference), the employer itself may be directly liable to a sexual harassment complainant on the basis of its own conduct. An alternative basis of liability—indirect liability—is provided by the common-law doctrine of *respondeat superior*.

A. Elements of the Doctrine

Under *respondeat superior*, a principal may be vicariously liable for torts committed by an agent of the principal. This liability may arise when the agent's act is expressly authorized by the principal, when the agent's act is committed within the scope of employment and in furtherance of the principal's business, or when the agent's act is ratified by the principal.[139]

Sexual harassment by an agent will rarely be authorized by the principal or in furtherance of the principal's business. In *Dockter v. Rudolf Wolff Futures*,[140] the employer was not vicariously liable for the sexually harassing acts of a supervisory employee, where the evidence demonstrated that the supervisor acted only for his own enjoyment and benefit.[141] Similarly, in *Davis v. Utah Power & Light Co.*,[142] the court found, as a matter of law, that the harasser's tortious acts—an off-duty, off-premises kiss and some late-night activity in the complainant's bedroom—were beyond his express scope of employment, not in furtherance of his employer's business, and otherwise outside the scope of employment.

Nonetheless, the scope of a manager's employment can be broad. In *Dias v. Sky Chefs*,[143] the employer was unable to disassociate itself from the retaliatory conduct of its general manager, even though his sexual harassment was not within the scope of his duties. Upholding a jury verdict of employer tort liability, the Ninth Circuit held that the jury reasonably could have concluded that the general manager's discharge of the plaintiff for complaining about sexual harassment was a misguided effort to exercise his managerial authority to remove an employee who was undercutting his authority.[144]

---

[139]*See* Restatement (Second) of Agency §§215–267 (1958); Brown v. Burlington Indus., 93 N.C. App. 431, 378 S.E.2d 232 (1989). See also Chapter 6, Harassment by Supervisors, Section IV.

[140]684 F. Supp. 532, 46 FEP Cases 1129 (N.D. Ill. 1988), *aff'd*, 913 F.2d 456, 53 FEP Cases 1642 (7th Cir. 1990).

[141]*Id.* at 536 (sexual misbehavior of supervisory employee not intended to, nor did it, benefit employer). *See also* Hunter v. Countryside Ass'n for the Handicapped, 710 F. Supp. 233, 49 FEP Cases 790 (N.D. Ill. 1989)(employer not liable under doctrine of *respondeat superior* for employee's sexual attack on co-worker); Valdez v. Church's Fried Chicken, 683 F. Supp. 596, 47 FEP Cases 1155 (W.D. Tex. 1988)(no *respondeat superior* liability because employee's assault and battery of female employee based on "purely personal motives"); Saulsberry v. Atlantic Richfield Co., 673 F. Supp. 811, 815, 45 FEP Cases 440 (N.D. Miss. 1987)(where complainant admitted sexual harasser's actions were not within course and scope of employment, doctrine of *respondeat superior* did not apply); Miller v. Lindenwood Female College, 616 F. Supp. 860, 861 (E.D. Mo. 1985)(no employer liability for infliction of emotional distress by employer's agent who, in making sexual overtures, was acting as "independent agent" not within scope of employment).

[142]53 FEP Cases 1047, 1049 (D. Utah 1990).

[143]919 F.2d 1370, 54 FEP Cases 852 (9th Cir. 1990), *vacated on other grounds*, 111 S.Ct. 2791 (1991).

[144]*Id.* at 1375–76. For conflicting views on whether a supervisor's sexual advances to a subordinate may be construed to be within the scope of employment, see the majority and dissenting opinions in *Davis v. United States Steel Corp.*, 779 F.2d 209, 39 FEP Cases 955 (4th Cir. 1985), discussed in Chapter 6, Harassment by Supervisors, Section IV.

The employer may also be liable where management personnel were aware of sexual harassment and consciously failed to respond,[145] where management could reasonably anticipate that intentional misconduct of the sort in question could occur,[146] or where the harasser acted with apparent authority.[146a]

Indirect liability may also attach, of course, to nonemployer organizations, such as unions, on the same principles as discussed above.[146b]

B. Liability for Punitive Damages

To state a claim for punitive damages, plaintiffs generally must show that the defendant acted willfully or with malice.[147] For pleading purposes, one state appellate court has ruled that an allegation sufficient to state a case for a sexually hostile environment "in and of itself pleads the evil motive necessary to support punitive damages."[148]

In some jurisdictions, employers may be liable for punitive damages even absent any participation in or ratification of the oppressive, willful, or malicious conduct.[149] In others, an officer, director, or managing agent of the corporation must participate in or ratify the conduct to render the employer liable for punitive damages.[150]

---

[145]Brown v. Burlington Indus., *supra* note 139; Spoon v. American Agriculturalist, 120 A.D.2d 857, 502 N.Y.S.2d 296, 298 (1986)(*respondeat superior* may apply where employer has pervasive knowledge of wrongful conduct and fails to take corrective action).

[146]*See generally* Restatement (Second) of Agency §231 (act may be within scope of employment even if consciously tortious). *Cf.* Bigoni v. Pay'N Pak Stores, 746 F. Supp. 1, 5 (D. Or. 1990)(employer awarded summary judgment on claim of intentional infliction of emotional distress based on harassing telephone calls attributed to individual defendant; any such calls were unrelated to individual's employment, "solely for his own perverse delight and benefit," and not reasonably foreseen by company management).

[146a]*Cf.* Davis v. Utah Power & Light Co., *supra* note 142, 53 FEP Cases at 1049–50 (no basis for tort liability on theory of apparent authority based on harasser's conduct alone; theory requires reliance on conduct of principal, not agent alone).

[146b]*See, e.g.,* Woods v. Graphic Communications, 925 F.2d 1195, 55 FEP Cases 242 (9th Cir. 1991)(union liable for tort of outrage for harassment by union agents under theory that union effectively ratified their conduct).

[147]*See, e.g.,* Dias v. Sky Chefs, *supra* note 143 (jury may award punitive damages for wrongful discharge if plaintiff proves willfulness and malice); Clemens v. Gerber Scientific, 1989 U.S. Dist. LEXIS 376 (E.D. Pa. 1989)(plaintiff permitted to recover punitive damages for sexual harassment-based wrongful discharge claim); Shrout v. Black Clawson Co., 689 F. Supp. 774, 780, 46 FEP Cases 1339, 1343 (S.D. Ohio 1988)(plaintiff recovered $50,000 in punitive damages under Ohio tort law where quid pro quo harassment was "malicious" and went unchecked for four years); Pease v. Alford Photo Indus., 667 F. Supp. 1188, 1192, 1203, 49 FEP Cases 497, 500, 509 (W.D. Tenn. 1987)(plaintiff entitled to $10,000 in punitive damages under theories of assault and battery, intentional infliction of emotional distress, invasion of privacy and outrageous conduct where she was repeatedly touched by employer in sexual manner and suffered migraines, skin rashes, and insomnia as result); Priest v. Rotary, 634 F. Supp. 571, 582–585, 40 FEP Cases 208, 216–18 (N.D. Cal. 1986)($15,000 exemplary damages awarded to plaintiff in sexual harassment action for battery, false imprisonment, and intentional infliction of emotional distress under California law); Wing v. JMB Property Mgmt. Corp., 714 P.2d 916, 919, 48 FEP Cases 111, 112 (Colo. Ct. App. 1985)(allegations of wanton, willful, malicious, and intentional actions of defendants sufficient to support claim for punitive damages).

[148]Fisher v. San Pedro Peninsula Hosp., 214 Cal. App.3d 590, 621, 262 Cal. Rptr. 842, 860, 54 FEP Cases 584 (1989). *See also* Monge v. Superior Court, 176 Cal. App.3d 503, 222 Cal. Rptr. 64 (1986)(complaint pleaded facts sufficient to show "oppression" and "malice" needed for purposes of punitive damages with allegation that corporate officers conspired to display the message, "How about a little head?" on complainant's computer terminal, and then systematically retaliated against her when she complained).

[149]*See* W. PROSSER, LAW OF TORTS §2 (4th ed. 1971); Note, *Liability of Employers for Punitive Damages Resulting from Acts of Employees,* 54 CHI.-KENT L. REV. 829, 931 (1978); Note, *The Assessment of Punitive Damages Against an Entrepreneur for the Malicious Torts of His Employees,* 70 YALE L.J. 1296 (1961).

[150]*See, e.g.,* Shrout v. Black Clawson Co., *supra* note 147, 689 F. Supp. at 783, 46 FEP Cases at 1346 (under Ohio law, employer may be assessed punitive damages because of malicious conduct of its employees if employer has authorized, ratified, participated or acquiesced in wrongdoing); Hart v. National Mortgage & Land Co., 189 Cal. App.3d 1420, 1432, 235 Cal. Rptr. 68 (1987)(under California Civil Code §3294,

There should be no liability for punitive damages in a sexual harassment case based on mere negligence.[151] Failure to correct known sexual harassment, however, may effectively ratify the harassing conduct, thereby entitling the complainant to punitive damages.[152] Ratification may be inferred from the fact that "the employer, after being informed of the employee's actions, does not fully investigate and fails to repudiate the employee's conduct by redressing the harm done and punishing or discharging the employee."[153]

---

employer is not liable for punitive damages based on acts of employee unless employer ratified wrongful conduct or was personally guilty of oppression, fraud, or malice); Clark v. World Airways, 24 FEP Cases 305, 309–10 (D.D.C. 1980)(in District of Columbia, plaintiffs may recover punitive damages against corporate employers only if they prove corporation, through directors and officers, participated in wrongful act or ratified conduct).

[151]See, e.g., Dias v. Sky Chefs, supra note 143 (plaintiff must show malice and oppression on part of defendant); Newsome v. Cooper-Wiss, Inc., 179 Ga. App. 670, 347 S.E.2d 619 (1986).

[152]Hart v. National Mortgage & Land Co., supra note 150 (employer could be liable for punitive damages for assault and battery and intentional infliction of emotional distress if employee proved that superior had knowledge of sexual harassment and failed to act); see also Newsome v. Cooper-Wiss, Inc., supra note 151 (employer may be liable for punitive damages if, after learning of alleged harassment by supervisor against employee, employer discharged employee and retained supervisor); Tretter v. Liquipak Int'l, 356 N.W.2d 713, 714, 43 FEP Cases 1522, 1524 (Minn. Ct. App. 1984)(employer liable for punitive damages where it permitted plaintiff to be harassed by supervisor for 6 months; conduct demonstrated willful indifference to plaintiff's rights and safety).

[153]Fisher v. San Pedro Peninsula Hosp., supra note 148. See also Shrout v. Black Clawson Co., supra note 147, 689 F. Supp. at 783, 46 FEP Cases at 1346 (that high-level managers knew or should have known of supervisor's four-year campaign of harassment and made no effort to investigate same justified $50,000 punitive damage award against employer); Rogers v. Loews L'Enfant Plaza Hotel, 526 F. Supp. 523, 534–35, 29 FEP Cases 828, 835–36 (D.D.C. 1981)(plaintiff can obtain punitive damage award against employer if she can prove that management knew about harassment by supervisor and took no action). In other cases, e.g., Fawcett v. IDS Fin. Serv., 41 FEP Cases 589 (W.D. Pa. 1986), and Ford v. Revlon, Inc., 734 P.2d 580, 43 FEP Cases 213 (Ariz. 1987), courts awarded punitive damages for intentional infliction of emotional distress rather than for ratification, but the analysis is similar under either theory.

CHAPTER 16

CRIMINAL LAW

I. OVERVIEW

Acts of sexual harassment may violate criminal statutes. In egregious cases of sexual harassment, complainants may consider contacting law enforcement authorities to explore criminal prosecution.

The effects of criminal prosecutions are qualitatively different from those of civil proceedings. Alleged harassers subject to criminal prosecution face possible incarceration, fines, restitution, and damage to personal reputation. Criminal prosecutions can also affect an alleged harasser's employer. Criminal prosecutions can tarnish a company's image, and lead to civil liability that will not be covered by insurance, which generally excludes claims resulting from intentional conduct.

This chapter discusses the crimes that most commonly occur in connection with sexual harassment in employment. It outlines how a criminal prosecution can benefit sexual harassment complainants and describes some of the problems and basic considerations for a complainant in pursuing an action in the criminal justice system. It also highlights the potential consequences to complainants and defendants who behave improperly in connection with a criminal complaint. Finally, this chapter offers suggestions for company counsel who are notified of possible criminal prosecutions for sexual harassment.

II. CRIMES COMMITTED BY SEXUAL HARASSERS

A. Rape and Sodomy

Proportionately few of the instances of sexual harassment in employment have involved rape,[1] although several of the reported cases have involved incidents of rape.[2] Most statutes define rape in terms of sexual intercourse

---

[1]About 1% of reported incidents of sexual harassment have involved rape or sexual assault. Pollack, *Sexual Harassment: Women's Experience v. Legal Definitions,* 13 HARV. WOMEN'S L.J. 35, 50 n.46 (1990).

[2]In *Meritor Sav. Bank v. Vinson,* 477 U.S. 57, 40 FEP Cases 1822 (1986), reproduced in Chapter 1, Overview, a former employee of the bank claimed that she was sexually harassed by a supervisor who forcibly raped her on several occasions. *See also* Valdez v. Church's Fried Chicken, 683 F. Supp. 596, 608, 47 FEP Cases 1155, 1160 (W.D. Tex. 1988)(defendant pushed plaintiff against wall, pulled down her pants, and attempted to have sexual intercourse); Gilardi v. Schroeder, 672 F. Supp. 1043, 1045, 45 FEP Cases 283, 287 (N.D. Ill. 1986)(drugging of plaintiff and forced sexual assault), *aff'd,* 833 F.2d 1226 (7th Cir. 1987).

accomplished with a person, against the victim's will, by means of force, violence, or fear of immediate and unlawful bodily injury.[3] Even consensual sex is criminalized as rape where the sexual activity is performed with one under a specified age.[4]

Sexual harassment can involve conduct that would constitute the crime of sodomy.[5] Sodomy, also referred to as deviant sexual intercourse, is generally defined in terms of sexual contact between the penis and the anus, the mouth and the penis, the mouth and vulva, or sexual contact with animals.[6] Whether this offense is a felony or a misdemeanor depends on the particular jurisdiction and whether the activity is consensual. Although consensual sodomy is rarely prosecuted, an employer may wish to evaluate the civil risks should it later be contended that the employer condoned criminal behavior that led to emotional or other damage to a complainant.[7]

B. Sexual Battery

Many states have enacted statutes that make it a felony or a misdemeanor to engage in conduct known as sexual battery. The California statute makes it a misdemeanor to touch an intimate part of another for the purpose of sexual arousal, gratification, or abuse, if done against the will of the person touched.[8] Touching is defined as physical contact either directly or through the clothing of the victim or of the person committing the offense. Intimate parts are the sexual organ, anus, groin, or buttocks of any person, and the breasts of a female. This conduct, which frequently forms the factual basis of sexual harassment

---

[3]*E.g.,* CAL. PENAL CODE §261 (West 1988); D.C. CODE ANN. §22-2801 (1989); N.Y. PENAL LAW §130.35 (McKinney 1987). The crime of rape most often is defined to apply only to sexual intercourse with someone other than the perpetrator's spouse. The absence of consent is generally shown by one of the following circumstances: (a) where a person is incapable, because of a mental disorder or developmental or physical disability, of giving legal consent; (b) where it is accomplished against a person's will by means of force, violence, or fear of immediate and unlawful bodily injury on the person of another; (c) where a person is prevented from resisting by any intoxicating or anesthetic substance, administered by or with the privity of the accused; (d) where a person is at the time unconscious and this is known to the accused; (e) where a person submits under the belief that the person committing the act is the victim's spouse; (f) where the act is accomplished against the victim's will by threatening to retaliate in the future against the victim or any person, where there is a reasonable possibility that the perpetrator will execute the threat (threatening to retaliate is restricted to mean a threat to kidnap or falsely imprison, or to inflict extreme pain, serious bodily injury or death); and (g) where the act is accomplished against the victim's will by threatening to use the authority of a public official to incarcerate, arrest, or deport the victim or another, and the victim has a reasonable belief that the perpetrator is a public official.

[4]*See, e.g.,* N.Y. PENAL LAW §130.25 (McKinney 1987)(17 years); ARIZ. REV. STAT. ANN. §13-1405 (1989)(18 years); IDAHO CODE §18-6101 (1987)(18 years). These statutes may apply in an employment setting in the context of part-time student employment or summer employment. While traditionally those under the age of 18 have been viewed as unable to give legal consent to sexual intercourse, the laws of the jurisdiction should be consulted to determine the precise age of consent in a particular locality.

[5]*E.g.,* Valdez v. Church's Fried Chicken, *supra* note 2, 683 F. Supp. at 608, 47 FEP Cases at 1160 (defendant pulled out his penis and attempted to force plaintiff to engage in oral copulation). *See generally* Brooms v. Regal Tube Co., 881 F.2d 412, 50 FEP Cases 1499 (7th Cir. 1989)(supervisor showed subordinate depiction of sodomy and told her that was what she had been hired for).

[6]*E.g.,* CAL. PENAL CODE §§286-87 (West 1988); N.Y. PENAL LAW §§130.00 and 130.38-.50 (McKinney 1987); D.C. CODE ANN. §22-3502 (1989).

[7]Local statutes should also be consulted in those jurisdictions that retain criminal adultery or fornication statutes. Classic adultery and fornication statutes are ILL. ANN. STAT. ch. 38, ¶¶11-7 and 11-9 (Smith-Hurd 1989) and FLA. STAT. ANN. §798.01 (West 1976), which punish as a misdemeanor sexual intercourse between unmarried individuals when the behavior is "open and notorious."

[8]CAL. PENAL CODE §243.4 (West 1988). Other jurisdictions have similar statutory schemes. *E.g.,* N.Y. PENAL LAW §130.00(3)(McKinney 1987); ARIZ. REV. STAT. ANN. §13-1404 (1989); GA. CODE ANN. §16-6-22.1 (1988).

charges,[9] rises to the level of a felony if the victim is restrained by the perpetrator or an accomplice at the time of the touching.[10]

C. Sexual Assault

When a perpetrator specifically intends to accomplish forcible nonconsensual sexual contact, but does not actually complete the act, a sexual assault has been completed. If the perpetrator is fought off while intending to commit rape, the crimes of attempted rape and, most probably, battery and sexual assault, have been completed. Sexual assault is historically prosecuted under one or more of these categories. The attempt to commit the most serious uncompleted act will almost always be included among the offenses charged. Attempt statutes universally provide that an individual perpetrates an attempt when, with intent to commit a specific offense, an individual does any act that constitutes a substantial step toward the commission of that offense.[11] Maximum possible sentences are usually those provided for the offense attempted, but statutory schemes vary considerably among jurisdictions.[12]

D. Obscene Telephone Calls

Many states forbid making telephone calls with the intent to harass or abuse the recipient of the call,[13] a problem that sometimes arises in sexual harassment cases.[14] Federal law prohibits obscene or harassing telephone calls whenever the interstate commerce jurisdictional element is present. Specifically, it is unlawful to

(1) make any comment, request, suggestion, or proposal that is obscene, lewd, lascivious, filthy, or indecent;

---

[9]*See, e.g.,* Waltman v. International Paper Co., 47 FEP Cases 671, 673–74 (W.D. La. 1988)(male co-workers touched and pinched complainant's breasts and thighs and placed air hose between her legs), *rev'd on other grounds,* 875 F.2d 468, 50 FEP Cases 179 (5th Cir. 1989); Garcia v. Williams, 704 F. Supp. 984, 1000, 51 FEP Cases 255, 267 (N.D. Cal. 1988)(employer allegedly touched complainant's "private parts"); Pease v. Alford Photo Indus., 667 F. Supp. 1188, 1190, 1203, 49 FEP Cases 497, 498, 505–9 (W.D. Tenn. 1987)(fondling complainant's breasts while she was at work); Langlois v. McDonald's Restaurants, 149 Mich. App. 309, 311, 316, 385 N.W.2d 778, 779, 781, 45 FEP Cases 134, 135, 137 (18-year-old restaurant worker called police after she was physically handled and propositioned by co-worker who "should have faced criminal responsibility for his actions").

[10]For examples of sexual harassment entailing this activity, see cases cited in note 24 *infra.*

[11]*See, e.g.,* ILL. ANN. STAT. ch. 38, ¶8-4 (Smith-Hurd 1989); ARIZ. REV. STAT. §13-1001 (1989); GA. CODE ANN. §16-4-1 (1988).

[12]In California, for example, an unsuccessful effort to commit a criminal act may be penalized with one-half of the maximum sentence called for by the statute covering the act that the attempt was designed to accomplish. *See* CAL. PENAL CODE §664 (West 1988). The offense of sexual assault with intent to commit rape has been eliminated from the Federal Assault Statute, 18 U.S.C. §113 (1988). That conduct may now be charged in the federal statutory scheme as an attempt under the appropriate sexual abuse statute. The federal sexual abuse statutes appear in 18 U.S.C. §§2241–45 (1988).

[13]*See, e.g.,* CAL. PENAL CODE §653m (West 1988); N.Y. PENAL LAW §240.30 (McKinney 1989); ARIZ. REV. STAT. ANN. §13-2916 (1989). For a general discussion of the obscene telephone call statutes, see Annot., *Validity, Construction and Application of the State Criminal Statutes Forbidding Use of Telephone to Annoy or Harass,* 95 A.L.R.3d 411 (1976).

[14]*E.g.,* Swentek v. USAir, 830 F.2d 552, 555, 44 FEP Cases 1808, 1810 (4th Cir. 1987)(obscene telephone call from person whose voice complainant recognized as that of a co-worker); Bigoni v. Pay 'N Pak Stores, 53 FEP Cases 697 (D. Or. 1990)(sexual harassment complainant warned by anonymous telephone caller not to press claim); Rogers v. Loews L'Enfant Plaza Hotel, 526 F. Supp. 523, 528, 29 FEP Cases 828, 831 (D.D.C. 1981)(plaintiff's employer allegedly made repeated telephone calls to plaintiff at home concerning her personal and sexual life); Disilva v. Polaroid Corp., 45 FEP Cases 639 (Mass. Dist. Ct. 1985)(defamation action by supervisor alleged to have made sexually harassing phone calls to hourly worker).

(2) make a telephone call, whether or not conversation ensues, without disclosing one's identity and with intent to annoy, abuse, threaten, or harass any person at the called number;

(3) make or cause another's telephone to ring repeatedly or continually, with intent to harass any person at the called number; or

(4) make repeated telephone calls, during which conversation ensues, solely to harass any person at the called number.[15]

E. Solicitation, Lewd Conduct, and Pandering

Some sexual advances, especially in the quid pro quo context, may be actionable as a classic solicitation of prostitution commonly prohibited by criminal statutes. The typical statute requires a solicitation to engage in any act of prostitution for money or other consideration.[16] Prostitution is commonly defined in terms of lewd or sexual acts between involved individuals,[17] and violations have traditionally been prosecuted as misdemeanors. Conditioning employment advancement or compensation on an exchange for sexual favors may fall within the ambit of these statutes.[18] Additionally, procuring another person for prostitution is usually deemed more serious than mere solicitation.[19] Procuring is prosecutable as a felony under statutes that prohibit pandering through means of promises, threats, coercion, scheme, or monetary or other persuasion.[20]

Most jurisdictions also prohibit as a misdemeanor any lewd or dissolute conduct, such as exposing oneself, in a public place or in a location open to public view.[21] The everyday workplace, of course, could constitute both a public place and a location where an individual's deviant behavior might be in the public view and, if so, prosecutable.[22]

---

[15]47 U.S.C. §223 (1988). For a discussion of the federal statute, see Annot., *Criminal Offenses Involving Use or Abuse of Communications Facilities*, 74 AM. JUR.2d TELECOMMUNICATIONS §206 (1974).

[16]*See, e.g.,* CAL. PENAL CODE §647(b)(West 1988); N.Y. PENAL LAW §230.02 (McKinney 1989); ARIZ. REV. STAT. ANN. §13-3208 (1989).

[17]*See, e.g.,* CAL. PENAL CODE §647(b)(West 1988); N.Y. PENAL LAW §230.00 (McKinney 1989); ARIZ. REV. STAT. ANN. §13-3211 (1989).

[18]*See, e.g.,* Lucas v. Brown & Root, Inc., 736 F.2d 1202, 35 FEP Cases 1855, 1857 (8th Cir. 1984)(Arkansas law)(requiring that complainant sleep with boss to keep job implicates statute that criminalizes prostitution, defined as exchanging "sexual activity" for a "fee": "A woman invited to trade herself for a job is in effect being asked to become a prostitute," although in a criminal prosecution perhaps the statutory term "fee" might not include a job); Fawcett v. IDS Financial Servs., 41 FEP Cases 589, 593 (W.D. Pa. 1986)(supervisor grabbed plaintiff and conditioned her promotion on submission to sexual relations); Rogers v. Loew's L'Enfant Plaza Hotel, *supra* note 14, 526 F. Supp. at 527, 29 FEP Cases at 829 (complainant alleged supervisor tried to force her either to submit or lose her employment).

[19]An excellent example of the type of factual setting that could be ripe for criminal prosecution appears in *Seritis v. Hotel & Rest. Employees,* 167 Cal. App.3d 78, 213 Cal. Rptr. 588, 590–91, 37 FEP Cases 1501, 1503–4 (1985)(case ordered not to be published), where waitresses were denied employment through union hiring-hall influence after they rejected a union officer's offers to be a "live-in sexual playmate" for two men, to provide sexual services at parties, to have sex with a dog in a stage show in Nevada, to work topless on a bus, to work as a prostitute at a convention, and to live with a lesbian.

[20]*See, e.g.,* CAL. PENAL CODE §266(i)(West 1988); D.C. CODE ANN. §22-2707 (1989); ARIZ. REV. STAT. ANN. §13-3202 (1989).

[21]*See, e.g.,* CAL. PENAL CODE §§314 and 647 (West 1988); N.Y. PENAL LAW §245.01 (McKinney 1989); D.C. CODE ANN. §22-1112 (1989).

[22]*E.g.,* Bailey v. Unocal Corp., 700 F. Supp. 396, 53 FEP Cases 1529 (N.D. Ill. 1988)(supervisor's alleged indecent exposure); Priest v. Rotary, 634 F. Supp. 571, 575, 40 FEP Cases 208, 209 (N.D. Cal. 1986)(defendant exposed genitals to plaintiff as she had coffee following end of her shift).

F. False Imprisonment

False imprisonment is the unlawful restraint of the personal liberty of another. The restraint need not be accomplished by violence or even physical contact—it may be accomplished by mere words, accompanied by a show of force or authority to which the victim submits.[23] False imprisonment generally is a felony if committed by violence, menace, fraud, or deceit.[24] It is seldom prosecuted singularly. In the usual case, a false imprisonment charge is coupled with a charge of completed or attempted rape, sodomy, solicitation, or other criminal sex act as a litigative tactic to encourage plea bargaining, to enhance potential penalties, and to provide juries with options in evaluating and judging alleged illicit behavior.

G. RICO

The Racketeer Influenced and Corrupt Organizations Act (RICO)[25] or one of its state law counterparts, can be the basis of both criminal and civil actions. Enacted to stem organized crime, the federal RICO statute prohibits the use of a "pattern of racketeering activity" to establish, operate, or invest in an "enterprise."[26] Proof of a pattern of racketeering requires proof of at least two predicate acts of "racketeering activity."[27] These acts include threats involving murder, extortion, obscene matter, and other subjects, but, with exceptions immaterial here, do not include sexual activity.[28] We are aware of no published authority applying criminal RICO provisions to sexual harassment. In *Hunt v. Weatherbee*,[29] a female carpenter was able to maintain a civil RICO action against her union, alleging that a long practice of sexual harassment by union officials formed the basis of a pattern of racketeering activity to coerce female union members, such as the plaintiff, into contributing to the union's political fund. The complainant alleged that union officers had committed the predicate

---

[23]*See, e.g.*, People v. Haney, 75 Cal. App.3d 308, 313, 142 Cal. Rptr. 186, 189 (1977); People v. Scalisi, 324 Ill. 131, 147–48, 154 N.E. 715, 722 (1926); Martin v. Houck, 141 N.C. 317, 54 S.E. 291, 293 (1906).

[24]*See, e.g.*, CAL. PENAL CODE §§236–37 (West 1988); ARK. STAT. ANN. §5-11-103 (1987); WASH. REV. CODE ANN. §9A.40.040 (1988). Absent aggravating circumstances, false imprisonment is usually a misdemeanor. *E.g.*, CAL. PENAL CODE §§236–37 (West 1988); IOWA CODE ANN. §710.7 (West 1979); MONT. CODE ANN. §45-5-301 (1987). The conduct found to exist in *Priest v. Rotary, supra* note 22, 634 F. Supp. at 583, 40 FEP Cases at 216–17, where an employer trapped the complainant between himself and another employee, preventing her escape while she was fondled, presents the classic false imprisonment situation. *See also* Hall v. Gus Constr. Co., 842 F.2d 1010, 1012, 46 FEP Cases 573 (8th Cir. 1988), reproduced in Chapter 2, Forms of Harassment (construction crew members cornered women co-workers between trucks and touched their breasts and thighs; one crew member picked up a woman and held her up to cab window so another man could touch her); Barrett v. Omaha Nat'l Bank, 584 F. Supp. 22, 24, 35 FEP Cases 585, 586 (D. Neb. 1983)(supervisor made sexual comments to employee while touching her breasts, thighs, and crotch while inside a vehicle from which she could not escape), *aff'd*, 726 F.2d 424, 35 FEP Cases 593 (8th Cir. 1984).

[25]18 U.S.C. §§1961–1968 (1988).

[26]An "enterprise" is defined by the statute as an individual, partnership, corporation, association, or other legal entity or any group of individuals associated in fact. 18 U.S.C. §1961(4).

[27]18 U.S.C. §1961(5).

[28]*See* 18 U.S.C. §1961(1). *Cf.* Puckett v. Tennessee Eastman Co., 889 F.2d 1481, 1489–90 (6th Cir. 1989)(affirming dismissal of civil RICO claim based on sexual harassment and employer's alleged cover-up; alleged interference with state fair employment practices agency investigating claims of sexual harassment did not qualify as a "racketeering activity"). For a discussion of RICO as a theory of recovery for sexual harassment, see Dworkin, Ginger & Mallor, *Theories of Recovery for Sexual Harassment: Going Beyond Title VII*, 25 SAN DIEGO L. REV. 125, 158 (1988).

[29]626 F. Supp. 1097, 39 FEP Cases 1469 (D. Mass. 1986).

acts of extortion and obstruction of justice in coercing her to withdraw a state-court complaint against a co-worker for sexual harassment.[30]

State RICO statutory schemes should be consulted to determine their possible use.[31]

III. CRIMES COMMITTED BY EMPLOYERS

A. Aiding, Abetting, and Conspiracy

Criminal statutes make all persons who knowingly and intentionally involve themselves in the commission of a crime chargeable as principals. Those who advise, encourage, aid, or abet the commission of a crime, including those historically classified as accessories before the fact, are also considered principals even though they may not physically or directly participate.[32] Although one may aid and abet a crime without sharing criminal intent, courts require specific criminal intent to impose criminal liability.[33] If an employer effected a plan of sexual harassment to induce the resignation of an employee, it could be prosecuted, along with its upper-level employees, if the involved lower-level employees committed criminal violations with the knowledge and approval of the employer.[34] To aid and abet another in committing sexual or other crimes, defendants must associate themselves with the venture, participate in it as in something they wish to bring about, and seek by their actions to make the venture succeed.[35] Because aiding and abetting the commission of a crime requires affirmative action, the mere knowledge and belief that a crime is being committed or likely to be committed and failure to take steps to prevent the crime do not amount to criminal conduct under traditional criminal assistance statutes. The test is whether the accused has, directly or indirectly, aided the perpetrator by acts or encouraged the perpetrator by words or gestures. Previous knowledge of what was about to transpire need not be proven to obtain a conviction, but that knowledge is often inferred from a defendant's actions at the time and place in question.[36] One may aid and abet in committing a crime without having previously conspired to commit it.

---

[30]For further discussion of RICO applications, in the civil context, see Chapter 11, Federal Constitutional Statutory and Civil Rights Law, Section VII.

[31]The Nevada RICO statute, for example, lists among the possible predicate acts that may form the basis of its pattern of racketeering activity the crimes of "sexual assault" and "statutory sexual seduction." NEV. REV. STAT. §207.360 (1986).

[32]See, e.g., CAL. PENAL CODE §27(3)(West 1988); N.Y. PENAL LAW §20.00 (McKinney 1987); D.C. CODE ANN. §22-105 (1989).

[33]See, e.g., Jefferson v. United States, 463 A.2d 681, 683 (App. D.C. 1983); People v. Bolden, 59 Ill. App.3d 441, 447–48, 375 N.E.2d 898, 903 (1978); People v. Durham, 70 Cal.2d 171, 181–86, 74 Cal. Rptr. 262, 268–71, 449 P.2d 198, 204–07, cert. denied, 395 U.S. 968 (1969).

[34]For illustrations of company responsibility for criminal acts, see United States v. Automated Medical Laboratories, 770 F.2d 399, 406–7 (4th Cir. 1985); United States v. Beusch, 596 F.2d 871, 877–78 (9th Cir. 1979); United States v. Gibson Prod. Co., 426 F. Supp. 768, 769 (S.D. Tex. 1976). These decisions impose corporate criminal responsibility for violations committed by employees acting within the scope of their employment or authority and for the benefit of the corporation even if the acts were against corporate policy or express company instructions.

[35]See, e.g., People v. Bunyard, 45 Cal.3d 1189, 1226–27, 249 Cal. Rptr. 71, 95–96, 756 P.2d 795, 819–20 (1988); Jefferson v. United States, 463 A.2d 681, 683 (App. D.C. 1983); People v. Lipton, 54 N.Y.2d 340, 349, 445 N.Y.S.2d 430, 435, 429 N.E.2d 1059, 1064 (1981).

[36]See cases cited in notes 33 and 35 supra. The cases make clear that mere presence at the scene of the crime does not make an accused a participant, and while an individual is not necessarily guilty if he does

Where an agreement does exist to commit the offense or assist in its commission, a participant may also be charged with the separate crime of conspiracy. A conspiracy violation requires that two or more individuals agree to commit a statutory offense, and that at least one of the conspirators knowingly and willfully performs some overt act to effect the object of the conspiracy.[37] The weight of authority suggests that for conspiracy purposes a corporate employer is not liable for conspiring with its own employees.[38]

Conspiracies are routinely charged in situations involving more than one defendant, whether there is a completed substantive offense or an unsuccessful attempt. This practice not only allows greater prosecutorial leeway in any plea-bargaining negotiations and jury flexibility in reaching possible compromise verdicts, but also maximizes the prosecution's evidentiary options.[39] Penalties for conspiracy violations, which constitute felonies, vary widely among jurisdictions.

B. Compounding, Concealing, and Obstructing

An employer and its personnel may incur criminal liability by engaging in conduct that conceals a crime. This conduct, known as compounding, commonly involves taking a bribe, or giving one, to conceal criminal activity.[40] For example, if a company having knowledge of a crime either takes or gives money in exchange for concealing the crime or withholding evidence of it, it may subject itself, as well as the individuals involved, to criminal prosecution for that behavior. A related crime—an endeavor to obstruct justice—results when one uses money or threats to induce a witness not to give testimony.[41] Another related crime—subornation of perjury—results when one induces a potential witness to give false testimony.[42] These related criminal violations are most often prosecuted as felonies.[43]

C. Accessories After-the-Fact

An accessory after-the-fact is one who, knowing a crime has been committed, helps the violator to escape justice. The various accessory statutes provide

---

not attempt to prevent the crime, these circumstances can be considered by a jury in passing on the question of guilt or innocence.

[37]See, e.g., CAL. PENAL CODE §§182 and 184 (West 1988); N.Y. PENAL LAW §§105.00–.20 (McKinney 1987); ARIZ. REV. STAT. ANN. §13-1003 (1989).

[38]See, e.g., Dombrowski v. Dowling, 459 F.2d 190, 196 (7th Cir. 1972); Nelson Radio & Supply Co. v. Motorola, 200 F.2d 911, 914 (5th Cir. 1952); Cole v. University of Hartford, 391 F. Supp. 888, 892–93, 10 FEP Cases 477, 478–80 (D. Conn. 1975).

[39]Rule 801(d)(2) of the Federal Rules of Evidence, for example, allows the admission into evidence, against all conspirators, of statements of co-conspirators made during the course and in furtherance of a charged conspiracy. These statements might otherwise be excluded, as against a nondeclarant, on the ground that they constitute inadmissible hearsay.

[40]Compounding is usually defined in terms of accepting or giving money or property to forgo proceeding with a prosecution or to forgo assisting an investigation of alleged illegal behavior. See, e.g., CAL. PENAL CODE §153 (West 1988); N.Y. PENAL LAW §215.45 (McKinney 1988); ARIZ. REV. STAT. ANN. §§13-2802 and 13-2803 (1989).

[41]See, e.g., D.C. CODE ANN. §§22-722 and 22-723 (1989); ARIZ. REV. STAT. ANN. §13-2409 (1989); ILL. ANN. STAT. ch. 38, ¶¶31-4 (Smith-Hurd 1977).

[42]See, e.g., CAL. PENAL CODE §§127 and 653(f)(West 1988); ILL. ANN. STAT. ch. 38, ¶32-3 (Smith-Hurd 1977); GA. CODE ANN. §16-10-72 (1988).

[43]Local statutory schemes will determine the applicability and severity of sanctions in a particular jurisdiction.

that one may not harbor, conceal, or aid a principal who has committed criminal conduct with the intent that the principal avoid or escape arrest, trial, conviction, or punishment.[44] In the employment context, an employer that protects an employee who has committed a sexual harassment-related crime could be found to be an accessory after-the-fact. Much of the activity covered by these accessory statutes is also covered by the previously discussed statutes concerning compounding, concealing, and obstructing justice. The accessory statutes, therefore, are most often used as catchalls to prosecute any behavior not covered in more specific statutes that aids a criminal perpetrator. They may also be used in less egregious circumstances because accessory-after-the-fact violations are usually misdemeanors. If an employer, for example, transferred an employee to another jurisdiction to help the employee evade prosecution, an accessory-after-the-fact statute might well be implicated. Thus, employers should consult with counsel once a sexual harassment complaint with criminal overtones is lodged, to determine how to handle information in the employer's possession and generally to guarantee appropriate conduct.[45]

IV. CRIMES COMMITTED BY COMPLAINANTS

A. Extortion

The traditional crime of extortion involves obtaining property from another through the wrongful use of force or fear, or under color of official right.[46] Whether designated extortion or blackmail, to demand compensation in exchange for not reporting criminal sexual activity will undoubtedly violate most statutory schemes. Extortion statutes may present traps for even well-meaning complainants who contemplate or participate in civil lawsuits. A traditional extortion statute may apply to any demand for money that is coupled with a threat to file a criminal complaint or to proceed with an already-initiated prosecution, even where the demand is made only to further one's legitimate advantage in civil litigation. Thus, while it is undoubtedly acceptable to demand civil damages where crimes involving acts of sexual harassment have been committed, a complainant must avoid threatening to press criminal charges if the employer or alleged harasser will not satisfy the complainant's demands for money.[47]

B. False Reporting

Any person who falsely reports to a law enforcement official that a sexual or other crime has been committed, knowing the report to be untrue, is, in

---

[44]*See, e.g.,* CAL. PENAL CODE §32 (West 1988); D.C. CODE ANN. §22-106 (1989); IDAHO CODE §§205–6 (1987).

[45]For more general discussion of the employer's response, see Chapters 19, Responding to Internal Complaints, and 22, Employer's Litigation Strategy.

[46]*See, e.g.,* CAL. PENAL CODE §§518–19, 523 (West 1988); N.Y. PENAL LAW §155.05 (McKinney 1988); D.C. CODE ANN. §22-3851 (1989).

[47]An attorney who threatens criminal action to enhance the prospects of settlement in a civil lawsuit acts contrary to Disciplinary Rule 7-105 of the American Bar Association Code of Professional Responsibility, which provides that "[a] lawyer shall not present, participate in presenting, or threaten to present criminal charges solely to obtain an advantage in a civil matter."

most jurisdictions, guilty of a misdemeanor.[48] If the information reported is material and the report is made with the knowledge that it is false, the statute will have been violated. Although false reporting will often violate several statutes such as those prohibiting attempted extortion, the false report itself constitutes a distinct violation chargeable either by itself or in conjunction with any greater crime to which it may relate.[49] A false-reporting violation could become the predicate for a subsequent civil cause of action alleging malicious prosecution.[50]

C. Concealing Criminal Activity

Virtually every criminal statutory scheme forbids one who, knowing of a crime, takes money or any other reward pursuant to an understanding to abstain from prosecution, or to conceal or withhold evidence of the crime.[51] Where a defendant offers to compensate the complainant if criminal charges are dropped, the offer itself may constitute a crime, as may any acceptance by the complainant. Because criminal activity is prosecuted by governmental entities, a complainant retains no legal authority to decide unilaterally how pending cases should be resolved. In most instances, while the court will usually follow the prosecution's recommendation, the authority to dismiss a case rests ultimately with the court. Refusal by a sexual harassment complainant to proceed with an already-initiated criminal prosecution in exchange for a cash settlement by the defendant could result in the complainant becoming a defendant in a separate compounding prosecution. Thus, civil settlement negotiations, especially in situations involving a corresponding criminal prosection, should be handled only in consultation with counsel familiar with the criminal judicial process.

V. CONSIDERATIONS FOR THE COMPLAINANT

A. Benefits of a Criminal Prosecution

1. Vindication in a Public Forum

A sexual harassment complainant may often be damaged emotionally to an extent far greater than any economic loss. The criminal justice system, despite its recognized problems in dealing with sexual misconduct, may nonetheless offer special benefits. During the criminal investigation and trial, the

---

[48]*See, e.g.,* CAL. PENAL CODE §148.5 (West 1988); N.Y. PENAL LAW §210.45 (McKinney 1988); GA. CODE ANN. §16-10-26 (1988). *See also* 18 U.S.C. §1001, which forbids making a false statement to any agency of the United States concerning any matter within its jurisdiction.

[49]Section 170 of the California Penal Code additionally punishes as a misdemeanor any person who maliciously and without probable cause causes a search or arrest warrant to be issued and executed by law enforcement authorities.

[50]For general discussions of the issues relating to the termination of a criminal prosecution as a prerequisite to a malicious prosecution action, see Annot., *Termination of Criminal Prosecution as Result of Compromise or Settlement of Accused's Civil Liability as Precluding Malicious Prosecution Action,* 26 A.L.R.4th 565 (1983); Annot., *Discharge in Habeas Corpus Proceedings Constituting Favorable Termination of Civil Proceedings Requisite to Maintenance of Malicious Prosecution Action,* 30 A.L.R.2d 1128 (1953).

[51]*See, e.g.,* CAL. PENAL CODE §153 (West 1988); N.Y. PENAL LAW §215.45 (McKinney 1988); ARIZ. REV. STAT. ANN. §§13-2802 and 13-2803 (1989).

prosecutor's office, or governmental agencies associated with it, can guide the complainant to crisis centers and victim support groups that can be of assistance before, during, and after the legal proceedings.[52] Trained professionals may accompany the complainant to court, provide counseling and follow-up, and generally, without significant monetary expense, take emotionally rehabilitating steps on the complainant's behalf.[53] A conviction of the harasser often enables the complainant to establish fault and reestablish honor or credibility in a public forum in a way that may not be possible in civil litigation.[54]

2. Evidentiary Protections

Criminal cases that allege sexual offenses may afford evidentiary protections for the complainant that are not available in civil proceedings. Evidence of the complainant's prior sexual misconduct with others is often not admissible in a criminal case,[55] but more likely could be the subject of exploration, at least in discovery, in civil litigation.[56] Some states will prohibit proof, in criminal litigation, that a complainant has received professional help from a psychologist or psychiatrist and, correspondingly, many courts will deny a request for, or are precluded from ordering, a psychiatric examination of the complainant.[57] The rationale for this protection is the need to encourage sexual abuse victims to report criminal conduct to law enforcement authorities.

3. Advantages for the Complainant's Parallel Civil Case

Where a complainant chooses to proceed both civilly and criminally against an alleged harasser, a criminal prosecution may make the civil case far easier to litigate. A conviction will eliminate many liability issues in the corresponding civil litigation.[58] The availability of evidence gathered by law enforcement authorities at no cost to the complainant may mean a more effective, highly expeditious, and less expensive civil lawsuit. Because the criminal prosecution will virtually always proceed at a substantially quicker pace than its corresponding civil litigation, these significant benefits, almost without exception, will become available to the civil complainant who can use the criminal investigative and judicial process.

---

[52]In addition to those services specifically available to local prosecutorial and investigative agencies, a variety of assistance services are generally available to sexual abuse victims. In California there is the Victims of Crimes Resource Center (1-800-842-8467). In New York there is the Victims Service Agency (1-212-577-7777). In Illinois there is the City of Chicago Rape Hot Line (1-312-744-8418) and Rape Victim Advocates (1-312-733-6954).

[53]In many jurisdictions, counseling costs for victims resulting from criminal sexual behavior may even be reimbursable as part of a court-imposed restitution order.

[54]Civil cases may not be resolved for years. Criminal cases get priority in terms of judicial resolution. Further, civil settlement agreements are often confidential and expressly disavow wrongful conduct by the harasser.

[55]See, e.g., Rules 404(b) and 412 of the Federal Rules of Evidence; CAL. EVID. CODE §1103(b)(1); ILL. ANN. STAT. ch. 38, ¶115–7 (Smith-Hurd 1989).

[56]For a discussion of evidentiary and discovery issues on this matter in civil litigation, see Chapters 25, Evidence, and 26, Discovery.

[57]See, e.g., CAL. PENAL CODE §1112 (West 1988); ILL. ANN. STAT. ch. 38, ¶115-7.1 (Smith-Hurd 1990); Note, Psychiatric Examinations of Sexual Assault Victims: A Reevaluation, 15 U.C. DAVIS L. REV. 973 (1982). See also Annot., Necessity or Permissibility of Mental Examination to Determine Competency or Credibility of Complainant in Sexual Offense Prosecution, 45 A.L.R.4th 310 (1986).

[58]By contrast, a loss in the criminal case will not prejudice the complainant's civil case because the criminal standard of proof is higher than the civil standard of proof.

The effectiveness of a law enforcement investigation should not be under-estimated. Law enforcement agencies have resources and tactical advantages well beyond the ordinary reach of civil litigants. Law enforcement activity can lend credibility to an accusation as well as a feeling of security to those who cooperate with the police or prosecutor. This feeling may not be present were witnesses to believe that their security depended only on the complainant's private attorney or investigator. Law enforcement officials have special tools at their disposal. When federal jurisdiction is implicated, investigators can monitor and tape-record conversations that private people often cannot.[59] The same is often true under state law,[60] although court-authorized electronic sur-veillance is seldom, if ever, used in traditional sex crime investigations. Further, federal or local enforcement officers who investigate sexual misconduct in the workplace may induce employers and employees, under threat of obstruction of justice or perjury prosecutions, to cooperate in a forthright manner and to come forward when they may otherwise have remained silent. Police officers, through the use of subpoena power, can also compel testimony before an investigating grand jury. The prosecuting agency may also grant immunity to witnesses to compel their testimony when they otherwise would be reluctant to testify.[61] Once a conviction has been obtained, a convicted defendant, in an effort to influence the sentence, may reveal evidence relating to other potential defendants.

Once criminal charges have been brought, most courts will condition an alleged sexual harasser's release on bail, which often will be economically prohibitive, upon an agreement to avoid contact with the complainant. Viola-tion of this condition will result in the bail's revocation. The complainant may thereafter enjoy a level of confidence that additional sexual harassment will not be forthcoming.

B. Disadvantages of a Criminal Prosecution

Involvement in a criminal proceeding can be frustrating and time-consuming. With the exception of rape, sodomy, and aggravated battery, crimes related to sexual harassment may often be perceived as less serious than others being processed in the criminal justice system. Although obscene telephone calls can often be recorded and traced, other crimes of sexual harassers are often difficult to corroborate. In the employment setting, the harasser may be liked and respected by supervisors or fellow employees and may appear to live an essentially normal life. The complainant may not be liked or may be a low-level employee. Under these circumstances, harassers typically can credibly deny guilt, with significant support from their business and personal colleagues.

Accordingly, in all but the most egregious cases, if there has been no physical sexual assault, or if the crime has not evolved into repeated harass-ment, such as continual abusive telephone calls, prosecutors may decline to

[59]*See* 18 U.S.C. §§2510–2519.
[60]*See, e.g.,* N.Y. CRIM. PROC. LAW §§700.05 *et seq.* (McKinney 1984); FLA. STAT. ANN. §§934.01 *et seq.* (West 1986); COLO. REV. STAT. §§16-15-101 *et seq.* (1985).
[61]A grant of criminal immunity protects a witness only against criminal liability while leaving the witness exposed to the civil liability that the testimony may help establish.

prosecute sexual harassment crimes, placing their priorities elsewhere. More than one viable criminal action has been declined in view of ongoing or contemplated civil litigation that is viewed as a sufficient forum in which to resolve the dispute. Whenever possible, therefore, the potential litigant should at least consider delaying civil litigation until after the charging of criminal violations, or until the criminal investigation has otherwise culminated.

VI. CONSIDERATIONS FOR THE EMPLOYER

Allegations of sexual impropriety relating to the workplace should trigger a variety of concerns for management personnel. In the usual situation, an employer learns of an investigation of potentially criminal conduct on short notice. Under those circumstances, it may be difficult to assess the legal risks soon enough to avert an intrusive criminal investigation. Because early impressions of the investigating law enforcement agency can be critical, it is important to take all appropriate steps to influence that agency's perceptions as to the employer and its innocent personnel, while fulfilling the obligations to protect both itself and the rights of all individual employees.

When informed of a criminal inquiry, the employer should consider retaining experienced criminal counsel.[62] Counsel should then contact all employees whose conduct appears to bear on the matter under review to determine exactly what the individuals know and what they will say if questioned during the investigation, and to advise employees that they may be approached by law enforcement officers outside the workplace or at home without prior notice. The surprise visit is a technique often chosen by investigating officers, and effectively so, to prevent potential witnesses or defendants from consulting with others or preparing for interviews. From the employer's standpoint, this investigative technique carries the potential for damage as it often results in answers from employees based on insufficient knowledge, unreliable hearsay, or mere personal impressions that may be inaccurate.

Investigating officers seldom advise their subjects not to speculate, and often encourage them to impress their listeners with the scope of their knowledge. In the event of civil litigation against the employer, these statements carry a potential for untold problems. If interviewees have already discussed the matter with counsel, however, they can be alerted against the possible pitfalls of the interview while maintaining their obligation to be truthful.

The safest course for both the employer and any employees contacted for an interview in a criminal investigation is for the employer to notify the potential witnesses in writing that an investigation may be or is being conducted and that it is the employer's position to cooperate to the fullest extent. A written document evidences proper conduct by the employer and management personnel toward potential witnesses in the event that this conduct is challenged as a conflict of interest or an obstruction of justice. The potential witness should

---

[62]As in all specialized areas of the law, consultation with experienced criminal counsel can provide additional helpful information, assist in devising effective work plans for dealing with an investigation, and maximize the employer's legal position when confronted with collateral effects of a criminal inquiry or prosecution.

be informed in writing that counsel for the employer would like to be notified by the employee of any forthcoming interviews and would like to attend. The employee should be further advised of the right to retain private counsel and that, in any event, the employer's counsel is available to answer questions and is monitoring the investigation. Finally, the employee should be informed in the letter that investigators will not draw adverse inferences from being told that the employee has no objection to speaking with them, but requests a delay in order to speak with counsel, inasmuch as the matter potentially relates to legal positions of the employer.

A letter such as this should sufficiently protect the potential interviewee, other company employees, and counsel as well, unless counsel knows information that implicates the employee in wrongdoing. In those cases, because of the clear conflict of interest, the employee should be directed without delay to an outside attorney of the employee's own choosing or from a list that can be furnished by the employer.[63] It remains in the employer's best interests, for purposes of civil liability and public relations, to distance itself from those it has reason to believe have engaged in criminal sexual behavior that could in any way implicate the employer.

If counsel attends interviews by criminal investigators, detailed notes should be taken, for they may be crucial in evaluating employer liability, recognizing conflicts of interest, and dealing with events as they arise in the course of an investigation. If not present at the interview, counsel should, soon thereafter, question the interviewed employee in detail and in the presence of an independent witness, such as an outside private investigator, regarding the scope of the questioning and answers given.

Counsel should immediately initiate contact with either the assistant district attorney or other prosecutor directing the investigation, or, in their absence, the supervising officer who is conducting it. An open line of communication can result in concessions not normally granted to those with whom there is no rapport. Through this means counsel may avoid having employees served with grand jury subpoenas at home or contacted at embarrassing times, may keep at least generally abreast of the progress of the investigation, and may anticipate possible problems involving company employees.

When contacting the investigating agency, counsel should attempt to learn whether the employer or any of its employees are targets[64] or subjects[65] of the investigation, provide the assurance that the employer wants to cooperate, and emphasize its wish to be notified of interviews of company employees and to be present at those interviews. While investigators do not like counsel present, they will often acquiesce in order to get the interview done, especially if independent contact with an employee also results in a request for counsel's presence.

---

[63]For a discussion of the potential conflict of interest between the employer and the alleged harasser, see Chapter 22, Employer's Litigation Strategy.

[64]To most prosecutors, a "target" is someone who is linked by substantial evidence to the commission of a crime and who is thus a potential defendant.

[65]A "subject" is one who is being considered as a possible defendant but about whom insufficient information exists to classify him or her as either a target or someone who will not be prosecuted.

Positive early contact with the investigating agency can result in the employer avoiding search warrants directed at the premises. Searches can be disruptive, affect company morale, and result in adverse or embarrassing publicity. Prosecutors generally use search warrants where there is some reason to doubt the integrity of evidence procured through a direct request or subpoena.

If a search warrant is used, most employers should have no hesitation in granting law enforcement personnel access to the premises or to any company documentation that may be relevant. Whenever use of a search warrant can be anticipated, all relevant employer documents or other company materials should be marked and stored apart from other business records. Law enforcement personnel who pay a surprise visit to the premises can be informed that the desired records are kept in a designated location and directed to that location to permit control of the documents without disturbing employer operations unnecessarily by rummaging through unrelated files. Rummaging can often create the need for monstrous organizational clean-ups.

VII. Considerations for the Alleged Harasser

Those accused of sexual harassment, especially in a potentially criminal context, must decide whether and how to cooperate with the employer in its investigation of the charges. Intelligent exercise of an informed choice by alleged harassers generally will not be possible without consulting a criminal attorney. Alleged harassers who consent to an interview with the employer or with law enforcement officials without prior consultation with an attorney may prejudice themselves in criminal proceedings with admissions or inadvertent statements.

The alleged harasser often will want to cooperate fully with the employer, which may insist on an interview without the presence of counsel and even without prior consultation of counsel. The alleged harasser nonetheless should request a short delay before any interview for the purpose of consultation.

In any interview by the employer or employer's counsel, the alleged harasser should be aware that the employer and employer's counsel are primarily acting in the interest of the employer, and owe no duty of loyalty and no duty of confidentiality to the alleged harasser. Thus, the alleged harasser's statements will not be privileged and may be turned over to law enforcement officials.

In the course of consultation with counsel, the alleged harasser should investigate to determine whether an insurance policy covers legal fees and monetary liability. With the aid of counsel, the alleged harasser should also investigate to determine whether the employer owes a duty of indemnification on the ground that the conduct complained of arguably occurred within the scope of the alleged harasser's employment.[66]

---

[66]Of course, a criminal act rarely would be within the scope of the harasser's employment. But the legal proceeding may entail claims for related conduct that arguably involves the harasser's scope of employment. For a discussion of related concerns of an alleged harasser in a civil context, see Chapter 23, The Alleged Harasser as Defendant. For the interrelated concerns of the employer and the alleged harasser, see Chapter 22, Employer's Litigation Strategy.

CHAPTER 17

COLLECTIVE BARGAINING AGREEMENTS AND UNION OBLIGATIONS

I. Overview

Long before Title VII, employers and unions were dealing with sexual harassment in the organized work force. Employers traditionally have disciplined employees for harassing conduct regardless of whether the basis of the harassment was sexual. Arbitrators have upheld the discipline on the basis of shop rules, the common law of the shop, and the employer's interest in maintaining common decency. These sources of authority make it unnecessary to determine whether harassment is sexual in nature.[1]

By far the most important arbitral developments regarding sexual harassment have occurred with the impetus of Title VII,[2] which has encouraged arbitrators to incorporate the developments in sexual harassment law into the arbitral concepts of just cause and acceptable workplace conduct.

The arbitration forum will continue to play an important role in enforcing standards relating to sexual harassment. While union-represented complainants need not limit their claims of sexual harassment to the grievance and arbitration procedure, they are free to invoke it.[3] The more significant source of arbitral law on sexual harassment has been the grievances of union-represented employees who are disciplined for sexual harassment. Their claims are generally limited to the grievance and arbitration procedure.[4] With respect to these

---

[1]Arbitrator Sanford Cohen noted in *Anaconda Copper Co.*, 78 LA 690, 694 (1982):
   Had the Company taken disciplinary action against the Grievant because of his harassment of a co-worker, there would be no need to further extend this opinion. The reason for discharge, however, was "sexual harassment toward co-worker." By so charging the Grievant, the Company assumed a burden of showing sexual harassment.
Cf. Ohio Dep't of Transp., 90 LA 783 (1988)(Duda, Arb.)(bumping female co-worker was not sexual harassment but still was subject to discipline as impermissible horseplay).
   [2]Early discussions of sexual harassment issues in labor arbitration noted very few reported arbitration decisions. Greenbaum & Fraser, *Sexual Harassment in the Workplace*, Arb. J. 30, 36 (December 1981); Marmo, *Arbitrating Sexual Harassment Cases*, Arb. J. 35, 35 (March 1980). Many more sexual harassment arbitration decisions have been reported since that time. *See, e.g.,* decisions cited in Jennings & Clapp, *A Managerial Tightrope: Balancing Harassed and Harassing Employees' Rights in Sexual Discrimination Cases*, 40 Lab. Law J. 756 (1989).
   [3]A complainant may grieve, for example, the failure of her employer to prevent or correct sexual harassment. See Section VI. *infra. See generally* Nelson, *Sexual Harassment Title VII, and Labor Arbitration*, 40 Arb. J. 55 (1985)(arguing that arbitration is superior to Title VII litigation as a means of addressing sexual harassment).
   [4]See Section VII. *infra.*

claims, arbitrators must develop and apply standards concerning sexual harassment to decide the ultimate question of whether there was just cause for the employer's disciplinary action.[5]

II. PROHIBITIONS AGAINST SEXUAL HARASSMENT IN THE LAW OF THE SHOP

A. Shop Rules

Employers have taken steps to curtail employee harassment or intimidation (sexual or otherwise) by developing rules that govern the conduct of employees in the workplace. Employees who violate these rules are subject to discipline, up to and including discharge. While they do not always specifically address sexual harassment, these rules often cover most conduct that constitutes sexual harassment.

The long-standing shop rules that apply to the hourly work force at the General Motors plant in Kansas City, Kansas, are representative of the shop rules found throughout American industry. These rules prohibit:

  •Distracting the attention of others, or causing confusion by unnecessary shouting, catcalls, or demonstration in the plant.
  •Horseplay, scuffling, running, or throwing things.
  •Threatening, intimidating, coercing or interfering with employees or supervision at any time.
  •Restricting output.
  •The initiating or publishing of false, vicious, or malicious statements concerning any employee, the supervisor, the Company, or its products.
  •Abusive language to any employee or supervisor.
  •Immoral conduct or indecency.

Employees engaged in sexual and other forms of harassment may be disciplined for breach of these rules. In *Perfection American Co.*,[6] the grievant was a man who entered the women's rest room in order "to see what it was like in there." A female employee was in the women's rest room at the time. The grievant was suspended without pay for violating the shop rule against any conduct that violates common decency or morality. Similarly, the grievant in *Powermatic/Houdaille*[7] was suspended for violation of the shop rule prohibiting immoral conduct after the employer learned that he had approached a female employee, placed his finger through the fly in his pants, and said, "Hey, big mama, look what I have for you."[8]

---

  [5]The vast majority of all reported arbitration cases involving sexual harassment issues are brought to arbitration as a result of grievances filed by employees who have been discharged or disciplined for sexual harassment conduct. Nowlin, *Sexual Harassment in the Workplace: How Arbitrators Rule,* ARB. J. 43, 31 (December 1988).
  [6]73 LA 520 (1979)(Flannagan, Arb.).
  [7]71 LA 54 (1978)(Cocalis, Arb.).
  [8]*Id.* at 55. *See also* Hannaford Bros. Co., 93 LA 721, 723 (1989)(Chandler, Arb.)(sustaining discharge, under employer's broad no-harassment policy, of male employee who repeatedly referred to co-worker by such names as "slug" and "fudgepacker" and by written sayings on the wall such as, "if you want a blow job see ___ ").

B. Common Law of the Shop

One line of arbitral authority holds that sexual harassment is inherently impermissible conduct, allowing employers to subject offenders to discipline, including discharge, without any reference to a specific shop rule. This concept is most clearly set forth in *Mengel Co.*:[9]

> In the arbitrator's judgment, no doubt may be reasonably entertained that a fundamental and essential component and corollary of the employment relationship is that every male employee who in the course of his employment comes in contact with female employees implicitly covenants and contracts with his employer to conduct himself in a decent and seemly manner. Clear and convincing proof that a male employee has laid his hands on the person of a female co-employee in an indecent manner and/or has otherwise molested her, establishes and constitutes a breach of his employment contract and the commission of grievous misconduct furnishing just cause for his dismissal.[10]

In deciding the propriety of discharge as a penalty for a grievant's forcibly grabbing a female co-worker's buttocks and kissing her, the arbitrator in *Dover Corp.*[11] stated: "Under the unusual nature of the instant matter, the Grievant cannot complain of receiving no express warnings; such male versus female aggressions on the job predate the very first collective bargaining contract and such a prohibition remains part of the unwritten law of the shop."[12]

C. Employer's Duty

In fashioning standards to govern discipline for harassment, arbitrators have relied on the employer's obligation to provide employees with a workplace free from harassment and intimidation. In *Monsanto Chemical Intermediates Co.,*[13] the arbitrator discussed the merits of a sexual harassment discipline case, noting: "equally important is the protection of the female employees from real sexual harassment. The balance is precarious at best. In this case, the Company was obligated to maintain 'a workplace free from fears of threats and intimidation.' "[14] Similarly, the arbitrator in *Care Inns*[15] stated: "Employees have the right to be safe from abusive actions and it is the duty and responsibility of the Company to give them this protection and, further, to discipline and even discharge those Employees whose misconduct justifies such a penalty."[16]

This affirmative employer obligation, which is similar to the obligations set forth in the EEOC Guidelines on Sexual Harassment,[17] was developed independently of Title VII.

---

[9]36 LA 618 (1961)(Turkus, Arb.).
[10]*Id.* at 620.
[11]78-2 ARB ¶8465 (1978)(Haemmel, Arb.).
[12]*Id.* at 5164.
[13]75 LA 592 (1980)(Penfield, Arb.).
[14]*Id.* at 596.
[15]81 LA 687 (1983)(Taylor, Arb.).
[16]*Id.* at 694. *See also* Rockwell Int'l Corp., 85 LA 246 (1985)(Feldman, Arb.); United Elec. Supply Co., 82 LA 921 (1984)(Madden, Arb.).
[17]29 C.F.R. §1604.11, reproduced in Appendix 1. In 1980, after notice and comment, the EEOC issued its Guidelines on Discrimination Because of Sex, 29 C.F.R. §1604, one part of which (§1604.11) was on sexual harassment. The EEOC Guidelines are nonbinding but "constitute a body of experience and informed judgment to which courts and litigants may properly resort for guidance." Meritor Sav. Bank v. Vinson, 477 U.S. 57, 65, 40 FEP Cases 1822, 1826 (1986), reproduced in Chapter 1, Overview (citations omitted).

III. COLLECTIVELY BARGAINED PROCEDURAL LIMITS TO DISCIPLINE FOR SEXUAL HARASSMENT

Employers subject to a collective bargaining agreement requiring just cause for discharge are required to provide employees with procedural due process before imposing discipline. The procedure generally includes notice to the employee as to what conduct is prohibited, an adequate factual basis to conclude that prohibited conduct has occurred, and an opportunity for the employee or the union to present the employee's side of the story. Arbitrators often consider procedural due process to be an integral part of the just cause requirement.[18]

A. Failure to Give Notice of Allegations and Opportunity to Respond

In *Kiddie, Inc.*,[19] the grievant previously had been suspended for sexual harassment, with a warning that any recurrence would be cause for dismissal. Several months later, another claim of sexual harassment was made against the grievant. The employer immediately suspended the grievant pending an investigation. The claims of sexual harassment were made by a female co-worker, with no corroborating witness. The company interviewed the complainant but did *not* interview the grievant or even notify him of the nature of the claims against him. After this abbreviated investigation, the company discharged the grievant. Although the testimony of the complainant was credible, the arbitrator reduced the discharge to a suspension because of the employer's failure to allow the grievant to present his side of the story before the discharge decision was made:

> Was this error in procedure a harmful error to Grievant . . .? In the fact situation at hand, credibility of witnesses was obviously a question Management should have considered. Three specific incidents were cited at the arbitration as reasons for the discharge, but these incidents were not cited to the Grievant or Union prior to the discharge decision. The facts of the incident involving the lead male employee might have certainly been clarified by Grievant's testimony, if it had been received prior to the discharge decision. There was obviously harmful error by Management's failure to obtain Grievant's side of the story. In each of the three incidents which Management cited, the Grievant and one other employee were the only direct participants. It is grossly unjust to accept one person's testimony "hook, line and sinker" while assuming that another person directly involved in the incident will not tell the truth. For this reason, alone, if for no other, the discharge cannot be upheld.[20]

---

[18]*See generally* Jennings & Clapp, *A Managerial Tightrope: Balancing Harassed and Harassing Employees' Rights in Sexual Discrimination Cases*, 40 LAB. LAW. J. 756 (1989). In *Enterprise Wire Co.*, 46 LA 359 (1966), Arbitrator Carroll R. Daugherty set forth the now-famous seven tests for just cause. These tests involve procedural requirements such as notice as to prohibited conduct; proper investigation to determine if the employee actually engaged in the prohibited conduct; fair and objective investigation; consistent application of the rules and penalties. For a complete treatment of this issue, see F. ELKOURI & E.A. ELKOURI, HOW ARBITRATION WORKS 673–75 (4th ed. BNA 1985).

[19]86 LA 681 (1985)(Dunn, Arb.)

[20]*Id.* at 683. For similar comments as to an inadequate investigation and failure to allow grievant an opportunity to present his side of story, see *King Soopers, Inc.*, 86 LA 254 (1985)(Sass, Arb.).

B. Failure to Give Notice of Standard

While the offensive nature of conduct constituting sexual harassment in most cases seems readily apparent, there are some circumstances where it may not be known that certain conduct is considered offensive. When such circumstances arise, an employee must be put on notice as to the offensive conduct before any form of disciplinary action is appropriate under a just cause standard. One arbitrator explained this requirement as follows:

> Before turning to [Ms. R.'s] testimony, the Arbitrator would like to comment on the testimony of [Ms. P.] and [Ms. C.]. It took courage and conviction for those women to come forward and what they had to say provided an education to everyone in the hearing room. Each employee is entitled to a work environment that is free of sexual harassment and, within reasonable limits, what is sexually harassing and what is not is determined from the viewpoint of the "victim"—not from the viewpoint of the "harasser." *But,* unless the conduct is of such a nature that it is automatically recognized as sexual harassment by almost anyone, it is not the sort of thing that an employee can be disciplined for *unless* that employee has been made aware that his/her conduct is considered objectionable and they persist in doing it anyway.[21]

C. Double Jeopardy

Arbitrators frown upon discipline that subjects employees to double jeopardy or multiple penalties for the same conduct. In *DeVry Institute of Technology,*[22] the grievant, an instructor in accounting and a professional photographer on the side, had been warned about asking several female students to pose for him in the nude. Part of the warning informed the grievant that in the event that there were any further substantiated sexual harassment claims against him, he would be discharged. Subsequently, the administration discovered other claims by students of sexual harassment, which had occurred before the warning letter. Because of these additional claims the grievant was discharged. Even though the claims came to the attention of the administration after the first warning, the arbitrator concluded that the grievant could not be discharged for incidents that occurred prior to any warning.

D. Reliance Upon Later-Discovered Evidence

The arbitrator in *DeVry Institute of Technology* rejected the employer's attempt to rely upon evidence of post-discharge complaints about the grievant's pre-discharge conduct. The arbitrator cited the "clear weight of arbitral opinion" that the propriety of a discharge must be evaluated based upon the evidence used by the employer to make the discharge determination; information acquired after that determination may not be used to support the discharge.[23]

---

[21]King Soopers, Inc., *supra* note 20, 86 LA at 259 (emphasis in original)(suspension overturned where grievant's comments about a frozen dinner still being "hard" were about the inadequacy of a microwave oven and were not a crude reference to a male sex organ).

[22]87 LA 1149 (1986)(Berman, Arb.).

[23]*Id.* at 1158–59. An employer's ability to rely upon after-acquired evidence was an issue in *Paperworkers v. Misco,* 484 U.S. 29, 126 LRRM 3113, 3117–18 (1987), where the Supreme Court held that whether

IV. THE RELATIONSHIP BETWEEN TITLE VII AND ARBITRAL AUTHORITY

Since the late 1970s, arbitrators have drawn upon judicial and administrative developments relating to sexual harassment under Title VII. The 1980 EEOC Guidelines on Sexual Harassment[24] are most commonly used for guidance.[25]

Labor arbitrators and the courts have long struggled with the relationship between external statutory or common law and the terms of the collective bargaining agreement. In reaching decisions pursuant to a grievance and arbitration procedure contained in a collective bargaining agreement, arbitrators must rely upon the terms of the agreement between the parties. If there is a conflict between external law and the terms of the agreement, then the arbitrator must enforce the intent of the parties under the contract, rather than enforce the external law.[26] Where there is no conflict between external law and the terms of the collective bargaining agreement, the arbitrator is free to examine external law in interpreting a collective bargaining agreement.[27]

In *Alexander v. Gardner-Denver,* the Supreme Court invited arbitrators in appropriate cases to consider Title VII when dealing with discrimination issues.[28] Title VII principles proscribing discrimination in the workplace are now incorporated into every collective bargaining agreement either because specific nondiscrimination provisions appear in the agreement, or because the principles of Title VII and principles of just cause are now merged.[29] As early as 1967, arbitrator Edgar A. Jones, Jr. stated:

> The coincident existence of the proscriptions of the Civil Rights Act superimposes no discrimination policy of the bargaining relationships which has not already been rather widely recognized for some time by arbitrators to be an incident of

---

arbitrators are free to ignore such evidence is a procedural matter to be left to the determination of the arbitrator.

[24]*Supra* note 17.

[25]Hyatt Hotels Palo Alto, 85 LA 11 (1985)(Oestreich, Arb.); United Elec. Supply Co., 82 LA 921 (1984)(Madden, Arb.); Louisville Gas & Elec. Co., 81 LA 730 (1983)(Stonehouse, Arb.); Dayton Power & Light Co., 80 LA 19 (1982)(Heinsz, Arb.); Anaconda Copper Co., 78 LA 690 (1982)(Cohen, Arb.), reproduced *infra;* University of Mo., 78 LA 417 (1982)(Yarowsky, Arb.).

[26]Alexander v. Gardner-Denver, 415 U.S. 36, 57, 7 FEP Cases 81, 89 (1974).

[27]The Supreme Court has specifically recognized that it was proper for an arbitrator to review external law for assistance in interpreting a collective bargaining agreement. Steelworkers v. Enterprise Wheel & Car Corp., 363 U.S. 593, 597 (1960).

[28]The Court stated:
We adopt no standards as to the weight to be accorded an arbitral decision, since this must be determined in the court's discretion with regard to the facts and circumstances of each case. Relevant factors include the existence of provisions in the collective-bargaining agreement that conform substantially with Title VII, the degree of procedural fairness in the arbitral forum, adequacy of the record with respect to the issue of discrimination, and the special competence of particular arbitrators. Where an arbitral determination gives full consideration to an employee's Title VII rights, a court may properly accord it great weight. This is especially true where the issue is solely one of fact, specifically addressed by the parties and decided by the arbitrator on the basis of an adequate record. But courts should ever be mindful that Congress, in enacting Title VII, thought it necessary to provide a judicial forum for the ultimate resolution of discriminatory employment claims. It is the duty of courts to assure the full availability of this forum.
415 U.S. at 60 n.21, 7 FEP Cases at 90.

[29]Centerville Clinics, 85 LA 1059, 1062 (1985)(Talarico, Arb.)("The contract involved in this matter contains a typical provision prohibiting the discharge or discipline of an employee, except for just and sufficient cause. The principle that discriminatory acts by employers violate such clauses long predates Title VII. For decades, labor arbitrators have overturned employer actions taken for reasons such as those now prohibited by law"); Alameda-Contra Costa Transit Dist., 75 LA 1273, 1280 (1980)(Randall, Arb.)(same).

the employment relationship to be vindicated through the arbitral tribunal created by the parties.[30]

V. ARBITRAL FINDINGS OF SEXUAL HARASSMENT

The varieties of sexual harassment analyzed by arbitrators fall into several broad categories: (A) vulgar hostile work environment, (B) nonvulgar but unwelcome sexual advances, and (C) harassment of nonemployees.

A. Vulgar Hostile Work Environment

1. Verbal and Visual Harassment

Arbitrators have routinely supported management's decision to discipline employees for sexual harassment in the form of vulgar conduct such as sexual or crude language directed at co-worker,[31] obscene sexual gestures,[32] exposing one's self to a female co-worker,[33] intentionally entering a women's restroom with a woman co-worker present,[34] and spreading false stories about the sexual activities of a co-worker.[35]

ANACONDA COPPER CO.

78 LA 690 (1982)(Cohen, Arb.)

Issue

COHEN, Arbitrator: — Was the discharge of S___ for just cause and, if not, what is the appropriate remedy?

---

[30]Kaiser Foundation Hosps., 48 LA 1138, 1142 (1967)(Jones, Arb.).

[31]Phillip Morris, USA, 94 LA 826 (1990)(Baroni, Arb.)(grievants made repeated catcalls and other animal sounds to female co-worker and repeatedly referred to her husband as a "faggot"); Flexsteel Indus., 94 LA 497 (1990)(Briggs, Arb.)(male grievant called female co-worker a "fucking cunt"; other female employees reported the statement; grievant had been previously warned about such vulgar speech); Can-Tex Indus., 90 LA 1230 (1988)(Shearer, Arb.)(repeated reference to female co-worker as a "fat ass" and "bitch"); Tampa Elec. Co., 88 LA 791 (1986)(Vause, Arb.)(grievant discharged for graphically describing sexual acts he would like to perform with female co-worker who had previously rejected requests for dates and had informed grievant she was married and who was visibly shaken after her encounter with the grievant); Anaconda Copper Co., 78 LA 690 (1982)(Cohen, Arb.), reproduced *infra* (repeated lewd comments and obscene sexual gestures directed at female co-worker; grievant discharged after numerous warnings); Sunshine Mining Co., 77 LA 1259 (1981)(Runkel, Arb.); Rochester Tel. Corp., 45 LA 538 (1965)(Duff, Arb.)(obscene remarks to female co-worker justified discipline, but not discharge).

[32]Can-Tex Indus., *supra* note 31; New Indus. Techniques, Inc., 84 LA 915 (1985)(Gray, Arb.)(discharge upheld for pattern of lewd conduct including rubbing against hips and breasts of female co-workers); Todd Shipyards, 86-1 ARB ¶8072 (1985)(Koven, Arb.)(simulated masturbation); Borg-Warner Corp., 78 LA 985 (1982)(Neas, Arb.)(grievant rotated his genitals in such a fashion as to exhibit them to a female employee); Kroger Co., 72 LA 540 (1979)(Sabella, Arb.)(male employee "mooning" a female employee); Powermatic/ Houdaille, 71 LA 54 (1978)(Cocalis, Arb.)(male employee put his finger through the fly in his pants and said to female employee, "Hey, big mama, look what I have for you").

[33]Porter Equip. Co., 86 LA 1253 (1986)(Lieberman, Arb.)("pulling female employee's hand toward grievant's exposed penis"); Hyatt Hotels Palo Alto, 85 LA 11 (1985)(Oestreich, Arb.)(grievant exposed his penis to female employee).

[34]Island Creek Coal Co., 87 LA 844 (1986)(Stoltenberg, Arb.); Consolidation Coal Co., 79 LA 940 (1982)(Stoltenberg, Arb.); Perfection Am. Co., 73 LA 520 (1979)(Flannagan, Arb.)(male employee intentionally entered female restroom and told occupant that he "always wanted to know what it looked like in here").

[35]Social Security Admin., 81 LA 459 (1983)(Cox, Arb.)(grievant falsely claimed to have engaged in sexual activity with co-worker); Schlage Lock Co., 88 LA 75 (1986)(Wyman, Arb.)(discharge of union steward who left anonymous note in female co-worker's locker room and mailed letter to her husband accusing her of sexual affair with her supervisor).

Background

S___, the grievant, was hired by the Company on July 11, 1977. He worked at various jobs and in various locations within the Company's facility and was a journeyman mill operator in the Leach Department when his employment was terminated. He was discharged on April 3, 1981 for sexual harassment of employee M___. S___ grieved the discharge and the matter, not resolved through the grievance procedure, was carried to arbitration.

Position of the Company

The Company contends that the Grievant was properly discharged for violation of Company policy which forbids harassment, sexual or otherwise, of one employee by another. Company policy on sexual harassment is based on requirements of federal law as set forth in the Equal Employment Opportunity Commission Final Guidelines on Sexual Harassment in the Work Place (29 CFR Part 1604). The Grievant's offending conduct, according to the Company, continued in the face of warnings and successive work reassignments made to move him some distance from M___. When these efforts to direct the Grievant to modify his behavior failed, the Company concluded that obligations to its work force and obligations imposed by federal law left no recourse other than to discharge S___.

The Company argues that the Grievant's pattern of behavior over a two and one-half year span had the purpose or effect of "creating an intimidating, hostile, or offensive working environment" for M___. Throughout this period, during the time they worked together and at other times when their immediate work contacts had ceased, "Grievant engaged in an open campaign consisting of lewd comments and gestures, replete with sexual innuendo, and evoking fear in M___ whenever she was in his company."

The Company refers to specific incidents of harassment, the earliest of which occurred over two years before the Grievant's discharge. On February 3, 1979, foreman Kenneth Ray (now employed elsewhere) observed the Grievant making an obscene gesture to M___ and heard him refer to her as "a lazy bitch". Ray warned the Grievant verbally that further use of such language and signs would result in a written warning.

M___ testified that she complained to foreman Jesse King in October 1980 of continuing verbal harassment by the Grievant. She alleged that, among his other taunts, the Grievant called her a "vieja pinche puta."

M___ alleged that on one occasion, around October 1980, the Grievant called her a "vieja pinche puta" and raised his fist as if he were going to strike her when she attempted to leave the lunchroom. She claimed that, at another time, when she had finished work and was waiting for her relief to arrive, the Grievant started swinging at her with his fists and started to kick at her. She held her lunchpail in front of her for protection. She complained about this incident to mill supervisor Thomas Simpson who warned the Grievant that his job would be on the line if he did not leave M___ alone. Shortly afterward, Simpson moved the Grievant to another building in order to physically separate S___ and M___ who, up to this time, had been working together. After M___ complained that she was still being harassed, the Grievant was transferred a second time in a further effort to limit his opportunity to bother her.

The events summarized above, as well as others, came to the attention of the Employee Relations Department in March 1981 and, in a meeting held on March 24, 1981, M___ made formal charges of sexual harassment. Georgia Laird, Manager of Employee Relations, investigated the matter further and recommended that the Grievant be discharged.

The Company holds that even if there were no EEOC guidelines on sexual harassment, the Grievant's actions would still have been a flagrant and continuing violation of Anaconda's posted policy prohibiting employee discrimination and harassment. Furthermore, even if there were no company policy regarding harassment, the Grievant's actions amounted to a vicious, relentless and purposeless tormenting of a fellow employee which was "repulsive to any standard of behavior in the work place".

The Company concludes that it terminated the Grievant for just cause. He had been counseled by management personnel and warned that further harassment would result in adverse employment action. His harassment of M___ was not simply a personality conflict arising from the work relationship between the two, as the Union contends, nor was it horseplay of a sort that is common in the plant. Rather, it was a campaign of terror which continued over time. • • • The Company's action was consistent with EEOC policy and with its own internal policy against sexual harassment.

Position of the Union

The Union contends that S___ did not engage in sexual harassment on the basis of sex or because of sex. The Union admits that there was a personality conflict between S___ and M___ but it notes that M___ is old enough to be the mother of S___ and the Company has not contended in its allegations that any of the Grievant's actions had the purpose or effect of promoting or encouraging any kind of sexual conduct. The Union maintains that the Company's argument disregards the basic premise of EEOC Guidelines Section 1604.11 which is that in order to find sexual harassment there must be harassment "on the basis of sex." According to the Union, this means that harassment must be undertaken ". . . in order to promote sexual conduct or because of the sex of the person being harassed". Thus, verbal or physical conduct of a sexual nature, not otherwise prohibited, does not become sexual harassment merely because of the sex of the involved parties. The object of the conduct is critical to a determination of the presence of sexual harassment.

The Union challenges Company interpretation of the several specific episodes referred to by M___. In the incident of February, 1979, the Union cites Foreman Ray's testimony to the effect that the Grievant complained that M___ was a lazy bitch, that she was not doing her share of the work, and, as a result, the Grievant had to do more work. Ray also testified that hand gestures such as throwing a finger are made frequently during working hours by both male and female employees and vulgar language is commonly used in the mine and mill by both sexes. The Union emphasized Ray's testimony that S___'s hand gesture was an expression of anger with no sexual implications.

The Grievant admits to calling M___ a lazy SOB, a "vieja" and a "vieja pinche" but he denies calling her a "puta" as she alleges. Union witnesses Mike Limos and Fernie Rodriguez did not corroborate M___'s allegations that S___ clenched his fist as if to strike her and called her a "vieja pinche puta" when she attempted to leave the lunchroom. • • •

The Union cites Kyriazi v. Western Electric Co. (18 FEP Cases 924) wherein District Court Judge Stern found sexual harassment of the plaintiff by male co-workers but was careful to note that the harassment was done to humiliate the plaintiff "as a woman." (Id., FEP Cases at 953, 964) In the instant case, then, to show sexual harassment, the Company must show that the alleged harassing conduct was directed to M___ as a woman, i. e., because of her being a woman. If M___ had been a man who was not holding up his end of the job, S___ could have, and probably would have, called him an old bastard, given him the finger, or made body gestures [to] him.

The Union emphasizes that a work place, such as a mine/mill, is not a parlor room. It is commonplace for the rougher edges of humanity to be revealed in such a site. While true sexual harassment cannot be condoned, it is fundamentally wrong to say that an employee's sex insulates him or her from personality conflict and hostile behavior on the part of other employees.

The Union relies on Hill v. BASF Wyandotte Corp (Mere personality conflicts between supervisor and employee do not rise to the level of illegal race or sex discrimination. 27 FEP Cases 66) and Halpert v. Wertheim & Co (Coarse language in a particular market place with frequent references to genitalia and sexual activity did not constitute harassment or demonstrate an intent to discriminate. 27 FEP Cases 21)

In Halpert, the Court recognized the realities of the market place which often, as here, include rough language, gestures and rough horseplay. The Union claims that the record in the instant dispute will not support the conclusion that the motivating factor in the alleged harassment of M___ by S___ was the fact that M___ is a woman.

The Union argues, finally, that even if S___ had been engaged in sexual harassment, the Company should have followed its progressive discipline policy by issuing a written reprimand and a suspension prior to discharge.

Discussion

Three major questions surface from the record of this dispute. These are (1) did the Grievant or did M___ present a more credible description of the nature of their workplace relationship throughout a period of approximately two and one-half years; (2) did a series of actions by S___ amount to a running harassment of M___; (3) if such actions were harassment, are they properly construed as sexual harassment.

M___ accuses the Grievant of relentless and continuing harassment expressed by obscene gesture, verbal slur, and, in at least one instance, physical assault. The Grievant denies that he addressed M___ by obscene gesture, denies, in part, her allegation of verbal slur, contends that the alleged incident of physical assault was, in fact, a "fooling around" situation, and claims that she either misinterpreted and/or falsified her description of other specific incidents.

We have at the threshold, then, a question of credibility. The Grievant admits that he harbored feelings of hostility against M___ and he describes their relationship as one of "personality conflict." His testimony *in toto,* however, does not provide a picture of relentless harassment over a long period of time such as is alleged by M___.

• • •

The Grievant consistently denied that he had ever made any obscene gesture toward M___, but I take note of the fact that is it part of the general Union position that gestures such as "throwing a finger" or pelvic movements carry no sexual connotation when made in the Company's work areas. In the February 1979 incident, however, S___ denied making any gesture, sexual or otherwise. His denial was straightforward and clear. He claimed no memory problems. His full testimony on the incident was detailed and presented without hesitation.

I give weight to the testimony of Foreman Ray who was not shown as harboring any hostility toward the Grievant and who, not now in the employment of the Company, is without incentive to be anything other than neutral in a dispute between two employees whom he supervised for a very brief time. I take note, also, of the fact that the Union does not deny that the Grievant make a gesture but argues, instead, that the gesture had no sexual implications.

For a second test of credibility, I rely on what the Parties refer to as the "lunchpail incident." The record is not entirely clear as to when this incident occurred but it appears to have been in late 1980. The Grievant and M___ were in the lunchroom at the end of the work shift and waiting for their reliefs to arrive. According to M___, she said something about leaving because the relief person was arriving whereupon S___ told her that she ". . . could get the hell out of there" and started swinging at her with his fist. She testified that she put her lunchpail in front of her for protection and he then started to kick at her.

• • •

For a final test on credibility, I rely on testimony concerning M___'s allegation that she was the object of an uncomplimentary physical gesture by S___ made in the Company's parking lot. • • •

• • •

On the basis of the incidents detailed above, as well as other matter in the record, I am able to conclude that M___'s description of the relationship between herself and the Grievant is more accurate than the version presented by the Grievant.

Waiving at this point the question of whether gestures such as throwing a finger and pelvic body movements and use of certain coarse language constitute sexual harassment, I have no problem in concluding that the Grievant did harass M___ and that such harassment continued over an extended period of time. As noted above, the Grievant's denial that he made any obscene gestures toward M___ must be weighed in light of the Union position that various hand and other gestures are not obscene. Obscene or otherwise, the gestures were made frequently and continued after Grievant had been warned against such conduct. The Grievant, furthermore, admitted that he was always getting after M___ and cussing at her.

Apart from the Grievant's actions, I find harassment on the basis of what appears to me to be a Union admission that his conduct toward M___ was hostile: ". . . it is fundamentally wrong to say that an employee's sex insulates him or her from personality conflict and hostile behavior of other employees. The first step is to show that the hostile conduct is engaged in on the basis of sex or because of sex". I take this statement as an admission, not only of harassment, but also that the Company had cause to discipline the Grievant since it is not tenable to argue that an employee who is the target of hostile actions on the part of another employee has no right to remedy because the hostile actions grow out of personality conflict. Had the Company taken disciplinary action against the Grievant because of his harassment of a co-worker, there would be no need to further extend this opinion. The reason for discharge, however, was "sexual harassment toward co-worker". By so charging the Grievant, the Company assumed a burden of showing sexual harassment.

• • •

The dispute under arbitration is unusual in that there is absent even the slightest hint of any interest on the part of the Grievant in sexual favors from M___. S___ admittedly did not like M___. His verbal slurs were demeaning and uncomplimentary. He repeatedly referred to her as an old lady. (She is, in fact, middle-aged but about twice the age of the Grievant.) The dispute is also unusual in that hostile actions against a female employee were undertaken by only one male coworker. In the more usual case, shunning, teasing, practical jokes, etc. are perpetrated by groups of male coworkers.

• • •

The Union argues that sexual harassment can only be found when harassment is undertaken (1) to promote sexual conduct or (2) because of the sex of the person being harassed. According to the Union, the object of the conduct is critical in a determination of whether sexual harassment is present.

The Company holds that it properly followed EEOC Guidelines on Discrimination Because of Sex. Since neither Party charges that the Grievant sought sexual favors, the relevant section of the Guidelines is found in 1604.11 (3).

1604.11 Sexual harassment.

(a) Harassment on the basis of sex is a violation of Sec. 703 of Title VII. Unwelcome sexual advances, requests for sexual favors, and other verbal or physical conduct of a sexual nature constitute sexual harassment when . . .

(3) such conduct has the purpose or effect of unreasonably interfering with an individual's work performance or creating an intimidating, hostile or offensive working environment.

The language in 1604.11 is not free of ambiguity. It is sufficiently clear, however, to support the conclusion that the Union's test is not on a par with guideline language. In the type of dispute under arbitration here, the Union would ask only whether harassment was undertaken because of the sex of the harassed. Under the guidelines, the test for sexual harassment is more complex. First, there must be verbal or physical conduct of a sexual nature. This is a necessary but not a sufficient condition. It becomes sexual harassment if it has the purpose or the effect of (1) unreasonably interfering with an individual's work performance or (2) creating an intimidating, hostile, or offensive working environment.

Under the guideline test, thus, we first look for verbal or physical conduct of a sexual nature and then seek to determine the purpose or effect of such conduct. Once this latter determination is made, we are able to conclude as to whether the verbal or physical conduct is violative of EEOC Guidelines. Under the guidelines, the fact that harassment is undertaken because of the sex of the harassed is, in a sense, immaterial. The harassment, even if so motivated, does not become sexual harassment unless it has the purpose or effects set forth in sub-section (3) of 1604.11. And if the harassment has any one of the effects set forth in sub-section (3), the intent of the harassment is immaterial.

Pursuant to the language in 1604.11 (3) we must first examine the record for evidence of verbal or physical conduct of a sexual nature. The Company finds such in the frequent hand gestures and body movements which S___ directed toward M___ and in his various verbal slurs against her, most of which he admitted to. The Union responds to the Company charge with the argument that obscene gestures and coarse language are commonplace in the mine/mill. As put by Union Representative Sam Tafoya, women were going to have to adjust to working conditions that involved obscene gestures and vulgar language. This, he testified, was "Equal rights". As already noted, the Union finds the situation in the Company analagous to that described in Halpert v. Wertheim where the Court ruled that coarse language in general use at the work place did not constitute sexual harassment when directed at the plaintiff.

Is there any basis for differentiating M___'s experience from that described in Halpert? Do we have an instance of overly sensitive ears and over-reaction to commonplace plant behavior or is something more involved?

Although the Grievant denies that he ever gestured toward M___ in an obscene way, his contention is impeached by his testimony on the February 1979 incident. I defer to M___'s testimony and find that she was the object of frequent obscene gestures by S___ over a lengthy time period. We have less disagreement between the Parties on the matter of verbal slurs. The Grievant admits to calling M___ a lazy son-of-a-bitch, a vieja, and a vieja pinche. He denies calling her a vieja pinche puta, as alleged by M___. He admits to telling supervisor Jesse King that he was "always getting after her, always cussing her."

A vieja is the Spanish term for old woman or old lady. The several witnesses for both parties were unable to agree upon a single meaning for vieja pinche but they did agree that it was a demeaning reference. S___ indicated that to him it meant "the old bag". (In its original Castilian meaning, pinche was a kitchen boy or scullion. At a later time the usage was extended to include female kitchen help. The Diccionario de Americanismos and the Dictionary of Chicano Spanish give "lowly," "abject," "insignificant," "poor," "contemptible," and "worthless" as examples of contemporary usage in Latin America and the Southwest part of the United States.)

The word "puta" means whore or prostitute. M___ alleges that S___ called her a vieja pinche puta (roughly translated as worthless old whore) on several occasions. S___ denies that he ever called her a puta.

We are not given an explicit motive for the Grievant's verbal and gesturing attacks against M___. He was clearly unhappy with her performance when the two worked as a team in SX and testified that she made his job more difficult through her failure to perform press work rapidly enough and by her need of his assistance to open certain valves. S___ complained to Supervisor King about her work performance "every time we had something hard to do." However, if S___'s attacks reflected his dissatisfaction with M___'s work, we are still left without explanation as to why he continued the attacks after he was transferred to another job for the express purpose of separating him from M___.

The Union would hold that whatever it was that motivated S___, his hostility toward M___ was not unlike hostile relationships that are common among fellow plant workers and his language and gestures were within the linguistic range of everyday floor level communications among all employees.

In evaluating the Union argument, I ask whether sexually tinged language and gestures are permanently neutered by frequency of usage. Do physical gestures with sexual connotation lose such connotation in all circumstances because they have lost them in some and, similarly, do insults that comment on the quality of a woman cease to be sexually demeaning regardless of context because they are made frequently, flippantly, or casually in plant or office or schoolyard?

I believe that the Union erroneously emphasizes form rather than context. If "verbal conduct of a sexual nature" can be expressed in perfectly elegant language, can we tenably argue that it can no longer be expressed through baser language? It is not the elegance or coarseness of language that is at issue. The question, instead, is whether language—and gesture which is a form of language—is used in a way that can reasonably be construed as verbal conduct of a sexual nature.

S___ persisted in his harassment of M___ over a period of several years. He harassed by means of gesture, language and, allegedly, by physical assaults or threat of assault. A substantial part of the record consists of testimony on what the Parties refer to as the "lunchpail incident," the "tailgating incident" and the "lunchroom" incident. In all of these incidents where physical assault is alleged, we have conflicting testimony and questions of credibility are present. While these incidents would certainly be significant episodes in a pattern of harassment as such. I do not see in them a presence of "physical conduct of a sexual nature" and I exclude them from my determination of whether sexual harassment occurred. For the latter determination I look only at the pattern of the physical gestures and verbal assaults.

The "one on one" nature of the Grievant's harassment of M___ is sufficient to differentiate the instant dispute from Halpert. We do not have here a situation where coarse expression is woven into the web of work place communications. S___ was not instructing, directing, reprimanding, or even arguing with M___. He was, purely and simply, harassing her.

I find guidance for the instant dispute in Gray v. Greyhound Lines, 13 FEP Cases 1401 (A pattern of racial slurs violates Title VII rights to a nondiscriminatory environment); U.S. v. City of Buffalo, 19 FEP Cases 776 (Black employees are entitled to a work environment free of racial abuse and insult); Compton v. Borden, Inc., 17 FEP Cases 310 (Demeaning religious slurs by supervisor violate Title VII).

I find that S___ did engage in verbal conduct of a sexual nature on the basis of what appears to me the clear message of the cited rulings but, more importantly, because of his relentless harassment of M___ through obscene gesture and demeaning slurs against the quality of her womanhood. Under the circumstances of the S___-M___ relationship, S___ cannot take refuge in the fact that he used language and gesture common in the work place. Constant, exaggerated and gratuitous reference to M___'s age and decrepitude, punctuated by obscene gesture, is verbal conduct of a sexual nature.

Did such verbal conduct have the effect of creating an intimidating, hostile, or offensive working environment for M___? On the basis of the record, I find that it clearly did. Although reluctant to do so, M___ was eventually driven to complain to her supervisors and finally to make a formal charge of sexual harassment to the Employee Relations Department. Along the way she sought advice from a municipal judge and appealed to the Grievant's father and the Grievant's wife for assistance. I accept as credible her testimony that she was afraid of S___ and note that on one occasion she decided not to apply for a job transfer because the transfer, if granted, would have placed her in a work location closer to the Grievant.

The final Union contention is that the discharge of the Grievant was improper because the Company failed to follow its policy of progressive discipline prior to taking the discharge action. The Company holds that its use of progressive discipline is dependent on the severity of an offense.

The Union has not shown either through reference to contract language or established past practice that progressive discipline was mandatory. Our question here asks whether discharge was reasonable in light of the circumstances of the dispute. In an effort to resolve the harassment problem, the Grievant was given a job transfer and verbally warned that if he continued to bother M___ his job was in jeopardy. When the transfer failed to have the hoped for result, the Grievant was transferred once more, this time to a work location even more removed from where M___ worked. Both transfers were lateral in nature and the Grievant suffered no loss of pay or benefits. The Grievant was discharged on April 3, 1981 pursuant to M___'s complaints that the harassment continued.

• • •

On the basis of these findings, I conclude that the Company's decision to terminate the Grievant without further resort to progressive discipline was not unreasonable.

AWARD

The grievance is denied.

2. Physical Contact

Arbitrators are especially reluctant to overturn discipline when the sexual misconduct involves offensive physical contact.[36] In *Care Inns*,[37] the grievant was discharged for grabbing the arm of a nurse's aide and kissing her on the cheek while she was preparing a patient for a bath. In evaluating the conduct of the grievant, the arbitrator relied extensively on Title VII precedent in determining that discharge was the appropriate penalty:

> In this case I feel that it is abundantly clear that the discharge penalty is justified. In this case the Employee is guilty of explicit sexual harassment. He forcefully grabbed B___'s arm, leaned over, and kissed her on the cheek. The complainant expressed fear, and she became nervous, upset, and hysterical. This testimony stands unrefuted. After supervision was made aware that sexual harassment did, indeed, occur then it has every right to move aggressively to deal with the offending male Employee. Sexual harassment is a serious offense and Management must move to deal with it accordingly. Certainly supervision is not required to stand by and let such conduct become progressively worse before the cause is removed. Furthermore, the Company has a legal obligation to provide a safe place for its female Employees to work.[38]

A similar result occurred in *Zia Company*,[39] where the grievant had grabbed, kissed, and hugged the complainant against her will on three occasions. Even though the grievant had worked for the employer for 24 years and had an unblemished work record, the arbitrator upheld the discharge.

Not all sexual harassment that involves unwanted touching is considered sufficient to constitute just cause for discharge. In deciding whether discharge is the proper penalty, arbitrators will consider the total facts and circumstances surrounding the misconduct, the effect on the complainant, the work record of the grievant, the length of service of the grievant and, in general, the egregiousness of the misconduct. In *Dayton Power & Light*,[40] the arbitrator found that the grievant's conduct, which included pinching a female co-worker on the breast while making kissing sounds, violated the employer's work rules and

---

[36]Porter Equip. Co., 86 LA 1253 (1986)(Lieberman, Arb.)(grievant grabbed victim's arm and pulled it toward grievant's exposed penis); Rockwell Int'l Corp., 85 LA 246 (1985)(Feldman, Arb.)(offensive touching of three female co-workers by a male employee); New Indus. Techniques, Inc., 84 LA 915 (1985)(Gray, Arb.)(discharge sustained after several warnings about touching female co-employees); United States Army Signal Ctr., 78 LA 120 (1982)(Hall, Arb.)(five-day suspension for more-than-accidental touching of breasts of six female soldiers while giving instructions); Mengel Co., 36 LA 618 (1961)(Turkus, Arb.)(grievant discharged for lewd comments and touching victim in unduly familiar manner despite victim's request to stop).

[37]81 LA 687 (1983)(Taylor, Arb.).

[38]*Id.* at 694.

[39]82 LA 640 (1984)(Daughton, Arb.) This case has a very peculiar procedural history. The complainant reported the first two incidents of harassment to the first level of management. The first-level supervisors did nothing to remedy the situation except request the complainant to take the matter to a higher level of management, which the complainant did not do. After the third incident, the complainant did report all three incidents to upper management. The company conducted an investigation and could not determine exactly what had happened since the company could not determine which party was telling the truth. The grievant was transferred to a different crew and was no longer complainant's supervisor. The complainant then filed a sexual harassment charge with the New Mexico Human Rights Commission against the employer. The Commission issued a determination of probable cause that sexual harassment had occurred. Subsequently, the complainant filed a federal court discrimination action against the company, the grievant, and two members of management. The court entered a judgment against the company and specifically found that the complainant had been sexually assaulted by the grievant. Based upon this decision, the company then discharged the grievant, who then filed the grievance which became the subject of the arbitration.

[40]80 LA 19 (1982)(Heinsz, Arb.).

constituted sexual harassment under Title VII. Nonetheless, in light of the grievant's 28 years of employment with the company, his good work with no prior disciplinary problems, and the complainant's failure to report the incident to management, the arbitrator reduced the discharge penalty to a seven-month suspension without pay:

> Under all the facts of this case, the Arbitrator determines that the discharge of the Grievant was too harsh a penalty. Such a conclusion should not be construed to lessen the seriousness of the misconduct which occurred on July 21 or to in any way minimize the problem of sexual harassment in American industry. Further, the Arbitrator certainly understands the Company's reaction in this case to terminate the Grievant. Not only does sexual harassment violate the Company's internal work rules but it is also plainly a violation of Title VII of the Civil Rights Act. Moreover, the EEOC Guidelines on Sexual Harassment in the Workplace specifically placed the responsibility upon the employer to prevent harassment which the employer authorizes, knows or should have known about. 29 C.F.R. §1604.11. Courts and arbitrators have upheld this responsibility on the part of employers and found them liable when they have condoned harassment in the workplace. *Henson v. City of Dundee,* 29 FEP Cases 787 (11th Cir. 1982); *Bundy v. Jackson,* 641 F.2d 934, 24 FEP Cases 1155 (D.C. Cir. 1981); *Hayden v. Cox Enterprises,* 28 FEP Cases 1315 (N.D. Ga. 1982); *University of Missouri Health Sciences Center,* 82-1 ARB ¶8134 (Yarowsky, 1982). Thus the Company was required to rigidly enforce its rules.[41]

Similarly, the discharge of the grievant by the employer in *Boys Markets*[42] was found to be too severe. It was determined that the grievant had moved his finger in an upward movement between the buttocks of a female co-worker. The arbitrator found the conduct reprehensible and a violation of the standards of conduct to be expected in the workplace. Nevertheless, the arbitrator found discharge simply too harsh. He reduced it to a disciplinary layoff without pay: "Although the EEOC Guidelines place upon the Employer the responsibility for immediate and appropriate action in situations of known sexual harassment it does not follow that discharge is necessarily the appropriate action in every incident."[43]

In *Sugardale Foods,*[44] the discharge imposed for touching the crotch of a female co-worker was reduced to a long-term suspension. The grievant came up behind the female co-worker and put his arms around the lower part of her body. He admitted to the touching but disputed the location of the touch. The arbitrator found that the grievant's hand was in the crotch area and that his conduct, coupled with his intrusive behavior toward the complainant, was serious sexual harassment. The arbitrator did not believe, however, that such conduct justified the discharge penalty. The grievant was reinstated without back pay, because:

> 1. There is no showing that Employees have received any express notice or indication that sexual harassment, at least harassment not involving actual physical contact, was prohibited.

---

[41]*Id.* at 21.
[42]88 LA 1304 (1987)(Wilmoth, Arb.).
[43]*Id.* at 1306.
[44]86 LA 1017 (1986)(Duda, Arb.).

2. The total period of harassment was a maximum of ten minutes. In that time, K___ felt uncomfortable and imposed upon, but the intense harassment stemming from the touching was of very short duration. Although serious, Grievant's conduct was significantly less severe and less heinous than many reported sexual harassment cases for which discharge was imposed.

3. There is no evidence or suggestion that Grievant had ever been involved in sexual harassment prior to September 29, 1985.

4. Discipline short of discharge is adequate to demonstrate to all Employees the Company's firm resolve in respect to sexual harassment.

5. A long extended suspension is adequate to deter Grievant from any repeat of sexual harassment.

6. Grievant had been employed for over 25 years at the time of his discharge. There is no claim that he had been an exemplary Employee. As a matter of fact, within the prior two years he had received two disciplines, one for absenteeism and another for using a Company phone for personal use. Both of these offenses, subject to progressive discipline, are qualitatively different than sexual harassment.[45]

In *GTE Florida*,[46] the grievant was discharged for the sexual harassment of an employee of a subcontractor. The grievant bit the victim on the buttocks, lifted her off a ladder and carried her around, finally putting her down on a desk top and kissing her neck. The arbitrator carefully reviewed the facts, including evidence derived from the employer's investigation that the grievant had been involved in other incidents of sexual harassment in the workplace. Although concluding that the grievant had engaged in serious sexual harassment, the arbitrator did not believe that the conduct justified discharge. Of significance to the arbitrator was that the employer had previously allowed, or at least had ignored, horseplay in the workplace. Even one of the complainants admitted to participating in some of the horseplay in the past. Under these circumstances, the arbitrator found a long-term suspension with reinstatement appropriate, conditioned on the understanding that any future sexual harassment on the part of the grievant would be grounds for immediate discharge.

B. Nonvulgar but Unwelcome Sexual Advances

Employees who knowingly make unwelcome amorous advances toward other employees engage in conduct that, while not crude or physical, is subject to discipline when it is persistent, annoying, and unwelcome. These cases sometimes require the arbitrator to distinguish harmless ineffectual romantic conduct from obsessive and compulsive behavior that may indicate serious psychological problems. In *IBP, Inc.*,[47] the grievant was a 41-year-old recent immigrant from Romania who became infatuated with a 21-year-old co-worker. Even in the face of her rejection and clear directions from management to cease bothering her, the grievant continued to write letters to her, send her gifts and flowers, and call her on the telephone. The company repeatedly warned the grievant to stop his conduct, even going so far as to place him on leave so that

---

[45]*Id.* at 1022.

[46]92 LA 1090 (1989)(Cohen, Arb.). *See also* Meijer, Inc., 83 LA 570 (1984)(Ellmann, Arb.)(discharge converted to ten-month suspension for embracing male co-worker and giving a "little bit of a hump motion").

[47]789 LA 41 (1987)(Eisler, Arb.). *See also* Ohio Dep't. of Transp., 90 LA 783 (1988)(Duda, Arb.)(reducing from 30 to 5 days a suspension based upon sexual harassment consisting of touching a female co-worker's abdomen and upper thigh with a flagpole).

he could be treated by a psychologist. When the grievant failed to see the psychologist, he was discharged for violation of the work rule against "coercion, obscene, abusive or threatening language, interference or threat of injury to any person, members of their families or their property."

The arbitrator upheld the discharge. Even though the discharge was for violation of a work rule, the arbitrator justified the discharge in terms of the employer's duty to prevent sexual harassment:

> Further, without some kind of action on the Employer's part, a case of sexual harassment could possibly have been made out against the employer under existing statutory and regulatory authority. *Meritor Savings Bank v. Vinson,* 40 FEP Cases 1822 (1986); *Barrett v. Omaha National Bank,* 726 F.2d 424, 35 FEP Cases 593 (8th Cir., 1984); EEOC Guidelines, 29 C.F.R. 1604.11. Indeed, if the Employer had discharged Grievant for sexual harassment of a co-employee, the result would have been the same, since the Employer has the obligation to free the workplace from intimidating, hostile or offensive work environments brought on because of advances made by one employee to another. *United Electric Supply Company,* 82 LA. 921 (1984, Madden); *Hyatt Hotels Palo Alto,* 85 LA. 11 (1985, Oestreich); *New Industrial Techniques, Inc.,* 84 LA. 915 (1985, Gray); *Rockwell International Corp.,* 85 LA. 246 (1985, Feldman).[48]

In the case of *United Electric Supply*[49] the grievant was also discharged for his persistent and repeated unwelcome advances to female co-workers. Prior to imposing discharge, the employer warned the grievant several times. While the grievant was persistent, neither vulgar language nor offensive touching was involved. In evaluating the conduct of the grievant to determine whether discharge was the appropriate penalty, the arbitrator relied extensively on Title VII precedent:

> Sexual harassment can occur without any touching in circumstances in which unwelcome sexual advances are made, so long as the advances are not reciprocated or provoked. *Gan v. Kepro Circuit Systems, Inc.,* 24 EPD 32,379, 28 FEP Cases 639 (ED Mo. 1982).

> In the present case, while the female employees were tardy in making a complaint about the grievant's advances, there was no evidence whatever, that the employees welcomed such advances or engaged in any similar conduct of their own. Grievant's case is clearly distinguishable from those cases in which there is a single, isolated instance of offensive conduct, those cases in which rude, sexually distasteful, or obscene words are not personally directed, those cases where the distasteful approach receives a response in kind and those cases in which an atmosphere prevails which is in accord with the conduct to which objection is made.

> There is, however, no question but that his advances were persistent, continued, and would have been construed to be unwelcome by any reasonable man. All of the complainants, except the one who worked in the warehouse, testified that they tried to avoid the grievant and some hesitated to go into the warehouse for fear of encountering him.

> Grievant had by means of unwelcome advances created an offensive working environment. *See* EEOC Decisions 82-2 and 81-18.[50]

---

[48]*Id.* at 45.
[49]82 LA 921 (1984)(Madden, Arb.).
[50]*Id.* at 925–26.

C. Harassment of Customers, Clients, and Other Nonemployees

Under the law of the shop, employees must not only refrain from sexually harassing their co-workers, but must also refrain from harassing customers, clients, and other nonemployees with whom they deal in their employment. Employees have been disciplined for making offensive comments to a passing citizen,[51] making sexual advances toward the teenage daughter of a customer,[52] and for making sexually oriented jokes and comments to clients.[53] Employees have also been disciplined for improperly touching the breast of a sales representative of another company,[54] making sexual propositions to the employer's customers,[55] and sexually assaulting a customer.[56] The factors used by arbitrators in these cases to evaluate the propriety of the discipline are no different from those used in co-worker harassment cases.

VI. CONDUCT FOUND NOT TO CONSTITUTE SEXUAL HARASSMENT

Arbitrators have recognized that not all questionable comments or horseplay between men and women will be considered sexual harassment sufficient to constitute just cause for discipline. As suggested by the EEOC Guidelines, arbitrators consider the circumstances surrounding the conduct, as well as the conduct and attitude of the complainant, in determining whether there has been sexual harassment.

The arbitrator in *Louisville Gas & Electric Co.*[57] held that the grievant had not engaged in sexual harassment where he showed a female co-worker a metal rod and said, "How would you like this stuck up your ass and have your temperature taken?" It was significant that the co-worker did not report the matter to management; rather, a bystander did. When the female co-worker was questioned about the incident, she stated she had considered the comment a joke. In evaluating the conduct the arbitrator concluded:

> The key here is the intent of the Grievant. It must be found that there was no intent to intimidate or harass a fellow employee beyond the sort of joking and

---

[51]City of Rochester, 82 LA 217 (1984)(Lawson, Arb.)(grievant, employed by city and working on a street project, yelled to a woman passing on her way to the offices of Planned Parenthood, "Hey baby come over here and talk to me!" and made other crude noises. Discharge was reduced to long-term suspension, the arbitrator finding that the comments, while offensive and vulgar, were not obscene or prurient).

[52]Pepco, 83 LA 449 (1984)(Kaplan, Arb.)(where grievant hired the 17-year-old daughter of a customer to clean his apartment and then touched her, made sexually suggestive remarks, and asked her to pose for nude photographs, discharge was reduced to long-term suspension only because of grievant's long-term service and unblemished record).

[53]County of Ramsey, 86 LA 249 (1986)(Gallagher, Arb.)(where grievant, an employment guidance counselor, suggested prostitution as possible career path for several clients for the apparent purpose of trying to initiate a sexual relationship with them, discharge converted to 30-day suspension).

[54]Fisher Foods, Inc., 80 LA 133 (1983)(Abrams, Arb.)(suspension sustained where grievant, a stock man for a food company and assigned to a specific grocery store, approached visiting sales representative from behind, picked her up, and twirled her around, placing his hand inside her blouse and on her breast).

[55]Nabisco Food Co., 82 LA 1186 (1984)(Allen, Arb.)(discharge sustained where grievant repeatedly made sexual propositions and abused customers at various retail stores where he delivered employer's product); DeVry Institute of Technology, 87 LA 1149 (1986)(Berman, Arb.)(faculty member making sexual propositions to students).

[56]Communications Workers v. Southeastern Elec. Co-op., 882 F.2d 467, 132 LRRM 2381 (10th Cir. 1989)(affirming summary judgment for union that enforced an arbitrator's decision to reinstate with one-month suspension an employee who had been discharged for kissing and offensive touching of a customer in her home).

[57]81 LA 730 (1983)(Stonehouse, Arb.).

needling that goes on daily among friends who work together. One can hardly find any sexual overtones in an anal temperature reading. If there was some indication of intent to harass or intimidate and it was done in some repetitive, persistent manner, the outcome herein would be different and more severe discipline would be in order.[58]

Similarly, the arbitrator in *Washington Scientific Industries*[59] held that a single statement about sex ("I suppose you don't even like sexual intercourse") did not constitute sexual harassment; nor did the comment violate the shop rule prohibiting obscene or abusive language. An arbitrator in *Bakery and Confectionery Union*[60] also refused to find sexual harassment when one employee passed an obscene, sexually explicit note to a fellow employee. The recipient of the note was not offended and had simply torn it up and thrown it in the waste basket. The arbitrator observed that, under the EEOC Guidelines, conduct is considered to be sexual harassment only if it was "unwelcome." Because the employer had not demonstrated the "unwelcome" nature of the grievant's conduct, the arbitrator reasoned that there was no sexual harassment, noting that "the EEOC guidelines recognize that in on-the-job interpersonal relationships between the sexes the focus necessarily must be on what the individual employee finds objectionable."[61]

VII. GRIEVANCES FILED BY COMPLAINANTS

A limited number of grievances are brought by employees subjected to sexual harassment. As long as the employer is responsive, a formal grievance may not be required. Review of sexual harassment arbitration decisions suggests that complainants in unionized workplaces often have not needed to file formal grievances in order to obtain employer assistance in remedying the situation. Instead, once the complainant or another employee has informed the employer of the problem, management generally reacted positively with an investigation and took steps to eliminate the problem.

A. Intangible Job Detriments

One of the few reported decisions involving a formal grievance charging sexual harassment is *County of Oakland*.[62] In order to comply with state requirements for special inmates, a county sheriff relocated behavior modification unit cells fitted with glass doors and windows. The cells were positioned across an open corridor from the booking area to permit constant observation of inmates by male and female deputies located in the booking office. Following the relocation, female booking clerks filed a grievance on the basis that they were exposed to nudity and obscene gestures by the male inmates.

---

[58]*Id.* at 733. These remarks resemble comments by the Supreme Court in *Meritor Sav. Bank v. Vinson*, 477 U.S. 57, 67–68, 40 FEP Cases 1822, 1827 (1986), reproduced in Chapter 1, Overview.

[59]83 LA 824 (1984)(Kapsch, Arb.).

[60]81-2 ARB ¶8567 (1981)(Harkless, Arb.).

[61]*Id.* at ¶5492. On the other hand, when the victim is overly sensitive and imaginative as to what constitutes sexual harassment, the victim's personal perceptions will not prevail. King Soopers, Inc., 86 LA 254 (1985)(Sass, Arb.).(male employee's comment that female co-employee's uncooked TV dinner was still hard after being in a microwave oven was not sexual harassment).

[62]94 LA 451 (1990)(Daniel, Arb.).

In denying the charge of sexual harassment, the arbitrator noted that the booking clerk job is open to both genders:

> The arbitrator has carefully considered the argument of the parties in terms of sexual harassment and discrimination and finds that there is no basis for such claim in the grievance. The group involved here is not appropriately identifiable. Simply because all of the current members of the group of booking clerks are female does not make it an exclusively female group. It is open at any time to inclusion of males; in fact, males have been employed in the past in such capacity. The definition of sexual harassment concerns personal confrontations or advances. That criterion is not met here because the conduct of the inmates is not shown to be directed to booking clerks or the grievant in particular. Nor is it shown that such is done for the purpose of interfering with their work or to create a hostile or offensive work environment. The fact that such may be the result does not satisfy the requirement of showing actual intent or purpose. There is no proof that the employer has purposely created the condition so as to bring about such a result.[63]

Another case, *Island Creek Coal Co.*,[64] resulted from a prior grievance filed by a sexual harassment complainant. Three male employees had opened the door of a women's dressing room to watch the female complainant, who then reported the incident to management. Nevertheless, she declined to identify the employees involved, opting to pursue the matter solely through the union. When that process failed to resolve the issue, she filed a grievance and named the three employees. The employer conducted an investigation, which resulted in five-day suspensions for all three men. That action resolved the complainant's grievance, although it led to a new grievance by the disciplined employees.

Similarly, the genesis of *Rockwell International Corp.*[65] was a grievance filed by a female employee claiming that the employer was not protecting her from sexual harassment. The grievance prompted an extensive investigation by the employer, which revealed that two other female employees had also been sexually harassed by the same male employee. The employer then discharged him, leading to his grievance and arbitration.[66]

B. Tangible Job Detriments

Female employees have grieved adverse employment actions on the basis that they resulted from sexual harassment. In *Amoco Texas Refining Co.*,[67] the grievant was dismissed during her probationary period because she failed to learn and could not perform the duties of her job. The grievant claimed that sexual harassment during her training period had so upset her that she was unable to study and learn the requirements of her position. She further contended that the numerous incidents of sexual harassment were known to the

---

[63]*Id.* at 456.
[64]87 LA 844 (1986)(Stoltenberg, Arb.).
[65]85 LA 246 (1985)(Feldman, Arb.).
[66]*See also* S-P Drug Co., 44 LA 730 (1965)(Kornblum, Arb.)(discharge sustained for sexual harassment, even though complaining female employees indicated to arbitrator that they did not desire grievant's discharge).
[67]78-2 ARB ¶8415 (1978)(Gowan, Jr., Arb.).

employer, the employer took no action to eliminate the harassment, and, there-fore, the employer was responsible for her failure.[68]

The arbitrator recognized the force of this argument but found that the employer had insufficient knowledge of the harassment to hold it responsible:

> It seems to the arbitrator that an essential element in any case of alleged discrimi-nation is not only that it occurred but that it occurred on the part of the Company who is the party complained of. In this case it cannot be denied there were acts of discrimination and that these acts formed a pattern of conduct reasonably designed to discourage Grievant's continued employment on the Ultracracker Unit. However, it must be determined if these were the acts of the Company. Clearly, they were the acts of the employees and that may, but does not necessar-ily, require a finding that they were also the acts of the Company. For this pattern of discrimination to fall on the shoulders of the Company there must be some positive showing that the acts were condoned, endorsed or encouraged by the Company. For that to be true it must be shown that the Company knew of the acts of harassment because it cannot condone, endorse or encourage that which is unknown. However, mere knowledge does not in and of itself make a complete case that the acts were condoned, endorsed or encouraged. Additional evidence to that effect would be required. The point being made here is that the entire chain of proof begins with knowledge. Without it there is no case of any kind.[69]

The arbitrator denied the grievance because the grievant reported only the last of a series of incidents to the employer, which then acted promptly to address the conduct.[70]

In *EZ Communications*,[71] another case involving loss of job benefits, the arbitrator sustained a grievance protesting a radio station's denial of severance pay to a female newscaster who walked off the job after a long series of on-air jokes about her sexual proclivities. The grievant's job was to read the news during a morning radio show featuring two male disc jockeys. Over a period of two years the disc jockeys made on-air comments, intended to be in jest, to the effect that the grievant suffered from sexually transmitted diseases and regularly performed promiscuous oral sex with large numbers of casual ac-quaintances, including members of the Pittsburgh Penquins hockey team and the United States Marine Corps. Despite her complaints, the remarks and jokes directed toward her continued on a regular basis, with the final straw being a joke to the effect that a tattoo on her forehead read, "Let go of my ears, I'm doing the best I can." Hearing the joke shortly before she was to read the news, the grievant was too distressed to go on the air and left the station, which resulted in her discharge for flagrant neglect of duty and the denial of her claim for severance pay, which was due under the collective bargaining agreement if she was terminated on a "noncause" basis.

Considering the employer's assertion of the principle of "obey now, grieve later," the arbitrator noted that while arbitral law abhors self-help, there

---

[68]For a similar claim, see *National Archives*, 73 LA 737 (1979)(Maller, Arb.), where a female employee grieved a poor performance appraisal, claiming her supervisor had downgraded her performance in retaliation for her rejection of sexual advances. The arbitrator only addressed the arbitrability issue and did not evaluate the merits of the grievance.

[69]78-2 ARB ¶8415 at 4949.

[70]The language of the arbitrator's analysis—that mere knowledge plus inaction is not enough to create employer liability for co-worker sexual harassment—is at odds with the EEOC Guidelines and the *Meritor* decision, which would impose employer liability in such a situation.

[71]91 LA 1097 (1988)(Talarico, Arb.).

are exceptions to the principle. Among the exceptions are circumstances where the duty to obey orders "would humiliate the employee or invade some personal right which is considered inviolable."[72] In determining whether this exception applied, the arbitrator acknowledged that the nature of the grievant's job, in the entertainment industry, required her to participate in "banter and interplay with the other on-air talent," and that the First Amendment protects even jokes that are "lewd, offensive, sophomoric, in bad taste." He concluded, however, that an employee need not tolerate free speech imposed as a condition of employment, for federal employment law protects employees from jokes, suggestions, and comments of a sexual manner that create a hostile working environment.[72a] Accordingly, the arbitrator held that the grievant was relieved of the responsibility to "obey now, grieve later":

> [T]he grievant's action of walking off the job was not only understandable, but more importantly, was justifiable. The conduct on the part of the disc jockeys was degrading, humiliating and a serious invasion of her personal rights and dignity. I would find it unreasonable to require the grievant to have remained on the job after being subjected to such vile and lewd insults and be expected merely to file a grievance. These circumstances are a narrow exception to the self-help rule and justify the grievant's actions.[73]

In *Paccar, Inc.*,[74] a female employee was terminated near the end of her probationary period. The grievant claimed that she had been terminated as a result of her repeated refusal to date and "party with" her supervisor. The arbitrator denied the grievance after finding the testimony of the foreman and general foreman credible as to the grievant's ability to perform her job. The evidence as to the foreman's sexual advances was uncorroborated and was also deemed to be unpersuasive in the light of the strong evidence relating to job performance.

VIII. RELATIONSHIP BETWEEN ARBITRAL AND JUDICIAL JURISDICTION

Since the Supreme Court's rulings in the *Steelworkers Trilogy*,[75] it has generally been held that arbitration is the exclusive remedy for employees covered by a collective bargaining agreement that provides for final and binding arbitration.

A. Claims by Sexual Harassment Complainants

Notwithstanding the general exclusiveness of the collective bargaining remedy, sexual harassment complainants typically are free to bring civil actions against their employers, either with or without a previous grievance, so long as the action is based on legal standards—such as the public policy against

---

[72]*Id.* at 1100.

[72a]For a discussion of First Amendment issues, see Chapter 27, Asserted Defenses, Section VII.

[73]*Supra* note 71, 91 LA at 1101.

[74]72 LA 769 (1979)(Grether, Arb.).

[75]Steelworkers v. American Mfg. Co., 363 U.S. 564 (1960); Steelworkers v. Warrior & Gulf Navigation Co., 363 U.S. 574 (1960); Steelworkers v. Enterprise Wheel & Car Corp., 363 U.S. 593 (1960).

employment discrimination—that may be applied without any need to interpret the terms of the collective bargaining agreement.[76]

B. Claims by Alleged Harassers Subjected to Discipline

When union-represented employees are disciplined or discharged for sexual harassment, their right to challenge such company discipline generally is limited to the grievance and arbitration procedures of the collective bargaining agreement. Absent a specific basis in some established public policy,[77] most claims of bargaining-unit employees are preempted by federal labor law, which requires claimants to proceed exclusively through the grievance and arbitration procedure.[78]

---

[76]*See* Perugini v. Safeway Stores, 935 F.2d 1083 (9th Cir. 1991)(common-law claims of on-the-job harassment regarding plaintiff's pregnancy not preempted because claims did not require reference to collective bargaining agreement but rather depended on inquiry into conduct and motive of employer); Cook v. Lindsay Olive Growers, 911 F.2d 233 (9th Cir. 1990)(claim of religious discrimination premised on California public policy against religious discrimination not preempted); Garibaldi v. Lucky Food Stores, 726 F.2d 1367 (9th Cir. 1984)(employee's claim of wrongful discharge in retaliation for reporting shipment of adulterated milk to health officials not preempted even though employee had filed grievance processed through arbitration and arbitrator had found that employee had been discharged for just cause, since employee had a right to separate proceeding on the public policy wrongful discharge claim); Ackerman v. Western Elec. Co., 860 F.2d 1514 (9th Cir. 1988)(employee's California state handicap discrimination claim not preempted); Chmiel v. Beverly Wilshire Hotel Co., 873 F.2d 1283 (9th Cir. 1989)(age discrimination claim for wrongful termination under California state law not preempted); Wells v. General Motors, 881 F.2d 166 (5th Cir. 1989)(claim that individual promises were fraudulently made by employer to induce employees to opt for voluntary termination plan in midst of layoffs not preempted); Dougherty v. Parsec., Inc., 872 F.2d 766 (6th Cir. 1989)(claim for tortious interference with contractual relations not preempted); Smolarek v. Chrysler Corp., 879 F.2d 1326 (6th Cir. 1989)(claims for discharge in violation of public policy and discrimination not preempted), *cert. denied,* 110 S.Ct. 539 (1989); Nelson v. Central Ill. Light Co., 878 F.2d 198 (7th Cir. 1989)(state-law retaliatory discharge claim for filing workers' compensation claim not preempted); Rintone v. Southern Bell Tel. & Tel. Co., 865 F.2d 1220 (11th Cir. 1989)(state-law wrongful discharge claim of retaliatory discharge for filing workers' compensation claim not preempted); Merchant v. American S.S. Co., 860 F.2d 204 (6th Cir. 1988)(state-law claim of retaliatory discharge for filing a Jones Act personal injury case not preempted); Wolfe v. Central Mine Equip. Co., 850 F.2d 469 (8th Cir. 1988)(state-law wrongful discharge claim of retaliatory discharge for filing workers' compensation claim not preempted); Jackson v. Southern Cal. Gas Co., 881 F.2d 638 (9th Cir. 1989)(preemption of contractual and emotional distress claims upheld; claims for employment discrimination, wrongful discharge in violation of public policy and defamation not preempted); Romero v. Mason & Hanger-Silas Mason Co., 55 EPD ¶40,362 (D.N.M. 1990)(sexual harassment plaintiff permitted to pursue state tort claims even though conduct complained of was also protected against by collective bargaining agreement). *But see* Noyes v. Ford Motor Co., 47 FEP Cases 1843 (E.D. Mich. 1988)(handicap harassment claim preempted where clause in collective bargaining agreement forbade handicap discrimination and claim depended on analysis of agreement).

[77]*See* note 75 *supra.*

[78]*Preempted Claims:* Terwilliger v. Greyhound Lines, 882 F.2d 1033 (6th Cir. 1989)(employee's claim that employer committed fraud by failing to rehire him expresses right set forth in labor contract and is preempted); Douglas v. American Information Technologies Corp., 877 F.2d 565 (7th Cir. 1989)(state-law claim for intentional infliction of emotional distress preempted); Vacca v. Viacom Broadcasting of Mo., 875 F.2d 1337 (8th Cir. 1989)(breach-of-contract action based on pre-employment promises preempted); De Lapp v. Continental Can Co., 868 F.2d 1073 (9th Cir. 1989)(claim for breach of oral contract preempted); Shane v. Greyhound Lines, Inc., 868 F.2d 1057 (9th Cir. 1989)(claims for wrongful withholding of wages, defamation, intentional infliction of emotional distress and wrongful death preempted); Jackson v. Liquid Carbonic Corp., 863 F.2d 111 (1st Cir. 1988)(state-law claim that employer's drug testing violated employee's privacy was preempted), *cert. denied,* 109 S.Ct. 3158; Knafel v. Pepsi Cola Bottlers of Akron, 850 F.2d 1155 (6th Cir. 1988)(state-law claims of physical injury and intentional infliction of emotional distress preempted); Evans v. Einhorn, 855 F.2d 1245 (7th Cir. 1988)(state-law claim based on state wage payment statute preempted); Hanks v. General Motors Corp., 859 F.2d 67 (8th Cir. 1988)(employee's state-law claim of being wrongfully discharged for refusing to work with foreman who molested her daughter preempted); Hyles v. Mensing, 849 F.2d 1213 (9th Cir. 1988)(employee's state-law claims of emotional distress and defamation preempted); Laws v. Calmat, 852 F.2d 430 (9th Cir. 1988)(employee's claim that employer's drug testing program violated state constitutional right to privacy preempted); Newberry v. Pacific Racing Ass'n, 854 F.2d 1142 (9th Cir. 1988)(employee's state-law claims for breach of implied covenant of good faith and fair dealing and intentional infliction of emotional distress preempted); Utility Workers of Am. v. Southern Cal. Edison Co., 852 F.2d 1083 (9th Cir. 1988)(employee's claim that employer's drug-testing program violated a state constitutional right to privacy preempted).

C. Judicial Review of Arbitration Awards

The standards for judicial review of an arbitration award are extremely narrow and limited.[79] Courts are not free to substitute their interpretation of the labor agreement for that of an arbitrator. So long as the award draws its essence from the agreement between the parties, the court has no authority to review the merits of the award. Only if the decision does not draw its essence from the labor contract may the court vacate the award on the basis that the arbitrator exceeded his or her authority, and the proof that the arbitrator exceeded that authority must be very clear, because the court will assume that the arbitrator acted within the prescribed authority. This rule was recently reaffirmed by the Supreme Court in *Paperworkers v. Misco.*[80]

A narrow exception to this rule applies if the arbitration award is contrary to public policy. The Supreme Court discussed this exception to the general rule of finality in *W.R. Grace & Co. v. Rubber Workers,*[81] where the Court stated:

> As with any contract . . . , a court may not enforce a collective bargaining agreement that is contrary to public policy. [The arbitrator's] view of his own jurisdiction precluded his consideration of this question, and, in any event, the question of public policy is ultimately one for resolution by the courts. . . . Kaden, *Judges and Arbitrators: Observations on the Scope of Judicial Review,* 80 Colum. L. Rev. 267, 287 (1980). If the contract as interpreted by [the arbitrator] violates some explicit public policy, we are obliged to refrain from enforcing it. Such a public policy, however, must be well defined and dominant, and is to be ascertained "by reference to the laws and legal precedents and not from general considerations of supposed public interest."[82]

Federal circuit courts have differed in invoking public policy to vacate an arbitration award. Some circuits hold that an arbitration award must require

---

[79]Steelworkers v. Enterprise Wheel & Car Corp., 363 U.S. 593, 46 LRRM 2423 (1960).

[80]The *Misco* Court stated:

Collective-bargaining agreements commonly provide grievance procedures to settle disputes between union and employer with respect to the interpretation and application of the agreement and require binding arbitration for unsettled grievances. In such cases, and this is such a case, the Court made clear almost 30 years ago that the courts play only a limited role when asked to review the decision of an arbitrator. The courts are not authorized to reconsider the merits of an award even though the parties may allege that the award rests on errors of fact or on misinterpretation of the contract. "The refusal of courts to review the merits of an arbitration award is the proper approach to arbitration under collective bargaining agreements. The federal policy of settling labor disputes by arbitration would be undermined if courts had the final say on the merits of the awards." *Steelworkers v. Enterprise Wheel & Car Corp.,* 363 U.S. 593, 596, 46 LRRM 2423 (1960). As long as the arbitrator's award "draws its essence from the collective bargaining agreement," and is not merely "his own brand of industrial justice," the award is legitimate. *Id.* at 597.

108 S.Ct. 364, 126 LRRM 3113, 3116 (1987).

[81]461 U.S. 757, 113 LRRM 2641 (1983).

[82]461 U.S. 766, 113 LRRM 2645 (citations omitted). In *Paperworkers v. Misco, supra* note 80, the Supreme Court again declared the public policy basis for vacating an arbitration award to be extremely narrow:

Two points follow from our decision in *W.R. Grace.* First, a court may refuse to enforce a collective-bargaining agreement when the specific terms contained in that agreement violate public policy. Second, it is apparent that our decision in that case does not otherwise sanction a broad judicial power to set aside arbitration awards as against public policy. Although we discussed the effect of that award on two broad areas of public policy, our decision turned on our examination of whether the award created any explicit conflict with other "laws and legal precedents" rather than an assessment of "general considerations of supposed public interests." At the very least, an alleged public policy must be properly framed under the approach set out in *W.R. Grace,* and the violation of such a policy must be clearly shown if an award is not to be enforced.

108 S.Ct. 364, 126 LRRM at 3119 (citation omitted).

a party to violate the law before the award will be vacated.[83] Other circuits have held that public policy can justify vacating an arbitration award even though no party is subjected to a violation of law by the terms of the award.[84]

Not widely addressed to date has been the matter of workplace sexual harassment as a public policy issue to be considered by courts in lawsuits seeking to vacate an arbitration award. In *Newsday v. Long Island Typographical Union*,[85] the Second Circuit vacated an arbitration award reinstating an employee who had been terminated for sexual harassment in the workplace. The grievant had a long history of sexually harassing his female co-workers. Prior to the discharge, the grievant had been suspended for sexual harassment, and this suspension had been sustained by an arbitrator who had noted that any further sexual harassment should be grounds for immediate discharge. The grievant did not discontinue his offensive conduct. After several reported incidents of sexual harassment, the employer discharged the grievant. When he grieved his discharge, the arbitrator, although noting that the grievant had repeatedly engaged in extremely offensive sexual harassment subsequent to his suspension, determined that the grievant had not been discharged for just cause and that progressive discipline should have been used. The arbitrator ordered the grievant reinstated without back pay.

The arbitrator's award was vacated by a federal district court on the basis that the award contravened the public policy against sexual harassment in the workplace in that the award would require the employer to reinstate a chronic sexual harasser. Affirming this decision, Judge J. Edward Lumbard stated:

> [The] award of reinstatement completely disregarded the public policy against sexual harassment in the workplace. The arbitrator has also disregarded [the earlier arbitration] ruling that any further acts of harassment by [the employee] would be grounds for discharge. Instead, [the arbitrator's] award condones [the grievant's] latest misconduct; it tends to perpetuate a hostile, intimidating and offensive work environment. [The grievant] has ignored repeated warnings. Above all, the award prevents [the employer] from carrying out its legal duty to eliminate sexual harassment in the work place.[86]

The Tenth Circuit was more deferential to the arbitral process in *Communications Workers of America v. Southeastern Electric Cooperative*,[87] in which Judge John P. Moore declined to vacate an arbitration award that reinstated an employee who had sexually assaulted a female customer in her home. The arbitrator determined that, although the assault occurred, the penalty of discharge was too severe in light of the harasser's nineteen years of service and his good work record. The arbitrator determined that the discharge should be converted to a one-month suspension without pay. The arbitrator considered that the employer, in a case involving a sexual offense by another employee,

---

[83]*E.g.,* Postal Workers v. Postal Serv., 789 F.2d 1, 122 LRRM 2094 (D.C. Cir. 1986); Northwest Air Lines v. Airline Pilots Ass'n Int'l, 808 F.2d 76, 124 LRRM 2300 (D.C. Cir. 1987); Bevles Co. v. Teamsters Local 986, 791 F.2d 1391, 122 LRRM 2666 (9th Cir. 1986); Stead Motors v. Machinists Lodge 1173, 886 F.2d 1200, 132 LRRM 2689 (9th Cir. 1989).

[84]*E.g.,* Delta Airlines v. Airline Pilots Ass'n Int'l, 861 F.2d 665, 130 LRRM 2014 (11th Cir. 1988); Iowa Elec. Light & Power Co. v. Teamsters Local 204, 834 F.2d 1424, 127 LRRM 2049 (8th Cir. 1987); Postal Service v. American Workers Union, 736 F.2d 822, 116 LRRM 2870 (1st Cir. 1984).

[85]915 F.2d 840, 135 LRRM 2659 (2d Cir. 1990), *cert. denied,* 111 S.Ct. 1314, 59 U.S.L.W. 3636 (1991)(Lumbard, Kearse & Mines, JJ.).

[86]*Id.* at 845, 135 LRRM at 2663.

[87]882 F.2d 467, 132 LRRM 2381 (10th Cir. 1989)(Moore, Anderson & Brorby, JJ.).

had warned the employee that if such conduct recurred the employee would be discharged.

When the employer sought to vacate the award as contrary to public policy, the federal district court refused to vacate the award and entered another enforcing the decision. Affirming, the Tenth Circuit stated:

> We are satisfied ... the arbitrator fully considered the evidence before him at the time of the discharge. Our reading of the record and hearing transcript reveals the arbitrator entertained substantially conflicting evidence and tangential considerations while observing the demeanor of the witnesses and evaluating their credibility. Albeit preventing the sexual assault and abuse of women is of paramount importance, we believe the just cause determination fully incorporated this important concern under all of the circumstances. Thus, we cannot substitute our understanding of the workplace and judgment of [the grievant's] conduct to conclude the conduct was an "employment decision" in which the complained of acts were "integral to the performance of his employment duties." *Delta Air Lines,* 861 F.2d at 665. The arbitrator recognized that this was a one-time offense and specifically noted Mr. Gray's "penitent and apologetic attitude" in response to his act. Based on the Agreement, the arbitrator premised his award on the principle that "[p]enalties are designed to correct if possible." The arbitrator concluded, "This leaves us with a long-time employee—about 19 years—with a good to excellent work record and no prior conduct involving a sexual offense, and of course ... no prior warnings of discharge if such an offense were repeated. I believe that correct discipline should be applied."[88]

IX. UNION OBLIGATIONS

A. Duty of Fair Representation

Relatively few sexual harassment complainants pursue their claims through collective bargaining agreement grievance and arbitration procedures. Nonetheless, nothing precludes a complainant from simultaneously pursuing both a grievance and a charge of discrimination filed under Title VII. Complainants have every right to pursue claims of sexual harassment through the grievance procedure, and the union is bound by the duty of fair representation toward all the employees it represents.[89]

A union that breaches its duty to fairly represent a member of a collective bargaining unit may be liable for compensatory and punitive damages. Such a breach occurs when a union's conduct toward a member of the collective bargaining unit is arbitrary, discriminatory, or in bad faith. While the duty of fair representation does not require the union to pursue every meritorious grievance, a union may not arbitrarily ignore a meritorious grievance or process it in a perfunctory fashion.[90]

Under this standard, a union that fails to protect women employees from harassment while it does protect men employees from similar mistreatment could be violating its duty of fair representation by discriminating on the basis

---

[88]*Id.* at 469, 470, 132 LRRM at 2383.

[89]Vaca v. Sipes, 386 U.S. 171, 64 LRRM 2369 (1967). For a complete treatment of the subject, see C. MORRIS, THE DEVELOPING LABOR LAW (2d ed. BNA 1983), Chapter 28.

[90]Vaca v. Sipes, *supra* note 89, 386 U.S. at 190, 191, 195, 64 LRRM at 2376–78.

of gender.[91] A union might also breach its duty if it simply fails to combat sexual harassment generally in that this failure could be attacked both as arbitrary and as having an unjustified discriminatory impact on women employees, who are affected disproportionately by sexual harassment.

In *Seritis v. Hotel & Restaurant Employees*,[92] the court held that a union may also breach its duty of fair representation by the discriminatory operation of its hiring hall. The two plaintiffs in *Seritis* were waitresses who were assigned to jobs from the union hiring hall. An officer of the union made several sexual advances toward the plaintiffs. One of the plaintiffs was fired through union influence after she rejected certain job opportunities the union officer made available to her, such as a monthly salary for being a "live-in sexual playmate" for two men, providing sexual services for parties, and having sex with a dog in a stage show in Nevada. The union denied the other plaintiff access to waitress jobs after she declined the union officer's offers to work as a topless waitress on a bus, work as a prostitute at a convention, live with a lesbian, and have sex with a dog as part of a Las Vegas stage show.

In entering a judgment of $200,000 against the union and its officer for intentional infliction of emotional distress and breach of the duty of fair representation, the trial court concluded:

> A Union has both a statutory and contractual duty of fair representation of workers whose livelihood depends on the Union, and if it acts arbitrarily, discriminatorily or in bad faith in failing to represent a member-employee, its conduct is actionable. On the evidence presented the Court has concluded that defendant Local did breach its duty of fair representation of plaintiff Seritis in discriminatorily removing her from her job, and discriminated against both plaintiffs ... and exhibited bad faith in failing to accord them the benefit of the same job placement services given others similarly situated, solely by reason of their having spurned [the union official's] sexual advances.[93]

B. Title VII

Labor organizations, like employers, are forbidden by Title VII from discriminating on the basis of sex.[94] Normally, an employee who sues for harassment in the workplace names as defendants the employer and, sometimes, the individual employees personally responsible for the harassment. The union, too, can be implicated in sexual harassment in the workplace, especially where union officials are reluctant to take action that may require discipline of union members. The possibility that a union will not always share the interests of its individual members in contesting employment discrimination claims was noted by the Supreme Court in *Alexander v. Gardner-Denver*, in its explanation of why union-represented employees need not submit their Title VII claims to arbitration:

---

[91]*See, e.g.,* Perugini v. Safeway Stores, 935 F.2d 1083 (9th Cir. 1991)(employee denied light duty despite her pregnancy had triable claim against union for breach of duty of fair representation with allegation that union failed to represent her when it would have represented a temporarily disabled male).

[92]30 FEP Cases 423 (Cal. Super. Ct. 1980), *aff'd*, 167 Cal. App.3d 78, 213 Cal. Rptr. 588, 591, 37 FEP Cases 1501, 1503 (1985). In denying review of this case, the California Supreme Court ordered that it not be cited in any legal proceeding.

[93]30 FEP Cases at 424.

[94]Section 703(c), (d), 42 U.S.C. §2000e-2(c), (d).

A further concern is the union's exclusive control over the manner and extent to which an individual grievance is presented. . . . [H]armony of interest between the union and the individual employee cannot always be presumed, especially where a claim of racial discrimination is made. . . . In arbitration, as in the collective-bargaining process, the interests of the individual employee may be subordinated to the collective interests of all employees in the bargaining unit. . . . And a breach of the union's duty of fair representation may prove difficult to establish. In this respect, it is noteworthy that Congress thought it necessary to afford the protections of Title VII against unions as well as employers. See 42 U.S.C §2000e-2(c).[95]

Title VII liability for a union may result where (1) the union intentionally has failed to file a grievance concerning workplace harassment,[96] (2) the union has failed to impose discipline on union members who engaged in the harassment,[97] (3) union agents have engaged in the harassment,[98] or (4) the union has acquiesced in the harassment.[99] The union's duty is only enhanced when the collective bargaining agreement it has negotiated with the employer provides, as such agreements typically do, that the employer will not discriminate on the basis of sex.

Exemplifying many of these bases for liability, in a racial harassment case, was *Woods v. Graphic Communications,*[100] in which a black union member who had sued his employer and his union for a racially hostile environment pressed his suit against the union alone after settling his dispute with his employer. The complainant had been subjected to racial jokes, comments, and other forms of hostility by his co-workers, who included a union steward and a union committeeman. The union filed no grievance on the complainant's behalf despite his three requests. Nor did the union discipline any union member for racial harassment. The trial court, in a decision upheld on appeal, found that the union, aware of the racial harassment but intentionally failing to take any action concerning it, was liable for violating the state fair employment practices statute.[101]

---

[95]415 U.S. 36, 59 n.19, 7 FEP Cases 81, 89 (1974).

[96]Goodman v. Lukens Steel Co., 482 U.S. 656, 667 (1987)(union's deliberate failure to bring race-based claims was itself discrimination in violation of Title VII). Streeter v. Joint Industry Board of the Electrical Industry, 1991 U.S. Dist. LEXIS 8468 (S.D.N.Y.)(denying motion to dismiss sexual harassment claim against unions and electricians' apprenticeship program who allegedly failed to take action to stop sexually hostile environment suffered by electrician's apprentices on various construction work sites); *See also* Driscoll v. Carpenters Dist. Council, 579 A.2d 863, 53 FEP Cases 1297 (Pa. 1990)(NLRB is not exclusive forum for employment discrimination claims against a union; plaintiffs could pursue claims of sexual discrimination against union under fair employment practices statutes).

[97]Woods v. Graphic Communications, 925 F.2d 1195, 1198, 1202, 55 FEP Cases 242 (9th Cir. 1991)(citing union failure to discipline members for harassment in upholding finding that union had effectively ratified harassment).

[98]*Id.* at 1202 (union liable for racial harassment by its steward and committeeman, where union was aware of harassment and failed to act, thereby ratifying it).

[99]Bonilla v. Oakland Scavenger Co., 697 F.2d 1297, 1304 (9th Cir. 1982)(union has affirmative duty to oppose employment discrimination against its members and if instead it acquiesces in employer's discriminatory practices then the union, too, is liable).

[100]925 F.2d 1195, 55 FEP Cases 242 (9th Cir. 1991)(Wright, Beezer, Trott, JJ.).

[101]The plaintiff's Title VII claim was untimely. The union was also liable for breach of the duty of fair representation, violation of 42 U.S.C. §1981, and the tort of outrage under Washington law.

Part IV

PREVENTIVE, INVESTIGATIVE, AND REMEDIAL ACTION

CHAPTER 18

TAKING PREVENTIVE ACTION

I. OVERVIEW

The best way to minimize the incidence and impact of sexual harassment is to have a positive program designed to discourage harassment and to take prompt corrective action when any incident occurs. The EEOC Guidelines generally prescribe methods to prevent sexual harassment:

> An employer should take all steps necessary to prevent sexual harassment from occurring, such as affirmatively raising the subject, expressing strong disapproval, developing appropriate sanctions, informing employees of their right to raise and how to raise the issues of harassment under Title VII, and developing methods to sensitize all concerned.[1]

A well-designed sexual harassment program will have several components:

(A) A written policy directed specifically against sexual harassment that defines what unlawful harassment is and states that sexual harassment will not be tolerated;

(B) A complaint procedure calculated to encourage victims of harassment to come forward;

(C) Effective methods of communicating the policy to all employees;

(D) Training and education programs to sensitize supervisors and employees to sexual harassment concerns;

(E) A prompt and thorough investigation of every complaint;

(F) Prompt corrective action, including appropriate sanctions if it is determined that unlawful harassment has occurred; and

(G) An assessment of supervisory support of the company's sexual harassment program and regular auditing to assure that the program is understood and effectively implemented.[2]

---

[1]29 C.F.R. §1604.11(f), reproduced in Appendix 1. Section 1604.11 is part of the EEOC Guidelines on Discrimination Because of Sex, 29 C.F.R. §§1604.1–.11, issued in 1980. The EEOC Guidelines are nonbinding but "constitute a body of experience and informed judgments to which courts and litigants may properly resort for guidance." Meritor Sav. Bank v. Vinson, 477 U.S. 57, 65, 40 FEP Cases 1822, 1826 (1986)(citations omitted).

[2]*See generally* Meritor Sav. Bank v. Vinson, 477 U.S. 57, 40 FEP Cases 1822 (1986), reproduced in Chapter 1, Overview (inquiry concerning employer liability should focus on (1) whether employer had

Strong preventive[3] and remedial[4] action by an employer will not only assist in defending a claim of unlawful harassment and avoid or minimize the employer's liability, it may diminish the incidence of harassment. The greater the extent to which employees are aware of their rights and are confident of potential disciplinary measures for transgressors, the less likely it is that sexual harassment will occur.

II. ELEMENTS OF AN EFFECTIVE SEXUAL HARASSMENT POLICY

A. Develop a Written Policy

Employers must "take all steps necessary to prevent sexual harassment."[5] The importance of adopting, publicizing, and enforcing a written sexual harassment policy, separate from general antidiscrimination policies, was emphasized by the Supreme Court in *Meritor Savings Bank v. Vinson,* where Justice William Rehnquist observed that the defendant's "general nondiscrimination policy did not address sexual harassment in particular, and thus did not alert employees to their employer's interest in correcting that form of discrimination" and that the employer's defense might have been "substantially stronger if its procedures were better calculated to encourage victims of harassment to come forward."[6]

There are certain minimum elements to include in a sexual harassment policy.[7] First, the policy language should make clear that sexual harassment

---

established and specific policy prohibiting sexual harassment in the workplace, (2) whether the policy was communicated to employees, (3) whether and when employer learned of the alleged harassment, and (4) if employer knew of the conduct, whether employer's response was adequate); Spencer v. General Elec. Co., 703 F. Supp. 466, 471 n.13, 51 FEP Cases 1709, 1712 (E.D. Va. 1989)(employer policy adequate where it encompassed all employees, provided specific complaint procedure that bypassed employees' immediate supervisors if necessary, provided for direct communications with all employees concerning sexual harassment matters and was provided to all employees), *aff'd,* 894 F.2d 651, 51 FEP Cases 1725 (4th Cir. 1990). Some employers, as part of injunctive relief, have been ordered to implement further aspects of an antiharassment policy, such as a procedure for "a formal evidentiary hearing" and notice to the complainant of the right to file a Title VII charge if the complainant is dissatisfied. *See, e.g.,* Arnold v. City of Seminole, 614 F. Supp. 853, 40 FEP Cases 1539, 1553 (E.D. Okla. 1985). For further discussion of injunctive relief in sexual harassment cases, see Chapter 28, Injunctive and Affirmative Relief.

[3]Bell v. St. Regis Paper Co., 425 F. Supp. 1126, 16 FEP Cases 1429 (N.D. Ohio 1976)(employer repeatedly published its harassment policies to all employees and held meetings to remind employees of responsibility to avoid harassment; held that employer did everything it reasonably could be expected to have done to prevent harassment). For further discussion of the importance of a complaint procedure, see Chapter 19, Responding to Internal Complaints.

[4]*See* Swentek v. USAir, 830 F.2d 552, 44 FEP Cases 1808 (4th Cir. 1987)(airline responded to flight attendant's complaint of harassment by pilot by issuing written reprimand); Dornhecker v. Malibu Grand Prix Corp., 828 F.2d 307, 44 FEP Cases 1604 (5th Cir. 1987)(employer assured employee less than 12 hours after she complained that she would not have to work with co-worker after current project ended); Barrett v. Omaha Nat'l Bank, 726 F.2d 424, 35 FEP Cases 593 (8th Cir. 1984)(bank conducted adequate investigation of complaint when bank officials interviewed complaining employee, alleged harasser and potential witnesses).

[5]29 C.F.R. §1604.11(f), *supra* note 1. A sample policy appears in Appendix 6. For an example of an extraordinarily detailed policy and procedure, said to be that of the Massachusetts Port Authority, see *Policy Against Sexual Harassment,* 7 CORP. COUNS. Q. 105 (1991). For another comprehensive policy, imposed after a finding of employer liability for hostile environment harassment, see Appendix 7 (reproducing order entered in Robinson v. Jacksonville Shipyards, 760 F. Supp. 1486, 1541–46 (M.D. Fla. 1991)). See also Ingulli, *Sexual Harassment in Education,* 18 RUTGERS L.J. 281 (1987)(with appendices containing sexual harassment policies from various universities).

[6]*Supra* note 2, 477 U.S. at 72–73, 40 FEP Cases at 1829.

[7]*See, e.g.,* California Dep't of Fair Employment & Hous. v. Madera County, FEHC Dec. 90-3 at 39

will not be tolerated. The policy should state that offenders will be subject to discipline up to and including discharge.[8] Second, because employees and supervisors may be confused about what constitutes sexual harassment, the policy should define it and provide examples of sexually harassing conduct, to ensure that employees do not misinterpret offensive sexual conduct as harmless teasing or practical joking.[9] Third, the policy statement should require that supervisors and employees promptly report any sexually harassing conduct that they experience or witness, while assuring all employees that no one will be retaliated against for any honest report. Prompt reporting may allow the company to eliminate the unlawful harassment at an early stage and reduce or eliminate any resulting harm.

B. Implement an Effective Complaint Procedure

Every sexual harassment program should include an internal grievance procedure. Employees who believe they have been the victims of sexual harassment must be able to report their complaints to management and have them investigated.[10]

A well-designed internal grievance procedure may serve a number of useful purposes. First, if complainants perceive that they can receive fair redress within the company, they will allow complaints to be resolved internally and will be less likely to file charges of discrimination with outside agencies or through private attorneys. Dealing with complaints internally is less expensive than being involved in government investigative proceedings or litigation. Second, a well-developed complaint program should encourage earlier reporting and investigation of problems. As a result, the employer may be in a better position to take immediate action to cure the problem or remedy the harm to the complainant. Third, prompt resolution of complaints may limit the scope of potential damages. Finally, the employer will reduce economic costs of

---

(1990), where the Department required the employer to implement a formal, written policy that contained at least the following elements:

   a. A clear and comprehensive description of the kinds of conduct that constitute harassment because of sex, race, ancestry, or any other protected basis, and a forceful statement that such conduct is prohibited by the employer's rules and by state and federal law;

   b. A clear statement of any employee's right to complain about harassment due to sex or any other protected basis without fear of retaliation, and a procedure for making such complaints;

   c. A procedure for promptly, fully, and objectively investigating complaints of harassment due to sex or other protected basis and determining their merit; and

   d. A statement that forceful and appropriate measures will be taken to punish offenders and to redress the harm done to their victims, and guidelines and procedures for doing so.

   [8]29 C.F.R. §1604.11(f), *supra* note 1. *See* Meritor Sav. Bank v. Vinson, *supra* note 2, 477 U.S. at 72–73, 40 FEP Cases at 1829; Spencer v. General Elec. Co., *supra* note 2, 703 F. Supp. at 471, 51 FEP Cases at 1712. Policy language of this sort may well create contractual liability for the employer, in that the policy amounts to a promise that the employer will take reasonable steps to promptly remedy sexual harassment. In rare cases where for some reason a statutory discrimination claim is unavailable, this contractual liability could be significant. See Chapter 15, The Common Law, Section IX.

   [9]*See generally* Steele v. Offshore Shipbldg., 867 F.2d 1311, 49 FEP Cases 522 (11th Cir. 1989)(affirming finding of hostile environment where supervisor made suggestive remarks to two female subordinates, although complainants themselves had participated in sexually oriented joking with the supervisor and had presented him with sexually explicit gift).

   [10]29 C.F.R. §1604.11(f), *supra* note 1 (employer should take all steps necessary to prevent sexual harassment from occurring, such as affirmatively raising the subject, expressing strong disapproval, developing appropriate sanctions, informing employees of their right to raise and how to raise issue of harassment, and developing methods to sensitize all concerned).

sexual harassment in the form of diminished employee morale, reduced productivity, increased absenteeism, and higher turnover rates.

1. Designating Where to File the Complaint

The complaint procedure should designate a specific department or position to handle sexual harassment complaints.[11] The designated persons should be trained to follow an effective investigative procedure and should be authorized by top management to make the necessary inquiries. Whenever practical, the designated recipient of complaints should be the same department or person normally charged with investigating personnel-related matters, to help ensure that sexual harassment complaints are treated like other allegations of misconduct.

The complaint procedure should allow complainants to file complaints with at least one easily accessible person who is outside the chain of command.[12] A policy that gives the supervisor the exclusive responsibility for receiving reports and correcting the harassment will "necessarily discourage reporting and diminish an employee's faith in the system" when the supervisor is the alleged harasser.[12a] Similar problems may befall a policy that requires complaints to go directly to upper management.[13] The employer should also consider, where the sexual harassment complainant is embarrassed by the unwelcome incident, whether the employer has available a qualified investigator who is of the same sex as the complainant.

2. Assuring Against Retaliation

The written complaint procedure should include a clause informing employees that they have a right to complain without fear of retaliation. The company must ensure that complainants are not treated as "troublemakers." Otherwise, it will be subject to claims of retaliation, and other employees may be discouraged from using the complaint procedure in the future. In *Shrout v. Black Clawson Co.*,[14] Judge S. Arthur Spiegel admitted expert testimony that a harassed woman could reasonably fail to use an open door policy, where the policy did not specifically address sexual harassment and did not assure complainants that no retaliation would occur.

---

[11]*Id.*

[12]For example, the designated person could be in the company's human resources organization. Even here an optional alternative reporting structure would be desirable, for fox-in-the-chicken-coop cases are surprisingly common. *See, e.g.,* Brooms v. Regal Tube Co., 881 F.2d 412, 50 FEP Cases 1499 (7th Cir. 1989)(white supervisor harassing black subordinate with sexual and racial comments and pornographic pictures of interracial sodomy and bestiality was company's human resources manager); Barnes v. Costle, 561 F.2d 983, 15 FEP Cases 345 (D.C. Cir. 1977), reproduced in Chapter 1, Overview (harasser was director of employer's EEO division); Kouri v. Liberian Servs., 55 FEP Cases 124 (E.D. Va. 1991)(complainant was secretary romanced by her boss, the Director of Personnel); Delgado v. Lehman, 665 F. Supp. 460, 462, 43 FEP Cases 593 (E.D. Va. 1987)(complainant, a naval EEO specialist, was harassed by the head of the naval EEO office); Stewart v. Thomas, 538 F. Supp. 891 (D.D.C. 1982)(EEOC litigation department).

[12a]Yates v. Avco Corp., 819 F.2d 630, 635, 43 FEP Cases 1595, 1599 (6th Cir. 1987); Meritor Sav. Bank v. Vinson, *supra* note 2, 477 U.S. at 73, 40 FEP Cases at 1829.

[13]*See, e.g.,* Shrout v. Black Clawson Co., 689 F. Supp. 774, 777, 46 FEP Cases 1339, 1341–42 (S.D. Ohio 1988) (company's "open door policy" too broadly worded and "intimidating for lower-echelon women who were harassed by their supervisors . . . because it required them to complain directly to the (male) president").

[14]*Supra* note 13.

C. Communicate the Policy to All Employees

The sexual harassment policy should be made known to each employee,[15] either independently or with the distribution of other employee materials, such as an employee handbook.[15a] Many employers collect written acknowledgments from employees that they have received a copy of the employer's policies, including the policy against sexual harassment, as proof that the employer's policies have in fact been disseminated, read, and understood. The written policy is often supplemented by personal meetings and further written material.

D. Sensitize Concerned Persons

Many harassers do not believe that they are sexually harassing others. Some supervisors do not know what kind of conduct to look for or what to do when sexually oriented conduct occurs in their organization.[16] Training programs can enhance employees' understanding of how to identify and deal with sexual harassment.

Training programs are also an effective means of demonstrating the company's commitment to eradicating sexual harassment. These programs inform supervisors in detailed terms of the kinds of conduct that may be viewed as sexual harassment. Because the language of the EEOC Guidelines is rather vague in this respect,[17] it is appropriate to make clear that sexual harassment may include such actions as lewd or profane speech; sexually oriented verbal kidding, teasing, or jokes; subtle pressure for sexual activity; physical contact such as patting, pinching, or brushing against another's body; or the display of sexually suggestive objects, pictures, statements, or graffiti.

Training programs may be enhanced through the use of discussion groups involving male and female workers. Role-playing and dramatizations of sexual harassment situations are often more effective than simple lectures in sensitizing employees and supervisors to the nature of sexual harassment. Films on this subject are available for rental or purchase.

The training should impress upon supervisors and employees the economic consequences of sexual harassment—adverse effects on productivity, corporate reputation, and job turnover—in addition to the investigation and litigation costs that episodes of sexual harassment may create. The training

---

[15]29 C.F.R. §1604.11(f), *supra* note 1. *See* Shrout v. Black Clawson Co., 689 F. Supp. 774, 46 FEP Cases 1339 (S.D. Ohio 1988)(employer's protestation that it had policy against sexual relationships between male managers and female subordinates unavailing when policy was not communicated to all managers).

[15a]Posting the sexual harassment policy on a bulletin board can be a highly effective device. At least one court has criticized, however, any method of distribution that does not give a sexual harassment policy at least equal stature with other personnel policies. Robinson v. Jacksonville Shipyards, 760 F. Supp. 1486, 1510 (M.D. Fla. 1991)(faulting employer's posting of policy on bulletin boards because policy not also included in company rulebook).

[16]*E.g.*, Wirig v. Kinney Shoe Corp., 448 N.W.2d 526, 51 FEP Cases 885 (Minn. Ct. App. 1989)(lack of employer policy or managerial training led to inappropriate attempts by supervisor to remedy harassing situation by pushing harasser up against a wall and threatening to fire him if he continued harassment). For a later proceeding in the same case involving an unrelated issue (plaintiff's ability to maintain claim for battery concurrently with state statutory claim), see *Wirig v. Kinney Shoe Corp.*, 54 FEP Cases 352 (Minn. 1990).

[17]29 C.F.R. §1604.11(a), *supra* note 1.

might also address the social attitudes that underlie cases of sexual harassment.[18]

E. Investigate Thoroughly

The sexual harassment policy should ensure that the employer will promptly and thoroughly investigate complaints of sexual harassment.[19] Wherever possible, claims of sexual harassment should be reduced to writing and signed by the complainant. Often, the complainant may need, and should be offered, assistance in formulating the written complaint. The interviewer should make sure that the written complaint is complete and records the allegations fairly so that the complainant is fully satisfied. The complaint should embody all of the relevant details and perceptions of the complainant. Written complaints assist the employer by ensuring a thorough investigation. If litigation follows, it may be helpful to have preserved a record of precisely what was alleged in the original complaint.

F. Take Prompt Corrective Action Upon Investigation

The sexual harassment policy should call for prompt corrective action if harassment is found. In *Barrett v. Omaha National Bank,* the employer avoided liability when it immediately investigated claims and, within four days of the report of unlawful harassment, reprimanded the alleged harassers, informed them that their conduct would not be tolerated, and told one of them that he would be fired for any further misconduct.[20] Judge Myron H. Bright concluded for the Eighth Circuit panel that the company had taken appropriate remedial action to ensure the plaintiff a working environment free of future harassment.[21]

It is also important for employers to follow up on individual cases to ensure that the corrective action is having the desired effect. Where a finding of harassment has warranted disciplinary action, the employer's internal program should provide for advising the complainant of that action and of the right to report any further harassment.[22]

If the company finds insufficient evidence to conclude that sexual harassment has occurred, then all parties involved should be notified. In addition, the complainant and the alleged harasser should be counseled that even though the employer was unable to conclude whether sexual harassment occurred, any future allegations of sexual harassment should be promptly reported, and that unwelcome conduct, whether unlawful or not, is unacceptable behavior and will result in disciplinary action.

---

[18]For a discussion of the sexual and economic implications of sexual harassment, see Chapter 1, Overview.

[19]For a discussion of the investigation of sexual harassment complaints, see Chapter 19, Responding to Internal Complaints.

[20]726 F.2d 424, 35 FEP Cases 593 (8th Cir. 1984)(Lay, Bright & Hanson, JJ.).

[21]For a more detailed discussion of taking remedial action, see Chapter 19, Responding to Internal Complaints. See also cases cited in note 4 *supra.*

[22]*See, e.g.,* California Dep't of Fair Employment & Hous. v. Madera County, FEHC Dec. 90-3 at 25–26 (1990)(finding employer liability for co-worker harassment where no one informed complainant of corrective action taken or assured her that further discipline would occur if harassment continued or otherwise kept "her informed as events progressed").

G. Assess Commitment to and Effectiveness of Program

Supervisory commitment to eradicating sexual harassment in the workplace is an essential element of a successful plan to combat harassment. Supervisors should know that their work performance is evaluated, in part, on their enforcement of the employer's sexual harassment policy and program. Factors that may be considered include (1) demonstrated commitment to the employer's equal employment opportunity and anti-sexual-harassment objectives; (2) demonstrated respect for the differing sexual attitudes of others, and avoiding the harassment of others on sexual grounds; and (3) actions taken to prevent harassment of employees by supervisors, co-workers, and nonemployees.

Employee surveys or workplace audits can measure the workplace atmosphere and create a more positive environment. Through surveys or interviews, the employer can measure the extent to which employees understand the sexual harassment policies and procedures and the nature of sexually harassing conduct, and learn if employees are aware of any sexual harassment within the company. Thus, the employer can evaluate its overall sexual harassment compliance and identify specific behaviors requiring immediate correction. The results may then be used for training programs to clarify any misunderstandings concerning the definition of sexual harassment and the employer's policies and procedures on the subject.

III. Reviewing Related Policies

A. Policies Involving Social Intercourse

Title VII does not outlaw all sexual relationships in the workplace or prohibit all types of sexual favoritism.[23] Title VII does forbid *unwelcome* sexual conduct that is made a condition of obtaining or retaining a job benefit, or that is so severe or pervasive as to render the work environment hostile.[24]

Nonetheless, consensual sexual relationships between supervisors and their subordinates raise concerns for employers. These relationships raise productivity concerns when they demoralize other employees in the work group and undermine efficiency. They raise legal concerns with respect to possible claims of favoritism by disadvantaged co-workers[25] and claims of sexual harassment by the subordinate, should the romance end.[26]

---

[23]EEOC Policy Guidance on Employer Liability for Sexual Favoritism, Fair Empl. Prac. Man. (BNA) at 405:6817 (Jan. 12, 1990), reproduced in Appendix 2, and EEOC Guidelines, 29 C.F.R. §1604.11(g), *supra* note 1. *See also* Chapter 5, Claims by Third Parties.

[24]29 C.F.R. §1604.11(a), *supra* note 1.

[25]*Compare* DeCintio v. Westchester County Medical Ctr., 807 F.2d 304, 42 FEP Cases 921, reproduced in Chapter 5, Claims by Third Parties (male respiratory therapists cannot pursue Title VII claim based on promotion of woman employee who had voluntary, romantic relationship with supervisor)(2d Cir. 1986), *cert. denied,* 484 U.S. 825 (1987) *and* Miller v. Aluminum Co. of Am., 679 F. Supp. 495, 45 FEP Cases 1775 (W.D. Pa. 1988), *aff'd,* 856 F.2d 184 (3d Cir. 1988)(where males treated no differently than female plaintiff, employer not liable for more favorable treatment of co-workers engaged in sexual relationship with supervisor) *with* King v. Palmer, 778 F.2d 878, 35 FEP Cases 1302 (D.C. Cir. 1985)(nurse, passed over for promotion because doctor promoted second nurse with whom he had special relationship, assumed by court to have cause of action). *See also* Note, *The Dehumanizing Puzzle of Sexual Harassment: A Survey of the Law Concerning Harassment of Women in the Workplace,* 24 Washburn L.J. 574, 593–94, 613 (1985)(suggesting ban on social fraternization to forestall claims of preferential treatment). For a discussion of claims alleging sexual favoritism, see Chapter 5, Claims by Third Parties.

[26]*See generally* Huebschen v. Wisconsin Dep't of Health & Social Servs., 716 F.2d 1167, 32 FEP Cases

Many employers attempt to protect themselves by simply banning social relationships between supervisors and employees.[27] Several reasons are advanced for imposing such a ban. Promulgation of an antifraternization policy emphasizes the employer's intent to enforce its sexual harassment policy,[28] and reduces the potential liability an employer assumes when it gives a supervisor the discretion to decide whether to make social invitations to a subordinate, welcome or not. A well-publicized antifraternization policy might encourage earlier reporting of potentially harassing situations by subordinate employees receiving unwelcome invitations.

With an antifraternization policy in place, an employer need not inquire deeply into the nature of ongoing relationships between supervisors and subordinates. As if to illustrate the difficulty of such an inquiry, one court has held that social invitations and flirting, even if "uncomfortable," are not sexual harassment,[29] while another court has found that a single invitation to dinner is enough to establish a Title VII violation.[30] A classic example of the risk an employer runs in tolerating apparently consensual romances between supervisors and subordinates appeared in *Meritor,* where the plaintiff had voluntary but allegedly unwelcome sexual intercourse with her boss forty to fifty times,[31] and where the Supreme Court held that her acquiescence would not necessarily defeat her sexual harassment claim.[32] Thus, even consensual sexual relationships can lead to claims of sexual harassment whenever an employee decides to end an affair and the supervisor either continues attentions that no longer are "welcome"[33] or makes an employment decision adverse to the subordinate.[34]

Antifraternization rules may also prevent sex discrimination and hostile environment claims by third-party employees not involved in the intracompany sexual relationship who believe that the employee who submits to sexual conduct with the supervisor receives more favorable treatment.[35]

1582 (7th Cir. 1983)(male subordinate alleged that he was demoted because he discontinued sexual relationship with female supervisor).

[27]*E.g.,* Sears v. Ryder Truck Rental, 596 F. Supp. 1001, 41 FEP Cases 1347 (E.D. Mich. 1984)(female employee not constructively discharged when employer enforced policy against co-worker sexual relationships); Wilson v. Swing, 463 F. Supp. 555 (M.D.N.C. 1978)(plaintiff properly disciplined for having extramarital affair with another police officer); Ward v. Frito-Lay, 95 Wis.2d 372, 290 N.W.2d 536 (Wis. 1980)(romantic on-the-job conduct with fellow employee caused dissension in workplace; employee termination upheld). *See generally* Note, *supra* note 25, 24 WASHBURN L.J. at 613 (1985)(suggesting ban on social fraternization as means of minimizing potential employer liability). *But see* Briggs v. North Muskegon Police Dep't, 563 F. Supp. 585, 1 IER 195 (W.D. Mich. 1983)(dismissal of police officer for cohabiting with married woman not his wife violated constitutional rights of association and privacy, absent showing that living arrangements adversely affected performance of his duties), *aff'd,* 746 F.2d 1475 (6th Cir. 1984), *cert. denied,* 473 U.S. 989 (1985).

[28]*See generally* Hill & Behrens, *Love in the Office: A Guide for Dealing With Sexual Harassment Under Title VII,* 30 DE PAUL L. REV. 581, 616 (1981).

[29]*E.g.,* Scott v. Sears, Roebuck & Co., 605 F. Supp. 1047, 1056, 37 FEP Cases 878, 884 (N.D. Ill. 1985), *aff'd on other grounds,* 798 F.2d 210 (7th Cir. 1986).

[30]*E.g.,* Blessing v. County of Lancaster, 609 F. Supp. 485, 37 FEP Cases 1721 (E.D. Pa. 1985).

[31]Meritor Sav. Bank v. Vinson, 477 U.S. 57, 60, 40 FEP Cases 1822, 1824 (1986), reproduced in Chapter 1, Overview.

[32]*Id.* at 68, 40 FEP Cases at 1827. *See also* Shrout v. Black Clawson Co., 689 F. Supp. 774, 46 FEP Cases 1339 (S.D. Ohio 1988)(despite plaintiff's earlier voluntary sexual relationship with supervisor, later advances coerced and thus unwelcome); EEOC Dec. 84-1, 33 FEP Cases 1887 (1983)("acquiescence in sexual conduct at the workplace may not mean that the conduct is welcome to the individual").

[33]*See, e.g.,* Shrout v. Black Clawson Co., *supra* note 32.

[34]See Chapter 3, Quid Pro Quo Harassment.

[35]See authorities cited in note 25 *supra;* see generally Chapter 5, Claims by Third Parties.

Antifraternization rules raise special problems of their own. The past practices of an employer, or the nature of its work, may make such a policy untenable, as may legal or moral concerns about interfering with the private conduct of individuals.[36] Moreover, if an employer prohibits the relationships, they may still exist but be clandestine, so that the company lacks witnesses to the relationship's voluntariness. Nevertheless, companies still have strong reasons to consider a policy requiring supervisors and subordinate employees who become romantically involved to request the transfer of one of the parties so as to sever the supervisory relationship.[37]

B. "No-Spouse" Rules

A variation of an anti-nepotism policy, the "no-spouse" policy may be adopted to combat co-worker complaints of unfair favoritism based on spousal relationships. As long as policies against hiring or continuing the employment of employee spouses are equally applied to male and female employees, and do not have an adverse impact on women, they are lawful under Title VII.[38]

No-spouse policies have two basic formulations. Companies may ban the employment of married couples entirely, or require that married couples work in different departments or otherwise have no supervisory relationship with each other.

If one employee must change jobs, the selection of the spouse to be affected must be made without regard to gender. One method is to allow the employees to choose which one will resign or be transferred, and impose the employer's choice only if the couple fails to decide.[39] If the employer decides, it should do so on some nongender basis, such as seniority.[40]

---

[36]Employees have challenged antifraternization policies on privacy grounds. *Compare* Patton v. J.C. Penney Co., 301 Or. 117, 719 P.2d 854, 122 LRRM 2445 (1986)(upholding dismissal of employee who was fired for refusing to break off romance with female co-worker, rejecting any personal right of privacy that could be asserted against private employer) *with* Rulon-Miller v. IBM Corp., 162 Cal. App.3d 241, 208 Cal. Rptr. 524 (1984)(affirming $300,000 jury award for employee fired for dating employee of competitor in violation of employer's conflict-of-interest rules; rules as applied invaded plaintiff's privacy rights).

[37]A policy that uniformly requires that the transfer involve the lower-level or lower-paid employee, typically a woman, may constitute unlawful sex discrimination. Less subject to question, although also less practical, would be a policy that transfers the least senior employee, perhaps after first permitting the employees themselves to choose which of them will transfer.

[38]*See generally* Yuhas v. Libbey-Owens-Ford Co., 562 F.2d 496, 16 FEP Cases 891 (7th Cir. 1977)(business necessity justified no-spouse rules where purpose was to prevent situations that could undermine employee morale and efficiency), *cert. denied,* 435 U.S. 934 (1978); Harper v. Trans World Airlines, 525 F.2d 409, 11 FEP Cases 1074 (8th Cir. 1975)(company rule preventing husband and wife from working in same department not a violation of Title VII, even where in four out of five couples affected by the rule, couple selected the woman to be terminated); EEOC v. Rath Packing Co., 787 F.2d 318, 40 FEP Cases 580 (8th Cir.)(no-spouse rule subject to "compelling need" standard when work force is predominantly male), *cert. denied,* 479 U.S. 910 (1986); Thomas v. Metroflight, 814 F.2d 1506, 43 FEP Cases 703 (10th Cir. 1987)(evidence insufficient to establish that no-spouse rule had disparate impact on women); McCluskey v. Clark Oil & Ref. Corp., 147 Ill. App.3d 822, 498 N.E.2d 559, 1 IER 1422 (1986)(no discharge in violation of public policy because plaintiff married co-worker); Linebaugh v. Auto Leasing Co., 18 FEP Cases 752 (D.C. Ky. 1978)(employer's anti-nepotism rule violated Title VII where employer disqualified a woman under rule after exceptions were made for male applicants); Southwestern Community Action Council v. Community Servs. Admin., 462 F. Supp. 289 (S.D.W. Va. 1978)(no violation of Title VII by employer's policy of prohibiting employment of family members in positions in which family members had same supervisor); Kilgo v. Bowman Transp. Co., 576 F. Supp. 600, 40 FEP Cases 1412 (N.D. Ga. 1984)(defendant enjoined from enforcing anti-nepotism rule against female spouses of employees).

[39]*See* Thomas v. Metroflight, *supra* note 38; Harper v. Trans World Airlines, *supra* note 38; George v. Farmers Elec. Coop., 715 F.2d 175, 32 FEP Cases 1801 (5th Cir. 1983)(deciding which spouse to terminate based on sex-related stereotypes, such as who is the head of household, is discriminatory).

[40]*See* Harper v. Trans World Airlines, *supra* note 38.

Employers must take care to research the governing state law before implementing anti-nepotism policies. Many state statutes prohibit discrimination on the basis of marital status, and some of these laws are interpreted to ban anti-nepotism rules.[41] State laws on marital status discrimination also may bar, anomalously, the application of such policies to married couples, but not to unmarried couples living together.

C. Dress Codes

Concerns about sexual harassment may also influence an employer's dress code policy. Dress standards are generally not prohibited under Title VII. Employers can implement different standards for each sex, if the standards are not based on offensive or demeaning sex stereotypes.[42] Thus, employers can require men, but not women, to wear ties,[43] and prohibit women from wearing pant suits in the executive office.[44] However, where the appearance requirement is based on offensive or demeaning sex stereotypes or would cause an employee to "be subjected to sexual harassment on the job," a Title VII violation is likely to be found.[45] The Seventh Circuit has held that Title VII forbids a dress policy that requires uniforms for female employees but only appropriate business attire for male employees.[46]

---

[41]*Cf.* Miller v. C.A. Muer Corp., 420 Mich. 355, 362 N.W.2d 650, 43 FEP Cases 1195 (1984)(protected class covered by Michigan law did not include married persons who desire to work with spouses); Manhattan Pizza Hut v. New York State Human Rights Appeal Bd., 51 N.Y.2d 506, 415 N.E.2d 950 (1980)(New York restriction predicated not on marital status but identity or position of one spouse); Thomson v. Sanborn's Motor Express, 154 N.J. Super. 555, 382 A.2d 53, 30 FEP Cases 33 (1977)(employer's policy prohibiting employment of spouse in same department does not constitute discrimination because of marital status). *But see* Kraft, Inc. v. State of Minn., 284 N.W.2d 386, 30 FEP Cases 31 (1979)(anti-nepotism rule discriminates unfairly on basis of marital status).

[42]*See* Craft v. Metromedia, 766 F.2d 1205, 38 FEP Cases 404 (8th Cir. 1985)(television station permitted to apply differing appearance standards for men and women anchors), *cert. denied*, 475 U.S. 1058 (1986). *But see* note 44 *infra*.

[43]Fountain v. Safeway Stores, 555 F.2d 753, 15 FEP Cases 96 (9th Cir. 1977).

[44]Lanigan v. Bartlett & Co., 466 F. Supp. 1388, 19 FEP Cases 1039 (W.D. Mo. 1979)(employer may ban pant suits for women).

[45]EEOC v. Sage Realty Corp., 507 F. Supp. 599, 609, 24 FEP Cases 1521, 1529–30 (S.D.N.Y. 1981)(employer may not impose dress requirements on employees that could expose employees to unreasonable sexual harassment); Priest v. Rotary, 634 F. Supp. 571, 40 FEP Cases 208 (N.D. Cal. 1986)(plaintiff established prima facie violation of Title VII by showing that defendant had removed her from position as cocktail waitress because she refused to wear sexually suggestive clothes); Marentette v. Michigan Host, Inc., 506 F. Supp. 909, 24 FEP Cases 1665 (E.D. Mich. 1980)(sexually provocative dress required as condition of employment that subjects cocktail waitresses and restaurant employees to sexual harassment could violate Title VII); EEOC Dec. 81-17, 27 FEP Cases 1791 (1981)(requirement that employee wear revealing costume while entertaining for employer, which exposed her to sexual harassment, unreasonably interfered with her work and was sexual harassment). For further discussion of cases on dress code requirements prompting sexual harassment, see Chapter 8, Harassment by Nonemployees.

[46]Carroll v. Talman Fed. Sav. & Loan Ass'n, 604 F.2d 1028, 1032, 20 FEP Cases 764, 768 (7th Cir. 1979)("[e]mployees performing the same function are subjected on the basis of sex to two entirely separate dress codes—one including a variety of normal business attire and the other requiring a clearly identifiable uniform"), *cert. denied*, 445 U.S. 929 (1980); *see also* Tamimi v. Howard Johnson Co., 807 F.2d 1550, 42 FEP Cases 1289 (11th Cir. 1987)(Title VII violated by requiring pregnant woman to wear makeup).

Chapter 19

RESPONDING TO INTERNAL COMPLAINTS

I. Overview

The EEOC Guidelines indicate that an employer must take "prompt remedial action reasonably calculated" to end sexual harassment.[1] This action entails an investigation of sexual harassment complaints to determine their merits and to fashion appropriate remedies designed to end any sexual harassment.[2] However, an employer must be cautious in its response to a harassment claim, as the response itself may lead to a legal proceeding by the alleged harasser.[3]

An adequate investigation into a claim of sexual harassment can identify instances of harassment, guide the appropriate employment decisions regarding the harassment, avoid or minimize employer liability,[4] reduce damages for the complainant,[5] protect potential future victims of sexual harassment, and forestall injunctive relief.[6]

Conversely, an inadequate investigation may fail to verify a meritorious claim and subject the employer to liability for harassment claims that the employer should have known about,[7] increase the damages for a harassment victim,[8] encourage a court to order injunctive relief,[9] or fail to identify a false

---

[1]29 C.F.R. §1604.11(d) and (e), reproduced in Appendix 1. In 1980, after notice and comment, the EEOC issued its Guidelines on Discrimination Because of Sex, 29 C.F.R. §§1604.1–.11, one part of which, §1604.11, is on sexual harassment. The EEOC Guidelines are nonbinding but "constitute a body of experience and informed judgments to which courts and litigants may properly resort for guidance." Meritor Sav. Bank v. Vinson, 477 U.S. 57, 65, 40 FEP Cases 1822, 1826 (1986), reproduced in Chapter 1, Overview (citations omitted).

[2]*Supra* note 1, at §1604.11(f). For related discussions of the appropriate response to internal complaints, see Chapters 4, Hostile Environment Harassment; 6, Harassment by Supervisors; 7, Harassment by Co-Workers; 8, Harassment by Nonemployees; 18, Taking Preventive Action; and 20, The Agency Investigation.

[3]See Chapters 15, The Common Law; 17, Collective Bargaining Agreements and Union Obligations; and 24, The Alleged Harasser as Plaintiff.

[4]Prompt remedial action typically will avoid liability altogether in cases of co-worker harassment, see Chapter 7, Harassment by Co-Workers, and typically will minimize liability already incurred in cases of harassment by any agent of the employer, see Chapter 6, Harassment by Supervisors.

[5]*E.g.,* Spencer v. General Elec. Co., 894 F.2d 651, 655, 51 FEP Cases 1725, 1727 (4th Cir. 1990)(quick transfer of complainant supports finding of no tangible loss due to harassment and award of nominal damages of one dollar), *aff'g* 697 F. Supp. 204, 51 FEP Cases 1696 (E.D. Va. 1988).

[6]*Id.* at 660, 51 FEP Cases at 1732 (trial court properly rejected injunctive relief based on comprehensive anti-sexual harassment policy and fact that alleged harasser no longer worked for employer).

[7]For a discussion of constructive employer knowledge of sexual harassment, see Chapters 4, Hostile Environment Harassment, Section VIII., IX.C.1.b.; and 7, Harassment by Co-Workers, Section IV.B.

[8]For a discussion of monetary relief, see Chapters 15, The Common Law, and 29, Monetary Relief.

[9]For a discussion of injunctive relief in a sexual harassment case, see Chapter 28, Injunctive and Affirmative Relief.

charge of sexual harassment and subject the employer to liability for erroneous discipline of the alleged harasser.[9a]

II. CIRCUMSTANCES GIVING RISE TO THE DUTY TO INVESTIGATE AND TAKE INTERIM CORRECTIVE ACTION

A. Duty to Investigate

Once a sexual harassment complaint arises, an employer has an affirmative duty to investigate.[10] This duty may arise without regard to whether the complaint is made formally through a preestablished grievance procedure, or made informally outside of the established employer procedures.[11] Courts have held that the duty to investigate exists without regard to whether the complainant has agreed that the employer need not investigate certain reported incidents of harassment.[12]

Even if no actual complaint is made, an employer can have constructive knowledge of a sexually hostile environment upon a showing of "the pervasiveness of the harassment, which gives rise to the inference of knowledge or constructive knowledge."[13] The Fifth Circuit, in *Waltman v. International Paper Co.*,[14] held that the employer's failure to investigate the authorship of widespread sexual graffiti about one female employee raised a triable issue regarding the adequacy of the employer's remedial measures.[15] Thus, to reduce the risk of exposure, it would be prudent for an employer to investigate incidents of sexual harassment whether they are brought to its attention directly by the complainant or by other circumstances.

Scoffing at an employee's complaint obviously increases the risk of liability. Judge H. Lee Sarokin observed:

[9a]See Chapter 24, The Alleged Harasser as Plaintiff.

[10]Heelan v. Johns-Manville Corp., 451 F. Supp. 1382, 1390, 20 FEP Cases 251, 256 (D. Colo. 1978)("If employers have reason to believe that sexual demands are being made on employees they are obligated under Title VII to investigate the matter and correct any violations of the law"). *See* Munford v. Barnes & Co., 441 F. Supp. 459, 466, 17 FEP Cases 107, 112 (E.D. Mich. 1977)(failure to investigate sexual harassment complaint may constitute official ratification of harassment). While in some jurisdictions an employer's failure to investigate an employee's claim of sexual harassment "is not in and of itself a civil rights violation," Sumner v. Goodyear Tire & Rubber Co., 427 Mich. 505, 545, 398 N.W.2d 368, 385–86, 47 FEP Cases 621, 634 (1986)(to permit independent cause of action for failure to investigate "would allow a plaintiff to state a cause of action against an employer and indeed win damages even where there has been no harassment"), in other jurisdictions a failure to investigate may be an independent violation.

[11]Meritor Sav. Bank v. Vinson, *supra* note 1, 477 U.S. at 72, 40 FEP Cases at 1829 (existence of grievance procedure and policy against discrimination, coupled with complainant's failure to invoke that procedure, while relevant, not necessarily dispositive as to whether employer insulated from liability); Waltman v. International Paper Co., 875 F.2d 468, 481, 50 FEP Cases 179, 189 (5th Cir. 1989)(employee's failure to follow employer's sexual harassment grievance procedure did not alone support summary judgment for employer). See Chapter 27, Asserted Defenses, Section IV.

[12]*See* Waltman v. International Paper Co., *supra* note 11, 875 F.2d at 472, 50 FEP Cases at 182 (complainant's written agreement did not necessarily excuse employer's failure to investigate); Hollis v. Fleetguard, 668 F. Supp. 631, 637 n.14, 44 FEP Cases 1527, 1532 (M.D. Tenn. 1987)("in most cases, a supervisor has a duty to investigate reported instances of sexual harassment, with or without an employee's consent"), *aff'd*, 848 F.2d 191 (6th Cir. 1988).

[13]Henson v. City of Dundee, 682 F.2d 897, 905, 29 FEP Cases 787, 794 (11th Cir. 1982), reproduced in Chapter 4, Hostile Environment Harassment; Swentek v. USAir, 830 F.2d 552, 558, 44 FEP Cases 1808, 1813 (4th Cir. 1987). See Chapters 4, Hostile Environment Harassment, and 7, Harassment by Co-Workers.

[14]*Supra* note 11, 875 F.2d at 478, 50 FEP Cases at 187.

[15]*Id.* at 480, 50 FEP Cases at 189. The existence of graffiti on lockers, in bathrooms, on walls, and in elevators also created a factual issue of whether the employer had notice of the alleged harassment.

Serious consideration and treatment of complaints of sexual harassment by employers is essential to the eradication of this all too common and degrading practice .... To greet complaints of sexual harassment with humor or ridicule serves to exacerbate the injury rather than remedy it. Those in a supervisory role who react in this fashion contribute to the atmosphere which encourages such humiliation.[16]

Other employer conduct compounding rather than addressing sexual harassment has included telling the complainant not to let the offensive conduct bother her,[17] counseling the complainant to expect such behavior from male co-workers,[18] and advising the complainant that an investigation of the complaint would harm her.[19]

Thus, even if a claim of sexual harassment appears to be fabricated by the complainant as a preemptive device to forestall an anticipated disciplinary action, the wisest course is to investigate the claim seriously.[20]

Some form of responsive action (such as an instruction to the alleged harasser to steer clear of the complainant) is not necessarily a substitute for an investigation. In *Watts v. New York City Police Department*,[21] Judge Robert W. Sweet rejected the employer's motion for judgment on the pleadings, finding the alleged facts sufficient to conclude that the NYPD had failed to take adequate action. In *Watts* a police officer trainee alleged that she was subjected to several sexually abusive physical attacks, that the NYPD took no action respecting her complaints of harassment, that the NYPD twice denied her requests to be reassigned to another available class that would have separated her from her attacker for several days, and that the NYPD at most told the alleged attacker to stay away from her.[22] The court concluded:

[O]nce an employer learns of claims of discriminatory acts, it cannot rest idly on hopes that such acts will not be repeated, whether by the same employee or any other. It has an obligation to investigate whether acts conducive to the creation of an atmosphere of hostility did in fact occur .... .[23]

---

[16]Owens v. Turnage, 681 F. Supp. 1095, 1099 (D.N.J.)(federal employee supervisors denied "official immunity" for acts that attempted to persuade complainant to drop complaint), *aff'd*, 865 F.2d 251 (3d Cir. 1988).

[17]Katz v. Dole, 709 F.2d 251, 31 FEP Cases 1521 (4th Cir. 1983), reproduced in Chapter 7, Harassment by Co-Workers (supervisor apprised by complainant of co-worker's sexual advance suggested she solve problem by acquiescing in proposition); Henson v. City of Dundee, *supra* note 13 (same); Robson v. Eva's Super Market, 538 F. Supp. 857, 861–62, 30 FEP Cases 1212, 1216 (N.D. Ohio 1982)(summary judgment for employer denied when record failed to establish employer did anything to investigate complainant's harassment complaint except to instruct her "not to allow the offensive conduct [to] bother her"); Arnold v. City of Seminole, 614 F. Supp. 853, 862–63, 40 FEP Cases 1539, 1545 (E.D. Okla. 1985)(police chiefs told female police officer she was letting acts of male police officers "bother her too much" and that she was "too picky," held liable for sexual discrimination and harassment under Title VII).

[18]Continental Can Co. v. State, 297 N.W.2d 241, 22 FEP Cases 1808 (Minn. 1980)(liability found where supervisor, told by complainant that co-workers had grabbed and patted her and that one had expressed wish that "slavery days would return so that he could sexually train her [to] be his bitch," said to complainant she had to expect that behavior while working with men).

[19]Waltman v. International Paper Co., *supra* note 11, 875 F.2d at 479–80, 50 FEP Cases at 188–89 (allegations that employer discouraged use of grievance procedure by citing procedure's "detrimental" effect sufficient to deny summary judgment for employer on its theory that employee waived claim).

[20]*See, e.g.,* Grand Rapids, 86 LA 819, 826 (Frost, Arb.)(even though harassment charge made only days before alleged harasser was to fire complainant, arbitrator found that "ample opportunity" existed for management to investigate and determine its validity of claims, particularly since alleged discriminator would be relied on in management's decision to retain or fire employee).

[21]724 F. Supp. 99, 107 (S.D.N.Y. 1989).

[22]*Id.*

[23]*Id.* at 108.

B. Interim Corrective Action

In some circumstances an employer may increase the risk of liability if it does not utilize interim measures to prevent serious harassment before the conclusion of its investigation. These measures might include temporary transfers or placing the alleged harasser on a nondisciplinary leave of absence with pay pending the conclusion of the investigation. In *Baker v. Weyerhaeuser Co.*,[24] the employer, although ultimately firing the alleged harasser after an internal investigation, engaged in such delay that a court found its conduct violative of Title VII and that a jury considered an "outrageous" act sufficient to impose liability for intentional infliction of emotional distress.

Factors determining whether an employer's interim response is adequate include the employer's objective difficulty in framing a response and the potential interim harm to the complainant. In *Dornhecker v. Malibu Grand Prix Corp.*,[25] the employer's contract consultant "playfully" choked the complainant at a business convention after she had objected to him dropping his pants in public and touching her breasts. When she complained to the employer's president the next morning, she was assured that she would not have to work with the consultant any further and that the convention would last only one and a half more days. Believing the employer's assurance was unresponsive, the complainant resigned immediately. From these facts Judge Edith H. Jones concluded that the employer's response was "unusually prompt":

> Where the offending conduct spanned only two days to begin with, it is not unreasonable for the company to offer ending it virtually overnight. And, although we do not condone [the harasser's] conduct, it was not as aggressive or coercive as that underlying a number of hostile sexual environment claims that have been unsuccessful in court. Mrs. Dornhecker was not propositioned, she was not forced to respond to [the harasser], she was not placed in any threatening situation. The company's remedy to Mrs. Dornhecker's complaint may be assessed proportionately to the seriousness of the offense. A company's lines of command, organizational format and immediate business demands cannot be wholly extracted from the analysis of its manner and promptness in resolving a claim of sexual harassment. The remedy was prompt.[26]

Judge Jones added that "one cannot reasonably demand the employer to ignore its [valuable past business experience] with the alleged offender or to examine a charge of sexual harassment based on one side of the story, in a vacuum."[27]

Implicit in the decision in *Watts v. New York City Police Department*[28] is the thought that an employer's failure to take action, particularly easily and immediately available action such as permitting a trainee to transfer to another class even before completing an investigation, unnecessarily exposes the complainant to continued and serious harassment. Similarly, one employer's failure

---

[24]903 F.2d 1342, 1347–48, 52 FEP Cases 1872, 1876–77 (10th Cir. 1990)(affirming verdict for $49,000 actual damages and $49,000 punitive damages for intentional infliction of emotional distress based on employer's knowledge of harassment and failure to act).

[25]828 F.2d 307, 308, 44 FEP Cases 1604, 1605 (5th Cir. 1987)(Gee, Garwood & Jones, JJ.).

[26]*Id.* at 309, 44 FEP Cases at 1605.

[27]*Id.* at 309–10, 44 FEP Cases at 1606.

[28]*Supra* note 21.

to remove offensive cartoons about a female employee from the men's restroom within one day was found neither prompt nor adequate.[29]

III. CONDUCTING THE INVESTIGATION

A. Choosing an Appropriate Investigator

1. Importance of the Investigator

The employer's choice of persons to investigate a claim of sexual harassment can determine whether the employer has an adequate antiharassment policy and whether it took prompt and adequate remedial steps to end the sexual harassment. Choosing the wrong investigator can discourage harassment victims from reporting meritorious claims and may cause the employer to make a decision based on faulty or incomplete information gleaned from an inadequate investigation. Consequently, the wrong investigator may create liability and increase damages stemming from that liability.

The investigator's role is a demanding one. The most effective investigator is a person with a high level of personal integrity who has the respect and backing of both employees and upper-level management, who is adept in the art of interviewing witnesses, and who possesses the proper mix of intellectual and interpersonal skills. To be most effective, the investigator should not appear to be an advocate for either the complainant or the alleged harasser; neutrality and objectivity in investigating and finding facts will enhance the credibility and effectiveness of the investigation. To achieve the best results, the investigator must understand the issues under investigation, have time to devote to the investigation, and be willing and able to get immersed in the details. The most effective investigators are tough enough to ask the hard questions and sensitive enough to engender the confidence necessary to draw out honest answers. An investigator with these qualities will be a credible and effective witness should it be necessary for the employer to support the findings of the investigation in a legal proceeding.

2. Providing an Alternate Investigator

Because the department or person designated to receive and investigate reports of sexual harassment might conceivably be implicated in the charge, it is prudent to identify an alternate investigator.[30] Normally, sexual harassment policies allow the complainant either to contact persons up the chain of command or to contact a designated official in the human resources department.[31]

---

[29]Bennett v. Corroon & Black Corp., 845 F.2d 104, 105–6 (5th Cir. 1988), *cert. denied,* 489 U.S. 1020 (1989).

[30]*See, e.g.,* Brooms v. Regal Tube Co., 881 F.2d 412, 416, 50 FEP Cases 1499, 1500 (7th Cir. 1989)(complainant accused human resources manager of repeated instances of grossly offensive conduct). For further discussion of this point, see Chapter 18, Taking Preventive Action, Section II.B.1.

[31]For a sample sexual harassment policy, see Appendix 6. For a more comprehensive policy, imposed on an employer after findings of liability for sexual harassment, see the order in *Robinson v. Jacksonville Shipyards,* 760 F. Supp. 1486 (M.D. Fla. 1991), reproduced in Appendix 7.

3. Considering an Outside Investigator

In some cases employers should consider retaining an independent fact finder. Exercising this option will allay suspicion that the employer's investigation favored the more highly valued employee, or reflected the personal bias of the company employee who investigated. The retention of outside counsel or a professional fact-finder to investigate a sexual harassment complaint occurs most often when the alleged harasser is a particularly high-level executive, and there is concern that the company investigator may appear to feel constrained to protect the executive.

4. Investigation by an Attorney

Employers should always consider whether to conduct the investigation under the protection of the attorney-client privilege and the attorney work product-doctrine.[32] An investigation covered by privilege may keep the results of the investigation private and prevent disclosure of poorly written or incomplete investigative reports.[33]

Keeping the investigation privileged, however, will make it more difficult for the employer to show that it acted properly and promptly to stop the harassment. The employer might still protect the investigation as privileged and later waive the privilege if disclosing the contents of the investigation becomes necessary or desirable.[34]

---

[32]The attorney-client privilege applies to communications made in confidence between a client and an attorney for the purpose of seeking or providing legal advice. This privilege protects the contents of the communication, but not the fact that the communication was made. Application of the attorney-client privilege to corporations under federal law is currently governed by the Supreme Court's decision in *Upjohn Co. v. United States,* 449 U.S. 383 (1981). The Court in *Upjohn* held that the application of the privilege to corporations should be determined on a case-by-case basis, in light of several factors:

    (1) whether the communications were made by employees to corporate counsel at the direction of corporate superiors in order to secure legal advice;

    (2) whether the communications concerned matters within the scope of the employee's corporate duties;

    (3) whether the information sought by counsel to provide legal advice was unavailable from higher-level management;

    (4) whether the employees were aware that the information was sought to allow the corporation to obtain legal advice; and

    (5) whether the communications were directed to be confidential and were kept confidential.

Id. at 394–96.

    The work product privilege is designed to protect the "written statements, private memoranda and personal recollections prepared or formed by an adverse party's counsel in the course of his legal duties." Hickman v. Taylor, 329 U.S. 495, 510 (1947). *See also* FED. R. CIV. P. 26(b)(3).

[33]For a discussion of making a written record of the investigation, see Section III.C. *infra.*

[34]*See* Brooms v. Regal Tube Co., *supra* note 30, 881 F.2d at 421–22, 50 FEP Cases at 1505 (prior to trial, defendant company successfully protected report, written by attorney whom defendant had hired as "impartial outsider" to investigate employee's allegations of harassment, based on attorney-client privilege and work product doctrine, but trial court deemed privileges waived at trial when defendant's opening statements asserted the reasonableness of the decision to hire "impartial outsider" to investigate employee's complaint). A "limited waiver" may be difficult to define or structure. *See* Diversified Indus. v. Meredith, 572 F.2d 596, 611 (8th Cir. 1978)(production of internal investigation report in response to agency subpoena did not waive attorney-client privilege for all purposes, because finding such waiver would discourage corporations from undertaking such investigations). *But see* Martin Marietta Corp. v. Pollard, 856 F.2d 619, 625 (4th Cir. 1988)(court found with respect to third parties broad subject-matter waiver of all of company's nonopinion work product relating to investigation, but found "limited implied waiver" applying only to opinion work product for pure mental impressions severable from underlying data), *cert. denied,* 109 S.Ct. 1655 (1989). For a more detailed discussion of the discoverability of the defendant's investigative file, see Chapter 26, Discovery.

B. Conducting the Investigation

The extent and adequacy of an employer's investigation of a harassment claim will be considered in determining whether the employer took prompt remedial action reasonably calculated to end the harassment.[35] Accordingly, while recognizing that the truth of every allegation of sexual harassment may prove impossible to determine, the aim of every investigation is to determine certain basic facts: what happened, who the alleged harassers were, where and when the incident took place, how the complainant's work was affected, whether anyone else witnessed the incident, whether the incident was isolated or part of a continuing practice, what the reaction of the complainant was, how the complainant has been affected, whether the complainant has talked to anyone else about the incident, and whether there is any documentation of the incident.

The law provides no per se rules as to what constitutes a proper investigation; the adequacy of an investigation will be judged on the facts and circumstances of each situation. Employers should nonetheless adopt a standard procedure for investigating complaints. While the investigator should not be tied to a set procedure where circumstances warrant a variation, the use of a standard procedure can reduce the likelihood that the investigation will be questioned as inadequate.

1. Interview With the Complainant

Ideally, the initial interview with the complainant determines, as to each incident of alleged harassment, when and where the incident occurred,[36] what precisely was said or done by both parties, whether there were any witnesses, the effects of the incident, whether there are any documents containing information about the alleged incident, and whether the complainant has knowledge of any other target of harassment. The complainant's statements should be made available to the complainant upon request.[37]

It is highly desirable to assure the complainant of protection from any unlawful reprisal, and to advise that the employer will limit disclosure of the information obtained during the investigation to those with a legitimate need to know.[38] The complainant should be advised, however, that it may be necessary

---

[35]Waltman v. International Paper Co., 875 F.2d 468, 479, 50 FEP Cases 179, 188 (5th Cir. 1989)(appropriateness of employer's response to sexual harassment charges was question of fact); Paroline v. Unisys Corp., 879 F.2d 100, 106–7, 50 FEP Cases 306, 312 (4th Cir. 1989), reproduced in Chapter 9, Constructive Discharge (same), *aff'd in part and vacated in part,* 900 F.2d 27, 52 FEP Cases 845 (4th Cir. 1990)(*en banc*).

[36]When the incidents occurred on the employer's premises, and whether they occurred during business hours, can be relevant in determining the employer's liability in certain circumstances. *See* Yates v. Avco Corp., 819 F.2d 630, 636, 43 FEP Cases 1595, 1600 (6th Cir. 1987)(where harassment took place at office during working hours and carried out by supervisor, easier to impute harasser's own knowledge to employer and employer's duty to inquire about problem created earlier).

[37]*Cf.* Yates v. Avco Corp., *supra* note 36, 819 F.2d at 635 (implicitly faulting employer who took taped testimony from sexual harassment complainants and then denied their requests for copy of their testimony: "An effective antiharassment policy does not operate this way").

[38]Suggesting to a complainant that widespread exposure of the incident will result from the claim could represent evidence of an employer's failure to take appropriate action to end the harassment. Waltman v. International Paper Co., *supra* note 35, 875 F.2d at 480, 50 FEP Cases at 189 (summary judgment denied in part because employer informed complainant that investigation of sexual harassment complaints would be detrimental to her; "[t]his evidence suggests that [the employer] attempted to dissuade her from seeking an investigation").

to discuss that information with the alleged harasser and others.[39] Investigating charges of sexual harassment will almost always require that the identity of the complainant be revealed to the alleged harasser. It often will be possible, however, to avoid disclosure of the complaint's identity to third-party potential witnesses.

If the complainant is reluctant to divulge names and details, the investigator should record any information that is available and proceed on that basis. The complainant's failure to cooperate should also be noted, for it bears on the reasonableness of the scope of the employer's response.[40]

2. Interview With the Alleged Harasser

Interviews with alleged harassers should occur without undue delay. The alleged harasser may be quite forthright, particularly if he thinks his behavior was trivial or misinterpreted. The investigator should advise the alleged harasser of the purpose of the investigation, the fact that no conclusion has been made regarding the investigation, and that the same rules of confidentiality that apply to the complainant apply to the alleged harasser. The investigator should explain the harassment allegations in enough detail for the alleged harasser to be able to respond fully to the claim.[41] The alleged harasser should be made aware, of course, that truthful cooperation in the investigation is required by the employer, that the alleged harasser must avoid any reprisal against the complainant, and that breach of these requirements could serve as any independent basis for discipline up to and including discharge.

Ideally, the interview of the alleged harasser will disclose the time, place, and circumstances of each incident as well as information on relevant witnesses and documents. If the alleged harasser believes that the complainant has a motive to lie, the facts supporting that belief should be explored.[42] If the alleged harasser denies that the acts claimed to be harassment were "unwelcome," all facts supporting that denial should be obtained.

3. Additional Interviews

It is often necessary to interview third-party potential witnesses to obtain a full picture of the claim.[43] It is prudent to interview all persons with knowl-

---

[39]While it is important to maintain confidentiality to the extent practicable, it is not unlawful retaliation to disclose the complainant's identity. Whitaker v. Carney, 778 F.2d 216, 220–21, 39 FEP Cases 987 (5th Cir. 1985), *cert. denied,* 479 U.S. 813 (1986). *See also* EEOC Dec. 86-6, 40 FEP Cases 1890, 1892 (1986)(questioning victim of harassment and co-workers to determine whether employer needed to take remedial action not unlawful retaliation).

[40]*See* Hollis v. Fleetguard, 668 F. Supp. 631, 637, 44 FEP Cases 1527, 1532 (M.D. Tenn. 1987)(employer's "meager" response, merely to monitor situation rather than confront alleged harasser, reasonable given that plaintiff had vague allegations, refused to divulge names of other women propositioned by alleged harasser, and maintained "she could handle the problem"), *aff'd,* 848 F.2d 191 (6th Cir. 1988).

[41]*See* Marsh v. Digital Equip. Corp., 675 F. Supp. 1186, 1191, 44 FEP Cases 1192, 1195 (D. Ariz. 1987)(employee fired for sexually harassing several employees recovers punitive damages where employer failed to tell alleged harasser who had made charges or to give him any details of accusations). *Cf.* Lawson v. Boeing Co., 58 Wash. App. 261, 792 P.2d 545, 548 (1990)(upholding summary judgment against fired harasser's negligence claim that employer withheld written statements of complainants where he was fully advised of their contents). For further discussion of the alleged harasser's legal claims, see Chapter 24, The Alleged Harasser as Plaintiff.

[42]One obvious motivation would be to discredit any negative job performance appraisal that the complainant has received from the alleged harasser.

[43]*See* Brooms v. Regal Tube Co., *supra* note 30, 881 F.2d at 421 n.5, 50 FEP Cases at 1504 (affirming finding that employer failed to take reasonable remedial measures in part because of failure to conduct

edge of the facts, including all witnesses identified by the complainant.[44] The investigator may also want to re-interview the complainant to obtain a response to the alleged harasser's or witnesses' recollections of events. In serious cases it is very useful to take written statements not only from the complainant, but also from all significant witnesses.

An investigation typically will include a final interview with the alleged harasser, particularly in a very serious charge, so that all parties will have a full opportunity to rebut adverse statements. Tentative determinations about the truth of a harassment claim should be discussed with the alleged harasser, who should be required to confirm or deny each charge.

4. Reaching a Conclusion

In arriving at a result, the investigator should focus on whether the facts given are based on firsthand knowledge, attributed hearsay, rumors, or gossip.[45] The investigator should also assess the parties' motives to lie or embellish,[46] and assess the credibility of all persons interviewed.[47]

C. Recording the Investigation

The employer must decide whether to keep a written record of the investigation. Creating a complete and accurate record can evidence that the employer took prompt and appropriate action. Creating a record that is incomplete or inaccurate, however, may undermine the adequacy of the investigation and taint the employer's response to the sexual harassment claim.[48] A written record creates the additional issue of whether the investigative record will be discoverable should litigation follow.[49]

Where an employer finds that sexual harassment has occurred and takes responsive disciplinary action, the employer should record the investigation

---

follow-up investigation after interviewing only alleged victim and harasser); College-Town v. Massachusetts Comm'n Against Discrimination, 400 Mass. 156, 508 N.E.2d 587, 46 FEP Cases 1406, 1411 (1987)(affirming finding of inadequate investigation based on failure to question potential witnesses individually and to conduct follow-up interviews with alleged victim and harasser after receiving additional information).

[44]*Compare* Barrett v. Omaha Nat'l Bank, 726 F.2d 424, 427, 35 FEP Cases 585 (8th Cir. 1984)(no liability where employer, within four days of complaint, interviewed all potential witnesses, informed employees no harassment would be tolerated, and disciplined alleged harasser) *and* Howard v. National Cash Register, 388 F. Supp. 603 (S.D. Ohio 1975)(no liability where employer investigated complaints of racial harassment, disciplined one employee for using word "nigger" in plaintiff's presence, told workers that harassment was subject to discipline, and transferred plaintiff to different shift when employer's investigation met with denials) *with* Heelan v. Johns-Manville Corp., 451 F. Supp. 1382, 1388, 20 FEP Cases 251 (D. Colo. 1978)(single telephone call to alleged harasser not adequate investigation) *and* Zabkowicz v. West Bend Co., 585 F. Supp. 635, 35 FEP Cases 610, 613 (E.D. Wis. 1984)(publicizing antiharassment policy alone insufficient response where harassment continued after complaint).

[45]*See, e.g.,* Kestenbaum v. Pennzoil Co., 766 P.2d 280, 288, 4 IER Cases 67, 73 (N.M. 1988), *cert. denied,* 109 S.Ct. 3163 (1989)(employee fired for sexually harassing co-workers awarded damages because discharge based on investigative report that failed to differentiate "between firsthand knowledge, attributed hearsay, or mere gossip or rumor"). For further discussion of the alleged harasser's legal claims, see Chapter 24, The Alleged Harasser as Plaintiff.

[46]*See, e.g.,* Martin v. Norbar, Inc., 537 F. Supp. 1260, 1262, 30 FEP Cases 103, 104 (S.D. Ohio 1982)(reasonableness of decision to reject allegations of harassment may depend on whether employer considered motives of parties to lie or alleged harasser's reputation for sexually harassing women).

[47]*See, e.g.,* Kestenbaum v. Pennzoil Co., *supra* note 45 (investigation inadequate if it fails to assess credibility of those interviewed).

[48]*Id.*

[49]See Chapters 21, Complainant's Litigation Strategy; 22, Employer's Litigation Strategy; 25, Evidence; and 26, Discovery.

and witness statements to guard against the possibility that the alleged harasser will challenge the action taken.[50] Similarly, if an employer finds insufficient evidence of harassment and thus has no ground for discipline, the employer's defense to any sexual harassment suit will require full access to the statements of all witnesses to show that its decision was well-founded.

The investigative file is typically kept in the offices of corporate or outside counsel, while a copy of the investigation result is kept in the personnel file of the alleged harasser.

IV. TAKING PROMPT CORRECTIVE ACTION

A. Responding to the Investigation

At the conclusion of the investigation, some specific action should occur. First, the results of the investigation should be communicated to the involved parties[51] including the alleged harasser, and may also warrant communication to others in the workplace to clarify or reinforce the employer's sexual harassment policy. The employer should be mindful of potential liability for defamation when disseminating information about specific sexual harassment allegations, and should not disseminate any information concerning the events beyond those persons with a direct "need to know."[52]

If the investigator determines that the claim was not a legitimate interpretation of events but rather was a deliberate falsehood designed to damage the standing of another company employee, the employer must decide what, if any, disciplinary action to take against the complainant.[53]

B. Where the Employer Cannot Determine Whether Sexual Harassment Has Occurred

Where factual accounts differ, the employer should not reflexively credit either the alleged harasser or the complainant, but should consider factors relevant to the disputants' credibility, such as their reputations, their motives to fabricate, and the observations of other employees.[54]

If the employer cannot determine whether sexual harassment has occurred, it should advise the parties in a neutral manner that no conclusion was reached. The complainant should be assured that although no finding could be made

---

[50]*See, e.g.,* Heublein, Inc., 88 LA 1292 (1987)(Ellmann, Arb.)(employee discharged for sexually harassing co-worker reinstated with back pay where employer failed to provide evidence that other employee witnesses had given statements to support complainant's allegation and alleged harasser had no opportunity to respond to specific charges against him).

[51]*See, e.g.,* Department of Fair Employment & Hous. v. Madera County, Cal. FEHC Dec. 90-03 at 25–26 (April 26, 1990)(employer criticized for failing to inform complainant of warning given to alleged harasser).

[52]See Section VI. *infra* and Chapter 24, The Alleged Harasser as Plaintiff, Section II.

[53]See Section V. *infra.*

[54]*See generally* Martin v. Norbar, Inc., *supra* note 46 (adequacy of employer's response at issue where record was silent as to whether factors mentioned in text had been considered).

on the claim, the employer intends to protect the complainant and all employees against unlawful harassment and reprisal, and that any future instance of harassment should be reported promptly. The alleged harasser should be advised that although the truth of the claim has not been determined, all employees are expected to comply with the company's policy against sexual harassment and retaliation. In addition, the employer may take the opportunity to review its sexual harassment policy and complaint procedures in light of the claim and investigation to ensure effectiveness and accessibility. The employer may also wish to communicate its policies in a general way to ensure that there is no misunderstanding that might flow from not taking any individual action.

The employer should also investigate the feasibility of transfers or reassignments of work to prevent future contact between the complainant and the alleged harasser.[55] An employer might be required to consider some "balance of hardships," as well as the credibility of the parties, before deciding how to react to the complaint.[56]

A diligent investigation leading to no conclusion may preclude liability even if it turns out that sexual harassment in fact occurred. In *Poe v. Haydon*,[57] the Sixth Circuit held that, under 42 U.S.C. §1983,[58] an employer should not be found liable merely because the findings of an adequate investigation proved inconclusive. Judge Danny J. Boggs noted that the complainant "did not have a clearly established constitutional or statutory right to a specific outcome following an investigation of her complaint of sexual harassment."[59] Similarly, in *Watts v. New York City Police Department*,[60] Judge Robert W. Sweet held that while the employer had a duty to remedy a hostile environment once it knew of one, it was not necessarily liable for every act of sexual harassment committed by its employees.

C. Where the Employer Determines That Sexual Harassment Has Occurred

1. General Considerations

Where the employer determines that harassment has occurred, it must promptly take action, including (1) sanctions against the alleged harasser, no matter how minor the infraction, and (2) advising the complainant of the action taken. The employer's action should be "reasonably calculated to end the

---

[55]See Section IV.C.2. *infra*.

[56]Martin v. Norbar, Inc., *supra* note 46 (by rejecting plaintiff's story, employer forced her to choose between riding in truck with alleged harasser or quitting, while crediting her claim would simply have required reassignment with presumably no great hardship on employer).

[57]853 F.2d 418, 52 FEP Cases 80 (6th Cir. 1988)(Lively, Jones, & Boggs, JJ.), *cert. denied,* 488 U.S. 1007 (1989).

[58]For a discussion of sexual harassment cases under §1983, see Chapter 11, Federal Constitutional, Statutory, and Civil Rights Law.

[59]*Supra* note 57, 853 F.2d at 427, 52 FEP Cases at 87 (citing Davis v. Holly, 835 F.2d 1175, 1180 (6th Cir. 1987)).

[60]724 F. Supp. 99, 107 (S.D.N.Y. 1989).

harassment."[61] Whether the remedial action is prompt[62] and adequate is a question of fact.[63]

One important matter to consider, quite apart from any disciplinary action to be taken against the putative harasser, is how best to assure that the complainant will not take precipitate action such as quitting the job and feeling the need to file a legal action. Possibilities include offering the complainant some time off with pay, offering to pay for counseling for the complainant, and urging the complainant not to quit.[64]

Most important, the employer must select disciplinary action appropriate under the circumstances. Several factors should guide that selection: (1) the severity of the conduct,[65] (2) the pervasiveness of the conduct, (3) the harasser's overall record of employment and employment history, (4) the complainant's employment history, (5) the notice that the harasser had of the employer's policy prohibiting sexual harassment, (6) the discipline imposed for previous cases of sexual harassment and for violations of other company policies, and (7) other company policies, such as any progressive discipline policy.

The discipline itself may range from an oral warning to the termination of employment. In determining the appropriate sanction, it may be helpful to ask the complainant whether the employer can do anything more to assist in keeping the complainant's work environment free of harassment.[66] After discipline has been imposed, the employer should promptly notify the complainant of the actions that it has taken to remedy the situation.[67]

---

[61]Katz v. Dole, 709 F.2d 251, 256, 31 FEP Cases 1521, 1524 (4th Cir. 1983), reproduced in Chapter 7, Harassment by Co-Workers. *See also* Sanchez v. City of Miami Beach, 720 F. Supp. 974, 981 (1989)(quoting *Katz v. Dole*)(employer must do more than indicate existence of official policy against sexual harassment); Paroline v. Unisys Corp., 879 F.2d 100, 107, 50 FEP Cases 306, 312 (4th Cir. 1989), reproduced in Chapter 9, Constructive Discharge (reasonable fact-finder could infer from head of office openly joking about female employee's sexual harassment complaints, after ostensibly warning supervisor and other male employees not to engage in sexual harassment, that employer did not intend to take serious action to stop harassment), *aff'd in part and vacated in part,* 900 F.2d 27, 52 FEP Cases 845 (4th Cir. 1990)(*en banc*). *See generally* EEOC Policy Guidance on Sexual Harassment (March 19, 1990), FAIR EMP. PRAC. MAN. (BNA) 405:6681, 6700, reproduced in Appendix 3.

[62]Rabidue v. Osceola Ref. Co., 805 F.2d 611, 621, 42 FEP Cases 631, 638–39 (6th Cir. 1986), reproduced in Chapter 2, Forms of Harassment ("The promptness and adequacy of the employer's response to correct instances of alleged sexual harassment . . . must be evaluated on a case by case basis"), *cert. denied,* 481 U.S. 1041 (1987); Dornhecker v. Malibu Grand Prix Corp., 828 F.2d 307, 309–10, 44 FEP Cases 1604, 1605 (5th Cir. 1987)(employer's remedial action taken within 12 hours of incident decided case for employer); Bennett v. New York City Dep't of Corrections, 705 F. Supp. 979, 987–88, 49 FEP Cases 134, 141 (S.D.N.Y. 1989)(employee's claim survived summary judgment in part because employer took four weeks to respond to incident).

[63]Waltman v. International Paper Co., 875 F.2d 468, 479–80, 50 FEP Cases 179, 188 (5th Cir. 1989)(appropriateness of employer's response to sexual harassment charges was question of fact); Paroline v. Unisys Corp., *supra* note 62, 879 F.2d at 106, 50 FEP Cases at 312.

[64]*See, e.g.,* Paroline v. Unisys Corp., 879 F.2d 100, 50 FEP Cases 306, 318 (4th Cir. 1989), reproduced in Chapter 9, Constructive Discharge (dissenting opinion of Judge Wilkinson, later adopted by Fourth Circuit *en banc,* emphasizing kinds of acts mentioned in text in arguing that employer entitled to summary judgment on issue of constructive discharge), *aff'd in part and vacated in part,* 900 F.2d 27, 52 FEP Cases 845 (4th Cir. 1990).

[65]Carosella v. United States Postal Serv., 816 F.2d 638, 43 FEP Cases 845 (Fed. Cir. 1987)(discharge justified when supervisor touched employees offensively and repeatedly asked them for dates); Hostetter v. United States, 739 F.2d 983, 35 FEP Cases 693 (4th Cir. 1984)(discharge justified when supervisor repeatedly touched employees offensively and made sexual remarks).

[66]*See* Department of Fair Emp. & Hous. v. Madera County, *supra* note 51, at 25–26 (failure of employer to ask complainant for ideas regarding steps to make work environment more tolerable supports determination that employer failed to take "immediate and appropriate corrective action" in response to complaint).

[67]*See* Wheeler v. Southland Corp., 875 F.2d 1246, 1250, 50 FEP Cases 86, 89 (6th Cir. 1989)(constructive discharge found where plaintiff who reported to management was told to "hang in there" rather than

Employers who carefully document the steps taken in determining the correct level of discipline are in the best position to defend against either a discrimination or wrongful discharge suit[68] or a grievance filed in opposition to the discipline.[69] The documentation might include a written acknowledgement of the company's sexual harassment policy from each employee counseled at the conclusion of the investigation, which could be placed in the employee's personnel file.

2. Ensuring That Discipline Is Adequate

Each disciplinary act must be calculated to deter future harassment.[70] In all cases, regardless of the discipline imposed, the employer should follow through to ensure that discipline has been effective, the situation has been remedied, and the complainant has not been subjected to retaliation.[71] If the discipline has not been effective, the employer should impose harsher sanctions. The employer is much less likely to be held liable for sexual harassment if the remedy proves effective.[72]

Decisions that discuss intermediate disciplinary steps demonstrate that substantial penalties may be imposed on harassers when initial discipline fails to deter harassment.[73] Consequently, employers should proceed cautiously and follow through after the initial discipline to ensure that no harassment or retaliation is recurring.

a. Oral and written warnings. Where the conduct complained of is minor, an oral warning may be sufficient to insulate the employer from liability. At the very least, the employer should remind all involved employees about its

---

being told when harassing supervisor would be replaced); Department of Fair Emp. & Hous. v. Madera County, *supra* note 51, at 26, 44 (commission criticized employer for failing to inform complainant of warnings it had given alleged harasser; failure contributed to complainant's feelings of powerlessness and subsequent emotional difficulties; commission ordered full disclosure of incident to all county employees, with notice posted in all offices to state that sexual harassment had occurred and county ordered to pay complainant back pay).

[68]For a discussion of the alleged harasser's legal rights, see Chapter 24, The Alleged Harasser as Plaintiff.

[69]For a discussion of the collective bargaining rights of a union-represented alleged harasser, see Chapter 17, Collective Bargaining Agreements and Union Obligations.

[70]Steele v. Offshore Shipbldg., 867 F.2d 1311, 1317, 49 FEP Cases 522, 526 (11th Cir. 1989)(employer not liable where, after it promptly issued reprimand, harassment stopped); Swentek v. USAir, 830 F.2d 552, 558, 44 FEP Cases 1808, 1813 (4th Cir. 1987)(after employer issued written warning, no more complaints were received; warning was adequate remedial action); Brooms v. Regal Tube Co., 881 F.2d 412, 421, 50 FEP Cases 1499, 1505 (7th Cir. 1989)(employer held liable even though it made supervisor apologize to victim, postponed merit salary increase, and threatened supervisor with termination, because a few weeks following these actions harassment began anew).

[71]EEOC Policy Guidance on Sexual Harassment, FAIR EMP. PRAC. MAN. (BNA) 405:6681, 6700, reproduced in Appendix 3. Watts v. New York City Police Dep't, *supra* note 60 (employer potentially liable if, after imposing discipline against initial harasser, it failed to investigate actions of other harassers).

[72]*Compare* Huddleston v. Roger Dean Chevrolet, 845 F.2d 900, 904, 46 FEP Cases 1361, 1363 (11th Cir. 1988)(oral threat of discharge sufficient) *and* Steele v. Offshore Shipbldg., *supra* note 70 (oral reprimand effective) *and* Barrett v. Omaha Nat'l Bank, 584 F. Supp. 22, 26, 35 FEP Cases 585, 588 (D. Neb. 1983)(reprimand and 90-day probation proved effective), *aff'd,* 726 F.2d 424, 35 FEP Cases 593 (8th Cir. 1984) *with* Department of Fair Employment & Hous. v. Madera County, Cal. FEHC Dec. 90-03 at 25 (April 26, 1990)(harassment continued after warnings) *and* Waltman v. International Paper Co., *supra* note 64, 875 F.2d at 479–80, 50 FEP Cases at 188–89 (adequacy of remedy remained question of fact where harassment continued after oral request that foreman stop making sexual comments over PA system and after supervisor required to read sexual harassment policy).

[73]*See, e.g.,* Maturo v. National Graphics, 722 F. Supp. 916, 922–24 (D. Conn. 1989)(complainant "constructively discharged" when employer failed to respond effectively to claim of sexual harassment by supervisor; despite alleged harasser's arrest for two counts of sexual assault, employer merely demoted him and he continued to work with and harass complainant).

policy prohibiting sexual harassment, tell them what conduct or communications constitute sexual harassment, and warn them that violation of the employer's sexual harassment policy may result in severe disciplinary action up to and including termination. The employer should make and retain a record in the alleged harasser's personnel file, as well as in the investigative file, of having administered the oral warning.

Employers will not necessarily escape liability simply by admonishing employees to act more professionally,[74] telling them to cease "horseplay,"[75] or reminding them of company rules prohibiting harassment or abusive language.[76] In *Ellison v. Brady*,[76a] the Ninth Circuit faulted an employer who simply told an alleged harasser, accused of sending the complainant bizarre love notes, to leave the complainant alone:

> [W]e cannot say that the [employer's] response was reasonable under Title VII. The ... employer ... did not reprimand [the alleged harasser], did not put him on probation, and did not inform him that repeated harassment would result in suspension or termination. ... Title VII requires more than a mere request to refrain from discriminatory conduct. ... Employers send the wrong message to potential harassers when they do not discipline employees for sexual harassment. If ... the [employer] failed to take even the mildest form of disciplinary action, the district court should hold that the [employer]'s initial remedy was insufficient under Title VII.[76b]

Sometimes a mere oral warning will suffice. In *Huddleston v. Roger Dean Chevrolet*,[77] the Eleventh Circuit held that an oral threat to discharge a harasser was sufficient where the acts of harassment consisted solely of derogatory comments and name-calling. Similarly, in *Steele v. Offshore Shipbuilding*,[78] the Eleventh Circuit held that where the plaintiffs' supervisor had engaged in sexually oriented joking and jocular requests for sexual favors, the employer was not liable when it orally reprimanded the harasser and the reprimand proved effective.[78a]

In general, a written reprimand is preferable, for it creates a record of the employer's action. The reprimand should warn the harasser that the conduct observed was improper and that recurrence may result in more serious discipline up to and including discharge. In *Barrett v. Omaha National Bank*,[79] a district court held that an employer was not liable for sexual harassment of the plaintiff by two co-workers where, within four days of the complaint, both co-workers were reprimanded and one was placed on ninety days of probation.[80]

---

[74]Moffett v. Gene B. Glick Co., 621 F. Supp. 244, 256, 41 FEP Cases 671, 677 (N.D. Ind. 1985).

[75]Morris v. American Nat'l Can Corp., 730 F. Supp. 1489, 1496, 52 FEP Cases 210, 217 (E.D. Mo. 1989).

[76]Katz v. Dole, *supra* note 61, 709 F.2d at 256, 31 FEP Cases at 1524; Zabkowicz v. West Bend Co., 589 F. Supp. 780, 785, 35 FEP Cases 610, 613 (E.D. Wis. 1984).

[76a]924 F.2d 872, 54 FEP Cases 1346 (9th Cir. 1991)(Beezer & Kozinski, JJ., with Stephens, J., dissenting).

[76b]*Id.* at 882.

[77]*Supra* note 72 (first female auto sales associate in car dealership subjected to harassment by male sales associates calculated to get her to leave dealership).

[78]*Supra* note 70.

[78a]*Id.*

[79]584 F. Supp. 22, 35 FEP Cases 585 (D. Neb. 1983), *aff'd*, 726 F.2d 424, 35 FEP Cases 593 (8th Cir. 1984).

[80]*Id.* at 30, 35 FEP Cases at 591–92.

Where an employer knows that a warning has not deterred further harassment, the employer must increase the severity of the discipline.[81] One state fair employment practices commission has found even repeated and progressive oral and written warnings to be insufficient where the harassing conduct was pervasive and repeated.[82]

b. Suspensions and demotions. Incidents of sexual harassment often may not warrant immediate discharge but do warrant stronger discipline than a mere warning. Although reported decisions rarely discuss intermediate forms of discipline, suspensions and demotions are options to consider before dismissing an offending employee. These forms of discipline may allow employers to deter future harassment, protect the dignity and security of the complainant, educate the work force, and permit the "rehabilitation" of an offending employee who is otherwise valuable and not a disciplinary problem.

Suspensions are one possibility. Labor arbitration decisions have consistently upheld suspensions where the employer can prove that the disciplined employee actually engaged in the sexual harassment of a co-worker.[83]

An employer might also consider demoting the employee. In *Spencer v. General Electric Co.*,[84] a supervisor was demoted from a management position to a position as an artist in the graphics department. His pay was not reduced, and he received his next yearly raise without incident. When investigation of a sexual harassment complaint revealed that the former supervisor had lied about consensual sexual relations that he had maintained with other female employees, he was asked to resign. Upholding the remedy, the reviewing court concluded that the employer had taken the appropriate remedial steps.[85] A demotion, of course, may not be appropriate if it allows the harasser to continue working with the complainant.[86]

---

[81]*See, e.g.,* Arnold v. City of Seminole, 614 F. Supp. 853, 859–60, 40 FEP Cases 1539, 1543 (E.D. Okla. 1985)(memoranda to all police officers directing them to refrain from directing immoral comments and objects to other officers was insufficient response to public display of pornographic pictures directed at plaintiff and other forms of harassment, where harassment continued with no effective employer response).

[82]Department of Fair Emp. & Hous. v. Madera County, *supra* note 72, at 25–26 (harassing supervisor originally terminated for extreme physical harassment but reinstated after appeal to Civil Service Commission; warnings received following reinstatement proved inadequate, for he continued sexually harassing conduct). *Cf.* Waltman v. International Paper Co., *supra* note 63 (question of fact existed as to adequacy of defendant's response where, despite numerous incidents of harassment of plaintiff, only actions taken by employer were to request that foreman stop making sexual comments over PA system and to require that all supervisors read company's sexual harassment policy).

[83]*E.g.,* Sealtest Foods, 89 LA 27 (1987)(Goldstein, Arb.) (three-day suspension proper under progressive discipline system for employee who wrote sexually degrading and racially discriminatory comments in his personal copy of in-house magazine, then showed comments to male co-workers); Social Security Admin., 81 LA 459 (1983)(Cox, Arb.)(two-day suspension upheld for male employee found to have falsely "boasted" that he had touched a female co-worker's breasts and buttocks); Fisher Foods, 80 LA 133 (1983)(Abrams, Arb.)(three-day suspension upheld for touching breast of outside sales representative temporarily working in employer's store). For further discussion of discipline upheld in arbitration, see Chapter 17, Collective Bargaining Agreements and Union Obligations.

[84]697 F. Supp. 204, 51 FEP Cases 1696 (E.D. Va. 1988), *aff'd,* 894 F.2d 651, 51 FEP Cases 1725 (4th Cir. 1990).

[85]*Id.* at 216, 219, 51 FEP Cases at 1706, 1709.

[86]Waltman v. International Paper Co., 875 F.2d 468, 479, 50 FEP Cases 179, 188 (5th Cir. 1989)(harassment continued when complainant's supervisor was demoted and assigned to work next to complainant); Department of Fair Emp. & Hous. v. Madera County, *supra* note 72, at 26 (employee demoted and suspended, but working in same office, continued to harass complainant). *Cf.* Paroline v. Unisys Corp., 879 F.2d 100, 106–17, 50 FEP Cases 306, 312 (4th Cir. 1989), reproduced in Chapter 9, Constructive Discharge (question of fact whether denying harasser's access to sensitive-material facility, which resulted in more potential contact between complainant and accused harasser, was appropriate remedy), *aff'd in part and vacated in part,* 900 F.2d 27, 52 FEP Cases 845 (4th Cir. 1990)(*en banc*).

A leading case on the adequacy of discipline for sexual harassment is *Department of Fair Employment & Housing v. Madera County*.[87] Initially, the harasser, a supervisor, was dismissed for his explicit sexual advances to a female subordinate. On his appeal, a civil service commission reduced the discipline to a one-step demotion and a thirty-day suspension without pay. The harasser returned to the same workplace, where he engaged in additional acts of harassment against the complainant. Although the complainant reported the continuing harassment, the employer, feeling its hands tied by the commission's order of reinstatement, did no more than issue a warning. The complainant eventually suffered considerable emotional difficulty and left her job. In her employment discrimination suit, the complainant was awarded substantial monetary damages, and the employer was ordered to engage in extensive remedial measures to educate all of its employees concerning its policy against sexual harassment and the procedures for dealing with future problems.

Madera County illustrates the desirability of considering more severe discipline when intermediate sanctions fail to deter harassment. Consequently, employers, in considering disciplinary actions short of termination, should consider not only the length of prior employment, the severity of the conduct that led to the complaint, and any prior disciplinary actions, but also the overall effectiveness of the disciplinary action in deterring harassment.

c. Transfers, reassignments, and restructuring the workplace. Transfers, reassignments, and restructuring of the work environment are other possible intermediate steps in the disciplinary process. The *Madera County* decision alludes to the possibility of restructuring the work environment:

> [N]o one ever asked complainant for any ideas she might have or steps which could be taken—such as, perhaps, rearranging the office to further minimize contact between complainant and [her reinstated harasser]—which might have made her daily work environment more tolerable.
>
> These communications, or actions similar to them, would have been simple for the County to take. Their absence, however, had severe ramifications in that they left complainant feeling insecure and powerless.[88]

A proposed transfer was considered adequate in *Dornhecker v. Malibu Grand Prix Corp.*,[89] where the employer offered to transfer the alleged harasser the day after the complainant informed the employer of the offensive conduct. By the same token, rejection of the complainant's request for transfer raised an issue as to the adequacy of the employer's response in *Martin v. Norbar, Inc.*,[90] where a female over-the-road truck driver complained to her terminal manager that her male co-driver had told lewd stories and made unwelcome sexual advances to her during a long-distance run. The terminal manager credited the male driver's denial of these allegations and rejected the plaintiff's request for reassignment. The plaintiff quit her job and sued. The employer moved for summary judgment. Judge S. Arthur Spiegel, while agreeing with

---

[87]*Supra* note 72, at 25–26.

[88]Department of Fair Emp. & Hous. v. Madera County, *supra* note 72, at 25.

[89]828 F.2d 307, 44 FEP Cases 1604 (5th Cir. 1987). *But see* Waltman v. International Paper Co., *supra* note 86, 875 F.2d at 479–80, 50 FEP Cases at 188 (question of fact raised as to adequacy of employer's response where only response was to transfer employee to another shift).

[90]537 F. Supp. 1260, 30 FEP Cases 103 (S.D. Ohio 1982).

the employer that it could be liable for co-worker harassment only if it knew or should have known of the harassment and failed to take appropriate action, denied the motion for summary judgment because there was an issue of fact as to whether it was "reasonable" for the employer to credit the male driver's story over the plaintiff's. The federal district court indicated that the employer would have to demonstrate that it considered such factors as the motives that either party had to lie, and the reputation of the alleged harasser for sexual harassment.[91] The court suggested that the employer could have easily credited the plaintiff's story and required a reassignment to prevent her from having to ride again with the alleged harasser. The court indicated that an employer might be required to consider some "balance of hardships," as well as the degree of the complainant's credibility, before deciding how to react to the complaint.[92]

Transfer of the complainant is not necessarily an adequate response. In one case,[93] the complainant was offered a transfer to another facility and then was dismissed when she failed to accept the transfer. In finding the dismissal to be retaliatory, the court chided the employer for moving the complainant while failing to consider moving the supervisor.[94] Indeed, transferring the complainant to a less desirable position may be inadequate as a matter of law, at least where the evidence of sexual harassment is strong.[95]

d. Other forms of discipline. Examples of other forms of discipline are those taken by the employer in *Paroline v. Unisys Corp.*[96] In *Paroline* the employer not only gave the alleged harasser a written warning but delayed his planned promotion and salary increase, instructed him to seek counseling, told him to limit his contact with female employees to official company business, and terminated his access to certain facilities. These intermediate forms of discipline were emphasized by the full Fourth Circuit in affirming a summary judgment for the employer on the issue of constructive discharge.[96a]

e. Termination of employment. Many complaints of sexual harassment lead to the dismissal of the alleged harasser. In the unionized setting, dismissals on this basis have been met with mixed acceptance by labor arbitrators.[97] A substantial number of arbitration decisions convert "improper" discharges for sexual harassment into lengthy suspensions without pay, generally extending from the original termination to the date of the arbitrator's decision.[98] An

[91]*Id.* at 1262, 30 FEP Cases at 104.
[92]*Id. See also* Wheeler v. Southland Corp., 875 F.2d 1246, 1248, 50 FEP Cases 86, 89 (6th Cir. 1989)(employer liable where it did not promptly inform complainant that alleged harasser would be replaced as supervisor).
[93]College-Town v. Massachusetts Comm'n Against Discrimination, 400 Mass. 156, 508 N.E.2d 587, 46 FEP Cases 1406 (1987).
[94]*Id.,* 46 FEP Cases at 1412. *Cf.* Waltman v. International Paper Co., *supra* note 86 (question of fact raised as to adequacy of employer's response where only response was to transfer employee to another shift). For further discussion of retaliation against a complainant, see Chapter 10, Retaliation.
[95]Guess v. Bethlehem Steel Corp., 913 F.2d 463, 465, 53 FEP Cases 1547 (7th Cir. 1990)(dictum)(transfer that leaves complainant worse off in terms of benefits or prospects for promotion necessarily ineffective).
[96]879 F.2d 100, 50 FEP Cases 306 (4th Cir. 1989), reproduced in Chapter 9, Constructive Discharge, *aff'd in part and vacated in part,* 900 F.2d 27, 52 FEP Cases 845 (4th Cir. 1990)(*en banc*).
[96a]See *id.,* 50 FEP Cases at 318 (dissenting opinion of Judge J. Harvie Wilkinson, later adopted by the Fourth Circuit *en banc*).
[97]See Chapter 17, Collective Bargaining Agreements and Union Obligations.
[98]*E.g.,* Boys Markets, 88 LA 1304 (1987)(Wilmoth, Arb.) (discharge reduced to 10-month suspension where employee "goosed" fellow employee); Sugardale Foods, 86 LA 1017 (1986)(Duda, Arb.)(discharge

employer's failure to conduct an adequate investigation can taint its conclusion of sexual harassment, leading to the discharge being found improper and reinstatement ordered with full back pay.[99] However, a substantial number of arbitrators have upheld dismissals for acts ranging from oral harassment to the exposing of genitalia.[100]

Dismissals for sexual harassment following thorough investigations frequently withstand scrutiny. In *Johnson v. International Minerals & Chemical Corp.*,[101] the employer fired three supervisors for subjecting female subordinates to sexual harassment that included forcibly kissing and fondling the complainants, pinching their breasts, and making lewd remarks.[102] After the complainants filed administrative charges, the employer settled their claims and investigated the allegations.[103] In denying the alleged harassers' claim for wrongful discharge and breach of the implied covenant of good faith and fair dealing, Judge Richard H. Battery held that the defendant employer "acted in good faith when it conducted a thorough investigation of the sexual harassment and sexual discrimination charges against plaintiffs prior to making a final decision to discharge them."[104]

---

converted to seven-month suspension for employee who hovered around female employee and momentarily touched her upper thigh while in restricted area that was semi-dark due to power failure); Hyatt Hotels Palo Alto, 85 LA 11 (1985)(Oestreich, Arb.)(discharge converted to 15-day suspension for exposing genitalia to two female co-workers on more than one occasion); Meijer, Inc., 83 LA 570 (1984)(Ellmann, Arb.)(discharge converted to 10-month suspension for embracing co-worker and giving "little bit of a hump motion"); Dayton Power and Light Co., 80 LA 19 (1983)(Heinsz, Arb.)(discharge reduced to seven-month suspension for employee who pinched female co-worker on the breast while making kissing sounds).

[99]Discharges found improper and reinstatement ordered with full back pay: Heublein, Inc., 88 LA 1292 (1987)(Ellmann, Arb.)(employer never adequately informed employee of precise details of any of alleged misconduct before discharging him); DeVry Institute of Technology, 87 LA 1149 (1986)(Berman, Arb.)(faculty member given one warning, then fired when new allegations were raised involving conduct that occurred prior to warning); Washington Scientific Indus., 83 LA 824 (1984)(Kapsch, Sr., Arb.)(discharge reversed with full back pay for employee who, in frustration, remarked to co-worker, "I don't think you would even enjoy sex").

[100]*E.g.,* Can-Tex Indus., 90 LA 1230 (1988)(Shearer, Arb.)(21-year employee whose constant and pervasive verbal sexual harassment of co-workers was unaffected by warnings); Tampa Elec. Co., 88 LA 791 (1986)(Vause, Dominguez, and Sugg, Arbs.)(use of crude, explicit language describing sexual fantasies about co-worker while she, alone, was driving him to isolated work sites in company vehicle); Schlage Lock Co., 88 LA 75 (1986) (Wyman, Arb.)(discharge of union steward who left anonymous note in female worker's locker and mailed letter to worker's husband accusing worker of sexual affair with supervisor); Porter Equip. Co., 86 LA 1253 (1986)(Lieberman, Arb.)(employer pulled hand of co-worker toward his exposed penis); New Indus. Techniques, 84 LA 915 (1985)(Gray, Arb.)(union lead set-up man discharged, after two verbal warnings, for making lewd remarks and grabbing, hugging, and kissing co-worker on three occasions); United Elec. Supply Co., 82 LA 921 (1984)(Madden, Arb.)(warehouseman discharged for persistent advances to several co-workers, even where advances did not involve offensive language or touching); Anaconda Copper Co., 78 LA 690 (1982)(Cohen, Arb.)(employee made obscene gestures and sexually demeaning slurs even after warnings and successive work reassignments); University of Mo., 78 LA 417 (1982)(Yarowsky, Arb.)(discharge upheld after three-day suspension proved insufficient to deter supervisor from "throwing kisses," "glaring suggestively," and casually touching subordinate female employees); St. Regis Paper Co., 74 LA 1281 (1980)(Kaufman, Arb.)(male employee discharged following argument between two co-workers where female employee threatened to have male employee fired and, in response, male employee threatened to rape her).

[101]40 FEP Cases 1651 (D.S.D. 1986).

[102]*Id.* at 1652.

[103]*Id.* at 1652–53.

[104]*Id.* at 1653. *See* Westinghouse Elec. Corp., 120 LRRM 1295 (1985)(NLRB reversed administrative law judge and approved employer's discharge of employee accused of sexual harassment); Hostetter v. United States, 739 F.2d 983, 35 FEP Cases 693 (4th Cir. 1984)(court affirmed dismissal of civilian air force employee which was "supported by substantial evidence"); Rivera v. Division of Employment Sec., 34 FEP Cases 894 (La. Civ. Dist. Ct. 1984)(alleged harasser properly denied unemployment compensation where facts established employee terminated for harassment); French v. Mead Corp., 33 FEP Cases 635 (S.D. Ohio

Before dismissing an alleged harasser, the employer should attempt to ensure that the investigation was adequate, that the discipline is not excessive, and that the results are not too broadly disseminated.[105]

V. WHERE THE EMPLOYER DETERMINES THAT FALSE REPORTING HAS OCCURRED

A primary goal of Title VII is a work environment free of harassment. Any discipline for false reporting may discourage employees from making justified complaints, thereby undermining this goal. Thus, even though an internal investigation may indicate that the complainant has lied about the incidents, the employer should proceed with great caution when imposing any discipline, lest it incur liability for retaliation.[106]

A. Internal Investigation

Employers who are considering any disciplinary action against the complainant for an internal false report must distinguish between instances where the employee knowingly makes a false report and one where there is an honest difference of interpretation about the incident that gave rise to the claim. An honest difference in perception should not warrant any disciplinary action, for under those circumstances the complainant may be protected from any form of discipline by both federal and state statutes that prohibit retaliation for the filing of a claim, participating as a witness, or opposing a practice made unlawful by fair employment practices laws.[107]

Where the employer concludes that the claim of sexual harassment was made in bad faith, the employer generally should apply the same level of disciplinary action against the complainant as it would for similar forms of dishonesty. In doing so, the employer should evaluate the degree of discipline applied in other contexts and apply an equal degree of discipline for the false reporting of sexual harassment. The employer should document its evaluation of similar disciplinary actions.

B. Agency Investigation

An employer should not take any disciplinary action against a complainant for filing a charge with the EEOC or a state fair employment practices agency.

1983)(court rejected white male supervisor's Title VII action where facts established he was discharged for sexually harassing female subordinates), *aff'd,* 758 F.2d 652, 37 FEP Cases 1408 (6th Cir. 1985)(Title VII case), *cert. denied,* 474 U.S. 820 (1985); Matter of Chapter 13, 19 Bankr. 713, 33 FEP Cases 1871 (W.D. Wash. 1982)(bankruptcy trustee properly removed where evidence showed he was sexually harassing employees).

[105]See Chapter 24, The Alleged Harasser as Plaintiff.

[106]For a more thorough discussion of situations in which an employer may incur liability for its reaction to complaints of sexual harassment, see Chapter 10, Retaliation.

[107]For a general discussion of Title VII prohibitions on retaliation, see Chapter 10, Retaliation.

Statements made during agency investigations may be protected under federal and state law even if they are deliberately false.[108]

C. Defamation Actions Against the Complainant

Bringing a defamation action against a complainant who has made a false claim of sexual harassment is a theoretical option for the employer or the alleged harasser.[109] This option, while not necessarily unlawful,[110] must be approached with caution inasmuch as it may be prohibited by the antiretaliation provisions of federal or state law.[111]

VI. BALANCING THE NEED TO DETER HARASSMENT WITH THE NEED TO AVOID EXCESSIVE PUBLICATION

The investigation of sexual harassment claims and any related discipline raise obvious issues of defamation.[112] While truth is a defense to defamation, a false complaint of sexual harassment may lead to a possible defamation suit by the alleged harasser.[113] The alleged harasser could also base defamation claims on the statements of any witness who supplied exaggerated details or characterizations.[114] Additionally, either the complainant or the alleged harasser may well be tempted to go beyond the truth and defame the reputation of the other or the reputations of other witnesses.

A. Cautionary Instructions

An internal investigation should aim to protect the reputations of both the complainant and alleged harasser, mindful of potential liability for defamation on the part of the investigator, witnesses, and the parties directly involved. The investigator should limit access to the investigative file to those persons required to have access. The allegations and information obtained should be discussed only with the involved parties. Each witness interviewed should be admonished not to discuss the matter with others, and should be informed of

---

[108]*See* Proulx v. Citibank, 659 F. Supp. 972, 44 FEP Cases 371 (S.D.N.Y. 1987), discussed in Chapter 10, Retaliation.

[109]For a discussion of defamation suits by the alleged harasser, see Chapter 24, The Alleged Harasser as Plaintiff; for a discussion of defamation actions by the complainant, see Chapter 15, The Common Law. The employer's qualified privilege is discussed in Section VI. *infra.*

[110]*See* Proulx v. Citibank, *supra* note 108, 659 F. Supp. at 979, 44 FEP Cases at 376–77 ("[t]he employer's remedy is to defeat the employee's claim on its merits . . . and then, if so advised for purposes of specific or general deterrence, attempt a suit against the employee for defamation").

[111]For a discussion of retaliation, see Chapter 10.

[112]Restatement (Second) of Torts §558 (1976)(one is liable for unprivileged publication to a third person of a false statement tending to harm reputation of another). For a discussion of principles of defamation in the sexual harassment context, see Chapters 15, The Common Law, and 24, The Alleged Harasser as Plaintiff.

[113]*See, e.g.,* EEOC v. Levi Strauss & Co., 515 F. Supp. 640, 644, 27 FEP Cases 346, 349–50 (N.D. Ill. 1981)(court rejected EEOC's attempt to enjoin as violation of Title VII state court defamation action by accused harasser against complainant).

[114]*See, e.g.,* Oetzman v. Ahrens, 145 Wis.2d 560, 427 N.W.2d 421, 423 (affirming judgment for supervisor libeled by union representatives who accused supervisor of making "requests for sexual favors," where supervisor had simply said there was a "sexual overtone" to a meeting, had offered female employee a ride to work, and had told employee he would kiss her if she showed up for work), *review denied,* 145 Wis.2d 917, 430 N.W.2d 351 (1988).

the risk of defamation if the incident is discussed outside the confines of the investigation.[115]

Emphasizing the need for truthfulness and confidentiality should not result in intimidating the complainant or supporting witnesses. A court could conceivably reason that overzealous witness admonitions chill the communication of useful information and thus undermine Title VII's goal of eliminating sexually discriminatory conduct. At the same time, principals and witnesses should not be told that their statements will be kept "off the record." While it is important to assure witnesses of as much confidentiality as is practicable, complete confidentiality can never be assured, and a written record of the recollection of witnesses may be essential.[116]

B. Qualified Privilege

1. During the Investigation

Allegations of sexual harassment must inevitably be shared to some extent during the investigation of the charge. Statements made during investigations may be protected by a qualified privilege.[117] Although the law will vary from state to state, a qualified privilege generally protects company investigators and witnesses who make defamatory statements in good faith and for a proper purpose to one who has a legitimate interest in or duty to receive the information.[118]

---

[115]*See, e.g.,* EEOC v. Southern Publishing Co., 894 F.2d 785, 787 (5th Cir. 1990)(complainant sought intervention in EEOC's suit to present defamation claims against employer and alleged harasser); Rudow v. City of New York, 822 F.2d 324, 329–30, 44 FEP Cases 229, 232–33 (2d Cir. 1987)(individual found guilty of sexual harassment by municipal FEP commission brought action for injury to reputation against commission, staff attorney and city); Babb v. Minder, 806 F.2d 749 (7th Cir. 1986)(former employee successfully established defamation claim against employer); Clark v. Yosemite Community College Dist., 785 F.2d 781 (9th Cir. 1986)(college instructor accused of sexually harassing female students sued for alleged defamatory statements placed in his personnel file and communicated to outside parties seeking to hire him); Otto v. Heckler, 781 F.2d 754, 39 FEP Cases 1754 (9th Cir.)(complainant, whose individual sexual harassment complaint was dismissed pending resolution of her participation in class-action EEOC complaint, sued for defamation), *modified in other part,* 802 F.2d 337, 42 FEP Cases 64 (9th Cir. 1986); Stockley v. AT&T Information Sys., 687 F. Supp. 764, 47 FEP Cases 28 (E.D.N.Y. 1988)(alleged harasser brought defamation action based on statements published by employer during sexual harassment investigation).

[116]*See generally* Whitaker v. Carney, 778 F.2d 216, 222, 39 FEP Cases 987, 989 (5th Cir. 1985)(antiretaliation provisions of Title VII do not prevent employer from disclosing complaints to alleged harasser), *cert. denied,* 479 U.S. 813 (1986).

[117]In *DiSilva v. Polaroid Corp.,* 45 FEP Cases 639 (Mass. Dist. Ct. 1985), a Massachusetts appellate court held that an employer was protected by a qualified privilege to publish defamatory statements made in an investigation into alleged sexual harassment of an employee by a supervisor. The court based this privilege not only on state law but on Title VII, federal regulations, and cases prohibiting sexual discrimination. Noting that the employer could be held liable for failure to investigate and remedy sexual harassment, the court held that by investigating the harassment, the employer was fulfilling its legal duty and thus all statements made in the investigation were conditionally privileged as a matter of law. The court noted that the privilege may be lost if abused by publication that was excessive or in bad faith. The plaintiff admitted that the statements made in the course of the investigation were not made with malice and were made by persons "simply doing their job." *Id.* at 643.

[118]*See, e.g.,* Kasachkoff v. City of New York, 107 A.D.2d 130, 485 N.Y.S.2d 992 (N.Y. App. Div. 1985)(statements made during employee counseling session and labor-management meeting regarding employee's work performance and general physical appearance were privileged; evidence of falsity, if proven, insufficient to raise issue of malice), *aff'd,* 68 N.Y.2d 654, 505 N.Y.S.2d 67, 496 N.E.2d 226 (1986); Judge v. Rockford Memorial Hosp., 17 Ill. App.2d 365, 150 N.E.2d 202 (1958)(letter asking Nurses' Registry not to assign named nurse to hospital again because medication was lost during her shift was privileged, absent showing of malice, even if statements were untrue).

Statements that are not made for good cause but are made maliciously or recklessly will abuse the privilege and thus result in the loss of the privilege.[119] Whether the privilege has been abused is a question of fact.[120]

Courts have applied the qualified privilege to exonerate investigators and witnesses from liability for statements made in employment-related investigations that, even if false, were made in good faith and for a proper purpose by a person with a duty to report to a person having a legitimate interest in the subject matter.[121]

2. Communicating the Results of the Investigation

An employer may sometimes want to communicate that it has enforced its policy against sexual harassment. At least one court has recognized that it is in the "common interest" of the employer and employees for the employer to communicate the circumstances that led to a dismissal for sexual harassment, and that a qualified privilege therefore attaches to publications that fulfill an employer's duty to publicize its policy against sexual harassment.[122]

Accordingly, an employer may be privileged to report investigation results in a way that is calculated either to deter further harassment, to inform any complainants that their rights have been adequately addressed, or to address a company policy to the entire work force.[123]

---

[119]See, e.g., Babb v. Minder, supra note 115, 806 F.2d at 756 (where defendant manager's accusations that plaintiff had "mooned" one employee and offered sexual favors to another, although conditionally privileged, were made with reckless disregard of truth or falsity of those statements, the facts, including lack of investigation of allegations, supported jury's finding of actual malice overcoming manager's qualified privilege under Illinois law); O'Brien v. Papa Gino's, 780 F.2d 1067, 1074 (1st Cir. 1986)(employer lost qualified privilege by purposefully misrepresenting reason for employee's dismissal where part of reason was personal grudge on employer's part); Loughry v. Lincoln First Bank, 67 N.Y.2d 369, 502 N.Y.S.2d 965, 969, 494 N.E.2d 70, 74 (1986)(affirming finding of slander where co-worker told plaintiff's supervisor that plaintiff had misappropriated bank's property and sold illegal drugs; privilege abused because statements were false and made with intent to injure plaintiff and employer liable for slander committed by its agents in course of their employment).

[120]See Gonzalez v. CNA Ins. Co., 717 F. Supp. 1087, 1090 (E.D. Pa. 1989)("If defendant acted out of malice, or published the information for a purpose other than that for which the privilege was given, or published it to a person not needed to accomplish the purpose of the privilege, or if the publication contained matter not necessary to accomplish the purpose of the privilege, the court may find an abuse of the privilege"); Glynn v. City of Kissimmee, 383 So.2d 774, 776 (Fla. Dist. Ct. App. 1980)("Whether the privilege exists or has been exceeded in some manner creates a mixed question of law and fact which should be determined by the trier of fact").

[121]See, e.g., Dwyer v. Smith, 867 F.2d 184, 195–96, 48 FEP Cases 1886, 1893–94 (4th Cir. 1989)(communications by department employees that accused plaintiff of being untruthful made in good faith are qualifiedly privileged); Holland v. Marriott Corp., 34 FEP Cases 1763, 1767–68 (D.D.C. 1984)(where discharged employee failed to demonstrate malice, court properly granted employer's motion for summary judgment); Bratt v. IBM Corp., 392 Mass. 508, 467 N.E.2d 126 (1984)(applies Massachusetts law at request of First Circuit to hold that qualified privilege cannot be lost upon showing of mere negligence in publication of statement); Zuniga v. Sears, Roebuck & Co., 100 N.M. 414, 671 P.2d 662 (security guard's report to store manager about employee's attempted theft held to be privileged; statements, even if false, made for proper purpose), cert. denied, 100 N.M. 439 (1983).

[122]Garziano v. E.I. du Pont de Nemours & Co., 818 F.2d 380, 388, 43 FEP Cases 1790, 1797 (5th Cir. 1987). See also Rouly v. Enserch Corp., 835 F.2d 1127, 1130 (5th Cir. 1988)(under Garziano, company had qualified privilege to tell employees plaintiff violated company's conflict-of-interest policies, because "all employees have an interest in their employer's termination policies and grounds for termination").

[123]See also Porterfield v. Burger King Corp., 540 F.2d 398, 403 (8th Cir. 1976)(internal crime loss theft report naming plaintiff as person involved protected by qualified privilege under Missouri law); Jackson v. J.C. Penney Co., 616 F. Supp. 233, 235 (E.D. Pa. 1985)(informing interested employees that plaintiff was fired for theft protected by qualified privilege under Pennsylvania law); Glynn v. City of Kissimmee, supra note 120, 383 So.2d at 774 (defamatory statements made in employment-related context privileged under Florida law).

The employer can try to reduce the risk of defamation by publicizing its policy against sexual harassment without disclosing specific charges against a former employee. One employer, having dismissed an employee for sexually harassing a co-worker, responded to workplace rumors by issuing a bulletin describing the actions taken and the EEOC Guidelines on sexual harassment. These actions were protected by a qualified privilege.[124]

C. Avoiding Excessive Publication

The qualified privilege is exceeded by statements beyond the scope of the investigation, or to persons who have no need to know about the sexual harassment claim.[125] The privilege may thus be lost by the malicious publication of defamatory statements where a proper purpose for the publication is not shown.[126]

---

[124]Garziano v. E.I. du Pont de Nemours & Co., *supra* note 122, 818 F.2d at 383–84, 43 FEP Cases at 1793 (while bulletin did not mention plaintiff by name, it was clear to everyone what incident had prompted it). The bulletin is reprinted as an appendix to the opinion. *Id.* at 396, 43 FEP Cases at 1803–14

[125]*See generally* W.P. KEETON, D. DOBBS, R. KEETON & D. OWEN, PROSSER AND KEETON ON TORTS, §115 at 832 (5th ed. 1984).

[126]*See* Porterfield v. Burger King Corp., *supra* note 123 (crime loss theft report required by parent company to be mailed to corporate insurance department upon discovery of theft that was read by two employees of company and retained in its files qualifiedly privileged); Jackson v. J.C. Penney Co., *supra* note 123, 616 F. Supp. at 234–35 (manager's accusation in presence of two security guards that employee attempted theft was privileged where one guard was investigating and other guard escorted employee out of store, because all persons shared common interest); Stockley v. AT&T Information Sys., 687 F. Supp. 764, 768–70, 47 FEP Cases 28, 32–34 (E.D.N.Y. 1988)(statements made by defendant's employees in course of investigation into sexual harassment charges against plaintiff protected by qualified privilege where defendant had a duty to investigate charges and allegedly defamatory statements were made to persons responsible for carrying out such duty); Judge v. Rockford Memorial Hosp., *supra* note 118, 150 N.E.2d at 206–17 (1958)(letter by defendant's director of nurses to nurses' professional registry requesting that plaintiff not be assigned to defendant's hospital, implying plaintiff's responsibility for missing drugs, is qualifiedly privileged under Illinois law as communication made in good faith by person having interest or duty to another person having interest or duty); Kasachkoff v. City of New York, *supra* note 118 (under New York law, good faith accusations that plaintiff appeared at work intoxicated and unable to perform professional duties, communicated during counseling session with plaintiff, her union representative, director of administrative affairs, and rehabilitation psychologist, were qualifiedly privileged as communications between parties with an interest or duty with respect to subject matter).

CHAPTER 20

THE AGENCY INVESTIGATION

I. FILING THE CHARGE

A. Preliminary Procedure

The EEOC's administrative process commences with the filing of a charge of discrimination, in writing under oath or affirmation.[1] The procedure by which an EEOC investigator works with an aggrieved individual to file a charge is termed the intake process. The EEOC has endorsed the use of testers— persons who pose as job applicants for the purpose of gathering evidence of discrimination, and testers have been used in sexual harassment cases.[2]

Upon arrival at the EEOC office,[3] the individual first completes a questionnaire identifying the parties, describing the circumstances of the alleged sexual harassment, and identifying any witnesses and any other victims. The EEOC investigator then meets with the complainant to discuss the allegations. If the circumstances are particularly sensitive or embarrassing and the complainant is reluctant to discuss them with an investigator of the opposite sex, the complainant is given the option of talking to someone of the same sex.[4]

The EEOC investigator will review the information provided to ensure that the charge states a valid claim under the statute and that the EEOC has

---

[1]For a complete discussion of the EEOC administrative process, see B.L. SCHLEI & P. GROSSMAN, EMPLOYMENT DISCRIMINATION LAW, Chapter 26 (2d ed. 1983) and Five-Year Supplement (1989). EEOC investigations are guided in large part by the EEOC Compliance Manual, some portions of which are general in application and procedure, and some portions of which, *e.g.,* §615, deal specifically with issues pertaining to sexual harassment. Section 615 is reproduced in Appendix 4. EEOC interpretations are also guided by EEOC policy guidances, one of which deals generally with sexual harassment, EEOC Policy Guidance on Sexual Harassment, 8 FAIR EMPL. PRAC. MAN. (BNA) 405:6681–6701 (March 19, 1990), reproduced in Appendix 3, and one of which deals with sexual favoritism, EEOC Policy Guidance on Employer Liability for Sexual Favoritism, 8 FAIR EMPL. PRAC. MAN. (BNA) 405:6817–21 (Jan. 12, 1990), reproduced in Appendix 2.

[2]*See, e.g.,* 111 DAILY LAB. REP. A-12 (June 10, 1991)(reporting on use of female testers by civil rights advocacy group in suit against employment agency that allegedly suggested females pay for agency's services in the form of sexual favors).

[3]A person may also file charges without visiting an EEOC office. When an aggrieved individual provides sufficient information by telephone or by mail, the EEOC will draft a formal charge and mail it for signature. *See* EEOC COMPL. MAN. §§2.2, 2.3, *reprinted in* EEOC COMPL. MAN. (BNA) p. 2:0001–2. "[A] charge is sufficient when the EEOC receives from the person making the charge a written statement sufficiently precise to identify the parties, and to describe generally the action or practice complained of." EEOC Procedural Regulations, 29 C.F.R. §1601.12(b)(1990). In states that have entered into a worksharing agreement with the EEOC, filing with the state fair employment practices agency is deemed filing with the EEOC. EEOC COMPL. MAN., §5.2 at 5:0001.

[4]EEOC COMPL. MAN., *supra* note 3, §2.4(j) at 2:0006.

jurisdiction. This review will include a determination that the person or entity charged—the "respondent"—is covered by Title VII.[5]

B. Determination of Timeliness

The investigator then reviews the timeliness of the charge. A charge must be filed within 180 days of the alleged discrimination, or within 300 days in a state with a fair employment practices statute prohibiting discrimination.[6] Two principles can relax the strict time limits for filing a charge: equitable tolling and the theory of continuing violation.

1. Equitable Tolling

In some cases, equitable circumstances can excuse the late filing of a charge; if so, the time period for filing is deemed tolled for the duration of these circumstances. Tolling was allowed in *Llewellyn v. Celanese Corp.*,[7] where a charging party suffered severe psychological problems as a result of sexual harassment that affected her ability to file a charge.[8]

2. Continuing Violations

The theory of continuing violation applies to a pattern of unlawful conduct that continues over a period of time. It does not actually excuse a late filing; there still must be actionable conduct within the charge-filing period.[9] Where the harassing conduct is part of a pattern that began outside of the charge-filing period and continued into that period, however, some courts hold that the charge may lawfully include the entire history of harassment.[10]

The Fifth Circuit has described some of the factors that help identify whether the continuing violation theory applies:

> The first is subject matter. Do the alleged acts involve the same type of discrimination, tending to connect them in a continuing violation? The second is frequency. Are the alleged acts recurring (*e.g.,* a biweekly paycheck) or more in the nature of an isolated work assignment or employment decision? The third factor, perhaps of most importance, is the degree of permanence. Does the act have the degree of permanence which should trigger an employee's awareness that the continued existence of the adverse consequences of the act is to be expected without being dependent on a continuing intent to discriminate?[11]

---

[5]An employer is covered if it employs 15 or more employees for 20 or more calendar weeks in the current or preceding year. Section 701(b) of Title VII, 42 U.S.C. §2000e-(b).

[6]Section 706(e) of Title VII, 42 U.S.C. §2000e-5(e). Section 706(c) of Title VII provides that state or local agencies have an initial period of exclusive jurisdiction. 42 U.S.C. §2000e-5(c). When the EEOC receives a charge that has not been filed with the state or local agency, it is "deferred" to the appropriate agency. *See* EEOC Procedural Regulations, 29 C.F.R. §1601.13. In most instances, these agencies have a worksharing agreement with the EEOC, which allocates primary investigative responsibility for charges. *See* SCHLEI & GROSSMAN, *supra* note 1, at Chapter 28.

[7]693 F. Supp. 369, 47 FEP Cases 993 (W.D.N.C. 1988).

[8]*Cf.* Barnell v. Paine Webber Jackson & Curtis, 44 EPD ¶37,437 (S.D.N.Y. 1987)(tolling not permitted where complainant could function in society and protect her legal rights despite psychiatrist's diagnosis that she suffered from anxiety neurosis).

[9]*See, e.g.,* Abrams v. Baylor Medical College of Medicine, 805 F.2d 528, 42 FEP Cases 806 (5th Cir. 1986)(plaintiff must show that one incident of harassment occurred within the 180-day period).

[10]For an extended discussion of the theory of continuing violation in the context of a sexual harassment claim, see Chapter 27, Asserted Defenses, Section II.B.5.

[11]Berry v. Board of Supervisors, 715 F.2d 971, 32 FEP Cases 1567 (5th Cir. 1983), *cert. denied,* 479

C. EEOC's Intake Process

If the investigator believes that there are jurisdictional problems, the investigator will try to counsel the complainant not to file a charge. The complainant, however, has a statutory right to file, and if the complainant insists, a charge will be taken.

The investigator will draft the formal charge from the information given by the complainant. The charge will contain the name and address of the parties, the date of the alleged discrimination, and a short statement of the discrimination alleged, including the harm suffered by the complainant.

Following signature by the complainant, the charge will be reviewed to determine if expedited processing is required. Title VII authorizes the EEOC to seek preliminary relief in United States District Court.[12] Charges that allege continuing sexual harassment are potential candidates for an expedited investigation and for an application for a temporary restraining order and preliminary injunction from the court.[13] For this reason, an EEOC attorney reviews incoming charges in most EEOC district offices.

II. THE INVESTIGATION

A. The Respondent's Position Statement

The investigation begins with the service of the charge. Title VII requires that a respondent be provided within ten days with notice that a charge has been filed.[14] In the usual case, service of the charge will be accompanied by a request that the respondent provide a position statement setting forth its response to the allegations of the charge. Like an answer to a court complaint, the position statement, in conjunction with the charge, will define what is at issue and, therefore, what needs to be investigated.

The position statement is vital to the respondent's defense of a sexual harassment charge. If thoughtfully prepared and persuasive, the statement may substantially assist the respondent's cause; if it is inaccurate or overstated, the statement may be counterproductive. Once the respondent response has been submitted to the EEOC, it will be extremely difficult for the respondent to change its theories of defense without compromising its credibility. If the EEOC finds reasonable cause to believe that sexual harassment has occurred, and efforts at conciliation fail, the position statement will be included in the materials submitted to the general counsel and commissioners when the decision whether to litigate is made, and will be made available to the complainant.

The position statement should offer a narrative of the facts. If there is some uncertainty surrounding the relationship of the complainant to any alleged

---

U.S. 868 (1986), *quoted in* Waltman v. International Paper Co., 875 F.2d 468, 475, 50 FEP Cases 179 (5th Cir. 1989).

[12]Section 706(f)(2), 42 U.S.C. §2000e-5(f)(2).

[13]For a discussion of injunctive relief, see Chapter 28, Injunctive and Affirmative Relief. The EEOC has prepared a model brief for use by EEOC attorneys in seeking temporary restraining orders and preliminary injunctions in sexual harassment cases. See 52 DAILY LAB. REP. A-4 (March 18, 1991).

[14]Section 706(b), 42 U.S.C. §2000e-5(b).

harasser, the position statement should clarify the relationship. The determination of the respondent's liability may depend on the nature of this relationship.[15] The statement should also describe the respondent's sexual harassment policy and detail any steps taken under that policy with respect to the complainant's allegations.[16]

It will be helpful to support all major factual statements either by attached documents or affidavits. Sexual harassment cases depend heavily upon credibility. The respondent can increase its chances of prevailing if it can demonstrate that one or more of the complainant's assertions conflict or are inconsistent with objective, credible fact.

B. Requests for Information

Following receipt of the employer's position statement, the investigator will frequently send the employer a written request for information (RFI). An RFI is analogous to an interrogatory or a request for production of documents in litigation. Examples of information typically sought in a sexual harassment RFI include:

(1) identification of previous complaints of sexual harassment;
(2) a copy of any existing policy on sexual harassment, including the procedure by which an employee may complain;
(3) a description of how employees are informed of the policy;
(4) a description of management training on how to handle sexual harassment; and
(5) the personnel files of the charging party, the alleged harasser, and other employees who have complained of sexual harassment.

In quid pro quo cases where the complainant alleges a tangible job detriment, the investigator will request documentation of the relevant employment decisions.

C. Witness Interviews

Testimony in the form of affidavits is critical to any employment discrimination investigation, but is particularly important in sexual harassment charges. The testimony of the complainant will be taken at intake. Witnesses identified by the complainant may be interviewed as soon as they can be located. Respondent's witnesses are typically interviewed at the work site.

To avoid influence by the parties, the investigator is instructed to "[i]nterview witnesses under conditions which assure privacy."[17] While the respondent's attorney has the right to attend the interview of management officials,

---

[15]EEOC investigators are required to determine this relationship. See Section III.B. *infra*.

[16]The role of respondent's policy and response in the EEOC investigation are discussed in Sections II.B. and III.D. *infra*. For a complete discussion of these issues, see Chapters 18, Taking Preventive Action, and 19, Responding to Internal Complaints.

[17]EEOC COMPL. MAN., *supra* note 3, §23.6(b) at 23:0003.

the investigator will seek to conduct interviews of nonmanagement employees only in private.[18]

EEOC investigators are instructed to "question the charging party and the alleged harasser in detail. ... Supervisory and managerial employees, as well as co-workers, should be asked about their knowledge of the alleged harassment."[19]

If the employer fails to respond to an RFI or refuses to allow the investigator to interview necessary witnesses, the EEOC may issue an administrative subpoena, which is judicially enforceable.[20]

D. Resolution of the Charge

When the investigator has obtained sufficient evidence to determine whether the charge has merit, the investigator may conduct a "pre-determination interview" with whichever party would not prevail in the determination.[21] During this interview, the investigator will review the evidence obtained, inform the party of the proposed determination, and invite the submission of additional evidence.

Thereafter, the EEOC will issue its determination. Title VII directs that the EEOC determine whether there is reasonable cause to believe the charge is true.[22] Thus, determinations that the charge is meritorious are termed "cause" findings; determinations that the charge is without merit are termed "no cause" findings. Under Rule 803(8)(C) of the Federal Rules of Evidence, these determinations are generally admissible at trial as factual findings of a public agency.[23]

If the EEOC finds cause, Title VII requires that the agency attempt to resolve the matter informally by conciliation.[24] Conciliation of a sexual harassment charge would typically include instituting an appropriate policy, providing relief to the complainant and any other victims, and disciplining the harasser. If conciliation is not successful, the EEOC may file an enforcement action in federal district court,[25] or advise the charging parties of their right to file a private suit within 90 days.[25a]

---

[18]*Id.*, §23.6(c) at 23:0003.

[19]EEOC Policy Guidance on Sexual Harassment, *supra* note 1, at 405:6687.

[20]Sections 709(a), 710 of Title VII, 42 U.S.C. §§2000e-8(a) and -9. For a complete discussion of EEOC subpoena authority, see SCHLEI & GROSSMAN, *supra* note 1, at Chapter 26, Section III.

[21]EEOC COMPL. MAN., *supra* note 3, §27 at 27:0001.

[22]Section 706(b) of Title VII, 42 U.S.C. 2000e-5(b).

[23]*See, e.g.,* Barfield v. Orange County, 911 F.2d 644 (11th Cir. 1990)("no cause" determination admissible in jury trial); Smith v. Universal Servs., 454 F.2d 154 (5th Cir. 1972)(EEOC findings are "highly probative"); Plummer v. Western Int'l Hotels, 656 F.2d 502, 26 FEP Cases 1292 (9th Cir. 1981)("plaintiff has a right to introduce an EEOC probable cause determination").

[24]Settlement is also possible before issuance of a cause determination. Such a resolution is termed a pre-determination settlement (PDS). EEOC COMPL. MAN., *supra* note 3, §15 at 15:0001–5.

[25]Section 706(f)(1) of Title VII, 42 U.S.C. §2000e-5(f)(1).

[25a]For a discussion of the timely filing of a lawsuit, see Chapter 27, Asserted Defenses, Section II.G.

III. INVESTIGATORY ISSUES IN SEXUAL HARASSMENT CHARGES

In its latest statement of policy on sexual harassment,[26] the EEOC has provided guidance to its investigators on how to address the special issues posed by sexual harassment charges.

A. Unwelcomeness

The threshold issue in many charges is whether the conduct complained of was unwelcome.[27] Recognizing that "sexual attraction may often play a role in the day-to-day social exchange between employees," the EEOC requires its investigators to determine unwelcomeness from the totality of the circumstances.[28] When unwelcomeness is seriously at issue, evidence of contemporaneous protest is viewed as particularly persuasive. "Generally, victims are well-advised to assert their right to a workplace free from sexual harassment."[29] Such a protest is not a necessary element of a claim, for sometimes victims may fail to protest out of a reasonable fear of reprisal. However, if there was no protest, the investigator must ascertain the reasons why the complainant did not complain.[30]

B. Charging Party's Relationship to the Alleged Harasser

In both quid pro quo and hostile environment cases, it is necessary to establish the relationship between the complainant and the alleged harasser. EEOC investigators are instructed to request information that will permit them to identify whether the alleged harasser was a supervisory employee, a co-worker, or a nonemployee. Establishing this relationship is critical in determining the employer's responsibility.[31] The EEOC uses common-law principles of agency in fixing the employer's liability.[32]

A supervisory relationship in a quid pro quo case may lead to a finding of direct employer liability if the underlying harassment claim is established. If the alleged harasser was not a supervisor of the complainant, but rather a co-worker or a nonemployee, the investigator will determine whether the employer knew or should have known of the alleged sexual harassment. The investigator will inquire whether the complainant or others made contemporaneous objections or reports concerning the conduct of the alleged harasser, or if a management employee knew or should have known of the alleged conduct. This information will help to determine if any illegal conduct can be imputed to the employer even in the absence of a direct supervisory relationship between the alleged harasser and the complainant.

---

[26]EEOC Policy Guidance on Sexual Harassment, 8 FAIR EMP. PRAC. MAN. (BNA) 405:6681–6701 (March 19, 1990), reproduced in Appendix 3.

[27]For a more thorough discussion of the concept of unwelcomeness, see Chapters 3, Quid Pro Quo Harassment, and 4, Hostile Environment Harassment.

[28]EEOC Policy Guidance on Sexual Harassment, *supra* note 26, at 405:6685.

[29]*Id.*

[30]*Id.*

[31]See Chapters 6, Harassment by Supervisors; 7, Harassment by Co-Workers; and 8, Harassment by Nonemployees.

[32]EEOC Policy Guidance on Sexual Harassment, *supra* note 26, at 405:6693–94.

C. Determination of Hostile Environment

In a hostile environment case, the EEOC has adopted the "reasonable person" standard for determining whether the harassment is sufficiently severe or pervasive to violate Title VII.[33] "[I]f the challenged conduct would not substantially affect the work environment of a reasonable person, no violation should be found."[34] In applying this standard, a pattern of offensive conduct is generally required to find a violation; a single incident usually will not suffice unless it is egregious.[35] Sexual touching is presumptively severe enough to be actionable: "[t]he Commission will presume that the unwelcome, intentional touching of a charging party's intimate body areas is sufficiently offensive to alter the conditions of her working environment and constitute a violation of Title VII."[36]

In evaluating allegations of verbal harassment, the EEOC investigator will determine the nature, frequency, context, and intended target of the remarks. The investigator will consider whether the alleged harasser singled out the complainant, whether the complainant participated, the relationship between the complainant and the alleged harasser, and whether the remarks were hostile and derogatory.[37]

D. Respondent's Internal Response to Complaint

If the employer asserts that its internal response remedied the situation, the investigator will try to determine whether the employer conducted a prompt and thorough investigation of the allegations and, if warranted, took prompt and appropriate corrective action.[38] The investigator will seek to learn what steps were taken, when they were taken, and whether the steps fully remedied the conduct without adversely affecting the complainant's employment status.[39] "If the Commission finds that the harassment has been eliminated, all victims made whole, and preventive measures instituted, the Commission normally will administratively close the charge because of the employer's prompt remedial action."[40]

---

[33]*Id.* at 405:6689.

[34]*Id.*

[35]*Id.* at 405:6690.

[36]*Id.* at 405:6691.

[37]*Id.*

[38]For a discussion of the employer's response to internal complaints, see Chapter 19, Responding to Internal Complaints.

[39]EEOC COMPL. MAN., §615.4(a)(9), *reprinted in* EEOC COMP. MAN. (BNA) p. 615:0013. The manual cites as inadequate a remedy that gives the complainant less desirable hours of work or a less desirable worksite. Investigators must be alert to these types of detrimental "cures" because the employer may be tempted to remedy the situation by limiting contact between the harasser and the complainant. This "cure" may result in retaining alleged harassers with more important roles in the organization in convenient headquarters locations, while the complainant is sent to a remote outpost or a less desirable shift. The employer will be required to submit the reasons it has for these actions.

[40]EEOC Policy Guidance on Sexual Harassment, *supra* note 26, at 405:6701.

Part V

SPECIAL LITIGATION ISSUES

CHAPTER 21

COMPLAINANT'S LITIGATION STRATEGY

I. PRE-FILING INVESTIGATION

A thorough investigation of the facts underlying a complainant's allegations should precede the filing of any action for sexual harassment. Rule 11 of the Federal Rules of Civil Procedure[1] and state-law counterparts[2] require a person filing a complaint to certify a belief, based on a reasonable inquiry, that the allegations in the complaint are well-grounded in fact. When agreeing to represent a complainant, counsel may want to consider reciting in a letter the factual representations that formed the basis of the agreement to represent, as well as the range of monetary and equitable relief to be sought consistent with the factual representations. This letter may be important in securing the complainant's cooperation in a less favorable resolution if discovery puts the case in a different factual posture.[3]

A. Initial Interview of the Complainant

An extensive initial interview of the complainant should be undertaken at the earliest possible time. It should elicit as much detail as possible about each alleged incident of harassment. The complainant should be asked for specific information concerning the time, place, and setting of each incident, any events leading up to or triggering the incident, the position and background of each person who was involved or who was present, the exact statements and actions of each person present, the identities of others not present who are aware of the incident, and the identity of any others who have been subjected to similar behavior.

---

[1]Rule 11 provides in part: "The signature of an attorney or party constitutes a certificate by the signer that the signer has read the pleading, motion, or other paper; that to the best of the signer's knowledge, information, and belief formed after reasonable inquiry it is well grounded in fact . . . ." For a discussion of cases where sanctions have been imposed for failure to make reasonable inquiry prior to filing, see Note, *Rule 11 of the Federal Rules of Civil Procedures and the Duty to Withdraw a Baseless Pleading*, 56 FORDHAM L. REV. 697 (1988); ABA SECTION OF LITIGATION, SANCTIONS, RULE 11 AND OTHER POWERS (2d ed. 1988).

[2]More than half the states have court rules or statutes patterned after Rule 11 or designed to serve a similar purpose, *e.g.*, CAL. CODE CIV. PROC. §128.5 (West 1985); ILL. ANN. STAT. ch. 110, ¶2-611 (Smith-Hurd 1986); VA. CODE ANN. §8.01-271.1 (1987). For a complete list, see LAW. MANUAL ON PROF. CONDUCT 61:165 (ABA/BNA 1990).

[3]To protect themselves, some plaintiffs' attorneys also ask the complainant to provide a detailed written account of the events giving rise to the allegations. To ensure that the written account is not discoverable, they advise the complainant to address the document to the attorney and to show it to no one else.

It is essential to determine the complainant's response to the harassment and whether the complainant made a contemporaneous internal report of the incident to management or others in the workplace. Because the adequacy of the employer's response to a complaint can affect liability,[4] counsel should find out the precise nature of any complaint made, when and to whom it was made, the reaction of the person receiving the complaint, and the adequacy and timeliness of any remedial actions taken by the employer. If no internal complaint was made, counsel should explore the reasons for this failure.[5]

Counsel should obtain information about the complainant to assess credibility and evaluate possible defenses. A complete work history should be developed, with emphasis on the complainant's position and progression within the company, reporting relationships, and any performance difficulties, personality clashes, or failed expectations that could supply a motive for a fabricated claim. Similarly, counsel should explore personal matters such as pertinent personal relationships; psychological and physical history; history of filing legal actions, particularly against the current or any former employers; and pressures from the complainant's spouse or family. The complainant's willingness to have personal matters exposed to public view, and an understanding of how a lawsuit could affect the complainant's career, should also be discussed at this initial stage.

Because the filing of a timely charge is a prerequisite to a lawsuit under Title VII and many state FEP statutes,[6] counsel must ascertain whether charges have been filed with the appropriate agencies and take steps to rectify any omission in that regard.

If a complainant cannot or will not provide documentary evidence or the names of any corroborating witnesses, it may be wise not to take the case. Counsel who have serious doubts about accepting a sexual harassment complainant as a client have the option of advising the complainant to file a charge with the EEOC and the appropriate state fair employment practices (FEP) agency,[7] which will assist the complainant regardless of whether the complainant has counsel. The case can always be reevaluated following an agency investigation. Counsel should also advise the complainant if the statute of limitations on any of the claims may run before the agency investigation is completed. Complainants may want to consider filing a complaint, but not serving it during the pendency of the agency investigation, to preserve their options.

---

[4]See Chapters 4, Hostile Environment Harassment, Section IX.C.2.; 6, Harassment by Supervisors, Section IV; and 7, Harassment by Co-Workers, Section V.

[5]A failure to make a contemporaneous complaint not only may raise questions as to the plaintiff's credibility and motives, but in some cases also may mean that the employer had no notice and no liability. See Chapters 4, Hostile Environment Harassment, Section IX.C.2.; 6, Harassment by Supervisors, Section IV.; and 7, Harassment by Co-Workers, Section IV.

[6]Under Title VII a complainant has 90 days from receipt of a right-to-sue letter to file a complaint, §706(f)(1), 42 U.S.C. §2000e-5(f)(1). See B.L. SCHLEI & P. GROSSMAN, EMPLOYMENT DISCRIMINATION LAW 1058–71 (2d ed. 1983), Five-Year Supplement 402–4 (1989), and Chapter 27, Asserted Defenses, Section II.B.

[7]Because of the differences in both the jurisdictional prerequisites for filing suit and in the available remedies, complaints should be filed whenever possible with both the EEOC and the FEP agency.

B. Documentary Investigation

As part of the preliminary investigation, counsel should request copies of all relevant documents in the complainant's possession. Often the complainant will have made personal or desk calendar notes or diary entries concerning the events in question. The complainant usually will have a copy of the employee handbook or brochure, and may have a copy of personnel and benefits policies, including the policy on sexual harassment.

Counsel should immediately obtain copies of any papers filed with the EEOC or state FEP agency and any findings that have been issued, and should request a copy of the right-to-sue letter and collect any evidence establishing when it was received by the complainant. If the EEOC investigation has been completed, counsel is entitled to—and should—review the EEOC's investigative file before filing a complaint.[8] Some state agencies may also permit this review.[9]

A copy of the complainant's personnel file should be sought from the employer. Some state laws grant employees access to at least some part of their personnel files upon written request.[10] Even in the absence of a legal requirement, an employer may voluntarily make the file available in the hope of deflecting a lawsuit. The file may reveal the employer's version of the events at issue and is likely, in any event, to contain evidence of the complainant's performance and disciplinary record, general policies and practices of the employer, and other potentially relevant documents such as time cards, logs, attendance records, medical history, and workers' compensation claims. It may be wise for the complainant to review the file to freeze its contents. Where an employee cannot make copies of what is in the file, the complainant should make a careful listing, including the number of pages of each document and the last entry on each document. Even a barren personnel file may be useful to show employer laxity in personnel matters.

A computer search of pending and decided cases involving the employer and other potential defendants is often helpful. Documents filed in prior litigation can provide substantial data concerning the employer's structure, procedures, and policies. Computer services also provide access to nonlitigatory filings such as Securities and Exchange Commission Forms 10-K and 10-Q, proxy materials, and secretary-of-state corporate filings, which contain valuable information about the employer's operations and finances.

C. Interviews With Other Witnesses

The complainant should prepare a list of potential witnesses, both favorable and unfavorable, including background information that would be useful

---

[8]*See* EEOC v. Associated Dry Goods Corp., 449 U.S. 590, 603, 24 FEP Cases 1356 (1981)(pre-litigation disclosure to charging party of information in EEOC file not "public" disclosure prohibited by §§706(b) and 709(e) of Title VII); EEOC v. University of Pittsburgh, 643 F.2d 983, 987, 25 FEP Cases 508 (3d Cir.), *cert. denied*, 454 U.S. 880 (1981).

[9]*See, e.g.,* FLA. STAT. ANN. §760.10(14)(West 1986)("all complaints filed with the [state FEP agency] . . . and all records and documents . . . which relate to and identify a particular complainant, employer, employment agency . . . shall be confidential and shall not be disclosed by the commission, *except to the parties*" (emphasis added)). *Cf.* IDAHO CODE §67-5907(2)(1989)(before lawsuit is filed, parties cannot have direct access to documents or statements of witnesses or opposing parties except to the extent they are incorporated into written findings; complainants may, however, obtain copies of answers and attachments).

[10]For reference to the state laws, see FAIR EMP. PRAC. MAN. (BNA) 8A, 8B.

in interviewing them or in taking a deposition. A careful interview of the complainant and a review of available documents may identify additional potential witnesses. In particular, the complainant's co-workers may be able to corroborate or controvert the claim and provide evidence of their own behavior, which may bear on the issue of "unwelcomeness."[11] Co-workers may also identify other employees who have been victimized by the same harasser or have observed similar behavior, or who have taken actions sufficient to put management on notice of the harassment.[12]

II. COMMUNICATION WITH THE DEFENDANT'S EMPLOYEES

Although co-worker witnesses may provide invaluable assistance in the pre-complaint stage, there are legal and ethical constraints on counsel's freedom to conduct *ex parte* interviews with employees of an adverse corporate party. A violation of *ex parte* communication rules could lead to sanctions, disqualification of counsel, or rulings precluding the use of admissions obtained through an improper employee interview.[13] Before contacting any present or former employee of the defendant employer, therefore, the complainant's counsel must determine whether the particular contact is permissible under the governing ethical rules and court decisions of the jurisdiction.

A. Rules Forbidding Ex Parte Contacts

Disciplinary Rule 7-104(A)(1) of the Model Code of Professional Responsibility prohibits a lawyer from communicating with a party who is known to be represented by counsel in the matter in question without the consent of the party's attorney or other legal authorization.[14] Rule 4.2 of the Model Rules of Professional Conduct contains a similar prohibition.[15] The disciplinary rules lack the force of law and are not binding on courts, but are frequently cited in rulings on issues presented by *ex parte* communications.[16]

---

[11]See Chapters 3, Quid Pro Quo Harassment, Section V., and 4, Hostile Environment Harassment, Section V.A.

[12]For a discussion of employer notice, see Chapter 7, Harassment by Co-Workers, Section IV. For a discussion of the admissibility of evidence of sexual harassment in the employer's workplace not directed at the complainant, see Chapters 5, Claims by Third Parties, Section V., and 25, Evidence, Section VI.

[13]See Section II. *infra.*

[14]Disciplinary Rule 7-104(A) provides:

During the course of his representation of a client, a lawyer shall not: (1) Communicate or cause another to communicate on the subject of the representation with a party he knows to be represented by a lawyer in that matter unless he has the prior consent of the lawyer representing such other party or is authorized by law to do so.

The Model Code of Professional Responsibility (Model Code) was originally adopted by the American Bar Association (ABA) in 1969. After amending the Model Code several times, the ABA replaced it in 1983 with the Model Rules of Professional Conduct (Model Rules). Most states still follow the Model Code rather than the Model Rules. For a reproduction of the Model Code and the Model Rules, with digests of judicial and bar-association opinions and state statutory provisions on ethical issues, see LAW. MANUAL ON PROF. CONDUCT (ABA/BNA 1990).

[15]Model Rule 4.2 provides: "In representing a client, a lawyer shall not communicate about the subject of the representation with a party the lawyer knows to be represented by another lawyer in the matter, unless the lawyer has the consent of the other lawyer or is authorized by law to do so."

[16]*E.g.,* J.P. Foley & Co. v. Vanderbilt, 523 F.2d 1357, 1360 (2d Cir. 1975)(Gurfein, J., concurring). *See generally* Annot., *Right of Attorney to Conduct Ex Parte Interviews With Corporate Party's Nonmanagement Employees,* 50 A.L.R.4th 652 (1986); Leubsdorf, *Communicating With Another Lawyer's Client: The Lawyer's Veto and the Client's Interest,* 127 U. PA. L. REV. 683, 708 (1979).

Neither Disciplinary Rule 7-104 nor Model Rule 4.2 defines the term "party." While it is clear that the rules forbid the complainant's lawyer from unilaterally approaching an individual defendant who is represented by counsel, it is less clear who is protected from unilateral contact when the opposing party represented by counsel is a corporation. The rules obviously treat at least some current employees of the defendant corporation as the corporate "party," but do not clearly identify which employees so qualify.

Courts considering this issue must accommodate strong competing interests. Permitting the complainant's counsel to conduct *ex parte* employee interviews may weed out frivolous claims, reduce the delay and expense of formal discovery, neutralize the employer's "unfair" advantage in having informal access to its own employees, and eliminate any intimidation of a witness caused by the presence of counsel representing the witness's employer. However, *ex parte* employee interviews invade the employer's interest in having its counsel regulate the release of information garnered by employees in the course of employment, and create risks of invading the corporation's attorney-client privilege and extracting admissions from lay persons whose statements may be binding on the corporation.[17]

B. Current Employees

1. Restriction as to All Current Employees

The most restrictive standard, adopted in a few court or bar-association opinions, defines the corporate party expansively and thereby prohibits *ex parte* interviews with *any* current employee of a represented corporate defendant.[18] Most courts, however, have refused to declare all current employees off-limits to opposing counsel, reasoning that such a broad definition of the corporate party unduly hampers the search for truth and is unnecessary to protect legitimate corporate interests.[19]

---

[17]Under Rule 801(d)(2)(D) of the Federal Rules of Evidence, a statement is admissible against a party if the statement is "by the party's agent or servant concerning a matter within the scope of the agency or employment, made during the existence of the relationship." Many state evidence rules are similar. For a list of states that have adopted the substance of Rule 801(d)(2), see 2 G. JOSEPH, S. SALTZBURG, & TRIAL EVIDENCE COMMITTEE OF THE ABA SECTION OF LITIGATION, EVIDENCE IN AMERICA: THE FEDERAL RULES IN THE UNITED STATES §56(2)(1987).

[18]*See generally* Miller & Calfo, *Ex Parte Contact With Employees and Former Employees of a Corporate Adversary: Is It Ethical?*, 42 BUS. LAW. 1053 (1987)(urging adoption of clear rule forbidding *ex parte* contacts concerning subject of controversy with all current employees). *See, e.g.,* Cagguila v. Wyeth Laboratories, 127 F.R.D. 653, 53 FEP Cases 11 (E.D. Pa. 1989); Nassau County Bar Ass'n Comm. on Prof. Ethics, Op. 89-2 (1989)(summarized in LAW. MANUAL ON PROF. CONDUCT, *supra* note 14, at 901:6267); L.A. County Ethics Comm., Formal Op. 410 (1983) summarized in LAW. MANUAL ON PROF. CONDUCT, *supra* note 14, at 801:1709; N.Y. Law. Ass'n, Op. 528 (1964); Bobele v. Superior Court, 199 Cal. App.3d 708, 713, 245 Cal. Rptr. 144, 147, 52 FEP Cases 428, 430 (1988)(plaintiffs could not conduct *ex parte* interviews with current employees or with former employees who remain members of the corporate "control group"). *Bobele* was based on an ethical rule since superseded by Rule 2-100 of the California Rules of Professional Conduct. See note 20 *infra*.

[19]*See, e.g.,* Niesig v. Team I, 76 N.Y.2d 363, 558 N.E.2d 1030, 1034, 559 N.Y.S.2d 493, 497 (1990)(despite contrary bar association opinions, New York's highest court explicitly rejected blanket rule prohibiting contact with all corporate employees because it forecloses all avenues of informal discovery and is unnecessary to safeguard corporation's interests in that employer's counsel can prepare employees in advance not to make improvident disclosures); Porter v. ARCO Metals Co., 642 F. Supp. 1116 (D. Mont. 1986)(nonmanagerial corporate employees may be contacted directly); Frey v. Department of Health & Human Servs., 106 F.R.D. 32, 36, 50 FEP Cases 1381 (E.D.N.Y. 1985)(extending term "party" to include all employees would bar civil rights plaintiffs from inexpensive access to vast numbers of potential witnesses and might frustrate individual's right to pursue legal relief).

2. Restriction as to Managerial Employees

Under most decisions, adverse counsel is permitted informal access to employee witnesses whose acts or statements cannot bind the employer.[20] Courts and bar associations issuing these decisions thus would permit *ex parte* contacts with all employees except managerial employees or others whose acts or omissions in the matter under inquiry are binding on the corporation or can be imputed to the corporation for purposes of liability.[21]

A variation of this second standard, reflecting a concern for protecting the corporation's attorney-client privilege, extends the prohibition on *ex parte* communications to employees who are responsible for effecting the advice of counsel in the matter that is the subject of the communication.[22]

Recognizing that statements of lower-level employees concerning matters within the scope of their employment could be admissible against the corporation under Federal Rule 801, even if the employee's own acts or omissions are not in issue, some courts have taken the precaution of ruling in advance that any statements obtained in *ex parte* interviews will not be treated as admissions binding on the corporation.[23]

---

[20]This rule is largely consistent with the interpretation of the corporate party set forth in the ABA Comment to Model Rule 4.2, *reprinted in* LAW. MANUAL ON PROF. CONDUCT, *supra* note 14, at 01:158, which identifies three categories of current employees shielded from *ex parte* contact:

> In the case of an organization, this Rule prohibits communications by a lawyer for one party concerning the matter in representation with [1] persons having a managerial responsibility on behalf of the organization, and with any other person [2] whose acts or omission in connection with that matter may be imputed to the organization for purposes of civil or criminal liability or [3] whose statement may constitute an admission on the part of the organization.

Along these lines is new Rule 2-100 of the California Rules of Professional Conduct, which forbids *ex parte* communications with an employee of an adverse corporate party "if the subject of the communication is any act or omission of [the employee] . . . which may be binding upon or imputed to the organization for purposes of civil or criminal liability or whose statement may constitute an admission on the part of the organization."

[21]*Decisions under Model Rule 4.2:* E.g., University Patents v. Kligman, 737 F. Supp. 325 (E.D. Pa. 1990)(Model Rule 4.2 forbids *ex parte* communications with all employees whose acts or omissions could bind or impute liability to employer or whose statements could be used as admissions against employer); Bey v. Arlington Heights, 50 FEP Cases 1375 (N.D. Ill. 1989)(restrictions of Model Rule 4.2 apply only to employees who have "speaking authority," *i.e.,* whose statements are attributable to and binding upon corporation, and not to lower-echelon employees).

Decisions under Model Code DR 7-104: Niesig v. Team I, *supra* note 19 (corporate "party" under DR 7-104 includes employees whose acts or omissions in matter under inquiry are binding on corporation or imputed to it for liability purposes or who implement advice of counsel); Wright v. Group Health Hosp., 103 Wash.2d 192, 691 P.2d 564, 569 (1984)("employees are considered parties under DR 7-104 if they have managing authority sufficient to give them the right to speak for, and bind, the corporation").

Bar Association Opinions: ABA Informal Op. 1410 (1978); Colo. Bar Ass'n Comm. on Ethics, Op. 69 (1985)(summarized in LAW. MANUAL ON PROF. CONDUCT, *supra* note 14, at 801:1905); Bar of Ga., Formal Advisory Op. 87-6 (1989)(summarized in LAW. MANUAL ON PROF. CONDUCT, *supra* note 14, at 901:2702); Bar of the State of Me. Prof. Ethics Comm., Bd. of Overseers, Op. 94 (1989)(summarized in LAW. MANUAL ON PROF. CONDUCT, *supra* note 14, at 901:4207); Ohio State Bar Ass'n Comm. on Legal Ethics and Prof. Conduct, Op. 81-5 (1981)(summarized in LAW. MANUAL ON PROF. CONDUCT, *supra* note 14, at 801:6827); Philadelphia Bar Ass'n Prof. Guidance Comm., Guidance Inquiry 88-30 (1988)(summarized in LAW. MANUAL ON PROF. CONDUCT, *supra* note 14, at 901:7523); Va. State Bar Standing Comm. on Legal Ethics, Op. 905 (1987)(summarized in LAW. MANUAL ON PROF. CONDUCT, *supra* note 14, at 901:8718).

[22]Niesig v. Team I, *supra* note 19, 558 N.E.2d at 1035, 559 N.Y.S.2d at 497–98.

[23]Chancellor v. Boeing Co., 678 F. Supp. 250, 45 FEP Cases 1808 (D. Kan. 1988)(in action challenging denial of promotions, plaintiff's counsel permitted to conduct *ex parte* interviews with all employees except those having any managerial responsibility or possible involvement in challenged promotion denials, but any statements so obtained not admissible under Fed. R. Evid. 801); Frey v. Department of Health & Human Servs., *supra* note 19 (plaintiff's counsel permitted to interview nonmanagerial employees without power to bind defendant governmental agency, but statements so obtained would not be treated as admissions of a party and would not be admissible under Fed. R. Evid. 801); B.H. by Monahan v. Johnson, 128 F.R.D. 659 (N.D. Ill. 1989)(plaintiff's counsel could conduct interviews with low-level employees but would not be permitted to use informally gathered evidence as admissions of party opponent).

3. Restriction as to Control Group

Under an even less restrictive standard, the corporate party has been defined very narrowly by adopting the "control group" test, which limits the corporate party to those members of senior management who make ultimate decisions on behalf of the corporation, or those who advise the decision-makers.[24] The "control group" test has been rejected by most courts as unfairly exposing the corporate defendant to potential breaches of the attorney-client privilege and to risks of unsupervised admissions.[25]

4. Case-By-Case Approach

In a few jurisdictions, courts have declined to specify any definition of the corporate party, preferring instead to balance the competing needs of plaintiffs and defendants on a case-by-case basis. In these jurisdictions, an *ex parte* communication is permissible to the extent that the plaintiff's need for informal investigation outweighs the defendant corporation's interests in shielding employees from contact with adverse counsel.[26]

C. Former Employees

Although some courts have applied the bar on *ex parte* contacts to all former employees,[27] ethical proscriptions on contact with a "party" generally

---

[24]Shealy v. Laidlaw Bros., 34 FEP Cases 1223 (D.S.C. 1984)(permitting *ex parte* contact with all employees of corporate defendant who are not officers, directors, or managing agents, despite possibility of damaging admissions); Fair Automotive Repair v. Car-X Serv. Sys., 128 Ill. App.3d 763, 471 N.E.2d 554, 560 (1984)("control group," which includes top management with final decision-making responsibility and their advisers, defines scope of corporate party for purposes of Disciplinary Rule 7-104 of Model Code).

[25]*E.g.,* Niesig v. Team I, *supra* note 19, 558 N.E.2d at 1034–35, 559 N.Y.S.2d at 497–98(control group test rejected because corporate employees other than senior management can bind corporation). *See also* Morrison v. Brandeis Univ., 125 F.R.D. 14, 16–17, 52 FEP Cases 473, 474–76 (D. Mass. 1989)(control group test rejected because Fed. R. Evid. 801(d)(2)(D) does not limit admissibility of statements against corporation to statements made by officers, directors, or managing agents); Chancellor v. Boeing Co., *supra* note 23, 678 F. Supp. at 251–52 ("based upon the [*Upjohn Co. v. United States,* 449 U.S. 383 (1981)] decision, the court believes the 'control group' test is a disfavored legal concept that is no longer appropriate as a definition of 'party' in DR 7-104(A)(1)"); Massa v. Eaton Corp., 109 F.R.D. 312, 313–14, 39 FEP Cases 1211, 1212 (W.D. Mich. 1985)(control group test is "unduly restrictive," at least to extent it allows middle- or upper-level management employees to be interviewed *ex parte,* because their admissions or statements might bind corporation under Fed. R. Evid. 801(d)(2)(D), and because communications between mid-level managers and corporation's attorney probably privileged under *Upjohn*); Mills Land & Water Co. v. Golden West Ref. Co., 186 Cal. App.3d 116, 230 Cal. Rptr. 461 (1986)(rejecting control group test in light of *Upjohn*).

[26]*See, e.g.,* B.H. by Monahan v. Johnson, *supra* note 23, 128 F.R.D. at 660–63 (rejecting formal test and adopting case-by-case balancing approach, permitting *ex parte* contact with caseworkers in suit against director of family services agency with proviso that statements of these employees not admissible against defendant under Fed. R. Evid. 801); Morrison v. Brandeis Univ., *supra* note 25, 125 F.R.D. at 16–18, 52 FEP Cases at 475–76 (rejecting "managing speaking" test, "control group" test, and test contained in comment to Model Rule 4.2, in favor of case-by-case balancing analysis under DR 7-104); Frey v. Department of Health & Human Servs., *supra* note 19, 106 F.R.D. at 36, 50 FEP Cases at 1383 (balancing search for truth against possible burdens and dangers to defendant, court permitted interviews with all employees except high-level managers with proviso that interviewed employees not treated as parties capable of making admissions); Mompoint v. Lotus Dev. Corp., 110 F.R.D. 414, 418–19, 45 FEP Cases 1810 (D. Mass. 1986)(in race discrimination case, employer defended on basis that reason for discharge was plaintiff's improper sexual advances toward employees, and plaintiff's counsel sought to interview *ex parte* current female employees who allegedly reported advances; court weighed competing interests of parties and found that "degree of need" for corporate counsel to be present at interviews was low relative to need of complainant's counsel to discuss facts freely with these employees).

[27]Public Serv. Elec. & Gas Co. v. Associated Elec. & Gas Ins. Servs., 745 F. Supp. 1037, 1042–43 (D.N.J. 1990)(forbidding all *ex parte* contact with former employees, finding bright-line test necessary to avert harm to organizations).

do not cover contacts with former employees of an adverse corporate party.[28] Courts may, however, restrict informal *ex parte* contacts with former members of management or former employees who participated in the acts giving rise to the claim,[29] or who have an ongoing relationship with the corporate defendant.[30]

Further, quite apart from the prohibition against *ex parte* contact with a represented opposing party, contact with a former employee is improper if counsel induces the former employee to violate the corporation's attorney-client privilege,[31] or otherwise violates ethical prohibitions concerning dealings with unrepresented persons.[32]

D. Mechanics of Ex Parte Communications

Given the difficulty of determining whether the adverse corporate party includes a particular employee, it is usually inadvisable to approach any corporate employee without the consent of the corporation's lawyer. Several courts have held that it is improper for the complainant's counsel to make a unilateral

---

[28]ABA Comm. on Ethics and Professional Responsibility, Formal Opinion 91-359 (1991)(Model Rule 4.2 does not cover contacts with former employees of an opposing corporate party); Wright v. Group Health Hosp., *supra* note 21 (*ex parte* contact with former employees proper because they cannot speak for corporation); Niesig v. Team I, *supra* note 19 (*ex parte* communications with former employees permitted); Polycast Technology Corp. v. Uniroyal, 129 F.R.D. 621, 628 (S.D.N.Y. 1990)(disciplinary rules did not prohibit *ex parte* contacts with former employee of defendant, but protective order prohibiting disclosure of any privileged information might be appropriate); Oak Indus. v. Zenith Indus., 1988 WL 79614 (N.D. Ill. 1988)("plain meaning of the word 'party,' as used in DR 7-104 and Model Rule 4.2, does not include persons who are no longer associated with the employer at the time of the litigation," and even *ex parte* communications with former general counsel of defendant not prohibited absent disclosure of confidential communications); Di Ossi v. Edison, 1990 WL 81976 (Del. Super. 1990)(Model Rule 4.2 "intended to preclude *ex parte* communications with those who could currently bind or admit liability for the represented entity," and does not apply to former employees who could not bind corporation by their acts). *See also* Fla. State Bar, Proposed Advisory Op. 88-14 (1988)(summarized in LAW. MANUAL ON PROF. CONDUCT, *supra* note 14, at 901:2507; Mass. State Bar, Formal Op. 82-7 (1982)(summarized in LAW. MANUAL ON PROF. CONDUCT, *supra* note 14, at 801:4607); Ill. State Bar Ass'n, Op. 85-12 (1986)(summarized in LAW. MANUAL ON PROF. CONDUCT, *supra* note 14, at 901:3001–2); Alaska State Bar, Formal Op. 88-3 (1988)(summarized in LAW. MANUAL ON PROF. CONDUCT, *supra* note 14, at 901:1303); Colo. Bar, Op. 69 (Revised)(1987)(summarized in LAW. MANUAL ON PROF. CONDUCT, *supra* note 14, at 901:1901); Md. Bar, Op. 86-13 (1985)(summarized in LAW. MANUAL ON PROF. CONDUCT, *supra* note 14, at 801:4363).

[29]Frey v. Department of Health & Human Servs., *supra* note 19 (permitting *ex parte* informal contacts with former employees except high-level managerial employees responsible for employment decision at issue); Porter v. Arco Metals Co., 642 F. Supp. 1116 (D. Mont. 1986)(*ex parte* contacts with former employees who had managerial responsibilities concerning matter in litigation prohibited); Bobele v. Superior Court, *supra* note 18 (prohibition against *ex parte* communication with "party represented by counsel" does not extend to former employees of corporation who were not and are not members of corporation's "control group").

[30]Mills Land & Water Co. v. Golden West Ref. Co., *supra* note 25, 186 Cal. App.3d at 133, 230 Cal. Rptr. at 470 (counsel disqualified because of *ex parte* communications with former president and current director of corporate defendant). The current rule in California, Rule 2-100 of the California Rules of Professional Conduct, appears inferentially to permit *ex parte* communication with the former employees of an adverse corporate defendant, but under some circumstances that communication may nonetheless be improper.

[31]*See* Amarin Plastics v. Maryland Cup Corp., 116 F.R.D. 36, 41 (D. Mass. 1987)(denying defendant's motion for protective order and sanctions against counsel who interviewed former corporate officer, without prejudice to renewal if defendant could demonstrate that plaintiff's counsel sought in any way to cause former employee to divulge corporate attorney-client communications or work product); In re Home Shopping Network, 1989 WL 201085 (M.D. Fla. 1989)(order permitting former employees to be interviewed but prohibiting them from discussing any privileged communications); Bobele v. Superior Court, *supra* note 18 (order inviting defendant to seek protective order with respect to any former employee who was privy to privileged information, if defendant believes there is real danger of disclosure in *ex parte* interview).

[32]ABA Formal Opinion 91-359, *supra* note 28 (while counsel is free under Model Rule 4.2 to communicate unilaterally with former employee of corporation, communication is subject to Model Rules such as 4.1, 4.3, and 4.4, regarding duties to be truthful, to disclose client's identity and interest, and to respect rights of others, including their attorney-client privilege).

determination of the applicability of the *ex parte* communication rules.[33] Notice to the defendant's attorney allows the corporation to seek specific protective orders, and the court to formulate appropriate conditions on the contact.[34]

Improper *ex parte* interview can lead to sanctions, including disqualification,[35] production to the defendant of notes, written materials or other information relating to the interview,[36] or an order limiting the use of evidence, particularly admissions, obtained in the interviews.[37] Deliberate misconduct is not necessary for the imposition of sanctions; the ethical rules also forbid inadvertent overreaching.[38]

When *ex parte* interviews are conducted, certain safeguards must be observed. Counsel should advise the prospective witness that the attorney is not disinterested but represents the complainant, and that the witness may decline to be interviewed, is entitled to have a personal attorney or the defendant's counsel present, and should not reveal any information protected by the attorney-client privilege.[39] Apart from warning the witness, counsel has an affirmative obligation not to intrude upon the employer's attorney-client privilege or other protected information.[40]

III. CHOICE OF CLAIMS AND CHOICE OF FORUM

A. Advantages of Non–Title VII Claims

In sexual harassment cases, the same core allegations will often support not only a federal claim under Title VII, but a claim under a state FEP statute[41] and one or more common-law claims.[42]

---

[33]*See* Mills Land & Water Co. v. Golden West Ref. Co., *supra* note 25, 186 Cal. App.3d at 131, 230 Cal. Rptr. at 469 (attorney may not make unilateral determination on application of ethics rule when corporate party is involved); Cagguila v. Wyeth Laboratories, 127 F.R.D. 653, 654, 53 FEP Cases 11 (E.D. Pa. 1989)("In such an uncertain area of ethical conduct, we believe that a prudent attorney would have given notice to opposing counsel of the intent to take such a statement"); University Patents v. Kligman, *supra* note 21, 737 F. Supp. at 329 (counsel's conduct inappropriate where he "imprudently proceeded with the interviews unilaterally without regard for the potential legal and ethical ramifications").

[34]Bobele v. Superior Court, *supra* note 18 (order prohibiting inquiry into privileged communications); Mompoint v. Lotus Dev. Corp., *supra* note 26, 110 F.R.D. at 420, 45 FEP Cases at 1814 (order establishing general guidelines for conduct of *ex parte* interviews and prohibiting plaintiff's presence); Frey v. Department of Health & Human Servs., *supra* note 19 (advance ruling that statements made by "nonparty" employees of defendant in *ex parte* interviews not admissible under Fed. R. Evid. 801(d)(2)(D)).

[35]Mills Land & Water Co. v. Golden West Ref. Co., *supra* note 25 (individual attorney representing plaintiff, but not entire law firm, disqualified after interviewing *ex parte* former president and current director of corporate defendant). In similar cases, however, other courts have concluded that disqualification is too harsh a sanction. University Patents v. Kligman, *supra* note 21; Cagguila v. Wyeth Laboratories, *supra* note 33, 127 F.R.D. at 655, 53 FEP Cases at 12.

[36]University Patents v. Kligman, *supra* note 21; Massa v. Eaton Corp., *supra* note 25.

[37]Chancellor v. Boeing Co., *supra* note 23; University Patents v. Kligman, *supra* note 21; Cagguila v. Wyeth Laboratories, *supra* note 33.

[38]Bobele v. Superior Court, *supra* note 18 (citing Mitton v. State Bar, 71 Cal.2d 525, 534, 78 Cal. Rptr. 649, 455 P.2d 753).

[39]These types of guidelines are frequently embodied in orders permitting the plaintiff's counsel to conduct *ex parte* interviews. *See, e.g.,* Mompoint v. Lotus Dev. Corp., *supra* note 26; Bey v. Arlington Heights, *supra* note 21; *In re* Home Shopping Network, *supra* note 31; Frey v. Department of Health & Human Servs., *supra* note 19.

[40]*In re* Home Shopping Network, *supra* note 31 (counsel must terminate inquiry in *ex parte* interview if it becomes apparent that information subject to corporation's attorney-client privilege is being divulged); Amarin Plastics v. Maryland Cup Corp., *supra* note 31 (any attempt by counsel to induce employee to divulge privileged communications in *ex parte* interviews "might well constitute sufficiently abusive conduct to impose sanctions").

[41]See Chapter 12, Fair Employment Practices Statutes.

[42]See Chapter 15, The Common Law. See also Chapters 11, Federal Constitutional, Statutory, and Civil Rights Law, and 13, Unemployment Compensation Statutes.

1. Damages

In determining which claims to plead, a complainant should consider that state FEP statutes generally authorize not only the injunctive and back-pay relief afforded by Title VII, but also the unlimited recovery of tort-like damages.[42a] State common-law tort claims likewise allow for the recovery of punitive and compensatory damages not fully available under Title VII.[42b]

2. Jury Trial

State-law actions typically afford the complainant the right to a jury trial. Under the Civil Rights Act of 1991, the same is now true of Title VII actions.[43]

The sexual harassment complainant will tend to prefer a jury trial for the same reasons that individuals suing corporations usually prefer a jury trial: the natural sympathies and biases of the average juror will favor the individual plaintiff.[44] This advantage can justify the greater complexity, length, and expense of a jury trial, although there may be unusual cases in which the plaintiff's behavior is so potentially offensive to a jury that the plaintiff will prefer to have the case heard by a sympathetic judge.[45]

In conducting *voir dire* of the jury panel, it will be essential to elicit the attitudes of prospective jurors concerning sexual harassment and, in the process, to achieve the incidental effect of educating them about the subtle forms and the emotional consequences of sexual harassment.[46]

An issue in jury selection is whether a party is free to use peremptory challenges in an attempt to exclude jurors on the basis of sex. In *Dias v. Sky*

[42a]See Chapter 12, Fair Employment Practices Statutes, Section V.A.

[42b]See Chapter 15, The Common Law, Section XIII.B. As amended by the Civil Rights Act of 1991, see Appendix 8, Title VII now permits limited compensation and punitive damages.

[43]See Appendix 8. The Supreme Court observed in 1979: "Because [Title VII] expressly authorizes only equitable remedies, the courts have consistently held that neither party has a right to a jury trial." Great Am. Fed. Sav. & Loan Ass'n v. Novotny, 442 U.S. 366, 375, 19 FEP Cases 1482, 1485 (1979). That trend continued: "Every circuit . . . has held or noted in dictum that Title VII implicates no jury right." Comment, *Beyond The Dicta: The Seventh Amendment Right to Trial by Jury Under Title VII*, 38 U. KAN. L. REV. 1003, 1003 (1990)(quoted in Snider v. Circle K Corp., 923 F.2d 1404, 1407 (10th Cir. 1991). Bucking that trend was a series of spirited decisions by District Judge William M. Acker, Jr., *e.g.*, Beesley v. Hartford Fire Ins. Co., 717 F. Supp. 781, 50 FEP Cases 782 (N.D. Ala. 1989)(Seventh Amendment requires jury trial in Title VII case by sexual harassment complainant claiming back pay), *reconsidered* at 723 F. Supp. 635, 51 FEP Cases 27 (N.D. Ala. 1989); Walton v. Cowin Equip. Co., 733 F. Supp. 327 (N.D. Ala. 1990); Walker v. Anderson Elec. Connectors, 736 F. Supp. 253 (N.D. Ala. 1990); *See also* Jenouri v. WAPA-TV, 54 FEP Cases 65 (D.P.R. 1990)(jury trial permissible in Title VII case).
   The Eleventh Circuit reversed in *Walton v. Cowin Equip. Co.,* 56 EPD ¶40,610 (11th Cir. 1991), holding in an officially unpublished decision that Title VII actions were in equity and as such do not entitle litigants to trial by jury. *See also* Lorillard v. Pons, 434 U.S. 575, 16 FEP Cases 885 (1978)(recognizing jury trial under ADEA while contrasting "legal" right available under ADEA with exclusively "equitable" relief available under Title VII).

[44]See generally P. TOBIAS & S. SOBERS, LITIGATING WRONGFUL DISCHARGE CLAIMS §10.21 (1987).

[45]*See, e.g.,* Thoreson v. Penthouse, 55 EPD ¶40,457 (N.Y. Sup. Ct. 1990), reproduced in Chapter 2, Forms of Harassment, in which a judge sitting without a jury held in favor of a magazine model—a former *Penthouse* "Pet of the Year"—who voluntarily had sex with the defendant's business associates over several months. The court found that this conduct resulted from economic coercion and awarded $4.06 million in compensatory and punitive damages. Query whether a jury sitting in that case would have avoided the temptation to rule against the plaintiff on the basis of a moral judgment about her conduct.

[46]For a list of sample plaintiff's questions for *voir dire* in a sexual harassment case, see A. CONTE, SEXUAL HARASSMENT IN THE WORKPLACE: LAW AND PRACTICE 447–51 (1990), Appendix B.

Chefs,[47] a Ninth Circuit panel acknowledged that a gender-based exercise of peremptory challenges raises constitutional issues of equal protection, but rejected a defendant corporation's argument on appeal that the complainant had acted improperly in striking three males from the jury venire to leave an all-female jury. Writing for the panel, Judge Warren Ferguson suggested several rationales for not interfering with this use of peremptory challenges: (1) the defendant, as a corporation, did not belong to the class excluded from the jury—males; (2) males, unlike blacks in criminal cases, might not be "a constitutionally cognizable 'suspect class,' " and nothing in equal protection jurisprudence suggests that corporations themselves are such a class; and (3) the corporation lacked standing to assert the rights of the excluded venire members.[48]

Dias was vacated in light of *Edmonson v. Leesville Concrete Co.*,[48a] in which the Supreme Court held that using peremptory challenges to exclude jurors on the basis of their race was unconstitutional in civil cases just as it long has been in criminal cases, and that an opposing litigant has standing to raise the prospective juror's equal protection right not to be excluded on a racial basis.[48b] The *Edmonson* holding, presumably applicable to sex-based challenges as well as race-based challenges, would require that peremptory challenges used disproportionately against male or female jurors be explained on a neutral basis by facts relating to the particular case.[48c]

B. Selecting State or Federal Court

Because state courts have concurrent jurisdiction over Title VII claims[49] and federal courts may exercise pendent jurisdiction over state-law claims when joined with a federal (such as a Title VI) claim,[50] the complainant often will have the option of suing in either federal or state court. In addition, even complaints asserting purely state-law claims may be filed in federal court if the requirements of diversity jurisdiction are met.[51]

The choice between federal and state court may involve important strategic considerations. Among the factors to be considered are the personalities of the judges on the state and federal benches in the jurisdiction, their relative

---

[47]919 F.2d 1370, 54 FEP Cases 852 (9th Cir. 1990); *vacated and remanded in light of Edmondson v. Leesville Concrete Co.*, 111 S.Ct. 2077 (1991).

[48]*Id.* at 1377–80, 54 FEP Cases at 858–59.

[48a]111 S.Ct. 2077 (1991).

[48b]*Id.* at 2080, 2087.

[48c]*See, e.g.,* DiDonato v. Sanini, 232 Cal. App.3d 721, 283 Cal. Rptr. 751 (1991)(reversing jury verdict in suit between former spouses where former husband had used seven of his eight peremptory challenges to remove female jurors to leave a jury of four females and eight males).

[49]Yellow Freight Sys. v. Donnelly, 110 S.Ct. 1566, 52 FEP Cases 875 (1990)(Title VII jurisdiction is concurrent in state and federal courts).

[50]United Mine Workers v. Gibbs, 383 U.S. 715, 725 (1966)(federal courts have discretion to exercise pendent jurisdiction over state-law claims joined with a federal claim when state and federal claims derive from "a common nucleus of operative fact" such that plaintiff would ordinarily be expected to litigate them in the same proceeding).

[51]Federal courts have original jurisdiction over disputes between citizens of different states when the amount in controversy exceeds $50,000. 28 U.S.C. §1332.

expertise in sexual harassment litigation, the tenor of any controlling decisions, the likely composition of juries, and the docket conditions that will affect the time to trial in each forum. Differing discovery procedures and rules of evidence in each jurisdiction may critically affect the complainant's ability to develop and prove the case. Standards applied on motions for summary judgment or dismissal should also be reviewed to determine whether the choice of forum will enhance or reduce the employer's ability to dispose of the case without a trial.

If systemic prospective relief is sought, state courts sometimes are better able to provide that relief without the necessity of federal class-action procedural requirements.[52] Further, state class actions often are not subject to the strict standing and Article III requirements of a federal class action.[53] In federal court, by contrast, systemic relief beyond what is necessary to protect the individual plaintiff would require class certification, which in many sexual harassment cases would be difficult to obtain.[54]

Absent special circumstances, such as a need for prompt adjudication and a relatively light federal docket, counsel for sexual harassment complainants usually have preferred to use state court systems.

C. Removal of State Court Actions

Although a complainant may choose a state forum in the first instance, that choice may be defeated if the employer has a statutory right to remove the action to federal court.[55] In general, the defendant is entitled to remove any state court action if (1) the action is founded on a claim or right arising under a federal law such as Title VII, the Constitution, or treaties of the United States;[56] or (2) there is diversity of citizenship among the parties and more than $50,000 in controversy and the defendant is not a citizen of the forum state.[57]

The benefits to the complainant of asserting a federal claim in a state-court action may not justify the risk that making this claim will permit the employer

---

[52]For example, California provides for injunctive relief, private attorney general style, for unfair business practices under Business & Professions Code §17,200 *et seq.* and, in some circumstances, through a California Code of Civil Procedure §526 injunctive and through a California Code of Civil Procedure §1085 mandamus action.

[53]Mendoza v. Tulare County, 128 Cal. App.3d 408, 180 Cal. Rptr. 347 (1982).

[54]*Compare* Meiresonne v. Manoff Corp., 124 F.R.D. 619, 49 FEP Cases 52 (N.D. Ill. 1989)(implying hostile environment case could be class action) *and* Fazier v. Southeastern Pa. Transp. Auth., 123 F.R.P. 195, 49 FEP Cases 856 (E.D. Pa. 1988)(class certified included sexual harassment allegations) *with* UAW v. LTV Aerospace & Defense Co., 55 FEP Cases 1078, 1091 (N.D. Tex. 1991)(denying certification of class of female employees of defendant who have been sexually harassed because of their sex, in that claims, ranging from rape to workplace display of photographs of nude women, are "very individual and varied" and subject to "very fact-specific" defenses, rendering "this form of discrimination . . . not amenable to class treatment") *and* Holden v. Burlington Northern, Inc., 665 F. Supp. 1398 (D. Minn. 1987)(refusing to certify class on sexual harassment because claims too individualized).

[55]28 U.S.C. §1441, which states in relevant part:
Except as otherwise expressly provided by Act of Congress, any civil action brought in a State court of which the district courts of the United States have original jurisdiction, may be removed by the defendant or the defendants, to the district court of the United States for the district and division embracing the place where such action is pending.

[56]28 U.S.C. §1331.

[57]*Id.* at §1332.

to remove the case to federal court, thereby depriving the complainant of the choice of the state-court forum.[58] The complainant therefore will consider omitting a Title VII or other federal claim in order to prevent removal on "federal question" grounds.[59] Because federal courts may construe the complaint to determine whether an apparent state-law claim is in fact grounded in a federal statute or constitutional provision,[60] the remaining state-law claims should be carefully drafted to avoid indirect reliance on federal statutes or constitutional rights.

The complainant is less able to control removal based on diversity because a corporate employer is deemed a citizen only of its state of incorporation and the state where it has its principal place of business, which may be different from the state where the complainant lives and works.[61] Where diversity exists between the complainant and the employer, a complainant may avoid removal by naming an individual defendant who is a citizen of the same state as the complainant, or a citizen of the state where the action is brought.[62] Adding an additional defendant will not defeat removal, however, if the joinder of the nondiverse defendant is deemed to be fraudulent or a sham.[63]

The complainant may also attempt to defeat diversity removal by not serving the complaint until one year after filing it, because the removal statute provides that a case may not be removed on the basis of diversity jurisdiction more than one year after the "commencement of the action."[64] In some jurisdictions, the strategy of defeating diversity by filing the complaint and then delaying service of the complaint may not be feasible, because court rules require service within a relatively short period (e.g., 120 days) after filing. In other jurisdictions, courts have read the one-year limit to apply only to cases removed on the basis of some post-complaint developments and not to apply to cases removed on the basis of the complaint itself.[64a]

---

[58]See Chapter 22, Employer's Litigation Strategy.

[59]"The plaintiff is the master of his or her own complaint and is free to ignore the federal cause of action and rest the claim solely on a state cause of action." Garibaldi v. Lucky Food Stores, 726 F.2d 1367, 1370 (9th Cir. 1984), cert. denied, 471 U.S. 1099 (1985).

[60]See, e.g., Stokes v. Bechtel N. Am. Power Corp., 614 F. Supp. 732, 740–44 (N.D. Cal. 1985)(wrongful discharge claim found not to be covered by federal nuclear regulatory law, and thus plaintiff's motion to remand granted).

[61]A corporate defendant is a "citizen" of the state in which it is incorporated and the state where it has its principal place of business. 28 U.S.C. §1332(c); New Alaska Development Corp. v. Guetschow, 869 F.2d 1298, 1301 (9th Cir. 1989).

[62]The removal statute specifically prohibits removal on diversity grounds if one of the defendants is a citizen of the state in which the action is brought. 28 U.S.C. §1441(b). For a discussion of the factors to consider in naming an individual defendant, see Section IV. infra.

[63]E.g., Tedder v. FMC Corp., 590 F.2d 115, 117 (5th Cir. 1979)(upholding denial of plaintiff's motion to remand following removal where fellow employees named as resident defendants immune from liability as a matter of law); but see Coker v. Amoco Oil Co., 709 F.2d 1433, 32 FEP Cases 702 (11th Cir. 1983)(court held that defendant failed to carry burden of showing either that there was no possibility that plaintiff would be able to establish cause of action against resident defendant in state court or that there had been outright fraud in plaintiff's pleadings of jurisdictional facts).

[64]28 U.S.C. §1446(b). In most states an action commences upon filing of the complaint.

[64a]Compare Rezendes v. Dow Corning Corp., 717 F. Supp. 1435, 1437–39 (E.D. Cal. 1989)(even though it may be unfair to defendant the one-year limitation applies to all removals based on diversity jurisdiction) with Greer v. Skilcraft, 704 F. Supp. 1570, 1582 (N.D. Ala.)(en banc)(one-year limitation applies only if case stated by the initial pleading is not removable).

D. Federal Court and the Exercise of Supplemental Jurisdiction

The complainant may file state-law claims in federal court when the requirements of diversity jurisdiction are met[65] or the state claims are "pendent" or "supplemental" to a federal claim.[66] The exercise of supplemental jurisdiction is discretionary, however, permitting a federal court to dismiss supplemental state claims. The exercise of jurisdiction may be declined if, for example, the state claims present novel issues of state law, their trial with nonjury claims would cause jury confusion, the state issues will predominate in a joint proceeding, or other interests of judicial economy, convenience, and fairness will not be served by the exercise of supplemental jurisdiction.

If there is a substantial concern that the federal court will decline to exercise jurisdiction over state-law claims, the complainant might commence the action in state court initially, allowing the employer to exercise its right of removal. This course might be wisest because, in removed actions, the federal court has the power to remand state-law claims to the state court in which they were brought,[67] while state-law claims originally filed in federal court must be dismissed if the court declines to entertain them. Unless the state law has a savings provision, the statute of limitations could run on the dismissed state-law claims during the pendency of the federal action, or in the time that it takes to reinstitute an action in the state court.[68]

Whether the federal court remands the state-law claims or dismisses them, the complainant will be faced with the additional burden and expense of litigating on two fronts. The complainant's counsel should be alert to the possibility that an adverse determination on the complainant's claims in federal court could bar the complainant's remaining claims in state court.[69]

IV. Naming Individual Defendants

If an alleged harasser is subject to liability under Title VII or the state FEP statute and a complainant expects to sue that person individually, the alleged harasser should be named initially as a respondent in the underlying EEOC and state FEP charges.[70] Failing to name the alleged harasser at the administrative stage could foreclose the complainant's option to sue the alleged harasser individually in a subsequent judicial action.[71] Courts may be reluctant to allow suits, particularly against supervisory personnel unnamed in an EEOC

---

[65]*Id.* at §1331.

[66]United Mine Workers v. Gibbs, *supra* note 50. For a more thorough discussion of the grounds upon which the court may decline to exercise supplemental jurisdiction, see Chapter 22, Employer's Litigation Strategy, Section III.

[67]Carnegie-Mellon Univ. v. Cohill, 484 U.S. 343, 45 FEP Cases 1163 (1988).

[68]*See id.* at 352, 45 FEP Cases at 1166–67.

[69]*See, e.g.,* Gamble v. General Foods Corp., 229 Cal. App.3d 893, 280 Cal. Rptr. 457, 55 FEP Cases 1248 (1991)(federal Title VII judgment adverse to complainant barred her wrongful termination action in state courts).

[70]See Chapter 23, The Alleged Harasser as Defendant, Section IV.A.

[71]Rio v. Presbyterian Hosp., 561 F. Supp. 325, 326, 31 FEP Cases 1344 (S.D.N.Y. 1983)(plaintiff ordinarily required to name each defendant in ADEA charges filed with EEOC to ensure each defendant has notice); Wasilchuk v. Harvey's Wagon Wheel, 610 F. Supp. 206, 208, 39 FEP Cases 237 (D. Nev. 1985)(in ADEA and Title VII actions, "plaintiff may not maintain an action against a defendant whom the plaintiff has not named previously in a charge filed with the EEOC"). *Cf.* Rabouin v. Colorado Dep't of Law, 54

charge, where full monetary relief is available from the employer and injunctive relief will bind incumbent supervisors.[72]

Even if the alleged harasser is not subject to suit under the discrimination laws, the complainant often will be able to assert state common-law tort claims against the alleged harasser.[73]

Once it is determined that an individual is subject to suit on one or more causes of action, the complainant must then weigh the advantages and disadvantages of asserting claims against that person.

A. Effect on Settlement

The assertion of claims against an individual defendant often raises the value of a settlement with the employer, if the individual remains the employer's employee. The employer cannot avoid publicity and internal disruption unless there is a global settlement disposing of all claims, including those against the alleged harasser. Even though the employer's own monetary exposure may be limited,[74] the employer may be forced to settle on terms that take into account compensatory and punitive tort damages sought against the alleged harasser.

On the other hand, naming individuals sometimes injects an emotional element that could undermine settlement opportunities. If the goal is to settle a case expeditiously, it may be more productive not to name an alleged harasser in the initial complaint, or to provide the defendants with a copy of the complaint, which will not be filed until settlement attempts have failed. Once publicly accused, an alleged harasser may feel compelled to clear his or her name, and if the alleged harasser is a particularly valuable employee, the employer may honor that wish.

B. Other Considerations

In many instances, complainants will want to sue alleged harassers to hold them accountable for their conduct and to deter future harassment by them or by others who fear similar public exposure. In addition, it is sometimes necessary to name an individual to ensure full recovery. Some common-law tort claims may not lie against the employer;[75] for others, there may be technical

---

FEP Cases 1225, 1227–28 (D. Col. 1990)(Title VII claim may be maintained against individuals not named in EEOC charge where individuals had actual notice of charge and had interests "virtually synonymous" with those of charged employer). For a discussion of when naming an individual defendant in an administrative charge is a jurisdictional prerequisite, see B.L. SCHLEI & P. GROSSMAN, EMPLOYMENT DISCRIMINATION LAW 1094–1103 (2d ed. 1983), Five-Year Supp. 415–18 (1989).

[72]White v. North La. Legal Assistance Corp., 468 F. Supp. 1347, 19 FEP Cases 307 (W.D. La. 1979)(president of legal assistance organization could not be sued under Title VII when not named in charge, had no notice, and no opportunity to participate in conciliation attempts); Pate v. Alameda-Contra Costa Transit Dist., 21 FEP Cases 1228 (N.D. Cal. 1979)(personnel manager not "employer" within meaning of Title VII). *But see* Mills v. Fox, 421 F. Supp. 519, 13 FEP Cases 1009 (E.D.N.Y. 1976)(union president and district representative "agents" of "labor organization" and therefore could be named as defendants).

[73]See Chapter 15, The Common Law.

[74]Where tort claims do not lie against the employer, the employer's monetary liability may be limited to injunctive relief. See Chapters 28, Injunctive and Affirmative Relief; 29, Monetary Relief; and 30, Attorney's Fees and Costs.

[**Editor's Note:** The Civil Rights Act of 1991, discussed in Appendix 8, authorizes recovery of limited compensatory and punitive damages for violations of Title VII.]

[75]See Chapter 15, The Common Law.

defenses, such as workers' compensation exclusivity, that may preclude recovery in a civil action against an employer.[76] Occasionally, an alleged harasser will be the sole or controlling shareholder, and naming the harasser protects against transfers of assets or other manipulative devices that may complicate a complainant's ability to recover on a judgment.

Naming an individual defendant, however, may not always be the best strategy choice. First, jurors who are reluctant to identify with a corporate defendant may well sympathize with an individual defendant. A complainant could receive a reduced award, or be denied punitive damages, if jurors fear that the individual defendant will bear the cost of the award. Of related concern, the individual defendant may retain independent defense counsel, whose presence may prolong discovery and trial proceedings and strengthen the defendants' overall defense.

Second, if a complainant does not prevail, then the court will be more likely to award attorney's fees to an individual defendant than to an employer.[77] A related concern is the increased likelihood that substantial Rule 11 sanctions will be awarded against the complainant or the complainant's counsel if the court believes that the complainant pursued frivolous claims to the injury of another individual.[78]

Third, suing an alleged harasser individually is likely to magnify the intensity of that person's adversity to the complainant. Although an individual directly involved in wrongful conduct is unlikely to cooperate with a plaintiff in any event, employees who were less directly involved might provide useful assistance. Before naming a marginal actor, counsel should consider whether a fruitful avenue of fact development is being foreclosed. Further, an alleged harasser's co-workers who are no longer employed by the employer might be more willing to assist the complainant if the alleged harasser is not a named defendant.

Finally, consider the possibility that the alleged harasser will no longer be employed by the employer when the trial occurs. If this is the case, and the alleged harasser has not been placed at risk personally, the alleged harasser may be less inclined to cooperate with the former employer. When the complainant's claims are based on one-on-one conduct, the alleged harasser's absence could leave the complainant's version of events effectively unrebutted at trial.

---

[76]See Chapter 27, Asserted Defenses, Section IV.

[77]Courts are usually reluctant to award costs to an employer defendant even where the plaintiff's claims are clearly improper. *See, e.g.,* Obago v. Union of Am. Hebrew Congregations, 52 FEP Cases 509 (S.D.N.Y. 1989)(institutional defendants not awarded sanctions although plaintiff's attorney asserted §1983 claim for second time without legal basis and filed Title VII claim without receiving right-to-sue letter).

[78]In *Jackson-Colley v. Army Corps of Eng'rs,* 655 F. Supp. 122, 126–28, 43 FEP Cases 617 (E.D. Mich. 1987), the court found that the plaintiff's hostile environment allegations "bordered on the malicious," and ordered the plaintiff to pay the defendants' costs and actual attorney's fees while assessing sanctions against the plaintiff's counsel. Although the alleged harasser, her supervisor, was not named as a defendant, the court was offended by the humiliation to which he was subjected. The court found the plaintiff's allegation that her supervisor fondled his genitals in her presence "mean-spirited," because the supervisor had a medical problem that caused serious itching in his groin area. Similarly, the court noted that the plaintiff's claim that her supervisor "gawked" at her was explained by a vision disorder that caused his eye to wander.

C. Effect on Defense Strategy

Naming an individual as a defendant often presents an employer with difficult choices and potential conflicts. The employer will be forced to investigate and commit itself to a factual theory at an earlier stage of the proceeding. If the employer concludes that the alleged harasser is likely to be found culpable, it may choose to defend on the ground that the harasser's conduct was outside the scope of employment and was not known or condoned by the employer, rather than focusing on an attack on the complainant's account of events.[79]

This defense posture would call for the alleged harasser to be represented by separate counsel.[80] In many instances, the employer will bear the cost of separate counsel, an increased expense that should make settlement more attractive. The appointment of separate counsel complicates any coordinated defense efforts and raises the possibility that separate defense counsel will assert different factual or legal positions, to the plaintiff's advantage.

V. Use of Publicity

Sexual harassment cases pose unique issues of publicity. Because sexual harassment allegations are a public relations nightmare for many employers, it has become a common practice for the complainant's counsel to invite settlement discussions before an action is filed by sending the employer a draft complaint detailing the charges.[81] With many employers, receipt of an explicit draft complaint is sufficient to raise the specter of adverse publicity and to generate substantial interest in a quiet settlement before litigation commences.

Some attorneys advocate an aggressive use of publicity, arguing that explicit threats of media involvement are a potent tool in obtaining earlier and larger settlements. The use of publicity, however, presents practical, legal, and ethical issues that should be analyzed before deciding whether to publicize allegations.

A. Practical Considerations

The efficacy of threatened publicity in forcing settlement depends to a large degree on the standing of the employer in the community. Large employers who are sensitive to their public image obviously are more susceptible to this tactic.

---

[79]See Chapter 23, The Alleged Harasser as Defendant.

[80]For a discussion of conflicts of interest between the individual and employer, see Chapter 22, Employer's Litigation Strategy, Section II.B.

[81]It is generally permissible to threaten a prospective party with legal action as long as the threat is made in good faith and the charges are well-founded. *See, e.g.,* Lerette v. Dean Witter Org., 60 Cal. App.3d 573, 131 Cal. Rptr. 592, 594 (1976)(recognizing "well established legal practice to communicate promptly with a potential adversary, setting out the claims made upon him, urging settlement, and warning of the alternative of judicial action"). Baseless threats to bring legal action may result in disciplinary sanctions. *See* Model Code of Professional Responsibility DR 7-102(A)(2)(1985)(attorney may not knowingly advance claim that is unwarranted under existing law). Criminal charges are another matter. A threat to file criminal charges if settlement fails is unethical and may itself constitute a criminal offense. For a discussion of criminal-law aspects of a sexual harassment complaint, see Chapter 16, Criminal Law.

The timing of any threat is also critical. Because newsreporters in many communities routinely track court dockets, the mere filing of a complaint may trigger media coverage, depriving the complainant's counsel of control over the timing and content of the first public report. Once charges have been made public, the employer may decide that it has little to lose by proceeding with a defense. Thus, a pre-filing threat is often more effective in achieving a settlement, because the employer is still in a position to bargain for confidentiality.

Counsel who have gone beyond threats to actual publicity generally agree that this tactic works only once. Thus, counsel must choose the optimal moment to go public. If there are other complainants represented by separate counsel, publicity should be coordinated.

In some instances, the threat of publicity may be counterproductive. Many defense counsel and employers perceive publicity threats as a form of blackmail used by unscrupulous opponents to pressure an employer into settlement without regard to the validity of the accusations. Overt or heavy-handed threats to try the case in the press may destroy any chance of settlement. Further, publicity also can be damaging to the complainant, in terms of the complainant's emotional well-being and future career prospects.

B. Ethical Considerations

In some circumstances, an attorney's communication with the press or other third parties can violate the rules of professional responsibility. An attorney has a general ethical duty to refrain from inflicting needless injury on an opposing party,[82] and publicizing proposed or pending charges has been held to be inconsistent with that duty.[83] In addition, bar association rules[84] and the local rules of many United States district courts[85] specifically prohibit certain extrajudicial statements by an attorney during the investigation or litigation of a matter. These prohibitions, designed to prevent publicity that could interfere with a fair trial, generally apply to any comment by an attorney

---

[82]*See* Model Code, EC 7-10, reproduced in Law. Manual on Prof. Conduct (ABA/BNA 1990), which provides: "The duty of a lawyer to represent his client with zeal does not militate against his concurrent obligation to treat with consideration all persons involved in the legal process and to avoid the infliction of needless harm."

[83]Green Acres Trust v. London, 141 Ariz. 609, 688 P.2d 617 (1984); Ind. St. Bar Ass'n Legal Ethics Op. No. 6 (1980)(summarized in Law. Manual on Prof. Conduct, *supra* note 82, at 801:3302).

[84]Disciplinary Rule 7-107(G) of the Model Code, *supra* note 82, provides:

A lawyer or law firm associated with a civil action shall not during its investigation or litigation make or participate in making an extrajudicial statement, other than a quotation from or reference to public records, that a reasonable person would expect to be disseminated by means of public communication and that relates to: (1) Evidence regarding the occurrence or transaction involved. (2) The character, credibility, or criminal record of a party, witness, or prospective witness. (3) The performance or results of any examinations or tests or the refusal or failure of a party to submit to such. (4) His opinion as to the merits of the claims or defenses of a party, except as required by law or administrative rule. (5) Any other matter reasonably likely to interfere with a fair trial of the action.

Model Rule 3.6, *supra* note 82, provides in part: "A lawyer shall not make an extrajudicial statement that a reasonable person would expect to be disseminated by means of public communication if the lawyer knows or reasonably should know that it will have a substantial likelihood of materially prejudicing an adjudicative proceeding."

[85]*E.g.*, U.S. Dist. Ct. Ala. Gen. R. 33 ("Free Press—Fair Trial in Civil Cases"); U.S. Dist. Ct. Ariz. R. 40 ("Conduct of Attorneys"); U.S. Dist. Ct. S.D. Fla., Gen. R. 21A ("Release of Information in Criminal and Civil Proceedings"); U.S. Dist. Ct. N.D. Ga. Gen. R. 115.2(a) & 3 ("Release of Information in Criminal and Grand Jury Proceedings and in Widely Publicized or Sensational Civil and Criminal Cases"); U.S. Dist. Ct. S.D. Ohio R. 2.7 ("Publicity and Disclosures").

on the evidence, witnesses, or merits of the claims or defenses, except by reference to a public record.

These "no comment" rules in civil cases may be unconstitutionally broad in their prohibition of speech.[86] While recognizing that the right to a fair trial may justify some restriction on counsel's speech, courts have held that "prior restraint" rules, such as Disciplinary Rule 7-107(G), are overly broad because the protracted nature of civil litigation may restrain comment for years, and because some civil cases involve questions of public concern in which lawyers can enlighten public debate.[87] Although a broad "no comment" rule thus may be constitutionally unenforceable, counsel should not overlook the court's power to remedy a publicity violation by other means—such as a change in venue, delay in trial, or extensive screening of jurors—that could adversely affect the complainant's case.[88]

C. Potential Defamation Liability

Apart from ethical concerns, extrajudicial disclosure of sexual harassment charges may expose both the attorney and the complainant to tort claims, particularly claims of defamation. Although truth is an ultimate defense, defamation litigation can be costly and embarrassing. A critical question is whether a proposed communication will be protected by an absolute or qualified privilege, thus subjecting a potential defamation claim to an early dismissal.

An attorney or witness normally enjoys an absolute privilege from defamation claims premised on defamatory statements made in pleadings or during the course of a judicial proceeding,[89] regardless of later publication by the media. Many jurisdictions extend this absolute privilege to an attorney's out-of-court statements if they are incident to the institution or conduct of litigation, and pertinent to its subject matter.[90] The privilege has been recognized for pre-lawsuit communications, but only if the communication is directed to a potential participant or other interested party and bears a relationship to proposed judicial proceedings that are contemplated in good faith.[91]

---

[86]Hirschkop v. Snead, 594 F.2d 356 (4th Cir. 1979)(Virginia rule, comparable to DR 7-107 prohibiting extrajudicial comments, held to be overly broad); Chicago Council of Lawyers v. Bauer, 522 F.2d 242 (7th Cir. 1975)(local rule similar to DR 7-107 held overly broad and unconstitutional), *cert. denied*, 427 U.S. 912 (1976); Shadid v. Jackson, 521 F. Supp. 85 (E.D. Tex. 1981)(disciplinary rule prohibiting lawyers from making extrajudicial statement that reasonable person would expect to be disseminated an unconstitutional prior restraint on its face).

[87]Hirschkop v. Snead, *supra* note 86.

[88]Shadid v. Jackson, *supra* note 86.

[89]Green Acres Trust v. London, *supra* note 83, 688 P.2d at 621 (defense is absolute and not affected by speaker's motive, purpose or reasonableness in uttering false statement); *see also* Restatement (Second) of Torts §586 (1977).

[90]*See* Restatement (Second) of Torts §586 (1977); Hoover v. Van Stone, 540 F. Supp. 1118, 1123 (D. Del. 1982)(communications to potential witnesses sufficiently related to underlying lawsuit to come within scope of absolute privilege); Froess v. Bulman, 610 F. Supp. 332 (D.R.I. 1984)(in custody controversy, attorney's letter to psychologist's superior questioning his qualifications held privileged as letter was pertinent to custody controversy and attorney was advocating rights of his client), *aff'd mem.*, 767 F.2d 905 (1st Cir. 1985); Penny v. Sherman, 101 N.M. 517, 684 P.2d 1182 (1984)(attorney's letter to employer of nursing home employee privileged as reasonably related to attorney's efforts to marshal assets in probate proceedings). *But see* Asay v. Hallmark Cards, 594 F.2d 692, 698 (8th Cir. 1979)(privilege did not apply automatically to "witness interrogatories" sent to other present and former employees of defendant in course of investigating possibility of class action).

[91]Lerette v. Dean Witter Org., 60 Cal. App.3d 573, 578, 131 Cal. Rptr. 592, 595 (1976)(demand letter by attorney to chairman of board of bank held privileged, because written in preparation of threatened judicial

There is substantial authority that an attorney or litigant's direct communications with the news media or members of the general public do not come within this absolute privilege for judicial proceedings.[92] Thus, while out-of-court communications with the harasser's employer, potential witnesses, or other third parties having a direct interest in the matter may be absolutely privileged, communication of the same information to the media or members of the general public is generally not so protected.

Some jurisdictions recognize a separate privilege, either qualified or absolute, for publication of filed pleadings or "fair and true reports" of their contents.[93] Where applicable, this privilege can preclude a defamation claim based on the issuance of a press release announcing that a complaint has been filed, delivery of the actual pleading to the press, or other communications that do no more than fairly and accurately report on a pending judicial action. Caution is in order, however, because the scope and application of this privilege varies considerably among jurisdictions.

In some jurisdictions, the "fair report" privilege may be afforded only to publication by news media and other disinterested persons; attorneys and litigants who publicize their own pleadings are not covered.[94] The privilege is generally lost where a communication is made with malice or for collateral purposes such as retribution.[95] Decisions also vary as to whether the mere filing of the complaint triggers the "fair report" privilege, with some courts holding that further judicial action is required.[96]

---

proceeding against bank); Larmour v. Campanale, 96 Cal. App.3d 566, 569, 158 Cal. Rptr. 143, 144 (1979)(copy of demand letter to escrow holder with interest in controversy held privileged). *But see* Rosen v. Brandes, 105 Misc.2d 506, 432 N.Y.S.2d 597 (1980)(letter by attorney representing wife in proposed matrimonial action, sent to husband's law partner, not absolutely privileged because no action yet pending); Kenny v. Cleary, 47 A.D.2d 531, 363 N.Y.S.2d 606 (1975)(communication by attorney on behalf of client before action commenced protected only by qualified, not absolute, privilege); Smith v. Suburban Restaurants, 374 Mass. 528, 373 N.E.2d 215 (1978)(where no judicial action then contemplated, attorney's letters to police indicating patron no longer welcome in client's restaurant held not absolutely privileged).

[92]Asay v. Hallmark Cards, *supra* note 90 (plaintiff's dissemination of complaint to news media not privileged because not connected with pending judicial proceeding); Bridge C.A.T. Scan Assocs. v. Ohio-Nuclear, 608 F. Supp. 1187, 1195 (S.D.N.Y. 1985)(delivery of copy or report of complaint to press is neither essential nor relevant to, nor statement made in course of, judicial proceeding, and therefore not protected by absolute privilege); Green Acres Trust v. London, *supra* note 83 (attorney's distribution of draft complaint to media and press conference three days before action commenced not protected by absolute privilege accorded to statements made in course of judicial proceeding); Timmis v. Bennett, 352 Mich. 355, 89 N.W.2d 748 (1958)(attorney's letter to members of community not absolutely privileged).

[93]*See generally* Restatement (Second) of Torts §611 (1977)("the publication of defamatory matter concerning another in a report of an official action or proceeding . . . is privileged if the report is accurate and complete or a fair abridgement of the occurrence reported"). *See, e.g.,* American Dist. Tel. Co. v. Brink's, 380 F.2d 131 (7th Cir. 1967)(press release describing lawsuit and quoting allegations of complaint protected by qualified privilege to report judicial proceedings); Phillips v. Murchison, 252 F. Supp. 513 (S.D.N.Y. 1966)(issuance of press release concerning complaint in pending judicial action absolutely privileged under New York statute protecting fair and true reports of judicial proceeding, but plaintiff's distribution of allegedly sham complaint to individuals not privileged), *aff'd in part and rev'd in part on other grounds,* 383 F.2d 370 (2d Cir. 1967), *cert. denied,* 390 U.S. 958 (1968).

[94]*Compare* Restatement (Second) of Torts §611, comment (c)(1977) *and* Green Acres Trust v. London, *supra* note 83 ("One exception to the privilege to fairly and accurately report about public proceedings is the speaker who by design uses the privilege to republish defamation he previously made during the public proceeding") *with* American Dist. Tel. Co. v. Brink's, *supra* note 93 (applying privilege to report judicial proceedings to press release issued by plaintiff describing complaint).

[95]*See, e.g.,* American Dist. Tel. Co. v. Brink's, *supra* note 93, 380 F.2d at 133 (under Illinois law, privilege lost if report published solely to defame, not to inform public); Bridge C.A.T. Scan Assocs. v. Ohio-Nuclear, *supra* note 92, 608 F. Supp. at 1195 (for plaintiff purposely and maliciously to stimulate press coverage and wide publicity of complaint with its allegedly false and malicious statements is beyond pale of protection).

[96]*Compare* American Dist. Tel. Co. v. Brink's, *supra* note 93 (press release setting forth details of complaint held to be accurate report of contents of complaint and not actionable) *and* Langford v. Vanderbilt

The risk to the attorney of publicizing allegations is well-illustrated by *Green Acres Trust v. London.*[97] In *Green Acres,* a defamation claim was allowed to stand against a group of attorneys who invited a newsreporter to their offices three days before a class action was filed, provided her with a copy of the draft complaint, and held a private "press conference" to explain the charges. The Supreme Court of Arizona held that these communications were not within the scope of any recognized privilege, and reversed a grant of summary judgment originally in the attorneys' favor.

The *Green Acres* court first held that the attorneys' communications with the reporter were insufficiently related to the prospective judicial proceeding to come within the absolute privilege.[98] Nor were the communications within the "fair report" privilege, because no proceeding was yet pending and the privilege does not extend to a speaker who republishes the speaker's own defamatory pleading.[99] The court also held that the attorneys had no qualified privilege because they had no obligation to communicate with the press and had no "special relationship" with the reporter that supplied a common interest in the subject matter.[100] In so holding, the court noted that the attorneys' conduct was inconsistent with ethical rules requiring a lawyer to avoid causing needless injury to an opponent[101] and prohibiting an attorney from making extrajudicial statements that are likely to interfere with the fairness of an adjudicative proceeding.[102]

A lawyer therefore must proceed cautiously in the use of publicity. Before making any public statements, counsel should carefully review controlling ethics provisions and local court rules as well as the potential for a defamation claim.

VI. THE COMPLAINANT'S EXPERT WITNESSES

Complainants in sexual harassment cases have used expert testimony to good advantage.* Experts commonly used are psychotherapists, medical doctors, sociologists or social workers, and employment professionals, each of whom is qualified to help the trier of fact understand the evidence or find a fact because of the expert's knowledge, skill, experience, training, or education in the area in question.[103] Experts are regularly permitted to testify in such

---

Univ., 199 Tenn. 389, 287 S.W.2d 32 (1956)(right of newspapers to publish without liability for damages extends to mere contents of filed pleadings though no judicial action has been taken thereon) *with* Restatement (Second) of Torts §611 comment (e)(1977)("publication . . . of the contents of preliminary pleadings such as a complaint or petition, before any judicial action has been taken is not within the rule") *and* Nixon v. Dispatch Printing Co., 101 Minn. 309, 112 N.W. 258 (1907)(distinguishing between complaint and judicial proceeding, former being *ex parte,* filed by the plaintiff, and not subject to control of court in first instance).

[97]*Supra* note 83.

[98]*Id. See also* Asay v. Hallmark Cards, *supra* note 90.

[99]Green Acres Trust v. London, *supra* note 83.

[100]*Id.*

[101]*Id.*

[102]*Id.*

*[**Editor's Note:** Under the Civil Rights Act of 1991, discussed in Appendix 8, expert's fees may be recovered as part of reasonable attorney's fees.]

[103]*E.g.,* Eide v. Kelsey-Hayes Co., 154 Mich. App. 142, 397 N.W.2d 532, 47 FEP Cases 1043, 1048 (1986)(expert qualified as sexual harassment expert because he taught in the area for a number of years, published books and articles on the subject, and was familiar with extensive body of research and literature regarding sexual harassment), *aff'd in part and rev'd in part,* 431 Mich. 26, 427 N.W.2d 488, 47 FEP Cases 1050 (1988). For an extended discussion of admissibility of expert testimony in sexual harassment cases, see Chapter 25, Evidence, Section VIII.

fields as medicine and psychology. However, an expert's opinion may be inadmissible if the question at issue is not so technical as to exceed the jury's ken. For example, a court may reasonably conclude that the issue of whether gender was the basis of differential treatment is not so technical as to require the aid of an expert.[104] Furthermore, expert testimony is no substitute for effective evidence.[105]

A. Mental Health Expert

1. Pre-Trial Referral

The preparation of any sexual harassment case will usually involve the help of a mental health expert—a psychiatrist, psychologist, or therapist. Initially, counsel should determine whether the complainant has been evaluated or treated by a mental health professional and, if so, immediately obtain all relevant information. If the complainant has not sought professional help, counsel should consider referring the complainant for psychological evaluation and treatment.

Counsel should recognize, however, that any history, treatment notes, physical examinations, and psychological testing created by the treating professional may become discoverable if the complainant makes mental state an issue in the case.[106] The complainant should also understand that claiming damages for psychological trauma or emotional distress and obtaining treatment may permit defense counsel to depose the psychotherapist or call the psychotherapist as a witness at the trial.[107] Courts have also ordered psychological examination of sexual harassment complainants by a defense expert, which can be ordered to occur outside the presence of the complainant's counsel.[108]

---

[104]See, e.g., Ward v. Westland Plastics, 651 F.2d 1266, 1270, 23 FEP Cases 128, 130–31 (9th Cir. 1980)(upholding trial court's exercise of discretion to exclude expert testimony on whether defendant discriminated against plaintiff because of sex).

[105]Bohen v. City of E. Chicago, 622 F. Supp. 1234, 1243 n.4, 39 FEP Cases 917 (N.D. Ind. 1985)(expert testimony ineffective regarding complainant's behavior that led to lawful termination where more probative evidence may have been testimony from friends or children regarding gradual change in complainant's demeanor), aff'd in part, rev'd in part on other grounds, 799 F.2d 1180, 41 FEP Cases 1108 (7th Cir. 1986); EEOC v. Domino's Pizza, 34 FEP Cases 1075, 1078 (E.D. Mich. 1983)(fees and expenses of plaintiff's expert denied because testimony was not relevant to issues).

[106]See, e.g., Caesar v. Mountanos, 542 F.2d 1064, 1069 (9th Cir. 1976)(plaintiff waived psychotherapist-patient privilege when she placed her mental or emotional condition in issue by claiming damages for mental and emotional distress), cert. denied, 430 U.S. 954 (1977); Ferrell v. Brick, 678 F. Supp. 111, 112, 46 FEP Cases 502 (E.D. Pa. 1987)(sexual harassment plaintiff waived physician-patient privacy right with respect to subpoenaed records of psychiatric treatment by placing her mental condition in issue); Lowe v. Philadelphia Newspapers, 101 F.R.D. 296, 298, 44 FEP Cases 1224 (E.D. Pa. 1983)(so long as plaintiff seeks damages by reason of physical, mental or emotional harm or distress, defendant is entitled to ask plaintiff's physicians and psychiatrists about plaintiff's past history). But see Broderick v. Shad, 117 F.R.D. 306, 309, 43 FEP Cases 532, 534 (D.D.C. 1987)(production of plaintiff's medical records not required despite alleged physical and mental manifestations of harassment where plaintiff submitted sworn statement that she had received no medical treatment for conditions alleged in complaint and no relevant medical records existed); Jennings v. D.H.L. Airlines, 101 F.R.D. 549, 551, 34 FEP Cases 1423, 1425 (N.D. Ill. 1984)(production not required where plaintiff did not claim mental distress and hence her psychological well-being not in issue).

[107]See, e.g., Mitchell v. Hutchings, 116 F.R.D. 481, 485, 44 FEP Cases 615, 618 (D. Utah 1987)(plaintiff's psychologists may be deposed regarding extent of plaintiff's emotional trauma, its causes, all information upon which opinion was based, and how certain information would affect opinion).

[108]Compare Vinson v. Superior Court, 43 Cal.3d 833, 845, 239 Cal. Rptr. 292, 301, 740 P.2d 404, 44 FEP Cases 1174, 1176 (1987)(court-ordered psychiatric examination of sexual harassment plaintiff outside presence of counsel) with Zabkowicz v. West Bend Co., 585 F. Supp. 635, 636, 35 FEP Cases 209, 210 (E.D. Wis. 1984)(sexual harassment plaintiff entitled to presence of counsel or use of recording device during mental examination by defendant's expert). For further discussion of mental examinations, see Chapter 26, Discovery, Section IV.

2. Expert Mental Health Testimony

If the complainant claims mental or emotional injury caused by sexual harassment, an expert can help establish both the existence and severity of the complainant's emotional distress[109] and the connection between that condition and the sexual harassment.[110] Evidence of a positive psychological evaluation prior to the onset of the sexual harassment may be particularly persuasive.[111] In addition, expert testimony is a guide to the amount of damages that the complainant may recover.[112] Where there are continuing psychological effects requiring treatment, the mental health professional can testify as to the anticipated time and cost of the therapy necessary to overcome the psychological trauma.[113]

When a sexual harassment complainant seeks damages for a psychological injury, defendants can be expected to argue that the complainant had a preexisting mental or psychological problem. A mental health professional may be useful to show that the prior condition made the complainant vulnerable to harassment, but that the clinically significant condition occurred only after the harassment.[114] To achieve this goal, the mental health expert should see the complainant soon after the events occur and should follow through with additional visits to confirm the validity of the conclusions.[115]

The complainant's mental health expert should be prepared to face defense attacks as to credibility and conclusions.[116] In particular, a psychotherapist

---

[109]See, e.g., Spencer v. General Elec. Co., 688 F. Supp. 1072, 1076 (E.D. Va. 1988)(where rape victim sued under Title VII and state tort law, expert testimony as to post-traumatic stress admitted to establish damages although excluded as proof that rape actually occurred), aff'd, 894 F.2d 651, 51 FEP Cases 1725 (1990); Moffett v. Gene B. Glick Co., 621 F. Supp. 244, 264–65, 41 FEP Cases 671, 684 (N.D. Ind. 1985)(expert testimony of certified psychologist concerning plaintiff's well-being established significant emotional and psychological harm as result of sexual harassment and termination); Alphonso v. Charity Hosp., 413 So.2d 982 (La. 1982)(evidence of post-traumatic stress disorder where rape victim sued hospital for damages used as basis for $50,000 award for emotional damages), cert. denied, 415 So.2d 952 (1982). For an extended discussion of expert testimony in sexual harassment cases, see Chapter 25, Evidence, Section VIII.

[110]See, e.g., Phillips v. Smalley Maintenance Servs., 711 F.2d 1524, 1528, 1537, 32 FEP Cases 975, 978, 986 (11th Cir. 1983)(relying upon testimony that plaintiff's chronic anxiety caused by defendant's wrongful intrusion or invasion and not by physical problems); Valdez v. Church's Fried Chicken, 683 F. Supp. 596, 611, 47 FEP Cases 1155, 1163 (W.D. Tex. 1988)(expert testimony admitted for purpose of determining cause of plaintiff's injuries and damages sustained); Shrout v. Black Clawson Co., 689 F. Supp. 774, 776, 46 FEP Cases 1339 (S.D. Ohio 1988)(testimony of three psychological experts established defendant's sexually harassing conduct at least one cause of plaintiff's emotional distress).

[111]See, e.g., Moffett v. Gene B. Glick Co., supra note 109.

[112]See, e.g., Valdez v. Church's Fried Chicken, supra note 110 (expert testimony on post-traumatic stress disorder (PTSD) admitted to determine cause of injuries alleged by plaintiff and damages in sexual harassment suit brought under Title VII and state law; plaintiff awarded $10,000 for mental anguish); Bohen v. City of E. Chicago, supra note 105 (plaintiff awarded compensatory damages of $25,000 for mental distress for 42 U.S.C. §1983 claim).

[113]Moffett v. Gene B. Glick Co., supra note 109, 621 F. Supp. at 265, 41 FEP Cases at 684 (expert testified plaintiff would require two years of semi-weekly therapy to overcome "psychological trauma" caused by harassment).

[114]See Broderick v. Ruder, 685 F. Supp. 1269, 1273, 46 FEP Cases 1272 (D.D.C. 1988), reproduced in Chapter 2, Forms of Harassment (psychiatrist testified plaintiff's developmental and relationship problems had not reached level of clinical diagnosis prior to employment); Valdez v. Church's Fried Chicken, supra note 110 (psychological testimony presented that plaintiff was more vulnerable to psychological injury because of prior marital difficulties).

[115]See Barrett v. Omaha Nat'l Bank, 584 F. Supp. 22, 27 n.10, 35 FEP Cases 585 (D. Neb. 1983)(doctor's testimony found to be of "marginal relevance" because diagnosis made more than one year after events complained of), aff'd, 726 F.2d 424, 35 FEP Cases 593 (8th Cir. 1984).

[116]McCandless & Schickman, In Sexual Harassment Cases Examining the Psychotherapist at Trial, 18 BRIEF 41 (Spring 1989).

should do a thorough case history that considers possible alternative causes of the complainant's symptoms, and should form opinions and conclusions that are consistent with both the complainant's medical records and any professional standards upon which the mental health expert relies.

3. Expert Medical Testimony

Doctors may be used to testify regarding the physiological as well as psychological effects of sexual harassment.[117] A complainant who has had any physical symptoms of sexual harassment[118] should be encouraged to seek medical treatment as soon as possible. Evidence of this treatment, like evidence of psychotherapy, may assist in establishing both the source and extent of the complainant's damages.

B. Sociological Experts

A sociological expert may be used to establish that a hostile environment existed.[119] The sociological expert can also link the hostile environment to the injuries suffered by the complainant by opining on the stress effects of harassment on those in the complainant's position.[120] Sociological expert testimony concerning the negative effects of sexual harassment on job performance may be useful to rebut the employer's claims of poor job performance.[121] Finally,

---

[117]*See* Howard University v. Best, 484 A.2d 958, 982, 36 FEP Cases 482, 497 (D.C. App. 1984)(court cited plaintiff's physician's testimony that defendant's harassment had elevated plaintiff's blood pressure from normal levels to level requiring hospitalization and medication). *See also* Zabkowicz v. West Bend Co., *supra* note 108, 589 F. Supp. at 783, 35 FEP Cases at 612 (diagnosis by plaintiff's gynecologist that diarrhea, vomiting, severe nausea, and cramping was "psychophysiological gastrointestinal disease due to harassment at work" considered by court in awarding judgment for plaintiff).

[118]Common effects include "depression, insomnia or excessive fatigue, gastrointestinal problems, fibroid tumors, alcohol or drug abuse, increased or resumed cigarette consumption, persistent bladder or urinary tract infections, arrythmia, and/or migraine headaches." Other symptoms typically include clinical depression, suicidal tendencies, and traumatic stress disorders. See *Attorney Discusses Role of Work Atmosphere in Successful Sexual Harassment Suits*, DAILY LAB. REP. (BNA) No. 158 at A-2 (Aug. 16, 1988). *See, e.g.,* Ford v. Revlon, Inc., 153 Ariz. 38, 734 P.2d 580, 583, 43 FEP Cases 213, 215 (1987)(complainant developed "high blood pressure, a nervous tic in her left eye, chest pains, rapid breathing, and other symptoms of emotional stress, . . . felt weak, dizzy, and generally fatigued . . . [and] consulted a physician about her condition"); Bohen v. City of E. Chicago, *supra* note 105, 622 F. Supp. at 1243, 39 FEP Cases at 923 (expert on sexual harassment testified that "harassment may lead to tension, anxiety, loss of sleep, feelings of diminished self-worth, nausea, cramps, and headaches").

[119]*Compare* Robinson v. Jacksonville Shipyards, 760 F. Supp. 1486 (M.D. Fla. 1991), reproduced in Chapter 2, Forms of Harassment (psychologist testified on sexual stereotyping to effect that permitting sexual joking and pornographic material in workplace is form of discrimination against women that contributes to sexually hostile environment) *and* Eide v. Kelsey-Hayes Co., *supra* note 103 (sociological testimony admitted to describe type of environment that existed and sexual connotations of acts complained of) *with* Lipsett v. University of P.R., 740 F. Supp. 921, 54 FEP Cases 257 (D.P.R. 1990)(denying expert witness status to social worker and social psychologist offered by plaintiff to testify as to existence of hostile environment sexual harassment; their education and experience did not rise to level of specialized knowledge necessary to qualify them as experts; jurors need no enlightenment through testimony on occurrences that they know through everyday experience and attitudes toward sexual matters; proposed expert testimony would bring nothing to jury that lawyers could not present in argument).

[120]Broderick v. Ruder, *supra* note 114, 685 F. Supp. at 1273, 46 FEP Cases at 1277 (social worker testified as to both general effects of sexual harassment and particular effects of hostile environment on plaintiff and her associates).

[121]Moffett v. Gene B. Glick Co., *supra* note 109, 621 F. Supp. at 262, 41 FEP Cases at 682 (expert testified, based on personal counseling experience and sexual harassment studies, that women subject to sexual harassment will have increases in on-the-job errors).

sociological expert testimony can be used to explain why women victimized by sexual harassment may acquiesce in it or fail to report it.[122]

Thus, expert sociological testimony, when properly grounded,[123] may be an effective tool to educate the jury and to explain, or to some extent validate, the actions of the complainant.

C. Employment Professionals

Employment professionals such as personnel or human resource specialists can provide expert testimony on the practices, policies, and procedures that an employer could have adopted to protect employees from sexual harassment.[124] This testimony may illustrate that the employer did not do all it reasonably could have done to prevent sexual harassment in the workplace.

Similarly, if the defense claims that the complainant failed to use the employer's internal grievance procedures, expert testimony may help to show that the lack of a formal complaint was reasonable under the circumstances.[125]

VII. INSURANCE COVERAGE CONSIDERATIONS

In drafting the complaint, the complainant's counsel should consider all of the causes of action that can be pleaded in good faith that might trigger coverage under a defendant's insurance policies. The involvement of an insurance carrier not only provides a fund for ultimate damage recoveries but also helps settlement negotiations to proceed on the basis of economic realities, including litigation costs, rather than emotions.

Whether a particular claim will trigger insurance coverage depends on the types of policies maintained by the defendants, any exclusions from those policies, and state laws governing indemnification for intentional wrongs and punitive damages.[126] In drafting the complaint without full knowledge of available insurance, counsel may assume that negligence claims based on failure to supervise the alleged harasser, or to investigate complaints of harassment,

---

[122]*See, e.g.,* Robinson v. Jacksonville Shipyards, *supra* note 119, 760 F. Supp. at 1506–7 (consultant opined that under typical coping strategies women may not complain about sexual harassment because of fear, embarrassment, and feelings of futility); Bohen v. City of E. Chicago, *supra* note 105, 622 F. Supp. at 1240, 39 FEP Cases at 920 ("expert witness testified that reticence about complaining and a diminished sense of self-worth are common in cases of sexual harassment").

[123]*Cf.* Perkins v. General Motors Corp., 129 F.R.D. 655, 666–68 (W.D. Mo. 1990)(analysis of proper and improper uses of expert sociological testimony); Lipsett v. University of P.R., *supra* note 119, 740 F. Supp. at 925 (proffered expert sociological testimony that work environment was "so heavily charged with sexism that it was intimidating, hostile, and offensive" excluded because it would usurp role of jury as fact-finder); Bushell v. Dean, 781 S.W.2d 652, 655, 52 FEP Cases 746, 748 (Tex. Ct. App. 1989)(expert testimony regarding "profile" of sexual harasser improper because developed from case files and facts unrelated to present suit).

[124]*See* Robinson v. Jacksonville Shipyards, *supra* note 119, 760 F. Supp. at 1519 (expert testimony on elements of effective sexual harassment policy); Shrout v. Black Clawson Co., *supra* note 110, 689 F. Supp. at 777, 46 FEP Cases at 1341–42 (citing testimony of human resources consultant to determine defendant's "open-door policy" inadequate as sexual harassment policy).

[125]*See* cases cited in note 124 *supra. See generally* Meritor Sav. Bank v. Vinson, 477 U.S. 57, 72, 40 FEP Cases 1822, 1829 (1986), reproduced in Chapter 1, Overview; EEOC v. Hacienda Hotel, 881 F.2d 1504, 1576, 50 FEP Cases 877, 886 (9th Cir. 1989).

[126]For a detailed discussion of these insurance coverage issues, see Chapter 22, Employer's Litigation Strategy.

are more likely to be covered than intentional torts or disparate treatment discrimination claims.[127] Similarly, psychological trauma coupled with physical injury is more likely to be covered than mere emotional distress.

Soon after the action is commenced, the complainant should seek detailed discovery of each defendant's insurance coverage.[128] Counsel should be aware of the types of insurance policies that may provide a defendant with coverage for a sexual harassment claim: comprehensive general liability; comprehensive personal liability; errors and omissions; workers' compensation; directors, officers, and partners' general liability; and homeowners' liability. Once the scope of potential coverage is known, counsel should consider amending the complaint to maximize coverage.

An important cautionary note in drafting a complaint with an eye toward insurance coverage is that an insurance carrier's duty to defend is broader than the duty to pay claims. In general, an insurer must provide a defense to all allegations in a complaint if it has a duty to defend against any of the allegations, even though some of them might eventually result in recovery of damages that are not covered by the policy.[129] Therefore, including claims with little chance of success may, as a practical matter, relieve the defendants of their costs and attorney's fees without enhancing the complainant's ability to collect on a judgment.

---

[127]*See* Seminole Point Hosp. Corp. v. Aetna Cas. & Sur. Co., 675 F. Supp. 44, 45 FEP Cases 929 (D.N.H. 1987).

[128]Discovery of a party's insurance coverage is specifically provided for in Rule 26(b)(2) of the Federal Rules of Civil Procedure and in corresponding state discovery provisions, *e.g.*, CAL. CODE CIV. PROC. §2017(b).

[129]California Union Ins. Co. v. Club Aquarius, 113 Cal. App.3d 243, 247, 169 Cal. Rptr. 685, 687 (1980).

CHAPTER 22

EMPLOYER'S LITIGATION STRATEGY

I. PRELIMINARY STEPS

A. Prompt Remedial Action

An employer should investigate and take prompt remedial action upon any report of sexual harassment—even before a charge or suit is filed.[1] An employer's effective response to complaints of sexual harassment may minimize monetary damages and obviate the need for a court to impose injunctive relief.[2] Courts may award injunctions against sexual harassment[3] unless the employer can demonstrate that it is unlikely to recur.[4] Thus, courts have granted injunctive relief when a hostile work environment continues to exist[5] or when an employer has taken corrective action only after being sued.[6] The employer's assurance that its employees have been educated about sexual harassment and that it will not recur may be insufficient.[7]

---

[1]For a discussion of the employer's prompt corrective action, see Chapters 4, Hostile Environment Harassment, Section IX.C.2.; 6, Harassment by Supervisors, Section IV; 7, Harassment by Co-Workers, Section V; and 19, Responding to Internal Complaints, Section IV.

[2]For a discussion of injunctive relief in sexual harassment cases, see Chapter 28, Injunctive and Affirmative Relief.

[3]*See* EEOC v. Goodyear Aerospace Corp., 813 F.2d 1539, 1544–45, 43 FEP Cases 875, 879 (9th Cir. 1987)(district court abused discretion by refusing to grant injunctive relief without finding that defendant was unlikely to repeat offensive actions). *See generally* B.L. SCHLEI & P. GROSSMAN, EMPLOYMENT DISCRIMINA- TION LAW 1415–16 & n.61 (2d ed. 1983), Five-Year Supp. 523–24 (1989).

[4]*See generally* County of Los Angeles v. Davis, 440 U.S. 625, 632–33, 19 FEP Cases 282 (1979)(where interim events have completely and irrevocably eradicated effects of alleged violation and no reasonable expectation violation will recur, action for injunctive relief moot). *Cf.* James v. Stockham Valves & Fittings Co., 559 F.2d 310, 354–55, 15 FEP Cases 827, 863–64 (5th Cir. 1977)(absent clear and convincing proof of no reasonable probability of future violations, injunctive relief should be granted), *cert. denied*, 434 U.S. 1034 (1978).

[5]*See* Sanchez v. City of Miami Beach, 720 F. Supp. 974, 982 (S.D. Fla. 1989); *see also* Bundy v. Jackson, 641 F.2d 934, 946 n.13, 24 FEP Cases 1155, 1162 (D.C. Cir. 1981)(no certainty that harassment would not recur, in part because "all the harassing employees still work for the agency").

[6]*See* EEOC v. Hacienda Hotel, 881 F.2d 1504, 1519, 50 FEP Cases 877, 889 (9th Cir. 1989)("appellant did not take prompt remedial action upon notification of the sexual harassment allegations against it . . . . Appellant's recent efforts to train managerial employees regarding discrimination problems and the absence of further EEOC charges in recent times are encouraging and laudable; however, the district court did not abuse its discretion by awarding permanent injunctive relief on the facts of this case"); EEOC v. Goodyear Aerospace Corp., *supra* note 3, 813 F.2d at 1544–45, 43 FEP Cases at 879 ("[a]n employer that takes curative actions only after it has been sued fails to provide sufficient assurances that it will not repeat the violation to justify denying an injunction"); James v. Stockham Valves & Fittings Co., *supra* note 4 (same). *But cf.* Spencer v. General Elec. Co., 894 F.2d 651, 660, 51 FEP Cases 1725, 1732 (4th Cir. 1990)(rejecting plaintiff's contention that remedial measures undertaken by defendant after instigation of litigation will never be adequate to obviate injunctive relief).

[7]*See* Bundy v. Jackson, *supra* note 5 (injunctive relief not moot simply because conduct has ceased;

The types of injunctive relief granted by courts illustrate the affirmative steps that an employer should consider taking before they are imposed by court order. Courts have required defendants to notify employees that sexual harassment is unlawful and against company policy,[8] to develop a plan outlining steps to prevent sexual harassment,[9] to develop effective grievance procedures for complainants[10] and disciplinary measures for harassers, to notify employees that offenders will be disciplined,[11] to train and educate supervisors and other employees,[12] and even to hire an equal employment opportunity expert to evaluate and recommend steps to enhance a defendant's future compliance.[13]

B. Unconditional Offer of Reinstatement

In a discharge or constructive discharge case, the employer may be able to limit back-pay and front-pay awards by an unconditional offer of reinstatement. In *Ford Motor Co. v. EEOC*,[14] a sex discrimination case, the Supreme Court held that unreasonable rejection of the employer's unconditional "good faith" offer of reinstatement to a position "substantially equivalent" to the plaintiff's former position ended the accrual of potential back-pay liability.

To help ensure that the offer of reinstatement will be understood as unconditional, the employer may expressly state that accepting the offer will not waive the complainant's right to pursue legal claims.[15] To help ensure that the proffered job is "substantially equivalent," the employer may wish to make clear that the job is comparable to the job that the complainant has left in terms of promotional opportunities, status, responsibilities, working conditions, and compensation.[16]

---

must be "no reasonable expectation that conduct will recur" or interim events must have " 'completely and irrevocably eradicated the effects of the alleged violation' ")(citations omitted).

[8]*E.g.,* Arnold v. City of Seminole, 614 F. Supp. 853, 871–73, 40 FEP Cases 1539, 1553–54 (E.D. Okla. 1985)(defendant ordered to notify all employees and supervisors through individual letters and permanent postings in prominent locations in all offices that sexual harassment—as explicitly defined by court's decree—violates Title VII, EEOC Guidelines, and policies of the employer); Broderick v. Ruder, 685 F. Supp. 1269, 46 FEP Cases 1272 (D.D.C. 1988), reproduced in Chapter 2, Forms of Harassment (ordering defendant "to take reasonable steps to advise its employees that sexually harassing other Commission employees is prohibited"). For an example of a specific form of notice, see *EEOC v. Fotios,* 671 F. Supp. 454, 466, 43 FEP Cases 1712, 1714 (W.D. Tex. 1987).

[9]*E.g.,* Boyd v. James S. Hayes Living Health Care Agency, 671 F. Supp. 1155, 1169, 44 FEP Cases 323, 344 (W.D. Tenn. 1987).

[10]*E.g.,* Arnold v. City of Seminole, *supra* note 8 (defendant required to develop "clear and effective procedures" for having complaints of sexual harassment promptly and thoroughly investigated by neutral factfinder and informal as well as formal processes for hearing, adjudication, and appeal of complaints); *see also* Sanchez v. City of Miami Beach, *supra* note 5 (defendant ordered to "design anew or re-formulate and thereafter stringently implement a comprehensive system to safeguard against all kinds of discriminatory conduct").

[11]*E.g.,* Broderick v. Ruder, *supra* note 8.

[12]*E.g.,* Arnold v. City of Seminole, *supra* note 8; Broderick v. Ruder, *supra* note 8.

[13]*E.g.,* Broderick v. Ruder, *supra* note 8. For a more thorough discussion of injunctive relief, see Chapter 28, Injunctive and Affirmative Relief.

[14]458 U.S. 219, 29 FEP Cases 121 (1982). *See also* Morris v. American Nat'l Can Corp., 730 F. Supp. 1489, 1497, 52 FEP Cases 210 (E.D. Mo. 1989), reproduced in Chapter 2, Forms of Harassment (plaintiff in Title VII constructive discharge case entitled to back pay from date of resignation until unconditional offer of re-employment).

[15]Toledo v. Nobel-Sysco, Inc., 892 F.2d 1481, 1493, 51 FEP Cases 1146 (10th Cir. 1989)(employee's rejection of offer did not toll accrual of back pay where offer was conditioned on employee dropping claim and passing polygraph test and physical examination), *cert. denied,* 110 S.Ct. 2208 (1990); Davis v. Ingersoll Johnson Steel Co., 39 FEP Cases 1197, 1199–1200 (S.D. Ind. 1985)(employer's offer tolled accrual of back pay where it was not conditioned on employee dropping claims).

[16]*E.g.,* Ford Motor Co. v. EEOC, *supra* note 14, 458 U.S. at 231, 29 FEP Cases at 127 n.16 (plaintiff need not enter another line of work, accept demotion, or take position with conditions substantially more

Any offer of reinstatement works best if made early. A long delay between the termination of employment and the offer of reinstatement may lead to increased back-pay liability, make reinstatement less feasible,[17] and make the employee's rejection of the offer seem more reasonable. To determine whether the plaintiff's rejection of the offer is "reasonable," courts examine the circumstances surrounding the rejection, including the reasons for the rejection and the terms of the offer.[18]

Rejection may be considered reasonable if the alleged harasser remains in the workplace.[19] This difficulty may be avoided, however, if the employer can offer the complainant a "substantially equivalent" job at a different location.[20] The employer will also remove objections by agreeing to expunge from the complainant's personnel file any information relating to the facts and circumstances of the harassment charge or proceedings and the complainant's resignation or discharge.[21]

---

onerous than prior position); Rasimas v. Michigan Dep't of Mental Health, 714 F.2d 614, 624, 32 FEP Cases 688 (6th Cir. 1983)("substantial equivalent" of position from which claimant was discharged must afford claimant "virtually identical promotional opportunities, compensation, job responsibilities, working conditions and status"), *cert. denied,* 466 U.S. 950 (1984); *cf.* Shore v. Federal Express Corp., 777 F.2d 1155, 1158, 39 FEP Cases 809, 811 (6th Cir. 1985)(offer with very different job responsibilities not comparable), *aff'd mem.,* 875 F.2d 867, 49 FEP Cases 1640 (6th Cir. 1989); EEOC v. Exxon Shipping Co., 745 F.2d 967, 979, 36 FEP Cases 330, 340 (5th Cir. 1984)(position requiring work every weekend not comparable to job that did not require such weekend work); Oldfather v. Ohio Dep't of Transp., 653 F. Supp. 1167, 1179, 48 FEP Cases 607, 616 (S.D. Ohio 1986)(job offer requiring plaintiff to commute three hours a day not substantially equivalent); Walters v. City of Atlanta, 610 F. Supp. 715, 728, 42 FEP Cases 369, 379 (N.D. Ga. 1985)(offer of lower-paying position not comparable), *aff'd in part, rev'd in part, and dismissed in part,* 803 F.2d 1135, 42 FEP Cases 387 (11th Cir. 1986); Donovan v. Commercial Sewing, 562 F. Supp. 548, 555 (D. Conn. 1982)(offer of full-time position not substantially equivalent to part-time position plaintiff held before unlawful discharge); Coates v. National Cash Register Co., 433 F. Supp. 655, 662–63 n.2, 15 FEP Cases 222, 228–29 (W.D. Va. 1977)(plaintiffs justified in rejecting offers for positions in different locations, especially when many offers were for nonexistent jobs).

[17]Where reinstatement is not feasible because of a hostile or unsuitable work environment, substantial front-pay awards may be granted in lieu of reinstatement. *E.g.,* Fitzgerald v. Sirloin Stockade, 624 F.2d 945, 956–57, 22 FEP Cases 262 (10th Cir. 1980)(front-pay awarded where evidence established atmosphere of hostility); Sowers v. Kemira, Inc., 701 F. Supp. 809, 827, 46 FEP Cases 1825, 1838 (S.D. Ga. 1988)(same); EEOC v. Pacific Press Publishing Ass'n, 482 F. Supp. 1291, 1320–21, 21 FEP Cases 848 (N.D. Cal. 1979)(six months' front pay awarded where litigation generated antagonism and there was likelihood of future litigation), *aff'd,* 676 F.2d 1272, 28 FEP Cases 1596 (9th Cir. 1982).

[18]Giandonato v. Sybron Corp., 804 F.2d 120, 124, 42 FEP Cases 219, 222 (10th Cir. 1986)(not valid to reject offer of reinstatement for personal reasons such as ill spouse or not wanting to work under particular supervisor). *See* Ford Motor Co. v. EEOC, *supra* note 14, 458 U.S. at 234–39; Claiborne v. Illinois Cent. R.R., 583 F.2d 143, 153, 18 FEP Cases 536 (5th Cir. 1978), *cert. denied,* 442 U.S. 934 (1979)(whether an employee was reasonable in rejecting reinstatement must be determined on individual basis); Boomsma v. Greyhound Food Mgmt., 639 F. Supp. 1448, 1456, 41 FEP Cases 1365 (W.D. Mich. 1986)(back pay tolled where plaintiff rejected reinstatement because, *inter alia,* "he liked his new job"). For a discussion of the plaintiff's duty to mitigate damages by seeking new employment, see Chapter 29, Monetary Relief.

[19]*See* Maturo v. National Graphics, 722 F. Supp. 916, 924 (D. Conn. 1989)(although defendant's reinstatement offer provided that alleged harasser would no longer be complainant's supervisor, rejection of defendant's reinstatement offer did not toll accrual of back-pay liability where supervisor continued to work for defendant).

[20]*See* Taylor v. Faculty-Student Ass'n, 40 FEP Cases 1292 (W.D.N.Y. 1986)(plaintiff's damages minimal where she rejected defendant's offer of reinstatement to her position at different location); Davis v. Western-Southern Life Ins. Co., 34 FEP Cases 97, 102 (N.D. Ohio 1984)(by rejecting offer to return to position at different location, plaintiff waived right to any relief subsequent to offer). *But see* Oldfather v. Ohio Dep't of Transp., *supra* note 16; Coates v. National Cash Register Co., *supra* note 16.

[21]Section 642.4 of the EEOC conciliation standards provides that in conciliation the employer should agree:

> to remove from its records and files any notations, remarks, or other indications evidencing that the service performed by the Charging Party prior to termination was other than or anything less than satisfactory. The Company further agrees that, in furnishing oral or written references concerning the Charging Party as may be requested by same or by prospective future employers, it will mention only the nature and duration of Charging Party's employment.

EEOC COMPL. MAN. (BNA) at 915:0002. *Cf.* Yates v. Avco Corp., 819 F.2d 630, 635, 43 FEP Cases 1595

The unreasonable rejection of an offer of reinstatement may be the basis for a summary judgment motion as to damages[22] or for negotiating a favorable settlement. In constructive discharge cases, a good-faith unconditional offer of reinstatement that does not re-expose the complainant to a harassing environment may also buttress a defense argument that the employer did not previously know about the alleged conduct, and has now taken appropriate steps to remedy it.[23] A rejection of the offer would bolster a defense contention that the complainant had left the job for reasons other than an intolerable work environment.

An unconditional offer of reinstatement could obviously be counterproductive where it would complicate an employer defense that the complainant was discharged for misconduct or poor performance.[24]

C. Offer of Judgment

If the complainant takes an unrealistic view of the potential recovery, the employer may attempt to exert pressure with an offer of judgment under Rule 68 of the Federal Rules of Civil Procedure or the appropriate state-law counterpart.[25] Under Rule 68, a plaintiff who rejects an offer of judgment that turns out to be more favorable than the judgment the plaintiff finally obtains is not entitled to collect costs incurred after the offer of judgment was made.[26] Because attorney's fees are recoverable costs under Title VII,[27] an offer of judgment may exert considerable settlement pressure on a plaintiff.[28]

Unless the employer is willing to pay the plaintiff's reasonable costs and attorney's fees without knowing precisely what they are, an offer of judgment should expressly state that the amount offered includes all costs and fees. If the plaintiff accepts an offer of judgment that is silent on this point, the court may hold that the plaintiff is entitled to the amount of the offer plus costs and attorney's fees.[29]

(6th Cir. 1987)(employer should not refuse to document complaints of sexual harassment in personnel file of complainant; that refusal protects employer and harasser, not complainant).

[22]See, e.g., Hopkins v. Shoe Show, 678 F. Supp. 1241, 1246 (S.D.W. Va. 1988)(partial summary judgment granted on issue of back pay where plaintiff did not offer any evidence to contradict claim that she unreasonably rejected unconditional offer of reinstatement).

[23]See Davis v. Western-Southern Life Ins. Co., supra note 20 (plaintiff offered reinstatement to position at different location unable to establish Title VII case where she never advised supervisors of alleged sexual harassment).

[24]Evidence of an unconditional offer of reinstatement could be introduced by either party at trial. Admission against the employer is not barred by Rule 408 of the Federal Rules of Evidence (barring admission of settlement offers), for by definition the unconditional offer of reinstatement is not an offer to settle the lawsuit.

[25]Approximately 40 states have rules similar to Rule 68 in their rules of procedure. For a more detailed discussion of offers of judgment, see Chapter 31, Settlement, Section V.

[26]See Marek v. Chesny, 473 U.S. 1, 5, 38 FEP Cases 124, 126 (1985); Spencer v. General Elec. Co., supra note 6, 894 F.2d at 662–64, 51 FEP Cases at 1733–35 (Rule 68 does not undercut policy goals of Title VII). See generally Klawes v. Firestone Tire & Rubber Co., 572 F. Supp. 116, 118 (E.D. Wis. 1983)(Rule 68 offer of judgment is procedural and thus state rule regarding offers of judgment inapplicable in diversity case in federal court).

[27]42 U.S.C. §2000e-5(k).

[28]For further discussion of Rule 68 offers, see Chapter 31, Settlement, Section V.

[29]Sas v. Trintex, 709 F. Supp. 455, 458, 49 FEP Cases 842 (S.D.N.Y. 1989)(plaintiff accepting Rule 68 offer is prevailing party entitled to costs and attorney's fees, even if offer did not expressly include costs; denying defendant's motion to rescind or modify judgment and awarding $7,500 in attorney's fees plus disbursements where offer of judgment had been for $5,000); Shorter v. Valley Bank & Trust Co., 678 F. Supp. 714, 718, 46 FEP Cases 155, 158–60 (N.D. Ill. 1988)(defendant who offered monetary sum plus "costs" manifested no intent to include attorney's fees in offer).

D. Rule 11 Letter

Rule 11 of the Federal Rules of Civil Procedure and comparable state rules provide for sanctions, including an award of attorney's fees, for filing a pleading that is not well-grounded in law or fact.[30] If, after review of the complaint and a thorough inquiry into the facts and law, it appears that the plaintiff's allegations are frivolous, defense counsel should consider sending the plaintiff's attorney a letter explaining why the case lacks merit and, in appropriate cases, giving notice of the defendant's intention to seek sanctions if the action is pursued. In addition to setting forth the relevant facts, it may be helpful to attach key documents, such as poor performance evaluations, that support the employer's position.[31]

II. THE JOINT DEFENSE OF THE EMPLOYER AND AN INDIVIDUAL DEFENDANT

Sexual harassment complainants often sue not only the employer, but also the individual alleged harasser.[32] In that event the employer and the individual defendant must decide whether to present a joint defense. A joint defense, while promoting coordination and minimizing litigation costs, creates potential conflicts of interest and raises issues of attorney-client privilege and attorney work product.

A. Joint Defense Strategy Issues

1. Relevant Considerations

Evaluating the desirability of a joint defense requires a thorough investigation of any complaint of sexual harassment. This investigation entails interviews of the complainant, the alleged harasser, and all appropriate witnesses. Additional interviews may be needed to deal with discrepancies or inconsistencies in the information received.[33]

The employer must then decide whether it believes that the alleged harassment actually occurred. This decision will determine whether the theory of the defense will be "it didn't happen" or "it's the harasser's fault."

---

[30]Taylor v. Prudential-Bache Secs., 594 F. Supp. 226 (N.D.N.Y.)(harassing, vexatious, and oppressive conduct of lawsuit warrants sanctions), *aff'd mem.*, 751 F.2d 371 (2d Cir. 1984). *Pro se* litigants, however, may be treated more leniently. *See* Connor v. Merit Sys. Protection Bd., 1988 U.S. Dist. LEXIS 3105 (E.D. Pa. 1988). A party moving for costs under Rule 11 has a duty to mitigate expenses and should gauge the response to the pleading to the merits of the claims asserted. *See* Thomas v. Capital Sec. Servs., 836 F.2d 866, 879 (5th Cir. 1988)(court must inquire into extent movant's expenses and fees could have been avoided). For more discussion of Rule 11, see Chapter 21, Complainant's Litigation Strategy, Section I.

[31]This tactic should be used with caution, because sanctions also may be awarded against an attorney who improperly invokes Rule 11. *See, e.g.,* Brown v. Capitol Air, 797 F.2d 106 (2d Cir. 1986)(defendant who won summary judgment denied Rule 11 sanctions when it used removal to bifurcate litigation more economically resolved as single proceeding); Kirby v. Allegheny Beverage Corp., 811 F.2d 253, 1 IER Cases 1580 (4th Cir. 1987)(signing of pleading in state court proceeding that is later removed to federal court cannot support Rule 11 sanctions); Foval v. First Nat'l Bank of Commerce, 841 F.2d 126 (5th Cir. 1988)(outlining standards for imposing Rule 11 sanctions; Rule 11 does not apply to conduct occurring in state court).

[32]For a discussion of the alleged harasser as an individual defendant, see Chapter 23, The Alleged Harasser as Defendant.

[33]For a discussion of how to minimize liability once notice of a sexual harassment complaint is received, see Chapter 19, Responding to Internal Complaints.

If the investigation establishes that the claim is true, the employer's strategy should be that "it's not our fault." Any other position would suggest that the employer approves of the conduct and would increase the employer's potential liability. Although selecting this strategy will entail disciplining and probably alienating the alleged harasser, the employer's object should be to direct the complainant's focus where it belongs—on the harasser.

If the investigation establishes that the claim is false, the defense strategy is again clear—"it didn't happen." This strategy should secure the cooperation of the alleged harasser and thus increase the probability that the correct result will be reached. Should the strategy prove to be factually erroneous, the chance of significant employer liability increases. That, however, is a risk that cannot be avoided.

The more difficult question arises when, as often happens, the alleged harasser denies the allegations and the only evidence is the complainant's allegation. It is generally impractical to defend a doubtful claim on the basis that "it's the harasser's fault," for that defense encourages the alleged harasser to assert claims against the employer.[34] Moreover, the employer has thereby assured itself that it will not have the alleged harasser's cooperation, but will have instead two hostile parties arrayed against it.

The employer response to doubtful claims usually will be that "we don't know what happened" at least until convincing evidence is produced as to what did happen. This strategy should help assure the employer of the alleged harasser's cooperation with the defense while it enables the employer to avoid a final conclusion until the matter is resolved in an independent forum.

If the judicial decision-maker ultimately rules against the employer and the alleged harasser, the complainant will certainly claim that the employer should be punished all the more. The employer can ameliorate this situation by cautioning the alleged harasser, after the earlier inconclusive investigation, that sexual harassment will not be tolerated and that if it is determined that the sexual harassment did occur, proper and prompt disciplinary action will be taken.[35]

2. Investigative Procedures

An employer's strategy alternatives will dictate its investigative procedures. Unless the evidence from the investigation pursued through other sources is unusually convincing and enables the employer to decide even before interviewing the alleged harasser, the employer's counsel should not commit the employer to any position at the time of counsel's initial investigative interviews following the filing of a lawsuit. Counsel generally advises the alleged harasser that counsel represents only the employer. Counsel should explain that the employer may decide to offer legal representation in the future, after all of the facts are gathered, but that joint representation will not be offered if there is a serious question of the alleged harasser's liability. Some counsel also advise

---

[34]For a discussion of the alleged harasser as a wrongful termination plaintiff, see Chapter 24, The Alleged Harasser as Plaintiff.

[35]The alleged harasser might be so advised in writing, to evidence the corrective action. For a discussion of taking appropriate corrective action, see Chapter 19, Responding to Internal Complaints.

that the alleged harasser has the right to retain separate counsel, both for general representation purposes and at the initial investigatory interview; that they might be sued and found liable for compensatory and punitive damages; and that in extreme cases there is the possibility of criminal action. Some counsel prefer to place these cautions in writing for alleged harassers to acknowledge.

Once the facts have been gathered, the employer should decide which strategy to follow. If litigation commences and the alleged harasser is named as an individual defendant, the employer must decide whether to offer joint representation. If the conclusion is that "it's the harasser's fault," joint representation should not be offered, without regard to whether the employee is a supervisor. Indeed, the employer will normally be taking corrective action, including discipline, and thus the alleged harasser is not likely to be cooperative in the subsequent defense by the employer.

The question of joint representation is more difficult where the claim is false or uncertain. The most cautious approach is for each defendant to retain separate counsel. This approach will ensure that each defendant will have counsel who can act on behalf of the client without facing any conflict of interest. The alleged harasser would then be able to confide fully in counsel without fear that disclosure will lead to discharge or other disciplinary actions. Independent counsel could also tell a more personalized story to the trier of fact.

Nonetheless, in the case of a false or uncertain claim, most employers offer an alleged harasser joint representation. First, a joint defense will offer cost advantages, for if an individual defendant retains independent counsel, the employer may be obliged to pay the individual defendant's attorney's fees.[36] Second, a joint defense permits the defendants to adopt one common approach toward the litigation. Third, a joint defense may seem preferable, particularly when the claim arose from the employment relationship and the individual defendant is a supervisor, because the employer may conclude that it would likely be found liable if the claim is sustained against the individual.[37]

If the individual defendant is a nonsupervisory employee, the question of joint representation is more difficult. A joint defense should increase the level of the alleged harasser's cooperation. However, because a co-worker harasser is less likely to be found to be an agent of the employer, the potential for employer liability, and thus the incentive to provide an employer-paid defense, is diminished.[38]

B. Conflicts of Interest

An attorney who jointly represents an employer and an alleged harasser has two separate clients, each of whom deserves the attorney's independent representation, even though it may be that the employer is paying the fees for defending the individual defendant. Rule 1.7 of the Model Rules of Professional

---

[36]For a discussion of indemnity of an individual defendant, see Chapter 23, The Alleged Harasser as Defendant, Section IV.C. McCandless & Sullivan, *Defending the Alleged Sexual Harasser*, 20 BRIEF 28 (Spring 1991).

[37]For a discussion of the employer's liability for sexual harassment by supervisors, see Chapter 6, Harassment by Supervisors.

[38]See Chapters 6, Harassment by Supervisors, and 7, Harassment by Co-Workers.

Conduct of the American Bar Association provides that a lawyer shall not represent a client if the representation will be "directly adverse to another client," unless the lawyer reasonably believes there is no such adversity and "each client consents after consultation."[39]

The joint defense of an employer and an individual defendant presents several potential conflicts of interest, particularly where (1) the causes of action differ as to the different defendants, or (2) a defense available to one defendant has the effect of shifting liability to the other.[40] For example, if the facts support the complainant's allegations of harassment by the individual defendant, it would be in the employer's interest, and against the alleged harasser's, to adduce proof that the alleged harasser was acting beyond the scope of employment or that the employer disciplined the alleged harasser for the conduct.[41] The employer may even decide to seek indemnification from the alleged harasser if the employer is found vicariously liable because of the alleged harasser's misconduct.[41a]

A lawyer may represent more than one client in a particular matter only if the interests of each client can be adequately represented *and* all clients consent to the representation after a full disclosure of the implications of multiple representation.[42] Counsel should inform the parties in writing, before undertaking representation, of the potential conflicts and the fact that subsequently developed conflicts may require one or both parties to obtain new counsel, which will cost both time and money. The initial disclosure should include all material facts and an explanation of their legal significance.[43] The test of whether counsel made an adequate disclosure is objective, measured by what a reasonable lawyer would disclose to a client under the circumstances.[44] Counsel should also explain which party, if any, counsel will con-

---

[39]The Model Code of Professional Responsibility (Model Code) was originally adopted by the American Bar Association (ABA) in 1969. After amending the Model Code several times, the ABA replaced it in 1983 with the Model Rules of Professional Conduct (Model Rules). Most states still follow the Model Code rather than the Model Rules. For a reproduction of the Model Code and the Model Rules, with digests of judicial and bar-association opinions and state statutory provisions on ethical issues, see LAW. MANUAL ON PROF. CONDUCT (ABA/BNA 1990).

[40]*See generally* Model Code, *supra* note 39, Canon 5. For a discussion of multiple representation in a civil rights case, see *Smith v. Daggett County Bd. of Educ.,* 650 F. Supp. 44 (D. Utah 1986)(lawyer representing school board allowed to represent each member of board in civil rights case after interviewing each member and deciding no conflict existed). For an Informal Opinion by the ABA Committee on Ethics and Professional Responsibility on joint representation of an employer and its employee, see ABA Informal Opinion 1476 (August 11, 1981).

[41]*See generally* Shadid v. Jackson, 521 F. Supp. 87, 89 (E.D. Tex. 1981)(attorney could not jointly represent city and city police officer accused of unconstitutionally brutalizing plaintiff in that officer likely could contend he acted in good faith within his official duties, while city might avoid liability by proving officer acted outside scope of his duties and in that attorney "might find it difficult" to preserve officer's confidences while also serving city). The *Shadid* court saw no ethical problem, however, in one attorney jointly representing the city and a county sheriff, where the city would necessarily be liable for the conduct attributed to the sheriff. *Id.* at 90–91.

[41a]Biggs v. Surrey Broadcasting Co., 56 FEP Cases 289, 290–91 (Okla. Ct. App. 1991)(employer who settled sexual harassment claim by employee based on conduct of co-worker could sue co-worker under theory of implied indemnity and recover to extent settlement was reasonable and employer was not a joint tortfeasor).

[42]*E.g.,* Ames v. Putz, 495 S.W.2d 581 (Tex. Civ. App. 1973).

[43]*See* Model Code, *supra* note 39, EC 5-16. The employer who retains counsel for the employee should reserve the employer's right to disassociate itself from the employee if it appears that the employee has acted outside the course and scope of his or her authority, or with malice, or for personal reasons not in the interest of the employer.

[44]Burien Motors v. Balch, 9 Wash. App. 573, 513 P.2d 582 (1973), *review denied,* 83 Wash.2d 1005 (1974).

tinue to represent in the event of a conflict. After fully disclosing potential conflicts, counsel should obtain each party's written consent to joint representation. The consent must demonstrate that the party assumes the risks associated with withdrawal, be it voluntary or by disqualification.

Joint representation may not always be appropriate, notwithstanding receipt of a written consent following full disclosure. When there is a potential conflict of interest, ethical concerns may require an attorney to advise the joint clients not to enter into a joint representation agreement.[45] Should an actual conflict of interest develop between the employer and the alleged harasser, counsel may be forced to discontinue representation of either or both parties.[46]

An actual conflict of interest for counsel will arise if it is discovered that the alleged harasser did engage in the wrongful conduct alleged. In those circumstances, the employer may decide to sever the joint defense to diminish its exposure to liability for the alleged harasser's conduct. Thus, the employer may seek to show that the alleged harasser is entirely responsible for the alleged conduct and that the conduct occurred without the knowledge or approval of the employer.

Once representation of the alleged harasser ceases, the employer's counsel may not, without the alleged harasser's consent, represent the employer in the same or a substantially related matter in which the employer's interests are materially adverse to those of the alleged harasser.[47] Thus, the employer providing a joint defense must, as a practical matter, seek the alleged harasser's written waiver of the subsequent disqualification of counsel in the event of a conflict. If the alleged harasser expressly waives any objection to the possibility of adverse representation after consultation and explanation by counsel, some courts have permitted continued representation of the employer in the same or other matters.[48] Continued representation of the employer will leave counsel, however, with a dilemma concerning how to use any privileged information received from the alleged harasser during the joint representation.[49]

C. The Attorney-Client Privilege

1. During Joint Representation of the Employer and the Individual Defendant

The attorney-client privilege may be maintained in a joint defense of an employer and an alleged harasser so long as the defendants share a "common interest."[50] A joint defense common-interest privilege requires a showing "that

---

[45]For example, if an employer seeks joint representation even though it understands that the harassment occurred, counsel should advise against joint representation because it will be almost impossible for counsel to exercise unfettered judgment on behalf of both clients. *See* Model Rules, *supra* note 39, Rule 1.7 comment. Because ethics rules differ from state to state, a thorough study of applicable ethical rules of conduct is essential for any attorney representing the interests of both the employer and an individual named in the action.

[46]*See* Model Rules, *supra* note 39, Rule 1.7; McCandless & Sullivan, *supra* note 36.

[47]*Id.*, Rule 1.9.

[48]*See* Melamed v. ITT Continental Baking Co., 592 F.2d 290, 294 (6th Cir. 1979)(no disqualification of counsel where client received full disclosure of potential conflicts before or after actual conflict developed).

[49]For a discussion of representation of the employer after joint representation has ended, see Section III.C.2. *infra*.

[50]*See* Eisenberg v. Gagnon, 766 F.2d 770, 787 (3d Cir.)(joint-defense privilege protects communications that are "part of an on-going joint effort to set up a common defense strategy"), *cert. denied,* 474 U.S. 946 (1985); United Coal Cos. v. Powell Constr. Co., 839 F.2d 958, 965 (3d Cir. 1988)("Where, as here, an attorney represents two clients, the privilege applies to those clients as against a common adversary").

(1) the communications were made in the course of a joint defense effort, (2) the statements were designed to further that effort, and (3) the privilege has not been waived."[51]

The common-interest privilege covers communications to counsel in the presence of a co-party as well as communications between parties jointly represented by a single attorney.[52] Those communications are not discoverable by adverse parties even though the presence of a third party ordinarily would negate the requisite intent that the communication be made in confidence.[53] Moreover, jointly represented clients need not have common interests in toto, so long as the communication deals with a matter in which the parties share a common purpose.[54]

The common-interest privilege may cover communications during the earliest stages of an investigation before a complaint has been filed. Several courts have ruled that the common-interest privilege can apply even when parties only contemplate or seek to avoid litigation.[55] It is essential, however, for the party claiming a common-interest privilege to show that the parties not only were pursuing a common interest, but had agreed to do so.[56] The parties would support that showing by promptly signing a written consent form.

2. After Joint Representation Has Ended

A more difficult problem of attorney-client privilege occurs when the joint defense ends.[57] The question will then focus on the employer's right to use, in

---

[51]*In re* Bevill, Bresler & Schulman Asset Mgmt. Corp., 805 F.2d 120, 126 (3d Cir. 1986)(citation omitted).

[52]E. EPSTEIN & M. MARTIN, THE ATTORNEY-CLIENT PRIVILEGE AND THE WORK-PRODUCT DOCTRINE 48 (2d ed. 1989).

[53]Nonetheless, the presence of multiple clients at a single conference may create an undue risk, in that a client's statements extraneous to the common interest would be admissible as admissions. The preferred approach is individual consultation and a pooling of information through counsel.

[54]*See* Eisenberg v. Gagnon, *supra* note 50, 766 F.2d at 787–88 (even though defendants' interests partially adverse, correspondence between one individual defendant and counsel for corporate defendant's insurer about another more culpable individual defendant privileged where communication dealt with matter on which defendants had common purpose); United States v. McPartlin, 595 F.2d 1321, 1336–37 (7th Cir.)(even though co-defendants had conflicting interests in general, communications privileged where co-defendants had common interest), *cert. denied,* 444 U.S. 833 (1979). *See generally* Hunydee v. United States, 355 F.2d 183 (9th Cir. 1965)(attorney-client privilege applied where statements dealt with matter of common interest between parties even though statements encompassed potential conflict of interest).

[55]*E.g.,* Davis v. Costa-Gavras, 580 F. Supp. 1082, 1098–99 (S.D.N.Y. 1984) (attorney-client privilege applied where book author present at "prepublication libel review" could "hardly be characterized as 'one who stands in a neutral or adverse position vis-à-vis the subject of the communication,' such that his presence destroys the presumption of attorney-client confidentiality"); SCM Corp. v. Xerox Corp., 70 F.R.D. 508, 513 (D. Conn. 1976)("privilege need not be limited to legal consultations . . . in litigation situations"); *In re* Grand Jury Subpoena Duces Tecum, 406 F. Supp. 381, 389–92 (S.D.N.Y. 1975)(attorney-client privilege held to apply to parties jointly consulting attorneys in connection with pending SEC investigation in which they had been advised that SEC contemplated civil and criminal proceedings).

[56]*Cf. In re* Bevill, Bresler & Schulman Asset Mgmt. Corp., *supra* note 51 (court denied privilege where party claiming privilege produced no evidence that parties had agreed to pursue joint-defense strategy); United States v. Melvin, 650 F.2d 641 (5th Cir. 1981)(although disputed statements made to enlist co-defendant in common defense, they were not protected; co-defendant had not yet agreed to cooperate with others); *In re* Colocotronis Tanker Sec. Litig., 449 F. Supp. 828, 830–32 (S.D.N.Y. 1978)(lead bank could assert privilege against other banks as to communications between lead bank and its law firms, even though other banks had paid part of attorney's fees, given no showing of "a relationship of trust, confidence and mutual reliance" between other banks and firms).

[57]This may occur, for example, when the employer, after first undertaking a joint defense, receives convincing evidence that the sexual harassment claim is true.

its own defense, what it learned during the joint defense. The general rule that confidential client-attorney communications retain the protection of the attorney-client privilege beyond termination of the attorney-client relationship[58] applies to a joint representation of an employer and an alleged harasser. Thus, whether separate counsel is retained for each of the formerly jointly represented parties or whether the former joint counsel continues to represent one of the parties, the privileged nature of the earlier disclosures must, absent the former client's consent, be retained throughout the litigation.[59] Although the employer should be able to use any unprivileged evidence that has confirmed the complainant's allegations,[60] privileged information obtained directly from the alleged harasser must remain confidential.

Once a waiver of the attorney-client privilege has occurred, the privilege is generally treated as completely relinquished.[61] In addition, when a client waives the attorney-client privilege with respect to a particular communication, the waiver generally extends to all communications on the same subject matter.[62]

A lawyer may reveal a confidence or secret of a former client if the client consents following a full disclosure.[63] That disclosure will describe all of the material facts and their legal significance. Before joint representation commences, employers generally attempt to obtain the individual defendant's specific voluntary consent to use of information acquired during the joint representation.[64]

---

[58]*See* Kevlik v. Goldstein, 724 F.2d 844, 849 (1st Cir. 1984)(attorney-client privilege existed between former client and former counsel regarding communications made before client dismissed counsel); United States v. Kleifgen, 557 F.2d 1293, 1297 (9th Cir. 1977) (attorney-client privilege would apply to any confidential communications between defendant and former attorney after attorney-client relationship ended); *see also* ABA Informal Op. 1301 (1975)("duty of the lawyer not to divulge confidential communications, information and secrets imparted to him by his client or acquired by the lawyer during their professional relations . . . continues after the relation of a lawyer and client has ceased").

[59]*See* K. Ryburn, Jr., & M. Mallery, Ethical Considerations in the Joint Representation of Supervisors and Employers in Sexual Harassment Cases, presented at the Sixth Annual Multi-State Labor and Employment Seminar sponsored by Southern Methodist University School of Law and the Multi-State Bar Association (May 5, 1988). However, if the employer and alleged harasser assume adversarial positions in subsequent litigation, any privilege otherwise applying to information obtained during the joint representation may be deemed to be waived.

[60]Of course, factual issues could arise as to whether the information sought to be used actually came from a privileged disclosure.

[61]*See* United States v. Krasnov, 143 F. Supp. 184, 190–91 (E.D. Pa. 1956)(when attorney-client privilege has been waived, it cannot be regained), *aff'd sub. nom.* Oppenheimer v. United States, 355 U.S. 5 (1957); United States v. Kelsey-Hayes Wheel Co., 15 F.R.D. 461, 464 (E.D. Mich. 1954)(privilege waived at first trial may not be claimed at second trial, because "after the first publication the communication is no longer confidential and there is no reason for recognizing the privilege").

[62]*See* Detection Sys. v. Pittway Corp., 96 F.R.D. 152, 156 (W.D.N.Y. 1982)("once a party has made a voluntary disclosure of part of a privileged communication, the privilege is lost for all communications relating to the same subject matter"); Handgards, Inc. v. Johnson & Johnson, 413 F. Supp. 926, 929 (N.D. Cal. 1976)("[v]oluntary disclosure of part of a privileged communication is a waiver as to the remainder of the privileged communication about the same subject").

[63]Model Code, DR 4-101(C), reproduced in LAW. MANUAL ON PROF. CONDUCT (ABA/BNA 1990). Although the Model Code does not explain the standard required for "full disclosure," it appears that counsel must take each client's individual circumstances into account. *See, e.g.,* ABA Comm. on Ethics and Professional Responsibility, Informal Op. 1287 (1974).

[64]*See In re* Grand Jury Subpoenas, 902 F.2d 244, 248–49 (4th Cir. 1990)(attorney-client joint defense privilege). Whether a prospective waiver of this sort is fully effective is subject to doubt, in that by definition the waiver is sought at a time in which a fully informed choice by the waiving party may not be possible.

D. The Work Product Doctrine

1. Generally

The work product doctrine absolutely protects from disclosure an attorney's mental impressions, conclusions, opinions, and legal theories.[65] The work product doctrine also prevents discovery of all other documents or tangible things prepared by or for a party, or by or for the party's representative, in anticipation of litigation or for trial,[66] except to the extent that an adverse party can show (1) substantial need and (2) an inability to obtain the substantial equivalent by other means without undue hardship.[67]

2. During Joint Representation of the Employer and the Individual Defendant

In contrast to the attorney-client privilege, the work product doctrine is not waived by mere disclosure to a third party.[68] The doctrine is designed not to protect confidential communications, but to promote the adversary system by safeguarding the fruits of an attorney's trial preparation from the discovery attempts of an opponent.[69] For disclosure to constitute a waiver of the work product privilege, it must be found to be " 'inconsistent with the maintenance of secrecy from the disclosing party's adversary.' "[70]

Pursuant to these principles, attorneys representing different clients with common interests may exchange work product materials without waiving the protections of the doctrine.[71] Similarly, two parties jointly represented by the same counsel may use their attorney's work product for their mutual benefit without the threat of waiver. In the latter situation, one party may not voluntarily waive the work product privilege as it relates to the common interests of another represented party. The party opposing disclosure may seek a protective order against the disclosure of the work product.[72]

---

[65]Fed. R. Civ. P. 26(b)(3); Hickman v. Taylor, 329 U.S. 495 (1947).

[66]*Id.*

[67]Fed. R. Civ. P. 26(b)(3). *See, e.g.,* EEOC v. General Motors Corp., 1988 WL 170448 (D. Kan. 1988)(disclosure warranted where documents contained information concerning eight potential witnesses who might be able to assist plaintiff in proving defendant's knowledge of sexual harassment and failure to take remedial action, because four potential witnesses unable to answer certain questions due to lack of memory and three indicated they might have made relevant records that were lost or destroyed). For further discussion of the work product doctrine in sexual harassment litigatory see Chapter 26, Discovery, Section V.B.

[68]Castle v. Sangamo Weston, Inc., 744 F.2d 1464, 1466–67, 36 FEP Cases 113 (11th Cir. 1984)(in age discrimination case, work product protection not waived when plaintiff gave work product to EEOC while both preparing for joint trial); United States v. American Tel. & Tel. Co., 642 F.2d 1285, 1299 (D.C. Cir. 1980)(corporations suing AT&T did not waive work product privilege by disclosing documents to government, which later filed civil antitrust suit against AT&T).

[69]Shields v. Sturm, Ruger & Co., 864 F.2d 379, 382 (5th Cir. 1989).

[70]United States v. American Tel. & Tel. Co., *supra* note 68, 642 F.2d at 1299 (footnotes omitted). *See also In re* Grand Jury Subpoenas, 561 F. Supp. 1247, 1257 (E.D.N.Y. 1982)("Disclosure of work product to a third party does not waive its protection unless it substantially increases the opportunity for potential adversaries to obtain the information").

[71]United States v. American Tel. & Tel. Co., *supra* note 68 ("So long as transferor and transferee anticipate litigation against a common adversary on the same issue or issues, they have strong common interests in sharing the fruit of trial preparation efforts"); Duplan Corp. v. Deering Milliken, Inc., 397 F. Supp. 1146, 1172 (D.S.C. 1974)("sharing of information between counsel for parties having common interests does not destroy the work product privilege, during the course of the litigation").

[72]*See, e.g.,* National Union Fire Ins. Co. v. Continental Ill. Group, 1987 U.S. Dist. LEXIS 9105 (N.D. Ill. 1987)(granting protective order with respect to documents to extent they reveal position, strategy, or opinion of movant's counsel even if documents created by disclosing party's counsel).

Because co-defendants need not be represented by the same counsel to wage a joint defense and to enjoy the protections of the work product doctrine, a separately represented alleged harasser and the alleged harasser's employer, to the extent they retain a community of interest in the litigation, may share work product materials without waiver of work product protection.[73]

3. After Joint Representation Has Ended

There is little authority concerning whether one co-defendant may withhold from the other co-defendant work product that was generated when both defendants had the same counsel. The court in *Rudow v. Cohen*[74] held that the individual co-defendant may obtain the work product of the employer's counsel that was created before the interests of the individual defendant and the employer diverged. The alleged harasser in *Rudow* successfully invoked the joint defense exception to obtain protected documents prepared by his former, and the employer's current, counsel. Documents prepared by the employer concerning the employer's dismissal of the harasser, however, were not discoverable because they did not relate to the subject matter of the joint representation or the common interest of the employer and harasser.

The court in *Rudow* emphasized the difficulties in determining when the interests of the employer and alleged harasser diverged, observing that a united defense may continue even after the alleged harasser consults separate counsel.[75] Employers should be alert to when their interests diverge from those of an individual defendant, because any work product created prior to that time may be discovered by the alleged harasser. Similarly, once it appears that the interests of the alleged harasser and the employer may diverge, the employer should be reluctant to disclose work product to the alleged harasser, because of the risk that voluntary disclosure could constitute a waiver of work product protection.

III. ISSUES OF FORUM, PENDENT JURISDICTION, AND JURY TRIAL

Sexual harassment complainants who have invoked federal jurisdiction by virtue of their Title VII claim commonly assert pendent state-law claims.[76] These claims include statutory claims,[77] tort claims, and contract claims.[78] The

---

[73]See cases cited in note 71 *supra*.

[74]WL 13746 (S.D.N.Y. 1988).

[75]In *Rudow,* the court found that the attorney-client relationship was severed as of the date of a letter from the employer's in-house counsel to the individual defendant, urging him to obtain his own attorney and discussing the circumstances of the conflict of interest. Thus, when such a conflict arises, it may be advisable for counsel to prepare a similar letter unequivocally informing each co-defendant of the conflict.

[76]*See, e.g.,* Stewart v. Thomas, 538 F. Supp. 891, 894–97, 30 FEP Cases 1609 (D.D.C. 1982)(state-law torts not preempted by Title VII). For a discussion of the complainant's strategy considerations in this regard, see Chapter 21, Complainant's Litigation Strategy, Section III.

[77]For a discussion of fair employment practices statutes, see Chapter 12.

[78]*See generally* Montgomery, *Sexual Harassment in the Workplace: A Practitioner's Guide to Tort Actions,* 10 GOLDEN GATE U.L. REV. 879 (1980); Guyette v. Stauffer Chem. Co., 518 F. Supp. 521, 524–25, 26 FEP Cases 634 (D.N.J. 1981)(sexual harassment as theory of liability "bears distinct similarities to" and "arises out of" several common-law forces). For a discussion of tort and contract claims, see Chapter 15, The Common Law.

inclusion of state-law claims presents the employer's counsel with several strategic options relating to the forum in which claims will be tried.

A. Supplemental Jurisdiction

If the complainant files a Title VII claim in federal court along with state-law claims, defense counsel may consider moving to dismiss the state-law claims. The primary strategic reasons to seek dismissal of the state-law claims are to limit the federal court case to Title VII remedies[79] and to disrupt the complainant's litigation strategy. In some instances, the complainant's counsel may decide that the burden and expense of litigating in two courts does not justify pursuing the dismissed claims independently in state court. Even if the complainant does bring a second suit in state court, the federal court proceeding may be concluded first, with determinations adverse to the complainant. The complainant may then be deterred from further investigation or collaterally estopped on some issues in the state case.

Although a federal court has the power to hear state-law claims whenever it is also hearing related federal claims, its exercise of jurisdiction is discretionary. Before the Judicial Improvements Act of 1990,[80] which introduced the term of "supplemental" jurisdiction, the federal court's power to hear state-law claims in the absence of diversity jurisdiction was analyzed in terms of "pendent" jurisdiction. In *United Mine Workers v. Gibbs*,[81] the Supreme Court identified the following factors to help a federal district court decide whether to exercise discretion to hear pendent state claims: (1) considerations of judicial economy, convenience, and fairness to litigants; (2) whether a presumably "surer-footed" reading of applicable state law could be obtained in a state court; (3) whether state issues predominate in terms of proof, scope of issues raised, or comprehensiveness of remedies sought; and (4) whether divergent state and federal principles are likely to cause jury confusion.[82]

If the complainant had demanded a jury trial on the pendent tort claims, the employer could argue for dismissal on the basis that the jury trial threatened to interfere with the expeditious resolution of the Title VII claim.[83] This argument was strongest where the Title VII claim was not joined with any federal

---

[79]For a discussion of the limitations inherent in Title VII remedies, see Chapter 29, Monetary Relief. Under the Civil Rights Act of 1991, discussed in Appendix 8, monetary and punitive damages are limited.

[80]28 U.S.C. §1367.

[81]383 U.S. 715, 725–26 (1966).

[82]*Id.* at 726–27. Some of these factors are now codified in 28 U.S.C. §1367(c)(1)–(3), which identifies the reasons a district court may use to decline "supplemental jurisdiction," which includes pendent and ancillary jurisdiction, as follows:

(1) the claim raises a novel or complex issue of state law,

(2) the claim substantially predominates over the claim or claims over which the district court has original jurisdiction,

(3) the district court has dismissed all claims over which it has original jurisdiction, or

(4) in exceptional circumstances, there are other compelling reasons for declining jurisdiction.

See generally H.R. Rep. No. 101-734 at 27–30, reprinted in U.S. CONG. & ADMIN. NEWS 6873–76 (1991).

[83]*See, e.g.,* Matthews v. North Slope Borough, 646 F. Supp. 943, 944, 43 FEP Cases 327, 328 (D. Alaska 1986)(Title VII claims could be tried more quickly if state claims dismissed, and jury confusion likely if all claims tried together); Alveari v. American Int'l Group, 590 F. Supp. 228, 232, 47 FEP Cases 778, 781 (S.D.N.Y. 1984)(dismissing New York FEP statutory claim and tort claim because exercise of

claim, such as a §1983 claim, that would be tried before a jury. In that event only the pendent state-law claims would create the need for a jury trial.[84]

The existence of different elements of proof, as well as wide disparities between the limited equitable relief then available under Title VII and the compensatory and punitive relief available under some state-law causes of action, also have led courts to conclude that the pendent claims will predominate over the federal claims or result in jury confusion.[85] Dismissal of pendent state-law claims was particularly likely when an unsettled question of state law was raised, so that a "surer-footed" reading of state law could be obtained in state court.[86]

---

pendent jurisdiction would "inevitably add to the proof in this case and complicate what can be a simple, straightforward nonjury case"); Mongeon v. Shellcraft Indus., 590 F. Supp. 956, 959–60, 38 FEP Cases 1532, 1535 (D. Vt. 1984)(exercise of pendent jurisdiction over state statutory and common-law claims, and resultant jury trial, conflicted with congressional intent for "prompt as well as effective remedy under Title VII"); Bennett v. Southern Marine Mgmt. Co., 531 F. Supp. 115, 117, 38 FEP Cases 437, 439 (M.D. Fla. 1982)(dismissing state-law tort claims supporting "right to jury trial, exercise of which would confuse and delay determination of the Title VII claim"); Jong-Yul Lim v. International Inst. of Metro. Detroit, 510 F. Supp. 722, 725–26, 25 FEP Cases 1517, 1520 (E.D. Mich. 1981)(jury trial and broadening of issues from pendent state statutory and common-law claims would "frustrate the express congressional intent . . . of having employment discrimination cases under Title VII resolved in the most expeditious manner possible").

[84]*See* Jong-Yul Lim v. International Inst. of Metro. Detroit, *supra* note 83 (if Title VII claim joined with claim under §1981, which provides for both legal and equitable relief, same jurisdictional concerns would not be raised); Van Hoomissen v. Xerox Corp., 368 F. Supp. 829, 6 FEP Cases 1231 (N.D. Cal. 1973)(denying leave to amend to add state claim for intentional infliction of emotional distress after §1981 claim stricken from complaint); Catania, *State Employment Discrimination Remedies and Pendent Jurisdiction Under Title VII: Access to Federal Courts,* 32 AM. U.L. REV. 777, 808 (1983); *cf.* Russell v. Moore, 714 F. Supp. 883, 50 FEP Cases 409 (M.D. Tenn. 1989)(exercising pendent jurisdiction over state claims, because no additional delay would result where companion §1983 claim entitled plaintiff to jury trial). For a discussion of §1983 claims, see Chapter 11, Federal Constitutional, Statutory, and Civil Rights Law, Section III.

[85]*See, e.g.,* Bouchet v. National Urban League, 730 F.2d 799, 805–6, 34 FEP Cases 545, 549 (D.C. Cir. 1984)(state-law claims for legal relief "would be pendent to this Title VII litigation much as a dog is pendent to its tail"); Coleman v. Wirtz, 745 F. Supp. 434 (N.D. Ohio 1990)(pendent state claims dismissed where "state law claims have broader and different elements and remedies than the federal claims, [and] there is a risk of jury confusion"); Malekian v. Pottery Club of Aurora, 724 F. Supp. 1279, 1281–82, 52 FEP Cases 121, 123 (D. Colo. 1989)("consideration of the outrageous conduct claim in conjunction with plaintiff's Title VII claim may lead to jury confusion"); Burger v. Health Ins. Plan, 684 F. Supp. 46, 50 (S.D.N.Y. 1988)(dismissing state age discrimination and other state claims upon finding that jury confusion could result from "[p]lacing . . . plaintiff's mental state and defendant's malice that are irrelevant to an ADEA claim, before the jury"); Brown v. Miami Beach, 684 F. Supp. 1081, 1083, 46 FEP Cases 1849, 1851 (S.D. Fla. 1988)(where state-law cause of action provides for damages unavailable under Title VII, "there is a great risk of jury confusion"); Matthews v. North Slope Borough, *supra* note 83, 646 F. Supp. at 945, 43 FEP Cases at 329 ("there is a high likelihood of jury confusion because of the divergent legal theories for the state and federal claims"); Spencer v. Banco Real, 623 F. Supp. 1008, 1013 (S.D.N.Y. 1985)("because relief available in a Title VII action is limited, the state law claims may become the predominant elements of the suit and may cause jury confusion"); Mongeon v. Shellcraft Indus., *supra* note 83, 590 F. Supp. at 961, 38 FEP Cases at 1536 (state-law issues would involve additional evidence regarding emotional distress claim); Lettich v. Kenway, 590 F. Supp. 1225, 1226, 35 FEP Cases 1289, 1290 (D. Mass. 1984)(" 'likelihood of confusion' resulting from trial of the state and federal [age discrimination] claims together far outweighs considerations of 'judicial economy, convenience and fairness to litigants' ")(citation omitted). *But see* Jones v. Intermountain Power Project, 794 F.2d 546, 41 FEP Cases 1 (10th Cir. 1986)(no statutory intent to negate pendent jurisdiction); Gilardi v. Schroeder, 833 F.2d 1226, 45 FEP Cases 346 (7th Cir. 1987)(district court properly awarded damages for state-law battery and intentional infliction of emotional distress claims); Bowersox v. P.H. Glatfelter Co., 677 F. Supp. 307, 45 FEP Cases 1443 (M.D. Pa. 1988)(damages for intentional infliction of emotional distress and loss of consortium under state law were proper). The impact of a "jury confusion" argument in cases subject to the Judicial Improvements Act of 1990 is uncertain. See notes 82 and 86a and accompanying text.

[**Editor's Note:** Under the Civil Rights Act of 1991, discussed in Appendix 8, either party to a Title VII case may now demand a jury trial where the plaintiff seeks compensatory and punitive damages.]

[86]*See, e.g.,* Coleman v. Wirtz, *supra* note 85, 745 F. Supp. at 441 (pendent state claims dismissed where state-law claims predominate and there will be "a surer-footed reading of state law in state court"); Bennett v. Steiner-Liff Iron & Metal Co., 714 F. Supp. 895, 898 (M.D. Tenn. 1989)(pendent jurisdiction declined,

The Judicial Improvements Act of 1990 and the Civil Rights Act of 1991 have superseded much of the foregoing authority in a way that has yet to be fully determined. The Judicial Improvements Act states that federal district courts shall have "supplemental jurisdiction" over all claims not within original federal jurisdiction that "are so related to claims in the action with such original jurisdiction that they form part of the same case or controversy," and identifies a limited number of reasons a federal court may use to dismiss a state-law claim over which the court has supplemental jurisdiction.[86a] The Civil Rights Act of 1991 will further complicate any motion to dismiss supplemental claims by providing for jury trial in Title VII cases.

B. Removal of State-Court Actions

In *Yellow Freight System v. Donnelly*,[87] the Supreme Court held that state and federal courts have concurrent jurisdiction over Title VII claims, thereby dispelling the notion that federal courts have exclusive jurisdiction over Title VII claims. As a result, plaintiffs now may choose to file Title VII claims in a state court, either alone or in conjunction with state claims.

If a Title VII or other federal claim is asserted in a state-court action, the defendant has the right to remove the entire case to federal court based on federal-question jurisdiction.[88] A pure state-law action is also removable if federal jurisdiction exists on the basis of diversity of state citizenship between the parties, if the claim exceeds $50,000 and if the defendant is not a citizen of the state where the action was commenced.[89] Because removal must be effected within thirty days of receipt of the complaint,[90] defense counsel should immediately evaluate whether grounds for removal exist, and, if so, whether a state or federal forum is preferable.

---

given unsettled questions of state law and fact that issues relating to broader relief will predominate at trial and may confuse jury); Robles v. Cruz, 670 F. Supp. 54, 58, 45 FEP Cases 113, 116 (D.P.R. 1987)(fact that plaintiff's state statutory claims alleging sexual harassment "would involve the Court in needless decisions of state law is reason to decline to exercise pendent jurisdiction over those claims"); Nystul v. Northwestern Tel. Sys., 623 F. Supp. 494, 498, 43 FEP Cases 402, 405 (D. Mont. 1985)(pendent claim dismissed because "employment discrimination law in Montana is largely a creature of judicial evolution, and a surer-footed reading of the law can be obtained in state court"); Benedict v. Sky Chefs, 38 FEP Cases 1127, 1129–30 (M.D. Tenn. 1985)(dismissing claims under Tennessee fair employment practices statute in part because of "the unsettled nature of the state statutory remedy relied upon by the plaintiff"); Alveari v. American Int'l Group, *supra* note 83, 590 F. Supp. at 232, 47 FEP Cases at 780–81 (declining to exercise jurisdiction over state discrimination claim because of surer-footed reading available on election of remedies provision); Mongeon v. Shellcraft Indus., *supra* note 83, 590 F. Supp. at 961, 38 FEP Cases at 1536 (pendent claims dismissed where significant questions existed concerning right to jury trial and relief available under those claims); Duva v. Bridgeport Textron, 632 F. Supp. 880, 886, 40 FEP Cases 1388 (E.D. Pa. 1985)(state law unsettled as to workers' compensation bar to intentional infliction of emotional distress claim).

[86a]See note 82 *supra*. 28 U.S.C. §1367(c).

[87]110 S.Ct. 1566, 52 FEP Cases 875 (1990).

[88]28 U.S.C. §1441(a). Removal on the basis of a federal claim is not an option if the plaintiff, although having a viable federal claim, chooses to rely solely on state-law claims. *See, e.g.,* Wood v. Vermont Ins. Mgmt., 54 FEP Cases 510 (D. Vt. 1990)(defendant sued under state-law tort theories for sexual harassment could not remove case to federal court in nondiversity action; plaintiff has right to rely exclusively on state law and case may not be removed to federal court on basis that plaintiff might also have cited federal law in support of claims).

[89]28 U.S.C. §1441(a), (b).

[90]*Id.* at §1446(b).

Federal courts generally are more attractive for employers who share the widespread belief that federal judges and magistrates have greater resources to handle Title VII cases than do their state judicial counterparts,[91] and who perceive procedural advantages in federal court, such as its case-management system and its liberal summary-judgment procedure.[92]

If the case is removed on federal question grounds, a defendant may be able to persuade the court not to entertain the supplemental state-law claims, thus forcing the plaintiff to fight on two fronts.[93] Other factors informing the decision of whether to remove include the effect of the respective forums on the time that it will take for the case to reach trial, the availability of discovery devices, and dismissal strategies.[94]

IV. INSURANCE COVERAGE

As soon as the employer has notice of a sexual harassment claim, it should collect and review all pertinent insurance policies. Several kinds of liability insurance policies may cover claims associated with sexual harassment. The plaintiff's counsel may have drafted the complaint with an eye toward triggering insurance coverage.[95] In light of the significant costs associated with sexual harassment litigation, the need to investigate potential insurance coverage cannot be overstated.

A. Notice to the Insurer

If it appears that a policy may provide coverage, the insurer should be notified promptly, before any deadline for filing a proof of loss. If the insurer

---

[91]*See, e.g.,* Yellow Freight Sys. v. Donnelly, *supra* note 87, 110 S.Ct. at 1570, 52 FEP Cases at 878 (that federal judges will have more experience in Title VII litigation is "a factor that plaintiff may weigh when deciding where to file suit, or that may motivate a defendant to remove a case to federal court"). The federal judiciary's Title VII experience may also weigh in favor of a federal forum even with respect to state discrimination claims. *See, e.g.,* Bennett v. Corroon & Black Corp., 517 So.2d 1245, 1246, 48 FEP Cases 675 (La. Ct. App. 1987)(Title VII may be used as guidance in ascertaining liability under a state discrimination law).

[92]Many counsel believe that federal judges are more apt to grant summary judgment in close cases, for several reasons: (1) some states have law and motion judges who do not themselves try the cases they refuse to dismiss and thus have little incentive to grant a summary judgment on which they will risk reversal; (2) state court judges generally lack the law-clerk talent available to federal judges; (3) some state courts discourage summary judgments by reversing the burden of proof in summary judgment procedures, requiring a defendant to disprove elements of a case that the plaintiff will be required to prove at trial.

[93]In a removed case, the federal court has discretion to remand state-law claims rather than dismiss them. Although 28 U.S.C. §1441(c) provides for only the discretionary remand or dismissal of a "separate and independent" claim, the Supreme Court in *Carnegie-Mellon Univ. v. Cohill,* 484 U.S. 343, 45 FEP Cases 1163 (1988), held that where it would be inappropriate for the federal court to retain jurisdiction over a removed case, the federal court would have discretion under the doctrine of pendent jurisdiction to remand the pendent claims to the state court where the case had initially been filed. Thus, where the statute of limitations has run on supplemental state claims, the federal court may exercise its discretion to remand the case rather than dismiss it so that the state claims will not be time-barred.

[94]The state court forum may also offer some advantages for the employer. In some states, for example, the joinder of requests for equitable relief (such as reinstatement) and claims for damages constitutes a waiver of the right to a jury trial. *See, e.g.,* Kaplan v. Long Island Univ., 116 A.D.2d 508, 497 N.Y.S.2d 378, 40 FEP Cases 431 (1986)(plaintiff waived right to jury trial under New York Human Rights law where complaint sought reinstatement in addition to money damages); Panarella v. Penthouse Int'l, 64 A.D.2d 545, 406 N.Y.S.2d 850 (1978).

[95]See Chapter 21, Complainant's Litigation Strategy, Section VII.

denies coverage, counsel should review any contractual limits on the insured's time to sue on the policy and take the necessary steps to preserve the employer's right to recover under the policy.[96]

B. Duty to Defend Broader Than Duty to Indemnify

An employer faced with costly litigation should remember that an insurance policy typically creates two separate obligations for the insurer: a duty to defend claims and a duty to indemnify for liability for those claims.[97] The duty to defend is broader than the duty to indemnify, meaning that an insurer must defend against a lawsuit if the complaint alleges any facts that, if proven, would trigger liability covered by the policy, even though the insurer would not be obligated to pay a judgment if the facts ultimately determined by a court or jury bring the case within a policy exclusion.[98] Even unpleaded theories of liability may trigger a duty to defend if facts known to the insurer suggest a potential liability, so long as the theory of liability is not "tenuous and far fetched."[99]

By assuming defense of its insured, the insurer generally acquires the right to control the defense and select defense counsel. However, the insurer must pay the reasonable fees of the insured's own selected counsel if there is an irreconcilable conflict of interest between insurer and insured. In some states such a conflict arises whenever the insurer reserves its rights as to coverage of liability for the underlying claim.[100]

C. Potentially Applicable Policies

Comprehensive general liability insurance typically covers the insured employer's liability for any "occurrence," typically defined as an "accident" that the insured employer "neither expected nor intended," that causes "bodily injury" or property damage. Whether these policies cover sexual harassment claims generally depends on the court's view of (1) whether the acts in question constituted an unexpected "occurrence," and (2) whether any psychological

---

[96]See generally B. OSTRAGER & T. NEWMAN, HANDBOOK ON INSURANCE COVERAGE DISPUTES 69–102 (2d ed. 1989).

[97]NPS Corp. v. Insurance Co. of N. Am., 213 N.J. Super. 547, 517 A.2d 1211, 1212–13, 44 FEP Cases 224, 224–25 (1986); Runyan v. Continental Casualty Co., 233 F. Supp. 214 (D. Or. 1964). See also Grinnell Mut. Reinsurance Co. v. Friedrich, 79 Ill. App.3d 1146, 399 N.E.2d 252 (1979)(insurer has duty to defend against complaint alleging conduct both within and beyond coverage of policy). See generally B. OSTRAGER & T. NEWMAN, supra note 96, at 105–44; Annot., Refusal of Liability Insurer to Defend Action Against Insured Involving Both Claims Within Coverage of Policy and Claims Not Covered, 41 A.L.R.2d 434 (1955).

[98]Continental Casualty Co. v. Parker, 161 Ga. App. 614, 288 S.E.2d 776 (1982)(although insurer obligated to defend, jury finding of intentional harm might eliminate insurer's duty to pay any judgment); Montgomery v. Hawkeye Sec. Ins. Co., 52 Mich. App. 457, 217 N.W.2d 449 (1974)(homeowner insurer had duty to defend against assault and battery action, but issue whether intentional-acts exclusion would preclude payment was mixed question of law and fact for jury).

[99]American Guar. & Liability Ins. Co. v. Vista Medical Supply, 699 F. Supp. 787, 793–94 (N.D. Cal. 1988).

[100]See generally Kennedy & Roberts, Insurance Coverage for Wrongful Termination Claims, 10 EMPL. REL. L.J. 654, 667 (1984); McCulloch & Barsky, How to Use Corporate Insurance Policies to Help Pay for Litigation, 14 EMPL. REL. L.J. 191, 196–97 (1988). California has addressed some of the issues involved by legislation. CAL. CIV. CODE §2860 (insured may select independent counsel at insurer's expense where conflict of interest exists, but insured has duty to keep insurer informed and consulted and attorney's fees may be limited to rates insurer pays in defense of similar actions).

damage and emotional distress incident to sexual harassment constitute a "bodily injury."

Errors and omissions liability policies cover risks inherent in the practice of a particular profession and may be construed to cover some intentional torts.[101]

Excess and umbrella liability policies provide coverage in areas that might not be included in basic coverage, or liabilities that exceed the insured's primary policy limits.

Directors' and officers' liability and general partners' liability policies cover the actions of a company's directors, officers, and certain managerial or executive employees while acting within the scope of their authority.[102]

Comprehensive personal policies and homeowner's policies may also cover the actions of individual defendants without regard to whether such actions were within the scope of their authority.[103]

Finally, employers should review their workers' compensation policy to determine if it covers some or all of the damages alleged by the complainant. These policies are not necessarily limited to claims brought under workers' compensation statutes.[104]

D. Coverage of Sexual Harassment Claims

1. Issue of Intentional Conduct

Many liability insurance policies do not cover injuries that are intentionally caused by an insured party, either because the act in question is not considered an accidental "occurrence" or because it falls within a policy exclusion for intentional acts. Accordingly, sexual harassment claims are not likely to trigger insurance coverage to the extent that they are litigated under a theory of intentional tort or under the disparate treatment theory of employment discrimination.[105] For the same reason, insurance coverage likely will be

---

[101]*See, e.g.,* Okehi v. St. Paul Fire & Marine Ins. Co., 161 Ga. App. 851, 289 S.E.2d 810 (1982)(physician's professional liability policy defined personal injury to include coverage for false arrest, detention, and imprisonment).

[102]*See, e.g.,* Royal Globe Ins. Cos. v. Fletcher, 123 N.H. 189, 459 A.2d 255 (1983)(policy covered allegation that company president breached supervisory duties by failing to ensure employee's safety on job).

[103]For a discussion of insurance coverage for the individual defendant, see Chapter 23, The Alleged Harasser as Defendant, Section V.

[104]*E.g.,* Republic Indem. v. Superior Court, 224 Cal. App.3d 492, 273 Cal. Rptr. 331 (1990)(insurer obligated under "employer's liability endorsement" of workers' compensation policy to defend employer on claim of failing to reasonably accommodate employee's handicap, because plaintiff needs to prove only unreasonable conduct, not intent to injure).

[105]*See, e.g.,* American Guar. & Liab. Ins. Co. v. Vista Medical Supply, *supra* note 99 (sexual harassment consisted of intentional acts not covered by insurance policy); Continental Ins. Co. v. McDaniel, 772 P.2d 6, 48 FEP Cases 522 (Ariz. App. 1988)(sexual harassment constitutes intentional act not covered by insurance policy); Merced Mutual Ins. Co. v. Mendez, 213 Cal. App.3d 41, 261 Cal. Rptr. 273 (1989)(forcible oral copulation intentional act outside homeowner's policy's coverage for "accident"); Terrio v. McDonough, 16 Mass. App. 163, 450 N.E.2d 190 (homeowner insurance carrier not obliged to defend action arising from insured's sexual assault of victim where policy excluded bodily injury either expected or intended by insured and victim expressly disavowed any cause of action sounding in negligence), *review denied,* 390 Mass. 1102, 453 N.E.2d 1231 (1983); Mary & Alice Ford Nursing Home Co. v. Fireman's Ins. Co., 86 A.D.2d 736, 446 N.Y.S.2d 599 (injuries alleged by plaintiff among damages intended or expected by insured and hence not covered by general liability or umbrella policies), *aff'd,* 57 N.Y.2d 656, 439 N.E.2d 883, 454 N.Y.S.2d 74 (1982); School Dist. v. Mission Ins. Co., 58 Or. App. 692, 650 P.2d 929 (1982)(reversing order requiring insurer to defend disparate treatment claims), *petition denied,* 294 Or. 682, 662 P.2d 725 (1983); Vermont Mut. Ins. Co. v. Malcolm, 128 N.H. 521, 517 A.2d 800 (1986)(sexual assault of victim not an "occurrence"

denied in a pure quid pro quo case where the offending supervisor is the employer's agent authorized to take the challenged personnel action.

When a complaint alleges that a company owner, manager, partner, or corporate officer committed an intentional tort as a managing agent of the insured corporate defendant, an insurer may have no duty to defend if the individual's intentional conduct is imputed to the insured.[106]

On the other hand, if an individual harasser is acting to further personal interests and not those of the insured corporation's, as typically is the case in sexual harassment, the intentional tort should not be imputed to the corporation for purposes of denying coverage, and coverage may be based on the corporation's potential negligence in supervision.[107] Coverage is most likely in a hostile environment case where an offender may be shown to have acted beyond supervisory authority.[108] Coverage is also more likely if the alleged harasser is a nonmanagement employee, for then it is not likely that the employee's intentional tort will be imputed to the employer for purposes of excluding coverage under the employer's policy.[109]

2. Issue of Bodily Injury

Coverage under the occurrence/bodily injury formula may be denied if the plaintiff alleges only emotional distress of a nonphysical nature. Some courts do not recognize such distress as a "bodily injury."[110] Further, even where emotional distress is recognized as a form of bodily injury, coverage

---

within meaning of homeowner's liability policy, because policy conditioned coverage on fortuitous nature of victim's injury and because assaults inherently injurious); E-Z Loader Boat Trailers v. Travelers Indem. Co., 106 Wash.2d 901, 726 P.2d 439 (1986)(sex discrimination excluded from coverage because it was not accidental). *Cf.* Solo Cup Co. v. Federal Ins. Co., 619 F.2d 1178, 22 FEP Cases 883 (7th Cir.)(insurer had duty to defend where complaint could proceed on disparate impact theory challenging facially neutral employment practices), *cert. denied,* 449 U.S. 1033 (1980); Jostens, Inc. v. CNA Ins., 36 N.W.2d 544 (Minn. 1983)(insurer conceded policy afforded coverage for unintentional sex discrimination). *But see* Mutual Serv. Casualty Ins. Co. v. Co-op Supply, 699 F. Supp. 1438, 1441 (D. Mont. 1988)(termination of employment resulting in unintended bodily injury is "occurrence" for purposes of insurance coverage); MacKinnon v. Hanover Ins. Co., 124 N.H. 456, 471 A.2d 1166 (1984)(homeowner's liability policy apparently covered insured's sexual assault of his stepdaughter). *See generally* Annot., *Construction and Application of Provision of Liability Insurance Policy Expressly Excluding Injuries Intended or Expected by Insured,* 31 A.L.R.4th 957 (1984); Annot., *Liability Insurance: Assault as an "Accident," or Injuries Therefrom as "Accidentally" Sustained, Within Coverage Clause,* 72 A.L.R.3d 1090 at §9 (1976).

[106]*See, e.g.,* Roberts v. R & S Liquor Stores, 164 So.2d 533 (Fla. Ct. App. 1964)(general manager's assault on bar patron imputed to corporate insured, thereby excluding coverage).

[107]*See* Seminole Point Hosp. Corp. v. Aetna Cas. & Sur. Co., 675 F. Supp. 44, 47, 45 FEP Cases 929, 931 (D.N.H. 1987)(coverage not excluded where president and executive officer not authorized to sexually harass employee and where harassment not to serve corporation).

[108]*Compare* Steele v. Offshore Shipbldg., 867 F.2d 1311, 1316–17, 49 FEP Cases 522 (11th Cir. 1989)(quid pro quo sexual harassment imputed to employer where supervisor acted as employer's agent within authority to "hire, fire, discipline or promote," but employer not necessarily liable for hostile environment where supervisor acting beyond scope of authority). *See also* Solo Cup Co. v. Federal Ins. Co., *supra* note 105; Jostens, Inc. v. CNA Ins., *supra* note 105.

[109]*See, e.g.,* Sterling Ins. Co. v. Hughes, 187 So.2d 898 (Fla. Ct. App.)(assault by "beach boy" patrolling beach not within exclusion for intentional torts, absent proof that insured had authorized him to assault persons who trespassed on its property), *cert. denied,* 194 So.2d 622 (Fla. 1966).

[110]*Compare* EEOC v. Southern Pub. Co., 894 F.2d 785, 789 (5th Cir. 1990)("bodily injury" present where sexual harassment complainant alleged that defendant's employees engaged in "persistent grabbing" of complainant's "private parts," causing "physical pain") *and* NPS Corp. v. Insurance Co. of N. Am., *supra* note 97, 517 A.2d at 1212 ("bodily injury" includes "emotional and psychological sequelae") *with* Mutual Serv. Casualty Ins. Co. v. Co-op Supply, *supra* note 105, 699 F. Supp. at 1440 ("bodily injury" does not include humiliation, pain, and mental and emotional distress) *and* Presidential Hotel v. Canal Ins. Co., 188 Ga. App. 609, 611, 373 S.E.2d 671, 672 (1988)("bodily injury" means just that—"bodily injury," not nonphysical, emotional, or mental harm).

has been denied on the basis of a policy exclusion for "bodily injury to any employee of the insured arising out of and in the course of employment."[111]

3. Other Bases for Coverage

Although insurance policies generally do not cover intentional acts, some policies expressly cover "personal injury" liability in connection with such claims as libel, slander, defamation, and false arrest.[112]

Even where the policy itself would appear to provide coverage, the public policy of some states may prohibit the insurer from indemnifying the insured for willful acts of discrimination.[113] Thus, even if an insurer is funding the defense, the employer may still be liable for damages.

Coverage for punitive damages raises special issues. While some states forbid coverage for these damages on public-policy grounds, other states do permit insurance coverage for punitive damages, at least with respect to vicarious liability.[114]

V. DEPOSITION OF THE COMPLAINANT

In a sexual harassment case the deposition of the complainant is the cornerstone of the defense strategy. The deposition serves several objectives: preparing for trial; creating a record on which to base a summary adjudication motion; persuading the complainant that the case has no merit by confronting the complainant with inconsistencies in testimony or other information not previously disclosed; and demonstrating to the complainant and the complainant's counsel that litigation is a major commitment of time, energy, and emotions.[115] Not all of these objections are compatible with each other. Stressing

---

[111]Omark Indus. v. Safeco Ins. Co. of Am., 590 F. Supp. 114 (D. Or. 1984)(finding insurance coverage for emotional distress caused by sex discrimination but then applying bodily injury exclusion quoted in text, despite employer's argument that exclusion should apply only to workers' compensation claims).

[112]*See, e.g.,* American Guar. & Liability Ins. Co. v. Vista Medical Supply, *supra* note 99 (defamation claim of sexual harassment complainant covered by "personal injury" coverage); Federal Ins. Co. v. Applestein, 377 So.2d 229 (Fla. Ct. App. 1979)(slanderous statements covered unless made with specific intent to harm equivalent to actual malice); Employers Commercial Union Ins. Co. v. Kottmeier, 323 So.2d 605 (Fla. Ct. App. 1975)(personal injury included libel, slander, defamation or statements invasive of an individual's right to privacy, except when maliciously published or uttered by, at the direction of, or with the consent of, insured). *See also* Continental Casualty Co. v. Canadian Ins. Co., 54 FEP Cases 1606, 1609–10 (1st Cir. 1991)(unusual "personal injury" definition covered "bodily injury, sickness, mental anguish, mental injury, and humiliation" and thereby covered complainant's claim that she was retaliated against for reporting sexual harassment by another employee); Levinson v. Aetna Casualty & Sur. Co., 42 A.D.2d 811, 812, 346 N.Y.S.2d 428, 430 (1973)(exclusion of acts "committed by or at the direction of the insured with intent to cause personal injury" did not eliminate insurer's duty to defend action for malicious prosecution, libel, slander, false arrest, and extortion).

[113]*See, e.g.,* Ranger Ins. Co. v. Bal Harbour Club, 549 So.2d 1005 (Fla. 1989); City Products Corp. v. Globe Indem. Co., 88 Cal. App.3d 31, 151 Cal. Rptr. 494 (1979); American Sur. Co. v. Gold, 375 F.2d 523 (10th Cir. 1966). *See generally* Annot., *Liability Insurance as Covering Accident, Damage, or Injury Due to Wanton or Willful Misconduct or Gross Negligence,* 20 A.L.R.3d 320, §5[a] (1968).

[114]B. OSTRAGER & T. NEWMAN, *supra* note 96, at §12.02. *See, e.g.,* Scott v. Instant Parking, 105 Ill. App.2d 133, 245 N.E.2d 124 (1969)(because policy covered injuries caused by willful and wanton misconduct, insurer liable for punitive damages); Ohio Casualty Ins. Co. v. Welfare Fin. Co., 75 F.2d 58 (8th Cir. 1934)(coverage of willful acts did not violate public policy where insured was liable only on basis of *respondeat superior*), *cert. denied,* 295 U.S. 734 (1935).

[115]Although deposition examinations will generate additional stress, there is some authority that those damages are not recoverable. *See* School Dist. v. Nilsen, 271 Or. 461, 534 P.2d 1135, 16 FEP Cases 1203, 1212 (1975)(anxiety and emotional distress suffered by plaintiff were normal results of being litigant).

inconsistencies, for example, may undermine defense trial strategy by providing a preview of the cross-examination, and should therefore be used with discretion if settlement is not the primary objective.

It is extremely important before the deposition to conduct a thorough investigation, including interviews of all employees who witnessed or should have witnessed the alleged harassment; who had an opportunity to observe either the complainant or the alleged harasser in the workplace; who were likely to have been taken into the complainant's confidence; or who may have received complaints from the complainant. The employer should also request a copy of the EEOC's investigation file under the Freedom of Information Act.[116] Any records available from the complainant's treating physicians and therapists should also be studied carefully before the deposition.

The deposition of a sexual harassment complainant should address all facts relevant to establishing a prima facie case of sexual harassment and any defenses that the employer may raise, such as lack of knowledge of the alleged harassment. Following are some of the topics explored at a complainant's deposition.

A. The Harassing Conduct

It is crucial to question the complainant thoroughly about the alleged acts of harassment, including their nature and frequency,[117] and where the acts occurred. This set of inquiries is particularly significant where the defense seeks to prove that the sexual advances were not "unwelcome." The nuances of conversation and the circumstances of any physical contact may determine the issue of unwelcomeness. The questioning should explore in detail such matters as who suggested what, what was said, where the alleged incident(s) occurred, for how long, and whether the complainant made efforts to terminate the sexual conduct. The examination should also seek the identity of all witnesses to the conduct.[118]

B. Effect on the Complainant's Employment

To be actionable sexual harassment, the conduct in question must affect a term or condition of the complainant's employment.[119] Thus, in a quid pro

---

[116]5 U.S.C. §552 *et seq.* Each party has the right to review information available to the EEOC during its investigation. B.L. SCHLEI & P. GROSSMAN, EMPLOYMENT DISCRIMINATION LAW 969–76 (2d ed. 1983), Five-Year Supp. 377–79 (1989).

[117]To establish a hostile environment case of sexual harassment, the conduct must be sufficiently severe or pervasive to have the effect of unreasonably interfering with the plaintiff's work performance and creating an intimidating, hostile, or offensive working environment that seriously affects the psychological well-being of the plaintiff. Henson v. City of Dundee, 682 F.2d 897, 903–5, 29 FEP Cases 787 (11th Cir. 1982), reproduced in Chapter 4, Hostile Environment Harassment. Thus, the severity and frequency of the conduct may be a critical issue.

[118]The availability of corroborative testimony is often crucial in a sexual harassment case. *Id.* at 912 n.25 ("in a case of alleged sexual harassment which involves close questions of credibility and subjective interpretation, the existence of corroborative evidence or the lack thereof, is likely to be crucial"). *See* EEOC Dec. 82-13, 29 FEP Cases 1855 (1982)(uncorroborated allegations cannot form basis for probable cause finding); Harris v. Bolger, 599 F. Supp. 1414, 39 FEP Cases 483 (C.D. Cal. 1984)(plaintiff's uncorroborated testimony of harassment failed to make prima facie case); *see also* Sardigal v. St. Louis Nat'l Stockyards Co., 42 FEP Cases 497 (S.D. Ill. 1986).

[119]Although a plaintiff may not be able to demonstrate a tangible job detriment, the state of psychological well-being has been held to be a term, condition, or privilege of employment. Henson v. City of Dundee,

quo case,[120] the deposition should address the relationship between the alleged harasser and the complainant, the nature of any sexual advances made, and why the complainant contends that employment decisions were based upon her response to the alleged harassment. In this regard, the examiner should seek admissions as to the accuracy of any adverse performance evaluations or criticisms of the complainant's job performance.

In a hostile environment case involving constructive discharge, it is important to explore whether there are other reasons why the complainant left the job, such as school, family plans, or a better job offer. If the complainant is alleging severe emotional stress, counsel should seek to establish that the complainant continued to function well in other aspects of life.

C. The Complainant's Conduct

The examiner should also explore the complainant's social and sexual conduct to undercut the claim that the advances were unwelcome. In *Meritor Savings Bank v. Vinson*,[121] the Supreme Court expressly held that facts such as the complainant's dress and speech might be relevant to the issue of "unwelcomeness."[122] If a defendant can show that the plaintiff who complains of vulgar comments and other conduct by a supervisor or co-workers was also sexually aggressive or engaged in sexually explicit conduct, the sexual advances that follow may not meet the "unwelcome" criteria.[123]

Also useful are questions about the complainant's nonsexual behavior toward the alleged harasser, such as sending gifts or notes, or other conduct reflecting affectionate or friendly feelings.[124] Conversations with others, including relatives and friends, should also be explored to identify other potential witnesses and to secure admissions as to the nature of the relationship.

The complainant may claim that although there was initial consent to the conduct, the conduct continued after consent was withdrawn. The defendant should inquire about the method and manner in which the complainant

---

supra note 117, 682 F.2d at 901; Rogers v. EEOC, 454 F.2d 234, 238, 4 FEP Cases 92 (5th Cir. 1971), *cert. denied*, 406 U.S. 957 (1972).

[120]See Chapter 3, Quid Pro Quo Harassment.

[121]477 U.S. 57, 40 FEP Cases 1822 (1986), reproduced in Chapter 1, Overview.

[122]Although the Court recognized that evidence may be relevant, it held that trial courts must decide on a case-by-case basis whether the evidence would be more probative than prejudicial. *Id.* at 69, 40 FEP Cases at 1828. *See, e.g.,* Priest v. Rotary, 98 F.R.D. 755, 32 FEP Cases 1064 (N.D. Cal. 1983)(discovery into plaintiff's past sexual conduct inadmissible to prove propensity to engage in such conduct).

[123]*See, e.g.,* Gan v. Kepro Circuit Sys., 28 FEP Cases 639 (E.D. Mo. 1982)(plaintiff actively contributed to distasteful working environment by her own profane and sexually suggestive conduct); Mitchell v. Hutchings, 116 F.R.D. 481, 44 FEP Cases 615 (D. Utah 1987)(workplace conduct of plaintiff, if known to defendant, bears on what conduct defendant thought was welcome); Reichman v. Bureau of Affirmative Action, 536 F. Supp. 1149, 1164, 30 FEP Cases 1644 (M.D. Pa. 1982)(plaintiff behaved in very flirtatious and provocative manner around alleged harasser by asking him to dinner, despite his repeated refusals, and continuing to behave in provocative manner after alleged harassment); McLean v. Satellite Technology Servs., 673 F. Supp. 1458, 45 FEP Cases 523 (E.D. Mo. 1987)(plaintiff possessed lusty libido and was no paragon of virtue); Meritor Sav. Bank v. Vinson, *supra* note 121 (Court noted plaintiff twice refused transfers to other offices located away from alleged harasser); *see also* Ukarish v. Magnesium Elektron, 31 FEP Cases 1315 (D.N.J. 1983); Ferguson v. E.I. du Pont de Nemours & Co., 560 F. Supp. 1172, 31 FEP Cases 795 (D. Del. 1983).

[124]*See, e.g.,* Sardigal v. St. Louis Nat'l Stockyards Co., *supra* note 118 (plaintiff's allegations not credible because she visited alleged harasser at hospital and at his brother's home and allowed him to come into her home alone at night after alleged harassment occurred).

communicated that the conduct was no longer welcome,[125] and whether the alleged harassment ceased upon that request.[126]

The deposition might also reveal any motive that the complainant might have to fabricate or exaggerate the alleged harasser's conduct. Some common hypotheses are that the complainant had a conflict with the alleged harasser on business issues, that the complaint was made to preempt or discredit an adverse job performance evaluation, that the complainant wanted to take the alleged harasser's job, or that the complainant was hurt or embarrassed by being sexually rejected by the alleged harasser.[127]

D. Failure to Use Grievance Procedure

Where the complainant failed to notify the employer immediately upon first experiencing what is now claimed to be harassing conduct, the examiner should inquire into the extent of the notice that the complainant had concerning the company's sexual harassment complaint procedure,[128] when and how, if at all, it was used, and why it was not used promptly. The complainant should be asked to acknowledge receipt of any literature describing the employer's procedures for filing an allegation of harassment, and to acknowledge the failure to follow them. The complainant's unreasonable failure to invoke the complaint procedure will bear on welcomeness and the employer's notice, and also may undermine the complainant's credibility as to the pervasiveness of the alleged harassment, if not as to whether it occurred at all.[129]

If the complainant did report harassment to the employer, the examiner should explore any explanation for any delay in the report. The complainant should be asked to describe exactly the complaint that was finally made. The examiner should also inquire as to the complainant's response, if any, when approached by management about the alleged problem. Nonchalance or indifference on the part of the complainant may serve as a defense or grounds for dismissal.[130]

E. Lack of Sex-Based Harassment

Counsel may wish to question the complainant about the harasser's conduct toward male as well as female employees. If the harasser was abusive to

---

[125]*See* Loftin-Boggs v. City of Meridian, 633 F. Supp. 1323, 1326–27, 41 FEP Cases 532 (S.D. Miss. 1986)(plaintiff's burden to show that any further sexual conduct was unwelcome, work-related harassment; if plaintiff later found conduct offensive, she should have conveyed this by her own conduct and reaction to co-worker's conduct)(citing Henson v. City of Dundee, *supra* note 117, 682 F.2d at 903–4, for elements of plaintiff's proof), *aff'd mem.*, 824 F.2d 971, 51 FEP Cases 1832 (5th Cir. 1987), *cert. denied*, 484 U.S. 1063 (1988). *See also* EEOC Dec. 84-1, 33 FEP Cases 1887 (1983)(simply ceasing to participate is insufficient to show that continuing activity no longer welcome).

[126]*See* Price v. Lawhorn Furn. Co., 24 FEP Cases 1506 (N.D. Ala. 1978)(no employer liability where, in part, harassment subsided upon plaintiff's request).

[127]*See, e.g.,* Huebschen v. Wisconsin Dep't of Health & Social Servs., 716 F.2d 1167, 32 FEP Cases 1582 (7th Cir. 1983)(female supervisor jilted by male subordinate).

[128]For a discussion of policy and complaint procedures, see Chapter 18, Taking Preventive Action, Section II.

[129]*See* Meritor Sav. Bank v. Vinson, *supra* note 121, 477 U.S. at 72, 40 FEP Cases at 1829 (although plaintiff's failure to utilize grievance procedure will not insulate against employer liability, it is relevant).

[130]*See* Highlander v. KFC Nat'l Mgmt. Co., 805 F.2d 644, 650, 42 FEP Cases 654, 658 (6th Cir. 1986)(unsuccessful sexual harassment complainant had told supervisor his conduct "was [not] that big of a deal" and she did not want to make a "big stink about it").

males and females alike, it is relevant to whether the harassment was because of the complainant's sex.[131]

F. Intent

The alleged harasser's intent to harm the complainant may be relevant where the claims include intentional torts, such as intentional infliction of emotional distress,[132] or where the exclusive remedy for a work-related injury may be under the state workers' compensation laws.[133] Intent may also be relevant to the question of insurance coverage.[134]

Associated with the issue of intent may be the relationship between the complainant and the alleged harasser. The existence of a good relationship before and after the alleged harassment may provide strong support for a defense.[135]

G. Emotional Distress

When claims of emotional injury or adverse effects on psychological well-being are made, the examiner should inquire into the complainant's emotional condition and any psychological treatment prior to the alleged harassment, the current claimed symptoms, and their onset and severity. The complainant should be questioned about treatment by physicians in addition to therapists, any medication being taken, and why it was prescribed. There may be an argument that the medication or the underlying condition being treated is an independent source of emotional stress.

As to treatment of the mental condition itself, counsel should structure the examination around any therapist's notes of the complainant's history and treatment sessions to develop inconsistencies between the information upon which any diagnosis was based and the complainant's current sworn version of events.

The defense may seek to show that other events or circumstances caused the complainant's alleged emotional distress. Because causation is an element of the complainant's proof,[136] other possible causes of emotional distress, for a period of years before or after the alleged harassment, are relevant.[137] Areas

---

[131]See Hill v. K-Mart Corp., 699 F.2d 776, 31 FEP Cases 269 (5th Cir. 1983)(manager treated male and female assistants with equal indifference); Henson v. City of Dundee, *supra* note 117 (where conduct complained of is equally offensive to male and female workers, no claim for sexual harassment). *But see* Bennett v. Corroon & Black Corp., 845 F.2d 104, 106, 46 FEP Cases 1329 (5th Cir. 1988)(conduct directed at both males and females could still be offensive to females only), *cert. denied,* 489 U.S. 1020 (1989).

[132]For a discussion of these torts, see Chapter 15, The Common Law.

[133]See, e.g., Eide v. Kelsey-Hayes Co., 154 Mich. App. 142, 397 N.W.2d 532, 542, 47 FEP Cases 1043, 1050 (1986)(for alleged acts of sexual harassment, exclusive remedy was workers' compensation), *aff'd in part and rev'd in part,* 431 Mich. 26, 427 N.W.2d 488, 47 FEP Cases 1050 (1988). For a discussion of this defense, see Chapter 27, Asserted Defenses, Section IV.

[134]For a discussion of the availability of insurance coverage, see Section IV. *supra.*

[135]See Scott v. Sears, Roebuck & Co., 798 F.2d 210, 214, 41 FEP Cases 805 (7th Cir. 1986)(that plaintiff still considered alleged harasser her friend was factor in affirming summary judgment for defendant).

[136]See, e.g., Rosario v. Amalgamated Ladies' Garment Cutters' Union, Local 10, 605 F.2d 1228, 1245 (2d Cir. 1979), *cert. denied,* 446 U.S. 919 (1980); Huntley v. Community School Bd., 579 F.2d 738, 742 (2d Cir. 1978)(evidence of alternative causes of plaintiff's alleged emotional distress relevant); Vance v. Southern Bell Tel. & Tel. Co., 672 F. Supp. 1408, 1416, 44 FEP Cases 1079, 1087 (M.D. Fla. 1987), *aff'd in part and rev'd in part,* 863 F.2d 1503, 50 FEP Cases 742 (11th Cir. 1989).

[137]See Ferrell v. Brick, 678 F. Supp. 111, 113, 46 FEP Cases 502, 504 (E.D. Pa. 1987)(psychiatric records ordered produced because evidence of other stressful situations in plaintiff's personal history, whether

of inquiry should include family relationships, personal relationships, traumatic experiences, moving of residence, deaths of parents or others, job-related stress, other incidents of harassment, illness, and any other possible sources of tension or stress.

H. Timeliness of Federal and State Claims

A prerequisite to suit under Title VII is the filing of a charge with the EEOC within 180 days of the last discriminatory act.[138] In "deferral states"—those with an approved state fair employment practices agency—the filing period is extended to 300 days.[139] To determine whether the charge was timely filed,[140] the complainant should be asked to identify the date of each particular act of harassment. Counsel similarly should establish facts to determine whether the state discrimination law and tort claims are barred by applicable statutes of limitations.[141]

The defendant can also inquire whether a Title VII suit was filed within ninety days of the complainant's receipt of the right-to-sue letter.[142] Because the ninety-day period may be tolled by misrepresentations or errors by the complainant or defendant, it is important for the defendant to discover any reasons that the complainant may have had for filing suit late.[143]

I. Mitigation

Sexual harassment complainants, like other plaintiffs, have a duty to mitigate damages.[144] In actual or constructive discharge cases, complainants

---

related or unrelated to job performance, relevant to emotional distress claim); Davis v. Ross, 107 F.R.D. 326, 329 (S.D.N.Y. 1985)(when damages for emotional or mental injuries sought, "health of the plaintiff *before* and after the accident may be inquired into")(quoting Miller v. Colonial Refrigerated Transp., 81 F.R.D. 741, 742 (M.D. Pa. 1979)); Lowe v. Philadelphia Newspapers, 101 F.R.D. 296, 298–99, 44 FEP Cases 1224, 1226 (E.D. Pa. 1983)(defendant permitted to depose plaintiff's psychiatrist and other witnesses concerning past personal history to show emotional distress damages not job-related). For further discussion of these issues, see Chapter 26, Discovery, Section III.

[138]42 U.S.C. §2000e-5(e); Delaware State College v. Ricks, 449 U.S. 250, 256, 24 FEP Cases 827 (1980).

[139]42 U.S.C. §2000e-5(e); Mohasco Corp. v. Silver, 447 U.S. 807, 23 FEP Cases 1 (1980). For a discussion of the defense that the complainant failed to exhaust the administrative process, see Chapter 27, Asserted Defenses, Section II.

[140]The plaintiff may claim the violations are continuing in nature. See Valentino v. United States Postal Serv., 674 F.2d 56, 65, 28 FEP Cases 593 (D.C. Cir. 1982)(plaintiff must show "a series of related acts, one or more of which falls within the limitation period, or a maintenance of a discriminatory system both before and during the [limitations]"); see also Roberts v. North Am. Rockwell Corp., 650 F.2d 823, 827–28, 25 FEP Cases 1615 (6th Cir. 1981). For discussion of the theory of continuing violation, see Chapter 27, Asserted Defenses, Section II.B.5.

[141]Because the rights vindicated under state tort laws are different than the Title VII right of nondiscrimination in the workplace, the filing of a Title VII charge does not toll the state claims. See Arnold v. United States, 816 F.2d 1306, 43 FEP Cases 1256 (9th Cir. 1987); Stewart v. Thomas, 538 F. Supp. 891, 895, 30 FEP Cases 1609 (D.D.C. 1982); Johnson v. Railway Express Agency, 421 U.S. 454, 465, 10 FEP Cases 817 (1975)(statute of limitations for claim brought under 42 U.S.C. §1981 not tolled by filing Title VII charge with EEOC).

[142]The defendant may have to obtain a copy of the return receipt that accompanied the notice of right-to-sue letter by making a request to the EEOC under the Freedom of Information Act, 5 U.S.C. §522 *et seq.* Where the agency does not retain return receipts, the defendant should check the date of delivery with the post office where the plaintiff resides.

[143]The defense of laches may be raised where there is an inexcusable delay between the filing of a discrimination charge and the complaint. See EEOC v. Star Tool & Die Works, 699 F. Supp 120, 47 FEP Cases 39 (E.D. Mich. 1987)(inexcusable delay by EEOC); Whitfield v. Anheuser-Busch, 820 F.2d 243, 43 FEP Cases 1534 (8th Cir. 1987)(suit filed promptly after notice of right to sue, but ten years after alleged discriminatory layoff, barred by doctrine of laches).

[144]Title VII provides: "interim earnings or amounts earnable with reasonable diligence . . . shall operate to reduce back pay otherwise allowable." 42 U.S.C. §2000e-5(g).

should be questioned thoroughly about their efforts to find new employment and, if they have secured a new position, about their new salary, fringe benefits, and other conditions of employment. It is important to establish when a complainant obtained other employment with comparable pay and working conditions,[145] or stopped seeking employment,[146] in order to define and limit the period of potential back-pay liability.

VI. EXPERT WITNESSES

A. The Complainant's Expert

1. General Use of Expert Testimony

Although all aspects of a sexual harassment case, even a case alleging emotional distress, can be proved without the use of expert testimony,[147] sexual harassment complainants frequently use experts for a variety of issues.[148]

Complainants may offer expert testimony to prove that the sexually harassing conduct adversely affected their psychological well-being.[149] This proof is particularly relevant in a constructive discharge case where the complainant was allegedly compelled to resign due to the psychological effects of the harassment.[150] Expert testimony may also be offered to show that the wrongful conduct was the proximate cause of the injuries complained of and to establish the damages suffered.[151]

2. Medical/Psychological Witnesses

A sexual harassment complainant who alleges emotional distress likely will offer the expert testimony of a mental health professional. Thorough

---

[145]*See, e.g.,* Di Salvo v. Chamber of Commerce, 568 F.2d 593, 20 FEP Cases 825 (8th Cir. 1978)(back-pay period terminated when plaintiff obtained job with salary in excess of former job).

[146]*See, e.g.,* Thorne v. El Segundo, 802 F.2d 1131, 46 FEP Cases 1651 (9th Cir. 1986)(back-pay period ceased where plaintiff testified that she planned to leave work force for four years to care for her children).

[147]*E.g.,* Block v. R.H. Macy & Co., 712 F.2d 1241, 1245, 32 FEP Cases 609 (8th Cir. 1983)(race discrimination case) ("because of the difficulty of evaluating the emotional injuries which result from deprivations of civil rights, courts do not demand precise proof to support a reasonable award of damages for such injuries"); Smith v. Anchor Bldg. Corp., 536 F.2d 231 (8th Cir. 1976)(humiliation or mental distress established by plaintiff's own testimony); Catalina Beach Club v. State Div. of Human Rights, 95 A.D.2d 766, 463 N.Y.S.2d 244, 246 (1983)("mental anguish may properly be established by the testimony of the complainant alone"). *But see* Perez v. Rodriguez Bou, 575 F.2d 21, 25 (1st Cir. 1978)(in absence of "medically cognizable psychological distress," loss of employment, or harm to plaintiff's reputation, "courts are not inclined to award compensatory damages for general mental distress" in civil rights employment actions)(citations omitted); Stolberg v. Members of Bd. of Trustees, 474 F.2d 485, 488–89 (2d Cir. 1973)(in §1983 action, without medical evidence of pain and suffering apart from plaintiff's own testimony of being "upset," damages for humiliation and distress "too speculative to be compensable"), *aff'd,* 541 F.2d 890 (2d Cir.), *cert. denied,* 429 U.S. 897 (1976).

[148]See Chapters 21, Complainant's Litigation Strategy, Section VI., and 25, Evidence, Section VIII.

[149]*See generally* Henson v. City of Dundee, 682 F.2d 897, 904, 29 FEP Cases 787 (11th Cir. 1982), reproduced in Chapter 4, Hostile Environment Harassment ("state of psychological well-being is a term, condition, or privilege of employment within the meaning of Title VII")(citing Rogers v. EEOC, 454 F.2d 234, 238, 4 FEP Cases 92 (5th Cir. 1971), *cert. denied,* 406 U.S. 957 (1972)).

[150]*See* Ross v. Twenty-Four Collection, 681 F. Supp. 1547, 1551–52, 48 FEP Cases 1590 (S.D. Fla. 1988)(expert testimony regarding exacerbation of plaintiff's Crohn's disease because of sexual harassment established that harassment affected plaintiff's psychological well-being, forcing her to resign), *aff'd mem.,* 875 F.2d 873, 50 FEP Cases 600 (11th Cir. 1989). *Cf.* Vinson v. Superior Court, 43 Cal.3d 833, 840, 239 Cal. Rptr. 292, 297, 44 FEP Cases 1174 (1987)(simple sexual harassment claim asking for compensation for having to endure oppressive work environment or for wages lost following unjust dismissal would not normally create controversy regarding plaintiff's mental state). For a discussion of constructive discharge, see Chapter 9.

[151]Valdez v. Church's Fried Chicken, 683 F. Supp. 596, 612, 47 FEP Cases 1155 (W.D. Tex. 1988).

pre-trial preparation and deposition testimony is the key to effective cross-examination at trial.

Through written discovery, or at the deposition of the expert, the defense should obtain a detailed statement of the diagnosis of the complainant's condition, the basis for that diagnosis, and the expert's view of the complainant's prognosis.[152] Whether the complainant's expert is the treating mental health professional or an expert who has evaluated the complainant only for purposes of the litigation, the task of the defendant's attorney is to obtain all of the available information about the complainant's condition.

Each of the complainant's treating physicians and therapists should be identified, and complete treatment records and medical history should be obtained either through a medical release signed by the complainant or by subpoena. Most courts will permit discovery of this material on the ground that the complainant waives any physician-patient privilege by placing her mental condition at issue.[153] Some courts that are more hesitant to conclude that the physician-patient privilege is waived have required defendants to obtain information from alternative sources[154] and have referred the evaluation of the complainant's psychiatric record to an independent forensic expert.[155]

If available, treatment notes, psychological evaluations, and medical histories may reveal facts about the complainant's personal life that may bear on liability or damages. The defense attorney should be especially alert to any evidence of a preexisting condition that may have contributed to the symptoms that the complainant now attributes to sexual harassment.

At trial, neutralizing the complainant's expert, especially in front of a jury, can be critical to a successful defense. Defense counsel should investigate the possibility of attacking the credentials of the expert witness or impeaching the expert on cross-examination with prior unreliable testimony.[156] The defense should investigate the expert's background, including all prior testimony and publications that may contain statements or opinions favorable to the defense.

---

[152]A diagnosis should be made in accordance with the specific criteria set forth in DIAGNOSTIC AND STATISTICAL MANUAL OF MENTAL DISORDERS OF THE AMERICAN PSYCHIATRIC ASSOCIATION (3d ed. 1987), known as DSM-III-R.

[153]*See, e.g.,* Ceasar v. Mountanos, 542 F.2d 1064, 1070 (9th Cir. 1976)(plaintiff waived psychotherapist-patient privilege when she placed mental or emotional condition in issue by claiming damages for mental and emotional distress), *cert. denied,* 430 U.S. 954 (1977); Ferrell v. Brick, *supra* note 137 (sexual harassment plaintiff waived physician-patient privacy right with respect to subpoenaed records of psychiatric treatment by placing mental condition in issue); Lowe v. Philadelphia Newspapers, *supra* note 137 (so long as plaintiff seeks damages by reason of physical, mental, or emotional harm or distress, defendant entitled to ask physicians and psychiatrists about plaintiff's past history). In addition, if the defense obtains a mental examination of plaintiff pursuant to Rule 35 of the Federal Rules of Civil Procedure, the plaintiff may obtain a report of that examination, and the defense is then entitled to any similar reports in the hands of the plaintiff. For further discussion of these issues, see Chapter 26, Discovery, Sections III. and IV.

[154]*E.g.,* Jennings v. DHL Airlines, 101 F.R.D. 549, 551, 34 FEP Cases 1423 (N.D. Ill. 1984)(to extent complainant's "interactions with her co-workers and her reactions to defendant's conduct" are important, defendant can obtain information short of obtaining psychological records).

[155]*E.g.,* Ferrell v. Brick, *supra* note 137, 678 F. Supp. at 113 ("parties agreed with court's proposal to refer the question to an independent forensic expert, whose opinion may be utilized in deciding whether the information should be protected from discovery"). For further discussion of evidentiary and discovery questions concerning a plaintiff's medical history, see Chapters 25, Evidence, Section IV., and 26, Discovery, Sections III. and IV.

[156]*See, e.g.,* United States v. Terry, 702 F.2d 299, 316 (2d Cir. 1983)(no prosecutorial misconduct where "voice expert" cross-examined regarding occasion when his testimony criticized by judge as being unworthy of belief and "guessing under oath"), *cert. denied,* 461 U.S. 931 (1983).

Because an expert opinion is no more reliable than the facts that it assumes, an important objective of cross-examination is to examine the facts
assumed by the complainant's expert. The expert should be questioned about
all of the steps that the expert has taken to become familiar with the facts on
which the opinion is based. In many instances, the expert will not have heard
the entire story.[157] The significance of prior matters not considered by the
expert, including traumatic events that might explain or contribute to the
complainant's current emotional state, should be explored in an attempt to
discredit the expert's conclusions.[158]

3. Sociological Experts

Complainants may also offer sociological experts to establish the existence of a hostile environment and to link it with the injuries suffered. When
confronted with this proposed testimony, the first consideration should be
whether it can be excluded or limited in subject matter. Unlike psychological
testimony, which is routinely admitted in sexual harassment cases, sociological
testimony may be controversial.[159] If the testimony cannot be excluded, defense
counsel should seek to rebut the testimony with any available evidence of bias,
failure to consider all of the relevant facts, or prior inconsistent or helpful
statements.

B. The Defendant's Expert

The decision of whether to use a defense expert on emotional distress or
physical injury issues can often be postponed until after deposing the complainant's expert, when defense counsel is better able to determine the extent of the
complainant's proof. If the complainant has a professional expert witness likely
to function as an advocate, the defendant should counteract the impact of that

---

[157]*See generally* Price Waterhouse v. Hopkins, 109 S.Ct. 1775, 1813 n.5, 49 FEP Cases 954, 981 (1989)
(Kennedy, J., dissenting)(criticizing plurality's enthusiasm for conclusions of plaintiff's expert on sexual
stereotyping, where expert "purported to discern stereotyping in comments that were gender neutral—*e.g.,*
'overbearing and abrasive'—without any knowledge of the comments' basis in reality and without having
met the speaker or subject. . . . Today's opinions cannot be read as requiring factfinders to credit testimony
based on this type of analysis").

[158]*See, e.g.,* Ferrell v. Brick, 678 F. Supp. 111, 113, 46 FEP Cases 502, 504 (E.D. Pa. 1987)(in
ascertaining causes of emotional distress in sexual harassment case, defendant entitled to inquire of witnesses,
including physicians or psychiatrists, as to plaintiff's past history, whether or not same was directly related
to her job); Mitchell v. Hutchings, 116 F.R.D. 481, 485, 44 FEP Cases 615 (D. Utah. 1987)(sexual harassment
defendant may inquire in hypothetical form or otherwise how certain information, if known to expert, would
affect his opinion). *But see* Valdez v. Church's Fried Chicken, *supra* note 151, 683 F. Supp. at 613–14 n.12,
47 FEP Cases at 1164 (due to pre-trial stipulation, defendant precluded from eliciting revised opinion from
expert after presenting him with new evidence of plaintiff's traumatic childhood).

[159]*Compare* Eide v. Kelsey-Hayes Co., 154 Mich. App. 142, 397 N.W.2d 532, 538, 47 FEP Cases 1043,
1047 (1986)(admitting sociological testimony to describe environment and sexual connotations of challenged
conduct) *and* Broderick v. Ruder, 685 F. Supp. 1269, 1273, 46 FEP Cases 1272 (D.D.C. 1988), reproduced
in Chapter 2, Forms of Harassment (admitting testimony as to both general effects of sexual harassment and
particular effects on plaintiff) *and* Moffett v. Gene B. Glick Co., 621 F. Supp. 244, 262, 41 FEP Cases 671,
684 (N.D. Ind. 1985)(admitting testimony of social worker that victims of sexual harassment will experience
problems) *with* Lipsett v. University of P.R., 740 F. Supp. 921, 924 (D.P.R. 1990)(ruling *in limine* that
proposed sociological experts did not have level of specialized knowledge to qualify them as experts and did
not possess professional safeguards ensuring objective testimony) *and* Perkins v. General Motors, 129 F.R.D.
655, 667 (W.D. Mo. 1990)(social worker never offered as expert after unsuccessful day-long attempt to
qualify her on broad range of issues). For an extended discussion of admissibility of expert testimony, see
Chapter 25, Evidence, Section VIII.

testimony with its own professional advocate.[160] If the complainant's witness, however, is a treating therapist, that sort of expert witness may be sufficiently candid to provide as much helpful information as could be obtained from an independent expert. A defendant may be just as effective in undermining the complainant's expert with additional facts unknown to the expert when the expert's opinion was formed. Testimony helpful to the defendant will, of course, be more persuasive if it comes from the complainant's own witness. However, where sexual harassment claims win the sympathy of the court or jury, a battery of unopposed plaintiff experts may dramatically increase the prospects for and the amount of a damage award.

Another factor in deciding whether to retain a defense expert is whether the critical factual issue is (1) the cause of the complainant's emotional distress or (2) whether the complainant actually suffered emotional distress. Ordinarily, an expert who has not seen a patient frequently over a lengthy period of time cannot testify definitively about the cause of the stress, but only as to the nature and extent of the problem.

If the evaluation of the case suggests that a defense expert is advisable or necessary, a request for a mental examination pursuant to Rule 35 of the Federal Rules of Civil Procedure or a state-law counterpart should be considered.[161] Rule 35 provides that the court may, "for good cause shown," order a party to submit to a mental examination by a physician when the "mental condition" of the party is "in controversy." Most courts will find that plaintiffs have placed their mental condition at issue when they seek to recover damages for mental distress.[162] Because Rule 35 requires that the report of the examination *must* be provided to the plaintiff on request,[163] the risk that the report may include harmful conclusions must be carefully weighed by the defense. Generally, plaintiffs are not entitled to have counsel present during mental examinations.[164] Where the potential for abuse exists, however, the court may permit

---

[160]Expert opinions may be discredited with less-biased expert opinions. *See, e.g.,* Tate v. Dravo Corp., 623 F. Supp. 1090, 1096, 39 FEP Cases 1544 (W.D.N.C. 1985)(court discredited plaintiff's expert's testimony when employer's conflicting evaluation of expert's opinion confirmed by independent certified analyst); Kresko v. Rulli, 432 N.W.2d 764, 767 (Minn. Ct. App. 1988)(court accepted defense experts' conclusions, based on review of plaintiff's psychological records and four-hour examination, that plaintiff's relationship with alleged harasser was not traumatic enough to cause post-traumatic stress syndrome, and that plaintiff welcomed supervisor's sexual advances). *See also* Shrout v. Black Clawson Co., 689 F. Supp. 774, 776, 46 FEP Cases 1339 (S.D. Ohio 1988)(court rejected testimony of one psychologist defense expert who found that sexual harassment had no measurable impact on plaintiff's psychological condition, but accepted testimony of other defense expert who testified that harassment *may* have contributed to plaintiff's present emotional state).

[161]Rule 35 examinations are discussed in more detail in Chapter 26, Discovery, Section IV.

[162]*See* text accompanying note 153 *supra.*

[163]*E.g.,* Lowe v. Philadelphia Newspapers, 101 F.R.D. 296, 301, 44 FEP Cases 1224 (E.D. Pa. 1983)(in race discrimination case, court ordered plaintiff to submit to psychiatric examination and psychiatrist to "prepare a full written report of such examination and his conclusions, if any, and provide a copy thereof to plaintiff's counsel").

[164]*Id.* at 299 (plaintiff's counsel not allowed to be present during psychiatric examination); Brandenberg v. El Al Israel Airlines, 79 F.R.D. 543, 546 (S.D.N.Y. 1978)("it has been consistently held, in connection with physical examinations under Rule 35, that counsel for the party being examined are not entitled to be present"); Dziwanoski v. Ocean Carriers Corp., 26 F.R.D. 595, 598 (D. Md. 1960)("presence of the lawyer for the party to be examined is not ordinarily either necessary or proper; it should be permitted only on application to the court showing good reason therefor").

plaintiffs to have their attorney, psychiatrist, or medical expert present as an observer.[165]

The defense should also consider the usefulness of expert testimony on nonmedical issues. Where the effectiveness and accessibility of internal grievance procedures are challenged by a complainant, a human resources consultant may be helpful to offset or discredit such testimony. Similarly, where an employer based its decision to discharge a complainant on performance evaluations, or seeks to use them at trial for other means, a human resources expert can endorse both the procedures in general and the ways in which they were applied to the complainant. In cases where the nature of the work environment is at issue, sociologists or industrial psychologists also may be of assistance.

In addition, EEOC investigators have been permitted to testify concerning EEOC findings in determinations admitted into evidence.[166] Where suit is filed after a "no-cause" determination has been issued by the EEOC, the defendant may want to produce the EEOC investigator as an expert witness regarding the agency's findings. The weight given to an EEOC "no-cause" determination will vary with the circumstances.[167]

---

[165]See, e.g., Zabkowicz v. West Bend Co., 585 F. Supp. 635, 636, 35 FEP Cases 209 (E.D. Wis. 1984)(sexual harassment plaintiffs entitled to have third party, including counsel, or recording device present during defendants' psychiatric examination, because "there are numerous advantages . . . which the defendants might unfairly derive from an unsupervised examination"); Lowe v. Philadelphia Newspapers, *supra* note 163, 101 F.R.D. at 299 (although plaintiff's counsel was not permitted to attend psychiatric examination, plaintiff may have own psychiatrist or medical expert present solely to observe and not for purpose of advising her). *But see* Swift v. Swift, 64 F.R.D. 440, 443 (E.D.N.Y. 1974)(presence of even party's own physician at psychiatric examination denied). For a further discussion of medical examination of plaintiffs, see Chapter 26, Discovery, Section IV.

[166]See Gillin v. Federal Paper Board Co., 479 F.2d 97, 5 FEP Cases 1094 (2d Cir. 1973).

[167]See, e.g., Robinson v. Jacksonville Shipyards, 760 F. Supp. 1486, 1517 (M.D. Fla. 1991), reproduced in Chapter 2, Forms of Harassment (discounting "no cause" determination where investigation apparently was "cursory" and where leading case at time may have provided "misleading impression" of law). For further discussion of admissibility of EEOC determinations, see Chapter 20, The Agency Investigation, section II.E.; and B.L. SCHLEI & P. GROSSMAN, EMPLOYMENT DISCRIMINATION LAW 977 (2d ed. 1983), Five-Year Supp. 379 (1988).

CHAPTER 23

THE ALLEGED HARASSER AS DEFENDANT

I. OVERVIEW

The anger of a sexual harassment complainant often will be directed at the individual alleged harasser, particularly where the allegations include physical abuse or quid pro quo harassment. In addition, the complainant's counsel may perceive tactical advantages in naming the alleged harasser individually as a defendant. Accordingly, sexual harassment complainants often name alleged harassers individually in administrative charges and lawsuits.[1] The employer will also be named as a defendant, but primarily because of its ability to respond financially.

Although courts have found alleged harassers individually liable for sexual harassment, the number of cases in which individual liability is discussed is small in comparison to the total number of sexual harassment cases. Those cases that have addressed the question of individual liability generally have provided no clear analytical framework for determining when it should be imposed. Usually the issue arises as an afterthought, once employer liability has already been found to exist.

The liability of an individual is evident where that individual performs an intentionally wrongful act, as in the case of a supervisor who is guilty of quid pro quo harassment or who creates a "hostile environment."[2]

Individual liability is less clear where "hostile environment" liability rests upon an individual's failure to prevent or remedy the misconduct of the complainant's co-workers. Nonetheless, for any corporate employer to be liable there must be *some* employee who has breached the employer's legal duty to use due care to prevent and remedy a sexually hostile environment, and whose breach of that duty triggers the corporate employer's vicarious liability.[3] The fact that an upper-level manager is acting as an agent of the corporate employer

---

[1]See Chapter 21, Complainant's Litigation Strategy. Naming an individual defendant in the administrative charge may be a jurisdictional prerequisite to naming that person in later litigation under Title VII. See Chapter 27, Asserted Defenses, Section II.C.; B.L. SCHLEI & P. GROSSMAN, EMPLOYMENT DISCRIMINATION LAW, Chapter 30, Section II (2d ed. 1983), Five-Year Supp. (1989). For a discussion of considerations involved in whether the corporate defendant and individual defendant should have a joint defense, see Chapter 22, Employer's Litigation Strategy.

[2]*E.g.,* Steele v. Offshore Shipbldg., 867 F.2d 1311, 1314, 49 FEP Cases 522, 523 (11th Cir. 1989)(individual supervisor liable for creating hostile environment).

[3]Hunter v. Allis-Chalmers Corp., 797 F.2d 1417, 1422, 41 FEP Cases 721, 724 (7th Cir. 1986)("to say that the 'corporation' has committed some wrong ... simply means that someone at the decision-making

in failing to prevent or remedy harassment does not foreclose individual liability.[4]

Thus, in theory, individual liability exists in every case where Title VII is violated. The rarity of suits against individual employees who are not themselves alleged to be harassers arguably reflects the absence of any tactical advantage of naming the individual as a defendant rather than any inherent legal difficulty in doing so.

Liability of an individual for failing to prevent harassment is most likely where the individual defendant is a member of management who has an affirmative duty to act against harassment by co-workers. First-line supervisors or co-workers are less likely to be individually liable, as their omissions may not breach a duty owed to a complainant by individuals in their position.[5]

II. INDIVIDUAL LIABILITY UNDER TITLE VII

Title VII imposes liability on an "employer."[6] The term is defined as an entity employing fifteen or more persons, and also as any "agent" of the employer.[7] Thus, an individual may be liable under Title VII as an "employer" if under the circumstances that individual has acted as an "agent" of an employer.

Whether an employee is individually liable for sexual harassment depends on whether (A) the employee's position makes the employee an "agent" of an employer in a general sense, and (B) the employee's personal involvement in the alleged harassment (or personal responsibility to prevent it) is sufficient.

A. When an Individual Qualifies as a Title VII Employer

Nowhere in Title VII is the term "agent" defined.[8] Courts most commonly define the term as "a supervisory or managerial employee to whom employment decisions have been delegated by the employer."[9] Employer "liability attaches only against individuals who exercise effective control in the workplace—

---

level in the corporate hierarchy has committed the wrong"); Kinnally v. Bell of Pa., 748 F. Supp. 1136, 1142, 54 FEP Cases 329, 333 (E.D. Pa. 1990)(Louis H. Pollak, Jr., J.)("inaction of executive and management personnel may serve as a basis for liability under Title VII even where these high-level employees have played no direct role in the alleged discrimination"). *Cf.* Restatement (Second) of Agency §219(c)(master liable for torts outside scope of employment if conduct violated nondelegable duty of master).

[4]*See* Restatement (Second) of Agency §351: "An agent who directs or permits conduct of another under such circumstances that he should realize that there is an unreasonable risk of physical harm to others . . . is subject to liability for harm resulting from a risk which his direction or permission creates."

[5]The fact that such a low-level employee has breached the employer's policy on sexual harassment would not mean that the employee thereby breached duty to the complainant: "An agent is not liable for harm to a person other than his principal because of his failure adequately to perform his duties to his principal . . . ." Restatement (Second) of Agency, §352. *See also id.* at §357 (agent not liable for economic harm caused to third parties by negligent failure to perform duties to principal).

[6]Section 706(b), 42 U.S.C. §2000e-5(b), provides that a charge may be filed against "an employer, employment agency, labor organization, or joint labor-management committee controlling apprenticeship or other training or retraining, including on-the-job training programs."

[7]Section 701(b), 42 U.S.C. §2000e(b). See SCHLEI & GROSSMAN, *supra* note 1, Chapter 27, Sections IV and V.

[8]Barger v. Kansas, 630 F. Supp. 88, 89 (D. Kan. 1985).

[9]York v. Tennessee Crushed Stone Ass'n, 684 F.2d 360, 362 (6th Cir. 1982). *See also* Smith v. Prudential Fin. Servs., 739 F. Supp. 1042, 1043 (D.S.C. 1990)("employer" is "officer, director or supervisor of Title VII employer or otherwise involved in managerial decisions").

those persons who make or contribute meaningfully to employment decisions."[10]

The clearest case for "employer" status exists where the employer has delegated to a general manager or upper-level supervisor the employer's traditional rights to hire, fire, and direct the work force.[11] Employer status may also exist even where the employer has delegated only one important employer function, such as hiring[12] or the setting of compensation.[13]

"Employer" status may exist both for those who actually made the challenged personnel decision[14] and for those who, while themselves lacking the decision-making power, had power to affect the decision.[15]

Nonsupervising employees who are merely senior co-workers with training responsibilities and a few additional privileges do not qualify as agents of the employer under Title VII.[16]

---

[10]Robinson v. Jacksonville Shipyards, 760 F. Supp. 1486, 1527 (M.D. Fla. 1991), reproduced in Chapter 2, Forms of Harassment. *See also* Kolb v. State of Ohio Dep't of Mental Retardation, 721 F. Supp. 885, 891, 50 FEP Cases 1418, 1422 (N.D. Ohio 1989)(individuals charged with responsibility to make or contribute to employment decisions for defendant employer may be liable as Title VII "agents"); McAdoo v. Toll, 591 F. Supp. 1399, 1406, 35 FEP Cases 833, 837–38 (D. Md. 1984)(same).

[11]*See, e.g.,* Harvey v. Blake, 913 F.2d 226, 227 (5th Cir. 1990)(supervisors are "employers" when delegated the employer's traditional rights, such as hiring and firing, and may be liable for sexual harassment); Paroline v. Unisys Corp., 879 F.2d 100, 104, 50 FEP Cases 306, 310 (4th Cir. 1989), reproduced in Chapter 9, Constructive Discharge (individual qualifies as employer under Title VII if serving in supervisory position and exercising significant control over plaintiff's hiring, firing or conditions of employment), *aff'd in material part en banc,* 900 F.2d 27, 52 FEP Cases 845 (4th Cir. 1990); Sparks v. Pilot Freight Carriers, 830 F.2d 1554, 1560, 45 FEP Cases 160, 164 (11th Cir. 1987), reproduced in Chapter 2, Forms of Harassment (terminal manager vested with employer's authority to alter complainant's job status acting as agent and thus "employer" when he used threats of discharge to assist harassing efforts). *See generally* Note, *Sexual Harassment and Title VII: The Foundation for the Elimination of Sexual Cooperation as an Employment Condition,* 76 MICH. L. REV. 1007, 1030–31 (1978).

[12]Aguilera v. Cook County Police & Corrections Merit Bd., 21 FEP Cases 731 (N.D. Ill. 1979)(county personnel board selecting employees for police department is "agent" of police department), *rev'd and remanded on other grounds mem.,* 661 F.2d 937, 26 FEP Cases 1416 (7th Cir. 1981); EEOC Dec. 73-0458, 19 FEP Cases 1785 (1972)(booking agents signing musicians for work in hotels were "employers" because of delegation to them of hiring authority).

[13]Hannahs v. Teachers' Retirement Sys., 26 FEP Cases 527 (S.D.N.Y. 1981)(governing board of public retirement system employer because it, in addition to school district, controls some aspect of plaintiff's compensation at issue and may be regarded as "arm" of school district).

[14]Howard v. Temple Urgent Care Center, 53 FEP Cases 1416, 1417 (D. Conn. 1990)(supervisor who participates in managerial decisions, without power to hire or fire, may be employer for purposes of Title VII; "employer" includes any party who significantly affects employees' job responsibilities and working conditions); Kolb v. State of Ohio Dep't of Mental Retardation, *supra* note 10 (individuals charged with making and/or contributing to employment decisions may be liable as employer's agents under Title VII); Cleary v. Department of Pub. Welfare, 21 FEP Cases 687, 690 (E.D. Pa. 1979)(Secretary of Department of Public Welfare with ultimate responsibility for hiring employees liable under Title VII as agent of employer).

[15]Vance v. Southern Bell Tel. & Tel. Co., 863 F.2d 1503, 1515 (11th Cir. 1989)(imposing individual liability on basis of role played in discipline, grievances, personnel changes; "agency standard which looks solely to the degree of authority the harasser wields over the plaintiff is not particularly useful in a hostile environment case such as this"; necessary to "examine any evidence bearing on the overall structure of the workplace, including the relative positions of the parties involved"). *Cf.* Huebschen v. Wisconsin Dep't of Health & Social Servs., 716 F.2d 1167, 1170, 32 FEP Cases 1582, 1584 (7th Cir. 1983)(immediate supervisor of sexual harassment complainant not Title VII "employer"); Smith v. Sentry Ins., 674 F. Supp. 1459, 1466, 45 FEP Cases 716, 721 (N.D. Ga. 1987)(individual defendant could not be liable for age discrimination claim arising from decision in which he had no part); Harris v. First Nat'l Bank, 680 F. Supp. 1489, 1494, 46 FEP Cases 189, 192–93 (D. Kan. 1987)(statement that chairman of board of directors was to remain active member of management team insufficient to show involvement in particular employment decisions so as to support discrimination against him).

[16]*E.g.,* Robinson v. Jacksonville Shipyards, *supra* note 10, 760 F. Supp. at 1521–22 (quartermen and leadermen are not employers, because they are not formally delegated authority to resolve disputes between employees and because they are excluded from formal supervisory structure); Smith v. Prudential Fin. Servs., 739 F. Supp. 1042, 1043 (D.S.C. 1990)(complainant's fellow sales agent not liable under Title VII for sexual harassment in that he lacked "supervisory authority" over her); Guyette v. Stauffer Chem. Co., 27 FEP Cases 483, 484–85 (D.N.J. 1981)(senior laboratory technician who trained two employees and enjoyed some

B. When an Individual "Employer" Is Liable for Sexual Harassment

1. Source of Individual Liability

"Employer" status alone does not make an individual liable for sexual harassment even if the complainant was harassed under that person's supervision, and even if the harassment has been such that the corporate employer is liable. Nonetheless, as noted previously, in every case in which a corporate defendant is liable, there must be *some* person at some level of the corporation who potentially is individually liable.[17] This principle flows from the application of general agency principles that are to be applied in Title VII sexual harassment cases.[18]

Under general principles of agency law, an employer may be liable in tort to third parties either directly or indirectly. The employer may be *directly* liable by virtue of the employer's own wrongful conduct. For example, an unincorporated employer may be directly liable for a battery that the employer commits on a third party, and an employer, whether an individual or a corporation, may also be directly liable for negligently supervising an employee.[19]

The employer is *indirectly* liable, under the doctrine of *respondeat superior,* when an employee of the employer commits a tort, such as a battery, within the scope of the employer-employee agency relationship.[20]

Where the employer is a corporation, employer liability is always "indirect" in the sense that a corporation can act only through its agents. Corporate liability can result under the doctrine of *respondeat superior* only because an employee of the corporation is directly liable because of that employee's own wrongful conduct that may be intentional or negligent. Thus, the offending employee must necessarily also be liable as an individual, because individual liability is the predicate for invoking the doctrine of *respondeat superior.* An employee is not relieved of liability on the ground that the employer is also liable: "An agent who does an act otherwise a tort is not relieved from liability by the fact that he acted at the command of the principal or on account of the principal . . . ."[21]

Individual liability for sexual harassment under Title VII has been found in three situations: active participation in the harassment, acquiescence, and failure to prevent or remedy the harassment.

2. Liability for Active Participation

The most obvious case of individual liability under Title VII is where an individual, vested with sufficient employer-delegated authority to be an

---

privileges and responsibilities because of greater seniority and experience not "supervisor" and therefore may not be sued under Title VII where no showing of actual control over employment opportunities).

[17]See Section III. *infra.*

[18]Meritor Sav. Bank v. Vinson, 477 U.S. 57, 72, 40 FEP Cases 1822, 1829 (1986), reproduced in Chapter 1, Overview (Congress wanted courts to resort to general agency law principles in determining employer liability issues in sexual harassment cases). For a more detailed discussion of employer liability, see Chapter 6, Harassment by Supervisors.

[19]Restatement (Second) of Agency §§213, 219(b). See also Chapter 15, The Common Law.

[20]*See generally Id.* at §219. The fact that the employee's act was outside the scope of employment, and even contrary to the employer's instructions, does not foreclose the employer's liability if the employee was aided in accomplishing the tort by the existence of the agency relation. *Id.* at §219(d) & Comment e.

[21]*Id.* at §343.

"employer," engages in the harassment. In *Steele v. Offshore Shipbuilding,* a supervisor was held individually liable under Title VII for creating a hostile environment. He had engaged in "sexually oriented joking" with his female subordinates, including requests for sexual favors. The joking promptly stopped upon the complainants' internal complaint. In an unusual result, the court found the employer free of liability because it promptly stopped the harassment once it was reported, but found the individual liable under Title VII, as an "employer," both for nominal damages and for over $15,000 in attorney's fees.[22]

3. Liability for Acquiescence

Short of active participation, a supervisor may be held liable, as in *Robson v. Eva's Super Market,* where the supervisor "acquiesces [in] or condones" sexual harassment.[23] The complainant's supervisor in *Robson* responded to her early allegations of harassment by instructing her to ignore the alleged harasser and "not let him bother you." Later the supervisor laughed when the alleged harasser responded to the complainant's allegations "in a threatening and profane manner." Finally, when the complainant demanded that her supervisor either put a stop to the harassment or accept her resignation, the supervisor accepted the complainant's resignation. The federal district court found that the supervisor, while he did not directly participate in any of the alleged acts of misconduct, could be held individually liable for sexual harassment because he acquiesced in the unlawful acts of his subordinate.

4. Liability for Failure to Take Prompt Corrective Action

Where an individual has responsibility for administering the employer's antiharassment policy, that individual may be liable for its failure: "[t]he inaction of executive and management personnel may serve as a basis for liability under Title VII even where these high-level employees have played no direct role in the alleged discrimination."[24]

The most extensive discussion to date of individual liability for failing to prevent or remedy a sexually hostile environment appears in Judge Howell

---

[22]Steele v. Offshore Shipbldg., 867 F.2d 1311, 1313–14, 1316–17 & n.1, 49 FEP Cases 522, 523, 525–26 (11th Cir. 1989). The court did not explain how the individual could be liable under Title VII, which necessarily meant that he was a Title VII employer, while at the same time finding the employer itself not liable, on the ground that the individual's harassment was outside the scope of his agency. For a more traditional active participation case, see *Maturo v. National Graphics,* 722 F. Supp. 916, 55 FEP Cases 325, 331 (D. Conn. 1989)(leadman with supervisory responsibilities individually liable under Title VII for his own harassment, while corporation and higher managers also liable).

[23]538 F. Supp. 857, 863, 30 FEP Cases 1212, 1217 (N.D. Ohio 1982).

[24]Kinnally v. Bell of Pa., 748 F. Supp. 1136, 1142, 54 FEP Cases 329, 333 (E.D. Pa. 1990)(plaintiff survived summary judgment motion with evidence that defendant president of corporation knew of sexual harassment complaints by plaintiff yet refrained from having her or her co-workers interviewed). *See also* Hall v. Gus Constr. Co., 842 F.2d 1010, 1016, 46 FEP Cases 573, 577 (8th Cir. 1988), reproduced in Chapter 2, Forms of Harassment (foreman who was aware of incidents of harassment individually liable for failing to investigate and take remedial steps to end them); Maturo v. National Graphics, *supra* note 22 (president and manager of corporation both individually liable because they had notice of harassment and failed to correct it). *But see* Hendrix v. Fleming Cos., 650 F. Supp. 301, 303, 42 FEP Cases 461, 462 (W.D. Okla. 1986)(dismissing individual defendants who simply knew or should have known about harassment and did nothing to stop it); Ponton v. Newport News School Bd., 632 F. Supp. 1056, 1068, 42 FEP Cases 83, 91–92 (E.D. Va. 1986)(only two of seven school district officials individually liable where plaintiff forced to leave job as teacher because she was single and pregnant; two individual defendants initiated personnel policy and one defendant communicated decision to plaintiff while other defendant implicitly approved policy).

Melton's decision in *Robinson v. Jacksonville Shipyards*. The decision discusses the potential liability of six individual defendants—the company president, the vice president of operations, the industrial relations manager, a middle manager, a facility superintendent, and a foreman:

> Having determined that the first four elements of a sexual harassment claim have been satisfied, the Court faces the task of assessing the liability of the employers in the case. The corporate employer, JSI, is subject only to vicarious liability, an issue more fully developed *infra*. The individual employers, however, pose a distinct liability issue.
>
> The principles of employer liability for individual corporate officers are broad. It has been described as "inconceivable that Congress intended to exclude from liability the very persons who have engaged in the employment practices which are the subject of the action." *Dague v. Riverdale Athletic Ass'n*, 99 F.R.D. 325, 327 (N.D. Ga. 1983). Instead, a liberal interpretation of Title VII works to hold responsible "those who control the aspects of employment accorded protection" by that law. *Spirt v. Teachers Ins. & Annuity Ass'n*, 475 F. Supp. 1298, 1308 (S.D.N.Y. 1979), *aff'd in relevant part*, 691 F.2d 1054 (2d Cir. 1982), *vacated*, 463 U.S. 1223 (1983), *reinstated as modified*, 735 F.2d 23 (2d Cir.), *cert. denied*, 469 U.S. 881 (1984).
>
> "It may seem odd that an individual occupying a supervisory position could be held liable for the acts of his underlings when the employer of both can also be held liable, particularly where the supervisor had no personal involvement in the discriminatory acts of those working for him. However, placing an affirmative duty to prevent discriminatory acts on those who are charged with employment decisions appears to be consistent with the aims of Title VII." *McAdoo v. Toll*, 591 F. Supp. 1399, 1406 (D. Md. 1984). Because these principles are so broad, however, they should be applied with an eye toward finding liability only against individuals who exercise effective control in the workplace—those persons who make or contribute meaningfully to employment decisions. *See, e.g., Kolb v. Ohio*, 721 F. Supp. 885, 891 (N.D. Ohio 1989); *McAdoo*, 591 F. Supp. at 1406. Thus, lower level supervisory employees who qualify as employers should be exonerated from liability when they do no more than follow the policies established by their superiors. Individual liability attaches, if at all, to the generals, not their soldiers.
>
> McIlwain [President of defendant corporation] is not liable for the hostile work environment to which Robinson [plaintiff] was subjected. He did not personally participate in any sexually harassing behavior that affected Robinson and he was not personally presented with her complaints of sexual harassment. Indeed, his status as an employer derives from his status as an agent of JSI. The responsibility for handling sexual harrassment complaints was delegated to supervisory personnel below McIlwain. While Robinson suggests that this delegation creates an agency relationship between McIlwain and the supervisory personnel responsible for remedying sexual harassment, her argument does not account for the source of McIlwain's authority to delegate. The delegation is done on behalf of the corporation, within McIlwain's agency relationship with JSI, and it therefore creates an agent-principal relationship between the delegatees and JSI, not the delegatees and McIlwain. *See* Brown [v. City of Miami Beach], 684 F. Supp. [1081], 1085–86 [(S.D. Fla. 1988)]; *see also* Restatement (Second) of Agency §5 comment a (1985); *id.* §222. Accordingly, JSI, not McIlwain, incurs liability when the actions (or inactions) of the delegatees create the circumstances for the application of respondeat superior.
>
> Brown [Vice President for Operations] is liable for the hostile work environment to which Robinson was subjected. His responsibility extended to the creation and implementation of JSI's sexual harassment policies. Their failure is his failure. Additionally, he personally intervened in Robinson's complaint and directed that no remedial action be taken.

Stewart [Industrial Relations Manager] is liable for the hostile work environment to which Robinson was subjected. He held responsibility for the day-to-day administration of the sexual harassment complaint machinery. Its failure is his failure. Additionally, he personally intervened in Robinson's complaint and directed that no remedial action be taken.

Ahlwardt [Vice President of the facility where plaintiff worked] is not liable for the hostile work environment to which Robinson was subjected. He stood in a middle management position and did no more or less than implement the order of his superiors, albeit with little finesse or compassion.

Owens [a superintendent at the facility where plaintiff worked] is not liable for the hostile work environment to which Robinson was subjected. He also stood too far down on the ladder of authority to [incur] individual liability for the state of the workplace.

Lovett [a foreman] is not liable for the hostile work environment to which Robinson was subjected. Not only did he stand too far down on the ladder of authority, he did not exercise control directly over Robinson.

Defendants argue that they cannot be held liable unless they personally participated in sexually offensive conduct, citing *Brown v. City of Miami Beach,* 684 F. Supp. 1081, 1085–86 (S.D. Fla. 1988), *judgment rendered sub nom. Sanchez v. City of Miami Beach,* 720 F. Supp. 974 (S.D. Fla. 1989), and *Hendrix v. Fleming Cos.,* 650 F. Supp. 301, 302–03 (W.D. Okla. 1986). The Court disagrees with the limiting force of defendants' proposition. Active participation in sexually harassing behavior is a sufficient but not a necessary condition to the imposition of Title VII liability. An individual employer who ratifies the sexually harassing conduct of another is surely as culpable as if the employer actively participated. *See McAdoo,* 591 F. Supp. at 1406. One method of ratification is an individual employer's failure or refusal to act to remedy a valid complaint of sexual harassment presented to that individual for which the individual has a duty to respond. *See Morris v. American Nat'l Can Corp.,* 730 F. Supp. 1489, 1496–97 (E.D. Mo. 1989); *Maturo v. National Graphics, Inc.,* 722 F. Supp. 916, 923–24 (D. Conn. 1989).[25]

C. Remedies

Damage assessments against individual defendants under Title VII vary according to the nature of the alleged conduct and the requested relief. When an individual defendant and an employer are found jointly liable, the court may exercise its discretion to apportion liability between them.[26] Courts generally, however, have declined to assess back-pay liability against individual defendants.[27] Judge Melton addressed this point in *Robinson v. Jacksonville Shipyards:*[28]

Binding precedent holds that public officials cannot be held personally liable for backpay under Title VII, *see Clanton v. Orleans Parish School Bd.,* 649 F.2d 1084, 1099 & n.19 (5th Cir. Unit A July 1981); persuasive authority extends this

---

[25]*Supra* note 10, 760 F. Supp. at 1527–28 (paragraph numbers and footnotes omitted).

[26]*See generally* Russell v. American Tobacco Co., 528 F.2d 357, 366, 11 FEP Cases 395, 399 (4th Cir. 1975), *cert. denied,* 425 U.S. 935 (1976)(holding union and employer jointly liable for racially discriminatory employment practices).

[27]Robinson v. Jacksonville Shipyards, *supra* note 10, 760 F. Supp. at 1533 (individual defendants not personally liable for back pay). *But see* Steele v. Offshore Shipbldg., *supra* note 22, 867 F.2d at 1311, 49 FEP Cases at 522 (individual held liable for nominal damages and attorney's fees).

[28]*Id.*

principle to individual employer defendants in private corporations,[11]*see Seib v. Elko Motor Inn, Inc.,* 648 F. Supp. 272, 274 (D. Nev. 1986); *Pree v. Stone & Webster Eng'g Corp.,* 607 F. Supp. 945, 950 (D. Nev. 1985). On this basis ... the nominal damages should be awarded against JSI only. Alternatively, backpay liability also may be limited for equitable reasons tailored to the circumstances of the individual's involvement, *see, e.g., Altman v. Stevens Fashion Fabrics,* 441 F. Supp. 1318, 1321 (N.D. Cal. 1977). The circumstances in this case do not show [the individual defendants found liable for the harassment] to be motivated by any ill will or bad faith; they appear to have acted on their belief concerning the best interests of JSI. The Court thus also finds equitable grounds to limit the assessment of ... damages to JSI alone.

---

[11]*Seib* and *Pree* reach this conclusion deductively from *Clanton* and other cases. The same result may be produced from a different approach. Backpay is part of the equitable remedy of reinstatement. *See, e.g., Harkless v. Sweeny Indep. School Dist.,* 427 F.2d 319, 324 (5th Cir. 1970), *cert. denied,* 400 U.S. 991 (1971). It makes little sense to speak of reinstatement by the individual defendants; the corporate defendant bears the burden of that remedy. Accordingly, since backpay follows from reinstatement, the liability for backpay falls on the shoulder of the employer who reinstates the victim of discrimination, the corporate employer defendant.

III. INDIVIDUAL LIABILITY UNDER OTHER LEGAL THEORIES

A. 42 U.S.C. §1983

State and local government employees may sue their superiors individually for committing or tolerating sexual harassment, subject to special rules and defenses discussed elsewhere.[29]

B. Tort Claims

The primary common-law tort claims[30] stated against individual defendants are for infliction of emotional distress,[31] invasion of privacy,[32] assault and battery,[33] defamation,[34] and false imprisonment.[35] In each of these cases complainants will attempt to prove direct action by the individual defendants who invaded their rights. Sexual harassment complainants need not prove a

---

[29]For a discussion of personal liability of individual harassers acting under color of state law, see Chapter 11, Federal Constitutional, Statutory, and Civil Rights Law, Section III.

[30]For a discussion of common-law causes of action, see Chapter 15, The Common Law.

[31]*E.g.,* Stewart v. Thomas, 538 F. Supp. 891, 894, 30 FEP Cases 1609, 1610 (D.D.C. 1982)(alleging emotional distress based on insulting and demeaning remarks, abusive language and sexual advances by plaintiff's direct supervisor). For further discussion, see Chapter 15, The Common Law, Section II.

[32]*E.g.,* Rogers v. Loews L'Enfant Plaza Hotel, 526 F. Supp. 523, 528, 29 FEP Cases 828, 830–31 (D.D.C. 1981)(improperly intrusive and sexually suggestive telephone calls from plaintiff's supervisor). For further discussion, see Chapter 15, The Common Law, Section V.

[33]*E.g., id.* at 529, 29 FEP Cases at 831–32 (assault and battery based on unwanted advances and touching by plaintiff's supervisor). For further discussion, see Chapter 15, The Common Law, Section III.

[34]*E.g.,* Schomer v. Smidt, 113 Cal. App.3d 828, 833–35, 170 Cal. Rptr. 662, 664–66 (1980)(affirming jury verdict against airline captain for slandering airline flight attendant when, after she rebuffed his sexual advances, captain told other co-workers that he had seen plaintiff engaged in lesbian activity with another flight attendant). For further discussion, see Chapter 15, The Common Law, Section VI.

[35]*See* Priest v. Rotary, 634 F. Supp. 571, 583, 40 FEP Cases 208, 216 (N.D. Cal. 1986)(defendant picked up plaintiff against her will and detained her and fondled her body). For further discussion, see Chapter 15, The Common Law, Section IV.

violation of Title VII or other antidiscrimination statutes in order to receive general tort damages.[36]

C. Remedies

If the complainant can establish the individual defendant's liability, the complainant may recover not only general damages for any resulting harm, but also, in appropriate cases, compensatory damages for pain and suffering and, upon a showing of malicious conduct, punitive or exemplary damages.[37] While the potential liability for these claims is significant, the practical limitation is that the individual defendant is unlikely to be able to respond to large damages awards. In most jurisdictions, the jury, in evaluating the amount of damages necessary to "punish" the defendant, will consider evidence of the individual's net worth.[38]

IV. Defenses of the Individual Defendant

A. Basic Defenses

If an individual defendant is a rank-and-file employee or a low-level supervisor, that individual defendant probably has the jurisdictional defense of not being an "agent" of an employer and hence not an employer subject to suit under Title VII.[39] If the alleged violation consists of a failure to prevent or remedy hostile environment harassment, the individual defendant may also have the defense of lacking any duty to discharge the employer's obligation to provide a workplace free of harassment.[40]

In a Title VII case the individual defendant may consider the further jurisdictional defense of not being named in the underlying charge of discrimination.[41] Courts have been reluctant to allow suits against supervisory personnel unnamed in an EEOC charge where full monetary relief is available from the employer and injunctive relief will bind incumbent supervisors.[42]

---

[36]*E.g.,* Clark v. World Airways, 24 FEP Cases 305 (D.D.C. 1980)(sexual harassment plaintiff awarded $52,000 in tort damages even though unsuccessful on Title VII claim). Indeed, the complainant need not sue the employer at all. *E.g.,* Schomer v. Smidt, *supra* note 34.

[37]*See* Valdez v. Church's Fried Chicken, 683 F. Supp. 596, 611, 47 FEP Cases 1155, 1162–63 (W.D. Tex. 1988)(punitive damages may be awarded in sexual harassment claim where malice found on part of defendant); Rogers v. Loews L'Enfant Plaza Hotel, *supra* note 32, 526 F. Supp. at 532, 29 FEP Cases at 836 (where plaintiff alleged sexual harassment under common-law tort theories, punitive damages recoverable when defendant engaged in outrageous conduct such as maliciousness, wantonness, gross fraud, recklessness and willful disregard for another's rights). For further discussion of punitive damages, see Chapter 29, Monetary Relief.

[38]*See generally* Bertero v. National Gen. Corp., 13 Cal.3d 43, 65, 118 Cal. Rptr. 184 (1975)("wealthier the wrongdoing defendant, the larger the award of exemplary damages need be"); Ferraro v. Pacific Fin. Corp., 8 Cal. App.3d 339, 349, 87 Cal. Rptr. 226 (1970)(jury invited to consider financial condition of defendant for purpose of determining appropriate punitive damages to be awarded plaintiff).

[39]*See* Section II.A. *supra.* See B.L. Schlei & P. Grossman, Employment Discrimination Law, Chapter 27, Sections IV and V (2d ed. 1983), Five-Year Supp. (1989).

[40]See text at notes 24–25 *supra.*

[41]For an extensive discussion of this issue, see Chapter 27, Asserted Defenses, Section II.C.; Schlei & Grossman, *supra* note 39, Chapter 30, Section II.

[42]White v. North La. Legal Assistance Corp., 468 F. Supp. 1347, 1349, 19 FEP Cases 307, 308–9 (W.D. La. 1979)(president of legal assistance organization could not be sued under Title VII where not named in charge, no notice, and no opportunity to participate in conciliation attempts); Pate v. Alameda-Contra Costa

Where the suit is by a federal employee, some courts have held that Title VII preempts any discrimination claim brought against individuals.[42a]

In addition, some courts have held that an individual "agent" of the employer may not be joined as a defendant unless the employer is also a named party to the litigation.[43]

Otherwise, the defense of the individual defendant will involve basically the same considerations as the defense of the employer.[44]

B. Indemnification

The individual defendant's limited ability to respond in damages will usually induce the complainant to attempt to hold the employer responsible for the individual defendant's acts. When an individual defendant is held liable for sexual harassment under one or more common-law tort theories, state law may require an employer to indemnify the individual defendant for losses incurred as the direct consequence of the individual defendant's discharge of employment duties, even though unlawful, unless the individual defendant, at the time of obeying the directions of the employer, believed the requested activity to be unlawful.[45]

Where the individual defendant is the alleged harasser, indemnity generally would not cover acts of sexual harassment that are not known to the employer, because there is ordinarily no duty to indemnify for losses arising from an unauthorized or negligent act.[46] Where the individual conduct was intentional and willful, one court has specifically ordered the employer not to indemnify the individual defendants for punitive damages.[47] Where an employer has an established policy prohibiting sexual harassment, indemnity for tort liability is highly unlikely.

Transit Dist., 21 FEP Cases 1228 (N.D. Cal. 1979)(personnel manager not "employer" within meaning of Title VII). *But see* Mills v. Fox, 421 F. Supp. 519, 13 FEP Cases 1009 (E.D.N.Y. 1976)(union president and district representative "agents" of "labor organization" and therefore could be named as defendants).

[42a]*See* Wood v. United States, 55 FEP Cases 1220, 1222 (D. Mass. 1991)(collecting conflicting cases on this point).

[43]Rogero v. Noone, 704 F.2d 518, 31 FEP Cases 969 (11th Cir. 1983)(county tax collector could not be sued as agent of county unless county also joined as party).

[44]For discussion of the defenses of qualified and official immunity in §1983 cases, see Chapter 11, Federal Constitutional Statutory, and Civil Rights Law, Section III.F. For a discussion of defenses generally, see Chapter 27, Asserted Defenses. For a discussion of the potential conflicts of interest that arise when the same attorney represents both the corporate employer and individual defendants, see Chapter 22, Employer's Litigation Strategy.

[45]*See, e.g.,* CAL. LAB. CODE §2802 (West 1991)(employer shall indemnify employee for "all that the employee necessarily expends or loses in direct consequence of the discharge of his duties as such, or of his obedience to the directions of the employer, even though unlawful, unless the employee, at the time of obeying such directions, believed them to be unlawful"); CAL. CORP. CODE §317 (West 1991)(providing for indemnification of officers, directors, and employees if they acted in good faith and in manner they reasonably believed to be in best interest of corporation).

[46]*See generally* Restatement (Second) of Agency §440(a) at 334 (1987)(principal not required to indemnify agent "for pecuniary loss or other harm, not of benefit to the principal, arising from performance of unauthorized acts or resulting solely from agent's negligence or other fault").

[47]*See* Kyriazi v. Western Elec. Co., 476 F. Supp. 335, 341, 26 FEP Cases 413, 418 (D.N.J. 1979)(court ordered employer could not indemnify employees for individual assessments of $1,500 in punitive damages because that would "entirely circumvent" purpose of punitive damages, which were awarded to punish despicable conduct).

C. Contribution

Pro rata contributions may be required among several individual defendants when the facts show joint participation in the harassment.[48] Where a complainant brings a Title VII action against the employer or the individual, but not both, the unsuccessful defendant has no right to contribution or indemnity against a party who could have been a defendant in the original action but was not joined.[49] Thus, if the complainant names only the employer, and the employer determines that liability should lie, if at all, with the alleged harasser, then the employer might consider joining the alleged harasser as a defendant and filing cross claims against him.[50] A cross claim of this sort is unlikely unless the employer determines that the liability of the alleged harasser is quite certain.

V. Insurance Coverage for the Individual Defendant

A. The Employer's Coverage

Most employer liability insurance policies cover the acts of employees only when they occur within the course and scope of the employee's employment.[51] Unauthorized acts of sexual harassment do not fall within the boundaries of liability coverage.[52] Harm caused by the willful act of an insured's employee may by definition be excluded from coverage where the policy expressly covers only the negligence of the insured.[53] Thus, under the language of most employer liability policies, an employer's insurance would not cover an individual employee's intentional acts of harassment.[54]

An employer's liability policy coverage normally excludes harm that occurs away from the employer's business premises; it may be operative only with respect to employees who are injured on the premises of the employer or at other places specified in the policy.[55] Absent a state statute that invalidates such an exclusion, where the alleged harassment does not occur at the workplace,

---

[48]*See, e.g.,* Hartford Accident & Indem. Co. v. R. Herschel Mfg. Co., 453 F. Supp. 1375, 1379 (D.N.D. 1978) (contribution is remedy securing right of one who has discharged more than his fair share of common liability or burden to recover from another who is also liable for proportionate share that other should pay or bear, based on principles of equity).

[49]*See* Northwest Airlines v. Transport Workers Union, 451 U.S. 77, 25 FEP Cases 737 (1981)(no right of contribution for Title VII claims).

[50]*See* Schlei & Grossman, *supra* note 39, at 647–51 (discussing cross claims between employer and union defendants in Title VII cases).

[51]*See* O'Connor v. McDonald's Restaurants of Cal., 220 Cal. App.3d 25, 29, 269 Cal. Rptr. 101 (1990)(master liable where servant acts in course of employment, not on "frolic of his own").

[52]Pryor v. United States Gypsum Co., 585 F. Supp. 311, 314–15, 47 FEP Cases 159, 162–63 (W.D. Mo. 1984)(claim of sex-based harassment based on purely personal and private quarrels did not arise out of course of employment); Murphy v. ARA Servs., 164 Ga. App. 859, 50 FEP Cases 572 (1982)(sexual assault did not arise in course of employment because alleged conduct not directed against plaintiff in furtherance of supervisor's duties of employment, but because of abusive personal reasons).

[53]G. Couch, Couch on Insurance §44:276 at 429 (2d ed. 1982).

[54]*See generally* Skinner v. Papania's, 425 So.2d 318 (La. App. 1982)(employer's insurance policy did not cover liability for injuries sustained in fight with co-employee since policy contained assault and battery exclusion); City of Newark v. Hartford Accident & Indem. Co., 134 N.J. Super. 537, 342 A.2d 513 (1975)(city's liability policy covered claim of false arrest, malicious prosecution, and assault and battery arising out of arrest, but coverage not extended to extortion claim arising out of acts of police officers).

[55]G. Couch, *supra* note 53, §44:170 at 324.

coverage under the employer's policy for injury to the employee may be denied on that ground.

The duty of an insurer to defend its insured, however, is broader than the duty to indemnify. An insurer ordinarily must provide a defense when there is any claim, and sometimes where there is a potential but currently unpleaded claim, that may seek damages within the applicable policy.[56] This obligation is based upon the potential for coverage under the policy created not only by the allegations in the complaint, but also by facts learned from any source.[57] Accordingly, an employer's insurer may be required to provide the defense for the individual defendant in a sexual harassment case if there is any possibility that the employer will be vicariously liable for that individual's acts.

B. The Individual Defendant's Coverage

It is unlikely that individual defendants would receive liability coverage under the individuals' own insurance, for almost no individual carries general liability insurance. Even under an "all risk" homeowners policy, which many individuals do purchase, a loss due to liability for sexual harassment is unlikely to be covered. State statutes generally provide that insurance cannot cover willful torts.[58] In cases of alleged sexual molestation, therefore, insurance coverage will not extend even to cases of accidental harm, for the willful-torts exemption is based upon the intent to do the act that causes the damage, rather than whether there was an intent to cause the damage itself.[59] Thus, where a homeowners' policy excludes losses expected or intended by the insured, the insurer has no duty either to provide the defense or to cover liability for sexual harassment or molestation.[60]

Furthermore, homeowners' coverage ordinarily would not apply where the loss occurred away from the covered property.[61]

---

[56]*See* Gray v. Zurich Ins. Co., 65 Cal.2d 263, 276, 54 Cal. Rptr. 104 (1966)(insurer must defend suit that *potentially* seeks damages within coverage of policy).

[57]*See* CNA Casualty v. Seaboard Sur. Co., 176 Cal. App.3d 598, 610, 222 Cal. Rptr. 276 (1986)(facts alleged and learned—rather than denomination of plaintiff's complaint—create duty to defend).

[58]*See, e.g.,* CAL. INS. CODE §533 (West 1991)(prohibiting insurance coverage for willful acts); CAL. CIV. CODE §1668 (West 1991)(contract exempting one from responsibility for willful injury unlawful).

[59]*See* Morton v. Safeco Ins. Co., 905 F.2d 1208, 1211 (9th Cir. 1990)(inference of specific intent to injure from fact of sexual misconduct may not be overcome by evidence of lack of subjective attempt to harm); United States Fidelity & Guar. Co. v. American Employers' Ins. Co., 159 Cal. App.3d 277, 284, 205 Cal. Rptr. 460 (1984)(same).

[60]*See* State Farm Fire & Casualty Co. v. Estate of Jenner, 874 F.2d 604, 607 (9th Cir. 1989)(insured's acts of sexual molestation fall within homeowners' policy exclusion for bodily injury expected or intended by the insured); State Farm Fire & Casualty Co. v. Robin R., 216 Cal. App.3d 132, 137, 264 Cal. Rptr. 326 (1989)(clause in homeowners' policy expressly excluding losses expected or intended by insured relieved insurer of any duty to defend civil action for sexual molestation); Allstate Ins. Co. v. Kim W., 160 Cal. App.3d 326, 333, 206 Cal. Rptr. 609 (1984)(homeowners' policy provides no coverage for sexual assaults). *But see* MacKinnon v. Hanover Ins. Co., 124 N.H. 456, 471 A.2d 1166 (1984)(exclusion for "bodily injury . . . intended by the insured" refers to actual intent of insured regarding bodily injury, not intent regarding insured's actions; implying homeowner's policy could cover claim of sexual assault, especially where insured was intoxicated at time).

[61]*See* G. COUCH, *supra* note 53, §42:3 at 149. A homeowner's policy almost invariably describes the covered premises as the insured's residence. Although the alleged conduct in a sexual harassment case sometimes does occur at the individual defendant's home, that event is rare.

CHAPTER 24

THE ALLEGED HARASSER AS PLAINTIFF

I. OVERVIEW

An employer's prompt remedial action to prevent sexual harassment will often include the discharge or other significant discipline of alleged harassers. Because of the serious nature of any allegation of sexual harassment, an employee dismissed for sexual harassment may suffer not only the obvious economic harm attending a discharge, but a loss of reputation within the company, the community, and the industry in which the employee works.

Alleged harassers who feel that they have been unjustly accused or unfairly treated during the investigation or disciplinary process have sued their employers on two basic claims: that the employer's discipline was improper, and that the alleged harasser was defamed during the investigation or thereafter.

II. CHALLENGES TO DISCIPLINE FOR SEXUAL HARASSMENT

Those accused of sexual harassment have challenged disciplinary actions taken against them under several different legal theories: (A) they have sued their employers for common-law claims of breach of public policy, breach of contract, intentional infliction of emotional distress, and have sued co-workers or subcontractors for interference with contractual relationships; (B) they have claimed that charges of sexual harassment were used as a pretext for unlawful discrimination; and (C) government employees have claimed that they were denied procedural due process or that the merits of their cases did not justify the action taken. Other challenges have asserted that the discipline was improper under a collective bargaining agreement.[1]

A. Common-Law Claims

1. Breach of Public Policy

Alleged harassers have not succeeded in challenging discipline for sexual harassment as a breach of public policy.[2] At-will employees generally may be

---

[1]Arbitration decisions are discussed separately in Chapter 17, Collective Bargaining Agreements and Union Obligations.

[2]*E.g.*, Patton v. J.C. Penney Co., 301 Or. 117, 719 P.2d 854, 122 LRRM 2445 (1986)(employee failed to state tort claim for wrongful discharge where employee had been discharged for fraternizing with co-worker); Willis v. Ideal Basic Indus., 484 So.2d 444 (Ala. 1986)(employer's decision to discharge alleged

discharged for any reason not forbidden by statute. An at-will employee will find it difficult to prove the existence of a public policy against discharging an employee alleged to have committed acts of sexual harassment.[3]

2. Breach of Contract

To maintain a breach of contract action, the alleged harasser must demonstrate, first, a contract of employment that restricted the employer's right to discipline the harasser[4] and second, that the discipline was a breach of that contract.[5]

In *Martin v. Baer*,[5a] a supervisor for General Motors (GM), whom two women employees accused of sexual harassment, sued GM after its investigation of the accusations produced insufficient evidence either to confirm the accusations or to find the supervisor innocent of harassment. The supervisor claimed that GM had damaged him by failing to follow its own policy against sexual harassment, which advised the personnel department to conduct a "complete investigation." The Eleventh Circuit, affirming a summary judgment, rejected the supervisor's argument that the policy created an implied contractual duty to protect him as the person accused of sexual harassment.[5b] The court concluded that any contractual duty to be inferred from such a policy runs to victims of sexual harassment, not to those accused of it.[5c]

When a contract specifies the grounds for dismissal, its terms must be considered.[6] If the contract requires cause for dismissal, the alleged harasser may emphasize mitigating circumstances, such as his prior work and disciplinary record, and any evidence that management may have condoned or contributed to the sexual harassment.[7]

Sexual harassment may qualify as good cause for dismissal wherever "good cause" is the standard[7a] and even as "misconduct" or "gross conduct"

---

sexual harasser does not fall within public policy exception to employment-at-will doctrine, therefore employee failed to state claim for wrongful discharge).

[3]Willis v. Ideal Basic Indus., *supra* note 2 (employer not liable for discharge of alleged sexual harasser where there was at-will employment contract).

[4]*Cf.* Willis v. Ideal Basic Indus., *supra* note 2 (at-will employee failed to state cause of action for wrongful discharge); Johnson v. International Minerals & Chem. Corp., 122 LRRM 2652, 2654, 40 FEP Cases 1651, 1654 (D.S.D. 1986)(absent express representations concerning duration of employment or other material contract terms, there was no contract in existence that employer could breach).

[5]Anderson v. Hewlett-Packard Corp., 694 F. Supp. 1294, 47 FEP Cases 1009 (N.D. Ohio 1988)(discharge proper where supervisor sexually harassed female subordinates, conditioning employment on submission to sexual advances; court therefore need not address supervisor's breach-of-contract claim).

[5a]928 F.2d 1067 (11th Cir. 1991)(Fay, Johnson & Peck, JJ.).

[5b]*Id.* at 1072 (finding plaintiff's argument an "attenuated and unwarranted stretch of the language of GM's sexual harassment policy.")

[5c]*Id.*

[6]*See, e.g.,* Jones v. Intermountain Power Project, 794 F.2d 546, 41 FEP Cases 1 (10th Cir. 1986)(manager who sexually harassed female employees prevailed on breach-of-contract claim when he demonstrated that employment contract was intended to continue until completion of a particular project).

[7]*See generally* Jennings & Clapp, *A Managerial Tightrope: Balancing Harassed and Harassing Employees' Rights in Sexual Discrimination Cases,* 40 LAB. L.J. 756, 762 (1989).

[7a]*See, e.g.,* Westinghouse Elec. Corp., 120 LRRM 1295 (1985)(NLRB reversed administrative law judge and approved employer's discharge of employee accused of sexual harassment); Hostetter v. United States, 739 F.2d 983, 35 FEP Cases 693 (4th Cir. 1984)(affirming dismissal of civilian Air Force employee that was "supported by substantial evidence"); Rivera v. Division of Empl. Sec., 34 FEP Cases 894 (La. Civ. Dist. Ct. 1984)(alleged harasser properly denied unemployment compensation where facts established that employee was terminated for harassment); French v. Mead Corp., 33 FEP Cases 635 (S.D. Ohio 1983)(rejecting white male supervisor's Title VII action where facts established that supervisor was discharged for

that would justify discharge under the terms of a written employment contract.[7b]

A key issue in any case alleging breach of contract or breach of the implied covenant of good faith and fair dealing will be the adequacy of the defendant's investigation.[8] In *Johnson v. International Minerals & Chemical Corp.,*[9] three supervisors allegedly forcibly kissed and fondled the complainants, pinched their breasts, and made lewd remarks.[10] After the complainants filed administrative charges, the employer settled their claims, then independently investigated the allegations and discharged the alleged harassers.[11] In denying the alleged harassers' claim for wrongful discharge and breach of the implied covenant of good faith and fair dealing, the court held that the employer "acted in good faith when it conducted a thorough investigation of the sexual harassment and sexual discrimination charges against plaintiffs prior to making a final decision to discharge them."[12]

3. Intentional Infliction of Emotional Distress

Jurisdictions that recognize a claim for intentional infliction of emotional distress[13] generally follow the Restatement (Second) of Torts §46: "One who by extreme and outrageous conduct intentionally or recklessly causes severe emotional distress to another is subject to liability for such emotional distress, and if bodily harm to the other results from it, for such bodily harm."[14] Those employees who are disciplined for sexual harassment have understandable difficulty establishing that the discipline constitutes "extreme and outrageous conduct."[15]

---

sexually harassing female subordinates), *aff'd,* 758 F.2d 652, 37 FEP Cases 1408 (6th Cir. 1985), *cert. denied,* 474 U.S. 820; *In re* Chapter 13, 19 Bankr. 713, 33 FEP Cases 1871 (W.D. Wash. 1982)(bankruptcy trustee properly removed where evidence showed he was sexually harassing employees).

[7b]Scherer v. Rockwell Int'l, 56 FEP Cases 215, 219–21 (N.D. Ill. 1991)(rejecting contract claims of company executive discharged for sexual harassment for "misconduct" under written employment agreement).

[8]For a discussion of investigating sexual harassment complaints, see Chapter 19, Responding to Internal Complaints.

[9]*Supra* note 4.

[10]*Id.* at 1652.

[11]*Id.* at 1652–53.

[12]*Id.* at 1653. *See also* Scherer v. Rockwell Int'l, *supra* note 7b, 56 FEP Cases at 222 (employer could discharge employee without proving misconduct by a preponderance of evidence so long as employer made good faith determination, even if employer was also motivated by desire to terminate expensive employment contract).

[13]Johnson v. International Minerals & Chem. Corp., *supra* note 4, 122 LRRM at 2655, 40 FEP Cases at 1654 (questioning whether Wyoming law recognizes claim).

[14]Patton v. J.C. Penney Co., *supra* note 2, 301 Or. at 122, 719 P.2d at 857 (elements of emotional distress claim are (1) intent to inflict severe mental or emotional distress, intent beyond the intent to act in a way that causes such distress; (2) actual causation of severe mental or emotional distress; and (3) conduct that is outrageous, that exceeds any reasonable limit of social toleration). In *Patton,* a male managerial employee terminated for fraternizing with a female co-worker failed to state a claim for emotional distress; employer's actions did not constitute extreme and outrageous conduct. For a discussion of a complainant's charge of emotional distress, see Chapter 15, The Common Law.

[15]Martin v. Baer, *supra* note 5a (not outrageous but merely negligent at most for employer to fail to investigate as fully as plaintiff claimed it should have); Johnson v. International Minerals & Chem. Corp., *supra* note 4 (no outrageous conduct when employee was terminated for engaging in sexual harassment); Patton v. J.C. Penney Co., *supra* note 2 (no outrageous conduct).

4. Intentional Interference With Contract

Alleged harassers have sued third parties, such as co-workers or subcontractors, for intentional interference with economic relations.[16] In *Jones v. Intermountain Power Project*,[17] the alleged harasser sued representatives of a construction firm who recommended to his engineering firm that he be discharged for sexual harassment. In *Jordan v. Hudson*,[18] the alleged harasser sued co-workers who complained of sexual harassment. In both cases, the court held that the third parties' actions were privileged.

B. Discrimination

Employees have challenged disciplinary actions taken for sexual harassment by arguing that it was a pretext for discrimination forbidden by an employment discrimination statute. These claims have included allegations of discrimination on the basis of race,[19] age,[20] gender,[21] ethnicity,[22] and religion.[23] An employee has also claimed, without success, that he suffered unlawful retaliation when his employer fired him after he retained a lawyer to contest a written reprimand for sexual harassment.[23a]

The success of a discrimination claim generally will depend on whether the employer can substantiate the allegations of sexual harassment,[24] and whether other similarly situated employees who engaged in similar conduct were subject

---

[16]The elements of this tort generally require the plaintiff to prove (1) that the defendant intentionally interfered with the plaintiff's existing or potential economic relations, (2) for an improper purpose or by improper means, (3) causing injury to the plaintiff, and (4) without privilege to do so. *See, e.g.*, Jones v. Intermountain Power Project, *supra* note 6, 794 F.2d at 554, 41 FEP Cases at 6.

[17]*Id.*

[18]690 F. Supp. 502, 47 FEP Cases 583 (E.D. Va. 1988), *aff'd*, 879 F.2d 98, 50 FEP Cases 813 (4th Cir. 1989).

[19]Bush v. Metropolitan Transit Auth., 54 EPD ¶40,182 (D. Kan. 1989)(granting summary judgment against black bus driver accused of sexually harassing five co-workers; no evidence to show defendant's reliance on pattern of sexual harassment was pretext for race discrimination); Baker v. McDonald's Corp., 686 F. Supp. 1474, 45 FEP Cases 1505 (S.D. Fla. 1987)(Title VII and Civil Rights Act claims), *aff'd*, 865 F.2d 1272 (11th Cir. 1988), *cert. denied*, 110 S. Ct. 57 (1989); Jackson v. City of Albuquerque, 890 F.2d 225, 51 FEP Cases 669 (10th Cir. 1989)(42 U.S.C. §§1981, 1983, U.S. Const. Amend. XIV); Marsh v. Digital Equip. Corp., 675 F. Supp. 1186, 44 FEP Cases 1192 (D. Ariz. 1987)(black employee fired for sexually harassing white women awarded damages for race discrimination where white men charged with more serious conduct not fired).

[20]Johnson v. Perkins Restaurants, 815 F.2d 1220, 43 FEP Cases 830 (8th Cir. 1987)(ADEA); Crimm v. Missouri Pac. R.R., 750 F.2d 703, 36 FEP Cases 883 (8th Cir. 1984)(ADEA).

[21]Baker v. McDonald's Corp., *supra* note 19; French v. Mead Corp., 33 FEP Cases 635 (S.D. Ohio 1983)(Title VII); Jackson v. St. Joseph's State Hosp., 840 F.2d 1387, 47 FEP Cases 1580 (8th Cir. 1988)(Title VII), *cert. denied*, 488 U.S. 892 (1988); Crawford v. Charlotte-Mecklenburg Bd. of Educ., 641 F. Supp. 571, 41 FEP Cases 1100 (W.D.N.C. 1986)(Title VII); Erickson v. Marsh & McLennan Co., 117 N.J. 539, 569 A.2d 793, 55 FEP Cases 1179 (1990)(male plaintiff had no sex discrimination claim under state fair employment practices statute when superior fired him to promote superior's girlfriend).

[22]Valdez v. Church's Fried Chicken, 683 F. Supp. 596, 47 FEP Cases 1155 (W.D. Tex. 1988)(Title VII).

[23]Levitt v. University of Tex., 847 F.2d 221, 47 FEP Cases 90 (5th Cir.)(Title VII), *cert. denied*, 488 U.S. 984 (1988).

[23a]Erickson v. Marsh & McLennan Co., *supra* note 21, 55 FEP Cases at 1186–87 (no retaliation under New Jersey FEP statute to fire alleged harasser for opposing discipline).

[24]*See* Baker v. McDonald's Corp., *supra* note 19, 686 F. Supp. at 1477–78, 45 FEP Cases at 1508–10 (discharge appropriate where employer's investigation resulted in numerous affidavits from victims of alleged harasser, and alleged harasser admitted that certain incidents had occurred).

to similar discipline.[25] In *Coen v. Elco Chevrolet*,[25a] the plaintiff failed to state a claim of sex discrimination with his allegation that he was fired, without a fair investigation of the sexual harassment charge against him, because the employer was afraid that otherwise it would be sued by the woman who had accused him of sexual harassment. Judge Edward L. Philippine reasoned that while the plaintiff might have other grounds for contesting his discharge, he had not pleaded facts to indicate that he was discharged because of his gender.[25b]

At least one court has rejected a claim that a person who is disciplined for sexual harassment has suffered handicap discrimination.[26]

C. Claims by Government Employees

Government employees disciplined for sexual harassment may assert violation of procedural due process.[27] In *Huff v. County of Butler*,[28] a federal district court held that an employee who was forced to resign amid allegations of sexual harassment and was not provided a hearing stated a claim for deprivation of liberty without due process,[29] even though the employee had no property interest in his at-will employment contract.[30]

A property interest was involved, however, where the alleged harasser was discharged during a one-year employment contract.[31] The Ninth Circuit held that a midterm contract termination, without a prior hearing, deprived the employee of both property and liberty interests without due process.[32]

Federal employees subject to civil service protection may challenge discipline for sexual harassment through the Merit Systems Protection Board.[33] On

---

[25]Jackson v. City of Albuquerque, *supra* note 19 (discharge overturned where evidence demonstrated that Hispanic employee who engaged in alleged sexual harassment was treated differently than black employee); *compare* Valdez v. Church's Fried Chicken, *supra* note 22 (facts supported inference that alleged harasser was singled out because of national origin, when other employees accused of sexual harassment not treated similarly and plaintiff's discharge violated employer's de facto policy of tolerating sexual harassment) *and* Marsh v. Digital Equip. Corp., *supra* note 19 *with* Baker v. McDonald's Corp., *supra* note 19 (black plaintiff failed to prove that two white male supervisors had sexually harassed female employees but had not been discharged).

[25a]756 F. Supp. 414, 54 FEP Cases 1358 (E.D. Mo. 1991).

[25b]*Id.* at 415, 54 FEP Cases at 1359.

[26]Blanton v. AT&T Comm., 52 FEP Cases 19 (D. Mass. 1990)(black employee dismissed for sexually harassing white females unsuccessfully argued that employer "should have recognized that this conduct constituted an aberration from his normal behavior and qualified him as a handicapped person"; no analysis needed to determine that "person who sexually harasses other persons is not handicapped"). *See generally* Americans with Disabilities Act of 1990, §511, 42 U.S.C. §12211 (exempting from definition of disabilities protected from discrimination such conditions or activities as pedophilia, homosexuality, bisexuality, transvestism).

[27]For a discussion of constitutional bases on which an employee may challenge the actions of a government employer, see Chapter 11, Federal Constitutional, Statutory, and Civil Rights Law. Private employers are generally immune from constitutional restrictions. Hurst v. Farmer, 40 Wash. App. 116, 697 P.2d 280 (1985).

[28]524 F. Supp. 751, 27 FEP Cases 63 (W.D. Pa. 1981).

[29]*Id.* at 753–54, 27 FEP Cases at 64–66.

[30]*Id.* at 753, 27 FEP Cases at 64. For discussion of a due process claim by an employee complaining of sexual harassment, see Chapter 11, Federal Constitutional, Statutory, and Civil Rights Law.

[31]Vanelli v. Reynolds School Dist., 667 F.2d 773 (9th Cir. 1982).

[32]*Id.* at 779.

[33]*See, e.g.,* Howard v. Department of Air Force, 877 F.2d 952, 50 FEP Cases 939 (Fed. Cir. 1989)(removal appropriate); Carosella v. United States Postal Serv., 816 F.2d 638, 43 FEP Cases 845 (Fed. Cir.

appeals from Merit Systems Protection Board decisions, courts reviewing disciplinary action have considered the credibility of the witnesses, the degree of proof of the alleged harassment, the frequency and nature of the alleged harassment, mitigating circumstances such as the alleged harasser's prior work record, and due process or procedural issues.

Some courts apparently feel that sexual harassment involving physical contact warrants greater discipline than mere verbal harassment.[34] Repeated incidents of harassment have justified greater discipline than isolated occurrences. The Federal Circuit has stated that "[w]hen disciplining an employee for sexually harassing conduct, the government must prove, at a minimum, that the conduct is 'sufficiently severe or pervasive' to 'create an abusive working environment.' "[35] In *Downes v. Federal Aviation Administration*,[36] the Federal Circuit overturned a demotion and reassignment even though the alleged harasser had made potentially offensive sexual remarks. The court ordered his reinstatement because the alleged harasser had never used the complainant's response to his requests for sexual favors as the basis for employment decisions affecting the complainant, the incidents were isolated and trivial, and he had touched the complainant only once, and then in a nonsexual manner.[37]

The Federal Circuit has also stated, however, that "[a]n employer is not required to tolerate the disruption and inefficiencies caused by a hostile workplace environment until the wrongdoer has so clearly violated the law that the victims are sure to prevail in a Title VII action."[38]

The discipline is more likely to be upheld if there are witnesses to the alleged harassment, or if more than one complainant has been involved.[39] Courts will also consider whether the information upon which the employer based the disciplinary action was based on firsthand knowledge, attributed hearsay, rumors, or gossip.[40] Other factors considered by courts include any

---

1987)(same); Downes v. Federal Aviation Admin., 775 F.2d 288, 39 FEP Cases 70 (Fed. Cir. 1985)(demotion and reassignment overturned); Jackson v. Veterans Admin., 768 F.2d 1325, 39 FEP Cases 100 (Fed. Cir. 1985)(penalty of removal was excessive); Snipes v. United States Postal Serv., 677 F.2d 375, 30 FEP Cases 1257 (4th Cir. 1982)(discharge affirmed). *See also* Hostetter v. United States, 739 F.2d 983, 35 FEP Cases 693 (4th Cir. 1984)(reinstatement denied); Petties v. New York State Dep't of Mental Retardation, 93 A.D.2d 960, 463 N.Y.S.2d 284, 31 FEP Cases 1164 (App. Div. 1983)(discharge appropriate).

[34]Carosella v. United States Postal Serv., *supra* note 33 (discharge justified when supervisor touched employees offensively and repeatedly asked them for dates); Hostetter v. United States, *supra* note 33 (discharge justified when supervisor repeatedly touched employees offensively and made sexual remarks).

[35]Howard v. Department of Air Force, *supra* note 33, 877 F.2d at 956 (quoting Carosella v. United States Postal Serv., *supra* note 33). *See also* Jackson v. Veterans Admin., *supra* note 33 (court evaluates MSPB decisions under "substantial evidence" standard).

[36]775 F.2d 288, 39 FEP Cases 70 (Fed. Cir. 1985).

[37]*See also* Jackson v. Veterans Admin., *supra* note 33 (when supervisor repeatedly asked for but never required nor received kiss from employee, discharge not justified but some lesser discipline appropriate).

[38]Carosella v. United States Postal Serv., *supra* note 33, 816 F.2d at 643. By contrast, in *Downes, supra* note 33, the court held that when an employer disciplines an employee for alleged sexual harassment, the employer must be held to the same standard the complainant would face in bringing such a claim.

[39]*Compare* Carosella v. United States Postal Serv., *supra* note 33 (six different victims) *with* Jackson v. Veterans Admin., *supra* note 33 (one victim) *and* Downes v. Federal Aviation Admin., *supra* note 33 (one victim).

[40]*See, e.g.,* Kestenbaum v. Pennzoil Co., 766 P.2d 280, 288 (N.M. 1988), *cert. denied*, 109 S.Ct. 3163 (1989)(employee fired for sexually harassing co-workers awarded damages on ground that employer did not have reasonable grounds to believe good reason existed to justify termination because it was based on investigative report that failed to differentiate "between firsthand knowledge, attributed hearsay, or mere gossip or rumor").

motive a witness has to lie or embellish[41] and the credibility of all persons whose information was considered in deciding upon the disciplinary action.[42]

III. Defamation

A. Elements of a Claim

Those accused of sexual harassment have sued their employers and co-workers for libel and slander on the basis of defamatory statements made during the investigation of the alleged harassment or as a result of the discipline imposed on the alleged harasser.[43] Defamation consists of:

(a) a false and defamatory statement concerning another;
(b) an unprivileged publication to a third party;
(c) fault amounting to at least negligence on the part of the publisher; and
(d) either actionability of the statement irrespective of special harm or the existence of special harm caused by the publication.[44]

Allegations of offensive sexual conduct sufficient to warrant discipline often will constitute a prima facie case of defamation.[45] However, the Eighth Circuit has narrowly defined "publication to a third party" to exclude intracorporate communications among corporate officers.[46]

B. Defenses

1. Truth

True statements are not actionable.[47] Historically, the truth of a statement has been accepted as an affirmative defense of justification in civil defamation cases[48] and, therefore, must be pleaded by the defendant as such. Eleven states have provided, by constitutional or statutory provision or by judicial decision,

---

[41]*See, e.g.,* Martin v. Norbar, Inc., 537 F. Supp. 1260, 1262, 30 FEP Cases 103, 104 (S.D. Ohio 1982)(employer may not assert that it could not determine truthfulness of allegations of harassment if there was reasonable basis to believe one person over another based on motives of parties to lie, or alleged harasser's reputation for sexually harassing women).

[42]*See, e.g.,* Kestenbaum v. Pennzoil Co., *supra* note 40 (investigation inadequate if it fails to assess credibility of those interviewed).

[43]*See, e.g.,* Garziano v. E.I. du Pont de Nemours & Co., 818 F.2d 380, 43 FEP Cases 1790 (5th Cir. 1987)(recognizing cause of action and discussing qualified privilege); Stockley v. AT&T Information Sys., 687 F. Supp. 764, 47 FEP Cases 28 (E.D.N.Y. 1988)(same); Barnes v. Oody, 514 F. Supp. 23, 28 FEP Cases 816 (E.D. Tenn. 1981) (recognizing cause of action and discussing absolute privilege); Corporon v. Safeway Stores, 708 P.2d 1385 (Colo. Ct. App. 1985)(recognizing that discharged employee could state claim for defamation, but not elaborating on merits of claim or whether privilege applied); Hurst v. Farmer, *supra* note 27 (discussing absolute privilege). For a discussion of the risks of defamation an employer runs in investigating sexual harassment complaints and in taking remedial action, see Chapter 19, Responding to Internal Complaints.

[44]Restatement (Second) of Torts §558 (1977).

[45]*Id.* at §574, comment; Scherer v. Rockwell Int'l, 56 FEP Cases 215, 224 (N.D. Ill. 1991)(accusations of sexual harassment on the job so obviously impugn integrity in discharge of job duties that such accusations constitute defamation per se).

[46]In *Halsell v. Kimberly-Clark Corp.,* 683 F.2d 285, 288–89, 29 FEP Cases 1185, 1187 (8th Cir. 1982), *cert. denied,* 459 U.S. 1205 (1983), the Eighth Circuit, applying Wisconsin law, held that written communications "between officers of a corporation or between different branches of the same corporation, in the course of corporate business, do not constitute publications to third parties."

[47]Restatement (Second) of Torts §581A (1977); Barnes v. Oody, *supra* note 43, 514 F. Supp. at 25, 28 FEP Cases at 818 (where complainant's statements were true, harasser had no basis for defamation claim).

[48]W.P. Keeton, D. Dobbs, R. Keeton & D. Owen, Prosser & Keeton on Torts, §116 at 840 (5th ed. 1984).

that truth in itself is not a defense to defamation where the statement has been published for malicious reasons or for unjustifiable ends.[49]

2. Qualified Privilege

Some defamatory statements, even though protected by a qualified privilege, are actionable if the privilege has been abused.[50] A qualified privilege applies where the circumstances lead to a reasonable belief that (1) the information affects an important interest of the publisher and the recipient's knowledge of the information protects that interest;[51] (2) the information affects an interest of the recipient or a third party, and the recipient is one to whom the publisher is under a legal duty to publish the defamatory matter or is a person to whom its publication is within generally accepted standards of decent conduct;[52] or (3) another person sharing the common interest is entitled to know the information.[53]

Nonetheless, statements subject to a qualified privilege may be actionable if the qualified privilege has been abused (1) because of the publisher's knowledge or reckless disregard as to the falsity of the defamatory statement;[54] (2) because the statement was published for a purpose other than the one that the privilege was designed to protect;[55] (3) because of excessive publication, *i.e.,* publishing the statement to persons other than those whose receipt of the statement would be privileged;[56] or (4) because the publisher did not reasonably believe the publication was necessary to accomplish the purpose of the privilege.[57] Further, statements "actuated by express malice or actual ill-will"[58] are not immunized from liability. Accordingly, persons accused of sexual misconduct may maintain defamation actions on the basis of defamatory statements where a proper purpose for the publication was not shown.[59]

In *Garziano v. E.I. du Pont de Nemours & Co.,*[60] the plaintiff was dismissed for sexually harassing a co-worker. In response to questions from employees, the employer issued a "Sexual Harassment" bulletin, which stated that an employee (not identified) had been discharged for deliberate, repeated,

---

[49]*Id.* at 841.
[50]Restatement (Second) of Torts §593 (1977).
[51]*Id.* at §594.
[52]*Id.* at §595.
[53]*Id.* at §596.
[54]*Id.* at §600.
[55]*Id.* at §603.
[56]*Id.* at §604.
[57]*Id.* at §605.
[58]Stockley v. AT&T Information Sys., *supra* note 43, 687 F. Supp. at 770, 47 FEP Cases at 34–35 (plaintiff failed to present evidence of malice).
[59]*Compare* Babb v. Minder, 806 F.2d 749, 756 (7th Cir. 1986)(defendant manager's accusations that plaintiff had "mooned" one employee and offered sexual favors to another, although conditionally privileged, were made with reckless disregard of truth or falsity of those statements and facts supported jury's finding of actual malice overcoming manager's qualified privilege under Illinois law) *with* Stockley v. AT&T Information Sys., *supra* note 43, 687 F. Supp. at 768–70, 47 FEP Cases at 32–34 (statements by defendant's employees in course of investigation into sexual harassment charges against plaintiff were protected by qualified privilege where defendant had duty to investigate charges and allegedly defamatory statements were made to persons responsible for carrying out such duty) *and* DiSilva v. Polaroid Corp., 45 FEP Cases 639, 642–43 (Mass. Dist. Ct. 1985)(employer had qualified privilege under common law and Title VII to repeat to management allegations of female employee that plaintiff, an alleged harasser, had made obscene telephone calls to her home).
[60]818 F.2d 380, 43 FEP Cases 1790 (5th Cir. 1987)(Garza, Williams & Gerwood, JJ.).

and unsolicited physical contact and for significant verbal abuse. The bulletin also quoted definitions of sexual harassment from the EEOC Guidelines. The bulletin went to all supervisors, with instructions that they discuss key points in the bulletin with employees. The Fifth Circuit, applying Mississippi law, reversed the jury's $93,000 verdict for defamation. Judge Reynaldo G. Garza held that a qualified privilege protected the statements in the bulletin:

> A communication made in good faith and on a subject matter in which the person making it has an interest, or in reference to which he has a duty, is privileged if made to a person or persons having a corresponding interest or duty, even though it contains a matter which without this privilege would be slanderous, provided the statement is made without malice and in good faith.[61]

According to the court, the bulletin fell within the qualified privilege because, in issuing the bulletin, the employer believed it was complying with its legal duty to protect workers from sexual harassment.[62]

The *Garziano* court noted that the employer could have abused the privilege by making statements beyond those necessary to protect its interest, or by excessive publication. Because the bulletin did not describe the incident in detail and limited the language in the bulletin to the EEOC definition of harassment,[63] the court held that the statement did not go beyond what was necessary to protect the employer's interest. While the Fifth Circuit remanded the case to determine whether the employer had abused the privilege by excessive publication, it noted that the employer's distribution of the bulletin to supervisors, rather than posting or generally distributing it, was a most restrictive means of communication and reasonable as a matter of law. So long as the supervisors did not discuss the contents of the bulletin with anyone other than employees and limited their discussion to the information contained in the bulletin, the privilege was not abused even if the employees subsequently discussed the bulletin with nonemployees.[64]

3. Absolute Privilege

In *Hurst v. Farmer*,[65] an employee discharged for sexual harassment brought defamation claims against co-workers who testified against him during administrative agency proceedings. The court held that statements made during administrative agency proceedings are absolutely privileged and cannot support a defamation action.

4. Official Immunity

An absolute privilege to defame applies to federal officials with discretionary responsibilities and protects them from civil liability for statements made within the scope of their duties.[66]

---

[61]*Id.* at 385, 43 FEP Cases at 1794 (citation omitted).
[62]*Id.* at 387–88, 43 FEP Cases at 1797.
[63]The bulletin is reprinted as an appendix to the court's decision.
[64]*Supra* note 60, 818 F.2d at 393–95, 43 FEP Cases at 1802–03.
[65]40 Wash. App. 116, 697 P.2d 280 (1985).
[66]Barnes v. Oody, 514 F. Supp. 23, 25, 28 FEP Cases 816, 818 (E.D.Tenn. 1981)(statements made by sexual harassment complainants during investigation were absolutely privileged)(citing Barr v. Matteo, 360 U.S. 564 (1959)).

CHAPTER 25

EVIDENCE

I. OVERVIEW

This chapter discusses evidentiary issues of particular importance to sexual harassment litigation; the next chapter focuses on issues of discovery. Discussions of evidence and discovery will inevitably overlap because both subjects address the same questions of admissibility of evidence at trial. The issues of evidence discussed in this chapter also pertain to discovery, and some material placed for purposes of convenience in the next chapter will relate equally to evidence.[1]

A sexual harassment case involves many different categories of evidence. The primary evidence consists of the complainant's testimony that the alleged harasser actually engaged in offensive conduct, and the defendant's denial or explanation. The complainant will also seek corroborating testimony to avoid a swearing match that simply pits the complainant's word against the alleged harasser's.[1a]

Other evidence typically includes the timing and nature of the complainant's report of unwelcome conduct, the presence or absence of changes in the complainant's behavior noticed by co-workers and friends following the incident(s), the sexual atmosphere of the workplace in question, expert testimony as to whether behavior by the complainant is consistent with sexual harassment, the complainant's prior conduct, the alleged harasser's prior conduct, and facts that bear on the credibility of the alleged harasser and the complainant.

The admissibility of these types of evidence is a function of not only their probative value but the degree to which the admission of evidence will invade a party's legitimate interests in preserving privacy and avoiding undue prejudice. Thus, in deciding questions of admissibility, courts try to balance the need for complete information against the privacy rights of the individual parties. For example, a broad inquisition into the complainant's prior conduct

---

[1]*See generally* Klein, *A Survey of Evidence and Discovery Rules in Civil Sexual Harassment Suits with Special Emphasis on California Law,* 11 INDUS. REL. L.J. 540 (1989).

[1a]Typical swearing-match cases are *Hall v. F.O. Thacker Co.,* 24 FEP Cases 1499 (N.D. Ga. 1980)(court forced to decide between secretary who claimed boss privately offered her $5000 a week to be his "woman" and boss who denied any sexual proposition or touching whatsoever; court found boss more credible) and *Phillips v. Smalley Maintenance Servs.,* 711 F.2d 1524, 32 FEP Cases 975 (11th Cir. 1983)(court forced to decide between maintenance employee who claimed that boss demanded oral sex in his closed office, and boss, who denied it; court, with advisory verdict by jury, found complainant more credible).

may provide substantive evidence in a given case, but could discourage valid lawsuits.[2] Alternatively, broad rules forbidding discovery of prior history could exclude valuable information from review by the trier of fact.[3]

II. Federal Rules of Evidence

A. Balancing Relevance Against Unfair Prejudice (Rule 403)

Generally, a party may introduce any evidence relevant to any element of a sexual harassment claim or defense.[4] Thus, a party can be expected to introduce evidence concerning such issues as whether
- the complained-of conduct occurred;
- the conduct was reasonably regarded as offensive;
- the complainant actually took offense;
- the conduct was directed toward the complainant because of the complainant's gender;
- the alleged harasser knew or should have known that the conduct would be unwelcome;
- the conduct affected terms and conditions of employment;
- the conduct was committed by an "agent" of the employer;
- the employer had actual or constructive knowledge of the conduct;
- the employer took prompt remedial action in response to knowledge of the conduct;
- the employer had nondiscriminatory reasons for any adverse job action taken against the complainant.

The Supreme Court in *Meritor Savings Bank v. Vinson*[5] interpreted Title VII to permit the broad admissibility of evidence of prior workplace activities in a sexual harassment case, except insofar as evidence of the prior activities would be unfairly prejudicial. The *Meritor* Court indicated that relevant evidence could be excluded under Rule 403 of the Federal Rules of Evidence[6] if its potential for unfair prejudice outweighed its probative value.[7]

For evidence to be excluded, it must be more than merely prejudicial; it must create unfairness to a party that substantially outweighs the probative value of the evidence.[8] An example of unfairly prejudicial evidence might be

---

[2]Kreiger & Fox, *Evidentiary Issues in Sexual Harassment Litigation*, 1 Berkeley Women's L.J. 115, 117 (1985).

[3]Tanford & Bocchino, *Rape Victim Shield Laws and the Sixth Amendment*, 128 U. Pa. L. Rev. 544 (1980). Although this article concerns rape and not sexual harassment, many of the concerns expressed are the same in both of these fields of law.

[4]Evidence is "relevant" if it has any tendency to make the existence of any fact that is of consequence to the determination of the action more probable or less probable than it would be without the evidence. Fed. R. Evid. 401.

[5]477 U.S. 57, 40 FEP Cases 1822 (1986), reproduced in Chapter 1, Overview.

[6]Rule 403 states:
Exclusion of Relevant Evidence on Grounds of Prejudice, Confusion, or Waste of Time: Although relevant, evidence may be excluded if its probative value is substantially outweighed by the danger of unfair prejudice, confusion of the issues, or misleading the jury, or by considerations of undue delay, waste of time, or needless presentation of cumulative evidence.

[7]*Supra* note 5, 477 U.S. at 68–69, 40 FEP Cases at 1827–28.

[8]*See, e.g.,* Rauh v. Coyne, 744 F. Supp. 1181, 1183 (D.D.C. 1990)(evidence of employer's racial discrimination excluded in sex discrimination case in view of "the weak correlation between the two types of discrimination" and the "very great potential for prejudice").

evidence of the sexual promiscuity of the complainant in a quid pro quo case where welcomeness is at issue: although sexual promiscuity may bear on whether a sexual advance to the complainant was welcome,[9] sexual promiscuity may also unfairly prejudice the jury against the complainant and confuse the issues at stake.

B. The Ban on Character Evidence (Rule 404)

1. General Prohibition

As stated in Rule 404(a) of the Federal Rules of Evidence, character evidence—whether in the form of reputation, opinion, or evidence of past acts—generally is inadmissible to prove that a person acted in conformity therewith on a particular occasion.[10] The traditional reason for excluding character evidence is that although it has probative value, that value is outweighed by the risks of unfair prejudice. The risk is that the finder of fact will rule against a party because he or she is a bad person, regardless of the facts in the present case. As explained by McCormick:

> Evidence that an individual is the kind of person who tends to behave in certain ways almost always has some value as circumstantial evidence as to how he acted ... in the matter in question.... Yet, evidence of character in any form— reputation, opinion from observation, or specific acts—generally will not be received to prove that a person engaged in certain conduct . . . .[11]

Accordingly, character evidence—whether it concerns the complainant or the alleged harasser—must enter the record, if at all, through one of the exceptions to the general rule against its admission.

2. Common Exceptions to the Ban on Character Evidence

a. Rebuttal. Rule 404(a)(1) permits the use of character evidence offered either by "an accused" or by "the prosecution" to rebut previously admitted character evidence. Although this language indicates that Rule 404(a)(1) applies only in criminal cases,[12] some courts have held that it also applies in civil cases.[13] Rule 404(a)(1) could apply in the sexual harassment context if, for example, an alleged harasser wished to introduce evidence that he has always been a faithful husband and therefore did not harass the complainant. Where the alleged harasser so testified, the complainant would be permitted to introduce character evidence in rebuttal.

---

[9]At one time, issues of dress or promiscuity of the prosecutrix were considered probative and relevant on the issue of consent in cases of rape. Berger, *Man's Trial, Women's Tribulation: Rape Cases in the Courtroom,* 77 Colum. L. Rev. 1 (1977).

[10]Rule 404(a) provides in part: "*Character evidence generally.* Evidence of a person's character or a trait of character is not admissible for the purpose of proving action in conformity therewith on a particular occasion." Fed. R. Evid. 404(a).

[11]E. Cleary, McCormick on Evidence §188 at 554 (3d ed. 1984).

[12]The Advisory Committee notes are ambiguous on its application in civil cases.

[13]Carson v. Polley, 689 F.2d 562, 575–76 (5th Cir. 1982)(Rule 404(a) applies to civil cases when central issue in case is "close to one of a criminal nature"; in case alleging excessive use of police force, sheriff's testimony that it was impossible for him to lose his temper did not sufficiently place his character at issue to justify admission of extrinsic evidence to attack his character).

b. Habit. Rule 406 of the Federal Rules of Evidence permits the use of character evidence to prove a "habit."[14] Because a habit is one's regular response to a repeated specific situation, it would seem to have little relevance in sexual harassment litigation.[15] In *Priest v. Rotary*,[16] the defense counsel attempted to justify use of the complainant's sexual history by characterizing her asserted promiscuity as a habit. Judge Thelton Henderson rejected this argument: "In absence of exceptional circumstances ... repeated instances of living with other persons for economic benefit will not establish a habit within the contemplation of Rule 406."[17] The court reasoned that the conduct of personal relations is a volitional activity that does not constitute an invariably regular, semiautomatic "habit" within the meaning of Rule 406.[18]

Conceivably, in appropriate cases, a party's addictive or obsessive need for sexual conquest could be characterized as a habit,[19] but the success of any such argument would still leave the proponent of the evidence vulnerable to a Rule 403 argument that the evidence would be unfairly prejudicial.

c. Motive, opportunity, intent, preparation, and other bases on which to admit evidence of prior acts. Rule 404 permits evidence of prior acts to prove motive, opportunity, intent, preparation, plan, knowledge, identity, or the absence of mistake or accident. The court in *Priest v. Rotary*[20] discussed "motive" as a possible basis for the defendant to justify admitting evidence of the complainant's sexual history. The defendant sought to prove that the complainant, a waitress in the defendant's restaurant and bar, had engaged in sexual relationships for economic gain and had a "motive" to solicit men at the defendant's bar, which was the reason the defendant had articulated for discharging her. The court ruled that the proferred evidence created too weak an inference that the complainant "picked up men" to overcome the prejudicial effect of such evidence.[21]

C. The Analogy to Rape Litigation (Rule 412)

When resisting an inquiry into their prior conduct, particularly their sexual history, complainants have emphasized the similarities between claims of sex-

---

[14]Rule 406 provides:
   Habit; Routine Practice: Evidence of the habit of a person or of the routine practice of an organization, whether corroborated or not and regardless of the presence of eyewitnesses, is relevant to prove that the conduct of the person or organization on a particular occasion was in conformity with the habit or routine practice.
   See generally E. CLEARY, MCCORMICK ON EVIDENCE, *supra* note 11, at §195.
[15]*But see* Chomicki v. Wittekind, 128 Wis.2d 188, 381 N.W.2d 561 (Wis. Ct. App. 1985), discussed in text accompanying notes 85–87 *infra*.
[16]98 F.R.D. 755, 32 FEP Cases 1064 (N.D. Cal. 1983).
[17]*Id.* at 759.
[18]*Id.* at 758–59. *Accord* Mitchell v. Hutchings, 116 F.R.D. 481, 44 FEP Cases 615, 618 (D. Utah 1987).
[19]See THE AMERICAN PSYCHIATRIC ASSOCIATION, DIAGNOSTIC AND STATISTICAL MANUAL OF MENTAL DISORDERS 296 (3d ed. 1987)(DSM-III-R), §302.90(2).
[20]*Supra* note 16.
[21]*Supra* note 16, 98 F.R.D. at 760–61, 32 FEP Cases at 1068. The court also concluded that proof of the plaintiff's relationships for economic gain could not show she was "motivated" to retaliate against the defendant for rejecting her own alleged advances, because the alleged relationships could suggest only that she was the one who had made advances and thus amounted to nothing more than circumstantial character evidence, banned by Rule 404(a). *Id.* at 759–60.

ual harassment and claims of rape.[22] One observed parallel between rape and sexual harassment litigation is the defendant's interest in proving the sexual promiscuity of the complainant, on the theory that sexual promiscuity shows a willingness to participate in the sexual activities complained of.[23] Another observed parallel is the defendant's interest in portraying the complainant as a blackmailer, a gold digger, a jilted lover, or a lunatic.[24] Other defenses seen in both kinds of litigation include the argument that the complainant's behavior led the alleged harasser to believe that the actions were welcome[25] and the corollary defense that any sexual relationship was consensual.[26] If the abuse was verbal, the defendant may argue that the behavior was widely accepted in the workplace and therefore welcome,[27] that the alleged harasser was only joking and thus the behavior was not severe or pervasive,[28] or that the victim was hypersensitive, perhaps because of an unhappy sexual history, and that the conduct would not have affected the condition of a reasonable person's employment.[29]

Rule 412 of the Federal Rules of Evidence specifically addresses the use of evidence of a complainant's sexual behavior in a criminal rape case. It forbids use of reputation or opinion evidence[30] and evidence of the complainant's "past sexual behavior," except under certain limited circumstances.[31]

---

[22]Various courts and commentators have discussed this similarity. *See, e.g.,* Priest v. Rotary, *supra* note 16, 98 F.R.D. at 761–62, 32 FEP Cases at 1069–70; Department of Fair Empl. & Hous. v. Fresno Hilton Hotel, Cal. FEHC Case 84-03 at 19–25 (1984)(relying on rape analogy to exclude evidence of complainant's sexual conduct with persons other than alleged harasser offered to show lack of offense or absence of emotional injury; defendant thus not permitted to show that complainant participated in sexual banter and sexual harassment); O'Neil, *Sexual Harassment Cases and Law of Evidence: A Proposed Rule,* 1989 U. Chi. Legal Found. 219.

[23]The common law linked sexual promiscuity with willingness to submit to sexual acts. Judge Cowan, in the oft-quoted rape case of *People v. Abbot,* distinguished between a woman "who has already submitted herself to the lewd embraces of another, and the coy and modest female severely chaste and instinctively shuddering at the thought of impurity" (cited in Berger, *supra* note 9, 77 Colum. L. Rev. at 16.)

[24]*See, e.g.,* Priest v. Rotary, *supra* note 16 (complainant alleged to have habit of picking up men in bars and trading sexual favors for living expenses); Neeley v. American Fidelity Assurance, 17 FEP Cases 482 (W.D. Okla. 1978)(complainant alleged to be mentally ill); Evans v. Mail Handlers, 32 FEP Cases 634 (D.D.C. 1983)(complainant allegedly made claims as revenge for failed romance).

[25]*See, e.g.,* Swentek v. USAir, 830 F.2d 552, 44 FEP Cases 1808 (4th Cir. 1987)(alleged harasser claimed he thought he could grab crotch of flight attendant because she had grabbed crotch of pilot); Gan v. Kepro Circuit Sys., 28 FEP Cases 639 (E.D. Mo. 1982)(grabbing breast of complainant claimed to be provoked by her pinching buttocks of alleged harasser).

[26]*See, e.g.,* Moylan v. Maries County, 792 F.2d. 746, 40 FEP Cases 1788 (8th Cir. 1986)(defense claimed that alleged rape victim agreed to sexual activity by removing her boots).

[27]*See, e.g.,* Rabidue v. Osceola Ref. Co., 805 F.2d 611, 42 FEP Cases 631 (6th Cir. 1986), reproduced in Chapter 2, Forms of Harassment (assessment of hostile environment must consider "lexicon of obscenity" that pervaded environment both before and after plaintiff entered it), *cert. denied,* 481 U.S. 1041 (1987).

[28]*See, e.g.,* Highlander v. KFC Nat'l Mgmt. Co., 805 F.2d 644, 42 FEP Cases 654 (6th Cir. 1986)(response to complainant seeking promotion that matter could be settled if they went to motel across street claimed to be just a joke).

[29]*See* Neeley v. American Fidelity Assurance, *supra* note 24 (allowing evidence that complainant had been hospitalized for mental problems, including poor relationships with men, as bearing on credibility of reports of harassment).

[30]Rule 412 states in part:
Sex Offense Cases; Relevance of Victim's Past Behavior (a) Notwithstanding any other provision of law, in a criminal case in which a person is accused of an offense under Chapter 109(A) of Title 18, United States Code, reputation or opinion evidence of the past sexual behavior of an alleged victim of such offense is not admissible.

[31]Evidence of past sexual history may be admitted if it is evidence of past sexual behavior with persons other than accused offered by the accused (1) upon the issue of whether the accused was a source of semen, or (2) as evidence of past sexual behavior with the accused offered to show consent. Fed. R. Evid. 412(b)(2)(A) & (B). Evidence of past sexual history may also be used under Rule 412(c)(1) after a proper evidentiary hearing.

Rule 412 ended a long tradition of permitting inquiry into a rape victim's prior sexual history.[32]

Although Rule 412 applies only in criminal rape cases, the analogies between rape and sexual harassment[33] have supported arguments that courts should also exercise their discretion to exclude evidence of prior sexual conduct in sexual harassment litigation.[34] To the extent that the issue of welcomeness in the sexual harassment context resembles the issue of consent in rape cases, the same policy reasons exist for denying the admission of prior sexual history.[35] It remains to be seen how far the protection of sexual harassment complainants from research into their sexual histories will expand through both the common law[36] and statute.[37]

III. BEHAVIOR OF THE COMPLAINANT

The prior behavior of the complainant is relevant to whether the alleged conduct was welcome and to whether the alleged conduct occurred at all. If the prior behavior consists of "sexual conduct," a discovery shield statute might apply.[38] In any event, the complainant's prior behavior may, depending on the circumstances, be excluded as unduly prejudicial.

A. The Decision in *Meritor*

In *Meritor Savings Bank v. Vinson,* the Supreme Court held that the workplace conduct of the complainant, such as sexually provocative speech and dress and "publicly expressed sexual fantasies," is "obviously relevant"

---

[32]*See, e.g.,* People v. Collins, 25 Ill.2d 605, 186 N.E.2d 30 (1962), *cert. denied,* 373 U.S. 942 (1963). For discussions of Rule 412, see Berger, *supra* note 8, 77 COLUM. L. REV. 1; Ordover, *Admissibility of Patterns of Similar Sexual Conduct: The Unlimited Death of Character for Chastity,* 63 CORNELL L. REV. 90 (1977).

[33]See authorities cited in note 22 *supra.*

[34]Applying a version of Rule 412 in sexual harassment cases would not implicate issues under the Sixth Amendment (permitting criminal defendant to confront accusers), as rape shield laws have. Tanford & Bocchino, *Rape Victim Shield Laws and the Sixth Amendment,* 128 U. PA. L. REV. 544 (1980).

[35]O'Neil, *supra* note 22, 1989 U. CHI. LEGAL FOUND. at 237. Plaintiffs' advocates believe that by protecting the complainant with a judge-made rule of evidence similar to Rule 412, a greater number of legitimate sexual harassment suits will be brought. O'Neil cites Terpstra & Baker, *A Hierarchy of Sexual Harassment,* 121 J. OF PSYCHOLOGY 599 (1987), for the contention that 42 to 90% of all women have encountered sexual harassment at the workplace. *Id.* at 239.

[36]*E.g.,* Department of Fair Employment & Hous. v. Fresno Hilton Hotel, *supra* note 22; Priest v. Rotary, 98 F.R.D. 755, 32 FEP Cases 1064 (N.D. Cal. 1983).

[37]Forty-six states have enacted rape shield laws very similar to Federal Rule of Evidence 412. Tanford & Bocchino, *supra* note 34 (appendix of rape shield statutes). California has enacted similar shield statutes for sexual harassment plaintiffs. Cal. Evid. Code §1106 and Cal. Gov't Code §11513 provide that in civil actions and administrative proceedings alleging sexual harassment, sexual assault, or sexual battery, certain evidentiary rules apply: (1) opinion evidence, reputation evidence, and evidence of specific instances of plaintiff's sexual conduct, or any of such evidence, is not admissible by the defendant in order to prove consent by the plaintiff or the absence of injury to the plaintiff, unless the injury alleged by the plaintiff is in the nature of loss of consortium; (2) the foregoing exclusion does *not* apply to evidence of the complainant's sexual conduct with the alleged harasser; (3) if the complainant introduces evidence that relates to the complainant's sexual conduct, the defendant may cross-examine the witness who gives the testimony and offer relevant evidence limited specifically to the rebuttal of the evidence introduced by the complainant.

Evidence of sexual conduct is admissible to attack the credibility of the complainant, under Cal. Evid. Code §783, but only if the defendant (1) first moves in writing for an order, with an offer of proof of the relevancy of evidence of the sexual conduct, (2) the court finds that the offer of proof is sufficient and holds a hearing out of the presence of the jury to allow the questioning of the complainant regarding the offer of proof, and (3) the court finds that evidence of sexual conduct is relevant and not unfairly prejudicial.

[38]See note 37 *supra.*

to whether particular conduct was unwelcome,[39] and thus admissible, in the discretion of the trial court.[40] The D.C. Circuit in *Meritor* had concluded that testimony about the complainant's dress and publicly expressed personal fantasies "had no place in this litigation."[41] Rejecting that view, Justice William H. Rehnquist stated that "[w]hile 'voluntariness' in the sense of consent is not a defense to such a claim [of sexual harassment], it does not follow that a complainant's sexually provocative speech or dress is irrelevant as a matter of law in determining whether he or she found particular sexual advances unwelcome."[42] The Court concluded that although this evidence creates a risk of unfair prejudice and must be carefully weighed before it is admitted, it could not be excluded categorically.[43]

B. Behavior With the Alleged Harasser

Courts routinely admit evidence of a complainant's behavior toward the alleged harasser to discredit a claim that the conduct was unwelcome.[44] Thus, it would be admissible that the complainant had an affair with her supervisor when she claims to have been fired for spurning his advances,[45] that the complainant visited the alleged harasser in nonemployment contexts and allowed him to enter her home alone at night after the alleged harassment occurred,[46] that the complainant was otherwise friendly toward the alleged harasser in a consensual off-premises setting,[47] and that the complainant presented a "sexually explicit gift" to the alleged harasser.[48]

C. Behavior With Others in the Workplace

In a hostile environment case, a defendant may show that the complainant engaged in the same general sexual conduct cited in the complaint, to show that the harassment of the complainant was prompted by the complainant's

---

[39]Meritor Sav. Bank v. Vinson, 477 U.S. 57, 69, 40 FEP Cases 1822 (1986), reproduced in Chapter 1, Overview.

[40]This evidence would seem to bear more on whether the *alleged harasser* reasonably should have thought the plaintiff would be offended by the advances than on whether the plaintiff actually was offended. *See, e.g.,* Swentek v. USAir, 830 F.2d 552, 44 FEP Cases 1808 (4th Cir. 1987)(evidence that plaintiff publicly grabbed genitals of pilot and issued frank sexual invitation to him bears on whether another pilot reasonably thought a sexual advance by him would be unwelcome).

[41]Vinson v. Taylor, 753 F.2d 141, 146 n.36, 36 FEP Cases 1423, 1427 (1985), *rev'd in relevant part sub nom.* Meritor Sav. Bank v. Vinson, 477 U.S. 57, 40 FEP Cases 1822 (1986).

[42]*Supra* note 39, 477 U.S. at 69. For a criticism of considering workplace dress in determining whether a complainant has been harassed, see O'Neil, *supra* note 22; Department of Fair Empl. & Hous. v. Fresno Hilton Hotel, *supra* note 22.

[43]*Supra* note 39, 477 U.S. at 71 (citing Rule 403).

[44]*Cf.* FED. R. CIV. P. 412(b)(2)(B)(court, on noticed motion, may admit evidence of alleged rape victim's past sexual behavior with accused to prove consent).

[45]Bigoni v. Pay'N Pak Stores, 48 FEP Cases 732 (D. Or. 1988)(employer entitled to inquire whether plaintiff had affair with assistant manager whom she accused of harassment).

[46]Sardigal v. St. Louis Nat'l Stockyards Co., 42 FEP Cases 497 (S.D. Ill. 1986)(complainant visited alleged harasser at hospital and at his brother's house); Reichman v. Bureau of Affirmative Action, 536 F. Supp. 1149, 1172, 30 FEP Cases 1644, 1666 (M.D. Pa. 1982)(complainant invited alleged harasser to home-cooked dinner on several occasions).

[47]*See, e.g.,* Evans v. Mail Handlers, 32 FEP Cases 634 (D.D.C. 1983)(off-premises consensual sexual relations relevant to issue of whether advances unwelcome); Laudenslager v. Covert, 163 Mich. App. 484, 415 N.W.2d 254, 45 FEP Cases 907 (1987)(off-premises activities relevant to whether sexual advances were welcome), *appeal denied,* 430 Mich. 865 (1988).

[48]Steele v. Offshore Shipbldg., 867 F.2d 1311, 49 FEP Cases 522, 523 (11th Cir. 1989).

own conduct or was otherwise welcome. In *Gan v. Kepro Circuit Systems*,[49] it was admissible that the complainant had frequently used crude and vulgar language, had initiated sexually oriented conversations with male and female co-workers, had frequently asked male employees about their marital and extramarital sexual relationships, and had volunteered intimate details about her own marital and premarital sexual relationships.[50] The court also admitted evidence that the complainant had called a co-worker "nigger" and on one occasion had pinched him on the buttocks, and that the co-worker, in retaliation, grabbed the plaintiff by her breasts. There was also evidence that when male employees compared the complainant to the female subjects of photographs in sexually oriented magazines, she had opined that she was much prettier.[51]

The *Gan* court also admitted evidence of nonsexual acts by the complainant, such as incidents of "horseplay" and associations at lunch with members of the opposite sex, as further proof that sexual advances were welcome. The court also emphasized that the complainant had volunteered information about her menstrual cycle to her co-workers.[52]

Courts generally hold, with the *Gan* court, that workplace behavior by complainants is probative on the welcomeness issue.[53]

D. Behavior With Third Parties Outside the Workplace

Courts generally have excluded evidence of the complainant's sexual behavior with third parties as being too remote in time or place to the working environment.[54] In a leading case, *Priest v. Rotary*,[55] a waitress claimed that her employer had fired her for rejecting his sexual advances. The employer sought to discover the name of each sexual partner the waitress had in the past ten years to show that she was the sexual aggressor and that she was fired for trying to "pick up" male customers in the defendant's bar. The court held that the employer was seeking inadmissible character evidence.[56]

Even where admitted, evidence of a complainant's sexual behavior toward persons other than the alleged harasser has received little weight for the purpose

---

[49]28 FEP Cases 639 (E.D. Mo. 1982).

[50]*Id.* at 641.

[51]*Id.* at 640.

[52]*Id. See also* Ukarish v. Magnesium Elektron, 31 FEP Cases 1315 (D.N.J. 1983)(where complainant claimed she was sexually harassed by co-worker, court admitted evidence she returned his sexual and vulgar remarks in kind).

[53]In *Swentek v. USAir, supra* note 40, 44 FEP Cases at 1811, the complainant, a flight attendant, placed a "dildo" in her supervisor's mailbox to "loosen her up," urinated in a cup and passed it to another employee pretending that it was a drink, and grabbed the genitals of a pilot and made a frank sexual invitation to him. Although the court said that use of foul language and sexual innuendo in a consensual setting does not waive legal protections against unlawful harassment, these activities tended to prove that the alleged harassment was in fact welcome. *See also* McLean v. Satellite Technology Servs., 673 F. Supp. 1458, 1459, 45 FEP Cases 523 (E.D. Mo. 1987)(alleged harasser made no sexual overture to complainant but, had he done so, her workplace behavior, which included lifting her dress to show supervisor an absence of undergarments, indicated that the advance would have been welcome). *Cf.* Wyerick v. Bayou Steel Corp., 887 F.2d 1271, 51 FEP Cases 491 (5th Cir. 1989)(complainant, a crane operator, had triable claim of hostile environment based upon sexually offensive remarks about her breasts and her recent physical examination, notwithstanding her own occasional resort to sexual comments).

[54]*E.g.,* Mitchell v. Hutchings, 116 F.R.D. 481, 44 FEP Cases 615, 617 (D. Utah 1978)(quashing depositions of complainant's sexual partners and of photographer said to have snapped sexually suggestive photographs of one of the complainants).

[55]98 F.R.D. 755, 32 FEP Cases 1064 (N.D. Cal. 1983).

[56]*Id.* at 762.

of showing that sexual advances were welcome. In *Swentek v. USAir*,[57] Judge James Wilkinson, III, emphasized that a complainant's "use of foul language or sexual innuendo in a consensual setting does not waive 'her legal protection against unwelcome harassment,'" and that the trial judge must determine whether the complainant welcomed the particular conduct in question from the alleged harasser.[58]

Nonetheless, courts have occasionally admitted evidence of the complainant's prior sexual activity,[59] especially where the complainant has testified as to the sexual conduct.[60]

IV. PSYCHOLOGICAL HISTORY AND MEDICAL EVIDENCE

For the same reasons that defendants will have difficulty proving a complainant's general sexual history,[61] they may have difficulty attacking the credibility of the complainant's story with evidence that the complainant had been sexually assaulted as a child or has a history of imagining sexual assaults or overreacting to trivial actions.[62]

The complainant's physical symptoms following the alleged harassment will be probative of whether the complainant found the alleged harassment unwelcome. The evidence might include unusual nervousness, crying, vomiting, sleeplessness, nightmares, headaches, or other common symptoms of stress-related disorders.[63] If the complainant must remain on the job for economic reasons, and thus sees no alternative but to endure the abuse, evidence of

---

[57]*Supra* note 40.

[58]*Supra* note 40, 830 F.2d at 557, 44 FEP Cases at 1812. The court was quoting *Katz v. Dole,* 709 F.2d 251, 254 n.3, 31 FEP Cases 1521 (4th Cir. 1983), reproduced in Chapter 7, Harassment by Co-Workers, which had noted that a plaintiff's use of sexual nicknames with a co-worker was unknown to the harasser. *Id.* at 557. The court in *Mitchell v. Hutchings, supra* note 54, also emphasized that the plaintiff's consensual sexual activity with third parties was unknown to the harasser. Why the harasser's awareness is crucial is unclear. In *Mitchell* and *Swentek,* where the plaintiffs made state-law claims for intentional infliction of emotional distress, the defendants' awareness of plaintiffs' sexual activity with others was probably relevant to whether they intentionally inflicted distress. That is, to the extent that the alleged harassers knew of the plaintiffs' conduct toward co-workers, that evidence might show that the harassers believed their conduct would not be offensive.

[59]*See, e.g.,* Gan v. Kepro Circuit Sys., *supra* note 49 (fact that plaintiff had been fired from previous job for propositioning married man relevant to whether plaintiff was sexual aggressor).

[60]*See, e.g.,* Kresko v. Rulli, 432 N.W.2d 764 (Minn. Ct. App. 1988)(where plaintiff alleged that supervisor forced her to have intercourse while visiting her at home, defendant could cross-examine plaintiff regarding her subsequent sexual relationships, including alleged incident of date rape.) *Cf.* Crimm v. Missouri Pac. R.R., 750 F.2d 703, 707–8, 36 FEP Cases 883, 886 (8th Cir. 1984)(plaintiff, allegedly fired because he sexually harassed subordinate, may not, to show alleged victim's untruthfulness, cross-examine her regarding drug use two years before).

[61]See Section III. *supra.*

[62]*See, e.g.,* Knoettgen v. Superior Court, 224 Cal. App.3d 11, 273 Cal. Rptr. 636 (1990)(although plaintiff, in reporting sexual assault by co-worker, had mentioned sexual assaults suffered in childhood, defendant employer not permitted to inquire as to childhood experiences because of California statutes shielding privacy of sexual harassment complainants and because of general discovery provisions protecting witnesses from unwarranted intrusiveness, despite opinion of employer's psychiatric expert that childhood trauma could be alternative source of emotional distress that plaintiff would attribute to defendant employer). *See generally* Roberts v. Saylor, 230 Kan. 289, 637 P.2d 1175 (1980)(where plaintiff has exaggerated and unreasonable reaction to conduct, no liability unless actor knew that plaintiff was particularly susceptible). *Accord* Restatement (Second) of Torts §46(1), comment f (1965). For more information regarding the discoverability of the complainant's sexual history, see Chapter 26, Discovery.

[63]*See, e.g.,* Priest v. Rotary, 634 F. Supp. 571, 40 FEP Cases 208, 216 (N.D. Cal. 1986)(stress-related symptoms, mostly after complainant's discharge, ostensibly stemming from fear of defendant, admissible to show unwelcomeness of conduct as well as damages).

adverse psychological reactions may be the only evidence to support the allegation that the sexual advances were submitted to under duress.

Courts routinely permit inquiries, addressed to the complainant or others, as to the psychological reaction of the complainant to the alleged abuse as relevant to whether the conduct actually occurred and whether it was welcome.[64]

V. THE COMPLAINANT'S REPORTS OF SEXUAL HARASSMENT

A. Reports to Management

1. Absence of Complaints

The absence of timely reports to management regarding misconduct is relevant to whether the complained-of conduct was welcome, whether it ever occurred, and whether in any event the employer knew or should have known about it.[65] The absence of a report is particularly probative, of course, where the employer had a grievance procedure that provided an effective avenue to report sexual harassment.

2. Complaints to Management

Reports of sexual harassment to management are admissible under any of several theories. Most commonly, a report to management is admissible as nonhearsay evidence to show that the employer had notice of the misconduct that it then failed to correct.[66] To the extent that any prior report conflicts with the complainant's testimony in deposition or at trial, the defendant may use the prior statement to impeach the complainant's testimony.[67]

If the report is excessively tardy or closely follows some disciplinary action against the complainant, these circumstances would be admissible to show that the report is unreliable and perhaps influenced by improper motive.[68]

---

[64]*See, e.g.,* Meritor Sav. Bank v. Vinson, 477 U.S. 57, 40 FEP Cases 1822 (1986), reproduced in Chapter 1, Overview (testimony by co-workers as to discussions by plaintiff about her sexual fantasies); Swentek v. USAir, 830 F.2d 552, 44 FEP Cases 1808 (4th Cir. 1987)(testimony that plaintiff was vindictive person who threatened suits against co-workers over imagined wrongs and who bragged she was going to get alleged harasser fired); Phillips v. Smalley Maintenance Servs., 711 F.2d 1524, 32 FEP Cases 975, 977 (11th Cir. 1983)(psychiatric testimony of chronic anxiety following boss's demands for oral sex in his office; complainant so upset after sexual advances that she could not work and went home early); Gan v. Kepro Circuit Sys., *supra* note 49 (allowing evidence of lewd conduct of plaintiff in workplace and at previous job).

[65]*See, e.g.,* Evans v. Mail Handlers, *supra* note 47, 32 FEP Cases at 637 (failure of plaintiff to complain until consensual affair soured admitted to show conduct welcome at time it occurred).

[66]*See, e.g.,* Bundy v. Jackson, 641 F.2d 934, 24 FEP Cases 1155 (D.C. Cir. 1981)(evidence that plaintiff complained to supervisor admissible to show liability of employer as well as unwelcome nature of advances being made).

[67]*See generally* FED. R. EVID. 613 (implying prior inconsistent statements of witness may be admitted provided witness has chance to explain). *See, e.g.,* Highlander v. KFC Nat'l Mgmt. Co., 805 F.2d 644, 42 FEP Cases 654 (6th Cir. 1986)(fact that plaintiff made light of alleged pass when it occurred held admissible on whether comment was actually unwelcome).

[68]*See, e.g.,* Evans v. Mail Handlers, 32 FEP Cases 634, 637 (D.D.C. 1983)(failure to complain about prior sexual advances by supervisor until consensual sexual affair had soured admitted as evidence that actions not unwelcome when they occurred); Neeley v. American Fidelity Assurance, 17 FEP Cases 482, 485 (W.D. Okla. 1978)(failure to complain about sexual joking and touching of shoulder until weeks after termination of employment admissible on whether conduct unwelcome at time).

3. Reports to Co-Workers and Others

The court will generally admit the complainant's evidence of statements to co-workers or others only if the statements would qualify either as an excited utterance exception to the hearsay rule[69] or as a statement of the complainant's then-existing mental state.[70] The complainant may also seek the admission of such reports as a prior consistent statement, where the defense has suggested that the witness fabricated the story and the prior consistent statement was made before there would have been any motive to fabricate.[71]

Rule 613 of the Federal Rules of Evidence may justify the admission of the prior unsworn statements of a witness who subsequently claims an inability to recall the facts.[72] Complainants might use prior statements of witnesses still employed by the employer who have changed or forgotten their stories. Employers might use prior statements of employees who, bitter over some adverse personnel action, see things differently now than they did when the matter was originally investigated.

4. Complaints to the Alleged Harasser

The complainant's proof that conduct was unwelcome often will include evidence of a contemporaneous objection expressed to the alleged harasser.[73] The evidence might be a written objection, testimony of co-workers or customers as to an oral objection, medical evidence of injuries incurred by either party while the complainant resisted an advance, and psychological or medical evidence of physical or emotional distress caused by the harassment.[74]

VI. The Alleged Harasser's Knowledge or Behavior

A complainant often will offer evidence of the knowledge or conduct of the alleged harasser and of harassment of other employees by other alleged

---

[69]FED. R. EVID. 803(2). *See, e.g.,* E. CLEARY, MCCORMICK ON EVIDENCE, §272 at 580 (3d ed. 1984). *See also* Priest v. Rotary, *supra* note 63, 40 FEP Cases at 209 (admitting evidence that plaintiff would say "keep your hands off" in response to grab at her breasts); United States v. Bailey, 834 F.2d 218 (1st Cir. 1987) (statement by juror to neighbor within three minutes of being offered bribe by party in case in which juror was sitting held admissible as excited utterance).

[70]FED. R. EVID. 803(3). *See, e.g.,* Priest v. Rotary, *supra* note 63. Statements made in a written report to management shortly after the occurrence may fall within the recorded recollection exception to the hearsay rule. FED. R. EVID. 803(5); Morris Jewelers v. General Elec. Credit Corp., 714 F.2d 32, 34–35 (5th Cir. 1983)(complaints by angry customers regarding mishandling of their accounts admissible to show state of mind of customers in suit for loss of goodwill due to botched credit transactions).

[71]*See, e.g.,* United States v. Lanier, 578 F.2d 1246, 1255–56 (8th Cir. 1977)(any witness may testify to prior consistent statement of witness once testimony of that witness has been assaulted as fabrication), *cert. denied,* 439 U.S. 856 (1978).

[72]*See* note 67 *supra.* In *United States v. Causey,* 834 F.2d 1277 (6th Cir. 1987), *cert. denied,* 486 U.S. 1034 (1988), the court permitted an investigator to testify as to statements made by a witness before trial, when the witness had testified at trial that she could not recall anything regarding her conversation with the investigator. The Court held that an inconsistent statement can be found in silence or a claimed inability to recall, with the result that rebuttal testimony in the form of testimony by the investigator as to prior statements by the witness made to the investigator can be introduced, presumably to show that the witness was lying and did recall what was said.

[73]*See, e.g.,* Priest v. Rotary, *supra* note 63, 40 FEP Cases at 209 (complainant's repeated objection to grabbing by owner).

[74]*See* Phillips v. Smalley Maintenance Servs., *supra* note 64 (admitting psychological evidence to show that complainant found conduct unwelcome).

harassers. Although this evidence will raise issues of privacy, undue prejudice, and the ban against the admission of character evidence,[75] such evidence often is admissible.

A. Evidence of the Harasser's Intent

As evidence that the alleged harasser's conduct was because of the complainant's sex, prior conduct of the alleged harasser with respect to both the complainant and co-workers may be admissible notwithstanding its nature as character evidence.[76] Evidence of the complainant's severe financial straits, and the alleged harasser's knowledge of same, may be admissible to show motive, opportunity, and intent with respect to threatened job loss if sexual favors were not extended.[77] In a tort case, this evidence could also bear on issues such as the nature of the alleged harasser's conduct and the availability of punitive damages.[78]

B. Evidence of Plan

In *Phillips v. Smalley Maintenance Services,*[79] a quid pro quo case, the complainant was fired after rejecting her boss's demand for oral sex. Before the complainant forced her way out of his office, her boss had told her that part of her job was to give him oral sex three times a week and had begun to put paper over the window of his office door to prevent anyone from seeing inside.[80] The court admitted testimony by another female employee that she had been subjected to treatment "similar" to that alleged by the complainant,[81] and by another witness that he had seen other female employees leave the alleged harasser's office when there was paper over the window of the office door.[82]

C. Evidence of Habit

At least one court has upheld the use of an alleged harasser's sexual history as "habit" evidence. In *Chomicki v. Wittekind,*[83] where the jury found that the defendant landlord terminated the plaintiff's tenancy for spurning his sexual advances, the trial court, relying upon a state rule of evidence modeled upon Rule 406,[84] admitted testimony from three other female tenants and one female

---

[75]See Section II.B. *supra.*

[76]Federal Rule of Evidence 404(b) states that although evidence of prior acts generally is not admissible for the purpose of proving action in conformity therewith on a particular occasion, that evidence is admissible to prove motive, opportunity, intent, preparation, plan, knowledge, identity, or absence of mistake or accident.

[77]*E.g.,* Phillips v. Smalley Maintenance Servs., *supra* note 64, 32 FEP Cases at 981.

[78]*See, e.g.,* Priest v. Rotary, *supra* note 63, 40 FEP Cases at 216 (harasser's knowledge of complainant's economic dependence on job showed outrageousness for purposes of tort of intentional infliction of emotional distress).

[79]*Supra* note 64.

[80]*Supra* note 64, 32 FEP Cases at 977.

[81]*Id.* at 981.

[82]*Id.* at 981 n.5.

[83]128 Wis.2d 188, 381 N.W.2d 561 (Wis. Ct. App. 1985).

[84]For a discussion of Rule 406, see Section II.B.2.6. *supra.*

tester, about four incidents over a two-year period that showed a "routine practice of demanding sexual favors."[85]

D. Evidence of Hostile Environment

Evidence that the alleged harasser sexually harassed other employees in addition to the complainant is routinely admitted in hostile environment cases.[86] The D.C. Circuit in *Meritor* explained that evidence of the alleged harasser harassing others as well can demonstrate that the incidents of harassment were pervasive rather than isolated.[87]

This evidence may also be introduced for the related purpose of showing the effect of the conduct on the complainant's working conditions. Judge Howell Melton, in *Robinson v. Jacksonville Shipyards*,[88] admitted evidence concerning the harassment of the complainant's co-workers because, among other grounds, the perception of a hostile environment may be "influenced by the treatment of other persons of a plaintiff's protected class, even if that treatment is learned second-hand."[89] One court even found that a supervisor's "widespread reputation" as a "womanizer" helped create a hostile environment.[90]

---

[85]*Supra* note 83, 381 N.W.2d at 563–64. *But see* Priest v. Rotary, 98 F.R.D. 755, 758–59, 32 FEP Cases 1064, 1067 (N.D. Cal. 1983)("characteristics of one's personal relationships" do not constitute habits); Kresko v. Rulli, 432 N.W.2d 764, 767–79 (Minn. Ct. App. 1988)(rejecting plaintiff's argument that testimony of other women employees should have been heard before jury to show defendant's "habit" of sexually harassing subordinates). Although it would likely be excluded as unfairly prejudicial, an argument could be made that evidence of a party's addictive or obsessive need for sexual conquest could be characterized as habit evidence. See text accompanying note 19 *supra*.

[86]*E.g.,* Dockter v. Rudolf Wolff Futures, 456 F.2d 913 (7th Cir. 1990)(other female workers corroborated complainant's assertions of sexual harassment in that they were subjected to sustantially same treatment); Henson v. City of Dundee, 682 F.2d 897, 899, 29 FEP Cases 787, 788–89 (11th Cir. 1982), reproduced in Chapter 4, Hostile Environment Harassment; Rauh v. Coyne, 744 F. Supp. 1181, 1183 (D.D.C. 1990)(finding admissible evidence of complaints of sexual harassment occurring after plaintiff had left defendant's employ but within 15 months of that time, where alleged harasser was "ultimate decisionmaker in all the incidents"); Rudow v. New York City Comm'n on Human Rights, 123 Misc.2d 709, 474 N.Y.S.2d 1005, 41 FEP Cases 1402, 1407 (N.Y. Sup. Ct. 1984)(two women other than complainant permitted to testify that company officer had fondled them in his office while discussing business, just as complainant testified he had done with her), *aff'd,* 109 A.D.2d 1111, 487 N.Y.S.2d 453, *appeal denied,* 66 N.Y.2d 605 (1985).

[87]Vinson v. Taylor, 753 F.2d 141, 146 n.40, 36 FEP Cases 1423, 1427 (D.C. Cir. 1985)(*dictum*)("Even a woman who was never herself the object of harassment might have a Title VII claim if she were forced to work in an atmosphere in which such harassment was pervasive"), *rev'd on other grounds sub nom.* Meritor Sav. Bank v. Vinson, 477 U.S. 57, 40 FEP Cases 1822 (1986), reproduced in Chapter 1, Overview. *See also* Waltman v. International Paper Co., 875 F.2d 468, 477, 50 FEP Cases 179, 187 (5th Cir. 1989)(evidence of graffiti directed toward others admissible in complainant's own hostile environment claim); Hicks v. Gates Rubber Co., 833 F.2d 1406, 1415–26, 45 FEP Cases 608, 615 (10th Cir. 1987)(trial court on remand must consider "incidents of sexual harassment at employees other than plaintiff" to decide question of hostile environment); Broderick v. Ruder, 685 F. Supp. 1269, 1277, 46 FEP Cases 1272, 1280 (D.D.C. 1988)("Evidence of general work atmosphere, involving employment other than the plaintiff, is relevant to the issue of whether there exists an atmosphere of hostile work environment"). *But see* Jones v. Flagship Int'l, 793 F.2d 714, 721 n.7, 41 FEP Cases 358 (5th Cir. 1986)(sexual harassment reported by other female employees "does not bear on Jones' individual claim of sexual harassment in the absence of evidence that such incidents affected Jones' psychological well-being"), *cert. denied,* 479 U.S. 1065 (1987).

[88]760 F. Supp. 1486, 1499–1501 (M.D. Fla. 1991), reproduced in Chapter 2, Forms of Harassment.

[89]*Id.* at 1499. *See also* EEOC v. Gurnee Inn Corp., 48 FEP Cases 871, 878 (N.D. Ill. 1988)("[o]bservance of sexual harassment of others can . . . create a hostile environment"), *aff'd,* 914 F.2d 815, 53 FEP Cases 1425 (7th Cir. 1990), and cases cited in note 99 *infra. But see* Fisher v. San Pedro Peninsula Hosp., 54 FEP Cases 584, 592 (Cal. Ct. App. 1989)(one who is not personally subjected to offensive remarks and touchings must show she "personally witnessed" the harassing conduct "in her immediate work environment"); Langlois v. McDonald's Restaurants, 149 Mich. App. 309, 385 N.W.2d 778, 781–82, 45 FEP Cases 134, 137 (complainant cannot rely on incidents of sexual harassment of which she was unaware to establish hostile environment claim), *appeal denied,* 426 Mich. 867 (1986).

[90]Jones v. Lyng, 669 F. Supp. 1108, 1115 (D.D.C. 1986).

Pervasive sexual conduct toward persons other than the complainant can also create a hostile work environment even if the targets of the conduct welcome it and even if little or no sexual conduct is directed at the plaintiff.[91]

E. Evidence of Sex Discrimination

Evidence of the harassment of employees other than the complainant may also be admitted as evidence of the employer's sexually discriminatory motive in making an employment decision.[92] This kind of evidence is, in fact, the very essence of one form of sexual harassment—making the sexual submission of employees a general condition of employment.[93]

Evidence of a sexually charged workplace has also been admitted to show that job decisions adverse to the complainant were motivated by the complainant's gender.[94]

F. Evidence of Employer Notice

Evidence of the alleged harasser's harassment of other employees may also be admitted to show that the employer knew or should have known of the problem and is liable for its failure to correct the harassment.[95] In *Hunter v. Allis-Chalmers Corp.*,[96] Judge Richard Posner explained that evidence of pervasive harassment by co-workers will support a finding that the employer is directly liable either because the employer acted negligently in failing to stop the harassment or because it actually condoned the harassment.[97]

The complainant thus may introduce evidence of earlier complaints by other employees regarding actions of the alleged harasser to show that the company had notice and yet did not take appropriate steps to end the harassment.[98]

---

[91]*E.g.,* Spencer v. General Elec. Co., 703 F. Supp. 466, 51 FEP Cases 1725 (E.D. Va. 1989)(evidence of supervisor's affairs and pervasive sexual horseplay with female subordinates establishes Title VII violation), *aff'd,* 894 F.2d 651, 51 FEP Cases 1725 (4th Cir. 1990); Shrout v. Black Clawson Co., 689 F. Supp. 774, 776, 46 FEP Cases 1339 (S.D. Ohio 1988)(current and former employees' testimony that pervasive sexual advances by male managers and affairs between managers and subordinates supports judgment for plaintiff); Broderick v. Ruder, 685 F. Supp. 1269, 46 FEP Cases 1272 (D.D.C. 1988), reproduced in Chapter 2, Forms of Harassment (plaintiff and several other witnesses testified to widespread sexual favoritism that they found offensive). *But see* Evans v. Mail Handlers, 32 FEP Cases 634, 635, 637 (D.D.C. 1983)(judgment for defendant where plaintiff was found to welcome supervisor's overtures despite evidence that workplace was pervaded with sexual activity and sexual innuendo).

[92]Morgan v. Hertz Corp., 542 F. Supp. 123, 128, 27 FEP Cases 990, 994 (W.D. Tenn. 1981)("history of vulgar and indecent language tolerated by management and directed toward women employees" leads to conclusion that sex played role in decision to promote men rather than women to manager jobs), *aff'd,* 725 F.2d 1070, 33 FEP Cases 1237 (6th Cir. 1984).

[93]For a discussion of this theory, see Chapter 5, Claims by Third Parties, Section II.A.1.

[94]*E.g.,* Contardo v. Merrill Lynch, 54 FEP Cases 1269, 1270 (D. Mass. 1990)(female securities broker subjected to sexually hostile environment and denied work opportunities).

[95]*See generally* cases cited in notes 86–90 *supra.*

[96]797 F.2d 1417, 1423–24, 41 FEP Cases 721 (7th Cir. 1986).

[97]*See also* Katz v. Dole, 709 F.2d 251, 31 FEP Cases 1521 (4th Cir. 1983), reproduced in Chapter 7, Harassment by Co-Workers (evidence of pervasive harassment by co-workers and lack of action by supervisors to correct was admissible to show intent of employer to discriminate on basis of sex); Spencer v. General Elec. Co., *supra* note 91 (plaintiff demonstrated that employer should have known of harassment given its pervasiveness).

[98]*See* Paroline v. Unisys Corp., 879 F.2d 100, 50 FEP Cases 306, 309 (4th Cir. 1989), reproduced in Chapter 9, Constructive Discharge (alleged harasser had been subject of complaints by others), *aff'd in part and rev'd in part,* 900 F.2d 27, 52 FEP Cases 845 (4th Cir. 1990); Yates v. Avco Corp., 819 F.2d 630, 635–36, 43 FEP Cases 1595, 1599 (6th Cir. 1987)(alleged harasser's long history of harassing women suggests notice to employer as well as "additional proof" that employer's antiharassment policies "not

　　　The complainant may introduce evidence that the alleged harassment was so pervasive that knowledge of the harassment, and presumptive discriminatory intent, can be imputed to the employer.[99] Evidence of harassing conduct by other supervisors may be admissible to show that the employer knew or should have known of the unreasonable working conditions or that the employer failed to take reasonable steps to correct the problems after it became aware of them.[100]

VII. THE EMPLOYER'S RESPONSE TO REPORTS OF HARASSMENT

　　　An employer has every incentive to offer evidence of its response to the complainant's allegations to show that it did not authorize the harassment and took prompt remedial action to correct it. The evidence will include facts concerning the employer's investigation of a sexual harassment complaint and disciplinary actions taken by the employer against the alleged harassers.[101]

　　　It is less clear whether a complainant can offer proof of the employer's reactions to complaints of sexual harassment.[102] Rule 407 of the Federal Rules of Evidence prohibits evidence of subsequent remedial measures designed to prove "negligence or culpable conduct."[103] The Rule sometimes permits, however, evidence of remedial actions when offered to prove control over the matters at issue or the feasibility of precautionary measures.[104]

---

functioning properly"); Bundy v. Jackson, 641 F.2d 934, 24 FEP Cases 1155, 1157 (D.C. Cir. 1981)(evidence of harassment of others admitted to show harassment was "standard operating procedure"); Ross v. Double Diamond, 672 F. Supp. 261–73, 45 FEP Cases 313, 322 (N.D. Tex. 1987)(previous suit by another complainant accusing alleged harasser of sexual harassment put employer "on notice" and should have resulted in policy to prevent harassment of sort found in current case).

　　Conversely, an employer may introduce evidence that its male employee had never before harassed female co-workers to show that discipline short of firing was adequate remedial action. Barnett v. Omaha Nat'l Bank, 584 F. Supp. 22, 30, 35 FEP Cases 585, 592 (D. Neb. 1983), aff'd, 726 F.2d 424, 35 FEP Cases 593 (8th Cir. 1984).

　　[99]See, e.g., Hall v. Gus Constr. Co., 842 F.2d 1010, 46 FEP Cases 573, 576 (8th Cir. 1988), reproduced in Chapter 2, Forms of Harassment (evidence of sexual harassment directed at employee other than plaintiff relevant to show hostile environment); Bundy v. Jackson, supra note 98 (allowing evidence of multiple acts of harassment by multiple parties to show sexual harassment was standard operating procedure); Shrout v. Black Clawson Co., supra note 91 (testimony by present and former employees of pervasive sexual advances by male managers and numerous affairs between managers and subordinates permitted to show acquiescence by employer in discrimination by supervisors). Accord Katz v. Dole, supra note 97; Hunter v. Allis-Chalmers Corp., supra note 96. But see Langlois v. McDonald's Restaurants, supra note 89 (plaintiff could not, in hostile environment case, introduce evidence about incidents of which she was unaware); Kresko v. Rulli, supra note 85 (excluding evidence of pattern of behavior of supervisor toward other employees as irrelevant); Jones v. Flagship Int'l, supra note 87 (other incidents admissible in hostile environment case only where plaintiff can show that they affected her psychological well-being).

　　[100]See cases cited in note 99 supra.

　　[101]See Huddleston v. Roger Dean Chevrolet, 845 F.2d 900, 46 FEP Cases 1361 (11th Cir. 1988)(evidence admitted that general manager threatened alleged harassers with discharge); Swentek v. USAir, 830 F.2d 552, 44 FEP Cases 1808 (4th Cir. 1987). Similarly, the employer may introduce evidence that the complaints were insufficient to warrant taking any disciplinary action. See, e.g., Highlander v. KFC Nat'l Mgmt. Co., 805 F.2d 644, 42 FEP Cases 654 (6th Cir. 1986)(fact that plaintiff made light of alleged pass at time and asked that management take no action held admissible on issue of whether employer was justified in taking no action).

　　[102]The plaintiff might wish, for example, to show that the employer improved its antiharassment policy after the incidents in question, to show that the employer's previous policy was inadequate.

　　[103]Rule 407 provides: "When, after an event, measures are taken which, if taken previously, would have made the event less likely to occur, evidence of the subsequent remedial process is not admissible to prove negligence or culpable conduct in connection with the event." This rule does not exclude such evidence, however, if it is offered to impeach or to prove ownership, control or feasibility of precautionary measures, if controverted.

　　[104]See, e.g., Kenny v. Southeastern Pa. Transp. Auth., 581 F.2d 351 (3d Cir. 1978), cert. denied, 439 U.S. 1073 (1979)(where defendant claimed it exercised reasonable care with respect to lighting of area where

VIII. EXPERT TESTIMONY

Rule 702 of the Federal Rules of Evidence authorizes opinion testimony by an expert who is qualified by knowledge, skill, experience, training, or education to help the trier of fact understand the evidence or find a fact in issue.[105] Admissibility of expert testimony is a matter in the discretion of the trial judge, whose decision will not be overturned unless it is clearly erroneous or an abuse of discretion.[106]

Expert testimony has been admitted on several issues in sexual harassment litigation, although some issues, such as whether the alleged harasser's conduct was on the basis of gender, often will not require the aid of an expert.[107] The admissibility of expert testimony may depend upon whether a jury will hear the case. For example, arguably jurors can rely on their common experience to determine whether the offensive conduct reasonably would have affected the work of a person in the complainant's place, while a court conducting a bench trial would both appreciate expert guidance and be less likely to be led too far astray by it.[108]

A. Whether Harassment Occurred

Expert testimony has been admitted as to whether the complainant reacted in a manner consistent with a person who has suffered sexual abuse.[109]

One Texas court has held that a plaintiff may not, however, use expert psychological testimony that the alleged harasser fit the "profile" of a person who would have a tendency to harass.[110] The trial court had admitted the expert

---

plaintiff was raped and claimed its inspections were adequate, plaintiff could introduce evidence of later repairs inconsistent with claims of defendant). *Cf.* Shrout v. Black Clawson Co., *supra* note 91, 689 F. Supp. at 778 (admitting evidence that, after alleged harassment, employer changed procedure for reporting incidents of harassment; evidence showed that employer's previous "open-door" policy was inadequate, so that harassed employee could reasonably fail to use it to report harassment).

[105]*See generally* Aloe Coal Co. v. Clark Equip. Co., 816 F.2d 110, 114 (3d Cir. 1987)(expert testimony liberally permitted if it will properly aid trier of fact), *cert. denied,* 484 U.S. 853 (1987); Federal Crop Ins. Corp. v. Hester, 765 F.2d 723, 728 (8th Cir. 1985)(witness may testify as expert if expert's knowledge of subject matter will most likely assist trier of fact in arriving at truth).

[106]*E.g.,* Davis v. Combustion Eng'g, 742 F.2d 916, 35 FEP Cases 975 (6th Cir. 1984)(age discrimination).

[107]*See* Ward v. Westland Plastics, 651 F.2d 1266, 1270, 23 FEP Cases 128 (9th Cir. 1980)(expert testimony properly excluded by trial court in its broad discretion in that question of whether differential treatment was based on sex was not so technical as to require an expert); *see also* Bohen v. City of E. Chicago, 622 F. Supp. 1234, 1243 n.4, 39 FEP Cases 917 (N.D. Ind. 1985)(expert testimony ineffective regarding plaintiff's behavior that led to lawful termination, where more probative evidence may have been testimony from friends or children regarding gradual change in demeanor), *aff'd in part, rev'd in part on other grounds,* 799 F.2d 1180, 49 FEP Cases 1108 (7th Cir. 1986); EEOC v. Domino's Pizza, 34 FEP Cases 1075, 1078 (E.D. Mich. 1983)(fees and expenses of plaintiff's expert denied because his testimony not relevant to issues).

[108]*Compare* Robinson v. Jacksonville Shipyards, *supra* note 88 (permitting consultant to testify as expert on common patterns of and responses to sexual harassment in bench trial, where court would "risk injustice" by applying "reasonable woman" standard without assistance) *with* Lipsett v. University of P.R., 740 F. Supp. 921, 54 FEP Cases 257 (D.P.R. 1990)(denying motion to have same expert testify in jury trial).

[109]*See* Robinson v. Jacksonville Shipyards, 760 F. Supp. 1486, 1506–7 (M.D. Fla. 1991), reproduced in Chapter 2, Forms of Harassment (consultant opined that under typical coping strategies women may not complain about sexual harassment because of fear, embarrassment, and feelings of futility); McCalla v. Ellis, 180 Mich. App. 372, 446 N.W.2d 904, 51 FEP Cases 569, 579 (1989)(complainant's experts could testify about characteristics found in sexually abused adult and could opine on ultimate issue of whether unwelcome sexual conduct occurred, but had no basis for such opinion in present case and could not in any event opine on complainant's truthfulness), *appeal denied,* 434 Mich. 893 (1990).

[110]Bushell v. Dean, 781 S.W.2d 652, 52 FEP Cases 746 (Tex. Ct. App. 1989)(reversed on procedural

to say some "general things that are true about a person who harasses." The appellate court reasoned that such evidence should be excluded because its probative value was substantially outweighed by the prejudice to the defendant, and because it amounted to inadmissible character evidence.

B. Causation

Testimony by an expert mental health professional may be admissible on whether the complainant has experienced emotional distress caused by sexual harassment.[111]

C. Damages

If there are continuing psychological effects that will require treatment, such as post-traumatic stress disorder (PTSD),[112] the expert may testify to the anticipated time and cost of therapy to overcome the psychological trauma

---

ground that objection to expert testimony not adequately preserved at trial), *rev'd on other grounds,* 54 FEP Cases 864 (Tex. 1990).

[111]*See, e.g.,* Hirschfeld v. New Mexico Corrections Dep't, 916 F.2d 572, 54 FEP Cases 268, 275–76 (10th Cir. 1990)(expert psychiatric testimony on whether sexual harassment caused plaintiff's medical depression); Phillips v. Smalley Maintenance Servs., 711 F.2d 1524, 32 FEP Cases 975 (11th Cir. 1983)(expert testimony by family practice physician and psychiatrist admissible as to whether distress caused by harassment or preexisting physical problems and surgery); Moffett v. Gene B. Glick Co., 621 F. Supp. 244, 264–65, 41 FEP Cases 671, 684 (N.D. Ind. 1985)(psychologist, psychiatrist, and counselor testified about plaintiff's psychological damages and their causal connection to harassment at work); Broderick v. Ruder, *supra* note 91, 46 FEP Cases at 1276–77 (plaintiff's and defendant's psychiatrists disagreed whether plaintiff suffered post-traumatic stress disorder from sexual harassment or had paranoid personality disorder evidenced by pervasive suspicion of all supervisors); Neeley v. American Fidelity Assurance Co., 17 FEP Cases 482 (W.D. Okla. 1978).

[112]The American Psychiatric Association Diagnostic and Statistical Manual of Mental Disorders (3d ed. 1987)(DSM-III-R), in diagnostic category 309.89, describes PTSD:

The essential feature is the development of characteristic symptoms following a psychologically traumatic event that is generally outside the range of usual human experience. The characteristic symptoms involve reexperiencing the traumatic event; numbing of responsiveness to, or reduced involvement with, the external world; and a variety of autonomic, dysphoric, or cognitive symptoms.

The diagnostic criteria include:

A. The person has experienced an event that is outside the range of usual human experience and that would be markedly distressing to almost anyone, *e.g.,* serious threat to one's life or physical integrity; serious threat or harm to one's children, spouse, or other close relatives and friends; sudden destruction of one's home or community; or seeing another person who has recently been, or is being, seriously injured or killed as the result of an accident or physical violence.

B. The traumatic event is persistently reexperienced in at least one of the following ways:

(1) recurrent and intrusive distressing recollections of the event (in young children, repetitive play in which themes or aspects of the trauma are expressed)

(2) recurrent distressing dreams of the event

(3) sudden acting or feeling as if the traumatic event were reoccurring (includes a sense of reliving the experience, illusions, hallucinations, and dissociative [flashback] episodes, even those that occur upon awakening or when intoxicated)

(4) intense psychological distress at exposure to events that symbolize or resemble an aspect of the traumatic event, including anniversaries of the trauma

C. Persistent avoidance of stimuli associated with the trauma or numbing of general responsiveness (not present before the trauma), as indicated by at least three of the following:

(1) efforts to avoid thoughts or feelings associated with the trauma

(2) efforts to avoid activities or situations that arouse recollections of the trauma

(3) inability to recall an important aspect of the trauma (psychogenic amnesia)

(4) markedly diminished interest in significant activities (in young children, loss of recently acquired development skills such as toilet training or language skills)

(5) feeling of detachment or estrangement from others

(6) restricted range of affect, *e.g.,* unable to have loving feeling

(7) sense of a foreshortened future, *e.g.,* does not expect to have a career, marriage, or children, or a long life

D. Persistent symptoms of increased arousal (not present before the trauma), as indicated by at least two of the following:

caused by the harassment. Several courts have relied on expert testimony about sexual harassment as a basis for determining the amount of damages to be awarded.[113]

D. Remedial Steps

Consultants have given expert testimony on what steps are reasonably designed to prevent and remedy sexual harassment in the workplace.[114]

E. Sexual Attitudes and Stereotypes

Courts have admitted testimony of expert witnesses on sexual attitudes in various contexts. In *EEOC v. Sears, Roebuck & Co.,*[115] a professional historian testified for the defense in a pay discrimination case that women, because of historical conditions, generally have preferred lower-paying, noncommission sales jobs.[116] In *Hopkins v. Price Waterhouse,*[117] Justice William Brennan, Jr., approved the use of testimony by a social psychologist that a female partner,

---

    (1) difficulty falling or staying asleep
    (2) irritability or outbursts of anger
    (3) difficulty concentrating
    (4) hypervigilance
    (5) exaggerated startle response
    (6) physiologic reactivity upon exposure to events that symbolize or resemble an aspect of the traumatic event (*e.g.,* a woman who was raped in an elevator breaks out in a sweat when entering any elevator)
    E. Duration of the disturbance (symptoms in B, C, and D) of at least one month.
Id. at 250–51. See also Burstein, *Posttraumatic Flashbacks, Dream Disturbances, and Mental Imagery,* 46 J. CLINICAL PSYCHIATRY 374 (1985)(discussing flashbacks of traumatic experience, precipitating dangerous or potentially dangerous situation).
    [113]*See, e.g.,* Valdez v. Church's Fried Chicken, 683 F. Supp. 596, 47 FEP Cases 1155 (W.D. Tex. 1988)(expert testimony on PTSD admitted to show cause of injuries alleged by plaintiff and damages in sexual harassment suit brought under Title VII and state law; plaintiff, a female worker in a fast-food restaurant subjected to continuous sexual harassment culminating in attempted rape, awarded $10,000 for mental anguish and symptoms such as nightmares, feeling need to shower two or three times daily, fear of men, difficulty sleeping, frequent crying spells, and clumsiness); Moffett v. Gene B. Glick Co., *supra* note 111, 41 FEP Cases at 684 (psychiatrist's estimate of need for more than $16,000 in psychological therapy); Arnold v. City of Seminole, 614 F. Supp. 853, 40 FEP Cases, 1539, 1548–49 (E.D. Okla. 1985)(psychiatric testimony that plaintiff suffers from post-traumatic stress syndrome and will require at least several years of weekly psychiatric sessions to reach stable status); Bohen v. City of E. Chicago, *supra* note 107 (plaintiff awarded compensatory damages of $25,000 for mental distress and $4,150 for medical expenses for Title VII and 42 U.S.C. §1983 claims against municipal fire department for sexual harassment; expert testified that sexual harassment may lead to tension, anxiety, loss of sleep, diminished self-worth, nausea, cramps, and headaches).
    In rape cases, most courts have allowed expert testimony on the psychological effect of rape, usually PTSD, for the purpose of assessing damages. *See, e.g.,* Spencer v. General Elec. Co., 688 F. Supp. 1072 (E.D. Va. 1988)(rape victim brought Title VII claim for sexual harassment and state tort claim for assault and battery and intentional infliction of emotional distress against former supervisor and employer; expert testimony that she suffered from PTSD not admitted as proof that rape actually occurred but was admitted to establish damages); White v. Violent Crimes Compensation Bd., 76 N.J. 368, 388 A.2d 206 (1978)(where rape victim sought recovery for injuries from the New Jersey Criminal Injuries Compensation Board, evidence of PTSD admissible to establish damages); Alphonso v. Charity Hosp., 413 So.2d 982 (La. Ct. App.)(where plaintiff raped twice in defendant's psychiatric hospital, evidence of PTSD supported award of $50,000 for emotional damages), *cert. denied,* 415 So.2d 952 (La. 1982).
    [114]Robinson v. Jacksonville Shipyards, *supra* note 109, 760 F. Supp. at 1519; Shrout v. Black Clawson Co., 689 F. Supp. 774, 777, 46 FEP Cases 1339, 1341–42 (S.D. Ohio 1988)(human relations consultant qualified as expert on corporate policy and procedure on sexual harassment; court relied on testimony to determine that defendant's "open-door policy" was inadequate and did not qualify as sexual harassment policy).
    [115]628 F. Supp. 1264 (N.D. Ill. 1986).
    [116]*Id.* at 1308.
    [117]490 U.S. 228, 49 FEP Cases 954 (1989).

denied partnership in an accounting firm, was evaluated in a process that was infected with sexist attitudes.[118]

Sociologists have been permitted to give expert testimony on "the sexual connotations of several of the acts of which plaintiff complained."[119] Psychologists have been permitted to testify on sexual stereotyping to the effect that permitting sexual joking and the display of pornographic material in the workplace is a form of discrimination against women and contributes to a sexually hostile environment.[120]

---

[118]The expert in *Hopkins*, Dr. Susan Fiske, was also the plaintiff's expert witness on sexual stereotyping in *Robinson v. Jacksonville Shipyards*.

[119]*E.g.*, Eide v. Kelsey-Hayes Co., 154 Mich. App. 142, 397 N.W.2d 532, 538, 47 FEP Cases 1043, 1047 (1986)(sociologist familiar with research and literature on sexual harassment qualified to testify about subtle forms of sexual harassment, which included use of nicknames and sexually suggestive posters in workplace), *aff'd in part and rev'd in part on other grounds,* 431 Mich. 26, 427 N.W.2d 488, 47 FEP Cases 1050 (1988).

[120]*E.g.*, Robinson v. Jacksonville Shipyards, *supra* note 109.

CHAPTER 26

DISCOVERY

I. Overview

This chapter focuses on the discovery problems that are particularly important in sexual harassment cases, such as the discovery of an individual's sexual or psychological history. In large part the law of evidence will determine a party's ability to discover information from adverse parties.[1] Discovery also involves certain procedural issues involving medical examinations[2] and protective orders. This chapter also discusses the attorney-client and related evidentiary privileges that typically are resolved before trial.

II. Behavior of the Complainant

Courts will prohibit discovery into the sex life of complainants, or into the identity of their sexual partners, unless there is a strong showing of the need for this information.[3] Courts have expressed concern that unnecessary inquiries into the sex lives of sexual harassment complainants may discourage valid complaints.[4]

A. Behavior With the Alleged Harasser

Virtually any interaction between the complainant and the alleged harasser is plainly relevant to the issue of welcomeness. Thus evidence of a complainant's sexual behavior toward the alleged harasser is generally admissible[5] and therefore discoverable.

---

[1]*See, e.g.,* FED. R. CIV. P. 26(b)(1)(discovery generally is permitted of all information reasonably calculated to lead to discovery of admissible evidence). Evidentiary issues are discussed in Chapter 25, Evidence.

[2]*See, e.g.,* FED. R. CIV. P. 26(c).

[3]*See generally* Berger, *Man's Trial, Woman's Tribulation: Rape Cases in the Courtroom,* 77 COLUM. L. REV. 1 (1977); FED. R. EVID. 412 (excluding most evidence of the prior sex life of complainant in criminal case); Klein, *A Survey of Evidence and Discovery Rules in Civil Sexual Harassment Suits with Special Emphasis on California Law,* 11 INDUS. REL. L.J. 540 (1989); *But see* Feldman, *Sexual Offense Prosecutions: The Defendant's Right to Obtain a Mental Examination of the Complaining Witness,* 24 TENN. B.J. 22 (1988); Tanford & Bocchino, *Rape Victim Shield Laws and the Sixth Amendment,* 128 U. PA. L. REV. 544 (1980).

[4]*See* Priest v. Rotary, 98 F.R.D. 755, 32 FEP Cases 1064, 1069 (N.D. Cal. 1983)(defense discovery tactics "might intimidate, inhibit or discourage Title VII plaintiffs").

[5]See Chapter 25, Evidence, Section III.B.

B. Off-Premises Behavior With Third Parties

Evidence of the complainant's sexual activity outside of the workplace with third parties is generally inadmissible,[6] and hence not discoverable. In *Mitchell v. Hutchings*,[7] a suit brought by several complainants for sexual harassment and emotional distress, the court quashed depositions of co-workers with whom the complainants allegedly had engaged in sexual behavior. Judge David K. Winder ruled that the alleged harasser could not use evidence of the complainants' sexual activity to show that they welcomed his advances or that they did not suffer damage from his overtures: "Past sexual conduct does not, as defendants would argue, create emotional calluses that lessen the impact of unwelcomed sexual harassment. The fact that plaintiffs may welcome sexual advances from certain individuals has no bearing on the emotional trauma they may feel from sexual harassment that is unwelcome."[8]

The leading federal case on the discoverability of a complainant's sexual history is *Priest v. Rotary*.[9] The complainant, a waitress in a restaurant and bar, claimed that her employer fired her for rejecting his sexual advances. The defendant sought the name of each sexual partner that the complainant had had over the past ten years to support a claim that she was the sexual aggressor and that she had been trying to "pick up" male customers at the defendant's bar. Judge Thelton E. Henderson granted the complainant's motion for a protective order to block this discovery, relying on the ban against character evidence,[10] and also ruling that even if the discovery were reasonably calculated to lead to admissible evidence, a protective order under Rule 26(c) would be appropriate because of the court's "deep[] concern[] that civil complaints based on sexual harassment in the workplace will be ... inhibited, if discovery tactics such as the one used by defendant herein are allowed to flourish."[11]

Similarly, the California Supreme Court, in *Vinson v. Superior Court*,[12] ruled that the defendant's psychiatrist could not inquire during a pre-trial medical examination into the sexual history, habits, and practices of a complainant whose sexual harassment suit claimed that she was fired for spurning the advances of the defendant's manager. The court relied on California law specifically addressing issues of discovery[13] and the admissibility of evidence in civil actions for sexual harassment.[14] The court held that the defendants had neither established specific facts justifying an intrusion into the complainant's

---

[6]See *id*. at Section III.D.

[7]116 F.R.D. 481, 44 FEP Cases 615 (D. Utah 1987).

[8]*Id*. at 485.

[9]*Supra* note 4.

[10]See Chapter 25, Evidence, Section II.B.

[11]*Supra* note 4, 98 F.R.D. at 762. The court relied heavily on the policy behind Federal Rule of Evidence 412 and the "rape shield" laws enacted to prevent abusive interrogation of victims in rape prosecutions. *Id*. at 761–62. For a discussion of Rule 412, see Chapter 25, Evidence, Section II.C.

[12]43 Cal.3d 833, 239 Cal. Rptr. 292, 44 FEP Cases 1174 (1987).

[13]CAL. CODE CIV. PROC. §2017(d):

In any civil action alleging conduct that constitutes sexual harassment, sexual assault, or sexual battery, any party seeking discovery concerning the plaintiff's sexual conduct with individuals other than the alleged perpetrator is required to establish specific facts showing good cause for that discovery, and that the matter sought to be discovered is relevant to the subject matter of the action and reasonably calculated to lead to the discovery of admissible evidence.

[14]CAL. EVID. CODE §§783, 1106, discussed in Chapter 25, Evidence, Section II.C.

privacy rights nor shown how the discovery sought would lead to relevant evidence.[15]

The same result occurred in *Mendez v. Superior Court*,[16] where the complainant sued her employer for sexual assault, battery, and intentional infliction of emotional distress. The defendants sought discovery of the complainant's sexual history with co-workers and her sexual activities outside of work. The court denied the discovery because of the privacy rights of the complainant and her sexual partners, and because the defendants showed no "compelling need" for the information, as required by California law.[17] The court ruled that any evidence of the complainant's infidelity could not be used to prove either (a) that the infidelity, rather than the alleged assault, caused her emotional distress, or (b) that infidelity caused some of her distress and that damages should be reduced accordingly.[18]

In *Knoettgen v. Superior Court*,[19] the complainant successfully resisted discovery into the sexual assaults that she had suffered as a child even though the defendant's forensic psychiatrist opined that the childhood incidents bore upon her current perceptions. The court concluded that the discovery was unduly intrusive and that it was not justified by the good cause required for such discovery under the California shield statute.

C. Complainant's Statements

The defendant is entitled to discover whether the complainant made prior inconsistent statements, which may be admissible under the Federal Rules of Evidence.[20] Accordingly, the defendant should have broad latitude to inquire in discovery into the identity of persons with whom the complainant discussed the incidents, what was said, and when it was said. These individuals, in turn, may be questioned regarding their conversations with the complainant and the reports made by the complainant as to the incident.

III. PSYCHOLOGICAL OR MEDICAL RECORDS

Where sexual harassment claims have placed the complainant's medical and psychological history at issue, the defendant may seek access to medical or psychological records of prior similar symptoms and stress-related disorders

---

[15]Vinson v. Superior Court, *supra* note 12, 44 FEP Cases at 1177–78.

[16]206 Cal. App.3d 557, 253 Cal. Rptr. 731 (1988).

[17]*Id.* at 573–74, 253 Cal. Rptr. at 741. The plaintiff took away some of the defendant's best arguments for discovery by stipulating that she would not seek damages for any harm done to the stability of her marriage or the quality of her sex life. *Id.* at 570.

[18]*Id.*, 253 Cal. Rptr. at 739–41. The court also rejected the defendant's arguments that the plaintiff's sexual history was relevant to her credibility and that discovery was necessary to attack the credibility of sexual partners who might appear as witnesses. *Id.* at 741–42.

[19]224 Cal. App.3d 11, 273 Cal. Rptr. 636 (1990).

[20]*See* FED. R. EVID. 806 (credibility of hearsay declarant or of party admission may be attacked by evidence admissible if declarant had actually testified); *cf.* FED. R. EVID. 613 (witness may be examined about any prior statement, written or not, and extrinsic evidence of prior statement can be admissible if witness offered opportunity to explain or deny and opposing party permitted to interrogate, or if justice otherwise requires).

to discover other stressful events that could have caused the complainant's symptoms.[21]

Defendants often seek information from mental health professionals who have treated a complainant for emotional trauma caused by sexual harassment. If the claim does not seek compensatory relief, mental health records arguably are irrelevant because the complainant's mental state is not in controversy. If there is a claim for emotional distress damages, however, an examination generally would be appropriate.[22]

In *Jennings v. DHL Airlines*,[23] a federal district court, citing a psychotherapist-patient privilege, quashed the defendant's subpoena of the records of the complainant's psychologist.[24] Although the Federal Rules of Evidence do not enumerate a patient-psychotherapist privilege, Rule 501 permits courts to recognize privileges under federal common law,[25] and in *Jennings* Judge Prentice H. Marshall reasoned that such a privilege was justified.[26]

A physician-patient or psychotherapist-patient privilege is qualified rather than absolute; psychological or medical records of the complainant may be discoverable on the ground that the complainant has placed the issue of mental health in controversy.[27] The court in *Jennings* held that a sexual harassment complainant suing solely under Title VII has *not* placed the issue of mental or physical health in controversy:* "whether [the harassment] unreasonably interfered with plaintiff's ability to perform her job ... can be determined without violating plaintiff's confidences to her psychotherapist."[28]

---

[21]*See, e.g.,* Vinson v. Superior Court, *supra* note 12 (allowing discovery and psychological exam where plaintiff claimed severe emotional problems arising from harassment). *But see* Cody v. Marriott Corp., 103 F.R.D. 421, 44 FEP Cases 1228 (D. Mass. 1984)(claims of transient psychological distress insufficient, as matter of public policy, to allow wide-ranging inquiries into mental health of Title VII plaintiff).

[22]Mitchell v. Hutchings, 116 F.R.D. 481, 485, 44 FEP Cases 615 (D. Utah 1987)(defendant may take deposition of plaintiff's treating psychologist and may inquire into all information on which psychologist relied in reaching expert opinion of extent of plaintiff's emotional trauma and its causes).

[23]101 F.R.D. 549, 34 FEP Cases 1423 (N.D. Ill. 1984).

[24]For discussion of the psychiatrist-patient privilege, see *In re Zuniga,* 714 F.2d 632 (6th Cir.) (psychotherapist-patient privilege mandated by "reason and experience," but courts must apply it on case-by-case basis), *cert. denied,* 464 U.S. 983 (1983). The privilege is advocated by several commentators. See J. WEINSTEIN & M. BERGER, WEINSTEIN'S EVIDENCE, ¶504[03] (1990) and authorities cited therein.

[25]Rule 501 provides that evidentiary privileges are a matter of federal common law, except with respect to an element of a claim or defense governed by state law, in which case the privilege is determined by state law. Proposed Rule 504, approved by the Supreme Court, would recognize a patient-psychotherapist privilege, which would apply so long as the holder of the privilege has not placed his or her "mental or emotional condition" in issue.

[26]The rationale for the privilege was articulated by the Group for the Advancement of Psychiatry:

Among physicians, the psychiatrist has a special need to maintain confidentiality. His capacity to help his patients is completely dependent upon their willingness and ability to talk freely. This makes it difficult if not impossible for him to function without being able to assure his patients of confidentiality and, indeed, privileged communication. Where there may be exceptions to this general rule ... there is wide agreement that confidentiality is a *sine qua non* for successful psychiatric treatment. The relationship may well be likened to that of the priest-penitent or the lawyer-client. Psychiatrists not only explore the very depths of their patients' conscious, but their unconscious feelings and attitudes as well. Therapeutic effectiveness necessitates going beyond a patient's awareness and, in order to do this, it must be possible to communicate freely. A threat to secrecy blocks successful treatment.

Report No. 45, Group for the Advancement of Psychiatry 92 (1960), quoted in Advisory Committee's Notes to Proposed Rules, 56 F.R.D. at 242. Many states have enacted some form of the privilege. See *In re Zuniga, supra* note 24, 714 F.2d at 639 n.3.

[27]*See* FED. R. CIV. P. 26; Jennings v. DHL Airlines, *supra* note 23, 34 FEP Cases at 1425 n.1 (privilege would not apply to extent plaintiff made emotional state part of claim).

*[**Editor's Note:** Under the Civil Rights Act of 1991, discussed in Appendix 8, it is now possible to seek compensatory damages for violations of Title VII.]

[28]Jennings v. DHL Airlines, *supra* note 23, 34 FEP Cases at 1425. *Cf.* Broderick v. Shad, 117 F.R.D. 306, 43 FEP Cases 532 (D.D.C. 1987)(where plaintiff alleged insomnia and nervousness because of harassment, inquiry permitted as to medical records reflecting any such conditions reported to physician).

IV. MENTAL EXAMINATION OF THE COMPLAINANT

Rules 26 and 35 of the Federal Rules of Civil Procedure, as well as corresponding state rules, provide that under certain circumstances a defendant may be entitled to an order that compels the complainant to undergo a mental examination.[29] Rule 26(a) identifies the "mental examination" as a legitimate form of discovery, and Rule 35 specifies the criteria governing whether the complainant must submit to a mental examination: (1) the "mental condition" of the plaintiff must be "in controversy," and (2) there must be "good cause shown" for the examination.[30] Rule 35 also addresses the scope and conduct of any examination and requires that the defendant deliver the examiner's findings to the complainant before trial.[31]

In the leading case on Rule 35 examinations, *Schlagenhauf v. Holder,*[32] the Supreme Court held that each motion to compel a mental examination is decided on a case-by-case basis, under all of the relevant circumstances.[33]

A. The "Mental Condition in Controversy" Requirement

The defendant's motion for an order of examination may be analyzed differently depending on whether a complainant claims only equitable relief,[34] or also asserts a claim that would entitle the complainant to emotional distress damages. A defendant moving for an order of examination obviously has a better argument that the complainant's "mental condition is in controversy" where the complainant claims emotional distress damages. Nonetheless, in determining whether mental condition is in controversy, the factor of whether the plaintiff is claiming emotional distress damages is not necessarily dispositive with all courts.

1. Claims for Noncompensatory Relief Only

Even as to causes of action in which the complainant does not claim emotional distress damages, the complainant may wish to present psychologi-

---

[29]We use "mental examination" to mean both psychiatric and psychological evaluations. The defendant may not compel other kinds of examinations. *See, e.g.,* Acosta v. Tenneco Oil Co., 913 F.2d 205, 54 FEP Cases 31, 34–35 (5th Cir. 1990)(defendant not entitled to have employment discrimination plaintiff, who allegedly failed to mitigate damages, interviewed by vocational rehabilitation expert; Rule 35 authorizes only mental examinations, by physician or psychiatrist).

[30]FED. R. CIV. P. 35(a).

[31]Federal Rule of Civil Procedure 35 reads in part:
  (a) When the mental condition of a party ... is in controversy, the court ... may order the party to submit to ... a mental examination by a physician or psychologist .... The order may be made only on motion for good cause shown ... and shall specify the time, place, manner, conditions, and scope of the examination and the person or persons by whom it is to be made.
  (b) ... [T]he party causing the examination to be made shall deliver to the requestor a copy of a detailed written report of the examining physician or psychologist setting out the physician's findings
  ....

[32]379 U.S. 104, 117–20 (1964)(discussing "in controversy" and "good cause" requirements for mental examination).

[33]The requirements are not met by mere conclusions in the pleadings—nor by mere relevance—but require an affirmative showing by the movant that each condition for which the examination is sought is really and genuinely in controversy and that good cause exists for ordering each particular examination. *Id.* at 118.

[34]Under the Civil Rights Act of 1991, discussed in Appendix 8, plaintiffs now may seek compensatory damages.

cal evidence to the effect that the events actually occurred as alleged (*i.e.,* that the complainant's behavior was consistent with having experienced harassment) and that they unreasonably interfered with the complainant's work by causing psychological harm.[35] In those situations, the defendant arguably is entitled to obtain evidence relating to the mental condition of the complainant, including an independent mental examination.[36]

Nonetheless, in *Robinson v. Jacksonville Shipyards,*[37] the first reported case of a hostile environment claim seeking solely Title VII equitable relief in which an employer sought a mental examination, Judge Howell Melton denied the employer's motion to compel. The complainant in *Robinson* alleged that a hostile environment was created by, among other things, pervasive workplace pornography offensive to female employees and to the complainant in particular. The employer made two arguments in support of its motion. First, the complainant had placed her mental condition in controversy in that her hostile environment claim required proof both that an objective "reasonable person" would have been affected by the workplace pornography and that the "complainant herself was no more sensitive to the alleged conduct than the average female shipyard worker."[38] Second, the complainant had placed her mental condition in controversy by seeking back pay for work days lost because of emotional distress caused by the harassment.[39]

Judge Melton rejected both arguments. First, the complainant's alleged hypersensitivity to pornography was not relevant, because the focus of sexual harassment is the employer's conduct viewed by an objective standard, which could be applied without regard to the complainant's own mental condition.[40] Second, the complainant's claim for back pay under Title VII did not place her mental condition in controversy, because that claim required proof of an "intermittent constructive discharge," which again would involve an objective standard that requires no inquiry into the plaintiff's mental state.[41]

Judge Melton reinforced his holdings with the public-policy concern that endorsing mental examinations in every hostile environment case would cause

---

[35]*See generally* Phillips v. Smalley Maintenance Servs., 711 F.2d 1524, 32 FEP Cases 975 (11th Cir. 1983) (psychological expert regarding emotional distress caused by harassment); Arnold v. City of Seminole, 614 F. Supp. 853, 857, 867, 40 FEP Cases 1539 (E.D. Okla. 1985)(plaintiff introduced psychiatric testimony on inability to return to work); Neeley v. American Fidelity Assurance, 17 FEP Cases 482 (W.D. Okla. 1978)(defendant introduced medical and psychological records of plaintiff, and testimony from psychologist, to effect that plaintiff suffered from schizophrenia); Lowe v. Philadelphia Newspapers, 101 F.R.D. 296, 298–99, 44 FEP Cases 1224 (E.D. Pa. 1983)(allowing mental exam by defendant's expert in racial discrimination suit where plaintiff planned to use psychological expert); Zabkowicz v. West Bend Co., 585 F. Supp. 635, 35 FEP Cases 209, 209 (E.D. Wis. 1984)(defendant entitled to have psychiatrist examine plaintiff alleging Title VII sexual harassment at place of employment because plaintiff alleged emotional distress), *aff'd in part and rev'd in part,* 789 F.2d 540 (7th Cir. 1986).
[36]*See* cases cited in note 35 *supra. But see* Vinson v. Superior Court, 43 Cal.3d 833, 840, 239 Cal. Rptr. 292, 297, 44 FEP Cases 1174, 1176 (1987)(dictum)("simple sexual harassment claim asking compensation for having to endure an oppressive work environment or for wages lost following an unjust dismissal would not normally create a controversy regarding the plaintiff's mental state").
[37]118 F.R.D. 525, 54 FEP Cases 83 (M.D. Fla. 1988).
[38]*Id.* at 529.
[39]*Id.*
[40]*Id.* at 531 (quoting Jennings v. DHL Airlines, *supra* note 23, 101 F.R.D. at 551, 34 FEP Cases at 1425): "focus of the question of sexual harassment should be on the defendant's conduct, not the plaintiff's perception or reaction to the defendant's conduct. . . . If defendant's conduct was sufficiently extreme to violate Title VII, then plaintiff's reaction to or interpretation of that conduct is unimportant. If, on the other hand, defendant's conduct did not unreasonably interfere with plaintiff's working environment, her perception of defendant's conduct does not suffice to create a violation of Title VII."
[41]*Supra* note 37, 118 F.R.D. at 531.

complainants to face sexual denigration and thereby discourage claims of discrimination, "undercutting the remedial effect intended by Congress in enacting Title VII."[42]

2. Tort Claims

Where tort claims for emotional distress damages are brought in addition to or instead of Title VII claims, courts generally will order an examination on the basis that the mental state of the complainant has been placed in controversy.[43] The only case to the contrary, *Cody v. Marriott Corp.*,[44] is a sparsely reasoned decision that would have granted the defendant's Rule 35 motion for a mental examination had the plaintiff alleged specific psychiatric or mental injuries or had the plaintiff retained her own psychiatrist or psychologist for trial.[45]

B. Good Cause

"Good cause" for a mental examination requires a showing that the examination could adduce specific facts relevant to the cause of action and necessary to the defendant's case.[46] In sexual harassment cases, defendants may assert (1) a need to show that the complainant was "oversensitive" to sexual banter, (2) a need to show a psychological condition that caused the complainant to imagine that sexual advances were being made,[47] or (3) a need to probe the complainant's allegations of severe emotional distress.[48]

"Good cause" has sometimes required a showing that the defendant has no other method available for discovering the relevant information; failure to show that other less intrusive means are not possible may be grounds to deny the motion.[49]

---

[42]*Id. See also* Vinson v. Superior Court, 43 Cal.3d 833, 239 Cal. Rptr. 292, 296, 44 FEP Cases 1174 (1987)(hostile environment claims themselves do not place mental condition in controversy, for "otherwise [it] would mean that every person who brings such a suit implicitly asserts that she is mentally unstable, obviously an untenable proposition").

[43]*See* Vinson v. Superior Court, *supra* note 42 (mental exams generally appropriate whenever sexual harassment plaintiff asserts claim for compensatory damages arising from emotional distress, but not appropriate when only claim is under Title VII for equitable relief).

[44]103 F.R.D. 421, 44 FEP Cases 1228 (D. Mass. 1984).

[45]*Id.,* 44 FEP Cases at 1229. The court's reasoning resembles that used in sexual assault cases, where courts have been reluctant to allow mental examinations of the complainant absent proof that actual mental condition is in controversy. Note, *Psychiatric Examination of Sexual Assault Victims: A Reevaluation,* 25 U.C. DAVIS L. REV. 973 (1982).

[46]*See generally* Schlagenhauf v. Holder, *supra* note 32, 379 U.S. at 118–19.

[47]Robinson v. Jacksonville Shipyards, *supra* note 37, 118 F.R.D. at 529. *Cf.* Jennings v. DHL Airlines, 101 F.R.D. 549, 550, 34 FEP Cases 1423 (N.D. Ill. 1984)(defendant sought examination of plaintiff's psychologist to obtain similar information).

[48]*See, e.g.,* Arnold v. City of Seminole, *supra* note 35 (plaintiff introduced psychiatric testimony on inability to return to work). In *Vinson, supra* note 42, 239 Cal. Rptr. at 297, the California Supreme Court held that a psychiatric examination could produce relevant evidence because the plaintiff had alleged diminished self-esteem, reduced motivation, sleeplessness, loss of appetite, fear, loss of social contacts, and mental anguish.

[49]Marroni v. Matey, 82 F.R.D. 371 (D. Pa. 1979)(defendant must try other methods before seeking mental exam). *See, e.g.,* Petition of Trinidad Corp., 238 F. Supp. 928 (E.D. Va. 1965)(personal injury case)(no exam to be ordered until after movant had deposed plaintiff or served interrogatories to determine conditions at issue and treatment received, and thus exactly what further data movant needed and how such could best be obtained). A court might also look for any prior discovery abuse by the defendant in deciding the "good cause" issue. See Krieger & Fox, *Evidentiary Issues for Sexual Harassment Litigation,* 1 BERKELEY WOMEN'S L.J. 115 (1985).

C. Conditions Placed on Mental Examinations

A party objecting to a motion to compel a mental examination may invoke the court's broad discretion to attach conditions concerning the "manner, conditions, and scope of the examination and the person or persons by whom it is to be made."[50]

1. Entitlement to Written Reports

The examined party, the examinee, is entitled, upon request, "to a detailed written report of the examining physician or psychologist setting out the physician's findings, including the results of all tests, diagnoses and conclusions, together with like reports of all earlier exams of the same condition."[51] If the examinee makes that request, the party moving to compel the examination, the movant, is entitled to reports by any physician or psychologist who treated the examinee for the same condition.

If the report is not furnished to the examinee, the testimony of the examiner may be excluded.[52] At least one court has held that the report must be made available if the examination proves to be favorable to the examinee and that the movant can be compelled to require the examiner to prepare a written report.[53]

2. Timing

Because of the need to exchange reports, courts typically will require that any examination be made in sufficient time so that all parties can have their respective written reports available well in advance of trial.[54] However, in unusual circumstances, such as where the mental condition of the plaintiff is placed in issue only at trial, the court has the discretion to order a mental examination of the plaintiff even during trial.[55]

3. Subject Matter of Inquiry

In *Vinson v. Superior Court,* the California Supreme Court held that a court may require the movant to outline the scope of the examination in advance to show that each area of questioning during an examination is "directly related to complainant's allegations and essential to the fair resolution of the lawsuit."[56] The *Vinson* court limited the questioning permitted during the mental

---

[50]FED. R. CIV. P. 35. The party may also move for a protective order under Rule 26(c), which permits the court to place conditions upon the examination or to obtain some type of preliminary indication as to the nature of the inquiry being sought. *See, e.g.,* Priest v. Rotary, 98 F.R.D. 755, 32 FEP Cases 1064 (N.D. Cal. 1983).

[51]FED. R. CIV. P. 35(b)(1).

[52]*Id.* ("if a physician fails or refuses to make a report the court may exclude his testimony if offered at trial").

[53]*See* Salvatore v. American Cyanamid, 94 F.R.D. 156, 157–58 (D.R.I. 1982)(examinee entitled, at examinee's expense, to have report prepared by movant's medical examiner who was not to be called as witness and who apparently was told by movant, after giving movant oral report, not to bother preparing written report).

[54]*See, e.g.,* Shapiro v. Win Sum Ski Corp., 95 F.R.D. 38 (E.D.N.Y. 1982).

[55]*See, e.g.,* Kresko v. Rulli, 432 N.W.2d 764 (Minn. Ct. App. 1988).

[56]*Supra* note 42, 239 Cal. Rptr. at 299. This ruling is in line with the arguments of commentators that courts need to limit the breadth and scope of the examination to avoid discouraging victims of sexual harassment from reporting these incidents. Krieger & Fox, *supra* note 49, 1 BERKELEY WOMEN'S L.J. at 125.

examination of the complainant to exclude her prior sexual history and practices.[57]

4. Presence of Observers

Generally, all third parties are excluded from a mental examination[58] because the purpose of the examination is to solicit information from the complainant in a nonadversarial environment.[59] Thus, courts generally will not permit counsel to be present.[60]

Nonetheless, the court has the discretion to allow the examinee to bring an observer to the examination, provided that this will not be unduly disruptive.[61] In *Lowe v. Philadelphia Newspapers,* Judge Donald W. VanArtsdalen ordered a Rule 35 psychiatric examination of a racial discrimination plaintiff on the condition that she could bring her own physician to observe the examination.[62]

Courts also have allowed various other regulatory devices, such as having an independent court reporter present,[63] permitting the complainant to tape-record the examination for review by counsel,[64] and permitting the plaintiff's counsel to take the deposition of the defendant's medical examiner to determine if evidence from the examination should be excluded at trial on the basis that the plaintiff was questioned improperly.[65]

D. Selection of Experts

Neither party may dictate who will conduct the mental examination; the court may choose the examiner if the parties disagree.[66] However, the examinee must articulate a legitimate reason for objecting to the movant's examiner; the examinee may not refuse to be examined by a given examiner without good

---

[57]*Id.,* 239 Cal. Rptr. at 297. *See also* Hughes & Anderson, *Discovery: A Competition Between the Right to Privacy and the Right to Know,* 23 U. FLA. L. REV. 289 (1971)(court may exclude inquiries irrelevant or whose marginal relevance is outweighed by invasion of complainant's privacy); Kreiger & Fox, *supra* note 49, 1 BERKELEY WOMEN'S L.J. at 126–27 (court may exclude inquiries regarding sexual history irrelevant to claims being made).

[58]*E.g.,* Ewing v. Ayres, 129 F.R.D. 137 (N.D. Miss. 1989).

[59]*See, e.g.,* Schempp v. Reniker, 809 F.2d 541 (8th Cir. 1987)(upholding dismissal without prejudice of sex abuse claim where mother refused to permit psychiatric exam of child in sex abuse case; her presence could distort results of exam); Wheat v. Biesecker, 125 F.R.D. 479, 480 (N.D. Ind. 1989)(majority rule is that plaintiff's attorney may not attend Rule 35 exam). A further rationale for excluding attorneys is that their observations during examinations might make them witnesses at trial, and present them with the ethical dilemma (or unfair advantage) of being a material witness and counsel in the same case.

[60]Brandenberg v. El Al Israel Airlines, 79 F.R.D. 543, 546 (S.D.N.Y. 1978)("it has been consistently held, in connection with physical examinations under Rule 35, that counsel for the party being examined are not entitled to be present").

[61]*See, e.g.,* Zabkowicz v. West Bend Co., 585 F. Supp. 635, 636, 35 FEP Cases 209, 210 (E.D. Wis. 1984)(court permitted sexual harassment plaintiff option of having lawyer present, having independent observer attend, or tape-recording exam), *aff'd in part and rev'd in part,* 789 F.2d 540 (7th Cir. 1986); Lowe v. Philadelphia Newspapers, 101 F.R.D. 296, 44 FEP Cases 1224, 1228 (E.D. Pa. 1983)(allowing plaintiff to have own psychiatrist attend Rule 35 psychiatric exam).

[62]*Supra* note 61; *but see* Swift v. Swift, 64 F.R.D. 440, 443 (E.D.N.Y. 1974)(court denied request to have even plaintiff's physician attend examination).

[63]DiBari v. Incaica Cia Armadora, 126 F.R.D. 12 (E.D.N.Y. 1989).

[64]Vinson v. Superior Court, 43 Cal.3d 833, 740 P.2d 404, 239 Cal. Rptr. 292, 44 FEP Cases 1174 (audio tape is unobtrusive measure that will permit evidence of abuse to be presented to court).

[65]Wheat v. Biesecker, *supra* note 59.

[66]See 4A MOORE'S FEDERAL PRACTICE ¶35.04.

reason.[67] If the examinee fails to report for the examination as ordered, the court has the discretion to dismiss the action or impose other discovery sanctions.[68]

E. Confidentiality Orders

In addition to obtaining protective orders relating to the availability and terms of any psychological examination, the parties may desire to obtain protective orders that prohibit general public dissemination of information obtained during the course of discovery. Rule 26(c) permits the court wide discretion to issue orders that protect a party from potential embarrassment as a result of the disclosure of private information. Thus, to the extent that discovery is permitted with respect to the sexual activities of either the complainant or the alleged harasser, courts likely will freely entertain motions to limit the availability of such information to the parties and their counsel and to prohibit general dissemination of such sensitive data to third parties.

V. PRIVILEGES INVOKED REGARDING INTERNAL INVESTIGATIONS

Employers who investigate sexual harassment complaints will often engage in communications and accumulate documents that may be discoverable in subsequent litigation.[69] Various privileges may justify nondisclosure of some aspects of the investigation, although, as a practical matter, the employer may choose to permit discovery because it will want to prove that an extensive investigation occurred.

A. The Attorney-Client Privilege

The Supreme Court in *Upjohn Co. v. United States*[70] held that communications between legal counsel for a corporation and its employees are protected by the attorney-client privilege if the communications are at the direction of corporate superiors in order to secure the legal advice of counsel. In determining the extent to which internal sexual harassment investigations are privileged, two issues are most problematic. The first is whether an attorney-client relationship existed. The relationship does not necessarily exist between a company attorney and the employees whom the attorney interviews. If the attorney is acting solely as legal counsel for a corporate employer, the communications will not be privileged unless the employee had corporate knowledge or stature sufficient to make that employee's speech the speech of the corporation on the

---

[67]*See* Gale v. National Transp. Co., 7 F.R.D. 237 (S.D.N.Y. 1946)(failure to support objection to examination by defendant's expert resulted in denial of objection).

[68]*E.g.,* Schempp v. Reniker, *supra* note 59 (dismissal of suit on behalf of child for alleged sexual abuse proper where mother refused to permit child to be examined). *See generally* FED. R. CIV. P. 37 (detailing sanctions for refusing to permit court-ordered discovery).

[69]For a discussion of employer investigations, see Chapters 18, Taking Preventive Action, and 19, Responding to Internal Complaints.

[70]449 U.S. 383, 394 (1981). *E.g.,* Price v. County of Erie, 40 FEP Cases 115, 117 (W.D.N.Y. 1986)(documents of employee investigation maintained by law department protected under attorney-client privilege in later age discrimination suit).

subject matter in question.[71] Further, if the investigation is conducted by nonattorneys, no attorney-client relationship may be found.[72]

A second problematic factor is the capacity in which the attorney functioned. Courts have held that neither the attorney-client privilege nor the work-product doctrine provide protection when the attorney is acting as a business adviser or an investigator for the employer.[73] These protections are available only when the attorney is acting as a legal adviser.

B. Work Product Immunity

1. Absolute Protection for Mental Impressions

The work-product doctrine, codified in Rule 26(b)(3) of the Federal Rules of Civil Procedure,[74] absolutely protects from disclosure any documentation of an attorney's mental impressions, conclusions, opinions, and legal theories prepared in anticipation of litigation.[75]

2. Qualified Protection for Other Material Prepared in Anticipation of Litigation

The work-product doctrine gives *qualified* protection to materials, such as notes of witness interviews, prepared in anticipation of litigation.[76] Some courts have indicated, however, that factual accounts of the events at issue in a case will not be protected by the work-product doctrine.[77]

a. When qualified protection applies. An employer's internal investigation may be protected by the work-product doctrine if the investigation was conducted in anticipation of imminent litigation arising from the same facts as those under investigation.[78] Litigation may be anticipated before the filing of

---

[71]*See generally* Upjohn Co. v. United States, *supra* note 70 (communications by employees to counsel privileged where communications concerned matters within scope of employees' corporate duties and employees aware they were being questioned so corporation could obtain legal advice); EEOC v. Anchor Hocking Corp., 31 FEP Cases 1049, 1051 (S.D. Ohio 1981)(without discussing requisites of privilege, court held that communications between counsel and employees were privileged). *But see* Veatch v. Northwestern Memorial Hosp., 1989 WL 51161 (N.D. Ill. 1989)(communications in-house counsel has with employee or former employee not privileged where counsel represents company, not employee).

[72]Mercy v. County of Suffolk, 93 F.R.D. 520, 522 (E.D.N.Y. 1982)(where internal police department investigation conducted by police officer, not attorney, officer's narrative report and statements of interviews deemed beyond scope of attorney-client privilege).

[73]Brooms v. Regal Tube Co., 881 F.2d 412, 422, 50 FEP Cases 1499, 1505–6 (7th Cir. 1989)(attorney hired to investigate and advise employer concerning allegations of sexual harassment held to have been hired as investigator, not attorney, and no privilege arose to protect notes or reports at trial); Winfield v. St. Joe Paper Co., 20 FEP Cases 1100, 1102 (N.D. Fla. 1978)(documents relating to organization's policies, even though developed in part upon advice of counsel, not within scope of attorney-client privilege because not confidential communications for purpose of securing legal advice).

[74]For a discussion of the work-product doctrine, see Chapter 22, Employer's Litigation Strategy.

[75]Rule 26(b)(3) provides that, even as to otherwise discoverable work product, "the court shall protect against disclosure of the mental impressions, conclusions, opinions, or legal theories of an attorney or other representative of a party concerning the litigation."

[76]Rule 26(b)(3) provides that where documents are "prepared in anticipation of litigation or for trial by or for [a] party or that party's representative," discovery may be had of the document "only upon a showing that the party seeking discovery has substantial need of the materials . . . and is unable without undue hardship to obtain the substantial equivalent of the materials by other means."

[77]*See, e.g.,* Broderick v. Shad, 117 F.R.D. 306, 308, 310, 43 FEP Cases 532, 533, 535 (D.D.C. 1987)(where sexual harassment plaintiff moved to compel production of "ethics file" compiled during counsel's investigation of alleged misconduct, court held factual data gathered in inquiry not privileged and ordered that segregable factual information be produced while any handwritten notes of counsel, recommendations, opinions, or conclusions be redacted).

[78]*See* Brooms v. Regal Tube Co., 42 FEP Cases 16, 17 (N.D. Ill. 1986)(interview notes and other documents prepared by outside counsel investigating sexual harassment charges not attorney-client communications

a formal legal complaint, and even before the filing of a formal charge with a state or federal agency.[79]

Although litigation is generally considered to be imminent once government charges have been filed,[80] at least one court has held that where there is nonetheless no real prospect of litigation, the doctrine does not apply.[81] Thus, if there is no substantial difference in the manner in which filed charges and informal claims are investigated, the employer may be unable to persuade the court that the employer viewed the charge as signaling that litigation was imminent.[82]

Courts will examine whether the employer's primary motivating purpose in conducting the investigation was to prepare for litigation that was expected to arise from the facts under investigation in the particular case.[83] If the investigation is conducted as an ordinary business practice or for business purposes—such as fostering employee relations or forestalling future litigation by identifying potential problems—and litigation is not expected, the doctrine does not apply.[84]

b. When disclosure is required. Where the qualified protection applies, documents prepared in anticipation of litigation must be disclosed only if the party seeking disclosure proves (1) a substantial need for the documents, and (2) an inability to obtain the substantial equivalent by other means.[85] When the

---

and thus not protected by attorney-client privilege, but protected from discovery by work-product doctrine because prepared after plaintiff's EEOC charge and in anticipation of litigation). Work-product materials may, however, be required to be produced at trial. Brooms v. Regal Tube Co., *supra* note 73 (attorney hired to investigate and advise employer concerning an employee's allegations of sex harassment held to have been hired as investigator, not attorney, and no privilege arose to protect notes or reports at trial). *Cf.* Star-Telegram v. Schattman, 784 S.W.2d 109, 110, 53 FEP Cases 1133, 1134–35 (Tex. Ct. App. 1990)(work-product doctrine not applicable to attorney's investigation of sexual harassment where no EEOC complaint filed, no evidence that employee was contemplating suit, attorney hired not a litigator admitted in jurisdiction, and sole purpose of investigation to advise employer how to comply with federal law, principally by taking corrective action).

[79]*See, e.g.,* Rauh v. Coyne, 744 F. Supp. 1181 (D.D.C. 1990)(documents prepared during attorney-conducted investigation of sexual harassment complaint before filing of charges held to be created in anticipation of litigation where suit related to identical facts already filed; protection not waived by employer's disclosure that its investigation could not determine truth of sexual harassment complaint).

[80]Brown v. Marriott Corp., 33 FEP Cases 550 (N.D. Ga. 1983)(where employee threatened litigation and filed EEOC charges, subsequent investigation constitutes work product); EEOC v. Anchor Hocking Corp., *supra* note 71, 31 FEP Cases at 1050 (work-product doctrine protected notes of attorney hired to conduct investigation after EEOC complaint filed).

[81]EEOC v. General Motors Corp., 47 EPD ¶38,262 (D. Kan. 1988)(materials assembled in ordinary course of business not protected).

[82]*Id. See also* EEOC v. Commonwealth Edison, 119 F.R.D. 394, 395, 46 FEP Cases 598, 599 (N.D. Ill. 1988)(where equal employment administrator investigated approximately 100 discrimination claims and admittedly expected very few, if any, to result in litigation, work-product doctrine did not apply).

[83]Resnick v. American Dental Ass'n, 95 F.R.D. 372, 375, 31 FEP Cases 1359, 1361 (N.D. Ill. 1982)(where personnel study and establishment of employee relations committee undertaken for business purposes, work-product privilege did not apply, despite fact that they were initiated with advice of counsel), *cert. denied,* 479 U.S. 813 (1986).

[84]EEOC v. Commonwealth Edison, *supra* note 82; Resnick v. American Dental Ass'n, *supra* note 83 (where (1) broad-ranging personnel practices study was management-oriented and role of counsel was tangential and (2) establishment of employee relations committee designed for overall business reasons and did not arise from threat of particular lawsuit, documents not protected by work-product doctrine, despite fact work initiated with advice of counsel and counsel advised of progress); Mercy v. County of Suffolk, *supra* note 72 (work-product privilege did not apply where investigation was to determine whether disciplinary action should be taken).

[85]In *EEOC v. General Motors Corp., supra* note 81, the court found disclosure was warranted where the documents contained information concerning eight potential witnesses who might be able to assist the plaintiff in proving the defendant's knowledge of the complaint of sexual harassment and failure to take remedial action. Since four of the potential witnesses were unable to answer certain propounded questions

complainant is free to question the same individuals that the employer has interviewed, no compelling need overcomes the work-product immunity.[86]

C. Critical Self-Analysis Privilege

To encourage corporate self-examination, courts sometimes protect internal materials from discovery under the critical "self-analysis" privilege.[87] Three factors support application of the self-analysis privilege: (1) the materials have been prepared for mandatory government reports; (2) the materials are subjective and evaluative, not objective, data; and (3) the policy favoring exclusion clearly outweighs the complainant's need for discovery.[88]

In employment discrimination cases, courts have considered whether self-evaluative materials required by law to be filed with affirmative action plans are discoverable.[89] Many courts have precluded discovery of the self-evaluation portions of those materials, permitting discovery of objective data only. Mental impressions and recommendations have been protected.

Employers have analogized other internal investigative material to affirmative action plans in order to avoid disclosure.[90] Where an employer voluntarily conducts an investigation, however, the privilege may not apply.[91] Similarly, because investigative reports are not literally required by Title VII,[92] investigations of sexual harassment claims arguably are not subject to a self-analysis privilege.[93]

D. Ombudsman's Privilege

Another common-law privilege of potential application in a sexual harassment case is the "ombudsman's privilege." This privilege was applied in *Kientzy v. McDonnell Douglas Corp.*,[94] where a Title VII plaintiff challenging

---

because of lack of memory and three of them indicated they might have made relevant records that had been lost or destroyed, the court held that the plaintiff had demonstrated substantial need and that the substantial equivalent could not be obtained.

[86]Rauh v. Coyne, *supra* note 79.

[87]Granger v. National R.R. Passenger Corp., 116 F.R.D. 507, 510 (E.D. Pa. 1987)(nonlawyer's investigation of train accident); Banks v. Lockheed-Georgia Co., 53 F.R.D. 283, 285, 4 FEP Cases 117, 118 (N.D. Ga. 1971)(employee research team's report on company's equal employment opportunities problems); *but see* Webb v. Westinghouse Elec. Corp., 81 F.R.D. 431, 20 FEP Cases 1231 (E.D. Pa. 1978)(critical self-analysis privilege does not protect objective data).

[88]Webb v. Westinghouse Elec. Corp., *supra* note 87, 81 F.R.D. at 434, 20 FEP Cases at 1233.

[89]According to *Stevenson v. General Elec. Co.,* 18 FEP Cases 746 (S.D. Ohio 1978), authority is split over access to affirmative action plans. Some courts have held that affirmative action plans are discoverable. *E.g.,* Ligon v. Frito-Lay, 19 FEP Cases 722, 723 (N.D. Tex. 1978); EEOC v. ISC Fin. Corp., 16 FEP Cases 174, 179 (W.D. Mo. 1977).

[90]Stevenson v. General Elec. Co., *supra* note 89 (request for names of employees who had previously filed complaints internally or with government agencies deemed analogous to affirmative action plans and not discoverable); Hoffman v. United Telecommunications, 117 F.R.D. 440, 442–43 (D. Kan. 1987)(where plaintiffs sought to depose attorney concerning his opinion based on reviewing EEO-1 report filed by company with EEOC on need to hire females, court held questions not protected by self-criticism privilege because deponent asked about his own opinion; discovery concerning analysis performed in preparation of the EEO-1 report, however, was protected).

[91]*See* Whitaker v. Carney, 778 F.2d 216, 218, 39 FEP Cases 987, 988 (5th Cir. 1985)(allowing disclosure of sexual harassment complaints lodged under employer's grievance procedure); Resnick v. American Dental Ass'n, *supra* note 83 (where personnel practices study and employee relations committee documents not prepared for mandatory government reports, critical self-analysis privilege did not apply).

[92]29 C.F.R. §1604.11 (1990), reproduced in Appendix 1.

[93]Star-Telegram v. Schattman, *supra* note 78 (investigatory reports not privileged; such reports not required by EEOC Guidelines).

[94]133 F.R.D. 570 (E.D. Mo. 1991).

her dismissal from employment sought to inquire into what the defendant's employees had told the corporate ombudsman who had been assigned to her case. The ombudsman was a person the corporation directed to "receive communications and to remedy workplace problems, in a strictly confidential atmosphere." The court held that communications to the ombudsman were protected from disclosure, reasoning that an ombudsman's privilege was appropriate to recognize in light of four "cardinal factors" informing determinations of common-law privilege: (1) the communication was made in the belief that it would not be disclosed, (2) confidentiality was essential to the relationship of the parties, (3) the relationship is worthy of being fostered, and (4) the injury caused by disclosure would be greater than the benefit gained in the correct resolution of the litigation.

An ombudsman's privilege will likely be of little practical effect. Recognition of the privilege in *Kientzy* rested upon factors that are not likely to recur often. First, the Ombudsman Office was solely a mediation, not a decision-making, office within the company, was independent of the human resources department, and had direct access to the company president. Second, the ombudsman was bound by the Code of Ethics of the Corporate Ombudsman Association, which requires confidentiality, and kept records confidential even from the company. Third, the defendant was a large government contractor, a fact the court noted in emphasizing the social benefits of the privilege.

VI. ENTITLEMENT OF THE ALLEGED HARASSER TO DISCOVERY FROM A CO-DEFENDANT EMPLOYER

Few decisions address the extent to which an alleged harasser may discover an employer's investigatory materials.[95] In an attempt to obtain discovery, an alleged harasser may invoke the joint-defense exception to the attorney-client privilege. Under the joint-defense exception, an alleged harasser named as a co-defendant with the employer may obtain an employer's investigatory materials created before the interests of the alleged harasser and the employer diverged.[96] One court has noted the difficulties in determining the moment of that divergence, finding that a joint defense may continue even after the alleged harasser consults separate counsel.[97]

---

[95]Of course, documents may be discoverable if they are not protected by the attorney-client privilege, the work-product doctrine, or the self-criticism privilege. Foore v. Crumpton, 43 FEP Cases 638, 640 (D. Or. 1987)(where investigation of alleged harasser not conducted for lawsuit but to determine if he was derelict in his duties, investigatory documents discoverable). At least one court has held that Title VII itself does not permit the employer to claim the need to protect its employees as a basis for refusing to comply with discovery demands by the alleged harasser. Whitaker v. Carney, *supra* note 91, 778 F.2d at 222, 39 FEP Cases at 991 (former employee accused of sexual harassment entitled to see evidence against him under Texas Open Records Act; Title VII does not require employer to withhold documentary evidence of employee reports of Title VII violations).

[96]Rudow v. Cohen, 1988 WL 13746 (S.D.N.Y. 1988)(alleged harasser successfully used obtained privileged documents prepared by former employer's counsel even though harasser did not participate in privileged communications; documents prepared by employer concerning termination of harasser, however, did not relate to subject matter of joint representation and were not discoverable). For further discussion of the individual defendant's rights vis-à-vis the corporate defendant, see Chapters 22, Employer's Litigation Strategy, and 23, The Alleged Harasser as Defendant.

[97]*Id.*

VII. OTHER DISCOVERY ISSUES

A. Evidence of Other Harassment

The complainant's as well as the defendants' discovery may be limited in scope by considerations of undue embarassment or invasion of privacy. In *Boler v. Superior Court*,[98] a California appellate court upheld an alleged harasser's refusal to answer deposition questions about female employees with whom he had had sexual relations. The questions were assertedly relevant to such issues as the employer's knowledge of a propensity to coerce sexual favors from subordinates, but the court held that the inquiries were unduly invasive of the privacy of not only the harasser but of the women in question. The court indicated, however, that it would permit discovery of a list of the women who had worked for the employer during the relevant time frame.

In *Cook v. Yellow Freight System*,[99] a Title VII sexual harassment case, the complainant requested the names, addresses, and telephone numbers of each female office employee who had worked with the alleged harasser. Citing "an embryonic movement" toward recognizing a federal common-law right of privacy in litigation, and using state-court cases as a "useful referent,"[100] the federal district court denied the plaintiff's motion to compel the discovery. The *Cook* court recognized that the information sought was "highly relevant" to a claim that the alleged harasser had a history of harassing women in the workplace and that the employer had failed to respond appropriately, but held that the privacy interests of the absent third parties—the women whose identities were sought—could be asserted by the defendant employer, and that they justified narrowing the discovery to be ordered. The court ordered that the complainant submit a letter for court approval to be sent to the women in question, that the defendant provide the complainant with mailing addresses for the purposes of allowing her to mail the court-approved letter, and that "further discovery of the [women] and their files [be] subject to their individual consent and . . . be used solely for the purpose of this lawsuit."[101]

B. Identity of the Parties

Because of embarrassing details sometimes alleged and discovered in sexual harassment lawsuits, the parties may wish to limit the full public access generally obtaining in judicial proceedings. In *Doe v. Hallock*,[102] a sexual harassment complainant moved for a protective order sealing the records to ensure the confidentiality of all parties, pleadings, and witnesses.[103] The court

---

[98]201 Cal. App.3d 467, 247 Cal. Rptr. 185 (1987).

[99]53 FEP Cases 1681 (E.D. Cal. 1990).

[100]*Id.* at 1682–83. The court cited cases decided under California constitutional law, which recognizes a right to privacy that limits discovery in litigation. *Id.*

[101]*Id.* at 1684.

[102]119 F.R.D. 640 (S.D. Miss. 1987).

[103]In the alternative, the plaintiff sought to sue anonymously under the name of "Jane Doe." The court held that she could not proceed anonymously, for she failed to show any real danger as a result of disclosing her identity. The court discounted evidence of the retaliation the plaintiff had already suffered, reasoning that the source of any harassment apparently was already aware of her identity and that it was the plaintiff's burden to show that further danger would result from disclosure of her identity.

denied the complainant's motion, concluding that her feelings of embarrassment did not outweigh the public policy of "judicial openness."

C. Employer-Alleged Harasser Settlement

In *Cook v. Yellow Freight System,*[104] Judge Hollows denied the complainant's request for documents concerning settlement negotiations between the defendant employer and the alleged harasser, who allegedly was dismissed as a result of the complainant's reports of sexual harassment. The court ruled that withholding these documents was justified by a "right of privacy" as well as by Rule 408 of the Federal Rules of Evidence, which excludes evidence of compromises, and evidence of conduct or statements in compromise negotiations, when offered to prove liability for or the invalidity of the claim being compromised.[105]

D. Discovery Abuses

In *Sanders v. Circle K Corp.,*[106] the complainant served a Rule 30(b)(6) notice of deposition on the corporate defendant, requiring it to designate as a deponent its representative most knowledgeable about the events of the sexual harassment alleged in the complaint. The corporate defendant designated the human resources official who investigated the report of harassment and had only second-hand knowledge regarding it. The complainant was sanctioned for filing a motion to compel the corporate defendant to designate the alleged harasser as its representative. The court reasoned that the corporation had a conflict of interest with the alleged harasser, in that the corporation was denying that he was its officer director, or managing agent, or acting within the scope of his employment, and could not reasonably be expected to name him as its representative.

In *McKenna v. Ward,*[107] the court denied a defense motion that a sexual harassment complaint be dismissed because of the complainant's discovery misconduct. The complainant, a police officer who alleged sexual harassment so severe that it had caused her psychological problems, repeatedly knifed her former supervisor in the back during one of the depositions in the case. Judge John F. Keenan, noting that the supervisor's wounds were not serious and that the complainant was willing to abide by any reasonable security measures in the future, concluded that dismissal of the lawsuit, even if it were within his authority, would not be appropriate.

---

[104]*Supra* note 99.

[105]*Id.* at 1684–86. The court acknowledged that a completed settlement between the alleged harasser and the defendant, as opposed to "the existence of unaccepted proposals," would be admissible to show bias of the alleged harasser; but settlement discussions short of that have only "marginal relevance," "outweighed by the privileged nature of settlement discussions." *Id.* at 1688.

[106]55 FEP Cases 1356 (D. Ariz. 1991).

[107]52 FEP Cases 1770 (S.D.N.Y. 1990).

CHAPTER 27

ASSERTED DEFENSES

I. OVERVIEW

A sexual harassment claim is subject to a number of common defenses, both factual and legal. Some of these defenses lend themselves well to a separate discussion and are addressed in this chapter. These defenses include the complainant's failure to file a timely complaint and to exhaust administrative remedies,[1] the exclusive nature of a state fair employment practices statute,[1a] the exclusive-remedies provision of a state workers' compensation statute,[1b] the complainant's failure to abide by an agreement to arbitrate,[1c] and potential constitutional restrictions on the government's ability to forbid certain forms of sexual harassment.[1d]

Other defenses, both legal and factual, are best discussed in conjunction with the specific claims to which they relate and therefore are discussed elsewhere. These defenses include the complainant's failure to invoke the employer's internal grievance procedure,[1e] the welcome nature of the conduct complained of,[1f] the employer's nondiscriminatory reasons for its challenged employment decisions,[1g] the employer's prompt remedial action,[1h] official and sovereign immunity,[1i] failure to mitigate damages,[1j] "unclean hands"[1k] and other equitable defenses,[1l] and accord and satisfaction.[1m]

---

[1]See Section II. *infra* and Chapter 23, The Alleged Harasser as Defendant, Section IV.A.

[1a]See Section III. *infra.*

[1b]See Section IV. *infra.*

[1c]See Sections V. and VI. *infra.*

[1d]See Section VII. *infra.*

[1e]See Chapters 4, Hostile Environment Harassment, Section IX.C.1., and 6, Harassment by Supervisors, Section IV.D.

[1f]See Chapters 3, Quid Pro Quo Harassment, Section V.B., and 4, Hostile Environment Harassment, Section V.A.

[1g]See Chapters 3, Quid Pro Quo Harassment, Section IX.B., and 10, Retaliation, Section VII.

[1h]See Chapters 4, Hostile Environment Harassment, Section IX.C.2.; 6, Harassment by Supervisors, Section IV.C.; 7, Harassment by Co-Workers, Section V.; 8, Harassment by Nonemployees, Section III.; 9, Constructive Discharge, Section V.A.2.; and 19, Responding to Internal Complaints, Section IV.

[1i]See Chapter 11, Federal Constitutional, Statutory, and Civil Rights Law, Section III.

[1j]See Chapter 29, Monetary Relief, Section II.B.2.b.

[1k]See Chapter 28, Injunctive and Affirmative Relief, Section III.C.

[1l]For defenses unique to injunctive relief, see Chapters 28, Injunctive and Affirmative Relief, Section III.C.; 29, Monetary Relief, Section II.E.; and *Robinson v. Jacksonville Shipyards,* 760 F. Supp. 1486, 1537 (M.D. Fla. 1991)(addressing and rejecting defense that injunctive relief would contravene collective bargaining mandates of National Labor Relations Act).

[1m]See Chapter 31, Settlement, Section II.

II. FAILURE TO EXHAUST ADMINISTRATIVE REMEDIES

A. Introduction

A jurisdictional prerequisite to suit under Title VII is the exhaustion of administrative remedies. This process includes (1) filing a timely administrative charge and (2) filing a timely complaint in court.[2] If the alleged discrimination occurred in a state where a fair employment practices (FEP) agency has authority to seek redress for employment discrimination, a charge must first be filed with the state FEP agency before it can be filed with the EEOC.[3] Pursuant to agreements between the EEOC and most state FEP agencies, a charge of discrimination filed with the EEOC automatically is filed simultaneously with the state FEP agency.[3a] Most agencies investigate only those charges that are filed directly with them.

Similarly, to sue under a state FEP statute, in most states a complainant must first exhaust the administrative remedies available under the state FEP statute.[4]

B. Untimely Charge

1. Timeliness Requirements

A charge of discrimination under Title VII must be filed with the EEOC within 180 days of the alleged unlawful employment practice.[5] In "deferral" states, in which the plaintiff must initially proceed with a state FEP agency, the time period for filing with the EEOC is extended to 300 days.[6]

2. Commencement of the Charge-Filing Period

Sexual harassment cases raise special issues concerning when the alleged unlawful employment practice occurred and thus when the limitations period begins to run. The general principle, enunciated by Justice Lewis F. Powell, Jr., in *Delaware State College v. Ricks*,[7] is that the commencement of the filing period is the time of the discriminatory acts, not the time at which the consequences of the acts become most painful.[8]

---

[2]*See, e.g.,* Alexander v. Gardner-Denver Co., 415 U.S. 36, 47, 7 FEP Cases 81, 85 (1974)(complainant suing private employer must file EEOC charge within 180 or 300 days and file judicial action within 90 days of receiving notice of right to sue from EEOC); B.L. SCHLEI & P. GROSSMAN, EMPLOYMENT DISCRIMINATION LAW 1014–15 (2d ed. 1983).

[3]Section 706(c), 42 U.S.C. §2000e-5(c); see 29 C.F.R. §1601.74 (listing state and local agencies authorized to receive charges).

[3a]See SCHLEI & GROSSMAN, *supra* note 2, at 941–42.

[4]For a discussion of exhaustion of FEP remedies, see Section III. *infra.*

[5]Section 706(e), 42 U.S.C. §2000e-5(e).

[6]*Id.* For an extended discussion of the Title VII timeliness requirement, see SCHLEI & GROSSMAN, *supra* note 2, at 1013–72, Five-Year Supp. at 393–405. For a more recent case on the interplay of state and EEOC filings, see EEOC v. Commercial Office Prods., 486 U.S. 107, 46 FEP Cases 1265 (1988).

[7]449 U.S. 250, 24 FEP Cases 827 (1980).

[8]*Id.* at 257, 24 FEP Cases at 830. *See also* O'Connor v. North American Phillips, 1989 U.S. Dist. LEXIS 11338 (N.D. Ill. Sept. 25, 1989)(claim untimely because sexual harassment and constructive discharge occurred before statutory period and it was irrelevant that complainant's severance payments ended within statutory period). *Cf.* Bertoncini v. Schrimpf, 712 F. Supp. 1336, 1338 (N.D. Ill. 1989)(charge filed 15 months after sexual advances ended was timely because charge was not predicated on sexual advances but upon discriminatory campaign that began well after plaintiff rebuffed employer's sexual advances).

The complainant's perception of when the discrimination began is often important in determining timeliness,[9] yet the date on which sexual harassment first occurred may be difficult to fix. Welcome conduct at some point may become unwelcome, and trivial conduct may at some point become severe or pervasive. Moreover, incidents that collectively constitute a hostile environment are not routinely recorded in business records as are the promotions or discharges or pay changes that may be involved in more traditional Title VII cases.

In a quid pro quo case the timeliness issue is complicated if the tangible job detriment does not closely follow the unwelcome sexual advances. In *Weide v. Mass Transit Admin.,*[10] a complainant filed a charge of sexual harassment in 1984, within 300 days of a negative performance evaluation from a supervisor who allegedly made an unwelcome sexual advance in 1981. Although the charge was filed more than 300 days after the advance, the court found the charge to be timely because the filing was within 300 days of the negative evaluation, which allegedly was in retaliation for the complainant's rejection of the sexual advance.[11]

3. Amended Charges

If the complainant amends the EEOC charge, an issue arises as to whether the timeliness of the charge is determined by the date of the amendment, or instead relates back to the date of the filing of the original charge. To "relate back" to the original date, an amended charge must (1) simply "cure technical defects or omissions, including failure to verify the charge, or to clarify and amplify allegations," or (2) allege "additional acts which constitute unlawful employment practices related to or growing out of the subject matter of the original charge."[12] The Fifth Circuit, in *Hornsby v. Conoco,*[13] held that a plaintiff's amended charge adding allegations of sexual harassment was time-barred because it did not relate back to her original, timely, charge of failure to promote because of sex and age discrimination. Judge E. Grady Jolly reasoned that the sexual harassment charge was based on facts "independent" of the sex and age discrimination claims, in that the sexual harassment allegations consisted of a claim that the plaintiff's supervisor had physically held her and inquired if she could still get pregnant, allegations that did not appear in the original charge.[14]

---

[9]Bertoncini v. Schrimpf, *supra* note 8.

[10]628 F. Supp. 247, 38 FEP Cases 1501 (D. Md. 1985).

[11]*Id.* at 249, 38 FEP Cases at 1503. The court did not find it necessary to rely on a theory of "continuing violation." *Id.* For a discussion of the continuing violation theory as it relates to timeliness of sexual harassment charges, see Section II.B.5. *infra.*

[12]29 C.F.R. §1601.12(b)(EEOC procedural regulations).

[13]777 F.2d 243, 39 FEP Cases 766 (5th Cir. 1985)(Politz, Garwood & Jolly, JJ.).

[14]*Id.* at 247, 39 FEP Cases at 768–69 (distinguishing *Sanchez v. Standard Brands,* 431 F.2d 455, 2 FEP Cases 788 (5th Cir. 1970), where amended charge alleging national origin discrimination based on same facts in original charge of discrimination).

4. Tolling the Limitations Period

The deadline for filing an administrative charge under Title VII[15] and also under many state FEP statutes[16] is not jurisdictional; it is like a statute of limitations, and as such is subject to equitable tolling, estoppel, and waiver.

5. Continuing Violations

a. General rule. Generally, a complainant may state a claim only for discrimination that occurred within the statutory limitations period. An exception may apply if the court recognizes a theory of a "continuing violation" of Title VII. Under this theory, some courts have held that a claim may proceed on the basis of *all* of the alleged incidents, if "at least one incident of harassment occurred within the [limitations] period."[17]

The complainant may attempt to establish a continuing violation in one of two basic ways: (1) by showing the maintenance of a discriminatory system both before and during the limitations period,[18] or (2) by showing a series of related acts, at least one of which falls within the limitations period.[19]

---

[15]*See, e.g.,* Zipes v. Trans World Airlines, 455 U.S. 385, 393, 28 FEP Cases 1, 4 (1982)(regarding EEOC filing period); Llewellyn v. Celanese Corp., 693 F. Supp. 369, 379, 47 FEP Cases 993, 1000–1001 (W.D.N.C. 1988)(sexual harassment complainant entitled to have statute tolled for 11 months until date she retained attorney who advised her to file claim, when she was mentally disabled by hostile environment and where employer failed to post legally sufficient notice of statutory rights and obligations); Stutz v. Depository Trust Co., 497 F. Supp. 654, 655–57, 24 FEP Cases 63, 63–65 (S.D.N.Y. 1980)(plaintiff given wrong advice by state FEP agency has statute of limitations tolled and is given 60 days beyond date of opinion to file discrimination charge).

[16]*See, e.g.,* EEOC v. Commercial Office Prods., *supra* note 6, 486 U.S. at 124, 46 FEP Cases at 1271 (Colorado's 180-day deadline not jurisdictional). *But see* Williams v. Pacific Mutual Life Ins. Co., 186 Cal. App.3d 941, 231 Cal. Rptr. 234, 48 FEP Cases 619, 622 (1986)(California's one-year limitations period is "condition on a substantive right" rather than "procedural limitation period").

[17]*Compare* Waltman v. International Paper Co., 875 F.2d 468, 474–77, 50 FEP Cases 179, 184–86 (5th Cir. 1989)(continuing violation issue raised where incidents of discrimination all involved sexual harassment, had sufficient continuity, and raised material issue as to quality or permanence with respect to plaintiff's awareness that her rights had been violated) *and* Shrout v. Black Clawson Co., 689 F. Supp. 774, 778–79, 46 FEP Cases 1339, 1342–43 (S.D. Ohio 1988)(upholding claim of sexual harassment based on withholding of pay as last act of continuing violation in sexual harassment charge) *with* Robinson v. Caulkins Indiantown Citrus, 701 F. Supp. 208, 211, 49 FEP Cases 459, 461–62 (S.D. Fla. 1988)(dismissing claim predicated upon continuing violation theory where discriminatory acts did not involve same subject matter, acts not sufficiently continuous—being separated by intervals of five to ten years, and plaintiff should have been apprised of permanence of acts at earlier date) *and* Barrett v. Florida Power & Light Co., 42 FEP Cases 1816 (S.D. Fla. 1987)(prior denials of pay raises were "discrete, isolated and completed acts" and not so closely related to pay decision within statutory period as to constitute continuing violation).

[18]*Compare* Streeter v. Joint Industry Board of the Electrical Industry, 1991 U.S. Dist. LEXIS 8468, slip op. at 16 (S.D.N.Y. 1991)(complainants could sue for acts beyond 300-day limitations period because they alleged "continuous practice and policy of sexual harassment" that included similar acts of harassment and that culminated in discharges that occurred during the limitations period); Porta v. Rollins Envtl. Serv., 654 F. Supp. 1275, 1281–82, 50 FEP Cases 11, 14 (D.N.J. 1987)(hostile environment claim timely even though only plaintiff's discharge fell within limitations period, because of allegations of continuing company policy of discriminating against women), *aff'd mem.,* 845 F.2d 1014, 50 FEP Cases 96 (3d Cir. 1988) *and* Scott v. City of Overland Park, 595 F. Supp. 520, 525, 41 FEP Cases 1211, 1214–15 (D. Kan. 1984)(claim timely because sexual harassment alleged to be part of illegal system or policy of employer) *with* Hoover v. Stauffer Communications, 1989 U.S. Dist. LEXIS 8499 (D. Kan. 1989)(claim untimely because allegations of illegal system or policy of harassment contradicted by defendant's antiharassment policy and swift action, prior to statutory period, in demoting and suspending alleged harasser upon plaintiff's complaints).

[19]SCHLEI & GROSSMAN, *supra* note 2, at 1042–43. *Cf.* Silverberg v. Baxter Healthcare Corp., 52 FEP Cases 1848, 1852 (N.D. Ill. 1990)(continuing violation theory of hostile environment fails when last act occurred 500 days before filing).

Because the continuing violation exception undermines the strict time requirements of Title VII, courts look carefully at continuing violation arguments.[20] The Supreme Court has admonished that mere continuity of employment, without more, does not prolong the life of a cause of action for employment discrimination.[21] Courts that have heard continuing violation arguments have been reluctant to reject them without allowing plaintiffs an additional opportunity to prove or replead their theories.[22]

b. The Waltman *test.* The Fifth Circuit, in *Waltman v. International Paper Co.,*[23] a hostile environment case, provided an analytical framework for applying the continuing violation doctrine in sexual harassment cases. *Waltman* involved a hostile environment claim based on incidents of harassment that had first occurred three years before the complainant's filing of her EEOC charge. The court identified three factors that can help determine whether the complainant has alleged a continuing violation: (1) identity of subject matter; (2) frequency of incidents alleged; and (3) quality of permanence.

The *Waltman* court found the first factor, identity of subject matter, present because each of the acts alleged involved "sexual harassment."[24] The *Waltman* court did not address whether quid pro quo and hostile environment harassment would be considered the same or separate subject matters.

The second *Waltman* factor is whether the acts of sexual harassment are sufficiently frequent; a series of isolated incidents do not constitute a continuing violation.[25] Determining the frequency of the harassment is not "a mechanical calculation," but rather requires the court to "review the pattern and frequency of the harassment and determine whether a reasonable person would feel that the environment was hostile throughout the period that formed the basis of the plaintiff's claim."[26] Incidents of harassment are not necessarily isolated merely because (1) of large gaps of time between incidents, (2) the incidents involved different harassers, (3) no conspiracy exists among the harassers, or (4) no company policy permitted sexual harassment.[27] The facts alleged in *Waltman* constituted sufficiently frequent harassment because co-workers directed sexual comments to the complainant on a weekly basis, and

---

[20]Some courts have required that the theory first be asserted in the administrative charge. *E.g.,* Miller v. IT&T Corp., 755 F.2d 20, 25, 37 FEP Cases 8, 11–12 (2d Cir.)(commencement of limitations period may be delayed until last discriminatory act if "a continuing violation is clearly asserted both in the EEOC filing and in the Complaint"), *cert. denied,* 474 U.S. 851 (1985).

[21]Delaware State College v. Ricks, *supra* note 7, 449 U.S. at 257, 24 FEP Cases at 830.

[22]*E.g.,* Stack v. Turnage, 690 F. Supp. 328, 331 (M.D. Pa. 1988)(deferring judgment on continuing violation theory of sexual harassment complainant). In *Vermett v. Hough,* 606 F. Supp. 732, 37 FEP Cases 1624 (W.D. Mich. 1984), the complainant was permitted an opportunity to prove her allegations of continuing hostile environment violation leading to her constructive discharge, *id.* at 738, 37 FEP Cases at 1628, but ultimately was unable to substantiate "on-going and continuous" harassment as opposed to a single incident. Vermett v. Hough, 627 F. Supp. 587, 608–9, 42 FEP Cases 1432, 1448–49 (W.D. Mich. 1986).

[23]*Supra* note 17, 875 F.2d at 475, 50 FEP Cases at 184–85 (citing Berry v. Board of Supervisors, 715 F.2d 971, 981, 32 FEP Cases 1567 (5th Cir. 1983), *cert. denied,* 479 U.S. 868 (1986)). *Cf.* Green v. Los Angeles County Superintendent of Schools, 883 F.2d 1472, 1480, 50 FEP Cases 1233, 1240 (9th Cir. 1989)(rejecting continuing violation claim of sexual harassment complainant where incidents of co-worker harassment prior to limitations period involved "separate form" of discrimination from that alleged in later period, which involved her discharge).

[24]*Id.* at 475, 50 FEP Cases at 184.

[25]*Id.* at 475–76, 50 FEP Cases at 184.

[26]*Id.* at 476, 50 FEP Cases at 185.

[27]*Id.* at 475–76, 50 FEP Cases at 185–86. Judge Edith Jones, dissenting on liability issues, argued that these factors strongly militated against liability. *Id.* at 483–84 & n.4, 50 FEP Cases at 191.

because sexually explicit notes, graffiti, and pictures were distributed throughout the workplace.[28]

The third *Waltman* factor is whether the incidents of harassment possessed a quality of "permanence" sufficient to alert the complainant that her rights had been violated.[29] The court observed that acts of hostile environment harassment "generally do not have the same degree of permanence" as would, for example, a discriminatory denial of promotion.[30]

c. Cases accepting continuing violation arguments. In *Sampayo-Garraton v. Rave Inc.*,[31] the complainant alleged that she endured repeated unwelcome sexual advances, including touching and requests for sexual relations, before finally being dismissed from her job because of her sex. The dismissal, but not the incidents of harassment, occurred within the 300-day filing period. The court concluded that if a claim of continuing violation were proven, then the court would "have jurisdiction to remedy all those practices."[32]

d. Cases rejecting continuing violation arguments. When complainants have asserted claims that involve a series of unrelated acts, they have been unsuccessful in meeting the continuing violation test.[33] In *Blesedell v. Mobil*

---

[28]*Id.* at 471, 476, 50 FEP Cases at 181, 185.

[29]*Id.* at 476, 50 FEP Cases at 185–86.

[30]*Id.* Taking the factors together, the *Waltman* court reversed a summary judgment for the employer on the ground of untimeliness. The court concluded that the complainant had alleged sufficient facts to create a genuine issue of material fact as to whether there was a continuing violation. *Id.*

[31]726 F. Supp. 18, 51 FEP Cases 994 (D.P.R. 1989).

[32]*Id.* at 20–21, 51 FEP Cases at 996. *Accord* Ravinskas v. Karalekas, 53 FEP Cases 909, 910 (D.D.C. 1990)(claim timely under state FEP statute because, even though initial sexual advance occurred beyond statutory period, defendant alleged to engage in further ongoing discrimination and retaliation); McLaughlin v. State of N.Y. Gov't. Office of Employee Relations, 739 F. Supp. 97, 107–8, 53 FEP Cases 410, 418–19 (N.D.N.Y. 1990)(upholding continuing violation claim of continuing pattern of sexual harassment over four-year period); Shrout v. Black Clawson Co., *supra* note 17, 689 F. Supp. at 778–79, 46 FEP Cases at 1342 (charge timely because only act during 180-day period—denial of pay increase—was continuation of discriminatory pattern of sexual harassment); Porta v. Rollins Envtl. Serv., *supra* note 18 (allowing plaintiff to complain of series of hostile comments and actions; "as long as she files a timely complaint as to one of those actions," claim as to all related acts deemed timely); Clay v. Quartet Mfg. Co., 644 F. Supp. 56, 59, 45 FEP Cases 51, 53 (N.D. Ill. 1986)(upholding claim based on continuous course of sexual remarks and offensive touching when last related act occurred within filing period); *Cf.* Scott v. City of Overland Park, 595 F. Supp. 520, 525–26, 41 FEP Cases 1211, 1214–15 (D. Kan. 1984)(plaintiff claimed continuing sexual harassment, failure to train, and retaliation, but plaintiff not to be compensated on claims exceeding back-pay recovery period of two years). *See also* Starrett v. Wadley, 876 F.2d 808, 822 (10th Cir. 1989)(remanding for district court to decide if unwelcome advances and threats to discharge, occurring beyond statutory period, constituted continuing violation that culminated in plaintiff's discharge).

[33]*E.g.*, Green v. Los Angeles County Superintendent of Schools, *supra* note 23 (continuing violation theory inapplicable to pre-termination conduct; plaintiff's charge addressed post-termination conduct); James v. IBM Corp., 737 F. Supp. 1420, 1424–25, 52 FEP Cases 1858, 1860 (E.D. Pa. 1990)(no continuing violation shown by "isolated, although unfortunate" separate acts of discrimination and harassment by small number of management and nonmanagement employees over seven-year period); O'Connor v. North American Phillips Lighting Co., 1989 U.S. Dist. LEXIS 11338 (N.D. Ill. 1989)(rejecting plaintiff's argument that violation continued with continuing severance benefits during statutory period; severance payment irrelevant to earlier claims of harassment and termination of employment); Blesedell v. Mobil Oil Co., 708 F. Supp. 1408, 1414–15, 1417–18, 53 FEP Cases 391, 395, 397–98 (S.D.N.Y. 1989)(discussed in text at notes 34–36 *infra*); Escott v. City of Chicago, 1988 U.S. Dist. LEXIS 8521 (N.D. Ill. June 10, 1988)(dismissing continuing violation claim where only act within statutory period was layoff that had no connection to earlier alleged incidents of sexual harassment), *aff'd mem.*, 892 F.2d 81 (7th Cir. 1989); DiMaggio v. U.S. Postal Serv., 643 F. Supp. 1, 7–8, 40 FEP Cases 1684, 1689 (D. Conn. 1984)(differentiating between isolated completed acts of unwelcome sexual advances and continuing pattern and practice of discrimination); Quillen v. U.S. Postal Serv., 564 F. Supp. 314, 319, 32 FEP Cases 1631, 1635 (E.D. Mich. 1983)(act within statutory period—denial of reinstatement—was "separate and discrete" from earlier acts of alleged sexual harassment and related discharge); Johnson v. Ramsey County, 424 N.W.2d 800, 46 FEP Cases 1686, 1693–94 (Minn. Ct. App. 1988)(continuing violation theory does not apply to sexual harassment claim when harassment occurred only before statutory period and no actionable harassment occurred thereafter).

Oil Co.,[34] the court rejected the continuing violation arguments of two sexual harassment complainants. In the case of complainant Bate, the court found that she could not sue for discrete instances of harassment, occurring five years apart and involving different individuals, that did not relate to acts that her supervisor had committed within the statutory period.[35] Complainant Blesedell, who was suing for unwelcome sexual advances made within the statutory period, likewise could not sue for earlier derogatory sexual comments or for an earlier unwelcome sexual advance, which had occurred four years before.[36]

Even where complainants have failed to establish a continuing violation, incidents of sexual harassment occurring before the limitations period may be admissible for purposes of showing employer knowledge and intent. In *Ferguson v. E.I. du Pont de Nemours & Co.,*[37] Judge Murray Schwartz, although questioning whether the continuing violation theory even applied in a nonclass action such as the case before him,[38] stated that "past practices, even though not separately actionable, constitute evidence relevant to discriminatory intent and recovery."[39]

C. Inadequate Charge

An EEOC charge must state the facts constituting the alleged sexual harassment, identify the parties charged, and the time period in which the harassment allegedly occurred.[40]

1. Facts Not Alleged in Charge

A subsequent court action generally cannot encompass facts or issues that do not relate to or grow out of the subject matter of the original charge.[41] However, EEOC charges are liberally construed.[42] The few reported decisions on this subject indicate that the complainant need not specify details in the charge, so long as sexual harassment allegations are indicated and the employer

---

[34]*Supra* note 33.

[35]*Id.* at 1415, 53 FEP Cases at 395–96.

[36]*Id.* at 1417, 53 FEP Cases at 397. Blesedell's claims of physical sexual harassment were also deemed untimely as failing to satisfy the continuing violations test because they involved unrelated acts committed by unrelated people. *Id.* at 1418, 53 FEP Cases at 398.

[37]560 F. Supp. 1172, 31 FEP Cases 795 (D. Del. 1983).

[38]*Id.* at 1191 n.42, 31 FEP Cases at 807.

[39]*Id.* at 1191, 31 FEP Cases at 807. *See also* Robinson v. Jacksonville Shipyards, 760 F. Supp. 1486, 1494–95 (M.D. Fla. 1991), reproduced in Chapter 2, Forms of Harassment (incidents preceding statutory period considered (1) to determine whether "more recent conduct may be dismissed as an aberration or must be considered to be part of the work environment" and (2) to assess reasonableness of defendants' responses to plaintiff's complaints).

[40]*See, e.g.,* Clay v. Quartet Mfg. Co., *supra* note 32, 644 F. Supp. at 59, 45 FEP Cases at 54 (sexual harassment); 29 C.F.R. §1601.12(a)(3).

[41]B.L. SCHLEI & P. GROSSMAN, EMPLOYMENT DISCRIMINATION LAW 1110–24 (2d ed. 1983), Five-Year Supp. 419–21 (1989). *See also* Nicol v. Imagematrix, 767 F. Supp. 744, 56 FEP Cases 911, 917–19 & n.11 (E.D. Va. 1991)(dismissing sexual harassment claim as beyond scope of EEOC charge, which alleged only pregnancy discrimination, and suggesting "a more bright line test" based on whether civil allegations name categories of discrimination not named in or implicit in EEOC charge); Sherman v. Standard Rate Data Serv., 709 F. Supp. 1433, 1441–42, 50 FEP Cases 1132, 1139 (N.D. Ill. 1989)(retaliatory discharge separate and distinct from original sex discrimination charge).

[42]*See, e.g.,* Bailey v. Unocal Corp., 700 F. Supp. 396, 398, 53 FEP Cases 1529, 1530–31 (N.D. Ill. 1988)(denying motion to strike allegation that supervisor had exposed himself to complainant, an allegation absent from EEOC charge; allegation was "reasonably related" to "sexual harassment" allegation of charge).

and the nature of the allegations being made are identified.[43] Further, under the "single filing" rule, it is possible that a complainant who has not even filed an administrative charge may join an action brought by someone else who has filed an administrative charge alleging similar discriminatory treatment in the same time frame.[43a]

2. Parties Not Named in Charge

In determining whether an individual defendant not named in the EEOC charge may be named as a defendant in the judicial complaint, courts have considered such factors as (1) whether the role of the unnamed party could reasonably be ascertained by the complainant when the charge was filed, (2) whether the interests of a named party are so similar to those of the unnamed party for purposes of obtaining conciliation and compliance that it would be unnecessary to include the unnamed party in the EEOC proceedings, (3) whether absence from the EEOC proceedings resulted in actual prejudice to the interests of the unnamed party, and (4) whether the unnamed party has in some way represented to the complainant that his relationship with the complainant is to be through the named party.[44]

D. Untimely Notice of Charge

The EEOC should serve a notice of the sexual harassment charge upon the respondent within ten days after the charge is filed.[45] The respondent cannot successfully assert the untimely service of the charge as a defense in private litigation by an individual claimant, unless the respondent can demonstrate actual prejudice.[46] The EEOC's failure to serve notice of the charge within ten

---

[43]*E.g.,* Bailey v. Unocal Corp., *supra* note 42 (permitting plaintiff to litigate allegation that supervisor "expos[ed] himself to plaintiff," even though EEOC charge itself alleged only "sexual harassment, including 'suggestions and advances' which 'create an environment that made it impossible to work' and which resulted in 'extreme emotional and physical distress and anxiety' "); Clay v. Quartet Mfg. Co., *supra* note 32, 644 F. Supp. at 59–60, 45 FEP Cases at 54 (although EEOC charge merely alleging sexually discriminatory wage policy may not support court action for sexual harassment, which "does not necessarily 'grow out of' a pay differential based on sex," charge, as amended to include sexual harassment, did adequately support subsequent complaint on that theory).

[43a]Streeter v. Joint Indus. Bd. of the Elec. Indus., 1991 U.S. Dist. LEXIS 8468, slip op. at 6, 7 (S.D.N.Y. 1991)(defendant named by first but not second complainant in administrative charge may be sued by both complainants in sexual harassment complaint that for both complainants "outlines nearly identical patterns of sexual discrimination and harassment").

[44]*E.g.,* Romero v. Union Pacific R.R., 615 F.2d 1303, 22 FEP Cases 338 (10th Cir. 1980). *Accord* Rabouin v. Colorado Dep't of Law, 54 FEP Cases 1225, 1227–28 (D. Colo. 1990)(applying *Romero* factors in declining to dismiss three individual Title VII defendants not named in EEOC charge); Scott v. City of Overland Park, *supra* note 32, 41 FEP Cases at 1213–14 (applying *Romero* factors in refusing to dismiss two individual defendants in sexual harassment case not named in EEOC charge). *See also* Maturo v. National Graphics, 55 FEP Cases 325, 331–32 (D. Conn. 1989)(permitting sexual harassment suit to proceed against individual defendants under *Romero*-like factors); Weide v. Mass Transit Admin., 628 F. Supp. 247, 38 FEP Cases 1501, 1503 (D. Md. 1985)(denying motion of alleged harasser for dismissal for failure to name him in EEOC charge; "failure to name a defendant in an EEOC charge does not bar the maintenance of a subsequent court action if the purpose of the naming was substantially met"). *See generally* SCHLEI & GROSSMAN, *supra* note 41, at 1094–96, Five-Year Supp. at 415–19. For an additional discussion of defenses peculiar to individual defendants in a Title VII sexual harassment case, see Chapter 23, The Alleged Harasser as Defendant.

[45]§706(b), 42 U.S.C. §2000e-5(b); EEOC v. Shell Oil Co., 466 U.S. 54, 81, 34 FEP Cases 709, 721–22 (1984); EEOC COMPL. MAN. (BNA) §3.1, p. 3:0001; SCHLEI & GROSSMAN, *supra* note 41, at 942–43, Five-Year Supp. at 371.

[46]SCHLEI & GROSSMAN, *supra* note 41, at 942–43, 1140–41. *See, e.g.,* Smith v. American President Lines, 571 F.2d 102, 107 n.8, 16 FEP Cases 712, 715 (2d Cir. 1978).

days thus is not jurisdictional, although some courts have intimated that such failure could bar an action by the EEOC itself.[47]

E. Failure to Conciliate

The EEOC cannot sue unless it first finds reasonable cause to believe that Title VII has been violated and then exhausts reasonable efforts at conciliation to resolve the violation.[48] Where conciliation fails, the EEOC must "so notify the respondent in writing."[49]

An individual complainant may sue once a right-to-sue letter is received, even if the EEOC has not found reasonable cause to believe that discrimination has occurred and even if there has been no effort to conciliate.[50]

F. Right-to-Sue Letter

The complainant may not maintain a Title VII lawsuit without a right-to-sue letter.[51] A plaintiff is entitled to a right-to-sue letter after one of four events: (1) an EEOC finding of no jurisdiction or other reasons for administrative closure;[52] (2) in the discretion of the EEOC, upon the plaintiff's written request, made before completion of the administrative process;[53] (3) an EEOC finding of no reasonable cause;[54] or (4) an EEOC finding of reasonable cause, failure of conciliation, and a determination by the EEOC that it will not itself bring suit.[55]

G. Untimely Lawsuit

A Title VII lawsuit against a private employer is untimely if filed more than 90 days after the plaintiff has received a right-to-sue letter.[56] The 90-day period runs from the plaintiff's actual receipt of notice.[57] This period, like the

---

[47]*Compare* Healen v. Eastern Air Lines, 8 FEP Cases 917, 922 & n.18 (N.D. Ga. 1973)(defendant not served with notice of charge prior to suit; although EEOC's dereliction might be considered jurisdictional in EEOC suit, EEOC's administrative oversight should not jeopardize rights of individual claimant) *with* SCHLEI & GROSSMAN, *supra* note 41, at 1140–41 (collecting cases to effect that EEOC may sue even with tardy notice of charge, absent bad faith or substantial prejudice to defendant).

[48]§706(b), 42 U.S.C. §2000e-5(b), 29 C.F.R. §1601.24. If conciliation succeeds, the charging party, the respondent, and the EEOC may enter into a conciliation agreement. For further discussion, see SCHLEI & GROSSMAN, *supra* note 41, at 965–67, 1142–44, Five-Year Supp. at 377, 431.

[49]29 C.F.R. §1601.25.

[50]*See* 29 C.F.R. §1601.28(b)(issuance of notice of right to sue).

[51]SCHLEI & GROSSMAN, *supra* note 41, at 1058–59, Five-Year Supp. at 400. *E.g.,* Puckett v. Tennessee Eastman Co., 889 F.2d 1481, 51 FEP Cases 580, 585–86 (6th Cir. 1989)(complainant cannot maintain Title VII action without right-to-sue letter where she did not request letter but merely requested withdrawal of EEOC charges). *But see* Wrighten v. Metropolitan Hosps., 726 F.2d 1346, 1351, 33 FEP Cases 1714, 1717 (9th Cir. 1984)(receipt of letter *after* filing suit will suffice absent showing of prejudice to defendant).

[52]29 C.F.R. §§1601.18 (grounds for dismissal of charge), 1601.28(b)(3), (d).

[53]*Id.* at §1601.28(a). Courts have split on whether a plaintiff may sue with a prematurely issued right-to-sue letter. SCHLEI & GROSSMAN, *supra* note 41, at 1060–61, Five-Year Supp. at 401.

[54]*Id.* at §§1601.19(b)(1), 1601.28(b)(3), (d).

[55]*Id.* at §1601.28(b)(1). In certain cases involving governmental respondents, the Attorney General will issue the right-to-sue letter. *Id.* at §1601.28(d). SCHLEI & GROSSMAN, *supra* note 41, at 967.

[56]§706(f)(1), 42 U.S.C. §2000e-5(f)(1); *cf.* Baldwin County Welcome Center v. Brown, 466 U.S. 147, 149–50, 34 FEP Cases 929, 930 (1984)(filing of right-to-sue letter insufficient to "commence" district court action).

[57]Motley v. Bell Tel. Co., 562 F. Supp. 497, 32 FEP Cases 1050, 1050 (E.D. Pa. 1983)(rejecting defense argument that period runs from date shown on notice and stating it begins upon actual or constructive notice); *cf.* Banks v. Rockwell Int'l N. Am. Aircraft Operations, 855 F.2d 324, 326, 47 FEP Cases 1147, 1152 (6th

period for filing an EEOC charge,[58] is subject to equitable tolling principles.[59]

The Supreme Court in *Baldwin County Welcome Center v. Brown*[60] indicated that equitable tolling may occur where (1) the plaintiff has received inadequate notice of her rights, (2) the court has misled the plaintiff into believing that she had fulfilled all procedural requirements, (3) the defendant, through affirmative misconduct, lulled the plaintiff into inaction, or (4) the plaintiff's motion for appointment of counsel is still pending.

III. State FEP Statutory Exhaustion

Most state FEP statutes, following the Title VII model, require sexual harassment complainants to exhaust administrative procedures before filing a suit under a state FEP statute.[61] In some states, the state FEP statute provides the exclusive state-law remedy for harassment, precluding common-law tort theories, particularly those claims that rely upon a public policy forbidding sexual harassment.[62] In other states, the FEP statute is treated as simply an additional remedy for acts that would constitute sexual harassment.[63]

IV. Workers' Compensation Preclusion

A. Overview

Each state has a statutory workers' compensation system designed to compensate employees for workplace injuries.[64] State systems typically provide that workers' compensation benefits are the employee's exclusive state-law remedy for workplace injuries.[65] The language of the Utah statute is an example of an exclusivity provision:

> The right to recover compensation [under this statute] . . . shall be the exclusive remedy against the employer and . . . shall be in place of any and all other civil liability whatsoever, at common law or otherwise, . . . on account of any accident

---

Cir. 1988)(90-day period began five days after notice was mailed, where plaintiff had moved and neither he nor counsel notified EEOC of new address). Receipt by complainant's attorney amounts to receipt by complainant. Irwin v. Veterans Admin., 111 S.Ct. 453, 456 (1990)(construing 42 U.S.C. §2000e-16(c), applicable to federal employee lawsuits).

[58]See text accompanying notes 15–16 *supra.*

[59]*Cf.* Baldwin County Welcome Center v. Brown, *supra* note 56, 466 U.S. at 151, 34 FEP Cases at 930–31 (filing right-to-sue letter did not toll period for commencing action); Gantt v. Green, 1987 U.S. Dist. LEXIS 11144 (D. Kan. 1987)(dismissing case for untimely filing despite claim that EEOC lulled complainant into inaction by sending copy of right-to-sue letter to her attorney).

[60]*Supra* note 56, 466 U.S. at 151, 34 FEP Cases at 930–31. However, the Court found each of these factors to be absent and admonished: "One who fails to act diligently cannot invoke equitable principles to excuse that lack of diligence." *Id.*

[61]For a discussion of exhaustion of administrative remedies under state FEP statutes, see Chapter 12, Fair Employment Practices Statutes, Section V. In some states, such as New York, no exhaustion is required and the complainant may elect to sue under the FEP statute directly in court.

[62]For a discussion of various state-law approaches to FEP preemption of common-law claims, see Chapter 12, Fair Employment Practices Statutes, Section III.

[63]*E.g.,* Rojo v. Kliger, 52 Cal.3d 65, 276 Cal. Rptr. 130, 54 FEP Cases 1146 (1990).

[64]For a discussion of state workers' compensation statutes, see Chapter 14.

[65]*See generally* Love, *Actions for Nonphysical Harm: The Relationship Between the Tort System and No-Fault Compensation,* 73 CAL. L. REV. 857, 865 (1987)(discussing statutory and judicially created exceptions to workers' compensation exclusivity); Schoenheider, *A Theory of Tort Liability for Sexual Harassment in the Workplace,* 134 U. PA. L. REV. 1461, 1490–94 (1986)(discussing workers' compensation barriers to

or injury or death, in any way ... incurred by such employee in the course of or because of or arising out of his employment, and no action at law may be maintained against an employer ... based upon any accident, injury or death of an employee.[66]

A state workers' compensation statute may thus bar an employee's state-law suit based on work-related conduct. In some states the defense bars only suits against the employer,[67] while in other states the exclusivity bar also applies to suits against co-workers.[68] The exclusivity defense bars only state-law claims,[69] although an analogous federal-law defense could apply with respect to injuries of federal employees who are covered by a federal workers' compensation system.[70]

B. Application of Workers' Compensation Exclusivity

In a sexual harassment case, the defense of workers' compensation exclusivity is most often successful against common-law claims of employer negligence.[71] Courts have also held that workers' compensation exclusivity bars a

---

tort recovery for sexual harassment). For a state-by-state survey of cases deciding whether tort claims for sexual harassment are barred by the workers' compensation system, which discusses several cases in detail, see Stauffer, *Sexual Harassment in the Workplace: Developments in State Law,* 1988 ANN. SURV. AM. L. 779.

[66]UTAH CODE ANN. §35-1-60 (1988). Analogous language in the California statute provides: "[where] conditions of compensation ... concur, the right to recover such compensation is ... sole and exclusive remedy of the employee or his or her dependent against the employer." CAL. LAB. CODE §3602 (West 1989).

[67]*E.g.,* Fields v. Cummins Employees Federal Credit Union, 540 N.E.2d 631, 53 FEP Cases 1613, 1618 (Ind. Ct. App. 1989)(claim against supervisor not barred because sexual harassment did not arise from his employment); Pryor v. United States Gypsum Co., 585 F. Supp. 311, 313, 47 FEP Cases 159 (W.D. Mo. 1984)(sexual harassment complainant could maintain assault and battery claim against six individual defendants, and husband could maintain claim for loss of consortium, because existence of workers' compensation act remedy against employer is no shield for individual defendants).

[68]*E.g.,* CAL. LAB. CODE §3602.

[69]A state-law defense obviously would not bar a claim under Title VII, 42 U.S.C. §1983, or other federal law. *E.g.,* Rosa v. Contrell, 705 F.2d 1208, 1221 (10th Cir. 1982)(exclusive remedy of state workers' compensation statute cannot interfere with "enforcement of federal civil rights"), *cert. denied,* 104 S.Ct. 85 (1983).

[70]*Compare* Clay v. United States, 1990 U.S. Dist. LEXIS 6414 (S.D.N.Y. 1990)(federal employee's exclusive remedy for injuries incurred in course of employment is provided by Federal Employees Compensation Act (FECA), therefore barring action for sexual harassment under Federal Tort Claims Act) *with* Nichols v. Frank, 732 F. Supp. 1085, 1089 (D. Or. 1990)(FECA no bar to Title VII sexual harassment claim, but any Title VII back-pay award would be offset by earlier recovery of federal workers' compensation benefits).

[71]*Arizona:* Irvin Investors v. Superior Court, 54 FEP Cases 954, 955–56 (Ariz. Ct. App. 1990)(employer entitled to summary judgment against negligent hiring, supervision, and retention claim that complainant was sexually molested by co-worker at place of employment; stress sustained by complainant was compensable as complainant was sexually harassed within course and scope of *her* employment, even if harasser not acting within scope of *his*);

Hawaii: Lui v. Intercontinental Hotels Corp., 634 F. Supp. 684, 687–88, 47 FEP Cases 99, 102 (D. Haw. 1986)(complaint of hotel employee who alleged multiple sexual assaults and batteries during working hours barred by exclusivity provisions);

Indiana: Fields v. Cummins Employees Federal Credit Union, *supra* note 67, 53 FEP Cases at 1617 (claim against employer for negligent retention barred because premised on negligence in employment relationship);

New Jersey: Cremen v. Harrah's Marina Hotel Casino, 680 F. Supp. 150, 155–59 (D.N.J. 1988)(claims against employer for negligent hiring and retention barred because incident compensable and negligence claim not within "intentional wrong" exception to exclusivity);

Utah: Davis v. Utah Power & Light Co., 53 FEP Cases 1047, 1049 (D. Utah 1990)(common-law claims premised upon negligence, including claim that employer failed adequately to train, supervise, or control alleged sexual harasser, barred by exclusive remedy provision);

Wisconsin: Busse v. Gelco Express Corp., 678 F. Supp. 1398, 1400 (E.D. Wis. 1988)(claim for negligent infliction of emotional distress barred where defendant employer failed to take corrective action after plaintiff complained about supervisor's abusive language and sexual advances).

Contra North Carolina: Hogan v. Forsyth Country Club, 340 S.E.2d 116, 124, 1 IER Cases 1026, 1032 (N.C. Ct. App.)(negligent retention claim not barred, as emotional injury suffered by plaintiff because of

sexual harassment complainant's claims of assault and battery[72] and intentional infliction of emotional distress.[73] Exclusivity is far less likely to bar common-law claims for dignitary harms, such as defamation or false imprisonment,[74] or claims that are asserted under a state FEP statute.[75]

---

co-employee's profanity and sexual advances not "natural and probable consequence or incident of the employment"), *review denied,* 317 N.C. 334, 346 S.E.2d 141, 6 IER Cases 480 (1986); cases cited notes 80–89 *infra.*

[72]*Florida:* Studstill v. Borg-Warner Leasing, 806 F.2d 1005, 1007, 50 FEP Cases 427 (11th Cir. 1986)(barring claim for assault and battery based on physical sexual harassment of supervisor);

Hawaii: Lui v. Intercontinental Hotels Corp., *supra* note 71 (barring complaint of hotel employee who alleged multiple sexual assaults and batteries during working hours);

Minnesota: Parker v. Tharp, 409 N.W.2d 915 (Minn. Ct. App. 1987)(barring claim against employer for assault by co-worker);

New Jersey: Cremen v. Harrah's Marina Hotel Casino, *supra* note 71, 680 F. Supp. at 156–59 (barring claim for injuries from assault and harassment by supervisor);

New York: Crespi v. Ihrig, 472 N.Y.S.2d 324 (1st Dep't), *aff'd,* 63 N.Y.2d 716, 480 N.Y.S.2d 205 (1984)(barring claim of assault by co-worker);

Wyoming: Baker v. Wendy's of Montana, 687 P.2d 885 (Wyo. 1984)(barring assault and battery claims against employer for emotional injuries arising out of offensive sexual touching by co-worker).

Contra Massachusetts: O'Connell v. Chasdi, 400 Mass. 686, 511 N.E.2d 349, 50 FEP Cases 574 (1987)(assault and battery claims against co-worker not barred in that policies behind exclusivity do not support immunizing co-worker for intentional torts not related to interests of employer);

Missouri: Pryor v. United States Gypsum Co., *supra* note 67, 585 F. Supp. at 316, 47 FEP Cases at 162–63 (denying employer's motion to dismiss assault and battery claims because court could not say as matter of law that sexual harassment arose out of employment and that female employee should expect sexual harassment as part of job).

[73]*Hawaii:* Lui v. Intercontinental Hotels Corp., *supra* note 71 (barring emotional distress claim of hotel employee who alleged multiple sexual assaults during working hours);

Illinois: Juarez v. Ameritech Mobile Communications, 53 FEP Cases 1722, 1729 (N.D. Ill. 1990)(barring action seeking to hold employer derivatively liable for sexual harassment by complainant's boss);

Missouri: Miller v. Lindenwood Female College, 616 F. Supp. 860, 861, 40 FEP Cases 510, 511 (E.D. Mo. 1985)(college not liable for emotional distress caused by its agent's alleged sexual overtures because if agent acted within scope of employment relief would lie exclusively under workers' compensation law); Harrison v. Reed Rubber Co., 603 F. Supp. 1456, 37 FEP Cases 1544, 1545 (E.D. Mo. 1984)(barring claims for negligent and intentional infliction of emotional distress where sexual harassment occurred at complainant's place of work and arose out of and in the course of her employment);

New York: Hart v. Sullivan, 445 N.Y.S.2d 40, 37 FEP Cases 1808 (3d Dep't 1981)(emotional distress claim against employer based on co-worker's sexual harassment barred, absent facts to trigger intentional tort exception to exclusivity), *aff'd,* 55 N.Y.2d 1011, 449 N.Y.S.2d 481, 37 FEP Cases 1809 (1982);

Virginia: Haddon v. Metropolitan Life Ins. Co., 389 S.E.2d 712, 713–14, 52 FEP Cases 478, 479 (Va. 1990)(barring claim for emotional distress caused by sexual harassment of complainant by branch manager as injury caused by "accident," which Virginia has defined as event unexpected by person to whom it happens); Kelly v. First Virginia Bank, 404 S.E.2d 723 (1991)(following *Haddon* in sexual harassment case but with three justices dissenting);

Wisconsin: Zabkowicz v. West Bend Co., 789 F.2d 540, 544, 40 FEP Cases 1171, 1173–75 (7th Cir. 1986)(as to employer, emotional distress caused by sexual harassment was "mental or physical harm to employee caused by accident" and thus was exclusively compensable under workers' compensation act; it sufficed if injury itself is unexpected);

Wyoming: Baker v. Wendy's of Montana, *supra* note 72 (barring claims for intentional infliction of emotional distress arising out of offensive touching and obscene language by co-worker).

Contra Massachusetts: O'Connell v. Chasdi, *supra* note 72 (emotional stress claim against sexually harassing supervisor not barred in that intentional torts are not accepted risk of doing business);

North Carolina: Hogan v. Forsyth County Club, *supra* note 71, 1 IER Cases at 1028–29 (intentional infliction not barred because it involves "an entire class of civil wrongs" beyond scope of workers' compensation act).

[74]*See generally* Love, *supra* note 65, 73 CAL. L. REV. at 858. *See, e.g.,* Pryor v. United States Gypsum Co., *supra* note 67, 47 FEP Cases at 162 (no bar to claims like false arrest or slander where damages are humiliation and diminished reputation instead of industrial injury). *Compare* Haddon v. Metropolitan Life Ins. Co., *supra* note 73 (barring sexual harassment complainant's claims for infliction of emotional harm, defamation, "insulting words," tortious interference with contract, and breach of contract) *with* Snead v. Harbaugh, 6 IER Cases 661, 661–62 (Va. 1991)(action alleging solely reputational damage and avoiding claims for physical or emotional injury or medical costs is not a claim for "injury" within meaning of workers' compensation act and therefore is not barred by exclusivity provisions).

[75]*California:* Jones v. Pan American World Airways, 53 FEP Cases 1092, 1096–97 (N.D. Cal. 1990)(emotional distress claims brought under FEP statute "carry an implied exception from the exclusivity provisions [of the Workers' Compensation Act]"); Meninga v. Raley's, 216 Cal. App.3d 79, 51 FEP Cases 902 (1989)(sex discrimination plaintiff could seek emotional distress damages under FEP statute notwithstanding

C. Rationales for Not Applying Workers' Compensation Exclusivity

Although a finding of coverage for purposes of workers' compensation will generally lead to a finding of exclusivity, judges may construe the language or the purpose of the workers' compensation statute to create exceptions to exclusivity with respect to particular injuries and particular causes of action.

Sexual harassment claims, while precluded by workers' compensation exclusivity in some states with respect to some causes of action,[76] have been permitted to proceed under various rationales.

1. Sexual Harassment as Causing a Nondisabling Injury

Where the complainant has alleged only nonphysical, nondisabling harm, some courts have rejected the application of the exclusivity bar on the basis that the workers' compensation system is designed to address only physical disabilities.[77] In *Hogan v. Forsyth Country Club*,[78] where the complainants alleged that sexual harassment caused severe emotional distress but not physical injuries resulting in disability, the court concluded that because the complainants had alleged injuries not compensable under workers' compensation, their claims could not be barred by the exclusivity doctrine.[79]

2. Sexual Harassment as Causing a Special Form of Injury

a. Sexual harassment as not a "normal risk" of employment. In determining whether an injury is compensable as arising out of and during the course of employment—and thus whether it is potentially subject to an exclusive remedy under the workers' compensation system—some courts ask if the injury

---

workers' compensation exclusivity; two statutes had distinct goals); Watson v. Department of Rehabilitation, 212 Cal. App.3d 1271, 1285–87, 53 FEP Cases 1203 (1989)(discrimination actions do not involve conduct "expected normally to occur in the workplace and . . . part of the employment risk"); Jones v. Los Angeles Community College Dist., 198 Cal. App.3d 794, 807–9, 51 FEP Cases 413 (1988)(emotional distress claims under FEP statute not barred);

Massachusetts: College-Town v. Massachusetts Comm'n Against Discrimination, 400 Mass. 156, 508 N.E.2d 587, 46 FEP Cases 1406, 1412 (1987)(emotional distress damages not compensable exclusively under workers' compensation act);

Michigan: Boscaglia v. Michigan Bell Tel. Co., 362 N.W.2d 642, 43 FEP Cases 1155, 1157–59 (Mich. 1984)(workers' compensation and FEP acts aim at different evils and not intended to modify or supersede each other regardless of whether disability involved).

[76]See cases cited in notes 71–73 *supra.*

[77]*Arizona:* Ford v. Revlon, Inc., 734 P.2d 580, 586, 43 FEP Cases 213, 218 (Ariz. 1987)(claim of intentional infliction of emotional distress not barred, given jury finding that injury caused by sexual harassment not "unexpected" and essentially nonphysical in nature);

District of Columbia: Coleman v. American Broadcasting Cos., 38 FEP Cases 65, 69 (D.D.C. 1985)(no bar where sexual harassment complainant not disabled);

Georgia: Cummings v. Walsh Constr. Co., 561 F. Supp. 872, 880–81 (S.D. Ga. 1983)(no bar because mental trauma alone not compensable under Georgia workers' compensation act and supervisors' sexual advances caused embarrassment, anger, anxiety and great worry, but not physical disability);

Hawaii: Lapinad v. Pacific Oldsmobile-GMC, 679 F. Supp. 991, 994–95, 50 FEP Cases 752 (D. Haw. 1988)(no bar to claim for intentional infliction of emotional distress because workers' compensation provides no remedy for nondisabling emotional injury);

But see Wisconsin: Zabkowicz v. West Bend Co., *supra* note 73 (barring claim for emotional distress caused by sexual harassment because workers' compensation act permits recovery for "mental or physical harm to employee caused by accident or disease"); Busse v. Gelco Express Corp., *supra* note 71 (claim for negligent infliction of emotional distress, which alleged sexual harassment while employed, barred by exclusive remedy provision of Wisconsin workers' compensation act, which covers mental injuries).

[78]*Supra* note 71.

[79]*Supra* note 71, 340 S.E.2d at 120, 1 IER Cases at 1028–29.

has resulted from a risk that one would normally expect in the workplace. Courts that employ this analysis are reluctant to hold that the risk of sexual harassment is a normal workplace risk. These courts conclude that because a complainant's injuries caused by sexual harassment are not covered by workers' compensation, the state-law claim against the employer may proceed unimpeded by the exclusivity provisions.[80]

In *Bennett v. Furr's Cafeterias*,[81] the court employed this workplace risk analysis to permit the complainant to maintain claims of assault, battery, and outrageous conduct under Colorado law. The complainant, a management trainee, alleged that her supervisor sexually assaulted her during business trips. The employer moved for summary judgment on the ground that workers' compensation provided the exclusive remedy. Denying the motion, the court reasoned that the workers' compensation act would bar the complainant's common-law claims only if her injuries had been caused by employment-related risks.[82] The court concluded that the acts and the "emotional trauma alleged to have been caused thereby" did not "result from risks inherent to the position of 'management trainee.' "[83] Similarly, in *Hart v. National Mortgage Land Co.*,[84] where the claim was that the complainant's supervisor grabbed his testicles, pinched his buttocks, mounted him, and showed him a dildo, the California Court of Appeal held that the workers' compensation act was no bar to an emotional distress claim because this behavior was not a risk, incident, or normal part of the employment relationship.[85]

b. Sexual harassment as causing a distinct type of injury. Another rationale for permitting sexual harassment claims to proceed, notwithstanding workers' compensation exclusivity, is that employment discrimination and workers' compensation laws address distinct injuries and should be read to provide supplemental rather than exclusive remedies. The rationale is that workers'

---

[80]*E.g., Arizona:* Ford v. Revlon, Inc., *supra* note 77, 43 FEP Cases at 221 (Feldman, J., concurring)("exposure to sexual harassment is not an inherent or necessary risk of employment, even though it may be . . . endemic");

California: Jones v. Pan American World Airways, *supra* note 75 (discrimination and retaliation not normal incidents of employment); Hart v. National Mortgage & Land Co., 189 Cal. App.3d 1420, 1430, 235 Cal. Rptr. 68 (1987)(discussed in text at notes 84–85 *infra*);

Colorado: Bennett v. Furr's Cafeterias, 549 F. Supp. 887, 890, 30 FEP Cases 93, 95 (D. Colo. 1982)(discussed in text at notes 81–83 *infra*);

North Carolina: Harrison v. Edison Bros. Apparel Stores, 724 F. Supp. 1185, 1191 (M.D.N.C. 1989)(emotional injuries from sexual harassment not natural and probable consequence or incident of employment); Hogan v. Forsyth Country Club, *supra* note 71 (no bar to claim for negligent retention of male co-employee who sexually harassed female employee because emotional injury caused by sexual harassment did not "arise out" of employment as sexual harassment not natural and probable consequence or incident of employment);

Oregon: Carr v. U.S. West Direct Co., 779 P.2d 154, 156–57 (Or. Ct. App.)(no bar where no causal link between occurrence of injury and risk connected with employment), *review denied,* 784 P.2d 1101 (1989);

Virginia: Paroline v. Unisys Corp., 879 F.2d 100, 50 FEP Cases 306, 315–16 (4th Cir. 1989), reproduced in Chapter 9, Constructive Discharge (no bar to claim for employer's failure to warn and reckless endangerment in connection with sexual harassment that occurred away from office when complainant not performing work for employer, because harassment not in "course of her employment"), *aff'd in part and vacated in part,* 900 F.2d 27, 52 FEP Cases 845 (4th Cir. 1990); *see also* City of Richmond v. Braxton, 230 Va. 161, 335 S.E.2d 259, 289 (1985)(plaintiff's injuries not compensable under workers' compensation act because employment not contributing cause to injuries caused by supervisor's harassment).

[81]*Supra* note 80.

[82]*Id.* at 890, 30 FEP Cases at 95.

[83]*Id.*

[84]*Supra* note 80.

[85]*Supra* note 80, 189 Cal. App.3d at 1430.

compensation systems are designed to provide an exclusive remedy for persons incapacitated by workplace injuries, not for injuries to intangible personal rights that inflict emotional stress and that may not cause physical or mental incapacity.[86] Courts reason that it is these intangible injuries that the sexual harassment victim seeks to vindicate through statutory discrimination claims and common-law intentional tort claims.

By this reasoning, the exclusivity provisions do not bar discrimination and common-law tort claims based on sexual harassment, because these claims address injuries separate from those covered under worker's compensation. The Florida Supreme Court, in *Byrd v. Richardson-Greenshields Securities,*[87] indicated that a sexual harassment complainant may sue an employer under state-law tort theories and antidiscrimination statutes notwithstanding the general exclusivity of the workers' compensation act as a remedy for workplace injuries.[88] The court noted that while workers' compensation addresses the economic consequences of a workplace injury, sexual harassment robs the victim of dignity and self esteem, injuries that are not covered by workers' compensation: "[T]o the extent these injuries are separable, we believe that they both should be, and can be, enforced separately."[89]

3. Sexual Harassment as an Intentional Act

In many states, a factor determining whether the workers' compensation act provides an exclusive remedy is whether the harassment was "intentional" instead of "accidental." This factor may arise in one of two contexts. First, in those states requiring that a compensable injury be "accidental," this factor bears on whether the workers' compensation act applies at all. Second, in those states providing for an intentional-acts exception to exclusivity, this factor may determine whether a tort claim will be permitted to proceed, notwithstanding workers' compensation coverage.

a. Sexual harassment as not a compensable "accident." Many states include the terms "accident" or "accidental" in the statute's coverage formula.[90] Some courts analyze these terms from the complainant's perspective: if the injury is unexpected to the complainant, the injury is compensable and the exclusivity provision bars the complainant's common-law claims.[91] Other courts analyze the term "accidental" from the alleged harasser's perspective:

---

[86]*See, e.g.,* cases applying state FEP statutes cited in note 75 *supra.*

[87]552 So.2d 1099, 51 EPD ¶39,446 (Fla. 1989).

[88]The torts at issue were assault and battery, intentional infliction of emotional distress, and negligent hiring and retention.

[89]*Id.* at 1104, 51 EPD ¶39,446.

See also Florida: Ramada Inn Surfside v. Swanson, 560 So.2d 300 (Fla. Ct. App. 1990)(affirming award of workers' compensation benefits for injuries caused by sexual harassment, while stating that other laws may address intangible injury to personal rights caused by sexual harassment);

Michigan: Eide v. Kelsey-Hayes Co., 397 N.W.2d 532, 540, 47 FEP Cases 1043, 1049 (Mich. Ct. App. 1986)(refusing to allow credit against FEP award of workers' compensation benefits already received, because FEP and workers' compensation claims are "independent"), *aff'd in part and rev'd in part on other grounds,* 427 N.W.2d 488, 47 FEP Cases 1050 (Mich. 1988).

[90]For a discussion of workers' compensation coverage, see Chapter 14, Workers' Compensation Statutes.

[91]*E.g.,* Haddon v. Metropolitan Life Ins. Co., *supra* note 73, 389 S.E.2d at 713–14, 52 FEP Cases at 479 (barring common-law claims because Virginia courts have consistently defined accident as event that is unusual and not expected by person to whom it happens); Zabkowicz v. West Bend Co., *supra* note 73, 789 F.2d at 545, 40 FEP Cases at 1175 (injuries from sexual harassment could be accidental because "it is

if the harassment is intentional and injuries resulting from harassment are foreseeable,[92] the injuries are not compensable and the exclusivity provisions are avoided.

    b. Sexual harassment as an intentional tort. Some state workers' compensation statutes provide that even if the sued-for injuries are compensable under the workers' compensation system, the exclusivity provisions do not apply where the employer has engaged in an "intentional tort" or "intentional wrong" to injure the complainant.[93] Courts have applied this exception to permit a sexual harassment complainant to avoid workers' compensation exclusivity.[94] Some courts have limited this exception to instances where the employer intended the specific injury,[95] or have not applied the exception to torts committed by a co-worker.[96] This more restricted interpretation has led

---

sufficient if the injury itself is unexpected"); Miller v. Lindenwood Female College, *supra* note 73, 616 F. Supp. at 861, 40 FEP Cases at 511 (intentional acts of fellow employees causing emotional distress fall within statutory definition of "accident").

  [92]Ford v. Revlon, Inc., *supra* note 77, 734 P.2d at 586, 43 FEP Cases at 218 (no bar to claims of sexual assault and battery where acts of harasser intentional, not accidental); Cline v. GE Capital Auto Lease, 55 FEP Cases 498, 504–5 (N.D. Ill. 1991)(injury not "accidental" and sexual harassment complainant may sue employer for battery by manager where employer authorization of battery could be inferred from employer's decision to tolerate manager's mistreatment of employees because his department performed well); Pursell v. Pizza Inn, 786 P.2d 716, 717 (Okla. Ct. App. 1990)(allegations of supervisors' intentional or willful sexual misconduct took plaintiff's claims outside exclusive remedy provision; workers' compensation act not designed to shield employers or co-workers from willful, intentional, or violent conduct).

  [93]*E.g.*, ALA. CODE §25-5-11 (1986); ARIZ. REV. STAT. ANN. §23-1022 (1983); KY. REV. STAT. ANN. §342.610 (Michie/Bobbs-Merrill 1988); MD. CODE ANN. §101-44 (1985); MONT. CODE ANN. §39-71-413 (1989); OHIO REV. CODE ANN. §4121.80 (1989 Supp.); OR. REV. STAT. §656.156(2)(1989); WASH. REV. CODE §51.24.020 (1990); W. VA. CODE §23-4-2 (1985). California workers' compensation law, while generally precluding common-law suits even for intentional acts, *Cole v. Fair Oaks Fire Protection Dist.,* 43 Cal.3d 148, 233 Cal. Rptr. 308 (1987), provides an exception from workers' compensation exclusivity in the case of "willful physical assault by the employer," CAL. LAB. CODE §3602 (West 1989).

  [94]*E.g., Louisiana:* Waltman v. International Paper Co., 47 FEP Cases 671, 678 (W.D. La. 1988)(while nonintentional employer torts are barred, intentional employer torts are not, and employer may be liable for intentional tort of complainant's co-worker if he was acting in course and scope of his employment), *rev'd on other grounds,* 875 F.2d 468, 50 FEP Cases 179 (5th Cir. 1989);

    Massachusetts: O'Connell v. Chasdi, 400 Mass. 686, 511 N.E.2d 349, 50 FEP Cases 574 (1987)(no bar to claim for assault and battery and intentional infliction of emotional distress in connection with sexual advances by co-worker on business trip);

    New Jersey: Cremen v. Harrah's Marina Hotel Casino, 680 F. Supp. 150, 156–59 (D.N.J. 1988)(no bar to claims for battery and intentional infliction of emotional distress, given employer's "cavalier" response to employee's report of sexual attack by supervisor, employer's retention of supervisor in position of direct authority over plaintiff, and employer's inadequate internal investigation);

    New York: Spoon v. American Agriculturalist, 502 N.Y.S.2d 296, 299 (3d Dep't 1986)(intentional tort claims based on sexual harassment not barred on motion given factual issue as to whether employer authorized intentional tort by failing to correct conduct); Hart v. Sullivan, 445 N.Y.S.2d 40, 37 FEP Cases 1808 (3d Dep't 1981)(intentional tort exception not established with mere allegation of agency and liability under *respondeat superior;* no allegation that employer knew or acquiesced in the harassment), *aff'd,* 55 N.Y.2d 1011, 449 N.Y.S.2d 481, 37 FEP Cases 1809 (1982);

    Oregon: Palmer v. Bi-Mart Co., 758 P.2d 888, 891 (Or. Ct. App. 1988)(no bar where supervisor's harassment showed specific intent to harm).

  [95]*E.g.*, Eide v. Kelsey-Hayes Co., *supra* note 89, 397 N.W.2d at 542, 47 FEP Cases at 1050 (barring claim of intentional infliction of emotional distress; intentional tort exception did not apply because plaintiff failed to allege employer intended injury itself instead of merely intending acts leading to injury).

  [96]*E.g., Connecticut:* Jett v. Dunlap, 179 Conn. 215, 425 A.2d 1263 (1979)(although employer might have subsequently condoned supervisor's battery of complainant, workers' compensation statute precluded tort action against employer where supervisor not alter-ego of employer);

    District of Columbia: Rustin v. District of Columbia, 491 A.2d 496 (D.C. 1985)(after employee killed by co-worker, wrongful death suit against employer barred by workers' compensation statute where no evidence that employer intended or conspired to injure decedent), *cert. denied,* 474 U.S. 946 (1985);

    Minnesota: Parker v. Tharp, 409 N.W.2d 915 (Minn. Ct. App. 1987)(intentional tort exception to exclusivity applies only to tort by employer, not to assault committed by co-employee, unless co-employee had policymaking authority or committed assault to further ends of employer);

    New York: Hart v. Sullivan, *supra* note 94 (claim for intentional infliction of emotional distress against employer and co-workers based on sexual harassment barred where no allegation of employer willfulness).

commentators to argue that the intentional tort exception is of little practical help to an injured employee.[97]

V. FAILURE TO ARBITRATE UNDER THE ARBITRATION PROVISION OF A COLLECTIVE BARGAINING AGREEMENT

A. *Alexander v. Gardner-Denver Co.*

An employer and the union representing its employees typically agree to submit employment disputes to mandatory, binding arbitration. This agreement, enforceable under the Labor Management Relations Act, provides the employer with a defense to many state-law claims on the basis that these claims are preempted by the federal law requiring the enforcement of the collective bargaining agreement.[98] A collectively bargained agreement to arbitrate cannot, however, be used to preclude or even defer claims under Title VII. A union-represented employee may choose to seek arbitration of a Title VII claim under the collective bargaining agreement, but the decision of the arbitrator is not binding as to the grievant's Title VII claims. Notwithstanding the arbitrator's ruling, the grievant can pursue judicial remedies for discrimination under Title VII. Further, the grievant may choose to bypass the grievance and arbitration procedure and rely solely on Title VII.

The Supreme Court made those rulings in 1974 in *Alexander v. Gardner-Denver Co.*[99] The plaintiff, having been discharged for producing too many defective parts, filed a grievance under the collective bargaining agreement and thereafter filed an administrative charge of discrimination. At the arbitration determining whether there was just cause for his discharge, one contention by the grievant was that the discharge was racially motivated in breach of provisions of the collective bargaining agreement. The arbitrator, without reference to this contention, upheld the discharge. The grievant then filed a Title VII claim in federal court.

A unanimous Supreme Court held that the plaintiff's right to sue under Title VII was unaffected by the arbitration. Justice Lewis F. Powell, Jr., emphasized three basic concepts: (1) Title VII authorizes enforcement by courts, which cannot be divested of jurisdiction by the arbitration forum;[100] (2) Title VII grants rights to be exercised by individuals as opposed to the union-

---

[97]*See* Love, *Actions for Nonphysical Harm: The Relationship Between the Tort System and No-Fault Compensation,* 73 CAL. L. REV. 857, 865 (1987)(discussing statutory and judicially created exceptions to workers' compensation exclusivity); Schoenheider, *A Theory of Tort Liability for Sexual Harassment in the Workplace,* 134 U. PA. L. REV. 1461, 1490–94 (1986)(discussing workers' compensation barriers to tort recovery for sexual harassment).

[98]For a discussion of preemption of state-law claims under a collective bargaining agreement, see Chapter 17, Collective Bargaining Agreements and Union Obligations.

[99]415 U.S. 36, 7 FEP Cases 81 (1974).

[100]Justice Powell explained:

Arbitral procedures, while well suited to the resolution of contractual disputes, make arbitration a comparatively inappropriate forum for the final resolution for the rights created by Title VII. This conclusion rests first on the special role of the arbitrator, whose task is to effectuate the intent of the parties rather than the requirements of enacted legislation. Where the collectively bargained agreement conflicts with Title VII, the arbitrator must follow the agreement. . . . [O]ther facts may still render

exercised rights granted under a collective bargaining agreement; and (3) an arbitration implicates rights under a collective bargaining agreement, while a Title VII lawsuit asserts independent statutory rights provided by congressional enactment.[101]

Gardner-Denver was followed by similar decisions in *Barrentine v. Arkansas-Best Freight System*[102] and *McDonald v. City of West Branch*.[103] In *Barrentine* the Supreme Court held that claims under the Fair Labor Standards Act (FLSA), like claims under Title VII, are independent of rights under collective bargaining agreements and may be pursued independently from collective bargaining agreement grievances concerning the same issue.[104] Similarly, in *McDonald* the Supreme Court stated that an arbitration award should have no *res judicata* or collateral estoppel effect in a §1983 action:

> Our rejection of a rule of preclusion in *Barrentine* and our rejection of a rule of deferral in *Gardner-Denver* were based in large part on our conclusion that Congress intended the statutes at issue in those cases to be judicially enforceable and that arbitration could not provide an adequate substitute for judicial proceedings in adjudicating claims under those statutes.[105]

Under *Gardner-Denver, Barrentine,* and *McDonald,* employees covered by a collective bargaining agreement that prohibits sex discrimination may pursue claims of sexual harassment under both the applicable grievance and arbitration clause and the enforcement procedures of Title VII.

There is an obvious tension between the *Gardner-Denver* decision and the increased judicial deference to arbitration of all claims, including statutory claims.[106] The decision departed from a line of decisions deferential to the arbitration process, especially in the collective bargaining area.[107] One commentator has argued that this departure "makes sense only when one considers ... the Court's distrust, based on a lengthy record of failure to prosecute, of

---

arbitral processes comparatively inferior to judicial processes in the protection of Title VII rights. Among these is the fact that the specialized competence of arbitrators pertains primarily to the law of the shop, not the law of the land.
Id. at 55–56, 7 FEP Cases at 89.

[101]Justice Powell stated:
[T]he federal policy favoring arbitration of labor disputes and the federal policy against discriminatory employment practices can best be accommodated by permitting an employee to pursue fully both his remedy under the grievance-arbitration clause of a collective-bargaining agreement and his cause of action under Title VII. The federal court should consider the employee's claim *de novo*. The arbitral decision may be admitted as evidence and accorded such weight as the court deems appropriate.
Id. at 59–60, 7 FEP Cases at 90.

[102]450 U.S. 728 (1981).

[103]466 U.S. 284 (1984).

[104]*Supra* note 102, 450 U.S. at 745. Further, an arbitration award on an FLSA issue would not bar an FLSA suit. *Id.* at 743–45.

[105]*Supra* note 103, 466 U.S. at 289.

[106]*See, e.g.,* Alford v. Dean Witter Reynolds, 905 F.2d 104, 106, 53 FEP Cases 529, 529 (5th Cir. 1990)(reluctantly following *Gardner-Denver,* noting if issue were open "we might well interpret Title VII consistent with these recent decisions [favoring enforcement of statutory remedies by contractual arbitration]"), *vacated and remanded in light of* Gilmer v. Interstate/Johnson Lane Corp., 111 S.Ct. 2050 (1991).

[107]*E.g.,* the *Steelworkers Trilogy:* United Steelworkers v. Enterprise Wheel & Car Corp., 363 U.S. 593 (1960); United Steelworkers v. Warrior & Gulf Navigation Co., 363 U.S. 574 (1960); United Steelworkers v. American Mfg. Co., 363 U.S. 564 (1960). Collectively, the three decisions created a presumption, absent an express exclusion, of arbitrability of grievances. As Justice William O. Douglas noted: "In the absence of any express provision excluding a particular grievance from arbitration, we think only the most forceful evidence of a purpose to exclude the claim from arbitration can prevail, particularly where, as here, the exclusion clause is vague and the arbitration clause quite broad." United Steelworkers v. Warrior & Gulf Navigation Co., 363 U.S. at 584–85.

the sincerity of unions in dealing with racial grievances."[108] Nevertheless, *Gardner-Denver* remains the dominant discrimination/arbitration case, and its central analysis of the separateness of statutory and contractual rights continues to control decisions.[109]

B. Significance of the Arbitration Decision

The *Gardner-Denver* Court suggested that an arbitral award should be admitted in a Title VII action for such weight "as the court deems appropriate."[110] In footnote 21 of its decision, the Supreme Court instructed trial courts to assign weight to arbitral decisions on a case-by-case basis in accordance with the following factors: (1) whether the decision applied collectively bargained provisions in substantial conformance with Title VII; (2) the degree of procedural fairness in the arbitral forum; (3) the adequacy of the record with respect to the discrimination issue; and (4) the special competence of the particular arbitrator.[111]

Courts addressing the issue after *Gardner-Denver* have generally given "considerable" or "great" weight to the arbitrator's findings, but have not found them to be conclusive.[112]

VI. FAILURE TO ARBITRATE UNDER INDIVIDUAL AGREEMENT TO ARBITRATE

A. Introduction

Just as an employer and a union may collectively bargain to arbitrate employment disputes, an employer and its employees may individually agree to arbitrate employment disputes.[113] The cases reported to date typically have considered individual arbitration agreements that appear in forms that securities representatives file with the New York Stock Exchange.[114] Yet a similar agreement to arbitrate could also appear in an individual written employment contract or even in an employment application or employee handbook.

---

[108]Citron, *Deferral of Employee Rights to Arbitration: An Evolving Dichotomy by the Burger Court?*, 27 HASTINGS L. J. 369 (1975)(cited in Nicholson v. CPC Int'l, 877 F.2d 221, 49 FEP Cases 1678, 1689 (3d Cir. 1989)(Becker, J., dissenting)).

[109]*See, e.g.,* Utley v. Goldman Sachs & Co., 883 F.2d 184, 187, 50 FEP Cases 1087 (1st Cir. 1989)("[The *Gardner-Denver*] reasoning, based upon a recognition of Title VII's unique nature, continues to be valid"), *cert. denied,* 110 S.Ct. 842 (1990). *But see* text accompanying note 130b *infra.*

[110]*Supra* note 99, 415 U.S. at 60, 7 FEP Cases at 90.

[111]*Id.* at 60 n.21, 7 FEP Cases at 90.

[112]B.L. SCHLEI & P. GROSSMAN, EMPLOYMENT DISCRIMINATION LAW 1084–85 (2d ed. 1983), Five-Year Supp. 407 (1989).

[113]Employers have various reasons for preferring arbitration, including cost containment, speedier resolution, greater privacy, potential limitation on remedies, and avoidance of a jury trial. Some of these are advantages for the employee as well.

[114]*E.g.,* Alford v. Dean Witter Reynolds, *supra* note 106; Steck v. Smith Barney Harris Upham & Co., 661 F. Supp. 543, 43 FEP Cases 1736 (D.N.J. 1987); Utley v. Goldman Sachs & Co., *supra* note 109. The Supreme Court majority in *Gilmer v. Interstate/Johnson Lane Corp.,* 111 S.Ct. 1647 (1991), distinguished between registration agreements and employment agreements. Justice John Paul Stevens, in dissent, argued that because the plaintiff had to sign the registration agreement as a condition of employment it was immaterial that there was no "specific contract of employment."

Employers seeking to enforce individual agreements to arbitrate have invoked the Federal Arbitration Act (FAA),[115] which provides that an "agreement in writing to submit to arbitration an existing controversy arising out of such contract . . . shall be valid, irrevocable and enforceable."[116] Similar state statutes likewise authorize the enforcement of arbitration agreements.[117]

A threshold issue is whether the FAA covers arbitration agreements that appear in employer-employee contracts. The issue of coverage arises because §1 of the FAA expressly excludes from coverage the "contracts of employment of seamen, railroad employees or any other class of workers engaged in foreign or interstate commerce."[118] Lower courts have split on this issue of coverage.[119]

In *Gilmer v. Interstate/Johnson Lane Corp.,*[120] the scope of the exclusion-from-coverage language in §1 of the FAA was argued but not decided. The Supreme Court, although addressing whether a claim under the Age Discrimination in Employment Act (ADEA)[121] was subject to compulsory arbitration under the FAA, did not resolve the §1 exclusion-from-coverage issue, because the issue was not raised on appeal and because the arbitration agreement in *Gilmer* appeared only in the employee's application for registration with the New York Stock Exchange and thus was not, strictly speaking, in a written "contract of employment."[122] The Court in *Gilmer* went on to rule, 7–2, that an ADEA claim can be subjected to compulsory arbitration under the FAA.[123]

B. The Impact of *Gilmer v. Interstate/Johnson Lane Corp.*

In cases decided before *Gilmer,* plaintiffs generally had been successful in urging that an FAA-governed agreement to arbitrate was no bar to a judicial

---

[115]9 U.S.C. §1 *et seq.*

[116]The full text of FAA §2, 9 U.S.C. §2, states:

A written provision in any maritime transaction or a contract evidencing a transaction involving commerce to settle by arbitration a controversy thereafter arising out of such contract or transaction, or the refusal to perform the whole or any part thereof, or an agreement in writing to submit to arbitration an existing controversy arising out of such a contract, transaction, or refusal, shall be valid, irrevocable, and enforceable, save upon such grounds as exist at law or in equity for the revocation of any contract.

[117]*E.g.,* CAL. CODE CIV. PROC. §1281.2 (party to arbitration agreement may move to compel arbitration absent such exceptions as a party's waiver of the right to compel arbitration, or grounds to revoke agreement to arbitrate). *Compare* Fregara v. Jet Aviation Business Jets, 1991 WL 88448 (D.N.J. 1991)(employee bound under New Jersey law by arbitration scheme set forth in employee handbook) *and* Suburban Hosp. v. Dwiggins, 573 A.2d 835 (Md. Ct. App. 1990)(same under Maryland law) *with* Jacobsen v. ITT Financial Servs. Corp., 55 FEP Cases 1189, 1192–93 (E.D. Tenn. 1991)(Tennessee Uniform Arbitration Act does not apply to claims of sex discrimination and sexual harassment brought under state FEP statute) *and* Anderson v. Dean Witter Reynolds, 449 N.W.2d 468, 51 FEP Cases 1075 (Minn. Ct. App. 1989)(same as to Minnesota arbitration and FEP statutes). *Cf.* Renny v. Port Huron Hosp., 398 N.W.2d 327 (Mich. 1987)(arbitration scheme not binding because it lacked "elemental fairness" under Michigan law).

[118]9 U.S.C. §1. This exclusion reflects the lobbying of union groups, such as the Seamen's Union, which were suspicious of arbitration. Textile Workers Union v. Lincoln Mills, 353 U.S. 448, 467 (1957)(Frankfurter, J., dissenting).

[119]*Compare* Miller Brewing Co. v. Brewery Workers' Local 9, 739 F.2d 1159, 1162 (7th Cir. 1984)(FAA excludes only workers employed in transportation industry and applies to other employees), *cert. denied,* 469 U.S. 1160 (1985) *with* Bacashihua v. United States Postal Serv., 859 F.2d 402, 404 (6th Cir. 1988)(FAA does not apply to labor contracts) *and* Copley v. NCR Corp., 55 EPD ¶40,533 (W.Va. 1990)(FAA does not apply to employment contracts of workers engaged in interstate commerce).

[120]*Supra* note 114.

[121]29 U.S.C. §621 *et seq.*

[122]*Supra* note 114, 111 S.Ct. at 1651–52 n.2.

[123]*Id.* at 1652–56.

action for employment discrimination.[124] The basis of those decisions was that *Alexander v. Gardner-Denver Co.*[125] and subsequent employment arbitration cases[126] were controlling in statutory employment claims, even though the Supreme Court had broadly construed the FAA to require arbitration of various legal claims, including federal antitrust and racketeering claims, between parties to commercial contracts.[127]

Thus, in *Alford v. Dean Witter Reynolds*,[128] the Fifth Circuit had permitted a sexual harassment claim to proceed under Title VII even though there was an individual agreement to arbitrate and even though the "enforcement of statutory remedies by means of contractual arbitration has ... become the norm rather than the exception for contracts governed by the ... FAA." Judge Edith Jones stated that "[i]f the issue were open to us to evaluate afresh, we might well interpret Title VII consistent with these recent decisions."[129] Nonetheless, the court assumed that the issue was not open because the *Gardner-Denver* rationale appeared to cover any arbitration of Title VII claims.[130] The Supreme Court has upset that assumption by directing that *Alford* be reconsidered in light of *Gilmer*.[130a] The Fifth Circuit itself determined in *Alford*, on remand, that "Title VII claims, like ADEA claims, are subject to arbitration under the FAA."[130b]

The Supreme Court in *Gilmer* had several reasons not to follow *Gardner-Denver*. First, it dismissed as outmoded the view expressed in *Gardner-Denver*

---

[124]*E.g.*, Utley v. Goldman Sachs & Co., *supra* note 109, 883 F.2d at 186 (sexual harassment claim); Alford v. Dean Witter Reynolds, *supra* note 106 (sexual harassment claim). *See generally* Nicholson v. CPC Int'l, 877 F.2d 221, 49 FEP Cases 1678 (3d Cir. 1989); Swenson v. Management Recruiters Int'l, 858 F.2d 1304, 47 FEP Cases 1855 (8th Cir. 1988)(involving allegations of employment discrimination but not sexual harassment), *cert. denied*, 110 S.Ct. 143 (1989); Cooper v. Asplundh Tree Expert Co., 836 F.2d 1544, 1553, 45 FEP Cases 1386 (10th Cir. 1988)(ADEA case).

[125]415 U.S. 36, 7 FEP Cases 81 (1974).

[126]See cases cited in notes 102–5 *supra*.

[127]The Supreme Court's commercial arbitration cases—*Rodriguez de Ouijas v. Shearson/American Express*, 109 S.Ct. 1917 (1989), *Shearson/American Express v. McMahon*, 482 U.S. 220 (1987), and *Mitsubishi Motors Corp. v. Soler Chrysler-Plymouth*, 473 U.S. 614 (1985)—broadly construed the FAA to require arbitration of various legal claims pursuant to investment agreements or commercial contracts. Emphasizing the FAA's "federal policy favoring arbitration," *Shearson/American Express v. McMahon*, 482 U.S. at 226 (citations omitted), the Court held that even federal statutory claims are presumptively arbitrable:

> The burden is on the party opposing arbitration ... to show that Congress intended to preclude a waiver of judicial remedies for the statutory rights at issue. [S]uch an intent 'will be deducible from [the statute's] text or legislative history,' ... or from an inherent conflict between arbitration and the statute's underlying purposes.

Id. at 227.

[128]905 F.2d 104, 53 FEP Cases 529 (5th Cir. 1990)(Clark, Thornberry & Jones, JJ.), *vacated and remanded in light of* Gilmer v. Interstate/Johnson Lane Corp., 111 S.Ct. 2050 (1991).

[129]*Id.* at 105, 53 FEP Cases at 529.

[130]*Id.* at 107, 53 FEP Cases at 531 (citations omitted). *See also* Utley v. Goldman Sachs & Co., 883 F.2d 184, 185–86, 50 FEP Cases 1087, 1088–89 (1st Cir. 1989)(Supreme Court "has done nothing to disturb" *Gardner-Denver* decision); Swenson v. Management Recruiters Int'l, *supra* note 124, 858 F.2d at 1306, 47 FEP Cases at 1857 (*Gardner-Denver* suggests "Congress did not intend federal judicial proceedings in discrimination cases to be preempted by employment arbitration agreements enforceable under the FAA," given lack of arbitral expertise); Benestad v. Interstate/Johnson Lake Corp., 56 EPD ¶40,620 (D. Fla. 1991)(arbitration agreement does not waive Title VII suit); Borenstein v. Tucker, 55 FEP Cases 259, 261 (D. Conn. 1991)(Title VII claim not suited to arbitration because arbitrators cannot enjoin future discrimination and are not regulated to ensure their adequacy; besides, holdings in *Gardner-Denver* and *Barrentine* have never been overruled explicitly or implicitly); Bierdeman v. Shearson Lehman Hutton, 54 EPD ¶40,329 (N.D. Cal. 1990)(denying motion to compel arbitration of Title VII claim on basis of employment arbitration agreement).

[130a]See note 106 *supra*.

[130b]939 F.2d 229, 230, 56 FEP Cases 1046, 1047 (5th Cir. 1991).

that arbitration was inferior to litigation as a way to resolve statutory claims.[131] The *Gilmer* court also distinguished *Gardner-Denver* on several grounds: *Gardner-Denver* (1) did not involve the enforceability of an agreement to arbitrate statutory claims but rather "the quite different issue" of whether the arbitration of contract-based claims precluded later judicial resolution of statutory claims; (2) involved arbitration in the context of a collective bargaining agreement, where exclusive union representation of the grievant created "tension between collective representation and individual statutory rights"; and (3) did not involve the FAA, which reflects a " 'liberal policy favoring arbitration agreements.' "[132]

Under *Gilmer,* a plaintiff seeking to enforce a federal statutory claim must abide by an FAA-governed agreement to arbitrate the claim, unless the plaintiff can prove that "Congress intended to preclude a waiver of a judicial forum."[133] That proof may take the form of either statutory language or the existence of an "inherent conflict" between arbitration and the underlying purpose of the federal statute.[134]

The plaintiff in *Gilmer* could not point to any language in the ADEA that precludes arbitration, but argued that arbitration and the ADEA were in "inherent conflict." The Court was not convinced. No inherent conflict between arbitration and the ADEA was shown by the fact that the ADEA furthered important social policies or that the EEOC is involved in enforcing the ADEA.[135] Nor was the *Gilmer* Court persuaded that arbitral procedures were inadequate as compared to the procedures available in a lawsuit to enforce the ADEA.[136] Justice Byron R. White made clear that the Court was willing to compel arbitration even where arbitration procedures are not as elaborate as judicial procedures, in that an arbitration agreement by its nature " 'trades the procedures and opportunity for review of the courtroom for the simplicity, informality, and expedition of arbitration.' "[137]

The rationale of *Gilmer* would appear to apply to a Title VII claim fully as much as to an ADEA claim. Accordingly, after *Gilmer,* where a sexual harassment complainant has entered into an agreement to arbitrate that is governed by the FAA, that agreement is likely to be enforced, even if the claim is made under a federal statute such as Title VII.[138] Enforcement of an

---

[131]The *Gilmer* court cited post-*Gardner-Denver* cases to conclude that "we are well past the time when judicial suspicion of the desirability of arbitration and of the competence of arbitral tribunals inhibited the development of arbitration as an alternative means of dispute resolution." *Supra* note 114, 111 S.Ct. at 1656 n.5 (quoting Mitsubishi Motors Corp. v. Soler Chrysler-Plymouth, 473 U.S. 614, 626–27 (1985)).

[132]*Supra* note 114, 111 S.Ct. at 1657 (quoting Mitsubishi Motors Corp. v. Soler Chrysler-Plymouth, 473 U.S. 614, 625 (1985)).

[133]*Id.* at 1652.

[134]*Id.*

[135]*Id.* at 1653.

[136]The Court emphasized that the New York Stock Exchange rules provide for protections against the selection of biased arbitrators, for discovery such as information requests and depositions, for written decisions, and for award of "damages and/or other relief." *Id.* at 1654–55.

[137]*Id.* at 1655 (quoting Mitsubishi Motors Corp. v. Soler Chrysler-Plymouth, 473 U.S. 614, 628 (1985)).

[138]There was limited authority to this effect even before *Gilmer. E.g.,* Roe v. Kidder Peabody & Co., 52 FEP Cases 1865, 1867–70 (S.D.N.Y. 1990)(staying Title VII action pending arbitration under contract covered by the FAA); Coulson, *Fair Employment: Voluntary Arbitration of Employee Claims,* 33 ARB. J. 23, 25 (Sept. 1978) ("often-cited holding in *Alexander v. Gardner-Denver Co.* . . . would not be applicable [to arbitration outside of the collective bargaining context], except as dictum")(cited in Nicholson v. CPC Int'l, 877 F.2d 221, 232, 49 FEP Cases 1678, 1687 (3d Cir. 1989) (Becker, J., dissenting)).

FAA-governed agreement to arbitrate is even more likely to be applied to claims made under a state FEP statute[139] or under the common law.[140]

VII. First Amendment Issues

A. Freedom of Speech

1. Introduction

Much of the sexual harassment described in the reported cases is accomplished through verbal or visual messages. The message in a classic quid quo pro case is a statement that the complainant must comply with a superior's demand for sexual favors or suffer job detriments.[141] The message in a classic hostile environment case is a series of gender-demeaning remarks, often to the effect that women do not belong in the workplace.[142]

From a First Amendment perspective the distinction between these two categories of harassing speech is crucial. Quid pro quo cases ordinarily involve no difficult First Amendment problem. In contrast, some hostile environment cases will present free speech issues that are both perplexing and novel.

---

[139]A state statutory claim is less likely to escape the FAA-created presumption of arbitrability because the plaintiff generally will not be able to rely on any congressional intent to preclude waiver of judicial remedies.

    E.g., California: Hall v. Nomura Securities, 219 Cal. App.3d 43, 48, 268 Cal. Rptr. 45, 52 FEP Cases 824, 826 (1990)(enforcing agreement to arbitrate employment claims and barring court remedies for age and handicap discrimination, finding no "express congressional intent" to defeat presumption of arbitrability under FAA)(citing Perry v. Thomas, 482 U.S. 483 (1987)(FAA required enforcement of agreement to arbitrate employee's action for unpaid commissions, notwithstanding state statutory provision invalidating arbitration agreements in wage-collection cases)); Cook v. Barratt Am., 219 Cal. App.3d 1004, 268 Cal. Rptr. 629 (1990)(depublished opinion not to be cited officially)(staying sex discrimination action under state FEP statute because of FAA-governed agreement to arbitrate employment disputes), *cert. denied,* 111 S.Ct. 2052 (1991);

    New Jersey: Steck v. Smith Barney Harris Upham & Co., 661 F. Supp. 543, 43 FEP Cases 1736 (D.N.J. 1987)(ordering arbitration of state FEP claim pursuant to an FAA-governed agreement to arbitrate: "where, as here, the statute in question is a state statute, such that no Congressional intent is involved, the [FAA] must be strictly enforced."

    But see Minnesota: Swenson v. Management Recruiters Int'l, *supra* note 124, 858 F.2d at 1309 n.12, 47 FEP Cases at 1859–60 (Title VII "preclude[s] waiver of judicial remedies for violation of both federal Title VII rights and parallel statutory rights, thereby exempting state statutes from the provisions of the [FAA]" and ADEA cases do not apply, because "the ADEA does not contain the same recognition of state procedural remedies as does Title VII"); Anderson v. Dean Witter Reynolds, 51 FEP Cases 1075, 1076 (Minn. Ct. App. 1989)(FAA did not require sexual harassment complainant to arbitrate state FEP claim because, under *Swenson,* Title VII claim is unaffected by agreement to arbitrate enforceable under FAA, and "no reason to have a different rule available under the Minnesota Human Resources Act when that statute appears to be modeled after Title VII and the purposes of the two statutes are the same");

    Tennessee: Jacobsen v. ITT Financial Servs. Corp., 55 FEP Cases 1189, 1192 (E.D. Tenn. 1991)(following reasoning of *Swenson* to hold that claim under Tennessee FEP statute is exempt from FAA).

[140]*See generally* Dean Witter Reynolds v. Byrd, 470 U.S. 213, 217 (1985)(even if federal court will in any event assert jurisdiction over federal-law claim, FAA "requires district courts to compel arbitration of pendent arbitrable claims . . . even when the result would be the possibly inefficient maintenance of separate proceedings in different forums"). *E.g.,* Steck v. Smith Barney Harris Upham & Co., *supra* note 139, 661 F. Supp. at 547, 43 FEP Cases at 1740 ("even where the relevant state law at issue expressly precludes waiver of the judicial forum, if the parties have nevertheless executed a binding arbitration agreement, the Supremacy Clause requires that the [FAA] supersede the state law").

[141]*E.g.,* Sparks v. Pilot Freight Carriers, 830 F.2d 1554, 45 FEP Cases 160, 161 (11th Cir. 1987), reproduced in Chapter 2, Forms of Harassment (terminal manager repeatedly importuned billing clerk for sexual favors while reminding her that "your fate is in my hands").

[142]*E.g.,* Hall v. Gus Constr. Co., 842 F.2d 1010, 46 FEP Cases 573, 574 (8th Cir. 1988), reproduced in Chapter 2, Forms of Harassment (male construction crew members called female co-workers names such as "Herpes" and "Cavern Cunt" and flashed pictures of oral sex).

2. Quid Pro Quo Harassment

Quid pro quo harassment is a species of threat or extortion, invoking as it does the employer's power to grant or deny job benefits. Generally speaking, the free speech clause of the First Amendment does not protect threats or extortion.[143] Commentators might disagree about the rationale for excluding threats and extortion from First Amendment protection,[144] and some threats and extortion might be protected speech.[145] Nonetheless, threats to have a person fired for resisting sexual advances would not qualify for protection under the First Amendment.[146]

3. Hostile Environment Harassment

More difficult free speech issues arise with respect to the prohibition or punishment of sexual speech that "has the purpose or effect of unreasonably interfering with an individual's work performance or creating an intimidating, hostile, or offensive working environment."[147] In light of the verbal and visual nature of environmental harassment, one might think that the First Amendment would be a common defense. Yet the first reported Title VII case in which a First Amendment defense was asserted and ruled upon was the 1991 federal district court decision in *Robinson v. Jacksonville Shipyards*.[148]

---

[143]*E.g.*, United States v. Kelner, 534 F.2d 1020 (2d Cir.)(no First Amendment protection for televised threat by member of Jewish Defense League to kill Yassar Arafat), *cert. denied*, 429 U.S. 1022 (1976). *See also* Rankin v. McPherson, 483 U.S. 378, 386–87 (1987)("statement that amounted to a threat to kill the President would not be protected by the First Amendment"). *Cf.* Watts v. United States, 394 U.S. 705, 708 (1969)(statement by antiwar protester that "if they ever make me carry a rifle, the first man I want to get in my sights is L.B.J." is protected "political hyperbole" because it is not a "true threat" against the President, which would not be protected speech).

[144]*See* K. GREENAWALT, SPEECH, CRIME AND THE USE OF LANGUAGE 90–109 (1989)(discussing various justifications).

[145]For example, telling your colleague that you will inform his wife that he is having an affair unless he immediately breaks off the extramarital relationship. K. GREENAWALT, *supra* note 144, at 95.

[146]Any detailed doctrinal justification for excluding quid pro quo harassment from First Amendment protection is beyond the scope of this treatise. Suffice it here to say that whatever rationale for protecting speech might be invoked—be it the search for truth, promotion of democracy, or protection of individual autonomy—the prohibition of threats and coercion will affect only tenuously the employer's ability to express ideas. On the other side of the free speech equation, the government has a strong interest, rooted in preventing gender discrimination in the work force, in prohibiting speech that forces employees to choose between their livelihoods and their right to reject unwanted sexual advances. *See generally* Pittsburgh Press Co. v. Human Relations Comm'n, 413 U.S. 376 (1973)(upholding prohibition of gender-designated help-wanted advertisements in newspapers for jobs covered by sex discrimination ordinance). For a comprehensive attempt to distinguish protected threats from unprotected ones, see K. GREENAWALT, *supra* note 144.

[147]29 C.F.R. §1604.11(a)(3)(EEOC interpretation of sexual conduct that constitutes sex discrimination in violation of Title VII). *See generally* Browne, *Title VII as Censorship: Hostile Environment Harassment and the First Amendment*, 52 OHIO ST. L.J. 481 (1991). For a comprehensive constitutional analysis of broad-based restrictions on verbal and visual harassment, see Strauss, *Sexist Speech in the Workplace*, 25 HARV. C.R.-C.L. L. REV. 1, 7–11 (1990)(four categories of sexist speech in employment: (1) sexual solicitation; (2) sexually explicit language directed at a woman; (3) gender-degrading language directed at a woman; (4) sexually explicit or degrading expression seen or heard by but not directed at a woman).

[148]760 F. Supp. 1486 (M.D. Fla. 1991), reproduced in Chapter 2, Forms of Harassment. An earlier case in which a free speech defense was raised, apparently *sua sponte* by the court, is *Rabidue v. Osceola Ref. Co.*, 584 F. Supp. 419, 36 FEP Cases 183 (E.D. Mich. 1984), *aff'd on other grounds*, 805 F.2d 611, 42 FEP Cases 631 (6th Cir. 1986), *cert. denied*, 481 U.S. 1041 (1987). The complainant alleged that vulgar language of a sexual nature used by her supervisor and pictures of nude women displayed by co-workers constituted sexual harassment. The court noted that a First Amendment issue was raised by this claim but found it unnecessary to address the free speech defense because the vulgar remarks and pornographic pictures did not constitute sexual harassment in violation of Title VII. *Id.* at 433, 36 FEP Cases at 1920 ("can Title VII prohibit people from verbally expressing themselves with language that is not 'obscene' under the legal definition of the term?"). *See also* Scandinavian Health Spa v. Ohio Civil Rights Comm'n, 1990 Ohio App. LEXIS 757 (1990)(summarily rejecting employer's defense that offensive sexual speech was protected under First Amendment).

One possible explanation for the lack of free speech litigation in hostile environment cases is that the remarks in these cases are rarely made by an employer defendant itself,[149] and Title VII regulates only the speech of the employer, not that of employees.[150] This explanation is inadequate, however, because an employer required by the government to suppress speech should be permitted to assert the rights of workers whose speech is in question.[151]

Another possible explanation for employers failing to assert First Amendment defenses is that environmental harassment is actionable under Title VII only if it is so severe or pervasive that it affects a "term, condition or privilege" of employment.[152] By usually requiring outrageously demeaning or insulting remarks to have been directed at the complainant before a hostile environment claim succeeds,[153] courts have in effect incorporated First Amendment concerns into the definition of sexual harassment.[154]

Nevertheless, findings of a hostile environment occasionally appear to rely in part on speech that, at least viewed in isolation, arguably warrants constitutional protection. One court, in interpreting the Title VII bar on hostile environments, went so far as to opine that the law requires that employers "take prompt action to prevent ... bigots from expressing their opinions in a way that abuses or offends their co-workers," so as to "inform[] people that the expression of racist or sexist attitudes in public is unacceptable."[155] Yet, as

---

[149]The most common "hostile environment" suit based on speech involves remarks made to the complainant by a co-worker, with the employer's liability being predicated not on the employer's own speech but on the employer's failure to prevent or remedy the harassment. *E.g.,* Hall v. Gus Constr. Co., *supra* note 142. A claim of hostile environment based on employer speech was filed in November 1991 by Minnesota female employees against the maker of Old Milwaukee Beer, based upon the beer maker's television advertisements featuring the five full-bodied members of the "Swedish Bikini Team" delivering beer to male outdoor enthusiasts.

[150]*Cf.* Robinson v. Jacksonville Shipyards, *supra* note 148, 760 F. Supp. at 1534 (no First Amendment concern present "when the employer has no intention to express itself").

[151]The employer could argue that government-mandated employer restraints on the speech of workers would violate those employees' free speech rights fully as much as would direct government restraints. *See generally* L. TRIBE, AMERICAN CONSTITUTIONAL LAW 137 (2d ed. 1988)("litigant's claim that complying with a duty imposed upon him would prevent another from exercising a constitutional right presents a clearly justiciable issue about the permissibility of the choice the government seeks to impose upon the litigant"). It is therefore not sufficient to assert, as did the court in *Robinson v. Jacksonville Shipyards, supra* note 148, that the employer has no intention in expressing *itself* through the sexually offensive pictures or comments of its employees.

Similarly, state action exists and the employees' free speech rights are at issue where a court, to enforce an antidiscrimination statute, issues an order requiring an employer to restrict certain forms of expression in the workplace. *See, e.g.,* Robinson v. Jacksonville Shipyards, *supra* note 148, 760 F. Supp. at 1542 (injunctive relief ordering defendant to forbid unwelcome sexually oriented remarks or jokes; displays of "sexually suggestive" pictures, calendars, or graffiti; and even possession on company premises of "sexually suggestive" reading material). Of course, a private employer may, insofar as the First Amendment is concerned, prohibit any speech it chooses, even the most innocuous sexually oriented expression. At issue here is whether it is consistent with the First Amendment for the government to *require* that the employer prohibit sexually oriented speech.

[152]*See* Meritor Sav. Bank v. Vinson, 477 U.S. 57, 67, 40 FEP Cases 1822, 1827 (1986), reproduced in Chapter 1, Overview. *Cf.* Minteer v. Auger, 844 F.2d 569, 46 FEP Cases 1173 (8th Cir. 1988)(harassment of female prison guard through unwelcome remarks by co-workers not sufficiently severe or pervasive to alter conditions of employment).

[153]*E.g.,* Hall v. Gus Constr. Co., *supra* note 142. An employer would ordinarily not have a valid First Amendment defense to a Title VII claim based on such directed expression. See text accompanying notes 143–46 *supra.*

[154]*E.g.,* Rabidue v. Osceola Ref. Co., *supra* note 148 (supervisor's habitual use of vulgar language, including such sexually explicit words such as "cunt," "pussy," and "tits," which were apparently not directed toward plaintiff, as well as occasional displays by male co-workers in their work areas of pictures of nude or partially clad women, did not constitute sexual harassment in violation of Title VII). *But see* Robinson v. Jacksonville Shipyards, *supra* note 148, discussed in text at notes 158–60 *infra.*

[155]Davis v. Montsanto Chem. Co., 858 F.2d 345, 350, 47 FEP Cases 1825, 1829 (6th Cir. 1988), *cert. denied,* 109 S.Ct. 3166 (1989). *See also* Volk v. Coler, 845 F.2d 1422, 1426, 46 FEP Cases 1287, 1290 (7th

one commentator has pointed out, "the right to express one's social views is generally considered to be at or near the core of the first amendment's protection of free expression."[156] Courts have yet to address the difficult question of whether sexually harassing, but arguably protected, speech should lose whatever constitutional protection it otherwise might have on the ground that it was part of a persistent pattern of verbal and physical harassment.[157]

The recent *Jacksonville Shipyards* case presented precisely this question. In that case the plaintiff was a female welder who worked in a shipyard where a large majority of the employees were male. Her Title VII hostile environment claim relied in part on pictures of nude and partially nude women in sexually suggestive poses that pervaded the workplace.[158] The claim also was based on "sexually demeaning remarks and jokes made by male workers."[159] The district court agreed that the pictures and the remarks created a hostile environment in violation of Title VII, and, in an extended analysis, expressly rejected the employer's First Amendment defense to the claim for injunctive relief:

> The first amendment guarantee of freedom of speech does not impede the remedy of injunctive relief. • • •
>
> First, JSI has disavowed that it seeks to express itself through the sexually-oriented pictures or the verbal harassment by its employees. No first amendment concern arises when the employer has no intention to express itself, *see Sage Realty,* 507 F.Supp. at 610 & n. 17, and JSI's action in limiting the speech options of its employees in the workplace • • • establishes that the company may direct an end to the posting of materials without abridging its employees' free speech rights • • •.
>
> Second, the pictures and verbal harassment are not protected speech because they act as discriminatory conduct in the form of a hostile work environment. *See Roberts v. United States Jaycees,* 468 U.S. 609, 628, 104 S.Ct. 3244, 3255, 82 L.Ed.2d 462 (1984) ("[P]otentially expressive activities that produce special harms distinct from their communicative impact ... are entitled to no constitutional protection."); *Hishon v. King & Spalding,* 467 U.S. 69, 78, 104 S.Ct. 2229, 2235, 81 L.Ed.2d 59 (1984); Strauss, *Sexist Speech in the Workplace,* 25 HARV.C.R.–C.L.L.REV. 1, 38–41 (1990). In this respect, the speech at issue is indistinguishable from the speech that comprises a crime, such as threats of violence or blackmail, of which there can be no doubt of the authority of a state to punish. • • • *See also* Smolla, *Rethinking First Amendment Assumptions About Racist and Sexist Speech,* 47 WASH. & LEE L.REV. 171, 197 (1990) (transactional setting of sexual harassment opens sexist speech to regulation) • • •.
>
> Third, the regulation of discriminatory speech in the workplace constitutes nothing more than a time, place, and manner regulation of speech. *See* Strauss, *supra,* at 46 ("[B]anning sexist speech in the workplace does not censor such speech everywhere and for all time."). The standard for this type of regulation requires a legitimate governmental interest unrelated to the suppression of speech, content neutrality, and a tailoring of the means to accomplish this interest. • • •
> The eradication of workplace discrimination is more than simply a legitimate

---

Cir. 1988)(relying in part on comment by supervisor to plaintiff's co-worker that "if it wasn't for you filling [the plaintiff] with the women's lib . . . , she'd be staying at home with her old man where she belongs").

[156]Browne, *supra* note 147, 52 OHIO ST. L.J. at 483.

[157]*See* Browne, *supra* note 147, 52 OHIO ST. L.J. at 544 (protected speech should be excluded from evidence in hostile environment case so that complainant alleging supervisor sexually touched her should not be permitted to adduce fact that he had *Playboy* pin-ups on his office wall).

[158]*Supra note* 148, 760 F. Supp. at 1495–98.

[159]*Id.* at 1522.

governmental interest, it is a compelling governmental interest. *See Rotary Int'l v. Rotary Club of Duarte,* 481 U.S. 537, 549, 107 S.Ct. 1940, 1947, 95 L.Ed.2d 474 (1987) (eliminating discrimination against women is compelling governmental interest); *Roberts,* 468 U.S. at 626, 104 S.Ct. at 3254 (compelling governmental interest lies in removing barriers to economic advancement and political and social integration that have historically plagued women). Given the circumstances of the JSI work environment, the method of regulation set forth in this order narrowly tailors the regulation to the minimum necessary to remedy the discrimination problem. To the extent that the regulation here does not seem entirely content neutral, the distinction based on the sexually explicit nature of the pictures and other speech does not offend constitutional principles. • • •

Fourth, female workers at JSI are a captive audience in relation to the speech that comprises the hostile work environment. "Few audiences are more captive than the average worker.... Certainly, if employer-employee relations involve sufficient coercion that we justify regulation in other contexts, then this coercion does not suddenly vanish when the issue is submission to racist or sexist speech." Balkin, *Some Realism About Pluralism: Legal Realist Approaches to the First Amendment,* 1990 DUKE L.J. 375, 423–24. The free speech guarantee admits great latitude in protecting captive audiences from offensive speech. • • •

Fifth, if the speech at issue is treated as fully protected, and the Court must balance the governmental interest in cleansing the workplace of impediments to the equality of women, the latter is a compelling interest that permits the regulation of the former and the regulation is narrowly drawn to serve this interest. *Cf. United States v. Paradise,* 480 U.S. 149, 171–85, 107 S.Ct. 1053, 1066–74, 94 L.Ed.2d 203 (1987) (performing similar analysis for race-conscious remedy to race discrimination). Other first amendment rights, such as the freedom of association and the free exercise of religion, have bowed to narrowly tailored remedies designed to advance the compelling governmental interest in eradicating employment discrimination. • • •

Sixth, the public employee speech cases lend a supportive analogy. If this Court's decree is conceptualized as a governmental directive concerning workplace rules that an employer must carry out, then the present inquiry is informed by the limits of a governmental employer's power to enforce workplace rules impinging on free speech rights. In the public employee speech cases, the interests of the employee in commenting on protected matters is balanced against the employer's interests in maintaining discipline and order in the workplace. *See, e.g., Finch v. City of Vernon,* 877 F.2d 1497, 1502 (11th Cir.1989). When an employee's exercise of free expression undermines the morale of the workforce, the employer may discipline or discharge the employee without violating the first amendment. • • • Analogously, the Court may, without violating the first amendment, require that a private employer curtail the free expression in the workplace of some employees in order to remedy the demonstrated harm inflicted on other employees. *Cf. McMullen v. Carson,* 568 F.Supp. 937, 943–45 (M.D.Fla.1983) (finding no first amendment violation in discharge of KKK member from police force because *inter alia* internal discipline and morale were threatened by potential for racial confrontations), *aff'd,* 754 F.2d 936 (11th Cir. 1985); *accord Rankin,* 483 U.S. at 391 n. 18, 107 S.Ct. at 2901 n. 18.

Finally, defendants' reliance upon *American Booksellers Ass'n v. Hudnut, 771 F.2d 323 (7th Cir.1985), sum. aff'd,* 475 U.S. 1001, 106 S.Ct. 1172, 89 L.Ed.2d 291 (1986), is misplaced. Two concerns dominate that case. One is the broad definition of "pornography" in the Indianapolis ordinance. *See* 771 F.2d at 332. This issue is not present in this case because the affected speech, if it is speech protected by the first amendment, is reached only after a determination that a harm has been and is continuing to be inflicted on identifiable individuals. The second concern raised in *Hudnut* is the underlying proposition of the Indianapolis ordinance that pornography conveys a message that is always inappropriate and always subject to punishment, regardless of the context in which it appears.

See id. at 327–32. In this case, the context of the speech is the heart of the cause of action and the remedy goes no further than to regulate the time, place, and manner of the offensive speech. *Cf. Bryson,* 888 F.2d at 1567 (public employee may be discharged lawfully for uttering on-job speech which would be protected fully if uttered off-duty and in private).[160]

In light of the severity and pervasiveness of the pornography and sexual commentary, some of which was directed at the plaintiff,[161] the district court's conclusion that the plaintiff established actionable sexual harassment that was not protected by the First Amendment seems correct. Nonetheless, the court's First Amendment analysis is not satisfying.[162] The court failed to distinguish between pornography that was thrust on the plaintiff and pornography that the plaintiff could easily avoid,[163] or between those gender-degrading remarks that were directed to the plaintiff and those that were not.[164]

When sexually explicit or gender-demeaning remarks are directed at the complainant, a free-speech defense would ordinarily lack merit. As one commentator has stated, where "an employer, supervisor or co-worker tells a woman she is a 'cunt,' or makes suggestive remarks about her sex life, the state's interest in preventing this behavior should outweigh any first amendment interests."[165] This is so because a gender-demeaning remark directed to an employee is usually much more likely to interfere with the ability to work than is an equally obnoxious remark that the employee just happens to overhear.[166] For the same reason, an employee does not have a First Amendment right to place unsolicited pornography in another employee's locker or desk.

Gender-demeaning or sexually explicit speech that is *not* directed at the complaining employee has a much better claim to First Amendment protection. Two male employees may well have a constitutional right to share sexually explicit jokes so long as a female employee who finds the jokes objectionable can easily remove herself from earshot. Similarly, a male worker may have a First Amendment right to keep a *Playboy* centerfold on the inside of his locker

---

[160]*Id.* at 1534–37.

[161]*E.g., id.* at 1499 (making complainant in her presence butt of joke about sodomous rape, leaving graffiti such as "lick me you whore dog bitch" in complainant's work area) and *id.* at 1498 (telling complainant, in presence of pictures of nude or partially nude women, "Hey pussycat, come here and give me a whiff").

[162]For extended criticism of the various constitutional rationales used by the court, see Browne, *supra* note 147.

[163]The court cited not only publicly displayed posters of nude women in gynecological poses, 760 F. Supp. at 1495–98, but also what the court called "girlie" magazines (such as *Playboy*) kept in the desk drawer of an outside machine shop trailer, *id.* at 1501.

[164]The court cited not only words heard and pictures seen by plaintiff, but words heard and pictures seen by other women in the workplace and experienced by the plaintiff only through hearsay reports, 760 F. Supp. at 1499–1501.

[165]Strauss, *Sexist Speech in the Workplace,* 25 HARV. C.R.-C.L. L. REV. 1, 44–45 (1990).

[166]Thus, in *Cohen v. California,* 403 U.S. 15, 20 (1971), the Supreme Court emphasized the distinction between offensive language "directed to the person of the hearer" and offensive language that is not a "direct personal insult." *Cf.* Chaplinsky v. New Hampshire, 315 U.S. 568 (1942)(certain insults directed at an individual are "fighting words" that are not protected by First Amendment). Although a crucial factor in determining whether the speaker has a First Amendment right to make a gender-demeaning remark to an employee is whether the remark was directed to the complaining employee, the fact that the remark was so directed does not automatically strip the remark of First Amendment protection. Thus a male employee presumably has a First Amendment right to inform a woman co-worker of his view that she should be home with her children rather than working, while he presumably lacks the right to taunt her with repeated expressions of this view. *Cf.* Strauss, *supra* note 165 ("An employee told once that she should be at home would probably not suffice to establish discrimination under Title VII. Persistent and pervasive taunts, however, to the same effect may be illegal.").

door.[167] A female co-worker who is offended by the display can avoid further offense "simply by averting [her] eyes" whenever the locker door is open.[168]

Somewhere between the situation in which offensive expression is directed to an employee and the situation in which the offensive expression can be easily avoided is offensive expression that is not directed toward the plaintiff but that is so pervasive that the plaintiff cannot possibly avoid it. The pornography at issue in *Jacksonville Shipyards* was primarily of this nature—calendars in plain view that depicted nude women in "sexually suggestive or submissive poses."[169] Whether government, through a statute such as Title VII, can rid the workplace of such expression consistent with the First Amendment is a vexing problem.

The primary rationale invoked by the court in *Jacksonville Shipyards* to justify prohibiting the pornography at issue was that the pictures were not in fact expression but rather "discriminatory conduct."[170] It is not uncommon to try to finesse difficult First Amendment analysis by characterizing disagreeable expression as "conduct."[171] But categorizing the pictures as "conduct" obscures the expressive value of the pictures in question. Although workplace pornography might resemble conduct in its power to interfere with a woman's job performance, the fact remains that displaying pornographic pictures is expression, particularly if it is intended to offend and demean female co-workers.

A more constitutionally tenable justification cited by the court in *Jacksonville Shipyards* is that employees are "captive audiences." The Supreme Court has stated that the First Amendment "permits the government to prohibit offensive speech as intrusive when the 'captive' audience cannot avoid the objectionable speech."[172] However, because this concept would be "dangerously encompassing" if used to prohibit any speech that a member of the "captive audience" might find offensive, "the Court has properly been reluctant to accept its implications whenever a regulation is not content neutral."[173]

---

[167]*See* Strauss, *supra* note 165, 25 HARV. C.R.-C.L. L. REV. at 47. *But see* Robinson v. Jacksonville Shipyards, *supra* note 148.

[168]Cohen v. California, *supra* note 166, 403 U.S. at 21.

[169]Robinson v. Jacksonville Shipyards, 760 F. Supp. 1486, 1490 (M.D. Fla. 1991). For descriptions of the poses, see *id.* at 1495–99.

[170]*Id.* at 1535.

[171]*See, e.g.,* F. SCHAUER, FREE SPEECH: A PHILOSOPHICAL INQUIRY 181 (obscenity is not speech but "a sex aid, no more and no less"); MacKinnon, *Not a Moral Issue,* 2 YALE L. & POL'Y REV. 321, 340 (1984)(pornography is subordination of women, not speech); Texas v. Johnson, 109 S.Ct. 2533, 2553 (1989)(Rehnquist J., dissenting)("flag burning is the equivalent of an inarticulate grunt or roar that . . . is most likely to be indulged in not to express any particular idea, but to antagonize others"); Cohen v. California, *supra* note 166, 403 U.S. at 27 (Blackmun, J., dissenting)(First Amendment does not bar punishment of antiwar protester for wearing jacket that said "Fuck the Draft" because this "absurd and immature antic . . . was mainly conduct and little speech").

[172]*See, e.g.,* Frisby v. Schultz, 487 U.S. 474 (1988)(upholding against constitutional challenge a ban on picketing in front of particular residence). *See also* Strauss, *supra* note 165 (rejecting various constitutional rationales for banning speech-based harassment, but ultimately endorsing "captive audience" and equality-interest rationales for banning directed sexist speech and, on a case-by-case basis, for banning non-directed sexist speech).

[173]L. TRIBE, AMERICAN CONSTITUTIONAL LAW §§12–19, 950 n.24 (2d ed. 1988)(citing *Erznoznik v. Jacksonville,* 422 U.S. 205, 210 (1975)(ordinance barring nudity in movies on drive-in screens visible from street could not be upheld in order to protect sensibilities of involuntary passers-by). Thus the only case in which the Court has invoked the "captive audience" rationale to uphold a content-oriented regulation was *FCC v. Pacifica Foundation,* 438 U.S. 726, 748–49 (1978)(opinion of the Court); *id.* at 759–60 (concurring opinion). Both the Court and the concurrence, however, also invoked the need to protect children as a rationale for sustaining an FCC prohibition of the broadcast of sexually vulgar words during certain times of the day. *Id.* at 749–50, 757–59. This additional rationale ordinarily would not apply in the workplace.

Prohibition of gender-demeaning expression in the workplace is not content-neutral because this prohibition does not cover all speech that employees might find offensive, but only sexually explicit expression that is demeaning to women.[174]

Indeed, it is this lack of content neutrality that belies the *Jacksonville Shipyards* court's characterization of the prohibition of "discriminatory speech in the workplace" as "nothing more than a time, place, and manner regulation of speech."[175] As the Supreme Court has repeatedly emphasized, to qualify as a "time, place, and manner" regulation entitled to a relatively deferential standard of judicial review, the regulation must be content-neutral.[176]

A better justification for excluding pornography from the workplace is that the workplace, unlike the speaker's corner at the local park or the opinion page of the local newspaper, is not a place devoted primarily to public discourse. Many have argued that the primary purpose of the First Amendment is to disable government from interfering with the content of public discourse.[177] Under this theory, images of women, be they empowering or demeaning, are protected from government interference when expressed in books, films, plays or discussions in a public forum, because such expression is crucial to the functioning of public discourse in a democracy.[178]

Although some speech in the workplace might be "public discourse" and thus entitled to heightened First Amendment protection,[179] ordinarily expression in the workplace will not be of this nature, and a display of pornography will almost never be. Thus, a strong argument can be made that pornography in the workplace not constituting public discourse can be prohibited, consistent with the First Amendment to further the state's significant interest in removing

---

[174]*See* American Booksellers Ass'n v. Hudnut, 771 F.2d 323, 332 (7th. Cir. 1985), *sum. aff'd*, 475 U.S. 1001 (1986)(ordinance creating civil liability for distribution of pornography that is demeaning to women not content-neutral).

[175]*Supra* note 170, 760 F. Supp. at 1535.

[176]*See, e.g.*, Police Dep't v. Mosley, 408 U.S. 92, 99 (1972); Frisby v. Schultz, *supra* note 172, 487 U.S. at 481; City Council v. Taxpayers for Vincent, 466 U.S. 789, 804 (1984). Although justifying the prohibition of pornography as content neutral "time, place, and manner" regulation, the court in *Jacksonville Shipyards* admits that "the regulation here [might] not seem entirely content neutral." The court, however, goes on to state that in any event "the distinction based on the sexually explicit nature of the pictures and other speech does not offend constitutional principles" (citing Renton v. Playtime Theatres, 475 U.S. 41, 48–49 (1986)). The Supreme Court in *Renton* held that an ordinance that singled out "adult theatres" for special zoning restrictions was not aimed at "the *content* of the films . . . but rather at the *secondary effects* of the theatres," such as increased crime and decreased property values in the surrounding community. *Id.* at 47. It could be argued that the prohibition of pornography in the workplace is similarly aimed at "secondary effects," *i.e.*, the interference with women's ability to perform their jobs. However, because the ill effects of pornography in the workplace stem from the demeaning *message* the pornography conveys, the discrimination that pornography in the workplace produces should be considered a primary rather than a secondary effect.

[177]*See, e.g.*, Post, *The Constitutional Concept of Public Discourse: Outrageous Opinion, Democratic Deliberation and Hustler Magazine v. Falwell*, 103 HARV. L. REV. 601 (1990); Hustler Magazine v. Falwell, 485 U.S. 46, 54 (1988); *compare* New York Times v. Sullivan, 376 U.S. 254 (1964)(strong First Amendment protection for speech critical of public official) *with* Dun & Bradstreet v. Greenmoss Builders, 472 U.S. 749 (1985)(plurality decision)(speech "on matters of purely private concern" entitled to less First Amendment protection than speech on "matters of public concern").

[178]*See* American Booksellers v. Hudnut, *supra* note 174. *Cf.* Post, *Racist Speech, Democracy, and the First Amendment*, 32 WM. & MARY L. REV. 267, 289 (1991)("even if the First Amendment were to immunize from legal regulation racist ideas in newspapers, it would not follow that the expression of those same ideas could not be restrained by the government within the workplace, where an image of dialogue among autonomous self-governing citizens would be patently out of place").

[179]Post, *supra* note 178, 32 WM. & MARY L. REV. at 289 n.112. Public discourse might include a lunchtime conversation on the role of women in society in which a male worker, and perhaps even the employer, has a First Amendment right to express his view that a woman's place is in the home, not in the workplace.

workplace inequalities. Accordingly, a key inquiry is the degree to which pornography in the workplace actually impedes women's ability to perform their jobs.[180] But in making this inquiry, a court should be careful not to confuse an assessment of what actually impedes women's ability to work with that court's own notions of what is "proper" expression.[181]

The nature and purpose of the workplace serves to distinguish Title VII workplace regulations from university codes that prohibit racist and sexist speech on campus. Thus, a recent decision finding a campus prohibition on racial and sexual harassment to violate the First Amendment[182] is not necessarily persuasive in a Title VII context. From a First Amendment standpoint, there is a very important difference between the college campus and the workplace: The primary purpose of a college campus—especially the classroom—is learning through the exploration of ideas. Although the exploration of ideas is not always foreign to the workplace, that is not its primary purpose. Thus the First Amendment standards for judging prohibitions of speech on college campuses should for the most part be more rigorous than the standards used for measuring speech prohibitions in the workplace.[183]

B. Freedom of Religion

In *Black v. Snyder*,[184] a former associate pastor of the Lutheran Church sued her church, her synod, and her former supervising pastor on the basis of allegations that the supervising pastor had made unwelcome sexual advances toward her, touched her in a sexual manner, and insisted over her objections that he accompany her outside the workplace, and that church authorities had failed to take appropriate remedial action. She also challenged her discharge, which had been for her asserted failure "to conduct the pastoral office efficiently." The Minnesota appellate court upheld the dismissal of the wrongful-discharge aspects of the lawsuit, holding that inquiry into reasons for the discharge would impermissibly involve the state in matters of religious doctrine. The complainant was entitled to pursue her claim of a pre-discharge sexually hostile environment, however, because that claim was "unrelated to

---

[180]An interesting question in this regard is the standard to apply. Should it be an objective "reasonable woman" standard, or is it sufficient that the plaintiff's ability to work was substantially impeded by the pornography even if the majority of women in the workplace were not adversely affected by it? For a discussion of the reasonable woman standard, see Chapter 4, Hostile Environment Harassment, Section VI.C.3.

[181]*See* Bruhwiler v. University of Tenn., 859 F.2d 419, 423 (6th Cir. 1988)(Nelson, J., dissenting)("One can only conclude that [the defendant's] sin lay in his having forgotten that it was a lady he was talking to, and not a man. That may have been a breach of etiquette . . . but it was hardly evidence of [sex discrimination].").

[182]Doe v. University of Mich., 721 F. Supp. 852 (E.D. Mich. 1989).

[183]See Weinstein, *A Constitutional Roadmap to the Regulation of Campus Hate Speech*, 38 WAYNE L. REV. ___ (1991)(arguing that EEOC definition of "hostile environment" is inappropriate for college campuses in light of difference in purpose of workplace and college campuses). Thus the court in *Doe v. University of Michigan, supra* note 182, while striking down the campus code on First Amendment grounds, expressly noted that "[m]any forms of sexually abusive and harassing conduct are sanctionable" consistent with the First Amendment, including quid pro quo harassment in the workplace and speech that is so "extreme and pervasive . . . as to create a hostile or offensive working environment." *Id.*, 721 F. Supp. at 862.

[184]56 FEP Cases 539 (Minn. Ct. App. 1991).

pastoral qualification or issues of church doctrine" and because the government was entitled to require that a church adhere to generally applicable, facially neutral statutes. The dissenting judge on the three-judge panel argued that the complainant should be able to sue the offending pastor alone, and not the church, because the lawsuit was a challenge to the way that the church supervises its religious personnel and, if permitted to proceed, would lead to an excessive state entanglement with religion.

CHAPTER 28

INJUNCTIVE AND AFFIRMATIVE RELIEF

I. STATUTORY AUTHORITY

Section 706(g) of Title VII provides in relevant part:

If the court finds that the respondent has intentionally engaged in or is intentionally engaging in an unlawful employment practice charged in the complaint, the court may enjoin the respondent from engaging in such unlawful employment practice, and order such affirmative action as may be appropriate, which may include, but is not limited to, reinstatement or hiring of employees ... or any other equitable relief as the court deems appropriate.[1]

Although the language of §706(g) appears to require a specific finding that the discrimination was intentional, this requirement has been, to a large degree, judicially eliminated. Relying upon the conclusion in *Griggs v. Duke Power Co.* that Title VII focuses on "the *consequences* of employment practices, not simply the motivation,"[2] numerous courts have interpreted "intentionally" to mean simply that the practices are not "accidental"; these courts have not required proof that the practices reflect an intent to discriminate.[3]

II. FACTORS INFLUENCING THE GRANT OR DENIAL OF INJUNCTIVE RELIEF

A. Preventing Future Discrimination

In sexual harassment cases, as in Title VII cases generally, where a violation is found "a court has the power, and indeed the obligation, to award those equitable remedies necessary 'to advance the dual statutory goals of eliminating the effects of past discrimination and preventing future discrimination.' "[4]

---

[1]42 U.S.C. §2000e-5(g). For a more extensive discussion of injunctive and affirmative relief in employment discrimination actions, see B.L. SCHLEI & P. GROSSMAN, EMPLOYMENT DISCRIMINATION LAW, Chapter 37 (2d ed. 1983) and Five-Year Supplement (1989).

[2]401 U.S. 424, 432, 3 FEP Cases 175, 178 (1971)(emphasis in original).

[3]SCHLEI & GROSSMAN, *supra* note 1, at 1395 n.2.

[4]Spencer v. General Elec. Co., 703 F. Supp. 466, 468–69, 51 FEP Cases 1709, 1710 (E.D.Va. 1988)(citing Albemarle Paper Co. v. Moody, 422 U.S. 405, 418, 10 FEP Cases 1181, 1187 (1975) and quoting Pitre v. Western Elec. Co., 843 F.2d 1262, 1274, 51 FEP Cases 656, 665 (10th Cir. 1989)), *aff'd*, 894 F.2d 651, 51 FEP Cases 1725 (4th Cir. 1990).

Until recently* a monetary award under Title VII required proof of tangible economic loss,[5] and because plaintiffs often endured environmental harassment for years without being terminated or suffering a tangible employment loss,[6] injunctive relief was the only form of relief available in many sexual harassment cases.[7]

In determining whether injunctive relief is appropriate, courts generally have held that a person subjected to employment discrimination is entitled to an injunction against future discrimination[8] "unless the employer proves that it is unlikely to repeat the practice."[9] Thus, courts have granted injunctive relief when a hostile work environment continues to exist[10] or when an employer has taken curative action only after being sued.[11] Some courts have determined that the sexual harassment claim is moot where the individual harasser has left the defendant's employ,[12] unless the unlawful conduct was

---

*[**Editor's Note:** Under the Civil Rights Act of 1991, discussed in Appendix 8, a plaintiff proving a violation of Title VII may now be entitled to a limited recovery of compensatory and punitive damages.]

[5]Brooms v. Regal Tube Co., 881 F.2d 412, 423, 50 FEP Cases 1499, 1506 (7th Cir. 1989)(in "hostile environment" case, court may award back pay to plaintiff "only as an equitable remedy, *i.e.,* if a plaintiff can demonstrate that the defendant discharged him or her either actually or constructively"); see also Chapter 29, Monetary Relief, Section II.

[6]*See, e.g.,* Spencer v. General Elec. Co., 894 F.2d 651, 654–55, 51 FEP Cases 1725, 1731–32 (4th Cir. 1990)(plaintiff proved that defendant maintained sexually hostile working environment but was awarded only nominal damages because she could not prove tangible loss resulting from harassment); Huddleston v. Roger Dean Chevrolet, 845 F.2d 900, 905, 46 FEP Cases 1361, 1363 (11th Cir. 1988)(although plaintiff established sexual harassment, she left job voluntarily and was not constructively discharged, and therefore not entitled to monetary award); *see also* Staton v. Maries County, 868 F.2d 996, 997, 49 FEP Cases 309, 311 (8th Cir. 1989)(plaintiff, a county employee, asserted hostile environment claim in that she was raped by county sheriff, but because sheriff did not offer job benefits in return for sex nor take retaliatory measures, district court not clearly erroneous in finding rape did not sufficiently affect conditions of plaintiff's employment).

[7]*See* Meritor Sav. Bank v. Vinson, 477 U.S. 57, 77, 40 FEP Cases 1822, 1831 (1986), reproduced in Chapter 1, Overview (concurring opinion)("[i]n the 'pure' hostile environment case, where an employee files an EEOC complaint alleging sexual harassment in the workplace, the employee seeks not money damages but injunctive relief"); *see also* Zowayyed v. Lowen Co., 735 F. Supp. 1497, 1504, 52 FEP Cases 1350, 1356 (D. Kan. 1990)("a plaintiff who has no economic damages . . . but who demonstrates the existence of a hostile work environment, may be entitled to an injunction against a continuation of the harassing conduct").

[8]*See* EEOC v. Hacienda Hotel, 881 F.2d 1504, 1519, 50 FEP Cases 877, 889 (9th Cir. 1989)("victims of employment discrimination generally are entitled to an injunction against future discrimination"); Nanty v. Barrows Co., 660 F.2d 1327, 1333 & n.6, 27 FEP Cases 410, 414 (9th Cir. 1981)(plaintiff in race discrimination case who proved his claim of unlawful discrimination "entitled to injunction against future or continued discrimination").

[9]EEOC v. Goodyear Aerospace Corp., 813 F.2d 1539, 1544, 43 FEP Cases 875, 879 (9th Cir. 1987)(abuse of discretion to deny injunction absent finding of no likely recurrence). *See also* James v. Stockham Valves & Fittings Co., 559 F.2d 310, 354–56, 15 FEP Cases 827, 863–64 (5th Cir. 1977)("absent clear and convincing proof of no reasonable probability of further noncompliance with the law a grant of injunctive relief is mandatory"), *cert. denied,* 434 U.S. 1034 (1978); Los Angeles County v. Davis, 440 U.S. 625, 633, 19 FEP Cases 282 (1979)(where interim events have completely and irrevocably eradicated effects of alleged violation and there is no reasonable expectation that violation will recur, action for injunctive relief is moot). *See generally* B.L. SCHLEI & P. GROSSMAN, *supra* note 1, at 1415–16 & n.61.

[10]*See* Sanchez v. City of Miami Beach, 720 F. Supp. 974, 979, 982 (S.D. Fla. 1989)(steps taken by employer were inadequate and did not prevent continuing sexual harassment); *see also* Bundy v. Jackson, 641 F.2d 934, 946 n.13, 24 FEP Cases 1155, 1162 (D.C. Cir. 1981)(finding no certainty that harassment would not recur, in part because "all the harassing employees still work for the agency").

[11]*See* EEOC v. Hacienda Hotel, *supra* note 8 ("appellant did not take prompt remedial action upon notification of the sexual harassment allegations against it"; employer's "recent efforts to train managerial employees regarding discrimination problems and the absence of further EEOC charges in recent times are encouraging and laudable; however, the district court did not abuse its discretion by awarding permanent injunctive relief on the facts of this case"); EEOC v. Goodyear Aerospace Corp., *supra* note 9, 813 F.2d at 1544–45, 43 FEP Cases at 879 ("employer that takes curative actions only after it has been sued fails to provide sufficient assurances that it will not repeat the violation to justify denying an injunction"); James v. Stockham Valves & Fittings Co., *supra* note 9 (same). *But cf.* Spencer v. General Elec. Co., *supra* note 6, 894 F.2d at 660, 51 FEP Cases at 1732 (rejecting contention that remedial measures undertaken by employer after instigation of litigation will never be adequate to obviate injunctive relief).

[12]*See* Walker v. Anderson Elec. Connectors, 742 F. Supp 591, 595 (N.D. Ala. 1990)(*dicta* that injunctive relief unnecessary because employer "has already rid itself of the highest profile sexual harasser"); Spencer

not limited to one harasser.[13] The employer's assurance that its employees have been educated with regard to sexual harassment and that the problem will not recur, standing alone, is insufficient to preclude the issuance of injunctive relief.[14]

B. Continued Employment of Complainant

Where the complainant is no longer employed, courts generally have denied injunctive relief, finding that termination either deprives the complainant of standing[15] or renders the matter moot.[16] Exceptions to mootness exist where the complainant has challenged the dismissal in legal proceedings that are still pending,[17] the case is litigated as a class action, or where the EEOC is a party to the action.[18]

---

v. General Elec. Co., *supra* note 4, 703 F. Supp. at 470, 51 FEP Cases at 1711 (termination of harasser not dispositive but relevant, and "weighs against the necessity for injunctive relief where, as here, there is no evidence that the illegal conduct was widespread"); Spencer v. General Elec. Co., 697 F. Supp. 204, 219, 51 FEP Cases 1696, 1709 (E.D. Va. 1988)("[i]njunctive relief is also inappropriate, given that [harassing supervisor] no longer works at GE"). *But see* Showalter v. Allison Reed Group, 56 FEP Cases 989, 996 (D.R.I. 1991)(ordering employer to refrain from sexual harassment even though harasser no longer employed, in that employer still lacked grievance procedure for harassed employees).

[13]*See* EEOC v. Gurnee Inn Corp., 914 F.2d 815, 817, 53 FEP Cases 1425, 1426 (7th Cir. 1990)(upholding injunction against company's claim that "the unlawful conduct was limited to one man," since fired, and agreeing with district court that because manager who knew of but failed to control harassment was still employed, discrimination resulted both from supervisor's behavior and company's "continued toleration of that behavior").

[14]*See* Bundy v. Jackson, *supra* note 10, 641 F.2d at 946 n.13, 24 FEP Cases at 1162 ("[a]ppellee has argued that an injunction is improper and unnecessary in this case since Bundy has complained of no instances of sexual harassment since 1975 and there is therefore no reason to think further harassment will occur. Common sense tells us that the men who harassed Bundy may well have ceased their actions solely because of the pendency of her complaint and lawsuit. Moreover, the law tells us that a suit for injunctive relief does not become moot simply because the offending party has ceased the offending conduct, since the offending party might be free otherwise to renew that conduct once the court denied the relief"); EEOC v. FLC & Bros. Rebel, Inc., 663 F. Supp. 864, 870–71, 44 FEP Cases 362, 368 (W.D. Va. 1987)(court discounted employer's assurances in light of testimony and other evidence), *aff'd,* 846 F.2d 70 (4th Cir. 1988).

[15]Davis v. Marsh, 876 F.2d 1446, 1450–51 (9th Cir. 1989)(plaintiff discharged from army "lacks standing to seek injunctive relief, as she has virtually no chance of suffering future sexual harassment by army officers").

[16]Swanson v. Elmhurst Chrysler Plymouth, 882 F.2d 1235, 1237, 50 FEP Cases 1082, 1083 (7th Cir. 1989)("Since Swanson was no longer an employee, the court could not exercise its equitable powers to enjoin the employer from engaging in unlawful conduct, since injunctions are available only to restrain present or threatened unlawful conduct"), *cert. denied,* 110 S.Ct. 758 (1990); McKinney v. Illinois, 720 F. Supp. 706, 709, 50 FEP Cases 1625, 1627 (N.D. Ill. 1989)(plaintiff no longer employed and "nothing in the complaint suggests that . . . [the] alleged sexual harassment . . . will recur"); Valdez v. Church's Fried Chicken, 683 F. Supp. 596, 621, 47 FEP Cases 1155, 1171 (W.D. Tex. 1988)(plaintiff no longer worked for employer and "request for injunctive relief is moot because there is no reasonable expectation that the conduct will recur"); Christoforou v. Ryder Truck Rental, 668 F. Supp. 294, 301–2 n.3, 51 FEP Cases 98, 104 (S.D.N.Y. 1987)("[a]ny claim for injunctive relief on plaintiff's hostile environment claim would be moot as to plaintiff since she is no longer employed by Ryder and she does not wish to be so employed"); *cf.* Alexander v. Yale Univ., 631 F.2d 178, 184 (2d Cir. 1980)(Title IX case)(sexual harassment claims deemed moot because plaintiffs had graduated from the university and thus "[n]one of these plaintiffs at present suffers from the alleged injury. Nor would the grant of the requested relief aid these plaintiffs in the slightest"). An action is moot if the issues are no longer live or the parties lack a legally cognizable interest in the outcome. Sample v. Johnson, 771 F.2d 1335, 1338 (9th Cir. 1985), *cert. denied,* 475 U.S. 1019 (1986). Federal courts lack jurisdiction over moot actions because their constitutional authority is limited to actual cases or controversies. *Id.*

[17]*See* Katz v. Dole, 709 F.2d 251, 253 n.1, 31 FEP Cases 1521 (4th Cir. 1983).

[18]*See* EEOC v. Hacienda Hotel, *supra* note 8 (case not moot where EEOC a party even though none of the individuals still employed; EEOC is "not merely a proxy for the victims of discrimination, but acts also 'to vindicate the public interest in preventing employment discrimination' "). *See generally* General Tel. Co. v. EEOC, 446 U.S. 318, 22 FEP Cases 1196 (1980)(EEOC may seek classwide relief). The EEOC is authorized by §706 of Title VII to seek injunctive relief to prevent any violation of Title VII. 42 U.S.C. §2000e-5(f). For the role of the EEOC in seeking preliminary injunctive relief in a sexual harassment case, see Section IV.B *infra.*

III. NATURE OF THE INJUNCTIVE RELIEF

A. Enjoining Practices Found Unlawful

Courts in sexual harassment cases have enjoined various forms of conduct: sexual harassment generally,[19] causing, encouraging, creating, or condoning the creation of a sexually hostile environment,[20] refusing to take proper steps to investigate complaints,[21] refusing to consider discipline of those found responsible for sexual harassment,[22] giving negative references to prospective employers of the complainant,[23] communicating in any way with former employees who are complainants,[24] and retaliating against complainants.[25] Some courts have simply framed injunctive relief in language borrowed from the EEOC Guidelines.[26]

B. Compelling Preventive or Affirmative Action

Section 706(g) also expressly authorizes courts to "order such affirmative action as may be appropriate."[27] Thus, in addition to prohibiting certain conduct, employers in sexual harassment cases have been ordered to prevent harassment through such measures as notifying employees that sexual harassment

---

[19]*See, e.g.,* EEOC v. Hacienda Hotel, *supra* note 8, 881 F.2d at 1518, 50 FEP Cases at 889 (defendant enjoined from "engaging in any employment practice which discriminates on the basis of sex"); EEOC v. Fotios, 671 F. Supp. 454, 465, 43 FEP Cases 1712, 1713 (W.D. Tex. 1987)(defendant enjoined from "engaging in sexual harassment of its employees (past, present, or future) and/or otherwise violating Title VII"); EEOC v. FLC & Bros. Rebel, Inc., *supra* note 14, 663 F. Supp. at 871, 44 FEP Cases at 368 (same); Arnold v. City of Seminole, 614 F. Supp. 853, 872–73, 40 FEP Cases 1539, 1553 (E.D. Okla. 1985)(same). Because violations of injunctions are punishable by contempt, respondents should object to any proposed injunction that lacks specificity with respect to what is prohibited or required, or that incorporates by reference material not set forth in the injunctive order. *See* FED. R. CIV. P. 65(d); *see also* Davis v. City & County of San Francisco, 890 F.2d 1438, 1450, 51 FEP Cases 1542, 1551 (9th Cir. 1989)(noting that "primary purpose of Rule 65(d) is to assure adequate notice to parties faced with possibility of contempt").

[20]*See, e.g.,* Bundy v. Jackson, *supra* note 10, 641 F.2d at 948 n.15, 24 FEP Cases at 1163 (*dictum* suggested by court of appeals for consideration by district court on remand); Sanchez v. City of Miami Beach, 720 F. Supp. 974, 982 (S.D. Fla. 1989)(defendant enjoined from "continuing or maintaining any policy, custom, practice, or usage which creates or maintains sexual harassment"); Arnold v. City of Seminole, *supra* note 19, 614 F. Supp. at 872, 40 FEP Cases at 1553 (defendant enjoined from "causing, encouraging, condoning, or permitting the practice of sexual harassment of female employees by male supervisors"); Broderick v. Ruder, 46 EPD ¶38,042 (D.D.C. 1988)(approving injunctive relief proposed jointly by parties); Morgan v. Hertz Corp., 542 F. Supp. 123, 128, 27 FEP Cases 990 (W.D. Tenn. 1981)(injunction should issue against supervisors making "sexually indecent comments to female employees" such as "Did you get any over the weekend?"), *aff'd,* 725 F.2d 1070, 33 FEP Cases 1237 (6th Cir. 1984).

[21]Broderick v. Ruder, *supra* note 20.

[22]*Id.*

[23]EEOC v. Fotios, *supra* note 19, 671 F. Supp. at 465, 43 FEP Cases at 1712–13.

[24]*Id.*

[25]*Id. See also* Broderick v. Ruder, *supra* note 20.

[26]*See, e.g.,* Bundy v. Jackson, *supra* note 10, 641 F.2d at 948, 24 FEP Cases at 1163; Sanchez v. City of Miami Beach, *supra* note 20; Arnold v. City of Seminole, *supra* note 19, 614 F. Supp. at 872, 40 FEP Cases at 1552–53. In *Bundy,* the D.C. Circuit suggested the following injunctive language for consideration by the district court on remand:

The court decrees that the defendant Delbert Jackson, Director of the District of Columbia Department of Corrections, along with his supervising employees, agents, and all those subject to his control or acting in concert with him, are enjoined from causing, encouraging, condoning, or permitting the practice of sexual harassment of female employees by male supervisors and employees within the Department: to wit, any unwelcome sexual advances, requests for sexual favors, or other verbal or physical conduct of a sexual nature when submission to such conduct is explicitly or implicitly a requirement of the individual's employment, or used as a basis for any employment decision concerning that individual, or when such conduct has the purpose or effect of unreasonably interfering with the individual's work performance or creating an intimidating or hostile or offensive work environment.

[27]42 U.S.C. §2000e-5(g).

is unlawful, against policy, or otherwise prohibited,[28] outlining steps it will take to prevent sexual harassment,[29] developing effective grievance procedures,[30] developing appropriate sanctions and disciplinary measures for those who are found to have sexually harassed other employees,[31] notifying employees that offending employees will be disciplined,[32] developing and implementing training and education for supervisors and other employees,[33] and even hiring an equal employment opportunity expert to recommend to the court any steps to be taken to enhance a defendant's future compliance.[34] Many of these features appear in a particularly broad order of injunctive relief issued by the United States District Court in *Robinson v. Jacksonville Shipyards*.[34a]

Courts have also provided for periodic reports[35] and monitoring procedures.[36] One court ordered the defendant to investigate the actions of specified individuals, to consider whether discipline should be imposed on those individuals, and to advise the court of its actions.[37]

---

[28]*See* Arnold v. City of Seminole, *supra* note 19, 614 F. Supp. at 871–73, 40 FEP Cases at 1553–54 (defendant ordered to "notify all employees and supervisors in the offices and departments of the city, through individual letters and permanent posting in prominent locations in all offices that sexual harassment [as explicitly defined in the prohibitive portion of the court's decree] violates Title VII . . . and regulatory guidelines of the [EEOC], and the policies of the City of Seminole"); *see also* Bundy v. Jackson, *supra* note 10, 641 F.2d at 948, 24 FEP Cases at 1163 (D.C. Cir. 1981)(same, in language suggested by Court of Appeals for consideration by district court on remand, except that notice and posting requirements limited to department in which plaintiff worked); Broderick v. Ruder, *supra* note 20 (ordering defendant "to take reasonable steps to advise its employees that sexually harassing other Commission employees is prohibited"); EEOC v. FLC & Bros. Rebel, Inc., *supra* note 14, 663 F. Supp. at 871 (defendant ordered to give notice to "all employees of their rights under [Title VII] and advising the employees that sexual harassment and sex discrimination will not be condoned"). For an example of a specific form of notice, see *EEOC v. Fotios, supra* note 19, 671 F. Supp. at 466, 43 FEP Cases at 1714, app. A.

[29]*See* Boyd v. James S. Hayes Living Health Care Agency, 671 F. Supp. 1155, 1169, 44 FEP Cases 332, 344 (W.D. Tenn. 1987)(defendant ordered to present to court "a plan outlining steps it will take to prevent sexual harassment from occurring").

[30]Arnold v. City of Seminole, *supra* note 19, 614 F. Supp. at 873, 40 FEP Cases at 1553 (defendant required to "develop clear and effective procedures by which employees complaining of sexual harassment may have their complaints promptly and thoroughly investigated (by a neutral fact-finder) and informal as well as formal processes for hearing, adjudication, and appeal of the complaints"); *see also* Sanchez v. City of Miami Beach, *supra* note 20, 720 F. Supp. at 982 (defendant ordered to "design anew or re-formulate and thereafter stringently implement a comprehensive system to safeguard against all kinds of discriminatory conduct").

[31]*See, e.g.,* Arnold v. City of Seminole, *supra* note 19, 614 F. Supp. at 873, 40 FEP Cases at 1553 (defendant required to "develop appropriate sanctions or disciplinary measures for supervisors or other employees who are found to have sexually harassed female employees, including warnings to the offending person and notations in that person's employment record for reference in the event future complaints are directed against that person, and dismissal where other measures fail"). *Cf.* Guess v. Bethlehem Steel Corp., 913 F.2d 463, 464, 53 FEP Cases 1547, 1548 (7th Cir. 1990)(plaintiff sought injunctive relief in the form of order requiring that employee who harassed her be fired; injunction denied on facts of case).

[32]*See, e.g.,* Broderick v. Ruder, *supra* note 20.

[33]*See e.g.,* Arnold v. City of Seminole, *supra* note 19, 614 F. Supp. at 873, 40 FEP Cases at 1553 (defendant required to develop "proposed plan of education and training for all employees of the City" that should include training in "detection, correction, and prevention of discriminatory practices"); Broderick v. Ruder, *supra* note 20; Department of Fair Empl. & Hous. v. Livermore Joe's, Cal. FEHC Dec. 90-07 at 27 (1990)(company to implement training program for all employees and to inform them of remedies available under company's antiharassment policy and under federal and state law).

[34]*See, e.g.,* Broderick v. Ruder, *supra* note 20.

[34a]760 F. Supp. 1486, 1541 (M.D. Fla. 1991), reproduced in Appendix 7.

[35]*See, e.g.,* Arnold v. City of Seminole, *supra* note 19, 614 F. Supp. at 873, 40 FEP Cases at 1553–54 (ordering defendant to "return to this Court within ninety days to report on the steps it has taken in compliance with this Order and to present its plans for the additional measures required [*i.e.*, develop grievance procedure, disciplinary measures, and means of educating employees]").

[36]*See, e.g.,* EEOC v. Fotios, *supra* note 19, 671 F. Supp. at 465, 43 FEP Cases at 1712–13 (providing for monitoring through inspection of company's premises, private interviews with employees, and review of personnel records, documents, and files).

[37]*See, e.g.,* Broderick v. Ruder, *supra* note 20.

C. Relief for Victims of Unlawful Practices

In *Franks v. Bowman Transportation Co.*,[38] the Supreme Court confirmed judicial authority to order reinstatement, with no loss in seniority, of identifiable victims of discrimination. In sexual harassment cases, courts have permitted such remedies as reinstatement,[39] transfer to a different company office,[40] promotion,[41] grant of a job title,[42] reimbursement of medical expenses,[43] reimbursement of equity interest in a car lost due to constructive discharge,[44] and even reinstatement of one of the alleged harassers under unique facts showing that the termination of that alleged harasser was actually due to national origin discrimination.[45] A court has discretion to deny reinstatement under appropriate circumstances.[45a]

Reinstatement might be resisted on equitable grounds. One court has denied relief on the ground that the sexual harassment complainant, who engaged in her own harassment against her former employer following her discharge, did "not come into this court of equity with clean hands" and therefore was entitled to no relief under Title VII.[45b] Other courts, while not expressly invoking the "unclean hands" doctrine, have nonetheless used equitable reasons to deny relief. Most notably, in *Summers v. State Farm Mutual Automobile Ins. Co.*,[45c] the Tenth Circuit upheld summary judgment for the defendant employer on the ground of the employer's post-discharge discovery that the plaintiff had materially falsified company records. The *Summers* court held that although the employer could not rely on such after-acquired evidence to

---

[38]424 U.S. 747, 12 FEP Cases 549 (1976).

[39]*See* Meritor Sav. Bank v. Vinson, 477 U.S. 57, 75, 40 FEP Cases 1822, 1830 (1986), reproduced in Chapter 1, Overview (concurring opinion)(noting that reinstatement is a Title VII remedy); Boyd v. James S. Hayes Living Health Care Agency, *supra* note 29, 671 F. Supp. at 1169, 44 FEP Cases at 343 (reinstatement appropriate remedy); EEOC v. FLC & Bros. Rebel, Inc., 663 F. Supp. 864, 871, 44 FEP Cases 362, 367 (W.D. Va. 1987)(ordering offer of reinstatement), *aff'd*, 846 F.2d 70 (4th Cir. 1988).

[40]*Cf.* Spencer v. General Elec. Co., 703 F. Supp. 466, 469, 51 FEP Cases 1709, 1710 (E.D.Va. 1988)(employer had "promptly transferred [plaintiff] to a similar position in a different GE office at the same pay level and with similar opportunities for advancement"), *aff'd*, 894 F.2d 651 (4th Cir. 1990). Transfer of the plaintiff instead of the harasser is appropriate only if the transfer does not make the plaintiff worse off. *See* Guess v. Bethlehem Steel Corp., 913 F.2d 463, 465, 53 FEP Cases 1547, 1549 ("A remedial measure that makes the victim of sexual harassment worse off is ineffective per se").

[41]*See* Bundy v. Jackson, 641 F.2d 934, 949–50, 24 FEP Cases 1155, 1166 (D.C. Cir. 1981)(*dicta* that promotion is an accepted remedy); *cf.* Broderick v. Ruder, 46 EPD ¶38,042 (D.D.C. 1988)(approving parties' joint proposal that plaintiff be promoted).

[42]*See* Broderick v. Ruder, *supra* note 41.

[43]*See* EEOC v. FLC & Bros. Rebel, Inc., *supra* note 39, 663 F. Supp. at 871, 44 FEP Cases at 368; *see also* Harrington v. Vandalia-Butler Bd. of Educ., 418 F. Supp. 603, 607, 13 FEP Cases 702 (S.D. Ohio 1976)(plaintiff not entitled to back pay or reinstatement is granted $1000 per year for six years of discriminatory working conditions; court has equitable power to grant some compensatory relief).

[44]*Id.*

[45]*See* Valdez v. Church's Fried Chicken, 683 F. Supp. 596, 637, 47 FEP Cases 1155, 1184 (W.D. Tex. 1988)(reinstatement ordered despite evidence that assistant manager had actually engaged in sexual harassment; court found that termination was result of "focused" investigation of anonymous complaint for which assistant manager could not have been guilty, that similarly situated managers had not been fired, and that termination was pretext for national origin discrimination).

[45a]*E.g.*, Lipsett v. Univ. of P.R., 759 F. Supp. 40, 55 FEP Cases 638, 652 (D.P.R. 1991)(sexual harassment plaintiff entitled to $525,000 in damages but denied reinstatement to surgical residency program).

[45b]Women Employed v. Rinella & Rinella, 468 F. Supp. 1123, 1128, 1129 (N.D. Ill. 1979)(*dictum*). *Cf.* Hargett v. Delta Automotive, Inc., 765 F. Supp. 1487 (N.D. Ala. 1991)(recognizing availability of "unclean hands" defense but finding that plaintiff's hands "are only smudged"). *See generally* Kirk v. Sullivan, 761 F. Supp. 58, 66 (N.D. Ill. 1991)(defense of "unclean hands" available to defendant in Title VII case but requires specificity under Rule 9(B) of the Federal Rules of Civil Procedure because factual basis of defense was that plaintiff defrauded employer by falsifying circumstances of leave of absence).

[45c]864 F.2d 700, 48 FEP Cases 1107 (10th Cir. 1988)(Logan, Moore & McWilliams, JJ.).

justify the plaintiff's discharge, the evidence was relevant to the plaintiff's claim of injury and justified a denial of relief. Judge Robert L. McWilliams explained:

> The present case is akin to the hypothetical wherein a company doctor is fired because of his age, race, religion, and sex and the company, in defending a civil rights action, thereafter discovers that the discharged employee was not a "doctor." In our view, the masquerading doctor would be entitled to no relief, and Summers is in no better position.[45d]

The *Summers* defense has been applied in sexual harassment cases.[45e]

IV. PRELIMINARY INJUNCTIONS

A. Rule 65 Preliminary Relief

Under Rule 65 of the Federal Rules of Civil Procedure, preliminary injunctions may be available even before state remedies are exhausted or before the EEOC has issued a right-to-sue letter.[46] Normal equitable standards apply, including the likelihood of prevailing on the merits, the existence of irreparable injury, the degree of harm to the defendant from the issuance and to the plaintiff from the denial of such injunctive relief, and consideration of the public interest.[47]

Where the plaintiff fails to make the necessary showing, relief will be denied.[48] Irreparable harm is not presumed and is seldom found from the mere loss of a job, since that loss ordinarily may be remedied by damages if the litigant prevails.[49] However, because sexual harassment plaintiffs often remain

---

[45d]*Id.* at 708, 48 FEP Cases at 1113.

[45e]*E.g.,* Churchman v. Pinkerton's, Inc., 756 F. Supp. 515, 55 FEP Cases 81, 84–86 (D. Kan. 1991)(granting summary judgment against Title VII sexual harassment complainant because of later-discovered material omissions on complainant's job application); Mathis v. Boeing Military Airplane Co., 719 F. Supp. 991, 50 FEP Cases 688 (D. Kan. 1989)(same). *See also* Washington v. Lake County, 55 FEP Cases 1298, 1300–1301 (N.D. Ill. 1991)(applying *Summers* defense in granting summary judgment motion and collecting cases following *Summers*).

[46]Aronberg v. Walters, 755 F.2d 1114, 1115, 45 FEP Cases 522, 523 (4th Cir. 1985)(where intent of Congress in enacting 1972 Amendments to Title VII extending its coverage to federal employment was to give public employees same rights as private employees, federal employee was not required to exhaust administrative remedies before obtaining injunctive relief to preserve status quo); Sheehan v. Purolator Courier Corp., 676 F.2d 877, 887, 28 FEP Cases 202, 209 (2d Cir. 1982)(where court eventually will have jurisdiction of substantive claims and administrative tribunal has preliminary jurisdiction, court has incidental equity jurisdiction to grant temporary relief to preserve status quo).

[47]*See, e.g.,* O'Connor v. Peru State College, 728 F.2d 1001, 1001, 34 FEP Cases 85, 86 (8th Cir. 1984); Shaffer v. Globe Protection, 721 F.2d 1121, 1123, 33 FEP Cases 450, 451 (7th Cir. 1983). Some courts have added special emphasis to the traditional analysis. *See* Duke v. Langdon, 695 F.2d 1136, 1137, 30 FEP Cases 1059, 1060 (9th Cir. 1983)(must demonstrate either probable success on the merits and irreparable harm, or that serious questions are raised and balance of hardships tips sharply in favor); Ferrell v. Durham Technical Inst., 569 F. Supp. 16, 19, 33 FEP Cases 855, 858 (M.D.N.C. 1983)(two most important factors are probable irreparable injury to plaintiff and likely harm to defendant).

[48]*See, e.g.,* Wickes v. Ward, 45 EPD ¶37,719 (S.D.N.Y. 1988)(motion for preliminary injunction denied because irreparable harm not demonstrated); *see also* Shaffer v. Globe Protection, *supra* note 47, 721 F.2d at 1124, 33 FEP Cases at 452–53 (no showing of irreparable injury).

[49]Sampson v. Murray, 415 U.S. 61, 88–91 (1974); *see also* O'Connor v. Peru State College, *supra* note 47, 728 F.2d at 1003, 34 FEP Cases at 86–87 (no showing of irreparable harm and balance of equities did not favor plaintiff).

at their jobs, particularly in hostile environment situations, preliminary and permanent injunctions may be more extensively used.[50]

B. Section 706(f)(2) Preliminary Relief

Section 706(f)(2) of Title VII provides in part:

> Whenever a charge is filed with the Commission and the Commission concludes on the basis of a preliminary investigation that prompt judicial action is necessary to carry out the purposes of this Act, the Commission ... may bring an action for appropriate temporary or preliminary relief pending final disposition of such charge. Any ... order granting preliminary or temporary relief shall be issued in accordance with rule 65 of the Federal Rules of Civil Procedure.[51]

Only the EEOC may seek relief under §706(f)(2). Courts disagree on whether the EEOC must meet the traditional test for preliminary relief by showing irreparable harm and likelihood of success, or whether a more relaxed standard is applicable.[52] The courts that adhere to the traditional standard hold that the irreparable injury may be shown either as to the charging party or the EEOC.[53] Irreparable injury to the EEOC is established by showing that the failure to grant preliminary relief will discourage other employees from cooperating with the EEOC's investigation or from filing their own claims.[54]

In sexual harassment cases, the most common type of §706(f)(2) relief sought by the EEOC is to prevent the employer from threatening to harm employees who object to sexual advances,[55] retaliating against employees who have complained to the EEOC, or otherwise preventing interference with the EEOC's investigation.[56]

---

[50]*Cf.* Wickes v. Ward, *supra* note 48 (preliminary injunction denied "before a court may grant injunctive relief, it must determine whether in a particular case the risk of irreparable harm exists as a result of a potential chilling effect. ... If the plaintiff had filed a complaint against her employer and was then harassed and suspended, she would have a stronger argument that denial of an injunction might inhibit policewomen from filing sexual harassment complaints for fear of retaliation"). *See also* EEOC v. Fotios, 671 F. Supp. 454, 465, 43 FEP Cases 1712, 1713 (W.D. Tex. 1987)(court previously issued preliminary injunction; ordered permanent injunction against continued sexual harassment of employees).

[51]42 U.S.C. §2000e-5(f)(2). The EEOC has prepared a model brief for use by EEOC attorneys in seeking temporary restraining orders and preliminary injunctions in sexual harassment cases. See 52 DAILY LAB. REP. A-4 (March 18, 1991).

[52]*Compare* EEOC v. Anchor Hocking Corp., 666 F.2d 1037, 27 FEP Cases 809 (6th Cir. 1981)(traditional standard) *and* EEOC v. Dravo Corp., 36 FEP Cases 1211 (W.D. Pa. 1984)(same) *and* EEOC v. City of Bowling Green, 607 F. Supp. 524, 37 FEP Cases 963 (W.D. Ky. 1985)(same) *and* EEOC v. Target Stores, 36 FEP Cases 543 (D. Minn. 1984) (same) *with* EEOC v. Pacific SW Airlines, 587 F. Supp. 686, 34 FEP Cases 1430 (N.D. Cal. 1984)(when EEOC requests preliminary injunction under §706(f)(2), court should presume existence of irreparable injury) *and* EEOC v. Credit Consultants, 532 F. Supp. 11, 28 FEP Cases 71 (N.D. Ohio 1981)(when EEOC seeks preliminary relief under §706(f)(2), traditional standard should be relaxed).

[53]*See, e.g.,* EEOC v. Target Stores, *supra* note 52; EEOC v. Howard Univ., 32 FEP Cases 331 (D.D.C. 1983).

[54]*Compare* EEOC v. ABC Rentals, 39 EPD ¶35,835 (N.D. Tex. 1985)(temporary restraining order granted to restrain defendant from harassing employees and interfering with investigation) *and* EEOC v. Work Connection, 40 EPD ¶36,393 (D. Minn. 1986)(preliminary injunction granted to prevent respondent from threatening witnesses to sexual harassment from participating in investigative process) *with* EEOC v. Howard Univ., *supra* note 53 (preliminary relief denied because EEOC failed to establish that alleged retaliation discouraged employees from cooperating with investigation).

[55]*See* EEOC v. Fotios, *supra* note 50, 42 FEP Cases at 1642–43.

[56]*Id. See also* EEOC v. ABC Rentals, *supra* note 54; EEOC v. Work Connection, *supra* note 54.

C. State Remedies

Where the actions of the alleged harasser are particularly onerous, state antiharassment remedies may enable the complainant to get an immediate protective order, such as an order barring telephone calls, touching, and other activities.[57]

---

[57]*See, e.g.,* California Code of Civil Procedure §527.6, which provides for a temporary restraining order and an injunction against "harassment" that consists of a willful course of conduct directed at a specific person which "seriously alarms, annoys, or harasses the person, and which serves no legitimate purpose," if the conduct is such as to cause "a reasonable person to suffer substantial emotional distress" and if it does actually cause substantial emotional distress.

CHAPTER 29

MONETARY RELIEF

I. STATUTORY AUTHORITY

Section 706(g) of Title VII provides:

> If the court finds that the respondent has intentionally engaged in or is intentionally engaging in an unlawful employment practice charged in the complaint, the court may ... order such affirmative action as may be appropriate, which may include, but is not limited to, reinstatement or hiring of employees, with or without back pay ... or other equitable relief as the court deems appropriate. Back pay liability shall not accrue from a date more than two years prior to the filing of a charge with the [EEOC]. Interim earnings or amounts earnable with reasonable diligence by the person or persons discriminated against shall operate to reduce the back pay otherwise allowable.[1]

As §706(g) states, monetary relief in the form of back pay is available within the framework of "equitable relief." Moreover, although back pay is the only monetary remedy specified in §706(g), courts have held that the power to grant appropriate equitable relief under Title VII also includes the power to grant other monetary remedies.[2] The Civil Rights Act of 1991 provides for further monetary relief in the form of limited compensatory and punitive damages.[3]

II. BACK PAY

In awarding back pay to victims of sexual harassment, courts rely upon case law dealing with back pay in Title VII actions generally, without regard to whether these cases have dealt specifically with sexual harassment.[4] The

---

[1]42 U.S.C. §2000e-5(g).

[2]The court's power to grant other forms of equitable monetary relief is discussed in Sections II.C., III., and V. *infra*.

[3]See Appendix 8.

[4]*See* EEOC v. Gurnee Inn Corp., 914 F.2d 815, 53 FEP Cases 1425 (7th Cir. 1990); Carrero v. New York City Hous. Auth., 890 F.2d 569, 580, 51 FEP Cases 596, 604 (2d Cir. 1989); Wheeler v. Southland Corp., 875 F.2d 1246, 1250–51, 50 FEP Cases 86, 90 (6th Cir. 1989); Horn v. Duke Homes, 755 F.2d 599, 607, 37 FEP Cases 228, 234–35 (7th Cir. 1985); Bundy v. Jackson, 641 F.2d 934, 948–53, 24 FEP Cases 1155, 1162–64 (D.C. Cir. 1981); Jones v. Wesco Investments, 1987 U.S. Dist. LEXIS 6873 (W.D. Mo. 1987), *aff'd,* 846 F.2d 1154, 46 FEP Cases 1431 (8th Cir. 1988). For further background on back pay under Title VII, see B.L. SCHLEI & P. GROSSMAN, EMPLOYMENT DISCRIMINATION LAW 1418–51 (2d ed. 1983), Five-Year Supp. 526–43 (1989).

Supreme Court noted in *Albemarle Paper v. Moody* that "back pay is not an automatic or mandatory remedy; like all other remedies under the Act, it is one which the courts 'may' invoke."[5] Despite this permissive language, Justice Potter Stewart also stated for the Court in *Albemarle Paper* that, consistent with Title VII's make-whole purpose,[6] "back pay should be denied only for reasons which, if applied generally, would not frustrate the central statutory purposes of eradicating discrimination throughout the economy and making persons whole for injuries suffered through past discrimination."[7]

The Court's decisions stand for the proposition that an award of back pay is the rule, not the exception.[8] Back pay is denied only in exceptional cases where "special factors" mitigate against its award.[9]

A. Requirement of Economic Loss

Nonetheless, in order to obtain back pay, the plaintiff must "demonstrate that the defendant discharged her, either actually or constructively," or that the plaintiff otherwise suffered a tangible economic loss.[10] A typical obstacle to an award of back pay in hostile environment cases, therefore, is the lack of any tangible economic detriment, *e.g.,* lost pay from a discharge, constructive discharge, or denial of promotion.[11]

---

[5]422 U.S. 405, 415, 10 FEP Cases 1181, 1186 (1975).

[6]According to its legislative history, Title VII is

intended to make the victims of unlawful employment discrimination whole, and . . . the attainment of this objective . . . requires that persons aggrieved by the consequences and effects of the unlawful employment practice be, so far as possible, restored to a position where they would have been were it not for the unlawful discrimination.

Section-by-Section Analysis of H.R. 1746, accompanying the Equal Employment Opportunity Act of 1972 Conference Report, 118 CONG. REC. 7166, 7168 (1972); *see also* Franks v. Bowman Transp. Co., 424 U.S. 747, 764, 12 FEP Cases 549, 555 (1976)(citing legislative history).

[7]*Supra* note 5, 422 U.S. at 421, 10 FEP Cases at 1189.

[8]*Id.* at 421 n.14, 10 FEP Cases at 1189 (if a district court should decline to award back pay, it must "carefully articulate" its reasons for doing so); *see also* Ford Motor Co. v. EEOC, 458 U.S. 219, 226–27, 29 FEP Cases 121, 125 (1982)(although "the power to award back pay is a discretionary power," this power must be exercised "in light of the large objectives of the Act"); Carrero v. New York City Hous. Auth., *supra* note 4 ("award of back pay is the rule, not the exception"); EEOC v. Hacienda Hotel, 881 F.2d 1504, 1517, 50 FEP Cases 877, 887–88 (9th Cir. 1989)(back pay awarded to victims of sexual harassment); Wheeler v. Southland Corp., 875 F.2d 1246, 1251, 50 FEP Cases 86, 90 (6th Cir. 1989)(same); Hall v. Gus Constr. Co., 842 F.2d 1010, 46 FEP Cases 573, 574 (8th Cir. 1988)(same), reproduced in Chapter 2, Forms of Harassment; Rasimas v. Michigan Dep't of Mental Health, 714 F.2d 614, 626, 32 FEP Cases 688, 696 (6th Cir. 1983), *cert. denied*, 466 U.S. 950 (1984)(same).

[9]*Compare* Le Beau v. Libbey-Owens-Ford Co., 727 F.2d 141, 149–50, 33 FEP Cases 1700, 1707 (7th Cir. 1984)(denying back pay when defendants' discriminatory practices found support in Illinois fair employment practices statute that conflicted with Title VII) *with* Horn v. Duke Homes, 755 F.2d 599, 606, 37 FEP Cases 228, 233 (7th Cir. 1985)(no "special factors" shown and, accordingly, "the district court did not have 'discretion' to deny back pay") *and* Rasimas v. Michigan Dep't of Mental Health, *supra* note 8 ("in the absence of exceptional circumstances, back pay should always be awarded when a Title VII violation is found").

[10]Brooms v. Regal Tube Co., 881 F.2d 412, 423, 50 FEP Cases 1499, 1506 (7th Cir. 1989). In *Brooms,* a sexual harassment case, the Seventh Circuit upheld the district court's finding of constructive discharge and award of back pay despite the plaintiff's failure to plead constructive discharge in her complaint. Back pay is also granted where the plaintiff can prove that the discharge was in retaliation for complaining of harassment. *See, e.g.,* Sahs v. Amarillo Equity Investors, 702 F. Supp. 256, 259, 48 FEP Cases 927, 929 (D. Colo. 1988). Back pay is also appropriate for a plaintiff who was *not* discharged but who sustained economic loss as a result of sexual harassment. *See, e.g.,* Broderick v. Ruder, 46 EPD ¶38,042 (D.D.C. 1988)(following liability determination, court approved settlement including back pay for plaintiff who was neither fired nor constructively discharged). *Cf.* Yates v. Avco Corp., 819 F.2d 630, 636–37, 43 FEP Cases 1595, 1600–1601 (6th Cir. 1987)(plaintiff awarded salary lost as result of harassment-induced sick leave, but denied additional damages because resignation not deemed constructive discharge).

[11]Steele v. Offshore Shipbldg., 867 F.2d 1311, 1314, 1317–18, 49 FEP Cases 522, 523, 527 (11th Cir. 1989)(only nominal damages awarded because plaintiffs left jobs voluntarily and were not constructively discharged); Huddleston v. Roger Dean Chevrolet, 845 F.2d 900, 905, 46 FEP Cases 1361, 1363–64 (11th

B. Computing the Back-Pay Award

As a general proposition, "[b]ackpay awards should completely redress the economic injury the claimant has suffered as a result of discrimination."[12] However, the calculation of back pay often is not straightforward, but rather is subject to different interpretations.

1. Elements of the Back-Pay Award

In accordance with Title VII's make-whole purpose, back pay encompasses more than an individual's lost "straight-time" pay; it includes overtime, shift differentials, and premium pay,[13] sales commissions,[14] cost-of-living increases, raises, bonuses,[15] promotional increases,[16] tips,[17] vacation and sick pay,[18] pension and retirement benefits,[19] severance pay,[20] profit-sharing,[21] uniform cleaning allowances,[22] and insurance.[23]

Cir. 1988)(despite existence of sexual harassment, no monetary award because plaintiff left job voluntarily and was not constructively discharged); Spencer v. General Elec. Co., 697 F. Supp. 204, 219, 51 FEP Cases 1696, 1708 (E.D. Va. 1988)(although complainant "forced to work in a hostile environment, she has not demonstrated that she suffered any tangible loss"), *aff'd,* 894 F.2d 651, 51 FEP Cases 1725 (4th Cir. 1990). *Cf.* Trautvetter v. Quick, 916 F.2d 1140, 1148, 54 FEP Cases 109, 115 (7th Cir. 1990)(*dictum*)("we are not sure that she has [a claim for equitable relief] for it is undisputed that [she] was neither affirmatively nor constructively discharged . . . and [she] has also failed to allege (or demonstrate) that . . . sexual advances infringed in some manner upon her ability to obtain a promotion or other job-related benefit").

[12]Rasimas v. Michigan Dep't of Mental Health, *supra* note 8.

[13]*E.g.,* Arnold v. City of Seminole, 614 F. Supp. 853, 871, 40 FEP Cases 1539, 1552 (E.D. Okla. 1985)(overtime, shift differential, fringe benefits); Ross v. Twenty-Four Collection, 681 F. Supp. 1547, 1552, 48 FEP Cases 1590, 1595 (S.D. Fla. 1988)(shift differential), *aff'd,* 875 F.2d 873, 50 FEP Cases 600 (11th Cir. 1989); Lamb v. Drilco Div., 32 FEP Cases 105, 107 (S.D. Tex. 1983)(overtime); Meyers v. ITT Diversified Credit Corp., 527 F. Supp. 1064, 1070, 27 FEP Cases 995, 1000 (E.D. Mo. 1981)(overtime); Macey v. World Airways, 14 FEP Cases 1426, 1430 (N.D. Cal. 1977)(overtime). *Cf.* Spencer v. General Elec. Co., 697 F. Supp. 204, 219, 51 FEP Cases 1696, 1708 (E.D. Va. 1988)(rejecting speculative claim for overtime hours), *aff'd,* 894 F.2d 651, 51 FEP Cases 1725 (4th Cir. 1990).

[14]*E.g.,* Huddleston v. Roger Dean Chevrolet, *supra* note 11, 46 FEP Cases at 1364; Gilchrist v. Jim Slemons Imports, 803 F.2d 1488, 1501, 42 FEP Cases 314, 315 (9th Cir. 1986)(last year of commission earnings used to estimate lost earnings).

[15]*E.g.,* Cox v. American Cast Iron Pipe Co., 784 F.2d 1546, 1562, 40 FEP Cases 678, 691 (11th Cir.)(bonuses), *cert. denied,* 479 U.S. 883 (1986); Sinclair v. Automobile Club of Okla., 733 F.2d 726, 729, 34 FEP Cases 1206, 1207 (10th Cir. 1984)(raises and bonuses); Taylor v. Jones, 495 F. Supp. 1285, 1292, 23 FEP Cases 1273, 1278 (E.D. Ark. 1980)(6% cost-of-living increase for each year of discrimination), *aff'd in part and rev'd in part on other grounds,* 653 F.2d 1193, 28 FEP Cases 1024 (8th Cir. 1981); Grindstaff v. Burger King, 494 F. Supp. 622, 625, 23 FEP Cases 1486, 1489 (E.D. Tenn. 1980)(5% cost-of-living raise).

[16]Parker v. Burnley, 693 F. Supp. 1138, 1153, 47 FEP Cases 587, 599 (N.D. Ga. 1988)(plaintiff "entitled to retroactive promotion . . . with an award of back pay"). *Cf.* Broderick v. Ruder, *supra* note 10 (following liability determination, court approved settlement including "award of back pay, based upon salary increases to which she would have been entitled had she been promoted on the [three] dates listed above"). *Cf.* Spencer v. General Elec. Co., 697 F. Supp. 204, 219, 51 FEP Cases 1696, 1708 (E.D. Va. 1988)(rejecting speculative claim for lost promotional opportunities), *aff'd,* 894 F.2d 651, 51 FEP Cases 1725 (4th Cir. 1990).

[17]*E.g.,* Priest v. Rotary, 634 F. Supp. 571, 579–80, 585, 40 FEP Cases 208, 213–14, 217 (N.D. Cal. 1986)(cocktail waitress entitled to tips as part of back-pay award).

[18]*E.g.,* Yates v. Avco Corp., 819 F.2d 630, 638, 43 FEP Cases 1595, 1601–2 (6th Cir. 1987)(sick leave); Pettway v. American Cast Iron Pipe Co., 494 F.2d 211, 263, 7 FEP Cases 1115, 1156 (5th Cir. 1974)(sick pay), *cert. denied,* 467 U.S. 1243 (1984); Meyers v. ITT Diversified Credit Corp., 527 F. Supp. 1064, 1070, 27 FEP Cases 995, 1000 (E.D. Mo. 1981)(vacation pay).

[19]*E.g.,* Meyers v. ITT Diversified Credit Corp., 527 F. Supp. 1064, 1070, 27 FEP Cases 995, 1000 (E.D. Mo. 1981)(pension benefits); EEOC v. Sage Realty Corp., 507 F. Supp. 599, 613, 24 FEP Cases 1521, 1532 (S.D.N.Y. 1981)(same).

[20]*E.g.,* Ross v. Twenty-Four Collection, *supra* note 13, 681 F. Supp. at 1556, 48 FEP Cases at 1598 (awarding severance pay in addition to back wages and fringe benefits).

[21]*E.g.,* EEOC v. Kallir, Philips, Ross, Inc., 401 F. Supp. 66, 74, 11 FEP Cases 241, 247 (S.D.N.Y. 1975)(profit-sharing awarded), *cert. denied,* 434 U.S. 920 (1977).

[22]*E.g.,* Laffey v. Northwest Airlines, 642 F.2d 578, 588–89, 23 FEP Cases 1628, 1635 (D.C. Cir. 1980)(uniform-cleaning allowance).

[23]*E.g.,* Kewin v. Board of Educ., 8 FEP Cases 125, 128 (Mich. Cir. Ct. 1974), *aff'd,* 65 Mich. App. 472, 16 FEP Cases 1586 (1975). Courts differ as to how plaintiffs should be compensated for insurance

2. *Deductions and Offsets*

a. Interim earnings. Section 706(g) of Title VII provides that "[i]nterim earnings or amounts earnable with reasonable diligence by the person or persons discriminated against shall operate to reduce the back pay otherwise allowable."[24] Accordingly, courts have deducted actual interim earnings from the back-pay award when those earnings substituted for employment with the defendant employer.[25] Where interim earnings exceed any possible back-pay award, back pay is properly denied.[26]

"Interim earnings" are not limited to net taxable income, but instead may include in-kind compensation for services rendered.[27] Courts differ, however, as to whether unemployment compensation benefits, Social Security benefits, or taxes should be deducted from the back-pay award. Some courts permit such deductions.[28] Other courts deny such deductions, either under the collateral source doctrine or general equitable principles.[29]

---

coverage. Options considered include: (1) compensation based upon the cost of the insurance to the employer; (2) compensation based upon the out-of-pocket expenses incurred by the plaintiff in obtaining substitute coverage; and (3) compensation based upon the losses incurred by the plaintiff that would have been covered by the insurance. *See* EEOC v. Rath Packing Co., 40 FEP Cases 576, 577 (S.D. Iowa 1984), *aff'd in part and rev'd in part,* 787 F.2d 318, 40 FEP Cases 580 (8th Cir.)(value of dental, vision, and prescription benefits included in back-pay award), *cert. denied,* 479 U.S. 910 (1986); Fariss v. Lynchburg Foundry, 769 F.2d 958, 965, 38 FEP Cases 992, 996–97 (4th Cir. 1985)(using amount of employer's premium, stating that if employee obtains substitute coverage, recovery of premiums permitted); Blackwell v. Sun Elec. Corp., 696 F.2d 1176, 1185, 30 FEP Cases 1177, 1184 (6th Cir. 1983)(plaintiff entitled to value of health benefits he would have received). One court has held that whichever of these three methods yields the largest amount should be used. EEOC v. Pacific Press Publishing Ass'n, 35 FEP Cases 322, 323 (N.D. Cal. 1982). *Cf.* Spagnuolo v. Whirlpool Corp., 550 F. Supp. 432, 433, 32 FEP Cases 1377, 1378 (W.D.N.C. 1982)(no compensation for value of insurance where plaintiff had not incurred any losses that would have been covered by insurance nor incurred out-of-pocket expenses to obtain substitute coverage), *aff'd in part and rev'd in part,* 717 F.2d 114, 32 FEP Cases 1382 (4th Cir. 1983).

[24]42 U.S.C. §2000e-5(g); *see also* EEOC v. FLC & Bros. Rebel, Inc., 663 F. Supp. 864, 44 FEP Cases 362 (W.D. Va. 1987), *aff'd,* 846 F.2d 70 (4th Cir. 1988); Joyner v. AAA Cooper Transp., 597 F. Supp. 537, 36 FEP Cases 1644 (M.D. Ala. 1983), *aff'd,* 749 F.2d 732, 41 FEP Cases 496 (11th Cir. 1984).

[25]*E.g.,* Horn v. Duke Homes, 755 F.2d 599, 608, 37 FEP Cases 228, 234–35 (7th Cir. 1985)(deducting earnings from housecleaning, sewing, and babysitting); Joyner v. AAA Cooper Transp., *supra* note 24 (interim earnings deducted); Sowers v. Kemira, Inc., 701 F. Supp. 809, 826, 46 FEP Cases 1825, 1838 (S.D. Ga. 1988)(interim wages and disability benefits deducted); Ross v. Double Diamond, 672 F. Supp. 261, 277, 45 FEP Cases 313, 325 (N.D. Tex. 1987)(interim wages reflected on W-2 deducted); Meyers v. ITT Diversified Credit Corp., *supra* note 19 (subtracting interim earnings).

[26]*See, e.g.,* EEOC v. New York Times Broadcasting Serv., 542 F.2d 356, 359, 13 FEP Cases 813, 815–16 (6th Cir. 1976); Butta v. Anne Arundel County, 473 F. Supp. 83, 89, 20 FEP Cases 24, 29 (D. Md. 1979).

[27]*E.g.,* Horn v. Duke Homes, *supra* note 25, 37 FEP Cases at 235 (income earned from babysitting, housecleaning, and sewing deducted); McCluney v. Joseph Schlitz Brewing Co., 540 F. Supp. 1100, 1103–4, 29 FEP Cases 1294, 1296–97 (E.D. Wis. 1982)(value of in-kind compensation at time received by plaintiff, not value at time of trial, is amount to be deducted from back-pay award), *aff'd,* 728 F.2d 924, 34 FEP Cases 273 (7th Cir. 1984).

[28]*E.g.,* EEOC v. Wyoming Retirement Sys., 771 F.2d 1425, 1431–32, 38 FEP Cases 1544, 1548–49 (10th Cir. 1985)(Social Security benefits deducted from back-pay award); Leonard v. Frankfort Elec. & Water Plant Bd., 752 F.2d 189, 195, 36 FEP Cases 1181, 1185 (6th Cir. 1985)(taxes deducted from back-pay award); Gilardi v. Schroeder, 672 F. Supp. 1043, 1047, 45 FEP Cases 283, 287 (N.D. Ill. 1986), *aff'd,* 833 F.2d 1226, 45 FEP Cases 346 (7th Cir. 1987)(unemployment compensation deducted from back-pay award); Lamb v. Drilco, 32 FEP Cases 105, 107 (S.D. Tex. 1983)(deduction of unemployment compensation in exercise of court's discretion); Meyers v. ITT Diversified Credit Corp., 527 F. Supp. 1064, 1070, 27 FEP Cases 995, 1000 (E.D. Mo. 1981)(unemployment compensation totaling $33,670.28 deducted from back pay); EEOC v. Sage Realty Corp., 507 F. Supp. 599, 613, 24 FEP Cases 1521, 1532 (S.D.N.Y. 1981)(unemployment insurance benefits deducted). *Cf.* Valdez v. Church's Fried Chicken, 683 F. Supp 596, 636, 47 FEP Cases 1155, 1183 (W.D. Tex. 1988)(no deduction for unemployment compensation because defendant failed to establish amount of compensation).

[29]*E.g.,* Guthrie v. J.C. Penney Co., 803 F.2d 202, 209, 42 FEP Cases 185, 190 (5th Cir. 1986)(no deduction for unemployment compensation benefits or Social Security benefits); Brown v. A.J. Gerrard Mfg. Co., 715 F.2d 1549, 1550, 32 FEP Cases 1701, 1702 (11th Cir. 1983)(*en banc*)(unemployment

b. Duty to mitigate. The complainant must make reasonable efforts to mitigate back-pay damages. The burden of proof as to whether the complainant has mitigated falls on the defendant, however, for failure to mitigate is an affirmative defense.[30]

The duty to mitigate damages may require that the complainant accept alternative employment that is "the substantial equivalent of the position from which the claimant was discriminatorily terminated."[31] The "substantial equivalent" test is not met if the new employment involves a different business paying substantially less money,[32] or requires more work for the same pay.[33]

Courts have justified a complainant's failure to obtain alternative employment when that failure appears to have resulted from the defendant employer's conduct.[34] Accordingly, some courts have excused a sexual harassment complainant's failure to find a new job where the harassment created special psychological obstacles to efforts to re-enter the workplace.[35] The rationale is

---

compensation benefits may not be deducted as matter of law); Rasimas v. Michigan Dep't of Mental Health, 714 F.2d 614, 627, 32 FEP Cases 688, 697 (6th Cir. 1983)(no deduction from back-pay award for taxes), *cert. denied*, 466 U.S. 950 (1984); Craig v. Y&Y Snacks, 721 F.2d 77, 82, 33 FEP Cases 187, 193 (3d Cir. 1983)(unemployment compensation may be recouped by state, but should not be deducted from back pay); EEOC v. Ford Motor Co., 645 F.2d 183, 195, 25 FEP Cases 774, 783–84 (4th Cir. 1981)(no deduction for unemployment compensation benefits), *rev'd on other grounds*, 458 U.S. 219 (1982); Boyd v. James S. Hayes Living Health Care Agency, 671 F. Supp. 1155, 1169, 44 FEP Cases 332, 343 (W.D. Tenn. 1987). *Cf.* Nichols v. Frank, 732 F. Supp. 1085, 1089, 52 FEP Cases 951, 953 (D. Or. 1990)(workers' compensation benefits deductible only to extent that benefits constitute double recovery).

[30]*See* 42 U.S.C. §2000e-5(g). *Accord* EEOC v. Gurnee Inn Corp., 914 F.2d 815, 818–19, 53 FEP Cases 1425, 1426–27 (7th Cir. 1990); EEOC v. Hacienda Hotel, 881 F.2d 1504, 1518, 50 FEP Cases 877, 888 (9th Cir. 1989)(employer failed to prove plaintiff's failure to mitigate where there was evidence she actively sought alternative employment); Horn v. Duke Homes, *supra* note 25, 37 FEP Cases at 234 (employer failed to prove nonmitigation); Sowers v. Kemira, Inc., *supra* note 25, 701 F. Supp. at 827 (employer failed to prove nonmitigation). For more extensive discussion of this requirement, see B.L. SCHLEI & P. GROSSMAN, EMPLOYMENT DISCRIMINATION LAW 1447–48 (2d ed. 1983), Five-Year Supp. 540 (1989).

[31]Rasimas v. Michigan Dep't of Mental Health, *supra* note 29, 714 F.2d at 624, 32 FEP Cases at 695; *see also* Ford Motor Co. v. EEOC, 458 U.S. 219, 228–29, 29 FEP Cases 121, 126 (1982)(employer not liable for back pay after plaintiffs failed to accept employer's unconditional offer of jobs previously denied plaintiffs); Walters v. City of Atlanta, 803 F.2d 1135, 42 FEP Cases 387 (11th Cir. 1986)(efforts to obtain one particular position insufficient; plaintiff obligated to seek employment in other fields when not awarded position in own field); Davis v. Western-Southern Life Ins. Co., 34 FEP Cases 97, 102 (N.D. Ohio 1984)(plaintiff who declined offer to return to former position at different location following resignation waived right to back pay); EEOC v. Domino's Pizza, 34 FEP Cases 1075, 1076 (E.D. Mich. 1983)(plaintiff not entitled to back pay for period after she voluntarily quit better-paying substitute job); Coley v. Consolidated Rail Corp., 561 F. Supp. 645, 651–52, 34 FEP Cases 129, 134–35 (E.D. Mich 1982)(back pay limited to eight months since alleged defensive attitude toward middle-aged men did not justify plaintiff's failure to seek employment beyond that period).

[32]Wheeler v. Snyder Buick, 794 F.2d 1228, 1235, 41 FEP Cases 341, 347 (7th Cir. 1986)(plaintiff not required to stay in job in different business paying substantially less money); *see also* Sowers v. Kemira, Inc., 701 F. Supp. 809, 826, 46 FEP Cases 1825, 1837–38 (S.D. Ga. 1988)(plaintiff not required to take position in different city).

[33]EEOC v. Exxon Shipping Co., 745 F.2d 967, 979, 36 FEP Cases 330, 340 (5th Cir. 1984)(plaintiff not required to accept position with same pay but requiring weekend work).

[34]*E.g.,* EEOC v. FLC & Bros. Rebel, Inc., 663 F. Supp. 864, 870, 44 FEP Cases 362, 367 (W.D. Va. 1987), *aff'd*, 846 F.2d 70 (4th Cir. 1988)(plaintiff who lost car as result of discharge not required to accept position at another location); Ross v. Twenty-Four Collection, 681 F. Supp. 1547, 1555, 48 FEP Cases 1590, 1597 (S.D. Fla. 1988)(employee who reasonably believed she was barred from seeking other employment because of noncompetition clause in contract with former employer relieved of obligation to seek such other employment), *aff'd*, 875 F.2d 873 (11th Cir. 1989).

[35]*E.g.,* Brooms v. Regal Tube Co., 881 F.2d 412, 423–24 n.8, 50 FEP Cases 1499, 1506–7 (7th Cir. 1989)(upholding district court's "determination that Brooms could not maintain a position until she completed therapy" and therefore including that period of time in the back-pay award); EEOC v. Gurnee Inn Corp., 48 FEP Cases 871, 882 (N.D. Ill. 1988)(considering plaintiff's "fear that she would run into the same situation again" in holding that plaintiff had not failed to mitigate damages and was entitled to back-pay award), *aff'd*, 914 F.2d 815, 53 FEP Cases 1425 (7th Cir. 1990); Arnold v. City of Seminole, 614 F. Supp. 853, 873, 40 FEP Cases 1539, 1554 (E.D. Okla. 1985)(awarding back pay and front pay for periods of psychological disability caused by sexual harassment where plaintiff was unable to work in order to mitigate damages).

that a person victimized by a sexually hostile environment or fired for failure to capitulate to sexual demands may be justifiably apprehensive about seeking comparable employment in the same field.[36]

3. Calculating Deductions and Offsets

The court may use the amount that the complainant would have earned absent the discriminatory conduct as the base award from which interim earnings are deducted.[37] Alternatively, the court may opt to subtract the plaintiff's interim earnings for each year from a figure equal to the last full year's salary earned with the defendant employer.[38] Still another method of determining the base back-pay award is to use the income history of another employee who was in the same position as the plaintiff at the time of termination.[39]

C. Interest

Although discretionary with the court,[40] both prejudgment and postjudgment interest generally are awarded in Title VII actions.[41] The method of computing interest is left to the court's discretion.[42]

---

[36]*See* EEOC v. Gurnee Inn Corp., *supra* note 30 ("it would not be unreasonable for a young woman having gone through the experience of these women to feel 'gun shy' about looking for a similar position"); *but cf.* Coley v. Consolidated Rail Corp., 561 F. Supp. 645, 652, 34 FEP Cases 129, 135 (E.D. Mich. 1982)(plaintiff's fear of middle-aged men insufficient to overcome defendant's evidence of plaintiff's nonmitigation).

[37]*E.g.,* Priest v. Rotary, 634 F. Supp. 571, 585, 40 FEP Cases 208, 217 (N.D. Cal. 1986).

[38]*E.g.,* Jenkins v. Orkin Exterminating Co., 646 F. Supp. 1274, 1279, 42 FEP Cases 152, 156 (E.D. Tex. 1986)(using this computation); Joyner v. AAA Cooper Transp., 597 F. Supp. 537, 544–45, 36 FEP Cases 1644, 1650 (M.D. Ala. 1983)(accord), *aff'd,* 749 F.2d 732, 41 FEP Cases 496 (11th Cir. 1984).

[39]*See, e.g.,* Ambrose v. United States Steel Corp., 39 FEP Cases 35, 38 (N.D. Cal. 1985). *Cf.* Brown v. Marsh, 713 F. Supp. 20, 23–24, 51 FEP Cases 844, 847 (D.D.C. 1989)(back-pay award for denial of multiple promotions based upon earnings of individual who received promotions, except no deduction for erroneous classification or demotion suffered by individual), *aff'd,* 1990 U.S. App. LEXIS 19656 (D.C. Cir. 1990).

[40]Donnelly v. Yellow Freight Sys., 874 F.2d 402, 411, 49 FEP Cases 1253, 1259 (7th Cir. 1989)("[t]he decision to grant or deny an award of prejudgment interest lies within the discretion of the district court"), *aff'd on other grounds,* 110 S.Ct. 1566 (1990).

[41]Loeffler v. Frank, 486 U.S. 549, 563–65, 46 FEP Cases 1659, 1663 (1988)(and cases collected in note 5 *supra*): "Respondent concedes, and apparently all the United States Courts of Appeals that have considered the question agree, that Title VII authorizes prejudgment interest as part of the backpay remedy in suits against private employers. This conclusion surely is correct". *See also* EEOC v. Gurnee Inn Corp., 48 FEP Cases 871, 880 (N.D. Ill. 1988)(adding prejudgment interest to back-pay awards of eight successful plaintiffs), *aff'd,* 914 F.2d 815, 53 FEP Cases 1425 (7th Cir. 1990); Hunter v. Allis-Chalmers Corp., 797 F.2d 1417, 1430, 41 FEP Cases 721, 731 (7th Cir. 1986)(awarding back pay plus interest); Sowers v. Kemira, Inc., 701 F. Supp. 809, 827–28, 46 FEP Cases 1825, 1838–39 (S.D. Ga. 1988)(awarding prejudgment interest); Pease v. Alford Photo Indus., 667 F. Supp. 1188, 1203, 49 FEP Cases 497, 509 (W.D. Tenn. 1987)(awarding postjudgment interest); Lamb v. Drilco Div., 32 FEP Cases 105, 107 (S.D. Tex. 1983)(awarding both prejudgment and postjudgment interest on back-pay award). *Cf.* Chamberlin v. 101 Realty, 915 F.2d 777, 786–87, 54 FEP Cases 101, 108–9 (1st Cir. 1990)(finding violation under both Title VII and state law, and awarding prejudgment interest for wrongful termination under state law). *But see* Boyd v. James S. Hayes Living Health Care Agency, 671 F. Supp. 1155, 1169, 44 FEP Cases 332, 343 (W.D. Tenn. 1987)(summarily holding that prejudgment interest not appropriate); Macey v. World Airways, 14 FEP Cases 1426, 1431 (N.D. Cal. 1977)(refusing to award interest as speculative).

[42]*See, e.g.,* Walters v. City of Atlanta, 610 F. Supp. 715, 728, 42 FEP Cases 369, 379 (N.D. Ga. 1985)(prejudgment interest on back-pay award computed under IRS adjusted prime interest rate; interest accrues quarterly), *aff'd,* 803 F.2d 1135, 42 FEP Cases 387 (11th Cir. 1986); Berndt v. Kaiser Aluminum & Chem. Sales, 604 F. Supp. 962, 967, 38 FEP Cases 182, 186 (E.D. Pa. 1985)(plaintiff awarded 8% interest rather than 11% rate suggested because he failed to show he could have invested money at higher rate), *aff'd,* 789 F.2d 253, 40 FEP Cases 1252 (3d Cir. 1986); Priest v. Rotary, 634 F. Supp. 571, 585, 40 FEP Cases 208, 218 (N.D. Cal. 1986)(plaintiff entitled to interest calculated from end of each calendar quarter, on "the amount when due and owing, at ninety percent (90%) of the average prime rate for the year in which the calendar quarter occurs").

As a result of recent amendments to the Back Pay Act, interest is available in Title VII actions against the federal government.[43] Courts are divided, however, on whether interest is available in suits against the government where the challenged conduct involves a denial of promotion not resulting in a reduction or cessation of compensation.[44]

Failure to follow procedural rules may result in denial of prejudgment interest.[45] However, a delay between the date of trial and entry of judgment does not relieve the defendant of the obligation to pay prejudgment interest.[46]

D. The Period of Recovery

1. Commencement of the Back-Pay Period

The period for which back pay is recoverable begins no earlier than two years before the EEOC charge was filed.[47] Cases of discharge or constructive discharge present the clearest instances for determining the commencement of the back-pay period. In these cases, courts hold that back pay accrues from the date of discharge or resignation.[48] In cases of failure to promote, the back-pay period would begin when the promotion would have become effective.[49] In a case where the complainant took an unpaid leave of absence because of sexual harassment, the back-pay period commences on the date that the unpaid leave started.[50]

---

[43]5 U.S.C. §5596(b)(2)(A)(1988).

[44]*Compare* Smith v. Brady, 744 F. Supp. 925, 928 (N.D. Cal. 1990)("Congress intended the waiver of sovereign immunity in the Back Pay Act to apply to back-pay awarded in Title VII actions" involving promotion claims) *and* Rollins v. Bennett, 48 FEP Cases 1172, 1175 (W.D. Wash. 1988)(same) *and* Parker v. Burnley, 693 F. Supp. 1138, 1153, 47 FEP Cases 587, 599 (N.D. Ga.), *as modified,* 703 F. Supp. 925, 926 (N.D. Ga. 1988)(same) *with* Mitchell v. Secretary of Commerce, 715 F. Supp. 409, 411 (D.D.C. 1989)(interest not available in denial of promotion case because challenged action did not result in "withdrawal or reduction" of compensation), *aff'd,* 1990 U.S. App. LEXIS 19656 (D.C. Cir. 1990) *and* Brown v. Marsh, 713 F. Supp. 20, 24–25, 51 FEP Cases 844, 898 (D.D.C. 1989), *aff'd,* 1990 U.S. App. LEXIS 19656 (D.C. Cir. 1990). The Supreme Court had previously expressly allowed prejudgment interest on a Title VII back-pay claim against the Postal Service under a waiver of sovereign immunity inferred by the Court from the Postal Reorganization Act. Loeffler v. Frank, 486 U.S. 549, 563–65, 46 FEP Cases 1659, 1663 (1988).

[45]Bunch v. Bullard, 795 F.2d 384, 399, 41 FEP Cases 515, 527–28 (5th Cir. 1986)(failure to appeal lower court's judgment precludes nonpromoted employees from challenging award that did not include prejudgment interest); Andre v. Bendix Corp., 38 FEP Cases 1817, 1819 (N.D. Ind. 1984)(former employee who waited two years to file Title VII claim not entitled to prejudgment interest because failure to obtain right-to-sue notice and promptly file suit substantially increased employer's back-pay liability), *vacated on other grounds,* 774 F.2d 786, 38 FEP Cases 1819 (7th Cir. 1985).

[46]Chamberlin v. 101 Realty, 915 F. Supp. 777, 787 n.16, 54 FEP Cases 101, 109 (1st Cir. 1990)("The two year interval between trial and the entry of judgment by the district court, while not to be encouraged, does not warrant reversal" of award of prejudgment interest).

[47]42 U.S.C. §2000e-5(g)(1982); *see also* Shrout v. Black Clawson Co., 689 F. Supp. 774, 782, 46 FEP Cases 1339, 1346 (S.D. Ohio 1988)(back pay accrues no more than two years prior to filing of EEOC charge). The two-year limitation period does not apply to suits by the EEOC or the Attorney General under 42 U.S.C. §2000e-6. *See also* SCHLEI & GROSSMAN, *supra* note 30, at 1430.

[48]*See, e.g.,* Horn v. Duke Homes, 755 F.2d 599, 607, 37 FEP Cases 228, 234 (7th Cir. 1985)(date of termination); Jones v. Wesco Investments, 1987 U.S. Dist. LEXIS 6873 (W.D. Mo. 1987)(date of constructive discharge), *aff'd,* 846 F.2d 1154, 46 FEP Cases 1431 (8th Cir. 1988).

[49]*See, e.g.,* Bundy v. Jackson, 641 F.2d 934, 948–49, 24 FEP Cases 1155, 1164–65 (D.C. Cir. 1981)(involving request for back pay to compensate plaintiff for delay in promotion due to refusal to accede to supervisor's sexual advances); *cf.* Broderick v. Ruder, 46 EPD ¶38,042 (D.D.C. 1988)(following liability determination, court approved settlement agreement that provided for plaintiff to receive back pay for multiple denials of promotions).

[50]Zabkowicz v. West Bend Co., 589 F. Supp. 780, 785, 35 FEP Cases 610, 613 (E.D. Wis. 1984), *aff'd in part and rev'd in part,* 789 F.2d 540, 40 FEP Cases 1171 (7th Cir. 1986).

2. Termination of the Back-Pay Period

Generally, the back-pay period terminates when the complainant is no longer suffering the economic effects of the discrimination. Courts have held that the back-pay period ends when all matters affecting the complainant's recovery have been resolved.[51] In individual cases, the back-pay period usually ends on the date that judgment is rendered.[52] The back-pay period may end sooner, however, if the plaintiff ceases to suffer adverse economic consequences, such as by acquiring a higher-paying job with earnings that exceed losses.[53]

The back-pay period may also end when the defendant offers the plaintiff unconditional and appropriate reinstatement.[54] Similarly, an employer may toll any period of back-pay liability by offering a sexual harassment complainant a transfer to another location. An offer of transfer, if rejected, may preclude a back-pay award.[55]

Finally, the back-pay period may end when the complainant voluntarily withdraws from the job market to pursue other interests.[56]

3. Back Pay for Periods of Disability

When the complainant can prove loss of earnings due to disability caused by sexual harassment, courts have awarded back pay for the period of disability.[57]

---

[51]*See, e.g.,* Arnold v. City of Seminole, 614 F. Supp. 853, 871, 40 FEP Cases 1539, 1552 (E.D. Okla. 1985)(termination of back-pay period occurs on date case was decided).

[52]*See, e.g.,* Anderson v. Group Hosp., 820 F.2d 465, 473, 43 FEP Cases 1840, 1847 (D.C. Cir. 1987); Nord v. United States Steel Corp., 758 F.2d 1462, 1472–73, 37 FEP Cases 1232, 1239 (11th Cir. 1985); Arnold v. City of Seminole, *supra* note 51.

[53]*See, e.g.,* Di Salvo v. Chamber of Commerce, 568 F.2d 593, 598, 20 FEP Cases 825, 828 (8th Cir. 1978)(end of back-pay period ended when plaintiff obtained employment at salary in excess of that to which she would have been entitled had she remained with defendant employer); EEOC v. Riss Int'l Corp., 35 FEP Cases 423, 425 (W.D. Mo. 1982)(no back pay for period in which interim earnings exceed wages that would have been earned).

[54]*See* Ford Motor Co. v. EEOC, 458 U.S. 219, 232, 29 FEP Cases 121, 127 (1982). For a discussion of unconditional offers of reinstatement, see Chapter 22, Employer's Litigation Strategy.

[55]*E.g.,* Davis v. Western-Southern Life Ins. Co., 34 FEP Cases 97, 102 (N.D. Ohio 1984)(plaintiff who rejected defendant's offer of transfer to same position in another company office was not entitled to back pay for period after offer). *Cf.* Spencer v. General Elec. Co., 894 F.2d 651, 655, 51 FEP Cases 1725, 1727 (4th Cir. 1990)("Because G.E. had quickly transferred Spencer and because Spencer had not missed any uncompensated days from work, the [district] court found that she could not prove any tangible loss due to the sexual harassment").

[56]*E.g.,* Miller v. Marsh, 766 F.2d 490, 492, 38 FEP Cases 805, 806–7 (11th Cir. 1985)(enrollment as full-time student in law school terminated back pay). *Cf.* Smith v. American Serv. Co., 796 F.2d 1430, 1432, 41 FEP Cases 802, 803 (11th Cir. 1986)(enrollment in cosmetology school did not terminate back pay because plaintiff had actively sought work without success); Nord v. U.S. Steel Corp., 758 F.2d 1462, 1471, 37 FEP Cases 1232, 1238 (11th Cir. 1985)(plaintiff who discontinued job search to assist husband in establishing psychology practice did not fail to mitigate damages because prior job search fruitless and plaintiff attempting to secure future economic security).

[57]*E.g.,* Brooms v. Regal Tube Co., 881 F.2d 412, 424 n.8, 50 FEP Cases 1499, 1507 (7th Cir. 1989)(upholding back-pay award that included period of time plaintiff could not maintain position because of therapy); Sowers v. Kemira, Inc., 701 F. Supp. 809, 827, 46 FEP Cases 1825, 1838–39 (S.D. Ga. 1988)(awarding back pay for period not worked due to psychological disability caused by sexual harassment); Arnold v. City of Seminole, 614 F. Supp. 853, 873, 40 FEP Cases 1539, 1554 (E.D. Okla. 1985)(back pay ordered for duration of plaintiff's psychological disability until reinstatement would be feasible through improvement of plaintiff's condition).

E. Equitable Defenses Limiting the Right to Back Pay for the Period of Recovery

1. Laches

A defendant may establish the equitable defense of laches by proving that the complainant engaged in an unreasonable delay that prejudiced the defendant.[58] The extent to which laches bars all or part of a back-pay claim depends entirely upon the specific facts of the case.[59]

2. Good Faith

Generally, the employer's "good faith" will not be a successful defense to a back-pay claim. As stated by the Supreme Court, "the mere absence of bad faith simply opens the door to equity; it does not depress the scales in the employer's favor."[60] The only exception appears to be when employers have relied upon state protective laws for women.[61]

3. Other Equitable Defenses

Back pay being an equitable remedy, it presumably is subject to the same equitable defenses that may apply to the complainant's claims for affirmative and injunctive relief. Courts have denied back pay to sexual harassment complaints for such equitable reasons as the complainant's material omissions in a job application and the complainant's counter-harassment following discharge.[61a]

III. QUASI-COMPENSATORY RELIEF

A few courts, recognizing the problems inherent in adequately compensating sexual harassment complainants, have used their discretion to tailor make-whole remedies that are not directly linked to back pay. Thus, courts have awarded lump-sum payments to allow the plaintiff sufficient time to obtain psychotherapy for trauma suffered as a result of sexual harassment and to find alternative employment,[62] medical expenses,[63] compensation for time spent

---

[58]*See, e.g.,* Sherman v. Standard Rate Data Serv., 709 F. Supp. 1433, 1441, 50 FEP Cases 1132, 1138–39 (N.D. Ill. 1989); Tunis v. Corning Glass Works, 698 F. Supp. 452, 454 (S.D.N.Y. 1988). *See generally* B.L. SCHLEI & P. GROSSMAN, EMPLOYMENT DISCRIMINATION LAW 1436–37 (2d ed. 1983). *See generally* Annot., *Laches as Defense to Actions under Title VII,* 52 A.L.R. FED. 218.

[59]*See, e.g.,* McLemore v. Interstate Motor Freight Sys., 33 FEP Cases 1384, 1391 (N.D. Ala. 1984)(laches found based on eight-year delay, dimming of memories of key witnesses, and destruction of some records); Raley v. Board of St. Mary's County Comm'rs, 1990 U.S. Dist. LEXIS 16,739 (N.D. Md. 1990)(seven-and-a-half-year delay while federal and local agencies retained charge justified); Sherman v. Standard Rate Data Serv., *supra* note 58, 709 F. Supp. at 1441, 50 FEP Cases at 1139 (laches not decided on summary judgment motion in sexual harassment case because further factual development required); Tunis v. Corning Glass Works, *supra* note 58, 698 F. Supp. at 454–55 (sexual harassment claim not barred by laches).

[60]Albemarle Paper Co. v. Moody, 422 U.S. 405, 422, 10 FEP Cases 1181, 1189 (1975).

[61]Alaniz v. California Processors, 785 F.2d 1412, 1416–17, 40 FEP Cases 768, 771 (9th Cir. 1986)(no back-pay liability for failure to hire women in jobs requiring heavy lifting when state protective laws in effect); Le Beau v. Libbey-Owens-Ford Co., 727 F.2d 141, 149–50 (7th Cir. 1984)(not an abuse of discretion to deny back pay when defendants' practices found support in Illinois Female Employment Act).

[61a]For citations to these and related authorities, see Chapter 28, Injunctive and Affirmative Relief, Section III.

[62]*E.g.,* Sowers v. Kemira, Inc., 701 F. Supp. 809, 827, 46 FEP Cases 1825, 1838 (S.D. Ga. 1988)(awarding nine-month lump sum payment). *Cf.* Broderick v. Ruder, *supra* note 49 (following liability determination, court approved settlement that included obligation to pay "reasonable costs of outplacement services" if used within two years).

[63]*E.g.,* EEOC v. FLC & Bros. Rebel, Inc., 663 F. Supp. 864, 870, 44 FEP Cases 362, 367 (W.D. Va.

preparing for trial,[64] and even an equity interest in a plaintiff's car that was repossessed for failure to make payments after an illegal discharge.[65] However, courts have denied damages for mental anguish[66] and physical injury[67] resulting from harassment.

IV. NOMINAL DAMAGES

Courts are divided over whether nominal damages may be awarded in Title VII actions. The issue of nominal damages has arisen when a complainant has established the existence of an unlawful sex-based hostile environment, but has failed to establish a right to back pay, injunctive relief, or any other equitable remedy available under Title VII.[68] Where no other remedy is available, some courts have dismissed the sexual harassment claim, despite evidence of a hostile environment, on the ground that no Title VII relief is possible.[69]

Some courts, however, have determined that their equitable powers under Title VII permit them to award nominal damages in circumstances where no other relief is available under Title VII.[70] The principal consequences of awarding nominal damages under such circumstances are the satisfaction it affords

---

1987), *aff'd*, 846 F.2d 70 (4th Cir. 1988). *Cf.* Bennett v. Corroon & Black Corp., 845 F.2d 104, 106, 46 FEP Cases 1329, 1331 (5th Cir. 1988), *cert. denied*, 489 U.S. 1020 (1989)(plaintiff submitted no evidence of medical expenses or other economic harm not previously compensated by employer); Broderick v. Ruder, *supra* note 49 (following liability determination, court approved settlement including an agreement "to pay for a maximum of 208 psychiatric counseling sessions over a two year period to the extent not covered by the plaintiff's insurance"); Meyers v. ITT Diversified Credit Corp., 527 F. Supp. 1064, 1070, 27 FEP Cases 995, 1000 (E.D. Mo. 1981). *But see* Bradford v. Guardsmark, Inc., 53 FEP Cases 1732, 1732–33 (N.D. Ind. 1990)(characterizing medical expenses as "compensatory damages" and therefore not recoverable under Title VII).

[64]Morris v. American Nat'l Can Corp., 730 F. Supp. 1489, 1497, 52 FEP Cases 210, 218 (E.D. Mo. 1989), reproduced in Chapter 2, Forms of Harassment.

[65]EEOC v. FLC & Bros. Rebel, Inc., 663 F. Supp. 864, 870, 44 FEP Cases 362, 367 (W.D. Va. 1987), *aff'd*, 846 F.2d 70 (4th Cir. 1988).

[66]*E.g.*, Bennett v. Corroon & Black Corp., *supra* note 63 (rejecting argument that plaintiff should obtain compensatory damages for "mental anguish and also punitive damages" because such relief is "unobtainable legal relief, not equitable relief"); Zowayyed v. Lowen Co., 735 F. Supp. 1497, 1503, 52 FEP Cases 1350, 1355 (D. Kan. 1990)(rejecting contention that damages for "mental anguish, embarrassment, humiliation, anger, and hurt" are authorized by Title VII).

[67]*E.g.*, Bradford v. Guardsmark, Inc., *supra* note 63. *Cf.* Guess v. Bethlehem Steel Corp., 913 F.2d 463, 465, 53 FEP Cases 1547, 1549 (7th Cir. 1990)(characterizing plaintiff's state-law tort claims as attempt to recast sexual harassment as intentional infliction of emotional distress in order to circumvent state court decision holding that physical or mental injuries resulting from sexual harassment are within exclusive jurisdiction of state workers' compensation statute).

[68]This situation may occur where the harassment has been completely eliminated, where the complainant is no longer employed by the defendant, and where the complainant did not suffer any economic loss.

[69]*E.g.*, Bennett v. Corroon & Black Corp., *supra* note 63, 845 F.2d at 106–7, 46 FEP Cases at 1331 (sexual harassment claim dismissed because employer voluntarily maintained salary and benefits of plaintiff until she obtained new job, and changed management promptly after sexually explicit cartoons caused plaintiff to resign); Guess v. Bethlehem Steel Corp., *supra* note 67, 913 F.2d at 464, 53 FEP Cases at 1548 (Title VII claim would have to be dismissed if no remedy available under that statute).

[**Editor's Note:** Congress has addressed the lack of a Title VII remedy in the Civil Rights Act of 1991, which provides for limited compensatory and punitive damages. See Appendix 8.]

[70]*E.g., Second Circuit:* Macko v. General Motors Corp., 1988 U.S. Dist. LEXIS 6928 (N.D.N.Y. 1988)(refusing to reduce attorney's fees because only nominal damages);

Fourth Circuit: Katz v. Dole, 709 F.2d 251, 253 n.1, 31 FEP Cases 1521, 1522 (4th Cir. 1983), reproduced in Chapter 7, Harassment by Co-Workers (*dicta* stating nominal damages and attorney's fees may be recoverable);

Fifth Circuit: Joshi v. Florida State Univ., 646 F.2d 981, 991 n.33, 26 FEP Cases 300, 308 (5th Cir. 1981)(on remand, court should consider whether plaintiff entitled to nominal damages and, therefore, attorney's fees), *cert. denied*, 456 U.S. 972 (1982); Jones v. Roswell, 40 FEP Cases 705, 706 (N.D. Ga. 1986)(plaintiff's one-dollar award establishes entitlement to attorney's fees because she brought harassment to light and obtained judgment of illegality beneficial to other women at workplace);

the harassed complainant, and, of more material benefit, the right to the attorney's fees that accompanies such an award.[71]

Other courts, however, have held that nominal damages are not available under Title VII.[72] In *Swanson v. Elmhurst Chrysler Plymouth*,[73] the plaintiff was denied relief because she had been discharged for reasons other than her reaction to sexual harassment. The Seventh Circuit refused to award nominal damages because those damages are legal rather than equitable remedies, and therefore not available under Title VII.[74]

V. FRONT PAY

Front pay is an award of future lost earnings to make a victim of discrimination whole.[75] Front pay is appropriate when a complainant would be entitled to reinstatement, but a suitable position is not available.[76] Front pay is also available if a hostile or otherwise unsuitable environment makes reinstatement unwise, which may often occur in the sexual harassment context.[77]

Sixth Circuit: Mitchell v. OsAIR, 629 F. Supp. 636, 644, 45 FEP Cases 580, 585 (N.D. Ohio 1986)(although plaintiff's termination did not constitute constructive discharge, plaintiff entitled to satisfaction of having prevailed by establishing hostile environment and entitled to attorney's fees);

Eighth Circuit: Dean v. Civiletti, 670 F.2d 99, 101, 29 FEP Cases 890, 892 (8th Cir. 1982)(sexual harassment plaintiff entitled to nominal damages and attorney's fees);

Tenth Circuit: Baker v. Weyerhaeuser Co., 903 F.2d 1342, 1344, 52 FEP Cases 1872, 1873 (10th Cir. 1990)(sexual harassment plaintiff entitled to nominal relief under Title VII);

Eleventh Circuit: Huddleston v. Roger Dean Chevrolet, 845 F.2d 900, 905, 46 FEP Cases 1361, 1364 (11th Cir. 1988)(remanding case to district court for consideration of nominal damages after holding that plaintiff established prima facie case of sexual harassment, but failed to establish damages that would entitle her to back-pay award); Henson v. City of Dundee, 682 F.2d 897, 905–6 & n.12, 29 FEP Cases 787, 794–95 (11th Cir. 1982)(same), reproduced in Chapter 4, Hostile Environment Harassment.

[71]*But see* Bohen v. City of E. Chicago, 622 F. Supp. 1234, 1245 n.5, 39 FEP Cases 917, 925 (N.D. Ind. 1985)(plaintiff's alleged entitlement to moral victory is only proper consideration because reliance upon potential attorney's fees would constitute impermissible "bootstrapping"), *aff'd in part and rev'd in part,* 799 F.2d 1180, 41 FEP Cases 1108 (1986).

[72]*See, e.g., Sixth Circuit:* Harrington v. Vandalia-Butler Bd. of Educ., 585 F.2d 192, 197, 18 FEP Cases 348, 352 (6th Cir. 1978)(female subjected to discriminatory work conditions, but, suffering no economic loss, not entitled to any recovery), *cert. denied,* 441 U.S. 932 (1979);

Seventh Circuit: Swanson v. Elmhurst Chrysler Plymouth, 882 F.2d 1235, 1239–40, 50 FEP Cases 1082, 1085–86 (7th Cir. 1989)(sexual harassment plaintiff not entitled to either nominal damages or attorney's fees), *cert. denied,* 51 FEP Cases 1224 (1990); Bohen v. City of E. Chicago, 799 F.2d 1180, 1189, 41 FEP Cases 1108, 1115 (7th Cir. 1986)(nominal damages not available under Title VII).

[73]882 F.2d 1235, 50 FEP Cases 1082 (7th Cir 1989), *cert. denied,* 51 FEP Cases 1224 (1990).

[74]*Id. Cf.* Texas State Teachers Ass'n v. Garland Indep. School Dist., 489 U.S. 782, 49 FEP Cases 465, 468 (1989)(plaintiff must obtain change in legal relationship with defendant to be prevailing party under 42 U.S.C. §1988); Hewitt v. Helms, 482 U.S. 755, 762, 44 FEP Cases 15, 17 (1987)("moral satisfaction of knowing that a federal court concluded that [a former prisoner's] rights had been violated" does not make plaintiff prevailing party). For a discussion of this point in the context of attorney's fees awards, see Chapter 30, Attorney's Fees and Costs, Section II.A.2.

[75]Pease v. Alford Photo Indus., 667 F. Supp. 1188, 1203, 49 FEP Cases 497, 509 (W.D. Tenn. 1987). For more extensive discussion of front pay, *see* SCHLEI & GROSSMAN, *supra* note 58, at 1434–36, Five-Year Supp. at 533.

[76]*See, e.g.,* Parker v. Siemens-Allis, Inc., 601 F. Supp. 1377, 1389, 37 FEP Cases 39, 50 (E.D. Ark. 1985)(plaintiff entitled to reinstatement and, if no such position exists, front pay until placed in comparable job).

[77]*See, e.g.,* Sowers v. Kemira, Inc., 701 F. Supp. 809, 827, 46 FEP Cases 1825, 1838 (S.D. Ga. 1988)("[f]ront pay is appropriate when a plaintiff is entitled to reinstatement, but a hostile or otherwise unsuitable work environment counsels against reinstatement"); Pease v. Alford Photo Indus., 667 F. Supp. 1188, 1203, 49 FEP Cases 497, 508 (W.D. Tenn. 1987)("award of front pay in this egregious case will aid in ending the sexual harassment of women at [the employer] and will aid in rectifying the harm caused Mrs. Pease"); Arnold v. City of Seminole, 614 F. Supp. 853, 873, 40 FEP Cases 1539, 1554 (E.D. Okla. 1985); Meyers v. ITT Diversified Credit Corp., 527 F. Supp. 1064, 1070, 27 FEP Cases 995, 1000 (E.D. Mo. 1981)(relationship between plaintiff and employer so strained after plaintiff brought action alleging sexual overtures by supervisor that reinstatement not a viable remedy; court instead awarded $3,000 in front pay). *Cf.* Cassino v. Reichhold Chem., 817 F.2d 1338, 1346, 47 FEP Cases 865, 870 (9th Cir. 1987)(same in age discrimination case), *cert. denied,* 484 U.S. 1047 (1988).

Front pay is the difference between what the plaintiff would have earned while employed by the defendant employer absent the unlawful employment practice, and what the plaintiff will earn at a new job, for the period of time until the plaintiff reaches a level of pay and responsibility equivalent to that of the former position.[78] The point at which front pay is terminated is within the discretion of the court.[79]

VI. COMPENSATORY AND PUNITIVE DAMAGES

A. Title VII

Until recently,* neither compensatory nor punitive damages were recoverable under Title VII.[80] Courts adhered to this prohibition in sexual harassment cases.[81]

Where the plaintiff requests both equitable relief (*e.g.*, reinstatement and back pay) and legal remedies (*e.g.*, compensatory and punitive damages under common-law theories), a right to a jury trial exists for the legal relief issues, with the question of equitable relief left to the court.[82]

---

[78]Briseno v. Central Tech. Community College Area, 739 F.2d 344, 348, 37 FEP Cases 57, 60 (8th Cir. 1984); Fitzgerald v. Sirloin Stockade, 624 F.2d 945, 956, 22 FEP Cases 262, 269 (10th Cir. 1980); Parker v. Siemens-Allis, Inc., 601 F. Supp. 1377, 1389, 37 FEP Cases 39, 50 (E.D. Ark. 1985).

[79]*See, e.g.,* Arnold v. City of Seminole, 614 F. Supp. 853, 873, 40 FEP Cases 1539, 1554 (E.D. Okla. 1985)(awarding front pay until plaintiff finds new job); Pease v. Alford Photo Indus., 667 F. Supp. 1188, 1203, 49 FEP Cases 497, 508 (W.D. Tenn. 1987)(awarding one year of front pay); Sowers v. Kemira, Inc., 701 F. Supp. 809, 827, 46 FEP Cases 1825, 1839 (S.D. Ga. 1988)(awarding nine months' front pay despite possibility that disability justifying front pay might last longer).

*[**Editor's Note:** Under the Civil Rights Act of 1991, discussed in Appendix 8, violations of Title VII may result in limited compensatory and punitive damages.]

[80]Shah v. Mt. Zion Hosp. & Medical Ctr., 642 F.2d 268, 272, 27 FEP Cases 772, 775 (9th Cir. 1981)("great weight of authority" against compensatory and punitive damages in Title VII cases). For a discussion of compensatory and punitive damage awards in discrimination suits generally, see B.L. SCHLEI & P. GROSSMAN, EMPLOYMENT DISCRIMINATION LAW 1452–53 (2d ed. 1983), Five-Year Supp. at 543. The 1990 Civil Rights Act, vetoed by President Bush, would have provided compensatory and punitive damages in cases of intentional discrimination, including sexual harassment. Conference Report on S. 2104, Civil Rights Act of 1990, Sec. 8, 136 CONG. REC. H8045, H8046 (1990).

[81]*E.g.,* Trautvetter v. Quick, 916 F.2d 1140, 1148, 54 FEP Cases 109, 115 (7th Cir. 1990)(harassment claim dismissed because it sought only unspecified damages, rather than equitable relief); King v. Board of Regents, 898 F.2d 533, 537, 52 FEP Cases 809 (7th Cir. 1990)(sexual harassment plaintiff could recover neither compensatory nor punitive damages under Title VII); Boddy v. Dean, 821 F.2d 346, 352, 45 FEP Cases 586, 590 (6th Cir. 1987)(same); Bohen v. City of E. Chicago, 799 F.2d 1180, 1184, 41 FEP Cases 1108, 1110 (7th Cir. 1986)(same); Zowayyed v. Lowen Co., 735 F. Supp 1497, 1504, 52 FEP Cases 1350 (D. Kan. 1990)(same); Glezos v. Amalfi Ristorante Italiano, 651 F. Supp. 1271, 1273, 45 FEP Cases 1097, 1098 (D. Md. 1987)(same); Arnold v. City of Seminole, 614 F. Supp. 853, 871, 40 FEP Cases 1539, 1552 (E.D. Okla. 1985). *But see* Beesley v. Hartford Fire Ins. Co., 723 F. Supp. 635, 650–52, 51 FEP Cases 27, 36–38 (N.D. Ala. 1989)("plaintiff in a Title VII action can recover intangibles, such as damages for psychological trauma" and "the question of entitlement to punitive damages under Title VII . . . is still open"). *See generally* Annot., *Award of Compensatory Damages, Aside From Backpay or Frontpay, For Violation of Title VII of Civil Rights Act of 1964,* 48 A.L.R. FED. 338 (1980 & Supp. 1988)); Note, *Relief for Hostile Work Environment Discrimination: Restoring Title VII's Remedial Powers,* 99 YALE L.J. 1611, 1615–16 (May 1990); Note, *Sexual Harassment Claims of Abusive Work Environment Under Title VII,* 97 HARV. L. REV. 1449, 1465 (1984).

[82]*See, e.g.,* Perkins v. Spivey, 911 F.2d 22, 34, 53 FEP Cases 973, 981 (8th Cir. 1990)(if plaintiff had been permitted to join legal claim against the individual defendant with equitable claim against employer, she would have been entitled to jury trial on legal claim). *But see* Beesley v. The Hartford Fire Ins. Co., *supra* note 81, 723 F. Supp. at 646–47, 51 FEP Cases at 33–34 (plaintiff entitled to jury trial on both Title VII and state tort claims where she sought compensatory and punitive damages for claims of assault and battery, false imprisonment, libel and intentional infliction of emotional distress, and front pay for Title VII claim; court characterizes front pay as legal damages). For further authorities pertaining to the availability *vel non* of a jury trial under Title VII, see Chapter 21, Complainant's Litigation Strategy.

B. Section 1983

Remedies available under §1983 include compensatory, punitive, and nominal damages.[83] Compensatory damages may be awarded for emotional distress[84] as well as for impaired reputation or humiliation.[85] Punitive damages are recoverable from supervisors in their individual and official capacities for conduct constituting reckless or deliberate indifference to a plaintiff's federal rights.[86] Nominal damages may be awarded to a plaintiff whose rights were violated, but who was unable to demonstrate a pecuniary loss.[87]

Municipalities may be liable for a compensatory damage award under §1983, but are immune to a punitive damage award.[88] Punitive damages are, however, available in suits against municipal officials personally.[89] Punitive damages have been awarded in sexual harassment suits even where only nominal actual damages were shown.[90]

C. State Fair Employment Practices Statutes

Fair employment practices statutes in about half of the states permit plaintiffs to recover compensatory damages in sexual harassment suits;[91] some also permit punitive damage awards.[92]

---

[83]*See, e.g.,* King v. Board of Regents, 898 F.2d 533, 537, 52 FEP Cases 809 (7th Cir. 1990)(plaintiff may recover compensatory and punitive damages under §1983 claim for environmental sexual harassment); Martinez v. Procunier, 354 F. Supp. 1092, 1094 (N.D. Cal. 1973)(*per curiam*), *aff'd,* 416 U.S. 396 (1974).

[84]Harris v. Harvey, 605 F.2d 330 (7th Cir. 1979), *cert. denied,* 445 U.S. 938 (1980).

[85]Memphis Community School Dist. v. Stachura, 477 U.S. 299, 307 (1986).

[86]Smith v. Wade, 461 U.S. 30, 52 (1983)(punitive damages available when conduct motivated by evil intent or motive or involved reckless or callous indifference to federal rights of others); *see, e.g.,* Goodwin v. Circuit Court, 729 F.2d 541, 547–48, 34 FEP Cases 347, 353 (8th Cir. 1984)(punitive damages appropriate under §1983 where defendant's derogatory comments about women showed his reckless indifference to plaintiff's right to be free from discrimination), *cert. denied,* 469 U.S. 1216 (1985); Murphy v. Chicago Transit Auth., 638 F. Supp. 464, 471–72, 49 FEP Cases 1514, 1519 (N.D. Ill. 1986)(supervisors liable for punitive damages because of deliberate indifference to plaintiff's complaints of frequent humiliating sexual remarks, requests, and touching).

[87]Carey v. Piphus, 435 U.S. 247, 266 (1978)(students suspended from school in violation of procedural due process rights would be entitled to nominal damages).

[88]City of Newport v. Fact Concerts, 453 U.S. 247, 271 (1981)(courts may not assess punitive damages against municipalities). *Cf.* Starrett v. Wadley, 876 F.2d 808, 824, 51 FEP Cases 608, 619 (10th Cir. 1989)(county initially assessed $75,000 in compensatory damages; court vacated liability determination and remanded on issue of damages).

[89]*See* Smith v. Wade, 461 U.S. 30 (1983). *See, e.g.,* Murphy v. Chicago Transit Auth., 638 F. Supp. 464, 471, 49 FEP Cases 1514, 1519 (N.D. Ill. 1986)(city transit authority supervisors liable for punitive damages for deliberate indifference to sexual harassment of female employee).

[90]Goodwin v. Circuit Court, *supra* note 86, 729 F.2d at 547–48, 34 FEP Cases at 353 (plaintiff entitled to punitive damages of $1,000 despite actual damage award of $1 where defendant showed "reckless indifference to [the plaintiff]'s right to be free from sex discrimination" by his derogatory comments about women), *cert. denied,* 469 U.S. 1216 (1984).

[91]*See* "Officials of NOW Say That Women Need Stronger Title VII Remedies," 1990 DAILY LAB. REP. (BNA) No. 39, at A-15 (Feb. 27, 1990). According to a preliminary assessment by the National Organization of Women (NOW), the states of California, Georgia, Idaho, Illinois, Iowa, Kentucky, Louisiana, Maine, Massachusetts, Michigan, Minnesota, Missouri, Montana, New Jersey, New Mexico, New York, Pennsylvania, Tennessee, Washington, West Virginia, and the District of Columbia all have fair employment practices statutes (modeled after Title VII) that permit plaintiffs to recover compensatory damages. *See, e.g.,* State Personnel Bd. v. Fair Empl. & Hous. Comm'n, 39 Cal.3d 422, 429 (1985)(in private actions under California's fair employment practices statute, courts may award compensatory and punitive damages); Glasgow v. Georgia-Pacific Corp., 103 Wash.2d 401, 51 FEP Cases 880, 881 (1985)(plaintiff recovered damages for emotional distress under Washington civil rights act for co-worker sexual harassment where supervisors knew of harassment and took no action to alleviate it); Coley v. Consolidated Rail Corp., 561 F. Supp. 645, 652, 34 FEP Cases 129, 135 (E.D. Mich. 1982)(plaintiff in verbal sexual harassment case recovered $5,000 in compensatory damages for mental anguish and humiliation under Michigan's civil rights act). *See generally* Annot., *On-the-Job Sexual Harassment as Violation of State Civil Rights Law,* 18 A.L.R.4th 328. For a discussion of state statutory claims, see Chapter 12, Fair Employment Practices Statutes.

[92]NOW identifies California, Minnesota, Missouri, and the District of Columbia as having such laws. *See, e.g.,* Wirig v. Kinney Shoe Corp., 448 N.W.2d 526, 530–31, 51 FEP Cases 885, 888–89 (Minn. Ct.

A number of state statutory schemes, however, expressly limit the amount of recoverable compensatory and punitive damages.[93] Plaintiffs in those states might be limited in the amount of their overall recovery for discrimination if the state fair employment practices statute is also held to preempt other causes of action.[94]

Some state fair employment practices statutes require a higher burden of proof for punitive damages,[95] and some require complainants to show that the defendant's conduct was willful or malicious.[96]

D. Common-Law Torts

Plaintiffs in sexual harassment cases rely on a variety of common-law tort theories[97] to obtain the unlimited compensatory and punitive damage remedies not presently available under Title VII,[98] including intentional infliction of emotional distress,[99] assault and battery,[100] false imprisonment,[101] invasion of privacy,[102] wrongful discharge,[103] and malicious interference with the complainant's employment.[104]

App. 1989)(punitive damages assessed under Minnesota Human Rights Act against employer because of its "willful indifference" to plaintiff's rights: employer terminated plaintiff because of uninvestigated allegation by harasser, did not have sexual harassment policy, and did not discipline harasser despite observation of conduct by all but one of its managers), *aff'd in part and rev'd in part*, 54 FEP Cases 352 (1990); Monge v. Superior Court, 176 Cal. App.3d 503, 510, 222 Cal. Rptr. 64, 67–68 (1986)(sexual harassment plaintiffs may recover punitive damages under California's fair employment practices statute provided plaintiffs plead and prove that defendant was guilty of oppression, fraud or malice). However, as of this printing, NOW's study is not complete. *See also* Dias v. Sky Chefs, Inc., 54 FEP Cases 1460 (D. Or. 1989)(plaintiff could be entitled to punitive damages under Oregon fair employment practices statute if jury finds defendant's conduct malicious and wanton), *aff'd*, 919 F.2d 1370, 54 FEP Cases 852 (9th Cir. 1990), *vacated on other grounds*, 111 S.Ct. 2791 (1991).

[93]Wirig v. Kinney Shoe Corp., *supra* note 92, 448 N.W.2d at 534 (court awarded plaintiff $6,000, maximum amount of punitive damages authorized under Minnesota Human Rights Act); Dias v. Sky Chefs, Inc., *supra* note 92 (compensatory damages under Oregon fair employment practices law limited to $250).

[94]Wirig v. Kinney Shoe Corp., *supra* note 92, 448 N.W.2d at 528 (plaintiff may not recover amount of punitive damages for statutory violation greater than that specified in statute). *But see* Dias v. Sky Chefs, Inc., *supra* note 92 (in a novel approach to preemption, the court ruled that because statutory damages insufficiently compensated plaintiff, her claim for retaliatory discharge was not preempted by Oregon antidiscrimination law). For a discussion of preemption of common-law claims by the state fair employment practices statutes, see Chapter 12, Fair Employment Practices Statutes.

[95]Wirig v. Kinney Shoe Corp., *supra* note 92, 448 N.W.2d at 534 (plaintiff met clear and convincing evidence standard required under Minnesota fair employment practices statute where co-worker harassed plaintiff for months while supervisors took no action).

[96]*See, e.g.*, Dias v. Sky Chefs, Inc., *supra* note 92 (plaintiff must show malice and oppression on part of defendant); Tretter v. Liquipak Int'l, 356 N.W.2d 713, 714, 43 FEP Cases 1522, 1524 (Minn. Ct. App. 1984)(employer liable for punitive damages where it permitted plaintiff to be harassed by supervisor for six months; such conduct demonstrated willful indifference to plaintiff's rights and safety).

[97]See Chapter 15, The Common Law.

[98]For a discussion of recent expansion of Title VII remedies, see Appendix 8.

[99]Shrout v. Black Clawson Co., 689 F. Supp. 774, 46 FEP Cases 1339 (S.D. Ohio 1988); Pease v. Alford Photo Indus., 667 F. Supp. 1188, 49 FEP Cases 497 (W.D. Tenn. 1987); Priest v. Rotary, 634 F. Supp. 571, 40 FEP Cases 208 (N.D. Cal. 1986); Gilardi v. Schroeder, 672 F. Supp. 1043, 45 FEP Cases 283 (N.D. Ill. 1986), *aff'd*, 833 F.2d 1226 (7th Cir. 1987); Arnold v. City of Seminole, 614 F. Supp. 853, 40 FEP Cases 1539 (E.D. Okla. 1985); Rogers v. Loews L'Enfant Plaza Hotel, 526 F. Supp. 523, 29 FEP Cases 828 (D.D.C. 1981).

[100]Valdez v. Church's Fried Chicken, 683 F. Supp. 596, 47 FEP Cases 1155 (W.D. Tex. 1988); Pease v. Alford Photo Indus., *supra* note 99; Priest v. Rotary, *supra* note 99; Gilardi v. Schroeder, *supra* note 99; Skousen v. Nidy, 90 Ariz. 215, 367 P.2d 248 (1961).

[101]Priest v. Rotary, *supra* note 99.

[102]Pease v. Alford Photo Indus., *supra* note 99; Priest v. Rotary, *supra* note 99; Rogers v. Loews L'Enfant Plaza Hotel, *supra* note 99.

[103]Dias v. Sky Chefs, Inc., *supra* note 92; Clemens v. Gerber Scientific, 1989 U.S. Dist. LEXIS 376 (E.D. Pa. 1989).

[104]Kyriazi v. Western Elec. Co., 476 F. Supp. 335, 26 FEP Cases 413 (D.N.J. 1979).

Courts have upheld claims of intentional infliction of emotional distress when the defendant's conduct included nonconsensual touching, kissing, fondling, or caressing the complainant's body[105] or exposing the alleged harasser's body.[106] In contrast, some courts have held that mere verbal harassment, without physical contact, is not sufficient to make out a claim of intentional infliction of emotional distress.[107]

Damages have also been awarded for assault and battery claims based upon the harasser's unwelcome touching and other sexual advances.[108] The touching need not be of sexual areas to warrant liability.[109]

Complainants have also been successful in obtaining tort damages on claims of invasion of privacy,[110] common-law wrongful discharge,[111] malicious interference with the complainant's employment,[112] and false imprisonment.[113]

To state a claim for punitive damages, plaintiffs generally must show that the defendant acted willfully or with malice.[114] A California appellate decision

---

[105]Shrout v. Black Clawson Co., 689 F. Supp. 774, 779–82, 46 FEP Cases 1339, 1343–46 (S.D. Ohio 1988)($75,000 in compensatory damages where conduct included "touch[ing] . . . intimately"); Pease v. Alford Photo Indus., *supra* note 99, 667 F. Supp. at 1190, 1203, 49 FEP Cases at 498, 507–9 ($2,500 in compensatory damages for complainant where conduct included "sexually harassing and humiliating touching of her body" and "fondling her breast while she was at work"); Priest v. Rotary, *supra* note 99, 634 F. Supp. at 578, 584, 40 FEP Cases at 212, 217 ($95,000 in compensatory damages where pattern of conduct included unwelcome touching of plaintiff's breasts and unzipping front of plaintiff's uniform); Gilardi v. Schroeder, *supra* note 99, 672 F. Supp. at 1047, 45 FEP Cases at 287 ($50,000 in compensatory damages for drugging, premeditated sexual attack, and being placed in bed with harraser's wife). *See also* Arnold v. City of Seminole, *supra* note 99, 614 F. Supp. at 857, 861, 40 FEP Cases at 1541, 1544 ($150,000 compensatory damage award where plaintiff pushed across room and into file cabinet).

[106]*See, e.g.,* Priest v. Rotary, *supra* note 99, 634 F. Supp. at 575, 40 FEP Cases at 209 (defendant "exposed his genitals to plaintiff . . . as [she] was having a cup of coffee following the end of [her] shift").

[107]*See* Polk v. Yellow Freight Sys., 801 F.2d 190, 41 FEP Cases 1279 (6th Cir. 1986)(construing Michigan law). *But cf.* Valdez v. Church's Fried Chicken, 683 F. Supp. 596, 612, 47 FEP Cases 1155, 1164 (W.D. Tex. 1988)(Texas courts recognize cause of action for mental anguish from sexual assault in absence of physical contact).

[108]Skousen v. Nidy, 90 Ariz. 215, 367 P.2d 248, 250 (1961)(actual and punitive damages assessed against defendant who placed hands on "private parts" of 65-year-old female employee and attempted to seduce her); Priest v. Rotary, *supra* note 99, 634 F. Supp. at 578, 584, 40 FEP Cases at 212, 217 (touching plaintiff's breasts and unzipping front of her uniform); Gilardi v. Schroeder, *supra* note 99, 672 F. Supp. at 1047, 45 FEP Cases at 287 (drugging of plaintiff and sexual assault); Wirig v. Kinney Shoe Corp., 54 FEP Cases 352 (Minn. 1990)(common-law battery claim for sexual harassment not preempted by state statute, but double recovery not permitted); Valdez v. Church's Fried Chicken, *supra* note 107, 683 F. Supp. at 608, 47 FEP Cases at 1160 (W.D. Tex. 1988)(defendant "pulled out his penis and attempted to force Plaintiff to engage in oral copulation . . . pulled down her pants, and attempted to have sexual intercourse with [her]"); Pease v. Alford Photo Indus., *supra* note 99, 667 F. Supp. at 1203, 49 FEP Cases at 508 (fondling plaintiff's breast).

[109]Newsome v. Cooper-Wiss, Inc., 179 Ga. App. 670, 347 S.E.2d 619, 621 (1986); *see also* Arnold v. City of Seminole, *supra* note 99, 614 F. Supp. at 861, 40 FEP Cases at 1544 (touching consisted of pushing plaintiff across room and into file cabinet).

[110]Pease v. Alford Photo Indus., *supra* note 99, 667 F. Supp. at 1203, 49 FEP Cases at 509; Priest v. Rotary, *supra* note 99, 634 F. Supp. at 582, 40 FEP Cases at 215 ("sexually suggestive comments to and about [plaintiff] in the presence of others which violated her right to privacy"). *Cf.* Rogers v. Loews L'Enfant Plaza Hotel, *supra* note 99, 526 F. Supp. at 528, 29 FEP Cases at 831 (allegations that defendant "called [plaintiff] at home, as well as at work when he was off duty" sufficient to state a claim for "intrusion").

[111]Dias v. Sky Chefs, Inc., *supra* note 92 (remedy provided by state antidiscrimination statute inadequate; court permitted plaintiff to assert common-law action for wrongful discharge for which jury may award punitive damages if plaintiff proves willfulness and malice); Clemens v. Gerber Scientific, *supra* note 103 (plaintiff permitted to recover punitive damages for wrongful discharge based on sexual harassment claim).

[112]Kyriazi v. Western Elec. Co., 476 F. Supp. 335, 336, 26 FEP Cases 413, 414 (D.N.J. 1979)(three of plaintiff's co-workers found liable for malicious interference with employment after plaintiff lost her job when work environment was made intolerable by their sexual harassment).

[113]Priest v. Rotary, *supra* note 99, 634 F. Supp. at 583, 40 FEP Cases at 216.

[114]*See, e.g.,* Dias v. Sky Chefs, Inc., *supra* note 92 (jury may award punitive damages for wrongful discharge if plaintiff proves willfulness and malice); Clemens v. Gerber Scientific, *supra* note 103 (plaintiff bringing wrongful discharge claim permitted to recover punitive damages for sexual harassment); Shrout v. Black Clawson Co., *supra* note 105, 689 F. Supp. at 780, 46 FEP Cases at 1343 ($50,000 in punitive damages under Ohio tort law where quid pro quo harassment was "malicious" and went unchecked for four years); Pease v. Alford Photo Indus., *supra* note 99, 667 F. Supp. at 1192, 1203, 49 FEP Cases at 500, 509 ($10,000

ruled that an allegation sufficient to state a case for a sexually hostile environment "in and of itself pleads the evil motive necessary to support punitive damages."[115]

In some jurisdictions, employers are liable for punitive damages even without their participation in or ratification of the oppressive, willful or malicious conduct.[116] In other jurisdictions, an officer, director, or managing agent of the corporation must participate in or ratify the conduct to render the employer liable for punitive damages.[117]

In a sexual harassment case, ratification may be inferred from the fact that "the employer, after being informed of the employee's actions, does not fully investigate and fails to repudiate the employee's conduct by redressing the harm done and punishing or discharging the employee."[118]

To calculate an award for emotional distress and related tort claims in bench trials, courts consider the duration and intensity of the harassment and the degree of emotional harm suffered by the plaintiff.[119]

---

in punitive damages under theories of assault and battery, intentional infliction of emotional distress, invasion of privacy and outrageous conduct where plaintiff repeatedly touched by employer in a sexual manner and suffered migraines, skin rashes, and insomnia as result); Priest v. Rotary, *supra* note 99, 634 F. Supp. at 582–85, 40 FEP Cases at 216–18 ($15,000 exemplary damages in sexual harassment action for battery, false imprisonment, and intentional infliction of emotional distress under California law); Wing v. JMB Property Mgmt. Corp., 714 P.2d 916, 919, 48 FEP Cases 111, 112 (Colo. App. 1985)(allegations of wanton, willful, malicious, and intentional actions of defendants sufficient to support claim for punitive damages).

[115]Fisher v. San Pedro Peninsula Hosp., 214 Cal. App.3d 590, 621, 262 Cal. Rptr. 842, 860 (1989). *See also* Fawcett v. IDS Fin. Servs., 41 FEP Cases 589, 594 (W.D. Pa. 1986)(allegations that supervisor grabbed plaintiff on two occasions and conditioned her promotion on submission to sexual relations sufficient to support claim for punitive damages).

[116]*See*, W. PROSSER, LAW OF TORTS §2 (4th ed. 1971); Note, *Liability of Employers for Punitive Damages Resulting from Acts of Employees*, 54 CHI.-KENT L. REV. 829, 931 (1978); Note, *The Assessment of Punitive Damages Against an Entrepreneur for the Malicious Torts of His Employees*, 70 YALE L.J. 1296 (1961).

[117]*See, e.g.,* Shrout v. Black Clawson Co., *supra* note 105, 689 F. Supp. at 783, 46 FEP Cases at 1346 (under Ohio law, employer may be assessed punitive damages because of malicious conduct of its employees if employer has authorized, ratified, participated, or acquiesced in the wrongdoing); Hart v. National Mortgage & Land Co., 189 Cal. App.3d 1420, 1432, 235 Cal. Rptr. 68 (1987)(under California Civil Code §3294, employer not liable for punitive damages based on acts of an employee unless employer ratified wrongful conduct or was personally guilty of oppression, fraud, or malice); Clark v. World Airways, 24 FEP Cases 305, 309–10 (D.D.C. 1980)(in the District of Columbia, plaintiffs may recover punitive damages against corporate employers only if they prove that corporation, through its directors and officers, either participated in the wrongful act or ratified the conduct).

[118]Fisher v. San Pedro Peninsula Hosp., *supra* note 115. *See also* Shrout v. Black Clawson Co., *supra* note 105, 689 F. Supp. at 783, 46 FEP Cases at 1346 (that high-level managers knew or should have known of supervisor's four-year campaign of harassment and made no effort to investigate same justified $50,000 punitive damage award against employer); Rogers v. Loews L'Enfant Plaza Hotel, *supra* note 99, 526 F. Supp. at 534–35, 29 FEP Cases at 835–36 (plaintiff can obtain punitive damage award against employer if she can prove management knew about harassment by supervisor and took no action).

[119]*E.g.,* Shrout v. Black Clawson Co., *supra* note 105, 689 F. Supp. at 782, 46 FEP Cases at 1345 (considering duration and intensity of harassment and degree of emotional distress, court awarded plaintiff $75,000 in compensatory damages; plaintiff was subject to frequent sexual remarks, offensive touching and leering and was harmed psychologically by this conduct); Priest v. Rotary, *supra* note 99, 634 F. Supp. at 584, 40 FEP Cases at 217 (in accordance with California Civil Code §§3281–3333, in assessing award of compensatory damages to person subjected to sexual harassment, "the trier of fact should consider the mental worry, grief, distress, and mortification suffered by the plaintiff, as well as her fright, nervousness, anxiety, shock, humiliation, indignity, and physical pain").

CHAPTER 30

ATTORNEY'S FEES AND COSTS

I. STATUTORY AUTHORITY

Prevailing parties in sexual harassment suits may recover their reasonable attorney's fees and costs. Section 706(k) of Title VII, as amended,* provides: "In any action or proceeding under this subchapter the court, in its discretion, may allow the prevailing party, other than the Commission or the United States, a reasonable attorney's fee (including expert fees) as part of the costs ...."[1]

Similarly, 42 U.S.C. §1988, codifying The Civil Rights Attorney's Fees Awards Act of 1976,[2] provides: "In any action or proceeding to enforce a provision of [42 U.S.C.] Sections 1981, 1982, 1983, 1985, and 1986 ... the court, in its discretion, may allow the prevailing party, other than the United States, a reasonable attorney's fee as part of the costs."

The standard for granting attorney's fees under §706(k) and §1988 is identical.[3] State fair employment practices statutes have similar standards.[4]

II. PREVAILING PLAINTIFFS

A. Judicial Proceedings

1. Determination of Whether Plaintiff Has Prevailed

A prevailing plaintiff in a sexual harassment suit is normally entitled to recover reasonable attorney's fees unless circumstances render such an award

---

*[**Editor's Note:** The Civil Rights Act of 1991, discussed in Appendix 8, added expert fees as recoverable attorney's fees.]

[1]42 U.S.C. §2000e-5(k).

[2]42 U.S.C. §1988. This Act, sponsored by Senator John Tunney, was enacted to overcome the effect of *Alyeska Pipeline Serv. Co. v. Wilderness Soc'y,* 421 U.S. 240, 10 FEP Cases 826 (1975)(under the American Rule, award of attorney's fees normally cannot be granted to prevailing parties absent specific statutory authorization).

[3]*See, e.g.,* Hanrahan v. Hampton, 446 U.S. 754, 758 n.4 (1980). For a discussion of attorney's fees awards in discrimination suits generally, see B.L. SCHLEI & P. GROSSMAN, EMPLOYMENT DISCRIMINATION LAW 1466–1522 (2d ed. 1983), Five-Year Supp. 549–61 (1989). Courts also have discretion to award attorney's fees and costs pursuant to rules generally applicable to civil litigation. *See, e.g.,* FED. R. CIV. P. 11, 28 U.S.C. §1912, 28 U.S.C. §1927, and FED. R. APP. P. 38.

[4]*See, e.g.,* Ackerman v. Western Elec. Co., 643 F. Supp. 836, 48 FEP Cases 1354 (N.D. Cal. 1986), *aff'd,* 860 F.2d 1514 (9th Cir. 1988)(discussing calculation of attorney's fee award under CAL. GOV'T CODE §12965(b)); Tretter v. Liquipak Int'l, 356 N.W.2d 713, 716, 43 FEP Cases 1522, 1524 (Minn. App. 1984)(under Minnesota Statute §363.14 subd. 3 (1982), prevailing party is entitled to recover reasonable attorney's fees). For a discussion of state fair employment practices statutes, see Chapter 12.

unjust.[5] In *Texas State Teachers Ass'n v. Garland Independent School District*,[6] the Supreme Court stated the test for determining a "prevailing party" under §1988 in cases where the plaintiff has prevailed on some, but not all, discrimination claims. The Court ruled that a party "prevails" if it succeeds "on any significant issue in the litigation which achieved some of the benefit that the [party] sought in bringing suit."[7] To be said to prevail, Justice Sandra Day O'Connor wrote, the plaintiff must " 'receive at least some relief on the merits of his claim.' ... Thus, at a minimum, ... the plaintiff must be able to point to a resolution of the dispute which changes the legal relationship between itself and the defendant."[8]

Under the Supreme Court's test, a plaintiff need not prevail on every claim, or even the most important claim, to be deemed the "prevailing party" for the purposes of an attorney's fees award.[9]

In *Texas State Teachers Ass'n*, the plaintiffs "prevailed" because they obtained summary judgment as to one of the defendant's policies and because their victory altered that policy.[10]

2. Nominal Damages

Whether a party must obtain back pay, injunctive relief, or at least voluntary action by the defendant in order to "prevail" for purposes of an attorney's fee award is still an open question.[11] Where no relief has been granted, several courts have awarded nominal damages in order to support an award of attorney's fees.[12] At least one court has awarded attorney's fees based solely on a finding of harassment, without any purported reliance upon a nominal damages

---

[5]*See* Newman v. Piggie Park Enter., 390 U.S. 400, 402 (1968)(race discrimination case; plaintiff acts as private attorney general).

[6]489 U.S. 782, 49 FEP Cases 465 (1989).

[7]*Id.*, 49 FEP Cases at 467.

[8]*Id.*, 49 FEP Cases at 468. Prior to *Texas State Teachers Ass'n*, the Fifth and Eleventh Circuits required a party to succeed on the "central issue" in the litigation and achieve the "primary relief sought" to be eligible for an attorney's fees award. *See, e.g.*, Simien v. San Antonio, 809 F.2d 255, 258, 42 FEP Cases 1657, 1660 (5th Cir. 1987); Martin v. Heckler, 773 F.2d 1145, 1149 (11th Cir. 1985)(*en banc*). Most other circuits merely required a party to succeed on a significant issue and receive some of the relief sought in the lawsuit to qualify for a fee award. *See, e.g.*, Gingras v. Lloyd, 740 F.2d 210, 212 (2d Cir. 1984); Lampher v. Zagel, 755 F.2d 99, 102 (7th Cir. 1985); Fast v. School Dist. of Ladue, 728 F.2d 1030, 1032–33 (8th Cir. 1984)(*en banc*); Lummi Indian Tribe v. Oltman, 720 F.2d 1124, 1125 (9th Cir. 1983); Nephew v. Aurora, 766 F.2d 1464, 1466 (10th Cir. 1985), *cert. denied*, 485 U.S. 976 (1988). In *Texas State Teachers Ass'n*, the Supreme Court expressly adopted the less demanding standard.

[9]*See* Starrett v. Wadley, 876 F.2d 808, 824–25, 51 FEP Cases 608, 619 (10th Cir. 1989)(plaintiff who prevailed on her §1983 sexual harassment claim but whose Title VII claim was erroneously dismissed and who abandoned her state tort claims was "prevailing party" for purposes of awarding attorney's fees under 42 U.S.C. §1988); Bucci v. Chromalloy Am. Corp., 53 EPD ¶39,882 (N.D. Cal. 1989)(awarding plaintiff attorney's fees under California fair employment practices statute where plaintiff prevailed on statutory sexual harassment claim but lost on common-law claims). *Cf.* Whatley v. Super Low Food Center, 1990 U.S. Dist. LEXIS 6271 (N.D. Ill. 1990)(plaintiff's loss on intentional infliction of emotional distress claim did not make sexual harassment claim frivolous and thereby entitled defendant to attorney's fees award).

[10]*Supra* note 6, 49 FEP Cases at 469.

[11]*Cf.* Moran v. Pima County, 474 U.S. 989 (1985)(White, J., dissenting from denial of *certiorari*)(noting split in circuits regarding whether award of nominal damages can itself support an attorney's fees award under §1988). *See also* Spencer v. General Elec. Co., 894 F.2d 651, 662, 51 FEP Cases 1725, 1733 (4th Cir. 1990)(reserving question whether nominal damages, absent further remedial action obtained in lawsuit, could support attorney's fee award).

[12]*See, e.g.*, Huddleston v. Roger Dean Chevrolet, 845 F.2d 900, 905, 46 FEP Cases 1361, 1364 (11th Cir. 1988)(awarding nominal damages and attorney's fees); Dean v. Civiletti, 670 F.2d 99, 101, 29 FEP Cases 890, 892 (8th Cir. 1982); Joshi v. Florida State Univ., 646 F.2d 981, 991 n.33, 26 FEP Cases 300, 308 (5th Cir. 1981), *cert. denied*, 456 U.S. 972 (1982). For a discussion of nominal damages, see Chapter 29, Monetary Relief, Section II.

award.[13] The Seventh Circuit, however, has refused to award either nominal damages or attorney's fees in the absence of other available relief.[14] The Seventh Circuit's position may find some support in the Supreme Court's requirement, in *Texas State Teachers Ass'n*, that there be some material alteration in the legal relationship between the parties before an attorney's fee award is proper.[15]

3. Voluntary Relief

a. Unilateral employer action. A lawsuit may prompt an employer to voluntarily provide the plaintiff with some or all of the relief sought. If the lawsuit causes the remedial action, a plaintiff may be found to be a prevailing party based upon the relief obtained outside the formal confines of a court's judgment.[16]

b. Settlements. A plaintiff who receives relief in exchange for a settlement of claims is generally entitled to attorney's fees.[17] To be the prevailing party in a settlement, a plaintiff's lawsuit must (1) be a catalyst or motivating factor in obtaining the favorable outcome and (2) be other than frivolous, unreasonable or groundless, so that the defendant's settlement was not wholly unrelated to the merits of the case.[18]

c. Accepting an offer of judgment. If the plaintiff accepts an employer's offer of judgment pursuant to Rule 68 of the Federal Rules of Civil Procedure, the plaintiff is the prevailing party if the judgment provides substantial relief on a major issue.[19] If the offer of judgment does not expressly provide for costs and attorney's fees, the plaintiff who accepts an offer of judgment is entitled to seek them in addition to the damages specified in the offer of judgment.[20]

B. Administrative Proceedings

Courts may award attorney's fees for work done in administrative proceedings that the plaintiff was required to exhaust in order to bring a Title VII

---

[13]*See* Mitchell v. OsAIR, 629 F. Supp. 636, 644, 45 FEP Cases 580, 585 (N.D. Ohio 1986)(awarding fees to plaintiff who voluntarily resigned but who was entitled to "satisfaction of having prevailed in her day in court"); *cf.* Bundy v. Jackson, 641 F.2d 934, 946 n.12, 24 FEP Cases 1155, 1162 (D.C. Cir. 1981)(remanding for award of attorney's fees and injunctive relief based upon finding of harassing environment).

[14]*See, e.g.,* Swanson v. Elmhurst Chrysler Plymouth, 882 F.2d 1235, 1239–40, 50 FEP Cases 1082, 1085–86 (7th Cir. 1989), *cert. denied*, 110 S.Ct. 758 (1990); Bohen v. City of E. Chicago, 799 F.2d 1180, 1189, 41 FEP Cases 1108, 1115 (7th Cir. 1986).

[15]*Supra* note 6, 49 FEP Cases at 468; *see also* Hewitt v. Helms, 482 U.S. 755, 762, 44 FEP Cases 15, 17 (1987)(declaration that prisoner's rights had been violated alone insufficient to support fee award under §1988).

[16]*See, e.g.,* Maher v. Gagne, 448 U.S. 122, 129 (1980)(§1988 case); Spencer v. General Elec. Co., 894 F.2d 651, 662, 51 FEP Cases 1725, 1733 (4th Cir. 1990)(fact that suit prompted defendant to revise its antiharassment policy made plaintiff "prevailing party" in Title VII hostile environment case).

[17]*See* Maher v. Gagne, 448 U.S. 122, 129 (1980).

[18]Nanetti v. University of Ill., 867 F.2d 990, 992–95, 52 FEP Cases 1775, 1776–78 (7th Cir. 1989)(faculty member who obtained salary increase after her attorney intervened in settlement negotiations was prevailing party on salary claim); *Cf. In re* Burlington N., 832 F.2d 422, 424–26, 53 FEP Cases 105, 107–9 (7th Cir. 1987)(law firms that obtained increased awards for their clients from settlement fund established by employer pursuant to consent decree were not prevailing parties because their efforts did not increase employer's liability).

[19]*See, e.g.,* David v. AM Int'l, 131 F.R.D. 86, 89, 53 FEP Cases 17, 18–19 (E.D. Pa. 1990).

[20]Said v. Virginia Commonwealth Univ., 130 F.R.D. 60, 63–64, 52 FEP Cases 339, 341–42 (E.D. Va. 1990); David v. AM Int'l, *supra* note 19 (plaintiff accepted offer of judgment of $27,000; court awarded costs and fees of $33,698 to plaintiff as prevailing party).

claim.[21] Courts are split, however, concerning attorney's fees awards for preliminary administrative proceedings not mandated by Title VII.[22]

In the §1983 context, the Supreme Court has stated that hours spent in optional state administrative proceedings conducted before the commencement of a successful related §1983 suit are compensable if the hours were reasonably expended for purposes of the subsequent litigation, because they were hours both useful and of a type ordinarily necessary to advance civil rights litigation.[23]

III. COMPUTING FEE AWARDS

A. General Principles

As in other types of employment discrimination suits,[24] courts set fees in sexual harassment suits by initially determining the "lodestar"—the number of hours reasonably expended multiplied by a reasonable hourly rate.[25] This figure may then be adjusted upward or downward.[26] In determining whether to adjust fees, courts often apply the twelve-factor analysis articulated by Judge Paul H. Roney in *Johnson v. Georgia Highway Express*.[27] The applicant has the burden of establishing the appropriate hourly rate and documenting the hours expended by submitting evidence supporting the hours worked and the rates claimed.[28] The burden is also on the requesting party to justify an upward adjustment to the lodestar.[29]

---

[21]New York Gas Light Club v. Carey, 447 U.S. 54, 22 FEP Cases 1642 (1980); Curtis v. Bill Hanna Ford, Inc., 822 F.2d 549, 552–53, 49 FEP Cases 1597, 1608–9 (5th Cir. 1987)(court erred in denying fees for time spent on EEOC hearings).

[22]*Compare* Manders v. Oklahoma, 875 F.2d 263, 267, 49 FEP Cases 1188, 1190 (10th Cir. 1989)(disallowing attorney's fees for optional internal grievance procedure for state employees because procedure is "an enforcement mechanism additional to, not a precondition of, Title VII enforcement, and is not an integral part of the Title VII scheme") *and* Renbarger v. South Bend School Corp., 52 FEP Cases 1795, 1799–1800 (N.D. Ind. 1990)(hours attributed to attorney's representation of laid-off teachers at school board hearings were not permitted because they were not type of hours ordinarily necessary to advance civil rights litigation) *with* Chrapliwy v. Uniroyal, 670 F.2d 760, 767, 28 FEP Cases 19, 25 (7th Cir. 1982), *cert. denied*, 461 U.S. 956 (1983)(prevailing plaintiffs permitted to recover for debarment proceeding because it contributed to "the ultimate termination of the Title VII action").

[23]*See* Webb v. County Bd. of Educ. of Dyer County, 471 U.S. 234, 243, 37 FEP Cases 785, 788–89 (1985)(denying attorney's fees for time spent during administrative appeal of school board termination decision because such time deemed too remote from subsequent action).

[24]For a more detailed analysis of the computation of attorney's fees awards in discrimination suits generally, see B.L. SCHLEI & P. GROSSMAN, EMPLOYMENT DISCRIMINATION LAW 1486–1511, Five-Year Supplement 554–58 (1989).

[25]Hensley v. Eckerhart, 461 U.S. 424, 433–34, 31 FEP Cases 1169, 1173 (1983).

[26]Blum v. Stenson, 465 U.S. 886, 896, 34 FEP Cases 417, 421 (1984).

[27]488 F.2d 714, 7 FEP Cases 1 (5th Cir. 1974). The 12 factors announced in *Johnson* and approved in *Blum* are (1) time and labor required, (2) novelty and difficulty of the case, (3) skill required, (4) preclusion of other employment caused by the case, (5) customary rate or fee, (6) contingent or fixed nature of the fee, (7) time limitation required by the case, (8) amount involved, (9) experience, reputation, and ability of the attorney, (10) desirability of the case, (11) nature and length of legal relationship, and (12) awards in similar cases. *Id.* at 717–19, 7 FEP Cases at 3–5.

[28]Hensley v. Eckerhart, *supra* note 25, 461 U.S. at 433, 437, 31 FEP Cases at 1173, 1175. *See also* Renbarger v. South Bend School Corp., *supra* note 22, 52 FEP Cases at 1805–6 (hours were reduced where time sheet entries included conferences, meetings, and telephone calls in which subject matter was not identified and descriptions were vague); Yates v. Avco Corp., 819 F.2d 630, 638, 43 FEP Cases 1595, 1602 (6th Cir. 1987)(trial court's award of one-half of requested fees reversed in light of total absence of documentation).

[29]Blum v. Stenson, *supra* note 26, 465 U.S. at 897, 34 FEP Cases at 421.

In exercising its discretion to award fees, the district court must articulate reasons for its decision and show its calculation.[30] If the court disallows certain fees, it must explain why an award of such fees would be improper.[31]

B. Applying the General Criteria

In *Blum v. Stenson*,[32] a §1988 case, the Supreme Court concluded that the lodestar figure establishes the presumptive amount to be awarded as a reasonable attorney's fee. The *Blum* Court reasoned that the novelty and complexity of the issues were fully reflected in allowable billable hours, and that the quality of representation and the skill and experience of the attorney ordinarily should be reflected in normal hourly billing rates.[33]

The *Blum* Court also stated that "in some cases of exceptional success an enhancement award may be justified."[34] The Court stated that, in certain cases, an enhancement may be made based upon the "contingent" nature of the attorney's fees, although the record in *Blum* did not support a "contingency" adjustment to the lodestar.[35]

1. Extent of Success

The Supreme Court held in *Hensley v. Eckerhart*[36] that "the extent of a plaintiff's success is a crucial factor in determining the amount of an award of attorney's fees." Courts have applied *Hensley* to reduce the total attorney's fees awarded where the plaintiff has prevailed on some but not all issues in a sexual harassment case.[37]

Where claims are unrelated, the work performed on unsuccessful claims is excluded from the award.[38] If the issues are sufficiently related, the court will disallow only repetitive or unrelated legal work and, if the claims are inextricably intertwined, the court will not reduce the fees at all.[39]

---

[30]Hensley v. Eckerhart, *supra* note 25, 461 U.S. at 433, 437, 31 FEP Cases at 1172, 1174–75.

[31]Steele v. Offshore Shipbldg., 867 F.2d 1311, 1318, 49 FEP Cases 522, 527 (11th Cir. 1989)(failure to articulate rationale for deductions requires reversal).

[32]*Supra* note 26.

[33]*Id.* at 900, 34 FEP Cases at 422.

[34]*Id.* at 897, 34 FEP Cases at 421.

[35]*Id.* at 901 n.17, 34 FEP Cases at 423.

[36]*Supra* note 25, 461 U.S. at 440, 31 FEP Cases at 1175–76.

[37]Zabkowicz v. West Bend Co., 789 F.2d 540, 553–54, 40 FEP Cases 1171, 1181–82 (7th Cir. 1986)(plaintiff entitled to recover attorney's fees for tort claims that sought to remedy same course of conduct that gave rise to Title VII action, but was prohibited from recovering fees for husband's tort claims and her voluntarily dismissed duty of fair representation claims); Carter v. Sedgwick County, 48 FEP Cases 1349, 1351 (D. Kan. 1988)(plaintiff's attorney's fees reduced by 40% to reflect partial success).

[38]*See* Zabkowicz v. West Bend Co., *supra* note 37, 789 F.2d at 553–54, 40 FEP Cases at 1181–82 (theories supporting plaintiff's husband's tort claims too dissimilar to permit recovery of attorney's fees expended on such claims); Carter v. Sedgwick County, *supra* note 37, 48 FEP Cases at 1350–51 (lodestar to be awarded to employee who prevailed on race harassment claim was reduced by 40% to account for failure to prevail on unrelated issues whether plaintiff was denied due process and subjected to sexual harassment); Bohen v. City of E. Chicago, 666 F. Supp. 154, 156, 53 FEP Cases 99, 100–101 (N.D. Ind. 1987)(employee who was successful on sex harassment claim but not on discharge claim awarded 90% of time spent by attorneys on harassment issue).

[39]Bucci v. Chromalloy Am. Corp., 53 EPD ¶39,882 (N.D. Cal. 1989)(plaintiff may recover for all claims, including dismissed tort claims, because all claims were based on "common core of facts and challenged a single course of conduct by defendant").

The amount of damages awarded to the plaintiff is not controlling as to the reasonableness of the fees,[40] and the amount of attorney's fees need not necessarily bear any relationship to the monetary award to the plaintiff.[41]

A special application of the extent-of-success issue arises when a plaintiff rejects an offer of judgment made by the defendant, pursuant to Rule 68 of the Federal Rules of Civil Procedure, and then prevails at trial but in an amount less than the amount of the offer.[42] Under those circumstances, Rule 68 provides that the plaintiff, even though the prevailing party, is not entitled to recovery of her post-offer costs. In *Marek v. Chesny*, the Supreme Court held that Rule 68 applies to attorney's fees awards under §1988.[43] Thus, a plaintiff who prevails in an amount less than the defendant's Rule 68 offer is not entitled to her post-offer attorney's fees.[44]

2. Contingent Nature of Attorney's Fees

Two Supreme Court decisions resolved issues concerning the contingent nature of attorney's fees in cases arising under §1988. In *Pennsylvania v. Delaware Valley Citizens' Council for Clean Air*,[45] the Court reversed an award of attorney's fees that had been adjusted upward because of the contingency factor. The plurality and Justice Sandra Day O'Connor, concurring in part, concluded that a contingency adjustment is appropriate only when the relevant market compensates contingent-fee cases, as a class, differently than other cases, and when the plaintiff would have encountered "substantial difficulties in finding counsel in the local or other relevant market" because of the difficult nature of the case.[46] Justice O'Connor's concurrence in *Delaware Valley* has been relied upon by some courts to permit upward adjustments based upon contingency risks in sexual harassment suits.[47]

In *King v. Palmer*, the D.C. Circuit, applying Justice O'Connor's two-part test, found that a 100 percent enhancement for a contingent fee case was appropriate because (1) the relevant legal market added this premium for contingency and (2) the plaintiff would have faced substantial difficulty in finding counsel absent an enhancement for risk. The *King* case was only

---

[40]City of Riverside v. Rivera, 477 U.S. 561, 574, 41 FEP Cases 65, 69 (1986).

[41]*Cf.* McHenry v. Chadwick, 896 F.2d 184, 189 (6th Cir. 1990)(prisoner rights case under §1983; court upheld attorney's fee award of more than five times damages, stating that "the value of the rights vindicated goes beyond the actual monetary award, and the amount of the actual award is not controlling").

[42]For a further discussion of Rule 68, see Chapter 31, Settlement.

[43]473 U.S. 1, 9, 11–12, 38 FEP Cases 124, 128–29 (1985). *See also* Spencer v. General Elec. Co., 894 F.2d 651, 663–64, 51 FEP Cases 1725, 1734 (4th Cir. 1990)(where defendant had offered $10,000 and injunctive and job-related relief and plaintiff recovered only $1 in nominal damages, defendant was not required to pay post-offer attorney's fees even though company meanwhile had instituted antiharassment policy; "judgment finally obtained" under Rule 68 is viewed literally and does not include relief plaintiff may obtain outside the judgment, such as voluntary antiharassment policy).

[44]The Civil Rights Act of 1990, vetoed by President Bush, would have amended Title VII to remove it from the scope of Rule 68, as interpreted by *Marek*. Section 9 of the Act would have excluded attorney's fees, "including expert fees and other litigation expenses," from the definition of Title VII "costs" governed by Rule 68 offers of judgment. *See* Conference Report on S. 2104, Civil Rights Act of 1990, 101st Cong., 2d Sess., 136 CONG. REC. H8045, H8046 (1990).

[45]483 U.S. 711, 45 FEP Cases 1750 (1987).

[46]*Id.* at 731, 45 FEP Cases at 1758. The Court also reversed the lower court's use of multipliers to reward exceptional success and restated its position in *Blum* that the lodestar is presumed to be the reasonable fee and should rarely be adjusted. *Id.* at 728, 45 FEP Cases at 1757.

[47]*See* King v. Palmer, 906 F.2d 762, 769 (D.C. Cir. 1990); Bucci v. Chromalloy Am. Corp., *supra* note 39.

partially contingent; the plaintiff had agreed to pay an attorney's fee of $5,000 regardless of the outcome of the case. The court ruled, however, that an enhancement was appropriate as to the contingent portion of the case.[48]

Similarly, in *Bucci v. Chromalloy America Corp.*,[49] the court ruled that a 100 percent enhancement to the lodestar in a contingency fee case was appropriate, given the market for legal services in San Francisco.

More recently, in *Blanchard v. Bergeron*,[50] the Supreme Court held that a contingent fee contract does not impose a ceiling on an award of attorney's fees under §1988, for to conclude otherwise would be inconsistent with the statute and its policy and purpose.[51]

C. Public Interest Law Firms

Most courts now hold that a public interest law firm should receive the same rates and be eligible for an upward adjustment of the lodestar to the same extent as similarly situated private attorneys in sexual harassment cases.[52]

IV. THE PREVAILING DEFENDANT'S RIGHT TO ATTORNEY'S FEES

In *Christiansburg Garment Co. v. EEOC*,[53] the Supreme Court ruled that a prevailing defendant may obtain attorney's fees under Title VII, but only if the plaintiff's suit was "frivolous, unreasonable or without foundation." A plaintiff's suit may qualify as such even if it is not brought in "bad faith." Courts have applied this standard to award attorney's fees to defendants in sexual harassment cases.[54] Although a finding of bad faith on the part of the plaintiff is not required for a prevailing defendant to obtain attorney's fees in a Title VII case, the plaintiff's motivation is one factor that the court may consider in determining the amount of fees to be awarded.[55] Another such factor, identified in *dicta* by one court, is the relative ability of the parties to absorb the cost of the litigation.[56]

---

[48]King v. Palmer, *supra* note 47, 906 F.2d at 766; *see also* Thompson v. Kennickell, 710 F. Supp. 1, 9 (D.D.C. 1989)(Richey, J.)($1,732,700 fee award at market rates with 100% enhancement to lodestar).

[49]*Supra* note 39.

[50]489 U.S. 87, 49 FEP Cases 1 (1989).

[51]*Id.* at 96, 49 FEP Cases at 5 ("The attorney's fee provided for in a contingent fee agreement is not a ceiling upon the fees recoverable under §1988").

[52]*E.g.*, Mammano v. Pittston Co., 792 F.2d 1242, 1245, 52 FEP Cases 794, 796 (4th Cir. 1986)(fact that firm is public interest law firm does not jeopardize its entitlement to fees in sexual harassment suit).

[53]434 U.S. 412, 16 FEP Cases 502 (1978).

[54]*See* Phillips v. TVA Eng'g Ass'n, 725 F.2d 684 (6th Cir. 1983), *cert. denied*, 469 U.S. 819 (1984)(not for full-text publication)(plaintiff's claim "frivolous" and defendant entitled to recover attorney's fees where plaintiff did not produce any corroborating testimony regarding charge of sexual harassment nor any evidence that she had ever complained of harassment and where evidence suggested that she had fabricated sexual harassment charge); *see also* Neidhardt v. D.H. Holmes Co., 583 F. Supp. 1271, 1277, 37 FEP Cases 1558, 1563 (E.D. La. 1984)(court granted award of attorney's fees against EEOC where EEOC had made finding of no reasonable cause as to one plaintiff, and then later supported that plaintiff's intervention and vigorously pursued her claim at trial, noting that the EEOC "at the very least should have known that [the intervenor's] claims were frivolous and without merit").

[55]*See, e.g.*, Hill v. BASF Wyandotte Corp., 547 F. Supp. 348, 354, 32 FEP Cases 1804, 1808–9 (E.D. Mich. 1982)(attorney's fees awarded to defendant where plaintiff produced no proof at trial to substantiate claims of sexual harassment and race discrimination).

[56]Kota v. Abele Tractor & Equip. Co., 52 FEP Cases 959, 960 (N.D.N.Y. 1990)(even if sex discrimination claim was viewed as frivolous, unreasonable, or meritless, court was not required to award employer attorney's fees; defendant, a small business, was in better position to absorb litigation costs).

Courts have also awarded attorney's fees against plaintiffs on the basis of general litigation standards apart from *Christiansburg*. In *Jackson-Colley v. Army Corps of Engineers*,[57] the court found that the plaintiff in a Title VII action had acted in bad faith by raising sexual harassment allegations that had not been raised in a prior administrative appeal of her performance-based termination. Moreover, the plaintiff's allegations had characterized as sexually motivated a supervisor's "gawking" and scratching of his groin, when in fact the supervisor had a vision problem and a medical condition that induced the scratching. Characterizing the plaintiff's allegations as "grossly aggrandized" and "mean-spirited," the court imposed costs and attorney's fees upon the plaintiff personally and an additional $500 upon the plaintiff's counsel pursuant to Rule 11. Courts have also relied upon 28 U.S.C §1927 to award attorney's fees against a plaintiff's counsel who, in a sexual harassment case, was found to have expanded the litigation vexatiously.[58]

V. COSTS

Costs are generally granted to the prevailing party in employment discrimination litigation. Rule 54(d) of the Federal Rules of Civil Procedure provides:

> Except when express provision therefor is made either in a statute of the United States or in these rules, costs shall be allowed as of course to the prevailing party unless the court otherwise directs; but costs against the United States, its officers, and agencies shall be imposed only to the extent permitted by law.[59]

"Costs" are defined in 28 U.S.C. §1920 as including:

(1) Fees of the clerk and marshal;
(2) Fees of the court reporter for all or any part of the stenographic transcript necessarily obtained for use in the case;
(3) Fees and disbursements for printing and witnesses;
(4) Fees for exemplification and copies of papers necessarily obtained for use in the case;
(5) Docket fees under Section 1923 of this title;
(6) Compensation of court appointed experts, compensation of interpreters, and salaries, fees, expenses, and costs of special interpretation services under Section 1828 of this title.

In *Crawford Fittings Co. v. J.T. Gibbons, Inc.*,[60] the Supreme Court held that courts may not award expert witness fees as part of costs, pursuant to 28

---

[57]655 F. Supp. 122, 136, 43 FEP Cases 617, 628 (E.D. Mich 1987); *see also* Matthews v. Freedman, 128 F.R.D. 194, 202–3, 53 EPD ¶39,756 (E.D. Pa. 1989)(attorney's fees and costs awarded against attorney as Rule 11 sanctions for bringing time-barred Title VII and frivolous Thirteenth Amendment sexual harassment and race discrimination claims).

[58]*See, e.g.*, Perkins v. General Motors Corp., 129 F.R.D. 655, 666 (W.D. Mo. 1990)(awarding fees against plaintiff and her counsel pursuant to Federal Rules of Civil Procedure 26(g) & 11, and 28 U.S.C. §1927 for multiple misrepresentations and abuses in pretrial discovery and filings); *see also* Ullman v. Olwine, 857 F.2d 1475 (6th Cir. 1988), *cert. denied*, 109 S.Ct. 1533 (1989)(awarding fees pursuant to 28 U.S.C. §1927 for improper challenge to settlement of sexual harassment claim); Smiga v. Dean Witter Reynolds, 766 F.2d 698, 708 (2d Cir. 1985), *cert. denied*, 475 U.S. 1067 (1986)(awarding fees pursuant to 28 U.S.C. §1927 for improper challenge to arbitration award independent of sexual harassment claim).

[59]FED. R. CIV. P. 54(d).

[60]482 U.S. 437, 439, 43 FEP Cases 1775, 1776 (1987).

U.S.C. §§1920 and 1821, except as expressly set forth in those statutes.* In cases in which a party is entitled to both costs and attorney's fees, however, lower courts have exercised their discretion to reimburse costs beyond those expressly provided in 28 U.S.C. §1920, provided only that such out-of-pocket expenses would normally and reasonably be charged to a client.[61] These expenses have included costs for postage, telephone, expert fees, travel, deposition transcripts, shipping, parking, lodging, and food.[62] In awarding such costs, courts have not always distinguished between costs awardable pursuant to §1920 and costs awardable as an element of attorney's fees.[63]

A plaintiff is the "prevailing party" for purposes of awarding costs in a sexual harassment action if the plaintiff is successful "on any significant issue in litigation which achieved some of the benefit that the [party] sought in bringing suit."[64] When the defendant prevails, courts have routinely awarded costs. Courts have explicitly rejected use of the *Christiansburg* standard to determine whether to award costs to the prevailing defendant.[65] The district court retains discretion, however, to disallow expenses that are unnecessary, unreasonable, or excessive.[66] Courts have also considered the limited financial means of plaintiffs in deciding whether to reduce a cost award.[67] Generally, courts do not award full costs where an action is based upon multiple individual claims or is brought by several plaintiffs where the plaintiffs have prevailed on some portion of their claims.[68]

---

*[**Editor's Note:** The Civil Rights Act of 1991, discussed in Appendix 8, amended Title VII to make expert fees recoverable as part of reasonable attorney's fees. See text accompanying note 1 *supra*.]

[61]*See, e.g.,* Henry v. Webermeier, 738 F.2d 188, 192 (7th Cir. 1984).

[62]*See* Danny Kresky Enters. Corp. v. Magid, 716 F.2d 215, 219–20 (3d Cir. 1983)(court reporter fees and shipping, copying, and telephone expenses); David v. AM Int'l, 131 F.R.D. 86, 90, 53 FEP Cases 17, 21 (E.D. Pa. 1990). The potential applicability of *Crawford Fittings* to these decisions is uncertain since *Crawford Fittings* did not involve a party entitled to both costs and attorney's fees. *Cf.* Crawford Fittings Co. v. J.T. Gibbons, Inc., *supra* note 60, 482 U.S. at 444–45, 43 FEP Cases at 1778 (Blackmun, J., concurring)(decision does not address costs recoverable under §1988). The proposed Civil Rights Act of 1990, vetoed by President Bush, would have overruled *Crawford Fittings* by including expert fees within the attorney's fees award. Conference Report on S. 2104, Civil Rights Act of 1990, 101st Cong., 2d Sess., 136 CONG. REC. H8045, H8046 (1990).

[63]*See, e.g.,* Henry v. Webermeier, *supra* note 61; Danny Kresky Enters. Corp. v. Magid, *supra* note 62.

[64]Texas State Teachers Ass'n v. Garland Indep. School Dist., 489 U.S. 782, 49 FEP Cases 465, 467 (1989); *see also* discussion of prevailing parties in Section II. *supra*.

[65]*See* Wrighten v. Metropolitan Hosp., 726 F.2d 1346, 1357, 33 FEP Cases 1714, 1722 (9th Cir. 1984)(declining to impose *Christiansburg* standard upon cost award); Poe v. John Deere Co., 695 F.2d 1103, 1108, 30 FEP Cases 827, 830–31 (8th Cir. 1982)(same); *Cf.* Matthews v. Allis-Chalmers Corp., 769 F.2d 1215, 1219, 38 FEP Cases 1118, 1121 (7th Cir. 1985)(declining to require bad faith to sustain cost award under ADEA).

[66]Zabkowicz v. West Bend Co., 789 F.2d 540, 553, 40 FEP Cases 1171, 1182 (7th Cir. 1986).

[67]Wrighten v. Metropolitan Hosp., *supra* note 65, 726 F.2d at 1357, 33 FEP Cases at 1722 (instructing court on remand to consider plaintiff's financial means).

[68]*See, e.g.,* Duke v. Uniroyal, 743 F. Supp. 1218, 1226–27, 53 FEP Cases 402, 409 (E.D.N.C. 1990); EEOC v. Colgate-Palmolive Co., 617 F. Supp. 843, 844, 51 FEP Cases 1601, 1602 (S.D.N.Y. 1985)(awarding one-third costs to EEOC and two-thirds costs to employer).

CHAPTER 31

SETTLEMENT

I. OVERVIEW

The congressional policy that favors the settlement of employment discrimination claims generally[1] applies to sexual harassment claims in particular.[2] Concerns about publicity, and the fact that testimony often is of a highly personal and sensitive nature, make sexual harassment cases particularly appropriate for resolution through settlement.[3] Employers and other respondents also enter into settlement agreements to avoid the costs of litigation, to avoid the loss of valuable time to the litigation process, and to obviate the risk of a finding of liability with the concomitant damage awards. Complainants enter into settlement agreements to obtain monetary and other benefits while avoiding the uncertainty and delay inherent in litigation. Thus, large numbers of sexual harassment cases are settled before trial, before the filing of a complaint, and even before charges of discrimination are filed with the EEOC.[4]

---

[1]Carson v. American Brands, 450 U.S. 79, 88 n.14, 25 FEP Cases 1, 4 (1981)(order refusing to enter consent decree is immediately appealable because of seriousness of possible loss of opportunity to settle; in enacting Title VII, Congress expressed "strong preference for encouraging voluntary settlement of employment discrimination claims"); Alexander v. Gardner-Denver Co., 415 U.S. 36, 44, 7 FEP Cases 81, 84 (1974)("Cooperation and voluntary compliance were selected as the preferred means for achieving this goal [equality of opportunity]. To this end, Congress created the Equal Employment Opportunity Commission and established a procedure whereby existing state and local equal employment opportunity agencies, as well as the Commission, would have an opportunity to settle disputes through conference, conciliation, and persuasion before the aggrieved party was permitted to file a lawsuit"); United States v. Allegheny-Ludlum Indus., 517 F.2d 826, 847, 11 FEP Cases 167, 183 (5th Cir. 1975)(noting deference to be accorded processes of voluntary conciliation and settlement as expressed in *Alexander v. Gardner-Denver Co.*), *cert. denied,* 425 U.S. 944 (1976).

[2]Harrison v. Edison Bros. Apparel Stores, 724 F. Supp. 1185, 1190 n.4 (M.D.N.C. 1989)(summary judgment granted in favor of employer on state-law claims for intentional infliction of emotional distress and battery premised on sexual harassment allegations, because plaintiff had voluntarily dismissed with prejudice claims against supervisor); Alexander v. Gardner-Denver Co., *supra* note 1 ("noting high premium placed by Congress on the voluntary private settlement of Title VII suits"); Holden v. Burlington N., 665 F. Supp. 1398, 1405 (D. Minn. 1987)(approved settlement of class action involving "across-the-board" sex discrimination claims including sexual harassment: "Federal courts look with favor on the voluntary resolution of litigation through settlement. This is especially true in Title VII class action litigation, where the public interest in voluntary resolution is great").

[3]For a general discussion of settling employment discrimination cases, see B.L. SCHLEI & P. GROSSMAN, EMPLOYMENT DISCRIMINATION LAW, Chapter 40 (2d ed. 1983).

[4]For a discussion of the negotiation of conciliation agreements following a cause determination by the EEOC, see Chapter 20, The Agency Investigation.

II. VALIDITY OF WAIVER OF SEXUAL HARASSMENT CLAIMS

Virtually all settlements of sexual harassment claims involve a release or waiver of claims by the complainant, for this, typically, is the most important element of consideration to the employer. A large body of Title VII case law has developed addressing the circumstances under which a privately negotiated release of claims will be upheld.

A. Knowing and Voluntary Waivers of Past Claims Are Valid

1. Waivers of Past Claims are Valid

Releases of preexisting claims have repeatedly been upheld by the courts. In *dicta* in *Alexander v. Gardner-Denver Co.,* Justice Lewis F. Powell, Jr., stated that an employee "presumably" may waive causes of action under Title VII as part of a voluntary settlement.[5] The Supreme Court noted, however that: "In determining the effectiveness of any such waiver, a court would have to determine at the outset that the employee's consent to the settlement was voluntary and knowing."[6]

In *United States v. Allegheny-Ludlum Industries,*[7] the Fifth Circuit ruled on a challenge to a proposed consent decree that provided for individual releases. Judge Homer Thornberry held that an employee may waive both monetary and injunctive relief on claims that "arise from antecedent discriminatory events, acts, patterns, or practices, or the 'continuing' or 'future' effects thereof so long as such effects are causally rooted—in origin, logic, and factual experience—in discriminatory acts or practices which antedate the execution of the release."[8] To decide otherwise, the court noted, would be to hold that Title VII lawsuits may be resolved only in the courtroom.[9] The court specified that the release must be "executed voluntarily and with adequate knowledge."[10]

2. Meaning of "Knowingly and Voluntarily"

Circuit courts have articulated two different "tests" to determine whether a waiver was executed "knowingly and voluntarily." The Fourth, Sixth, and Eighth Circuits apply "ordinary contract principles" in determining whether a release was given knowingly and voluntarily.[11] The Second, Third, Fifth, and

---

[5]*Supra* note 1, 415 U.S. at 52, 7 FEP Cases at 87.

[6]*Id.* at 52 n.15, 7 FEP Cases at 87.

[7]517 F.2d 826, 11 FEP Cases 167 (5th Cir. 1975) (Thornberry, Morgan & Clark, JJ.), *cert. denied,* 425 U.S. 944 (1976).

[8]*Id.* at 853, 11 FEP Cases at 187.

[9]"[W]e cannot conceive of how any employment discrimination dispute could ever be resolved outside, or indeed inside, the courtroom, if defendants were forbidden to obtain binding, negotiated settlements. No defendant would ever deliver money, promises, or any other consideration—not even a peppercorn— except after entry of a contested, final court order . . . ." *Id.* at 858–59, 11 FEP Cases at 192.

[10]*Id.*

[11]O'Shea v. Commercial Credit Corp., 930 F.2d 358, 362 (4th Cir. 1991)(better approach is to analyze waivers under ordinary contract principles); Lancaster v. Buerkle Buick Honda Co., 809 F.2d 539, 42 FEP Cases 1472 (8th Cir.)(ordinary contract principles to be applied), *cert. denied,* 482 U.S. 928 (1987); Pilon v. University of Minn., 710 F.2d 466, 32 FEP Cases 508 (8th Cir. 1983)(absent evidence of fraud or duress, court declined to adopt rule that even where waiver of Title VII rights is unambiguous, court must inquire

Tenth Circuits apply a "totality of the circumstances" standard.[12] The differences between the two tests may be more apparent than real. A close examination of the cases applying contract principles generally reveals a consideration of the circumstances surrounding the execution of the release[13] or a finding of a clear agreement entered into while the complainant was represented by counsel.[14]

Courts that apply the "totality of the circumstances" standard have found the following factors relevant:

> (1) the plaintiff's education and business experience, (2) the amount of time the plaintiff had possession of or access to the agreement before signing it, (3) the role of the plaintiff in deciding the terms of the agreement, (4) the clarity of the agreement, (5) whether the plaintiff was represented by or consulted with an attorney, (6) whether an employer encouraged or discouraged the plaintiff to consult an attorney, and (7) whether the plaintiff had a fair opportunity to consult an attorney.[15]

Congressional legislation in an analogous context[16] has suggested these general indicators of a knowing and voluntary waiver of an employment discrimination claim:

> (1) the waiver is part of an agreement between the individual and the employer that is written in a manner calculated to be understood by such individual or by the average individual;
>
> (2) the waiver specifically refers to statutory rights or claims;
>
> (3) the waiver does not apply to rights or claims that may arise after the date of the agreement;

---

into voluntariness of employee's consent); Runyan v. National Cash Register Corp., 787 F.2d 1039, 1044 n.10, 40 FEP Cases 807, 811 (6th Cir. 1986)(*en banc*)("In determining whether plaintiff knowingly and voluntarily waived his ADEA claims, we apply ordinary contract principles"), *cert. denied*, 479 U.S. 850 (1986).

[12]O'Hare v. Global Natural Resources, 898 F.2d 1015, 1016 (5th Cir. 1990); Coventry v. United States Steel Corp., 856 F.2d 514, 522, 47 FEP Cases 1560, 1566 (3d Cir. 1988)("In Title VII cases, the determination of whether a waiver has been 'knowingly and willfully' made has been predicated upon an evaluation of several indicia arising from the circumstances and conditions under which the release was executed"); Cirillo v. Arco Chem. Co., 862 F.2d 448, 48 FEP Cases 678 (3d Cir. 1988)(Becker, Stapleton & Greenberg, JJ.)(following *Coventry*); Bormann v. AT&T Communications, 875 F.2d 399, 49 FEP Cases 1622 (2d Cir. 1989)(adopting Third Circuit's "totality of the circumstances" standard), *cert. denied*, 110 S.Ct. 292 (1989); Torrez v. Public Serv. Co. of N.M., 908 F.2d 687, 53 FEP Cases 764 (10th Cir. 1990)(same).

[13]In *Coventry v. United States Steel Corp., supra* note 12, 856 F.2d at 522–23 n.9, 47 FEP Cases at 1567, the Third Circuit noted that while the Sixth Circuit in *Runyan, supra* note 11, had purported to apply contract principles, it really "considered other factors, among them the fact that plaintiff himself was a lawyer . . . knowledgeable in labor law and employment discrimination matters." In *Lancaster v. Buerkle Buick Honda Co., supra* note 11, the Eighth Circuit considered the fact that Lancaster had the agreement for five days, that it contained no ultimatums or deadlines, that it was clear and unambiguous, that Lancaster had input into its terms, and that Lancaster was a well-paid management employee who in his lifetime had signed numerous contracts.

[14]In *Pilon v. University of Minn., supra* note 11, the plaintiff was represented by an attorney, the release language was clear, and there was no evidence of fraud or duress. *See also* Riley v. American Family Mut. Ins. Co., 881 F.2d 368, 50 FEP Cases 668 (7th Cir. 1989)(settlement of sexual harassment case upheld absent evidence of fraud or duress where plaintiff was represented by experienced counsel).

[15]Riley v. American Family Mut. Ins. Co., *supra* note 14, 881 F.2d at 372, 50 FEP Cases at 671. For a slightly different listing of factors, see *EEOC v. American Express Publishing Corp.*, 681 F. Supp. 216, 219, 47 FEP Cases 1596, 1598–99 (S.D.N.Y. 1988)(identifying the additional factor of "whether the consideration given in exchange for the waiver exceeds employee benefits to which the employee was already entitled by contract or law").

[16]Older Workers Benefit Protection Act of 1990, Pub. L. No. 101-433 (1990)(amending Age Discrimination in Employment Act).

(4) the waiver is exchanged for consideration in addition to what the individual would already be entitled to receive;

(5) the individual is advised in writing to consult with an attorney prior to executing the agreement;

(6) the individual is given reasonable time in which to review the agreement.[17]

Courts have applied factors similar to these in determining whether to uphold challenged settlement agreements.[18] In *Cirillo v. Arco Chemical Co.,* Judge Walter K. Stapleton reproduced the release that employees were required

---

[17]This list reflects the Act's nontechnical requirements for assessing whether waivers under the Age Discrimination in Employment Act (ADEA) are knowing and voluntary. The Older Workers' Benefit Protection Act supersedes EEOC regulations on ADEA waivers. See 52 FED. REG. 32293, 32294 (Aug. 27, 1987)(proposed to be codified at 29 C.F.R. §1627.16(c)(1)–(3)), suspended by Act of Congress, Pub. L. No. 100-202, 101 STAT. 1329, 1329–31 (1987) and Pub. L. No. 100-459, 102 STAT. 2186, 2216 (1988). The relevant portions of the Act are to be codified at 29 U.S.C. §626(f)(1). Additional specific requirements are that the individual be advised to consult with an attorney, be given at least 21 days in which to consider the agreement, and be given the opportunity to revoke the agreement within seven days of executing it. *Id.*

[18]*Agreement upheld:*

Second Circuit: Bormann v. AT&T Communications, *supra* note 12, 875 F.2d at 403, 49 FEP Cases at 1625 (dismissal of ADEA claims upheld based upon district court's findings that appellants "were experienced executives familiar with reading and analyzing contracts," that "the release itself is written in clear and unambiguous language," that release specifically referred to age discrimination claims, that release stated that signer was aware of right to consult an attorney, that appellants had "sufficient time to consider the release," and that "there was no economic duress"; lack of opportunity to negotiate terms in and of itself did not require trial on issue of voluntariness).

Third Circuit: Cirillo v. Arco Chem. Co., *supra* note 12, 862 F.2d at 452–53, 48 FEP Cases at 681 (validity of release upheld even though plaintiff not represented by counsel; Cirillo was a "literate, well-educated man"; he had "ample period of time to deliberate about signing the release" where employees were not permitted to sign release for at least five days and Cirillo took considerably longer; release was "straightforward, clear and specific"; it "was presented to employees in a manner and context that signalled the importance of the matter, explained the nature of the claims that would be released, and counseled mature consideration with the help of an attorney").

Fifth Circuit: Rogers v. General Elec. Co., 781 F.2d 452, 39 FEP Cases 1581 (5th Cir. 1986)(affirming summary judgment predicated on finding that release in sex discrimination case was knowingly and voluntarily signed, since release was unambiguous and was labeled a release, plaintiff was advised both orally and in writing that she could consult an attorney and admitted that she had not been forced to sign release); Fulgence v. J. Ray McDermott & Co., 662 F.2d 1207, 27 FEP Cases 799 (5th Cir. 1989)(oral settlement agreement upheld where negotiated by attorney with plaintiff's approval and where there was no evidence of fraud, coercion, or overreaching or incompetence of counsel).

Sixth Circuit: Shaheen v. B.F. Goodrich Co., 873 F.2d 105, 49 FEP Cases 1060 (6th Cir. 1989)(release of ADEA claims upheld where plaintiff was given three months to decide among options and consulted with attorney; court found that release was supported by consideration independent of entitlements described in employee handbook); Runyan v. National Cash Register Corp., *supra* note 11, 787 F.2d at 1044, 40 FEP Cases at 811 (settlement upheld since Runyan was a "well-paid, well-educated, labor lawyer with many years of experience" who "tried to take advantage of the employer").

Seventh Circuit: Riley v. American Family Mut. Ins. Co., *supra* note 14, 881 F.2d at 373, 50 FEP Cases at 672 (settlement upheld where plaintiff signed unambiguous release, supported by consideration, while represented by counsel who actively negotiated its terms, despite fact that counsel may have inadequately conveyed effect of release or failed to adequately protect her rights, since latter may be remedied in malpractice action).

Eighth Circuit: Lancaster v. Buerkle Buick Honda, *supra* note 11, 809 F.2d at 541, 42 FEP Cases at 1473 (unambiguous release valid since Lancaster was a well-paid management employee with business experience who had executed many contracts, had five days to consider agreement, which had no ultimatums or deadlines, and who chose not to consult an attorney); Worthy v. McKesson Corp., 756 F.2d 1370, 37 FEP Cases 539 (8th Cir. 1985)(oral settlement agreement enforced where plaintiff represented by counsel who discussed settlement with him for more than an hour; court found that plaintiff had expressly agreed to a release of all claims and that other items, *e.g.,* confidentiality and no re-employment, were not so significant that they could be used to abrogate agreement); Pilon v. University of Minn., *supra* note 11 (affirming summary judgment that settlement agreement valid where waiver was unambiguous and plaintiff was represented by counsel).

Ninth Circuit: Stroman v. West Coast Grocery Co., 884 F.2d 458, 50 FEP Cases 1204 (9th Cir. 1989) (release of claims upheld despite absence of lawyers, court noting that agreement was unambiguous and that Stroman's army training and business management-related community college degree demonstrated he

to sign as a condition of receipt of an enhanced retirement package, characterizing it and its presentation as "well-designed."[19] The court stated that if the release were found to be an inadequate predicate for an effective waiver, "we would be hard-pressed to describe an adequate one."[20]

Settlement agreements and releases that are executed by an unrepresented complainant before litigation begins are more likely to be ruled invalid than agreements entered into by a represented complainant after a charge or complaint has been filed.[21] Particularly at the pre-litigation stage, employers who

---

possessed education and skills necessary to understand that he waived all legal claims), *cert. denied,* 59 U.S.L.W. 3247 (October 2, 1990).

Eleventh Circuit: Freeman v. Motor Convoy, 700 F.2d 1339, 31 FEP Cases 517 (11th Cir. 1983)(conciliation agreement binding upon employee who, although unrepresented by counsel, received advice from EEOC representative, read agreement, and obtained relief sought).

Agreement not upheld:

Third Circuit: Coventry v. United States Steel Corp., *supra* note 12, 856 F.2d at 524–25, 47 FEP Cases at 1568–69 (reversing district court finding that appellant had "knowingly and willfully" released age discrimination claims; appellant was given "Hobson's choice" of indefinite layoff or signing release to become entitled to early retirement, indicating choice was not free of duress, and there was no evidence that appellant had been encouraged to consult an attorney or that he had done so).

Fifth Circuit: Mosley v. St. Louis Sw. Ry., 634 F.2d 942, 24 FEP Cases 1366 (5th Cir.)(release held invalid where settlement terms did not address plaintiffs' discrimination claims and amounted to "precious little more" than promise of nonretaliation, which is statutory right, and where EEOC representative supervised execution of agreements even though she knew plaintiffs were represented by counsel, stating that to obtain benefit of agreements and avoid formal proceedings it was necessary that they sign immediately without conferring with counsel and intimating that if plaintiffs sued they might be held liable for attorney fees), *cert. denied,* 452 U.S. 906 (1981).

Sixth Circuit: Lyght v. Ford Motor Co., 643 F.2d 435, 25 FEP Cases 246 (6th Cir. 1981)(plaintiff's back-pay claims were not knowingly and voluntarily waived where plaintiff was unrepresented, did not participate in settlement negotiations, signed no release, and was never told that acceptance of promotion constituted waiver).

Tenth Circuit: Torrez v. Public Serv. Co. of N.M., *supra* note 12, 908 F.2d at 690, 53 FEP Cases at 766 (question of fact existed whether waiver was knowing and voluntary where employee stated that it did not occur to him that he was waiving possible discrimination claims, release did not mention employment discrimination, employee was high-school educated, unfamiliar with law and unrepresented, there was no opportunity to negotiate and unfair economic pressure may have existed).

[19]*Supra* note 12.

[20]The text of the release is as follows:

Notice: Various State and Federal laws prohibit employment discrimination based on age, sex, race, color, national origin, religion, handicap or veteran status. These laws are enforced through the Equal Opportunity Employment Commission (EEOC), Department of Labor and State Human Rights Agencies. If you feel that your election of the Atlantic Richfield Special Payment Allowance was coerced and is discriminatory, you are encouraged to speak with your Employee Relations representative or follow the steps described in the Employee Problem Resolution procedure. You may also want to discuss the following release language with your lawyer. In any event, you should thoroughly review and understand the effect of the release before acting on it. Therefore, please take this Release home and consider it for at least (5) working days before you decide to sign it.

General Release: In consideration for the Special Payment Allowance under the Atlantic Richfield Special Termination Plan offered to me by the Company I release and discharge the Company, its successors, subsidiaries, employees, officers, and directors (hereinafter referred to as the Company) from all claims, liabilities, demands, and causes of action known or unknown, fixed or contingent, which I may have or claim to have against the Company as a result of this termination, and do hereby covenant not to file a lawsuit to assert such claims. This includes but is not limited to claims arising under federal, state, or local laws prohibiting employment discrimination or claims growing out of any legal restrictions on the Company's rights to terminate its employees. This release does not have any effect on any claim I may have against the Company unrelated to this termination.

I have carefully read and fully understand all the provisions of this Separation Agreement and General Release which sets forth the entire agreement between me and the company and I acknowledge that I have not relied upon any representation or statement, written or oral, not set forth in this document.

Id. at 450, 48 FEP Cases at 679.

[21]An employer's unaccepted offer to "settle" all claims, made before any claims are actually asserted by a complainant, may possibly be admissible as evidence of discrimination, Rule 408 of the Federal Rules of Evidence notwithstanding. Cassino v. Reichhold Chems., 817 F.2d 1338, 47 FEP Cases 865 (9th Cir. 1987), *cert. denied,* 484 U.S. 1047 (1988). *Cf.* Mundy v. Household Fin. Corp., 885 F.2d 542 (9th Cir. 1989)(employer's unaccepted offer inadmissible under Rule 408, where it was made after termination of employment and employee had retained legal counsel).

seek to resolve sexual harassment claims in a binding fashion should (1) utilize a clear and unambiguous written release referring specifically to the sexual harassment claims; (2) allow the complainant a generous time period within which to consider whether to sign the agreement; (3) affirmatively encourage the complainant to consult with counsel, or, at a minimum, advise the complainant of the right to consult with an attorney and allow sufficient time for that to occur; and (4) respond accurately and completely to questions. It also will be helpful to retain a record of any negotiations regarding the language of the contract, in that complainant-suggested changes in the language or substance of an agreement clearly evidence the complainant's knowing and voluntary consent to it.

B. Prospective Waivers Are Invalid

In *Alexander v. Gardner-Denver Co.*,[22] the Supreme Court stated that "there can be no prospective waiver of an employee's rights under Title VII."[23] In *United States v. Allegheny-Ludlum Industries*,[24] the court upheld consent decrees in the steel industry but noted that "the release cannot preclude a suit for *any* form of appropriate relief for *subsequent* injuries caused by *future* acts or undertakings."[25] Accordingly, the court explained, defendants would be fully liable for any discrimination occurring after the dates of the releases executed by the employees.[26]

The settlement of a sexual harassment complaint should be entered into with full awareness that the employer will be liable for any future discrimination, including any future acts of harassment and retaliation against the complainant for pursuing the settled claim. Accordingly, an employer is well-advised to take appropriate steps to prevent retaliation and future acts of sexual harassment against the settling complainant.[27]

III. TERMS OF THE SETTLEMENT AGREEMENT

Careful crafting of the terms in the settlement agreement is critical for both the complainant and employer.[28]

A. The Defendant's Perspective

In almost all instances it is the complainant who challenges the validity of a settlement agreement or seeks to continue prosecution of claims that may appear to have been released. Accordingly, a settling employer should proceed

---

[22]415 U.S. 36, 7 FEP Cases 81 (1974).

[23]*Id.* at 51, 7 FEP Cases at 86.

[24]517 F.2d 826, 11 FEP Cases 167 (5th Cir. 1975), *cert. denied,* 425 U.S. 944 (1976).

[25]*Id.* at 854, 11 FEP Cases at 188 (emphasis added).

[26]*Id.* at 854–55, 11 FEP Cases at 188–89. *See also* Rogers v. General Elec. Co., *supra* note 18, 781 F.2d at 454, 39 FEP Cases at 1582 (release that waives prospective Title VII claims is invalid as violative of public policy); Williams v. Vukovich, 720 F.2d 909, 925, 33 FEP Cases 238, 251 (6th Cir. 1983)(consent decree containing waivers of future discrimination claims invalid).

[27]See Chapter 10, Retaliation, and Chapter 19, Responding to Internal Complaints.

[28]For a sample settlement agreement and general release, see B.L. SCHLEI & P. GROSSMAN, EMPLOYMENT DISCRIMINATION LAW 1553–58 (2d ed. 1983).

carefully to ensure that the scope of the release is as intended, that provisions establishing that the release was knowing and voluntary are included, and that other provisions protecting the employer's interests have been considered.

1. General and Special Releases

It is good practice to specify all statutory authority for the sexual harassment claims and all other possibly applicable claims covered by the release.[29] Failure to specify that statutory employment discrimination claims are being released may result in challenges that the complainant did not waive the claims knowingly and voluntarily.[30] If the parties are reluctant to specify the claims, well-drafted "standard" general release language may suffice.[31] If the employer feels that specifying claims in the release might "put ideas in the complainant's head," that is all the more reason to suspect that an unspecified release would not be executed knowingly.

It is also important that the release explicitly state whether it is a general release encompassing any and all claims of whatever nature.[32] Ambiguous or unusual language may result in a finding that the release covers a much narrower group of claims than the employer intended, and that the waiver is wholly or partially invalid.[33]

Clients should be specifically advised if there are any potential claims that, as a matter of law, may not be waived. For example, in certain states,

---

[29]For examples of release language, see *id.* at 1554–55 and note 20 *supra.*

[30]Torrez v. Public Serv. Co. of N.M., *supra* note 12, 908 F.2d at 690, 53 FEP Cases at 766 (material issues of fact precluded summary judgment in favor of defendant including fact that "[t]he language of the release, although clear and unambiguous, failed to mention specifically waiver of employment discrimination claims"); Mashman v. Universal Match Corp., 54 EPD ¶40,244 (E.D. Pa. 1989)(salesman's release of "all claims" rising out of employment did not bar age or handicap discrimination claims, which were not separately enumerated in release).

[31]*See* EEOC v. American Express Publishing Corp., *supra* note 15 (though issue of fact existed whether waiver was knowing and voluntary, court found release language itself did not suffer from ambiguity even though it did not explicitly mention that it was intended to apply to ADEA claims; "standard" general release language was utilized); Lancaster v. Buerkle Buick Honda Co., *supra* note 11, 809 F.2d at 540, 42 FEP Cases at 1472 (upholding release of ADEA claim despite fact that ADEA was not expressly mentioned in termination agreement; release extended to "each and every claim of any kind"); Stroman v. West Coast Grocery Co., *supra* note 18, 884 F.2d at 461, 50 FEP Cases at 1206 ("[A]n agreement need not specifically recite the particular claims waived in order to be effective").

[32]*See* Oglesby v. Coca-Cola Bottling Co., 620 F. Supp. 1336, 1341, 39 FEP Cases 327, 332 (N.D. Ill. 1985)(release of " 'any claim . . . with respect to employee benefits, insurance, salary or any other claim related to employment' may well be read as a release of claims limited to the types of emoluments of employment to which an employee is normally entitled . . . but not of claims related to allegedly illegal activity by the employer"; "on its face" the release was not "characterized as a 'general release,' nor is it phrased as such releases normally read").

[33]Kawatra v. Medgar Evers College, 700 F. Supp. 648 (E.D.N.Y. 1988)(while plaintiff relinquished right to initiate further suits, agreement did not explicitly address whether plaintiff was precluded from continuing then-pending complaints in judicial rather than administrative forum. "If the defendants wanted to make sure that the settlement agreement would bar any lawsuit growing out of the then-pending administrative proceedings, they could have made that crystal clear in the agreement. They did not. Accordingly, no such waiver will be inferred"); EEOC v. American Express Publishing Corp., *supra* note 15, 681 F. Supp. at 219 n.5, 47 FEP Cases at 1599 (summarizing collected cases as follows: "*Anderson v. Montgomery Ward & Co.,* 650 F. Supp. 1480, 1486, 47 FEP Cases 1455 (N.D. Ill. 1987)(waiver of 'all provisions of any compensation practices' could not be construed to apply to federal discrimination laws) [*vacated on other grounds,* 704 F. Supp. 162 (N.D. Ill. 1989)]; *Bernstein v. Consolidated Foods Corp.,* 662 F. Supp. 1096, 1106, 36 FEP Cases 1333 (N.D. Ill. 1984)(fact that agreement referred to 'right to renumeration' [sic] and 'compensation' rather than 'causes of action' or 'suits' creates genuine issue of material fact precluding summary judgment); *Oglesby v. Coca-Cola Bottling Co.,* 620 F. Supp. 1336, 1341, 39 FEP Cases 327, 332 (N.D. Ill. 1985)(release referring to 'any claim . . . with respect to employee benefits, insurance, salary or any other claim related to employment' was ambiguous, because it could reasonably be construed to relate only to employee benefits)").

workers' compensation claims may not be compromised without the approval of a workers' compensation judge. This is of particular concern in sexual harassment cases, because it is not uncommon for individuals who have been subjected to sexual harassment to seek workers' compensation benefits, especially in states that permit "stress claims."[34]

2. Dismissals and Withdrawals of Charges or Complaints

The settlement agreement should require that all pending litigation be dismissed with prejudice unless there is reason to except a specific matter from the scope of the settlement. If discrimination charges are pending before the EEOC or a state agency, the settlement agreement should require that the charging party submit a request for withdrawal,[35] with proof of submission provided to the defendant. Although withdrawal of an EEOC charge is not a matter of right, the EEOC's general policy is to permit the withdrawal of Title VII charges.[36] The requisite forms of pleadings for accomplishing the dismissal with prejudice of a lawsuit and withdrawals of pending charges should be prepared and agreed upon at the same time as the settlement agreement, and should be incorporated by reference into the agreement. It is advisable to include a provision that the complainant will execute such additional documents or take such actions as may reasonably be requested by the employer to accomplish any agreed-upon dismissals and withdrawals. In some instances, employers condition the payment of any sums upon receipt of a court order dismissing any pending case and upon receipt of approval from the EEOC and state agency of any requests for withdrawal.

3. Covenants Not to File Charges or to Assist in the Future Prosecution of Claims

In negotiating a settlement agreement, the employer will often bargain for a promise that the complainant will not cause any claim with the EEOC or any other federal, state, or local administrative agency to be filed on any matter related to the matters released in the settlement agreement. In *EEOC v. Cosmair,*[37] an employee filed a discrimination charge with the EEOC after executing a general release pursuant to which he had begun to receive severance payments to which he was not otherwise entitled. Cosmair ceased making payments, claiming that the employee breached the agreement by filing the charge. The employee then filed a retaliation charge. The EEOC, after finding that reasonable cause existed to believe that unlawful retaliation had occurred, filed for an injunction seeking, among other matters, an order barring Cosmair from continuing to refuse to pay severance. Judge Charles Clark found that the release did not, by its terms, bar the filing of the charge. Alternatively, however, the Fifth Circuit held that if the release had so provided, the waiver would

---

[34]For a discussion of workers' compensation claims based on sexual harassment, see Chapter 14, Workers' Compensation Statutes.

[35]The EEOC provides a form for requests for withdrawal. EEOC COMPL. MAN. §7, (BNA) p. 7:0005, reproduced in Appendix 4.

[36]*Id.* at 7:0001.

[37]821 F.2d 1085, 44 FEP Cases 569 (5th Cir. 1987)(Clark, Politz & Higginbotham, JJ.).

have been against public policy and therefore void. The court, in granting the requested preliminary injunction, reasoned that "[a]llowing the filing of charges to be obstructed by enforcing a waiver of the right to file a charge could impede EEOC enforcement of the civil rights laws."[38] The court, however, noted that while an agreement to waive the right to file a charge is void, the waiver of the employee's right to file suit and recover thereon, or to recover in a suit brought by the EEOC, is not void.[39]

Similar issues are raised by clauses containing a promise by the signatory employee not to counsel or assist in the prosecution of claims whether on behalf of the employee or others. The EEOC has successfully argued that such promises are contrary to public policy.[40]

4. Confidentiality

In sexual harassment cases, confidentiality clauses are frequently of substantial importance to the employer and the alleged harasser. Not only is there a desire to avoid adverse publicity, but employers also wish to discourage the filing of unmeritorious claims by others who hope to recover a monetary settlement.[41]

Confidentiality clauses should clearly define the scope of the obligation, specifying any exceptions such as disclosure for the purpose of obtaining tax or legal advice, disclosure in response to a court order, disclosure to enforce the settlement, or disclosure to the complainant's spouse. The settlement agreement should also oblige the complainant to instruct any individual who is permissibly advised about the settlement, including the complainant's counsel, to maintain the confidentiality of the information.

A confidentiality clause in a settlement agreement has limited value if the contents of the negotiations leading to the settlement have been widely discussed before execution of the agreement. Accordingly, at the commencement of negotiations, counsel for the defendant should consider advising the complainant's counsel that a term of considerable importance to the defendant is a representation by the complainant in the final agreement that the complainant has not discussed the negotiations with anyone other than counsel and other

---

[38]*Id.* at 1090, 44 FEP Cases at 573.

[39]*Id.* at 1091, 44 FEP Cases at 574. *But see* EEOC v. United States Steel Corp., 728 F. Supp. 1167 (W.D. Pa. 1989)(allowing recovery in action brought by EEOC).

[40]In *EEOC v. United States Steel Corp.,* 671 F. Supp. 351, 44 FEP Cases 1801 (W.D. Pa. 1987), the employer was enjoined from using and enforcing a provision in a release whereby an employee promised "not to counsel or assist in the prosecution of such claim whether on his behalf or on the behalf of others." *Id.* at 354, 44 FEP Cases at 1804. The court stated: "The mere possibility that this provision would deter individuals from participating in any ADEA claims is sufficient to render it violative of §4(d) [prohibiting retaliation] and public policy." *Id.* at 358, 44 FEP Cases at 1807. The court also found the promise of the employee not to file a claim under ADEA contrary to public policy, because the employee's pension benefits would be adversely affected if a claim were filed. *Id.* at 358–59, 44 FEP Cases at 1807–8. *But see* Hoffman v. United Telecommunication, 687 F. Supp. 1512 (D. Kan. 1988)(settlement with original named plaintiff in class action prohibited plaintiff from further participation in case, except that plaintiff could testify pursuant to subpoena; provision found lawful under circumstances given plaintiff's prior testimony, the many years case was pending, her availability to testify upon subpoena, and interest in settling her case and receiving monetary compensation).

[41]It may be difficult to negotiate a confidentiality provision if the EEOC is prosecuting the lawsuit. The EEOC General Counsel Memorandum, "Standards and Procedures for Consent Decrees and Settlement Agreements" (May 31, 1990) reprinted in 110 DAILY LAB. REP. (BNA) D-1, D-2 (June 7, 1990), provides: "Absent compelling circumstances, settlement of Commission civil actions must be made a matter of public record. All settlement *nondisclosure* provisions must be approved by the General Counsel."

agreed-upon individuals, if any. The complainant can then be counseled that negotiations should be kept confidential. In many instances, particularly if litigation has commenced, the parties should agree upon a statement[42] that they will use in response to questions about the matters resolved by the agreement.[43] To minimize any later dispute concerning what was said, employers should pre-record or read from a prepared text any statement they make to other employees. In appropriate high-visibility cases, a press release can be negotiated.

One of the concerns of defense counsel is the inability to effectively enforce compliance with a confidentiality clause once the complainant has received the agreed-upon monetary consideration. A liquidated damage clause can be negotiated as a deterrent to breach. In some agreements, payment of a portion of the monetary consideration is deferred to a future date and made subject to compliance with the terms of the agreement during the interim period.

If the employer is asked to agree to a confidentiality clause, the scope of the clause is again critical. Allowance must be made for reasonable intra-company communications and communications with third parties, including auditors, accountants, and legal counsel. Broad promises of confidentiality on behalf of all employees should not be made if the employer will be unable to ensure compliance. An alternative is to promise to instruct designated individuals to hold the matter in confidence.

5. Acknowledgment Concerning Legal Advice and Voluntariness

The agreement should reflect the fact that the complainant has consulted with an attorney, or, at a minimum, that the complainant is aware of the right to consult with an attorney and has had sufficient time to do so. If advice has been received from the EEOC or another agency, that fact should be reflected. The agreement should provide that the complainant has read the agreement, understands it, and is signing it voluntarily.

6. Additional Provisions

The agreement should state that it is not an admission of liability and that the settling defendants deny any wrongdoing and assert that they have at all times acted lawfully. Other commonly utilized provisions include an integration clause, a choice-of-law clause, an indemnity provision, a clause dealing with the subject of attorney's fees,[44] an "after-acquired facts" clause,[45] a clause

---

[42]*E.g.*, "The matter has been resolved to my satisfaction."

[43]It is most important that this statement be carefully crafted by counsel. For a discussion of the possibility of defamation actions arising out of allegations of sexual harassment, see Chapters 15, The Common Law; 19, Responding to Internal Complaints; and 24, The Alleged Harasser as Plaintiff.

[44]Ethical considerations can be presented by simultaneous negotiation of attorney's fees and the substantive terms of the settlement, resulting, for example, in an agreement that all parties are to bear their own attorney's fees and costs. *But see* Evans v. Jeff D., 475 U.S. 717, 40 FEP Cases 860 (1986)(class action settlement conditioned on waiver of fees does not violate Civil Rights Attorney's Fees Award Act of 1976, 42 U.S.C. §1988, and district court may approve consent decree with fee waiver provision, subject to state and local ethics considerations).

[45]In such a clause the parties acknowledge that additional facts may be acquired after entry into the settlement agreement and agree that the validity of the settlement will not be affected thereby.

providing for the severance of any unlawful provision and the continued validity of remaining provisions, and provisions for the resolution of any future
disputes concerning breach of the agreement, including the prevailing party's
entitlement to attorney's fees and the right of the defendant to respond with
an "offensive action" in the event a lawsuit is filed in breach of the settlement
agreement.[46] Arbitration clauses are being used with increasing frequency.

B. The Plaintiff's Perspective

1. General and Special Releases

Any claims that are to be excepted from the scope of the release should
be identified expressly and clearly; exception by implication should never be
relied upon. The complainant may also seek a release of all claims by the
employer or alleged harasser against the complainant. Because an employer
corporation does not have the authority to agree to a release of the individual
claims of its employees and agents, the agreement and signatures of specific
individuals should be obtained if the complainant wishes to obtain the release
of any claims, such as defamation, held by those individuals.

2. Monetary and Other Benefits

The time of payment should be clear. An acknowledgment of receipt,
which is incorporated in many standard forms of settlement agreements, should
never be signed until payment is actually received.

In sexual harassment cases, the negotiation of noncash benefits is often
particularly appropriate. If an employee has been or will be terminated, an
agreement that the employer pay the cost of COBRA continuation coverage
under the employer's medical plan for a specified time period, together with
other types of insurance coverage, can also be negotiated. Because many
medical plans do not provide for counseling or impose low maximum levels
on such benefits, it can be agreed that the employer will pay the cost of
counseling for the complainant and, in appropriate cases, for a spouse.[47]

It is also good practice for the settlement agreement to set forth the
complainant's statutory and contract entitlements if these matters have not

---

[46]The importance of preserving a right to sue for breach of a release was emphasized in *Isaacs v.
Caterpillar, Inc.*, 702 F. Supp. 711, 49 FEP Cases 607 (C.D. Ill. 1988), where plaintiffs signed a general
release in exchange for special payments but then filed suit for age discrimination, claiming the releases
were of no legal effect. Caterpillar counterclaimed for breach of the settlement agreement, seeking damages
in the amount of the special payments plus attorney's fees and costs. The court characterized the release as
purely "defensive" and dismissed the counterclaim, holding that Caterpillar should have drafted the release
to give it an "offensive" right of action in the event of a lawsuit if it wished to retain the right to sue for
damages. The court rejected Caterpillar's argument that this result would mean that it had received nothing
in exchange for its payments: "Caterpillar obtained Plaintiffs' departure from its employment, and it obtained
releases which, if valid, may be used to defend against litigation." *Id.* at 715, 49 FEP Cases at 610. In an
alternative holding, the court stated that the ADEA preempts any state law allowing recovery of damages
for breach of a defensive release, in that such a law would discourage ADEA plaintiffs from asserting their
rights.

[47]Other types of nonmonetary consideration vary greatly depending on the individual circumstances of
the complainant; these can include outplacement assistance, training, transfer, early retirement, relocation
assistance, and retention of company property after termination, including automobiles, car phones, club
memberships, computers, and computer software.

previously been resolved, including final wages, vacation pay, bonuses, post-termination commissions, and rights to continued insurance coverage.[48]

3. References

The wording of a reference letter can be negotiated and attached as an exhibit to the settlement agreement; the complainant should not rely on the employer's promise to prepare such a letter following the execution of the agreement. The complainant should ask the employer to prepare a draft of the letter in as positive a manner as possible, emphasizing the complainant's strengths; often the result is more persuasive than the letter that the complainant would have prepared. If the complainant cannot obtain a reference letter, the settlement agreement should provide that the employer will release no information other than the complainant's dates of employment and last position held.

C. Special Considerations Presented by Individual Defendants

Settlement agreements in sexual harassment cases often involve not only the employer and the complainant but also the alleged harasser. Difficult issues may arise if the employer wishes to settle when the alleged harasser does not, or when different views are held concerning settlement provisions. If defendants have conflicting settlement positions, separate representation may be advisable or necessary.[49]

IV. TAX CONSEQUENCES

The value of a monetary settlement to the plaintiff will be substantially greater if the employee is not required to pay taxes on all or a portion of the settlement. Thus, whether amounts paid pursuant to a settlement agreement are properly treated as income or can be excluded from income under the tax laws may be an important factor in the settlement negotiations.[50]

The Internal Revenue Code provides for exclusion from income of "damages received (whether by suit or agreement and whether as lump sums or as periodic payments) on account of personal injuries or sickness."[51] The Treasury Department has promulgated a regulation on the meaning of "damages" under the Code section: "The term 'damages received (whether by suit or agreement)' means an amount received (other than workmen's compensation)

---

[48]These preexisting entitlements are *not* consideration for the settlement agreement.

[49]See Chapter 23, The Alleged Harasser as Defendant.

[50]For more detailed discussions of the tax consequences of settlements of employment discrimination cases, see Kande, *Current Developments in Employment Litigation: Tax-Free Settlements of EEO Claims: A Reprieve,* 15 EMPL. REL. L.J. 577 (1990); Cuff, *Litigation Awards and Settlements,* L.A. LAW. 23 (June 1990); Ennis & Smolarek, *Tax Consequences of Court Awards and Settlement Payments Received in Employment Cases,* 6 LAB. LAW 395 (1990); Album & Joffe, *Tax Treatment of Settlement Payments in Employment Discrimination Cases,* 15 EMPL. REL. L.J. 209 (1989); Winslow, *Structured Settlements in Employment Litigation,* L.A. LAW. 19 (April 1988).

[51]I.R.C. §104(a)(2)(1990). Section 104(a) was recently amended by adding the following sentence: "Paragraph (2) shall not apply to any punitive damages in connection with a case not involving physical injury or physical sickness." Pub. L. No. 101-239, 103 STAT. 2106, 2379 (1989).

through prosecution of a legal suit or action based upon tort or tort type rights, or through a settlement agreement entered into in lieu of such prosecution."[52]

Whether settlement proceeds will be excluded from income depends upon the facts and the nature of the claim, not its effect or consequences. Thus, payments to settle a claim for lost income may not be taxable if the underlying claim is for tort or personal injury.[53]

The IRS has ruled that settlement payments under Title VII are includable as income and are to be treated as wages for purposes of FICA, FUTA, and income tax withholding.[54] The Tax Court has agreed, rejecting the taxpayer's argument that the purpose of Title VII is to assure recovery for personal injuries, and that the designation of the settlement amount as back pay is unimportant.[55]

Recently, however, circuit court decisions and at least one tax court decision have reflected a willingness to find amounts paid in settlement of civil rights and employment cases excludable from income. In *Rickel v. Commissioner,*[56] the Third Circuit held that the payments received by the taxpayer in settlement of his age discrimination lawsuit were excludable from income. After tracing the development of the law in this area and summarizing the relevant holdings of the circuit courts and the Tax Court,[57] Judge Robert E.

---

[52]Treas. Reg. §1.104-1(c)(as amended in 1970).

[53]*See* Threlkeld v. Commissioner, 848 F.2d 81, 84 (6th Cir. 1988), *aff'g* 87 T.C. 1294 (1986). Damages for malicious prosecution for damage to professional reputation were excludable from income as personal injury damages:

[W]e agree with the Ninth and the Third Circuit[s] that the nonpersonal consequences of a personal injury, such as a loss of future income are often the most persuasive means of proving the extent of the injury that was suffered, and that the personal nature of an injury should not be defined by its effect.

Similarly, the Tax Court stated:

[W]hether the damages received are paid on account of 'personal injuries' should be the beginning and the end of the inquiry. To determine whether the injury complained of is personal, we must look to the origin and character of the claim, and not to the consequences that result from the injury. No doubt a defamatory statement that injures a person's professional reputation will result in lost income. In such cases, the amount of income lost is an accurate measure of the damage sustained because of the injury to reputation. However, the extent to which income is decreased, even though this may be the best measure of loss, in no way changes the nature of the claim.

87 T.C. 1294, 1299 (citations omitted).

[54]*E.g.,* Rev. Rul. 72-341, 1972-2 C.B. 32 (payment in settlement of Title VII action that was based upon what earnings would have been absent discrimination are includable income and "wages" for purposes of FICA, FUTA, and federal income tax withholding); Rev. Rul. 72-572, 1972-2 C.B. 535 (amount paid in settlement of state discrimination complaint is "remuneration" for FICA and FUTA purposes and is subject to income tax withholding); Rev. Rul. 78-176, 1978-1 C.B. 303 (Title VII settlement payments to applicants who allegedly were wrongfully denied employment due to race discrimination are wages for FICA, FUTA, and income tax withholding).

[55]*See* Hodge v. Commissioner, 64 T.C. 616 (1975)(amounts received in settlement of Title VII race suit includable as income, noting complaint contained no allegations of personal injuries and formula used to arrive at settlement amount was based on pay disparities).

[56]900 F.2d 655, 52 FEP Cases 1389 (3d Cir. 1990)(Stoviter, Hutchinson & Cowen, JJ.), *aff'g in part and rev'g in part,* 92 T.C. 510 (1989).

[57]*See* Bent v. Commissioner, 835 F.2d 67 (3d Cir. 1987)(settlement payment received by taxpayer who contended his employment as teacher was terminated in violation of §1983 for exercise of First Amendment free speech was excludable from taxable income as damages received for personal injuries, though settlement based in part on lost wages), *aff'g* 87 T.C. 236 (1986); Byrne v. Commissioner, 883 F.2d 211, 46 FEP Cases 1372 (3d Cir. 1989)(payment in settlement of Fair Labor Standards Act retaliation claim that involved Equal Pay Act investigation and state-law claim for discharge in violation of public policy held excludable from income on basis claims were "tort-like"), *rev'g and remanding* 90 T.C. 1000 (1988); Thompson v. Commissioner, 866 F.2d 709, 48 FEP Cases 1649 (4th Cir. 1989), (award under Equal Pay Act taxable since "claim for back pay was essentially a contractual claim for accrued wages," but award of liquidated damages excludable from gross income as "compensation received through a tort or tort-type action for personal injuries"; "Sex discrimination actions in general are tort or tort-type actions and damages awarded for violation of that right are damages for personal injuries"), *aff'g* 89 T.C. 632 (1987). *Thompson* was distinguished by the court in *Rickel v. Commissioner, supra* note 56, 900 F.2d at 664 n.16, 52 FEP Cases at 1396.

Cowen held that an age discrimination claim is more analogous to a personal injury tort than to a breach-of-contract claim, and that the tortious nature of the claim, rather than the economic nature of its effects, should control "the nonpersonal, economic effects of the employer's act of discrimination, loss of wages, does [sic] not transform a personal tort type claim into one for nonpersonal injuries."[58]

In *Metzger v. Commissioner,*[59] the Tax Court considered the claim of a taxpayer who had received $75,000 in settlement of administrative charges of sex and national origin discrimination, and lawsuits alleging violations of Title VII, the Equal Pay Act, 42 U.S.C. §§1981, 1985(3) and 1986, a state employment discrimination statute, and breach of contract. The settlement agreement, without separately evaluating the causes of action, provided that $37,500 was in settlement of all wage claims (and thus taxable) and that the remaining $37,500 was in settlement of all claims other than wages (and thus not taxable). The Tax Court upheld this allocation on the ground that the violation of the taxpayer's constitutional and statutory right to be free from discrimination on the basis of sex and national origin was a claim for redress of personal injuries. Specifically, with regard to the Title VII claim, the court, noting that in *Johnson v. Railway Express Agency*[60] the Supreme Court had compared 42 U.S.C. §1981 and Title VII, reasoned that because §1981 claims are tort-like, both the plaintiff's §1981 and Title VII claims were for personal injuries.[61]

The extent to which the *Metzger* holding—that amounts paid in settlement of Title VII claims can be considered attributable to personal injuries and are excludable from income—will be followed by the Tax Court and the IRS is uncertain.[62]

In sexual harassment cases, common-law tort claims frequently accompany a statutory employment discrimination claim.[63] If consistent with the allegations in the case and the course of settlement negotiations, it is advisable to state expressly whether all or a portion of the settlement is allocable to the plaintiff's personal injury claims and to include a recitation of the tort claims being released.

If only a Title VII claim is settled, and if the settlement amount is measured by wage loss, it is currently uncertain whether a characterization of the claim as one for personal injury will be successful. The Sixth Circuit, in a split panel decision now pending review by the Supreme Court,[63a] has thrown its

---

[58]*Id.* at 662, 52 FEP Cases at 1394.

[59]88 T.C. 834, 44 FEP Cases 1505 (1987), *aff'd without published op.,* 845 F.2d 1013 (3d Cir. 1988).

[60]421 U.S. 454, 10 FEP Cases 817 (1975).

[61]Metzger v. Commissioner, *supra* note 59, 88 T.C. at 856, 44 FEP Cases at 1516.

[62]*See* Rickel v. Commissioner, *supra* note 56, 900 F.2d at 660 n.5, 52 FEP Cases at 1392 (noting inconsistency of Tax Court rulings in applying new *Threlkeld/Metzger* approach). In *Sparrow v. Commissioner,* T.C. Mem. 1989-315, 50 FEP Cases 197 (June 27, 1989), the Tax Court distinguished *Metzger* and noted that at least some of the statutes relied upon by the taxpayer in *Metzger* authorized recovery of damages for personal injuries. This reasoning is inconsistent with the reasoning of the court in *Metzger* concerning Title VII claims. In a private letter ruling, the IRS has stated that it has not acquiesced in the *Metzger* decision. Priv. Ltr. Rul. 8833014 (May 20, 1988).

[63]For a discussion of tort claims, see Chapter 15, The Common Law.

[63a]Burke v. United States, 929 F.2d 1119 (6th Cir. 1991)(Merritt & Jones, JJ., with Wellford, J., dissenting), *cert. granted,* 60 U.S.L.W. 3220 (Oct. 8, 1991)(granting review on whether damages received in settlement of Title VII suit are received " 'on account of personal injuries' " and thus excludable from gross income under IRC).

weight on the side of the taxpayer by ruling that the entire proceeds of a settlement of a Title VII claim for sex-based pay discrimination was not subject to tax. Judge Nathaniel R. Jones concluded for the panel majority that Title VII suits, like ADEA and other "tort type" suits, are suits for injury to the person.[64]

If a settlement amount from which no taxes were withheld is later found to constitute wage income, the necessary taxes will be due from both the employee and the employer. An employer can be held liable not only for the employer's portion of FICA and the required FUTA payments, but also for the employee's income taxes and FICA payment.[65] In addition, the parties are liable for interest payments and penalties.[66]

V. RULE 68 OFFERS OF JUDGMENT

A plaintiff who is confident of prevailing on at least some aspects of a case may have an incentive to litigate more speculative issues, with little incremental financial risk other than a diminution in the amount of attorney's fees to which the plaintiff will be entitled as the prevailing party.[67] Defendants can address this impediment to settlement with a Rule 68 offer of judgment.[68]

A Rule 68 offer allows the complainant to obtain judgment against the employer in a specified amount.[69] If a Rule 68 offer is not accepted within a period of ten days, it is deemed withdrawn, and subsequent settlement negotiations can proceed without reference to the offer of judgment. A Rule 68 offer of judgment need not be filed with the court unless accepted or until after trial, thereby not prejudicing the employer's case.

Rule 68 does not apply if the employer prevails.[70] However, where a complainant, in litigation following a Rule 68 offer of judgment, is insuffi-

---

[64]*Id.* at 1123–24.

[65]26 U.S.C. §§3403, 3102(b)(1990).

[66]26 U.S.C. §§6621, 6661 (1990).

[67]See Chapter 30, Attorney's Fees and Costs.

[68]Rule 68 of the Federal Rules of Civil Procedure provides:

At any time more than 10 days before the trial begins, a party defending against a claim may serve upon the adverse party an offer to allow judgment to be taken against him for the money or property or to the effect specified in his offer, with costs then accrued. If within 10 days after the service of the offer the adverse party serves written notice that the offer is accepted, either party may then file the offer and notice of acceptance together with proof of service thereof and thereupon the clerk shall enter judgment. An offer not accepted shall be deemed withdrawn and evidence thereof is not admissible except in a proceeding to determine costs. *If the judgment finally obtained by the offeree is not more favorable than the offer, the offeree must pay the costs incurred after the making of the offer.* The fact that an offer is made but not accepted does not preclude a subsequent offer. When the liability of one party to another has been determined by verdict or order or judgment, but the amount or extent of the liability remains to be determined by further proceedings, the party adjudged liable may make an offer of judgment, which shall have the same effect as an offer made before trial if it is served within a reasonable time not less than 10 days prior to the commencement of hearings to determine the amount or extent of liability. [Emphasis added.]

Most states have analogous provisions. *See, e.g.,* CAL. CODE CIV. PROC. §998 (Deering 1989).

[69]In *Marek v. Chesny,* 473 U.S. 1, 38 FEP Cases 124 (1985), the Supreme Court held that a Rule 68 offer can be made in one lump sum including attorney's fees, costs, and damages. A Rule 68 offer should specify whether it includes costs and attorney's fees. An offer silent on the question of fees may give the plaintiff an opportunity to accept the offer and later claim attorney's fees on the basis of being the prevailing party. One approach is to offer a specific dollar amount of substantive relief and in addition costs and reasonable attorney's fees in an amount to be set by the court.

[70]Delta Air Lines v. August, 450 U.S. 346, 25 FEP Cases 233 (1981). The *Delta* Court thus avoided the possibility of defendants routinely serving an offer of judgment for one cent and removing the discretion of

ciently successful—successful but in an amount less than the amount of the offer—the insufficiently successful plaintiff is not a "prevailing party." Accordingly, the plaintiff is not entitled to payment of post-offer costs and may not recover post-offer attorney's fees.[71]

Other effects of an improvident rejection of a Rule 68 offer is that by the language of Rule 68, the insufficiently successful plaintiff must pay the defendant's post-offer costs, and may be liable for the defendant's post-offer attorney's fees. Because §2000e-5(k) of Title VII states that reasonable attorney's fees may be "part of costs," a defendant can claim that its post-offer attorney's fees are part of the post-offer costs to which it is entitled under Rule 68 against an insufficiently successful plaintiff.[72]

A Rule 68 offer will not bar a Title VII plaintiff from amending the complaint to add non-Title VII claims, but the plaintiff may be subject to the operation of Rule 68 as to the Title VII claims in the original and amended complaint.[73]

The defendant may attempt to force the Rule 68 issue, in appropriate cases, by following its Rule 68 offer with a summary judgment motion that incorporates a partial confession of judgment on the same terms as the Rule 68 offer. If the motion succeeds, Rule 68 should entitle the defendant to post-offer costs (and deprive the plaintiff of an award for post-offer attorney's fees) just as if the plaintiff had been insufficiently successful at trial. The summary judgment in this context would be considered a judgment for the plaintiff.[74]

In comparing the offer of judgment with the final judgment, to determine whether the plaintiff has been sufficiently successful to avoid the effects of Rule 68, changes wrought by nonjudgment relief are irrelevant. This point may be important in sexual harassment actions where the plaintiff's lawsuit has induced the employer to modify its sexual harassment procedure but where that modification was not required by the final judgment.[75]

---

the Court to deny costs if the defendant prevailed. The Court also avoided the necessity of determining whether particular offers are "reasonable." However, the Court's decision in *Delta Air Lines* creates the anomalous result that a defendant who loses, but in an amount less than the Rule 68 offer, will recover its post-offer costs from the insufficiently successful plaintiff as a matter of right, whereas a defendant who prevails totally may, in the discretion of the trial court, be denied its costs.

[71]An insufficiently successful plaintiff may not recover post-offer attorney's fees where the underlying statute (42 U.S.C. §1988) defines recoverable "costs" to include attorney's fees. Marek v. Chesny, *supra* note 69, 473 U.S. at 7–8, 38 FEP Cases at 127–28.

[72]*See* Delta Air Lines v. August, *supra* note 70, 450 U.S. at 378–79, 25 FEP Cases at 245 (dissenting opinions).

[73]Ashby v. Butler County Memorial Hosp., 38 FEP Cases 1589, 1590 (W.D. Pa. 1985)(plaintiff did not act in bad faith by amending complaint to include claims under 42 U.S.C. §1981 following receipt of Rule 68 offer, but right to amend was conditioned upon Title VII claims in original and amended complaint being subject to operation of Rule 68).

[74]Liberty Mut. Ins. Co. v. EEOC, 691 F.2d 438, 35 FEP Cases 574 (9th Cir. 1982).

[75]Spencer v. General Elec. Co., 894 F.2d 651, 51 FEP Cases 1725 (4th Cir. 1990)(plaintiff who proved employer maintained sexually hostile environment and who served as catalyst for employer's voluntary development of comprehensive sexual harassment policy was prevailing party, but because judgment entailed no injunctive relief and payment of only one dollar, plaintiff was not entitled to fees incurred after defendant's Rule 68 offer of $10,000).

Part VI

APPENDICES

EEOC 1980 GUIDELINES ON SEXUAL HARASSMENT

Sec. 1604.11. Sexual Harassment

(a) Harassment on the basis of sex is a violation of Sec. 703 of Title VII. * Unwelcome sexual advances, requests for sexual favors, and other verbal or physical conduct of a sexual nature constitute sexual harassment when (1) submission to such conduct is made either explicitly or implicitly a term or condition of an individual's employment, (2) submission to or rejection of such conduct by an individual is used as the basis for employment decisions affecting such individual, or (3) such conduct has the purpose or effect of unreasonably interfering with an individual's work performance or creating an intimidating, hostile, or offensive working environment.

(b) In determining whether alleged conduct constitutes sexual harassment, the Commission will look at the record as a whole and at the totality of the circumstances, such as the nature of the sexual advances and the context in which the alleged incidents occurred. The determination of the legality of a particular action will be made from the facts, on a case by case basis.

(c) Applying general Title VII principles, an employer, employment agency, joint apprenticeship committee or labor organization (hereinafter collectively referred to as "employer") is responsible for its acts and those of its agents and supervisory employees with respect to sexual harassment regardless of whether the specific acts complained of were authorized or even forbidden by the employer and regardless of whether the employer knew or should have known of their occurrence. The Commission will examine the circumstances of the particular employment relationship and the job functions performed by the individual in determining whether an individual acts in either a supervisory or agency capacity.

(d) With respect to conduct between fellow employees, an employer is responsible for acts of sexual harassment in the workplace where the employer (or its agents or supervisory employees) knows or should have known of the conduct, unless it can show that it took immediate and appropriate corrective action.

(e) An employer may also be responsible for the acts of non-employees, with respect to sexual harassment of employees in the workplace, where the employer (or its agents or supervisory employees) knows or should have known of the conduct and fails to take immediate and appropriate corrective action. In reviewing these cases the Commission will consider the extent of the employer's control and any other legal responsibility which the employer may have with respect to the conduct of such non-employees.

(f) Prevention is the best tool for the elimination of sexual harassment. An employer should take all steps necessary to prevent sexual harassment from occurring, such as affirmatively raising the subject, expressing strong disapproval, developing appropriate sanctions, informing employees of their right to raise and how to raise the issue of harassment under Title VII, and developing methods to sensitize all concerned.

(g) Other related practices: Where employment opportunities or benefits are granted because of an individual's submission to the employer's sexual advances or requests for sexual favors, the employer may be held liable for unlawful sex discrimination against other persons who were qualified for but denied that employment opportunity or benefit.

---

*The principles involved here continue to apply to race, color, religion or national origin.

Reprinted from *Fair Employment Practices, Labor Relations Reporter,* The Bureau of National Affairs, Inc., Washington, D.C.

EEOC POLICY GUIDANCE ON EMPLOYER LIABILITY FOR SEXUAL FAVORITISM

Following is the text of an EEOC policy guide issued January 12, 1990, providing guidance to the Commission's field staff on the extent to which an employer should be held liable for discriminating against qualified individuals based on the employer's favoritism toward another individual who submitted to sexual advances or requests.

EEOC POLICY GUIDE

Subject Matter

Background

The Commission and the courts have declared that sexual harassment violates Section 703 of Title VII. *Meritor Savings Bank v. Vinson,* 477 U.S. 57, 64, 40 EPD ¶31,159 [40 FEP Cases 1822] (1986); EEOC's Guidelines on Discrimination Because of Sex, 29 C.F.R. §§1604.11(a). EEOC's Guidelines define two kinds of sexual harassment: "quid pro quo," in which "submission to or rejection of [unwelcome sexual] conduct by an individual is used as the basis for employment decisions affecting such individual," and "hostile environment," in which unwelcome sexual conduct "unreasonably interfer[es] with an individual's job performance" or creates an "intimidating, hostile or offensive working environment." 29 C.F.R. §§1604.11(a)(2) and (3).

Subsection (g) of EEOC's Guidelines provides:

> where employment opportunities or benefits are granted because of an individual's submission to the employer's sexual advances or requests for sexual favor, the employer may be held liable for unlawful sex discrimination against other persons who were qualified for but were denied that employment opportunity or benefit.

As discussed below, sexual favoritism in the workplace which adversely affects the employment opportunities of third parties may take the form of implicit "quid pro quo" harassment and/or "hostile work environment" harassment.

Discussion

A. Isolated Instances of Favoritism Towards a "Paramour" Not Prohibited

Not all types of sexual favoritism violate Title VII.[1] It is the Commission's position that Title VII does not prohibit isolated instances of preferential treatment based upon consensual romantic relationships. An isolated instance of favoritism toward a "paramour" (or a spouse, or a friend) may be unfair, but it does not discriminate against women or men in violation of Title VII, since both are disadvantaged for reasons other than their genders.[2] A female charging party who is denied an employment benefit because of such sexual favoritism would not have been treated more favorably had she been a man nor, conversely, was she treated less favorably because she was a woman. *See Miller v. Aluminum Co. of America,* 679 F.Supp. 495, 47 EPD ¶38,112 [45 FEP Cases 1775] (W.D. Pa.), *aff'd mem.,* 856 F.2d 184 (3d Cir. 1988);[3]

---

[1] The material in §615 of the Compliance Manual on subsection (g) of the Guidelines (at pp. 615-10 and 11) is superseded by this Policy Guidance.

[2] *See Benzies v. Illinois Dept. of Mental Health,* 810 F.2d 146, 148, 39 EPD ¶35,870 [42 FEP Cases 1537] (7th Cir.), *cert. denied,* 107 S.Ct. 3231 [43 FEP Cases 1896] (1987) (denial of promotion to woman is not violation if motivated by personal or political favoritism or a grudge); *Bellissimo v. Westinghouse Electric Corp.,* 764 F.2d 175, 180, 37 EPD ¶35,315 [37 FEP Cases 1862] (3d Cir. 1985), *cert. denied,* 475 U.S. 1035, 39 EPD ¶35,875 [40 FEP Cases 192] (1986) (discharge of female employee violates Title VII only if it is done on a basis that would not result in the discharge of a male employee).

[3] The plaintiff in *Miller* alleged that her supervisor treated her less favorably than her co-worker because the supervisor knew that the co-worker was engaged in a romantic relationship with the plant manager. *Miller,* 679 F.Supp. at 500-01. The lower court held that in order to establish a Title VII

Reprinted from *Fair Employment Practices, Labor Relations Reporter,* The Bureau of National Affairs, Inc., Washington, D.C.

DeCintio v. Westchester County Medical Center 807 F.2d 304, 42 EPD ¶36,785 [42 FEP Cases 921] (2d Cir. 1986), *cert. denied*, 108 S.Ct. 89, 44 EPD ¶37,425 (1987).[4] *But see King v. Palmer*, 778 F.2d 878, 39 EPD ¶35,808, [39 FEP Cases 877] *reh'g denied*, 39 EPD ¶36,036 [40 FEP Cases 190] (D.C. Cir. 1985).[5]

---

claim, the plaintiff would have to show that her employer would have or did treat males differently. *Id.* at 501. Since the plaintiff's male co-workers shared with her the same disadvantage relative to the co-worker who was engaged in the affair with the manager, the plaintiff could not show that she was treated differently than males. *Id.* On appeal to the Third Circuit, the Commission filed an amicus brief supporting the ruling of the district court on the basis that favoritism toward a female employee because of a consensual romantic relationship with a male supervisor is not sex discrimination against other female employees within the meaning of Title VII. The Court of Appeals summarily affirmed.

[4]In *DeCintio*, seven male respiratory therapists claimed that they were unlawfully disqualified for a promotion that went to a woman who was engaged in a romantic relationship with the department administrator. The court held that the department administrator's conduct, though unfair, did not violate Title VII. *DeCintio*, 807 F.2d at 308. The court reasoned that the prohibition of sex discrimination in Title VII refers to discrimination on the basis of one's sex, not on the basis of one's sexual affiliations; the therapists' claims were not cognizable under the Act since they were denied promotion because the administrator preferred his "paramour," rather than because of their status as males. *Id.* The court distinguished EEOC's Guidelines by stating that they address the granting of employment benefits because of an individual's "submission" to sexual advances or requests, and the word "submission" connotes a lack of consent. Since the department administrator did not force anyone to submit to sexual advances in order to win promotion, his conduct was not within the purview of the Guidelines. *Id.* at 307-08. *Accord, Handley v. Phillips*, 715 F.Supp. 657, 675, (M.D. Pa. 1989).

[5]In *King*, the plaintiff claimed she had been denied a promotion that went to a less qualified co-worker who was engaged in an intimate relationship with the selecting official. Although the issue of whether Title VII applied to preferential treatment was not raised on appeal, the court stated that it agreed with the lower court's conclusion that the case was within the purview of Title VII. *King*, 778 F.2d at 880. The court ruled in favor of the plaintiff on the basis of its finding that her co-worker was promoted because of the sexual relationship. *Id.* at 882. In a concurring opinion to the decision denying a suggestion for rehearing *en banc*, it was emphasized that the issue of whether Title VII applied to the facts of the case was

B. Favoritism Based Upon Coerced Sexual Conduct May Constitute Quid Pro Quo Harassment

If a female employee[6] is coerced into submitting to unwelcome sexual advances in return for a job benefit, other female employees who were qualified for but were denied the benefit may be able to establish that sex was generally made a condition for receiving the benefit.[7] Thus, in order for a woman to have obtained the job benefit at issue, it would have been necessary to grant sexual favors, a condition that would not have been imposed on men. This is substantially the same as a traditional sexual harassment charge alleging that sexual favors were implicitly demanded as a "quid pro quo" in return for job benefits.[8] For example, in *Toscano v. Nimmo*, 570 F.Supp. 1197, 1199-1201, 32 EPD ¶33,848 [32 FEP Cases 1401] (D. Del. 1983), the court found a violation of Title VII based on the fact that the granting of sexual favors was a condition for promotion. Although the individual who was granted preferential treatment was engaged in a consensual affair with her supervisor, there was evidence that the supervisor made telephone calls to proposition several female employees at home, phoned employees at work to describe his supposed sexual encounters with female em-

---

not raised on appeal or in the petition for rehearing. 39 EPD ¶36,036.

[6]Although this Policy Guidance uses female pronouns to refer to individuals who are treated favorably because they engage in sexual conduct, it also covers situations in which men are granted favorable treatment based on sexual conduct.

[7]The employer would also be liable for "quid pro quo" harassment with regard to the individual who was coerced into submitting to the advances.

[8]*See* Section 1604.11(1) of EEOC's Guidelines on Sexual Harassment, which states that a violation will be found when submission to unwelcome sexual conduct is made "either explicitly or implicitly" a term or condition of an individual's employment.

ployees under his supervision, and engaged in suggestive behavior at work.[9]

Many times, a third party female will not be able to establish that sex was generally made a condition for the benefit in question. For example, a supervisor may have been interested in only one woman and, thus, have coerced only her. Nevertheless, in such a case, both women and men who were qualified for but were denied the benefit would have standing to challenge the favoritism on the basis that they were injured as a result of the discrimination leveled against the woman who was coerced. *See* EEOC amicus brief (filed Sept. 30, 1988) in *Clayton v. White Hall School District*, 875 F.2d 676, 50 EPD ¶39,048 [49 FEP Cases 1618] (8th Cir. 1989), in which the Commission argued that a white employee had standing under Title VII to challenge her employer's decision to deny her an employment benefit pursuant to an employment policy which it allegedly enforced for the purpose of denying the same benefit to a black employee; although the plaintiff was not the object of racial discrimination, she was injured as a result of the race discrimination practiced against the black employee.[10] *See also DeCintio v. Westchester County Medical Center*, 807 F.2d at 307-08 (by implication) (male plaintiffs' claims of favoritism rejected not because of lack of standing but because the woman who received the favorable treatment was not coerced into submitting to sexual advances); *EEOC v. T.I.M.E.-D.C. Freight, Inc.*, 659 F.2d 690 n.2, 27 EPD ¶32,202 [27 FEP Cases 10] (5th Cir. 1981) (white plaintiffs could challenge discrimination against blacks provided that they could establish a personal injury); *Allen v. American Home Foods, Inc.*, 644 F.Supp. 1553, 42 EPD ¶36,911 [42 FEP Cases 407] (N.D. Ind. 1986) (males who lost their jobs due to their employer's discrimination against female coworkers suffered an injury as a result of the discrimination, and therefore had standing to sue under Title VII).

C. Widespread Favoritism May Constitute Hostile Environment Harassment

If favoritism based upon the granting of sexual favors is widespread in a workplace, both male and female colleagues who do not welcome this conduct can establish a hostile work environment in violation of Title VII regardless of whether any objectionable conduct is directed at them and regardless of whether those who were granted favorable treatment willingly bestowed the sexual favors. In these circumstances, a message is implicitly conveyed that the managers view women as "sexual playthings," thereby creating an atmosphere that is demeaning to women. Both men and women who find this offensive can establish a violation if the conduct is "sufficiently severe or pervasive 'to alter the conditions of [their] employment and create an abusive working environment.'" *Vinson*, 477 U.S. at 67, [quoting *Henson v. City of Dundee*, 682 F.2d 897, 904, 29 EPD ¶32,993 [29 FEP Cases 787] (11th Cir. 1982)),.[11] An analogy can be made to a situation in which supervisors in an office regularly

---

[9]*See also DeCintio v. Westchester County Medical Center*, 807 F.2d at 307, in which the court stated that the claim in *Toscano* was premised on the coercive nature of the employer's acts, and therefore that the case lent no support to the contention that a voluntary amorous involvement may form the basis of a Title VII claim.

[10]In *Clayton*, the court ruled that the plaintiff did have standing, but it based that standing on her allegation of a hostile work environment. 875 F.2d at 679.

[11]*See* EEOC's Policy Guidance on Current Issues of Sexual Harassment (10/25/88) at 13-18 for standards governing the determination of whether a work environment is "hostile." That Policy Guidance makes clear that the commission will evaluate the totality of circumstances or a case-by-case basis, employing the objective perspective of a "reasonable person" in the context in which the challenged conduct took place. Some factors that could be considered in determining whether a hostile environment is established are the number of incidents of favoritism, the egregiousness of the incidents, and whether or not other employees in the office were made aware of the conduct.

make racial, ethnic or sexual jokes. Even if the targets of the humor "play along" and in no way display that they object, co-workers of any race, national origin or sex can claim that this conduct, which communicates a bias against protected class members, creates a hostile work environment for them. *See Rogers v. EEOC*, 454 F.2d 234, 4 EPD ¶7597 [4 FEP Cases 92] (5th Cir. 1971), *cert. denied*, 406 U.S. 957, 4 EPD ¶7838 [4 FEP Cases 771] (1972) (discriminatory treatment of medical patients created hostile work environment for plaintiff employee); Commission Decision No. 71-969, CCH EEOC Decisions (1973) ¶6193 (supervisor's habitual use of racial epithet in referring to Black employees created discriminatory work environment for White Charging Party); Compliance Manual Volume II, Section 615.3(a)(3) Examples (1) and (2) (sexual harassment of females may create hostile work environment for other male and female employees).

Managers who engage in widespread sexual favoritism may also communicate a message that the way for a woman to get ahead in the workplace is by engaging in sexual conduct or that sexual solicitations are a prerequisite to their fair treatment.[12] This can form the basis of an implicit "quid pro quo" harassment claim for female employees, as well as a hostile environment claim for both women and men who find this offensive.[13]

---

[12]*See, e.g., Priest v. Rotary*, 634 F.Supp. 571, 39 EPD ¶35,897 [40 FEP Cases 208] (N.D. Cal. 1986), in which the defendant gave preferential treatment to his consensual sexual partner and to those female employees who reacted favorably to his sexual advances and other conduct of a sexual nature, and he disadvantaged those employees, including the plaintiff, who reacted unfavorably to his conduct. The court found a violation of Title VII in part because the defendant's conduct implied that job benefits would be conditioned on an employee's good-natured endurance of his sexually-charged conduct or sexual advances. *Id.* at 581.

[13]In *Miller v. Aluminum Co. of America*, 679 F.Supp. at 501-502, the court rejected a claim that sexual favoritism based on a consensual relationship can create a hostile environment for others in the workplace. The court found that the favoritism itself

The case of *Broderick v. Ruder*, 685 F.Supp. 1269, 46 EPD ¶37,963 [48 FEP Cases 232] (D.D.C. 1988) illustrates how widespread sexual favoritism can be found to violate Title VII. In *Broderick* a staff attorney at the Securities and Exchange Commission alleged that two of her supervisors had engaged in sexual relationships with two secretaries who received promotions, cash awards, and other job benefits. Another of her supervisors allegedly promoted the career of a staff attorney with whom he socialized extensively and to whom he was noticeably attracted. In addition, there were isolated instances of sexual harassment directed at the plaintiff herself, including an incident in which her supervisor became drunk at an office party, untied the plaintiff's sweater, and kissed her. The court found that the conduct of these supervisors "created an atmosphere of hostile work environment" offensive to the plaintiff and several other witnesses. It further stated that the supervisors' conduct in bestowing preferential treatment upon those who submitted to their sexual advances undermined the plaintiff's motivation and work performance and deprived her and other female employees of promotions and job opportunities. *Broderick*, 685 F.Supp. at 1278. While the court in *Broderick* grounded its ruling on the hostile environment theory, it is the Commission's position that these facts could also support an implicit "quid pro quo" harassment claim since the managers, by their conduct, communicated a message to all female employees in the office that job benefits would be awarded to those who participated in

did not violate Title VII since it was voluntary, and that "[h]ostile behavior that does not bespeak an unlawful motive cannot support a hostile work environment claim." *Id.* at 502. However, it is the Commission's position that had the sexual favoritism been widespread, the fact that it was exclusively voluntary and consensual would not have defeated a claim that it created a hostile work environment for other people in the workplace. As indicated above in n.11, the question of whether actions complained of are sufficiently widespread or egregious to constitute a hostile environment must be decided case-by-case.

sexual conduct. *See also Spencer v. General Electric*, 697 F.Supp. 204 (E.D. Va. 1988).[14]

Example 1 — Charging Party (CP) alleges that she lost a promotion for which she was qualified because the co-worker who obtained the promotion was engaged in a sexual relationship with their supervisor. EEOC's investigation discloses that the relationship at issue was consensual and that the supervisor had never subjected CP's co-worker or any other employees to unwelcome sexual advances. The Commission would find no violation of Title VII in these circumstances, because men and women were equally disadvantaged by the supervisor's conduct for reasons other than their genders. Even if CP is genuinely offended by the supervisor's conduct, she has no Title VII claim.

Example 2 — Same as above, except the relationship at issue was *not* consensual. Instead, CP's supervisor regularly harassed the co-worker in front of other employees, demanded sexual favors as a condition for her promotion, and then audibly boasted about his "conquest." In these circumstances, CP may be able to establish a violation of Title VII by showing that in order to have obtained the promotion, it would have been necessary to grant sexual favors. In addition, she and other qualified men and women who were denied the promotion would have standing to challenge the favoritism on the basis that they were injured as a result of the discrimination levelled against their co-worker.

Example 3 — Same as Example 1, except CP's supervisor and other management personnel regularly solicited sexual favors from subordinate employees and offered job opportunities to those who complied. Some of those employees willingly consented to the sexual requests and in turn received promotions and awards. Others consented because they recognized that their opportunities for advancement would otherwise be limited. CP, who did not welcome this conduct, was not approached for sexual favors. However, she and other female and male co-workers may be able to establish that the conduct created a hostile work environment. She can also claim that by their conduct, the managers communicated to all female employees that they can obtain job benefits only by acquiescing in sexual conduct.

Date: 1/12/90   Approved: _____

Clarence Thomas
Chairman

---

[14]In *Spencer*, the supervisor of an office engaged in virtually daily horseplay of a sexual nature with female subordinates. This behavior included sitting on their laps, touching them in an intimate manner, and making lewd comments. The subordinates joined in and generally found the horseplay funny and inoffensive. With the exception of one incident (which may have been time-barred and was not critical to the court's decision), none of the horseplay was directed at the plaintiff. The supervisor additionally engaged in consensual relations with at least two of his subordinates. The court found that the supervisor's conduct would have interfered with the work performance and would have seriously affected the psychological well-being of a reasonable employee, and on that basis it found a violation of Title VII. 697 F.Supp. at 218. Although *Spencer* did not involve sexual favoritism, the case supports the proposition that pervasive sexual conduct can create a hostile work environment for those who find it offensive even if the targets of the conduct welcome it and even if no sexual conduct is directed at the persons bringing the claim.

EEOC Policy Guidance on Current Issues
of Sexual Harassment

Following is the text of a March 19, 1990, policy guide issued to EEOC field office personnel that defines sexual harassment and establishes employer liability in light of recent court decisions. This policy statement replaces one issued October 17, 1988.

EEOC POLICY GUIDANCE

Subject Matter

This document provides guidance on defining sexual harassment and establishing employer liability in light of recent cases.

Section 703(a)(1) of Title VII, 42 U.S.C. §2000e-2(a) provides:

> It shall be an unlawful employment practice for an employer —
>
> ... to fail or refuse to hire or to discharge any individual, or otherwise to discriminate against any individual with respect to his compensation, terms, conditions, or privileges of employment, because of such individual's race, color, religion, sex, or national origin[.]

In 1980 the Commission issued guidelines declaring sexual harassment a violation of Section 703 of Title VII, establishing criteria for determining when unwelcome conduct of a sexual nature constitutes sexual harassment, defining the circumstances under which an employer may be held liable, and suggesting affirmative steps an employer should take to prevent sexual harassment. *See* Section 1604.11 of the Guidelines on Discrimination Because of Sex, 29 C.F.R. §1604.11 ("Guidelines") [403:213]. The Commission has applied the Guidelines in its enforcement litigation, and many lower courts have relied on the Guidelines.

The issue of whether sexual harassment violates Title VII reached the Supreme Court in 1986 in *Meritor Savings Bank v. Vinson,* 106 S.Ct. 2399, 40 EPD ¶36,159 [40 FEP Cases 1822] (1986). The Court affirmed the basic premises of the Guidelines as well as the Commission's definition. The purpose of this document is to provide guidance on the following issues in light of the developing law after *Vinson:*

— determining whether sexual conduct is "unwelcome;"

— evaluating evidence of harassment;

— determining whether a work environment is sexually "hostile;"

— holding employers liable for sexual harassment by supervisors; and

— evaluating preventive and remedial action taken in response to claims of sexual harassment.

BACKGROUND

A. Definition

Title VII does not proscribe all conduct of a sexual nature in the workplace. Thus it is crucial to clearly define sexual harassment: only unwelcome sexual conduct that is a term or condition of employment constitutes a violation. 29 C.F.R. §1604.11(a). The EEOC's Guidelines define two types of sexual harassment: "quid pro quo" and "hostile environment." The Guidelines provide that "unwelcome" sexual conduct constitutes sexual harassment when "submission to such conduct is made either explicitly or implicitly a term or condition of an individual's employment," 29 C.F.R. §1604.11(a)(1). "Quid pro quo harassment" occurs when "submission to or rejection of such conduct by an individual is used as the basis for employment decisions affecting such individual," 29 C.F.R. §1604.11(a)(2).[1] The EEOC's

---

[1]*See, e.g., Miller v. Bank of America,* 600 F.2d 211, 20 EPD ¶30,086 [20 FEP Cases 462] (9th Cir. 1979) (plaintiff discharged when she refused to cooperate with her supervisor's sexual advances); *Barnes v. Costle,* 561 F.2d 983, 14 EPD ¶7755 [15 FEP Cases 345] (D.C. Cir. 1977) (plaintiff's job abolished after

Reprinted from *Fair Employment Practices, Labor Relations Reporter,* The Bureau of National Affairs, Inc., Washington, D.C.

Guidelines also recognize that unwelcome sexual conduct that "unreasonably interfer[es] with an individual's job performance" or creates an "intimidating, hostile, or offensive working environment" can constitute sex discrimination, even if it leads to no tangible or economic job consequences. 29 C.F.R. §1604.11 (a)(3).[2] The Supreme Court's decision in *Vinson* established that both types of sexual harassment are actionable under section 703 of Title VII of the Civil Rights Act of 1964, 42 U.S.C. §2000e-2(a), as forms of sex discrimination.

Although "quid pro quo" and "hostile environment" harassment are theoretically distinct claims, the line between the two is not always clear and the two forms of harassment often occur together. For example, an employee's tangible job conditions are affected when a sexually hostile work environment results in her constructive discharge.[3] Similarly, a supervisor who makes sexual advances toward a subordinate employee may

communicate an implicit threat to adversely affect her job status if she does not comply. "Hostile environment" harassment may acquire characteristics of "quid pro quo" harassment if the offending supervisor abuses his authority over employment decisions to force the victim to endure or participate in the sexual conduct. Sexual harassment may culminate in a retaliatory discharge if a victim tells the harasser or her employer she will no longer submit to the harassment, and is then fired in retaliation for this protest. Under these circumstances it would be appropriate to conclude that both harassment and retaliation in violation of section 704(a) of Title VII have occurred.

Distinguishing between the two types of harassment is necessary when determining the employer's liability (*see infra* Section D). But while categorizing sexual harassment as "quid pro quo," "hostile environment," or both is useful analytically these distinctions should not limit the Commission's investigations,[4] which generally should consider all available evidence and testimony under all possibly applicable theories.[5]

---

she refused to submit to her supervisor's sexual advances); *Williams v. Saxbe*, 413 F.Supp. 665, 11 EPD 10,840 [12 FEP Cases 1093] (D.D.C. 1976), *rev'd and remanded on other grounds sub nom. Williams v. Bell*, 587 F.2d 1240, 17 EPD ¶8605 [17 FEP Cases 1662] (D.C. Cir. 1978), *on remand sub nom. Williams v. Civiletti*, 487 F.Supp. 1387, 23 EPD ¶30,916 [22 FEP Cases 1311] (D.D.C. 1980) (plaintiff reprimanded and eventually terminated for refusing to submit to her supervisor's sexual demands).

[2]*See, e.g., Katz v. Dole,* 709 F.2d 251, 32 EPD ¶33,639 [31 FEP Cases 1521] (4th Cir. 1983) (plaintiff's workplace pervaded with sexual slur, insult, and innuendo and plaintiff subjected to verbal sexual harassment consisting of extremely vulgar and offensive sexually related epithets); *Henson v. City of Dundee,* 682 F.2d 897, 29 EPD ¶32,993 [29 FEP Cases 787] (11th Cir. 1982) (plaintiff's supervisor subjected her to numerous harangues of demeaning sexual inquiries and vulgarities and repeated requests that she have sexual relations with him); *Bundy v. Jackson,* 641 F.2d 934, 24 EPD ¶31,439 [24 FEP Cases 1155] (D.C. Cir. 1981) (plaintiff subjected to sexual propositions by supervisors, and sexual intimidation was "standard operating procedure" in workplace).

[3]To avoid cumbersome use of both masculine and feminine pronouns, this document will refer to harassers as males and victims as females. The Commission recognizes, however, that men may also be victims and women may also be harassers.

[4]For a description of the respective roles of the Commission and other federal agencies in investigating complaints of discrimination in the federal sector, *see* 29 C.F.R. §1613.216. [403:692]

[5]In a subsection entitled "Other related practices," the Guidelines also provide that where an employment opportunity or benefit is granted because of an individual's "submission to the employer's sexual advances or requests for sexual favors," the employer may be liable for unlawful sex discrimination against others who were qualified for but were denied the opportunity or benefit. 29 C.F.R. §1604.11(g). The law is unsettled as to when a Title VII violation can be established in these circumstances. *See DeCintio v. Westchester County Medical Center,* 807 F.2d 304, 42 EPD ¶36,785 [42 FEP Cases 921] (2d Cir. 1986), *cert. denied,* 108 S.Ct. 89, 44 EPD ¶37,425 (1987); *King v. Palmer,* 778 F.2d 878, 39 EPD ¶35,808 [39 FEP Cases 877] (D.C. Cir. 1985), *decision on remand,* 641 F.Supp. 186, 40 EPD ¶36,245 (D.D.C. 1986); *Broderick v. Ruder,* 46 EPD ¶37,963 [48 FEP Cases 232] (D.D.C. 1988); *Miller v. Aluminum Co. of America,* 679 F.Supp. 495, 500-01 [45 FEP Cases 1775] (W.D. Pa.), *aff'd mem.,* No. 88-3099 (3d Cir. 1988). However, the Commission recently analyzed the is-

B. Supreme Court's Decision in Vinson

Meritor Saving Bank v. Vinson posed three questions for the Supreme Court:

(1) Does unwelcome sexual behavior that creates a hostile working environment constitute employment discrimination on the basis of sex;

(2) Can a Title VII violation be shown when the district court found that any sexual relationship that existed between the plaintiff and her supervisor was a "voluntary one"; and

(3) Is an employer strictly liable for an offensive working environment created by a supervisor's sexual advances when the employer does not know of, and could not reasonably have known of, the supervisor's misconduct.

1) Facts — The plaintiff had alleged that her supervisor constantly subjected her to sexual harassment both during and after business hours, on and off the employer's premises; she alleged that he forced her to have sexual intercourse with him on numerous occasions, fondled her in front of other employees, followed her into the women's restroom and exposed himself to her, and even raped her on several occasions. She alleged that she submitted for fear of jeopardizing her employment. She testified, however, that this conduct had ceased almost a year before she first complained in any way, by filing a Title VII suit; her EEOC charge was filed later (*see infra* at n.34). The supervisor and the employer denied all of her allegations and claimed they were fabricated in response to a work dispute.

2) Lower Courts' Decisions — After trial, the district court found the plaintiff was not the victim of sexual harassment and was not required to grant sexual favors as a condition of employ-

sues in its "Policy Guidance on Employer Liability Under Title VII for Sexual Favoritism" dated January 1990.

ment or promotion. *Vinson v. Taylor*, 22 EPD ¶30,708 [23 FEP Cases 37] (D.D.C. 1980). Without resolving the conflicting testimony, the district court found that if a sexual relationship had existed between plaintiff and her supervisor, it was "a voluntary one ... having nothing to do with her continued employment." The district court nonetheless went on to hold that the employer was not liable for its supervisor's actions because it had no notice of the alleged sexual harassment; although the employer had a policy against discrimination and an internal grievance procedure, the plaintiff had never lodged a complaint.

The court of appeals reversed and remanded, holding the lower court should have considered whether the evidence established a violation under the "hostile environment" theory. *Vinson v. Taylor*, 753 F.2d 141, 36 EPD ¶34,949, [36 FEP Cases 1423] *denial of rehearing en banc*, 760 F.2d 1330, 37 EPD ¶35,232 [37 FEP Cases 1266] (D.C. Cir. 1985). The court ruled that a victim's "voluntary" submission to sexual advances has "no materiality whatsoever" to the proper inquiry: whether "toleration of sexual harassment [was] a condition of her employment." The court further held that an employer is absolutely liable for sexual harassment committed by a supervisory employee, regardless of whether the employer actually knew or reasonably could have known of the misconduct, or would have disapproved of and stopped the misconduct if aware of it.

3) Supreme Court's Opinion — The Supreme Court agreed that the case should be remanded for consideration under the "hostile environment" theory and held that the proper inquiry focuses on the "unwelcomeness" of the conduct rather than the "voluntariness" of the victim's participation. But the Court held that the court of appeals erred in concluding that employers are always automatically liable for sexual harassment by their supervisory employees.

a) "Hostile Environment" Violates Title VII — The Court rejected the employer's contention that Title VII prohibits only discrimination that causes "economic" or "tangible" injury: "Title VII affords employees the right to work in an environment free from discriminatory intimidation, ridicule, and insult" whether based on sex, race, religion, or national origin. 106 S.Ct. at 2405. Relying on the EEOC's Guidelines' definition of harassment,[6] the Court held that a plaintiff may establish a violation of Title VII "by proving that discrimination based on sex has created a hostile or abusive work environment." *Id.* The Court quoted the Eleventh Circuit's decision in *Henson v. City of Dundee*, 682 F.2d 897 902 29 EPD ¶32,993 [29 FEP Cases 787] (11th Cir. 1982):

> Sexual harassment which creates a hostile or offensive environment for members of one sex is every bit the arbitrary barrier to sexual equality at the workplace that racial harassment is to racial equality. Surely, a requirement that a man or woman run a gauntlet of sexual abuse in return for the privilege of being allowed to work and make a living can be as demeaning and disconcerting as the harshest of racial epithets.

106 S.Ct. at 2406. The Court further held that for harassment to violate Title VII, it must be "sufficiently severe or pervasive 'to alter the conditions of [the victim's] employment and create an abusive working environment.'" *Id.* (quoting *Henson*, 682 F.2d at 904).

b) Conduct Must Be "Unwelcome" — Citing the EEOC's Guidelines, the Court said the gravamen of a sexual

harassment claim is that the alleged sexual advances were "unwelcome." 106 S.Ct. at 2406. Therefore, "the fact that sex-related conduct was 'voluntary,' in the sense that the complainant was not forced to participate against her will, is not a defense to a sexual harassment suit brought under Title VII .... The correct inquiry is whether [the victim] by her conduct indicated that the alleged sexual advances were unwelcome, not whether her actual participation in sexual intercourse was voluntary." *Id.* Evidence of a complainant's sexually provocative speech or dress may be relevant in determining whether she found particular advances unwelcome, but should be admitted with caution in light of the potential for unfair prejudice, the Court held.

c) Employer Liability Established Under Agency Principles — On the question of employer liability in "hostile environment" cases, the Court agreed with EEOC's position that agency principles should be used for guidance. While declining to issue a "definitive rule on employer liability," the Court did reject both the court of appeals' rule of automatic liability for the actions of supervisors and the employer's position that notice is always required. 106 S.Ct. at 2408–09.

The following sections of this document provide guidance on the issues addressed in *Vinson* and subsequent cases.

GUIDANCE

A. Determining Whether Sexual Conduct Is Unwelcome

Sexual harassment is "unwelcome ... verbal or physical conduct of a sexual nature...." 29 C.F.R. §1604.11(a). Because sexual attraction may often play a role in the day-to-day social exchange between employees, "the distinction between invited, uninvited-but-welcome, offensive-but-tolerated, and flatly rejected" sexual advances may well be difficult to discern. *Barnes v. Costle*, 561 F.2d 983, 999, 14 EPD ¶7755 [15 FEP Cases 345] (D.C. Cir. 1977) (MacKinnon J., con-

---

[6]The Court stated that the guidelines, " 'while not controlling upon the courts by reason of their authority, do constitute a body of experience and informed judgment to which courts and litigants may properly resort for guidance.'" *Vinson*, 106 S.Ct. at 2405 (quoting *General Electric Co. v. Gilbert*, 429 U.S. 125, 141-42, 12 EPD ¶11,240 [13 FEP Cases 1657] (1976), quoting in turn *Skidmore v. Swift & Co.*, 323 U.S. 134 (1944)).

curring). But this distinction is essential because sexual conduct becomes unlawful only when it is unwelcome. The Eleventh Circuit provided a general definition of "unwelcome conduct" in *Henson v. City of Dundee*, 682 F.2d at 903: the challenged conduct must be unwelcome "in the sense that the employee did not solicit or incite it, and in the sense that the employee regarded the conduct as undesirable or offensive."

When confronted with conflicting evidence as to welcomeness, the Commission looks "at the record as a whole and at the totality of circumstances...." 29 C.F.R. §1604.11(b), evaluating each situation on a case-by-case basis. When there is some indication of welcomeness or when the credibility of the parties is at issue, the charging party's claim will be considerably strengthened if she made a contemporaneous complaint or protest.[7] Particularly when the alleged harasser may have some reason (e.g., a prior consensual relationship) to believe that the advances will be welcomed, it is important for the victim to communicate that the conduct is unwelcome. Generally, victims are well-advised to assert their right to a workplace free from sexual harassment. This may stop the harassment before it becomes more serious. A contemporaneous complaint or protest may also provide persuasive evidence that the sexual harassment in fact occurred as alleged (*see infra* Section B). Thus, in investigating sexual harassment charges, it is important to develop detailed evidence of the circumstances and nature of any such complaints or protests, whether

to the alleged harasser, higher management, co-workers or others.[8]

While a complaint or protest is helpful to a charging party's case, it is not a necessary element of the claim. Indeed, the Commission recognizes that victims may fear repercussions from complaining about the harassment and that such fear may explain a delay in opposing the conduct. If the victim failed to complain or delayed in complaining, the investigation must ascertain why. The relevance of whether the victim has complained varies depending upon "the nature of the sexual advances and the context in which the alleged incidents occurred." 29 C.F.R. §1604.11(b).[9]

Example — Charging Party (CP) alleges that her supervisor subjected her to unwelcome sexual advances that created a hostile work environment. The investigation into her charge discloses that her supervisor began making intermittent sexual advances to her in June, 1987, but she did not complain to management about the harassment. After the harassment continued and worsened, she filed a charge with EEOC in June, 1988. There is no evidence CP welcomed the advances. CP states that she

---

[7]For a complaint to be "contemporaneous," it should be made while the harassment is ongoing or shortly after it has ceased. For example, a victim of "hostile environment" harassment who resigns her job because working conditions have become intolerable would be considered to have made a contemporaneous complaint if she notified the employer of the harassment at the time of her departure or shortly thereafter. The employer has a duty to investigate and, if it finds the allegations true, to take remedial action including offering reinstatement (*see infra* Section E).

[8]Even when unwelcomeness is not at issue, the investigation should develop this evidence in order to aid in making credibility determinations (*see infra* p. 12).

[9]A victim of harassment need not always confront her harasser directly so long as her conduct demonstrates the harasser's behavior is unwelcome. *See, e.g., Lipsett v. University of Puerto Rico*, 864 F.2d 881, 898, 48 EPD ¶38,393 (1st Cir. 1988) ("In some instances a woman may have the responsibility for telling the man directly that his comments or conduct is unwelcome. In other instances, however, a woman's consistent failure to respond to suggestive comments or gestures may be sufficient to communicate that the man's conduct is unwelcome"); Commission Decision No. 84-1, CCH EEOC Decisions ¶6839 (although charging parties did not confront their supervisor directly about his sexual remarks and gestures for fear of losing their jobs, evidence showing that they demonstrated through comments and actions that his conduct was unwelcome was sufficient to support a finding of harassment).

feared that complaining about the harassment would cause her to lose her job. She also states that she initially believed she could resolve the situation herself, but as the harassment became more frequent and severe, she said she realized that intervention by EEOC was necessary. The investigator determines CP is credible and concludes that the delay in complaining does not undercut CP's claim.

When welcomeness is at issue, the investigation should determine whether the victim's conduct is consistent, or inconsistent, with her assertion that the sexual conduct is unwelcome.[10]

In *Vinson*, the Supreme Court made clear that voluntary submission to sexual conduct will not necessarily defeat a claim of sexual harassment. The correct inquiry "is whether [the employee] *by her conduct* indicated that the alleged sexual advances were unwelcome, not whether her actual participation in sexual intercourse was voluntary." 106 S.Ct. at 2406 (emphasis added). *See also* Commission Decision No. 84-1 ("acquiescence in sexual conduct at the workplace may not mean that the conduct is welcome to the individual").

In some cases the courts and the Commission have considered whether the complainant welcomed the sexual conduct by acting in a sexually aggressive manner, using sexually-oriented language, or soliciting the sexual conduct. Thus, in *Gan v. Kepro Circuit Systems*, 27 EPD ¶32,379 [28 FEP Cases 639] (E.D. Mo. 1982), the plaintiff regularly used vulgar language, initiated sexually-oriented conversations with her co-workers, asked male employees about their marital sex lives and whether they engaged in extramarital affairs, and discussed her own sexual encounters. In rejecting the plaintiff's claim of "hostile environment" harassment, the court found that any propositions or sexual remarks by co-workers were "prompted by her own sexual aggressiveness and her own sexually-explicit conversations." *Id.* at 23,648.[11] And in *Vinson*, the Supreme Court held that testimony about the plaintiff's provocative dress and publicly expressed sexual fantasies is not *per se* inadmissible but the trial court should carefully weigh its relevance against the potential for unfair prejudice. 106 S.Ct. at 2407.

Conversely, occasional use of sexually explicit language does not necessarily negate a claim that sexual conduct was unwelcome. Although a charging party's use of sexual terms or off-color jokes may suggest that sexual comments by others in that situation were not unwelcome, more extreme and abusive or persistent comments or a physical assault

[10]Investigators and triers of fact rely on objective evidence, rather than subjective, uncommunicated feelings. For example, in *Ukarish v. Magnesium Electron*, 33 EPD ¶34,087 [31 FEP Cases 1315] (D.N.J. 1983), the court rejected the plaintiff's claim that she was sexually harassed by her co-worker's language and gestures; although she indicated in her personal diary that she did not welcome the banter, she made no objection and indeed appeared to join in "as one of the boys." *Id.* at 32,118. In *Sardigal v. St. Louis National Stockyards Co.*, 41 EPD ¶36,613 [42 FEP Cases 497] (S.D. Ill. 1986), the plaintiff's allegation was found not credible because she visited her alleged harasser at the hospital and at his brother's home, and allowed him to come into her home alone at night after the alleged harassment occurred. Similarly, in the *Vinson* case, the district court noted the plaintiff had twice refused transfers to other offices located away from the alleged harasser. (In a particular charge, the significance of a charging party's refusing an offer to transfer will depend upon her reasons for doing so.)

[11]*See also Ferguson v. E.I. DuPont deNemours and Co.*, 560 F.Supp. 1172, 33 EPD ¶34,131 [31 FEP Cases 795] (D. Del. 1983) ("sexually aggressive conduct and explicit conversation on the part of the plaintiff may bar a cause of action for [hostile environment] sexual harassment"); *Reichman v. Bureau of Affirmative Action*, 536 F.Supp. 1149, 1172, 30 FEP Cases 1644 (M.D. Pa. 1982) (where plaintiff behaved "in a very flirtatious and provocative manner" around the alleged harasser, asked him to have dinner at her house on several occasions despite his repeated refusals, and continued to conduct herself in a similar manner after the alleged harassment, she could not claim the alleged harassment was unwelcome).

will not be excused, nor would "quid pro quo" harrassment be allowed.

Any past conduct of the charging party that is offered to show "welcomeness" must relate to the alleged harasser. In *Swentek v. USAir, Inc.*, 830 F.2d 552, 557, 44 EPD ¶37,457 [44 FEP Cases 1808] (4th Cir. 1987), the Fourth Circuit held the district court wrongly concluded that the plaintiff's own past conduct and use of foul language showed that "she was the kind of person who could not be offended by such comments and therefore welcomed them generally," even though she had told the harasser to leave her alone. Emphasizing that the proper inquiry is "whether plaintiff welcomed the particular conduct in question from the alleged harasser," the court of appeals held that "Plaintiff's use of foul language or sexual innuendo in a consensual setting does not waive 'her legal protections against unwelcome harassment.' " 830 F.2d at 557 (quoting *Katz v. Dole*, 709 F.2d 251, 254 n.3, 32 EPD ¶33,639 [31 FEP Cases 1521] (4th Cir. 1983)). Thus, evidence concerning a charging party's general character and past behavior toward others has limited, if any, probative value and does not substitute for a careful examination of her behavior toward the alleged harasser.

A more difficult situation occurs when an employee first willingly participates in conduct of a sexual nature but then ceases to participate and claims that any continued sexual conduct has created a hostile work environment. Here the employee has the burden of showing that any further sexual conduct is unwelcome, work-related harassment. The employee must clearly notify the alleged harasser that his conduct is no longer welcome.[12]

---

[12]In Commission Decision No. 84-1, CCH Employment Practices Guide ¶6839, the Commission found that active participation in sexual conduct at the workplace, e.g., by "using dirty remarks and telling dirty jokes," may indicate that the sexual advances complained of were not unwelcome. Thus, the Commission found that no harassment occurred with respect to an employee who had joined in the telling of bawdy jokes and the use of vulgar language during

If the conduct still continues, her failure to bring the matter to the attention of higher management or the EEOC is evidence, though not dispositive, that any continued conduct is, in fact, welcome or unrelated to work.[13] In any case, however, her refusal to submit to the sexual conduct cannot be the basis for denying her an employment benefit or opportunity; that would constitute a "quid pro quo" violation.

B. Evaluating Evidence of Harassment

The Commission recognizes that sexual conduct may be private and unacknowledged, with no eyewitnesses. Even sexual conduct that occurs openly in the workplace may appear to be consensual. Thus the resolution of a sexual harassment claim often depends on the credibility of the parties. The investigator should question the charging party and the alleged harasser in detail. The Commission's investigation also should search thoroughly for corroborative evidence of any nature.[14] Supervisory and managerial employees, as well as co-workers, should be asked about their knowledge of the alleged harassment.

---

her first two months on the job, and failed to provide subsequent notice that the conduct was no longer welcome. By actively participating in the conduct, the charging party had created the impression among her co-workers that she welcomed the sort of sexually oriented banter that she later asserted was objectionable. Simply ceasing to participate was insufficient to show the continuing activity was no longer welcome to her. *See also Loftin-Boggs v. City of Meridian*, 633 F.Supp. 1323, 41 FEP Cases 532 (S.D. Miss. 1986) (plaintiff initially participated in and initiated some of the crude language that was prevalent on the job; if she later found such conduct offensive, she should have conveyed this by her own conduct and her reaction to her co-workers' conduct).

[13]However, if the harassing supervisor engages in conduct that is sufficiently pervasive and work-related, it may place the employer on notice that the conduct constitutes harassment.

[14]As the court said in *Henson v. City of Dundee*, 682 F.2d at 912 n.25, "In a case of alleged sexual harassment which involves close questions of credibility and subjective interpretation, the existence of corroborative evidence or the lack thereof is likely to be crucial."

In appropriate cases, the Commission may make a finding of harassment based solely on the credibility of the victim's allegation. As with any other charge of discrimination, a victim's account must be sufficiently detailed and internally consistent so as to be plausible, and lack of corroborative evidence where such evidence logically should exist would undermine the allegation.[15] By the same token, a general denial by the alleged harasser will carry little weight when it is contradicted by other evidence.[16]

Of course, the Commission recognizes that a charging party may not be able to identify witnesses to the alleged conduct itself. But testimony may be obtained from persons who observed the charging party's demeanor immediately after an alleged incident of harassment. Persons with whom she discussed the incident — such as co-workers, a doctor or a counselor — should be interviewed. Other employees should be asked if they noticed changes in charging party's behavior at work or in the alleged harasser's treatment of charging party. As stated earlier, a contemporaneous complaint by the victim would be persuasive evidence both that the conduct occurred and that it was unwelcome (see supra Section A). So too is evidence that other employees were sexually harassed by the same person.

The investigator should determine whether the employer was aware of any other instances of harassment and if so what was the response. Where appropriate the Commission will expand the case to include class claims.[17]

Example — Charging Party (CP) alleges that her supervisor made unwelcome sexual advances toward her on frequent occasions while they were alone in his office. The supervisor denies this allegation. No one witnessed the alleged advances. CP's inability to produce eyewitnesses to the harassment does *not* defeat her claim. The resolution will depend on the credibility of her allegations versus that of her supervisor's. Corroborating, credible evidence will establish her claim. For example, three co-workers state that CP looked distraught on several occasions after leaving the supervisor's office, and that she informed them on those occasions that he had sexually propositioned and touched her. In addition, the evidence shows that CP had complained to the general manager of the office about the incidents soon after they occurred. The corroborating witness testimony and her complaint to higher management would be sufficient to establish her claim. Her allegations would be further buttressed if other employees testified that the supervisor propositioned them as well.

If the investigation exhausts all possibilities for obtaining corroborative evi-

---

[15]In *Sardigal v. St. Louis National Stockyards Co.,* 41 EPD ¶36,613 at 44,694 [42 FEP Cases 497] (S.D. Ill. 1986), the plaintiff, a waitress, alleged she was harassed over a period of nine months in a restaurant at noontime, when there was a "constant flow of waitresses or customers" around the area where the offenses allegedly took place. Her allegations were not credited by the district court because no individuals came forward with testimony to support her.

It is important to explore all avenues for obtaining corroborative evidence because courts may reject harassment claims due to lack of corroborative evidence. *See Hall v. F.O. Thacker Co.,* 24 FEP Cases 1499, 1503 (N.D. Ga. 1980) (district judge did not credit plaintiff's testimony about sexual advances because it was "virtually uncorroborated"); *Neidhart v. D.H. Holmes Co.,* 21 FEP Cases 452, 457 (E.D. La. 1979), *aff'd mem.,* 624 F.2d 1097 (5th Cir. 1980) (plaintiff's account of sexual harassment rejected because "there is not a scintilla of credible evidence to corroborate [plaintiff's version]").

[16]*See* Commission Decision No. 81-17, CCH EEOC Decisions (1983) ¶6757 (violation of Title VII found where charging party alleged that her supervisor made repeated sexual advances toward her; although the supervisor denied the allegations, statements of other employees supported them).

[17]Class complaints in the federal sector are governed by the requirements of 29 C.F.R. §1613 Subpart F.

dence, but finds none, the Commission may make a cause finding based solely on a reasoned decision to credit the charging party's testimony.[18]

In a "quid pro quo" case, a finding that the employer's asserted reasons for its adverse action against the charging party are pretextual will usually establish a violation.[19] The investigation should determine the validity of the employer's reasons for the charging party's termination. If they are pretextual and if the sexual harassment occurred, then it should be inferred that the charging party was terminated for rejecting the employer's sexual advances, as she claims. Moreover, if the termination occurred because the victim complained, it would be appropriate to find, in addition, a violation of section 704(a).

C. Determining Whether a Work Environment Is "Hostile"

The Supreme Court said in *Vinson* that for sexual harassment to violate Title VII, it must be "sufficiently severe or pervasive 'to alter the conditions of [the victim's] employment and create an abusive working environment.'" 106 S.Ct. at 2406 (quoting *Henson v. City of Dundee*, 682 F.2d at 904. Since "hostile environment" harassment takes a variety of forms, many factors may affect this determination, including: (1) whether the conduct was verbal or physical, or both; (2) how frequently it was repeated; (3) whether the conduct was hostile and patently offensive; (4) whether the alleged harasser was a co-worker or a supervisor; (5) whether others joined in perpetrating the harassment; and (6) whether

---

[18]In Commission Decision No. 82-13, CCH EEOC Decisions (1983) ¶6832, the Commission stated that a "bare assertion" of sexual harassment "cannot stand without some factual support." To the extent this decision suggests a charging party can never prevail based solely on the credibility of her own testimony, that decision is overruled.

[19]*See, e.g., Bundy v. Jackson*, 641 F.2d 934, 953, 24 EPD ¶31,439 [24 FEP Cases 1155] (D.C. Cir. 1981).

---

the harassment was directed at more than one individual.

In determining whether unwelcome sexual conduct rises to the level of a "hostile environment" in violation of Title VII, the central inquiry is whether the conduct "unreasonably interfer[es] with an individual's work performance" or creates "an intimidating, hostile, or offensive working environment." 29 C.F.R. §1604.11(a)(3). Thus, sexual flirtation or innuendo, even vulgar language that is trivial or merely annoying, would probably not establish a hostile environment.

1) Standard for Evaluating Harassment — In determining whether harassment is sufficiently severe or pervasive to create a hostile environment, the harasser's conduct should be evaluated from the objective standpoint of a "reasonable person." Title VII does not serve "as a vehicle for vindicating the petty slights suffered by the hypersensitive." *Zabkowicz v. West Bend Co.*, 589 F.Supp. 780, 784, 35 EPD ¶34,766 [35 FEP Cases 610] (E.D. Wis. 1984). *See also Ross v. Comsat*, 34 FEP Cases 260, 265 (D. Md. 1984), *rev'd on other grounds*, 759 F.2d 355 (4th Cir. 1985). Thus, if the challenged conduct would not substantially affect the work environment of a reasonable person, no violation should be found.

> **Example** — Charging Party alleges that her co-worker made repeated unwelcome sexual advances toward her. An investigation discloses that the alleged "advances" consisted of invitations to join a group of employees who regularly socialized at dinner after work. The co-worker's invitations, viewed in that context and from the perspective of a reasonable person, would not have created a hostile environment and therefore did not constitute sexual harassment.

A "reasonable person" standard also should be applied to the more basic determination of whether challenged conduct is of a sexual nature. Thus, in the above example, a reasonable person would not consider the co-worker's invitations sexual in nature, and on that basis as well no violation would be found.

This objective standard should not be applied in a vacuum, however. Consideration should be given to the context in which the alleged harassment took place. As the Sixth Circuit has stated, the trier of fact must "adopt the perspective of a reasonable person's reaction to a similar environment under similar or like circumstances." *Highlander v. K.F.C. National Management Co.*, 805 F.2d 644, 650, 41 EPD ¶36,675 [42 FEP Cases 654] (6th Cir. 1986).[20]

The reasonable person standard should consider the victim's perspective and not stereotyped notions of acceptable behavior. For example, the Commission believes that a workplace in which sexual slurs, displays of "girlie" pictures, and other offensive conduct abound can constitute a hostile work environment even if many people deem it to be harmless or insignificant. *Cf. Rabidue v. Osceola Refining Co.*, 805 F.2d 611, 626, 41 EPD ¶36,643 [42 FEP Cases 631] (6th Cir. 1986) (Keith, C.J., dissenting), *cert. denied*, 107 S.Ct. 1983, 42 EPD ¶36,984 (1987). *Lipsett v. University of Puerto Rico*, 864 F.2d 881, 898 48 EPD ¶38,393 (1st Cir. 1988).

2) Isolated Instances of Harassment — Unless the conduct is quite severe, a single incident or isolated incidents of offensive sexual conduct or remarks generally do not create an abusive environment. As the Court noted in *Vinson*, "mere utterance of an ethnic or racial epithet which engenders offensive

feelings in an employee would not affect the conditions of employment to a sufficiently significant degree to violate Title VII." 106 S.Ct. at 2406 (quoting *Rogers v. EEOC*, 454 F.2d 234, 4 EPD ¶7597 [4 FEP Cases 92] (5th Cir. 1971), *cert. denied*, 406 U.S. 957, 4 EPD ¶7838 (1972)). A "hostile environment" claim generally requires a showing of a pattern of offensive conduct.[21] In contrast, in "quid pro quo" cases a single sexual advance may constitute harassment if it is linked to the granting or denial of employment benefits.[22]

But a single, unusually severe incident of harassment may be sufficient to constitute a Title VII violation; the more severe the harassment, the less need to show a repetitive series of incidents. This is particularly true when the harassment

---

[20]In *Highlander* and also in *Rabidue v. Osceola Refining Co.*, 805 F.2d 611, 41 EPD ¶36,643 [42 FEP Cases 631] (6th Cir. 1986), *cert. denied*, 107 S.Ct. 1983, 42 EPD ¶36,984 (1987), the Sixth Circuit required an additional showing that the plaintiff suffered some degree of psychological injury. *Highlander*, 805 F.2d at 650; *Rabidue*, 805 F.2d at 620. However, it is the Commission's position that it is sufficient for the charging party to show that the harassment was unwelcome and that it would have substantially affected the work environment of a reasonable person.

[21]See, e.g., *Scott v. Sears, Roebuck and Co.*, 798 F.2d 210, 214, 41 EPD ¶36,439 [41 FEP Cases 805] (7th Cir. 1986) (offensive comments and conduct of co-workers were "too isolated and lacking the repetitive and debilitating effect necessary to maintain a hostile environment claim"); *Moylan v. Maries County*, 792 F.2d 746, 749, 40 EPD ¶36,228 [40 FEP Cases 1788] (8th Cir. 1986) (single incident or isolated incidents of harassment will not be sufficient to establish a violation; the harassment must be sustained and nontrivial); *Downes v. Federal Aviation Administration*, 775 F.2d 288, 293, 38 EPD ¶35,590 [39 FEP CAses 70] (D.C. Cir. 1985) (Title VII does not create a claim of sexual harassment "for each and every crude joke or sexually explicit remark on the job.... [A] *pattern* of offensive conduct must be proved...."); *Sapp v. City of Warner-Robins*, 655 F.Supp. 1043, 43 FEP Cases 486 (M.D. Ga. 1987) (co-worker's single effort to get the plaintiff to go out with him did not create an abusive working environment); *Freedman v. American Standard*, 41 FEP Cases 471 (D.N.J. 1986) (plaintiff did not suffer a hostile environment from the receipt of an obscene message from her coworkers and a sexual solicitation from one co-worker); *Hollis v. Fleetguard, Inc.*, 44 FEP Cases 1527 (M.D. Tenn. 1987) (plaintiff's co-worker's requests, on four occasions over a four-month period, that she have a sexual affair with him, followed by his coolness toward her and avoidance of her did not constitute a hostile environment; there was no evidence he coerced, pressured, or abused the plaintiff after she rejected his advances).

[22]See *Neville v. Taft Broadcasting Co.*, 42 FEP Cases 1314 (W.D.N.Y. 1987) (one sexual advance, rebuffed by plaintiff, may establish a prima facie case of "quid pro quo" harassment but is not severe enough to create a hostile environment).

is physical.[23] Thus, in *Barrett v. Omaha National Bank*, 584 F.Supp. 22, 35 FEP Cases 585 (D. Neb. 1983), *aff'd*, 726 F.2d 424, 33 EPD ¶34,132 (8th Cir. 1984), one incident constituted actionable sexual harassment. The harasser talked to the plaintiff about sexual activities and touched her in an offensive manner while they were inside a vehicle from which she could not escape.[24]

The Commission will presume that the unwelcome, intentional touching of a charging party's intimate body areas is sufficiently offensive to alter the conditions of her working environment and constitute a violation of Title VII. More so than in the case of verbal advances or remarks, a single unwelcome physical advance can seriously poison the victim's working environment. If an employee's supervisor sexually touches that employee, the Commission normally would find a violation. In such situations, it is the employer's burden to demonstrate that the unwelcome conduct was not sufficiently severe to create a hostile work environment.

When the victim is the target of both verbal and non-intimate physical conduct, the hostility of the environment is exacerbated and a violation is more likely to be found. Similarly, incidents of sexual harassment directed at other employees in addition to the charging party are relevant to a showing of hostile work environment. *Hall v. Gus Construction Co.*, 842 F.2d 1010, 46 EPD ¶37,905 [46 FEP Cases 573] (8th Cir. 1988); *Hicks v. Gates Rubber Co.*, 833 F.2d 1406, 44 EPD ¶37,542 [45 FEP Cases 608] (10th Cir. 1987); *Jones v. Flagship International*, 793 F.2d 714, 721 n.7, 40 EPD ¶36,392 [41 FEP Cases 358] (5th Cir. 1986), *cert. denied*, 107 S.Ct. 952, 41 EPD ¶36,708 (1987).

3) Non-physical Harassment — When the alleged harassment consists of verbal conduct, the investigation should ascertain the nature, frequency, context, and intended target of the remarks. Questions to be explored might include:

— Did the alleged harasser single out the charging party?

— Did the charging party participate?

— What was the relationship between the charging party and the alleged harasser(s)?

— Were the remarks hostile and derogatory?

No one factor alone determines whether particular conduct violates Title VII. As the Guidelines emphasize, the Commission will evaluate the totality of the circumstances. In general, a woman does not forfeit her right to be free from sexual harassment by choosing to work in an atmosphere that has traditionally included vulgar, anti-female language. However, in *Rabidue v. Osceola Refining Co.*, 805 F.2d 611, 41 EPD ¶36,643 [42 FEP Cases 631] (6th Cir. 1986), *cert. denied*, 107 S.Ct. 1983, 42 EPD ¶36,984 (1987), the Sixth Circuit rejected the plaintiff's claim of harassment in such a situation.[25] One of the factors the court found

---

[23]The principles for establishing employer liability, set forth in Section D below, are to be applied to cases involving physical contact in the same manner that they are applied in other cases.

[24]*See also Gilardi v. Schroeder*, 672 F.Supp. 1043, 45 FEP Cases 283 (N.D. Ill. 1986) (plaintiff who was drugged by employer's owner and raped while unconscious, and then was terminated at insistence of owner's wife, was awarded $113,000 in damages for harassment and intentional infliction of emotional distress); Commission Decision No. 83-1, CCH EEOC Decisions (1983) ¶6834 (violation found where the harasser forcibly grabbed and kissed charging party while they were alone in a storeroom); Commission Decision No. 84-3, CCH Employment Practices Guide ¶6841 (violation found where the harasser slid his hand under the charging party's skirt and squeezed her buttocks).

[25]The alleged harasser, a supervisor of another department who did not supervise plaintiff but worked with her regularly, "was an extremely vulgar and crude individual who customarily made obscene comments about women generally, and, on occasion, directed such obscenities to the plaintiff." 805 F.2d at 615. The plaintiff and other female employees were exposed daily to displays of nude or partially clad women in posters in male employees' offices. 805 F.2d at 623-24 (Keith, J., dissenting in part and concurring in part). Although the employees told manage-

relevant was "the lexicon of obscenity that pervaded the environment of the workplace both before and after the plaintiff's introduction into its environs, coupled with the reasonable expectations of the plaintiff upon voluntarily entering that environment." 805 F.2d at 620. Quoting the district court, the majority noted that in some work environments, " 'humor and language are rough hewn and vulgar. Sexual jokes, sexual conversations, and girlie magazines may abound. Title VII was not meant to — or can — change this.' " Id. at 620-21. The court also considered the sexual remarks and poster at issue to have a "de minimis effect on the plaintiff's work environment when considered in the context of a society that condones and publicly features and commercially exploits open displays of written and pictorial erotica at the newsstands, on prime-time television, at the cinema, and in other public places." Id. at 622.

The Commission believes these factors rarely will be relevant and agrees with the dissent in Rabidue that a woman does not assume the risk of harassment by voluntarily entering an abusive, antifemale environment. "Title VII's precise purpose is to prevent such behavior and attitudes from poisoning the work environment of classes protected under the Act." 805 F.2d at 626 (Keith, J., dissenting in part and concurring in part). Thus, in a decision disagreeing with Rabidue, a district court found that a hostile environment was established by the presence of pornographic magazines in the workplace and vulgar employee comments concerning them; offensive sexual comments made to and about plaintiff and other female employees by her supervisor; sexually oriented pictures in a company-sponsored movie and slide presentation; sexually oriented pictures and calendars in the workplace; and offensive touching of plaintiff by a coworker. Barbetta v. Chemlawn Services

---

ment they were disturbed and offended, the employer did not reprimand the supervisor.

Corp., 669 F.Supp. 569, 45 EPD ¶37,568 [44 FEP Cases 1563] (W.D.N.Y. 1987). The court held that the proliferation of pornography and demeaning comments, if sufficiently continuous and pervasive, "may be found to create an atmosphere in which women are viewed as men's sexual playthings rather than as their equal coworkers." Barbetta, 669 F.Supp. at 573. The Commission agrees that, depending on the totality of circumstances, such as atmosphere may violate Title VII. See also Waltman v. International Paper Co., 875 F.2d 468, 50 EPD ¶39,106 Commission's position in its amicus brief that evidence of ongoing sexual graffiti in the workplace, not all of which was directed at the plaintiff, was relevant to her claim of harassment. Bennett v. Corroon & Black Corp., 845 F.2d 104, 46 EPD ¶37,955 (5th Cir. 1988) (the posting of obscene cartoons in an office men's room bearing the plaintiff's name and depicting her engaged in crude and deviant sexual activities could create a hostile work environment).

4) Sex-based Harassment — Although the Guidelines specifically address conduct that is sexual in nature, the Commission notes that sex-based harassment — that is, harassment not involving sexual activity or language — may also give rise to Title VII liability (just as in the case of harassment based on race, national origin or religion) if it is "sufficiently patterned or pervasive" and directed at employees because of their sex. Hicks v. Gates Rubber Co., 833 F.2d at 1416; McKinney v. Dole, 765 F.2d 1129, 1138, 37 EPD ¶35,339 [38 FEP Cases 364] (D.C. Cir. 1985).

Acts of physical aggression, intimidation, hostility or unequal treatment based on sex may be combined with incidents of sexual harassment to establish the existence of discriminatory terms and conditions of employment. Hall v. Gus Construction Co., 842 F.2d at 1014; Hicks v. Gates Rubber Co., 833 F.2d at 1416.

5) Constructive Discharge —
Claims of "hostile environment" sexual
harassment often are coupled with
claims of constructive discharge. If constructive discharge due to a hostile environment is proven, the claim will also
become one of "quid pro quo" harassment.[26] It is the position of the Commission and a majority of courts that an
employer is liable for constructive discharge when it imposes intolerable working conditions in violation of Title VII
when those conditions foreseeably would
compel a reasonable employee to quit,
whether or not the employer specifically
intended to force the victim's resignation. *See Derr v. Gulf Oil Corp.*, 796 F.2d
340, 343-44, 41 EPD ¶36,468 [41 FEP
Cases 166] (10th Cir. 1986); *Goss v. Exxon Office Systems Co.*, 747 F.2d 885, 888,
35 EPD ¶34,768 [36 FEP Cases 344] (3d
Cir. 1984); *Nolan v. Cleland*, 686 F.2d 806,
812-15, 30 EPD ¶33,029 [29 FEP Cases
1732] (9th Cir. 1982); *Held v. Gulf Oil Co.*,
684 F.2d 427, 432, 29 EPD ¶32,968 [29
FEP Cases 837] (6th Cir. 1982); *Clark v.
Marsh*, 665 F.2d 1168, 1175 n.8, 26 EPD
¶32,082 (D.C. Cir. 1981); *Bourque v. Powell Electrical Manufacturing Co.*, 617
F.2d 61, 65, 23 EPD ¶30,891 [22 FEP
Cases 1191] (5th Cir. 1980); Commission
Decision 84-1, CCH EEOC Decision
¶6839. However, the Fourth Circuit requires proof that the employer imposed
the intolerable conditions with the intent
of forcing the victim to leave. *See EEOC
v. Federal Reserve Bank of Richmond*,
698 F.2d 633, 672, 30 EPD ¶33,269 (4th
Cir. 1983). But this case is not a sexual
harassment case and the Commission believes it is distinguishable because specific intent is not as likely to be present
in "hostile environment" cases.

---

[26]However, while an employee's failure to utilize
effective grievance procedures will not shield an employer from liability for "quid pro quo" harassment,
such failure may defeat a claim of constructive discharge. *See* discussion of impact of grievance procedures later in this section, and section D(2)(c)(2),
below.

An important factor to consider is
whether the employer had an effective internal grievance procedure. (*See* Section
E, *Preventive and Remedial Action*). The
Commission argued in its *Vinson* brief
that if an employee knows that effective
avenues of complaint and redress are
available, then the availability of such
avenues itself becomes a part of the work
environment and overcomes, to the degree it is effective, the hostility of the
work environment. As Justice Marshall
noted in his opinion in *Vinson*, "Where a
complainant without good reason bypassed an internal complaint procedure
she knew to be effective, a court may be
reluctant to find constructive termination...." 106 S.Ct. at 2411 (Marshall, J.,
concurring in part and dissenting a
part). Similarly, the court of appeals in
Dornhecker v. Malibu Grand Prix Corp.,
828 F.2d 307, 44 EPD ¶37,557 [44 FEP
Cases 1604] (5th Cir. 1987), held the
plaintiff was not constructively discharged after an incident of harassment
by a co-worker because she quit immediately, even though the employer told her
she would not have to work with him
again, and she did not give the employer
a fair opportunity to demonstrate it
could curb the harasser's conduct.

D. Employer Liability for Harassment by Supervisors

In *Vinson*, The Supreme Court agreed
with the Commission's position that
"Congress wanted courts to look to agency principles for guidance" in determining an employer's liability for sexual
conduct by a supervisor:

> While such common-law princi-
> ples may not be transferable in all
> their particulars to Title VII, Con-
> gress' decision to define "employ-
> er" to include any "agent" of an
> employer, 42 U.S.C. §2000e(b),
> surely evinces an intent to place
> some limits on the acts of employ-
> ees for which employers under Ti-
> tle VII are to be held responsible.

106 S.Ct. at 2408. Thus, while declining to
issue a "definitive rule on employer lia-

bility," the Court did make it clear that employers are not "automatically liable" for the acts of their supervisors. For the same reason, the Court said, "absence of notice to an employer does not necessarily insulate that employer from liability." *Id.*

As the Commission argued in *Vinson*, reliance on agency principles is consistent with the Commission's Guidelines, which provide in section 1604.11(c) that:

> ... an employer ... is responsible for its acts and those of its agents and supervisory employees with respect to sexual harassment regardless of whether the specific acts complained of were authorized or even forbidden by the employer and regardless of whether the employer knew or should have known of their occurrence. The Commission will examine the circumstances of the particular employment relationship and the job functions performed by the individual in determining whether an individual acts in either a supervisory or agency capacity.

Citing the last sentence of this provision, the Court in *Vinson* indicated that the Guidelines further supported the application of agency principles. 106 S.Ct. at 2408.

1) Application of Agency Principles — "Quid Pro Quo" Cases — An employer will always be held responsible for acts of "quid pro quo" harassment. A supervisor in such circumstances has made or threatened to make a decision affecting the victim's employment status, and he therefore has exercised authority delegated to him by his employer. Although the question of employer liability for "quid pro quo" harassment was not at issue in *Vinson*, the Court's decision noted with apparent approval the position taken by the Commission in its brief that:

> where a supervisor exercises the authority actually delegated to him by his employer, by making

or threatening to make decisions affecting the employment status of his subordinates, such actions are properly imputed to the employer whose delegation of authority empowered the supervisor to undertake them.

106 S.Ct. at 2407–08 (citing Brief for the United States and Equal Employment Opportunity Commission as *Amicus Curiae* at 22).[27] *See also Sparks v. Pilot Freight Carriers, Inc.*, 830 F.2d 1554, 44 EPD ¶37,493 [45 FEP Cases 160] (11th Cir. 1987) (adopting EEOC position quoted in *Vinson* opinion); *Lipsett*, 864 F.2d at 901 (adopting, for Title IX of the Education Amendments, the *Vinson* standard that an employer is absolutely liable for acts of quid pro quo harassment "whether [it] knew, should have known, or approved of the supervisor's actions"). Thus, applying agency principles, the court in *Schroeder v. Schock*, 42 FEP Cases 1112 (D. Kans. 1986), held an employer liable for "quid pro quo" harassment by a supervisor who had authority to recommend plaintiff's discharge. The employer maintained the supervisor's acts were beyond the scope of his employment since the sexual advances were made at a restaurant after work hours. The court held that because the supervisor was acting within the scope of his authority when making or recommending employment decisions, his conduct

---

[27]This well-settled principle is the basis for employer liability for supervisors' discriminatory employment decisions that violate Title VII. 106 S.Ct. at 2408; *see, e.g., Anderson v. Methodist Evangelical Hospital, Inc.*, 464 F.2d 723, 725, 4 EPD ¶7901 [4 FEP Cases 987] (6th Cir. 1972) (racially motivated discharge "by a person in authority at a lower level of management" is attributable to employer despite upper management's "exemplary" record in race relations); *Tidwell v. American Oil Co.*, 332 F.Supp. 424, 436, 4 EPD ¶7544 [3 FEP Cases 1007] (D. Utah 1971) (upper level management's lack of knowledge irrelevant where supervisor illegally discharged employee for refusing to disqualify black applicant discriminatorily); *Flowers v. Crouch-Walker Corp.*, 552 F.2d 1277, 1282, 14 EPD ¶7510 [14 FEP Cases 1265] (7th Cir. 1977) ("The defendant is liable as principal for any violation of Title VII ... by [a supervisor] in his authorized capacity as supervisor.")

may fairly be imputed to the employer. The supervisor was using his authority to hire, fire, and promote to extort sexual consideration from an employee, even though the sexual advance itself occurred away from work.

2) Application of Agency Principles — "Hostile Environment" Cases

a) Vinson — In its *Vinson* brief the commission argued that the employer should be liable for the creation of a hostile environment by a supervisor when the employer knew or had reason to know of the sexual misconduct. Ways by which actual or constructive knowledge could be demonstrated include: by a complaint to management or an EEOC charge; by the pervasiveness of the harassment; or by evidence the employer had "deliberately turned its back on the problem" of sexual harassment by failing to establish a policy against it and a grievance mechanism to redress it. The brief argued that an employer should be liable "if there is no reasonably available avenue by which victims of sexual harassment can make their complaints known to appropriate officials who are in a position to do something about those complaints." Brief for the United States and Equal Employment Opportunity Commission as *Amicus Curiae* at 25. Under that circumstance, an employer would be deemed to know of any harassment that occurred in its workplace.

While the *Vinson* decision quoted the Commission's brief at length, it neither endorsed nor rejected its position.[28] 106 S.Ct. at 2407-08. The Court did state, however, that "the mere existence of a grievance procedure and a policy against discrimination, coupled with [the victim's] failure to invoke the procedure" are "plainly relevant" but "not necessarily dispositive." *Id.* at 2408-09. The Court further stated that the employer's argu-

ment that the victim's failure to complain insulated it from liability "might be substantially stronger if its procedures were better calculated to encourage victims of harassment to come forward." *Id.* at 2409.

The Commission, therefore, interprets *Vinson* to require a careful examination in "hostile environment" cases of whether the harassing supervisor was acting in an "agency capacity" (29 C.F.R. §1604.11(c)). Whether the employer had an appropriate and effective complaint procedure and whether the victim used it are important factors to consider, as discussed below.

(b) Direct Liability — The initial inquiry should be whether the employer knew or should have known of the alleged sexual harassment. If actual or constructive knowledge exists, and if the employer failed to take immediate and appropriate corrective action, the employer would be directly liable.[29] Most commonly an employer acquires actual knowledge through first-hand observation, by the victim's internal complaint to other supervisors or managers, or by a charge of discrimination.

---

[28]The Court observed that the Commission's position was "in some tension" with the first sentence of section 1604.11(c) of the Guidelines but was consistent with the final sentence of that section. (*See supra* at 21).

[29]*Barrett v. Omaha National Bank*, 584 F.Supp. 22, 30-31 [35 FEP Cases 593] (D. Neb. 1983), *aff'd*, 726 F.2d 424, 33 EPD ¶34,132 (8th Cir. 1984); *Ferguson v. duPont Corp.*, 560 F.Supp. 1172, 1199 (D. Del. 1983); Commission Decision No. 83-1, CCH EEOC Decisions (1983) ¶6834. "[A]n employer who has reason to know that one of his employees is being harassed in the workplace by others on ground of race, sex, religion, or national origin, and does nothing about it, is blameworthy." *Hunter v. Allis-Chalmers Corp.*, 797 F.2d 1417, 1422, 41 EPD ¶36,417 [41 FEP Cases 721] (7th Cir. 1986).

This is the theory under which employers are liable for harassment by co-workers, which was at issue in *Hunter v. Allis-Chalmers*. Section 1604.11(d) provides:

With respect to conduct between fellow employees, an employer is responsible for acts of sexual harassment in the workplace where the employer (or its agents or supervisory employees) knows or should have known of the conduct, unless it can show that it took immediate and appropriate corrective action.

Section E(2) of this paper discusses what constitutes "immediate and appropriate corrective action," and is applicable to cases of harassment by co-workers as well as supervisors.

An employer is liable when it "knew, or *upon reasonably diligent inquiry should have known,*" of the harassment. *Yates v. Avco Corp.,* 819 F.2d 630, 636, 43 EPD ¶37,086 [43 FEP Caes 1595] (6th Cir. 1987) (emphasis added) (supervisor harassed two women "on a daily basis in the course of his supervision of them" and the employer's grievance procedure did not function effectively). Thus, evidence of the pervasiveness of the harassment may give rise to an inference of knowledge or establish constructive knowledge. *Henson v. City of Dundee,* 682 F.2d 897, 905, 29 EPD ¶32,993 [29 FEP Caes 787] (11th Cir. 1982); *Taylor v. Jones,* 653 F.2d 1193, 1197-99, 26 EPD ¶31,923 [28 FEP Cases 1024] (8th Cir. 1981). Employers usually will be deemed to know of sexual harassment that is openly practiced in the workplace or well-known among employees. This often may be the case when there is more than one harasser or victim. *Lipsett,* 864 F.2d at 906 (employer liable where it should have known of concerted harassment of plaintiff and other female medical residents by more senior male residents).

The victim can of course put the employer on notice by filing a charge of discrimination. As the Commission stated in its *Vinson* brief, the filing of a charge triggers a duty to investigate and remedy any ongoing illegal activity. It is important to emphasize that an employee can always file an EEOC charge without first utilizing an internal complaint or grievance procedure[30] and may wish to pursue both avenues simultaneously because an internal grievance does not prevent the Title VII charge-filing time period from expiring.[31] Nor does the filing of an EEOC charge allow an employer to cease

action on an internal grievance[32] or ignore evidence of ongoing harassment.[33] Indeed, employers should take prompt remedial action upon learning of evidence of sexual harassment (or any other form of unlawful discrimination), whether from an EEOC charge or an internal complaint. If the employer takes immediate and appropriate action to correct the harassment and prevent its recurrence, and the Commission determines that no further action is warranted, normally the Commission would administratively close the case.

(c) Imputed Liability — The investigation should determine whether the alleged harassing supervisor was acting in an "agency capacity" (29 C.F.R. §1604.11(c)).[34] This requires a determination whether the supervisor was acting within the scope of his employment (*see* Restatement (Second) of Agency, §219(1) (1958)), or whether his actions can be imputed to the employer under some exception to the "scope of employ-

---

[30]Sexual harassment claims are no different from other types of discrimination claims in this regard. *See Alexander v. Gardner-Denver Co.,* 415 U.S. 36, 52, 7 EPD ¶9148 [7 FEP Cases 81] (1974).

[31]*See I.U.O.E. v. Robbins & Myers, Inc.,* 429 U.S. 229, 236, 12 EPD ¶11,256 [13 FEP Cases 1813] (1976).

[32]The Commission has filed suit in such circumstances, alleging that termination of grievance processing because a charge has been filed constitutes unlawful retaliation in violation of §704(a). *See EEOC v. Board of Governors of State Colleges & Universities,* 706 F.Supp. 1378, 50 EPD ¶39,035 [50 FEP Cases 126] (D. Ill. 1989) (denying EEOC's motion for summary judgment on ground that ADEA's retaliation provision is not violated if termination of grievance proceedings was done in good faith).

[33]*See Brooms v. Regal Tube Co.,* 44 FEP Cases 1119 (N.D. Ill. 1987), *aff'd in relevant part,* 881 F.2d 412 (7th Cir. 1989).

[34]The fact that an EEOC charge puts the employer on notice of sexual harassment means that the question of imputed employer liability under agency principles often will become of secondary importance. It figured critically in the *Vinson* case because the plaintiff never filed an EEOC charge before filing her Title VII lawsuit. Without having given any prior notice of the sexual harassment to anyone, she waited to file her lawsuit until almost a year after she admitted it had ceased. The sexual harassment was alleged to have taken place mostly in private, and she produced no witnesses either to the alleged harassment or to its adverse effects on her. Her case did not include a constructive discharge claim, and the district court found no "quid pro quo" harassment.

ment" rule (*Id.* at §219(2)). The following principles should be considered, and applied where appropriate in "hostile environment" sexual harassment cases.

1. Scope of Employment. — A supervisor's actions are generally viewed as being within the scope of his employment if they represent the exercise of authority actually vested in him. It will rarely be the case that an employer will have authorized a supervisor to engage in sexual harassment. *See Fields v. Horizon House, Inc.,* No. 86-4343 (E.D. Pa. 1987) (available on Lexis, Genfed library, Dist. file). *Cf. Hunter v. Allis-Chalmers Corp.,* 797 F.2d 1417, 1421-22, 41 EPD ¶36,417 [41 FEP Cases 721] (7th Cir. 1986) (co-worker racial harassment case). However, if the employer becomes aware of work-related sexual misconduct and does nothing to stop it, the employer, by acquiescing, has brought the supervisor's actions within the scope of his employment.

2. Apparent Authority — An employer is also liable for a supervisor's actions if these actions represent the exercise of authority that third parties reasonably believe him to possess by virtue of his employer's conduct. This is called "apparent authority." See Restatement (Second) of Agency, §§7, 8; 219(2)(d) (1958). The Commission believes that in the absence of a strong, widely disseminated, and consistently enforced employer policy against sexual harassment, and an effective complaint procedure, employees could reasonably believe that a harassing supervisor's actions will be ignored, tolerated, or even condoned by upper management. This apparent authority of supervisors arises from their power over their employees, including the power to make or substantially influence hiring, firing, promotion and compensation decisions. A supervisor's capacity to create a hostile environment is enhanced by the degree of authority conferred on him by the employer, and he may rely upon apparent authority to force an employee to endure a harassing environment for

fear of retaliation. If the employer has not provided an effective avenue to complain, then the supervisor has unchecked, final control over the victim and it is reasonable to impute his abuse of this power to the employer.[35] The Commission generally will find an employer liable for "hostile environment" sexual harassment by a supervisor when the employer failed to establish an explicit policy against sexual harassment and did not have a reasonably available avenue by which victims of sexual harassment could complain to someone with authority to investigate and remedy the problem. (*See* Section E.) *See also EEOC v. Hacienda Hotel,* 881 F.2d 1504, 51 EPD ¶39,250 [50 FEP Cases 877] (9th Cir. 1989) (finding employer liable for sexual harassment despite plaintiff's failure to pursue internal remedies where the employer's anti-discrimination policy did not specifically proscribe sexual harassment and its internal procedures required initial resort to the supervisor accused of engaging in or condoning harassment).

But an employer can divest its supervisors of this apparent authority by implementing a strong policy against sexual harassment and maintaining an effective complaint procedure. When employees know that recourse is available, they cannot reasonably believe that a harassing work environment is authorized or condoned by the employer.[36] If an employee failed to use an effective, available complaint procedure, the employer may

---

[35]*See also Fields v. Horizon House, supra* (an employer might be charged with constructive notice of a supervisor's harassment if the supervisor is vested with unbridled authority to retaliate against an employee).

[36]It is important to reemphasize, however, that no matter what the employer's policy, the employer is always liable for any supervisory actions that affect the victim's employment status, such as hiring, firing, promotion or pay. *See supra* at 21-22. Moreover, this discussion of apparent authority recognizes the unique nature of "hostile environment" sexual harassment claims and therefore is limited to such cases.

be able to prove the absence of apparent authority and thus the lack of an agency relationship, unless liability attaches under some other theory.[37] Thus, even when an employee failed to use an effective grievance procedure, the employer will be liable if it obtained notice through other means (such as the filing of a charge or by the pervasiveness of the harassment) and did not take immediate and appropriate corrective action.

Example — Charging Party (CP) alleges that her supervisor made repeated sexual advances toward her that created a hostile work environment. The investigation into her charge discloses that CP had maintained an intermittent romantic relationship with the supervisor over a period of three years preceding the filing of the charge in September of 1986. CP's employer was aware of this relationship and its consensual nature. CP asserts, however, that on frequent occasions since January of 1986 she had clearly stated to the supervisor that their relationship was over and his advances were no longer welcome. The supervisor nevertheless persisted in making sexual advances toward CP, berating her for refusing to resume their sexual relationship. His conduct did not put the employer on notice that any unwelcome harassment was occurring. The employer has a well-communicated policy against sexual harassment and a complaint procedure designed to facilitate the resolution of sexual harassment complaints and ensure against re-

taliation. This procedure has worked well in the past. CP did not use it, however, or otherwise complain to higher management. Even if CP's allegations are true, the Commission would probably not find her employer liable for the alleged harassment since she failed to use the complaint procedure or inform higher management that the advances had become unwelcome. If CP resigned because of the alleged harassment, she would not be able to establish a constructive discharge since she failed to complain.

In the preceding example, if the employer, upon obtaining notice of the charge, failed to take immediate and appropriate corrective action to stop any ongoing harassment, then the employer will be unable to prove that the supervisor lacked apparent authority for his conduct, and if the allegations of harassment are true, then the employer will be found liable. Or if the supervisor terminated the charging party because she refused to submit to his advances, the employer would be liable for "quid pro quo" harassment.

3. Other Theories — A closely rated theory is agency by estoppel. *See* Restatement (Second) of Agency at §8B. An employer is liable when he intentionally or carelessly causes an employee to mistakenly believe the supervisor is acting for the employer, or knows of the misapprehension and fails to correct it. For example, an employer who fails to respond appropriately to past known incidents of harassment would cause its employees to reasonably believe that any further incidents are authorized and will be tolerated.

Liability also may be imputed if the employer was "negligent or reckless" in supervising the alleged harasser. *See* Restatement (Second) of Agency §219(2)(6); *Hicks v. Gates Rubber Co.*, 833 F.2d 1406, 1418, 44 EPD ¶37,542 [45 FEP Cases 608] (10th Cir. 1987). "Under this standard,

---

[37]*Cf. Fields v. Horizon House* ("Apparent authority is created by and flows from the acts of the principal, not from the personal beliefs of the third party."). Moreover, as noted above, an employee would find it difficult to establish a constructive discharge in this situation because she could not show she had no alternative but to resign. Failure to complain also might undermine a later assertion that the conduct occurred or was unwelcome.

liability would be imposed if the employer had actual or constructive knowledge of the sexual harassment but failed to take remedial action." *Fields v. Horizon House, Inc.,* No. 86-4343 (E.D. Pa. 1987). This is essentially the same as holding the employer directly liable for its failure to act.

An employer cannot avoid liability by delegating to another person a duty imposed by statute. Restatement (Second) of Agency at §492 (1958), Introductory Note, p.435 ("liability follows if the person to whom the performance is delegated acts improperly with respect to it"). An employer who assigns the performance of a non-delegable duty to an employee remains liable for injuries resulting from the failure of the employee to carry out that duty. Restatement, 11214 and 219. Title VII imposes on employers a duty to provide their employees with a workplace free of sexual harassment. An employer who entrusts that duty to an employee is liable for injuries caused by the employee's breach of the duty. *See, e.g., Brooms v. Regal Tube Co.,* 44 FEP Cases 1119 (N.D. Ill. 1987) (employer liable for sexual harassment committed by the management official to whom it had delegated the responsibility to devise and enforce its policy against sexual harassment), *aff'd on other ground,* 881 F.2d 412, 240-21 (7th Cir. 1989).

Finally, an employer also may be liable if the supervisor "was aided in accomplishing the tort by the existence of the agency relation," Restatement (Second) of Agency §219(2)(d). *See Sparks v. Pilot Freight Carriers, Inc.,* 830 F.2d 1554, 44 EPD ¶37,493 [45 FEP Cases 160] (11th Cir. 1987); *Hicks v. Gates Rubber Co.,* 833 F.2d at 1418. For example, in *Sparks v. Pilot Freight Carriers,* the court found that the supervisor had used his supervisory authority to facilitate his harassment of the plaintiff by "repeatedly reminding [her] that he could fire her should she fail to comply with his advances." 830 F.2d at 1560. This case illustrates how the two types of sexual harassment can merge. When a supervisor creates a hostile environment through the aid of work-related threats or intimidation, the employer is liable under both the "quid pro quo" and "hostile environment" theories.

E. Preventive and Remedial Action

1) Preventive Action — The EEOC's Guidelines encourage employers to:

take all steps necessary to prevent sexual harassment from occurring, such as affirmatively raising the subject, expressing strong disapproval, developing appropriate sanctions, informing employees of their rights to raise and how to raise the issue of harassment under Title VII, and developing methods to sensitize all concerned.

23 C.F.R. §1604.11(f). An effective preventive program should include an explicit policy against sexual harassment that is clearly and regularly communicated to employees and effectively implemented. The employer should affirmatively raise the subject with all supervisory and non-supervisory employees, express strong disapproval, and explain the sanctions for harassment. The employer should also have a procedure for resolving sexual harassment complaints. The procedure should be designed to "encourage victims of harassment to come forward" and should not require a victim to complain first to the offending supervisor. *See Vinson,* 106 S.Ct. at 2408. It should ensure confidentiality as much as possible and provide effective remedies, including protection of victims and witnesses against retaliation.

2) Remedial Action — Since Title VII "affords employees the right to work in an environment free from discriminatory intimidation, ridicule, and insult" *(Vinson,* 106 S.Ct. at 2405), an employer is liable for failing to remedy known hostile or offensive work environments. *See, e.g., Garziano v. E.I. DuPont deNemours & Co.,* 818 F.2d 380, 43 EPD ¶37,171 [43 FEP Cases 1790] (5th Cir. 1987) (*Vinson* holds employers have an "affirmative duty to eradicate 'hostile or offensive' work environments"); *Bundy v. Jackson*, 641 F.2d 934, 947, 24 EPD ¶31,439 [24 FEP Cases 1155] (D.C. Cir. 1981) (employer violated Title VII by failing to investigate and correct sexual harassment despite notice); *Tompkins v. Public Service Electric & Gas Co.*, 568 F.2d 1044, 1049, 15 EPD 7954 [16 FEP Cases 22] (3rd Cir. 1977) (same); *Henson v. City of Dundee*, 682 F.2d 897, 905, 15 EPD ¶32,993 [29 FEP Cases 787] (11th Cir. 1982) (same); *Munford v. James T. Barnes & Co.*, 441 F.Supp. 459, 466, 16 EPD ¶8233 [17 FEP Cases 107] (E.D. Mich. 1977) (employer has an affirmative duty to investigate complaints of sexual harassment and to deal appropriately with the offending personnel; "failure to investigate gives tacit support to the discrimination because the absence of sanctions encourages abusive behavior").[38]

When an employer receives a complaint or otherwise learns of alleged sexual harassment in the workplace, the employer should investigate promptly and thoroughly. The employer should take immediate and appropriate corrective action by doing whatever is necessary to end the harassment, make the victim whole by restoring lost employment benefits or opportunities, and prevent the misconduct from recurring. Disciplinary action against the offending supervisor or employee, ranging from reprimand to discharge, may be necessary. Generally,

the corrective action should reflect the severity of the conduct. *See Waltman v. International Paper Co.* 875 F.2d at 479 (appropriateness of remedial action will depend on the severity and persistence of the harassment and the effectiveness of any initial remedial steps). *Dornhecker v. Malibu Grand Prix Corp.*, 828 F.2d 307, 309-10, 44 EPD ¶37,557 [44 FEP Cases 1604] (5th Cir. 1987) (the employer's remedy may be "assessed proportionately to the seriousness of the offense"). The employer should make follow-up inquiries to ensure the harassment has not resumed and the victim has not suffered retaliation.

Recent court decisions illustrate appropriate and inappropriate responses by employers. In *Barrett v. Omaha National Bank*, 726 F.2d 424, 33 EPD ¶34,132 [35 FEP Cases 593] (8th Cir. 1984), the victim informed her employer that her co-worker had talked to her about sexual activities and touched her in an offensive manner. Within four days of receiving this information, the employer investigated the charges, reprimanded the guilty employee, placed him on probation, and warned him that further misconduct would result in discharge. A second co-worker who had witnessed the harassment was also reprimanded for not intervening on the victim's behalf or reporting the conduct. The court ruled that the employer's response constituted immediate and appropriate corrective action, and on this basis found the employer not liable.

In contrast, in *Yates v. Avco Corp.*, 819 F.2d 630, 43 EPD ¶37,086 [43 FEP Cases 1595] (6th Cir. 1987), the court found the employer's policy against sexual harassment failed to function effectively. The victim's first-level supervisor had responsibility for reporting and correcting harassment at the company, yet he was the harasser. The employer told the victims not to go to the EEOC. While giving the accused harasser administrative leave pending investigation, the employer made the plaintiffs take sick leave,

---

[38]The employer's affirmative duty was first enunciated in cases of harassment based on race or national origin. *See, e.g., United States v. City of Buffalo*, 457 F.Supp. 612, 632-35, 18 EPD ¶8899 [19 FEP Cases 776] (W.D.N.Y. 1978), *modified in part*, 633 F.2d 643, 24 EPD ¶31,333 [24 FEP Cases 313] (2d Cir. 1980) (employer violated Title VII by failing to issue strong policy directive against racial slurs and harassment of black police officers, to conduct, full investigations, and to take appropriate disciplinary action); *EEOC v. Murphy Motor Freight Lines, Inc.*, 488 F.Supp. 381, 385-86, 22 EPD ¶30,888 [22 FEP Cases 892] (D. Minn. 1980) (defendant violated Title VII because supervisors knew or should have known of co-workers' harassment of black employees, but took inadequate steps to eliminate it).

which was never credited back to them and was recorded in their personnel files as excessive absenteeism without indicating they were absent because of sexual harassment. Similarly, in *Zabkowicz v. West Bend Co.*, 589 F.Supp. 780, 35 EPD ¶34,766 [35 FEP Cases 610] (E.D. Wis. 1984), co-workers harassed the plaintiff over a period of nearly four years in a manner the court described as "malevolent" and "outrageous." Despite the plaintiff's numerous complaints, her supervisor took no remedial action other than to hold occasional meetings at which he reminded employees of the company's policy against offensive conduct. The supervisor never conducted an investigation or disciplined any employees until the plaintiff filed an EEOC charge, at which time one of the offending co-workers was discharged and three others were suspended. The court held the employer liable because it failed to take immediate and appropriate corrective action.[39]

---

[39]*See also Delgado v. Lehman*, 665 F.Supp. 460, 44 EPD ¶37,517 [43 FEP Cases 593] (E.D. Va. 1987) (employer failed to conduct follow-up inquiry to determine if hostile environment had dissipated); *Salazar v. Church's Fried Chicken, Inc.*, 44 FEP Cases 472

When an employer asserts it has taken remedial action, the Commission will investigate to determine whether the action was appropriate and, more important, effective. The EEOC investigator should, of course, conduct an independent investigation of the harassment claim, and the Commission will reach its own conclusion as to whether the law has been violated. If the Commission finds that the harassment has been eliminated, all victims made whole, and preventive measures instituted, the Commission normally will administratively close the charge because of the employer's prompt remedial action.[40]

Date 3/19/90

Approved:

/s/R. Gaull Silberman
Vice Chairman

(S.D. Tex. 1987) (employer's policy inadequate because plaintiff, as a part-time teenage employee, could have concluded a complaint would be futile because the alleged harasser was the roommate of her store manager); *Brooms v. Regal Tube Co.*, 44 FEP Cases 1119 (N.D. Ill. 1987) (employer liable when a verbal reprimand proved ineffective and employer took no further action when informed of the harasser's persistence).

[40]For appropriate procedures, see §§4.4(e) and 15 of Volume I of the Compliance Manual.

APPENDIX 4

EEOC COMPLIANCE MANUAL SECTIONS
PERTAINING TO CHARGE OF SEXUAL HARASSMENT

SECTION 2
INTAKE OF CHARGES AND COMPLAINTS

(a) Coverage - Explain Title VII, ADEA, or EPA coverage as appropriate. If necessary, provide publications outlining these laws.
. . .

(b) Prohibited Discrimination - Explain the provisions of the applicable statutes and, in particular, the prohibition against retaliation.
. . .

(c) Confidentiality for Third Party Charges and Complaints - It is EEOC policy not to disclose the identity of persons on whose behalf a Title VII, concurrent (Title VII/ADEA or Title VII/EPA), or ADEA charge is filed or of ADEA/EPA complainants. Inform persons concerned about confidentiality of the option of filing a complaint or third party charge and advise that:

(1) Every effort will be made to avoid disclosure of their identity as an informant, unless required in a court action, without prior written consent (if it is later established that an investigation broad enough to protect their identity cannot be made, written consent will be obtained before proceeding - see §22.11);

(2) Even though the person has requested confidentiality, s/he may later permit EEOC to use his or her name in settlement efforts.
. . .

(e) Time limits for Obtaining Relief
(1) Title VII - Back pay may be obtained under Title VII for a period of up to two years before the filing of a charge, so long as the charge itself is timely filed pursuant to (d)(1) above and §605.7.
. . .

(g) Right to Sue
(1) Title VII - Persons who wish to sue under Title VII after a charge is filed must obtain a Notice of Right to Sue. Within 90 days of receipt of the Notice, suit may be filed for back pay, attorneys' fees, court costs, and appropriate make-whole or other injunctive relief.
. . .

(h) Deferral/Referral of Charges - In deferral/referral jurisdictions, explain that a copy of the charge will be sent to the FEPA, and, as appropriate, that the FEPA may investigate it in accordance with EEOC procedures (if the FEPA is certified, explain that EEOC will generally adopt its final finding unless the party asks for EEOC review within 15 days of receipt of the finding). Also explain as appropriate that a state court decision, whether initiated by the FEPA or either party, may bear a federal court suit.
. . .

(j) Sexual Harassment - When a party complains about a sensitive incident of alleged sexual harassment, but is embarrassed or reluctant to discuss the matter with an investiga-

Reprinted from *EEOC Compliance Manual,* The Bureau of National Affairs, Inc., Washington, D.C.

tor of the opposite sex, give the option of referral to an investigator of the same sex. If an investigator of the same sex is not immediately available, then an attorney or supervisor of the same sex may conduct the interview. If this situation only becomes apparent after referral to an investigator of the opposite sex, offer to arrange for completion of the interview by someone of the same sex. (However, deny requests to be interviewed by an investigator of the same sex, race, or national origin made for no apparent reason other than a belief that s/he may be better qualified or motivated to provide assistance.)

. . .

2.8 Charges Warranting Priority Handling - Immediately after intake, the RA should review a copy of every charge alleging retaliation or otherwise warranting preliminary relief (e.g., help-wanted ads for young executives, racial and/or sexual harassment, imminent destruction of records) for appropriate action.

(a) Retaliation Cases - Investigate all charges alleging retaliation on a priority basis. Identify on the face of the charge the statute under which retaliation is alleged to have occurred. See §614.3- - if it is found during the investigation that the charging party has been discriminated against because s/he filed the charge, then EEOC has authority to investigate the retaliation issue based on the original charge.

. . .

SECTION 615

HARASSMENT

Contents

SECTION 615

HARASSMENT

615.1 <u>Introduction</u> - This section discusses the issue of harassment in an employment context resulting from discrimination on a prohibited basis. The section addresses first sexual harassment (see §§615.2 through 615.5), then harassment which is based on sex but which does not constitute sexual harassment (see §615.6), and finally harassment based on race, religion, age, and national origin, respectively (see §§615.7 through 615.11). The section does not address the issue of retaliatory harassment in violation of §704(a) of Title VII, although there may be similarities between the types of discriminatory conduct described in this section and some forms of unlawful retaliation. (See §614, Section 704(a); see also §615.6(c) below.)

In investigating a charge of unlawful harassment, the EOS should be aware that a charging party may allege harassment on a combination of bases; for example, religion and national origin. Where a charge involves allegations of harassment on more than one basis, the EOS should still follow the basic investigative technique outlined in this section. If the issue of harassment on each specified basis considered separately is CDP, then harassment on the combined bases is CDP. If the issue of harassment on any one of the bases is non-CDP, then harassment on the combined bases is non-CDP. However, as an exception to this general rule, where a charging party alleges harassment on the combined bases of <u>race and sex</u>, that issue is non-CDP. This is so even though harassment based on race and harassment based on sex are CDP issues when considered separately. (See §615.7(d) below for the procedure to follow for such charges.)

The EOS, at any stage of charge processing, should also be aware that a harassment charge often presents a situation in which it would be appropriate, under §706(f)(2) of Title VII and §1601.13(d) of the Commission's Procedural Regulations, to bring an action in a U.S. district court seeking temporary or preliminary relief pending final disposition of the charge. For this reason, the EOS should refer a potential §706(f)(2) harassment charge to his/her supervisor without delay and follow the procedure established in the EEOC Compliance Manual, Volume I, §13.

As an example of this last point, preliminary relief in the form of a temporary restraining order (TRO) was granted to protect a charging party who had brought a charge of sexual harassment and who alleged that she was then discharged by her employer in retaliation for filing the first charge. The court ordered the employer to continue paying the charging party her salary without requiring her to return to the workplace pending a scheduled court hearing. The charge was successfully settled before the hearing date. <u>EEOC v. Golden State Glass Co.</u>, Civil Action No. CV 80-837 MML, 22 EPD ¶30,807 (C.D. Cal., TRO granted Mar. 6, 1980).

615.2 <u>Sexual Harassment</u>

(a) <u>Introduction</u> - The EEOC has long recognized that sexual harassment — like harassment on the basis of race, color, religion, or national origin — is an unlawful employment practice in violation of §703 of Title VII of the Civil Rights Act of 1964, as amended, 42 U.S.C. §2000e-2 (1976 & Supp.II 1978). In order to reaffirm its position that sexual harassment is sex discrimination, the Commission amended its existing Guidelines on Discrimination Because of Sex, 29 C.F.R. §1604.1 <u>et seq.</u> (1980), to add a new section, §1604.11, dealing specifically with sexual harassment. The Guidelines were amended on an interim basis, effective April 11, 1980. With minor modifications and one addition, the amended Guidelines were adopted in final form by the Commission and became effective upon publication in the Federal Register on November 10, 1980. 45 Fed. Reg. 74676 (1980) (to be codified in 29 C.F.R. §1604.11).

(b) <u>Recognizing Sexual Harassment</u> - A finding of sexual harassment does not depend on the existence of any one given set of facts. Sexual harassment can occur in a wide variety of circumstances and encompass many variables. Although the most widely recognized fact pattern is that in which a male supervisor sexually harasses a female employee, this form of harassment is not the only one recognized by the EEOC. The Commission's view of sexual harassment includes, but is not limited to, the following considerations:

(1) A man as well as a woman may be the victim of sexual harassment, and a woman as well as a man may be the harasser.

(2) The harasser does not have to be the victim's supervisor. (S)he may also be an agent of the employer, a supervisory employee who does not supervise the victim, a non-supervisory employee (co-worker), or, in some circumstances, even a non-employee.

(3) The victim does not have to be of the opposite sex from the harasser. Since sexual harassment is a form of sex discrimination, the crucial inquiry is whether the harasser treats a member or members of one sex differently from members of the other sex. The victim and the harasser may be of the same sex where, for instance, the sexual harassment is based on the victim's sex (<u>not</u> on the victim's sexual preference) and the harasser does not treat employees of the opposite sex the same way. (See Commission Decision No. 81-16, CCH Employment Practices Guide ¶6756, and §615.5(1) below.)

> <u>Example 1</u> - If a male supervisor of male and female employees makes unwelcome sexual advances toward a male employee because the employee is male but does not make similar advances toward female employees, then the male supervisor's conduct may constitute sexual harassment since the disparate treatment is based on the male employee's sex.
>
> <u>Example 2</u> - If a male supervisor harasses a male employee because of the employee's homosexuality, then the supervisor's conduct would not be sexual harassment since it is based on the employee's sexual preference, not on his gender. Title VII covers charges based on gender but not those based on sexual preference. (See Commission Decision Nos. 76-67 and 77-28, CCH Employment Practices Guide ¶¶6493 and 6578, respectively.)

(4) The victim does not have to be the person at whom the unwelcome sexual conduct is directed. (S)he may also be someone who is affected by such conduct when it is directed toward another person. For example, the sexual harassment of one female employee may create an intimidating, hostile, or offensive working environment for another female (or male) co-worker. (See §615.3(a)(3) below.)

(5) There is no requirement that the victim complain to the harasser or report the sexual harassment to his/her supervisor or employer in order for the employer to be held responsible for the unlawful conduct when the harassment is committed by a supervisor.

And while there is, likewise, no requirement that the victim complain to the harasser or report the sexual harassment where the act is committed by a co-worker or a non-employee, the employer will not be held responsible for the act unless it knew or should have known that the act occurred and failed to take appropriate corrective action. (See §615.3(d) below.)

(6) A finding of unlawful sexual harassment does not depend on the victim's having suffered a concrete economic injury as a result of the harasser's conduct. For example, improper sexual advances which do not result in the loss of a promotion by the victim or the discharge of the victim may, nonetheless, constitute sexual harassment where they unreasonably interfere with the victim's work or create a harmful or offensive work environment. (See Commission Decision No. 81-18, CCH Employment Practices Guide ¶6758.)

(c) Non-CDP Issue - The Commission will review charges of sexual harassment on a case-by-case basis, recognizing that actions which constitute sexual harassment in one factual context may not in another. With the narrow exceptions discussed below at §615.4(b), the issue of sexual harassment is non-CDP. Therefore, after completing the investigation of a charge alleging sexual harassment, the EOS should contact OPI for further instructions.

615.3 Sexual Harassment Guidelines - For purposes of the following discussion, the term "Guidelines" refers specifically to §1604.11 of the Commission's amended Guidelines on Discrimination Because of Sex. 45 Fed. Reg. 74676 (1980) (to be codified in 29 C.F.R. §1604.11). The Guidelines establish the criteria for determining when unwelcome sexual conduct, whether verbal or physical, constitutes sexual harassment and define the circumstances under which an employer is liable for such conduct. The Guidelines also describe how the Commission will review charges of sexual harassment. Because the Commission considers prevention to be the best means of eliminating sexual harassment, the Guidelines suggest affirmative steps an employer should take to prevent the occurrence of this unlawful employment practice. Finally, the Guidelines address an issue which is related to sexual harassment: how an employment decision based on sexual favors provided by one person may affect the employment rights of other persons. The provisions of each of the seven sections of the Guidelines are discussed in turn.

(a) Section 1604.11(a) - The first section of the Guidelines states that harassment on the basis of sex is a violation of §703 of Title VII. Sexual harassment is sex discrimination not because of the sexual nature of the conduct to which the victim is subjected but because the harasser treats a member or members of one sex differently from members of the opposite sex. However, it is the sexual nature of the prohibited conduct which makes this form of sex discrimination sexual harassment. (See §615.6 below.)

This section further states that unwelcome sexual advances, requests for sexual favors, and other verbal or physical conduct of a sexual nature constitute sexual harassment when any one of three criteria is met:

(1) Submission to such conduct is made either explicitly or implicitly a term or condition of an individual's employment.

> Example - If a female laborer complains to her foreman that the male workers on the job direct sexually suggestive remarks and gestures at her and the foreman tells her that such conduct is to be expected as part of the job, then her submission to the sexually harassing conduct is made an explicit term or condition of her employment.

No such overt statement is necessary to show that submission to sexual harassment is a term or condition of employment where a connection between employment and submission can be inferred. Such an inference could be made where, for example, other women workers had complained to the employer, either directly or through an agent or supervisor, and had been told that if they did not like the conduct they could find other jobs. Because submission to such sexual conduct is an additional term or condition of employment, one not imposed on employees of the opposite sex, it is sex discrimination and, specifically, sexual harassment.

(2) Submission to or rejection of such conduct by an individual is used as the basis for employment decisions affecting such individual.

> Example - If an employee's promotion depends on his or her granting certain sexual favors and the promotion is denied because the employee refuses to do so, then the employee is the victim of sexual harassment. The same result is reached if the employee does submit and consequently receives the promotion.

Basing any employment decision on whether the affected individual submits to or rejects unwelcome sexual conduct is sexual harassment where a similar decision affecting a member of the opposite sex is not so based. The decision need not have a concrete economic effect on the victim, although it often does, because the nature of the specific employment decision is irrelevant. Whether it involves promotion, discharge, transfer, training, work assignment, salary, overtime, or getting an office with a window — the decision cannot have a sexual string attached.

(3) Such conduct has the purpose or effect of unreasonably interfering with an individual's work performance or creating an intimidating, hostile, or offensive work environment.

> Example 1 - If a male co-worker of a female employee makes unwelcome sexual advances toward her, his conduct may depending on the total circumstances, unreasonably interfere with her ability to do her work. Likewise, his conduct may unreasonably interfere with the work performance of other employees, male or female.

> Example 2 - If certain male employees make sexual remarks, jokes, or gestures in the presence of or directed toward female employees, that conduct may make the work atmosphere intimidating or threatening for the female employees. The harassment of the female employees may also create an offensive work environment for other male employees.

In the examples, the objectionable conduct may not be such that submission to it constitutes a term or condition of employment, and submission to or rejection of the conduct may not be the basis of an employment decision. Nonetheless, the conduct is sexual harassment if it unreasonably interferes with an employee's work performance or creates a negative work environment, even if the conduct is not specifically directed at the person who is affected by it. This section is intentionally broad enough to encompass types of sexual harassment which might not be covered in other ways.

The section also reaffirms that, consistent with Title VII principles, an employee's work atmosphere should be free from harassment and intimidation based on sex. (See §§615.7 through 615:10 for a discussion of an employer's affirmative duty to maintain a working environment free from harassment on the basis of race, religion, or national origin.)

It should be noted that the conduct described in a charge of sexual harassment may meet more than one or even all three of the criteria established in §1604.11(a). For example, the act or acts alleged may be found to constitute an unlawful term or condition of employment and also to create an intimidating, hostile, or offensive work environment and/or to underlie an employment decision based on the victim's response to the conduct. By the same token, a specific example given in this section to illustrate one criterion may also overlap and serve to illustrate another criterion. (For a discussion of investigative procedure for determining whether alleged conduct constitutes sexual harassment, see §615.4(a) below.)

(b) Section 1604.11(b) - This section provides that, in reviewing a charge of sexual harassment, the Commission will examine the record in its entirety, considering the allegations in light of the total evidence presented. The final determination of whether the alleged conduct constitutes sexual harassment will be based on the specific facts of each case. The section recognizes that an action which is sexual harassment in one set of circumstances may, in another context, not be.

> Example - A female secretary works for two male supervisors, and each man invites her on repeated but separate occasions to go out for a drink or dinner after work. She considers the invitations of the first supervisor to be unwelcome and does not accept them, although he indicates that her job depends on her having a sexual relationship with him. However, she gladly accepts the invitations of the second supervisor, with whom she has an outside social relationship unrelated to their business relationship in the office.

As in the example, submission to a specific form of sexual conduct may be an unlawful condition of continued employment in one case. In another case, similar submission may be part of a voluntary personal relationship having no employment consequences. For this reason, the legality of a particular action will he determined on a case-by-case basis. (See §615.4(a) below on investigative procedure for sexual harassment charges.)

(c) Section 1604.11(c) - This section of the Guidelines specifies that the term "employer" refers to an employer, employment agency, joint apprenticeship committee, or labor organization. The section provides that an employer is responsible for its own acts of sexual harassment and those of its agents and supervisory employees. The responsibility exists regardless of whether the specific acts complained of were authorized or even prohibited by the employer and regardless of whether the employer knew or should have known of their occurrence. In sum, the section imposes strict liability on the employer for sexual harassment committed by it, its agents, or supervisory employees. The strict liability standard applied here is in keeping with Title VII principles and the general standard of employer responsibility for acts of agents and supervisors.

The section also provides that the Commission will determine whether an individual acts in an agency or supervisory capacity on the basis of the particular facts involved. Therefore, the Commission will look beyond a job description or title to examine the specific job functions performed by the individual. For example, if an individual who is temporarily assigned supervisory duties engages in sexual harassment of an employee, then the employer may be strictly liable for that individual's conduct while acting in a supervisory capacity. (See §615.4(a) below on investigative procedure and §615.4(b) below on the CDP issue of supervisory sexual harassment having economic impact.)

The term "agent" is used in the Guidelines in the same way as it is used in §701(b) of Title VII where "agent" is included in the definition of employer." (See §605.7(c), Jurisdiction.) The issue of whether an individual acts as an agent is non-CDP. Therefore, the EOS should contact OPI for further instructions whenever a harassment charge involves a determination of an individual's status as an agent of the employer.

(d) Section 1604.11(d) - This section defines an employer's liability for sexual harassment of an employee by a fellow employee. The section provides that the employer is responsible for the unlawful conduct where the employer, or its agents, or its supervisory employees knew or should have known of the conduct, unless the employer can show that it took immediate and appropriate corrective action. In contrast to the provisions of the preceding section holding an employer strictly liable for sexual harassment committed by it, its agents, or supervisory employees, this section does not impose strict liability on the employer for co-worker sexual harassment.

As discussed above, there is no requirement that the victim report the sexual harassment to his/her supervisor or employer. However, in the context of co-worker sexual harassment or non-employee sexual harassment, discussed below, employer responsibility depends, among other things, on a finding that the employer knew or had reason to know of the unlawful conduct. Therefore, a showing that the conduct was reported is one means of evidencing employer knowledge in such cases; but showing that the conduct was not reported does not automatically preclude a finding that the employer knew or had reason to know of the sexual harassment.

In accordance with the provisions of this section, an employer will be deemed to know or have reason to know of the sexual harassment if an agent or supervisor of the employer knows or has reason to know. Where the employer, its agents, and its supervisors do not know or have reason to know of the harassment, then the employer is not liable. Where the employer, its agents, or its supervisory personnel do know or have reason to know of the harassment, then the employer may still not be liable if the employer can show that it took immediate and appropriate corrective action. The Commission will determine on a case-by-case basis what constitutes "reason to know" and "immediate and appropriate corrective action." (See §615.4(a) below on investigative procedure.)

In holding an employer liable for co-worker sexual harassment in the stated circumstances, this section recognizes that co-worker conduct can have an impact on an employee's ability to successfully perform his/her job. For example, although a co-worker does not have authority to make employment decisions, his/her lack of cooperation may adversely affect a fellow employee's performance and, consequently, result in the employer's taking action against the fellow employee. (See, e.g., Commission Decision No. 71-2725, CCH EEOC Decisions (1973) ¶6290.) Co-worker sexual harassment can lead to the same result. Clearly, such harassment can also detrimentally affect the working environment.

(e) Section 1604.11 (e) - This section provides that an employer may also be responsible for the sexual harassment of an employee by a non-employee. The basic standard applied by this section is similar to that in the preceding section defining employer responsibility for co-worker sexual harassment. The employer may be responsible where the employer, or its agents, or its supervisory employees knew or should have known of the unlawful conduct and the employer failed to take immediate and appropriate corrective action. However, the difference between the two sections is that an employer is liable for co-worker sexual harassment if the two conditions (knowledge and failure to take remedial action) are met. An employer is potentially liable for non-employee sexual harassment in the same circumstances, but actual liability depends upon additional factors as well.

This section identifies these additional factors as the extent of the employer's control over the non-employee and any other legal responsibility which the employer may have with respect to the non-employee's conduct. The Commission will determine an employer's liability for non-employee sexual harassment on the basis of the total facts and circumstances of each case, including employer knowledge, corrective action, control, and other legal responsibility. (See §615.4(a) below on investigative procedure.)

> Example 1 - When the waitress asked if the four male customers seated at the table were ready to order, one man put his arm tightly around her waist and told her that what he wanted was not on the menu, prompting his companions to laugh and comment in the same vein. When she was finally able to finish taking their orders, the man removed his arm and patted her as she turned to leave. She went directly to the restaurant manager and reported the unwelcome sexual conduct. The employer may be responsible if, on learning of the sexual harassment, it failed to take immediate and appropriate corrective action within its control. Depending on the circumstances, such action might be as relatively simple as switching table assignments to have a waiter finish serving that table and making whatever arrangement might be necessary so that the waitress would not be financially or otherwise harmed by the

substitution (for instance, by losing the amount of a tip she could have earned).

Example 2 - An employer contracted to have the office duplicating machine serviced, which was frequently necessary. The female employee who was responsible for operating the machine dreaded service calls because the male service representative who repaired and maintained the machine made sexual advances toward her whenever he was in the office and she found his unwelcome behavior increasingly disturbing. When he told her that he would be unable to make a rush repair unless she "cooperated" by going out with him, she complained to her supervisor. As in the preceding example, the employer may be responsible in such circumstances if it failed to take corrective measures within its control once it knew or had reason to know of the sexual harassment.

It bears repeating that, although the victim in both of the examples reported the non-employee's sexual harassment, such reporting is not a requirement. However, it could have a bearing on the issue of employer knowledge. (See §615.3(d) above.)

Because the Commission will decide the liability issue on a case-by-case basis, evidence that the wrongful conduct was by a non-employee of a certain type or description (for example, a salesperson, or a repairperson, or a customer) will neither conclusively establish nor bar employer liability. Whether an employer is ultimately responsible will depend on the relationship between the employer and the non-employee as revealed by the specific factual context in which the allegedly unlawful conduct occurred.

(f) Section 1604.11(f) - This section emphasizes the Commission's position that the best means of eliminating sexual harassment is preventing its occurrence. Toward that end, the section provides that an employer should take all necessary steps to prevent sexual harassment and suggests several kinds of action an employer can take, including: affirmatively raising the subject, expressing strong disapproval, developing appropriate sanctions, informing employees how to raise and pursue their Title VII right to be free from sexual harassment, and sensitizing all concerned. The Commission recognizes that what constitutes appropriate preventive action depends on the nature of the particular workplace. Therefore, each employer should develop its own preventive program tailored to its individual circumstances. (See §615.4(a) below on investigative procedure.)

(g) Section 1604.11(g) - The final section of the Guidelines addresses an issue which does not involve sexual harassment but which the Commission recognizes as related to sexual harassment and governed by general Title VII principles. The section states that an employer may be liable for unlawful sex discrimination against persons who were qualified for but denied an employment opportunity or benefit which was granted to another person because that individual provided sexual favors to the person who granted the employment opportunity or benefit.

The person(s) to whom an employer may be liable under the provisions of this section depends on the specific factual circumstances.

Example - If a male supervisor recommends a promotion for a female employee (who may or may not be qualified) because she is engaged in a sexual relationship with him, then the supervisor's action may constitute sex discrimination against an eligible and qualified male employee who consequently lost the promotion opportunity.

However, the male in the example may not be the only employee who can allege sex discrimination in that context. Depending on the facts, a showing of sex discrimination may also be made by an eligible and qualified female employee who was likewise denied the promotion opportunity.

> Example - If such a female employee were to show, for instance, that sex is a factor in getting a promotion and that the employer traditionally only promotes male employees (this particular promotion notwithstanding because of the circumstances), then the fact that a woman was promoted would not preclude a finding of sex discrimination against the female employee who was denied the promotion.

In accordance with the provisions of this section, employer liability, if any is found to exist, is based on sex discrimination — which can affect males or females, employees or non-employees. The Commission will determine the liability issue involved in such charges on a case-by-case basis, closely examining the entire factual record. In sum, the Commission will follow the same procedure in this area as it follows in resolving questions which arise in the related area of sexual harassment.

615.4 <u>Investigating Charges of Sexual Harassment</u> - As indicated in the preceding discussion of the Guidelines, the Commission will decide charges of sexual harassment on a case-by-case basis. When a charge alleging sexual harassment is received for investigation, the EOS should follow the procedure outlined below. With the narrow exceptions specified in §615.4(b), the issue of sexual harassment is non-CDP. Therefore, unless the facts alleged in the charge fall within the exceptions, the EOS should contact OPI for further instructions when the investigation is completed.

(a) <u>Matter to Be Investigated</u> - In investigating a charge of sexual harassment, the EOS should:

(1) Specifically detail the conduct which is alleged to constitute sexual harassment. Include the type(s) of conduct, the frequency of occurrence, and the date(s) on which or the time period over which the conduct occurred.

(2) Ascertain the specific context(s) in which the conduct occurred. Include the nature and general description of the workplace and the specific location and circumstances in which the conduct occurred.

(3) Determine the effect of the conduct on the charging party: identify the type(s) of effect (e.g., economic, non-economic, and/or psychological), and detail the specific consequences involved. For example, if the charging party was discharged for rejecting the employer's sexual advances, determine whether and to what extent (s)he suffered economic harm (including wages lost less other income earned, benefits lost, and expenses incurred).

(4) Determine the time relationship between the occurrence of conduct and its effect on the charging party.

(5) Ascertain whether persons of the opposite sex from the charging party were subjected to similar conduct or were treated differently by the alleged harasser.

(6) Identify the relationship of the alleged harasser to the employer; i.e., determine whether the harasser was the employer, an agent of the employer, a supervisory employee, a non-supervisory employee (co-worker), or a non-employee. Make this determination on the basis of the total facts existing at the time of the alleged sexual harassment, not just on the basis of a job title or description. For example, if the harasser was a non-supervisory employee (co-worker of the charging party), ascertain whether (s)he was acting in a supervisory capacity when the conduct occurred.

In determining whether an individual was a supervisor or agent:

(i) Ascertain his/her job title;

(ii) Obtain a copy, if available, of his/her job description;

(iii) Ascertain the specific duties performed at the time of the alleged sexual harassment; and

(iv) Especially, note whether (s)he directed and had responsibility for the work of other employees; had authority to recommend, even if not to make, employment decisions affecting others (e.g., hiring, firing, promoting, granting, or denying leave); or was responsible for the maintenance of administrative records concerning others (e.g., time, attendance).

Such a determination is important in identifying the classification not only of the alleged harasser but also of a person who allegedly knew or should have known of the conduct.

Note, however, that the issue of whether an individual acted as an agent of the employer is non-CDP. (See §615.3(c) above.) Therefore, after obtaining the information listed above and otherwise completing the investigation, contact OPI for further instructions.

(7) If the alleged harasser was a non-employee, ascertain the extent of the employer's control over and legal responsibility for the conduct of the harasser.

(8) If the alleged harasser was a co-worker or a non-employee, determine whether the employer, an agent of the employer, or a supervisory employee knew or should have known of the alleged sexual harassment.

In this regard, ascertain whether:

(i) The charging party or any other individual reported or complained of the harasser's conduct to the employer, an agent, or supervisor;

(ii) The employer, an agent, or a supervisor observed or was in a position to observe the conduct; or

(iii) The employer, an agent, or a supervisor was or should have been otherwise alerted to the conduct (if, for example, the conduct was discussed in the presence of the employer, an agent, or a supervisor).

Obtain copies of any available documentation (e.g., letters, memoranda, reports, statements) which would support a conclusion that such persons knew or had reason to know of the sexual harassment.

(9) If the alleged harasser was a co-worker or a non-employee, also determine whether the employer took immediate and appropriate
corrective action.

In making this determination, ascertain:

(i) What action, if any, was taken;

(ii) When it was taken; and

(iii) Whether it fully remedied the conduct without adversely affecting the terms or conditions of the charging party's employment in some manner (for example, by requiring the charging party to work less desirable hours or in a less desirable location).

Also note whether the employer had a policy or practice designed to prevent the occurrence of sexual harassment and what specific steps, if any, the employer had taken to implement such a policy or practice.

(10) Obtain statements from witnesses or other persons, if any, who can corroborate or support any of the charging party's allegations. Such evidence is very important in a sexual harassment charge. Without it, the record often consists of the charging party's word against that of the employer; and the outcome depends on the credibility of the charging party.

(11) Obtain statements from other persons, if any, who are or have been victims of sexual 'harassment by the alleged harasser in the workplace. These people do not have to be working for the employer at the time of the investigation. They may, for example, have quit before charging party was hired in order to escape the sexual harassment.

(12) Obtain a statement from the alleged harasser. Also obtain statements from witnesses or other persons, if any, who can corroborate or support the employer's statements.

(13) If an adverse employment action was taken against the charging party, ascertain the employer's reason(s) for the action and obtain any information or documentation which would bear on the legitimacy of the reason given. In this regard, note that there may be a connection between the employment decision and the alleged harassment which is not readily apparent.

For example, if the employer discharges the charging party because of his/her deteriorating work performance or absenteeism and the charging party's poor record is the result of sexual harassment, the employer's reason may be a pretext for unlawful discrimination against the charging party if the employer knows of the sexual harassment. Where such an adverse action is taken, compare the charging party's performance or record before and after the alleged harassment and note whether the employer provided the charging party with any notice (e.g.. a written warning) prior to taking the adverse action.

(14) If the charging party alleges that (s)he was sexually harassed by more than one person, follow the investigative procedure outlined above with respect to each alleged harasser.

(b) CDP Issues - Two narrow exceptions exist to the general rule that sexual harassment is a non-CDP issue. It is CDP only where either of the two allegations listed below forms the basis for a sexual harassment charge. In such cases, the EOS should still follow the investigative procedure outlined above. However, upon completion of the investigation, the district office may issue an LOD without contacting OPI.

(1) Sexual harassment is CDP where the charge consists of an allegation by the charging party that (s)he suffered concrete economic harm as a result of rejecting his/her supervisor's unwelcome sexual advances or requests for sexual favors. (See Commission Decision No. 81-17, CCH Employment Practices Guide ¶6757.) The loss of wages due to denial of promotion or discharge is one example of such economic harm.

A cause LOD should be issued where the investigation reveals the following evidence:

(i) The charging party's supervisor made unwelcome sexual advances toward or requests for sexual favors from the charging party.

(ii) The charging party rejected the supervisor's sexual advances or requests.

(iii) As a result of the charging party's rejection of the supervisor's sexual advances or requests, the supervisor used his/her official position to take an adverse employment action against the charging party or the supervisor's conduct forced the charging party to take an action which was against the charging party's own employment interests (e.g., resigning).

(iv) The employment action resulted in economic injury to the charging party.

Note: If the charging party submitted to the advances or requests for sexual favors, the issue is non-CDP regardless of whether economic benefit or harm resulted from the submission.

(2) Sexual harassment is also CDP where the charge consists of an allegation that charging party's employer required him/her to wear a sexually provocative and revealing uniform and that a charging party was sexually harassed as a result of wearing the uniform. (See Commission Decision No. 77-36, CCH Employment Practices Guide ¶6588; Commission Decision No. 81-17, CCH Employment Practices Guide ¶6757; EEOC v. Sage Realty Corp., 507 F. Supp. 599, 25 EPD ¶31,529 (S.D. N.Y. 1981); and §619, Grooming Standards). Often charging party may further allege that the employer took an adverse employment action against him/her for refusing to continue to wear the uniform; however, such an allegation is not necessary for this issue to be CDP.

A cause LOD should be issued where the investigation reveals the following evidence:

(i) The charging party's employer required him/her to wear a sexually provocative and revealing uniform as a term or condition of employment.

(ii) The employer did not require employees of the opposite sex from the charging party to wear similarly sexually provocative and revealing uniforms.

(iii) As a result of wearing the uniform, the charging party was sexually harassed.

(iv) The charging party refused to continue wearing the uniform, and the employer took an adverse employment action against the charging party because of the refusal. (Note: These two elements are not essential to a cause determination but may form part of the findings supporting a cause LOD.)

615.5 Court Cases on Sexual Harassment - The body of federal case law on sexual harassment is of relatively recent origin. It was not until 1976 that a federal district court found that the discharge of a female employee for rejecting the sexual advances of her male supervisor constituted sex discrimination in violation of Title VII. Williams v. Saxbe, cited below. That decision laid the foundation for federal case law recognizing sexual harassment as a form of sex discrimination prohibited by Title VII. In the following year, 1977, three federal courts of appeals reversed lower court decisions which had held that sexual harassment claims were not within the scope of Title VII. Garber v. Saxon Business Products, Inc., (4th Cir.); Barnes v. Costle, (D.C. Cir.); and Tomkins v. Public Service Electric & Gas Co., (3d Cir.), cited below. In 1979, the Court of Appeals for the Ninth Circuit held that an employer is strictly liable for sexual harassment committed by a supervisor, applying the legal doctrine of respondeat superior. Miller v. Bank of America, cited below. In 1981, the Court of Appeals for the District of Columbia Circuit held, in a case involving sexual harassment of a female employee by various male supervisors, that an employer is liable for sexual harassment which creates a discriminatory working environment even if it does not result in economic harm to the victim. Bundy v. Jackson, cited below.

Although reported federal court decisions in sexual harassment cases are still few, the number is growing. However, with few exceptions, these cases have involved sexual harassment of a female employee by her male supervisor with resulting economic harm to the victim. Many sexual harassment issues in other factual contexts are yet to be directly addressed by the courts or successfully litigated. Moreover, courts have applied different standards in determining employer liability. The following list is not exhaustive but includes the leading cases in this area.

(a) Williams v. Saxbe, 413 F.Supp. 654, 11 EPD ¶10,840 (D.D.C. 1976), rev'd and remanded on other grounds sub nom. Williams v. Bell, 587 F.2d 1240, 17 EPD ¶8605 (D.C. Cir. 1978), decided on remand sub nom. Williams v. Civiletti, 487 F. Supp. 1387, 23 EPD ¶30,916 (D.D.C. 1980) (submission to supervisor's sexual advances was a term and condition of plaintiff's employment in violation of Title VII).

(b) Garber v. Saxon Business Products, Inc., 552 F.2d 1032, 14 EPD ¶7598 (4th Cir. 1977) (complaint alleged an employer policy or acquiescence in a practice of compelling female employees to submit to male supervisors' sexual advances in violation of Title VII).

(c) Barnes v. Costle, 561 F.2d 983, 14 EPD ¶7755 (D.C. Cir. 1977) (appellant established a prima facie case of sex discrimination by alleging that retention of her job was conditioned upon submission to sexual relations with her supervisor and that, but for her sex, such a condition would not have been imposed; generally, an employer is chargeable with Title VII violations committed by its supervisory personnel).

(d) Tomkins v. Public Service Electric & Gas Co., 568 F.2d 1044, 15 EPD ¶7954 (3rd Cir. 1977) (a Title VII violation is alleged where (1) a term or condition of employment has been imposed, and (2) it has been imposed by the employer, either directly or vicariously, in a sexually discriminatory fashion).

(e) Miller v. Bank of America, 600 F.2d 211, 20 EPD ¶30,086 (9th Cir. 1979) (the employer was not relieved of liability either because of its established policy against sexual harassment or because of the plaintiff's failure to use the personnel procedures available to her). The court concluded: ". . . [R]espondeat superior does apply here, where the action complained of was that of a supervisor, authorized to hire, fire, discipline or promote, or at least to participate in or recommend such actions, even though what the supervisor is said to have done violates company policy." 600 F.2d at 213 (emphasis added).

The decision in this case is particularly significant because, in the stated context, the plaintiff's Title VII claim was not dependent upon the employer's knowing or having reason to know of the sexual harassment and failing to take corrective action. The standard applied by the court is the same strict liability standard applied by the EEOC under §1604.11(c) of the Guidelines, defining employer responsibility for sexual harassment committed by the employer, its agents, or its supervisory employees.

(f) Bundy v. Jackson, 641 F.2d 934, 24 EPD ¶31,439 (D.C. Cir. 1981), rev'g and remanding Civil Action No. 77-1359, 19 EPD ¶9154 (D.D.C., Apr. 25, 1979) (the court reversed the lower court's conclusion that, although the plaintiff fully proved supervisory sexual harassment, she had not been discriminated against in any term or condition of employment, including promotions; the court ordered the employer to establish specific procedures for investigating and remedying sexual harassment).

Noting that violations of Title VII have been found where harassment on the basis of race or national origin creates a discriminatory work environment, the court applied the same principles in holding that such an atmosphere resulting from sexual harassment likewise violates Title VII. This important decision is consistent with the Commission's position and with §1604.11(a)(3) of the Guidelines.

(g) Munford v. James T. Barnes & Co., 441 F. Supp. 459, 16 EPD ¶8233 (E.D. Mich. 1977) (an employer has an affirmative duty to investigate sexual harassment complaints and deal appropriately with the offending personnel).

(h) Heelan v. Johns Manville Corp., 451 F. Supp. 1382, 16 EPD ¶8330 (D.Colo. 197K) (plaintiff established a prima facie case of sex discrimination by showing that (1) submission to her supervisor's sexual advances was a term or condition of employment, (2) this fact substantially affected her employment, and (3) employees of the opposite sex were not similarly affected. Plaintiff is not required to prove a policy or practices of the employer endorsing sexual harassment).

(i) Rinkel v. Associated Pipeline Contractors, Inc., Civil Action No. F77-19, 16 EPD ¶8331 (D. Alaska, Apr. 6, 1978) (plaintiff stated a cause of action under Title VII by alleging that she was denied another position with the defendant because she refused to perform sexual acts with a senior management official; plaintiff is not required to plead that the alleged incidents of sexual harassment involved a policy or continued practice on the part of the employer).

(j) Kyriazi v. Western Electric Co., 461 F. Supp. 894, 18 EPD ¶8700 (D.N.J. 1978) (sexual harassment of female employee by male co-workers included loud remarks of a sexual nature and the creation and dissemination of an obscene cartoon designed to embarass and humiliate her as a woman; supervisors' awareness and failure to take action implicitly encouraged the harassment).

(k) Equal Employment Opportunity Commission v. Sage Realty Corp., 507 F. Supp. 599, 25 EPD ¶31,529 (S.D. N.Y. 1981) (employer imposed a sexually discriminatory term or condition of employment by requiring female employee to wear a revealing and provocative uniform which subjected her to sexual harassment by the public).

(l) Wright v. Methodist Youth Services, Inc., _____ F. Supp. _____, 25 EPD ¶31,712 (N.D. Ill. 1981) (male plaintiff stated a cause of action under Title VII by alleging that he was discharged for rejecting his male supervisor's homosexual advances).

615.6 Harassment on the Basis of Sex and Related Conduct Not Constituting Sexual Harassment - Sexual harassment is one type of harassment based on sex. However, it is not the only type of unlawful harassment which is sex-based or which stems from sex discrimination. For proper processing and investigation of harassment charges, it is important to correctly distinguish sexual harassment from other forms of sex-based harassment and related conduct.

(a) Sexual Harassment Distinguished - Sexual harassment is a form of sex discrimination in which the prohibited conduct is sexual in nature, not just sex-based. Additionally, the allegedly discriminatory conduct must fall within the definition of sexual harassment set forth in §1604.11(a) of the Guidelines. If the alleged discrimination does not meet one or more of the criteria in §1604.11(a), then it is not sexual harassment. (See §615.3(a) above.)

(1) Verbal Conduct - In describing discriminatory conduct which may be sexual harassment, the Guidelines include unwelcome sexual advances and requests for sexual favors. Such forms of conduct are clearly sexual in nature. It is important to bear in mind that the discriminatory, unwelcome "verbal conduct" referred to in the Guidelines must also be of a sexual nature in order to constitute sexual harassment.

Other forms of verbal conduct or harassment (such as terms or expressions) may unlawfully discriminate on the basis of sex (gender) without being sexual in nature. For instance, an employer's practice of referring to male employees as "men" and female employees as "girls" discriminates against the women on the basis of their sex. As noted by the Commission, there is an implication of female inferiority inherent in such disparate treatment. Commission Decision No. 72-0679, CCH EEOC Decisions (1973) ¶6124.

However, such discriminatory verbal conduct is not sexual in nature and, therefore, is not sexual harassment. (See §613, Terms, Conditions, and Privileges.)

Similarly some forms of verbal conduct (such as specific words or some jokes) may involve sex or sexuality without discriminating on the basis of sex. That is, such conduct does not treat one sex either more or less favorably than the other sex. Without such disparate treatment, unwelcome verbal conduct of a sexual nature is not sex discrimination and, consequently, cannot be sexual harassment.

Verbal conduct — no matter how offensive — which neither discriminates on the basis of sex nor is sexual in nature clearly cannot be sexual harassment. Such conduct includes, for example, profanity or vulgar language of a non-sexual nature. If, however, such language were used in the presence of or directed toward members of one sex only, then the conduct would constitute sex discrimination but still not sexual harassment.

(2) Physical Conduct - The distinction drawn in the preceding discussion applies equally to discriminatory, unwelcome "physical conduct." It must be of a sexual nature to constitute sexual harassment. Physical conduct — such as obstructing a person's path, pushing him/her, grabbing his/her arm — is sex discrimination if it based on the sex of the person subjected to it. However, it is not sexual harassment unless the manner or context in which it occurs has sexual implications.

(b) Harassment on the Basis of Sex - As discussed above, some types of unwelcome verbal or physical conduct may constitute harassment or some other form of sex discrimination, although not sexual harassment. However, harassment on the basis of sex is not limited to discriminatory verbal or physical conduct. It also encompasses many other forms of unlawful conduct.

Berating an individual for mistakes, criticizing his/her work performance, keeping strict account of absence or tardiness, taking away duties or responsibilities, imposing additional work or burdensome conditions, forbidding conversation with co-workers, suggesting that (s)he quit are examples of conduct which may be harassment. A refusal to instruct or assist or to cooperate in work requiring team effort is still another example of conduct which may constitute unlawful harassment. If such conduct is directed at an individual because of his/her sex — whether by the employer, a supervisor, or a co-worker — it constitutes prohibited sex discrimination. (See, e.g., Commission Decision No. 71-2725, CCH EEOC Decisions (1973) ¶6290.) Under Title VII, an employer has an affirmative duty to maintain a working environment free from such harassment.

With one exception, harassment on the basis of sex (which is not sexual harassment) is a CDP issue. In investigating such an allegation, the EOS should follow the basic procedure outlined in §615.4(a) above. Because this issue is CDP, the district office may issue an LOD upon completion of the investigation without contacting OPI. Importantly, however, an allegation of harassment on the combined bases of sex and race presents a non-CDP issue. (See §615.7(d) below.)

(c) Harassment in Violation of §704(a) - Section 704(a) of Title VII prohibits an employer from retaliating against an individual for opposing unlawful employment practices or for filing a charge or otherwise participating in a Title VII proceeding. Harassment is one form of such prohibited retaliation and may involve, for example, the types of conduct described above to illustrate harassment on the basis of sex. (See, e.g., Commission Decision Nos. 70-661, 71-382, and 72-1883, CCH EEOC Decisions (1973) ¶¶6138, 6202, and 6375, respectively; and Commission Decision Nos. 74-93 and 74-133, CCH Employment Practices Guide ¶¶6426 and 6497, respectively.)

While such harassment violates §704(a), it does not constitute either sexual harassment or harassment on the basis of sex (which are both violations of §703 of Title VII), even if it stems from the victim's opposing sex discrimination. Retaliatory harassment is a separate and distinct violation. (See §614, Section 704(a).) However, a charge of sexual harassment or of harassment on the basis of sex (or on any other prohibited basis) may include a separate allegation of harassment in violation of §704(a) stemming from the charging party's opposition to the initial discriminatory conduct.

615.7 <u>Harassment on the Bases of Race, Religion, and National Origin</u>

(a) <u>Introduction</u> - As discussed above in the introduction to the topic of sexual harassment (see §615.2), the EEOC has long recognized that harassment on the basis of race, color, religion, or national origin is an unlawful employment practice in violation of §703 of Title VII of the Civil Rights Act of 1964, as amended, 42 U.S.C. §2000e-2 (1976 & Supp. II 1978). The Commission has held and continues to hold that, under Title VII, an employer has an affirmative duty to maintain a working environment free from such harassment, intimidation, or insult and that the duty encompasses a requirement to take positive action where necessary to eliminate such practices or remedy their effects. (See Commission decisions cited below, §§615.8 through 615.10.) The Commission's position on the issue of harassment has been upheld by the courts. (See, e.g., Rogers v. EEOC, 454 F.2d 234, 4 EPD ¶7597 (5th Cir. 1971), cert. denied, 406 U.S. 957, 4 EPD ¶7838 (1972); EEOC v. Murphy Motor Freight lines, Inc., 488 F. Supp. 381, 22 EPD ¶30,888 (D.Mn. 1980); and cases cited below in §§615.8 through 615.10.) However, as with sexual harassment, courts have applied differing standards in determining employer liability.

(b) <u>Applicable Principles and Standards</u> - As noted by the Commission in the first section of the amended Guidelines on Discrimination Because of Sex ("Guidelines," see §615.3 above), the principles involved with regard to sexual harassment continue to apply to harassment on the basis of race, color, religion, or national origin. By the same token, although the Commission's views expressed in §615.2(b) above concern sexual harassment, the underlying concepts have equal validity when applied to other types of unlawful harassment.

In conformity with §1604.11(b) of the Guidelines, the Commission will continue to determine on a case-by-case basis whether alleged conduct constitutes racial, religious, or national origin harassment, considering the circumstances and context in which the conduct occurred as reflected by the entire record. (See §615.3 above.) In determining whether an employer is liable for such harassment, the Commission has applied and will continue to apply the standards set forth in the Guidelines, §1604.11(c)-(e): an employer is strictly liable for harassment committed by it, its agents, or its supervisors; and an employer is responsible for co-worker harassment and may be responsible for non-employee harassment if the employer, its agents, or supervisors knew or should have known of the unlawful conduct and the employer failed to take immediate and appropriate corrective action. (See the discussion at §615.3 above.)

(c) <u>CDP Issues</u> - With one exception discussed below, all issues raised by allegations of racial, religious, or national origin harassment are CDP. In investigating such allegations, the EOS should follow the basic procedure outlined in §615.4(a) above, substituting the appropriate basis (i.e., race, religion, or national origin) in place of sex. Because these issues are CDP, the district office may issue an LOD upon completion of the investigation without contacting OPI.

(d) <u>Non-CDP Issue</u> - The one exception to the information given in the preceding paragraph is that an allegation of harassment based on race and sex raises a non-CDP issue. Consequently, before the district office may issue an LOD on such a charge, the EOS should contact OPI for further instructions once the investigation is completed.

> Example - A Black female employee alleges that her supervisor subjects her and/or other Black females to sexual harassment because of her/their race and sex but does not sexually harass White female employees.

615.8 <u>Racial Harassment</u>

(a) <u>Commission Decisions</u>

(1) Commission Decision No. YSF 9-061, CCH EEOC Decisions (1973) ¶6013 (Black employee was subjected to co-worker and supervisory harassment even after

employer signed conciliation agreement; mere announcement of policy against racial discrimination is insufficient where management has reason to believe racial discrimination is occurring).

(2) Commission Decision No. YSF 9-108, CCH EEOC Decisions (1973) ¶6030 (Title VII requires an employer to maintain a working environment free from racial intimidation, including taking positive action where necessary to redress or eliminate employee harassment; here, employer clearly had knowledge of supervisory and co-worker harassment of Black employee and, rather than aiding the victim, accommodated the wrongdoers by discharging their victim).

(3) Commission Decision No. 70-61, CCH EEOC Decisions (1973) ¶6059 (cause found where Black female supervisor was demoted for inability to perform supervisory duties as result of harassment by supervisors and subordinates).

(4) Commission Decision No. 71-969, CCH EEOC Decisions (1973) ¶6193 (White employee was "aggrieved" in fact and as a matter of law by supervisor's attitude toward and use of racial epithets in referring to Blacks; employer is responsible for behavior of its agents and failure to take reasonable steps calculated to maintain working environment free from racial intimidation or insult).

(5) Commission Decision No. 71-1442, CCH EEOC Decisions (1973) ¶6216 (employer is responsible for the actions of its supervisory personnel and is not relieved from liability for harassment by a disclaimer of responsibility for the personal bias of an employee and the promise to dismiss any individual not conforming to company policy of nondiscrimination).

(6) Commission Decision No. 71-2344, CCH EEOC Decisions (1973) ¶6257 (employer failed to take reasonable steps to prevent co-worker harassment of first Black employee assigned to a previously all-White locker room). (See also Commission Decision No. YME 9-068, CCH EEOC Decisions (1973) ¶6039.)

(7) Commission Decision No. 72-1561, CCH EEOC Decisions (1973) ¶6354 (employer failed to remedy supervisory and co-worker harassment on basis of race and national origin, including derogatory jokes, remarks, and publication; union was also responsible because it failed to take necessary affirmative action).

(8) Commission Decision No. 74-25, CCH Employment Practices Guide ¶6400 (fire department was responsible for race bias where Black firemen were harassed by co-workers and excluded from social and other functions; employer failed to take reasonable steps to eliminate such actions or remedy their effects).

(9) Commission Decision No. 76-09, CCH Employment Practices Guide ¶6604 (police department violated Title VII by failing to maintain working atmosphere free from racial harassment of Black officers, including: racial epithets over police radio, racially derogatory remarks, requiring multiple reports for routine incidents, building up adversely critical personnel files, using subjective evaluations by all-White supervisory staff).

(b) Court Cases

(1) Rogers v. Equal Employment Opportunity Commission, 454 F.2d 234, 4 EPD ¶7597 (5th Cir. 1971), cert. denied, 406 U.S. 957, 4 EPD ¶7838 (1972) (the court reversed the denial of EEOC's demand for access to defendant's patient records in connection with a charge investigation where the lower court based the denial on a determination that a Hispanic employee was not "aggrieved" by alleged racial discrimination against patients; the court stated that the relationship between an employee and his/her working environment is of such significance as to be entitled to statutory protection and that §703 of Title VII prohibits the practice of creating a working environment heavily charged with ethnic or racial discrimination).

(2) Anderson v. Methodist Evangelical Hospital, Inc., Civil No. 6580, 3 EPD ¶8282 (W.D. Ky., June 23, 1971), aff'd, 464 F.2d 723, 4 EPD ¶7901 (6th Cir. 1972) (employer was liable for failure to investigate and correct racial unfairness of Black plaintiff's discharge which was based on her inability to get along with racially prejudiced coworkers; employer had knowledge, through its agents, of the racial conflict).

(3) Harberson v. Monsanto Textiles Co., Civil Action No. 75-1626, 3 EPD ¶11,586 (D. S.C., Dec. 12, 1976) (no race discrimination in termination of White employee for making racially derogatory remarks to Black co-worker; employer acted lawfully and laudably in preserving non-racist working environment and enforcing policy of non-harassment).

(4) United States v. City of Buffalo, 457 F.Supp. 612, 18 EPD ¶8899 (W.D. N.Y. 1978) (numerous incidents of racial slurs and harassment of Black police officers disclosed a working environment heavily charged with racial discrimination; police department hid behind a paper policy of racial tolerance and failed to issue strong policy directive and take appropriate internal disciplinary action).

(5) De Grace v. Rumsfeld, 614 F.2d 796, 22 EPD ¶30,621 (1st Cir. 1980) (court reversed dismissal of Black plaintiff's claim of racial discrimination in his discharge for absenteeism and remanded case to provide plaintiff, a civilian firefighter with the Navy, an opportunity to show that racially offensive co-worker conduct created a reasonable fear for his personal safety, that employer knew or should have known of harassment but failed to take remedial measures, and that he himself acted reasonably and would have reported for duty but for his fear and the lack of corrective action; court stated that employer may not stand by and allow employee to be subjected to racial harassment by co-workers and must accept responsibility for supervisors' derelictions).

(6) Equal Employment Opportunity Commission v. Murphy Motor Freight Lines, Inc., 488 F. Supp. 381, 22 EPD ¶30,888 (D. Mn. 1980) (defendant's management and supervisors knew and should have known of numerous instances of co-worker harassment of Black employee but took inadequate steps to prevent racial harassment and company had no clear policy against it; employer was ordered to take affirmative action, including educating and sensitizing supervisory and management personnel and developing written disciplinary measures to be directed against offending employees and officials; court awarded harassed employee attorney's fees, finding that he deserved them for performing a valuable public service although he had not prevailed on all issues).

615.9 Religious Harassment

(a) Commission Decisions

(1) Commission Decision No. 71-685 (unpublished) (Title VII imposes on an employer the duty to protect its employees from harassment by either co-workers or supervisors where such harassment is because of or related to the employee's Title VII status).

(2) Commission Decision No. 71-764 (unpublished) (cause found where employer discharged charging party because four co-workers threatened to resign otherwise; the employer knew or should have known that the co-workers were motivated, at least in part, by charging party's having left the Amish faith).

(3) Commission Decision No. 72-1114, CCH EEOC Decisions (1973) ¶6347 (employer failed to provide working environment free of religious intimidation where supervisor harassed employees by preaching religion on the job; an employer is responsible for the actions of its supervisors, and charging parties had no obligation to inform higher level managerial personnel of their supervisor's conduct in order for the employer to be bound by the requirements of Title VII).

(4) Commission Decision No. 76-98, CCH Employment Practices Guide ¶6674 (cause found where Muslim prison guard was harassed and constructively discharged for practicing respect demanded by his religion, in absence of showing that charging party's religious practices impaired the performance of his duties or the operation of the institution).

(b) Court Cases and Other Decisions

(1) Compston v. Borden, Inc., 424 F.Supp. 157 (S.D. Ohio 1976) (supervisor's conduct calculated to demean employee because of his religion was held to be a Title VII violation).

(2) Rattner v. Trans World Airlines, City of New York Commission on Human Rights, Decision No. 4135-J (September 11, 1973) (Jewish airline employee was improperly harassed on the basis of his religion where he was singled out for unpleasant and exceptionally heavy work).

615.10 National Origin Harassment

(a) Guidelines - On December 29, 1980, the Commission published in the Federal Register a revision of its existing Guidelines on Discrimination Because of National Origin. 45 Fed. Reg. 85632 (1980) (to be codified in 29 C.F.R. §1606.1 et seq.). The revised Guidelines clarify and expand the prior Guidelines and reaffirm the Commission's position on national origin discrimination as expressed in Commission decisions and other legal interpretations.

Section 1606.8 of the revised Guidelines addresses the issue of harassment on the basis of national origin and basically follows the provisions of the Sexual Harassment Guidelines. (See §615.3 above.) Section 1606.8(b) provides that ethnic slurs and other verbal or physical conduct relating to an individual's national origin constitute harassment when this conduct: (1) has the purpose or effect of creating an intimidating, hostile, or offensive working environment; (2) has the purpose or effect of unreasonably interfering with an individual's work performance; or (3) otherwise adversely affects an individual's employment opportunities. Section 1606.8(c) through (e) sets out the standards for determining employer responsibility for national origin harassment in conformity with the corresponding provisions of the Sexual Harassment Guidelines. (See §615.3 above.)

(b) Commission Decisions

(1) Commission Decision No. 71-813 (unpublished) (employer knew or should have known that charging party's inability to supervise was directly attributable to the prejudice and harassment of her staff because of her Jamaican national origin; employer may not use the natural consequences of prohibited harassment as the basis for discharging the victim of that harassment).

(2) Commission Decision No. CL 68-12-43EU, CCH EEOC Decisions (1973) ¶6085 (cause found where employer, through supervisor, was aware of and tolerated incidents of coworker harassment of employee of Polish descent; harassment included vulgar names, jokes, and derogatory remarks about employee's ancestry).

(3) Commission Decision No. 70-683, CCH EEOC Decisions (1973) ¶6145 (cause found where two supervisors made derogatory and vulgar remarks about Hispanics). (See also Commission Decision No. 72-1561, CCH EEOC Decisions (1973) ¶6354.)

(4) Commission Decision No. 71-1874, CCH EEOC Decisions (1973) ¶6270 (cause found where foreman harassed Hispanic employee by imposing additional work, instructing other employees not to converse with charging party, and making statements expressing dislike of Hispanics).

(5) Commission Decision No. 72-0621, CCH EEOC Decisions (1973) ¶6311 (cab found where coworker harassed Hispanic employee and employer took no remedial action against harasser after charging party complained of the conduct but instead transferred and then discharged charging party for not getting along with fellow employees).

(6) Commission Decision No. 745, CCH EEOC Decisions (1983) ¶6387 (coworker and supervisory harassment and intimidation of Hispanic employee resulted in his constructive discharge; employer failed to maintain an atmosphere free of such intimidation and n or remedy the effects).

(7) Commission Decision No. 76-41, CCH EEOC decisions (1983) ¶6632 (employer failed to fulfill affirmative duty to act in response to Hispanic employee's complaint of coworker harassment and improper training).

(c) Court Cases

(1) Fekete v. United States Steel Corp., 353 F.Supp. 1177, 5 EPD ¶8569 (W.D. Pa. 1973) (Isolated incidents of co-worker harassment were not based on plaintiff's Hungarian

national origin; even if they had been, the employer would not have been liable since it took preventive and corrective steps with regard to those incidents of which its administrative and supervisory personnel knew or became aware).

(2) Cariddi v. Kansas City Chiefs Football Club, Inc., 568 F.2d 87, 15 EPD ¶8014 (8th Cir. 1977) (ethnic slurs about Italian-Americans made by plaintiff's supervisor were part of casual conversation and were not so excessive and disgraceful as to rise to the level of a Title VII violation).

(3) Morales v. Dain, Kallman and Quail, Inc., 467 F.Supp. 1031, 20 EPD ¶30,042 (D. Minn. 1979) (no evidence to support harassment allegation by Cuban plaintiff; supervisor's comments concerning "fast-thinking Latin Americans," which were not excessive or disgraceful, did not constitute a Title VII violation).

(4) St. J. Enriquez v. Transit Mixed Concrete Co., 492 F.Supp. 390, 23 EPD ¶31,057 (C.D. Cal. 1980) (Mexican-American plaintiff failed to prove national origin discrimination; although plaintiff was harassed by coworkers, it was never brought to the attention of employer or supervisors).

615.11 Age Harassment

a) Introduction - This subsection discusses the issue of employer harassment of an employee on the basis of age. As explained in the preceding subsections, the EEOC has long recognized that there are various types of employer harassment. For instance, sexual harassment, like harassment on the basis of race, color, religion, or national origin, is an unlawful employment practice prohibited by Title VII. Under Title VII, an employer has an affirmative duty to maintain a work environment free from any such harassment. Similarly, an employer has a duty under the ADEA to maintain a work environment free from harassment; this duty encompasses a requirement to take positive steps to eliminate age harassment taking the form of, for example, intimidation or insults in the workplace.

Although the EEOC has to date not addressed the issue of age harassment, Title VII case law and Commission Decisions serve as a guide in handling age harassment charges and complaints. Where ADEA precedent is lacking, substantive enforcement of the Act may be developed by borrowing and applying existing Title VII principles to particular facts. This is so because the substantive prohibitions of the ADEA were copied verbatim from Title VII, with the term "age" merely being substituted for "race, color, religion, sex or national origin." (See §801, Introduction.) Thus, when an age harassment action is filed, it will be accepted and investigated in much the same way as a Title VII charge. Title VII law and agency principles will guide the determination of whether an employer is liable for age harassment by its supervisors, employees, or non-employees.

b) Recognizing Age Harassment - Whether the conduct alleged in a charge or complaint constitutes age harassment must be determined on a case-by-case basis. The determination will he based on the circumstances and the context in which the conduct occurred, as reflected by the entire record. (See §615.3.)

> Example 1 - J works as a dock employee at a large meat packaging firm. He is the only dockhand over the age of 50 years old; all the other dock workers are in their late 20's or 30's. J complains that he is often harassed by his supervisor while working on the dock. For example, in the presence of co-workers, his boss often characterizes him as being "more accident prone than other employees, and unable to learn new tasks on his job because he is too old," and says that he "is less efficient than younger workers." On a number of occasions, the dock supervisor has said to J that "you can't teach an old dog new tricks" and refused to let him complete assignments. J files an ADEA harassment complaint alleging that as an older worker he is always characterized as more rigid, inefficient, lazy, and accident prone, while younger workers are not generally characterized by their supervisors in such harsh terms.

Example 2 - B works as a bank teller. She is the only teller over 50 years old. During work hours the other tellers frequently tell jokes and insult B about her age, poor health, and medical problems; they never discuss existing health or medical problems of younger workers. B does not enjoy hearing these jokes and particularly resents the insults. She complains about these jokes to her supervisor, who in turn tells her "not to be so sensitive." He then tells her a few age-related jokes of his own. Displeased with his response, B files an age harassment action against her employer. In her charge she alleges that her coworkers harass her at work and her employer tolerates this behavior. B alleges that her employer is responsible for maintaining a work environment free of harassment and that her employer must take positive steps to eliminate employee harassment. Since B's employer knew of the harassment and did not maintain a work environment free of harassment, the employer has violated the ADEA.

Example 3 - Same facts as in Example 2 above, but in this example CP's supervisor requires all employees to lift large and heavy boxes as part of their jobs. In addition to making age-related jokes and insults, B's coworkers leave her the heaviest boxes because they want to force B to retire from that job. Again, B's supervisor took no action after B complained about her coworkers' behavior. B files an age harassment complaint. Since B's coworkers harassed her by leaving the heavier boxes for her to lift with the intention of forcing her to retire and CP had complained to her supervisor of this harassment, the employer has violated the ADEA.

In the above examples, the coworkers' harassment of the charging party was motivated by a bias towards older individuals. In other situations, the motivation may be less one of bias and more of an economic nature. For example, the charging party in a situation like Example 3 may rank high on the seniority list. As a result, she may receive the pick of assignments, get better pay or, by her presence, be blocking the advancement of younger and less senior employees. Had there been no age-related jokes and insults, is seniority so closely related to age as to make the harassment (leaving B the heaviest boxes) a violation of the ADEA? Guidance on the issue of age-related factors such as seniority will be provided at a later date. Until that time, the issue is non-CDP. (See §603.)

Age-related harassment may lead to the resignation of the aggrieved individual, who may then bring an action alleging constructive discharge. Lewis v. Federal Prison Industries, 786 F.2d 1537, 40 EPD ¶36,110 (11th Cir. 1986). (See §§612, 812 and Commission Decision No. 84-1, CCH Employment Practices Guide ¶6839.)

Example 4 - K is a 60 year old restaurant worker; he works the night shift for R. He worked as a waiter without a mishap for 25 years, until a new supervisor became manager of the night shift. The new supervisor calls everyone over 50 years old who has gray hair "Pops." One time he said to K that "this business needs the old bags of the world to retire or rest in peace." When K's supervisor said this, a large group of customers were listening and K became extremely embarrassed. His supervisor would say similar things repeatedly in front of customers while K was on the floor serving them. K complained to the owner about the supervisor's behavior, but she failed to take any action and the remarks continued. In discomfort over these remarks, K quit his waiter job. K now brings an ADEA charge against his employer alleging age harassment and constructive discharge. If the record shows that K's supervisor subjected him to age-related harassment, there would be a violation of the ADEA. Further, if a reasonable person would have found the working conditions created by the harassment intolerable, and CF's resignation was in fact due to these conditions, then CF would have been constructively discharged in violation of the ADEA.

Example 5 - Same facts as in Example 4, but here K's supervisor assigns to him the least profitable tables for tips. His supervisor believes that if K's income drops dramatically over the next few months that this will force him to transfer to another restaurant in another part of town. K may bring an age harassment complaint against his employer because his supervisor gave him a less desirable work assignment in order to force him to accept transfer to another restaurant.

An employer may be liable for age harassment and sex discrimination or some other form of discrimination or harassment at the same time.

Example 6 - A 55 year old employee alleges that her supervisor subjects her and other female employees to sex and age harassment by repeatedly calling them "old biddies and old hoots." Their supervisor does not call men over 55 by these names, only the women who are all over 55 years old. However, the supervisor has been known to call all his employees over age 55 senile, out-worn, and members of the Geritol generation.

As in Example 6 above, given the appropriate circumstances, a charge or complaint may allege more than one type of harassment. In the example above, it would be appropriate to file an age and sex discrimination charge or complaint against the employer since the employer's alleged actions would violate both Title VII and the ADEA.

615.12 Cross References

(a) §613, Terms, Conditions, and Privileges

(b) §614, Retaliation

(c) §619, Grooming Standards

(d) §801, Introduction

619.4 Uniforms and Other Dress Codes in Charges Based on Sex

(a) Uniforms - The use of dress and grooming codes which are suitable and applied equally is not unlawful under Title VII, but where respondent maintains a dress policy which is not applied evenly to both sexes, that policy is in violation of Title VII.

Example - R has a dress policy which requires its female employees to wear uniforms. Men are only required to wear appropriate business attire. Upon investigation it is revealed that R requires uniforms for its female employees because it feels that women are less capable than men in dressing in appropriate business attire. R states that if it did not require its female employees to dress in uniforms, the female employees would come to work in styles which were in vogue; e.g., slit skirts and dresses, low cut blouses, etc. Based on either the additional cost to the employees that the purchase of uniforms imposes or the stereotypical attitude that it shows, the policy is in violation of Title VII. (See Carroll v. Talman Federal Savings and Loan Association, below.)

There may be instances in which the employer requires both its male and female employees to wear uniforms, and this would not necessarily be in violation of Title VII. But keep in mind that if this requirement is enforced against members of only one sex, race, national origin, or religion, the disparate treatment theory would apply and a violation may result.

The requirement of a uniform, especially one that is not similar to conventional clothes (e.g., short skirts for women or an outfit which may be considered provocative), may subject the employee to derogatory and sexual comments or other circumstances which create an intimidating, hostile, or offensive working environment based on sex. In some cases the mere requirement that females wear sexually provocative uniforms may by itself be evidence of sexual harassment. Since the employer is required to maintain an atmosphere which is free of sexual harassment, this may also constitute a violation of Title VII. (See Hasselman v. Sage Realty Corp., below. For processing a sexual harassment case see §615 of this manual.)

There may be situations In which members of only one sex are regularly allowed to deviate from the required uniform and no violation will result.

> Example - R requires all its employees to wear uniforms. R, however, allows female employees to wear regular maternity clothes when they are pregnant. CP (male) alleges sex discrimination because he was not allowed to deviate from the required uniform. CP alleged that the uniform made him uncomfortable. In view of the fact that pregnant women cannot wear conventional clothes when they are pregnant, R's policy cannot be said to result in disparate treatment or have an adverse impact on similarly situated males, so long as males are allowed to deviate from the uniform requirement when medical conditions necessitate a deviation.

(b) EEOC Decisions

In EEOC Decision No. 77-36, 2 CCH Employment Practices Guide ¶6588, charging party was required to wear provocative outfits as a term and condition of her employment. Charging party wore such outfits but refused to wear one "Bicentennial outfit" because when she wore that outfit, she was the target of sexually derogatory comments. Charging party was terminated for her refusal to wear this outfit. The Commission found sex discrimination because requiring charging party to wear such outfits as a condition of her employment made her the target of derogatory comments and inhibited rather than facilitated the performance of her job duties. Moreover, the Commission found that male workers performed similar job functions without having to wear sexually revealing uniforms. In analyzing the issue, the Commission stated that it had not held unlawful the use of dress and grooming codes which are suitable and applied equally, but where a dress policy reflects a stereotypical attitude toward one of the sexes, that policy will be found in violation of Title VII.

(c) Federal Court Cases

In Carroll v. Talman Federal Savings and Loan Association, 604 F.2d 1028, 20 EPD ¶30,218 (7th Cir. 1979), female bank employees were subjected to illegal sex discrimination when they were required to wear uniforms while male employees only had to wear suitable business attire. No evidence was presented that female workers had ever worn improper business attire on those days when they were permitted to wear "street clothes" so that the uniform could be cleaned. The court concluded that the justification given, i.e., that women were less capable than men in choosing appropriate business attire, was based on offensive stereotypes prohibited by Title VII.

Requiring female employees to wear sexually revealing uniforms which will subject them to lewd and derogatory comments also constitutes sex discrimination under Title VII. Hasselman v. Sage Realty Corp., _____ F.Supp. _____ Civil Action No. 78-CIV-4607 (S.D.N.Y. Sept. 24, 1980).

(d) Dress Codes Which Do Not Require Uniforms - There may also be instances in which an employer's dress code requires certain modes of dress and appearance but does not require uniforms. For example, the dress code may require male employees to wear neckties at all times and female employees to wear skirts or dresses at all times. So long as these requirements are suitable and are equally enforced and so long as the requirements are equivalent for men and women with respect to the standard or burden that they impose, there is no violation of Title VII.

> Example - R requires its male employees to wear neckties at all times. It also requires its female employees to wear dresses or skirts at all times. CP (female) was temporarily suspended when she wore pants to work. She files a charge alleging that the dress code requirement and its enforcement discriminate against her due to her sex. The investigation reveals that one male who had worn a leisure suit with an open collar shirt had also been suspended. There is no evidence of other employees violating the dress code. R also states that it requires this code of dress for each sex because it wants to promote its image. The investigation has revealed that the dress code is enforced equally against both sexes and that it does not impose a greater burden or different standard on the employees on the basis of sex. Therefore, there is not reasonable cause to believe that either R's dress code or its enforcement discriminates against CP because of her sex.

> Example - R prohibits the wearing of shorts by women who work on the production line and prohibits the wearing of tank tops by men who work on the production line. This is an equivalent standard.

(e) Federal Court Cases

No discrimination under Title VII was found in an employer dress code policy which required male employees to wear ties. There was a comparable standard for women Fountain v. Safeway Stores Inc., 555 F.2d 753 (9th Cir. 1977). Also, there was no discrimination in a policy which prohibited women from wearing slacks in the executive portion of defendant's offices. Lanigan v. Bartlett and Company Grain, 466 F.Supp. 1388 (W.D. Mo. 1979).

SEXUAL HARASSMENT IN CANADA

I. JURISDICTION OVER LABOR RELATIONS IN CANADA

Politically and geographically Canada is divided into ten provincial governments, two territories, and the federal government. Each has exclusive authority to regulate affairs coming within its own jurisdiction, as set out originally in the British North America Act.[1]

The question of who has legislative authority to pass laws dealing with labor relations and employment in Canada was settled in 1925. In *Toronto Electric Commissioners v. Snider*,[2] the Privy Council[3] was asked to determine the validity of the federal Industrial Disputes Investigation Act[4] of 1907, which was intended to provide for the settlement of labor disputes. The Privy Council determined that the Act was unconstitutional in that it purported to regulate industries that would not otherwise fall within federal jurisdiction.

The Industrial Disputes Investigation Act was subsequently amended so that its application was restricted to employment upon or in connection with undertakings or businesses that fell within the legislative authority of the Parliament of Canada.[5] Subsequent cases decided by the Supreme Court of Canada ultimately delineated the powers of the provincial governments so that all matters related to labor relations fell to the exclusive jurisdiction of the provinces, provided that they did not involve a federal undertaking. Consequently, unlike the United States, Canada does not have federal legislation that generally governs discrimination in private employment.

Each territory and province, however, administers its own human rights code or act and has its own human rights commission. In addition, the Federal Human Rights Commission hears complaints of federal government employees or persons employed on a federal undertaking.[6]

Individuals employed by a ministry, governmental department or crown corporation may file a complaint only under federal human rights legislation, while employees in private industry, universities, hospitals, and the like, have recourse only under relevant provincial legislation.

---

[1]British North America Act, 1867, 30 & 31 Victoria, c.3 (U.K.), R.S.C. 1985, Appendix II, No. 5.
[2](1925) 2 D.L.R. 5,(1925) A.C. 396, (1926) 1 W.W.R. 785 (P.C.).
[3]In 1925 the Privy Council was the highest judicial authority in Canada.
[4]S.C. 1907, c.20.
[5]*E.g.,* mining, interprovincial transportation, shipping, communication, navigation, and the like.
[6]Whether something is a federal undertaking is dependent on whether it is "necessarily incidental to" or "an integral part of" a federal operation or project. For a discussion by the Supreme Court of Canada of the standard for determining whether an activity is a federal undertaking, see *Quebec v. Canada* (1987), 51 D.L.R. (4th) 161 (S.C.C.).

Human rights complaints in Canada are adjudicated in the first instance by a single or tripartite board of inquiry. Resort to the courts from decisions of boards of inquiry, while possible under various human rights legislative provisions, are not common and generally involve serious questions of law or interpretation. Courts are otherwise reluctant to overturn decisions where findings of fact are made by a board of inquiry.

II. The Relationship Between Sexual Harassment and Sex Discrimination

All levels of government, both federal and provincial, have human rights legislation that prohibits sex discrimination. The federal government and the provinces of Ontario, Quebec, and Newfoundland have statutes specifically banning sexual harassment.

The federal Canadian Human Rights Act defines sexual harassment as follows:

Harassment

Section 14

(1) It is a discriminatory practice,
> (a) in the provision of goods, services, facilities or accommodation customarily available to the general public,
> (b) in the provision of commercial premises or residential accommodation, or
> (c) in matters related to employment, to harass an individual on a prohibited ground of discrimination.

Sexual harassment

(2) Without limiting the generality of subsection (1), sexual harassment shall, for the purposes of that subsection, be deemed to be harassment on a prohibited ground of discrimination.[7]

Sexual harassment is defined in the Ontario Human Rights Code as follows:

Section 4(2)
> Every person who is an employee has a right to freedom from harassment in the workplace by the employer or agent of the employer or by another employee because of race, ancestry, place of origin, color, ethnic origin, citizenship, creed, age, record of offences, marital status, family status or handicap.

Section 6(2)
> Every person who is an employee has a right to freedom from harassment in the workplace because of sex by his or her employer or agent of the employer or by another employee.

Section 6(3)
> Every person has a right to be free from,
> > (a) a sexual solicitation or advance made by a person in a position to confer, grant or deny a benefit or advancement to the person where the person making the solicitation or advance knows or ought reasonably to know that it is unwelcome; or
> > (b) a reprisal or a threat of reprisal for the rejection of a sexual solicitation or advance where the reprisal is made or threatened by a person

---

[7]Canadian Human Rights Act, S.C. 1976–77, c.33.

in a position to confer, grant or deny a benefit or advancement to the person.[8]

Newfoundland legislation deals with harassment and sexual solicitation as follows:

Harassment in establishment prohibited

No person in an establishment shall harass another person in the establishment because of the race, religion, religious creed, sex, marital status, physical disability, mental disability, political opinion, color or ethnic, national or social origin of that person.[9]

Sexual solicitation prohibited

(1) No person who is in a position to confer, grant or deny a benefit or advancement to another person shall engage in sexual solicitation or make a sexual advance to that person where the person making the solicitation or advance knows or ought reasonably to know that it is unwelcome.

(2) No person who is in a position to confer or deny a benefit or advancement to another person shall penalize, punish or threaten reprisal against that person for the rejection of a sexual solicitation or advance.[10]

In Quebec, the sexual harassment provision states as follows: "No one may harass a person on the basis of any ground mentioned in section 10." Section 10 includes, *inter alia,* sex.[11]

Even before the specific inclusion of sexual harassment in the above noted human rights legislation, human rights tribunals in all jurisdictions relied upon the general prohibition against discrimination on the basis of sex to adjudicate cases alleging sexual harassment.

The first Canadian decision that dealt with an allegation of sexual harassment acted in the absence of any specific prohibition against sexual harassment in the Human Rights Code. In *Bell & Korczak v. Aldas & Flaming Steer Steak House,*[12] the Board ruled that sexual harassment amounted to sex discrimination and as such was prohibited by the Ontario Human Rights Code as it existed at that time. In coming to that conclusion, the adjudicator reasoned that a woman who is being denied a job or promotion because of her unwillingness to participate in or endure sexual innuendo or conduct is in fact being discriminated against in her employment because of her sex:

The evil to be remedied is the utilization of economic power or authority so as to restrict a woman's guaranteed and equal access to the workplace, and all of its benefits, free from extraneous pressure having to do with the mere fact that she is a woman. Where a woman's equal access is denied or when terms and conditions differ when compared to male employees, the woman is being discriminated against. The forms of prohibited conduct that, in my view, are discriminatory run the gamut from overt gender based activity, such as coerced intercourse to unsolicited physical contact to persistent propositions to more subtle conduct such as gender based insults and taunting, which may reasonably be perceived to create a negative psychological and emotional work environment. There is no reason why the law, which reaches into the workplace so as to protect the work environment from physical or chemical pollution or extremes of temperature, ought not to protect employees as well from negative psychological and mental effects

---

[8]S.O. 1981, c.53
[9]Newfoundland Human Rights Code, 1988, S.N. 1988, §13.
[10]*Id.* at §14.
[11]Quebec Charter of Human Rights and Freedoms, R.S.Q. 1977, c.C.-12, § 10(1).
[12](1980), 1 C.H.R.R. D/155.

where adverse and gender directed conduct emanating from a management hierarchy may reasonably be construed to be a condition of employment.[13]

While most cases following the *Flaming Steer* decision ultimately adopted its reasoning, it was not without lengthy debate on the question of whether sex discrimination was indeed broad enough to encompass sexual harassment. When a Manitoba Court of Appeal, in *Janzen v. Platy Enterprises*,[14] departed from this reasoning and found that sex discrimination did not encompass sexual harassment, the issue finally was referred to the Supreme Court of Canada.[15]

The Supreme Court, concluding that sex discrimination is broad enough to include sexual harassment, relied on numerous Canadian as well as American authorities. The Court ruled that unwelcome sexual encounters in the workplace are tantamount to an abuse of power. Accordingly, such behavior creates an environment that exploits an individual who is economically dependent upon the person in a position of power to deprive that individual of livelihood.

The Supreme Court relied upon and accepted dictum in the American case of *Henson v. City of Dundee*.[16] Chief Justice Brian Dickson, writing for the Court, referred to the following quotation from *Henson:*

> Sexual harassment which creates a hostile or offensive environment for members of one sex is every bit the arbitrary barrier to sexual equality at the workplace that racial harassment is to racial equality. Surely, a requirement that a man or woman run a gauntlet of sexual abuse in return for the privilege of being allowed to work and make a living can be as demeaning and disconcerting as the harshest of racial epithets.[17]

The Chief Justice went on to define sexual harassment:

> Without seeking to provide an exhaustive definition of the term, I am of the view that sexual harassment in the workplace may be broadly defined as unwelcome conduct of a sexual nature that detrimentally affects the work environment or leads to adverse job-related consequences for the victims of the harassment. It is, as Adjudicator Shime observed in [*Flaming Steer*], and as has been widely accepted by other adjudicators and academic commentators, an abuse of power. When sexual harassment occurs in the workplace, it is an abuse of both economic and sexual power. Sexual harassment is a demeaning practice, one that constitutes a profound affront to the dignity of the employees forced to endure it. By requiring an employee to contend with unwelcome sexual actions or explicit sexual demands, sexual harassment in the workplace attacks the dignity and self-respect of the victim both as an employee and as a human being.[18]

The fact, therefore, that human rights legislation in the majority of jurisdictions in Canada does not specifically prohibit sexual harassment is no longer relevant. The tribunals that adjudicate matters of sexual harassment, and the courts of those provinces, are now bound by the ruling of the Supreme Court of Canada. As such there is no longer any question of whether an allegation of sexual harassment may be founded on the general prohibition of sex discrimination.

---

[13]*Id.* at D/156.
[14](1986), 8 C.H.R.R. D/3831 (Man. C.A.), *rev'g* (1985), 7 C.H.R.R. D/3309 (Q.B.), *aff'g* (1985), 6 C.H.R.R. D/2735 (Bd. Adj.), *rev'd* (1989), 25 C.C.E.L. 1, 59 D.L.R. (4th) 352 (S.C.C.).
[15]*Id.* The Supreme Court of Canada is now Canada's highest court.
[16]682 F.2d 897, 29 FEP Cases 787 (11th Cir. 1982), reproduced in Chapter 4, Hostile Environment Harassment.
[17]Janzen v. Platy Enterprises (1989), 25 C.C.E.L. 1, 32.
[18]*Id.* at 33.

III. THE NATURE OF SEXUAL HARASSMENT

Like American courts, Canadian boards of inquiry have struggled with the analysis of what constitutes sexual harassment in any given circumstance. Boards of inquiry have been concerned not to interfere with normal male-female interaction in the workplace. At the same time, they have been sensitive to the fact that what may appear to be perfectly normal and acceptable behavior to a male employee may be very offensive and coercive to a female employee. Similarly, what may be acceptable in one work environment may not be in another.

A. Quid Pro Quo Harassment

Being careful to balance these apparently differing perspectives, the adjudicator in the *Flaming Steer* case stated:

> The prohibition of such conduct is not without its dangers. One must be cautious that the law not inhibit normal social contact between management and employees or normal discussion between management and employees. It is not abnormal, nor should it be prohibited, activity for a supervisor to become socially involved with an employee. An invitation to dinner is not an invitation to a complaint. The danger or the evil that is to be avoided is *coerced or compelled social contact* where the employee's refusal to participate may result in the loss of employment benefits. Such coercion or compulsion may be overt or subtle, but if any feature of employment becomes reasonably dependent on reciprocating a social relationship proffered by a member of management, then the overture becomes a condition of employment and may be considered to be discriminatory.

> Again, The Code ought not to be seen or perceived as inhibiting free speech. If sex cannot be discussed between supervisor and employee neither can other values such as race, color or creed, which are contained in The Code, be discussed. Thus, differences of opinion by an employee where sexual matters are discussed may not involve a violation of The Code; it is only *when the language or words may be reasonably construed to form a condition of employment* that The Code provides a remedy. Thus, the frequent and persistent taunting by a supervisor of an employee because of his or her color is discriminatory activity under The Code and, similarly, *the frequent and persistent taunting of an employee* by a supervisor because of his or her sex is discriminatory activity under The Code.[19]

Thus, while an "invitation to dinner" is not an "invitation to a complaint," the fact remains that a superior who initiates social contact with an employee must be aware of the potential danger of being so involved. As stated in *Potapczyk v. MacBain:*

> Any social invitation in the evening by a male employer to a female employee, whether simply for the purpose of discussing business or not, is fraught with danger and evidences bad judgment at the least, when the employee is having problems (for whatever reason) in respect of her job functions. This is particularly so, when the employer, like Mr. MacBain, suddenly and drastically changes her duties, as he did in the next few days following her declining his dinner invitation on January 25th. The position of the employer's authority implies a possible coerced socializing, an intimation that compliance with the employer's invitation is, in effect, a condition of employment. Clearly, if the adverse changes in job function are a consequence of the refusal to meet socially, there is sexual harassment.[20]

---

[19]*Supra* note 13, at D/155, D/156 (emphasis added).
[20](1984), 5 C.H.R.R. D/2285 (Can. H.R. Trib.), §19321.

For there to be a finding of sexual harassment, the conduct must have verbal or physical sexual overtones. It must be unwelcome and unsolicited. It may be intentional or systemic, as in the case of sexual stereotyping. It need not be persistent, depending on the severity of the conduct. Finally, the sexual harassment may or may not have adverse job-related consequences.[21]

B. The Poisoned Work Environment

Because of the body of jurisprudence that has developed over the last decade, it is no longer necessary for an employee to show threatened job security to succeed in a sexual harassment complaint. Canadian boards of inquiry have adopted the concept of the "poisoned work environment" enunciated in the leading American case of *Bundy v. Jackson*.[22]

In dealing with the concept of a "poisoned work environment," boards of inquiry have held that the atmosphere contained within a workplace is just as much a term or condition of employment as are benefits, hours of work, rates of pay, and health and welfare benefits. Accordingly, conduct that makes the work environment hostile by reason of constant taunting, verbal exchanges, or statements directed at a person's gender is discrimination on the basis of sex.[23]

The much-publicized *MacBain* case,[24] involving a prominent politician, illustrates a subtle form of environmental harassment that arguably would not have been action-able had it been the first case in which Canadian courts considered this problem. The complainant was hired to work as special assistant to Mr. MacBain, a member of Parliament and Parliamentary Secretary to the Minister of Justice. The complainant testified that MacBain had a habit of coming too close when talking to her, so that their bodies would touch on occasion at the arm. This type of conduct was also experienced by two female co-workers in the office.

After working for MacBain for some ten months, the complainant felt she had been propositioned by him when he suggested they have dinner at her apartment in order to discuss her work. Perceiving this as a sexual advance, she declined.

A consultant hired by MacBain advised him to refrain from what he observed to be "excessive physical closeness" with his female staff. MacBain apparently did not consider this to be worthy of note and continued his behavior. The consultant heard MacBain make crude comments about the complainant as well as comments on the physical endowments of the other two female staff members in his office. There was no evidence that the three women were aware that these comments had been made. MacBain did, however, on a number of occasions, suggest to the other two staff members that he and the complainant might have been having a relationship outside of the office. There was also some evidence that he made comments to the two staff members about their personal appearance.

Ultimately, MacBain suggested that the complainant look for work elsewhere, and the complainant eventually quit her job and sued both for wrongful dismissal and lodged a complaint with the Canadian Human Rights Commission. MacBain attempted on two occasions to have the proceedings before the Canadian Human Rights Commis-

---

[21]In Ontario the prohibition against this classic type of sexual harassment (also known as "quid pro quo") has been codified in §6(3) of the Human Rights Code. See text accompanying note 8 *supra*.

[22]641 F.2d 934, 24 FEP Cases 1155 (D.C. Cir. 1981). Boards have cited *Bundy* not only for the proposition that an employee need not suffer tangible work repercussions for her to maintain an action for sexual harassment but also for the proposition that the employee need not show resistance to the harassing conduct in order to succeed in the claim. See Section III.B.2. *infra*.

[23]Giovandoudis (nee) Makri v. Golden Fleece Restaurant and Tavern Limited and Steve Carias (1984), 5 C.H.R.R. D/1967.

[24]*Supra* note 21.

sion stayed on the basis that the tribunal was not impartial. This motion was denied with the result that MacBain refused to participate in the proceedings or to present any evidence. Accordingly, the tribunal only had before it the undisputed and uncontradicted evidence set out above. Based on that evidence MacBain was found guilty of sexual harassment.

In *Aragona v. Elegant Lamp Co.,* while dismissing the complaint because the evidence of sexual banter and teasing did not amount to a condition of employment, the tribunal stated:

> Thus, sexual references which are crude or in bad taste, are not necessarily sufficient to constitute a contravention of section 4 of the Code on the basis of sex. The line of sexual harassment is crossed only where the conduct may be reasonably construed to create, as a condition of employment, a work environment which demands an unwarranted intrusion upon the employee's sexual dignity as a man or woman. The line will seldom be easy to draw, particularly where, as in the present case, there is considerable dispute as to what exactly was said and done.[25]

The adoption of the "poisoned work environment" concept has broadened the definition of sexual harassment and has had a significant impact on Canadian jurisprudence.

1. Frequency and Offensiveness

By definition, harass means to "worry, vex, weary by prolonged or often repeated molestation or importunity . . . to annoy, fatigue by incessant attacks."[26] In *Hanion v. T.G. Mobile Aerial Equipment Ltd.,*[27] the British Columbia Human Rights Council dismissed a complaint of sexual harassment for insufficient evidence of "poisoned work environment." The evidence was that the complainant's employer once touched her hand and asked her whether she slept in the nude, that the complainant had received a Christmas bonus, that she had received flowers from her employer and an invitation to lunch and subsequently had dinner with her employer and a client. The Board reasoned that, although the employer's action may have been offensive and perhaps in bad taste, it certainly did not constitute the kind of serious action that would create a "poisoned environment," rendering it a condition of employment for the complainant to endure as part of her day-to-day working life.

The issue of whether frequency of sexually oriented conduct or statements is required for a finding of sexual harassment was dealt with in *Watt v. Regional Municipality of Niagara:*

> The burden which must be discharged in order to bring a case within Section 4 is to establish that the incidents occurred with a combination of frequency and offensiveness which warrants the inference that exposure to such conduct was a discriminatory condition of employment.[28]

This language might be read to suggest that more than one act of impropriety is necessary to support a finding of sexual harassment. If a single act is socially repugnant or results in punitive withholding of employment benefits, however, then even one isolated act may constitute sexual harassment:

> It is likely that a single unrepeated act is not harassment unless it results in the denial or removal of a tangible benefit available or offered to other persons in

---

[25](1982), 3 C.H.R.R. D/1109, D/1110 (Ont. Bd. Inq.).

[26]*Webster's Universal Dictionary,* Unabridged International Edition, 1970.

[27](1986), 7 C.H.R.R. D/3475, D/3476.

[28](1984), 5 C.H.R.R. D/2453, D/2459 (Ont. Bd. Inq.).

similar circumstances, or *unless it amounts to an assault, or is a proposition of such a gross or obscene nature that it could reasonably be considered to have created a negative or unpleasant emotional or psychological work environment.* A "normal" proposition or suggestion would probably not have this result. . . . However, repetition of otherwise unactionable conduct may constitute harassment when it can reasonably be considered to have created a poisoned work environment.[29]

The case law attempts to attain the delicate balance between unlawful conduct and other conduct which, although boorish and crude, is not sexually harassing.

2. Unwelcome Conduct

While an overt rejection of any sexual advance or innuendo would clearly show that the sexual advances were unwelcome, the absence of an outright rejection is not fatal to a claim of sexual harassment. Determining, in the absence of such a rejection, whether conduct was unwelcome is perhaps the most difficult issue facing boards of inquiry. The issue is difficult because perceptions differ markedly not only between men and women, but among members of the same sex and ultimately between different adjudicators looking at the same facts.

Thus, in *Robichaud v. Brennan,*[30] the adjudicator in the first instance found that the complainant and the respondent's supervisor had engaged in a variety of sexual acts, including masturbation, fellatio, and fondling of genitals. Professor Abbot found that given the sexual activity there was far too much voluntary participation for him to be able to conclude that the sexual advances by the supervisor were unwelcome. On appeal, however, the Review Tribunal made a completely opposite finding of fact.

In the absence of a complainant's direct and categorical rejection of the sexual advance, a tribunal must make findings of fact and credibility. This onerous task is facilitated when the conduct complained of is very provocative and out of the norm. In *Gervais v. Agriculture Canada,*[31] the sexual conduct complained of amounted to a sexual assault, which caused the complainant to attend a rape crisis center the following day. Given this evidence, little weight attached to the fact that, on the day before the assault, the complainant told the harasser of her erotic dream in which he was the main protagonist, and the fact that the complainant displayed erotic photographs of male posteriors to her co-workers and participated in sexual activity in the workplace. The single act of sexual assault so clearly exceeded the bounds of acceptable social or workplace interaction that it was sufficient to support a finding of sexual harassment.

In attempting to determine whether conduct is welcome or unwelcome, the case of *Kotyk v. Canadian Employment & Immigration Commission* formulated a test:

> The test of whether the advances are unsolicited or unwelcome is objective in the sense that it depends upon the reasonable and usual limits of social interaction in the circumstances of the case. The Complainant should not need to prove an active resistance or other explicit reaction to the activity complained of, other than a refusal or a denial, unless such might reasonably be necessary to make the perpetrator aware that the activity was in fact unwelcome or exceeded the bounds of usual social interaction.[32]

---

[29]Kotyk v. C.E.I.C. (1983), 4 C.H.R.R. D/1416, D/1430 (Can. H.R. Trib.)(emphasis added).

[30](1982), 3 C.H.R.R. D/977 (Can. H.R. Trib.) *rev'd* (1983) 4 C.H.R.R. D/1272 (Can. H.R. Rev. Trib.) *aff'd* Treasury Board v. Robichaud (1985), 6 C.H.R.R. D/2695 (F.C.A.) *rev'd* Robichaud v. The Queen (1987), 8 C.H.R.R. D/4326, 40 D.L.R. (4th) 577 (S.C.C.).

[31](1988), 9 C.H.R.R. D/5002 (Can. H.R. Rev. Trib.).

[32]*Supra* note 30, at ¶12251.

This test unquestionably applies in sexual assault cases such as *Gervais*[33] or in cases involving touching or grabbing intimate body parts. It is, however, not as applicable in cases dealing with less overt conduct, such as that considered in *MacBain*,[34] where the complainant admittedly never advised Mr. MacBain that she felt uncomfortable because of his closeness. Furthermore, she acknowledged quite candidly that she did not believe that Mr. MacBain actually appreciated her discomfort. This admission did not preclude the tribunal from making a finding of guilt.

3. Culture of the Workplace

Individual sensitivities make it extremely difficult in some cases for tribunals to determine when the line has been crossed between mere banter and sexual harassment. Some men and women may consider sexual humor amusing and entertaining, while others may find it offensive and in poor taste. It is trite, therefore, to say that one must carefully consider the evidence regarding the sexual nature of the verbal conduct in question in order to assess, on a case-by-case basis, whether it created an offensive work environment.

Boards of inquiry must not only scrutinize conduct, but also the workplace setting, to determine what the norm of that workplace might be. In *Daigle v. Hunter*, the Board of Inquiry stated:

> I do not deny that there are some who find off-color humour offensive and they have every right to do so. They have the fundamental right to dignity in the workplace. *However, if the norm in their workplace is offensive to them, they have an obligation to overtly,* by words or actions, bring it to the attention of the offenders or management or both. If the offenders persist and particularly if they accelerate the offensive action and deliberately direct it at the individual, the "line" is crossed and that individual is being harassed contrary to the *Act*.[35]

The work environment was highly relevant to the ultimate disposition in *Rack v. The Playgirl Cabaret*.[36] The complainant was the former common-law spouse of the respondent, who hired her to work in one of his nightclubs. She worked for him for approximately one year before he discharged her for breaching a company policy against socializing and dating among employees.

The complainant filed a complaint with the British Columbia Human Rights Commission, alleging that the respondent was verbally abusive and maligned both her and other employees. The complainant also stated that since she started to date a co-worker, her hours were markedly decreased. The tribunal found that the respondent was in fact very crude and did engage in profanity. However, the tribunal further found that the employees, both male and female, reciprocated in kind.

The tribunal characterized the issue as follows: Does verbal abuse and verbal malignment constitute sexual harassment in these circumstances? It relied on dicta from *Grace Aragona v. Elegant Lamp Co.:*

> [T]he proven conduct was freely accepted and enjoyed by the other employees. In the circumstances, it could not "reasonably be perceived to create a negative psychological and emotional work environment." *Where there is general acceptance but where an individual employee does not care to participate, that feeling should be expressed directly and unambiguously.* The objective standard could then be applied to that individual in light of the additional fact of expressed disapproval.[37]

---

[33]*Supra* note 32.
[34]Potapczyk v. MacBain, *supra* note 21.
[35](1988), 10 C.H.R.R. D/5670, D/5677 (N.B. Bd. Inq.).
[36](1985), 6 C.H.R.R. D/2857 (B.C. Cncl. H.R.).
[37]*Supra* note 26, at D/1113 (emphasis added).

The tribunal in the *Rack* case was dealing with a respondent who operated three night clubs frequented predominantly by "rowdy males" who came to hear rock 'n' roll music while viewing erotic dancers and strippers. Given this workplace setting, the tribunal had no difficulty in concluding that in this case the crude language constituted nothing more than "ordinary banter."[38]

Canadian boards of inquiry, not unlike American courts, have been very careful to examine the particular facts in any given complaint of sexual harassment. What may be characterized as sexual harassment if the conduct occurs within the offices of a member of Parliament may not be construed as sexual harassment if the same conduct occurred in a striptease parlor. If a complainant working in a striptease parlor is particularly sensitive to crude comments or jokes that others engage in freely, she is required to make her objection known. Failing that, she risks the chance of having her complaint dismissed.

IV. EMPLOYER LIABILITY FOR ACTS OF SEXUAL DISCRIMINATION

A. Statutory Liability of Employer

In the landmark decision of *Robichaud v. Canada (Treasury Board)*,[39] a case interpreting the Federal Human Rights Act, the Supreme Court of Canada finally put to rest the question of employer liability. Until that point numerous tribunals and courts had grappled with the problem of whether the employer's liability in circumstances of sexual harassment was based on the theory of strict liability, vicarious liability, or some other form of liability.

The Court determined that "fault oriented" theories of liability were "beside the point," in that Human Rights legislation is not primarily intended to be punitive, but "to eradicate anti-social conditions without regard to the motives or intention of those who cause them."[40]

Given this reasoning Justice LaForest felt that theories of employer liability are not of much assistance when dealing with violations of human rights legislation:

> Hence, I would conclude that the statute contemplates the imposition of liability on employers for all acts of their employees "in the course of employment," interpreted in the purposive fashion outlined earlier as being in some way related or associated with the employment. It is unnecessary to attach any label to this type of liability; it is purely statutory. However, it serves a purpose somewhat similar to that of vicarious liability in tort, by placing responsibility for an organization on those who control it and are in a position to take effective remedial action to remove undesirable conditions.[41]

The Court concluded that the liability of an employer for acts of its employees is not based on concepts developed in tort or quasi-criminal law. The liability that attaches

---

[38]The Tribunal also stated that it would have dismissed the complaint in any event because the respondent used foul language equally to male as well as to female employees.

[39]*Supra* note 31.

[40]Page D/4330, paragraph 33938. It should also be noted that the Supreme Court of Canada was interpreting the Federal Human Rights Act (S.C. 1976–77, c.33). The principle that the legislation is not intended to be punitive applies to all jurisdictions in Canada that do not provide for exemplary damages. However, in Manitoba, for example, the Human Rights Code, S.M. 1987, c.45, s.43(3)(d) does give the adjudicator the power to award exemplary damages where the adjudicator considers this to be just and appropriate punishment for any malice or recklessness involved in the contravention of the Act. *See also* Yukon Territory's Human Rights Act, S.Y.T. 1987, c.3, Section 23(1)(e).

[41]Robichaud v. The Queen (1987), 8 C.H.R.R. D/4326, D/4333, 40 D.L.R. (4th) 577, *rev'g* Treasury Board v. Robichaud (1985), 6 C.H.R.R. D/2695 (F.C.A.), *rev'g* Robichaud v. Brennan (1983), 4 C.H.R.R. D/1272 (Can. H.R. Rev. Trib.) *rev'g* (1982), 3 C.H.R.R. D/977 (Can. H.R. Trib.).

is purely statutory and not founded on any fault-based models. While endorsing this "no-name" type of liability, the opinion of Justice LaForest draws the analogy to vicarious liability only for the purpose of placing the onus of responsibility upon those individuals who are in a position to control the acts of their employees. By so doing employers are required to take appropriate and necessary action in order to remove any conditions of employment that contravene the legislation. Failure to do so will result in a finding of liability.

B. Conduct of Employer As a Factor Affecting Remedy

While the conduct of the employer is not a relevant consideration for the purpose of assessing liability, it may nevertheless be a relevant factor in determining the degree of liability attributed to the employer. As Justice LaForest stated for the Court in *Robichaud:*

> I should perhaps add that while the conduct of an employer is theoretically irrelevant to the imposition of liability in a case like this, it may nonetheless have important practical implications for the employer. Its conduct may preclude or render redundant many of the contemplated remedies. For example, an employer who responds quickly and effectively to a complaint by instituting a scheme to remedy and prevent recurrence will not be liable to the same extent, if at all, as an employer who fails to adopt such steps. These matters, however, go to remedial consequences not liability.[42]

The Supreme Court of Canada appears to be saying that employers who endow managerial employees with certain powers to confer or withhold benefits ought to be mindful that they will be liable for any abuses of these powers by their employees. This is so without regard to whether they have knowledge of the abuses.

Similarly, the Supreme Court of Canada seems to be telling the lower courts and tribunals that an employer who is quick to respond to allegations of harassment by investigating, by instituting policies, and by dealing with harassers, ought not to feel the full blow of any remedial jurisdiction these tribunals may have.

V. REMEDIES BEFORE THE HUMAN RIGHTS TRIBUNALS

A. Mandated Apologies

Boards of inquiry have, albeit rarely, required respondents to issue a written apology to the complainant. In one case, the adjudicator stated:

> Any apology goes far beyond a confirmation of the personal vindication of the victim. It serves a broad educational function that can advance the purposes of the *Act:* it tells every employee throughout the country and abroad that a prominent institution and employer in our society stands firmly for equality in the workplace. By its very existence it acknowledges that it was a party to a serious affront to human dignity. It holds out the hope and commitment that the mistakes of the past will not be repeated in the future. We recognize that an apology under compulsion is somewhat diminished but nevertheless the gesture and words signal an important commitment to change.[43]

The tribunal, accordingly, not only ordered a formal apology to be given to the

---

[42]*Id.* at D/4334.
[43]Treasury Board v. Robichaud (No. 2)(1989), 11 C.H.R.R. D/194, D/203 (Can. H.R. Rev. Trib.).

complainant but also that this apology be posted throughout the various facilities operated by the Department of National Defense.

The same federal human rights tribunal came to an opposite conclusion regarding the question of a forced apology in *Potapczyk v. MacBain*.[44] There, the tribunal declined to make such an order, finding that in the circumstances of that case no useful purpose would be served given the notoriety of the case and the limited number of employees working for the respondent at that time.

B. Damages

The extent of a tribunal's jurisdiction to make remedial orders will depend upon the applicable human rights code for that province. Generally speaking, however, all human rights codes do provide for the making of restitution. The range for the payment of general damages, however, varies from $100 in Newfoundland to $10,000 in Ontario.

Tribunals take into account numerous factors in determining the amount of damages that it will order the employer to pay. Thus, where the complainant does not seem to have been severely affected by the harassment in that she would have continued working but for her termination, an award of $1,500 was given notwithstanding the persistent nature of the harassment.[45]

In determining the amounts of damages, boards of inquiry have also considered the age and vulnerability of the victim, whether the harassment was in the form of verbal or physical contact, the extent of the aggressiveness used in perpetuating the harassment, the frequency and ongoing nature of the harassment, and the psychological impact that the harassment may have had upon the victim.[46]

C. Other Relief

Along with the usual remedial powers to make awards for legal costs, loss of wages and pain and suffering, Canadian human rights tribunals have considered requests for relocation costs[47] and psychological counseling for the complainant.[48] While reinstatement is possible, it is rarely ordered, since by the time the parties have gone through lengthy litigation, very little of a viable employment relation remains intact, making reinstatement impractical.

In *Morano v. Company Garden Centre*,[49] after finding that the respondent was guilty of both verbal and physical harassment, the tribunal required the corporate respondent during the following two years to report to the Ontario Human Rights Commission every instance of a female employee leaving its work force[50] and to permit periodic monitoring by the Commission.

D. Costs to Respondent

Some jurisdictions also have provision for the payment of costs to the respondent. In Ontario, for example, where a board of inquiry finds a complaint to have been

---

[44](1984), 5 C.H.R.R. D/2285.
[45]Zarankin v. Johnstone (1984), 5 C.H.R.R. D/2274 (B.C. Bd. Inq.).
[46]Roseanna Torries v. Royalty Kitchenware Ltd. (1982), 3 C.H.R.R. D/176.
[47]Potapozyk v. MacBain (1984), 5 C.H.R.R. D/2285 (Can. H.R. Trib.), ¶ 19321.
[48]Deisting v. Dollar Pizza (1982), 3 C.H.R.R. D/898 (Alta. Bd. Inq.).
[49](1988), 9 C.H.R.R. D/4876 (Ont. Bd. Inq.).
[50]Further, the employer was required to provide the Ontario Human Rights Commission with the name, address, and reason for the discharge of any female employee and to permit periodic monitoring by the Commission.

frivolous or vexatious or made in bad faith, where this has caused undue hardship to the respondent, it may award costs payable by the Ontario Human Rights Commission.[51]

VI. Other Recourse for Sexual Harassment Complainants

Notwithstanding the human rights legislation prohibiting sexual harassment, victims of sexual harassment may seek relief in a forum other than the Human Rights Commission. Indeed, there is precedent for these disputes to be resolved in the courts or before privately established tribunals.

A. Exclusivity of Human Rights Board Remedies

A claim of sexual harassment, as such, must go to the Human Rights Board rather than directly to court. In *Board of Governors of Seneca College v. Bhaduria,*[52] the plaintiff commenced an action against her employer, not with the Ontario Human Rights Commission, but in the courts. The issue was whether the courts should recognize a new intentional tort of discrimination. In a unanimous decision, the Supreme Court of Canada held that in Ontario there is no separate civil cause of action on the grounds of discrimination. In overruling the Court of Appeal, the Supreme Court of Canada found that because the Ontario Human Rights Code sets out a mechanism by which it can deal effectively with allegations of discrimination, it thereby foreclosed any other civil causes of action based upon a breach of that statute. Thus, where there exists a provincial statute that prevents discrimination or harassment, that body appears to have the exclusive jurisdiction to deal with a complaint to the exclusion of the courts.

B. Effect of Collective Bargaining Agreements

Acts of sexual harassment may be the basis for a wrongful dismissal action, which generally can be brought directly in court. In *Foisy v. Bell Canada,*[53] a decision of the Quebec Superior Court, the plaintiff alleged successfully that she had been wrongfully dismissed because of noncompliance with sexual overtures by her supervisor. The plaintiff commenced an action claiming damages for psychological distress before the Quebec courts. The plaintiff, it should be noted, was a member of a union. Upon her dismissal a grievance was filed and was settled. The plaintiff was not a signatory to the settlement, which reinstated her to full employment and provided that she was precluded from taking any further action either before the courts or the Human Rights Tribunal. Notwithstanding the settlement, the plaintiff commenced an action before the Quebec Superior Court, claiming $15,000 in extracontractual damages arising out of her dismissal.

In assuming jurisdiction, in spite of the existence of a collective agreement, the court relied on the fact that the compensation being claimed by the plaintiff was for delictual damages arising out of an "abus de droit" and civil liability of the employer and its representatives:

> "Abus de droit" and offences do not fall within the realm of collective relations nor of the working conditions agreed to by the parties in a collective labor contract.

---

[51]Ontario Human Rights Code, S.O. 1981, c.53, as amended by S.O. 1984, c.58, s.39, and S.O. 1986, c.64, § 18.
[52](1981), 1 C.H.R.R. D/468, 124 D.L.R. (3d) 193, *rev'g* (1979), 105 D.L.R. (3d) 707 (Ont. C.A.).
[53](1984), 18 D.L.R. (4th) 222.

Furthermore, the union cannot waive the right to recourse on behalf of the individual, following a violation of this nature. This is personal damage involving the individual that the union has not the authority to either negotiate or settle. The individual concerned may do so . . .[54]

The damage award in this case in the amount of $3,000 was awarded for psychological trauma and "social and professional isolation."

C. Concurrent Actions

A defendant who is faced with both a court action as well as an action under the human rights legislation may seek to have one of the matters stayed. There is, however, usually a significant time delay from the time of filing the complaint to the time when it is actually served upon the respondent. Accordingly, situations arise where the employer is not aware that there is a concurrent human rights action, or vice versa.

In *MacBain*,[55] the complainant filed a human rights complaint as well as a judicial action for wrongful dismissal. When her wrongful dismissal action was settled, the employer was not aware that the complainant had also filed an action with the Human Rights Commission. The settlement of the wrongful dismissal action provided the complainant with ten weeks of severance pay. This amount exceeded the complainant's actual losses, since she commenced work with another employer within a month of leaving the employ of the respondent. The Canadian Human Rights Tribunal, in considering the request for additional costs, while expressing some concern that the respondent was not aware of the multiple actions against him, did nevertheless award an additional $1,500 to the complainant for pain and suffering resulting from what was characterized as the respondent's "callous, willful and reckless acts." The tribunal seemed to consider the complainant's failure to advise the respondent of the true state of affairs in settling the wrongful dismissal claim by denying the complainant's request for relocation costs.[56]

D. Private Tribunals

A very highly publicized case involving a professor at the University of Toronto was adjudicated before a private "sexual harassment hearing tribunal."[57] The respondent (commonly referred to in the press as the "Leering Professor") was found guilty of sexual harassment initially by the Sexual Harassment Hearing Board and ultimately by the Sexual Harassment Appeal Board. The finding of guilt was based on the university's sexual harassment policy and procedure, and, specifically, its provision proscribing "offensive staring or leering."

In essence, the professor would put on goggles and swim in the university swimming pool. A female student would also swim at the same swimming pool. She complained that while she swam the professor would leer at her both underwater and on the surface. The professor was found guilty and was precluded from using the swimming facilities for a period of five years. The order was also placed in the professor's personnel file for a period of one year. While this order was modified somewhat by the appeals board, the case is nevertheless proceeding to the Ontario Divisional Court for judicial review of the Appeal Board's ruling, and at publication time has yet to be heard.

---

[54]*Id.* at 229.

[55]*Supra* note 45.

[56]It should be noted that a recent Canadian decision in Ontario has stated that normal common-law principles governing reasonable notice in wrongful dismissal actions are not applicable to Human Rights cases. Airport Taxicab Ass'n. v. Piazza (1989), 10 C.H.R.R. D/6347.

[57]Torfason v. Hummel (13 Feb. 1989)(S.U.U. Bd.), aff'd (6 Dec. 1989)(S.H.A. Bd.).

VII. THE ALLEGED HARASSER AS PLAINTIFF

In cases of sexual harassment an employer may find itself in a "catch-22" situation: While an employer may fend off a potential wrongful dismissal suit or human rights complaint with swift disciplinary action, the same employer action may provoke a wrongful dismissal suit by the alleged harasser.

In *Tellier v. Bank of Montreal*,[58] the plaintiff, with 18 years of seniority, was dismissed for sexually harassing a subordinate. The court held that a dismissal for sexual harassment of a subordinate employee does in fact constitute just cause for dismissal. The court was very cognizant of the employer's responsibility to protect employees from sexual harassment and to take positive action when it occurs. Had the employer not done so, the court recognized that the employer would leave itself open for a charge of harassment under the relevant human rights legislation.

VIII. CONCLUSION

This discussion provides an overview of how tribunals and the courts deal with sexual harassment, rather than an exhaustive review of the law in Canada. To a large extent Canadian courts and tribunals have relied upon American jurisprudence in this regard. In each case, however, given the division of Canada into ten provinces and two territories, it is always necessary to refer to the actual wording in the respective human rights codes in order to ascertain a commission's jurisdiction over any given action, as well as the board of inquiry's remedial powers and jurisdiction.

On the whole, however, all of the jurisprudence clearly states that employers in Canada have a very substantial responsibility to ensure that their workplace is free from sexual harassment. Failure to do so can result in costly and lengthy litigation, as well as the possibility that tribunals may exercise their very broad remedial powers and impose affirmative action programs, reporting requirements and other nonmonetary but nonetheless restrictive business practices to ensure compliance with the human rights code.

Canadian employers, therefore, are wise to familiarize themselves with the obligations under the respective human rights codes and also to implement their own harassment policies.

---

[58] 17 C.C.E.L. 1 (Ont. Dt. Ct.).

SAMPLE ANTIHARASSMENT POLICY

The ABC Company is committed to maintaining a work environment that is free of discrimination. In keeping with this commitment, we will not tolerate harassment of ABC employees by anyone, including any supervisor, co-worker, vendor, client, or customer of ABC.

Harassment consists of unwelcome conduct, whether verbal, physical, or visual, that is based upon a person's protected status, such as sex, color, race, ancestry, religion, national origin, age, physical handicap, medical condition, disability, marital status, veteran status, citizenship status, or other protected group status. The Company will not tolerate harassing conduct that affects tangible job benefits, that interferes unreasonably with an individual's work performance, or that creates an intimidating, hostile, or offensive working environment.

Sexual harassment deserves special mention. Unwelcome sexual advances, requests for sexual favors, and other physical, verbal, or visual conduct based on sex constitute sexual harassment when (1) submission to the conduct is an explicit or implicit term or condition of employment, (2) submission to or rejection of the conduct is used as the basis for an employment decision, or (3) the conduct has the purpose or effect of unreasonably interfering with an individual's work performance or creating an intimidating, hostile, or offensive working environment. Sexual harassment may include explicit sexual propositions, sexual innuendo, suggestive comments, sexually oriented "kidding" or "teasing," "practical jokes," jokes about gender-specific traits, foul or obscene language or gestures, display of foul or obscene printed or visual material, and physical contact such as patting, pinching, or brushing against another's body.

All ABC employees are responsible to help assure that we avoid harassment. If you feel that you have experienced or witnessed harassment, you are to notify immediately Mr. _____ or Ms. _____ in the Department of Human Resources. The Company forbids retaliation against anyone for reporting sexual harassment, assisting in making a sexual harassment complaint, or cooperating in a sexual harassment investigation.

The Company's policy is to investigate all such complaints thoroughly and promptly. To the fullest extent practicable, the Company will keep complaints and the terms of their resolution confidential. If an investigation confirms that harassment has occurred, the Company will take corrective action, including such discipline, up to and including immediate termination of employment, as is appropriate.

ORDER OF INJUNCTIVE RELIEF
ROBINSON V. JACKSONVILLE SHIPYARDS

760 F. Supp. 1486 (M.D. Fla. 1991)

JACKSONVILLE SHIPYARDS, INC.
SEXUAL HARASSMENT POLICY

STATEMENT OF POLICY

Title VII of the Civil Rights Act of 1964 prohibits employment discrimination on the basis of race, color, sex, age or national origin. *Sexual harassment is included among the prohibitions.*

Sexual harassment, according to the federal Equal Employment Opportunity Commission (EEOC), consists of unwelcome sexual advances, requests for sexual favors or other verbal or physical acts of a sexual or sex-based nature where (1) submission to such conduct is made either explicitly or implicitly a term or condition of an individual's employment; (2) an employment decision is based on an individual's acceptance or rejection of such conduct; or (3) such conduct interferes with an individual's work performance or creates an intimidating, hostile or offensive working environment.

It is also unlawful to retaliate or take reprisal in any way against anyone who has articulated any concern about sexual harassment or discrimination, whether that concern relates to harassment of or discrimination against the individual raising the concern or against another individual.

Examples of conduct that would be considered sexual harassment or related retaliation are set forth in the Statement of Prohibited Conduct which follows. These examples are provided to illustrate the kind of conduct proscribed by this Policy; the list is not exhaustive.

Jacksonville Shipyards, Inc., and its agents are under a duty to investigate and eradicate any form of sexual harassment or sex discrimination or retaliation. To further that end, JSI has issued a procedure for making complaints about conduct in violation of this Policy and a schedule for violation of this Policy.

Sexual harassment is unlawful, and such prohibited conduct exposes not only JSI, but individuals involved in such conduct, to significant liability under the law. Employees at all times should treat other employees respectfully and with dignity in a manner so as not to offend the sensibilities of a co-worker. Accordingly, JSI's management is committed to vigorously enforcing its Sexual Harassment Policy at all levels within the Company.

STATEMENT OF PROHIBITED CONDUCT

The management of Jacksonville Shipyards, Inc., considers the following conduct to represent some of the types of acts which violate JSI's Sexual Harassment Policy:

A. *Physical assaults of a sexual nature, such as:*
(1) rape, sexual battery, molestation or attempts to commit these assaults; and
(2) intentional physical conduct which is sexual in nature, such as touching, pinching, patting, grabbing, brushing against another employee's body, or poking another employee's body.

B. *Unwanted sexual advances, propositions or other sexual comments, such as:*
(1) sexually-oriented gestures, noises, remarks, jokes, or comments about a person's sexuality or sexual experience directed at or made in the presence of any employee who indicates or has indicated in any way that such conduct in his or her presence is unwelcome;
(2) preferential treatment or promise of preferential treatment to an employee for submitting to sexual conduct, including soliciting or attempting to solicit any employee to engage in sexual activity for compensation or reward; and
(3) subjecting, or threats of subjecting, an employee to unwelcome sexual attention or conduct or intentionally making performance of the employee's job more difficult because of that employee's sex.

C. *Sexual or discriminatory displays or publications anywhere in JSI's workplace by JSI employees, such as:*
(1) displaying pictures, posters, calendars, graffiti, objects, promotional materials, reading materials, or other materials that are sexually suggestive, sexually demeaning, or pornographic, or bringing into the JSI work environment or possessing any such material to read, display or view at work.
A picture will be presumed to be sexually suggestive if it depicts a person of either sex who is not fully clothed or in clothes that are not suited to or ordinarily accepted for the accomplishment of routine work in and around the shipyard and who is posed for the obvious purpose of displaying or drawing attention to private portions of his or her body.
(2) reading or otherwise publicizing in the work environment materials that are in any way sexually revealing, sexually suggestive, sexually demeaning or pornographic; and
(3) displaying signs or other materials purporting to segregate an employee by sex in any area of the workplace (other than restrooms and similar semi-private lockers/changing rooms).

D. *Retaliation for sexual harassment complaints, such as:*
(1) disciplining, changing work assignments of, providing inaccurate work information to, or refusing to cooperate or discuss work-related matters with any employee because that employee has complained about or resisted harassment, discrimination or retaliation; and
(3) intentionally pressuring, falsely denying, lying about or otherwise covering up or attempting to cover up conduct such as that described in any item above.

E. *Other acts:*
(1) The above is not to be construed as an all inclusive list of prohibited acts under this policy.
(2) Sexual harassment is unlawful and hurts other employees. Any of the prohibited conduct described here is sexual harassment of anyone at whom it is directed or who is otherwise subjected to it. Each incident of harassment, moreover, contributes to a general atmosphere in which all persons who share

the victim's sex suffer the consequences. Sexually-oriented acts or sex-based conduct have no legitimate business purpose; accordingly, the employee who engages in such conduct should be and will be made to bear the full responsibility for such unlawful conduct.

SCHEDULE OF PENALTIES FOR MISCONDUCT

The following schedule of penalties applies to all violations of the JSI Sexual Harassment Policy, as explained in more detail in the Statement of Prohibited Conduct.

Where progressive discipline is provided for, each instance of conduct violating the Policy moves the offending employee through the steps of disciplinary action. In other words, it is not necessary for an employee to repeat the same precise conduct in order to move up the scale of discipline.

A written record of each action taken pursuant to the Policy will be placed in the offending employee's personnel file. The record will reflect the conduct, or alleged conduct, and the warning given, or other discipline imposed.

(A) *Assault*
Any employee's first proven offense of assault or threat of assault, including assault of a sexual nature, will result in dismissal.

(B) *Other acts of harassment by co-workers*
An employee's commission of acts of sexual harassment other than assault will result in non-disciplinary oral counseling upon alleged first offense, written warning, suspension or discharge upon the first proven offense, depending upon the nature and severity of the misconduct, and suspension or discharge upon the second proven offense, depending on the nature and severity of the misconduct.

(C) *Retaliation*
Alleged retaliation against a sexual harassment complainant will result in non-disciplinary oral counseling. Any form of proven retaliation will result in suspension or discharge upon the first proven offense, depending upon the nature and severity of the retaliatory acts, and discharge upon the second proven offense.

(D) *Supervisors*
A supervisor's commission of acts of sexual harassment (other than assault) with respect to any other employee under that person's supervision will result in non-disciplinary oral counseling upon alleged first offense, final warning or dismissal for the first offense, depending upon the nature and severity of the misconduct, and discharge for any subsequent offense.

PROCEDURES FOR MAKING, INVESTIGATING AND
RESOLVING SEXUAL HARASSMENT AND RETALIATION COMPLAINTS

A. *Complaints*
JSI will provide its employees with convenient, confidential and reliable mechanisms for reporting incidents of sexual harassment and retaliation. Accordingly, JSI designates at least two employees in supervisory or managerial positions at each of the Commercial and Mayport Yards to serve as Investigative Officers for sexual harassment issues. The names, responsibilities, work locations, and phone numbers of each Officer will be routinely and continuously posted so that an employee seeking such name can enjoy anonymity and remain inconspicuous to all of the employees in the yard in which he or she works.

The Investigative Officers may appoint "designees" to assist them in handling sexual harassment complaints. Persons appointed as designees shall not conduct investigation until they have received training equivalent to that received by the Investigative Officers. The purpose of having several persons to whom complaints may be made is to avoid a situation where an employee is faced with complaining to the person, or a close associate of the person, who would be the subject of the complaint.

Complaints of acts of sexual harassment or retaliation that are in violation of the sexual harassment policy will be accepted in writing or orally, and anonymous complaints will be taken seriously and investigated. Anyone who has observed sexual harassment or retaliation should report it to a designated Investigative Officer. A complaint need not be limited to someone who was the target of harassment or retaliation.

Only those who have an immediate need to know, including the Investigative Officers and/or his/her designee, the alleged target of harassment or retaliation, the alleged harasser(s) or retaliator(s) and any witnesses will or may find out the identity of the complainant. All parties contacted in the course of an investigation will be advised that all parties involved in a charge are entitled to respect and that any retaliation or reprisal against an individual who is an alleged target of harassment or retaliation, who has made a complaint or who has provided evidence in connection with a complaint is a separate actionable offense as provided in the schedule of penalties. This complaint process will be administered consistent with federal labor law when bargaining unit members are affected.

B. *Investigations*

Each Investigative Officer will receive thorough training about sexual harassment and the procedures herein and will have the responsibility for investigating complaints or having an appropriately trained and designated JSI investigator do so.

All complaints will be investigated expeditiously by a trained JSI Investigative Officer or his/her designee. The Investigative Officer will produce a written report, which, together with the investigation file, will be shown to the complainant upon request within a reasonable time. The Investigative Officer is empowered to recommend remedial measures based upon the results of the investigation, and JSI management will promptly consider and act upon such recommendation. When a complaint is made the Investigative Officer will have the duty of immediately bringing all sexual harassment and retaliation complaints to the confidential attention of the office of the President of JSI, and JSI's EEO Officer. The Investigative and EEO Officers will each maintain a file on the original charge and follow up investigation. Such files will be available to investigators, to federal, state and local agencies charged with equal employment or affirmative action enforcement, to other complainants who have filed a formal charge of discrimination against JSI, or any agent thereof, whether that formal charge is filed at a federal, state, or local law level. The names of complainants, however, will be kept under separate file.

C. *Cooperation*

An effective sexual harassment policy requires the support and example of company personnel in positions of authority. JSI agents or employees who engage in sexual harassment or retaliation or who fail to cooperate with company-sponsored investigations of sexual harassment or retaliation may be severely sanctioned by suspension or dismissal. By the same token, officials who refuse to implement remedial measures, obstruct the remedial efforts of other JSI employees, and/or retaliate against sexual harassment complainants or witnesses may be immediately sanctioned by suspension or dismissal.

D. *Monitoring*

Because JSI is under legal obligations imposed by Court order, the NOW Legal Defense and Education Fund, its designated representative, and, if one is appointed upon motion and a showing of need, a representative of the U.S. District Court for the Middle District of Florida are authorized to monitor the JSI workplace, even in the absence of specific complaints, to ensure that the company's policy against sexual harassment is being enforced. Such persons are not ordinarily to be used in lieu of the JSI Investigative Officers on investigations of individual matters, but instead are to be available to assess the adequacy of investigations. Any individual dissatisfied with JSI's investigation of a complaint may contact such persons in writing or by telephone and request an independent investigation. Such persons' addresses and telephone numbers will be posted and circulated with those of the Investigative Officers. Such persons will be given reasonable access by JSI to inspect for compliance.

PROCEDURES AND RULES FOR EDUCATION AND TRAINING

Education and training for employees at each level of the work force are critical to the success of JSI's policy against sexual harassment. The following documents address such issues: the letter to be sent to all employees from JSI's Chief Executive Officer/President, the Sexual Harassment policy, Statement of Prohibited Conduct, the Schedule of Penalties for Misconduct, and Procedures for Making, Investigating and Resolving Sexual Harassment and Retaliation Complaints. These documents will be conspicuously posted throughout the workplace at each division of JSI, on each company bulletin board, in all central gathering areas, and in every locker room. The statements must be clearly legible and displayed continuously. The sexual harassment policy under a cover letter from JSI's president will be sent to all employees. The letter will indicate that copies are available at no cost and how they can be obtained.

JSI's sexual harassment policy statement will also be included in the Safety Instructions and General Company Rules, which are issued in booklet form to each JSI employee. Educational posters using concise messages conveying JSI's opposition to workplace sexual harassment will reinforce the company's policy statement; these posters should be simple, eye-catching and graffiti resistant.

Education and training include the following components:

1. *For all JSI employees:* As part of general orientation each recently hired employee will be given a copy of the letter from JSI's Chief Executive Officer/President and requested to read and sign a receipt for the company's policy statement on sexual harassment so that they are on notice of the standards of behavior expected. In addition, supervisory employees who have attended a management training seminar on sexual harassment will explain orally at least once every six months at safety meetings attended by all employees the kinds of acts that constitute sexual harassment, the company's serious commitment to eliminating sexual harassment in the workplace, the penalties for engaging in harassment, and the procedures for reporting incidents of sexual harassment.

2. *For all female employees:* All women employed at JSI will participate on company time in annual seminars that teach strategies for resisting and preventing sexual harassment. At least a half-day in length, these seminars will be conducted by one or more experienced sexual harassment educators, including one instructor with work experience in the trades.

3. *For all employees with supervisory authority over other employees, including leadermen, quartermen, superintendents, and all employees working in a managerial capacity:* All supervisory personnel will participate in an annual, half-day-long training session on sex discrimination. At least one-third of each session (of no less than one and one-half hours) will be devoted to education about workplace sexual harassment, including training (with demonstrative evidence) as to exactly what types of remarks, behavior and pictures will not be tolerated in the JSI workplace. The president of JSI will attend the training sessions in one central location with all company supervisory employees. The president will introduce the seminar with remarks stressing the potential liability of JSI and individual supervisors for sexual harassment and the need to eliminate harassment. Each participant will be informed that they are responsible for knowing the contents of JSI's sexual harassment policy and for giving similar presentations at safety meetings to employees.

4. *For all Investigative Officers:* The Investigative Officers and their designees, if any, will attend annual full-day training seminars conducted by experienced sexual harassment educators and/or investigators to educate them about the problems of sexual harassment in the workplace and techniques for investigating and stopping it.

The training sessions for components 2–4 will be conducted by an experienced sexual harassment educator chosen jointly by JSI and the NOW Legal Defense and Education Fund after receiving bids. In the event of a disagreement between the parties, the parties will refer the matter to an arbitrator chosen by the parties.

THE CIVIL RIGHTS ACT OF 1991

In November 1991 Congress approved and President Bush signed the Civil Rights Act of 1991. The Act amended Title VII of the Civil Rights Act of 1964, the Civil Rights Act of 1866 (as codified in 42 U.S.C. §1981), the Attorney's Fees Awards Act of 1976, the Americans with Disabilities Act of 1990, and the Age Discrimination in Employment Act of 1967. A full summary and analysis of the Act appears in Daily Labor Report (BNA) Special Supplement No. 218. The discussion below focuses on the changes that will affect sexual harassment litigation.

I. Compensatory and Punitive Damages

Section 102(a) of the Act adds a new section after 42 U.S.C. §1981 to provide that in cases of "intentional discrimination" unlawful under Title VII, a party may recover compensatory and punitive damages in addition to back pay, interest on back pay, and any other relief already authorized by §706(g) of Title VII.

Section 102(b)(1) of the Act provides that punitive damages are available upon proof that "the respondent engaged in a discriminatory practice or discriminatory practices with malice or with reckless indifference to the federally protected rights of an aggrieved individual."

Section 102(b)(3) of the Act indicates that compensatory damages may be awarded for "future pecuniary losses, emotional pain, suffering, inconvenience, mental anguish, loss of enjoyment of life, and other nonpecuniary losses."

II. Cap on Total Compensatory and Punitive Damages

Section 102(b)(3) of the Act provides that the sum total of compensatory and punitive damages is subject to a cap that varies with the size of the respondent, as follows:

Number of Employees	Cap on Total Damages
15–100	$50,000
101–200	$100,000
201–500	$200,000
more than 500	$300,000

III. Trial by Jury

Section 102(c) of the Act provides that when compensatory or punitive damages are sought, any party can demand a jury trial. The court is forbidden to inform the jury about the cap on damage awards.

IV. EXPERT FEES

Section 113(b) of the Act amends Title VII to provide that an award of reasonable attorney's fees may include an award of expert fees.

V. ARBITRATION

Section 118 of the Act provides:

Where appropriate and to the extent authorized by law, the use of alternative means of dispute resolution, including settlement negotiations, conciliation, facilitation, mediation, factfinding, minitrials, and arbitration, is encouraged to resolve disputes arising under the Acts or provisions of Federal law amended by this title.

VI. RACIAL HARASSMENT

Section 101 of the Act amends 42 U.S.C. §1981 by providing that the right to "make and enforce contracts" includes "the enjoyment of all benefits, privileges, terms, and conditions of the contractual relationship." This amendment is intended to overrule the holding in *Patterson v. McLean Credit Union* that §1981 applied to the hiring and perhaps to the promotion process and did not prohibit racial harassment on the job.

VII. MIXED MOTIVE CASES

Section 107 of the Act amends Title VII to provide that where the plaintiff proves that a prohibited factor motivated an employment action, and where the employer proves that the same action would have been taken even absent the discriminatory motive, a violation of Title VII has been proven, with the employer's proof going to the issue of remedy rather than to liability. This change overrules a portion of *Price Waterhouse v. Hopkins*.

VIII. EFFECTIVE DATE

Section 402 of the Act states that absent specific provisions to the contrary, the Act takes effect upon enactment. The effect on pending cases is not specified.

TABLE OF CASES

Cases are referenced to chapter and footnote number(s); *e.g., 2:* 21 indicates the case is cited in chapter 2, footnote 21. Cases printed in full text are referenced by italicized page numbers that precede the chapter and footnote references. Alphabetization is letter-by-letter.

F

FAA; Downes v., 775 F.2d 288, 39 FEP Cases 70 (Fed. Cir. 1985) *4:* 21, 70; *24:* 33, 36, 38–39

Fact Concerts; City of Newport v., 453 U.S. 247 (1981) *29:* 88

Facteau; McClelland v., 610 F.2d 693 (10th Cir. 1979) *11:* 111

Faculty-Student Ass'n; Taylor v., 40 FEP Cases 1292 (W.D.N.Y. 1986) *4:* 188; *22:* 20

Fair v. Guiding Eyes for the Blind, 742 F. Supp. 151 (S.D.N.Y. 1990) *4:* 131, 163, 166; *5:* 84

Fair Automotive Repair v. Car-X Serv. Sys., 128 Ill. App.3d 763, 471 N.E.2d 554 (1984) *21:* 24

Fair Oaks Fire Protection Dist.; Cole v., 43 Cal.3d 148, 233 Cal. Rptr. 308 (1987) *27:* 93

Falwell; Hustler Magazine v., 485 U.S. 46 (1988) *27:* 177

Faris v. Henry Vogt Mach. Co., 813 F.2d 786 (6th Cir. 1987) *7:* 63

Fariss v. Lynchburg Foundry, 769 F.2d 958, 38 FEP Cases 992 (4th Cir. 1985) *29:* 23

Farmer; Hurst v., 40 Wash. App. 116, 697 P.2d 280 (1985) *24:* 27, 43, 65

Farmers Elec. Coop.; George v., 715 F.2d 175, 32 FEP Cases 1801 (5th Cir. 1983) *18:* 39

Farrell; Skadegaard v., 578 F. Supp. 1209, 33 FEP Cases 1528 (D.N.J. 1984) *11:* 39, 63

Fashion Centre, Ltd.; Berube v., 771 P.2d 1033 (Utah 1989) *15:* 101

Fast v. School Dist. of Ladue, 728 F.2d 1030 (8th Cir. 1984) *30:* 8

Favors v. Alco Mfg. Co., 186 Ga. App. 480, 367 S.E.2d 328 (1988) *15:* 111, 117, 119

Fawcett v. IDS Fin. Servs., 41 FEP Cases 589 (W.D. Pa. 1986) *9:* 29; *12:* 36; *15:* 86, 153; *16:* 18; *29:* 115

Fazier v. Southeastern Pa. Transp. Auth., 49 FEP Cases 856 (E.D. Pa. 1988) *21:* 54

FCC v. Pacifica Foundation, 438 U.S. 726 (1978) *27:* 173

Federal Crop Ins. Corp. v. Hester, 765 F.2d 723 (8th Cir. 1985) *25:* 105

Federal Express Corp.; Shore v., 777 F.2d 1155, 39 FEP Cases 809 (6th Cir. 1985), *aff'd mem.*, 875 F.2d 867, 49 FEP Cases 1640 (6th Cir. 1989) *22:* 16

Federal Ins. Co.

—v. Applestein, 377 So.2d 229 (Fla. Ct. App. 1979) *22:* 112

—Solo Cup Co. v., 619 F.2d 1178, 22 FEP Cases 883 (7th Cir.), *cert. denied,* 449 U.S. 1033 (1980) *22:* 105, 108

Federal Paper Board Co.; Gillin v., 479 F.2d

97, 5 FEP Cases 1094 (2d Cir. 1973) *22:* 166

Federal Prison Indus.; Lewis v., 786 F.2d 1537, 40 FEP Cases 998 (11th Cir. 1986) *2:* 54

Federal Reserve Bank of Richmond; EEOC v., 698 F.2d 633, 30 EPD ¶33,269, 30 FEP Cases 1137 (4th Cir. 1983) *9:* 47

Feeney; Personnel Adm'r v., 442 U.S. 256, 19 FEP Cases 1377 (1979) *11:* 66

FEHC, *see* other party

Fekete v. United States Steel Corp., 353 F. Supp. 1177 (W.D. Pa. 1973) *4:* 126, 165, 194

Feldleit v. Long Island R.R., 723 F. Supp. 892 (E.D.N.Y. 1989) *15:* 75

Ferguson v. E.I. du Pont de Nemours & Co., 560 F. Supp. 1172, 31 FEP Cases 795 (D. Del. 1983) *4:* 71; *10:* 24, 47, 49; *22:* 123; *27:* 37–39

Ferraro v. Pacific Fin. Corp, 8 Cal. App.3d 339, 87 Cal. Rptr. 226 (1970) *23:* 38

Ferrell v. Brick, 678 F. Supp. 111, 46 FEP Cases 502 (E.D. Pa. 1987) *21:* 106; *22:* 137, 158

Ferris v. Hawkins, 135 Ariz. 329, 660 P.2d 1256 (Ct. App. 1983) *13:* 58–59

Ficalora v. Lockheed Corp., 193 Cal. App.3d 489, 238 Cal. Rptr. 360, 48 FEP Cases 817 (1987) *12:* 33–34, 46–49

Fielder v. Southco, 699 F. Supp. 577, 48 FEP Cases 1895 (W.D. Va. 1988) *10:* 27

Fields

—v. Cummins Emp. Fed. Credit Union, 540 N.E.2d 631, 53 FEP Cases 1613 (Ind. Ct. App. 1989) *12:* 36; *14:* 12, 41; *15:* 41, 111, 115, 136; *27:* 67, 71, 76

—v. Horizon House, 1987 U.S. Dist. LEXIS 11315 (E.D. Pa. 1987) *6:* 58, 71–72

Fireman's Ins. Co.; Mary & Alice Ford Nursing Home Co. v., 86 A.D.2d 736, 446 N.Y.S.2d 599, *aff'd,* 57 N.Y.2d 656, 439 N.E.2d 883, 454 N.Y.S.2d 74 (1982) *22:* 105

Firestone Tire & Rubber Co.; Klawes v., 572 F. Supp. 116 (E.D. Wis. 1983) *22:* 26

First Interstate Bank; Leggett v., 86 Or. App. 523, 739 P.2d 1083, 111 LAB CAS. 56,040 (1987) *2:* 62

First Nat'l Bank; Harris v., 680 F. Supp. 1489, 46 FEP Cases 189 (D. Kan. 1987) *23:* 15

First Nat'l Bank of Commerce; Foval v., 841 F.2d 126 (5th Cir. 1988) *22:* 31

First Virginia Bank; Kelly v., 404 S.E.2d 723 (1991) *27:* 73, 76

Fisher

—v. San Pedro Peninsula Hosp., 214 Cal. App.3d 590, 262 Cal. Rptr. 842, 54 FEP

Schultz; Frisby v., 487 U.S. 474 (1988) *27:* 172, 176

Schwartz v. Zippy Mart, 470 So.2d 720, 50 FEP Cases 464 (Fla. Dist. Ct. App. 1985) *14:* 16

SCM Corp. v. Xerox Corp., 70 F.R.D. 508 (D. Conn. 1976) *22:* 55

Scott
—Estate of; v. de Leon, 603 F. Supp. 1328, 37 FEP Cases 563 (E.D. Mich. 1985) *11:* 39, 63
—v. City of Overland Park, 595 F. Supp. 520, 41 FEP Cases 1211 (D. Kan. 1984) *11:* 110, 128–29, 133; *27:* 18, 32, 44
—v. Instant Parking, 105 Ill. App.2d 133, 245 N.E.2d 124 (1969) *22:* 114
—v. Sears, Roebuck & Co., 605 F. Supp. 1047, 37 FEP Cases 878 (N.D. Ill. 1985), *aff'd,* 798 F.2d 210, 41 FEP Cases 805 (7th Cir. 1986) *4:* 70, 80; *6:* 2; *7:* 30; *18:* 29; *22:* 135

Scottsdale Mem. Hosp.; Wagenseller v., 147 Ariz. 370, 710 P.2d 1025 (Ariz. 1985) *15:* 95

Seaboard Sur. Co.; CNA Casualty v., 176 Cal. App.3d 598, 222 Cal. Rptr. 276 (1986) *23:* 57

Sealtest Foods, 89 LA 27 (1987)(Goldstein, Arb.) *19:* 83

Sears v. Ryder Truck Rental, 596 F. Supp. 1001, 41 FEP Cases 1347 (E.D. Mich. 1984) *18:* 27

Sears, Roebuck & Co.
—v. Florida Unemp. Appeals Comm'n, 463 So.2d 465 (Fla. Dist. Ct. App. 1985) *13:* 39–40, 45–46
—EEOC v., 628 F. Supp. 1264 (N.D. Ill. 1986) *25:* 115–16
—Holien v., 298 Or. 76, 689 P.2d 1292, 36 FEP Cases 137 (1984) *12:* 26, 34, 68–70, 107; *15:* 94
—Luft v., 117 LRRM 2704 (Iowa Dist. Ct. 1984) *13:* 60
—Scott v., 605 F. Supp. 1047, 37 FEP Cases 878 (N.D. Ill. 1985), *aff'd,* 798 F.2d 210, 41 FEP Cases 805 (7th Cir. 1986) *4:* 70, 80; *6:* 2; *7:* 30; *18:* 29; *22:* 135
—Zuniga v., 100 N.M. 414, 671 P.2d 662, *cert. denied,* 100 N.M. 439 (1983) *19:* 121

Secretary of Commerce; Mitchell v., 715 F. Supp. 409 (D.D.C. 1989), *aff'd,* 1990 U.S. App. LEXIS 19656 (D.C. Cir. 1990) *29:* 44

Sedgwick County; Carter v., 48 FEP Cases 1349 (D. Kan. 1988) *30:* 37–38

Seeman v. Little Crow Trucking, 412 N.W.2d 422 (Minn. Ct. App. 1987) *13:* 40

See's Candies; Pugh v., 116 Cal. App.3d 311, 171 Cal. Rptr. 917, 115 LRRM 4002 (1981) *15:* 101

Seminole, City of; Arnold v., 614 F. Supp. 853, 40 FEP Cases 1539 (E.D. Okla. 1985) *2:* 101; *4:* 95; *7:* 18, 65, 74, 112, 115; *15:* 25; *18:* 2; *19:* 17, 81; *22:* 8, 10, 12; *25:* 113; *26:* 35–36, 48; *28:* 19, 26, 28, 30–31, 33, 35; *29:* 13, 35, 51–52, 57, 77, 79, 81, 99, 105, 109

Seminole Point Hosp. Corp. v. Aetna Cas. & Sur. Co., 675 F. Supp. 44, 45 FEP Cases 929 (D.N.H. 1987) *10:* 62; *21:* 127; *22:* 107

Sentry Ins.; Smith v., 674 F. Supp. 1459, 45 FEP Cases 716 (N.D. Ga. 1987) *23:* 15

Sereni v. Star Sportswear Mfg., 24 Mass. Ct., 509 N.E.2d 1203, 53 FEP Cases 739 (1987) *12:* 19

Seritis v. Hotel & Rest. Employees, 30 FEP Cases 423 (Cal. Super. Ct. 1980), *aff'd,* 167 Cal. App.3d 78, 213 Cal. Rptr. 588, 37 FEP Cases 1501 (1985) *8:* 29, 31; *16:* 19; *17:* 92–93

Serruto Builders; Gray v., 110 N.J. Super. 297, 265 A.2d 404 (N.J. Sup. Ct. Ch. Div. 1970) *12:* 24

Sewall v. Taylor, 672 F. Supp. 542 (D. Me. 1987) *13:* 54, 60

Shad; Broderick v., 117 F.R.D. 306, 43 FEP Cases 532 (D.D.C. 1987) *21:* 106; *26:* 28, 77

Shadid v. Jackson, 521 F. Supp. 87 (E.D. Tex. 1981) *22:* 41

Shaffer v. National Can Corp., 565 F. Supp. 909, 34 FEP Cases 172 (E.D. Pa. 1983) *12:* 76

Shaheen v. B.F. Goodrich Co., 873 F.2d 105, 49 FEP Cases 1060 (6th Cir. 1989) *31:* 18

Shah v. Mt. Zion Hosp. & Medical Ctr., 642 F.2d 268, 27 FEP Cases 772 (9th Cir. 1981) *29:* 80

Shane v. Greyhound Lines, 868 F.2d 1057 (9th Cir. 1989) *17:* 78

Shapiro
—v. Holiday Inns, No. 89 C 7458, 1990 U.S. Dist. LEXIS 3801 (N.D. Ill. April 5, 1990) *2:* 40–41
—v. Win Sum Ski Corp., 95 F.R.D. 38 (E.D.N.Y. 1982) *26:* 54

Shapp; Robinson v., 23 Pa. Commw. 153, 350 A.2d 464 (1976), *aff'd,* 473 Pa. 315, 374 A.2d 533 (1977) *4:* 150

Shealy v. Laidlaw Bros., 34 FEP Cases 1223 (D.S.C. 1984) *21:* 24

Shearson/American Express
—v. McMahon, 482 U.S. 220 (1987) *27:* 127

Tucker; Borenstein v., 55 FEP Cases 259 (D. Conn. 1991) *27:* 130

Tulare County; Mendoza v., 128 Cal. App.3d 408, 180 Cal. Rptr. 347 (1982) *21:* 53

Tunis v. Corning Glass Works
—54 EPD ¶40,170 (S.D.N.Y. 1990) *4:* 186
—698 F. Supp. 452 (S.D.N.Y. 1988) *3:* 154; *29:* 58–59

Turnage
—Owens v., 681 F. Supp. 1095 (D.N.J.), aff'd, 865 F.2d 251 (3d Cir. 1988) *19:* 16
—Stack v., 690 F. Supp. 328 (M.D. Pa. 1988) *27:* 22

Turner v. United States, 595 F. Supp. 708 (W.D. La. 1984) *11:* 154e

Turpin v. Mailet, 591 F.2d 426 (2d Cir. 1979) *11:* 10

Tuttle v. ANR Freight Sys., 5 IER Cases 1103 (Col. Ct. App. 1990) *15:* 102

TVA Eng'g Ass'n; Phillips v., 725 F.2d 684 (6th Cir. 1983), cert. denied, 469 U.S. 819 (1984) *30:* 54

Twenty-Four Collection; Ross v., 681 F. Supp. 1547, 48 FEP Cases 1590 (S.D. Fla. 1988), aff'd mem., 875 F.2d 873, 50 FEP Cases 600 (11th Cir. 1989) *6:* 57; *9:* 13, 46; *22:* 150; *29:* 13, 20, 34

TYK Refractories Co.; Kelley v., 860 F.2d 1188 (3d Cir. 1988) *13:* 54

U

UAW v. LTV Aerospace & Defense Co., 55 FEP Cases 1078 (N.D. Tex. 1991) *21:* 54

Ukarish v. Magnesium Elektron, 31 FEP Cases 1315 (D.N.J. 1983) *4:* 27–28, 100; *7:* 73, 88–90; *22:* 123; *25:* 52

Ullman v. Olwine, 857 F.2d 1475 (6th Cir. 1988), cert. denied, 109 S.Ct. 1533 (1989) *30:* 58

Under 21 v. City of N.Y., 108 A.D.2d 250, 488 N.Y.S.2d 669 (1985) *4:* 150

Unemployment Compensation Bd.; United States Banknote Co. v., 575 A.2d 673 (Pa. Commw. Ct. 1990) *13:* 11

Unemployment Ins. Appeals Bd.
—Prescod v., 57 Cal. App.3d 29, 127 Cal. Rptr. 540 (1976) *13:* 30, 34
—Sanchez v., 36 Cal.3d 575, 685 P.2d 61, 205 Cal. Rptr. 501 (1984) *13:* 32

Union Carbide Corp.; Drinkwater v., 904 F.2d 853, 56 FEP Cases 483 (3d Cir. 1990) *4:* 23, 70, 138; *5:* 35, 45–45a, 64, 70–71; *10:* 20, 32; *12:* 11

Union of Am. Hebrew Congregations; Obago v., 52 FEP Cases 509 (S.D.N.Y. 1989) *21:* 77

Union Pacific R.R.; Romero v., 615 F.2d 1303,

22 FEP Cases 338 (10th Cir. 1980) *27:* 44

Uniroyal
—Charpliwy v., 670 F.2d 760, 28 FEP Cases 19 (7th Cir. 1982), cert. denied, 461 U.S. 956 (1983) *30:* 22
—Duke v., 743 F. Supp. 1218, 53 FEP Cases 402 (E.D.N.C. 1990) *30:* 68
—Polycast Technology Corp. v., 129 F.R.D. 621 (S.D.N.Y. 1990) *21:* 28

Uniroyal Chem. Corp.; Comeaux v., 849 F.2d 191 (5th Cir. 1988) *13:* 54, 60

Unisys Corp.; Paroline v., 879 F.2d 100, 50 FEP Cases 306 (4th Cir. 1989), aff'd in part, rev'd in part, and remanded, 900 F.2d 27, 52 FEP Cases 845 (4th Cir. 1990) *263; 4:* 21, 160, 191; *7:* 102; *9:* 54, 57–59, 61; *14:* 39; *15:* 28, 127; *19:* 35, 61, 63–64, 86, 96–96a; *23:* 11; *25:* 98; *27:* 71, 80; 63–64; 86; 96–96a

United Biscuit; Cripps v., 53 FEP Cases 519 (E.D. Tenn. 1989) *12:* 107

United Coal Cos. v. Powell Constr. Co., 839 F.2d 958 (3d Cir. 1988) *22:* 50

United Elec. Supply Co., 82 LA 921 (1984)(Madden, Arb.) *17:* 16, 25, 49; *19:* 100

United Ins. Co.; Rice v., 465 So.2d 1100, 36 FEP Cases 1641 (Ala. 1984) *15:* 33

United Mine Workers v. Gibbs, 383 U.S. 715 (1966) *21:* 50, 60

United Nuclear Corp.; Barela v., 462 F.2d 149, 4 FEP Cases 831 (10th Cir. 1972) *10:* 15, 68, 72

United States v., see other party

United States Banknote Co. v. Unemployment Compensation Bd., 575 A.2d 673 (Pa. Commw. Ct. 1990) *13:* 11

United States Dep't of Treasury; Blackwell v., 830 F.2d 1183, 44 FEP Cases 1856 (D.C. Cir. 1987) *4:* 152

United States Fidelity & Guar. Co.
—v. American Employers' Ins. Co., 159 Cal. App.3d 277, 205 Cal. Rptr. 460 (1984) *23:* 59
—Mead v., 442 F. Supp. 114, 18 FEP Cases 140 (D. Minn. 1977) *10:* 65

United States Gypsum Co.; Pryor v., 585 F. Supp. 311, 47 FEP Cases 159 (W.D. Mo. 1984) *14:* 34–35; *15:* 125; *23:* 52; *27:* 67, 72, 74, 76

United States Postal Serv.
—Bacashihua v., 859 F.2d 402 (6th Cir. 1988) *27:* 119
—Carosella v., 816 F.2d 638, 43 FEP Cases 845 (Fed. Cir. 1987) *19:* 65; *24:* 33–35, 38–39
—DiMaggio v., 643 F. Supp. 1, 40 FEP Cases 1684 (D. Conn. 1984) *27:* 33

Wittekind—*Contd.*
N.W.2d 561 (Wis. Ct. App. 1985) *25:* 15, 83, 85

Woerner v. Breczek, 519 F. Supp. 517, 26 FEP Cases 897 (N.D. Ill. 1981) *11:* 39, 63, 94

Wolf v. Burum, 1990 U.S. Dist. LEXIS 6700 (D. Kan. 1990) *4:* 70

Wolfe v. Central Mine Equip. Co., 850 F.2d 469 (8th Cir. 1988) *17:* 76

Wolk v. Saks Fifth Avenue, 728 F.2d 221, 34 FEP Cases 193 (3d Cir. 1984) *12:* 76; *15:* 98, 103

Womack v. Munson, 619 F.2d 1292, 22 FEP Cases 1079 (8th Cir. 1980), *cert. denied,* 450 U.S. 979 (1981) *10:* 20

Women Employed v. Rinella & Rinella, 468 F. Supp. 1123 (N.D. Ill. 1979) *28:* 45b

Wood
—v. United States, 55 FEP Cases 1220 (D. Mass. 1991) *11:* 154d–e; *23:* 42a
—v. Vermont Ins. Mgmt., 54 FEP Cases 510 (D. Vt. 1990) *22:* 88

Woodard Hotels; Kofoid v., 78 Or. App. 283, 716 P.2d 771 (1986) *12:* 36, 71–72, 74

Woods v. Graphic Communications, 925 F.2d 1195, 55 FEP Cases 242 (9th Cir. 1991) *12:* 12; *15:* 38a, 146; *17:* 97–98, 100

Woolley v. Hoffman-LaRoche, Inc., 99 N.J. 284, 491 A.2d 1257, *modified,* 101 N.J. 10, 499 A.2d 515 (1985) *15:* 102

Worcester Found. for Experimental Biology; Hochstadt v., 425 F. Supp. 318, 11 FEP Cases 1426 (D. Mass), *aff'd,* 545 F.2d 222, 13 FEP Cases 804 (1st Cir. 1976) *10:* 30, 66

Work Connection; EEOC v., 40 EPD ¶36,393 (D. Minn. 1986) *28:* 54, 56

Workers' Comp. Appeals Bd.; City of La Habra v., 48 Cal. Comp. Cas. 21 (Cal. Ct. App. 1983) *14:* 46

World Airways
—Clark v., 24 FEP Cases 305 (D.D.C. 1980) *15:* 150; *23:* 36; *29:* 117
—Macey v., 14 FEP Cases 1426 (N.D. Cal. 1977) *10:* 67; *29:* 13, 41

Worthy v. McKesson Corp., 756 F.2d 1370, 37 FEP Cases 539 (8th Cir. 1985) *31:* 18

W.R. Grace & Co. v. Rubber Workers, 461 U.S. 757, 113 LRRM 2641 (1983) *17:* 81–82

Wright
—v. Group Health Hosp., 103 Wash.2d 192, 691 P.2d 564 (1984) *21:* 21, 28
—v. Methodist Youth Servs., 511 F. Supp. 307, 25 FEP Cases 563 (N.D. Ill. 1981) *1:* 18; *3:* 114

Wrighten v. Metropolitan Hosp., 726 F.2d 1346, 33 FEP Cases 1714 (9th Cir. 1984) *27:* 51; *30:* 65, 67

W-S Equip. Co.; Hickman v., 176 Mich. App. 17, 438 N.W.2d 872, 51 FEP Cases 24 (1989) *5:* 35, 45a

Wunnicke; Jeppsen v., 611 F. Supp. 78, 37 FEP Cases 994 (D. Alaska 1985) *1:* 42; *6:* 20, 61

Wu v. Thomas, 863 F.2d 1543, 52 FEP Cases 3 (11th Cir. 1989) *10:* 70

Wyandot Mental Health Ctr. v. Kansas Employment Sec. Bd. of Review, No. 60,654 (Kan. 1988) *13:* 7

Wyerick v. Bayou Steel Corp., 887 F.2d 1271, 51 FEP Cases 491 (5th Cir. 1989) *4:* 37, 49, 95, 166; *25:* 53

Wyeth Laboratories; Cagguila v., 127 F.R.D. 653, 53 FEP Cases 11 (E.D. Pa. 1989) *21:* 18, 33, 35, 37

Wyoming Retirement Sys.; EEOC v., 771 F.2d 1425, 38 FEP Cases 1544 (10th Cir. 1985) *29:* 28

X

Xerox Corp.
—SCM Corp. v., 70 F.R.D. 508 (D. Conn. 1976) *22:* 55
—Van Hoomissen v., 368 F. Supp. 829, 6 FEP Cases 1231 (N.D. Cal. 1973) *22:* 84

Y

Yale Univ.; Alexander v., 631 F.2d 178 (2d Cir. 1980) *28:* 16

Y&Y Snacks; Craig v., 721 F.2d 77, 33 FEP Cases 187 (3d Cir. 1983) *3:* 163; *4:* 207; *6:* 9, 17; *29:* 29

Yates v. Avco Corp., 819 F.2d 630, 43 FEP Cases 1595 (6th Cir. 1987) *4:* 80, 170–71; *6:* 48, 68, 79; *9:* 10, 20, 22, 55–56, 69; *10:* 48; *18:* 12a; *19:* 36–37; *22:* 21; *25:* 98; *29:* 10, 18; *30:* 28

Yatvin v. Madison Metro. School Dist., 653 F. Supp. 945, 45 FEP Cases 1852 (W.D. Wis. 1987), *aff'd,* 840 F.2d 412, 45 FEP Cases 1862 (7th Cir. 1988) *5:* 35, 45–45a, 46–48

Yellow Freight Sys.
—Cook v., 53 FEP Cases 1681 (E.D. Cal. 1990) *26:* 99–101, 104
—Donnelly v., 874 F.2d 402 FEP Cases 1253 (7th Cir. 1989), *aff'd,* 110 S.Ct. 1566 (1990) *21:* 49; *22:* 87, 91; *29:* 40
—NLRB v., 930 F.2d 316 (3d Cir. 1991) *10:* 80
—Polk v., 801 F.2d 190, 41 FEP Cases 1279 (6th Cir. 1986) *3:* 115; *29:* 107

York v. Tennessee Crushed Stone Ass'n, 684 F.2d 360 (6th Cir. 1982) *23:* 9

Yosemite Community College Dist.; Clark v.,

INDEX

A

I

Q

About the Authors

Barbara Lindemann is an attorney with Seyfarth, Shaw, Fairweather & Geraldson in Los Angeles, the largest labor law firm in the United States, where she represents management in employment matters. She is an honor graduate of Yale Law School where she was a member of the Board of Editors of the Law Journal. She is a former Police Commissioner of the City of Los Angeles and served with the Equal Employment Opportunity Commission from 1965–1977 both in Washington, D.C., and as Regional Counsel to the Los Angeles office. She is a member of the U.S. Trade Representative's Service Policy Advisory Committee, having first been appointed by Clayton Yuetter and reappointed by Carla Hills. She also serves on the California Commission for Economic Development's Advisory Council on Asia. This is her fifth legal treatise. A nationally prominent civil rights lawyer, she is co-author of *Employment Discrimination Law*, the official publication of the American Bar Association that is widely regarded by scholars and judges to be the "Bible" in its field.

David D. Kadue is a partner in the Los Angeles office of Seyfarth, Shaw, Fairweather & Geraldson, where he has specialized in employment law counseling and litigation since 1983. He received his B.A. degree, with honors, from Yale University in 1975 and his J.D. degree, with honors, from the University of Minnesota Law School in 1978. He served as notes & comments editor on the Minnesota Law Review. Upon graduation from law school, he served for one year as an instructor at the University of Miami Law School in Coral Gables, Florida, and for the next two years as a law clerk, first to Circuit Judge Roy L. Stephenson of the United States Court of Appeals for the Eighth Circuit and then to Circuit Judge George E. MacKinnon of the United States Court of Appeals for the D.C. Circuit. He then joined the federal employment law practice of Seyfarth, Shaw, Fairweather & Geraldson in Washington, D.C., and continued with that practice upon his move to Los Angeles in 1983. In addition to his writings on sexual harassment, he has published several law journal articles on federal civil procedure, employment discrimination law, and the Americans With Disabilities Act of 1990.